A STAR CHAMBER COURT IN IRELAND

* Volumes 1–7 are published by Irish Academic Press.

The seal of Lord Deputy Wentworth, Marsh's Library, Dublin.

Marsh's Library, Dublin, MS Z.3.2.6, item 109, p. 305. Wentworth warrant of office to William Hilton. The personal seal of Thomas, Viscount Wentworth, was used to authenticate documents emanating from the viceroy, including those which authorized action before the court of castle chamber. A warrant granting the office of baron of the exchequer to William Hilton was signed by Wentworth at Dublin Castle on 2 January 1638. The chief governor sent word to the attorney general or solicitor general, making note of the death of Sir Launcelot Lowther, and conferring his former employment and its stipend on Hilton. The document was sealed with this wax image, containing Wentworth's seal, 'Thomae Vicecomitis Wentworth Sigillum', and the motto 'En Dieu Est Tout'.

A Star Chamber Court
in Ireland

THE COURT OF CASTLE CHAMBER, 1571–1641

JON G. CRAWFORD

FOUR COURTS PRESS
in association with
THE IRISH LEGAL HISTORY SOCIETY

Typeset in 10.5pt on 12.5pt EhrhardtMt by
Carrigboy Typesetting Services, County Cork for
FOUR COURTS PRESS LTD
7 Malpas Street, Dublin 8, Ireland
e-mail: info@four-courts-press.ie
and in North America for
FOUR COURTS PRESS
c/o ISBS, 920 N.E. 58th Avenue, Suite 300, Portland, OR 97213.

A catalogue record for this title is available
from the British Library.

ISBN 1–85182–934–2

This publication has received support from The Heritage Council
under the 2005 Publications Grant Scheme.

Printed by MPG Books Ltd, Bodmin, Cornwall.

Contents

PART ONE: THE WORLD OF THE COURT:
THE IRISH STAR CHAMBER IN ITS JUDICIAL CONTEXT

PART TWO: THE RISE AND FALL OF PREROGATIVE JUSTICE IN
IRELAND: THE IRISH STAR CHAMBER FROM 1534 TO 1641

Preface

IN ASSEMBLING THE MATERIALS for a history of the court of castle chamber, the researcher encounters many conflicting reports among rival authors, including clerks, judges, lawyers and other observers. Whereas attorneys general such as Sir John Davies and Sir Richard Bolton could agree on the need for a painstaking accumulation of legal knowledge to buttress the Irish judicial system, Justice William Saxey and Lord President Sir Richard Bingham despaired of equitable treatment at the hands of capricious jurors and ruthless chief governors. The Protestant earl of Cork and the Catholic attorney Patrick Darcy both complained against the persecution of Lord Deputy Sir Thomas Wentworth, who allegedly pursued both personal and political agendas with equal force. Yet, the caution of Lord Mountjoy as chief governor moved him to reprove his lord chancellor, Archbishop Adam Loftus, for prosecuting recusancy at a time of great peril during the Nine Years War. What do we make of these opposing strands in the implementation of common law rule in early modern Ireland?

The present work is an extension of my previous book in the Irish Legal History Society series, *Anglicizing the government of Ireland: the Irish privy council and the expansion of Tudor rule, 1556–1578* (1993). In that essay, I attempted to show that the court of castle chamber was a key instrument of early efforts to institutionalize the norms of Tudor administration in Ireland. The Irish court of star chamber originated in the schemes of Lord Deputies Sussex and Sydney, foundering until its inception in 1571. The court became a pillar of judicial administration in Ireland until its demise in 1641, and this is the first book-length history of the Irish star chamber and its context. The court of castle chamber was at the centre of royal policymaking in early modern Ireland; it was one of the most successful efforts to anglicize institutions of government; it was the celebrated target of numerous hostile petitions from opposition groups; and it was the instrument of Absolutism and religious despotism at various times in its regime of seventy years. The institution inspired many opposing chronicles of events, despite their common origin in the formal archive, leading to the complex and intricate picture of the tribunal that now emerges.

This is fundamentally a castle-centred history, since the extant documents are drawn from the judicial and administrative remnants of a central government that was evidently challenged by the increasing burden of archival records. It is important to acknowledge here the inherent bias of crown sources, and to affirm the caveat of Vincent Carey and David Edwards, among others, who caution against relying upon officially-derived narratives and justifications. Fortunately, the blazing partisanship of factions within the government prevented the sources from merely duplicating an authorized history of self-sanctioning apologias.

Mutual recriminations among crown servants throughout the entire period constitute a useful corrective to the belief that royal policy was coherent, compliant
and systematic; in fact, it was rarely so.

The surviving evidence for the court of castle chamber is taken from numerous
other legal sources. This has resulted in a pastiche of impressions that provides
insights into the Irish judicial framework, including the four courts, the quarter
sessions and the assizes. Fortunately, new work has already begun on the chancery
court and the presidency in Munster, while the municipal courts also merit
attention for their fascinating record of Irish social history. The present book
offers a profile of selected judges and attempts to demonstrate the importance of
this official group (who await their historian) at the centre of the Irish polity. The
primary documents for the court of castle chamber register only the orders and
decrees of the tribunal, so the important pleadings and interrogations of the
litigants and attorneys are largely missing. Suitors commonly petitioned the court
for mitigation of fine and sentence, or wrote to the crown for relief from castle
chamber enforcement, which often remained suspended as a result. A legacy of
unfinished business and tortuous wrangling plagued the court's entries during
much of its existence, and sources for the enforcement of its decrees are scant.

Nonetheless, we can learn much from the seven decades of castle chamber
litigation. The court was very busy at times, though it often suffered through
periods of apparent dormancy, caused by the lapsed attention of chief governors
preoccupied with crises such as war and insurrection. The court was incompletely
articulated from the Irish privy council, at times sharing with it the responsibility
for adjudication, a fact which made it difficult to identify which tribunal was
determining a case. Circumferencing the judicial system in Ireland, the court
became an active superintendent of junior tribunals and magistrates, punishing
the malfeasance of royal officers. At the fulcrum of English government in
Ireland, the court and its judges maintained close relationships with a succession
of secretaries of state, committees for Irish causes and royal favourites in London.
Litigants before the court were primarily from the landowning élite, though some
sued *in forma pauperis*. Property issues were, in fact, often at the heart of a suit,
though cloaked in other raiment such as riot, forgery and maintenance of jurors.
Policymaking and adjudication were mixed priorities before the court, and it was
frequently used to enforce proclamations or acts of state. However, the court was
often torn by internecine faction, occasionally expressed in openly rancorous
correspondence with the court in London, and, rarely, in episodes of violence at
meetings of the Irish privy council. While the court achieved a certain notoriety
when its work was condemned by a hostile opposition, leading to commissions of
inquiry and the undoing of a viceroy's regime, the routine operation of the
tribunal demonstrates a firm commitment to the correction of social violence, the
punishment of egregious dishonour and the punctilious maintenance of a legal
system challenged by social disorder and religious dissent. The court was
employed by some chief governors as the chosen instrument for policies of

persecution and intimidation, and its dénouement was tangled with the impeachment of Strafford and his successors. Paradoxically, the court was largely dormant
after 1639, when it appeared at the centre of a storm of controversy, its rulings
reversed on appeal and its members impeached in both England and Ireland,
fighting for their lives.

This work owes an unusual debt of gratitude to professional historians on
whom the author has relied. The labours of Herbert Wood and Sophie Lomas a
century ago provided a trail to the original documents and an explanatory framework for the court of castle chamber. The late David Quinn studied the sources
and offered an extremely helpful guide to conciliar records , along with personal
encouragement to the author that was very gratefully received. Among a host of
other scholars I must thank Raymond Gillespie, Nicholas Canny, Kenneth
Nicholls, Ciaran Brady, Colm Lennon, James Kelly, Steven Ellis, Mary O'Dowd,
Bernadette Cunningham, John McCafferty, Vincent Treadwell, John McCavitt,
Toby Barnard, Karl Bottigheimer, Vincent Carey, Jane Ohlmeyer, Aidan Clarke,
Patricia McCabe and Tom O'Connor for their ideas and inspiration. Two institutions
deserve much credit for allowing me time to pursue research and writing: Mars Hill
College (NC) and Roanoke College (VA) were very generous and patient during
some five years of writing and editing. I also acknowledge with thanks the
generous financial support of the Appalachian Colleges Association fellowship
during my sabbatical year 1997–98. During that time I was privileged to enjoy the
title of research associate at two fine institutions: the Institute of Historical
Research in London, and the Law Faculty of University College Dublin. Thanks
to the Institute's former Director, Patrick O'Connell, Dean Paul O'Connor and
colleagues Andrew Lyall, Kevin Costello and John O'Dowd for a memorable year of
strong support and good fellowship. To our special landlords in Dublin's over-heated
housing market, John and Emily Aherne, thanks for Sandycove and a patented
farewell anthem! From the libraries in England and Ireland, I received consistent
professionalism and reliable assistance: the British Library, Lambeth Palace Library,
the Institute of Historical Research, the Public Record Office, Chatsworth House,
Sheffield City Library, the Bodleian Library, and in Ireland, Trinity College Library,
the Royal Irish Academy, Marsh's Library, National Library, National Archives and
the University College Dublin Library. For obtaining interlibrary loans and endless
photocopies, I wish to thank Rebecca Heller, the late Patricia Scott, and librarian Stan
Umberger. My gratitude to Nial Osborough, editor of this series and indefatigable
researcher in legal history, cannot begin to acknowledge his constancy and friendship
over the past decade. At his urging, I was awarded a stipend in support of my
research by the Irish Legal History Society, for which I am also much obliged. For
the opportunity to address the Irish Historical Society on my topic, I wish to thank
Tom Bartlett and James Kelly. And for their forbearance with this struggle to
maintain two careers simultaneously, my children and my wife Robin deserve
more of my time and resources than I have been able to afford them since our
bittersweet departure from Dun Laoghaire in the spring of 1998.

The spelling of words in quotations has been left in the original, although I have extended contractions and added punctuation where necessary. I have also decided to leave the spelling of English surnames in the original, following the usage of the individual where practicable. The English, rather than the Gaelic, spelling of all place names and personal names has also been employed. The dates have been left in the original except that I used the Gregorian calendar to calculate the beginning of the year.

List of plates

appearing between pages 304 and 305

The seal of Lord Deputy Wentworth. Marsh's Library, Dublin: *Frontispiece*

List of abbreviations

Acts privy council	*Acts of the privy council of England*
AJLH	*American Journal of Legal History*
Anal Hib	*Analecta Hibernica*
Anc. rec. Dublin	*Calendar of ancient records of Dublin*, ed. Sir J.T. Gilbert and Lady Gilbert
Arm. Pub. Lib.	Armagh Public Library
Birmingham Hist Jn	*Birmingham Historical Journal*
BL	British Library
Bodl.	Bodleian Library, Oxford
Cal. Carew MSS	*Calendar of the Carew manuscripts preserved in the archiepiscopal library at Lambeth*
Cal. pat. rolls	*Calendar of the patent rolls* [of England]
Cal. pat. rolls Ire., Chas I	*Calendar of patent and close rolls of chancery in Ireland, Charles I, years 1–8*, ed. J. Morrin
Cal. pat. rolls Ire., Hen. VIII–Eliz.	*Calendar of patent and close rolls of Ireland, Henry VIII to 18th Elizabeth*
Cal. pat. rolls Ire., Jas I	*Irish patent rolls of James I: facsimile of the Irish record commissioners' calendar prepared prior to 1830*
Cal. S.P. dom.	*Calendar of state papers, domestic series*
Cal. S.P. Ire.	*Calendar of the state papers relating to Ireland*
Desid. cur. Hib.	[J. Lodge (ed.)], *Desiderata curiosa Hibernica: or a select collection of state papers*
DNB	*Dictionary of national biography*
Edwards, 'Poisoned chalice'	D. Edwards, 'The poisoned chalice: the Ormond inheritance, sectarian division and the emergence of James Butler, 1614–42', in T. Barnard and J. Fenlon, ed., *The dukes of Ormonde, 1610–1745*
EHR	*English Historical Review*
Fiants Ire., Eliz.	'Calendar to fiants of the reign of Elizabeth'
G.E.C., *Peerage*	G.E.C. [okayne], *The complete peerage of England, Scotland, Ireland, Great Britain and the United Kingdom*
Hand & Treadwell, eds.	G.J. Hand and V. W. Treadwell, 'His majesty's directions for 'ordering and settling the courts within his kingdom of Ireland, 1622', in *Analecta Hibernica*, no. 26 (1970)
Hist	*History* (the journal of the Historical Association)
Hist Jn	*Historical Journal*

HL	Huntington Library, San Marino, California
HMC	Historical Manuscripts Commission
IHR Bull	*Bulletin of the Institute of Historical Research*
IHS	*Irish Historical Studies*
IR	Irish Reports
Ir Econ Soc Hist	*Irish Economic and Social History*
Ir Jur	*Irish Jurist*
Ir Term Rep	Irish Term Reports
Jn Brit Stud	*Journal of British Studies*
Jn Eccl Hist	*Journal of Ecclesiastical History*
Jn Soc Archivists	*Journal of the Society of Archivists*
Kelly, *Duelling*	J. Kelly, '*That damn'd thing called honour*'; duelling in Ireland *1570–1860*
Liber mun. pub. Hib	R. Lascelles, *Liber munerum publicorum Hiberniae*
Louth Arch Soc Jn	*Journal of the County Louth Archaeological Society*
LPL	Lambeth Palace Library
LQR	*Law Quarterly Review*
N & Q	*Notes and Queries*
NAI	National Archives of Ireland
OED	*Oxford English dictionary*
Ormond deeds	*Calendar of Ormond deeds*, ed. E. Curtis
Pat. rolls. Ire., Jas I	*A repertory of the inrolments on the patent rolls of Chancery in Ireland commencing with the reign of James I*, ed. J.C. Erck
Perrott, *Chron. Ire., 1584–1608*	Sir James Perrott, *The chronicle of Ireland, 1584–1608*, ed. H. Wood
PP	*Past and Present*
PRO	Public Record Office, London (now the National Archives)
RIA	Royal Irish Academy
RIA Proc	*Proceedings of the Royal Irish Academy*
RSAI Jn	*Journal of the Royal Society of Antiquaries of Ireland*
Sidney SP	*Sidney state papers, 1565–70*, ed. T. Ó Laidhin
S.P. Hen. VIII	*State papers, Henry VIII*
Steele, *Tudor and Stuart*	R. Steele, ed., *Tudor and Stuart proclamations*
Stud Hib	*Studia Hibernica*
TCD	Trinity College, Dublin
TRHS	*Transactions of the Royal Historical Society*
WWM STR P	Sheffield Public Library, Wentworth Woodhouse Muniments, Strafford Papers

Introduction

> The Jurors of this kingdome, being for the most part Papistes, are soe mislead
> by their Priests, as they will seldome fine against anie of thier owne Religion
> in Criminall causes, though the evidence bee never soe pregnant and Direct.
> And therefore uppon Trialls in such causes, after they have brought in their
> verdicte in the negative, contrarie to Direct and plaine evidence in the
> affirmative, then, and not before, the kinges Counsell have sometymes told
> them that they did deserve to bee brought into the Starchamber.
>
> 'Appostiles to the Articles preferred by the Recusantes of
> Ireland to his matie touching the Disorder and abuses
> pretended to bee in the Civill government', n.d.[1]

THE COURT OF CASTLE chamber, a star chamber jurisdiction in Ireland,
functioned in the government of Ireland from its tentative inception in 1571 until
its apparent demise in 1641. The period witnessed an unusually dynamic transformation of the government, an anglicization of its core institutions. However,
the social and economic framework of Irish culture remained in many ways
traditional and conservative. Most provincial towns were commercial centres
dominated by a local merchant élite which strove to resist the Protestant
Reformation, while maintaining loyalty to the crown. The countryside in the
English Pale and the midland counties was gradually moving toward a settled
agricultural system patterned on the lowlands in England, and dominated by the
landed gentry. The Old English families vied with newcomers for possession of
profitable estates, and office-holding became an essential ingredient for, and
emblem of, security of tenure. In Ulster and Munster, the plantations were conceived in a more systematic manner than practical conditions would allow.
Dispossession of native landowning élites took longer than expected, and the
ability of Old English and Gaelic Irish landholders to retain their inheritances was
often tried at law. Nevertheless, the plantation policy created an atmosphere of
tension and mistrust, along with mountains of litigation.[2] The Ulster plantation

---

1. Bodl., Carte MS 61, f. 66. Probably a response by the privy council in Ireland to accusations made
   against the government of Chichester in 1613, focusing particularly on the plantation of Ulster
   and the lands escheated to the crown.
2. See N. Canny, *Making Ireland British, 1580–1650* (Oxford, 2001), pp. 121 et seq. Canny finds that
   the theoretical foundations for plantation were developed well before the Munster colony was
   established in the aftermath of the Desmond Rebellion (ending in 1583), yet the practical
   achievement was disappointing. Opportunity had to await the parliamentary act of attainder in
   1585–86, and the invitation to undertakers after 1586 was preceded by mapping and surveys,
   while Irish proprietors contested their dispossession in the courts. Canny explained that the use
   of the law to oppose plantation was encouraged by Ormond, causing potential settlers uncertainty
   and resulting in a lengthy investigation into the 'legal niceties' surrounding disputed ownership.

of 1609 introduced Scottish and English settlers in large numbers, while retaining Irish tenants despite the codicils designed to prevent this.[3] Some of the Gaelic Irish were gradually pushed to the frontiers of the western counties where poor land and mountainous terrain offered both refuge and opportunity to continue traditional practices, such as booleying their cattle by semi-nomadic creaghs with large herds. Whereas some leading Irish lords in Ulster and Connacht continued Gaelic traditions, maintaining bards and swordsmen and speaking the Irish language, the period also witnessed the creation of new Protestant towns, the importing of new industries and the rapid settlement of estates based on the English townland. As Dr Gillespie has observed, early modern Ireland was not yet a country, but rather a series of connected entities, united by social and legal ties, but divided by economic relations with the continent and the seaports of England and Scotland, as well as by cultural and historic distinctions unique to each region. In a recent essay, Gillespie has shown that negotiating the social order in early modern Ireland required a nimble exploitation of legal options and skilful balancing of local conflict with the priorities of the emerging commonwealth. The mixed polity which resulted from generations of intermarriage, land transfers and litigation was managed for the benefit of both Irish and newcomer élites, and the impact of the common law could be measured in the importation of core legal terms into the Irish language.[4]

The incomplete transformation of Irish society prior to the upheaval of civil war in 1641 caused the delay of political hegemony until the late seventeenth century. Nevertheless, the visitor to Ireland in 1625 might have found isolated new dwellings, such as the fortified Parke's Castle on the shore of Lough Gill, as testimony to the impact of Protestant settlement in the remoter regions of the west of Ireland. In 1610 Robert Parker established the fortified manor house on

Ibid., pp. 135–40. Isolated and struggling communities were overthrown rapidly in 1598 by Tyrone's confederates in Munster. In the midlands, arriviste officials like Sir Charles Coote, Viscount Ely and Lord Lambert expanded their new estates, sometimes at the expense of Elizabethan planters like the Cosbys and Hovendens who had become 'absorbed into their locale'. Ibid., pp. 372–73.

3. Ibid., pp. 184–87, 205–08. In Ulster, a campaign was launched in 1603 to challenge the lawful title of the rebel earls of Tyrone and Tyrconnell, led by Dublin officials and churchmen, and the lawyers Richard Hadsor and Sir John Davies, then solicitor general. Ibid., pp. 180–82. Hadsor sought to bring all Ulster into shire ground, so that litigation could proceed in the manors and freeholds, and Davies proceeded with the government's case to dismember the seignories of the earls into smaller tenancies in freehold. The legal process was interrupted in 1607 by the flight of the earls.

4. R. Gillespie, *Colonial Ulster* (Belfast, 1985), introduction; Gillespie and B. Cunningham, *Stories from Gaelic Ireland: microhistories from the sixteenth century Irish annals* (Dublin, 2003), pp. 178–94. Irish leaders saw the benefit of working through commissions of the peace, sought brokers in factional politics and turned to the presidency courts for solutions. 'What had begun as an attempt to impose authority and social order on the localities was transformed so that the provincial government became a pawn in the negotiation of social authority within the MacWilliam lordship.' *Stories from Ireland*, p. 194.

the foundation of an O'Rourke castle, with a moat and mullioned windows.⁵ The perambulating visitor would have been even more impressed with the country house of the Cork merchant, Walter Coppinger, who spent part of his fortune on a grand estate near Rosscarbery. Coppinger was a frequent castle chamber litigant, a recusant Catholic who possessed substantial political power and managed to thrive in the uncertain decades of the early Stuart dynasty in Ireland.⁶ The formidable Jacobean mansion of the earl of Clanricarde at Portumna stands today as an aristocratic symbol of dynastic ambition. In order to maintain his position in the quicksand politics of Charles I, Clanricarde spent most of his time and money in England, yet he managed to resist the power of Wentworth by cleverly delaying and compromising to avoid the threat of dispossession.⁷ Similarly, the earl of Antrim exploited English estate management practices to expand his castle and town of Dunluce in Ulster, adding Scots settlers and balancing the Irish, Scottish and English obligations of his far-flung possessions.⁸ Dr Canny has shown that early seventeenth-century landholders were often former soldiers and established crown officials, as well as new settlers. The natural convergence of interests within small communities was described by Canny thus: 'The intricate web of debt and obligation that bound natives and newcomers together in communities that had been refashioned by settlement is well illustrated by the list of debtors provided in the deposition of Richard Christmas, a cloth-maker', whose debtors included eight Protestants and fifteen Irish Catholics.⁹

5. T. Reeves-Smyth, *Irish castles* (Belfast, 1995), p. 64. Co. Fermanagh is dotted with these picturesque remains near Enniskillen, for example, including Crom Castle (1611, Michael Balfour), Castle Balfour (1619, Sir James Balfour), Enniskillen (1607, William Cole), Monea (1616, Revd Malcolm Hamilton) and Tully (1612, Sir John Hume).
6. Ibid., p. 24. Coppinger's Court was built after 1612 without fortification as a Jacobean mansion with hundreds of windows, nearly fifty chimneys and a Great Hall measuring 68 feet in length. The house was three storeys tall with gabled attics and elaborate machicolations for effect, surrounding an open courtyard.
7. Clanricarde was raised in England as ward of the earl of Essex, graduated from Christ Church, Oxford and fought with Mountjoy at the battle of Kinsale in 1601. He became earl in 1601 and married Frances Walsingham, widow of Essex and Sydney, adding English honours to his Irish inheritance. Portumna was completed around 1618 in the Jacobean fashion, with mullioned windows, three storeys, a large courtyard and a Great Hall measuring 87 feet in length. It was here that Wentworth threatened the Galway juries in the famed contretemps of 1638. M. MacMahon, *Portumna Castle and its lords* (Nenagh, 1983), pp. 7–8.
8. The resourceful Antrim was born in 1609 and in 1637 married Katherine, the duke of Buckingham's widow, but spent most of the time at the Caroline court trying to shore up his fortune as an improving landlord. He moved to the Ulster castle of Dunluce in 1639 with his wife, but suffered there the embarrassment of having the ancient kitchen fall into the sea, whereupon the duchess of Buckingham left for England. See J. Ohlmeyer, *Civil war and restoration in the three Stuart kingdoms: the career of Randal MacDonnell, marquis of Antrim, 1609–1683* (Cambridge, 1993), p. 68.
9. Canny, *Making Ireland British*, p. 338. Canny found settlers in Munster cooperated with each other and with the natives, learning Irish and borrowing money and materials. He added: 'Nor is this surprising since people of different religious, linguistic and national backgrounds who found themselves thrown together within the same localities quickly came to recognize the advantages of learning each other's language and cooperating in the interest of their individual profit and of communal solidarity.' Ibid., p. 454.

Dublin remained the capital of English officialdom, yet resistance to oppressive policies was most frequently sounded there by the loyal Old English families who were loath to see their traditional roles taken by arriviste clients and pensioners.[10] Further north, the town of Donegal exemplified the transitions which occurred. After the flight of the earls in 1607, the former seat of the O'Donnells was planted by Sir Basil Brooke, who modified the citadel in the style of a Jacobean mansion with a splendid banqueting hall and laid out the 'Diamond', Donegal's attractive marketplace.[11] The traveller in 1625 would have been welcomed in the earl of Thomond's famed Bunratty Castle, Co. Clare, a tower house updated with extravagant halls and gardens in which three thousand deer were said to roam. Thomond was a notable example of the more pliant among the oligarchy in Ireland, for he became a Protestant in order to safeguard his fortune. In the Co. Cork seaport of Youghal, traditional concerns about access to the quays preoccupied the municipal corporation, while the encroaching power of Richard Boyle, earl of Cork, led to a celebrated dispute in castle chamber over his rights to an ecclesiastical property in the walled town.[12] Within this volatile matrix of new settlements and competing authorities, the court of castle chamber was a barometer of change. The aggravated relations of the people living in Ireland created many opportunities for actions at law. Prior to 1640 it was this recourse to judicial solutions, more than military resistance, which increasingly characterized the Ireland of Elizabeth I and the early Stuarts.

In a recent study by Marjorie McIntosh, the arbitrary chronological boundaries of English legal history were re-conceptualized to include later medieval courts and communities which exhibited the same concern with varieties of misbehaviour that we commonly associate with Puritanism. McIntosh urges modern

10. Dr Lennon has shown that the prosecution of Dublin aldermen for recusancy in castle chamber effected a more vigorous Catholic resistance under Chichester's regime. Nonetheless, the recorder of Dublin in this period was the notable New English Protestant, Richard Bolton, who ultimately became lord chancellor under Wentworth. C. Lennon, *The lords of Dublin in the age of the Reformation* (Dublin, 1989), ch. 6, 'Recusancy and the defence of privilege, 1597–1613'. Lennon asserts that 'the response of the urban leaders to the assertion of state control in political and economic as well as ecclesiastical matters was shaped within the traditional mode of constitutional and legal procedure up to 1613 and beyond'. Ibid., p. 190.

11. Reeves-Smyth, *Irish castles*, p. 28. Brooke was granted the O'Donnell castle after the flight of the earls in 1607, remodelling it after 1623 in the English style with gabled roof and four-light mullioned windows.

12. *Corporation book of Youghal*, ed. R. Caulfield (Guildford, 1878). The corporation book preserved numerous proclamations of the Irish council requiring transgressors to be tried in the court of castle chamber. For example, violators of the proclamation against bringing gunpowder into Ireland were to answer for their offence in castle chamber after putting in security for their appearance. Ibid., p. 184. Boyle purchased the estates of Sir Walter Raleigh in Youghal and elsewhere, taking for himself the profits of the college which, in turn, led to his celebrated fine of £15,000 by the connivance of his adversary and superior, Lord Deputy Wentworth, who followed Boyle and Loftus, the lords justices, in 1633. See N. Canny, *The upstart earl; a study of the social and mental worlds of Richard Boyle, first earl of Cork, 1566 to 1643* (Cambridge, 1982), pp. 9–14.

scholars to re-consider the paradigm of Tudor and Stuart exceptionality. She points to studies of other early modern societies in Reformation Europe as models of the *longue durée*, enabling students to consider village and city life on their own terms.[13] In the case of Ireland, there is a need to escape from the seductive charms of religious division and national identity as explanatory modes when examining the past. Important as they are, high politics and crusading religion often obscure the durable realities which more typically governed the lives of most Irish men and women. Dr Gillespie has recently discussed the complex interaction that took place within local communities, and he concludes that the new power realities of early modern Ireland were subtly altered to permit the existing social order, dominated by local élites, to thrive under conditions of common law rule. Gillespie has shown that the native Irish resorted to the courts as suitors with great frequency, incorporated legal language into spoken Irish and served as sub-sheriffs, bailiffs and even justices of the peace.[14] It would be useful to analyze the fragmentary remains of local courts and councils in the early modern period, in works such as the corporation books of Youghal and Cork, to shed new light on the social history of Ireland, viewed from the bottom of society. To a limited extent, these local and personal concerns percolated up from Irish communities in the early modern period and garnered the attention of the highest tribunal, the court of castle chamber. However, the Irish star chamber jurisdiction was primarily concerned with matters of the greatest import. The current study will afford only occasional glimpses of that terra incognita for the Irish historian, ordinary life at the village level in the early modern period.

A EUROPEAN PERSPECTIVE

Early modern Ireland has rarely been systematically studied in a comparative European context.[15] While no attempt will be made here to remedy that omission,

13. M. McIntosh, *Controlling misbehaviour in England, 1370–1600* (Cambridge, 1999), pp. 1–16.
14. R. Gillespie, 'Negotiating order in early seventeenth-century Ireland' in M. Braddick and J. Walter, eds., *Negotiating power in early modern society: order, hierarchy and subordination in Britain and Ireland* (Cambridge, 2002), pp. 189, 191, 193, 199–203. Stressing the contingent nature of 'negotiated order', Gillespie argues for a more subtle and nuanced paradigm through which to view the Irish polity and its remarkable successes achieved through the expansion, and metamorphosis, of the common law. He concluded: 'The diffusion of the ideas of the common law throughout all the communities of Ireland meant that the law provided a common language through which social order could be negotiated and in some cases a venue for that negotiation in the quarter sessions or assize.' Ibid., p. 201.
15. Steven Ellis has done much to expand the historiography of Ireland recently, with forays into comparative history. See S.G. Ellis, *Tudor frontiers and noble power: the making of the British state* (Oxford, 1995); Ellis, 'The Pale and the far North: government and society in two early Tudor borderlands' (Galway, 1988) [O'Donnell lecture to National University of Ireland]; Ellis, 'Nationalist historiography and the English and Gaelic worlds in the late middle ages', *IHS*, xxv (1986), 1–18. He calls for 'modifications in the present Anglo-centric presentation of the late medieval English polity'.

we may hazard some observations with respect to the extension of royal authority to the periphery in the period under discussion. The French monarchy in 1562 was about to plunge into decades of religious war, pitting the minority Protestant Huguenots against the dominant Catholic majority, a violent and partisan blood-letting which ended only in 1598 with the settlement of the Edict of Nantes. In 1572 the Spanish throne was challenged by the Revolt of the Netherlands, another religious war in which the Dutch Protestant minority finally achieved practical independence in 1609. The Schmalkaldic War in Germany had just ended in 1555 with the Peace of Augsburg, and the long Thirty Years War (1618–1648) which so disrupted all of central Europe was still in the future. In comparison, the intermittent warfare of Elizabethan Ireland gave way to four decades of peace under James I and his successor. Seen in its larger British and European context, the court of castle chamber was apposite for the new pretensions of the Renaissance monarchy, struggling to achieve bureaucratic and constitutional hegemony in an age of sectarian conflict and rebellion. Grandiose in stature, but hampered in practice by the intrinsic limits of irregular communication and transportation, the court might be compared to the viceregal tribunals of Philip II in Brussels, or of Charles V in Vienna during the long absences of the monarch from their distant possessions. Useful comparisons might be made to the attempts by Henry IV and Richelieu to expand royal government throughout France, an incipient absolutism. However, the breakdown of French royal authority under Henry III and his predecessors would also be instructive, a sight which Elizabeth I witnessed with increasing concern from Westminster. It is important to state at the outset of this investigation that early modern Ireland was very much a part of European events and conditions; that the resistance in Ireland to anglicizing policies and institutions was mirrored in other European states which tried to impose regal power and an established religion on truculent provinces; and that the mixed results which occurred in Ireland between 1570 and 1640 were fairly typical of dynamic fluctuations in the early modern state.

Along with religious division, these late Renaissance kingdoms faced considerable resistance from distinct regions and provinces that strove to maintain their linguistic and cultural identities. Spain and its far-flung possessions required the use of provincial governors, military garrisons and sovereign courts. The development of absolutist institutions by the French monarchy in the seventeenth century was undertaken with minimal legislative opposition, a process which coincided very nearly with the Personal Rule of Charles I in England (1629–40) and the arbitrary government of Wentworth in Ireland (1633–40). Nevertheless, a proper understanding of the foundations of French royal despotism must take account of resistance from Breton, Basque, Alsatian, Flemish, Savoyard and other sources, including that of the restive Huguenots. When Ireland is compared to other European states in the period, it becomes clear that institutional expansion and religious uniformity were resisted vigorously everywhere. The process of state formation resulted in 'composite monarchies' incorporating minority populations, religions and cultures.[16] John Morrill has argued that 'Historians of these islands [Britain and Ireland] need to realise that the existence of several nations within a loosely structured polity is the norm in European history and not the exception'.[17] The difficult road to a unitary state, incorporating Ireland and Scotland along with England and Wales, was not dissimilar to the hazards encountered by the multiple kingdoms which slowly emerged on the continent.

A BRITISH PERSPECTIVE

The new British history offers another comparative perspective for the work of the early modern prerogative courts. Historians such as Steven Ellis have investigated a 'pattern of state formation' which evolved in different incarnations for each of the 'multiple kingdoms' after 1536. In particular, Ellis finds the model of southeastern England wholly unsuited to the borderlands of Britain and Ireland, which explains the bewildering array of militarized buffer zones, piecemeal annexations and marcher law that arrested the state-building process. Dr Ellis's conclusion that Ireland by 1603 had been only superficially integrated into Britain is certainly warranted. However, his judgement that tensions between the local élites and the unrepresentative cliques which dominated the Dublin government led inexorably to the crises of 1638–60 compresses too many of the tangents of subsequent history.[18] Stressing the incomplete, untidy and irritated nature of the process, John Morrill has explained that the concept of 'nation' in this period was inchoate, an imagined community which was exceedingly difficult to govern from the centre. Ellis and Morrill both cite the vulnerability of dynastic unions, and the fragility of 'horizontal comradeship' in the new composite monarchies as evidence of the unsettled nature of early modern kingship. Resistance to the development of a 'hegemonic metropolitan language' as well as legal and institutional ties was common throughout Europe, and hence state formation in Ireland should be seen as part of a European-wide process. Yet, while noting that Ireland was not visited by a British sovereign until 1689 in the early modern period, and there were no Irish coronations of Tudor and Stuart monarchs, Morrill finds the nature of Irish opposition staunchly legalistic, using unqualified respect for the processes and institutions of traditional British privileges and seeking constitutional guarantees of their liberties.[19] Irish legal history is particularly relevant to this evolving process

16. Michael J. Braddick, *State formation in early modern England, 1550–1700* (Cambridge, 2000), pp. 1–7, 16–25, 136.
17. John S. Morrill, 'The fashioning of Britain', in S.G. Ellis and S. Barber, eds., *Conquest and union: fashioning a British state, 1485–1725* (London, 1995), p. 11.
18. Ellis, 'Tudor state formation and the shaping of the British Isles' in Ellis & Barber, eds., *Conquest and union*, pp. 40, 44, 52, 56–60.
19. Morrill, 'Fashioning Britain', in Ellis & Barber, eds., *Conquest and union*, pp. 9–33. See also B. Bradshaw and J.S. Morrill, eds., *The British problem, c.1534–1707: state formation in the Atlantic archipelago* (London, 1996), pp. 1–38.

of 'incomplete estrangement and irritated coexistence' with the English monarchy.[20] The period prior to 1640 was one of interdependence and acculturation in which the centrifugal forces were gradually weakened militarily, while the judicial framework and opportunity for litigation steadily grew. Dr Canny has recently described the 'ordered conditions which prevailed in Ireland for most of the first half of the seventeenth century' which allowed the constitutional opposition among Irish Catholics to win important concessions from the Dublin administration. The outburst of violence in October 1641 'could not have been predicted even a few short months previously', and most people in Ireland were surprised by the suddenness of it.[21] Nonetheless, harmonizing the institutions of government was a hollow victory, since the tension between the divided spiritual communities in Ireland gave way to military confrontation in 1641.

THE TRANSFORMING ROLE OF THE COMMON LAW

Anglicizing the government of Tudor Ireland was complementary to similar initiatives for the principality of Wales from the latter years of Henry VIII. Nevertheless, Ciaran Brady has recently argued that the results were entirely different, owing to the resistance of the Old English of the Pale. Whereas Brady has found a quarry of Welsh expertise that veteran administrators hoped to mine for policy formation in Ireland, he challenged the assumption of Dr Quinn that 'gradual assimilation of Gaelic Ireland by means of legal and cultural reforms, similar to those applied in Wales, was being proposed in conscious opposition to alternative arguments, from outright dispossession and colonization, which were gaining ground in some circles in Elizabethan England'.[22] In contrast, Brady found that the many Irish crown officials who shared substantial experience in Wales used discordant voices in drawing blueprints for the reform of Ireland. In a cogent essay, he demonstrated the key differences among such experts as William Gerrard, Henry Sydney, James Croft and William Herbert. While admitting that Tudor Ireland had witnessed more systematic recourse to common law and appeals to English justice, Brady argued that the revival of English law and administration was 'a highly unstable process', prone to reversal and challenged by great lords as well as disgruntled Palesmen. Despite the explicit preference of English statesmen for a 'model English polity' in Ireland based on full assimilation

---

20. Morrill, 'Fashioning Britain', p. 38.
21. Canny, *Making Ireland British*, pp. 500–01. Canny rejects the notion that 'the Catholic people in Ireland were consciously working towards that outcome [rebellion]', arguing instead that 'most who remained in Ireland had been seeking rather to establish a niche for themselves within the social and governmental frameworks that had come into being in the aftermath of the Elizabethan conquest of the country'. Ibid., p. 403.
22. C. Brady, 'Comparable histories? Tudor reform in Wales and Ireland', in Ellis & Barber, eds., *Conquest and union*, p. 77.

with England, Brady concluded that the dichotomies which emerged under Elizabeth between coercion and conciliation finally led to wholesale resistance in the Tyrone Rebellion and undermined the potential for a Welsh-style condominium in politics and government. He argued that the colonizing of Irish offices by English officials and the imposition of cess finally alienated the Pale and compromised the rule of law.[23] All the strategists cited by Brady were unanimous in proposing legal remedies, from the reform of central courts and the revival of assizes, to the regular use of parliaments and the appointment of sheriffs. As we shall see, the resistance to anglicization of this sort was offset to a degree by working partnerships both in Dublin and the provinces. In the last analysis, the rule of law was unquestioned by the lawyerly constitutional opposition which formed at various times to oppose cess, the mandates and the tyranny of Wentworth.

Nevertheless, some writers have chosen to emphasize an older paradigm, that of military aggression and colonization. Despite the weight of evidence showing a general preference for the cheaper solution of common law governance, Dr Canny continues to assert the predominance of plantation and dispossession in official thinking. In his important review of Brady's work, *The chief governors*, Canny argued that the governors had dismissed the ideal of common law rule by the 1570s and thereafter worked to impose their will by arbitrary settlement, intimidation and a militarized presidency system in Munster and Connacht. Canny wrote, 'I still remain convinced that Sidney, and those associated with him, established it as a fixed principle of government that Ireland would be reformed only in the aftermath of a decisive military conquest followed by extensive plantation.'[24] Citing the work of Edmund Tremayne and Edmund Spenser as representative of official thinking, Canny denied that either man seriously believed in the relevance of English judicial norms to the reform of Irish society.[25] He reasserts the claim that Elizabethan administrators brought with them to Ireland an evangelizing Protestant bias and a commitment to proprietary colonies, notions which were quickly intensified when officials made contact with the truculent resistance of the

23. Brady, 'Comparable histories?', pp. 71–85. Brady's conclusion that the Palesmen became enemies of the state in the early Stuart period is unwarranted. They were more clearly a loyal opposition. Ibid., 85.

24. N. Canny, 'Revising the revisionist' [a review of Ciaran Brady, *The chief governors: the rise and fall of reform government in Tudor Ireland, 1536–1588* (Cambridge, 1994)], *IHS*, xxx (1996), 242–54.

25. Canny, *Making Ireland British*, ch. 1, 'Spenser sets the agenda'. Canny argues here that Spenserian fulminations against the rebel Irish constituted a serious set of proposals that levitated to grand strategy in the conservative court of Elizabeth I. While Canny is right to suggest that modern academic boundaries would have startled the Renaissance mind, it is difficult to prove the connection between Spenser's moral philosophy and Irish policymaking, just as it is hard to accept the argument he makes for 'poetry as politics', Placing Stuart policies of plantation and military conquest on the shoulders of a poet/bureaucrat who briefly held office in the provincial court of Munster during the Tyrone Rebellion is probably a weight too heavy for him to bear. This is especially true since Canny reveals that the unpublished manuscript circulated for decades before being published in 1633, when it was dedicated to Wentworth. See p. 58.

native population. He continued to argue 'that Sidney, even when he was aban-
doning his colonisation schemes and adopting temporising methods for governing
the country, still lacked confidence in the gradualist methods of his predecessors
and believed that Ireland could be reformed only in the aftermath of a miltary
conquest'.[26]

At the heart of the matter lies a fundamental truth. Common law governance
was discussed by every viceroy during the early modern period, and it was never
wholly dismissed as irrelevant to a 'contaminated' Irish society. Brady has argued
that the powerful chief governors used different means to achieve the consistent
purpose of common law rule in the provinces, although Chichester and St John
may have been more interested in profiteering.[27] The abiding question at issue was
when the Irish judicial establishment would become sufficiently mature and
confident to extend the protocols of common law governance throughout the
entire island. Since both Brady and Canny cite Tremayne as an Irish expert, and
yet draw from his work such different conclusions, we may be permitted to suggest that exasperated bureaucrats offered intemperate outbursts along with their
more reflective musings on the overarching issues which transcended day-to-day
administration. The ravings of Spenser during the crisis of war and rebellion in
1596 cannot be taken as dogma, though Canny cites his work often as a key to
Elizabethan planning.[28] Perhaps more germane in this context was the judicious
appraisal of Sir Richard Hadsor, written in 1604 after the Tyrone Rebellion,
which argued that 'justice may be duely mynistered throughout the Realme
according to the Lawes thereof by learned & sinceare Judges and Magistrates'.[29]

A study of the ideas of legal practitioners in Ireland from 1570 to 1640 might
offer new insight. Although the evidence is slender, an extensive review of
lawyers' and judges' considerations on the imposition and effectiveness of legal
remedies throughout Ireland in this period would prove a useful corrective to the
abstractions of literary men with military experience in Ireland. The occasionally
stiff constitutional opposition to royal policies in Ireland, which managed to
coexist with the steady and routine administration of justice in the countryside,
also deserves further examination. It will be instructive at that time to juxtapose
the combative idealism of Spenser with the cooperative practice of judges from

---

26. Ibid., p. 249.
27. Ciaran Brady, 'England's defence and Ireland's reform: the dilemma of the Irish viceroys,
    1541–1641' in Bradshaw & Morrill, eds., *The British problem, c.1534–1707*, pp. 91, 105–11. Brady
    sees an important hiatus in reform imperatives during the crisis of the 1590s and a military
    temperament which characterized the Jacobean viceroys, Chichester and St John.
28. Despite his preference for radical military solutions, Spenser was prepared to embrace the
    reform potential of humanist education and the common law as civilizing agents. In this manner,
    he was stating the Renaissance conventions of the Elizabethan court, concluding that 'society
    would best be reformed through the formal education of the sons of the elite'. Canny, *Making
    Ireland British*, pp. 45, 55.
29. 'Select documents XLVII: Richard Hadsor's "Discourse on the Irish state, 1604"', ed. Joseph
    McLaughlin, in *IHS*, xxx (1997), 350.

Sir Lucas Dillon to Sir Richard Bolton. Furthermore, in this case, a British perspective would be helpful. Canny argues, for example, that 'the deployment of the common law to promote reform was being questioned in official circles in Ireland' long before 1588, and cites Tremayne's fear that no Pale juries would be impartial due to 'the attachment of people there to their own narrow interests'.[30] But he has also discussed the dissension and division among the English Protestant administration itself, citing Sir Henry Wallop's observation that 'even our English that are planted to live here differ little from those that are of this country [by] birth'.[31] This apprehension could apply equally well in Devon as in Dublin, and Canny seems to rely less on anthropologically derived assumptions of cultural asymmetry for his magisterial work on Ireland before the Civil War. Finally, Tremayne's argument that soldier-settlers were no guarantee of anglicizing influence at the local level could also be used to assert the growing development of a hybrid population of Irish-influenced Englishmen whose self-interest would promote a level of security, rather than an instrument of tyranny, in the Pale and beyond it. A recent survey by Jane Ohlmeyer finds that the late Tudor efforts to extend the 'civilizing' influence of English law, education and language were largely successful by 1641and the marginal 'frontier' elements of Irish society were in decline. Despite the vitality of the Roman Catholic faith and the tentative manner in which some anglicized lords adapted to the new political milieu, the expanded English jurisdiction over most Gaelic areas prior to the Irish Rebellion was irreversible.[32] Canny has analyzed the veteran servitors on the frontier such as Nicholas Bagenal at Newry, William Piers at Carrickfergus, and Nicholas Malbie in Galway, finding that they made practical accommodations with the native élites, keeping Irish husbandmen as tenants and governing with a 'status and income such as was enjoyed by a Gaelic overlord'.[33]

Is it possible to re-imagine the early Stuart regime in the context of an 'Unrevolutionary Ireland' (with apologies to Conrad Russell)? Much has been written on the constitutional opposition to Stuart 'tyranny' in England, and Russell

30. Canny, 'Revising the revisionist', p. 247. If Tremayne were 'mouthing conventional platitudes about the efficacy of the common law in maintaining people in a civil condition', a fair analysis would give more weight to this affirmation than to the plots of private speculators whose schemes were so airy that they were sometimes transmitted orally and have hence disappeared as evidence. Ibid., pp. 248, 251.

31. Canny, *Making Ireland British*, pp. 112–13. He cites Loftus and Fenton as examples of careerist politicians who profited corruptly at the expense of the crown, noting they often cooperated with members of the Pale community and favoured recusants with preferment as an example of their 'degeneracy'. Ibid., pp. 116–17.

32. J. Ohlmeyer, '"Civilizing of those rude partes": colonization within Britain and Ireland, 1580s to 1640s,' in N. Canny and A. Low, eds., *Oxford history of the British Empire, vol. 1, Origins of the empire: British overseas enterprise to the close of the seventeenth century* (Oxford, 1998), pp. 124–45.

33. Canny, *Making Ireland British*, pp. 79–81. Piers, while closely linked to the Smith and Essex plantation projects, was also mayor of Carrickfergus and preserved good working relations with both the Gaelic and Scottish chiefs in northeast Ulster. Ibid., p. 89. Even the curmudgeonly Richard Bingham assigned both Old English and Gaelic Irish as bailiffs, tax-collectors, sheriffs and sub-sheriffs in Connacht. Ibid., pp. 96, 98.

has gone far to correct the bias toward incipient rebellion prior to 1640.[34] Draconian measures in Ireland, from the plantation of Ulster to the recusancy trials in castle chamber and the expulsion of leading Irish officials by Wentworth, indicate the sudden collapse of the Elizabethan policies of gradualism and incremental change after 1603. Aidan Clarke has shown that the lawyers and peers who sued to obtain royal sanction for the Graces were convinced of the reliability of settled law in their favour.[35] Hans Pawlisch claimed that Sir John Davies was the architect of a policy of legal imperialism which amounted to the legitimation of conquest by expropriation.[36] Hugh Kearney and, more recently, Canny, have blamed the government of Wentworth for high-handed and extra-legal Absolutist measures.[37] Yet other constitutionally dubious excesses in England and Scotland did not produce revolution, and in Ireland the underlying tensions of the society were exacerbated without leading to the expected conflagration. The clumsy failures of the Reformation in Ireland aggravated political conditions, yet the 'faith and fatherland' argument met with indifference or scepticism in most quarters.[38] Dr Russell himself has expounded on the matter, showing that the Queries proposed in 1641 to the English parliament by its sister parliament in Ireland were grounded upon assertions of common law and statute, by which they were bound and governed.[39] Despite substantial evidence that the rival communities in Ireland were becoming estranged by this point, Russell shows that they continued to pursue lawful means and sought political

---

34. C. Russell, *Unrevolutionary England, 1603–1642* (London, 1990), pp. ix–xxvi. Russell revises the 'struggle for sovereignty' concept which articulated a two-party division between court and country and saw parliament as a debating forum between opposition and government. His analysis shows many differing views and a strong royalist flavour to debates which usually occurred among courtiers. Principally, he tries to see the total picture of Stuart government, including the forces for comity as well as for dispute.

35. A. Clarke, *The Graces* (Dublin, 1976), pp. 4, 14–18, 23–24.

36. H. Pawlisch, *Sir John Davies and the conquest of Ireland: a study in legal imperialism* (Cambridge, 1985).

37. H. Kearney, *Strafford in Ireland, 1633–41: a study in Absolutism* (Cambridge, 1959); Canny, 'Anglicisation of Ireland', pp. 157–86. Dr Canny recently cited the view of James Dowdall of Queen's Co., writing before 1641, that 'both the English and the Irish lived like loving neighbours and the English mistrusted them not', as evidence that the insurrection came as a surprise to observers on all sides. Canny, *Making Ireland British*, p. 455. He has also shown the predominance in Gaelic Irish circles of Old English lawyers who opposed plantation, and relied on the crown and the courts to sustain their ancient privileges. Canny demonstrates the complexity of the Irish polity by showing that most of the Old English were conversant with the Irish language, and increasingly united through ties of marriage and commerce.

38. Michael MacCraith, 'Gaelic reaction to the Reformation', in Ellis & Barber, eds., *Conquest and union*, pp. 139 ff. See also Alan Ford, *The Protestant Reformation in Ireland, 1590–1640* (Frankfurt, 1987); Karl Bottigheimer, 'The failure of the Reformation in Ireland: *une question bien posée*', *Jn Eccl Hist*, xxxvi, no. 2 (1985), 196–207; and John MacCafferty, 'Protestant prelates and godly pastors: the dilemma of the early Stuart episcopate', paper presented at the Irish Reformation conference, University College Dublin, March, 1998.

39. C. Russell, 'The British background to the Irish rebellion of 1641', in Russell, *Unrevolutionary England*, p. 268.

gains through conventional channels. It is to be hoped that the early modern period down to 1641 can finally be judged on its own terms. Lacking foreknowledge, the disputants in Ireland under the first two Stuarts quarrelled and debated their positions with a zest borne of the assumption that their polity was secure, even if their lands were not. Decades after the end of the Tyrone Rebellion, Ireland remained tranquil, if unsettled. The road to civil war was unmapped and the angry voices raised in protest against Wentworth engaged in heated parliamentary debate rather than rousing the rabble, or conspiring against the crown. Using the paradigm of the new British history to view the archipelago as a composite kingdom, full of restive elements, we may justifiably regard early Stuart Ireland as discontented, but not alienated: in a word, 'unrevolutionary'.

THE RULE OF LAW

The rule of law in early modern England has been much discussed. While general agreement is still a distant prospect, there are certain fundamentals which inform the judgment we must make about the court of castle chamber. The court was authorized in an atmosphere which was suffused with lawyerly discussion and constitutional questions of great import. Its work continued for seventy years during a time of political tension, culminating in a rhetorical revolution against its arbitrariness. Geoffrey Elton has argued that the formation of the unitary state rested on parliamentary legislation, but 'Tudor lawyers … regarded the royal prerogative as a department of the common law, definable but not establishable by statute'.[40] He explained that the legislation governing the issuance of royal proclamations allowed sufficient flexibility to interpret the law, but denied the right to make new law. Beside the role of parliament, which added substantially to the corpus of English law, new courts were created to manage the transfer of ecclesiastical property; to offer access to legal remedy at reduced costs; to manage the wealth of heirs and heiresses; and to provide a venue for suits arising from navigation. These and other new tribunals multiplied the number of lawsuits in the century from 1540 to 1640. In addition, the number of lawyers and litigants increased exponentially. New forms of action evolved, including trespass on the case, and the increased caseload in the central courts required administrative brokering to eliminate the logjam. The growth of equity jurisdiction as managed in chancery and star chamber led to more opportunistic lawsuits; vexatious litigation was a source of much complaint. Lastly, the apparent rise in the crime rate led to the multiplication of criminal prosecutions at all levels. As Dr Brooks has suggested, it was 'a great age for lawyers'.[41]

40. G.R. Elton, 'The rule of law in sixteenth century England,' in G.R. Elton, *Studies in Tudor and Stuart politics and government, vol. 1* (Cambridge, 1974), p. 266.
41. C.W. Brooks, 'Litigants and attorneys in King's Bench and Common Pleas, 1560 to 1640' in J.H. Baker, ed., *Legal records and the historian* (London, 1978), pp. 45–46.

In the counties and towns of England, a substantial metamorphosis occurred. The courts leet and baron of manorial jurisdictions were abandoned in favour of royal courts. Ecclesiastical courts were subsumed under royal control and became instruments of a coherent state policy. E.W. Ives has found that the Tudor lawyers developed a closed society, a homogeneous and influential élite of like-minded individuals who governed in town and county as well as the metropolitan centre.[42] They shared a legal education, dominated lucrative posts and worked to achieve the prolongation of suits at all levels. James Cockburn declared that the assize courts were unique in their attempt to manage local disputes according to the constitutional norms established at Westminster. The judges visited the county towns twice yearly, operating on the basis of instructions from the lord chancellor in star chamber and thus empowered to administer a kind of official line in the provinces. Assize judges were masters of the law, above local faction and capable of hearing causes arising from inferior jurisdictions. The 'Star Chamber charge' to them amounted to a rehearsal of public policy on matters of law and order, a mandate with which to execute their responsibilities and a final source of coercion if needed for the correction of errant local officials. They were guardians of common law and tutors of the justices of the peace, and their work increased throughout the period. As 'translators of executive thinking' they were mainly successful, and the implementation of common law remedies in distant places such as Wales and the North is testimony to their effectiveness.[43] This was the model which was consciously employed in the creation of the court of castle chamber.

The court of castle chamber struggled to life after a decade of campaigning for it by two powerful chief governors, the earl of Sussex and Sir Henry Sydney. As the potent star chamber jurisdiction in Ireland, the new court was intended to provide judicial remedy at the highest level, articulating the executive and judicial roles of the Irish privy council. Charges of despotism which were levied against the court in the next century would have been untimely in the 1570s. In the first place, the court was instituted to formalize the work of the wide-ranging Elizabethan Irish council. Its caseload was reflective of this parochial mood, a reform which was designed to match the needs of a unique jurisdiction. Whether or not one accepts the view that it was inherently a colonial administration, the governing apparatus in Dublin increasingly mirrored the bureaucratic machinery in Westminster. Yet successive chief governors encountered a markedly different political culture and quickly saw the defects in using an English model to manage Irish affairs. The court of castle chamber was therefore also an instrument of change, a tool which political leaders employed in their determination to implement common law jurisdiction throughout Ireland. The wilful destruction of the Elizabethan *via media* and its delicate equilibrium can be traced in the work of the

---

42. E.W. Ives, *The common lawyers of pre-Reformation England: Thomas Kebell, a case study* (Cambridge, 1983), pp. 1–22, 194–208.
43. J.S. Cockburn, *A history of English assizes, 1558 to 1714* (Cambridge, 1972), pp. ix–xii, 5–8, 36–37.

castle chamber from 1604 to 1640. However, only the last period of its decrees under Wentworth might qualify the work of the court as tyrannical. In comparison with its continental contemporaries, the castle chamber was, more often than not, a quintessential Tudor compromise which was amended to suit the new fabric of the Stuart monarchy.

PROBLEMS OF INVESTIGATION

Unlike its parent institution in England, the Irish court of star chamber did not produce a veritable torrent of litigation during its seventy years of existence. Whereas the English star chamber records are highly routinized and ample, the documents of the court of castle chamber are surprisingly meagre and suffered from listless record-keeping.[44] The core of the court's business was the entry book, kept by the clerk and his assistants in Dublin Castle. This fragile document is now to be found among the manuscripts of the British Library in London and Appendix One of the current volume is a full record of its contents.[45] The entry

44. John Guy found that the English court's caseload increased from 150 per annum in 1547 to an apex of 732 lawsuits in the last year of Elizabeth's reign, then fell to an average of 358 per annum during James I. The archive was split into two parts after the court was abolished, and that which covered the reign of Charles I, and which also contained the entry books of orders and decrees has disappeared. The files of pleadings, interrogatories, recognizances and writs are contained in STAC 1⁻⁴ and STAC 10 in the Public Record Office, but here, too, the ravages of time have destroyed some evidence. Only STAC 10 contains miscellaneous material for the period to 1641. J. Guy, *The court of star chamber and its records to the reign of Elizabeth I* [PRO Handbooks, no. 21] (London, 1985), pp. 9, 19–29. Thomas G. Barnes has found that star chamber cases became inordinately clogged by procedural delays under Elizabeth and her successors, noting that an ordinary reading of one plea of some seven pages took over an hour of court time. T.G. Barnes, 'Due process and slow process in the late Elizabethan and early Stuart star chamber', *AJLH*, vi (1962), 236. Barnes has claimed that the original archive of star chamber was vast, consuming the work of seven under-clerks to the clerk of star chamber and teams of assistants during only 34 days of sitting each year. The books of orders and decrees are now lost, but subsequent copies from these originals would suggest that for the period 1552 to 1595 some 11 volumes of about 250 to 500 folios each summarized the work of the court. For the 1630s Barnes suggests the court may have produced two volumes of 800 folios each per year. T.G. Barnes, 'The archives and archival problems of the Elizabethan and early Stuart star chamber,' *Jn Soc Archivists*, ii (1963), 345–51. In 1608 one of the clerks turned over to his successor, Sir Francis Bacon, six calendars, one of which was in loose papers, indicating that a labyrinth of documents existed in convoluted disorder, a situation not often revealed in the official summaries which truncated much information about the court. In the same year, the clerk had four large presses of wainscot, with three partitions in each, constructed in the star chamber to hold its bountiful proceedings. The rest of the documents were kept in the court's office in Gray's Inn and have since disappeared. Given the court of castle chamber's problems with its venue and the lack of space for hearing causes, it is not surprising that a wayward lack of process vexed the compiling of its records. Ibid., 355, 360.

45. BL, Add. MS 47,172. Plate 15. The entry book is extremely fragile, its binding decayed and folios hardened to a brittle condition. The first folios are missing from the text, indicating a provenance of 1571 based on subsequent evidence dismissing several cases begun in that year in

book of orders and decrees tends to compress judicial business by omitting all the stages of deliberation except for the final order of the court. In contrast, the English star chamber records contain all the stages of pleading but often omit the culminating judgment of the tribunal. The consequence of this editorial trimming of castle chamber documents has left the researcher with several major problems. First, it is not clear how much litigation was commenced in the period that did not proceed to a final judgment of the court. Since there were many complaints about vexatious pleading, we may assume that a number of suits were begun at castle chamber which were also in litigation before other courts and which the plaintiff never intended to prosecute fully. Secondly, due to the lack of archival space in Dublin Castle, the incompetence of clerical assistants and the inattention of pluralist officeholders, the records were often dispersed, lost or removed from the court's jurisdiction. The clerks often provided only the barest details of each case, rendering the order of the court as a perfunctory formality rather than a carefully calculated rationale. Thirdly, the records show an inordinate sensitivity to political events which apparently interrupted the judicial work of the court. It must be remembered that the castle chamber was an incompletely articulated instrument of the executive body, the Irish privy council. Unlike its English parent, the Irish star chamber remained dependent on the temperament and availability of leading officials who also held military and financial roles in the government. The entry book demonstrates this interdependence in times of crisis, when the chief governor had to be involved in military campaigns, by periodic lapses of judicial activity. In fact, a long hiatus of seven years without a record in the entry book coincided with the height of the Nine Years War from 1597 to 1604. Lacking the chronicle of king's bench and other courts, we cannot simply assume that judicial work was merely transferred to other venues. Indeed, it is probable that the efforts to rule by common law were completely halted, perhaps even reversed, during this period. Finally, the clerks resorted to a convenient shorthand in their reporting of cases and thus compressed the deliberations of the judges, the filtering of evidence and the discussion of alternative outcomes into a neutered composite that refuses to yield an abundant harvest of judicial information.

   A further difficulty lies in the abrupt termination, without explanation, of the entry book in 1621. The last case recorded there was on 18 June 1621, a matter

castle chamber. The remainder of the document indicates that it lay about in a muniments room for many years, since it contains the scribbled words and graffiti of underclerks, two notes of indebtedness involving Thomas McTeige and Mr William Latties of Dublin [the latter dated in May 1660], and a reference to an earlier accusation against the clerk of the court for taking excessive fees. The worn leather binding has a curious circular emblem of uncertain origin and the title is scratched out though it may be read thus: 'Elizab__ at the ____ ____ 1570 [?] Castel Chamb __ _rela__.' There is no title page and the foliation has probably been altered five times, based on numbering of the first folio. An Elizabethan '15' appears at the top, and subsequent pages numbered 16–18 suggest a pagination of seven original folios which probably recorded several missing cases together with a title page and perhaps instructions for the court. This document was admirably calendared by Mrs Sophie C. Lomas for the Historical Manuscripts Commission in HMC, *Report on the manuscripts of the earl of Egmont*, vol. 1 (London, 1905).

involving aggravated assault against the aged mayor of Drogheda and his wife by a drunken rogue who was the younger brother of a local gentleman.[46] Aside from clerical notes regarding a debt incurred in 1660 and two fiants emanating from castle chamber fines in 1578, the entry book reveals no hint of a second volume, no reason for its sudden termination.[47] The simplest explanation, that the entry book was already a bulky 285 folios and thus substantially full, does not explain the omission to begin another one at this time. However, in 1621 certain events may help to explain the context in which this occurred. The viceregal administration of Oliver St John had come under fire from many quarters and the English privy council was already preparing his recall. Although this did not occur until the following April, the lame duck status of St John may have led to a decline in castle chamber litigation. The activist attorney general, Sir John Davies, who had authored many castle chamber indictments, left Ireland for an English appointment in 1619, but his replacement, Sir William Ryves, continued to pursue a vigorous prosecution of recusants and others. Perhaps most suggestive is the advent of the powerful commission on Irish causes which was sent to investigate multiple problems in the administration. The commission was authorized early in 1622, but it was adumbrated in England by a committee of the privy council for Irish causes which was designed to meet weekly. The correspondence in this period includes numerous Irish petitions to these commissioners, who included the former lord deputy, Chichester. One of the charges to the 1622 commission was 'To inquire into the courts of justice, and whether any causes are unduly drawn from the court to the Council table, and what is fit to be done'.[48] We may hazard a guess that this reforming group, which included the experienced legal scholar Sir Richard Hadsor, sought to improve Irish government by hearing certain causes in England. Certainly by this time a formidable array of experienced former Irish officials was resident in London and ready to assume such a role. They included the chief justices Sir James Ley and Sir Humphrey Winche, the attorney general Sir John Davies, and the clever lawyer Sir Humphrey May, who was Robert Cecil's principal advisor on Irish affairs.[49] Davies, in fact, rose to speak

46. BL, Add. MS. 47, 172, ff. 279–81.
47. Ibid., ff. 282–85. The note of a debt refers to a Mr William Latties of Dublin, dated 14 May 1660. The clerk inserted a note in Latin referring to a fine in the case of S.P. versus W.R. de Kilkenny in castle chamber on 2 September 1578. This case was not made part of the entry book, showing the existence of other litigation which did not proceed to a final conclusion. The last folios are actually part of the binding in vellum, containing clerical scribbles. The binding itself is now very stiff, the leaves crumbling with age, the vellum with some extraneous marks, holes for a leather strap and a curious circle motif repeated on the rear, showing geometrical leaf patterns evidently drawn with a compass, six leaves within a circle. There is no title on the outside of the document, indicating its existence as a clerical copy book rather than a formal public record.
48. *Cal. S.P. Ire.*, *1611–25*, p. 347. See also G.J. Hand and V. Treadwell, eds., 'His majesty's directions concerning the ordering and settling of his courts in Ireland, 1622', *Anal Hib*, no. 26 (1970), 179–212.
49. *Cal. S.P. Ire.*, *1611–25*, p. 354. See the recent article by Victor Treadwell, 'New light on Richard Hadsor, I: Richard Hadsor and the authorship of "Advertisements for Ireland", 1622/3', *IHS*,

on Irish affairs frequently during the parliament of 1621. It is worth noting that two other council books were ended at roughly the same time. A council book for the president and council of Munster was begun 20 August 1601 and the last case recorded was on 18 October 1620.[50] And the digest of the Irish privy council proceedings, commenced under Fitzwilliam in 1571, incorporated materials from other extant council books. This council book ended when St John, as Viscount Grandison was lord deputy in 1619.[51]

Fortunately, the records of the court of castle chamber are supplemented by a digest of its activities, made apparently for the incoming lord deputy, Thomas Wentworth, about the time of his appointment in 1632. Manuscript 852 in Trinity College Dublin contains an eclectic mix of early Stuart documents, bound together and described on the spine as 'Star-Chamber Tryals &c'.[52] The first folio is a petition to the king from John Elliott, containing pregnant references to the forced loan, the right to tax without the consent of the Commons, and other matters. The following folios deal with the calling of a parliament under Charles I, including forms of writ for the creation of a peer, the use of proxies, the correct order and descent of the upper house, and very precise instructions on how to proceed in reading of a bill and enrolling acts of parliament. The royal proclamation of 1 October 1625 which re-authorized the court of castle chamber is fully transcribed in the document, commanding the court to meet two days each week during the four legal terms, with extensive notes on the procedural basis for its adjudication. Following the articulation of all writs and fees of the court, folio 81 begins an extensive summary of its work, organized by topic. This important archive contains missing details of the judicial record from 1621 until 1632, as well as many references to cases which were more fully reported in the entry book. Following upon this, and without editorial comment, the document contains a form for Thomas Preston to be created Ulster King of Arms in Ireland in the presence chamber at 'Castle Chamber of Dublin', dated 1 November 1633. After detailing the role and responsibility of the herald king of arms, the document explains the use of certain writs, mainly ecclesiastical in nature, procedures for taking of recognizances, filing bills and pleadings, and other clerical details.[53]

The provenance of the document is unexplained, although it contains matters that would be critical to the new administration of Wentworth and his personal

xxx (1997), 305–36, for a review of his involvement in reform proposals and his advocacy of moderate judicial courses.

50. BL, Harleian MS 697, a book of some 208 folios.

51. BL, Add. MS 4792, ff. 136–44. For a fuller discussion see D.B. Quinn, ed., 'Calendar of the Irish council book 1581–1586' in *Anal Hib*, no. 24 (1967), 93–105. Ware's Chronicle of Ireland includes some of this material, collected in an arbitrary fashion, in BL, Add. MS 4813.

52. TCD, MS 852. The document is a bound volume containing some 153 folios referring to the holding of parliament, to the court of castle chamber and to ecclesiastical causes, which were then heard by a commission which the lord deputy customarily convened. Wentworth was chosen to be lord deputy as early as January 1632, but he did not arrive in Ireland until July 1633.

53. TCD, MS 852. Plate 16.

secretary, Sir Philip Perceval. The last case which was summarized for the new lord deputy was heard on 13 June 1632, one of significant portent. The defendants were fined, pilloried and imprisoned for having resisted arrest by the sheriff of Co. Westmeath, throwing great stones and hot water on the sheriff's party from the castle of Moyvanan.[54] The handwriting of the documents is not entirely consistent, so they may have been bound together at a later time, but the notation on the binding which refers to star chamber trials would suggest a more ample repository than the 19 folios of case work. The explicit references to castle chamber are many, yet the total of 153 folios has only about 25 folios on the court. The proclamation and the digest of cases have been transcribed as Appendix Two of this volume and they may be compared with cases in the entry book. For the most part, each case digest is a less formal compression of the judicial language of the original decree which omits some detail. Nonetheless, it is an invaluable supplement to the original entry book. The accuracy of the copies may be measured by comparing them with the fuller records still extant in the entry book. One case of 19 November 1602 shows that the apparent hiatus of judicial activity in the entry book itself from 1597 to 1604 did not mean that the court of castle chamber suspended its work.[55] Plainly, some of its final adjudication did not appear in the record of orders and decrees, along with a substantial portion of the pleadings of petitioners. The editing of cases also followed a didactic purpose for prospective judges who might refer by topic to the summary of castle chamber prosecutions. The original foliation and arrangement of cases have been followed in Appendix Two in order to articulate the logic of clerical and judicial decision-making. Since the total of 25 folios is evidently an abstract of the court's work (the entry book contains 285 folios, by comparison) there is no obvious way to assess the burden of its litigation in the period after 1621. Nonetheless, a memorandum to Dorchester penned about 1630 claimed that the castle chamber was 'abused for private ends' and spoke of a 'list of cases now pending in the court, being about 1,200 in number, "most of them of great consequence and very foul", which are and have been discountenanced'.[56] The existence of a second entry book is not mentioned and it has not come to light, although the summaries must have been taken from such a document in 1632. Oddly, the entry book and other key documents of the English court of star chamber are also missing from the archives for this period.

Wentworth intended to systematize Irish administration, and it is unlikely that his clerical staff failed to maintain an entry book of orders and decrees for the court of castle chamber. The absence of such a record may be explained by his sudden departure and the crises of the 1640s, but other sources do not refer to

54. Ibid., f. 84.
55. Ibid., f. 81.
56. *Cal. S.P. Ire., 1647–60*, p. 172. The anonymous note was described as 'A Brief Collection for His Highness' high court of castle chamber'. Asserting the benefits of the court for causes which the common law 'cannot take hold of', the author claimed plaintiffs were 'wresting and terrifying the poor' and finally compounding with delinquents without licence, abruptly ending suit with a loss to the crown of £1,000 a year in revenue.

such a document. Consequently, the last decade of the court's existence is full of paradox. While the lord deputy was frequently accused of tyrannical manipulation of the prerogative court for his own ends, there are only patchy judicial records from this period.[57] And the extensive documentation surrounding the case of Richard Boyle, earl of Cork, who was charged with misappropriation of ecclesiastical funds from the college of Youghal, belies the fact that his expected trial in the court of castle chamber never progressed beyond the initial stages of pleading.[58] Wentworth's arbitrary dismissal of officials such as Mountnorris and Loftus took place at the privy council but did not involve castle chamber adjudication. In the Mountnorris case he used the dubious venue of a court martial to find the financial officer guilty of treason. One of the few extant examples of castle chamber adjudication involved the Black Oath, a Wentworth expedient designed to humble Presbyterians into submission to the royal will. This decision was reversed on appeal by the English parliament after Wentworth's fall, and the besieged prerogative court became extremely edgy during the crisis of 1640–41.[59] Since all the members of the post-Wentworth court and council were charged with maladministration and summoned to England for a hearing, it is unlikely that the regular judicial terms were being followed. Indeed, when the English prerogative courts were formally abolished by parliament in the next year, the court of castle chamber was left untouched, perhaps a mark of its moribund and attenuated status. Strangely, and in spite of the furor over its proceedings, this royal court was allowed to lapse into desuetude during the heated atmosphere of the War of the Three Kingdoms.

In spite of the lack of an entry book for the important Wentworth regime in Ireland, we may use other documents for information regarding the court of castle chamber. There were many petitions presented to the lord deputy and Wentworth apparently read them with some diligence, penning his name to orders which were formulated by the clerks of the court. Three such petition books have been found which throw new light on the judicial temperament of the chief governor.[60] In each of them, Wentworth is seen as a reliable source of justice and fairness, one to whom petitioners might come for judicial remedy that was

---

57. Hugh Kearney and others have steadfastly argued that Wentworth increased the use of castle chamber and relied more heavily on conciliar government at the expense of the common law. Kearney, *Strafford in Ireland*, pp. xvii, 70–74.
58. Chatsworth, Lismore MSS, vol. 18, item 29: warrant from Wentworth dated 22 September 1634 ordering the earl of Cork to appear in castle chamber. After two years of delay, the earl agreed to pay a fine in lieu of trial and settled with the lord deputy in June 1636. Item 133, ff. 1–6.
59. Marsh's Library, Dublin, MS Z.3.2.6, item 116, p. 327; and item 117, p. 329, ordering the reversal of the castle chamber decree by the House of Lords dated 9 September 1642. The plaintiffs Henry Stewart and James Grey were awarded £1,500 by way of fine and the judges in castle chamber forced to pay damages.
60. BL, Harleian MS 4297, a petition book of 1634; BL, Harleian MS 430, a petition book of 1637; and NAI, MS 2448, a petition book of 1638. The latter volume in the National Archives in Dublin was purchased at Sotheby's in 1938 and was then described as 'Petitions and Decisions in Irish Law Courts 1638'. MS 2448A is a brief calendar of the petitions.

unavailable at common law. He commanded action in every case, from referral to a commission of inquiry to submission at the court of castle chamber. The enigmatic wording of these orders indicates that the lord deputy may have sought judicial flexibility in choosing the appropriate venues for further action at law. In October 1633 Wentworth signed an order in regard to a petition of Sir Henry Bealing for lands in Co. Wicklow, saying 'Let this petition bee delivered to the Clerke of the councell whome wee require to present it unto us at the Councell table and there wee will take the requests of it into our further consideracon'.[61] His predecessors had signed similar orders in the past, and these petition books are only oblique evidence for the work of castle chamber. Nonetheless, they show a continuous and systematic recourse to remedies at law and a rigorous review of administrative malfeasance. In that respect, the aims and policies of the court of castle chamber were given effect, regardless of whether adjudication was initiated before the court itself. However, it is possible to interpret the extensive judicial labours of Wentworth in another way. Demanding that petitioners 'appear before us at the Councill table' may have meant that the chief governor intended to function as a new incarnation of the medieval justiciar, dispensing justice by virtue of the royal will and convening a court without reference to the formality of castle chamber.[62] The impression of a tyrannical instrument in the hands of a bombastic satrap as viceroy is the legacy of both the historical record and the interpretations of that record by generations of scholars. In order to fill in the judicial profile of the court, it is therefore necessary to comb the records of its actors, from Wentworth himself to his rivals in office such as Richard Boyle, earl of Cork, and Adam Loftus, Viscount Ely, lord chancellor. The extensive self-justifying narratives which remain allow us to view the work of the court through a skewed and distorting mirror. But it is all we have.

An assortment of ancillary documents helps us to explain the role of the court of castle chamber, but here again unsystematic record-keeping, compounded by the accident of survival, compels us to see the court obliquely, through partisan accounts and subsequent accusations rather than a trove of court archives. Aside from the petition books for the tenures of chief governors Wentworth, Chichester and Falkland and fragments from the governments of Sydney and Perrot, we have the Acts of the Privy Council of England.[63] The latter is a very full record of proclamations, letters, orders and decrees which reflects a surprisingly active role in Irish affairs. At crucial times, and for extraordinary purposes, the English privy council simply took over the managements of Irish lawsuits for political reasons.

61. BL, Harleian MS 4297, f. 130v.
62. Ibid., f. 3. In the instant case of 23 June 1634 Wentworth may have intended to complete the work of an ecclesiastical court, in advance of the creation of the High Commission in Ireland on a permanent basis.
63. *Acts of the privy council of England*, new ser., vols. 7–28, for the reign of Elizabeth I. BL, Add. MSS 11033 and 18824 contain letter books of Lord Deputy Falkland; TCD, MS 746 is a letter book of Chichester for 1612–14; and the Sidney and Perrot papers have been published in *Analecta Hibernica* (see items in Bibliography).

During the reign of James I, the new commission for Irish causes siphoned Irish business to a special committee of the privy council, and its work is indifferently recorded in the state papers for Ireland.[64] Whereas the state papers are virtually complete for much of the period 1584 to 1640, the acts of the privy council are an unsatisfactory record of conciliar business for the early Stuarts. The privy council in Ireland has left a very slender account of itself, apart from the Council Book of Sussex and Sydney in the Royal Irish Academy for 1556 to 1571. Subsequent council books now survive only through calendars and these are too limited to allow an analysis of castle chamber litigation, apart from the recognizances taken in that court.[65] Finally, private family papers give a strongly parochial view of litigation, especially the rival archives in Derbyshire and Yorkshire, the Boyle manuscripts at Chatsworth and the Wentworth Woodhouse archive in Sheffield.[66]

This brings us to the crux of a constitutional question of great importance. When was the membership of the court of castle chamber not practically identical to the Irish privy council? We can surmise that proceedings heard before the council, whether in castle chamber or at council table, were judicial hearings and must be assessed as part of the overall conciliar jurisdiction which embraced both prerogative courts. In a petition brought before the court of castle chamber in 1635, making note of a prior hearing at that court, the petitioner cited the writs of habeas corpus as 'orders of the Councell Table and Courte of Starrchamber graunted to your peticoner', and later referred to another order of the 'Councell board & Castle Chamber' in the same document.[67] Wentworth signed the document and ordered, 'Lett this Peticon bee presented at ye Councell Table' on 12 July 1637.[68] The petition of an insider, John Dobb, who was marshal of the court of castle chamber offers another view of the reciprocal jurisdictions and identities of these two courts. He had been fined £10 for permitting a 'sudden noyse & rumor' during a hearing of the court by some indiscreet and disordered

---

64. Special committees and councils of war preceded, on an ad hoc basis, the formation of a committee for Irish causes of the English privy council. The Irish commission of 1622 led to this formalization, explained in detail by V. Treadwell, *Buckingham and Ireland, 1616–1628: a study in Anglo-Irish politics* (Dublin, 1998), pp. 190–211. The 'standing commission in England for Irish affairs' was established on 9 May 1623. See Treadwell, 'Richard Hadsor', 323.

65. RIA, MS 24 F. 17, transcribed by J.T. Gilbert in HMC, *Haliday MSS*, i. David Quinn published the 'Calendar of the Irish council book for 1581–86' in *Anal Hib*, no. 24 (1967), 93–180. The Ware manuscripts in the British Library, BL, Add. MS 4792, contain a very slender calendar of privy council activity and are practically mute on its judicial functions. A copy of the earlier red council book, ending in 1609, may be found in TCD, MS 843, pp. 3–20, along with a spare index by William Usher of conciliar activity commenced in the reign of James (n.d.) and extending to the Wentworth regime. TCD, MS 843, pp. 21–39. Neither document contains material relevant to the court of castle chamber, but the red council book originally ran to 372 folios and the successor document was at least 209 folios in length.

66. Chatsworth, Lismore MSS 1396–1774, 30 vols.; Sheffield City Library, Wentworth Woodhouse Muniments, Strafford Papers, vols. 24–25.

67. BL, Harleian MS 430, f. 57.

68. Ibid.

persons, but he protested that the disturbance was occasioned by the unruly behaviour of the guard at the door of the court, in the employ of the councillors themselves. Dobb claimed that he had been sick and was himself absent, noting in passing the 'great throng & multitude of people then in & aboute the said Court' as reason for the disquiet. Wentworth referred a decision about this castle chamber matter to the 'Councell table' for further direction.[69] Apparently, then, few distinctions were practicable between these two institutions. The membership was nearly identical, although the court might occasionally be strengthened by the addition of more junior members of the bench, and rarely used the military councillors in its deliberations. Since the work of the court was so closely aligned with that of the council board, it is important to use the records of both venues simultaneously, if not interchangeably.

The disputed reconstruction of events in this important period has suffered from the perception that the causes of the civil war and revolution must be sought in the records of Elizabeth I and the early Stuarts. When Patrick Darcy, the celebrated Galway lawyer and constitutional theorist, looked back upon Irish legal history in 1642 and conceived of a distinct sovereign jurisdiction, he was greatly influenced by the charged atmosphere of the moment.[70] The judicial reasoning of Sir John Davies, who came to the opposite conclusion in the first decades of the century, was conditioned by the demands of post-war reconstruction.[71] On the other hand, both men were actively engaged in the judicial work of the court of castle chamber and other tribunals, and it is in their routine, steady and unspectacular business that we might look for the impact of the common law on the Irish polity. Much has been made of the theatrical pronouncements of observers such as Barnaby Rich, but we may learn more from the correspondence of judicial drones like the careerists Dominic Sarsfield, Viscount Kilmallock, or Thomas Jones, archbishop of Dublin, both of whom spent many years on the bench in Ireland.[72] The

---

69. Ibid., f. 69v.
70. A. Clarke, 'Patrick Darcy and the Queries', in Jane Ohlmeyer, ed., *Political thought in seventeenth-century Ireland* (Cambridge, 2000), p. 47. See the new edition of the Queries in 'Patrick Darcy, an argument', ed. C.E.J. Caldicott, *Camden miscellany: xxxi*, Camden Soc., 4th series, vol. 44 (London, 1992), p. 191.
71. See, for example, Bodl., Carte MS 61, ff. 67–67v, in which Davies probably authored a defence of castle chamber proceedings against the recusants; and f. 83 where Ellesmere and Bacon respond to Davies on the proper course of proceeding in recusancy cases before castle chamber. His argument on impositions famously defended the prerogative rights of the crown. See TCD, MS 651, ff. 1–31. The definitive account is Hans Pawlisch, *Sir John Davies and the conquest of Ireland: a study in legal imperialism* (Cambridge, 1985).
72. Andrew Hadfield and John McVeagh, eds., *Strangers to that land: British perceptions of Ireland from the Reformation to the Famine* [Ulster editions and monographs, 5] (Gerrards Cross, Bucks., 1994) offers excerpts from Davies, Rich, Spenser and others, showing the animus of English observers against a supposed Irish barbarism. Sarsfield and Jones, on the other hand, represented an entrenched English interest in Ireland which sought the elusive *modus vivendi* and preferred their well-established family estates, often at the expense of the crown. See *Cal. S.P. Ire., 1611–25*, p. 98; and *1625–32*, pp. 133, 139–43.

remarkable tenures of two men named Adam Loftus as lords chancellor in Ireland gave continuity to the judicial hierarchy in this period, and yet both have been dismissed as egotistical, self-interested enemies of reform. The papers of Richard Bolton, the last lord chancellor in this period, sought to defend the peremptory judgements of the Wentworth court, but his work should be consulted along with that of Darcy, his adversary, to provide a balanced account of the pre-revolutionary context of the Irish judiciary. Bolton's painstaking digest of common law actions for the use of justices of the peace instanced punishments for the crimes of stealing cloth from a market booth; for killing a man by 'witchcraft, enchantment, charmes and sorcery'; and for riot committed in the cutting and carrying away of corn, or plowing in a close.[73] It is the aim of this volume to provide a more intensive reflection on the work of the Irish judges and the impact of the common law in Ireland in the seventy-year existence of the court of castle chamber. While the records are too uneven to permit a definitive account of its work, a judicial *longue durée*, we may reach some conclusions about the underlying constitutional basis for the kingdom of Ireland as well as the extent of common law rule in this period. At the local and provincial level, the surviving records of judicial activity for this era are scant. Nevertheless, we may use the evidence from the presidency system, the corporation books, and family papers to sketch the history of the court of castle chamber and its erratic performance in the enforcement of judicial decrees.

73. Richard Bolton published *A justice of the peace for Ireland* in 1638 (Dublin, Society of Stationers), the same year in which he joined in the dismissal of Lord Chancellor Adam Loftus, Viscount Ely, whom he replaced. Bolton was also impeached by the House of Commons in Ireland while he was speaker of that body and was thereupon suspended as a privy councillor. See F.E. Ball, *The judges in Ireland, 1121–1921*, 2 vols. (London, 1926), i, 331. See also Bolton's notes on litigation in the form of *aides memoire* in Armagh Public Library, fols. 1–46. These memoranda add little to the corpus of castle chamber cases, apart from notes on the subornation and corrupt verdicts of jurors and the prosecution of weavers in 1637. Bolton cited a proclamation of 21 December 1636 (not found in Steele) requiring all [weavers to produce woollens and 'frizes' of greater breadth, and six] weavers and merchants from Co. Wexford were (presumably) indicted in castle chamber; five of them were found guilty of producing or possessing the narrower cloth and censured after May 1637: Arm.Pub.Lib., Bolton papers, ff. 12, 16. Two similar proclamations of 30 June 1635 and 31 January 1637 required accused transgressors to appear before the court of castle chamber, or council board. R. Steele, *Tudor and Stuart proclamations, 1485–1714* (Oxford, 1910), ii, 35–36.

Part One

The world of the court: the Irish star chamber
in its judicial context

CHAPTER ONE

The court system in Ireland, 1571 to 1641

> The cheeffe thinge wantinge in that countrye is cyvillitye, and dutyfull obe-
> dience of the people to their soveraigne, which groweth partly through a desyre
> in the principall kindreds and septes to shake off all forreigne obedience and to
> governe acordinge to their owne lawes, which is their owne willes.
>
> John Dymmok, *A treatise of Ireland*.[1]

THE RULE OF LAW in early modern England was widely accepted as cardinal
doctrine, defined as a consistent and uniform reliance upon law and law-
determined processes, according to the late Dr Elton.[2] The concept embraced the
court system, the crown and the parliament, and there was substantial agreement
that prerogative justice, usually exercised in the form of royal proclamations, was
an appropriate use of sovereignty acting within legal boundaries. The court of
castle chamber, or star chamber in Ireland, was erected in about 1571 to manage
the judicial responsibilities of the Irish privy council in a more systematic fashion.
In order to study the prerogative court of castle chamber, it will be necessary to
sketch the court system in Ireland, and its relations with England, within which
this new tribunal acted. In Ireland, there was a clear intent to model the judicial
framework throughout the country on the more sophisticated court structure in
England. By the reign of Elizabeth, the four central courts of chancery, queen's
bench (or chief place, as it was sometimes called), common pleas and exchequer
were well-established, and certain Pale families like the Dillons dominated the
bench. The personnel of these tribunals resembled that of the English courts,
including the lord chancellor and master of the rolls, the two chief justices and
the chief baron of the exchequer. Unlike their English counterparts, however, all
of these men were also privy councillors in Ireland and as such constituted the
core of legal opinion available to the Irish privy council when it proceeded to
adjudication. They were assisted by the attorney general, the solicitor general and
the serjeant at law, as well as by second justices and barons in each of the courts.
In what follows, as Part One of this work, the judicature in which the court of
castle chamber operated during its seven decades of existence will be outlined,

---

1. John Dymmok, *A treatise of Ireland*, ed. by Richard Butler for the Irish Archaeological Society
   (Dublin, 1842), p. 6. Dymmok, apparently an Englishman attending Essex as lord lieutenant,
   wrote the essay about 1600. The original is now BL, Harleian MS 1291.
2. G.R. Elton, 'The rule of law in sixteenth century England', in Elton, ed., *Studies in Tudor and
   Stuart politics and government*, vol. i (Cambridge, 1974), p. 260.

along with the judicial personality of the court. While chief governors exerted a powerful influence, other officials also had a surprisingly effective role. A profile of the litigants and litigation before the court will conclude Part One, along with a summary of constitutional issues raised by the lawyerly opposition to the court at critical stages in its development.

THE CENTRAL COURTS

The centrality of the court of castle chamber within an expanding judicial matrix in Ireland allows us to view two concurrent operations between 1571 and 1641: (1) the framework of common law jurisdictions, which tended to remain stable; and (2) the steady growth of a parallel court structure, largely prerogative in nature, such as the courts of wards and admiralty, the commissions of defective titles and ecclesiastical, or high, commission which were then under way. Since the castle chamber court was the judicial arm of the Irish privy council and commonly met with either chief governor or the lord chancellor, or both, in attendance, it was the most powerful tribunal in Ireland. The court was given responsibility for the juridical superintendence of other courts in Ireland, from the commissions of the peace and municipal corporations to the provincial presidencies and the new courts of admiralty and wards. Consequently, it is necessary to review the legal infrastructure in Ireland in order to gain a sense of the court's unusual position at the head of government. In the constellation of common law and prerogative tribunals in Ireland, the court of castle chamber occupied a pre-eminent role. And, as conciliar authority expanded throughout Ireland, both the physical territory and the levels of judicial sophistication over which the court exercised authority grew alongside it. When the first blows were struck in the uncivil wars of the 1640s, the Irish judiciary was a fairly complete replica of the English system, a silhouette that concealed the deficient administration of the inferior courts.

The court of the lord chancellor in Ireland mirrored that of the English chancery, but the role of this senior official in Irish government loomed larger than that of his English counterpart.[3] By contrast, the new office of secretary of state in Ireland, established in 1560, failed to develop a parallel authority and remained largely subordinate to more senior officials, despite the management of an increasing flow of correspondence. As a result, Irish politics was in an arrested state of development, and the lord chancellor concentrated both titular and actual power as second in command to the viceroy. The chancellor was routinely chosen to serve the function of lord justice in the absence of the chief governor, and this complementary executive role frequently compromised relations with new viceroys. During the history of the court of castle chamber, the chancellors grew more powerful and more combative. In part, this judicial animosity grew out of

3. For an extensive account of chancery, see W.J. Jones, *The Elizabethan court of chancery* (Oxford, 1967).

the parallel jurisdictions of the two courts, since both used the principles of equity to resolve suits and thus relied heavily on the discretionary authority of the lead judge, the notorious 'length of the chancellor's foot'. The remarkable double tenure of the two English lord chancellors who shared the same name, Adam Loftus, archbishop of Dublin, and his namesake, Viscount Ely, was marked by their aggressive ambitions as powerful members of the New English élite. Both quarrelled with their respective successors as chief governor, and both witnessed the downfall of their nemeses, Perrot and Wentworth, after launching campaigns of vituperation and outright hostility. As we shall see, the parallel jurisdictions of chancery and castle chamber led to frequent appeals to the crown, occasionally undermining respect for both institutions in the process.

The chancery court was led by the lord chancellor, or in his absence, the lord keeper, and the master of the rolls. Clerical staff were limited to the clerks of the hanaper and the crown and the masters in chancery, so the opportunities for ample patronage at the court were limited. The master of the rolls took custody of the patent and close rolls, the fiants and inquisitions and other returns to chancery, and the commissions, decrees, bills, answers, replications and rejoinders of the court.[4] The tendency of clerks to hold offices in tandem, combining their responsibilities in other courts, was probably continued in the later Tudor period as it had been prior to 1534.[5] The Irish chancery followed the English example in offering exceptional judicial remedy, where fairness dictated an alternative to the more rigid practice of the common law. Consequently, equity jurisdiction was less routinized, rules of evidence were less formal, and litigants were admitted to plead without special writs, commencing by the simpler bill of complaint. This informality also dispensed with jury trial and permitted the liberal use of commissions of *dedimus potestatem*, deputizing minor officials and others to obtain evidence and hear testimony away from Dublin. Weaker and poorer litigants were attracted to the venue, but the opportunity for corruption led to numerous petitions to the crown and challenges in the Irish court of castle chamber throughout the period.[6] A recent essay by Mary O'Dowd has demonstrated that the Irish chancery court heard suits from female litigants in some 22% of its cases, the majority in conjunction with a husband. Vulnerability and ignorance of the law were frequently alleged in order to gain access to the equity jurisdiction of the court, with its speedier process unencumbered by arcane protocols. Ironically, the Irish chancery chose to enforce a strict interpretation of the common law instead of using the wider latitude of equity in order to assure Irish women protection of their property rights.[7] A promising study of early Stuart records of

---

4. S.G. Ellis, *Reform and revival: English government in Ireland, 1470–1534* (London, 1985), p. 166.
5. Ibid., p. 171
6. See K. Nicholls, 'A calendar of salved chancery proceedings concerning Co. Louth', *Louth Arch Soc Jn*, xviii (1972), 112–20.
7. M. O'Dowd, 'Women and the Irish chancery court in the late sixteenth and early seventeenth centuries', *IHS*, xxxi (1999), 472, 476–79, 485.

the Irish court of chancery was recently begun by Dr Jane Ohlmeyer, whose preliminary conclusions found a total of 1,135 litigants in the period 1627–1634 appearing before a well-trained Protestant bench.[8]

The lord chancellor sought to increase the business of his court and frequently was regarded as a proprietary champion who brought cases within his purview that more properly belonged to other jurisdictions. As a result, judicial oversight of the court was extended, not infrequently, by the crown and the court of castle chamber. In 1627 the king wrote to the viceroy to provide for a trial in chancery of the dispute between the earl of Ormonde and Captain Thomas Butler over the profits of two manors, commanding that the chancellor and master of the rolls be joined by the two chief justices, the chief baron and Justice Sibthorpe for the hearing. Though he commanded the parties to be satisfied with the decision, the king wrote again five years later to sanction another commission to resolve the issue, demonstrating that chancery decisions, even those enhanced by the presence of the senior bench, were not ultimately authoritative for wealthy and persistent litigants.[9] The chancellor himself was compelled to seek redress from the crown in 1629 to defend his reputation against his detractors, coming directly to England and obtaining royal favour. As a consequence, the court of castle chamber was required by Charles I to hear an action of slander and false information against the enemies of the chancellor, the king declaring:

> we being tender to the reputation of our good officers and servants, and knowing it to be our part to give them protection and punish false aspersions against them, do hold it very just and fit that all those that have preferred any scandalous and false informations or charges against our Chancellor, for his carriage in the execution of his office, be proceeded against in our High Court of Castle Chamber, and punished according to their demerits, and as by our laws in cases of that nature is provided.[10]

In a chancery case of 1618, the manor of Drimnagh Castle in Co. Dublin was contested by Sir Adam Loftus, by then master in chancery, against Peter Barnewall, based on a feoffment contracted in May 1597. The court of castle chamber became involved when Peter was accused of bribing a witness against his cousin, James Barnewall. The two courts thus shared the judicial record during extensive depositions taken in chancery pursuant to the settlement, showing the interdependence of the courts and the ways in which they could be manipulated to the advantage of a litigant with deep pockets.[11] Sir John Davies, commenting

---

8. J. Ohlmeyer, 'Records of the Irish court of chancery: a preliminary report for 1627–34', in D.S. Greer and N.M. Dawson, eds., *Mysteries and solutions in Irish legal history* (Dublin, 2001), pp. 30, 38.

9. *Cal. pat. rolls Ire., Chas. I*, pp. 281, 651. See Dr Edwards's essay, 'Poisoned chalice', pp. 64–69, for the struggles of the imprisoned Catholic earl of Ormond to maintain his estate.

10. *Cal. pat. rolls Ire., Chas. I*, p. 464

11. *Cal. pat. rolls, Ire., Jas. I*, pp. 327–29. The wily Loftus used his position to influence proceedings,

on this issue of shared responsibility in equity, said, 'Doth not the Kinges Councell of Estate & his highe Court of Chauncerie give a more speedy and sumary hearing unto the Causes of Merchantes then unto ye causes of others Subiectes.'[12]

Though his predecessors were often undistinguished, Lord Chancellor Sir William Gerrard took office in 1576 as part of the reforming milieu associated with Sir Henry Sydney, and immediately took stock of the judiciary. His caustic assessment of the veteran magistrates found them corrupt, partisan and frequently too ill to be of service to the crown. Gerrard used the office of chancellor to commence a sweeping reform of the judiciary, hearing all cases in chancery during his first year in office, but his energetic initiatives were blunted by the cess controversy and the onset of the Munster Rebellion, and he died in 1581.[13] The next opportunity for innovation came after the Nine Years War and it was sponsored by Lord Deputy Chichester, not the incumbent archbishop, Adam Loftus. As McCavitt has shown, assizes were systematically introduced throughout Ireland beginning in 1605 and quickly became a burden to the central judges as well as a popular venue for Irish landowners.[14] The noted controversy between chancery and common law over the status of equity jurisdiction was not played out in Ireland, although the lofty position taken by Lord Chancellor Ellesmere on the Jacobean assertion of prerogative law would have supported the ambitions of Chichester as viceroy against his detractors.[15] By 1628, the king wrote to Falkland that the court of chancery needed another examinator, in conformity with the English court, one for the plaintiff and another for the defendant, acknowledging that 'now peace has brought [more] litigation'.[16] Instead of the chancery, it was the court of castle chamber which became a lightning rod for opposition, based on its frequent assertion of crown rights to purveyance and the need for religious uniformity. At the end of the period, Lord Deputy Wentworth employed the court of castle chamber to intimidate his rivals and obtained the political downfall of the lord chancellor, installing his own client in the office by 1639.

despite the ample depositions in the case showing the property was enfeoffed to Maurice O'Cullen but regained by the Barnewalls. The clerk's order stated, 'Here follows the order for the publication of the depositions, as also for the interchange of evidence for the use of the castle-chamber and the court of chancery.— 26 May 15th [JamesI]' i.e. 1618. Ibid., p. 329. On 6 May 1618 Loftus obtained an injunction in chancery prohibiting Peter Barnewall from disturbing his possession of the ancient Barnewall manor pursuant to his 99-year lease of the property from the heirs of Marcus Barnewall. Ibid., p. 425. Plate 4.

12. TCD, MS 651, f. 24.
13. PRO, SP 63/56/105; LPL, Carew MS 628, ff.311v–14; 'Report on the state of Ireland by Lord Chancellor Gerrard', ed. C. McNeill, *Anal Hib*, no. 2 (1930), 93–291.
14. J. McCavitt, '"Good planets in their several spheares"; the establishment of the assize circuits in early seventeenth century Ireland,' *Ir Jur*, xxiv (1989), 248–78.
15. L. Knafla, *Law and politics in Jacobean England: the tracts of Lord Chancellor Ellesmere* (Cambridge, 1977), p. 68. Ellesmere took the view that the king could act by virtue of his private will and judgment, an exalted conception of royal power, mitigated in practice by inherited law that he was obliged to uphold. Ibid., pp. 70–73.
16. *Cal. S.P. Ire., 1625–32*, p. 308.

The court of castle chamber was, of course, the executive council acting in its judicial capacity, so it is no surprise that the court exercised an appellate role in its handling of litigation. Indeed, as the court extended its authority more fully to include the furthest counties in Ireland, it also expanded its superintendence over provincial jurisdictions and even the senior tribunals in Dublin. However, this claim of a right to judicial review did not afford the court of castle chamber genuine autonomy, for the English privy council demanded frequent accounting of its actions and occasionally reprimanded the Irish council for taking unauthorized steps. In rare cases, decisions rendered by castle chamber were reversed on appeal by the English privy council and remanded for a new trial. These were political revocations, for the most part, or intensely partisan judicial hearings. Yet the English executive found, in its readiness to superintend the viceroy and his Irish council, that suitors from Ireland frequented the court at Westminster with the expectation that any Irish decision could be nullified by a clever petition to the sovereign. In the 1590s the privy council could be heard saying two things at once. They noted the large number of Irish petitioners at Westminster and demanded that the lord deputy and council take up their causes, giving final orders and ending the steady stream of appeals to England. In June 1593, however, the English privy council heard a petition alleging injustice to the son of an Irish suitor and sent the case back for a change of venue before the lord deputy and council, even though the accused had been duly indicted for murder in queen's bench (see below, page 61).[17] In the same year, the English executive had earlier warned its Irish counterpart,

> that generallie all causes determinable in the Courtes of Chauncery, King's Bench, Common Pleas and the Exchequier may be heard and determined in those Courtes according to the lawes and customes of the same Courtes, and not to be drawn to be heard and ordered by the Lord Deputy and Counsell, except in such speciall cases as the heades and principal officers of the same Courtes shall thinke convenient for anie speciall respectes and furtherance of justice.[18]

Although the momentum for judicial reform lapsed under succeeding lord chancellors after 1581, the initiative passed to commissions of inquiry launched from England. Concerns about the handling of sensitive cases by Chichester and his successor led to separate reviews of executive and judicial conduct in 1613 and in 1622. In the latter year, a team of lawyers and Irish experts were authorized to examine the ecclesiastical and temporal state of Ireland on 20 March, and they published in August 'His Majesty's Directions for Ordering and Settling the Courts within his Kingdom of Ireland'. Combining the testimony of judges and

17. *Acts privy council, 1591–92*, p. 587; *1592*, p. 82; *1592–93*, p. 307.
18. *Acts privy council, 1592–93*, p. 219.

law officers with three lists of grievances from Irish lawyers like Sir John Everard, the 'Directions' were quickly approved in England and printed after enrolment in chancery.[19] The comprehensive set of instructions prepared for the courts began by establishing the boundaries of castle chamber and conciliar adjudication in the first clause, stating,

> It is his Mates pleasure that the Councell Table shall conteyne it self within its proper boundes in handling of matters of state & waight fit for that place, ... And that neither the lo: Deputy Governors nor Councell Table doe hereafter intermeddle nor trouble themselves with Comon business, that is within the Cognizance of the ordinarie Courtes, ... causes recommended from the councell table of England & special causes concerning the Church excepted.[20]

The Irish council was further instructed not to meddle in civil causes between party and party, nor the viceroy to grant pardons or protections alone. The compendium addressed the limiting of 'foreign trials', sometimes made necessary by the partiality of kinsmen for their families in regard to land titles in dispute, so that both chancery and council might initiate them without prejudice to the litigants. Chancery was given authority to issue orders by which cases might be remanded from other common law courts, but the secretary for Irish causes in London was directed to send no orders from England without explicit direction from the chief governor, thus limiting the appeals to the crown beyond Irish jurisdictions. Specific limitations were imposed on chancery to ban referral of causes to another court without written consent; the crossing of orders made by another court; meddling in proceedings determinable at common law; limiting writs of certiorari to remove causes from provincial courts into chancery; and the indiscriminate use of injunctions or relief in equity for cases of mortgage or forfeiture or to regain possession. Finally, the right to file writs of error upon judgement in king's bench in Ireland to the senior bench in England was limited to the 'meere pointe in lawe,whereuppon the Court gave their Judgement', noting how abuses of this privilege in law had increased.[21]

The other three principal courts in Tudor Ireland were modelled on their English counterparts, though they did not experience the flood of litigation so often remarked upon by contemporaries in England. The court of queen's bench was probably busier than the court of common pleas, though only the senior court had cases heard on appeal by the court of castle chamber, with which it shared a

19. TCD, MS 853, f. 139. See also G.J. Hand and V. Treadwell, eds., 'His majesty's directions for ordering and settling the courts within his kingdom of Ireland, 1622', *Anal Hib*, no. 26 (1970), 179–82. See also Treadwell, 'Richard Hadsor', 312–18.
20. TCD, MS 853, f. 145; Hand and Treadwell, eds., 'Directions for the courts', p. 190; Chatsworth, Lismore MSS, vol. 15, item 21.
21. TCD, MS 853, f. 149, and see ff. 147–49.

criminal jurisdiction. In a report prepared by Robert Legge for the arrival of Perrot as lord deputy, the courts of queen's bench, common pleas and exchequer were described as weak, corrupt and partisan. In particular, the informality of proceedings captured the attention of Legge, and he called for the proper robing of judges who 'sit like any common persons' in their courts. Likening the casual behaviour of the attorneys to 'any hundred court', Legge continued,

> Whereas these Irish officers use no order at all, neither in sitting in the court nor otherwise, but rather walk out of the court at their pleasure to talk with their friends, or with such as have any matter to be moved again, although it be against the Queen; they will be so instructed again [that] they come to their places as they will rather speak for the party than with the Queen, or else they will be silent altogether.[22]

Ellis has shown that in the early Tudor period king's bench was the more powerful venue, claiming that cases of debt and detinue might be pleaded in that court, and by the middle of the reign of Elizabeth the criminal cases taken up in her senior court had increased with the shiring of most Irish counties.[23] In two cases heard at castle chamber in 1610, juries empanelled before the king's bench were fined and imprisoned for giving corrupt verdicts against the evidence. In the case of the murder of Simon Barnwell, gentleman, during the notorious affray in Dublin between the retainers of Lord Howth and his rival, Sir Roger Jones, twelve jurors in king's bench acquitted eight of Howth's men, ignoring the judges' instruction that, by drawing their swords in the quarrel, they were equally guilty with the rest. The jurors protested in vain that 'yt was not proved unto them who yt was in Certaine and by name that did kill the said Simon Barnwell'.[24] In the second case, the jury's foreman, Cahir O'Toole, wilfully changed the verdict from murder to manslaughter in his report to king's bench, for which he was fined, pilloried and his ears cut off after conviction in the castle chamber court.[25]

The court of exchequer was governed by the chief baron as senior attorney in the treasury, his superior being a financial officer who frequently combined this service with previous military training (Sir Henry Wallop, for example). The court of upper exchequer was concerned with enforcement of the penal laws and had a parallel jurisdiction with queen's bench in the enforcement of crown rights.[26] While the court might take cognizance of the customs, or concealment of dutiable goods and the regulation of internal trade, foreign merchants more often came before the court of castle chamber or the council in Ireland itself.[27] Along

---

22. *Cal. Carew MSS, 1575–88*, p. 400. Perrot sought a new location for the court, finding it too near the prison called the 'Grate' and the powder magazine in Dublin Castle. Ibid., p. 409.
23. Ellis, *Reform and revival*, pp. 119–21.
24. BL., Add. MS 47,172, ff. 166–66v.
25. BL., Add. MS 47,172, ff. 168–68v.
26. Ellis, *Reform and revival*, p. 123.
27. Ibid., p. 127.

with the lord chancellor and master of the rolls, the two chief judges and the chief baron of the exchequer formed the core of judicial expertise on the council in Ireland and served, almost invariably, on the court of castle chamber in its mature phase from about 1584. As W.J. Jones has observed regarding the English court system, the early modern period witnessed a general growth of litigation, substantial interdependence and overlapping jurisdictions, and an interest in the devolution of judicial authority to commissions and local officials.[28]

The interdependence of the principal law courts became a marked feature of the Dublin government after 1603, when Chichester launched a campaign of dispossession in the wake of the Ulster plantation. In 1609 the new plantation in Co. Wexford threatened the estates of many landowners, both English and Irish, and the survey was challenged by the property owners and the juries called upon to affirm them. The septs of Cavanaughs, MacMurroughs and others challenged the re-distribution of some 66,800 acres of land near Arklow, but they were assured of equitable treatment and a writ of seizure was issued out of chancery in 1611 to take up lands for the king. A commission led by the bishop of Ferns was sent to Wexford in November 1611 but the jury offered a verdict of ignoramus, refusing to find the king's title, and they were bound over to appear in the court of exchequer. The jurors petitioned the viceroy and delayed their appearance until February when they appeared before commissioners including four chief judges, but five jurors refused to find the crown title and were censured in the court of castle chamber, with the rest of the jurors discharged. A new jury was then formed to appear in the court of exchequer in the next term and they heard testimony from the reign of Richard II, confirming the incumbents as rightful landowners. The court of chancery then ordered the patentees of the king to be put into possession by injunction from chancery court, enforced by the sheriff, and several leading councillors were granted large estates in the proceeding after the sheriff 'did break open the doors of such as resisted, and turned them out'.[29] The native Irish protested their loyalty and long possession of the estates, to no avail, while the undertakers were obliged to erect stone fortresses with battlements on the frontiers of the plantation. This judicial manipulation became the hallmark of the Chichester regime and demonstrated how the king's interest was sure to prevail by cooperation among the leading tribunals. On the other hand, clever petitioners such as Charles O'Doyne, master in chancery, could prolong suit to their advantage, switching venues and filing countersuits to weaken their adversaries. The viceroy and Irish council were brought into the suit between

---

28. W.J. Jones, 'Palatine performance in the seventeenth century', in P. Clark, A.G.R. Smith and N. Tyacke, eds., *The English Commonwealth, 1547 to 1640* (Leicester, 1979), pp. 192, 199. Jones found that the Welsh council heard up to 1500 cases a year, and one entry book for 1639–42 had over 1200 pages, while the chancery in London made 2,000 orders and decrees each year. Star chamber, however, recorded only about 300 bills annually. Ibid.

29. *Desid. cur. Hib.*, i, pp. 372–89. There were 667 listed freeholders among the native Irish, claiming to hold by gavelkind, who were subject to the writ of seizure out of chancery in June 1611. See also Canny, *Making Ireland British*, pp. 199, 249, 379–80.

O'Doyne and his elder brother, Teig, in 1608 over a contested inheritance, but the case moved slowly from the assize courts in 1606 to the chancery and finally to common law in 1612, without final determination.[30]

A gradual augmentation of central courts with prerogative powers enlarged the Dublin administration throughout the period 1571 to 1641. This evolution was not part of a grand design, but rather a spasmodic response to critical needs. The Irish court of admiralty was designed to regularize practice in Irish seaports and navigation, since abuses were often reported by public officials such as Perrot when he was president of the council in Munster. However, the establishment of an admiralty court in Dublin and a judge of the court in the 1570s did not lead to a substantial increase of litigation and there were constant quarrels with the English court over its jurisdiction. When the first judge, Ambrose Forth, died in 1610, he was succeeded by the ambitious Sir Adam Loftus in a climate of increasing piracy along the Irish coast. Loftus retained the judgeship of admiralty until his death in 1643, even though he became lord chancellor of Ireland after 1619, but the work of the court was diffused through a warren of local and provincial jurisdictions, as well as the senior court in London. In sum, the admiralty court suffered from inadequate and incomplete authority and its work was compromised by the inability to carry out reform.[31] In a similar manner, the Irish court of wards was delayed by the entrenched interests of incumbent administrators, the occasionally authorized escheators who were given the right to administer the legal rights of heirs who held directly of the crown. When a formal court of wards was sanctioned in the wake of the reforming commission of 1622, the court became a ready object of derision for its conduct of anti-recusant policies, including the education of wards in the Protestant academy of Trinity College, Dublin and the requirement to take the oath of supremacy before entering their estates. When Wentworth tightened the administration of the court in the 1630s with the aim of increasing income from feudal tenures, the court irritated both Protestants and Catholics alike. It collapsed in the crisis of the 1640s along with the short-lived prerogative court of high commission.[32] Again, the functions of this court were to enforce the Reformation and a series of commissions authorized Dublin officials to take steps in that direction from 1561 to 1593.[33] The spirited evangelizing policies of Davies and Chichester against recusants in the early Jacobean period were reversed under adverse diplomatic circumstances, so the

---

30. K.W. Nicholls, ed., *The O'Doyne manuscript* (Dublin, 1983), pp. 37, 61, 96, 108.
31. J.C. Appleby and M. O'Dowd, 'The Irish admiralty: its organisation and development, c. 1570–1640', *IHS*, xxiv (1985), 299–325.
32. H.F. Kearney, 'The court of wards and liveries in Ireland 1622–41', *RIA Proc*, lvii (1955), sect c, p. 29; V. Treadwell, 'The Irish court of wards under James I', *IHS*, xii (1960), 1 ff.
33. See 'Harris' Collectanea de rebus Hibernicis', ed. C. McNeill, *Anal Hib*, no. 6 (1934), 424. The high commission for ecclesiastical causes of 1593, authorized five leading judges and ecclesiastics to hear and determine all offences against the Elizabethan acts of uniformity, from seditious books and false rumours to adulteries, usuries, simonies and other ecclesiastical crimes.

court of high commission actually had to re-commence its campaign for uniformity when it was finally authorized in 1635 and began its work in 1638. Wentworth and Bramhall used the opportunity to attack nonconforming Protestants and so intensified the religious divisions in Ireland that the court was swiftly abolished in 1641. John McCafferty has explained that it was a busy court which exercised a national jurisdiction from Dublin, proceeding in much the same way as English courts did. He concluded: 'It ran alongside the other prerogative tribunals as part of an interlocking system at the centre of which lay a chief governor pursuing a coordinated programmme for church and state. The court of High Commission was, in many ways, a perfect miniature of the workings and assumptions of Wentworth's viceroyalty.'[34] In summary, we can see that the court of castle chamber was, in practice, the only prerogative central court which attained a fully articulated and consistently administered identity throughout this period, despite sporadic efforts to achieve a harmony of the judicial infrastructure between England and Ireland.[35]

Despite these superficial similarities with English practice, the court system in Ireland differed in several other ways. While there was no Irish equivalent of the court of requests, a tribunal meant to facilitate judicial access for the working poor and part of the Cromwellian reforms under Henry VIII, there were two novel Irish jurisdictions dealing with property matters. The first of these was the commission to investigate defective titles, a product of the uncertainties attending war, plantation and re-settlement.[36] The original policy of surrender and regrant was intended to substitute good title by formal terms of common law for the weaker claim by Gaelic law and tradition. English lawyers much preferred the legal certainties of primogeniture as opposed to the Irish custom of partible inheritance and the custom of tanistry whereby the strongest male kinsman replaced an ageing or disabled chief, overriding the claims of an eldest son. Furthermore, the terms of surrender and regrant brought the land and title within the conditions of wardship and offered potential profit to the crown in the case of a minor heir. Nevertheless, the time required to put in place this peaceable evolution of feudal property rights and obligations was unavailable in the later sixteenth century. Chief governors, impatient for progress, implemented instead a system of presidency courts which demanded immediate jurisdiction over Munster and Connacht, and when the Desmond and Tyrone Rebellions occurred after 1579 the property of some rebels was confiscated, while others regained some or all of their patrimony. Along with these unsettled conditions, the plantations of Munster and of Ulster strove to colonize new English and Scots

34. J. McCafferty, 'Bramhall and reconstruction of the Church of Ireland, 1633–41', Ph.D. dissertation, Cambridge University, ch. 3. The author wishes to thank Dr McCafferty for sharing his research on this subject.

35. For a study of the ecclesiastical courts and commissions of ecclesiastical causes from 1571 to 1641, see W.N. Osborough, 'Ecclesiastical law and the Reformation in Ireland' in his *Studies in Irish legal history* (Dublin, 1999), pp. 136–52.

36. Canny, *Making Ireland British*, pp. 169, 177.

settlers on land formerly held by Irish clans and septs with imperfect results. As a consequence, legitimate questions of title were many and James I issued commissions to examine defective titles in 1606 and 1615 to address these uncertainties. When Davies and others used these quasi-judicial investigations to settle land disputes, they invariably favoured the English claimant, leading to protests and further litigation over concealed lands. In 1634 Wentworth obtained a new commission of defective titles with statutory authority and laid claim to higher crown rents as well as religious discrimination in the court of wards, threatening the titles of Old English and new settlers alike. In the end, both the commissions for plantation and defective title allowed a process of proprietary doubtfulness to continue, aggravating the conditions for quiet government of the realm.[37]

Finally, the high court of parliament in Ireland was substantially attenuated during this period. The legislature was called to meet only four times between 1570 and 1640, and the parliaments of 1569–71, 1585–86, 1613–15 and 1634–35 were brief sessions that were brokered by the chief governor with uneven results.[38] Sir Henry Sydney attempted to get parliamentary assent to his reform proposals which offered financial compromise in lieu of the military cess, but the parliament balked at this and protested at the election of new English members who were not resident in Ireland.[39] The parliament of Perrot in 1585–86 failed when opponents of his composition scheme waylaid plans for a streamlined government in Connacht, despite the viceroy's successful packing of the house of commons with an official cadre of supporters.[40] Sir Arthur Chichester experienced the most truculent parliament in 1613 when the corpulent speaker, attorney general Davies, was physically placed in the chair in which the Old English nominee was already sitting. Recriminations about the creation of new parliamentary boroughs, most of them little more than villages in the plantations, led to a sustained campaign of opposition to the viceroy's anti-recusancy bills. Passage of the subsidy act did little to mask the minimal legislative outcome and James was confronted with a united opposition.[41] However, the Wentworth parliament of 1634 obtained agreement to a reform programme due to his manipulation of parliamentary boroughs and his cynical prior assent to the Graces, a modification of royal policy which never received legislative enactment.[42] These irritated

37. *Cal. pat. rolls Ire., Chas. I*, p. 299. This commission authorized seven officials, including most of the Irish privy council, to hear and determine all charges.
38. See J.P.Cooper, *Land, men and beliefs: studies in early modern history*, ed. G.E. Aylmer and J.S. Morrill (London, 1983) for an essay on the relationship of common law to parliament, suggesting that long intervals in parliamentary functioning would have strengthened the common law and prerogative justice. Ch. 5, p. 108.
39. Ellis, *Tudor Ireland*, pp. 258–59, 263–64.
40. V. Treadwell, 'Sir John Perrot and the Irish parliament of 1585–6', *RIA Proc*, lxxxv (1985), sect c, 286–305. Perrot interrogated his parliamentary adversaries in June 1585, jailed leaders such as the lawyer Netterville, and 'the rest were bound over to appear in the castle chamber.' Ibid., 289.
41. J. McCavitt, *Sir Arthur Chichester, lord deputy of Ireland, 1605–1616* (Belfast, 1998), pp. 190–207.
42. A. Clarke, *The Graces*, pp. 27–29; H.F. Kearney, *Strafford in Ireland, 1633–41: a study in absolutism* (Cambridge, 1989), chs. 6–7.

legislatures did not function as tribunals, although their meetings served as forums for the ventilation of criticism against the incumbent regimes. Importantly, the last parliament of Wentworth, called in 1640, initiated the most serious constitutional challenge to Stuart government in this period, leading to the impeachment of Wentworth himself and the assertion of a right of legislative independence and judicial control apart from either royal prerogative or parliament in Westminster. The ensuing war and rebellion made these arguments still more complex and heated until the Restoration, though Dr McCafferty in a recent article downplays the constitutional significance of the contretemps, saying it was primarily a sideshow for the linked attainder and execution of Strafford.[43] The English parliament did not interfere in Irish affairs until the crises of the 1640s when the king agreed to sanction a standing committee of parliament constructed to wage war against Irish rebels.[44]

The suitability of Dublin Castle as the venue for the Four Courts was compromised by its central function as an urban fortress, especially since the storage of gunpowder just below the judges' chambers presented an opportunity for accidental mayhem, or worse. This predicament, noted by chief governors from Perrot onwards, was presumably aggravated by the increasing resort of litigants to the courts of law under reformers like Gerrard.[45] Nonetheless, moving the central courts to more suitable quarters was delayed by the conflicts of the 1590s, which demanded that precious resources were devoted first to the military. The reign of James I began with adjournment of the courts due to plague in Dublin that required postponement and a midsummer session in Drogheda.[46] A fire and explosion in Dublin Castle punctuated Chichester's insistence upon removal of the courts, timed with the rapid expansion of the assize courts and an inspection of the former Blackfriars property by Chief Justice Ley and others in July 1606.[47]

43. Kearney, *Strafford in Ireland*, chs. 13–14; M. Perceval-Maxwell, *The outbreak of the Irish Rebellion of 1641* (Montreal, 1994); J. McCafferty, '"To follow the late precedents of England": the Irish impeachment proceedings of 1641', in D.S. Greer and N.M. Dawson, eds., *Mysteries and solutions in Irish legal history* (Dublin, 2001), pp. 51–72.

44. P. Little, 'The English parliament and the Irish constitution, 1641–9' in M. Ó Siochrú, ed., *Kingdoms in crisis: Ireland in the 1640s* (Dublin, 2001), pp. 108–09. Little traced the constitutional basis for English intervention to 1642, citing the commission of 1642 for Irish affairs that appropriated the role of the privy council itself. Ibid., pp. 110–11.

45. Sir John Perrot asserted 'there is here no place for the law, save only an old hall in this castle … and the same very dangerously over the munition and powder, where a desperate fellow by dropping down a match might haply mar all.' 'The Perrot papers', ed. C. McNeill, *Anal Hib*, no. 12 (1943), 8. He sought the use of St Patrick's for an inn of court, abusing the deanery there as the resort of 'idle singing men that cannot aptly pronounce an English word'. Ibid., p. 9.

46. *Cal. S.P. Ire, 1603–06*, pp. 142, 162. Watson's plan of Dublin Castle in 1606 showed the ample quarters of the chief governor against the south wall and the council chamber located in quarters adjacent to the north gates. In contrast, the crowded confines of the four courts were to be found in the corners of the Great Hall of the Upper Yard, bounded by the prison and the kitchen yard. See G.A. Hayes-McCoy, *Ulster and other Irish maps* (Dublin, 1964), pp. 29–31, and Plate 2.

47. C. Kenny, *King's Inns and the kingdom of Ireland: the Irish 'inn of court', 1541–1800* (Dublin, 1992), pp. 72–73; *Cal. S.P. Ire., 1603–06*, pp. 522–23. The Gunpowder Plot in England was

Since this would have meant moving the courts across the Liffey, a plan opposed by civic interests, the former chapter house of Christ Church cathedral was finally chosen as the site, and alterations to its buildings were made from 1606 to 1608 when the courts were temporarily shifted to Blackfriars. By May 1610 Sir John Davies could write to Salisbury that the courts of justice 'and all the legal proceedings therein' were better established than ever before.[48] Davies's evident satisfaction, however, may be contrasted with the protests of the dean and chapter of Christ Church over nonpayment of rent lasting for decades. Apparently the original agreement with Chichester for a yearly rent of £10 from 1608 was yet unpaid at Michaelmas term 1626, an amount to be augmented by the unpaid rent of 40s. per annum for the court of wards during the previous six years.[49] The English privy council responded on 29 November 1627, on the advice of the Irish commissioners, that the rent should be paid semi-annually from the profits of the courts and the arrears satisfied out of the casualties of the said courts.[50] When the judicial terms were suspended during the crises of the early 1640s, the Four Courts were still meeting in the precincts of Christ Church cathedral, some 300 yards from Dublin Castle.

The important judicial milieu in which lawyers and judges interacted in England was not replicated in Ireland, though such attempts were made throughout the period. The unsettled venue of the four courts, moving from Dublin Castle to Christ Church and continuously faced with unfunded projects for improvement, was mirrored by the unfinished establishment of the King's Inns. Though an ambitious programme of legal education in Ireland was envisioned in its first charter of 1541, and a second lease of 1567 was made to 25 Old English lawyers and officials, the institution did not thrive until its refounding in June 1607. The active involvement of Sir Arthur Chichester, who became a founding member himself as lord deputy, and of Sir John Davies, the attorney general who arranged for the new lease of Blackfriars, suggests that this re-establishment had serious policy implications. Dr Kenny has explained that the revival was sought in order to make use of the centre for exchanging information on the reinvigorated assizes, as well as cases pending in provincial courts.[51] The growing

revealed to Chichester in letters of 10 November 1605, at a time when his anti-recusant policy had stirred much opposition in Dublin. Ibid., p. 359.

48. *Cal. S.P. Ire., 1608–10*, pp. 451, 523. In 1609 he had complained that after the term had begun, and 'the town full of people', the courts were nearly empty and litigants deferred their suits at the behest of priests who spread rumours of war and trouble, despite the 'universal inward peace' at the time. Ibid., p. 204.

49. *The first chapter act book of Christ Church Cathedral, Dublin, 1574–1634*, ed. R. Gillespie (Dublin, 1999), p. 151. The petition humbly stated that this grant was made to the use of the Four Courts at a rent much less than might have been obtained for the place, citing as a consequence the ruinous state of the church itself.

50. Ibid., p. 153. The commissioners, including Irish experts Hadsor, Annesley, Denham, and William Jones, demanded, in return for the payment of arrears, a lease of 1,000 years for the rooms in question to the use of the said courts. Ibid., pp. 154–55.

51. Kenny, *King's Inns, 1541–1800*, p. 75. The two chief justices, the master of the rolls and the

importance of the King's Inns is suggested by the admission of honorary members from the earl of Thomond and Sir Adam Loftus to Richard Boyle, the future earl of Cork and a notorious litigant.[52] The Catholic lawyers were officially excluded from membership in 1614, when the heated debates in parliament were led by recusant lawyers, until 1628 when the Graces were largely accepted by the crown. On 18 June 1628, Patrick Darcy of Galway, the leading opposition lawyer in this period, was admitted to King's Inns, to be followed by numerous other recusants. However, the arrival of Wentworth in 1634 led to the colonizing of the King's Inns with senior officials beholden to the chief governor and to a reinstatement of the rule that all attorneys pleading throughout Ireland must become members of the inns and attend commons for at least one week in every term. While it is doubtful that this rubric was successfully implemented in 1637, it is nonetheless clear that efforts to create a judicial milieu in Dublin had reached a new threshold prior to the denouément of the chief governor in the troubled period 1640–41.[53]

RELATIONS WITH PROVINCIAL AND LOCAL COURTS

In tandem with establishment of the court of castle chamber, the installation of presidency courts in the provinces of Ireland was an integral part of the policies of Sussex and Sydney, an effort to bring all of Ireland under the rule of law. Anglicizing the government of Ireland in this way would bring tangible benefits including the local resolution of civil conflict, increased revenue to the crown, and a systematic military presence to keep watch on unruly Irish magnates who were reluctant to abandon Gaelic customs.[54] In the instructions meant for Sir Warham St Leger in 1566, Sydney and the council laid out the crucial dimensions of this policy. Leading magnates were named to attend the new lord president, though a regular working council was made up largely of civil administrators including the future master of the rolls, Nicholas White.[55] The admonition to hear and determine causes of action throughout Munster, including the liberties or

chief baron were all enrolled at the same time as the chief governor, and Sir James Ley gave the inn his full support. The three law officers were also enrolled three days later, giving the Irish inns a Protestant and orthodox complexion, though former recusant officials like John Everard and Patrick Sedgrave also won admission. Everard had been replaced as second justice of king's bench in the previous year, while Sedgrave was fined in a corruption case at castle chamber, heard in 1602, and dismissed as baron of the exchequer. Ibid., p. 81.

52. Ibid., pp. 87–89. Privy councillors like Sir Gerald Moore and Sir Henry Harrington also joined the inns in 1612.

53. Ibid., pp. 99–109. Wentworth populated the inns with the chief judges of the four courts, but added numerous cronies including his personal secretary, Sir George Radcliffe, as well as Christopher Wandesford and the vice treasurer, Sir Adam Loftus of Rathfarnham.

54. See J.G. Crawford, *Anglicizing the government of Ireland: the Irish privy council and the expansion of Tudor rule, 1556–1578* (Dublin, 1993), pp. 307 ff.

55. PRO, SP 63/16/40.

palatinates claimed by leading peers, included actions of real or personal property, inheritance, and criminal proceedings. The council was designed to offer the queen's impartial justice to persons who wished to sue powerful members of the landed élite, and to hear on appeal cases in which municipal courts had acted in a partisan manner. Owing to the queen's parsimony, the presidency was not established until 1570, in the midst of rebellion, and many writers have supposed that the court was, for this reason, subordinate to the martial law. However, the second lord president, Sir William Drury, took office in 1576, and proclaimed the need to establish a court of justice to hear suits and complaints.[56] He was assisted by James Dowdall, second justice of queen's bench, and Nicholas Walshe, who was to become chief justice of common pleas at the end of the reign. And despite the rocky start of the presidency in Connacht under the intemperate and unstable Sir Edward Fyton, his successor Sir Nicholas Malbie was commanded to proceed solely by commission of oyer and terminer in his instructions of May 1573.[57] Drs Gillespie and Cunningham have recently shown that Malbie won the confidence of the local élites, establishing his residence in stately Roscommon Castle and building a walled town. Malbie was honoured by the Irish annalists at his death in 1584 as the one who brokered arrangements among the powerful chiefs of Connacht and took his place among the Irish as a force for stability. Malbie's instructions of 1578, during a time of rebellion in Munster, addressed matters of judicial administration in 23 of its 34 clauses. The council was authorized to meet as a court in regular terms, to encourage the Irish to abandon brehon law, to sit for at least one month during every term of the year with six clerks learned in the law, and to expedite proceedings in the 'small causes of poor man's suits' by examining the case in the presence of both litigants and issuing an order immediately.[58]

There were, of course, other objectives for the new presidency system, and these included the goal of reining in the excessive power of feudal magnates. Earlier, the employment of seneschals such as Francis Agarde was used to enforce order among Irish septs known for their unruliness, such as the O'Byrnes and O'Tooles in Co. Wicklow. But the ultimate remedy for Irish unrest lay in the gradual acceptance of the rule of common law, even for the vexed province of Ulster.[59] These prerogative courts, authorized by instructions from the Irish privy council, had both criminal and civil jurisdiction, though much of the evidence for their adjudication stems from the resolution of cases of assault or wrongful distress, recovery of debt and quieting possession in the case of real property disputes.[60] It is difficult to accept the view of Ciaran Brady that the presidency courts had become 'unambiguously military institutions,' based on the excesses of

56. BL, Add. MS 4786, f. 49.
57. PRO, SP 63/40/124-25.
58. BL, Add. MS 4786, ff. 3-6. Gillespie & Cunningham, *Stories from Ireland*, pp. 190-94.
59. N. Canny, *The Elizabethan conquest of Ireland: a pattern established, 1565-1576* (New York, 1976), pp. 47-53, ch. 5; *Making Ireland British*, pp. 174-75.
60. L. Irwin, 'The Irish presidency courts, 1569-1672', *Ir Jur*, xii (1977), 107-13.

men such as Bingham and Carew during the height of the Nine Years War.[61] Dr O'Dowd has shown, for example, that the presidency of Connacht managed a gradual transition to English rule over time, despite the occasional ferocity of the Binghams and the dispossession of the Gaelic landowning élite. In the early seventeenth century, the county of Sligo witnessed the full implementation of English norms of justice, including regular visits of assize judges, and the dominant role of the presidency court had become a legal one.[62] Even the contemplated dispossession of the native élite in Munster following the Desmond Rebellion in 1585 generated a veritable flood of petitions, lawsuits, counterclaims and hearings before commissioners for the plantation, including members of the presidency court. Violent confrontation was avoided, and the resulting compromises allowed Old English merchants like Walter Coppinger of Cork to thrive in the Jacobean era.[63]

While the early development of the presidency courts was conditioned by rebellion in Munster and Connacht, leading some writers to conclude that their purpose was to superimpose an Elizabethan military regime on the feudal strongholds of her aristocratic enemies, it is also clear that renegade officials were restrained by the court of castle chamber.[64] Dr Edwards has recently claimed that Elizabeth pursued a systematic regime of 'state terror' through the use of commissions of martial law. The existence of these routine commissions, common enough in England itself, led neither to the 'pronounced aggression' of Sydney nor to the 'widespread use' of martial law, and Edwards offers no citation for his inflated charge against local officials that 'the more people they killed, the greater their profits'.[65] Indeed, the withdrawal of the queen's support for such a draconian policy after 1584 is chronicled by Edwards himself, and his discovery of her essential moderation in 1591 is actually three decades too late.[66] Nonetheless, a balanced view of local justice must acknowledge the survival of martial law as a tactical weapon in the ongoing struggle for a civil society well into the next century. A commission of martial law to Sir William St Leger as lord president in Munster put the case for martial law thus:

> Forasmuch as the wicked, malicious and disordered nature of sundry persons, being of vile and base conditions, not having whereon to live, and therefore less careful of their allegiance and obedience, doth require that we

61. C. Brady, *Chief governors*, pp. 137–40.
62. M. O'Dowd, *Power, politics and land in early modern Sligo, 1568–1688* (Belfast, 1991), pp. 54–55.
63. M. MacCarthy-Morrough, *The Munster plantation: English migration to southern Ireland, 1583–1641* (Oxford, 1986), pp. 89, 97, 152, 286. The author found that the mixed results of the plantation were 'not invariably charged with tension'. See also Canny, *Making Ireland British*, ch. 3.
64. Brady, *Chief governors*, p. 139; Ellis, *Tudor Ireland*, p. 261.
65. D. Edwards, 'Ideology and experience: Spenser's *View* and martial law in Ireland', in H. Morgan, ed., *Political ideology in Ireland, 1541–1641* (Dublin, 1999), pp. 131–33, and 137.
66. Ibid., p. 142.

should correct and repress the same by some more speedy and sharp means than by our common laws; and considering our martial law and orders thereof to be much necessary for the reforming of the naughty livers and idle vagabonds, such as do not cease to disquiet our liege people.[67]

The notorious machinations of Sir Richard Bingham as lord president in Connacht deserve mention as an extreme version of the proprietary and vengeful character of the presidency when its course was subverted by private ends. Bingham enriched himself and his brother with the estates of defeated enemies and conspired to undo them, yet his surrogate, the sheriff of Co. Roscommon,was hauled before the court of castle chamber by Perrot in 1586 and condemned for malfeasance in office. Henry Ealand was accused of tyrannical behaviour, hanging suspects without trial and taking money from landlords to construct stocks and gibbets in the shire.[68] Bingham complained loudly to the privy council in England and won a hearing, but his escape from imminent disgrace owed more to the emerging crises of the Nine Years War and the campaign to humiliate his despised rival, Perrot.[69] Bingham's contemporary in Munster, Sir Thomas Norris, was cautioned by the English privy council in 1597 to avoid complaints of unfairness and to prevent the continual recourse to Dublin courts on appeal.[70] Dr Edwards, in contrast, has stressed the re-emphasis on martial law in 1597, noting the rise of commissions during the heat of the Nine Years War, and declaring that the poet/ functionary Spenser had somehow vanquished the peace party at court.[71] That 'unrestrained martial government in Ireland' was coincident with the most savage events of the Tyrone Rebellion would hardly have surprised contemporaries, but Spenser's advocacy of 'ruthless imperial coercion' was out of step with the thinking of the queen and her last great general, Mountjoy himself.[72]

Finally, it is important to remember that these commissions of martial law included routine administrative matters as well as the banishment of 'all idle men, vagabonds, sturdy beggars, harpers, rymers and bards' on pain of death.[73] Such a commission was issued to the earl of Ormonde on 8 March 1585 for Kilkenny and Tipperary, commanding him as well to prosecute all who aided outlaws,

---

67. *Cal. pat. rolls, Ire., Chas. I*, p. 236.
68. *Cal. S.P. Ire., 1586–88*, pp. 493–94, 496; BL, Add. MS 47,172, ff. 82–82v. The charges against Ealand were brought by the Old English Theobald Dillon, an adventuring third son of the prominent Dillons of Meath who had obtained from the MacCostello clan the estate of Castlemore in Co. Mayo. Dillon had obtained office and land through Irish connnections, and in return authored the indictment against Bingham's henchman, demonstrating that competent provincial rule must navigate the hidden shoals of Irish social and political allegiances. Gillespie & Cunningham, *Stories from Ireland*, pp. 74–83.
69. *Acts privy council, 1588*, p. 10.
70. *Acts privy council, 1597–98*, p. 117.
71. Edwards, 'Martial law in Ireland', pp. 151–53.
72. Ibid., p. 155. Canny argues that Spenser influenced not only contemporaries but Wentworth himself some four decades later. *Making Ireland British*, ch. 1, p. 287.
73. *Ormond deeds, 1584–1603*, p. 16.

thieves, murderers and rebels. He was authorized to seize the goods of any who refused their assistance, to make reprisal for any robbery or spoil of goods, and to 'kill, plague or correct' offenders. In addition, the order required him to put in execution all statutes against grey merchants, makers of aquavitae, and unlicensed buyers and sellers of horses.[74] Significantly, this authority was often given to native landowners who were thus sanctioned to do what Irish chiefs had done for centuries. Paradoxically, they became the willing instruments of the policy of anglicization on their own estates. The mere authorization of a commission of martial law, without reference to its context or its purpose, fails to explain government policy in this period and tends to distort the consistent objective of the rule of common law.

The court of castle chamber was frequently engaged with the actions of the presidency system, buttressing its authority when called upon to do so. For example, Sir Nicholas Malbie wrote to Leicester on 12 July 1580 to complain of a riot in Galway by the townsmen, occasioned by drunkenness and the aggravation of billeting English troops on the city. He called for a star chamber fine and added, 'the governor and the English shall ever be in danger of those odious people upon every drunkard's quarrel'.[75] During the heat of the Nine Years War, Mountjoy demanded the forbearance of Sir George Carew in Munster, admonishing sheriffs to withhold serving process against men whose arrears were greater than they could pay and generally moderating the ordinary course of law.[76] On 25 September 1602, Mountjoy counselled Carew to delay open hearings and examinations of an accused nobleman:

> For, considering you are not ignorant of the aptness of this country people to raise accusations, sometimes out of malice and sometime of practice, and likewise what may be the danger to take hold of such matters in this looseness of time, which is now growing to a staidness and settling.[77]

The work of the lords president gradually became more settled and litigious, and they were often used on commissions to serve the interests of the crown. For example, the earl of Thomond was instructed by the Irish council on 21 February

---

74. Ibid. In his fine treatment of the Ormond lordship in Kilkenny, Edwards recently argued that it was the earl who supported common law courts and offered to prosecute rebels in the sessions of 1577. Lord Chancellor Gerrard arrived in Kilkenny to discover the county was in good order, used indifferent justice and accepted common law rule, blaming Sydney for excessive badgering of the Butler dominions. Edwards argued that Sydney preferred martial law remedies, having appointed Francis Cosbie as seneschal to challenge the local seignory; Henry Harrington as military governor of Leinster; and his servant Francis Lovell as commissioner for martial law in Kilkenny. D. Edwards, *The Ormond lordship in Co. Kilkenny, 1515–1642* (Dublin, 2003), pp. 218–24

75. *Cal. Carew MSS, 1575–88*, pp. 270–71

76. *Cal. Carew MSS, 1601–03*, p. 131.

77. Ibid., p. 341.

1617 to examine the liberties of the corporation of Waterford, along with the chief justice, Sir William Jones, in an effort to challenge the judicial autonomy of the Munster towns. It appeared that no recorder had been elected since the death of the loyal official Sir Nicholas Walshe in 1615, as a protest against taking the oath of supremacy: 'For the want of the said officers, all causes, suits, and plaints, depending in the courts of the city during the vacancies lay dormant, and no execution had thereupon, and that none of the offices were void by death during the two years, except the office of recorder.'[78] By 1622 the presidency courts had to be warned against exceeding their instructions, since the lords president had apparently reprieved prisoners who had been condemned before justices of assize and contended with chancery for jurisdiction in provincial suits. The 'Directions for ordering ... the courts' urged judicial restraint, censuring the provincial presidencies thus:

> Limitacon of presidencie Courtes. That the presidencie Courtes of Mounster & Connaght may by instruccon be limited not to intermeddle with any title of landes betweene party & party, other then to settle possessions, where a man hath ben quietly in possession for three yeares before or wher a man is forcibly or by fraude put out of possession. That they may have power to hold plea only of debtes , detinue, accons uppon the case & accompt where the Debt or Damage shall not exceede xl [li] Irish & in Replevins where the title of land shall not come in question & that they be restrayned to proceed uppon any penall statute in other sort then is prescribed by the statute.[79]

Under James I, the presidency court of Connacht was re-authorized as a tribunal, receiving a commission for civil government on 1 September 1604. Justices and commissioners were named to take recognizances, 'to hear, adjudicate and terminate all actions, suits, causes, controversies, complaints, pleas, petitions, contracts and conventions, reall, personnel and mixt', saving to the king all fines and amercements. Two further commissions of martial law allowed the lord president and provost marshal to proceed 'by fier and sworde' against the enemies of the crown.[80] A fuller set of instructions for the earl of Thomond as lord president of Munster listed officials of his government, naming six clerks in addition to the chief clerk. Attorneys of the court were instructed to prefer all

---

78. *Cal. Carew MSS, 1603–24*, pp. 335, 342. Protestantization of the shrievalty by Chichester in 1609 anticipated the harassment of juries, beginning with the appointment of Cyprian Horsfall, son of the Protestant bishop. In 1612, the assize judges Elliott and Denham tested the conformity of local officials in Kilkenny, and the mayor and city sheriffs resigned. Intimidation of jurors and local officials by castle chamber prosecution had a strong impact on the local order in Kilkenny, but did nothing to strengthen the cause of Protestant religion according to Edwards. See his *Ormond lordship*, pp. 270–78.

79. TCD, MS 853, f. 147. For the original policy statement, see Hand & Treadwell, eds., 'Directions for the courts', p. 198.

80. *Pat. rolls Ire., Jas. I*, ed. Erck, pt. 1, pp. 156, 262.

information in criminal causes and examine all persons accused, while the clerks were to endorse the backs of all petitions and bills to be reviewed by the lord president and his court. The council was ordered to give swift execution to all orders emanating from the castle chamber or privy council, and to punish errant jurors who found against their evidence, but to delay proceeding capitally against any offenders until the council and viceroy in Dublin were informed. The Munster court was ordered to proceed with commissions of oyer and terminer, to try all black rent, embracery, extortions and abuses of power by local officials, cases which were ordinarily within the purview of the castle chamber. Decorum was commanded by the court for 'comely and decent order' so the petitioners were ordered to wear English attire and to avoid wearing of weapons or armour in the court room. Particular offences were singled out for punishment by the court, such as notorious adulterers or those who left their wives to live with another woman, fornicators, and spreaders of false tales. Finally, the court was given special authority to restore quiet possession to anyone who was riotously dispossessed of his lands, though the aggrieved party had common law remedies available. This authority was akin to that employed by castle chamber on proof of the use of violence. In addition to the legal proceedings detailed in these extensive instructions, the court was given the extra-legal authority to use martial law against rebels and 'upon vehement suspicion and presumption of any great offence by any party committed against the king, or to the general disturbance of that province, to put the same party so suspected to tortures, as they shall think convenient, and cause shall require'.[81] The commission declared

> all the saide persons in all tymes of Sessions and sittinge tearmes do use and weare Englishe attyre & apparyle, punishinge by fine and imprisonment all such as shall appear before them attyred in Mantells and Rowles and punishe the wearer, and also to expell and Cutt all Glibbes: And also to take order that noe persons other then such as shall attend upon the Lo: President and councell and Sheriffe do duringe the tyme of the said Sessions or sittinge Terme weare any manner of weapons or Armor.[82]

The rare instructions to the presidency court and the slender resources available to the investigator prohibit us from seeing clearly into its work as a prerogative jurisdiction, yet the provincial tribunals were, theoretically at least, important as the judicial mirror of the more powerful court of castle chamber. The court of castle chamber, often acting through the privy council in Ireland, exercised supervisory jurisdiction over its junior partners, issuing definitive instructions for its work and commanding the execution of castle chamber decrees

---

81. TCD, MS 672, f. 54v (and see ff. 50–59). See also *Desid. cur. Hib.*, ii, p. 17, and see pp. 2–35 ('Instructions sent to the government of Munster').
82. TCD, MS 672, ff. 55–55v.

and orders. The admixture of martial law with prerogative justice was common in the period, but it is clear that the move to implement the presidency court aimed to provide judicial remedies in place of the more vigorous assertions of power by the seneschals prior to 1570. While some independent jurisdictions survived well into the seventeenth century, the presidency courts were destined to show the way to a more normative legal framework of common law and equity, though the courts themselves did not survive the legislative recriminations of the 1640s aimed at the policy of Thorough. The court of castle chamber frequently took up issues emanating from the provinces, but seldom addressed matters that had been heard and determined before the presidency courts. In 1606, however, the castle chamber court heard an allegation of wrongful dispossession and assault brought by Cahir O'Callaghan of Co. Cork. The plaintiff alleged that the chief justice of Munster, William Saxey, issued a writ of restitution to Brian McOwen for the possession of the castle of Dromynyn, then in the hands of O'Callaghan, despite the decision of the assize judges at Youghal (of which Saxey was one) to stay the writ. The sheriff corruptly refused to execute a writ of supersedeas obtained by O'Callaghan from the court of common pleas, and instead implemented the writ of restitution, joining the defendant in a midnight assault on the castle with scaling ladders, axes and pikes. The castle chamber court found both the sheriff, John Barry, and the defendant guilty, censuring the pluralist chief justice for issuing the writ 'contrarie to the Directions of the said Justices and the Caveat entred that no such writt shold be graunted'.[83]

The full implementation of assize courts took more time. After the caretaker regime of Sir William Fitzwilliam and his doting lord chancellor Sir Robert Weston, the return in 1576 of Sir Henry Sydney as viceroy and the installation as lord chancellor of Sir William Gerrard energized judicial reform. As we have already seen, Gerrard found the incumbent judges of the senior bench aged, infirm, partisan and corrupt, citing the four courts as 'onlie showes and shadowes of Cortes', and deciding to take the hearing of all causes in chancery whether or not they might be tried at common law.[84] The incapacity and partiality of the judiciary compromised Gerrard's strong ambition to reform the assize courts and to expand the reach of the common law. While Kenneth Nicholls has argued that the lack of local courts in unshired territories, the difficulty of finding impartial juries and the unique ability of equity jurisdiction to hear cases involving Irish customs drove suitors to chancery, it was Gerrard's purpose to implement the assizes regularly during four terms every year.[85] Gerrard laid out a scheme to require seasoned judges to conduct regular sessions in the principal towns of Connacht and Munster twice annually, while travelling throughout the provinces

83. BL, Add. MS 47,172, ff. 135–36.
84. PRO, SP 63/56/105. See Gerrard's report in LPL, Carew MS 628, ff. 311v–14, and below, pp. 210 ff. The printed edition may be found in 'Report on the state of Ireland, 1577–78, by Lord Chancellor Gerrard,' ed. C. McNeill, *Anal Hib*, no. 2 (1930), p. 124.
85. K. Nicholls, 'Calendar of salved chancery pleadings', *Louth Arch Soc Jn*, xxvii (1969–72), 250.

during the other two sessions, saying 'justice would be delivered to itinerant circuitinge the whole pale and everye other partie made counties twoe tymes in the yeare to deliver the same at the doores of such poore creatures as either for feare or wante of abilitie could not travell to Dublin'.[86] The proposal envisaged a system for holding sessions twice yearly in Newry for the unshired portions of Ulster, as well as naming the circuits each judge would travel on assize and requiring judges to pay for all their own victuals. He carefully detailed the costs of the scheme at £1,306 13s. 4d. and ridiculed the military option, concluding 'the pollecye to wade further to gayne territories is as it were to suffer the parties nier home to burne, and to seek to quenche a fyer afarr of[f]'.[87]

Unfortunately, Gerrard's proposals for assize circuits coincided with the crises over cess and the origins of the Desmond Rebellion, though he assured Walsingham in 1579 that he would go on circuit himself because the chief justices were too sick to travel. He laid out a plan to journey from Drogheda to Louth, Meath, West Meath, Longford and Offaly.[88] Gerrard's successor did nothing remarkable to further the plans for full imposition of the assizes, and the reform he envisaged had to await the end of the Nine Years War. Using the newly won opportunity to formalize the administration of English law throughout Ireland, Chichester reluctantly approved the use of recusant judges to further his design for the comprehensive edification of assize circuits as soon as practicable. Dr McCavitt has studied the impact of the assize courts established under Chichester from 1605, noting that he ran into unexpected resistance from the newly revived presidency courts in Munster and Connacht.[89] In 1606 the lord president of Munster, Sir Henry Brouncker, complained that the assize judges 'derogate much from the authority of my place', while in 1615 the future lord deputy, Sir Oliver St John, groused as vice president of Connacht that the assize judges 'deal in all those causes that are assigned to the president and council of the province, either by their commision or instructions and so we are left without power to control these people that were wont to resort to us for justice'.[90] McCavitt concluded that the successful dissemination of English law through the assize courts attracted a surprising number of Irish litigants, for whom the process was translated into Irish in Co. Antrim in 1605.[91]

Sir John Davies wrote to Salisbury in 1605 to describe the asymmetrical metamorphosis taking place in Ireland as a result of establishing the assize courts. As attorney general, he travelled with Chichester, Lord Chancellor Jones, Chief Justice James Ley, Sir Oliver Lambert and Sir Garrett Moore to the Irish

86. 'Gerrard's report', ed. McNeill, p.124.
87. Ibid., pp. 185–87.
88. Ibid.
89. J. McCavitt, '"Good planets in their several aphearom": the establishment of the assize circuits in early seventeenth century Ireland,' *Ir Jur*, xxiv (1989), 248–51.
90. McCavitt, '"Good planets"', 251; St John to Winwood, 3 Mar. 1615, PRO, SP 63/233/9, quoted in McCavitt, p. 258.
91. Ibid., p. 259; see also Gillespie, *Colonial Ulster*, p. 111.

countries now shired as Monaghan, Fermanagh and Cavan, finding them in a lapsed state of proprietary confusion, owing to the recent rebellion and the 'transitory' nature of Irish settlement there. Despite the shiring by Fitzwilliam and Perrot, these counties were in disarray, Irish customs had been revived, all covenants broken and freeholders driven out. Cavan in particular was incompletely reformed, and Davies searched the Dublin archives in vain for records of the commission to establish seven baronies there, a situation made more confusing by the dower suit won by an O'Reilly widow whose rights in law were found by Davies to be insufficient. In July 1605 the justices arrived in the village of Monaghan, settled with cabins and peopled by soldiers who had allowed the new castle to become derelict under the seneschal, Sir Edward Blayney. Chichester left to the assize judges and commissions of gaol delivery the hearing of petitions for debt and trespass, and after an inquisition into lands and title, travelled to the abbey of Fermanagh. Davies recounted that the party pitched tents near Lough Erne and held their sessions at the ruined abbey, condemning the sheriffs and justices of the peace for their negligence since nothing was prepared (there was no gaol) and all of the twenty men indicted were released due to lack of evidence. The attorney general rebuked the justices of the peace for omitting to bind accusers to prosecute the defendants, but noted there was no fixed village or market town in the entire county, so civil government was perforce delayed until a market town could be erected. Though he returned to Dublin from assizes in August, Davies was sent immediately on a new commission of assize with the chief justice to Waterford, Wexford, and Wicklow, finding there a more settled jurisdiction. He declared there was no further need for military officials in Co. Wexford, since the county was peaceable and the forms of civil government were in place. On the other hand, there were numerous corruptions in the church, the corporations and the government itself which had led to diminished revenue, the decay of impropriations, and other abuses.[92]

The court of castle chamber customarily reviewed cases that had begun in other common law jurisdictions, and once the assize courts were fully erected, the castle chamber court heard numerous cases in which their jurors were accused of corrupt verdicts, finding against the evidence. In an action heard at castle chamber on 21 November 1610, jurors empanelled before the justices of assize at Mullingar, Co. West Meath, were fined £20 each and imprisoned during pleasure for acquitting Turlogh Gallchowe, a 'notorious traitor'.[93] A similar fine was levied on 6 May 1612 against a jury empanelled at the assizes in Carlow that acquitted Donell Mackyn for relieving 'notorious rebels'.[94] In addition, the campaign against recusancy that was orchestrated by Chichester from the castle chamber court intimidated grand juries and assize juries alike, jurors being fined at Trim, Cashel, Mullingar, Clonmel, Cork, Monaghan, Longford, Wexford, Maryborough

92. TCD, MS 842, ff. 113–21, 125v–28, 156–57v.
93. BL., Add. MS 47,172, f.169.
94. Ibid., f. 184.

and Kilkenny from 1612 to 1614. The intimidation of jurors during the administration of St John 'greatly unsettled the local order' in Kilkenny, according to Dr Edwards. The city elected five mayors in less than six months during 1616, including the prominent Ormonde clients Lucas Shee, Clement Ragget and David Rothe, but each refused the oath of supremacy and resigned in protest.[95] On 29 April 1618 the court of castle chamber fined Melaghlen McGranell McLoghlin of Co. Leitrim for refusing to present recusants, noting that it was the second time he had been censured in the same court, and calling for forfeiture of his bond.[96] Davies's earlier findings that assize courts suffered from lax supervision led to numerous later reforms, embedded in the 'Directions for the courts' in 1622. For example, judges of assize were not to ride circuit where they were born or where they had a residence, and no judge's servant or follower could serve in court as an attorney, even where no attorney of record was available.[97] Although the records are silent on the matter, it is likely that the court of castle chamber issued a 'star chamber charge' to justices about to depart on assizes, similar to the one given by Lord Chancellor Ellesmere in England for Hilary term in the first year of James I. The principal aims of government were cited along with the need to avoid judicial delay, to maintain peace in remote parts and to keep dignified sessions each quarter.[98] As Dr Cockburn has demonstrated, assizes offered the potential for a detailed and comprehensive extension of the power of the early modern state, serving as the crown's representative and bringing a more assured and consistent version of common law rule to the provinces.[99]

Under Elizabeth I, new counties were shired under reforming governors like Sussex, Sydney and Perrot, and the entire country was shired by 1609 when the Ulster plantation began. Sheriffs were chosen to administer the counties, and superintendence of their work became a hallmark of the new vigilance exercised by the court of castle chamber. By 1625 the country was served by a full establishment of justices of the peace, constables, sub-sheriffs, bailiffs, gaolers, portreeves, recorders, sovereigns and other local functionaries essential to the task of carrying out litigation. They served writs and executed orders of the central courts, planned for twice yearly assizes and held commissions of the peace. Instructions to these junior officials were remarkably detailed, using the models provided by Lord Chancellor Ellesmere and others in England. The extensive litany of actions enumerated by Bolton in his instructions to justices of the peace demonstrated their ample jurisdiction. Justices were required to indict offenders for pulling out

95. Ibid., ff. 182–211. See Edwards, *Ormond lordship*, pp. 275–76. A calculated attempt to ruin the fortunes of leading Catholic families was traced by Edwards in the downfall of William Sweetman and his uncle, whose castle chamber fines were so onerous that they fell into financial ruin. Ibid.
96. BL, Add. MS 47, 172, f. 264.
97. TCD, MS 853, ff. 149v 150; Hand & Treadwell, eds., 'Directions for the courts', 207–08.
98. TCD, MS 862, f. 367.
99. J.S. Cockburn, *A history of English assizes, 1558–1714* (Cambridge, 1972), pp. 7–8, 36, 153–57.

a man's eyes, or cutting out of tongues; for buggery and sodomy; for assaulting a vicar; and for various pastoral offences including forcible entry to a barn or a cattle-pound, 'depasturing' of grass and fishing in a mill pond.[100] Expectations for the smooth transition to common law rule were unrealistically high, yet a remarkable number of litigants pursued their actions through the courts and showed a persistence at every level of adjudication. One signature of this new confidence in adjudication was the extraordinary length of cases pending, and the eagerness of suitors to continue their action on appeal. And, while some writers have insisted that a common law regime was unrealistic and unattainable because of local resistance and corruption, we should take notice of similar obstacles in the English countryside to the final triumph of common law.[101] Dr J.P. Cooper has reminded us of the Elizabethan efforts to prevent powerful magnates from employing their personal retainers as local officials in English shires, but he noted that this tendency persisted well into the next century. Jurors in particular followed the lead of local lords, and sheriffs acknowledged the force of the *noblesse de l'épée* in England.[102] In 1617 an advisory opinion by the justices of the peace in Co. Down titled 'Tracks in the County of Down' illustrated the extent to which commissions of the peace were devoted to the formalization of a common law regime in newly shired territories of Ulster.[103]

The court of castle chamber frequently took cognizance of actions at the lowest level of the judicial system, fining jurors, reprimanding sheriffs and recorders, censuring gaolers and dismissing recusant officials who had taken office without swearing the oath of supremacy. In this manner, the court blended its ambitious goals in policymaking and adjudication. The court of castle chamber was determined to hold sheriffs accountable for their excesses, and reform of the shrievalty began with injunctions to choose them with great care. In order to expedite justice and increase revenue to the crown, English procedure was to be followed. A public meeting of the chief governor, lord chancellor and judges heard the nomination of three men for each county, choosing a sheriff only from that list unless the three were determined to be unfit, in which case other names were to be submitted by circuit judges and the presidents of Munster and Connacht were to be informed.[104] Undersheriffs and bailiffs were then chosen by the sheriffs and sworn to duty in the locality. Justices of the peace were drawn from the local gentry, as in England, but the troubled Irish countryside frequently made this process impossible and military men were sometimes given exceptional

100. Bolton, *Justice of peace for Ireland*, pp. 72 ff. For the shiring of the country, see Plate 1.
101. C. Brady, 'The decline of the Irish kingdom', in Mark Greengrass, ed., *Conquest and coalescence; the shaping of the state in early modern Europe* (London, 1991), pp. 101, 111–12.
102. J.P.Cooper, *Land, men and beliefs: studies in early modern history*, ed. by G.E. Aylmer and J.S. Morrill (London, 1983), pp. 78, 88–89. Cooper reminded us that even Burghley kept retainers and employed them liberally in local administration.
103. *Cal. S.P. Ire., 1615–25*, pp. 153–54, cited in W.N. Osborough, 'The Irish custom of tracts', in his *Studies in Irish legal history* (Dublin, 1999), pp. 73–75.
104. TCD, MS 853, ff. 145v–146; Hand & Treadwell eds., 'Directions for the courts', 193–94.

authority as seneschals who could replace the commissioners of the peace. Commissions of gaol delivery and oyer and terminer were issued after 1605 with greater effect, and the corporate towns managed their affairs with an autonomy that was occasionally viewed with suspicion. In Ulster the devolution of power to local lords was like a marriage of convenience, with the marquis of Antrim, Sir James Hamilton and others taking responsibility for apprehending malefactors on their own estates and keeping gaols to hold suspects, while local officials were chosen only with their prior approval.[105] Dr Pawlisch has shown that the court of castle chamber also used its judicial muscle to threaten the Munster towns with the extinction of their corporate privileges.[106]

As Irish society became more litigious, the competition between tribunals was increasingly heated, even at the local level. The municipal courts in the Munster towns preserved a substantial record of their litigation, including a decree that citizens of Youghal could be fined by the mayor for suing another citizen in a court other than that of Youghal.[107] Just as the court of castle chamber took upon itself the defence of women, so the Youghal corporation fined 'lewd and incontinent persons' who through flattery and wickedness managed to deflower 'young and silly virgin maids' according to the social standing of the maiden so deflowered.[108] The local corporation was held responsible for publishing and implementing conciliar decrees, such as that issued by Grandison and the council prohibiting unlicensed alehouses. Pursuant to an act of state, the corporation required payment of a commission for keeping alehouses, to be chosen by justices of the peace who would determine the number and condition of the alehouses for lodging strangers and the provision of bread and beer. Common dicing or carding was proscribed, and a later proclamation cited the dangerous practice of establishing alehouses in bogs and woods, beyond the scrutiny of the corporation. The corporation censured behaviour that went well beyond the ultimate attention of the castle chamber court, including the crowding of ships along the quay and keeping misrule at an inn after midnight. Local officials cited the bailiff for failing to clean the dung from the quayside, and condemned two butchers for dressing pigs before their houses 'by which there riseth a great scent, to the hurt of the inhabitants'.[109]

The independent jurisdictions which gradually lost out to centralizing government included the courts of Irish lords and peers, who continued to maintain their manorial courts leet and baron, while the great earl of Ormonde maintained his palatinate court in Tipperary against the encroaching power of the

---

105. Gillespie, *Colonial Ulster*, pp. 90–93, 106–07.
106. H. Pawlisch, *Sir John Davies and the conquest of Ireland: a study in legal imperialism* (Cambridge, 1985), pp. 41–43, 47–49.
107. *Corporation book of Youghal*, ed. R. Caulfield (Guildford, 1878), p. 5.
108. Ibid. Fornicating with the mayor's daughter might lead to a fine of £40; with a groom's daughter only £5.
109. Ibid., pp. 75, 171. The corporation also noted 'That Edmond O Byrnne's wife and Marg[are]t Orrniell are notable scolds'. Ibid., pp. 30–31.

crown. In 1586 Lord Deputy Perrot was ordered by the privy council in England to maintain the Ormonde manors and lands in Kilkenny and Tipperary free from all cess, based on an earlier concordatum to the earl from Sydney. Although this was later confirmed by Mountjoy in 1603, Ormonde entered into an indenture with the queen and Fitzwilliam in 1592 to victual 100 soldiers by a composition to which he voluntarily agreed.[110] By the Jacobean period, two of the peers took office as lords president in Munster and Connacht, symbolizing their allegiance to crown prerogative and substituting common law forms of adjudication for traditional and indigenous ones. On the other hand, certain new English and Scottish peers developed a reputation for independence that frustrated even the most powerful chief governors. The earl of Antrim demanded in right of his wife an annual allowance of £200 out of an estate in Queen's County, holding forth against Wentworth and Lord President St Leger in 1637.[111] The well-connected Scot, James Hamilton, was awarded substantial estates in east Ulster, and quickly became an independent power in the province. The earl of Antrim and Hamilton, who became Viscount Claneboye in 1622, used their manorial courts to thwart sheriffs and refused to allow their tenants to be subpoenaed without their permission, citing them for debt or trespass in their own courts and intimidating the sheriffs at quarter sessions.[112] Dr Brady employs dual themes of decline and failure to describe the efforts to implement the common law at the local level, citing resistance even among the servitors of the crown in the Pale itself and suggesting that the effect of seventy years of reform was to drive the native communities apart. Brady argues that some like Captain William Piers in Carrickfergus and Sir Nicholas Malbie in Newry won the support of Irish chiefs, but their alliances drove them to subvert the common law rather than to support it, manipulating the courts to the advantage of their friends. He said, 'In the later sixteenth century , as confidence in the reform policy faltered amidst persistent administrative failure, an increasingly sceptical attitude toward the potency and value of the common law began to become apparent among English servitors in Ireland.'[113] However, the exploitation of advantage in adversarial pleading is the essential nature of common law process and in this way the actions of servitors were, paradoxically, in harmony with the very policy they allegedly tried to subvert.

The coexistence of traditional Irish law and common law jurisdictions persisted throughout the middle ages and well into the late sixteenth century. The two legal systems were not always at odds, since Irish chiefs sought the protection and security of title afforded by the common law, and by the early fourteenth century parliament offered most of the Irish of Ireland the right to plead in the

---

110. *Ormond deeds, 1584–1603*, pp. 26–28, 50.
111. J. Ohlmeyer, *Civil war and restoration in the three Stuart kingdoms: the career of Randal MacDonnell, marquis of Antrim, 1609–1683* (Cambridge, 1993), p. 68.
112. Gillespie, *Colonial Ulster*, pp. 100–06.
113. C. Brady, 'Decline of Irish kingdom', p. 111. See also Canny, *Making Ireland British*, pp. 78–100 on Piers, Malby, Bagenal and Bingham.

king's courts, at least in theory.[114] Indeed, as Dr Patterson has shown for the late sixteenth century, 'in the case of the O'Dorans [leading brehon lawyers in the Pale], their own decision was ... to accept shiring, primogeniture, capital punishment of felons and the whole package of institutional changes demanded by the crown in the hope of gaining crown protection against would-be planters and retaining their lands'.[115] Dr Morgan has stressed the militarization of Ulster as the explanatory thesis for the end of Gaelic culture there, and Dr Brady argued that Tudor ruthlessness was cloaked in rhetorical moderation, claiming that 'the Tudor pretension to peaceful reform was at heart vapid, a hopeless aspiration at best, and at worst a mere pretext for the management of affairs by power alone'.[116] However, Dr Cunningham and Dr Gillespie argue convincingly that the reception of English law and administration was not uniformly opposed and, in fact, evidence from the annalists demonstrates that lords president were welcomed by subordinate Irish chiefs in Connacht, where their arrival was viewed in traditional terms of dynastic collapse and renewal. They have explained that

> the increasing power of the English administration in Ireland [was] accepted as a logical and not necessarily unwelcome development ... [and] ... The holding of sessions and other features of the common law were noted in the annals, and it is evident that the native Irish were eager to use the machinery of the common law to resolve disputes among themselves.[117]

Cunningham and Gillespie have more recently shown that the Old English adventurer, Theobald Dillon, joined his fortunes to a client of MacWilliam Burke in order to advance his prospects in Connacht, a juncture of Irish and English forms of proprietary interest that was ultimately sanctioned by the common law despite the suspicions of Lord President Bingham.[118] Evidence of local resistance

114. J. Otway-Ruthven, 'The native Irish and English law in medieval Ireland,' *IHS*, vii (1950), 1–16.

115. N. Patterson, 'Gaelic law and the Tudor conquest of Ireland: the social background of the sixteenth century recensions of the pseudo-historical Prologue to the *Senchas mar*', *IHS*, xxvii (1991), 215.

116. C. Brady, 'Sixteenth century Ulster and the failure of Tudor reform' in C. Brady, M. O'Dowd and B. Walker, eds., *Ulster: an illustrated history* (London, 1989), p. 97; H. Morgan, 'The end of Gaelic Ulster: a thematic interpretation of events between 1534 and 1610', *IHS*, xxvi (1988), 8, 14–21, 23.

117. B. Cunningham and R. Gillespie, 'Englishmen in sixteeenth century Irish annals', *Ir Econ Soc Hist*, xvii (1990), 14. See also Gillespie, 'Negotiating order', pp. 191–93, 199–203; B. Cunningham, 'Native culture and political change in Ireland 1580–1640' in Brady and Gillespie, eds., *Natives and newcomers: essays on the making of Irish colonial society, 1534–1641* (Dublin, 1986), pp. 148ff, and K.W. Nicholls, 'Some documents on Irish law and custom in the sixteenth century', *Anal Hib*, no. 26 (1970), 103–29, showing the survival of brehon practices within the context of the Tudor chancery court in Ireland.

118. Cunningham and Gillespie, *Stories from Ireland*, pp. 59–74, 82. Dillon negotiated transfer of the castle of Castlemore from Sean MacCostello in 1586 as part of a bargain for land and influence

to the full implementation of common law regimes allows us to appreciate the nuanced, measured process of anglicization during the late sixteenth century. Dr Edwards has recently shown that the 'current orthodoxy' of reform government fails to account for the 'actual experience of Tudor rule' in the countryside, citing the MacGiollapadraigs (or Fitzpatricks) of Upper Ossory as a model of regional autonomy. Though raised to the Irish peerage and reared in England as a Protestant courtier alongside the future king, Edward VI, the 'outwardly anglicised' Barnaby Fitzpatrick 'offered the crown little beyond political collaboration'.[119] Edwards explained that the Gaelic lord proudly maintained a law school run by the O'Doran brehons, kept traditional control of his market town of Aghaboe and assessed levies on Upper Ossory consistent with the customary native Irish exactions. However, while using the brehons to determine causes in dispute, Fitzpatrick was also forced to acknowledge to Gerrard in 1576 that he possessed no deeds to his land since all his tenants were, in effect, serfs.[120] When Gerrard in 1577 insisted that Upper Ossory be shired within Butler-controlled Co. Kilkenny, Fitzpatrick used his influence to delay the proceedings and the lordship ultimately accepted incorporation into Queen's Co., attending sessions at Maryborough from at least 1602.[121] Yet, Edwards cites the imprisonment of the baron in 1580 after he had been charged with treason in the Kilkenny courthouse as evidence that the Dublin government accepted Kilkenny's jurisdiction over Upper Ossory at the time. The flawed argument that ordinary commissions of martial law, issued routinely to supporters of the regime like Upper Ossory, were meant to substitute for common law institutions in his territory obscures the fact that derogation of power in this manner was an accepted practice in the Tudor borderlands. In fact, the baron was a compliant and loyal captain of the kerne who consistently appeared for general hostings and obediently 'served the crown dependably and fiercely' on the borders of the Leix and Offaly plantation.[122] Edwards is certainly correct to argue the need for 'evidence of law courts and legal officials at work in the territories of the O'Briens of Thomond, the MacMahons of Monaghan, the O'Reillys of Breifne' before acknowledging the primacy of anglicization.[123] However, his blanket

in Connacht. MacCostello in turn sought the protection of common law governance against his overlords, the Burkes, and his estates were exempted from the composition of Connacht through the intervention of Dillon, who continued to support MacCostellos in their quarrels with Bingham and his henchman, Sheriff Henry Ealand.

119. D. Edwards, 'Collaboration without anglicisation: the MacGiollapadraig lordship and Tudor reform' in D. Edwards et al., eds., *Gaelic Ireland, c. 1250–c. 1650: land, lordship and settlement* (Dublin, 2002), pp. 77–80.

120. Ibid., pp. 85–88.

121. Ibid., pp. 88–90.

122. Ibid., pp. 90, 91–93.

123. Ibid., p. 96. Edwards offers the alternative paradigm of 'Gaelic survival' in lieu of reform for the late Tudor period. What he demonstrates, however, is a substantial hybridization of Gaelic practices in order to assure survival, a pragmatism that might equally apply to English stakeholders as well, who opted for a different sort of 'collaboration' with their Irish neighbours.

assertion that there was 'no "reform" in Upper Ossory during the Tudor era' is needlessly exclusive. As he has shown, the pliant and 'opportunist' Fitzpatrick chose to cooperate with the Dublin government on numerous important issues, and he was a classic example of the transition, however gradual and incomplete, to the predominance of the common law under the Stuarts.

In the early seventeenth century, the native Irish were frequently dispossessed in east Ulster, yet they commonly resorted to legal remedies and generally welcomed the protection of civil law. Dr Gillespie declared,

> It cannot be argued that the settlers dragged the Irish into the courts since two thirds of these suits [in chancery] were pursued entirely by natives. Given that a case in chancery was usually a last resort, the procedure being long, complex and costly, this is a high figure. Measured in this way, acceptance of the new order was, therefore, quite widespread. The native Irish generally resorted to the common law over a wide range of matters including theft and murder.[124]

What is more, as Professor Osborough has demonstrated, the Irish privy council constructed an act of state as early as 1552/3 to confirm the Gaelic practice of tracking stolen cattle. This aspect of brehon law was subsequently contained in instructions to justices of the peace, and endorsed by the lords president, and abolished only in 1640 by another act of state. Instructions for the lord president and council in Munster of 1616 declared,

> All and every his majesty's subjects ... being preyed, robbed, or spoiled ... [are to] presume not to seek their revenge by their accustomed Brehone laws, or restitution of their goods by arbitrary means, other than by complaint as aforesaid, to the lord president and council, or before the judges of assizes in their circuits, or justices of the peace in their quarter sessions, or as by his majesty's laws is appointed.[125]

The act of state which created this hybrid legal remedy, an Irish custom enforceable by officials of the common law regime, is a notable example of the slow process of anglicization at the local level that was inspired by the Irish council and, theoretically, supervised in its implementation by the court of castle

---

A study of the English captains and their efforts to settle estates within and near the Pale would offer similar rewards to the researcher. See also S.G. Ellis, *Tudor frontiers and noble power: the making of the British state* (Oxford, 1995); Ellis, 'England in the Tudor State', *Hist Jn*, xxvi (1983), 210–12.

124. One fourth of local cases brought to chancery in relation to Antrim and Down in the early seventeenth century, out of the 50 bills of pleadings that have survived, involved Irish plaintiffs. Gillespie, *Colonial Ulster*, p. 111.

125. *Desid. cur. Hib.*, ii, 16, quoted in Osborough, 'The Irish custom of tracts', in his *Studies in Irish legal history*, p. 75.

chamber. In 1612 Chichester wrote to Sir Humphrey May to explain that, paradoxically, the British undertakers had become devoted to the custom of tracks, using it to justify a financial settlement greater than the value of the lost animal.[126] The 'Directions for ordering ... the courts' in 1622 referred to the continuing practice of kencogus law, another remnant of an obsolescent brehon law, affirming that 'It is his maties pleasure yt it shold be contynued or left as shalbe found fittest to the Lo: Deputy & Councell. ... [and], so long as they contynue in use, be equally communicated aswell to the Irish as Brittish, or wholly taken away'.[127]

In the current state of research, it is difficult to say for Ireland that the systematic and comprehensive 'devolution of royal authority to private persons' that had obtained in England by the Jacobean period was in place by 1641.[128]

RELATIONS WITH ENGLISH COURTS AND COMMITTEES

The court of castle chamber maintained a symbiotic and dependent relationship with the crown, labouring to defend the honour of the sovereign while suffering in embarrassed silence when policy detours left the court politically exposed. Constitutional issues will be taken up in a later section, but it is important to recognize here certain essential features of the connection with the sovereign. First, the court was originally sanctioned by Elizabeth I after a decade of badgering by her first two lords deputy, Sussex and Sydney.[129] Both James I and Charles I re-authorized the court by charters at the commencement of their reigns, citing the need to maintain the course of prerogative justice in Ireland.[130] Secondly, the crown interfered directly in some legal proceedings on appeal from Irish magnates, suggesting that the jurisdiction of the castle chamber court was

126. Osborough, 'Custom of tracts', p. 72, quoting 'The letter book of Sir Arthur Chichester 1612–1614', ed. R.D. Edwards, *Anal Hib*, no. 8 (1938), 3 at 30–33.
127. TCD, MS 853, f. 149v, article 34. On the other hand, the council was also admonished to abolish by act of state certain Irish customs in conflict with English practice in the church, denying vicars and parsons the right to claim tithing and mortuaries to a certain valuable consideration, in lieu of tithes in specie. Ibid., f. 151. See also Hand & Treadwell, eds., 'Directions for the courts', 206, 211–12.
128. W.J. Jones 'Palatine performance in the seventeenth century' in P. Clark, A.G.R. Smith and N. Tyacke, eds., *The English commonwealth, 1547 to 1640* (Leicester, 1979), p. 189.
129. The queen authorized the court in 1562 in orders to Sussex and promised to send the orders of the court in 1566 to Sydney. *Cal. Carew MSS, 1515–74*, pp. 330, 342–43; PRO, SP 63/6/101; *Sidney state papers, 1565–70*, ed. T. Ó Laidhin (Dublin, 1962), pp. 19–20.
130. Documents preserved in Trinity College Library contain numerous commissions, charters and procedures from English star chamber. See TCD, MS 649. 'Star Chamber Cases', f. 1: 'An exact Compendium of the whole Course of the Court of Starr Chamber'; TCD, MS 722, titled 'A Treatise of the high Courte of Starchamber'; TCD, MS 721 for rules and star chamber cases under Charles I; TCD, MS 734 for a list of Elizabethan officials on her star chamber court; and TCD, MS 802 for the fees and orders of the court under Elizabeth.

circumscribed by political realities when dealing with the power élite. The frequent references to the privilege of tonnage and poundage for prise wines awarded to the earl of Ormonde is a recurring example of royal largesse, protected by appeal to prerogative justice; while the laboured explanation of his patrimony in defence of the title to the earldom of Clanricarde drew the attention of James I and his court to the incumbent, Richard Burke, and his conniving brothers, Thomas and John.[131] Thirdly, the crown was defended on all points of honour, particularly at times of war and rebellion, when treasonable words were punished as 'trayterous & sedicious speeches'. On 28 November 1593, for example, the court condemned Nicholas White of Co. Kildare for publishing a prophecy that O'Donnell would become king in Ireland when the pope sent an ancient crown from Rome. White was pilloried, whipped and both his ears cut off before he was imprisoned for the offence.[132]

Fourthly, the crown took action in cases where the chief governor was disgraced, or impeached, for offences that occurred during his Irish tenure, implicating the court of castle chamber. Sir John Perrot was arraigned for treason in London and certain decisions of the court of castle chamber were reversed on appeal as a result. The court heard allegations in 1591 that Perrot had called the queen a 'pyskitchen', aggravating his lengthy incarceration in London.[133] In 1590, the court under Fitzwilliam dutifully reversed its previous decision condemning Henry Bird for forgery of Perrot's signature, reinstating Bird to his office as register for the ecclesiastical commission.[134] The earl of Strafford's impeachment proceedings before the high court of parliament struck directly at his misuse of the court of castle chamber, while the king stood by impassively.[135] And finally, on

---

131. BL, Add. MS 47,172, ff 172–77. See also the challenge to the title of the earl of Kildare by Lady Lettice Fitzgerald, the ward of Queen Elizabeth, and her English husband Sir Robert Digby. Ibid., ff. 154–59.

132. Ibid., f 111. On 6 May 1597 Captain John Norris was fined 500 marks and given life in prison for uttering slanderous words and false rumours against the queen. Ibid., f 128. See also the case of Alexander Plunkett who declared in Co. Louth that the Spanish would return to Ireland and conquer it in the spring of 1588. He was pilloried and imprisoned for 'bearing a most disloyal hate unto the sacred Majesty of the Queen's most royal person'. Ibid., f. 89.

133. On 16 June 1591 John Delahide was condemned for reporting Perrot's slander of the queen. Ibid., f. 96. 'Pyskitchen' lacks a formal entry in the *OED*; however, given the context of slander and defamation, we can surmise the origin must have been from the place or room where one would 'piss'; and reference made to the place might infer that the person connected with it would have the duty of cleaning it. Common usage of the term 'kitchen' invited scurrilous forms from 'kitchen-wench' to 'kitchen-drudge' or even, 'kitchen-slut'. Alternatively, the use of kitchen as symbolic of the stomach might have referred in this instance to other body parts. Contemptuous and humorous renderings from the period often referred to 'kitchen-aphorisms' or 'kitchen-science', in this case a derogation of the crown's presumed majesty, power and wisdom; the word might also have reference to the chamber-pot, or the place where it was found.

134. Ibid., ff. 90v–92.

135. On this issue, now see J. MacCafferty, '"To follow the late precedents of England": the Irish impeachment proceedings of 1641', in D.S. Greer and N.M. Dawson, eds., *Mysteries and*

some core issues involving the royal prerogative, crown rights were defended by appeal for grace and favour directly to the sovereign. Sir Henry Sydney's undoing was caused by an appeal to the queen against the cess, or purveyance for the lord deputy and the army, by a delegation of Pale representatives who refused to be daunted by threats of prosecution in castle chamber.[136] And Lord Falkland was under constant pressure in 1627–29 to accord certain privileges known as the 'Graces' to the Old English, despite their recusant beliefs.[137] On other matters, such as the religious policy crafted by Chichester against recusancy under James I, the campaign began with a royal proclamation, read into the entry book of the court of castle chamber. The decree, citing nine defendants of the city of Dublin for an outrageous suggestion that 'wee for our parte have a purpose or inclination [to offer] libertie of Conscience and tolleration of religion unto our said Su[bjects]', rectified any misunderstanding by ordering all subjects to attend parish churches on Sundays, and condemned seminary priests who 'doe malitiously endeavor to alienate the hartes of our Subiects from us, by insinuatinge and breeding a distaste in them both of our Religion and Cyvill government'.[138] Later, it became neces-sary to rein in the truculent lord deputy when he employed the court of castle chamber as an instrument of royal tyranny against the wishes of the king and the advice of his senior ministers.[139]

Relations between the Irish privy council and the government in Westminster were profoundly important and deserve more attention than they will be afforded here. The secretaries of state in England devoted volumes of correspondence to Ireland, some of which addressed adjudication before the court of castle chamber. In cases that involved the crown directly, Cecil and his successors sent instructions to the lord deputy and council touching upon foreign merchants, English aristocrats, corporate towns and private undertakers in Ireland. Although the chief governors were immensely powerful in Ireland during this period and the petition books demonstrate the wide latitude of their discretionary authority, heightened scrutiny of their work was only a crisis away. The secretaries of state increased their vigilance over Irish matters throughout the period, adding layers of bureaucracy to handle matters ranging from the ecclesiastical administration to the plantations. Dr Brady's fine study of the Tudor viceroys acknowledged

solutions in Irish legal history (Dublin, 2001). For a full record of the Irish parliament proceed-ings and the Queries see TCD, MS 615, and TCD, MS 672, ff. 274–75.

136. See Crawford, Anglicizing, pp. 369–407 for a discussion. The queen was both offended at their temerity and conscious of their desperate financial straits. See Cal. Carew MSS, 1575–88, pp. 78–79, 105; PRO, SP 63/58/67.

137. See Clarke, The Graces, pp. 9–26.

138. BL, Add. MS 47,172, ff. 137–37v. The defendants were accused of contempt of the crown's statutes, proclamations and 'Royall prerogative' commanding regular attendance at church services. Ibid., f. 139v.

139. The entry book of orders and decrees was littered with recusancy fines against jurors and local officials under Chichester. See below, Part Two, Ch. 8. For a good discussion of the issue, see McCavitt, Chichester, ch. 7.

their skill and experience but, he claimed, the principal secretaries 'rarely functioned as independent policy-makers ... [and] ... were simply incapable of devoting the sustained effort which policy formulation and execution demanded'.[140] It was only when Strafford negotiated the terms of his viceregal government that appeals to the crown were forced back to Ireland for vetting by the lord deputy himself. And this in turn became one of the *causes de guerre* cited in the Queries by Darcy and his fellow critics of the Strafford regime, both in England and Ireland.

The English privy council closely superintended Irish affairs and kept up regular correspondence with Irish officials consistently throughout the period. Far from the 'chronic neglect of Ireland' mentioned by Dr Brady, the privy council took up days of work exclusively on Irish business, finally complaining that too many Irish suitors required their attention and creating committees for Irish matters. On 24 June 1592, for example, the privy council heard thirty Irish petitions.[141] In August 1592 the privy council wrote to the deputy and council in Dublin that the long suit of Nicholas Power against James, Lord Power should be left to trial at common law, observing, 'our meaning is not that any course be taken contrarie to justice or to the ordinarie course of tryall by the lawes in cases that shall so requier to be determined, or that any cause duely and orderly heard and ended there be, by our letters, reversed or recalled in question'.[142] The privy council affirmed their intention to streamline ordinary litigation in the Irish courts, warning the Irish privy council in May 1593 against diverting causes determinable in the ordinary courts, with rare exceptions.[143]

This useful clarification was almost immediately undermined by the privy council itself. On a petition of Alice Bowen of Queen's Co. on behalf of her son, Robert, aged 17, the English council found that a charge of wilful murder in queen's bench against the young offender was too severe. Robert was accused of wounding Richard MacMoyler in apprehending him on a charge of treason, after which Richard died in custody for want of care. The privy council ordered the viceroy to stay all proceedings against young Bowen in queen's bench and to enter a new examination of the case before the conciliar tribunal.[144] The undercurrent of distrust and suspicion accorded to Irish courts of law by the queen's senior ministers runs through much of the correspondence, despite overtures of respect for the administration of the common law. Knowing this, the earl of Thomond wrote to Burghley on 28 June 1593 to require Fitzwilliam to stay the bill of George Darsey against the earl in castle chamber.[145] The privy council expressed its frustration over long days spent in the hearing of Irish suits:

140. Brady, 'Court, castle, country', p. 32 and see p. 4; Brady, *Chief governors*, pp. 292–96.
141. *Acts privy council, 1591–92*, pp. 551–81. See Brady, 'Court, castle, country', p. 31. On 5 August 1587 nearly the entire meeting of the privy council was taken up with Irish affairs: *Acts privy council, 1587–88*, pp. 181–90.
142. *Acts privy council, 1592*, p. 179.
143. *Acts privy council, 1592–93*, p. 219.
144. Ibid., p. 307.
145. *Cal. S.P. Ire., 1592–96*, p. 110. No mention of this bill occurs in the entry book.

Theire Lordships in respecte of the multitude of Iryshe suitours that do repaire hether upon verye lighte occasion, whereof, as theire Lordships are informed, the greater parte aswell of Irishe birthe as of Englishe do not frequente the Churche and are therefore suche as deserve litle favor in theire suites.[146]

The privy council took note of the Byzantine proceedings in Irish courts of law, where multiple jurisdictions claimed the right to hear a cause, and petitioners changed venue with impunity. For example, in June 1624 the council chose to cut the judicial Gordian knot in the case of Florence McCarthy, imprisoned in England and unable to prosecute his suit for title to lands in Co. Cork. They remanded the case to the hearing of the lord deputy and council as a matter of equity, though more properly belonging to the common law.[147] On 28 January 1618 the privy council took up the cause of Sir Richard Fleetwood in a suit pending for seven years against David Condon for lands in Munster, despite many orders made in Ireland for speedy trial and determination of the dispute. Condon refused to appear at trial in the Irish exchequer court and appealed against a commission named by the viceroy and Irish council, so the privy council made an order favouring Fleetwood, putting Condon out of possession pending a final hearing in Ireland, and finding the latter in contempt.[148] On 31 July 1624 the privy council reviewed decrees made in the Irish court of chancery against the petitioner, Sir Thomas Fitzwilliam, after referring the matter to the English chief justices. They found that Fitzwilliam had received 'harde measure' and called upon the viceroy along with the chief justices and master of the rolls in Ireland to review the chancery decrees in question, a clear derogation of the Irish lord chancellor's authority.[149] In a similar check to a previous lord chancellor, the privy council on 19 December 1586 upbraided Loftus for his handling of a controversy between Thomas Colclogh and Thomas Williams, clerk of the check, over Tintern Abbey, charging that,

[he] proceeded against the said Williams with some severity; their Lordships thought good to praie his Lordship for the avoyding of suspicion to forbeare to proceed anie further to the hearing and ordering of the case, and that the same might either be commytted to be decyded at the Common Lawe, or els be hard befor the bodie of the Councell there.[150]

---

146. *Acts privy council, 1591–92*, p. 587. Written on 24 June 1592, the council ordered the clerk to administer the oath of allegiance to all suitors before them, and if they refused, to dismiss their suits. A later order required all suits determinable in Ireland by common law or equity to be returned there for remedy. *Acts privy council, 1592*, p. 82.

147. *Acts privy council, 1623–25*, p. 262.

148. *Acts privy council, 1618–19*, p. 23.

149. *Acts privy council, 1623–25*, p. 286.

150. *Acts privy council, 1586–87*, p. 269. In a subsequent letter to the chancellor, the matter was referred to arbitrators, forbidding any decree or order in chancery to disadvantage either party.

Although real property actions were not technically within the purview of the court of castle chamber, numerous suits were brought there alleging wrongful dispossession among other offences. Most of these actions were brought by, or on behalf of, members of the aristocracy in Ireland. The privy council often called upon the lord deputy and Irish council to deliberate on issues of inheritance, title, jointure and related claims inherent in the nature of a landed aristocracy. In March 1580, for example, the privy council required three of the Irish councillors to hear and determine the allegation of Lady Echingham that her rights to the abbey of Dunbrody were wrongfully withheld by Lady Williams of Thame, executrix of her late husband, the viceroy Sir William Drury.[151] The earl of Clancare came directly to the privy council in England in July 1588 to condemn the 'sinister practice' of Fynny MacCarty in abducting his only daughter and heir. Stating that she was enticed to leave his household, though very young and not of age to consent to a marriage contract, the earl sought a conciliar order to bring MacCarty before the viceroy and Irish council in Dublin and to restore the young lady to her father.[152] In granting this order, the privy council made note of the dishonour to the earl and, in so doing, took up a cause that was normally heard before the court of castle chamber. In 1613 the English councillors remanded to their Irish counterparts the hearing of a cause begun by Lady Inchiquin, wife of John FitzPatrick, who argued the award made between her husband and the baron of Upper Ossory was prejudicial to her jointure.[153] The privy council took up the ongoing controversy between the two feuding relations, Baron Brittas and his nephew, Baron Castleconnell, seeking a *via media* to honour the patrimony of the minor heir while securing title to the disputed estate of his uncle. Through the mediation of the attorney general and solicitor general and Richard Hadsor for the commission for Irish causes, a compromise was reached so that

> all suites betweene the said two Lordes and their servantes and other their followers in the Castle Chamber or elswhere to be discontinewed and discharged, for which purpose an Act of State is to be made and entred into the Councell Booke ther for performance thereof.[154]

Despite the studied interventions of the privy council, however, the two disputants were left to pursue the matter before the lord deputy and council in Ireland by an exasperated memorandum of December 1620.[155]

> The two chief justices, the master of the rolls, the chief baron and two attorneys were called upon to hear and determine the matter, while the council affirmed that it was 'not meaning hereby to bring into mistrust the said Lord Chauncellour's upright dealinges in maters of justice'. Ibid., pp. 291–92.

151. *Acts privy council, 1579–80*, p. 412; *1580–81*, p. 203.
152. *Acts privy council, 1588*, p. 147.
153. *Acts privy council, 1613–14*, p. 181.
154. *Acts privy council, 1619–20*, pp. 109–10.
155. Ibid., p. 325. The rents due for estates of the minor heir were at issue, as well as the point of

The constitutional ambivalence manifested by the privy council in its discussion of legal proceedings in Ireland occasionally touched the court of castle chamber directly. Efforts to steer the course of litigation appear not infrequently, alongside a stated reluctance to interfere in its equity jurisdiction. In rare situations, the court of castle chamber had become enmeshed in a politically charged gambit that involved the clash of senior government officials over policy. Sir John Perrot's eventual disgrace and treason trial led to the privy council's reversal of two highly disputed castle chamber decisions, taken while he was lord deputy in Ireland. In one such case, Henry Ealand, formerly sheriff of Co. Roscommon, had been condemned in the castle chamber court for malfeasance in office. This client of Perrot's hated rival, Sir Richard Bingham, president of the council in Connacht, was accused of tyranny and brutality by numerous Irish petitioners, but he was defended by Bingham who challenged the right of the court to try him during the hearing of sessions in Roscommon.[156] Since Ealand was tried and condemned at castle chamber in his absence, the privy council sought a review of the case in April 1588 when Fitzwilliam had replaced the fallen Perrot. The senior council 'marveled' at the 'hard sentence' given to Ealand while he was absent on the queen's service, yet not wishing to undermine the authority of the tribunal, and uncommonly aware of the judicial perimeter separating the council in Ireland from the court of castle chamber, they cautioned

> which re-examynacion and that which was further thereuppon by them to be don, their Lordships thought meet should be don at the Councell Borde and not in the Starr Chamber, because yt could not in their opinions stand with the honnour and reputacion of any soche Court of Justice after a judgment given in the same Court to have yt re-examyned and altered.[157]

The privy council asked for the full record to be made available to Ealand, required the Irish council to inform them of the result, and waited for the predictable reversal.

The cantankerous Bingham, meanwhile, pursued the cause on behalf of his minion with a flood of letters to the privy council, though he was personally under attack for acts of tyranny in Connacht and had to defend himself at two hearings before the Irish council in 1587 and 1589.[158] Curiously, this detour around the court of castle chamber was apparently sanctioned by the privy council itself, despite the fact that the castle chamber court routinely heard allegations of official misconduct. The explanation appears to lie in the seniority

---

honour noted by the council that a baron should not pay rent to another lord for his chief manor house, held directly of the king.

156. BL, Add. MS 47,172, ff. 82–82v; *Cal. S.P. Ire., 1586–88*, pp. 206–07, 493–95.

157. *Acts privy council, 1588*, p. 11. The entire case is discussed more fully below.

158. *Cal. S.P. Ire., 1586–88*, p. 267; *1588–92*, pp. 173, 223, 230, 262, 270, 274. He was acquitted on 4 December 1589 after six days of hearings from counties Galway, Mayo, Sligo and Roscommon.

and potency of Bingham's role, though the hearings seemed to follow the protocols normally reserved for the castle chamber venue. Writing to the viceroy in 1589, the privy council declared it was 'inconvenient' for the governor of the province to be charged for offences at general sessions, seeking rather to

> appoint to have the matter speedely heard before you and the whole Councell at Dublyn at suche tyme as you shall most speedely limitt, the said Governour being first warned and acquainted with the complaintes, and being sent for to come unto Dublyn, where also the complaintes against him maie be heard and duly examined, and pro[o]ffes produced for the verefying of the troth of the said accusactions.[159]

The senior council ordered that if Bingham were culpable the Irish council should inform them and the queen, but if he were not guilty the council was to publish the record of his innocence in the open sessions of Connacht. They were further ordered to reform the inferior officers of Connacht, addressing complaints there 'for even in the bowells within the Realme of England we fynd manie tymes causes of complaintes, thoughe not of soe barbarous condicions as those of Ireland seeme to ... be'.[160]

The enemies of Perrot prevailed against him a second time in the case of a reversal of the castle chamber judgement against the clerk for ecclesiastical causes, Henry Bird. Perrot had charged him with counterfeiting the deputy's name in the court of castle chamber in 1586, reading into the record of the court numerous long extracts from the alleged forgeries, whereupon he was duly condemned and sentenced.[161] However, Archbishop Loftus, the lord chancellor, dissented from the judgement since he was also head of the ecclesiastical commission, and the lone accuser of Bird was a renegade priest of doubtful reputation, Sir Denis O Roghan. When Perrot was under suspicion of treason in London, the case of Henry Bird was brought up for review by the privy council, seeking evidence from the castle chamber hearing by letters to the chancellor and deputy in August and September 1590. The senior council demanded to see matters proved in the court against Bird and O Roghan and writings pursuant to the case, calling for the priest to be sent to England for examination there. On 6 November 1590 the court of castle chamber heard the suit of Henry Bird for remission of his sentence in the same court, on grounds that the proceedings were not in due form and that the accuser, Perrot, was also present in the courtroom. Taking note of the letter from the privy council dated 17 August 1590, as well as the recantation of O Roghan, the court was persuaded that Henry Bird was innocent of the alleged forgery and proceeded to reverse its earlier verdict, setting Bird free 'without prejudice'.[162] The

159. *Acts privy council, 1588–89*, p. 431.
160. Ibid., p. 433.
161. BL, Add. MS 47,172, ff. 79–81.
162. Ibid., ff. 90v–92.

politically inspired reversal was highly unusual in the records of the court, but it demonstrates the close scrutiny of its work by the privy council in England and the availability of an appeal from castle chamber verdicts directly to the crown or the senior executive committee. The privy council condemned both the viceroy and chancellor in a stinging rebuke on 17 January 1591 for their 'over slite and carles manner of proceeding' in the Bingham case, demanding to know more about Perrot's alleged disloyal speeches.[163] Based on the litany of Irish suits and suitors heard in England, it is difficult to accept the notion that 'the government [of Ireland] was generally allotted a subordinate place in the priority lists of the great Tudor ministers until imminent danger forced it upon their attentions'.[164] Dr Brady has argued that

> the reform of Ireland through the gradual extension of English law through-
> out the whole island remained the officially declared objective of each suc-
> ceeding Tudor regime, [but] the policy itself was continually undermined
> by the fact that no one involved in the process was prepared to make a firm
> and determined commitment to it.[165]

Abundant evidence for the continual crown supervision of the Irish courts and direct intervention in their decisions would appear to make the opposite point.

Conciliar reproof from England of the castle chamber court extended as well to the work of the lord deputy and council, acting in its judicial capacity on matters beyond the purview of castle chamber. For example, in 1606 the Irish council had granted letters patent to Baron Delvin for the manor of Granard, compromising the rights of the crown to certain cows, rent, military service, and other benefits in socage tenure, including twenty marks by composition. Acting on the suit of the O'Ferralls, the privy council wrote to their counterparts in Ireland on 31 August to demand that the original intent of the king's grant be honoured:

> we do first send you informations against the same [his grant], whereby it
> may appear unto him, if they be true, that his grant is voidable, and so no
> wrong done unto him; if he will not yield to reason, whereof we desire your
> lordship so to make application, as his majesty may pass to the lord of
> Delvin those things which are reasonable, without doing that to others to
> whom his majesty intendeth no such course of severity.[166]

---

163. *Acts privy council, 1590–91*, p. 212. It was claimed that Perrot said he would send the council in
     Ireland out of the castle gate on coal staves.
164. Brady, 'Court, castle, country', p. 40.
165. Ibid., p. 41.
166. *Desid. cur. Hib.*, i, 503. The privy council added that they wished the councillors of Ireland who
     were best acquainted with these matters had 'made a good end'.

The privy council's reprimand of the council in Ireland in this case was tantamount to an appeal in law, suggesting that a parallel appellate jurisdiction for prerogative justice lay outside the common law, administered by the executive council and the crown. The privy council received a petition in December 1627 by one Christopher Draycott, gentleman, who had been convicted in the court of castle chamber on 23 June 1620 of an assault on Francis Roe, the mayor of Drogheda, and his wife.[167] Draycott had suffered long imprisonment in addition to his fine. It was noted that the lord deputy and council had subsequently reduced the fine of £500 and discharged Draycott, but the petitioner neglected to enter an order in the court of exchequer so that his fine remained on the record. The senior council referred the case to the commission for Irish causes, which recommended a reduced fine and this order was communicated to the viceroy and council in Ireland on 27 December 1627.[168] Viscount Falkland fell afoul of the privy council in 1628 when he appealed their decision favouring Phelim MacFeagh O'Byrne directly to the king. The English councillors took offence, finding his bitter recriminations a slander and dishonour to the privy council and noting that if an Irish subject had used like phrases and invectives he would have questioned them in the castle chamber court.[169]

In a rare example of the survival of a castle chamber case that was not recorded in the entry book, the privy council in England received a petition in 1628 on behalf of the litigious Sir Walter Coppinger of Co. Cork. Coppinger was a successful merchant and Old English public official who had appeared before the court as early as 1593 as an undersheriff of the county.[170] The plaintiff in the case, Sir Allen Apsley, sued Coppinger in castle chamber in Michaelmas term 1625, and the case was determined on behalf of the latter, who was acquitted. However, Apsley appealed to the king, who on 11 September 1627 wrote to Falkland as lord deputy to alter the decree of acquittal into one of censure of Coppinger.[171] The merits of the case were not discussed, but Coppinger sued to the privy council on 16 March 1628, complaining that he had been restrained since 29 November 1627 in the marshalsea of the court of castle chamber for no cause other than failure to bring in certain evidence in the dispute with Apsley over lands. The privy council heard that the evidence had been deposited in the castle chamber court but was afterward released to the respondent upon the final hearing of the issue, so Coppinger was not in contempt of the court, and the commission for Irish causes agreed.[172] Cautiously, the senior council wrote to the chief justices in Ireland for their opinion, particularly seeking testimony as to whether Coppinger pleaded the

---

167. BL, Add. MS 47,172, ff. 279–80.
168. *Acts privy council, 1627–28*, p. 201.
169. *Acts privy council, 1628–29*, p. 289. Falkland had been present at the hearing and was admonished to forbear taunts against 'this board'.
170. BL, Add. MS 47, 172, f. 106.
171. *Cal. S.P. Ire., 1625–32*, p. 270.
172. *Acts privy council, 1627–28*, p. 351.

general pardon as his principal defence, and ordering his release.[173] The king wrote to the viceroy and Irish council in May, however, to order the castle chamber decree altered from acquittal to censure, confirming this order in a subsequent letter of 21 November 1628.[174] Once again, the castle chamber court was reversed on appeal to the crown and privy council, though it is interesting to note that the English star chamber was never engaged in any of these judicial reviews. The case demonstrates the frequent use of the commission for Irish causes, and offers a glimpse of the substantial caseload of the court of castle chamber that remains unrecorded in the archives. By 1630 Apsley's continuous litigation against Coppinger resulted in an appeal to the crown over two assaults on the defendant's female relatives and neighbours. The king ordered Coppinger to appear in England, 'seeing how our Court of Castle Chamber was lately divided on this question, to have it tried before us and our Privy Council in our Court of Star Chamber.'[175]

The English privy council occasionally concerned itself with matters of protocol in Ireland, finding the allegations of dishonourable speeches made in the court of castle chamber by Lord Mountnorris at the trial of Patrick O Mulvany in 1630 to be groundless. Based on disputed examinations of the judges and counsel of that court, the privy council concluded that they did not intend to 'take advantage of such slippes as may be made in sodaine speaches when they may beare anie good construccion'.[176] On 21 April 1616 the privy council wrote to the lords justices on behalf of two attorneys appointed to the court of castle chamber in Ireland, in support of their petition for an increase of fees. The English privy council required that the clerk of the court of castle chamber effectively share the perquisites of his office in an equitable manner, according to the form established by English star chamber and formerly used in Ireland.[177] The privy council found that the fee of 10 shillings received by attorneys from every plaintiff and defendant for reading their pleadings and depositions was removed by an act of council for ease of the petitioners, at the urging of the recent parliament. So the councillors appealed for a reasonable solution, leaving it to the viceroys to find an equitable result.[178]

173. Six Irish judges wrote to the privy council in England on 16 May 1628 to show that Coppinger was acquitted of champerty on the merits of the case, though for other offences he pleaded the queen's pardon. *Acts privy council, 1628–29*, p. 127.

174. *Cal. S.P. Ire., 1625–32*, pp. 312, 341, 405. The privy council returned to the matter on 31 October 1628, noting that Coppinger should not have had the benefit of the pardon since his attorneys did not plead it, blaming this on the clerk's mishandling of the decree and referring in their decision to the need to preserve the honour of the court of castle chamber. *Acts privy council, 1628–29*, p. 217.

175. *Cal. S.P. Ire., 1647–60*, p. 163. And see below, p. 365. Coppinger was accused of striking out a tooth from Gennett Grant and throwing his neighbour's wife, Ellen O'Driscoll, into the sea.

176. *Acts privy council, 1630–31*, p. 133.

177. *Acts privy council, 1615–16*, p. 498.

178. Ibid.

Later, the privy council took note of the poverty of Cornelius Kelly of Co. Galway in his suit depending in the court of wards for nearly nine years, finding Kelly penurious and urging the lords justices in 1630 to allow him to plead *in forma pauperis* against the more powerful Viscount Clanmorris for his inheritance. This plea was often an avenue to the court of castle chamber, but no record of this suit exists in the entry book.[179] In sum, the omnicompetence of the privy council has been often remarked, and the evidence for its influence on the Irish council and the court of castle chamber is incontestable.

At times when the English privy council was out of harmony with the policy of the chief governor, they proceeded cautiously. This was particularly true of the tendentious policy of Chichester and his successors in their reckless prosecution of the king's Catholic subjects during the aftermath of the Tyrone Rebellion.[180] Recusant officials of the corporate towns had launched a campaign to safeguard their royal charters and in 1607 the king offered to compromise. Their lawsuits were opposed by *quo warranto* proceedings wherein learned counsel had found their claim of a right to tonnage and poundage was 'insufficient in law', invalidating not only their claims but decades of unlawful charges that the king proposed to collect from them. The privy council wrote to the viceroy and Irish council that the king moved them to stay the suit against the corporate towns until municipal officials had a chance to consider the crown offer to remit all previous charges in return for their willingness to pay subsidies of tonnage and poundage.[181] In this way, the crown offered to divert legal process in order to effect royal policy, holding up the proceedings in court until an answer was received on a matter of tax exemption. In 1616 the privy council ordered the corporate towns that had elected recusant magistrates to be fined and their officials imprisoned for ignoring the king's demand to elect more 'conformable' officials. They ordered proceedings against the royal charters of certain towns to be commenced, 'finding by experience that neyther admonition nor moderate correccion doth worcke the endes which hee aymeth at', but acknowledging that the legal proceedings would take years to conclude.[182] In the case of Waterford, the privy council worried in 1616 that the proud town would be governed as a village and ordered the Irish council to effect some interim solution until another charter was devised for it.[183] In July 1617 the king ordered proceedings to commence, and the judges found defects in charters and contempts in their administration, particularly in returning sheriffs and justices of the peace who refused the oath of supremacy. The privy council ordered the trial of a few of the principal persons along with deprivation of the town charter, yet they temporized

179. *Acts privy council, 1630–31*, p. 86, and see, too, pp. 44–45.
180. See below, Part Two, Ch. 8; McCavitt, *Chichester*, ch. 7; and *Desid. cur. Hib.*, i, 151: 'A Chronicle of Lord Chichester's government of Ireland containing … discourses for years 1612–1615'.
181. *Desid. cur. Hib.*, i, 510.
182. *Acts privy council, 1615–16*, p. 689.
183. *Acts privy council, 1616–17*, p. 91.

on more extreme proposals. While some agreed that priests might be confined in castles on safe islands under guard, it was imperative to avoid punishment so extreme that it would spark more controversy.[184] They further acknowledged that the need for credible persons required the employment of substantial men in office, avoiding 'persons of mean sort' even if they conformed, so the privy council ordered

> that you might for a tyme, till religion by the courses now in hande might be further wrought into the mynde of the better sorte, winke at the admission of some into those places of justices and sheriffes, whoe, though they take not the oath of supremacy, yet you finde them otherwise forwarrd and ready in all civill services and matters pertaynninge to justice.[185]

By 1619 the charters of the corporation of Waterford had been found invalid and negotiations were commenced to reinstate a new charter while the lord president in Munster, the earl of Thomond, governed in the absence of a municipal corporation.[186]

Finally, the privy council responded promptly when a member of its own board suffered calumny in Ireland. On 26 March 1618 they wrote to the viceroy and Irish council to condemn the 'lewd and slanderous report' of a priest named Verdon who had slandered the archbishop of Canterbury and was prosecuted for it in the Irish star chamber under the king's orders. Verdon reportedly claimed the primate of England was imprisoned in the Tower for saying that a foreigner should not be king of England, and for opposing the Spanish Match as a ruse whereby to ruin the English.[187] After Verdon was duly condemned, the privy council wrote in support of the castle chamber decree, offering the archbishop's mercy to the offender if he would acknowledge his crime.[188] In 1630, after nearly three decades of fruitless persecution of recusancy, the English privy council expressed outrage at an urban riot in Dublin apparently led by friars who were living under the protection of local notables. But the senior privy council again urged caution, saying 'we must leave to your owne discretions, whose particular knowledge of the present state of things can guide you best when and where to carry a soft or harder hand'.[189] The continued growth of correspondence concerning Irish affairs in the archives of the English privy council demonstrates a

---

184. Ibid., p. 311.
185. Ibid.
186. Ibid., p. 332; *1618–19*, pp. 94, 65.
187. *Acts privy council, 1618–19*, p. 83. Viscount Gormanston was also condemned as the one who had harboured and maintained Verdon in his household. The castle chamber suit was prosecuted on 15 May 1618 and Verdon was duly fined £500 and pilloried with loss of both his ears. BL, Add. MS 47,172, f. 270.
188. *Acts privy council, 1618–19*, p. 163.
189. *Acts privy council, 1629–30*, p. 259.

strong commitment to review the execution of crown policy in Ireland. Yet there is an erratic voice in the record and we must recognize that policymaking in Ireland was a species of shared governance, with the viceroy and council treading a safe path while the crown and executive committees deferred to their expertise and practical knowledge of affairs. The commissioners of 1622, sent to inquire into the condition of Irish courts, were notified of an action taken by castle chamber to end vexatious pleading that had consumed twelve years of litigation between David Gibbon and Gibbon FitzMorris Fitzgibbon of Co. Limerick. Petitions by both suitors were remanded to trial in the Irish king's bench, and after the verdict was handed down,

> [it] was afterwards ratified both by censure in the Castle Chamber and by Act of Councell and that [although] it was not usuall any way to interposse the authority of this Boarde in cases of this nature so fully and legally deter-myned; yet wee have ben moved aswell for the freeing of the said Gibbon

from further trouble at law.[190] The deluge of petitions and long attendance of Irish suitors finally led the Caroline privy council in 1629 to refer petitions to a committee of lawyers experienced in Irish affairs, with instructions to certify the council in writing with their opinions of the complaints.[191] In June 1630 the privy council angrily denounced a suitor, Lord Fitzwilliam, who had plagued them with years of agitation in the courts of justice in both England and Ireland. Despite final resolution, and orders by the king himself to forbear renewing of his petitions, Fitzwilliam rallied his judicial forces interminably.[192]

The English court of star chamber offered a well-developed model to the Irish court of castle chamber, but the original star chamber rarely intervened as an appellate jurisdiction, leaving its supervision to the crown and privy council. The more judicially settled English parent court lacked the policymaking mandate of the privy council, though it frequently dealt with Irish issues, particularly in the reign of Charles I. The beleaguered Viscount Falkland had to defend his stricken administration on numerous occasions, and some of his enemies petitioned for a hearing in the English star chamber, citing the lord deputy for corrupting justice. Falkland wrote in November 1629 to defend himself against the charges of Phelim McFeagh O'Byrne, promising to stay all proceedings against the latter and

190. *Acts privy council, 1621–23*, pp. 207–08. The suit concerned an estate which passed to the crown by attainder and ultimately became part of the endowment of Trinity College Dublin, from whom Gibbon FitzMorris held directly. On 24 June 1622 David Gibbon petitioned again to the privy council despite the efforts at a final order in castle chamber, noting that he sued *in forma pauperis*. Ibid., p. 260.

191. *Acts privy council, 1629–30*, p. 42.

192. *Acts privy council, 1630–31*, p. 13. See also the privy council orders of 1614 requiring a decree of the Irish council to confirm the final order for James Casie in his contest for the title of Rathmore against David Sheighan, castigating the latter for exploiting all legal forms in contempt of crown authority and the course of justice. *Acts privy council, 1613–14*, p. 638.

establishing a commission of inquiry into the events surrounding his trial. Falkland bitterly protested that the commissioners were more alert in investigating the lord deputy than they had ever been as impartial judges in other cases, suggesting that the lord chancellor was himself under suspicion and thus disqualified from sitting in judgment on the case. He challenged the witnesses who had actually partaken in the crimes of which O'Byrne was accused, and complained that his reputation and honour as a magistrate were unfairly impugned, especially in view of the fact that others had carefully managed the case without his intervention. Falkland concluded that the investigation would undermine all crown authority, and subvert the rule of law: 'The Judge will be in Danger to become corrupt, And all moste howe can yt be avoyded, when he shall see nothing but Disgrace & Danger yf he prosecute his Duty with honesty & upright mynd.'[193] The petition of O'Byrne laboured to prove that the jurors in his case, heard at Ballinasloe instead of Wicklow, were partisan and corrupt; that some of his witnesses were not called; and the jurors heard matters beyond the original petition, believing anything claimed by the plaintiffs, Richard Graham and his sons. In the end, the case involved a lengthy trial over the estates of the O'Byrnes in Co. Wicklow and their multiple efforts to defend their rights in law since 1625, with various permutations of the case heard in king's bench and at the Irish council board. O'Byrne authorized his son to take the case to the duke of Buckingham in England, where it languished while the latter was away in Spain. Buckingham and the duke of Richmond were to hear the suit based on testimony gathered by the commissioners for Irish causes, and Falkland worried that his role in the protracted dispute would imperil his administration.[194] He left Ireland under a cloud of suspicion in July 1629, nearly a year after the assassination of Buckingham, blaming O'Byrne and others for his fall from power.

The star chamber took up the causes of one Philip Bushen of Co. Kildare on two occasions in 1633, finding that the corruption of justice in his suits was so egregious that it demanded the attention of the senior tribunal. Bushen's father was accused of killing his own wife in 1629, though his accuser was a sworn enemy whose brother had been executed for stealing from Bushen's estate. His son accused the lord deputy of complicity in the elder Bushen's execution in order to exploit the opportunity to take possession of his estates. Bushen was joined in his charges by Arthur Savage, a former Irish councillor, and others, putting Lord Deputy Falkland on the defensive. The star chamber suit was heard over a period of six days, with the judges rendering their decisions in an extensive order that remains archived in the Wentworth papers. Sir Francis Cottington found Bushen 'the wretched son of a dead father' but censured him for defaming the viceroy without cause, and argued for a fine against Savage for abetting the suit of Bushen. Upon hearing the strained defence of the former viceroy, the

193. TCD, MS 843, p. 151.
194. Ibid., pp. 155, 167–78.

judges unanimously acquitted him of all charges.[195] The chief justice of king's bench added the accusation that an Irish judge, Dominic Sarsfield, Viscount Kilmallock, was gravely implicated in the case, especially since he apparently sought to gain the estate of the deceased. Sarsfield heard the case in private chambers, according to court testimony, refused to admit Bushen or other witnesses, and generally abused his judicial discretion. The chief justice cited him for allowing testimony to the jurors that a certain 'great man' had an interest in the case, attempting to subvert their neutrality.[196] Viscount Wentworth sided with Falkland, finding the whole episode a dreary repetition of the characteristic Irish bane of factionalism, but the lord keeper spoke for all the judges when he added,

> And if a Judge doe misbehave himself wee maye censure him heere; Sir John Trogmorton was censured in this Court for a cause not neere soe badd as this. It is ill order in a Judge to have the grand Jury come to his Chamber; Justice should be donne in open Court before the face of the world, and mens Lives not to bee taken awaye in private Chambers; In most causes the Jurors may give a privy verdict, but in case of Life & death there is not any admitted but they must give it in open Court, then the Judge makes a subscripcon to the indictment; you of the grand Jury are to fynde this Indictment and put his hande to it. [adding] Hee sende them [the jury] word how in his Circuite one of the Jurors that would not agree with the rest was by them beaten. These reasons enduce mee to thinke some thinge which I will not speake. Judges should not bee too prodigall of blood but good executioners of Justice, And I doe verely perswade my self that Bussyn dyed ynnocently.[197]

In a separate hearing in star chamber on 20 November 1633, Viscount Kilmallock was found guilty of judicial corruption in the case for allowing the sheriff, Henry Belling, and others to take advantage of Bushen's trial in order to possess his estate. The viscount was fined £5,000, imprisoned and deprived of office, and made to pay £2,000 in damages, effectively ending his career.[198]

Viscount Wentworth was intimately familiar with the star chamber jurisdiction well before he went to Ireland in 1633 as viceroy. In 1632 he prosecuted David Foulis of Yorkshire for scandalous words used against him as president of the council in the North. Foulis had agreed to a composition of £3,000 for taking up

---

195. TCD, MS 843, p. 411; see also TCD, MS 808, ff. 121–23. Falkland also defended his earlier nomination of Sarsfield as assize judge.
196. TCD, MS 843, pp. 411–24.
197. Ibid., p. 425.
198. *Cal. S.P. Ire., 1633–41*, p. 26. Sarsfield was a native of Cork, trained at the inns of court, who became chief justice in Munster in 1604 and married the daughter of Marshal Bagenall. Though he became chief justice of common pleas in 1612, he was a notorious pluralist, a lightning rod for accusations of corruption and an inveterate defender of his own interests in letters to the court. Ball, *Judges in Ireland*, i, 319.

his knighthood, but allegedly claimed that Wentworth took the money for himself, so the court fined him an additional £3,000, and Wentworth sued in 1634 to protest that Foulis had alienated the estates to his neighbours in frustration of the star chamber decree. By 1641 the heir of Foulis was back in star chamber to claim his rightful inheritance against the estate of the fallen lord lieutenant of Ireland.[199] Wentworth returned to the fray on 22 May 1639 when he accused Sir Piers Crosbie and Viscount Mountnorris, among others, for falsely charging that Wentworth had struck a ship's captain from Wexford, Robert Esmond, the kinsman of Lord Esmond, in a fury, causing his death. The celebrated case gained the attention of star chamber in part because the viceroy suffocated other judicial venues and the only path to vindication lay in the crown's prerogative court in England. Strangely, it was Wentworth who laid the charges, in contrast to the victimized Falkland, and he orchestrated the evidence to show that the alleged altercation was nothing other than an accident, a misunderstanding that arose because of his gout rather than his irascible temperament. The star chamber sat for five days in this hearing, finding three present and former Irish councillors guilty of scandalous dishonour to the lord deputy by falsely communicating that he had caused the death of the elderly Esmond. Crosbie was fined £4,000 and others paid nearly as much, but this treatment of Wentworth's former adversary was more about vengeance than vindication. Crosbie had become a cupbearer to James I and gentleman of the privy chamber to his son, but disputes with Lord Falkland in 1626 and Wentworth in the parliament of 1634 led the crown to sanction proceedings against him in the court of castle chamber on two occasions, though no record of either prosecution exists. The star chamber case against Crosbie began slowly with interrogations in 1636, after Wentworth escaped a potentially ugly review of his alleged misconduct in Ireland. After the star chamber decree, Crosbie acknowledged his guilt, obtained release from the Fleet and had his fine reduced to £1,000.[200]

Legal and political matters in Ireland earned the attention of the English privy council and the star chamber court in such magnitude after about 1570 that it became necessary to construct a conduit for the course of Irish business. This led, ultimately, to the creation of the more systematic commission for Irish causes under the Stuarts, but the Elizabethan solution to this novel intrusion of Irish business was to set aside entire days for Irish petitions and to complain that suitors should conclude their actions in Irish courts.[201] The lord deputy and council were

199. Sheffield Public Library, Wentworth Woodhouse Muniments, Strafford Papers, items 428–32. Hereafter cited as WWM STR P.
200. Though he appeared in France with a troop of mercenaries in 1640, Crosbie returned in 1641 to participate in the impeachment hearings against Wentworth and he was reinstated to the Irish privy council by Charles I in June. A. Clarke, 'Sir Piers Crosby, 1590–1646: Wentworth's "tawney ribbon"', *IHS*, xxvi (1988), 142–58; WWM STR P, items 461–75.
201. *Acts privy council, 1591–92*, p. 551. On 24 June 1592, as already remarked, they spent a long day on Irish causes, hearing 30 suits.

often called upon to act on behalf of suitors like Nicholas Power of Co. Waterford, who in April 1591 alleged wrongs and injuries daily against his lands by James, Lord Power, who had the ability to 'overwhelm his cause at common law'. The privy council required the council in Ireland to take up the cause, examine title and review the evidence, and it was this sort of judicial detour that led the English executive committee to revise its procedures in the next reign.[202] A certain ambiguity, however, parallels these complaints. Whereas the queen herself, on 28 July 1592, urged the Irish council to address all complaints of injustice, citing the availability of a comprehensive court system in Ireland, and ordered the dismissal of Irish suitors from the royal audience, one month later the privy council wrote on behalf of Philip O'Reilly to seek his release from prison. On a petition from his wife, the council wrote to order an end to O'Reilly's five-year imprisonment, noting that previous orders on the matter had been ignored by the viceroy and adding, 'so severe a manner of proceeding by continuall imprisonement without apparent matter of disloyalltie should not be used, and might breed a generall murmur and dislike amongst the rest'.[203] The privy council itself included former viceroys throughout much of the Tudor period and their expertise was summoned frequently, though the fall and disgrace of numerous lords deputy after 1580 deprived the government of a ready source of Irish expertise. After 1593 the Nine Years War consumed the attention of the privy council, so the project for a standing committee on Irish causes was deferred until the next reign.

The question of the emergence of expert committees as a function of conciliar government in the early modern period deserves further study. It is indisputable that the Tudor panels named by the privy council were primarily designed as commissions of inquiry, spurred by rumours of corruption within the Irish executive. While they occasionally looked into the management of the courts, it was their main function to seek out fiscal negligence and misgovernment. After 1603, a more methodical administrative refinement was developed, though lords deputy continued to suffer the intrusion of commissions of inquiry, such as those of 1613 and 1622. When Mountjoy retired to England in 1604 he enjoyed the more exalted title of lord lieutenant of Ireland, though Chichester governed in fact as lord deputy. Mountjoy continued to exercise great authority on Irish affairs until his death in 1606, a point Dr McCavitt has recently made clear.[204] Thereafter, the earl of Salisbury exercised effective control of Irish policy until his death in 1612, using such Irish experts as the groom of the privy chamber, Sir Humphrey May, to vet dispatches and petitions at a first reading.[205] The first commission for Irish causes was authorized by James I on 22 March 1611, naming six former judges and lawyers in Ireland to membership. They included three former chief justices of king's bench: Sir James Ley (who would become chief

---

202. *Acts privy council, 1591*, p. 56.
203. *Acts privy council, 1592*, pp. 129–30. O'Reilly was released on a bond of £2,000.
204. J. McCavitt, *Sir Arthur Chichester: lord deputy of Ireland, 1605–1616* (Belfast, 1998), pp.18–28.
205. Ibid., pp. 28–29.

justice in England in 1622); the elderly Sir Robert Gardener, then aged 71; and the incumbent, Sir Humphrey Winch, who was about to leave Ireland to take the other chief judgeship in England in 1612. The others were the former master of the rolls, Sir Anthony St Leger, who had recently retired to England; the veteran solicitor general, Sir Roger Wilbraham, who had pleaded numerous informations before the court of castle chamber; and Sir James Fullerton, a Scot who had served the king in Ireland before he came to the English throne.[206] To their number they soon added Sir George Carew, the former lord president of Munster, who joined them in a signed opinion of 5 June 1611. They recommended that the O'Byrnes in Co. Wicklow surrender their lands to the crown in return for a re-grant, assuring them that Captain Henry Harrington would also surrender his patent of office and receive a pension, slyly acknowledging the bad blood between the clan and their former seneschal.[207]

The Chichester regime was buffeted in response to its aggressive policies against the recusants and its ambitious plantations in Ulster and elsewhere, so it was no surprise that another commission was launched in 1611 to investigate financial matters. Sir George Carew was named to lead the commission of inquiry with a mandate to review the poor progress then under way in the Ulster plantation, as well as the means by which to reduce Irish expenditures.[208] Two years later, the parliament of 1613 launched a series of invectives against the Chichester government, leading to the appointment of still another commission to examine the charges. The veteran legists, Winch and Wilbraham, were named to this *ad hoc* committee, along with Sir Charles Cornwallis and Sir George Calvert. Their remit was to investigate grievances of the recusant petitioners who protested at the creation of new parliamentary boroughs to assure a Protestant majority in Chichester's first and only parliament, as well as other conditions in religion, finance and the military.[209] The king's response to their findings occurred on 20 April 1614 in a speech at the council chamber in Whitehall. He was willing to tolerate their complaints, but found their 'causeles expostulations' to be 'rude, disorderly, [and] inexcusable'.[210] In his instructions to Chichester of 5 June 1614 he authorized the viceroy and Irish council to proceed at their discretion against recusants, to restrain planters in Ulster from intermarrying with the Irish and to prosecute recusant officials who refused the oath of supremacy 'either at the council table or in the Castle Chamber there'.[211] In a further affront to the

---

206. *Cal. S.P. Ire., 1611–14*, p. 22; McCavitt, *Chichester*, p. 31. All of them save Wilbraham were also named councillors of state in Ireland in September of the same year. *Cal. S.P. Ire., 1611–14*, p. 102.
207. *Cal. S.P. Ire., 1611–14*, p. 69; McCavitt, *Chichester*, p. 32.
208. McCavitt, *Chichester*, p. 33.
209. *Cal. S.P. Ire., 1611–14*, pp. 426, 436. They were to report their findings to the English chancery by April 1614.
210. Ibid., pp. 474–75.
211. Ibid., p. 481. A privy council order of October 1613 required all those learned in the laws to take the oath of supremacy, including mayors and local officials. *Acts privy council, 1613–14*, pp. 223–25.

parliament, James wrote to Chichester in October 1615 that their petition to continue the legislature and not to be dissolved was unnecessary, because the most important matters could thereafter be dealt with by act of state or proclamation of the Irish privy council.[212]

Another commission was authorized on 20 March 1622 to investigate Irish causes, coinciding with the removal of St John as lord deputy. St John himself, now Lord Grandison, was named to the commission along with Lord Chancellor Loftus and nineteen others.[213] Sir Richard Hadsor, the veteran Irish lawyer resident in England, was named to this *ad hoc* committee and he helped to write the critical report, 'His Majesty's directions for ordering and settling the courts within his kingdom of Ireland'. Hadsor had become a notable adviser to Cecil after 1598, demonstrating moderation, loyalty, legal skills and facility in the Irish language. He attached himself successively to courtiers like the earl of Lennox and the duke of Buckingham prior to his death in 1635.[214] Hadsor examined details of the Ulster plantation and the flood of petitions to the crown, suggesting the practical remedy of a standing commission to be implemented at the outset of the Falkland regime, as well as the foundation of an Irish court of wards.[215] During 1622 and 1623 the new commission for Irish causes was organized along with a number of other *ad hoc* committees to examine the Ulster plantation and Irish finances.[216] In June 1622 the commission began its work, issuing specific orders to restrict judges of assize and presidency councils from certain forms of hearing, and forbidding the assize judges from riding circuit in countries of their birth or their residence.[217] The members of the commission at this time included former chief justices, Ley, Winch and John Denham; the former attorney general of Ireland, Sir John Davies; and the English officials Thomas Coventry, William Byrd and Henry Masters.[218] In July 1625 the commission, writing from Serjeants' Inn, offered expert legal opinion in two cases, requiring the Irish secretary of state, Sir Dudley Norton, to bring his action for debt to common law, rather than using the power of the council board, on which he sat. On the other hand, though they doubted the truth of her claim, they allowed Lady Raleigh to sue the earl of

212. *Cal. S.P. Ire., 1615–25*, p. 93.
213. Ibid., p. 346. See Canny, *Making Ireland British*, pp. 243–46.
214. Treadwell, 'Richard Hadsor', 309–21.
215. Ibid., 321–23. See also V. Treadwell, 'The Irish court of wards under James I', *IHS*, xii (1960), 19–21; Treadwell, *Buckingham and Ireland 1616–1628: a study in Anglo-Irish politics* (Dublin, 1998), pp. 186–205. See Canny, *Making Ireland British*, pp. 243–51 for related deliberations on plantation policy from interested servitors like Annesley and Parsons.
216. *Ad hoc* committees were named for the church, the revenue and plantation and the army, though an overlap of membership allowed some continuity, since most committees numbered 18 officials, including Chichester and Grandison. *Acts privy council, 1619–21*, p. 356.
217. *Cal. S.P. Ire., 1615–25*, pp. 354–55. For the full text, see Hand & Treadwell, 'Directions for the courts', pp. 179–212; a manuscript copy is in TCD, MS 853, f. 145 ff.
218. Ibid. For further discussion see Part Two, Ch. 9, below. The 46 clauses of the commission's report on handling Irish courts are detailed in TCD, MS 853, ff. 145–51, and see Hand & Treadwell, 'Directions for the courts'.

Cork before the council board in recognition of his personal influence in suits at common law.[219] In sum, the efforts to circumscribe the work of Irish judges and to streamline the process of petitioning the crown ended in further delays, a veritable glut of special pleading, and ample means by which to hamstring the crusty lord deputy.[220] It was the steady purpose of Wentworth to prevent appeals to the crown and his success in doing so meant the attenuated near-dormancy of the commission for Irish causes after 1633. In his contest with the Irish lord chancellor, Adam Loftus, Viscount Ely, Wentworth's dispatches were reviewed by the committee for Irish causes and his allegations of corruption in office supported with this notation: 'our further will is that in case the Lord Chancellor doe still continue his obstinacy to that our government you doe proceed against him for those misdemeanors by information in our castle chamber or otherwise as you shall see cause.'[221]

The relationship between the court of castle chamber and the other English courts was limited, though on occasion judicial opinions from England might be solicited for precedent there. For the most part, however, other Irish courts relied more notably on their respective English counterparts. As Professor Osborough has shown, requests for the written opinions of English judges on Irish legal questions were not altogether welcome, though in 1569 a panel of five judges agreed to examine the lease of ecclesiastical property from the archbishopric of Dublin to one Richard Brereton. The incumbent prelate, Adam Loftus, sued to invalidate the lease and appeared before the judicial panel in England, but they decided in favour of the lessee.[222] The treason trial of Brian O'Rourke, the lord of West Breifne, throws additional light on the mixed relationship of Irish and English courts. As Dr Morgan has demonstrated in an excellent article, O'Rourke was captured while in Glasgow seeking mercenary troops in 1591 and brought for trial to London by an arrangement between James VI and Elizabeth I. The question of jurisdiction in his case was referred to a panel of judges, including Sir Edward Coke and the chief justice of common pleas, Sir Edmund Anderson. Citing a statute of 35 Henry VIII, they justified trial in the English queen's bench

---

219. *Cal. S.P. Ire., 1625–32*, pp. 21–22. The commissioners especially demanded that the earl should be compelled to appear and plead before the council in this case.

220. *Cal. S.P. Ire., 1625–25*, pp. 275, 542, 547, 561, 579.

221. WWM STR P, item 475, f. 1. See also TCD, MS 843, p. 141, citing an order in May 1633 made by the committee for Irish affairs to cease all further action in the case of Dublin imposing a customs charge on foreign merchants.

222. Osborough postulated that the case might have been heard previously by the Irish council board, prior to the formal establishment of the court of castle chamber, but there is no evidence of that. W.N. Osborough, 'Letters to Ireland: professional enlightenment from the English bench', *Ir Jur*, xxxvii (1977), 228–33. In a note of Irish causes that were heard in England, it was stated the castle chamber was erected there 'for criminal causes, yet that does not disable his Majesty to hear them here if he pleases'. *Cal. S.P. Ire., 1647–60, addenda 1625–60*, p. 181. Professor J.H. Baker has confirmed, in correspondence with this author, that a writ of error to king's bench from Dublin would not have been appropriate for a court not of record, such as castle chamber. Baker to Crawford, 14 March 1998.

on the charge of treason committed 'out of this realm of England', despite the existence of a parallel case in 1584 in which the Irish council were assured by the judges in Dublin that the statute in question did not apply in Ireland, lacking confirmation by an Irish legislature. O'Rourke was duly tried and convicted in queen's bench on eight charges of treason, and executed at Tyburn on 3 November 1591.[223] As we have noted above, the charter of the city of Waterford was sent to England in 1617 where the former chief justices of king's bench, Sir Humphrey Winch and Sir John Denham, examined it prior to the punishment of the city by the viceroy and Irish council.[224] In 1622 the commissions of inquiry generated a formal statement of judicial review, including a specific order to limit appeals to the English king's bench from that in Ireland by writ of error. While acknowledging that the right to seek reversal by this means was enshrined in law, the directions cited vexatious pleading and delays in their order that 'meere pointe[s] in law' should not be the basis for the writ if the error were in form only.[225] The trial of Viscount Kilmallock for corruption as a judge brought forth a severe censure from the star chamber in 1633 (see above), but for the most part the relationship with the English judiciary was a quietly symbiotic one.

Until well into the reign of Charles I, most Irish lawyers were trained with their English counterparts at the inns of court for up to six years at a time, sharing both legal training and, presumably, London's attractions.[226] Service in Ireland was viewed by the English legal profession as an unwelcome deviation from their ambitions to achieve honour and wealth as senior magistrates, yet most of the leading English judges became members of the King's Inns in Dublin in the period under discussion. The development of the King's Inns after 1541 offered an Irish medium in which both English-born and Irish-born lawyers convened, socially and professionally, forming a nexus of convenience, short of marriage but linked by necessity. Numerous recusant lawyers who became leaders of the opposition were trained alongside their Protestant counterparts at the inns of court, and this English legal education was enforced by statute and by proclamation.[227] However, the King's Inns offered no readings, moots or other benefits

223. H. Morgan, 'Extradition and treason trial of a Gaelic lord: the case of Brian O'Rourke', *Ir Jur*, xxviii (1987), 285–95. Morgan asserts that the trial was a rehearsal for and essential prop of the treason trial of Sir John Perrot, who was languishing in the Tower at the same time.
224. *Acts privy council, 1616–17*, p. 332.
225. TCD, MS 853, f. 149.
226. D. Cregan, 'Irish Catholic admissions to the English inns of court, 1558–1625', *Ir Jur*, v (1970), 96ff.; J. Ohlmeyer, 'Irish recusant lawyers during the reign of Charles I', in M. Ó Siochrú, ed., *Kingdoms in crisis: Ireland in the 1640s* [Essays in honour of Donal Cregan] (Dublin 2001), p. 63 ff. Ohlmeyer found that at least 140 Irish recusants attended the English inns from 1625 to 1641, owing to the insecurity of land tenure and the widely accepted belief that legal training offered 'an exclusive finishing school', access to the royal court and important legal knowledge with which to defend title to land and honour. pp. 63–69.
227. Ohlmeyer found that the outbreak of rebellion in Ireland forced the expulsion of many recusants from the inns in England. By that time in 1641, however, two generations of well-trained Irish lawyers had developed their careers, pleading in chancery or serving magnates like

of academic law at this time. The re-edification of King's Inns was authorized by Chichester in 1607, when the viceroy himself became an honorary member, some 93 judges and lawyers were admitted to King's Inns within two years, including both John Everard and Patrick Sedgrave, two recusant judges who were dismissed from office in 1607 and 1602 respectively.[228] During a hiatus from 1613 to 1628 in the admission of Catholic lawyers, the King's Inns were nearly dormant, but the reforms of 1628 led to an order in the following year requiring that attorneys admitted to practice in the Dublin courts must first be admitted to the society.[229] Wentworth reinforced this order in 1635, extending the requirement to the provinces and in 1637 Dublin benchers were also ordered to attend at commons (a substantial meal, ordinarily) at least once a week during term time.[230]

CONCLUSION

The court of castle chamber thus found itself circumscribed by innumerable adjacent tribunals, both inferior and superior in stature. The role of the court as both an appellate jurisdiction and a prerogative instrument of royal authority demands that we consider its function within the larger constellation of lesser courts, both traditional and new. The high court of parliament itself took notice of the work of the castle chamber court on occasion, reversing on appeal the conviction of Henry Stewart and others for refusing the oath of supremacy during Wentworth's tenure.[231] The effects of these circumferential jurisdictions were many. In the first place, the castle chamber tribunal was petitioned directly

Clanricarde. The earl employed Patrick Darcy, James Donnellan and Richard Martin, among others. Ohlmeyer, 'Irish recusant lawyers', pp. 73–77. The lawyers of Confederate Ireland provided an experienced bench for a new judiciary, conceived its 'model of Civil Government' as a constitution, and Darcy served as its lord chancellor until 1644. Ibid., pp. 78–79. Brid McGrath has shown the importance of the lawyerly élite in the Confederate parliament, of whom at least 33 MPs had been admitted to the inns of court. Nicholas Plunkett, for example, was elected speaker of the Confederate general assembly in 1642 and 'worked consistently for a peaceful legal solution to the problems in Ireland'. McGrath, 'Parliament men and the confederate association', in M. Ó Siochrú, ed., *Kingdoms in crisis*, pp. 100–03.

228. Kenny, *King's Inns*, pp. 79–81. In contrast to the English inns of court, the Irish society was led by the senior judges and Dr Kenny has argued that 'most of those actually practising common law in the courts chose to join the restored society [after 1607]'. Ibid., p. 82.

229. Ibid., p. 100. A similar hiatus was imperfectly observed in the fifteenth century when the inns of court excluded Irish law students for a time. P. Brand, 'Irish law students and lawyers in late medieval England', *IHS*, xxxii (2000), 166–169.

230. Kenny, *King's Inns*, p. 117. Evidence that the privy councillors and their under-clerks frequented the Inns at this time demonstrates the close interaction of the legal profession, perhaps unique to Dublin, in this period.

231. The case of September 1639 was reversed in the English house of lords on 3 June 1642 after the impeachment of Wentworth and his allies. Parliamentary opposition to the court will be taken up in Ch.3, below. See also, Ch. 10 in Part Two. *Cal. S.P. Ire., 1633–41*, pp. 222, 325; Marsh's Library, Dublin, MS Z.3.2.6, item 117, p. 329.

by numerous suitors alleging various wrongs, as well as by the crown's attorneys, and these suits were often begun in other jurisdictions so that the complexity of competing venues was an added burden to litigation. In the second place, hearings of the court were frequently the result of failed proceedings in inferior courts, or failed petitions to the crown, so that castle chamber suits must have been inordinately lengthy, reciting not only the facts of the case but the long and tortuous judicial route to the senior court on appeal. In the third place, the court was obliged to balance its legal judgments with the reality of external political conditions in the case of powerful suitors, since the English privy council was prone to scrutinize its decisions and on some occasions ordered them reviewed. In the fourth place, the accretion of other courts of record gradually transformed the character and quantity of litigation before the castle chamber court, both expanding and contracting its business, and siphoning off some of the projected revenue from hearings on plantations, wards and other matters. And, finally, the court itself became embroiled in constitutional controversies from the cess dispute to the impeachment of its own members in 1641, demonstrating its importance and centrality to the events of early modern Ireland from 1571 to 1641. A summary of this sort is, of necessity, preliminary and tentative, though it is clear that the tribunal gradually amplified both its scope and its sophistication in the decades before 1641.[232] Ironically, just as the long-delayed formalization of the Irish judicial system had become nearly crystallized and a pattern of litigation emerged mirroring the active judicial processes in England itself, the entire institutional process of anglicization, so painstakingly prepared under Elizabeth, became the victim of Stuart clumsiness and the tyranny of Charles I's greatest viceroy. In a further irony, the most celebrated cases heard before the court of castle chamber under Wentworth entirely disappeared from the official record and must be pieced together from surviving fragments due to the sudden collapse of the regime in 1641.

232. Canny has shown that the British presence in Ireland 'exerted a major impact on the lives of all elements of the population of Ireland on a continuing basis,' by 1641, extending the 'administrative arm of the state' into the most remote provinces, including the enforcement of legal decisions. Canny, *Making Ireland British*, p. 309.

CHAPTER TWO

The court of castle chamber: its structure and judicial personality

> May it therefore please yor good L to dyrect yor lres to her maties learned [in the laws] remayning and every of them thearebye carefully and consyderately thearein to deale, So as the clarke bringinge to them any acte orr order drawen uppon any acte or order heretofore pronounced, and yet not entred into the bookes, or hearafter to be pronouncede, they do accordinglye wth suche expedicon correcte and perm[anen]tly forme for the beste advauntage of her matie and her good subyectes as the clarke may have suffycyent tyme theareuppon to enter the same into the bookes of the Court before the next court then to be holden.
>
> Laurence Holinshed, clerk of the castle chamber,
> to Lord Deputy Grey de Wilton, 1582[1]

THE COURT OF CASTLE chamber was held in a specially constructed room over the gateway to Dublin Castle. Like its parent institution in England, the Irish star chamber alternated meetings with the privy council and probably observed a similar routine, the preparations for which may have included a ceremonial green tapestry like that used in London. A red tapestry signified the meeting of the privy council in England, and a similar one may have also been used in Dublin. The rhythms of judicial life began each year with Candlemas term, followed by Trinity, Hilary and Michaelmas. When the court met to hear cases, a large volume of business had already been completed by its subordinate officials. Initial pleadings were taken by clerks who carefully observed the ritual fee-taking at each stage of proceeding. Writs were issued and testimony given at various stages, both in Dublin and in the countryside. Challenges were expected from defendants and delays were routine, particularly when witnesses had to make depositions. Litigants who could afford the cost often appealed beyond castle chamber directly to the crown, and in these cases further delays were unavoidable. Consequently, the famous 'slow process' that described star chamber proceedings in England applied with at least equal strength to the castle chamber in Ireland.

---

1. BL, Add. MS 47,172, f. 52.

THE INFRASTRUCTURE OF THE COURT OF CASTLE CHAMBER

The star chamber in England evolved from meetings of the king's council in the late medieval period and Dr Guy has established that it lacked statutory authority, despite the evidence of an act 'Pro camera Stellata' in 1487.[2] The design or mandate of the 'King's council sitting judicially' was to establish a forum for hearings by the late medieval council on local disorder and subversion, perversion of justice and official maladministration, yet there was no effective differentiation between council and court. A more sedentary council developed around Henry VIII's great ministers, Thomas Wolsey and Thomas Cromwell, and the former has been credited with the full articulation of a star chamber court with himself presiding as lord chancellor. The business of the court of star chamber under Wolsey increased tenfold to an average of 120 suits per annum, and Cromwell's development of a streamlined executive committee termed the 'privy council' led, after his downfall in 1540, to a more manageable record-keeping burden for the court, which then began a separate register of orders and decrees. Nonetheless, the membership of the court continued to embrace the full complement of privy councillors, assisted by expert justices, and this format continued in operation until the court's abolition in 1641. Despite the political turbulence of the mid-Tudor convulsions in the monarchy itself, the court of star chamber continued to hear about 150 suits in each year, culminating in the late Elizabethan period with a peak of 732 suits.[3]

The origins of the court of castle chamber in Ireland have been discussed more fully elsewhere,[4] and will be taken up below, in Part Two, Chapter 4. Though a star chamber jurisdiction, the castle chamber court manifested numerous important differences. In the first place, the original star chamber evolved gradually over a period of some five decades into a settled prerogative court, never far from the sovereign. By contrast, the court of castle chamber emerged some time after 1570 with a clear mandate, a full structure and a vigorous set of expectations. Unfortunately, the Irish court lacked the complementary judicial infrastructure of its parent in England. It took most of the next 70 years to create in Ireland a replica of the English court system, from the shires and presidency courts to the admiralty, wards and high commission. In the second place, the court of castle chamber was practically excluded from hearing matters concerning the Ulster plantation after 1609, while some of the greater magnates petitioned directly to the crown. Attenuated from its outset by inadequate enforcing power in the provinces, and handicapped by its distance from the crown, the court was, for much of its existence, only a silhouette of its more potent progenitor. In the third place, the castle chamber court suffered from an incomplete bifurcation with the

---

2. Guy, *The court of star chamber*, p. 2.
3. Ibid., pp. 2–9.
4. J.G. Crawford, 'The origins of the court of castle chamber: a star chamber jurisdiction in Ireland', *AJLH*, xxvi (1980), 22–55; *Anglicizing*, ch. 4.

Irish privy council. Membership in both council and court was effectively identical, and executive business of the Irish council took priority, especially when the lord deputy was on progress with senior members of the court in his retinue. As a consequence, judicial business in castle chamber was a fraction of that in the English star chamber. In the fourth place, the chief governors exercised a powerful influence on proceedings in the court of castle chamber, and there was no English counterpart of the Irish viceroy to prioritize and delimit hearings in the star chamber. The admixture of policymaking and adjudication was a striking feature of the castle chamber court, as we shall see below. Nonetheless, the creation of the court of castle chamber and its various reformulations under the Stuarts plainly conceived of a tribunal closely modelled on that of England.

The star chamber in Ireland, for such it was often termed, grew directly from the authority of the privy council in Ireland to judge cases and to exercise a superior, appellate jurisdiction over the other courts in Ireland. This prerogative court evolved within a judicial edifice which has been discussed at some length above. However, it is important to understand the amalgam of executive and judicial powers of the council in order to assess its constitutional role. The council in Ireland was an exceptional institution, endowed with the power to rule in the chronic absence of parliament, using proclamations and acts of state to govern. There were but four parliaments in the period under discussion: in 1569–71, 1585–86, 1613–15 and 1634–35. Each of them was called to address financial problems of the crown, and each witnessed a show of noisy opposition. In the long intervals between meetings of the legislature, the privy council in Ireland managed affairs, thus combining the unseparated powers of the early modern state. Since the Irish council could issue proclamations and then proceed to enforce them judicially, it was prone to abuses of its own authority. For that reason, the English privy council exercised virtually continual oversight of its proceedings. Early in the reign of James I, acting with the approval of the sovereign, the Irish privy council issued orders concerning religious conformity and then, sitting as the court of castle chamber, heard a number of cases involving those who refused to conform. The lord deputy sought and received authority to pursue a militant ecclesiastical policy, that of the Mandates. Despite hearing a number of cases involving public officials, ordinary parishioners and hidden priests, the court largely abandoned the policy after two decades of erratic enforcement, ending in futility.[5] Consequently, one must be cautious in imputing too much power to this well-endowed executive forum. The Irish privy council enjoined public rectitude by the employment of sovereign decrees and used the star chamber court to implement prerogative justice but its record of enforcement was not particularly impressive.

When the castle chamber court was first proposed by the earl of Sussex in the 1560s, the Irish privy council was already hearing many cases which would

5. McCavitt, *Chichester*, chs. 6 and 7. McCavitt has called it 'an aborted protestantising campaign'.

ultimately be handled separately by its star chamber jurisdiction. Apart from the allegations of riot, cases involving foreigners, and other charges specific to the court, the new venue was given primary responsibility for the management and supervision of the expanded judicial system in Ireland. In this regard, the court undertook the hearing of individual cases and the buttressing of common law justice throughout Ireland. From its inception in 1571, the court of castle chamber adjudicated upon malfeasance in office, and its various judges and attorneys continuously reported on the effectiveness of common law jurisdiction. The court of castle chamber commenced its work very slowly, after a decade of uncertainty concerning its independent legal authority and a tentative building of its slender clerical foundations. Upon the arrival of Lord Chancellor Gerrard, and the return of Sir Henry Sydney as viceroy in 1576, the court became embroiled in the constitutional crisis over the imposition of cess, commanding the attention of the crown and becoming the reluctant foil of a campaign by agents of the Pale. The Elizabethan court lacked a defining charter setting forth its mission, struggled to achieve institutional autonomy, and apparently lapsed into near-dormancy in times of military crisis. Yet the assertion of judicial predominance was central to the rationale of the star chamber jurisdiction. The late Elizabethan court was described thus:

> When Offendors shall finde that they shall not Aunswere their Offences anye further then at home, they wilbe more bold to offend. But when they looke upon the matter and justice of this Court, beinge a Parliament, and the punishment sharpe accordinge to the bitternes of their offences, they will the more feare and forbeare to offend, And it hath been often gravely sayd in Court upon such occasion, that the dreade of this Cort is a greater maintainer of the quiett Government and nippeth off in the budd as many enormities as the punishment of the inferrior Courtes doe … For that manye suites and offences are of such nature, as that punishments of inferrior Courtes are not Condigne to the outraigiousnes and exorbitancy of the Offences. But this Court inflicteth punishment with the highest of anye Lawe, and addeth new, according to the Noveltye and fowlnesse of the Offences And therein is unlimittable under life.[6]

Two Elizabethan-era compendia now held in the Manuscripts Department of the Library of Trinity College Dublin were probably drawn up to provide clarification and institutional support for the Irish court. One undated document rehearsed the records, judges and pleadings of the English star chamber court in the time of Sir Christopher Hatton, a justice of the star chamber whose office of lord chamberlain did not occur in Ireland. Other privy councillors were explicitly included as justices of the star chamber and the ordinary proceedings of the court were explained thus:

6. TCD, MS 649, f. 34.

The matter most commonly belonging to the Starr Chamber, there to be punished ... As in takeing away young Maydens within age, against the will of their parents or guardians ... All notable forgeries ... Counterfeting of Lres or Privy tokens ... All notable periuries ... slaundering of nobles and raysing seditious newes ... And all the tytle of Ryottes in the Collection of adiudgment of statutes made by Rastall. Allso notable deceipts and fraudulent dealings any where perpetrated.[7]

The second document offers a justification for the court, arguing the need for judicial flexibility in light of the unusual nature of some cases, such as offenders who were powerful members of the peerage; corrupt justices or civil officials; or poor men and women who were eligible to sue *in forma pauperis*. This document provides a wider juridical context for the prosecution of jurors who refused to follow their evidence, or who acquitted a 'heynous murderer'. The honour of the bench could be defended in star chamber, as when a judge, justice of the peace or officer of the court was slandered or libelled or 'contemptuously despited', and the reputation of the crown was similarly protected against offence.[8] Exceptional cases of conspiracy were also heard in star chamber, from the man of honour who secretly planned the assaulting of another person, to the corporations or townships that displaced an honest member, including the fraudulent undoing of young heirs by a kind of reverse sexual harassment.

If a coseninge Crewe shall entize a young man to the company of a Woeman, and cause him to be deprehended by one that pretendeth to be her husband, and soe for his redemption (he sealeth Leases of his Lands) or makes gifte of his goods.[9]

It was the clear purpose of these documents to expand the potential jurisdiction of the star chamber court, noting that the number of such misdemeanours was indeed infinite and that the special laws provided against all injustice and inequity could not possibly reach to every such contempt, while asserting the ancient right of the crown to try such cases.[10] On the other hand, the court was prepared to punish a counsellor at law who gave learned advice to a suitor solely for the purpose of advancing vexatious pleadings in the court, or to defraud the crown or break a statute law.[11]

---

7. TCD, MS 734, ff. 16–17v.   8.   TCD, MS 721, f. 338.
9. TCD, MS 721, ff. 341–41v. This Chaucerian episode was not unlike the litigation involving the abduction of women, discussed below.
10. Ibid.
11. Ibid., f. 340v. J.H. Baker has observed that the true achievement of the star chamber in England was in refining criminal libel, forgery, perjury, subornation of perjury, conspiracy and attempts to commit crimes, all important legacies of star chamber jurisdiction. Baker, *An introduction to English legal history*, 2nd ed. (London, 1979), p. 101.

Technical details marked the regulation of star chamber business in England, and it is reasonable to assume that exacting procedures were expected of counsel in all castle chamber proceedings as well. Lacking evidence for the pleadings of the Irish court, however, it is necessary to rely upon the English 'Course of the Court of Starr Chamber'.[12] This undated document served as a guide to filing bills of record, after which a subpoena was sued out. Allowing a plaintiff to renew the subpoena in the two next terms without an affidavit, and thereafter only with affidavit, served to extend the preliminary 'course' of pre-trial litigation at the instigation of the willing petitioner. The plaintiff was allowed to amend bills within a period of days, but subpoenas could be returned to the court only on certain days of the week, further delaying trial itself. A defendant had five days to appear upon a summons, and on the sixth day, an attachment was awarded for non-appearance on the basis of an affidavit showing the writ of summons was served, or left at his dwelling. If the defendant were to appear and make no exception to the writs, the plaintiff was required to put in interrogatories immediately, 'For he shall not take benefitt by his owne mistakinge to Cavill with his Adversarie, and inforce him to a double Journey'.[13] The defendant who put in his or her answer to the charges was forced to await the plaintiff's reply, since the latter was not bound to submit a replication until formally given notice of the defendant's appearance. But if the defendant were to depart from Dublin without licence, after the answer was given, then attachment might be awarded against him. A narrow procedural route was defined for both suitors in terms of the requirement to respond to pleadings, stating that neither party was to be examined on parts of the bill and answer that were demurred to, nor could the examination be amended after a copy was delivered to the other party. The plaintiff was allowed four days to wait for a defendant to rectify an insufficient answer, but then compelled to exhibit his articles.[14] The plaintiff's duty to give replication against multiple defendants did not allow him cause for delay, since he must continue his prosecution in the next term or allow the defendants who gave answer to plead for dismissal. But if the defendants pleaded not guilty to the whole bill, the replication was not allowed since it would merely delay proceeding to trial. The examining of witnesses in court was cumbersome, since they had to be questioned before both parties, cross-examined if necessary, and commissions of *dedimus potestatem*, deputizing minor officials and others to obtain evidence and hear testimony away from Dublin, slowed the process immeasurably. Plaintiffs were duly warned to be brisk about their litigation, filing pleas and responding promptly, and, 'If a plt shall dilatorilye prosecute, as to make some colourable prosecution once in three Tearmes to prevent dismission, and frustrate the Rules of the Court, The deft maye informe the Court thereof and obtaine his dismission for the Dalying with the court.'[15] Finally, the court expressed scepticism about the abuse of pleading *in forma*

---

12. TCD, MS 649, ff. 1–37v.
14. Ibid., f. 8.

13. TCD, MS 649, f. 3v.
15. Ibid., ff. 23–23v.

pauperis, saying: 'it is found out that the Subiects are Causelesslye vexed, and the dignitie of the Court blemished thereby; for not one amonge fortie of them come to any thinge But fall out triviall and clamorous and by color of the proces of the Suite, they vex the countrey and exact Monej to the dishonor of the Court.'[16]

The court of castle chamber offered to balance the rights of the defendant against the interest of the plaintiff, explaining that the awarding of 'sureties', or payment to guarantee appearance, tended to disenfranchise the poor suitor. The court declared,

> For that the Gates of Justice are open to all, and not to shutt the poore Man out which this device of Suerties doth, if he hath not credit to bringe them in. The plt sueth aswell for the kinge as himselfe, and in that Respect he hath the assistance and favor of the Court, for by his Costs and Travell are wrought fines to the kinge and examples to the Comon Wealth. It often falleth out that when plts are robbed of their estates by Oppression Ryotts &c and Complaine here for Reliefe, then the defendants fall upon this point of Suerties and thereby slipp the Coller and gett themselves dismissed and the plt goeth home Remedilesse. For those Reasons the Court hath ever ben tender in grauntinge such moc[i]ons.[17]

Indeed, the language of the court seemed to favour the plaintiff, although the use of *ore tenus* pleading, which often anticipated the confession of a defendant, was usually restricted to cases brought by the crown's learned counsel. The court explained that a defendant who confessed to his crime when brought to the bar, and willingly signed his examination, thereby waived his right to counsel: 'For it needeth not when his owne Mouth hath Condemned him already.'[18] But the rights of the defendant to a full hearing of the court were not thereby jeopardized, since he could withdraw his confession, or deny it, whereupon the case would be continued by way of pleading and proof. If the plaintiff found that the confession contained sufficient matter on which to ground sentence, he might waive further proceedings and go to hearing by plea of *super confessionem*, in which case the defendant was allowed counsel. However, if the defendant refused to answer the plaintiff's bill, the court allowed him time to answer or, if he defaulted, to be taken *pro confesso*, wherein the tribunal could pronounce him guilty of all matters and proceed to punishment.[19] Only when the defendant fully acknowledged the jurisdiction of the court might he or she proceed to examination of witnesses, using the plea of *secundum allegata et probata*, alternating replies with the king's attorney (who always had the last word).[20]

---

16. Ibid., f. 36.   17. Ibid., f. 34v.

18. Ibid., f. 37. *Ore tenus* refers to pleading orally, 'by word of mouth', at the bar of the court, and the majority of castle chamber cases after 1605 that were brought by the crown attorney initiated proceedings in this manner. In contrast, the written plea of a private complainant began by 'exhibiting information' at the court.

19. Ibid., f. 37v.

20. Ibid. *Super confessionem*, or upon confession, allowed proceedings to move to deliberation of the

In the aftermath of the Tyrone Rebellion, James I ordered a new commission re-establishing the court of castle chamber on 10 August 1603. A note of this document, signed by Robert Cecil and containing a list of all causes to be prosecuted by the court, was sent to Ireland along with a detailed schedule of fees and court officials.[21] This was the first royal charter for the court after its Elizabethan foundation; a further re-commissioning followed from Charles I on 1 October 1625.[22] Charles I's commission is addressed to the chief governor, lord chancellor, lord treasurer, vice treasurer, the two chief justices, the chief baron of the exchequer, the master of the rolls and the secretary of state. The crown directed that any four of the nine officials named above were to be 'our Commissioners and justices of our said Court of Castle Chamber', whereof the chief governor or lord chancellor, and less often the treasurer or vice treasurer, was to be one.[23] The court was authorized to hold its hearings during the four ordinary terms two days each week (customarily, Wednesday and Friday), and to augment its membership from the rest of the privy council or the justices of 'anie of our Benches within our said Realme of Ireland' and as many of the lords spiritual and temporal as the quadrumvirate 'shall thincke meete'.[24] The potentially inflated membership of the castle chamber court was seldom realized in practice, but this discretionary power to add judges, confined to the four leading officials in Ireland, meant the court was more than just a shadow of the English star chamber. Indeed, the royal order carefully defined the special role of the chief governor, who at his discretion might come in person to the court of castle chamber wherein he should have 'in our behalfe the full and whole power of Cheife head and principall Justicer and Determiner … and principall Judg' in all matters propounded in the court.[25]

The charters re-founding the court of castle chamber explicitly named star chamber precedent when defining the offences to be prosecuted and the pleadings and summons to be used. The list of unlawful acts indicted in star chamber was standardized by the reign of Charles I to include the corruption of juries, maladministration by local officials, riots and forcible entries, and other 'hatefull Disorders', misdemeanours and contempts.[26] Noting that the realm was 'well neare subverted' because these crimes went unpunished and approving his royal father's stern correction of 'such execrable and pernicious evills, contemptes and greifes', Charles I was content to continue the court, and his order defined in great detail how it should operate.[27] The court was authorized to receive bills of complaint, award ordinary process and summon evildoers to the discussion and determination of the disorders and offences complained of, fining and imprisoning

court; whereas the equity bill *pro confesso* allowed the plaintiff to obtain a decree according to the merits of the case by virtue of the defendant's failure to file an answer. For a fuller discussion of these procedural details see Guy, *Star chamber*, ch. 3, p. 37ff.

21. *Pat. rolls Ire.*, *Jas I*, ed. Erck, pt. 1, p. 38.

22. TCD, MS 852, ff. 74–76. This document is fully transcribed as Appendix Three, below, p. 570.

23. Ibid., f. 74v.   24. Ibid.

25. Ibid., f. 76.   26. Ibid., ff. 74–76.

27. Ibid., f. 74.

offenders according to the justices' discretions. Turning to the profits of the court, the royal decree ordered the court to be certain to tax to the crown's use all amercements, fines and penalties for default, departure without licence or other violations of castle chamber protocol and procedure. Suitors were duly warned that they would not be discharged without licence obtained in open court and entered in the book of orders and decrees of the court, a reasonable fine being assessed to the crown for the withdrawal of the charges. What is more, if any plaintiff failed to proceed with his or her suit, it was the privilege of the attorney general to prosecute the cause and the plaintiff could be sued in turn *per falso clamore*. Once fines were determined in the court, no reduction or qualification could be obtained but in open court on the last sitting day of the term (though this could be deferred to the next term, at the latest). Fines were payable within ten days of the end of the next term after they were imposed, a period of roughly four months in duration. Lastly, all bonds taken by the court were to be processed by the first remembrancer of the exchequer, a measure signalling the duty to execute castle chamber orders throughout the Irish administration.[28]

Once these preliminary pleadings were concluded, usually without the direct involvement of the court itself, publication was granted for a hearing of the matter and the court sat in judgment. The judges gave their opinion in reverse order of seniority, the youngest declaring his opinion and judgment first, and the decree was finally determined by the greater number in agreement. If the party were convicted, the court might order the offender to be imprisoned or fined, and costs awarded against him. However, if he were exonerated, costs might be awarded against the plaintiff. The court rarely operated with such speed, however. Extensive notes were added, requiring the sheriff to serve process and to commit the recalcitrant to ward, or to issue an attachment for his appearance on contempt charges before the court. If the party were not found after attachment and proclamation, a commission of rebellion might be issued against the offender, resulting in a tougher penalty and costs to the plaintiff. However, in many cases, a commission of *dedimus potestatem* was awarded to persons who took the defendant's answer by oath, examining him or her by authority of the court in recognition of the parties' infirmity or impotence and presenting an affidavit to the court explaining the reasons for non-appearance.[29] Fees were awarded to the clerk of the court for every warrant, entry, process, recognizance and commission. For dismissing any party and for admission to attorney, the clerk received two shillings, and for the appearance of every person at court he received twelve pence. The clerk took two shillings for examining every party and witness, and for copies of bills, answers, replications, rejoinders and depositions he earned twelve pence for every sheet of fifteen lines.[30] Given the bureaucratic genius for profit-making at the court, it is remarkable that litigants frequented the venue in such great numbers.

28. Ibid., ff. 74–76. 29. Ibid., f. 76.
30. Ibid., ff. 77v–78.

The court of castle chamber experienced long delays in the course of litigation, and some of this was caused by the cumbersome processes of the court itself. The Jacobean ordinances for the court of star chamber explained in excruciating detail the requirements for renewing of bills and process by the plaintiff, laying down that any new bill should set forth the original matter in addition to the amendment, and allowing two terms after the bill was exhibited before any process might be sued. If the defendant were to plead not guilty, the plaintiff had the whole next term to file a replication before dismissal, and this time was extended if all of the defendants had not been served. Plaintiffs were admonished to attend the court during two successive terms or their cases would be dismissed, while defendants were warned not to interfere with the plaintiff's right to demurrer and answer, extending the time for this to two whole terms. Defendants were allowed time to prepare their attorneys and counsel for both parties might negotiate an early publication of the proceedings. In addition, clerks of the court were admonished to write their orders in a timely fashion between terms, using under-clerks who were sworn to uphold the dignity and authority of the court. It was necessary to add that they 'shall not use anie idle repeticons or needelesse Circumstances in settinge downe ye same examinacons or deposicons' since the clerks were paid by the sheet of 15 lines, encouraging profitable verbosity.[31] The clerks were required to copy whatever was needed by the attorneys of both sides, searching the archives of the court and signing any official records, another potential obstacle to speedy trial. Defendants were given six to eight days to put in their answer after appearing to receive the plaintiff's bill; while the plaintiff had four days in which to put his or her interrogatories after the answer was certified to the court. Witnesses and interrogations then followed, often in the country, and both parties were assured they would not have to answer matters irrelevant to the cause of action.[32] Depositions, even in the most ordinary suits, created an abundance of paperwork. For example, in a case of July 1618, that of *Peter Barnewall* v. *James Barnewall*, the enrolment of depositions in chancery gave testimony from ten or more witnesses regarding the feoffment of the contested estate of Drimnagh, Co. Dublin, in May 1597. The castle chamber court was involved because Peter had allegedly bribed one witness five shillings to write on his behalf.[33]

In this manner, the court contributed to its own problem of chronic deferral of proceedings. It is likely that the Irish court, like that of its English parent, was similarly overwhelmed by procedural detail, a situation described by Dr Barnes as 'blind comprehensiveness at the proof stages, putting into their interrogatories scores of questions in search of every shred of relevant evidence'.[34] The customary

31. TCD, MS 802, ff. 104v–05.
32. TCD, MS 802, ff. 101–07. See also TCD, MS 649, ff. 1–21 for an extensive analysis of the pleadings in star chamber.
33. *Cal. pat. rolls Ire., Jas I*, pp. 327–29. Plate 4.
34. T.G. Barnes, 'The archives and archival problems of the Elizabethan and early Stuart star chamber', *Jn Soc Archivists*, ii (1963), 358. See also his 'Due process and slow process in the late Elizabethan and early Stuart star chamber', *AJLH*, vi (1962), 221–49, 315–45.

array of numerous defendants, facing a multiplicity of charges, also caused the proceedings to falter. In the first extant prosecution of the entry book of the court of castle chamber, 48 persons were named as co-defendants with the principal offender, Patrick Plunkett of Termonfeckin, a gentleman who was implicitly made responsible for riot and the plunder of a wrecked ship.[35] The usual consequence of this strategem was to multiply the answers, replications and rejoinders, allowing 'procedural skirmishes' to occur that slowed proceedings considerably.[36] In addition, the increasing rigidity of obligatory formulae complicated the work of the court and the attorneys.[37] The interlocutory pleading of motions to take exception to a point in law, suspending further progress on the case until the motion was properly settled, was a flexible and pernicious instrument available to wily counsel seeking to put off near-certain defeat in law.[38] However, the lacunae in the records of the castle chamber court prevent a confident analysis of its distinctive procedures, and we must wonder whether the 'constant course' observed so carefully by star chamber in England was equally injurious to proceedings in Ireland.[39]

The 'Directions for ordering ... the courts' in 1622 condemned the 'Councell Table' for exceeding its proper judicial bounds when acting as a court, though the court of castle chamber itself was not specifically mentioned. The patents of plantation were excepted from this prohibition as 'matters of state', to be heard and determined by the lord deputy and council, but the titles 'growne after those Patents granted' were to be left to adjudication in other courts. Apart from petitions remanded by the English privy council, or matters concerning the church in Ireland, the council was ordered to leave causes to ordinary trial at law.[40] On the other hand, a cautious allowance was inserted for 'foreign trials' to be authorized by chancery or the council table, a concession acknowledging the partiality of juries in the counties and the vulnerability of female and minor heirs to exploitation of their rights. In deference to the need for convenient trial of title, the 1622 commissioners recommended that those in continuous possession for thirty years should not be compelled to face trial outside the customary juris-diction, except in cases where the interest of the crown, infants or *femes coverts* might be affected.[41] The council was further required to limit its proceedings against offenders who violated proclamations, a step assuring that the accused was first called into the ordinary courts to answer his or her contempt, and so preventing the council from enforcing its own decrees without due process.[42] The reform of the Irish courts was set forth in a list of 46 clauses, yet the commission

35. BL, Add. MS 47,172, f. 1.   36. Barnes, 'Slow process', 232.
37. Ibid., 235.   38. Ibid., 236–38.
39. Ibid., 242.
40. TCD, MS 853, f. 145; Hand & Treadwell, eds., 'Directions for the courts', 190.
41. TCD, MS 853, f. 146; Hand & Treadwell, eds., 'Directions for the courts', 194–96. Further exceptions permitting the use of 'foreign trials' included the assertion of the rights of persons beyond the seas and those '*non sane memorie*'.
42. TCD, MS 853, ff. 149–49v; Hand & Treadwell, eds., 'Directions for the courts', 205.

has been viewed as a political failure rather than an institutional watershed.[43] A memorandum to Dorchester, penned about 1630, offered to explain why so many causes were discontinued in the castle chamber court. The anonymous author explained that poor suitors were 'wearied out by delays' while others of more ability were discouraged from bringing suit due to the wasting of resources in bringing a cause to censure. While the crown profited from fines, the plaintiff was awarded little or nothing in damages, and the clerks customarily reduced by up to one third the petitioner's bills for expenses, leaving him no means to recover his costs. Further alleging that wicked people brought suit against innocents in order to get a composition from them, knowing they would ultimately drop the case, the critic called upon the king to levy costs of court against the lands and goods of delinquents and prosecute them for refusal to pay.[44]

While the court of castle chamber was the subject of occasional censure in England, based on contentious accusations from its enemies in Ireland, it is also clear that the court received numerous judicial endorsements. A treatise on star chamber prepared for the English court under James I rehearsed the principled justification for the venue in a spirited defence of its actions that has relevance for its sister tribunal in Ireland. The author denied that star chamber was a usurpation of common law, *ad hoc* in nature and lacking continuous warrant. Quoting Egerton, he asserted that the law of England had always used an extraordinary and expedient course when the 'bleeding state' required speedy remedy, as well as a settled law. The author likened the star chamber to the court of chancery in its use of equity and prerogative justice, defending as well the unique form of *ore tenus* (described above), yet acknowledging that the taking of a confession was rife with potential for abuse and tyranny.[45] At the core of the argument was the classic statement of the character of royal justice:

> Theise Judiciall opinions both of moderne and ancient times, together with the Contynuall usage in the Raigne of all the kinges of this lande in succession and that the kinge whoe is the fountaine of all Justice must necessarily by the lawe have power to execute Justice himselfe which hee doth most properly in this Court.[46]

The star chamber court operated in similar fashion to the court of chancery, allowing a measure of flexibility to its proceedings and sometimes denying access to its jurisdiction to those who failed to observe the proper forms and pleadings. But the author acknowledged the need to maintain the court's dignity, noting that officers of the court were sometimes perfunctory in their management of its records and actions.[47] William Hudson's subsequent 'Treatise of the court of star

---

43. Treadwell, 'Richard Hadsor', 305–36; Hand & Treadwell, eds., 'Directions for the courts', 185ff; Treadwell, *Buckingham and Ireland*, ch. 5.

44. *Cal. S.P. Ire.,1647–60*, p. 158.   45. TCD, MS 722, ff. 5–7v, 114v–15v.

46. Ibid., f. 7.   47. Ibid., f. 7v.

chamber', published in 1621, defended both the legitimacy and the effectiveness of the court from the perspective of its most eminent barrister. Noting that the court was staffed with most of the senior judges, Hudson claimed that star chamber was the ultimate repository of legal knowledge, though he lamented the procedural complexity that gave rise to its 'luxuriant bureaucratic garden'.[48]

Charles I inherited an Irish privy council that was remarkable for its disgruntled bitterness, and he set out to remedy those defects by bringing the Irish executive into fuller conformity with his council in England. He gave orders to require Irish councillors to keep the hours of meeting punctually, to hear petitioners (who knelt at the upper end of the table) without discussing their causes except to question them, and to avoid giving their opinions until the parties had left the chamber. The councillors were particularly admonished to keep the confidence of court regarding any division, so that decisions were rendered 'by the whole board' without any subsequent reference to internal dispute. Councillors were ordered to stay in their respective places, to address the chief governor and not each other, and to absent themselves in cases which concerned their own interests. The clerks were to take their notes of all deliberations and orders of the court or council, then read the final order openly in court to correct any mistakes and reform them, drawing the final order from the amended draft and showing it to the chief governor before entering it in the record.[49] On 1 October 1629, the civil establishment for Ireland was further reformed to encourage the better behaviour of officials, with annual fees being delimited for all the clerks of the court. John Stoughton, clerk of the court of castle chamber, was awarded £13 6s. 8d. per annum, the same fee as his counterpart Robert Newcomen, marshal of the court.[50]

The reputation of the castle chamber court hinged on its employment of prerogative justice *in terrorem tantum*, yet the finality of its decrees rests at odds with the incompleteness of their enforcement. The Elizabethan star chamber suffered the same problems, despite efforts to award double damages, penal recognizances and supervised restitution.[51] While, on the one hand, the customary punishment of fine and imprisonment might be coupled with exemplary humiliations such as the pillory, nailing of ears to the stocks, and public confessions in the courts of the realm, it is also clear that offenders commonly won reduction of their fines at the end of the term or appealed to the crown to seek a new hearing. In 1618 the unfortunate Melaghlen McGranell McLoghlin of Co. Leitrim was found guilty by the court of failing to present recusants as member of a jury, but

---

48. T.G. Barnes, 'Mr Hudson's star chamber' in D. Guth and J.W. McKenna, eds., *Tudor rule and revolution* (Cambridge, 1982), pp. 285–308. Cockburn, in contrast, alleged that Egerton 'used star chamber prosecution as a means of intimidating and discrediting opponents'. J.S. Cockburn, 'The spoils of law: the trial of Sir John Hele, 1604', in Guth & McKenna, eds., *Tudor rule and revolution*, p. 341.

49. TCD, MS 672, ff. 163–66.   50. Ibid., ff. 217–20v.

51. The phrase '*in terrorem tantum*' enjoined the potent authority of the court acting with the full force of the crown's majesty. Guy, *Star chamber*, p. 50.

his fine was remitted upon his promise to repair to church himself. When he committed the same offence a second time, his bond was estreated, he was forced to stand on the pillory with a paper on his head declaring his offence, to acknowledge his crime publicly and to suffer imprisonment during pleasure.[52] Review of castle chamber decisions was not uncommon, but reversals were extraordinary, while some lengthy cases ended only with the death of the suitor. In 1582 the court records were swept clean of the accumulated judicial residue, with castle chamber arbitrarily dismissing numerous suits pending for up to ten years.[53] By the late Elizabethan era, the English star chamber courts had become the vehicle for vexatious pleading and thinly veiled attacks on real property.[54] In similar fashion, a gentleman named Thomas Fleming of Co. Cork won an award in castle chamber against the Kinsale merchant Philip Roche FitzPhillip and others in 1594, for trespassing and cutting wood on his lands. Roche paid a fine of £5 plus the costs of Fleming and was imprisoned during pleasure, while the remaining ten and more defendants paid twenty shillings each as a fine.[55] Though Chichester would add a strong policy dimension to castle chamber adjudication that was followed by his immediate predecessors, the court spent an inordinate amount of its time on peripheral matters such as local property disputes and questions of noble patrilineage.[56]

JUDICIAL PERSONALITY: THE JUDGES AND CLERKS OF THE COURT

Early modern Ireland witnessed a profound transformation in its legal establishment in the period from 1571 to 1641. At the beginning of Elizabeth's reign, the majority of privy councillors were Old English Catholic subjects who had served under three or more English sovereigns. By the time of Wentworth's execution in 1641, all the councillors were English-born officials. This meant that the senior bench of Irish-born lawyers who had been trained at the inns of court was slowly eliminated in favour of English office-seekers. Suspicions about the religious beliefs of stalwart Old English judges like Sir Lucas Dillon and Sir Nicholas White ended when they died in 1592 and 1593, and both were replaced by New English magistrates. The last of the recusants, the able Catholic second justice of king's bench, John Everard, was removed in 1607. He returned to haunt Lord

---

52. BL., Add. MS 47,172, f. 264.
53. Some sixteen cases of riot were dismissed by the court on a single day, 7 November. Ibid., ff. 65–74.
54. Guy, *Star chamber*, p 47. J.A. Guy has found that 80 per cent of cases in the Jacobean court had property at stake, or were connected with the action.
55. BL., Add. MS 47,172, ff. 117–17v.
56. Ibid., ff. 172–77. The protracted case of the earl of Clanricarde's disputed ancestry belonged more properly to the jurisdiction of chancery, or a crown commission.

Deputy Chichester in the parliament of 1613–15 when he challenged Sir John
Davies for the speakership of the house of commons and was physically humiliated
by the corpulent attorney general, who sat on him during a lively confrontation
over the speaker's chair. While Elizabeth rather half-heartedly insisted that all
Irish suitors and public officials take the oath of supremacy, her successor made
it clear that this entitling gesture of conformity would be the requirement for
service to the crown. In 1614 Lord Killeen and Sir Christopher Plunkett
petitioned the privy council in England on the matter:

> The gentlemen professing the common law in Ireland were debarred from
> practice this last Michaelmas term, to the great hindrance of the common
> people, whose suits depend on their endeavours; and they conceived that
> neither by the statute 2° of the late Queen, nor any other law, they may be
> so deprived. For matter of conveniency it is likewise offered to your con-
> sideration that the gentlemen being descended of English families have
> spent their time and patrimonies in the acquisition of knowledge of the
> common law, and by the benefit of that professsion both the gentlemen of
> this present age, and their predecessors, have done good service to the Crown,
> and by their long experience they have given exemplary encouragement to the
> ignorant multitude to embrace the fruition and freedom of the common
> laws, which, in comparison to the Brehon laws, is of inestimable value unto
> them. Their inhibition from practice is hurtful to the King's subjects, who
> depend on their advice. To this may be added the assurance of confidence
> and trust, being acquainted with the evidences and estates of most of the
> subjects of that kingdom, the community of language, and the poverty of
> the common sort, who, for want of great fees to retain others, are enforced
> to relinquish their rights.[57]

As Colum Kenny has shown, the effect of this penal law was not as dramatic as
it might first have appeared. Litigants required competent assistance and many
Irish lawyers continued to train at the inns of court in London, returning to serve
their communities in a variety of roles. Indeed, the opposition to crown policies
in this period was more often led by lawyers such as the tenacious Henry Burnell
than by rebels like O'Doherty.[58] When the Graces were drawn up for presentation
to the crown in 1628, one of the principal aims of the opposition was to restore
the right of Irish-born lawyers, who had trained for up to five years at the inns of
court, to be admitted to practice in Ireland after taking an oath of allegiance. It
was further recommended that at least one judge on assize should be a native
speaker of Irish, to assure the lives and property of those who must rely on
interpreters. The castle chamber court was to be enjoined not to summon jurors

---

57. *Cal. Carew MSS, 1603–24*, p. 304.
58. C. Kenny, 'The exclusion of Catholics from the legal profession in Ireland, 1537–1829', *IHS*,
    xxv (1988), 338–49.

or witnesses from the assize courts without strong evidence of corruption, treble damages being given against a relator whose accusation against them proved false.[59] In the Irish parliament of 1641 a strong remonstrance against the government of Wentworth as lord deputy was put forward with judicial acumen by a powerful union of Wentworth's Catholic and Protestant enemies. Furthermore, as Victor Treadwell has indicated, the court of James I had a potent advocate for Irish causes in the lawyer Richard Hadsor and the legal expert Sir Humphrey May.[60]

The predominance of the chief governors on the court of castle chamber has been noted above, and Part Two of this book will address the history of the court from the perspective of viceregal policy and personality. A straightforward narrative history of the tribunal is required, in part, because of the direct relationship between the policy-driven employment of the court to achieve certain ends, and the response of the court to external events such as war and rebellion. As we shall see below, the conduct of litigation at the court varied widely, depending on multiple factors. Any effort to compress the broad scope of its litigation over seven decades into a series of tables and graphs would risk distortion. What is more, the broken path of the court's record in its later years tends to highlight the 'show trials' of the period, diminishing the ordinary work of the tribunal at a time when it had gained a reputation for judicial tyranny. While it would appear that lords justices lacked the policy mandate of chief governors appointed with the full backing of the crown and privy council, some of the more ambitious and senior interim officials pursued an active judicial agenda, without striking out on new ground. The lame duck status of the lords justices after the departure of Wentworth, coupled with the parliamentary challenge to the conduct of the court, fatally compromised the prosecution of causes at the court of castle chamber and led to its extinction.

After 1590, it becomes more difficult to view the roles of particular justices since decrees in the entry book were no longer signed. Nonetheless, the lord chancellor in Ireland was usually at the forefront of proceedings, frequently signing the entries in the absence of the viceroy and occasionally challenging the jurisdiction of the conciliar court when his own tribunal was directly engaged with a suit pending in castle chamber. In what follows, a description of the judges and clerks of the court of castle chamber will complete the discussion of the court's structure and judicial personality. In 1571 the four courts of chancery, queen's bench, common pleas and exchequer were manned by experienced judges. The key role of lord chancellor of Ireland, however, had become troublesomely unstable. Successive lords chancellor were seen as the pawns of more powerful viceroys; the English John Alen was succeeded by the Old English Palesman Thomas Cusake

---

59. *Cal. S.P. Ire., 1625–32*, pp. 332–36.
60. Treadwell, 'Richard Hadsor', 305–17. Hadsor sponsored numerous Irish students at the Middle Temple during this period, including the Galway lawyer Patrick Darcy, admitted in 1617. When Hadsor died in 1635, Darcy was already pleading the case of the Galway jurors against Wentworth's relentless intimidation. Ibid., 330.

in 1546, and the latter maintained a continuous presence on the Irish council long after he was replaced as chancellor in 1555. Junior officials in England vied for the high office and two successive English incumbents, Hugh Curwen, archbishop of Dublin, and Robert Weston, former dean of the arches, were overshadowed in council by more seasoned veterans of Irish service. When Weston died in 1572 an unseemly conflict arose over possession of the great seal between the Old English Sir Nicholas White, master of the rolls, and the ambitious New English lord keeper, Adam Loftus, the new archbishop of Dublin. The recent history of the Catholic diocese of Dublin credits Weston, rather than Loftus, with the primary role in spearheading the early Reformation in Dublin under Elizabeth. The powerful local clergy successfully resisted reform and Loftus's mishandling of key initiatives such as the delayed founding of a Protestant university marked the final decades of the century.[61] The long-delayed instructions and implementation of the star chamber jurisdiction for Ireland was a welcome force for stability at a time when the chancery had failed to exercise its traditional role as the anchor of a judicial framework.

Perhaps the most remarkable lord chancellor in the history of the court of castle chamber was the redoubtable Sir William Gerrard, who had been Sydney's vice president in the council in the marches of Wales. Gerrard brought to the government both experience and energy, arriving in 1576 with a reformer's zeal and the judicial acumen of a secular legist who was determined to implement the rule of law. Though he spent only five years in Ireland, and was preoccupied with the dangers of rebellion and the controversy over cess, Gerrard managed the work of the conciliar tribunal along with that of his own chancery court, and corresponded frequently with England on his ambitious proposals for changes in the personnel of the Irish bench. His remarkable critique of the judiciary offered an unusual, and devastating, glimpse of the senior bench in Ireland, prompting him to hold most of the causes before him in chancery and going on the assize circuits himself upon his first arrival in Ireland. Finding the aged chief justices beyond service, 'overleapt as scarecrows' as he said, Gerrard charged the remainder with corruption and negligence, and set about finding English replacements.[62] Nonetheless, he commended the Old English justices Lucas Dillon and Nicholas White, whose proven loyalty and consistent attendance at the council table contrasted with the indifferent performance of their contemporaries. Gerrard occasionally acted alone in the castle chamber court to prompt judicial celerity, making orders and decrees that moved causes of action to a conclusion, but his programme of action was stymied by bureaucratic inertia, rebellion and the crisis over cess. He spent much of the final years of his tenure working in England, suffering from ill-health, while his place was taken by the aspiring Loftus.

61. J. Murray, 'The diocese of Dublin in the sixteenth century' in J. Kelly and D. Keogh, eds., *History of the Catholic diocese of Dublin* (Dublin, 2000), pp. 99, 106–09.
62. LPL, Carew MS 628, ff. 311v–14. Gerrard's compelling review of the ability, disposition and alliances of each of the princiapl law officers was never repeated by his successors in office. For a fuller discussion see my *Anglicizing*, pp. 210–16.

Archbishop Adam Loftus, the father of twenty children, was an active politician as lord chancellor and a partisan of religious conformity. Trained at Trinity College in Cambridge University, he had become chaplain to the earl of Sussex, travelling with him to Ireland in 1561 where he took up the first of many Irish livings in Co. Meath. The quarrelsome Loftus soon became archbishop of Armagh, though his diocese was so disturbed in 1561 that he lived in Dublin. Loftus took the degree of doctor of divinity in 1566 and returned to Ireland as archbishop of Dublin the next year. He retained that office until his death in 1605, becoming lord keeper on the death of Weston in 1572 and ultimately lord chancellor after Gerrard's demise in 1581. During the first decade of the court of castle chamber, Loftus was lord keeper on at least four separate occasions, yet he made no mark on the court during that time. He fought with the master of the rolls, Sir Nicholas White, for the right to the use of the great seal in 1572 and he was nearly overlooked for the role of chancellor in 1581 when Secretary Fenton recommended either Lucas Dillon or a secular lawyer from England in his place. As lord chancellor of Ireland for 24 years, Loftus rarely spoke of the need for judicial reform, attending to the interests of his family and the diocese of Dublin as his foremost responsibilities. The chancery court probably benefited from twinning of these responsibilities, since the court of castle chamber heard relatively few causes during his tenures as lord justice (1582–84, 1597–99, 1599–1600). Loftus argued with Lord Deputy Perrot over the founding of a Protestant university, since this would have denied him the profitable deanery of St Patrick's, and he took his revenge upon Perrot by undermining his support on the Irish council and spearheading the subsequent investigation at his treason trial in London. In a lengthy complaint to Burghley, written in December 1586, Loftus challenged Perrot on a number of issues, claiming that he wrongly took the naming of sheriffs from the chancellor's domain, overruled the new chief justice of queen's bench, and removed causes from other courts to be heard by himself. He concluded that

> It is an usual thing with my Lord Deputy to remove such causes as are begun in Chancery out of that Court, and to call the same before himself, to be ordered by him and his favourites of this Council. And in case any person by me, the Chancellor, be in Court committed, either for disobedience and contempt, or upon an execution after judgment, his Lordship at his pleasure releaseth the parties by his authority, which he supposeth is absolute, and neither can nor ought to be limited.[63]

Loftus further claimed the lord deputy appointed justices of assize from his own followers, and dishonoured the Irish councillors by calling them dunghill churles and beggars, terming the chief justices 'ten shilling knaves'.[64]

That Loftus became the first provost of Trinity College in 1592 was an ironic conclusion to the debate over its founding, though the rigid sectarianism of the

---

63. *Cal. S.P. Ire., 1586–88*, pp. 211–12.   64. Ibid.; Plate 7.

university's early years is a due reflection of his own predestinarian Calvinism. As Dr Lennon has shown, Loftus had the patronage of 17 of the 24 richest livings in the diocese and he used both clerical livings and politically astute marriages to endow his family's ample fortune.[65] Loftus was further distracted by his leadership of the occasional court of high commission, and his prosecution of the unfortunate Catholic archbishop, Dermot O'Hurley, in 1584 demonstrated the hard line he took as lord justice. In 1600, at the height of rebellion, he warned the English privy council against leniency, noting that the court of high commission had not met for four years, and pleading for strict observance of the law in the English Pale.[66] Despite his many years of service, Loftus had a doubtful reputation for judicial probity, and had to defend his conduct in a letter to Cecil of November 1600. He had agreed to grant St Leger, master of the rolls, the escheated Desmond seat of Askeaton in Munster, but the queen challenged his ill-advised 'insider trading'. Loftus then blamed the lord deputy for concealing the crown order that forbade passing such castles from the crown to her servitors. In the same letter he took pains to deny that he had profited from his office to the benefit of his children or sons-in-law, a belief widely held in Dublin circles.[67] He excused the St Leger transaction, saying the master of the rolls now stood ready to regrant the castle to the crown (though under duress, we must assume).[68] In 1586 Loftus was accused of 'severity' in a case involving the monastery of Tintern and charged with subverting common law. He was admonished to forbear proceeding in chancery and either to remit the cause to common law or else to be heard by the 'bodie of the Councell there'.[69] Despite his reputation for intransigence, he was chosen to lead the government during the transitions of the late sixteenth century, and he survived the queen to participate in the troubled first years of the Stuart regime. However, Loftus was directly challenged by Mountjoy in January 1603 for imprisoning seven aldermen of Dublin for recusancy, in his absence, stating that a 'violent course' would do little to win men's consciences, particularly at such a sensitive moment.[70]

The successor of Adam Loftus as archbishop of Dublin and lord chancellor of Ireland was his surrogate, Thomas Jones, who was brought to Ireland to live in Loftus's household after he was awarded master of arts at Cambridge in 1573. He

---

65. C. Lennon, *Sixteenth century Ireland: the incomplete conquest* (New York, 1995), p. 310. After the Baltinglas rebellion in the Pale, Loftus purchased the escheated Eustace property of Rathfarnham and built an Elizabethan manor house. With walls up to 5 feet thick and hidden gunports near the portico, he adapted the country house to unsettled Irish conditions and withstood several incursions of the Wicklow septs of O'Byrnes and O'Tooles. The bulky four-storey residence today retains Elizabethan features in the kitchen and the long gallery. It is in the care of the Irish government today. Plate 3.

66. *Cal. S.P. Ire., 1600*, pp. 78–79.   67. *Cal. S.P. Ire., 1600–01*, p. 25.

68. Ibid.

69. *Acts privy council, 1586–87*, pp. 269, 290–91.

70. *Cal. S.P. Ire., 1601–03*, pp. 555–56. Lennon, *Sixteenth century Ireland*, pp. 310, 318, 320. See also A. Ford, *The Protestant reformation in Ireland, 1590–1641* (Dublin, 1997), pp. 31–34, 38, 51–62.

became chancellor of St Patrick's and a commissioner for ecclesiastical causes in 1578; dean of St Patrick's in 1582; and bishop of Meath in 1584 with a seat on the Irish council. From that time forward until his death in 1619, he participated in decisions of the court of castle chamber. As Loftus's closest ally, Jones joined in the political campaigns against Perrot and White and Bingham, suffering censure for neglect of his diocese on several occasions. His Protestant zeal endeared him to Lord Deputy Chichester, who recommended him to become archbishop of Dublin and lord chancellor on the death of his mentor in 1605. Jones visited the dioceses of Leinster and Munster, joining Chichester on two occasions for surveying the plantation of Ulster, and he acted as speaker of the house of lords in the parliament of 1613–15. He acted as lord justice during Chichester's absence in 1614 and again in 1616, continuing the inquisitorial policy of the viceroy against recusancy. Though he was not a frequent correspondent with England, Jones was a pillar of the New English wing of advanced Protestant reform and his role as lord chancellor in the castle chamber court probably did much to sustain the ruthless determination of Chichester to punish offenders. His son, Roger Jones, became Viscount Ranelagh and was involved in a violent encounter with Lord Howth that brought them to the attention of castle chamber in 1611.[71] Remarkably, the court of castle chamber was powerfully influenced for over forty years by two Calvinist bishop-chancellors, double advocates who brokered the leading equity jurisdictions in a manner that brought frequent accusations of partisanship.[72]

Lord Chancellor and Archbishop Jones was replaced in 1619 by the equally contentious Sir Adam Loftus, the young nephew and namesake of the former archbishop and chancellor. Born in Yorkshire like his kinsman, Loftus proceeded to Cambridge and Lincoln's Inn, appearing in Ireland about 1592 as archdeacon of Glendalough. Using the patronage of his powerful uncle, Loftus became a master in chancery at the end of 1598 and married the widow of the dean of St Patrick's. He became a commissioner for ecclesiastical causes and his uncle's vicar general and he was knighted in Christ Church cathedral in 1604. As a member of the Irish privy council from 1609, he participated in the judgements of the castle chamber court for the next thirty years. By 1613 Loftus had become a wealthy landowner and member of parliament, with estates in Kildare, Wexford and King's County, along with his castle of Drimnagh, near Dublin, probably obtained through the manipulation of evidence in the court of chancery itself.[73] On the death of

71. *Cal. S.P. Ire., 1611–14*, pp. 49, 60–61; BL, Add. MS 47, 172, f. 166. The Jones monument in St Patrick's cathedral, little smaller than the bold construction of Boyle which faces it, was erected in 1628 to honour the family. The lord chancellor is depicted as a kneeling effigy in the upper portion, his son as recumbent knight in armour, along with figures representing his fourteen daughters. This confidently opulent memorial depicts Jones in his legal and secular role within the confines of his ecclesiastical domain. See Plate 9.

72. F.E. Ball, *The judges in Ireland, 1221–1921*, 2 vols. (London, 1926), i, 315–17.

73. *Cal. pat. rolls, Ire., Jas. I*, pp. 327–29, 425. As we have seen above, chancery depositions furnished evidence for the suit of Loftus in 1618 against Peter Barnewall who sought to dispossess him of the ancient manor of Drimnagh. Marcus Barnewall had inherited the estate

Archbishop Jones in 1619, he became the first secular lord chancellor of Ireland since 1581. Loftus was selected as lord justice on three occasions: serving as interim viceroy in 1622 when he was also created Viscount Ely; governing alongside the earl of Cork after the fall of Falkland, 1629–33; and acting in the absence of Wentworth in 1636. His career was marked by episodes of confrontation with Falkland, Cork, and Wentworth, along with many others. Loftus was accused of intense partisanship in favouring his relatives in the court of chancery and he had to defend his stewardship of office on charges of corruption in 1627. After a number of lesser quarrels, Wentworth charged him with breach of contract regarding the marriage portion of his son, a charge aggravated by his 'covert carriage' and disrespect to the viceroy that brought the attention of the council and castle chamber in 1638. Refusing to give up the great seal, he was sent to Dublin Castle as a prisoner, and his appeal to the crown was rejected. Finally allowed to leave for England under humiliating terms in 1639, Loftus's appeal was again denied and he was deprived as lord chancellor. Though his last appeal was accepted by the house of lords in 1642, his Irish estates were ruined and he died in England in the next year.[74]

The last lord chancellor of Ireland to attend the court of castle chamber was the noted lawyer, Sir Richard Bolton. He entered the Inner Temple in 1601 and thereafter appeared in Ireland as deputy recorder of Dublin in 1605. As recorder of Dublin and a freeman of the city from 1606 to 1613, Bolton enjoyed a high reputation for erudition and won the favour of Chichester, becoming a member of King's Inns in 1610. Bolton was knighted in 1618 by Grandison and became solicitor general in Ireland the following year, bringing numerous cases before the castle chamber court. He published his *Statutes of Ireland* in 1621 and *A justice of the peace for Ireland* in 1638, showing a remarkable knowledge of the Irish legal system. In 1622 he was appointed attorney of the new court of wards and three years later he became chief baron of the exchequer, a role which automatically conferred on him membership of the Irish privy council. After 1633, Bolton allied himself with the new lord deputy, Wentworth, the future earl of Strafford, and joined with him in managing the disgrace and fall of his predecessor, Adam Loftus. At the close of 1639, he became lord chancellor on the recommendation of Strafford and he acted as speaker in the house of lords in 1640–41, during the impeachment of his patron. In the wake of Strafford's execution, Bolton was named in the Irish impeachment proceedings along with his fellow councillors,

and its farflung possessions in Co. Dublin, enfeoffing Maurice O'Cullen with the lands of Drimnagh in 1597. O'Cullen then leased the lands to Loftus for 15 years in 1604, and Loftus successfully bargained for a 99-year lease from James Barnewall, the husband (and cousin) of Marcus's heir, Elizabeth. Many of the depositions purported to show that O'Cullen had previously re-enfeoffed the lands to Marcus, who took the deed to Goodman Hill and had a sod of earth placed on the red wax seal to symbolize his regaining of the property. Peter Barnewall was accused of intimidating the tenants and seeking the rent from Drimnagh and Ballythermott, as well as attempting to suborn witnesses in the case.

74. Ball, *Judges in Ireland*, i, 326–28; WWM STR P, items 475, 476.

Bishop Bramhall, Sir George Radcliffe and Sir Gerald Lowther. He was then suspended as speaker and the judicial work of the council was abated during the crisis of the Irish Rebellion. When parliament was prorogued in 1642, Bolton was restored to his position as lord chancellor, but he had lost both his estates and his salary and sought leave to go to England. He negotiated with Irish Catholics thereafter in 1643–44 and in 1646, but he was accused of injustice toward the native Irish and had to defend his impartiality. He died in England in 1648, a fitting symbol of the disastrous consequences of Strafford's government. The intellectual promise of his treatises, written in the anticipation of reforming the Irish judiciary, was frustrated by the dénouement of the regime. Ironically, the two chancellors most likely to institutionalize progress, Gerrard and Bolton, experienced the shortest tenures in this period and ended their lives in England during the midst of crises that drove them from Ireland.[75]

Along with the lord chancellor, the two chief justices sat on the court of castle chamber bench as well as their own. The court of king's bench was the senior criminal jurisdiction in Ireland as in England; it heard civil cases too, as did the court of common pleas. We have very little evidence for the work of these two courts, but we may surmise that they, like their English counterparts, vied for litigation through a series of judicial expedients, legal fictions and arcane pleadings. The court of castle chamber heard cases on appeal from the king's bench, but rarely intervened in questions before the court of common pleas. Chief justices of king's bench were often seen as judicial sinecurists, men for whom the judgeship represented advancement and profit rather than opportunity to extend the reach of the common law. Sir John Plunkett was named to the Irish council in 1556, becoming chief justice of queen's bench in 1559. He was the most active councillor in this period, attending nearly all the meetings until age and infirmity interrupted his service after 1577. In that year, his work on the bench was severely criticized by Lord Chancellor Gerrard and numerous proposals for his replacement by an English judge were the hallmark of his later years. Plunkett died in 1582, and his attenuated judgeship coincided with Gerrard's push for judicial reform and renewal. A transitional figure, James Dowdall, had been second justice of queen's bench in 1565 and was named the first chief justice of the new presidency

75. Ball, *Judges in Ireland*, i, 330–32. The 'Notes by Sir Richard Bolton, ... on cases in the Four Courts and Castle Chamber, 1621–53' in Arm. Pub. Lib., MS H. II. 4 hold interesting 'aide mémoires' of numerous cases from the period in which he was both attorney and judge. The memoranda on jurors possibly being tried before the castle chamber court for a corrupt verdict contain only fragments of the reasoning of the jurors in refusing to indict Hugh McArt of burglary, but illustrate an elusive process in castle chamber proceedings. The case is not dated and the venue not named specifically. Another case of 1636–37 deals with the enforcement of a proclamation concerning the official size of woollens and furzes, with comments of Bolton suggesting discharge of certain weavers and censure of the owners of the cloth. The scribbled observations are detached from the official record and preserve only the judicial impressions of the careful Bolton, so they do little to expand our knowledge of castle chamber litigation. See ff. 10, 12, 15–16.

court in Munster in 1570. He succeeded Plunkett briefly, from 1582 until his own death in 1585. Sir Robert Gardener succeeded Dowdall in 1586, ending a decade of near-dormancy in the senior bench. The rivalry on Perrot's council between the viceroy and his Old English supporters against the chancellor and his allies was soon heightened by the arrival of the New English Protestant Gardener, who participated actively in the undoing of Perrot's reform administration. A frequent correspondent with England, Gardener was engaged in negotiation with Tyrone in 1594 and again in 1596, finally serving as lord justice along with Loftus in 1597. Gardener served reluctantly in Ireland until 1603 when he was replaced by another English barrister, James Ley.[76] Gardener was the only chief justice to be named lord justice in the Elizabethan period. He served James I until his death in 1620, appearing as commissioner in the Channel Islands and advising the crown on Irish affairs in 1607.[77] In August 1593, Gardener was joined by three New English justices in the offices of master of the rolls, chief baron of the exchequer and chief justice of common pleas. This judicial coup temporarily brought an end to the Old English presence on the senior bench, though Judge Weston's tenure at common pleas was short lived.[78]

Sir James Ley was sent to Ireland to replace Gardener in 1603 at the age of 51, a senior barrister who had graduated from Oxford in 1574 and was called to the bar from Lincoln's Inn a decade later. This veteran bencher was selected for the Irish chief justiceship to spearhead a reform movement launched by Mountjoy and Chichester, joining the latter on assizes in Ulster in 1605.[79] Sir Patrick Barnewall, as leader of the Pale opposition during the Mandates controversy, charged that Ley withheld a copy of an indictment from defendants at his court of king's bench in 1605, making him 'hatefull to this whole kingdom & a scandall to the place which he holdeth'.[80] Ley participated actively in the castle chamber persecution of recusants until his departure from Ireland in 1608, a fact Barnewall must have considered in his charges against the chief justice. Known for his active role in the assize courts, he was also a commissioner for the plantation of Ulster in 1608, but he was finally allowed to resign as chief justice in that year and became a key adviser to the crown on Irish affairs. Ley was a governor of Lincoln's Inn, MP for Westbury and was created baronet in 1619, winning the position of chief justice of king's bench in England three years later. An ally of Buckingham after he married the duke's niece as his third wife, Ley was promoted to lord treasurer and became earl of Marlborough in 1626, three years before his death. His was an

---

76. Ball, *Judges in Ireland*, i, 210, 222–23.　　　77. Ibid.
78. *Cal. S.P.Ire., 1592–94*, pp. 143–44. Anthony St Leger, Robert Napier and William Weston arrived within a day of each other in June 1593. They sat only the last three days of the midsummer term before riding the assize circuits. St Leger then wrote to Burghley, asking that Gerrard's son be required to return the missing chancery records from his father's tenure as lord chancellor. Ibid.
79. McCavitt, *Chichester*, pp. 78, 85, 98–105.
80. TCD, MS 672, f. 27. The Irish council wrote to England at the same time to assure the privy council that Ley was an upright judge whose court was full of eager suitors.

extraordinarily powerful role as chief justice in both kingdoms and he was a prominent adviser on Irish affairs throughout the Jacobean period.[81]

Three legal scholars in succession replaced Ley as chief justice of king's bench in Ireland, and each of them subsequently became integral parts of the increasingly sophisticated network of commissions and committees on Irish affairs. Sir Humphrey Winch, born in 1555, was another veteran bencher of Lincoln's Inn who was selected for Irish service under James I, leaving for Ireland as the new chief baron of the exchequer in 1606. Promoted to chief justice of king's bench in 1608 on Ley's departure, he joined Chichester on a progress to Ulster in 1609, but complained of ill-health, inadequate support and a humiliating fee. He was finally released from the burden of his Irish judgeship in 1612 and became a judge of common pleas in England, but he remained active on the Irish committees in England, and he returned to Ireland as part of the commission of inquiry in 1613. Winch died in London in 1625. He was replaced as chief justice in Ireland in 1612 by Sir John Denham, a Londoner active in the business of Lincoln's Inn prior to being called to Ireland as chief baron of the exchequer in 1609. Denham was active on the assize circuit during his Irish tenure of seven years and served as lord justice in 1616, returning to England as a baron of the exchequer in the following year. He took a prominent role along with Ley and Winch on the committees for Irish affairs in England until his death in 1639, and he married as his second wife Eleanor Moore, the daughter of Garret, first Viscount Drogheda.[82] The last of this Jacobean triumvirate was the Welshman William Jones, a graduate of Oxford and bencher of Lincoln's Inn, who went to Ireland at the age of 51 to replace Denham as chief justice of king's bench. Like the others, he was active on the assize circuit and produced learned papers on the law and British antiquities, returning to England in 1620 where he became a judge in common pleas in the following year. He returned to Ireland as commissioner for Irish causes in 1622 and again in 1624, after which he became a judge of king's bench in England. He died in 1640, and was buried in Lincoln's Inn chapel, the fourth successive chief justice of Ireland from that inn.[83]

The last of the early Stuart chief justices of king's bench was Sir George Shurley, a graduate of Cambridge and the Middle Temple, who was sent to Ireland in 1620 at the age of 61 to replace Jones. He spent the next 26 years in Ireland, acting as a commissioner for the plantation of Ulster in 1622 and usually riding the assize circuit in Munster. As a member of the castle chamber court and the Irish council throughout this period, he would have been an important witness

81. Ball, *Judges in Ireland*, i, 312–14; *DNB*. Like Bolton and Davies, Ley was the author of a number of legal treatises and papers, demonstrating the quality of the reformed Irish judiciary at the senior level under the early Stuarts. See, for example, ' Of sterling money of the time when England was first divided into shires'; 'Of the antiquity of the office of the chancellor of England'; 'Of epitaphs', in T. Hearne, *A collection of curious discourses* (London, 1720); and *Reports of divers resolutions in law, arising upon cases in the courts of wards and other courts at Westminister ...* (London, 1659).

82. Ball, *Judges in Ireland*, i, 321–22.   83. Ibid., i, 325.

had he not remained largely silent on issues of contention among the leaders in Irish government, though his own dispute with the chief justice of common pleas over issues of precedence is chronicled in the State Papers. He died in England in 1647, an aged veteran of Irish government and a landowner in Co. Carlow who was, most probably, ruined in the turmoil of the Irish Rebellion.[84] Shurley's rival, the Cork-born careerist Dominic Sarsfield, took office as chief justice of common pleas in 1612, after attending New Inn and Middle Temple. He was named attorney general for Munster in 1600 and became chief justice of that province in 1604, using Munster as the base for his increasingly powerful network of estates and alliances. A notorious pluralist, he combined his Munster judgeship with that of a judge of king's bench in 1607 and won the reversion of the chief justiceship of common pleas on the basis of his adherence to the reformed church and the support of the wealthy earl of Cork, to whose daughter he had promised his son in marriage. Sarsfield was widely suspected of corruption, defending his reputation in England in 1615, but he was created a baronet and then Viscount Kinsale in 1625, setting off a series of disagreements on precedence. He quarrelled with Shurley over precedence as chief justice since he was now a peer, and disputed the title itself with Baron Courcy of Kinsale, finally settling for the new title of Viscount Kilmallock in 1628.[85] Sarsfield ended his flinty career as a judge when his corrupt verdict against an aged English planter, given while on assize in 1625, was challenged in the star chamber in London. He was duly convicted in 1633, committed to the Fleet, deprived of office, fined £2,000 and finally died in disgrace in 1636.[86] In contrast to the elevated and circumspect conduct of the chief judges in king's bench, their counterparts in common pleas generated an unenviable record. This may have been due, in part, to the presence in that court of a large number of Irish-born judges whose adherence to official church doctrine was constantly in doubt.[87]

Chief justices of common pleas were often at the centre of a storm of controversy during this period, after the recumbent Sir Robert Dillon died in office in 1580. Dillon was a member of the celebrated Pale family of Old English judges who dominated high office for over a century. His father was chief justice of king's bench under Henry VII and his son, Lucas, was chief baron of the exchequer (noted below). Dillon became chief justice in his own right in 1559, but rarely attended council meetings after 1571 and his office was usually executed by the second justice. He was the foremost target of Gerrard's judicial reforms after 1576, and his

84. Ibid., i, 328–29.

85. *Cal. S.P. Ire., 1625–32*, pp. 133, 139–40, 143. Courcy resisted trial in castle chamber, and pleaded for the intervention of the earl marshal in England, a request supported by the commission for Irish causes.

86. *Cal. S.P. Ire., 1633–41*, pp. 26–31; Ball, *Judges in Ireland*, i, 319–20. Kilmallock conspired with the sheriff Henry Belling to gain part of the estate of Philip Bushin, and he intimidated the jurors in private session after excluding everyone else from the courtroom.

87. Kilmallock was himself suspected of treason in 1631 and his son accused of recusancy in 1628. Ibid.

imminent replacement was expected for four years prior to his death. Competition to succeed him in office was intense, perhaps inflamed by the rebellions of Fitzmaurice, Desmond and Baltinglas in this period. His great-nephew and namesake, another Robert Dillon, was second justice of the common pleas in 1577 and considered for the senior post, but he was passed over in favour of his chief rival, Nicholas Nugent, scion of another important Pale family from whom many judges and lawyers had descended. Nugent was accused of complicity in the Pale rebellion of his kinsman, William Nugent, and in a hasty trial conducted at Trim under unusual circumstances, he was found guilty of treason and executed in 1582.[88] Dillon, who had quarrelled with Nugent when both were scholars at Lincoln's Inn, succeeded him in office. He had been a judge in Connacht in 1569 under the doomed presidency of Sir Edward Fyton, and chancellor of the exchequer in 1572, so his experience in office was extensive. He was commended for his learning by the sceptical Gerrard, championed for higher office by Wallop, and described by Waterhouse as 'one of the most sufficient in knowledge and judgment, and he is of very good hability to beare out the Countenance of a Counsailor, being born to fair living as the chief of that surname'.[89] However, he was also a lightning rod for trouble, accused of corruption and partiality by Bingham in the investigation of his presidency of Connacht, and finally deprived of office in 1592 when the Nugents won their vengeful campaign to destroy him.[90] Dillon fought to survive accusations of treason, felony and disloyalty in the maelstrom surrounding the disgrace and fall of Perrot, finally winning restoration to his seat on the council in 1593 and resumption of the chief justiceship two years later. He died at his important estate of Riverston, Co. Meath in 1597, reputedly among the wealthiest commoners in Ireland.[91]

Dillon was replaced as chief justice of common pleas by another veteran Irish-born judge, Sir Nicholas Walsh. Son of the mayor of Waterford, and a member of Lincoln's Inn, he was named recorder of Waterford and subsequently second justice of Munster in 1570, working with Sir John Perrot as president. A frequent correspondent of Burghley, he took office as chief justice of the presidency court in Munster in 1576. He was brought to Dublin as part of Perrot's regime in 1585 to become second justice of queen's bench. Walsh served as MP for Waterford and speaker of the house of commons in that year, earning the enmity of Loftus for his close relationship with the lord deputy. Indeed, Walsh enjoyed, uniquely, a seat on the Irish privy council as 'minister without portfolio', awaiting

---

88. H.C. Walshe, 'The rebellion of William Nugent, 1581', pp. 41–45, in R.V. Comerford et al., eds., *Religion, conflict and coexistence in Ireland: essays presented to Mgr Patrick J. Corish* (Dublin, 1990); Ball, *Judges in Ireland*, i, 217–18.

89. 'Gerrard's Report' in LPL, Carew MS 628, ff. 311v–14; Waterhouse to Cecil, 20 April 1580, PRO, SP 63/72/147.

90. *Cal. Carew MSS, 1589–1600*, pp. 62, 75. He was examined at St Patrick's by the chancellor, chief justice of queen's bench, and solicitor general along with Henry Bagenal.

91. Ball, *Judges in Ireland*, i, 218–19.

appointment to a senior judgeship. On the death of Sir Lucas Dillon in 1592, Walsh was recommended by Fitzwilliam as his successor, but Loftus had him removed from the council on suspicion of conspiring with Perrot and he was threatened with trial in the court of castle chamber. Nonetheless, he went on assizes in the next year and was restored to the council in 1593, becoming chief justice of common pleas in 1597. Walsh suffered the indignity of being attacked in Waterford during the uprising of the corporate towns in 1603. Nonetheless, he was an active participant in the new regime, attending the assize circuits with Sir John Davies in Munster and Leinster until he finally resigned his office, about the age of 70, in 1612.[92] A loyal Old English townsman in the mould of Sir Nicholas White, with whom he was brought up, Walsh personified both the difficulties and the determination of the important generation of Irish-born jurists who retained the support of key policymakers in England. The blighted career of his successor, Kilmallock (noted above), effectively ruined the carefully designed balancing act of Irish-born justices and their extensive network of judicial officeholding.

The last chief justice of common pleas in this period was also the first English-born officeholder, Sir Gerard Lowther, whose uncles Gerard and Lancelot Lowther had already made their judicial careers in Ireland in the courts of common pleas and exchequer, respectively. The younger Gerard attended Queen's College at Oxford and was called to the bar at Gray's Inn, appearing as a member of King's Inns in Dublin in 1619. He married the daughter of Sir Lawrence Parsons in 1621 at the earl of Cork's house in Lismore, becoming legal adviser to Cork, attorney general of Munster, and later succeeding his father-in-law as second baron of the exchequer in 1628. Cork intervened on his behalf to secure the chief justiceship of common pleas after the disgrace of Kilmallock in 1633, promising Wentworth £1,000 for the office, which he obtained in the following year. After this, Lowther became a staunch supporter of the lord deputy. Lowther assisted in planning for the plantation of Connacht in 1635, and aided in the overthrow of Lord Chancellor Loftus in 1638, becoming a core member of the Wentworth party on the Irish council. He attended the viceroy in London to oppose the chancellor's appeal to the king, but was subsequently impeached by the Irish parliament in 1641 along with Bolton and Bramhall for acts of treason. A survivor in the mould of the mid-Tudor pragmatists, Lowther negotiated for the crown with Confederate Catholics in 1644, treated with the London parliament for the relief of Dublin in 1646, and earned the favour of the Cromwellians after

92. Ball, *Judges in Ireland*, i, 221–22. Walsh died in 1613. Walsh, of Clonmore, was a notable Kilkenny client of the earl of Ormonde, having traditional lands in the south and effectively displacing the Kavanaghs after 1587 by leasing substantial lands from the sept. Along with Gerald Comerford, who became attorney for the presidency in Connacht, Walsh conformed to the state religion and was handsomely rewarded. According to Edwards, his kinsmen gradually blended Gaelic practice with English stewardship and triumphed in the seventeenth century through intermarriage with families such as Mastersons, Devereux, Powers, Sextons and Butlers. Edwards, *Ormond lordship*, pp. 61–62, 247.

1651 when he appeared as the president of the high court of justice until 1654.[93] In summary, the record of these judges in office was occasionally stained by their actions as politicians, yet they generally proved to be assiduous in their work as assize judges and agents of crown policy.

The tarnished careers of subordinate judges is even more notorious. The compromised pluralist William Saxey demonstrated the doubtful wisdom of employing ambitious English opportunists as judges in Ireland. He obtained the chief justiceship of Munster in 1594, departed for England without leave in 1597 to defend his corrupt and partisan handling of cases, and held concurrently a judgeship in common pleas from 1599 until he resigned all his offices prior to 1606.[94] The ethically-challenged Saxey returned to the lists with a memorandum on Irish government, designed to restore him to favour, written in the midst of the Rebellion in 1598. He called for the elimination of all native-born judges and the proscription of the native Irish from holding any office. He charged that recusants, soldiers and others without knowledge of the law conducted hearings at *nisi prius* and of *oyer and terminer*, blaming corrupt sheriffs for mishandling of process, and preferring 'professors of the law' as magistrates. Saxey particularly condemned the practice of suitors going to Dublin from the Munster courts, arguing that no writs for removal of a case should be returned without a certificate from the chief governor and council.[95] Saxey was condemned in 1600 for holding two judicial positions concurrently, since he could hardly be in Munster and Dublin at the same time and Nicholas Walsh before him had given up the inferior position. Saxey rarely attended as second justice of queen's bench and refused to name a deputy, though he kept the allowance of £100 per annum.[96] Corruption in office plagued Irish-born incumbents as well. Sir Robert Dillon's son-in-law, Patrick Sedgrave, was removed from his office of second baron of the exchequer in 1602 after a trial in castle chamber for conspiring with a plaintiff to share in the contested title to Donshaghlin, Co. Meath.[97]

The court of exchequer was led by the chief baron, an official with multiple roles as judge, privy councillor and financial officer. The notable career of Sir Lucas Dillon, chief baron from 1570 until his death in 1592, spanned the reforming governorships of Sussex, Sydney and Perrot. This talented son of the

---

93. Ball, *Judges in Ireland*, i, 332–34. Lowther died in 1660, aged 70 years.
94. Ball, *Judges in Ireland*, i, 226–27. The lord deputy and council wrote to England in February 1597 to condemn Saxey for departing without licence, charging him with 'intemperate and undecent proceedings' in a suit in Munster. The Irish council claimed that he was unqualified for office and generally disliked, and so should not be returned to Ireland. *Cal. S.P. Ire., 1596–97*, p. 230. Saxey had earlier defended his conduct arguing there was routine indiscipline during the judicial sessions in Munster towns. Ibid., p. 224.
95. *Cal. S.P. Ire., 1596–98*, pp. 394–97.
96. *Cal. S.P. Ire., 1600*, p. 411. It was reported that 'The Fathers of the law at Dublin are directly of opinion that it is against the law for one man to hold two such places'. Ball, *Judges in Ireland*, i, 226–27.
97. Ball, *Judges in Ireland*, i, 226; TCD, MS 852, f. 81.

chief justice of common pleas was an experienced former attorney general and son-in-law of the incumbent, James Bathe, when he took office as chief baron. He was viewed as the most loyal servant of the crown and an energetic reformer by the critical Gerrard, but having sided with Perrot in his quarrel with the lord chancellor, Loftus accused him of recusancy in 1590 and tried to ruin him in the campaign against his partisan cousin, the chief justice Robert Dillon in 1591.[98] He was succeeded on his death in 1592 by another Old English loyalist, Nicholas Walsh, until Walsh became chief justice of common pleas five years later. Like Dillon, Walsh was threatened with trial in castle chamber for suspicion of favouring the regime of Perrot, but he survived this assault on his fidelity and worked with Attorney General Davies in the next reign until he retired in 1612. Walsh was commended by Fitzwilliam in 1592 for his honesty as a judge, finding him 'upright' at the council board, though Fenton argued against replacing Dillon with another native-born justice, despite his favourable opinion of Walsh.[99] Walsh was succeeded as chief baron in 1593 by Sir Robert Napier, a bencher of the Middle Temple who had been a fellow of Exeter College in Oxford University. Napier proved unreliable, complaining of the insufficiency of his stipend, and returning frequently to England until superseded in 1601 by Sir Edmund Pelham. This fifth son of the former lord justice, Sir William Pelham, had entered Gray's Inn in 1563. Almost forty years later, he spent five years in Ireland, enduring sickness and making extensive visits on assize before he died in 1606 on his way back to Ireland.[100] The chief barons under the early Stuarts were remarkably able, energetic and dependable English legists. Sir John Denham became chief justice of king's bench and Sir Richard Bolton lord chancellor, while Sir William Methwold and Sir John Blennerhassett were industrious assize judges, returning numerous cases from the provinces to be heard in the court of castle chamber.[101]

Since the lord chancellor was exceptionally busy with multiple roles in government, including that of lord justice in the absence of the chief governor, much work in chancery was done by the master of the rolls. This senior official was consistently named as a privy councillor in Ireland and commonly sat on the castle chamber bench as judge. The redoubtable Old English servitor Nicholas White succeeded the new English bencher Henry Draycott as master of the rolls in 1572. White was a colourful and clever statesman, well-connected with the Butler family and a client of the earl of Ormonde. Nevertheless, he was removed from office on two occasions, once when he opposed the composition for cess in 1578 and again when his ally, Lord Deputy Perrot, was indicted in London for treason.[102] White

98. For further information see my *Anglicizing*, pp. 160–63.

99. *Cal. S.P. Ire., 1590–92*, pp. 518, 462, 471.

100. Ball, *Judges in Ireland*, i, 228. Pelham was over 60 years old when he died.

101. BL, Add. MS 47,172, f. 191. Methwold was holding assizes in Mullingar, Co. West Meath in 1612. See also ibid., ff. 193, 245. Blennerhassett held sessions in Tipperary in 1617, et seq. Ibid., f. 250.

102. Attorney General Snagge gave information against White for failing to account for the estreats of letters patent and writs from his office to the exchequer court, leading the Irish council to sequester him from his duties pending full examination. The privy council required the viceroy

was a well-informed correspondent of Lord Burghley on Irish affairs for two decades, in spite of the vicissitudes of his career in Dublin.[103] Anthony St Leger, nephew of the famous viceroy of mid-Tudor Ireland, succeeded White in 1593 and served with some reluctance until he retired to England in 1609. His place was taken by two remarkable Englishmen. Francis Aungier was already 51 years of age, an experienced reader at Gray's Inn, when he became master of the rolls in Ireland in 1609. Thereafter, he became involved in the plantations of Longford and Munster, an elder statesman on the privy council and in 1621 was created Baron Longford. On his death in 1632, Aungier was replaced by the ally of the new lord deputy, Christopher Wandesford, who worked to undermine the lord chancellor, Sir Adam Loftus, by now Viscount Ely. Within five years, Loftus was jailed for treason and Wandesford became lord justice, and then lord deputy when Wentworth was recalled to England. Wandesford died suddenly in December 1640, leaving a legacy of political havoc on the council and in the court of castle chamber.[104] Of the principal judges on the court of castle chamber, only that of common pleas thus remained in the hands of an Old English magistrate after 1603. The resulting loss of political equilibrium and judicial indifference may have compromised the work of the court and allowed the inquisitorial policies of Chichester free rein after 1605, as we shall see below.

The principal legal officers of the crown in Ireland were actively engaged in litigation before the court of castle chamber. For many, the positions of solicitor general, attorney general and serjeant at law were obvious stepping stones to the senior positions on the bench. During the reign of Elizabeth, the legal officers presented indictments and prepared cases which were driven more by the vicissitudes of Irish society and culture than by the imperatives of crown policy. In the decade after the inception of the court, five different men held the office of attorney general in routine, workmanlike fashion. Sir Charles Calthorpe, a bencher of Lincoln's Inn, became attorney general in 1584 and met with a relentless torrent of abuse for his conduct of the office. He was compromised by the attacks on Perrot in 1590 and accused of partisanship for favouring the causes of the native Irish, while Chichester reluctantly made him third justice of common pleas in 1606 after complaining that he was a weak official the previous year.[105] Facing imminent trial in castle chamber in 1592 for his role in the commission of inquiry against Perrot, he was forced to submit publicly in open court before the new viceroy, Fitzwilliam. He wrote pitifully to Burghley that he had been suspended from office, though he had been joined in his support of Perrot by eight other commissioners.[106]

to proceed with caution, naming the two chief justices to hear the case and allowing White and his counsel to plead his case along with Snagge. This would normally have been a castle chamber case, so the intervention of the privy council probably prevented a hearing at which White would have been both judge and accused. The correspondence was sent from the star chamber in England. *Acts privy council, 1578–80*, p. 119.

103. Ball, *Judges in Ireland*, i, 214.   104. Ibid., i, 322, 334–35.   105. Ibid., i, 317–18.
106. *Cal. S.P.Ire., 1588–92*, pp. 588–89. Calthorpe was subsequently restored to office and continued to plead before castle chamber, barely escaping the odium of the court in which he was often the principal prosecutor. Ibid.

Under James I, the notable efforts of Sir John Davies changed the role of attorney general. Davies became the advocate for interlocking policies designed to implement a systematic and seamless common law jurisdiction throughout Ireland. Bringing numerous recusancy cases before the court of castle chamber and leading commissions of assize to every province, the dynamic figure of Davies put his stamp on the judicial portrait of Jacobean Ireland during his tenure from 1603 to 1619.[107] His numerous reports to Cecil detail in suspiciously glowing terms the success of his policies, even when they occurred against the backdrop of the unexpected 'flight of the earls' in 1607. Davies wrote to Cecil in December that

> as soon as the term began by adjournment after Allhallowtide, there was an extraordinary concourse of people from all parts of the kingdom, soliciting and pursuing their causes with as much diligence as if no such accident had happened; especially the Irish, whereof divers have been at great charge to surrender their lands this term, and to take letters patent back again from the King, whereby their estates are established for ever according to the laws of England.[108]

On the other hand, Davies reluctantly supported the continued use of martial law, even when it appeared there had been grievous misuse of these extra-judicial protocols. In the spring of 1606 he wrote to Cecil about the assizes in Munster, explaining that an English soldier-settler named Downing had been accused of murder for peremptorily hanging a 'notorious fool' who was retained by the earl of Thomond, using the commission of martial law he had from the lord president, and claiming the right to execute 'vagabonds and idle men'. Downing was tried by an indifferent jury of English landholders and found guilty of murdering the 'idiot' follower of Thomond. The lord president took umbrage at this finding, since he had bestowed the commission of martial law, while Thomond appealed for justice to the privy council and chief governor. Davies's opinion was sought in the case, and he wrote, circumspectly,

> But in the meantime, we for our parts, though the fact was foul, and though our provost marshals are oftentimes too nimble and too rash in executing their commissions, so that it were not amiss that one or other of them did smart for it, and were made an example to all the rest, yet, because we would

---

107. See Pawlisch, *Sir John Davies*. Davies's blueprint for 'legal imperialism' was overstated by Pawlisch, according to John McCavitt in his recent study, *Chichester*, pp. 23–25, 74–90, 115–28. Davies's reports on the state of Ireland may be found in TCD, MSS 651, 672, 647 and 842. He wrote the noted poem 'Nosce te ipsum' (1599); *A dissertation on the progress and constitution of the legislature of Ireland* [A speech addressed to the lord deputy, 21 May 1613]; *Le primer report des cases & matters en ley resolved & adjudged en les courts del roy en Ireland* (Dublin, 1615; English ed., Dublin, 1762); and *A discoverie of the true causes why Ireland was never entirely subdued* ... (London 1612).

108. *Cal. S.P. Ire., 1606–08*, p. 355. See also p. 451 on the staffing of the central courts.

not utterly discountenance the martial law, which at that time and that place perhaps had been necessary, and because Downing had been a tall soldier, and performed good services in the late wars, we thought good to reprieve him, to the end my Lord Deputy may grant him His Majesty's pardon, if it so please his Lordship.[109]

Davies's successor William Ryves was equally assiduous in litigation before the central courts and on circuits of assize until promoted to second justice of king's bench in 1636.

The office of solicitor general was held by a number of active prosecutors before the castle chamber court, including Roger Wilbraham (1585–1603), Robert Jacob (1606–1618) and the son of the lord chancellor, Edward Bolton (1622–1640). Davies and Richard Bolton both held this position briefly before advancing to the more senior role.[110]

The king's serjeant at law was charged with defending or prosecuting royal interests in all the law courts and appeared frequently before the court of castle chamber in this period. On the other hand, the eclipse of his senior role by the other law officers had already begun by the late sixteenth century, as indicated by the substantially greater fees of the attorney general (£159 6s.8d. compared with the serjeant's fee of £27 6s. 8d.).[111] Sir Edward Fitzsymon became serjeant in 1574 after serving as attorney general, the last official to do so, and he remained in that role for twenty years, pleading some of the cases before the court of castle chamber. The serjeants often found themselves leading commissions of inquiry and giving testimony on points of law at the behest of the castle chamber court.[112] Fitzsymon was specifically called upon by Chancellor Gerrard to give his opinion on the important issue of the queen's prerogative right to the cess in 1577.[113] However, despite the appointment of a second serjeant in 1627 who was given precedence in the court of castle chamber, the serjeant's role was gradually diminished throughout the early Stuart period.[114] Nathaniel Catelyn found his dual role of recorder of Dublin and second serjeant nearly compromised his judicial integrity in 1629, temporarily costing him his job when he defended the corporation for refusing to admit the king's troops to quell a riot after the mass was held in Dublin.[115]

---

109. *Cal. S.P. Ire., 1603–06*, pp. 444, 470–71. Davies wrote that the commission of martial law was unfairly exploited by Downing, who probably knew the man was mentally challenged and hanged him on a Sunday morning, thus 'maliciously' transgressing his authority and committing murder. See D. Edwards, 'Two fools and a martial law commissioner: cultural conflict at the Limerick assizes', in D. Edwards, ed., *Regions and rulers in Ireland, 1100–1650: essays in honour of Kenneth Nicholls* (Dublin, 2004), pp. 237–65.

110. *Liber mun. pub. Hib.*, vol. 1, pt. ii, 73–75; Ball, *Judges in Ireland*, i, 330–31, 338.

111. A.R. Hart, *A history of the king's serjeants at law in Ireland: honour rather than advantage?* (Dublin, 2000), p. 44.

112. Ibid., pp. 39–47. Serjeant Finglas was granted an annuity of £10 Irish in anticipation of his service in the castle chamber court. Ibid., p. 45.

113. 'Gerrard's Report', *Anal Hib*, no. 2 (1931), p. 132.

114. Hart, *King's serjeants*, pp. 52–57.   115. Ibid., p. 55.

Although the role of lords chancellor and attorneys general in the court of castle chamber is made clear from the bulk of the evidence, the performance of other judges in that court is difficult to establish. Senior members of the bench were regularly included in the tribunal and litigation was sometimes commissioned to judges itinerant. Chief judges of both benches, acting with the master of the rolls and chief baron of the exchequer, were largely mute observers in the collective judgments of the court, despite the occasionally sharp recriminations of individual justices in correspondence with England. In contrast, the notable efforts of Sir John Davies highlighted the catalytic effects which attorneys general could have on the court. Davies, appearing as both solicitor and attorney general, presented information against the accused on no less than 68 occasions, making him the single most active participant in the history of the court.

Davies's predecessors Sir Roger Wilbraham and Sir Charles Calthorpe frequently appeared before the tribunal, though neither man was known for innovative actions at law. Wilbraham and Calthorpe prosecuted the noted case of Henry Bird, accused of forging the signature of Perrot as lord deputy, a suit extensively reported in the entry book, which later caused both men to regret their energetic pleading.[116] Wilbraham wrote infrequently to England, but his letter of 9 July 1586 to Burghley told much about the court. Explaining that the loyal Sir Hugh Magennis was coming to Dublin to give evidence against Tyrone, he added to the complaints against the arbitrary government of Bingham in Connacht:

> Some of the Irishry inhabiting in that country, and of some credit there (indeed dislikers of Sir Richard), say the cause of this trouble is because the country is grievously oppressed and spoiled daily by unlawful cesses and extortions of sheriffs since the composition, and not improbable; for upon our new late reviving of our Star Chamber Court, two several bills against two of the sheriffs in Connaught are preferred; the one of them containeth 24 articles of outrageous offences, as unlawful execution by martial law of gentlemen of living without cause, cess and grievous extortion, &c; by their punishment others will be warned, and henceforth we hope to draw in sheriffs to account, which innovation will hold back governor's men and councillor's friends from their eager desire to become sheriffs.[117]

Wilbraham ended his note with a commendation for Judges Walsh and Robert Dillon, among the wealthiest commoners in Ireland and the 'best deserving lawyers here'.[118] Despite the impact of Davies on the court and the judicial

---

116. BL, Add. MS 47,172, f. 79. Calthorpe appeared before the court to present an information against accused persons on 7 occasions; Wilbraham appeared 9 times. The serjeant at law, Fitzsymons, appeared only twice.

117. *Cal. S.P. Ire., 1586–88*, pp. 97–98.

118. Ibid., p. 100. He made note of the importance of castle chamber for suits of the poor subjects who would otherwise be 'oppressed with countenance'.

foundations of the government, his successors did not sustain the momentum for 'judge-made law' after his departure in 1619. Sir William Ryves, a bencher of the Middle Temple, was recommended to succeed Davies and went to Ireland in 1619, serving regularly as justice of assize and acting as speaker of the house of lords in 1641. He became second justice of king's bench in 1636, and remained a secondary figure after the star of Davies disappeared into the east.[119]

Membership on the court of castle chamber was limited to the privy councillors of Ireland, occasionally supported by common law judges who were not *ex officio* members of the Irish council. However, the members of the Irish privy council in this period varied greatly, sometimes including a number of peers and bishops, as well as lords president and others who appeared for specific purposes on commission from the crown. In practice, however, the regular meetings of the council and the court were held in the absence of the peers, such as Ormonde. In the Tudor period, the privy council often sat as a council of war, and the presence of the marshal and master of the ordnance was expected. However, the only two *ex officio* councillors who routinely served on the court of castle chamber throughout this period, apart from the senior judges, were the vice treasurer and the secretary of state.[120] The two Elizabethan mainstays as vice treasurer and treasurer-at-war, Sir Edward Fyton and Sir Henry Wallop, were highly partisan and combative as councillors. Fyton quarrelled endlessly with Fitzwilliam and Sydney, finding himself incarcerated and banished from council meetings on more than one occasion. He used his office to prevent the sealing of documents and tried to undermine viceregal authority by writing to Burghley and the queen at every opportunity.[121]

Sir Henry Wallop, likewise, joined forces with Loftus and others against numerous powerful viceroys, most particularly Sir John Perrot. Wallop served the queen as vice treasurer from 1579 to 1598 and was the contemporary of Sir Geoffrey Fenton, secretary of state from 1581 to 1608. Fenton succeeded the feeble John Chaloner and made the role of secretary into a powerful and demanding one, using his access to the crown and the English secretaries of state as the conduit for shaping policy, seeking patronage and damaging his adversaries. He, too, joined the Loftus connection in the council against Perrot, and he aided Richard Boyle in his quest to win estates in Munster, marrying his daughter to the future earl of Cork. Fenton shared his office of secretary with Sir Richard Cooke after 1603, and on the death of Cooke the office was awarded to the ambitious Sir Francis Annesley in 1618. Annesley coveted the estates and offices of more senior magistrates, ultimately winning the post of vice treasurer in 1625 and treasurer-at-war in 1632. En route to that victory, he worked to destroy the administration of Falkland and was nearly undone himself, though he won promotion to the Irish peerage as Baron Mountnorris in 1628. Falkland wrote in 1629 that Annesley should be sued in the star chamber for his breach of discipline in contradicting

---

119. Ball, *Judges in Ireland*, i, 336–37.   120. See my *Anglicizing*, pp. 37–45.
121. *DNB*; Crawford, *Anglicizing*, pp. 124–28, 268–69, 314–16, 455.

the viceroy over the case of Phelim McFeagh O'Byrne.[122] Wentworth found him obdurate and corrupt, finally winning a judicial victory over the treasurer-at-war by staging a court martial in which the viceroy was both accuser and judge. Mountnorris was sentenced to death for a slight to the honour of Wentworth, though he suffered no more than imprisonment with the loss of his office in 1635. Though the tribunal in the case was not the court of castle chamber, Wentworth's abuse of prerogative justice brought the court itself into disrepute by these means. Mountnorris spent much of his life attempting to regain his offices, and won the support of the commons in 1641 during the impeachment trial of Strafford, finally earning the title of Viscount Valentia on the death of Henry Power in 1642. The last secretary of state in this period was Wentworth's creature, Sir Philip Mainwaring, a sycophantic functionary who did the bidding of the viceroy in anticipation of reward.

A longitudinal study of the court's active membership is nearly unmanageable due to the fragmentary remains of the archive. For the reign of Elizabeth, there is a substantial record of the justices in attendance until about 1590. A smaller chronicle exists for James I, and practically nothing to show the court's membership for Charles I's reign, apart from the commission of 1625. Nonetheless, several trends become clear. First, the leading secular officials took the most active role. Under Elizabeth, the lord deputy presided over the court of castle chamber 34 times and the lord chancellor or lord keeper 20 times. The long tenures of Dillon and White as chief baron and master of the rolls, respectively, allowed them to become the most steady in attendance at the court, and to lead the largest number of commissions. Dillon was present 28 times and White 29 times in this period. In contrast, the enfeebled chief justices did not appear as often, though Robert Dillon the younger was an assiduous member after 1581. The chief justices of queen's bench sat on the court 12 times in the period, the chief justice of common pleas 17 times. The steady performance of the secretary of state is marked by attendance at 21 sessions of the court, the same number as the vice treasurer. Both Fenton and Wallop account for the largest part of these meetings. A very similar pattern may be observed in the reign of James I, so that the core of the active membership throughout the period was eight secular officials, of whom five were senior judges. For James I, the figures are: chief governor (9); lord chancellor (10); chief baron (8); master of the rolls (8); chief justices (5); secretary (6); vice treasurer (6). Second justices were also invited to appear, though rarely, as in the case of Judges Walsh, Dowdall, Everard and Comerford.

The court of castle chamber was the judicial forum of the privy council in Ireland, so it is not surprising to see the active membership of the court reflect this larger executive committee. However, the consistent participation of some officials is certainly due to the unique qualities of the incumbent, such as Hugh Brady or Thomas Jones as bishops of Meath, who met with the court on 17 occa-

122. Falkland to Conway, 24 March 1629: *Cal. S.P. Ire., 1625–32*, p. 443.

sions, or John Garvey as dean of Christ Church who attended 12 meetings of the court.[123] Less remarkable is the relatively infrequent attendance of military officials like the marshal or master of the ordnance, though Nicholas Bagenal attended 6 meetings during his long tenure as marshal. Seneschals and captains such as Francis Agarde, Henry Cowley and Thomas LeStrange occasionally enjoyed membership of the Irish council, but their attendance at castle chamber was rare indeed, each appearing only once. Again, the presence of lords president of provincial councils, such as Nicholas Malbie or George Carew, was made unlikely by the need to attend their own sessions during each legal term, though both made appearances at the court. On the other hand, the presence on 12 occasions of Sir Edward Waterhouse, Sydney's chancellor of the exchequer, was due largely to his personal influence rather than his office. Bishops of the established church rarely attended the court of castle chamber, though an assortment of bishops appeared at least once, including those of Kilmore, Ossory, Tuam, Down, Ferns, and Dromore. Finally, attendance by the peers of the realm at meetings of the court was predictably infrequent, though the earl of Thomond, Viscount Baltinglas and Barons Howth and Slane appeared at least twice. The others were, for James I, Baron Delvin, Viscount Fermoy, Viscount Roche, Baron Courcy and Baron Burke.[124]

A profile of all the judges of the court of castle chamber would require a prosopographical analysis of the entire membership of the early modern privy council in Ireland, a task well beyond the scope of this book. However, we can examine briefly the core membership of eight secular officials who were most commonly in attendance at the court. There were some sixty councillors who took up these posts in the seventy-year period under discussion. The ages of 43 men can be reasonably determined. The average age of justices (or councillors) was usually about 45 years when they earned the right to sit on the court of castle chamber. The elder Sir Robert Dillon was 80 years old when he died in office in 1580. Officials such as Sydney became councillors prior to the creation of the court. He was 46 when he entered his second term as lord deputy, though he was only 36 in his first regime there and became a councillor at a youthful 27 years. The senior judges tended to be older, having trained for up to a decade at the inns of court. Shurley was the eldest, taking office at 61 years of age in 1620, while Jones became lord chancellor at 60 in 1619, though he had entered the council 21 years before under the tutelage of Archbishop Loftus. Blennerhasset was 58 when he became a councillor one year after Shurley. However, this varied greatly since the long tenures of men like Archbishop Loftus and Secretary Annesley and Chief Baron Dillon gave the court a distinctly greying appearance over time.

---

123. See BL, Add. MS 47,172 as Appendix One, below. Jones also appeared frequently as archbishop of Armagh.

124. BL, Add. MS 47,172. Under James I a number of other secular officials appeared on more than one occasion. This can be explained by their membership in commissions of inquiry or for other *ad hoc* purposes. These men were Thomas Roper, Richard Morrison, Francis Stafford, James Fullerton, Garret Moore and Christopher Lambert.

Mountjoy, on the other hand, was a youthful 37 years old when he became viceroy in 1600. The relatively brief tenure of a judge like William Jones, who went to Ireland as chief justice of king's bench in 1617 and retired three years later, must be contrasted with the seniority of Francis Aungier, who went to Ireland as master of the rolls in 1609 and died in office in 1632 as Baron Longford, aged 74, founder of a important New English dynasty.

More important than the age of the justices was the average number of years they served in office while sitting on the court. This varied with the nature of the post, since the viceroy enjoyed a typically brief tenure of five years, despite the long decade of Chichester's service under James I (1605–1616). In contrast, the typical service of the secretary of state and the lord chancellor in the period lasted from eleven to twelve years for each incumbent. And, while the two chief justices served an average of nine to ten years in office, the masters of the rolls persevered for an average of seventeen years (only four men held the office throughout the period). The chief baron and vice treasurer averaged eight and nine years in office, respectively. The composite figure for all offices is an average of ten years of service while sitting on the bench of the court of castle chamber. At any given time, the court was likely to be led by a veteran judicial presence. During the 1580s, for example, apart from the viceroy who changed frequently, the seven incumbent officials were the four New English members: Loftus (24 years), Wallop (19 years), Gardener (20 years) and Fenton (27 years); frequently opposed by the three Old English members: Lucas Dillon (22 years), White (20 years) and Robert Dillon (23 years). During the 1620s the New English predominated, though a similarly veteran crew would have populated the bench if a snapshot were taken of them in 1625. The judges would have been, in order of seniority, Loftus (19 years of service), Annesley (who was by that time a pluralist as secretary of state and vice treasurer (18 years), Shurley (22 years), Sarsfield (the only remaining Old English judge in this period, 21 years), and Bolton (14 years). Thus, we may imagine that the combined judicial experience of the incumbent magistrates weighed heavily in the balance, despite the protocol that required the viceroy to be principal judge in the court of castle chamber. Finally, it is also important to remember the long experience of these judges prior to their elevation to the senior bench. Many of them were attorneys general, or other law officers, and in those roles had pleaded before the court prior to enjoying a seat on its bench. If an insular view of Irish politics and culture emerged from this entrenched magistracy, it would hardly be surprising, despite their considerable activities as assize judges throughout the early Stuart period.

The education of the principal justices of the court of castle chamber was appropriate to the offices they held, and generally improved throughout the period. Of the eight Elizabethan viceroys in this period, only three attended university (Mountjoy distinguished himself, taking a degree at Oxford and matriculating at the Inner Temple). Their Stuart successors, however, were more intellectually polished since all attended university and St John, Wentworth and

Wandesford also enrolled at an inn of court. Of the lords chancellor in this period, all attended either a university or an inn of court, though only Sir Adam Loftus, Viscount Ely, enrolled at both institutions (Jesus College, Cambridge and Lincoln's Inn). Throughout the history of the court, the chief justices were uniformly trained at an inn of court (only the first Robert Dillon is doubtful), usually Lincoln's Inn (10 of the 14 judges), while some of the early Stuart judges also attended a university (Ley, Winch, Jones and Shurley). Similarly, all the chief barons and masters of the rolls attended an inn of court (Aungier was most ambitious, enrolling at Trinity College, Cambridge before attending Gray's Inn). By contrast, the vice treasurers were generally military men or younger sons of the social élite who obtained office through favour and showed little inclination to letters. The secretaries of state varied widely in the quality of their learning, from the erudite scholar Fenton, who penned Latin translations for Mary Sydney, to the grasping sinecurist Annesley. Using a composite picture of the senior judges and law officers, we can assert with some confidence that the bench was not under-trained. Sir John Davies was perhaps the most remarkable for his learning, having been a notable poet and scholar before leaving for Ireland as solicitor general.

Membership on the court was remarkably stable. Some justices remained on the court for decades, moving from one senior position to another. Bolton was chief baron of the exchequer for fifteen years before becoming lord chancellor in 1638. Similarly, these senior offices were colonized by certain leading families. The venerable legal family of the Dillons laid claim to numerous offices based on their long tenures and resourceful marriages in the Pale. During the first decade of the castle chamber court's operation, Sir Robert Dillon and his son, Sir Lucas, were both sitting on the court as judges, while Sir Robert's namesake and nephew became second justice of common pleas, succeeding Nugent as chief justice of that court in the infamous judicial coup of 1581. Through generations of intermarriage with the families of Bathe, Sarsfield and Barnewall, the Dillons crystallized their power in the Pale, eventually winning titles of nobility under the Stuarts.[125] Old English families like the Nugents, Plunketts, Dowdalls and their many kinsfolk, however, were increasingly excluded from high office after 1590 and replaced by the New English officials like Adam Loftus, lord chancellor. Loftus, father of twenty children–as we have seen–and scion of a Yorkshire family, obtained offices and sinecures throughout the administration for his progeny and their relations. When Loftus became lord chancellor in 1581 after several earlier terms as lord keeper, he held the senior judgeship for 24 years, passing it on to his fellow archbishop and ally, Thomas Jones, for another 14 years of uninterrupted domination of that office. When Loftus's nephew, Sir Adam Loftus, Viscount Ely, rose to become chancellor in his own right in 1619, the Dublin-based clan of New English servitors retained the office for another generation until his removal in

---

125. Theobald Dillon became the first Viscount Costello-Gallen in 1622, while Lucas's eldest son James became Baron Dillon in 1620 and subsequently earl of Roscommon.

1638. In 1636 upon the fall of Mountnorris, Sir Adam Loftus of Rathfarnham, the archbishop's grandson, became vice treasurer.

Connexion mattered greatly in Irish politics and faction must have influenced the conduct of the court when it sat for hours at a time to hear its cases. Tension between the members of the court broke into the open repeatedly as testified by the heated correspondence with England. Consequently, opinions of the court may have been rendered in a divisive manner, though the tradition of secrecy and the requirement to reveal nothing of a divided judgement prevents us from gathering information about the conduct of the court in its chambers. The machinations surrounding the threat of castle chamber prosecution against the earl of Cork suggests that a good deal of negotiation went on outside the courtroom. The haughty former lord justice was served by a warrant from the clerk of castle chamber on 22 September 1634 for his appearance at the first sitting of the next term.[126] After eighteen months of prevarication, during which time the viceroy sent numerous delegations from the court to the earl seeking a final settlement of the fine for his misappropriation of funds for the college at Youghal, Cork was compelled to resolve the issue by threats from the lord deputy and the case was never adjudicated.[127] Numerous meetings in the corridors of Dublin Castle between the earl and the lord chancellor, the viceroy, Sir George Radcliffe, and others suggested that the business of the court might be conducted through informal channels, using secret covenants that undermined both the honour and credibility of the high court under Wentworth.[128]

Efforts by reforming chief governors to penetrate the web of nepotism that embraced the Irish judiciary usually came to nought. Sydney brought the activist Gerrard into the administration, and he began to address the issues of corruption and partiality, but Gerrard was replaced by the powerfully entrenched Loftus. Perrot's downfall was caused in part by the grasping Loftus and his allies, who contested the last great survivors of the Old English tradition on the council and the court, Dillon and White. Except for the tenuous grip of Walsh and Sarsfield well into the next century, the Old English judges were effectively excluded from the court with the death of Sir Robert Dillon the younger in 1597. In the next reign, Chichester and his successors made every effort to populate the judiciary with their minions, so that by the Wentworth era commencing in 1634 a tradition of factional power politics using the officeholding élite as the source of a power base in Ireland was well established. The Wentworth court witnessed numerous upheavals owing to the power struggles of the viceroy against his incumbent rivals, Cork, Loftus and Mountnorris, but his eventual victory in 1638 sealed off the court from any potential divergence of opinion. His creatures were close personal aides like Wandesford and Mainwaring from Yorkshire, though he also

---

126. Chatsworth, Lismore MSS, vol. 18, item 29. The conflict may be followed in *The Lismore papers*, ed. A.B. Grosart, 10 vols. (London, 1886–88).
127. Chatsworth, Lismore MSS, vol. 18, items 42, 58, 61, 67, 72, 83, 134.
128. Ibid.

fastened to his regime the obliging assistance of Bolton and his son, Edward; Cork's former ally, Chief Justice Lowther; the Dubliner, Sir Adam Loftus of Rathfarnham; and George Shurley, the pliant chief justice of king's bench.

Finally, it is worth noting that the court became increasingly the preserve of a wealthy and well-connected élite. The Elizabethan justices were more often wealthy commoners, including Sir Robert Dillon the younger, reputed to be the richest in Ireland, and Sir Nicholas Walsh of the prosperous Waterford family. They lacked titles of nobility and their income came from inherited estates rather than their fees or salaries. Their power, in turn, came from the embedded network of family and friendship within the government of Ireland. The New English often came to Ireland in this period to seek their fortunes, and men like Loftus and the earl of Cork succeeded beyond their wildest dreams. Indeed, by the end of our period, we can see the importance of a new social element, the well-established families of New English careerists who had been in Ireland for three generations and viewed with some suspicion the *arriviste* planters and adventurers. While it is important to note the displacement of Old English families in crown service by their Protestant rivals, it is also clear that some of the latter became part of the conservative orthodoxy of Ireland's landed élite, resistant to change and to reform. A number of the senior judges returned quickly to England to pursue their careers, men such as Ley, Winch, Denham and Jones, all chief justices of king's bench. Others, however, became highly successful men of affairs in Ireland, settling with their families and generating profitable networks and alliances. Men like Richard Bolton, George Shurley and Gerard Lowther succeeded in this manner, while some like Aungier won titles of nobility in recognition of their service. Aungier became Baron Longford; Annesley became Viscount Mountnorris; Sarsfield was named Viscount Kilmallock after his earlier title of lord of Kinsale was contested; and Loftus became Viscount Ely. The chief governors were generally powerful courtiers rather than journeyman military officers, though some of the latter served in times of crisis as lords justices. Under James I, all of the viceroys won the title of viscount upon leaving office, if not before. As these men of affairs gathered power and wealth during long years of service to the crown, it is difficult to imagine a judicial proceeding at which contention and conflict were far below the surface of the discourse. Joined with the inherent tensions that undergirded meetings of the Irish privy council in this period, mixing policy disputes with the flexing of political muscle, knowing that potent courtiers like Buckingham were seeking proxy advantage over rival factions at court through the workings of the Irish government, the meetings of the tribunal must have been highly volatile.

The clerical staff of the court of castle chamber was initially very small, owing to the delay in its formal implementation. Indeed, the first four clerks, appointed between 1563 and 1569, simply used the post as a sinecure, awaiting the formal foundation of the court by commission from the queen. When this document arrived in the summer of 1571, the clerks apparently were not yet up to speed,

since the entry book of the court records no business until 4 November 1573 apart
from two undated and unexplained memoranda of fines against some 40 defendants.[129] Anthony Wilcocks, Edmund Molyneux and Robert Kendall succeeded
each other in the office of clerk of the court between 1572 and 1581. Kendall was
upbraided for taking excessive fees at the court, but the Irish council praised his
work thus: 'At whose entrie into that office, he found the same in greate disorder,
by meanes of the often chaunges of the former officers which preceded hym,
thorough some of their remisfull usadgies in that chardge.'[130] On 13 November
1577 the court under Sydney took up a motion against Kendall, calling upon him
to testify. He defended the fines and charges as identical to those used previously
and warranted by the star chamber in England, but the court ordered him to
moderate the fees by taking Irish currency instead of sterling, allowing him to order
the marshal to arrest and detain those who refused to pay. The court's reasoning
reveals much about the efforts to bring reliable justice to the bench in Ireland:

> wee wei[gh]ing the disabilitie of a nomber of the sewtors followinge theyre
> Cauwses and sewtes in the saied Courte to be suche as yf some quallificacon
> of the rattes and ffees so formerlye ordered should not by us be sett downe
> and taxed in certaintie to avoyde the dislyke of the Complained excessy-
> venes, The same moughte in tyme growe to be overburdensome to those
> sewtors and ptyes sewed.[131]

In September 1611 Chichester returned to the matter of castle chamber fines,
ordering that the clerk of the court appear before the tribunal at the end of each term
to take note of the reducement and to estreat it into the exchequer, requiring all bills
to be prosecuted unless they had been withdrawn by permission of the court.[132]

The appearance of Laurence Holinshed as clerk of the court was a notable
exception to the bureaucratic routine. He earned the confidence of Lord Deputy
Grey after his examination of the records demonstrated the need for a complete

129. BL, Add. MS 47,172, ff. 1–3. Nonetheless, the clerk of castle chamber, John Harepenny,
    confidently sued to the queen to have full 21-year leases of tithes and estates, in which he
    already possessed an interest. The council wrote on his behalf, and in July 1571 the privy
    council confirmed this royal bequest of Cloughshalles, Bathenye and Hunstonne. *Acts privy
    council, 1571–75*, p. 35.
130. PRO, SP 63/60/152. Kendall sought a grant for life of his office of clerk of castle chamber, but
    the privy council rejected his request on 30 May 1578, suggesting he was already well
    compensated, and recommending he seek the favour of the lord deputy. *Acts privy council,
    1577–78*, p. 235. The pitiful revenue of the court identified by the exchequer in 1575 stood at
    £20, compared with £200 from wardships in the absence of a court of wards. *Cal. Carew MSS,
    1575–88*, p. 35.
131. BL, Add. MS 47,172, f. 23v. Two Latin entries at the end of the record book of the court appear
    to confirm that, in the case of 'Sir P[blank] versus W R de Kilkenny' at the court of castle
    chamber the fine was taken in legal money of England to the use of the crown, but the fees of
    the clerk were taken in legal money of Ireland. Ibid., f. 283.
132. *Cal. Carew MSS, 1603–25*, pp. 70, 96, 110–11.

overhaul, reconciling the active suits with the court calendar and preparing to dismiss over fifteen suits that were previously adjudicated or allowed to lapse.[133] On 5 July 1582 the court ordered all plaintiffs to give bond for the continuous prosecution of their suits, a Holinshed ploy to end the logjam of pending litigation. He argued at the time there were 30 or 40 causes ready to be heard before the court and 'farre greater number' pending, though plaintiffs were in Dublin and dallied in their suits.[134] Holinshed was a learned scholar with a deserved reputation for careful investigation, though he was rebuked for his impatience on more than one occasion.[135] Holinshed prepared the 1581 memorandum for Grey, entered in the record book of the court, which in turn launched a housekeeping revolution in the archive. Announcing that 'the actes and orders hearetofore pronouncyd in Corte have not bene entered in to the same [entry book] ... but set downe most commonly in Lewse papers, and by that meanes often cast aside and lost and so not at all enterd into the saide bookes', he sought Grey's permission to require a settled procedure of all the clerks.[136] When he resigned the post in 1586, the Stoughton family appropriated the office for their heirs and assigns, using the patronage system to undermine the honest labour of Holinshed. Anthony Stoughton sought the appointment as a sinecure, held it in his own right for 21 years and then shared the work with his son, John, in the next reign. John Stoughton obtained the clerkship in his own right in 1625 on the death of the elder Stoughton, and passed the job to his son Anthony, in 1626. This colonizing of the clerkship did little to maintain the rectitude of the office, and the disappearance of the new entry book that was probably commenced in 1620 or 1622 has never been explained. Despite the reforming energy of Wentworth and his determination to rectify abuses in Irish government, he was unable to jettison the Stoughton clan from the record office of the court. In contrast to the English star chamber, the Irish court apparently never developed the sophisticated infrastructure of its much busier parent.[137]

The minor officials of marshal and usher of the court of castle chamber were charged with assuring an orderly hearing before the court. William Kendall was

---

133. BL, Add. MS 47,172, ff. 65–76.
134. Ibid., f. 63. See *Anglicizing*, pp. 225–27.
135. BL, Add. MS 47,172, ff. 53–54, 76.
136. Ibid., f. 52. Holinshed referred to 'bookes of actes and orders', inferring the existence of several distinct records, and he blamed the underclerks 'being ignorant etc.' for incomplete orders that in turn led to reversals, reducing crown revenue and encouraging offenders. In 1581 Holinshed asked the council to authorize repair of a document entered in 1579. Ibid., f. 48.
137. See Barnes, 'Due process', pp. 340–43; Guy, *Star chamber*, pp. 10–17. By 1522 the English privy council had already nominated four of their number, assisted by two masters of requests, to sort through petitions and bills destined for star chamber, whereas the petition books to Wentworth show the viceroy sitting for hours at this task in the 1630s. Under Elizabeth a staff of specialized under-clerks was designated, and by 1615 there were four attorneys, each with about eight clerks, and four examiners assisted by a range of sub-clerks. Guy, *Star chamber*, p. 14; Barnes, 'Due process', p. 341.

awarded the office in 1578, two years after his kinsman, Robert, became clerk of the court. Thomas Beere, a scrivener by profession, held the post from 1583 until 1597 with a short hiatus in 1590–91. Beere was called to London to testify in Perrot's trial and removed as marshal of castle chamber, but the privy council rebuked Fitzwilliam for his arbitrary dismissal without cause shown, demanding that he be restored to his place and his fees resumed.[138] Samuel Molyneux (or Mullenax), had the dubious honour of serving as marshal during the seven year hiatus of the court, from 1597 until 1604, though he managed to retain the post until 1608. It was considered at the time that an usher was needless (the court was not regularly meeting during the Tyrone Rebellion), so the position was discontinued. On 6 February 1605, Molyneux sued in castle chamber to obtain his right to custody of those imprisoned by the court, against his rival, Tristram Caleston, constable of Dublin Castle. Both men claimed the same right, so the court commissioned the two chief justices and the chief baron to examine their patents. An investigation and hearing of counsel before this *ad hoc* commission failed to end the matter conclusively, so a full meeting of castle chamber set forth a compromise. Under these terms, the marshal of the court was given custody of the 'meaner sort', requiring that all peers of the realm, councillors, senior judges, lords of Irish countries, sheriffs, mayors, knights, deans and justices of the peace were to be committed by the constable.[139] Ten years later Molyneux surrendered the office of marshal to Richard Pemberton, by permission of the viceroy, with full rights to the fees, profits and perquisites.[140] Henry Southey replaced Pemberton in 1617, and he in turn was succeeded on his death in 1627 by Robert Newcomen and Robert Richards. Thomas Parry, another gentleman, took his patent in July 1639 and died in 1642. He was not replaced.[141] In 1623 the Irish council under Falkland took up the need to replace the recently deceased Gregory Holton, a messenger attending the council chamber who probably assisted in castle chamber duties as well. One Thomas Larke was chosen to succeed Holton and an act of state authorized him to have the same fee of £10 Irish.[142]

Although the court itself ceased to operate after 1641, it was expected that a re-foundation under Charles II was imminent, so a new bureaucracy of sinecurists was soon formed. Sir George Lane was duly paid his fee as clerk of the court of castle chamber each year from 1666 until 1672, while George Rutledge (1666–71) and William Robinson (1671–72) were similarly remunerated as the marshals of the defunct tribunal.[143] The presence of a fully articulated clerical infrastructure

---

138. *Acts privy council, 1592*, p. 48. The first two marshals were both gentlemen sinecurists, Thomas King (appointed 1563) and John Montaigne, who served for a time under King. *Liber mun. pub. Hib.*, vol. 1, pt. ii, 181.
139. BL, Add. MS 47,172, f. 133.
140. Bodl., Carte MS 62, f. 310. Order of Chichester, 20 November 1615.
141. *Liber mun. pub. Hib.*, vol. 1, pt. ii, 181.
142. TCD, MS 672, f. 114v.
143. *Liber mun. pub. Hib.*, vol. 1, pt. ii, 181. Charles Hildeyard held office briefly from December 1671 to March 1672.

nearly a decade before the establishment of the court, and over a decade after the Restoration failed to restore it, suggests that the court itself had a meagre connection with its staff. This may have been owing to the reciprocal, even redundant, functions of the clerk of the privy council and the marshals and ushers belonging to that august body. What is more, the largely independent work of the castle chamber bureaucrats during the intervals between legal terms, taking depositions and issuing subpoenas and summonses, forced them to take action on pleadings that were often years away from a hearing at the court. This disjuncture may have led to the early founding and late ending of the clerkships, since it might have been expected that they would have to receive petitions and issue preliminary documents well in advance of the work of the magistrates.[144]

CONCLUSION

The court of star chamber in Ireland was a potentially powerful tribunal that merged the judicial and executive functions of the Irish privy council. The use of its authority and the enforcement of its decrees, however, depended heavily on a judicial infrastructure that was inchoate under Elizabeth and incomplete until the permanent foundation of the court of high commission late in the final decade of its existence. Furthermore, the court experienced vicissitudes of potency and debility under a series of viceroys who, in turn, met with opposition from rival factions at court and from intransigent adversaries in Ireland. The court of castle chamber was no mere replica of the English star chamber, though it received its commissions directly from the crown and it was explicitly designed to provide the judicial forum for cases of riot, official malfeasance, the abduction of women, and other causes, much like the English court. Castle chamber was unique because it was led by a viceroy who enjoyed substantial independence of action; it was blended more fully with his privy council which included non-judicial officers of state, bishops and peers of the realm; it was hampered by factions that were unique to Ireland, including the presence of Old English judges until Sarsfield was removed in 1634; and it was sanctioned by the crown and the English privy council, an endorsement that could be withdrawn on appeal or whenever shifts in policy required a new tack. The settled infrastructure of the court did not assure efficient record-keeping, so that the archive, which was irregular and incomplete in Tudor times, lapsed entirely after 1632. What is more, the elaborate procedural technicalities assured that the tactic of vexatious pleading became routine, despite numerous efforts at reform. The complex judicial milieu of assize courts, presidency courts, oyer and terminer, admiralty, wards and other jurisdictions presented the castle chamber court with a maze of adjudication, some of which was siphoned off to the star chamber in England. The court's apparently thin record of business

144. H. Wood, 'The court of castle chamber or star chamber of Ireland', *RIA Proc*, xxxii (1914), sect. c, 170.

must be contrasted with external evidence of its regular operation, apart from times of war and rebellion. And, while internal faction must have compromised the work of the court under Perrot and Falkland, among others, castle chamber was readily identified with the striking longevity of its senior justices, some of whom served for entire generations on the Irish star chamber. The quality and competence of these justices was not altogether dissimilar to those of the English judiciary, and indeed, many of the Irish judges returned to England to become honoured members of the bench there.

CHAPTER THREE

Lawyers, litigants and litigation before the court of castle chamber

Memorandum qd Termino Sci Mich[aelm]is Anno Domini 1602 Sir Robert Digby, knight, and the Ladie Lettice, his wieff, Exhibited there Bill of Complainte into this honnorable Courte of Castle Chamber Against Garrett, now Earle of Kildare, Dame Mable, Countesse Dowager of Kildare, Sometime wieffe to Garret, Late Earle of Kildare, and Henry Burnell, Esqr, Deffendantes.

Entry book of the court of castle chamber[1]

THE COURT OF CASTLE chamber was originally designed to hear suits in precisely delineated categories. It was, in effect, a criminal jurisdiction and it offered, theoretically at least, a financially attractive, though sluggish, forum to poor petitioners. In practice, however, the litigants before the court came from every social class and sued for a wide variety of purposes. There were several reasons for this. First, it was the clear purpose of succeeding chief governors to expand the reach of the common law, and in attempting this, the court of castle chamber was often called upon to buttress the authority of local government officials, or, in contrast, to correct their abuses. This involved the court in local issues often far beyond the original mandate. Secondly, as the court provided a judicial remedy of a novel kind, it was used increasingly to harass rivals or to pursue causes that might not succeed elsewhere, ones alleging riot or slander as a cover for challenges to title, for example. Thirdly, the court willingly heard unusual causes such as those involving the abduction of women, or the threatened extinction of dower rights (as in *Digby* v. *Countess of Kildare*), or the accusation that a noble pedigree was corrupted. This willingness to expand the judicial horizons of the court was duly noted by lawyers, and castle chamber was sought out after 1603 by suitors from every province as a way to exploit the power of the court for the advantage of a weak cause of action in the locality where it originated. The court struggled against this opportunism without much success. Finally, the court was used by policymaking viceroys and English privy councillors to enforce proclamations and acts of state, involving the court in Reformation politics despite its lack of ecclesiastical standing. In the absence of a court of requests, and owing to the erratic operation of commissions for ecclesiastical causes, the castle chamber court took on itself a number of additional roles not originally envisioned for it.

1. BL, Add. MS 47,172, f. 54.

The design of this chapter is to explore the litigation of the court from several perspectives; a narrative history in Part Two discusses the court's business more fully in a chronological framework. First, the legal representation of petitioners and respondents demands attention, since the number of lawyers available to clients apparently grew smartly in this period, despite the intermittent ban on the employment of recusant counsel. Secondly, the litigants themselves were drawn from all walks of life, and attempts to characterize the 'typical' plaintiff or defendant are defeated by the wide range of possibilities. Some of the more striking cases of female suitors, noble claimants and petty slights will be discussed below, as well as the most numerous plaintiffs, the wronged Protestant ministers accusing their Catholic flocks of non-attendance at the established church under Chichester and his immediate successors. Thirdly, the litigation of the court metamorphosed in the period 1571 to 1641 from a concentration on riot and other disturbances to a broader focus on recusancy, dishonour, corruption and political 'show trials', as we shall see below. Finally, the court invited the attention of a well-connected lawyerly opposition, supported by Catholic peers of the realm, against policies crafted by the Irish council and enforced by the court of castle chamber.

LAWYERS

Lawyers appearing before the court were generally not named in the surviving book of orders and decrees, unless they were law officers of the crown (described in Chapter 2). In a few cases, the lawyers themselves were accused of corruption at the court and in those cases became defendants as well as counsellors. Also, leading Irish lawyers shared with Irish judges the familiar premises of the King's Inns in Dublin, and we may gain some knowledge of their interaction from a study of that institution. By 1571, at the inception of the court of castle chamber, the King's Inns had been operating in Dublin for three decades. This truncated Irish institution lacked the substantial pedagogical function of the English inns of court, and in fact membership of King's Inns was based upon prior satisfaction of a five-year tenure at the English inns. Irish students performed certain prescribed exercises although in most instances they were not formally called to the bar in England. Lawyers admitted to practice in Irish courts were called to the bar by the chief justices there, a distinction not found in English courts. The leading officers of King's Inns were the chief judges and law officers themselves, who in England were ineligible to continue as members after elevation to the bench. This unique feature apparently allowed the ordinary counsellors, barristers, attorneys and solicitors to mix socially at the inns with the senior legal officials of the crown, a situation peculiar to Ireland. Using the common dining-hall where fellows were required to spend a portion of their time during each legal term, probably allowed the lawyers and judges to become familiar with each other, to discuss legal principles and to ponder policy questions. The impact of this modicum of collegiality on the court of castle chamber is difficult to assess. However, it is not unlikely that common lawyers from both England and Ireland developed a functional network of professional relationships, if not mutual respect, despite the hierarchical configuration of the membership.[2] Writing in 1604, Richard Hadsor described the situation in an essay to the king:

> So as Ireland is governed by the comon Lawes of England & by certen auncyent Customes of that Realme & by the said Statutes, and the like Courtes & forme of the administracion of Justice are ordeyned there, accordinge to the said Lawes, and the judiciall recordes are made in Lattin, & the Judges & Lawyers doe pleade in english as they doe in England, The Irish lawyers doe studdy the Lawe in the Innes of Court in Englande, being alwaies such as are discended of English & not of the meere Irishe.[3]

Irish-born lawyers would have met their English counterparts at the inns of court during five years of training. The records show that the recusant leader Henry Burnell entered Lincoln's Inn in 1561 at a time when his fellow Irishman and future chief justice, Nicholas Walsh, was in residence, along with another future chief justice, the New English Robert Gardener, who entered in the next year.[4] Burnell signed the law students' protest against the cess in 1562 and eventually became a prominent agitator for the Pale in 1577–78, though this did not prevent his elevation to the bench of common pleas for a term in 1590.[5] His trial in castle chamber for fraudulent conveyancing on behalf of the dowager countess of Kildare is noted above. And, despite the gradual disappearance of native-born judges from the bench itself, the number of Irish students at the inns of court continued to grow in this period, a fact remarked upon by both Sir Henry Sydney and James Stanyhurst. Many of them returned to Ireland as leaders of the 'commonwealth' opposition, including the lawyers Burnell, Richard Netterville, Barnaby Scurlock, and Patrick Bermingham.[6] The nobles and gentry of the Pale who refused to subscribe to the cess were represented before the court of castle chamber by John Netterville and Christopher Fleming, as well as Nicholas Nugent, then second baron of the exchequer.[7] When Scurlock was imprisoned in May 1577 for agitating in London against the cess, it was learned that he had

2. Kenny, *King's Inns*, pp. 1–5.
3. 'Richard Hadsor's "Discourse" on the Irish state, 1604', ed. J. McLaughlin, in 'New light on Richard Hadsor, II', *IHS*, xxx (1997), 337.
4. Ball, *Judges in Ireland*, i, 222–23. Peter Palmer entered Lincoln's Inn in 1562 as well, becoming second justice of common pleas in 1600, a position he held for 21 years until his death in office. Ibid., i, 227.
5. Ball, *Judges in Ireland*, i, 223–24.
6. BL, Add. MS 47,172, ff. 26v–28.
7. Kenny, *King's Inns*, pp. 50–51. See C. Brady, 'Conservative subversives: the community of the Pale and the Dublin administration 1556–1586', in P.J. Corish, ed., *Radicals, rebels and establishments: Historical Studies XV* (Belfast, 1983), p. 28.

earlier threatened Garret Wesley, a sheriff of the Pale, saying he would indict him at law for treason if he proceeded to impose the cess on the countryside. The privy council then ordered the solicitor general to examine Scurlock in the Fleet, charging him with conspiring to overthrow the queen's royal prerogative, and demanding answer to the charges.[8] Dr Cregan has shown that a 'steady stream' of admissions to the London inns from Ireland occurred in the period 1558 to 1625, despite the fitful enforcement of anti-recusancy laws in England.[9] Important Jacobean lawyers and adversaries of crown policies, such as William Meade of Cork and Patrick Barnewall of Dublin, attended the inns of court, though the latter apparently did not become a lawyer, according to Kenny.[10]

When the King's Inns came up for a renewal of its lease in 1567, the 25 lawyers who joined in the lease included not merely the chief justice of common pleas and master of the rolls, but the three leading law officers. In addition, leading coun-sellors who later advised the adversaries of the cess in the Pale were named as lessees, including Barnaby Scurlock and William Bathe, as well as James Stanyhurst, recorder of Dublin and clerk of the crown in chancery. The privy councillor Nicholas White was named as lessee five years before becoming master of the rolls, along with the future king's serjeant, Edward Fitzsymon of Dublin. All of these native-born lawyers eventually pleaded before the court of castle chamber. When the King's Inns receded into the shadows after 1584, crown policy in favour of English Protestant judges gradually eliminated recusants from the senior bench, an initiative that became the hallmark of the Chichester regime and the source of heated agitation by Irish-born lawyers early in the Jacobean period. The revival of the King's Inns in 1607, nonetheless, allowed Irish lawyers to regain membership until the hiatus lasting from 1613 to 1628. Indeed, the Inns, now dominated by the viceroy himself and all the senior judges, may have required admission for all 'practicers, officers, attornies and others of the several courts'.[11] Despite omissions from the record, Kenny has argued, 'it seems likely that most of those actually practising common law in the courts chose to join the restored society. All counsellors who appeared in the major cases of the period reported by Sir John Davies were members.'[12] Kenny and others have pointed to the central role of lawyers in the period, showing that the pressure to restore Catholic coun-sellors to practice in 1628 was a reflection of the genuine need for legal representation throughout the country.[13] The humble petition of the Irish lawyers to the Irish privy council in 1614 cited the recent interruption of their right to practise at the bar, complaining that the chief governor misinterpreted the statute of 2 Elizabeth and alleging that they 'being descended of auncient English families have spent their tyme and thier patrimonyes in the industrious and painefull acquisicon of the said study of the Common Lawes'.[14] The lawyers continued their petition by

8. *Acts privy council, 1575–77*, p. 355 (29 May 1577).
9. Cregan, 'Irish Catholic admissions', 95–106.   10.   Kenny, *King's Inns*, pp. 52–53.
11. Kenny, *King's Inns*, pp. 54–58, 81–82.   12.   Ibid., p. 82.
13. Ibid., p. 99.   14.   Bodl., Carte MS 62, ff. 261–61v.

alleging the benefits to the crown of native-born advocates who understood the Irish language, offered professional advice to loyal subjects who depended on their expertise based on confidence and trust in their long service, and provided a superior alternative to the practice of the discredited brehon law.[15]

Two celebrated Galway lawyers who led the parliamentary opposition to the Wentworth regime in 1640 and after, Patrick Darcy and Nicholas Plunkett, were both admitted to the English inns in 1628, a year in which the admission of 48 members trebled the previous figures for any year since 1607. Dr Cregan has shown that Irish Catholic students continued to attend the London inns throughout the period. During James I's reign at least 101 were admitted; and in his son's reign approximately 250 Irish-born students enrolled, despite numerous obstacles in their path, not the least of which was a disordered curriculum lacking in basic principles or coherence. Nonetheless, the inns provided an important social and cultural setting as well as legal training for those who became the adversaries of crown policy during the Confederate period.[16] More recently, Dr Ohlmeyer found that at least 140 Irish recusants attended the inns of court from 1625 to 1641, encouraged by local powerbrokers such as Richard Shee of Kilkenny.[17] As Dr Barnard has concluded in his study of lawyers and the law,

> In seventeenth century Ireland the law increasingly defined and regulated relationships: between government and governed; between landlord and tenant; between master and servant; among the propertied; and even, by the end of the century, between Catholics and Protestants. This situation, similar to that throughout western Euope, signalled—at least superficially— England's success in assimilating Ireland. The system of courts, centred on Dublin and, through regular assizes and quarter sessions, borough, sheriffs', church and manorial courts, reaching deep into the localities, was celebrated as a prime benefit, as well as the principal means, of anglicisation.[18]

The impact of the court of castle chamber on the provinces gradually increased, along with the shiring of new Irish counties and the progress of the assizes. In turn, Irish lawyers in Dublin sought the business of the provincial courts, a rivalry condemned in a letter of the privy council in England to the president of Munster, Sir Thomas Norris, in November 1597. Citing the practice of attorneys, solicitors and other counsellors in the Dublin courts initiating process in the capital against Munster denizens, even though the cases had been adjudicated previously in the

---

15. Ibid. See also W.N. Osborough, 'The regulation of the admission of attorneys and solicitors in Ireland, 1600–1860' in his *Studies in Irish legal history* (Dublin, 1999), pp. 157–59.

16. D. Cregan, 'The Confederate Catholics of Ireland: the personnel of the Confederation, 1642–9', *IHS*, xxix (1995), 499–501.

17. Ohlmeyer, 'Irish recusant lawyers', pp. 63–67.

18. T.C. Barnard, 'Lawyers and the law in later seventeenth-century Ireland', *IHS*, xxviii (1993), 256. Barnard added that, despite attempts to deny them legal representation, Catholics willingly used the courts to seek satisfaction of their claims. Ibid.

locality, they cautioned Norris to restrain his own involvement in legal proceedings to avoid giving cause for appeal.[19] Three years later, at the height of the Tyrone Rebellion, Lord President Carew complained to the privy council that all the Munster towns had elected lawyers to be their magistrates, in place of merchants formerly chosen. The effect of this, according to Carew, was to stiffen the resistance of the towns to his governance, particularly in the form of support for the troops in the field. He cited Geoffrey Gallway, the new mayor of Limerick lately returned from a stint at the inns of court, as the source of opposition, noting he had advised the city to refuse supplies for Carew's retinue. Blaming the merchants for profiting from the war itself, and the lawyers for leading them in a form of civil disobedience, Carew defended his actions in fining Gallway and threatening others. Gallway had imprisoned a soldier in Limerick for petty larceny of a hatchet, and Carew sent warrants to free the soldier so he could be prosecuted by the council in Munster. This tactic was opposed by the mayor, who asserted the corporate privileges of the town in defending his jurisdiction against the intervention of the lord president.[20] Gallway appeared before the council in Munster, put himself on the 'grace of the court' and denied their authority to condemn him. As a result of his obstinacy, the townspeople refused to come to church, according to Carew, who feared a general municipal revolt. Gallway had advised the previous mayor to disarm all soldiers in his jurisdiction after an affray between the citizens and the soldiers had disturbed the peace, and Carew threatened to bring both men before the Irish council for punishment.[21] Carew listed the other legally-trained magistrates in Munster, finding them a seditious crew, and citing the contempts of mayors John Meade of Cork and Edward Gough of Waterford; one White, the sovereign of Clonmel; and the portreeve of Cashel, 'the profoundest man of learning for the civil law within the kingdom and as obstinate as learned'.[22] The beleaguered Carew was cautioned by Mountjoy, nonetheless,

> to forbear for a time all further open and public proceeding in that cause. For considering you are not ignorant of the aptness of this country people to raise acusations, sometimes out of maleice and sometime of practice, and likewise what may be the danger to take hold of such matters in this looseness of time, which is now growing to a staidness and settling, we are of mind that where such particular information, having but weak grounds, if they should be severely followed, would put in hazard to interrupt the quiet now growing to the general estate, it were not amiss to temporize with them for a while, till by time things might be more certainly discovered.[23]

---

19. *Acts privy council, 1597–98*, p. 117.   20. *Cal. Carew MSS, 1601–03*, p. 6.

21. Ibid. This letter was signed by Carew and Thomond, as well as by the judges of the provincial court, Saxey, Gerald Comerford, and Francis Barkeley.

22. He also cited an unknown official from Kinsale, who was 'brought up at the inns of court'. *Cal. Carew MSS, 1598–1600*, pp. 490–93.

23. Ibid., p. 341: lord deputy and council to Carew, 26 September 1602.

In most cases, the counsel for the defence or for private suitors was not named in the documentation for the court of castle chamber. It is far from clear how many of the recusants who trained at the inns of court prosecuted cases at castle chamber upon their return to Ireland. Indeed, most of them were primarily interested in advancing their families' fortunes and used legal strategies to preserve their estates. Bolton and others encouraged greater understanding of the common law as 'the provision and food of this commonwealth', and the legal dynasties such as the Barnewalls of Turvey and Crickstown and the Luttrells of Luttrellstown continued to send their sons to London until 1641.[24] Nonetheless, it is certain we shall not discover an Irish William Hudson, akin to the star chamber expert discussed at length by Barnes for the Jacobean period.[25] Sir John Davies's *Report* of cases adjudged in the courts of Ireland offers a glimpse of the work of lawyers in the central courts, though, again, the predominance of law officers occludes the presence of counsel for the defendants or private suitors. A case heard in the exchequer court concerned with the rights to proxies issued by the bishop of Meath involved as plaintiff Sir Ambrose Forth, doctor of civil law and a master in chancery, whose lawyer was Henry Lynch, of the Middle Temple.[26] In the *Case of tanistry* heard before king's bench in 1608, Davies mentioned that Richard Bolton, then recorder of Dublin, and John Meade, former magistrate of Cork, were of counsel for the plaintiff who sued a writ of *ejectione firmae* for the castle of Dromineen.[27] While the work of lawyers multiplied in this period, in direct proportion to the numerous courts and commissions established by the crown, it is possible to identify only the members of these bodies and rarely the counsel who appeared before them. For example, the commission for the remedy of defective titles named most of the leading councillors of Ireland, as well as the senior judges and law officers to its membership, but left no record of its proceedings.[28] Unlike the English star chamber, its Irish counterpart left a slender account of the attorneys, solicitors and barristers who carried on the 'legal campaigns' of their suitors in this period. Barnes found some 1,250 counsel who signed pleadings in star chamber cases for 1603–25, estimating the total at about 1,550 lawyers. The castle chamber figure would have been far less, probably under 100, though it is difficult to estimate.[29]

---

24. Ohlmeyer, 'Irish recusant lawyers', pp. 64–65, 70, 75. Dr Ohlmeyer found that the barristers all pleaded cases in chancery from the late 1630s, and we may surmise some of them also pleaded before castle chamber.
25. See Barnes, 'Mr. Hudson's Star Chamber', pp. 285–308.
26. J. Davies, *A report of cases and matters in law resolved and adjudged in the king's courts in Ireland* (Dublin, 1762), p. 1. See H. Pawlisch, 'Sir John Davies' *Law Reports* and the case of proxies', *Ir Jur*, xvii (1982), 368–83.
27. Davies, *A report of cases*, p. 115.
28. *Pat. rolls Ire., Jas. I*, ed. Erck, pt. 1, p. 299.
29. T.G. Barnes, 'Star chamber litigants and their counsel, 1596–1641', in J.H. Baker, ed., *Legal records and the historian* (London, 1978), pp. 23–27. See also C.W. Brooks, 'Litigants and attorneys in King's Bench and Common Pleas, 1560–1640', in Baker, ed., *Legal records*, pp. 45–57.

LITIGANTS AND LITIGATION

Owing to the erratic record-keeping of the court of castle chamber and the fact that only a portion of the entry book for this period survives, it is impossible to compile a definitive chronicle of litigants. Unlike the Jacobean star chamber in England, for which Dr Barnes compiled a statistical analysis of over 8,000 cases and 65,000 defendants, the court of castle chamber has left a meagre record of its proceedings.[30] Due to the gaps in the record, as opposed to the well-documented cases of historical importance, the resulting imbalance prevents the researcher from developing a longitudinal analysis of practice at the court. In what follows, then, we must rely on case studies rather than on statistical profiles of litigants and litigation. Further, most of the detail is lodged in the Appendices and the narrative of Part Two, so the digest of suitors and suits is rather a pastiche than a definitive account. Unlike the English privy council, which had refined the manner in which petitions were heard and diverted to other venues, the Irish privy council retained a quasi-judicial function for purposes of arbitration, apart from hearings at the court of castle chamber. Consequently, some of the litigation under review was actually resolved in the conciliar tribunal, having a residual function as a court, though hardly distinguishable in other ways from the castle chamber itself. This was particularly the case when senior judges were themselves involved in the suit, such as Sir Adam Loftus, Viscount Ely, who was tormented by Wentworth.

An integrated study of litigants and litigation, taken together, may be justified on a number of grounds. First, certain classes of litigants commonly sued, or were charged, at castle chamber for reasons having to do with their unique characteristics as a class. Aristocrats sued over title and matters of personal honour; women sued over dower rights; local officials were charged with malfeasance; merchants sued for restoration of goods; Protestant clergy proceeded against their parishioners for recusancy; and the gentry were charged with sedition for opposing the cess. In sum, the identity of the litigant and the nature of the litigation were often inseparable. Secondly, the important questions of why the suitors appeared before the court are most often answered by the nature of their litigation. Husbandmen, horseboys and cottagers appeared among long lists of defendants in riot cases because the outraged landowner attempted to compel his rival to take responsibility for their fines. His aim was to entangle his adversary in litigation, so the presence of members of the lowest social classes as 'litigants' was ancillary to their status as dependents of their social superiors. Lastly, a statistical profile of suitors and cases would rest on such slender evidence, concentrated in some years and lacking in other years, that the result would be a distorted picture of the court. The paradoxical absence of court records for the judicially active Wentworth era forces the researcher to compress the data into an artificial compendium.

---

30. Barnes, 'Star chamber litigants', pp. 8–10.

.Nonetheless, an effort will be made to gauge some representative characteristics of the court and its work over time.

The deficient entry book of the court of castle chamber, as explained above, commenced without an explanatory preamble or a commission from the crown. The first folio contains an unexplained record, citing the names of 37 men from Co. Louth who were found guilty of an unnamed offence, at an uncertain date. They were apparently connected with the second list of 46 men and one woman who were present 'at the spoyle of the said shippe,' along with Patrick Plunkett's 'howsehold men'.[31] Plunkett, the only gentleman named in both lists, who was almost certainly made responsible for the payment of many fines, was joined in the second group by two other gentlemen, including a kinsman, Edward Plunkett, along with Bele Mando, wife to George Fitzjohn, gentleman. The social class of other defendants in both lists was largely omitted, though some five were cottagers.[32] We may assume that a riot was committed when a ship was dashed ashore near Termonfeckin and that the locals scrambled to exploit their opportunity, perhaps violating the commandment of a local official to honour the property rights of the merchant owner. A commotion of this sort would have naturally engaged the attention of the court of castle chamber, but the suit was probably initiated to claim damages to the property, a tactic employed by the majority of suitors in the English parent court. In a subsequent case heard on 4 November 1573, the court found Daniel Roo and Patrick Taylor guilty of riot and fined them each forty shillings. They were, again, described as former servants to Edward Cusack, gentlemen, but their offence was not described. While we lack enough information, the pattern of suing in castle chamber to obtain a judgement against a rival gentleman might lie behind these actions, though the bill was of course introduced by the solicitor general, John Bathe.[33] On 30 January 1579, the suit of Walter McHarbarde FitzGeffrye against the gentleman, James Nugent of Donore, Co. West Meath, and 27 others was partially dismissed after eight gentlemen and two husbandmen pleaded the queen's pardon to a charge of riot.[34]

Private suitors also brought bills of riot against their neighbours, generally naming multiple defendants to disadvantage their adversaries and potentially increase the award if damages were assessed. William Clynche brought such an action against Nicholas Russell and five co-defendants, probably his kinsmen, and a similar suit was filed by James Fitzgarret of Co. Dublin against Edward FitzMorris of Co. Kildare and five co-defendants. In the latter case, FitzMorris

---

31. BL, Add. MS 47,172, ff. 1–1v.   32. Ibid.

33. Ibid., f. 2.

34. Ibid., f. 36v. Bolton articulated the connections between riot and property offences, such as riot in a park upon the keeper of the park and his servants (and hurting the servants with an arrow); riot in pulling down hedges and ditches; riot in stealing oats from a barn; riot in pulling down hedges and ditches; riot in rescue of cattle taken for damage feasant; and riot in entering and withholding possession of a messuage of land, and expelling the owner. *Justice of peace for Ireland*, pp. 72ff.

was a gentleman who was fined and forced to give bond for the appearance of the others.[35] However, Sir Morris Fitzgarold of Lecagh, brought a bill of riot against sixteen Irish servants of Owny McHugh of Ballybrittas, including others who did not appear. The court found for the plaintiff on 29 April 1574, ordering McHugh to bring in the other defendants, though he was not convicted of the offence. On 1 July 1574, the court took further note of the case, determining that McHugh had failed to bring in the defendants according to the court order, despite several 'dayes of respyte', so he was obliged to pay all the fines and costs of the court by the first day of the next term. This, in fact, was the probable intention of Sir Morris in bringing suit at castle chamber, a tactic much followed in the English court as well.[36] In another probable case of vexatious pleading, Edmund Butler of Callan, Co. Kilkenny was joined by Walter Archer in a suit against over twenty defendants including notable Kilkenny family names like Rothe, Ragged, and Purcell. The defendants, however, by their attorney Thomas Brownell, pleaded the queen's pardon and so were dismissed with costs by the court on 12 November 1574.[37]

The stubborn John Garrahall appeared before the court on three occasions, suing a bill of riot, along with Richard Fynn, against Tybbot Walshe and fifteen others without success, until he won a judgement (probably against the same defendants, without Walshe) on 5 November 1574. In the last case, Garrahall astutely sued a gentleman, William Ashepoole of Kenleston, who was made responsible for bringing in the defendants, paying the large fine of £20 himself, and accepting the burden of fines for those defendants he could not bring to justice.[38] In a rare exception to the petitions of the social élite, Joyce Adryan of Dublin, a leatherdresser, successfully sued eight tanners for a riot in which they assaulted him and his wife and carried away a 'dicker' [ten skins or hides] of tanned leather. The beating 'greavously hurt' Elizabeth, the wife of Adryan, 'by whiche misdemenors she was inforst to beare a dead borne child', and later died herself. The court of castle chamber on that occasion was manned by four senior judges who fined three of the defendants five marks apiece, dismissing the others, including two women (perhaps their wives) with costs of court.[39] On 2 July 1606, two Dublin bakers, James Browne and Patricke Englishe, were fined £40 each for refusing to attend divine service. This odd detour, fining ordinary tradesmen in addition to the aldermen and public officials of the city as part of Chichester's anti-recusancy campaign, was not explained by the court.[40]

Members of the peerage sued in castle chamber on numerous occasions, frequently to defend their inheritance. The earl of Clanricarde was forced to

---

35. BL, Add. MS 47, 172, ff. 3–4. The social class of Clynche and Fitzgarret was not mentioned in the suits.
36. Ibid., ff. 5–6.
37. Ibid., f. 8. The suit was commenced on 25 January 1573 and much delayed by the need for examining witnesses and counter-pleas.
38. Ibid., ff. 4v, 5v, 7–7v. The last case named 27 defendants, including one Thomas (not Tibbot) Walche. His original bill was brought on 7 October 1573.
39. Ibid., f. 90. The justices were Loftus, Gardener, White and Walsh.   40. Ibid., f. 145.

support his title in an action against his own brothers, Thomas and John Burke, defending his patrimony by calling witnesses to testify to the marriage of his parents and his subsequent birth five years after, thus defeating the charge of illegitimacy.[41] Lady Lettice Fitzgerald and her husband, Robert Digby, were continually at law trying to assert her rights to the estate of the late earl of Kildare, her grandfather. In February 1608, they sued and won in castle chamber against the dowager countess and her venerable counsellor, Henry Burnell, claiming that the lawyer had fraudulently changed the countess's dowager rights by forging the deed of the late earl made some forty years before.[42] In February 1624, the solicitor general sued on behalf of the earl of West Meath in a case of slander against one Humphrey Walsh of Co. Cavan. Apparently, Walsh had spread the news that the earl would become king of Ireland, just a year before the expected death of James I.[43] In another proxy suit heard in June 1628, a defence of the reputation of the duke of Buckingham was mounted, when the attorney general sued Richard Browne of Bromyard in England for saying that the duke was lodged in the Tower of London, accused of sending the king of Spain a basin and ewer to promote the Catholic faith in England.[44] The earl of Ormonde jealously guarded his rights to the prise wines, suing in castle chamber and chancery simultaneously to defend his privilege of the customs duty against both foreign merchants and local officials of Drogheda and Dublin.[45] The nobility were, however, more likely to take their petitions directly to the crown, and the jurisdiction of the court of castle chamber was rarely accepted as the court of last resort for aristocrats who lost their suit in that venue. The barons of Howth, however, fell foul of the law frequently. Baron Howth was convicted of the heinous manslaughter of his own daughter and contemptible brutality toward his wife and servants in 1579, while his grandson subsequently was accused of conspiring to murder Sir Roger Jones in an affray by a tennis court in Dublin.[46] In a similar case, on 9 May 1593 Baron Slane and his servants were assaulted in the High Street of Dublin by Viscount Gormanston and thirty retainers while on their way to a commission presided over by the lord chancellor.[47] The next year Lord Inchiquin was fined 100 marks for an assault on Sir Tirlough O'Brien on the quay of Dublin while making his way to the council chamber.[48]

Wealthy merchants were often suitors at the castle chamber, though tradesmen were far less likely to be involved. On 15 November 1622, the court heard the case of a fraudulent overvaluing of silver spoons by two goldsmiths in Dublin, a rare case of tradesmen's offences.[49] Since the well-off capitalist often purchased land

---

41. Ibid., ff. 172–77.
42. Ibid., ff. 154–59. The original bill of complaint was exhibited in 1602.
43. TCD, MS 852, f. 99v.   44. Ibid., f. 99.
45. BL, Add. MS 47,172, ff. 17–19.   46. Ibid., ff. 41v–43, 166.
47. Ibid., f. 109; TCD, MS 852, f. 97.
48. BL, Add. MS 47,172, f. 118 (8 June 1594). Inchiquin was also prosecuted for harbouring a known Jesuit priest, Nicholas Nugent, in 1616. TCD, MS 852, f. 90v.
49. TCD, MS 852, f. 93.

with his profit, the class of merchant suitors can be easily obscured. For example, the prosperous Cork merchant, Sir Walter Coppinger, had been a mayor and undersheriff, built a fine mansion near Rosscarbery, and became involved in numerous castle chamber suits. We might classify him thus as an official, a merchant and a landowner, although categorization of most litigants is less difficult. For example, Coppinger was witness for the prosecution in 1593, when undersheriff in Co. Cork;[50] he had been assaulted by the defendant whilst taking a distress from John Fitz Edmonds Fitzgerald. In February 1616, Coppinger was in turn sued at castle chamber for 'malicious indictments' brought against his New English neighbours, including an accusation of treason against Thomas Crooke and his tenants 'newly planted at Baltimore'.[51] More often, merchants were sued for customs or duties owed, or to recover damages. One George Clerck of Dublin confessed before the court on 26 November 1623 that he had unloaded his merchandise and goods at Custom House quay onto a barque and conveyed them to Wood quay without paying any custom.[52] And on 10 May 1616, a group of 21 Limerick merchants were sued in castle chamber for keeping the petitioner, Edmond Sexton, in continual suits at law to prevent him from purchasing more lands in the city. Twenty of the merchants were convicted for a riot in which they came to the new house of Sexton near Limerick, drove away his workmen, and pulled down the edifice. Among them were the late mayor, William Haly, and six aldermen, suggesting the case had wider implications than corporate envy.[53] On 26 June 1579, two merchants of Chester, John Fuller and Walter Foxe, sued the leaders of an unlawful assembly of 200 persons at Wexford who broke up and carried away the goods from their wrecked ship, refusing to cooperate in making restitution.[54] In a rare case of quiet sedition, Walter Cregg, a merchant of Scotland, was convicted in castle chamber on 3 May 1616 of transporting the Jesuit priests, Nicholas Nugent and William Malone, to Inch Katherine on the River Shannon.[55]

One of the largest classes of litigants before the court were the civil and military officials, charged with implementing royal policy in Ireland. From the mayors, recorders, sovereigns and portreeves accused of taking office without pledging the oath of supremacy during the early Stuart period, to the solitary cases of abuse of power such as that heard before Chancellor Gerrard, involving the seneschal of Wexford, Thomas Masterson, the court was busy with cases of official malfeasance.[56] The lowly jailer of Mullingar, Jane Hopp, was convicted of negligence and dereliction of duty for allowing dangerous prisoners to escape.[57] On the other hand,

50. BL, Add. MS 47,172, f. 106.
51. Ibid., f. 212.
52. TCD, MS 852, f. 93.
53. BL, Add. MS 47,172, f. 220.
54. Ibid., ff. 40v–41.
55. Ibid., f. 218. See a similar case in February 1618 of Martin Skerret of Galway who transported a friar. Ibid., f. 262.
56. Ibid., ff. 14–16. Masterson and Brian McCahir McArt Cavanaugh accused each other of various riots, murders and other felonies, so Chancellor Gerrard bound both of them to make restitution and to keep the peace pending their appearance before the court in the next term.
57. Ibid., f. 129.

Sir Richard Bingham and his henchmen in the presidency of Connacht were brought before the court for numerous charges involving the arbitrary execution of Irish landowners as well as of vagabonds.[58] Sir John Wolverston of Co. Wickow was involved as both petitioner and defendant. In 1612, he was sued by Denys Byrne of Dublin for driving away his cattle, and by Dermot McGylpatrick of Co. Wicklow for breaking up the harrows in his fields. However, four years later he petitioned as justice of the peace against Nicholas Walsh, who challenged him and assaulted him publicly, leading the court to humiliate the defendants at the next general sessions in Wicklow. Sir Richard Bolton demanded that justices of the peace in Ireland prosecute cases of riot skilfully, threatening them with a star chamber fine for committing an accused malefactor to ward without sufficient cause; or for failing to execute the law against riot, rout or unlawful assembly in the country.[59] The drunken assault by Christopher Draycott in June 1620 against Francis Roe, mayor of Drogheda, was viewed in similar terms of outrage by the court, accompanied as it was by coarse language and spitting in the face of the mayor.[60] Two military rivals in Carrickfergus, the constable Charles Egerton, and Captain Rice Mansfield, were engaged in an affray outside the town in April 1597 in which both were injured, though Egerton was the loser before the court when he was fined 100 marks and imprisoned. Oliver Scurlocke, former sheriff of Co. Donegal, was fined the same amount in 1605 for extortion in demanding that householders and herders pay him for their defence.[61] Gilbert Butler, sheriff of Co. Tipperary, was forced to pay a fine in 1619 for reprieving a notorious rebel who had been convicted at the assizes and sentenced to execution.[62] Celebrated cases under Wentworth, such as the trial of Mountnorris for dishonouring the lord deputy and the dismissal of Viscount Ely as lord chancellor, occurred outside the parameters of the court of castle chamber (they are dealt with in Part Two). The discharge of Patrick Sedgrave in 1602 as second baron of the exchequer on counts of bribery and corruption in a case heard before him was the lone example of a senior magistrate being punished before the court.[63]

Of all the litigants appearing in the court of castle chamber, local jurors were probably the most numerous. While not technically officials of the government, they were acting in a judicial capacity and the court used its power to punish corrupt verdicts frequently. What is more, when the juries refused to implement controversial government policies, allowing the accused to go unpunished, the court of castle chamber proceeded against the jurors themselves. Only in that way could the common law tradition of trial by one's peers be made to work in Ireland,

---

58. Ibid., f. 82.
59. Ibid., ff. 187–88, 235; Bolton, *Justice of peace for Ireland*, pp. 194–95. Bolton noted that no action of trespass on the case would lie against a judge of record, acting in his judicial role; but if he acted out of malice or corruption, the star chamber fine would be the appropriate recourse. He burdened the justices with the mandate to pursue rioters and arrest them, stating that justices in neighbouring counties shared the responsibility and faced a penalty in castle chamber for default.
60. BL, Add. MS 47, 172, ff. 279–80.　　61. Ibid., ff.127, 134.
62. Ibid., f. 275.　　63. TCD, MS 852, f. 81.

though it cannot be said the court was successful in this quest for jurors' con-formity to expectations. On 21 June 1577, the foreman of a jury in Co. Meath, Christopher Barnewall, gentleman, was indicted for corrupting the other jurors in the controversy over the cess. Appearing before the chief justice, he sought to protest against the imposition of purveyance for the victualling of soldiers, challenging the viceroy and council for 'misconstruing the laws'.[64] In the following year, three separate grand juries, empanelled before Drury and the presidency court of Munster in Kilkenny, were fined and imprisoned at castle chamber for returning an *ignoramus* to three bills for felony and treason committed in the shire.[65] The unrepentant Barnewall reappeared as foreman of another jury whose corrupt verdict was investigated at castle chamber on 5 May 1581. The jury considered evidence in the case of an estate claimed by the wife of the deceased, Richard Lynham, but the commissioners (including Sir Robert Dillon, the second justice of common pleas, and the solicitor general) had deter-mined the estate was left by knight service to the minor heir, in which case a substantial wardship and its profits would fall to the queen. All jurors were fined £50, with Barnewall and Christopher Hussey paying £100 for the offence, though six days later the fines were reduced after the jurors petitioned that their poor estates were unable to support such heavy penalties, claiming ignorance of the law.[66] Despite these essays in intimidation, jurors continued to find against the crown in controversial cases. On 7 February 1582, a jury empanelled before the court of king's bench was convicted of giving a corrupt verdict of innocent by the court of castle chamber. Summoned to try Morris FitzJames FitzGerald for high treason in aiding the Pale rebellion of Baltinglas, the jurors refused to comply.[67] The relentless campaign against corrupt verdicts slackened after 1582, and the castle chamber proceeded more circumspectly against jurors from Co. Kildare in 1587. They found a verdict of not guilty, contrary to the 'manifest evidence', but their case was reviewed by the two chief justices and the fines mitigated to ten shillings after long debate on the nature of their 'perjury'.[68] Bolton's instructions to justices of the peace made clear the determination of the court to punish recalcitrant jurors:

> And therefore where the Justices of peace are remisse herein, in not sufficently punishing such offenders by due fine and imprisonment, the Lords in the Starchamber, may and doe often assesse upon Riotters for the same riot (for which the justices of peace have formerly assessed a fine in the Countrey) a greater penalty, if they see cause, and yet in this case the offendors be not twice punished for one offence, but part of the due punishment is inflicted at one time and part at another.[69]

64. BL., Add. MS 47, 172, ff. 20–20v.   65. Ibid., ff. 33v–35v.
66. Ibid., ff. 44v–47v.   67. Ibid., ff. 49–49v.
68. Ibid., ff. 83–83v.
69. Bolton, *Justice of peace for Ireland*, p. 203. He added that if the riot could not be found by the

The remarkable crusade against recusancy launched by Sir Arthur Chichester, against the advice of his mentor and lord lieutenant, the earl of Devonshire, was the hallmark of the Jacobean court of castle chamber. Compared to a mere three cases in which jurors were fined for corrupt verdicts in the last twenty years of the Tudor period, Chichester led the court to an inquisition of jurors that lasted until Wentworth finally put a stop to it. While none of the Elizabethan juries were charged with refusing to present recusants indicted in the royal courts, the castle chamber became clogged with these dubious cases under the early Stuarts. Nonetheless, the prosecutions were condensed into operations that lasted for two years or more before crown policy changed direction. In the first case recorded at castle chamber for seven years, on 15 June 1604, a jury of Co. Cork, composed of leading men who had appeared before special commissioners at Youghal, was charged. They had refused to convict William Meade, the ringleader of Cork's recent defiance of the king's troops, who had declined to proclaim James I. The jurors, with the advice of counsel, answered only that they knew Meade did not intend treason, so the court of castle chamber convicted them of perjury, fining them £500 each.[70] After a formal proclamation requiring attendance at divine service, the viceroy issued writs, or mandates, to leading aldermen of Dublin to attend church or face punishment at castle chamber. Five cases were tried at court, which resulted in the fining of most of the leading officials and depriving them of office. A long hiatus ensued after 1607, during which the juries throughout the realm enjoyed a respite. However, in 1612 two juries were condemned at castle chamber for corrupt verdicts involving crown title to land and an acquittal 'against the evidence'. In May, six merchants of Dublin were convicted of giving fraudulent verdicts, refusing to join their fellow jurors in presenting recusants on the testimony of Protestant ministers for not attending divine service. They were imprisoned and fined 100 marks apiece.[71] On 25 November, three cases were heard on one day, resulting in the condemnation of grand juries from Co. West Meath, Co. Tipperary and Co. Meath for refusing to present recusants. In all, seven ringleaders were fined and imprisoned.[72] Chichester's campaign against recusancy was a *casus belli* during the turbulent parliament of 1613, when he attempted to use the threat of fine and imprisonment against recusants to intimidate them or to discourage them from serving in the legislature. Three juries suffered for their actions in 1613; four in 1614; and four more in 1615. In the latter year, another jury was punished for failing to convict Geoffrey Keating, who had relieved Piers Keating, the murderer of Henry Davells; and a jury empanelled before king's bench was punished for acquitting ten men of the charge of hearing mass at Navan.[73]

'perverseness' of the jurors, the justices of peace were to certify to the star chamber in Ireland or to the 'body and board of the privy Councell or into the kings Bench' the facts, circumstances and names of the offenders, on pain of a fine of £100. Ibid.

70. TCD, MS 852, f. 130.   71. Ibid., f. 186.
72. Ibid., ff. 191–93.   73. Ibid., ff. 206, 207.

The anti-recusant policies of Chichester were continued under his successor, with some refinements. Jurors were punished in castle chamber for the same offences, but in 1616 the local officials such as the mayor and sheriffs of Kilkenny were also prosecuted for taking up their offices without pledging the oath of supremacy. On the same date, 1 May, the sovereigns of Thomastown, Kilmallock, and portreeves of Gowran and Inistioge were fined for the same reasons. Two days later, the mayors of Limerick, Cork, Waterford and Clonmel suffered the like fate. Lord Deputy St John used the month of November 1616 to punish jurors and local officials for recusancy offences. In a period of two weeks, from 13 to 27 November, the court of castle chamber meted out punishments to 70 jurors and local officials in thirteen separate cases from Waterford, Limerick, Kilkenny, Clonmel, Fethard, Tipperary, Wexford, West Meath, Carlow, Kildare, Cashel, New Ross and Naas.[74] An undated memorandum of Ellesmere and Bacon to Davies offered their support of the prosecution of local officials in the court of castle chamber for taking up office without swearing the oath of supremacy.[75] The next year, 1617, was even worse, with twenty cases before the castle chamber, in which 68 persons were charged with various offences tinged with recusancy. In fact, the court did little else in this period, with eight of ten cases in 1618 being occupied with recusancy matters. By this time, the court had turned to charging merchants and others with harbouring friars and priests, providing them with shipping, or assisting them with their travels, culminating in the pathetic prosecution of Richard Nugent and his wife in April 1619 for illegally receiving letters from Irish students in Spain and Portugal, including their own son, John Nugent, in Lisbon.[76]

As the court of castle chamber was increasingly used as an instrument of judicial harassment for purposes of religious persecution, it was in turn robbed of the very dignity with which its founders had hoped to endow it. Nonetheless, for political reasons, the inquisition ebbed and flowed, without changing the attachment of loyal Catholic subjects to either their faith or their sovereign. In England, the judges offered a definitive resolution on the treatment of recusants in the Trinity term of 1626, suggesting that the handling of recusancy in Ireland was not more dictatorial than royal policy would allow. They addressed the question of a recusant who dwelt within a liberty, saying the person could be indicted in king's bench or at quarter sessions, but recommended the assizes for the county as the

---

74. Ibid., ff. 214–34. Dr Edwards has recently claimed that the anti-recusancy policy was focused on the Butler strongholds of Kilkenny and Tipperary, to weaken the Catholic earl of Ormonde. As a result of the replacement of four Catholic mayors of Kilkenny in 1616, Sir Cyprian Horsfall, the son of the Protestant bishop of Ossory, finally took office as the city's fifth mayor in that year. Edwards, 'The poisoned chalice: the Ormond inheritance, sectarian division and the emergence of James Butler, 1614–42' in T. Barnard and J. Fenlon, eds., *The dukes of Ormonde, 1610–1745* (Woodbridge, Suffolk, 2000), p. 65.

75. Bodl., Carte MS 61, f. 83. They confirmed that mayors and other local officials were crown officers 'mediately', but urged discretion in the prosecution of cases and suggested a period of 'dormancy' before launching an all-out campaign.

76. BL, Add. MS 47,172, f. 272, and see ff. 237–71.

best venue, noting the policies in effect and how to administer the fines for not attending divine service. The judges concluded with this recommendation for recusant women as femme coverts: '[She] maye by warrant bee taken out of hir howse, and Carryed to pryson ... And yf the Sherife, or other offycer knocke att the doore, it beinge shutt, thei maye Breake it open.'[77] Wentworth's policy of religious pragmatism stopped the prosecution of jurors and local officials, aiming instead to shore up the ecclesiastical establishment. His charge in castle chamber against the earl of Cork for expropriating the ecclesiastical living at the college of Youghal shifted attention to the administration of church offices and officials.[78]

The jury system was specially protected by the court of castle chamber through the prosecution of champerty and maintenance, traditional star chamber offences. Though few of these cases reached the final stage of order and decree, Sir John Burke, David Burke and Walter Oge McJames McMorris were convicted of champerty and maintenance in May 1621. Sir John and Walter Oge conspired to commence suit for the lands in question, with the latter promising to convey half the lands to Sir John in consideration for his secret financing of the prosecution and maintenance of the suit. David Burke, probably the son of Sir John, exacerbated the situation by 'riding post hast in a tempestuous night' to find the jury engaged in deliberation and there 'violently thrust into the Roome and privatly conferred with one of the Jurie'.[79] Another offence prosecuted in castle chamber was the subornation of witnesses, a jury-related crime in that reliable witnesses formed the basis of verifiable evidence for jurors' decisions. Thomas Nolan, esquire, and his son James were found guilty in castle chamber on 6 February 1627 of conspiring to suborn witnesses in a case heard in Co. Mayo. The plaintiff, Michael Cormack, was accused of treason in providing a pirate with munitions and victuals, but the witnesses to the alleged crime had all been secretly corrupted to offer perjured testimony at the assize court, perverting justice and threatening Cormack with defamation and loss of life. This subverting of the justice system was treated by castle chamber as a prime offence, so the punishment was severe. The Nolans were fined £1,000 with £300 damages to Cormack, while the witnesses were fined £500 each. All four were placed in the jail, pilloried in the market place, and had their ears nailed to the pillory.[80] In another case of perjured testimony, heard on 5 February 1629, Edward Fitzgerald of Dublin, gentleman, accused John Nolan, esquire, and others of conspiring to make a false accusation. Fitzgerald was accused of conspiracy to murder Nolan and steal his goods from his house in the high street of Dublin, upon which he was arrested by the mayor,

77. TCD, MS 802, f. 130.
78. Chatsworth, Lismore MSS, vol. 18, items 15, 29–32, 42, 58–61, 72, 83.
79. TCD, MS 852, f.81v. Sir John was fined £300, David £100 and Walter Oge £20, apparently in relation to their ability to pay.
80. Ibid., f. 82v. The Nolans had their ears cut off, while the witnesses were allowed to tear them free 'with their owne force'. In a subsequent case, it appeared that James Nolan managed to escape while en route back to the sessions in Co. Mayo, for which the subsheriff was found responsible. Ibid., f. 84v.

accused by the grand jury, but acquitted by the petit jury in king's bench. Castle chamber found Nolan guilty of perjury and conspiracy for setting up the unfortunate Fitzgerald, fining Nolan £200 with £100 damages to the plaintiff.[81]

Embracery was an offence by which a suitor attempted to subvert a juror's honest independence of judgement, a crime punished at castle chamber though seldom recorded in the entry book. Nicholas Wolfe of Kilcolman, Co. Kildare, gentleman, was prosecuted in the castle chamber court on 23 January 1626 for attempting to influence two jurors in a petit jury charged with the trial of four men on a life or death matter (undisclosed). Wolfe had met one of the bailiffs and, after providing him with drink, got the opportunity to speak with the jurors and gave his opinion that no one should be condemned upon the sole testimony of one 'notorious malefactor', apparently the only witness in the case.[82] On 22 November 1620, the solicitor general informed against Deran McBran, mother of a prisoner indicted for treason in Co. Wicklow, who was accused of procuring Teig McShane to write a letter to one of the jurors at the trial of her son. The letter was received by John McMorrough Byrne, who in turn communicated its contents to the rest of the jurors in an attempt to get their consent to an acquittal, a tactic that failed to sway them. The court fined all the offenders, humbling them with the pillory and forcing them to declare their crimes before all the four courts in Dublin and the sessions in Wicklow.[83] On 17 May 1620, the court fined Gerald Fitzmorris and others for bribing, soliciting and 'embracing' the jurors in king's bench to secure a verdict against the plaintiff at castle chamber, David Fitzgibbon.[84] The court of castle chamber concerned itself with the integrity of the judicial system, pun-ishing offenders severely, though it is difficult to glean from the records a sub-plot that may have strongly influenced the court's decision to take up selected cases. In any event, the relatively small number of cases of this type suggests the court did not give these matters of judicial rectitude the highest priority. On 11 November 1631, the court censured James McCarton, former sheriff of Co. Down, for threatening jurors in a case involving the claim of tithes owed to a local priest. The jurors doubted there was any just contract or debt owed in law, but the sheriff made them fast for several days and they finally capitulated, finding for the priest. The sheriff, apparently still dissatisfied with their performance, extorted fees from the repentant jurors without just cause.[85]

While the court of castle chamber laboured to punish official malfeasance at the local level, from the perjury of a clerk in the council of Connacht, to the extortion of collectors, the tribunal also punished malefactors who interfered with the administration of justice.[86] The court censured numerous defendants who attempted to subvert the work of sheriffs in the countryside, giving a kind of *ex*

81. Ibid., f. 83.
82. Ibid., f. 88v.
83. Ibid., f. 88.
84. BL, Add. MS 47,172, ff. 276–77. Fitzgibbon was acquitted in king's bench, and the censures of that court against the defendants in castle chamber were allowed to remain in force.
85. TCD, MS 852, f. 86v.
86. Ibid., ff. 85v, 94v.

post facto protection to the difficult work of imposing crown policy on a truculent and often unruly population.[87] In addition to its scrutiny of civil and military officials, the court extended its purview to the behaviour of ecclesiastical administrators, including bishops, local vicars and clerical staff. For example, the court censured the bishop of Killaloe in 1611 for providing Sieve Ny Carroll with fraudulent support for her claim of legitimate paternity on behalf of her bastard son, Christopher Blount. The mother had approached the bishop in Co. Clare to obtain such documentation for her suit in Co. Monaghan, but Bishop Maurice repented of his cooperation and the court lightened his punishment.[88] Lord Deputy Fitzwilliam took offence at the bishop of Leighlin in 1594, fining him in castle chamber for defying the viceroy over the appointment of a schoolmaster in his diocese. The bishop impudently claimed the chief governor had no jurisdiction and he would not accept Caesar's rule there, but he later apologized and his fine was reduced.[89] On 5 May 1592, the court fined and imprisoned the vicar of St Michael's in Co. Longford, Donogh McCary, for perjury.[90] And the celebrated case, mentioned above, of Henry Bird, register of the court of ecclesiastical causes, led the court into a maze of contradictions. Lord Deputy Perrot demanded the prosecution of Bird for forging his signature to a series of pardons, based on the testimony of a priest, Sir Denis O'Roghan. Perrot had ordered the documents to be written carefully into the entry book as evidence. Bird was condemned by the court in 1585, even though some argued the cause should more properly have been handled in an ecclesiastical tribunal. The privy council in England demanded that the verdict be reversed when Perrot himself was on trial in England for treason, and Bird was duly restored to office, his honour besmirched.[91]

As we have seen above in the campaign against recusancy, the court of castle chamber asserted a role in the implementation of Reformation policies. Apart from the recusancy issues identified above, however, this claim of responsibility for church administration was applied fitfully and was, primarily, a reaction to notable cases tinged with riot or subversion. On 1 June 1608, for example, the court heard the case of Thomas Meredith, vicar of Balrothery, Co. Dublin, against James Barnewell and other defendants accused of riot. During the height of Chichester's anti-recusancy campaign, on Sunday, 1 November 1607, Barnewell prepared to attend the funeral of his mother in Meredith's church. According to the testimony, the service was to be held in 'idolatrous' fashion which Meredith foolishly opposed, causing some 200 persons assembled at the church to assault the vicar and his pregnant wife. Barnewell and others were found guilty of the

---

87. Ibid., ff. 92, 92v.
88. BL, Add. MS 47,172, ff. 179–81. The bishop had signed and sealed the depositions of witnesses in the case.
89. Ibid., f. 114. The case was heard in castle chamber on the charge of disloyal speeches arising from the bishop's assertion of his ecclesiastical jurisdiction, a dangerous challenge to the statutory authority for the erection of schoolhouses and a repudiation of the lord deputy's warrant.
90. Ibid., f. 102.   91. Ibid., ff. 79–81, 90v–92.

riot, though most of the defendants were dismissed for lack of evidence. The gratuitous naiveté of Meredith went unnoticed by Chichester's court, though his predecessor would surely have commented on the lofty contempt shown to the grieving son and his family.[92] In a similarly oblique punishment of a recusancy offence, the court censured David Verdon, a priest, for scandalizing the archbishop of Canterbury on 15 May 1618. Verdon had claimed Archbishop Abbot was committed to the Tower of London for treason, having stated James I was an illegitimate ruler who sought a contract of marriage with the Infanta of Spain to overthrow the English, uniting the crowns in a single Catholic regime.[93] In an action of slander and sedition, heard on 29 May 1611, the court punished Symon Paulee for having published the news in Dublin that James I planned to make a declaration of toleration of religion in return for certain sums of money. Paulee was to be whipped from the Castle bridge to the Newgate prison, set on the pillory with his ears nailed to the device, and imprisoned in the Grate, a dungeon located in Dublin Castle.[94] While the court lacked a mandate to prosecute religious offences, and did so rarely under Elizabeth I, it became clear after 1603 that castle chamber might amplify its substantial purview to include the enforcement of the Reformation. A Protestant inquisition soon followed, as we have seen above, in the face of an intensified Counter-Reformation crusade led by priests and friars throughout the kingdom of Ireland. On 24 May 1620, the court convicted Patrick Plunkett of receiving a barrel of popish books and pictures from Jesuit priests 'knowne to be most malignant opposite to his Maties Civill government and the true Religion'.[95] The court of castle chamber provided only intermittent enforcement of the ban on seditious books, hearing only a handful of cases in the period.[96] On the other hand, the court took up the uncontroversial and non-sectarian case of the widow Jane Hamilton for forging the will of her dying husband, asserting its jurisdiction directly in support of the court of the prerogative and faculties of the diocese of Armagh, on 2 May 1632.[97]

In their important collection of essays on women in early modern Ireland, Mary O'Dowd and Margaret MacCurtain edited a valuable compendium that can be used to assess the status of women before the court of castle chamber. While

---

92. Ibid., 151–52.   93. Ibid., f. 270.

94. Ibid., f. 171.

95. TCD, MS 852, f. 91. See Ford, *Protestant reformation*, pp. 194, 204, 206–07; Colm Lennon, 'Mass in the manor house: the Counter Reformation in Dublin, 1560–1630', pp. 112–26; and J. Murray, 'The diocese of Dublin in the sixteenth century' in James Kelly and D. Keogh, eds., *History of the Catholic diocese of Dublin* (Dublin, 2000), pp. 99–109. Dr Gillespie's recent study of 'religiosity' in Catholic Ireland emphasizes the stability of communal life, describing 'a series of religious accommodations, though not compromises, … made at local level to ensure that religion was not a disruptive force'. R. Gillespie, *Devoted people: belief and religion in early modern Ireland* (Dublin, 1997), p. 4.

96. See M. Pollard, *Dublin's trade in books, 1550–1800* (Oxford, 1989), p. 12. No order from castle chamber that required the archbishop of Dublin to license books has been found in the records.

97. TCD, MS 852, f. 87v.

the castle chamber court did not figure prominently in their essay, it is clear from the records that female litigants were frequently before the tribunal, in a variety of guises. As Kenneth Nicholls has shown, women of property possessed certain basic rights in law and often sued to protect their estates. Nicholls detailed the comparative treatment of women at common law and in brehon law, finding that legitimacy of birth and written contract became the hallmarks of legally binding covenants to transfer property, though common law vested the wife's moveable property entirely in her husband.[98] In Ireland, the testator could not disinherit a wife or children, as their portions were lawfully determined by thirds. Nicholls suggests there was a mixed law in the Pale and elsewhere during the Tudor period, whereby women could be accepted as witnesses. Noble women could act as agents for their husbands and arbitrate in property disputes, use their share in lands to endow sons with marriage portions, and enter jointly into leases.[99] The payment of dowry by the father or family of a wife was sanctioned by canon law, as well as by Gaelic and civil law. Gaelic law allowed for divorce and repudiation of wives, so the Irish chancery court heard suits to regain dowries in kind well into the 1590s.[100] By the late sixteenth century, the English type of jointure, enjoyed exclusively by the widow during her life, was well established among the Irish, though there was pressure on women to release their claims to agnatic male heirs.[101] Dr Gillespie has shown that Irish women were less often prosecuted for crime than in England, though they appeared with some frequency at the castle chamber. Indictments for witchcraft were very few, and accusations of the notorious 'scold' and keeping of bawdy alehouses, especially by widows, were limited to the local venues. The socially cohesive Irish village managed its own problems of deviance, through the arbitration of Catholic clergy or the intervention of local lords in their courts leet and baron.[102]

Dr O'Dowd has recently determined that the Irish chancery court 'provided women with legal redress which would have been denied them at common law', although the Irish court lacked the procedural refinements with which the English chancery operated.[103] While married women could not sue at common law in their own name, chancery allowed women to sue independently in equity, the same legal principle used by the court of castle chamber. O'Dowd argues that the impact of chancery on the legal status of women in Ireland was to improve their rights to dower and estates in land, challenging the Gaelic practice of partible inheritance by which women were commonly excluded.[104] The substantial archive

---

98. K. Nicholls, 'Irishwomen and property in the sixteenth century' in M. O'Dowd and M. MacCurtain, eds., *Women in early modern Ireland* (Edinburgh, 1991), p. 17.

99. Ibid., pp. 18–19.

100. Ibid., p. 21.   101. Ibid., p. 24.

102. R. Gillespie, 'Women and crime in seventeenth-century Ireland', in O'Dowd & MacCurtain, eds., *Women in early modern Ireland*, pp. 43–48.

103. M. O'Dowd, 'Women and the Irish chancery court in the late sixteenth and early seventeenth centuries', *IHS*, xxi (1999), 470, 487.

104. Through this means, the Gaelic family holdings could be alienated by a widow who subsequently

of the chancery court, containing roughly 5,000 documents in a period similar to that of the court of castle chamber, allows for a more meaningful statistical analysis. O'Dowd has found that approximately 22 per cent of the legible bills and answers included women litigants, of which some 13 per cent describe the woman as plaintiff, the majority of whom were married or widows.[105] Unsettled title in the seventeenth century offered opportunity for exploitation, so women with claims to property were 'often the catalyst for litigation by a woman jointly with her husband', though a widow might appear in chancery as executrix as well.[106]

Given the frequency of women as litigants appearing before the Irish chancery court, it is understandable that they sued before the court of castle chamber since it offered similar advantages. Nonetheless, it is surprising, in some respects, to see women before the court at all. Women could not appear on juries nor hold civil or military or ecclesiastical office, so they would not have appeared as respondents in any of these actions. However, as heiresses, mothers, and victims of crime, they appeared in fairly large numbers throughout the period. Women were rarely accused in actions of riot (only once), but their sometimes clumsy efforts to manipulate the conveyance of property embroiled them in legal actions, and, more rarely, their defiance of laws against recusancy brought them before the castle chamber as well. In what follows, a digest of the treatment of women before the court of castle chamber will be suggested as a topic for further research, despite the dearth of evidence in comparison to that for the chancery court. The absence of a court of requests in Ireland to hear suits of the poor may have influenced the appearance of women as suitors *in forma pauperis*, but there is not enough evidence to support a conclusion in this regard.[107]

Riot was alleged in the great majority of cases involving women as plaintiffs, a stratagem often used to attract the attention of the court for the heinous nature of the alleged crime. Jennet Sarsfield, the aged wife of the former lord chancellor, Thomas Cusake, appeared often before the court. Her husband had died in 1571, and a year later she sued Margaret Howth of Corballies, Co. Meath in castle chamber for abduction, a charge unaccompanied in the record book by sufficient evidence to explain the circumstances of the case. As a dowager of some substance and a member of two important Pale families, she alleged the abduction occurred on 4 October 1571, and Howth was condemned along with others in a hearing on 30 January 1572.[108] A similar abduction occurred in 1620 when Margaret Cusack

remarried, or by an heiress whose marriage might permanently remove property from the sept or clan. Ibid., 486.

105. Ibid., 472. About 38 per cent of female plaintiffs sued independently, most as widows. Some of the 5,000 documents are merely 'charred remnants' from the fire of 1922, and the chance remains offer primarily the original bills of complaint (75 per cent of the documents) detached from the required answers. No continuous record of a suit is therefore possible, though 'few cases reached the decree stage'. This judicial aridity mirrored the lapsed causes brought before the castle chamber court, for similar reasons. Ibid., 471–72.

106. Ibid., 473, 475.   107. Ibid., 475–78.

108. TCD, MS 852, f. 95v. The case was apparently joined with others against Richard Nugent and

(perhaps a relation by marriage) appeared as plaintiff against Martin Plunkett and others for a conspiracy to carry her away to be married. The rowdy malefactors had taken the plaintiff and held her for three days, but the court initially considered that the cause should be heard in king's bench. Unable to resist the opportunity to correct this violent breach of the peace, however, they proceeded to fine, pillory and imprison Martin and his colleagues for their 'disordinat filthey and coveteous desire, by evill, inhumane and barbarous violence to ymprove and advance [their] own private fortunes'.[109] The moral outrage of the court was barely suppressed when considering the abduction of Frances, daughter of Robert Pipho, from her own house in 1594. Edmund Sutton and others had come to the house after ten at night with weapons drawn, entered and took Frances along with a chest of the goods of Robert, then locked the doors so he could not pursue them.[110] John Pentnye, a merchant of Dublin, sued in court on 23 October 1577 for the abduction of his wife, Thomazine, in Co. Louth, but the court dismissed the case since the defendant, Lawrence Taafe, pleaded the queen's pardon.[111]

Although women were infrequently named as independent plaintiffs in actions before the castle chamber court, they were privileged to sue there on their own behalf, particularly if they were of means. For example, Mary Pentny, widow of the late Dublin alderman, John Malone, sued Richard Stevenson and four others in castle chamber on 12 June 1594 for an assault in which she was beaten on the head with a club by Stevenson at Kilmainham. The court censured the defendant with a fine of £5, despite the egregious circumstances.[112] Katherine Barrett of Ballencolly, apparently on her own behalf, lodged a bill of riot against Cormock McDermod of Blarney in Co. Cork for assaulting her estate and castle, called Castlenyhinche, along with some 200 persons 'by way of insurrectione' in 1589. The suit alleged, on behalf of Barrett's retainers, that the defendants besieged Castlenyhinche for three days, threatening to cut off the heads of her servants unless they surrendered it. The court found for the plaintiff on 25 January 1594, five years later, imprisoning McDermod and fining him the small sum of £10 for the riot, surely an indication that the allegations of violence were somewhat overstated in the pleadings while slenderly supported in testimony.[113] Dame Alyson FitzLyons was named as defendant along with a probable kinsman, Olyver FitzGerald, in a case heard on 27 November 1577, the court finding her guilty of

Francis Birmingham, since three cases of riot involving 'Lady Cusake' were ultimately dismissed along with many others in 1582. BL, Add. MS 47,172, ff. 69–69v, 74.

109. BL, Add. MS 47, 172, f. 81.
110. TCD, MS 852, f. 96. For a study of the ritualized scheming to obtain the hand of an heiress, secure a marriage portion or sue for jointure, see A.P.W. Malcomson, *The pursuit of the heiress: aristocratic marriage in Ireland 1750–1820* (Belfast, 1982).
111. BL, Add. MS 47,172, f. 21.   112. Ibid., f. 119.
113. Ibid., f. 112. Four days later, Edmond Barrett, probably the husband of Katherine, sued an extortion case stemming from another forcible entry of his castle and barony of Ballencolly. He had filed suit in a previous case against Andrew Barrett in castle chamber on 24 November 1592, by which he obtained a writ of restitution. Ibid., f. 121.

a riot along with other defendants, making Olyver responsible for all of their fines.[114] The next year, on 25 April 1578, Dame Alyson was again before the court of castle chamber. In this case, Sir Thomas Fitzwilliams of Merrion and John Finglas, gentleman, feoffees of trust for her late husband, Roger Finglas, acting for Dame Alyson, sued William Conton and others for perjury in a case arising from a contested lease in chancery. Dame Alyson alleged that Conton (one of the plaintiffs in her former suit) gave perjured testimony in court favouring Simon Luttrell of Busserdston, Co. Dublin. Luttrell had claimed that Dame Alyson leased him the property for 21 years. The court found against Dame Alyson yet again, dismissing the charges and confirming the chancery award of the lease to Luttrell.[115]

In numerous other cases, the wife of a plaintiff was mentioned in actions in castle chamber, alleging the gravity of the offence by showing physical harm to a woman. In most of these cases the female was not joined in suit. For example, in the assault on Francis Roe, mayor of Drogheda, Lady Roe suffered 'a great blow on her face in her owne house, when she came only to pacifye him [Christopher Draycott, the defendant]'.[116] In the case of Henry Bennett of Dunbard's Island, Co. Wexford, gentleman, an allegation of riot included testimony that the defendants, John Deverox and others, entered the castle and assaulted Maryon, Bennett's wife, 'Caused the said Maryon Bennett to be dragged out of the said Castle and threwe hir Downe a payre of stayres,' and other outrages.[117] As we have seen above, the pregnant wife of Thomas Meredith, Protestant vicar of Balrothery, was assaulted during the hotly contested funeral of James Barnwell's mother in Meredith's church, being thrown to the ground.[118] And Jenet, the wife of James Edwards, farmer, of Co. Dublin, joined in an information of riot against Nicholas Begg and others on 31 January 1610. James was lying sick in his bed when eight or more men entered his house, threw him in the street, and violently thrust out Jennet and her eight children. The defendants were made to pay twenty marks in damages to Edwards, in addition to fine and imprisonment.[119]

The mixed action, seeking remedy at law in a variety of ways, was typical of the litigation before the court of castle chamber. For example, the jointure of Dermot McCarthy's mother-in-law was at issue in a complaint adjudicated on 1 June 1627, alleging a riot in taking away a distress from her lands in Co. Cork. McCarthy sued Sir Valentine Browne and others for coming with a company in the night to take over 50 cattle for arrearages of rent, then beating the tenants of the estate so that they left the lands waste for three years, causing great economic damage that was, in truth, at the heart of the allegation of riot.[120] Chichester,

---

114. Ibid., ff. 25–25v.   115. Ibid., ff. 32v–33.

116. Ibid., f. 279. Draycott was fined £500 and forced to submit to Lady Roe on his knees at the next sessions held in Drogheda, to ask for her forgiveness for striking a lady of her dignity and worth. Ibid.

117. Ibid., f. 147. In the case heard on 6 February 1606, John Deverox was punished on behalf of the others, his retainers and sons.

118. Ibid., ff. 151–52.   119. Ibid., f. 165.

120. TCD, MS 852, f. 97.

acting independently of the court, pardoned a woman for manslaughter of her husband when he accepted the testimony of the justices that 'her said housband, in som passion or heate of love, Did him in uppon the kniffe, which this woeman held in her hands at that tyme, & so was guilty of his owne Death'.[121] The jointure of Lady Mabel, dowager countess of Kildare, was at issue in a case we have encountered before, when the venerable Pale attorney, Henry Burnell, was accused in 1609 of fraudulently altering the original conveyance of the earl to favour the countess over another claimant, Lady Lettice Fitzgerald, wife of Sir Robert Digby, who sued as the legitimate heir of the estate. While the countess was held not responsible for the forgery of the will, Burnell was punished for acts that allegedly took place a generation before at the earl's house in Maynooth.[122] This protracted litigation in numerous venues carried on by the Digbys was a *cause célèbre* of the early Jacobean court, and the skirmish conducted in castle chamber was but one instalment, one relying on witnesses' accounts of events that had occurred in 1566. The case certainly defines the willingness of landed families to carry on their disputes at law on behalf of women claimants, while the incumbent earl of Kildare was left to sue both women for collusion. He alleged they had brought the weak case by 'fainte pleadinge' to discredit the deed by which he had gained possession of the Geraldine earldom.[123] Another case involving the jointure of Katherine Handcock, wife of the late Richard Lynham of Adamston, Co. Meath, gentleman, was brought before the court of castle chamber as a corrupt verdict. The jurors in Co. Meath had found for the widow over the claim of young Thomas Lynham, son and heir of Richard, who was a minor and thus a royal ward. Plainly, the case involved crown rights and the court was determined to assert them, fining the jurors for finding 'against their evidence' and remanding the case to be heard in another forum.[124] In February 1617, John Dobb and his wife, Margaret Dobb of Dublin, sued Jane Dalway and her son, James Walsh, for conspiring to destroy the legitimate evidence of deeds and letters patents, conveying to Margaret, as daughter and sole heir, all the estates of the deceased John Dalway of Carrickfergus. The court convicted Jane Dalway, the widow of John, of seeking to forge a counterfeit deed and arranging with a Dublin merchant to take custody of the great trunk that contained the last will and testament of John. It would appear that Jane was a second wife whose own natural children she sought to favour on the death of her late husband.[125] The widow Jane Hamilton

---

121. Bodl., Carte MS 62, f. 285.
122. BL, Add. MS 47,172, f. 154. O'Dowd has shown that the lack of a statute of uses in Ireland until 1635 made possible the conveyance of an estate by entail, using feoffments and jointures to assure provision for a spouse. O'Dowd, 'Women and Irish chancery', 483. Lettice was the daughter and heir of Lord Gerald, eldest son of the late earl, and a ward of the queen, who had married the Englishman Digby.
123. BL, Add. MS 47,172, f. 160. The earl's case against the countess and Lady Lettice was dismissed by the court on 3 February 1609.
124. Ibid., ff. 44v–45v.
125. Ibid., f. 261. The court left validity of the feoffment itself to trial at law in another forum.

was convicted in May 1632 of a similar forgery, in which she coerced her dying husband, William, to sign a codicil on his deathbed, effectively disabling the plaintiff, John Hamilton, from serving with her as executor of the will.[126]

Female representation at the bar of justice, both as plaintiffs and defendants, was largely a reflection of social class. The most egregious example of women as victims before the court of castle chamber was reported extensively in the brutal case of Lord Howth, noted above, who was convicted of beating his wife and daughter, causing them to lie sick and his daughter to lose her life. The case also implicated his butler, Nicholas Terrell, who assisted Howth in his unnatural cruelty and procured for him the company of a Dublin prostitute, Elizabeth Brymingham, then lied about the liaison.[127] The court of castle chamber prosecuted Terrell for perjury on 22 May 1579, before turning to the case of his master in July. Howth was accused of beating his fifty-year-old wife with a staff, flogging his butler for being over-familiar with his spouse, and striking his thirteen-year-old daughter over thirty times so that she fell ill and died of an ague. The court fined him for each offence (a total of £1,000, reduced in subsequent procedings of the court).[128] The two cases illustrate the Dublin court's genuine concern for matters of social violence, particularly those involving members of the aristocracy, expanding its putative jurisdiction to include cases that would normally have come before the king's bench, and using prerogative justice to supply a remedy when the facts of the case might not support a common law indictment (for manslaughter in this instance).

On the other hand, ordinary women were prosecuted at the local level for a myriad of lesser offences, and appeared as petitioners in a wide variety of cases before the lord deputy, few of which ever came before the court of castle chamber. The splendid Corporation Book of Youghal, mentioned above, details the local offences involving women, such as Ellen Magner, who kept misrule in her tavern; the frequent offence of deflowering young virgins, punished by fines levied by the corporation; and the wife of Edmond O Brynne accused as a 'notable scold'.[129] Judging from the heightened concern over ravishment of women expressed by Richard Bolton in his study of the statutory relationship between England and Ireland, we may assume that abduction was a frequent offence. Bolton sought legislative assurance that multiple forms of deceit and collusion would be prohibited in law in the aftermath of a sexual offence. He drafted a statutory remedy based on numerous scenarios, citing previous statutes of force in Ireland and England:

> If any man from hence foorth ravish any woman married, Lady, Damsell or other, with force where she did not Consent, neither before nor after, he shale have Judgment of life & member: And likewise where a man ravished a woman married, lady, Damsell or other with force, although she Consent

126. TCD, MS 852, f. 87v.   127. BL, Add. MS 47,172, ff. 39–39v.
128. Ibid., ff. 41v–43.
129. *Corporation book of Youghal*, ed. Caulfield, pp. 5, 30–31.

afterwards he shall have Judgment as aforesaid … [and] in Case the wife will fully forsake her husband & goe away & Continue with the Adulterer she shall be barred forever of action to demand her dower that she ought to have of her husbands estate if she be Convict[ed] thereuppon.[130]

Perhaps the most celebrated case of Wentworth's regime involved his aggressive suit against Lord Chancellor Loftus over the estate of Frances Rush, the wife of Loftus's eldest son, who also happened to be the sister-in-law of his brother, George.[131] Wentworth received hundreds of petitions seeking redress, some of which might have found their way to castle chamber court in earlier guises, but the records of Wentworth's court are largely missing. For example, on 20 June 1638, Wentworth heard the petition of Jennet White, widow of Rowland Plunkett of Co. Meath, esquire, who had recently re-married James White, 'takeing him to be a very careful Man and to have much joye and comfort of him in this her great age'. Jennet sued to regain her lost estate, claiming that White defrauded her, leaving her and her children nothing to live on while appropriating all the property of her late husband. Wentworth ordered James White 'to appear forthwith before us', but the venue of the castle chamber court was not mentioned and the viceroy often determined cases of this sort in his own peremptory fashion.[132] Wentworth took up cases in other venues that had formerly been adjudicated at castle chamber, employing for this purpose, for example, the committee for plantation affairs. In the case of Dorraghan McCoog and his wife, Margaret, their suit for possession of a house or cottage on the grounds of their castle of Newtown in Co. Galway, was referred to the plantation committee. The house had descended to Margaret, as sole daughter and heir of Hugh O'Madden, gentleman, but McCoog alleged that Daniel O'Madden and his wife, another Margaret, by the procurement of Donagh O'Madden, gentleman, entered the house and forcibly detained it. Despite an indictment before the justices of the peace, the O'Maddens wrested possession of the property from the tenants of McCoog, who claimed quiet title for fourteen years after the death of Margaret's father. The charge of riot would normally have gained the attention of the court of castle chamber, but Wentworth, who heard the petition on 20 June 1638, chose another executive committee of the Irish council to adjudicate upon the cause.[133] On 27 June 1638, Wentworth agreed to hear the cause of Elizabeth Talbott, sister of Adam Talbott, who petitioned on her behalf for remission of fees unlawfully withheld from her by the subsheriff of Co. Dublin. The small sum of £5 was at issue and the principle of enforcing the

---

130. TCD, MS 843, p. 72. The parliament in 1639 gave 'An act against Carnall knowledge of women Children [girls]' a third reading before deciding not to proceed with the legislation as written. TCD, MS 615, ff. 3–4.

131. The viceroy was charged by Loftus with being both accuser and judge in the case, heard before the members of the Irish council in 1638. *Strafforde's letters*, ed. Knowler, ii, 160–72, 176, 196, 227.

132. NAI, MS 2448, p. 22.

133. No further record of the disposition of the case exists. Ibid., pp. 11–12.

upright administration of justice against the allegedly corrupt defendant, William Pallice, would have ensured that such a case would normally have come before the court of castle chamber.[134] Wentworth agreed to hear a case against Dame Elizabeth Slingsby of Co. Sligo in July 1638, on a petition from her son-in-law William Dodwell, the high sheriff of the county, for trying to subvert her own daughter from the Protestant religion. The petitioner claimed that Dame Elizabeth came to his wife while he was away in Dublin, along with a priest, her two sons and another daughter. Seeking to 'regain her' to the church of Rome by 'perplexing her conscience' with books from the priest, they carried her away from his house. The anxious suitor sought the protection of the court for his wife's 'conscience' and punishment of the malefactors, three of whom had since fled the country. Though properly a matter for ecclesiastical courts, Wentworth took up the cause and demanded Lady Elizabeth attend him in Dublin for a hearing.[135]

The court of castle chamber heard numerous cases alleging scandal, usually brought by the law officers of the crown. These cases involved some public disgrace of civil or ecclesiastical officials or peers of the realm, thereby touching the sovereign in his or her regalian rights. While the possibility of expanding this category of litigation in order to terrorize opponents of the government was very real, the number and variety of actions were probably no greater than in England in the same period. Outrages to personal honour were notoriously *causes de guerre* among the aristocracy, so this class of suits was limited to persons of substance who balanced a delicate vulnerability to public shame with a careful sense of who was shaming them.[136] As the court took up a variety of breaches of the peace, it might well become involved in accusations of scandal while adjudicating a case of riot, such as the affray between Lord Howth and Sir Roger Jones in Dublin.[137] Normally, however, the scandals involved persons of higher rank and engaged the castle chamber in defending the honour of the state. Four cases of scandal against Elizabeth I were heard at castle chamber during the crises of the last decade of the Tudor century, each involving malicious words used against the queen. On two successive days in 1591 the court punished a gentleman named John Delahide for calling the queen a 'piskitchen'; and a husbandman named John Beagham for calling her a 'barren drone', the latter term in Irish.[138] In November 1593, Nicholas White of Co. Kildare was convicted of disloyal speeches for relating a prophecy that O'Donnell would be king in Ireland, noting an ancient crown in Rome was being sought by the Catholic bishops for this purpose.[139] On 31 January 1588, the court convicted Alexander Plunket of publicly anticipating the coming of the Spanish, by saying all the Irish would join them against the queen.[140] In 1597 the court found Captain John Norris guilty of using false and slanderous words against the queen, fining him £500 and sentencing him to prison for life.[141]

134. Ibid., p. 66.   135. Ibid., p. 128.
136. J. Kelly, *'That damn'd thing called honour': duelling in Ireland 1570–1860* (Cork, 1995), pp. 12–20.
137. Ibid., p. 27.   138. TCD, MS 852, f. 98v.
139. BL, Add. MS 47,172, f. 111.   140. Ibid., f. 89.   141. Ibid., f. 128.

The priest David Verdon was condemned for slandering the archbishop of Canterbury in 1618, and obliquely maligning the king (see above for details).[142]

As we have seen, the viceroys themselves regarded their position as a kind of regency in Ireland, so any hint of scandal against their reputation was punished severely. Perrot and Wentworth were particularly exercised by malicious accusations, and Lord Deputy Falkland had the attorney general present an information against Thomas Velden, a gentleman of Co. Meath, for reproaching the cess of the lord deputy's troops in June 1627. Velden told the soldiers they should be hanged for taking purveyance after Falkland had left his office, adding that a viceroy had been executed in the past for exceeding his instructions. Falkland and the court fined Velden £500 and had him pilloried in each of the four courts when they were in session.[143] Finally, cases of scandal against peers of the realm were brought before the court in rare instances, usually involving some questions of public policy. The case against Richard Browne, a gentleman of Bromyard, England, found him guilty of falsely stating the duke of Buckingham had been incarcerated in the Tower for, as we have already noted, sending a basin and ewer to the king of Spain.[144] In similar vein, one Humphrey Walsh was convicted in 1624 of spreading the false rumour that the earl of West Meath would be king in Ireland, even though the falsehood apparently began in an otherwise innocent conversation with a Scottish boy of fourteen years of age.[145]

Classifying suitors by family origin risks compounding the difficult questions surrounding Irishness and the Catholic religion in the early modern period. Defining the native Irish in terms of the spelling of their names in the court records is itself hazardous and incomplete; it may conceal the intermarriage of Irish and Old English families; and such a technique risks distortion since we often know nothing whatever about the litigants save their names in this record. The identity of the Old English, with recognizable names like Plunkett, Dowdall and Dillon and Talbott in the Pale, is nonetheless made difficult because they shared the same family origins as the New English. Consequently, this category is a rough approximation of the litigation of these suitors before the court. The native Irish appeared rarely as plaintiffs, and were named in numerous cases where upwards of ten other defendants were grouped in an accusation of riot or a charge against jurors of failing to present recusants.[146] This is not to say, how-

---

142. TCD, MS 852, f. 99.
143. Ibid., f. 99v. See also *Strafforde's letters*, ed. Knowler, ii, 332, 340. On 6 August 1639, Wentworth wrote to the king as follows: 'It is wonderful, how Men are inclined now-a-days to report all wherein I am concerned to the worse Sense … For I have been therein all along so damnably abused, as is almost above Patience to be born, and hath, to speak truth, more vexed me, than any Thing that ever befel me in all my Life.' Ibid., p. 376.
144. TCD, MS 852, f. 99. Browne was highly intoxicated, but the court refused to consider this as a mitigating circumstance. The case was heard in 1628, the year of Buckingham's assassination.
145. Ibid., f. 99v. Walsh spoke with the boy on the highway near Oldcastle, then foolishly spread the rumour in a subsequent conversation in Co. Cavan.
146. The first two cases in the entry book contained the names of some 83 defendants in linked cases, of whom 51 may be described as native Irish. BL, Add. MS 47,172, ff. 1–1v.

ever, that the native Irish were victimized by the court, since numerous examples could be cited of the punishment of Old English administrators for disadvantaging native Irish subjects of the crown. For example, on 28 August 1576, the court ordered the seneschal of Co. Wexford, Thomas Masterson, to cease harassment of the estates and retainers of Brian McCahir McArt Cavanagh, pending adjudication of matters in dispute between them.[147] On 19 May 1587, Ross O'Ferrall, gentleman, of Co. Longford was sued by his kinsman, Irriell O'Ferrall, sheriff of the county, for a riot and affray during which an accused traitor, Manus McShane O'Rourke, was allowed to escape. Ross alleged that Manus was a dutiful subject who had been a guest in his house.[148] And in 1605, Cahir O'Callaghan, a gentleman of Co. Cork, won a verdict against John Barry, the sheriff of the county, along with Brian McOwen and Conagher O'Callaghan, both gentlemen, for a riot in dispossessing Cahir of the castle of Dromynyn.[149] For the most part, however, native Irish were found in long lists of defendants in the cases of recusancy and riot, a tendency increased after the accession of James I in 1603. The admixture of both Old English and native Irish as suitors was also commonplace, as in the suit for defrauding the court brought against Sieve ny Carroll and her illegitimate son, Christopher Blount, for asserting his claim to the inheritance of her former lover.[150] Dr Ellis has recently argued that Gaelic Ireland was subsumed within a 'unitary kingdom of Ireland' as a result of the Tudor 'conquest' and that the 'mere Irish' enjoyed the full protections of English land law and administration, concluding 'Irish Gaeldom was anglicised more quickly and thoroughly than its Scottish counterpart'.[151] Dr Edwards, in contrast, has claimed that Gaelic lords like Barnaby Fitzpatrick, baron of Upper Ossory, signed agreements with the government which he cynically planned to void in practice, exploiting his role as an English-educated courtier while maintaining all the trappings of Gaelic lordship including the maintenance of brehon lawyers in his courts.[152]

Old English suitors appeared before the court of castle chamber as both petitioners and respondents throughout the period, since they were most likely to be residents of the Pale, local officials, recusant jurors, and members of the landed aristocracy. Until the seventeenth century, they were also to be found among the judiciary on the court itself. The New English litigants were summoned often as soldiers and civil officials, but the records do not show a pattern of judicial combat

---

147. Ibid., ff. 14–16.   148. Ibid., ff. 84–84v.

149. Ibid., f. 135.

150. Ibid., f. 179 . See also the case of *David Fitzgibbon* v. *Gerald and Gibbon FitzMorris, Nicholas Freeman, Donnogh O'Grady, Edmond Schoole, and others* for soliciting and embracing jurors in the king's bench. Ibid., f. 276.

151. S.G. Ellis, 'The collapse of the Gaelic world, 1450–1650', *IHS*, xxxi (1999), 468–69.

152. Edwards, 'Collaboration without anglicisation', pp. 79–81. His description of the glacial pace of accommodation, mixing hospitality for English judges with resistance to shiring Ossory within Kilkenny, balances the competing priorities of an Elizabethan lordship, though he exaggerates the extent of Fitzpatrick's 'military independence'. Ibid., p. 94.

between the *arriviste* planter class and the incumbent landowners. Among the most numerous Old English suitors were merchants from the loyal towns, who used the forum to defend their interests, both mercantile and personal. Denys Byrne, a merchant of Dublin, sued John Wolverston, Edmond McCavenagh, Donogh O'Broe, Edmond O'Doran, Patrick Neveagh and others for driving away thirty cows from his lands in Balleneparke, depriving his poor tenants of their only means of subsistence.[153] Another Dublin merchant, John Cage, was fined £200 for falsely accusing a privy councillor, Sir Edward Brabazon, of seizing the goods of a fugitive for debt and taking them into his own possession.[154] New English litigants often appeared at the court in the guise of reckless adventurers instead of cunning advocates. Sir Richard Graham and his brother Thomas were fined £10 each and imprisoned for threatening a commission of inquiry into their concealed lands in Co. Wicklow. They were convicted of beating witnesses, drawing their swords upon Charles Valentyne, gentleman, and threatening the king's counsel, Peter Delahyde, declaring they would pull the beard from his face.[155] Thomas Brookes, a soldier of Dublin, was convicted of making disloyal and contemptuous speeches, saying he cared not for the queen, the mayor of Dublin or the queen's watch.[156] In some cases, the New English battled each other, bringing their quarrels to the attention of the court of castle chamber. The assault of Charles Egerton, constable of Carrickfergus castle, upon Captain Ryce Mansfield – an episode already mentioned above – involved a notorious affray among the crown's servants.[157] The most common, and familiar, pattern that emerges from an analysis of cases based on family origins is that members of an extended family frequently sued one another for the estates, titles and chattels of their kinsmen. Both the earls of Kildare and Clanricarde were engaged in these contentions at the court of castle chamber, suggesting that the rule of law brought potential combatants from the field of battle to the courts of law in this period.[158] The role of the court of castle chamber as a civilizing agent for a violent society is distorted, in part, since allegations of riot were often exaggerated to gain the attention of the court. Yet, in 1604, Hadsor urged the new king that 'Noblemen and cyvill Gentry of quallity [being] Natives of the Country whose posterity the good or evill estate of that Realme shall most concerne, being capable thereof, may be used as Councellors of estate'.[159]

Finally, we must acknowledge, as Dr Barnes has shown for the Jacobean court of star chamber in England, that most of the suits initiated at the court were

153. BL, Add. MS 47,172, f. 187.
154. Ibid., f. 198.
155. Ibid., f. 189.
156. Ibid., f. 105.
157. Ibid., f. 127.
158. Ibid., ff. 154–59, 172–77. The work of Lawrence Stone on the English aristocracy has not been replicated for the Irish social élite, despite the substantial promise such an enterprise would offer. See Stone, *The crisis of the aristocracy, 1568–1640* (Oxford, 1965).
159. 'Hadsor's "Discourse"', ed. McLoughlin, 350. Hadsor added that men of Scotland, England and Ireland should be employed on the king's 'grand Councell of estate', meaning the privy council in England, suggesting the need for men 'of good experience in Ireland and well affected to the Country and the people thereof'. Ibid., 353.

crossing or collateral actions involving property[160]: for example, the Kildare case in castle chamber, already noted, in which Henry Burnell, the dowager countess's attorney, was accused of concealing a forgery of her jointure and thus defrauding Lady Lettice Fitzgerald of her inheritance.[161] Naturally, cases involving property brought litigants of some substance before the court, so the majority of instances involved merchants or landowners. As Barnes has indicated, most star chamber suits pursued 'essentially civil ends, albeit in criminal raiment'.[162] Crimes against property might take the form of forgery, fraud, extortion, embezzlement, disseisin and distraint of goods, abduction of heiresses, defamation, destruction of weirs and other chattels, forcible entry and numerous other charges. Crimes against the state involving riot were often, as we have seen, merely shoring actions to support other contentions involving property, and actions involving conspiracy were exploited to implicate witnesses or to impeach their testimony. Barnes portrays the subtlety thus:

> 'Riot' in Star Chamber proceedings had become virtually a term of art, an allegation for procedural advantage more often than a substantive charge ... The principal function of the Court of Star Chamber for the Jacobean litigant was to mount a collateral attack, either to shore up or to cross an action in another court, in furtherance of a large-scale strategy of litigation with the objective of winning a substantial prize. That prize was some form of property.[163]

Property cases and other suits were brought to the court from locations all over Ireland, though the castle chamber venue was most frequented by petitioners from the capital. From the extant evidence of some 260 orders and decrees, 15 per cent of cases originated in the city of Dublin (41); 10 per cent in Co. Dublin (27); and approximately 46 per cent came to the court from five counties of the Pale (120).[164] However, almost all the Irish counties were represented by at least one castle chamber suit before 1641.[165] The shiring of Ireland and the implementation

---

160. Barnes, 'Star chamber litigants', pp. 12–22.
161. BL, Add. MS 47, 172, ff. 154–59.
162. Barnes, 'Star chamber litigants', p. 13.
163. Ibid., p. 15. Guy has found a similar result for the early Tudor court of star chamber, with title to property involved in 41 per cent of the cases, though he argued 'the Elizabethan court did not try titles after the opening years of the reign had passed'. Guy, *Star chamber*, pp. 52, 57.
164. Data was compiled from the entry book of orders and decrees (to 1620), supplemented by information from TCD, MS 852 (to 1632) and a few cases from the Wentworth era. Evidence from the last decade would probably have changed the profile of cases to reflect greater concern with the provinces, particularly those areas being considered for new plantation such as Galway and Wicklow. Litigation from the Pale, Co. Wexford and Co. Cork remained consistent throughout the period, though a surge of new cases after 1603 was noted from Co. Tipperary (15) and Co. Wicklow (9).
165. The exceptions were Kerry, Clare, Fermanagh and Tyrone. Only twenty of 32 counties were named in cases before the court prior to 1603.

of assize circuits did much to bring this about. On the other hand, the liberties and franchises were often quasi-independent, reluctant to allow the embrace of castle chamber jurisdiction, while the Ulster plantation generated business for the committee on plantations rather than the castle chamber.[166] Dr Ohlmeyer has indicated the success of the earl of Antrim in bringing his suits directly to the attention of the crown and resisting the intrusion of assize judges in his territories, just as the O'Neills had done before him.[167] Distant counties with a predominantly native Irish population rarely appeared on the rolls of the court, though the sheriff of Co. Donegal, Oliver Scurlocke, was punished on 6 February 1605 for demanding ten shillings from every household that grazed cattle 'on the montaynes'.[168] The principal port towns and their respective hinterlands generated much of the business of the castle chamber court. Cork, Galway and Kilkenny provided most of the litigation, with fewer cases coming from Waterford and Youghal. The presidency courts sought to become the court of first instance for cases in the provinces, with some success, but issues of jurisdiction plagued relations with local officials in both Munster and Connacht. Among the new counties shired after 1603, Wicklow, Mayo and Down sent the most cases to the court of castle chamber, while Wexford set the standard with twenty cases, some 7 per cent of the total throughout the period.[169]

Finally, the enforcement of its orders and decrees bedevilled the court of castle chamber throughout its existence. Using fines and imprisonment as its principal means of punishment, abetted on occasion by the humbling of defendants at the pillory and accompanying mutilation, the court intended to 'terrify' malefactors. Yet, in many cases, the fines were nominal in amount, and nearly always the court allowed defendants to sue for a 'reduction' at the end of the term. While the prison was an unhappy detour for many convicted by the court, long sentences were usually mitigated in practice and even the degenerate Baron Howth was released and his fine reduced by half. The effectiveness of castle chamber decrees relating to property is difficult to trace, but the ongoing litigation by members of the peerage suggests that the court imposed interlocutory orders rather than definitive awards in these cases. Sending cases to arbitration was a favoured strategem, though, again, this tended to defer final resolution of each suit. The court occasionally revisited its own judgements, adjusting the award or the punishment, dismissing suits long pending, and, in rare circumstances, reversing itself. The lack of evidence prevents us from learning much about the post-litigation stage of orders and decrees, so the question of the court's effectiveness in resolving disputes cannot be answered satisfactorily. Litigants sued to receive just awards

---

166. See Edwards, 'Collaboration without anglicisation', pp. 85–91; Canny, *Making Ireland British*, p. 177.
167. Ohlmeyer, *Marquis of Antrim*, pp. 68, 91.
168. BL., Add. MS 47,172, f. 134.
169. Tipperary was not far behind with seventeen cases; Kilkenny was represented by fourteen cases in the period.

and expected a conclusive end to their complaints, but all early modern courts faced the problem of enforcement, lacking a police force and relying on local magistrates to compel compliance, often on their own neighbours. Measuring the effectiveness of the court by examining its end results is an elusive goal, but it should not bar the researcher from examining the question in its larger sense. The court of castle chamber heard petitions from all over the country, from all social classes and extended the ambit of its authority throughout the period, demonstrating that, at least, the court was an accessible instrument of prerogative justice. This is not to say, however, that determined local resistance in the form of Gaelic exactions, property relations and the keeping of kerne did not interrupt the process of legal and cultural assimilation, as Dr Edwards has recently shown in the case of the Fitzpatrick barons of Upper Ossory.[170]

ENFORCEMENT AND OPPOSITION

The court of castle chamber was partnered in a symbiotic relationship with the Irish privy council and this mutuality of function mixed policymaking with adjudication in a potentially explosive manner. The court was staffed by senior councillors, as we have seen, men who met as an indifferent tribunal to consider matters they had debated forcefully in the executive forum. Not surprisingly, the court was confronted by substantial opposition in its efforts to implement controversial policies set forth by the Irish council, from the critics of the cess in the 1570s to the advocates of the Queries in the 1640s. It is not the intention here to examine in detail the opposition to castle chamber, but rather, to study its reputation from the perspective of hostile external forces, grouped together to resist crown policies of various kinds. As we shall see, the core of each opposition movement was composed of Old English lawyers. While it is possible to see in these conservative blocs the politics of a nascent religious or nationalist resistance, the language and tone of the documents suggests, instead, that men like Burnell, Barnewall and Darcy intended to preserve their ancient inheritance by forcing the crown to accept the constitutional foundation for Irish rights to property, representation, judicial remedy and legislative autonomy. The history of the court was punctuated by constitutional crises, turbulent parliaments and commissions of inquiry. The court of castle chamber was frequently targeted at these times and a brief review of the issues will help to frame the interpretation of the Irish star chamber.

Lawyerly intransigence framed the debate over the cess from its origins in 1561–62, a decade before the inception of the court of castle chamber. Among the

---

170. Edwards, 'Collaboration without anglicisation', pp. 91–96. Bolton cited an array of condign punishments that could be employed by justices of the peace, such as the burning of a woman convicted of treasonable words against James I. At common law, a man could be hung, drawn and quartered for burning a house at night, or setting fire to a barn. However, castle chamber could not impose more than fine and imprisonment, despite the permitted use of torture during the interrogation of an accused. *Justice of peace for Ireland*, part III, pp. 12, 15.

law students who protested against the imposition of purveyance on the unwilling Pale were future leaders like Henry Burnell, Barnaby Scurlocke and Richard Netterville. In 1577 these native-born lawyers joined with the Pale aristocracy to campaign against Sydney's efforts to impose a radical new cess, designed to provide an extra-parliamentary source of revenue for the cash-strapped Dublin administration. Sydney and Gerrard strove to intimidate the Pale opposition by bringing an indictment against them in the court of castle chamber. In the first of these actions, Christopher Barnewall of Co. Meath was prosecuted on 21 May 1577 as foreman of a grand jury, alleging that he 'practised and devised howe he might touche and sclaunder the L deputie and Counsell for theire proceadinge with ymponinge of Cesse for the vyttlinge of the Soldiers and maintenance of the L deputies house'.[171] It was further alleged that he supported the journey of the lawyers to petition the queen against the cess, attempting to indict the lord deputy and council for illegally and 'extorcionslie' taxing the Pale, and slandering the viceroy by comparing his actions to those of Tressilian who was executed in the reign of Richard II for misinterpreting the laws.[172] Corrupt juries were frequently charged before the court of castle chamber, but rarely did they challenge the very foundations of prerogative right as administered by the Irish privy council. The court found that Barnewall had subverted the grand jury process, concealing his intentions from the other 'simple' jurors in his 'presompteous dealinge to touche the state, and namelie in a cause onelie concerninge the service of her matie which he can in no wise aunswere but rather practised of will to sowe discention, sclaunder the magistrate and hinder her matie of that which to her Roiall prerogative belongethe'.[173]

It was clearly the intention of the court of castle chamber to intimidate the opposition by this prosecution, imprisoning Barnewall and fining him £50 for his offence. This gambit failed, however, since the Palesmen temporized, bargained for time, offering numerous theoretical alternatives, while they appealed to the crown. Throughout the confrontation, the Pale lawyers drafted a number of position papers that took issue with the rights of the chief governor to tax the Palesmen. The three lawyers Burnell, Scurlock and Netterville responded to seven clauses, of which the first asked whether the chief governor, with the assent of the nobility and others of the Irish council, had customarily cessed the Pale for victuals at reasonable prices. They responded that the viceroy and council had done so for 29 years, but that the assent of the nobility was not always obtained, and the new cess imposed an onerous charge on the Pale due to higher prices for victuals and general dearth, concluding 'For that it is not accordinge unto the prescript rule of Law nor otherwise by any consent of those whose goodes are taken'.[174] Though Elizabeth imprisoned the agents of the Pale and closely interrogated them on the matter of the prerogative, she conceived doubts about Sydney's policy that were aggravated by the cautions of Ormonde and Kildare,

171. BL, Add. MS 47,172, f. 20. 172. Ibid.
173. Ibid. 174. TCD, MS 581, f. 45v.

and intensified by the scepticism of White and Gerrard on the Irish council itself.[175] Gerrard was sent to court by the Irish council to defend their actions, but he went beyond his instructions to seek a compromise with the obdurate Palesmen that would satisfy the queen.

Meanwhile, the court of castle chamber assumed the mantle of advocate for crown policy, fining the recalcitrant Palesmen and organizing a new form of purveyance. On 7 February 1578, the court took action against nineteen leaders of the Pale, acting by instructions received from the queen at the end of the previous October. The court cited the queen's order to call before them the nobility who refused to subscribe to the cess, then summoned the ringleaders to appear on 31 January, and read to them the royal instruction to 'allow of her Highness said prerogative of cess'.[176] Without their leader, Viscount Baltinglas, who pleaded sickness, the eighteen defendants sought additional time, and the next day offered a submission which the council found insufficient. A conference with the attorney general was then sought at which the two lawyers, John Netterville and Christopher Fleming, were joined by Lord Delvin and Nicholas Nugent, second baron of the exchequer. The compromise submission drafted by this group was rejected by the defendants after two further days of deliberation, and after a week of frustration all the defendants were fined by the court according to their ability to pay.[177] By taking upon itself the role of policy enforcer, the court compromised its judicial autonomy at an early stage in its development. The cess debate continued to bedevil future administrations well into the Perrot regime, causing the court to revisit its theoretical justification for taxation without representation on several occasions. By March 1578, the recall of Sydney was being rumoured and he left Ireland for the last time in the summer without having reached a final agreement with the Pale.

At the outset of the reign of James I in Ireland, the ports in Munster seized the opportunity to declare their corporate rights by refusing to declare James the lawful sovereign. Cork, in particular, took advantage of the unsettled aftermath of the Tyrone Rebellion to assert its municipal freedoms against the depredations of the soldiers stationed there, a reflection of the long decade of war and crisis rather than any formal declaration of independence. Prosecution in castle chamber of jurors who refused to convict William Meade, the recorder of Cork, for 'heynous treasons' was the first case in the reign of James I, heard in 1604.[178] Thereafter,

175. Brady, *Chief governors*, pp. 149, 152–57.
176. BL., Add. MS 47,172, f. 27 and see ff. 26v–28v.
177. Ibid. Viscount Baltinglas was excused by reason of sickness but the clerk of the court, Robert Kendall, was sent to him personally with the submission and he was to be fined £500 Irish if he refused to sign it. Two years later he was leading the rebellion in the Pale. Nugent was imprisoned and lost his seat on the bench in 1578 as a result, winning briefly the chief justiceship of common pleas in the next regime before losing his life after a questionable trial during the Baltinglas rebellion. The fines were imposed only on the landowners, but the lawyers for the defence were mentioned prominently in the trial, including the veteran adversary of the regime Barnaby Scurlocke, as well as Christopher Fleminge and John (or Richard) Misset.
178. Ibid., f. 130. See A.J. Sheehan, 'The recusancy revolt of 1603: a reinterpretation', *Archivium Hibernicum*, xxxviii (1983), 3–13.

the court of castle chamber acted against the corporate towns, depriving them of ancient freedoms and punishing their freely elected officers. Turning to Dublin itself, the Chichester regime pursued an aggressive anti-recusant policy designed to enforce religious conformity, using the court of castle chamber as the primary instrument of this sectarian tyranny. On 21 November 1605, the court fined and imprisoned nine leading Dublin aldermen for refusing to attend divine service, including in the entry book an extensive justification for their action that transcribed the full text of the proclamation.[179] The 'Mandates' requiring Old English Catholics to attend divine service sparked the second constitutional crisis of the period, one in which the Old English Palesman, Patrick Barnewall, took the lead. Barnewall and others sought an audience with the king to protest at the Irish council's mishandling of the new policy, asserting a traditionalist conservatism in the face of unrehearsed innovations by the chief governor. Charging the castle chamber court with operating unlawfully as a 'spiritual consistory', the opposition leaders, who included in their number the respected Henry Burnell, petitioned the crown directly and forced the court to engage in a lengthy and spirited justification of its work.[180]

In 'A Defence of the proceeding in the Castellchamber of Ireland upon the Mandates,' the court put forth a number of important arguments for prerogative justice. First, it asserted the right of the crown to demand that local officials attend the church in the presence of the lord deputy, as an 'ordinarie dutie of every Cittizen towards the Magestrate, especially of the Aldermen and best sorte of Cittizens'.[181] The 'Defence' argued that these were civil, and not spiritual, injunctions affirming the secular obedience to the crown 'and might have [been] done without preiudice to their Conscience', for which they were rightly punished in castle chamber.[182] The superior jurisdiction of the court was asserted over the attendance at divine service itself:

> the king being supreame head in Causes as well Ecclesiasticall as Civill his regal powre and prerogative doe extend as Lardge as doth his supremacy And the Statutes giveth power to Civill Maiestrates to enquire and punishe soe the same is become temporall or at least mixt and not meerly spirituall. Soe that since the kinge[s] prerogative in Causes of that Nature canne be gainesaid whie shold anie man demaund a former presedent of thexercise therof in speciall, When it Cannot be found that in [ms torn: either] of the kingdomes anie like Cause was at anie tyme since the Conquest given before.[183]

Citing Bracton as precedent, the court further defended its use of prerogative power to strengthen the common law at times when defiance of the law endangered the

---

179. BL, Add. MS 47, 172, ff. 137–40.
180. See McCavitt, *Chichester*, pp. 116–25; Pawlisch, *Davies*, pp. 108–15; BL, Add. MS 47,172, ff. 141–46, 148.
181. TCD, MS 843, p. 395.   182. Ibid.   183. Ibid., pp. 395–96.

viability of the judicial system itself. Finally, the 'Defence' justified the work of the court in pragmatic terms: 'And yet this Commaundement of the kinges extende not to Compell the hart and mind nor the religion of the partyes but onely the externall actes of the bodye which ought lawfully to be obeyed'.[184]

After nearly a decade of Chichester's inquisitorial policies, the parliament of 1613 witnessed a strongly worded petition that blamed much of the trouble on the court of castle chamber. In a list of the 'disorders' in civil government, the foes of the regime damned the practice of the Irish council in hearing causes between private parties, properly determinable by the ordinary course of law which was often suspended by warrant of the council. The petitioners added that 'in deciding of such causes at the council table, the same being put to voice (as the course ther is) the martial men (being the greatest number) having lessser skill, may over-rule the judges in law matters'.[185] They further challenged the star chamber practice of threatening jurors with prosecution there:

> it is great danger for any innocent man, if he be accused upon malice, or upon light ground of suspicion, the jurors being terrified through fear of imprisonment, of loss of their ears, and of their goods, may condemn him, and the rather for that it is an opinion publickly delivered, and maintained by the lord chief baron in the star chamber, that upon proof or evidence given by witness, the jurors are bound to go according to that, though it were contrary to their precise knowledge.[186]

The third constitutional crisis of the period evolved during the febrile administration of Lord Deputy Falkland, in which the Pale lawyers framed the debate around the restoration of fundamental rights called the Graces. Led by a group of Old English lawyers who resented their expulsion from the bar in 1614, an opposition movement appeared during the critical year 1628, when the Petition of Right was signed in England and the duke of Buckingham was assassinated. Among the most important assertions of the protagonists was the charge that the court of castle chamber had exceeded its authority, a challenge to prerogative justice itself. As Dr Clarke has shown, the negotiations for the Graces took place over three years, 1625–28, during a period of transition and instability.[187] Although they were finally confirmed by the crown in 1628, the parliamentary authorization by statute was frustrated by the incompetent Falkland who had

---

184. Ibid., p. 396. Dodging the accusation that the court merely enforced hypocrisy and engaged in sectarian compulsion, the author claimed that outward obedience was the standard it would accept. After two years of mutual recrimination in the courts of England and Ireland, the court of castle chamber suspended its prosecution of these cases, deferring a final decision on its legitimacy until the next reign. The Mandates are treated more fully in Part Two, Ch. 8.

185. *Desid. cur. Hib.*, i, 243.

186. Ibid. Petitioners also blamed the councillors who threatened jurors with star chamber in the assize courts, alleging they would rather accept a fine than serve on a jury.

187. Clarke, *Graces*, pp. 6–14.

failed to secure the proper review of proposed legislation according to Poynings' Law. For the conciliar court, the admonition to facilitate hearings of 'publique grievances' from gentlemen in the provinces who would 'modestly represent unto them misgovernment and abuses of the country where they are resident' was a direct criticism of judicial malfeasance by local officials.[188] Among the most important victories of the period was the reinstatement of the native-born Catholic lawyers to practice at the bar.[189] Article 43 of the Graces required that the court of castle chamber protect witnesses from malicious prosecution who testified in private suits at quarter sessions or assizes. If such witnesses were bound over to castle chamber by information against them, a relator was to be named to award damages to the witness in case the information against him or her were not proved.[190] Prosecution of jurors at castle chamber in cases of recusancy was not specifically mentioned, though the court was urged to limit its review of jurors' decisions to cases involving their 'corruption or partiality'.[191]

The penultimate challenge to the court of castle chamber arrived with the calling of the Irish parliament in 1640 and the constitutional defiance of the Dublin administration in the form of the Queries. On 20 November 1640, the humble remonstrance of the Irish house of commons against the government of Strafford was read to a committee of the English parliament. The second and third clauses condemned

> the Arbitrarie decision of all civill causes and controversies by paper peticons before the Lord Leivetennant and Lord Deputie and infinite other Judicatories uppon references from theim derived in the nature of all accons determinable at the Comon law, not lymited unto a certaine tyme, cause, reason or thing whatsoever.[192]

The grievances of the Irish parliament were soon translated into bills for enactment, seeking legal restraints upon the prerogative courts of high commission, wards and castle chamber in preference to the ancient courts of common law. The viceroy and Irish council were specifically enjoined not to hear private causes involving the lands or goods of loyal subjects. Citing the oppression of jurors in castle chamber and the intimidation of men's free conscience, the petition asked that

> his Matie may bee pleased to admitt the passinge of an Acte for prohibiteinge Jurors to bee bound to the Castle Chamber, or to bee their in any sorte questioned, except Combinacon Subornacon or other Corrupcon bee proved agt the Jurors soe bound over; And that the Evidence of persons convicte of Notorious offences & ill fame, bee noe byndinge Evidence to any

188. TCD, MS 672, f. 192v and see ff. 190–93.
189. TCD, MS 672, f. 193. See Ohlmeyer, 'Irish recusant lawyers', pp. 63ff.
190. Clarke, *Old English*, p. 251.   191. Ibid., p. 248.
192. TCD, MS 541, f. 83.

Jury to fynde agreeable to the testimony of such persons: ... And that noe Jurors in any case heerafter bee proceeded agt ore tenus nor bound over to appeare or be called into the Starchamber upon any pretence before the Informacon bee fyled of Record, And then a Subpena & the ordinary & subsequent proces to yssue & noe other compullsive course bee used, it beinge as is humbly conceaved contrary to lawe, yt that Subiecte should bee compelled or restrained to become bound to Aunswere matters of that kinde before there bee some presentement or informacon of Recorde to impeach them.[193]

The substance of accusations made by Pym and others against Strafford in November 1640 was that he 'Trayterously endeavoured to subvert the fundamentall Lawes and goverment of the Realmes of England and Ireland and instead thereof to introduce an arbitrary and tirannicall govermt against lawe'.[194] Specific charges were brought against him by his adversaries, including Cork and Loftus, for arbitrary proceedings in the court of castle chamber, whereby they were threatened, intimidated and dispossessed of their estates. Numerous other matters were introduced to show that Strafford corruptly subverted the process of the conciliar tribunal itself. In October 1635, he had ordered Dame Mary Hibbot, a widow, to relinquish her estate despite the majority opinion of the councillors then present. The property was conveyed to Sir Robert Meredith to the use of Strafford, according to the charge.[195]

The Queries were drawn up in Ireland by 13 February 1641 and delivered to the lords with the aim of indicting the Irish judges. In the context of accusations against Strafford's government, the Queries produced a fusillade of direct criticism against the court of castle chamber. While it is important to note that Patrick Darcy and the opposition lawyers who authored the document raised the issue of legislative independence for the Irish parliament, at least implicitly, Dr Perceval-Maxwell and others have rightly seen the twenty-one Queries as targeting specific measures and abuses to limit the arbitrary acts of the Irish council.[196] Moving through parliamentary committees simultaneously with the impeachment of four members of the Irish council, the Queries posed an immediate threat to conciliar government at a time when the court of castle chamber had practically ceased to operate. After affirming the rule of English common law in Ireland and the judicial imperative of allowing suitors to commence petitions freely in any of the king's courts, the authors attacked the basis for the conciliar tribunal itself.[197]

---

193. TCD, MS 808, f. 129. The king gave answer on 16 April 1641 to the grievances of the Irish parliament, offering a list of remedies to prohibit the 'extrajudiciall' hearings of the Irish council and the court of castle chamber. TCD, MS 808, ff. 135–36v, 138. The Irish legislation was never formally enacted owing largely to the subsequent crises of the rebellion in 1641.
194. TCD, MS 867, f. 4v.
195. Ibid., f. 303v. Strafford had initially recommended the petition of Thomas Hibbot against the widow.
196. M. Perceval-Maxwell, *The outbreak of the rebellion of 1641* (Toronto, 1994), pp. 172–76.
197. TCD, MS 843, pp. 63–64.

This challenge to the theoretical foundation of prerogative justice called into question the pattern of castle chamber decrees since the century began, and threatened to inculpate the justices of the court who, increasingly, under Wentworth, had exceeded their authority.

The Queries were vetted by parliamentary committee and when they were presented at nearly the same time as the impeachment of Bramhall, Lowther, Bolton and Radcliffe they had an explosive effect. Placing the Irish council immediately on the defensive, the opposition pressed its advantage, knowing it had the collaborative support of both Protestant and Catholic members of the parliament. Bramhall and Bolton penned defences of their actions in the Irish council and warned that the replacement of the lord chancellor as speaker would threaten the stability of the kingdom as well as the lawful proceedings of parliament. Three of the last charges in the Queries were inflammatory, accusing the court of castle chamber not merely of tyranny but of physical coercion. In an atmosphere of high drama, the charge of persecution denounced the humbling of jurors by the pillory and mutilation by branding or cutting off their ears after a fine in castle chamber.[198]

The response of the government was to temporize, proroguing the Irish parliament in August 1641 and playing for time while the Irish judges offered their timid responses to the robust challenge posed by Darcy and his colleagues. But the commencement of the Irish Rebellion in October 1641 brought a sudden end to the relevance of the Queries and the opportunity to resolve the central issues of prerogative law in relation to common law principles. In summary, the articulate and forceful opposition to practices of the court of castle chamber demonstrates both the viability of lawful resistance to excesses of prerogative justice and the ongoing dialogue in Ireland concerning fundamental questions of constitutional legitimacy. Peaceful opposition, led by native-born counsel for the Old English aristocracy, was thus a hallmark of the rule of law. As Dr McGrath has recently shown, the same lawyerly opposition became an effective force during the early years of the confederate association, led by Darcy, Nicholas Plunkett, Richard Martin and others.[199]

198. TCD, MS 615, no foliation (22 February 1641). A fuller study of the Queries in their context is taken up in Part Two of this work.
199. McGrath identified 104 men from the commons of 1641 who supported the confederate association, 33 of whom were admitted to the inns of court, and 14 to King's Inns. Nicholas Plunkett, counsel to the earl of Cork, was elected speaker of the confederate general assembly in 1642 and sat on every supreme council until 1649. Of him, McGrath wrote, 'Like the other old English lawyers, Plunkett was essentially a man of the gown, rather than the sword, and he worked consistently for a peaceful, legal solution to the problems in Ireland.' B. McGrath, 'Parliament men and the confederate association' in M. Ó Siochrú, ed., *Kingdoms in crisis: Ireland in the 1640s*, p. 100 and see pp. 91, 93, 96–100. See also Ohlmeyer, 'Recusant lawyers', pp. 78–84.

CONCLUSION

Part One has attempted to study the court in its bureaucratic matrix, examining the judicial framework for prerogative law in the period 1571 to 1641. In Part Two a chronological narrative treats the distinctive features of the court in relation to its political, social, religious and cultural milieu. While the first section of the book is devoted to matters of form, the incomplete development of a fully articulated court system in Ireland prevents the researcher from observing the court of castle chamber in a stable bureaucratic configuration over time. In addition, the court occasionally changed direction, turning from an official policy of judicial indifference toward recusancy to one of activist interference in the religious preferences of Irish subjects after 1605. Although it was not nearly as busy as the English star chamber, the castle chamber followed a similar career. The pattern of adjudication was roughly the same, at least until the reign of James I, and the judiciary present in the majority of decisions represented the senior courts of law. Both star chamber courts operated as appellate jurisdictions as well as courts of first instance. However, the chief governors in Ireland exercised strong influence on the court of castle chamber, a situation that had no parallel in the English court. Though a certain deference to the viceroy was expected, the Irish tribunal was dominated by men like Wentworth and Chichester, while others like Perrot and Falkland struggled against entrenched interests on the council board and the court. The world of the court constituted a lawyerly oasis in which perplexed laymen came for judicial relief and experienced instead lengthy delay compounded by fees, fines and collateral actions. The court was designed to hear public questions at issue, but it was often accused of considering private suits and indeed, most litigation involved property, title and honour in some way.

While it is possible to exaggerate the importance of the court and its efforts to implement common law governance throughout the kingdom, it is beyond doubt that the judicial infrastructure accommodated a steadily increasing appetite for litigation, spearheaded in meaningful ways by the court of castle chamber.[200] The lawyers and judges became permanent fixtures in the social élite during this period, and while some of them were notoriously corrupt, the majority worked continuously to superimpose a stabilizing judicial order in the most distant reaches of the kingdom. On the other hand, the number of cases heard from petitioners suing *in forma pauperis* was disappointingly small. Finally, it must be admitted that, while the rule of law was fully implemented by the end of the period, the court of castle chamber gradually became the *bête noire* of a constitutional opposition that found its anti-recusant policies repugnant and its leadership under Wentworth guilty of relentless bullying, and worse. Though it began life as a promising instrument of the Elizabethan compromise, it finally came to grief, its leaders impeached and its viceroy executed. The tyrannical regime of Wentworth

---

200. For a useful corrective see Edwards, 'Collaboration without anglicisation', pp. 77ff.

was unique in some respects, so the castle chamber court became an easy target for his enemies, and it is difficult to characterize the fractious body as an arbitrary tool of powerful chief governors throughout the period. Indeed, the constitutional opposition to the court, both within and outside the government, says much about the victory of the rule of law, and lawyers, prior to the events of 1641. The lamentable record of religious persecution by the court, however, substantially mitigates Protestant triumphalism and places in question whether common law principles raised the standard of legal practice, and its reputation for fairness and equity, prior to the Irish Rebellion. What is more, the recourse to adjudication favoured British undertakers and allowed new plantations to exploit juristic advantage over Irish landowners, undermining the civil objectives of the plantation of Leitrim and others.[201] Although the Irish Rebellion in October 1641 led to a regrettable cycle of violence and recrimination, it is important to remember that the four decades of peace in the early seventeenth century represented a triumph of sorts for the forms of judicial encounter and common law remedies, an 'unrevolutionary Ireland'.

201. B. MacCuarta, 'The plantation of Leitrim, 1620–41', *IHS*, xxxii (2001), 301–06, 317–20. 'A rural social order on the English model' with security of tenure guaranteed to the natives was, in practice, sabotaged by non-resident British landlords and corrupt dispossession of the native Irish, using legal chicanery before the commission for defective titles, and other courts. See also Canny, *Making Ireland British*, pp. 247–51.

Part Two

*The rise and fall of prerogative justice in Ireland:
the Irish star chamber from 1534 to 1641*

CHAPTER FOUR

The origins of the court of castle chamber

Imprimis, where hir matie hath ... appoynted certeyn noble men, principall officers, and others of good experience in that land to be of hir maties counsell there, hir matie willeth the sayd deputye to consider that the usuation of so many and so div[er]se is because, as the varietie of the cases may arise for hym to have advise, so maye he therein to make choise and yet, as the circumstance of thinges maye beare it, to comm[un]icate with as many of them as he shall think mete, that thereby the governance maye have the most partes both to ayde him and to allowe and maynteine determinacons passed, in wch poynte considering the forme[r] experience had of his wisedome hir maty thinketh it the lesse nedefull to enlarge any more, but to conclude, requireth hym to cherish and maynteine suche of them chiefly as he shall fynd careful, willing and paynefull.

Instructions from the Queen to the Lord Deputy, 10 July 1559[1]

THE TUDOR ORIGIN of the court of castle chamber has received little attention from historians, despite the court's notoriety under the Stuarts.[2] This is due, in part, to the erratic attempts to charter the court in Ireland, caused as well by the attenuated survival of archival records, and overshadowed by the frequent crises that shook the Tudor regime in the mid-sixteenth century. Since the star chamber court was the judicial arm of the Irish privy council, its origins must be traced to judicial functions of the medieval chief executive in Ireland, the justiciar, and his management of litigation. The situation in Ireland under the viceroy was analogous to that in England, where 'the Council which attended the king while he travelled about the country on progress, and that which met in Star Chamber, during the four law terms, were still protean forms of the same institution'.[3] The late fifteenth century witnessed a gradual ebbing of the tide of Gaelic resurgence in Ireland, despite the generous freedom of action granted to the powerful earls of Kildare with scant attention from London. Kildare was allowed practical independence in his choice of personnel, few councillors opposed him and most of the leading Pale families were firmly within his constellation of power.[4] Yet, the Irish

---

1 PRO, SP 63/1/104. See also *Cal. Carew MSS, 1515–1574*, pp. 279–81.
2. H. Wood, 'The court of castle chamber or star chamber of Ireland', *RIA Proc*, xxxii (1914), sect. c, 152; and Crawford, 'The origins of the court of castle chamber', 22.
3. Guy, *Star chamber*, p. 2.   4. Ellis, *Reform and revival*, pp. 31–33.

council after 1470 was becoming a compact body of officials who were called upon to confirm acts of the chief governor.[5] In 1514 two justices and the chief baron went to Trim to examine and determine a case based on a petition to the lord deputy, that was finally resolved two years later by the council. This model would be used by the court of castle chamber well into the mid-seventeenth century. After 1524, the Irish privy council became more sedentary, composed primarily of bureaucrats, and the council heard numerous cases by petition.[6] The other law courts were recovering business that had declined in the later middle ages, and by 1534 both the king's bench and common pleas courts were more active. The two chief justices sat on the privy council and this in turn required that the executive remain sedentary in Dublin. However, the judicial work of the privy council was spasmodic, and important cases such as the dispute over the earldom of Ormonde were taken up in the English star chamber, after preliminary hearing by the lord deputy and council in Ireland.[7]

HENRICIAN REFORM AND THE INCIPIENT COURT OF CASTLE CHAMBER

In 1534, Sir Thomas Cromwell was fully engaged with the orchestration of Henry VIII's Reformation in England, while simultaneously fashioning a remodelled state bureaucracy. Irish political thinkers and reformers were among the 'humanist' milieu that surrounded Cromwell and formed part of the dynamic core of Henrician strategic thinking. Dr Brendan Bradshaw has argued that a 'commonwealth strategy' of governance emerged in reform circles prior to the uprising in Ireland associated with the earl of Kildare in 1534.[8] As a part of the 'unitary sovereignty' that was designed to assimilate and integrate Ireland into Tudor administrative practice, Cromwell had published the Ordinances for the government of Ireland. Article eleven of the Ordinances required the lord chancellor to convene a special court,

> callyng to hym a juge of every of the kynges courtes, & such other of the lords and counsayle as shalbe present in terme tyme, shal syt twies every weke duryng terme season in the counsayle chambre, there to receyve and here such compleyntes as the kynges subjectes shal exhibite; and take order therein accordingly.[9]

5. Ibid., p. 36.
6. Ibid., pp. 42–44. There was no Irish Wolsey, however, to institutionalize star chamber procedures in Ireland. Guy, *Star chamber*, p. 5.
7. Ellis, *Reform and revival*, pp. 44, 109–35, 157–58, 208.
8. Bradshaw, *Irish constitutional revolution*, pp. 33, 49–54, 118–19. See also Bradshaw, 'Cromwellian reform and the origins of the Kildare rebellion, 1533–34', *TRHS, 5th ser.*, xxvii (1977), 73ff.
9. PRO, SP 60/2/66. The printed document of 14 sides included 41 separate articles. Other instructions to establish jails, assist judges coming to corporate towns, for royal judges to ride in

A comparison might be made here to the earlier determination by Wolsey in 1517 that star chamber in England should sit twice weekly, on Wednesday and Friday in term time, to differentiate the work of the privy council and deal with its case-load of about 120 suits per annum. By contrast, the Irish court never generated this kind of judicial business. The incomplete bifurcation of the English star chamber and privy council was mirrored in Ireland by meetings of the lord deputy and council that continued to deliberate judicial suits alongside military matters, estate management and financial accounts.[10]

Herbert Wood found that the Cromwellian Ordinances for the government of Ireland included 'the germ of the court which was afterwards to develop into the Court of Castle Chamber'.[11] This compendium made for Cromwell has more recently been characterized by Ellis as a series of well-known platitudes repro-duced from earlier fifteenth-century documents. He has shown that the Irish privy council was already acting in a judicial capacity by 1516, adjudicating disputes involving peers and the loyal towns, acting as arbitrators and creating *ad hoc* courts to handle its judicial business.[12] Furthermore, if a star chamber jurisdiction were created by the ordinances of 1534, evidence of its work as a prerogative court would be expected in the aftermath of rebellion. Instead, evidence of a 'Tudor despotism' is minimal, and the capital executions in Co. Kildare itself amounted to only six persons at one session in 1535.[13] Nonetheless, the Cromwellian recon-struction of the Irish council achieved its aim in the harnessing of independent viceroys, and this in turn made judicial action part of their joint responsibility, laying the groundwork for a later refinement of the privy council as a star chamber in the reign of Elizabeth.[14]

Brendan Bradshaw has argued that 'It took the Irish crisis of 1534 to produce an Irish policy'.[15] A generation of humanist reform thinking, characterized by Bradshaw as 'commonwealth liberalism', began in the English Pale and spread to the court in London, where Cromwell inaugurated the reform period in 1534 with the aid of experienced Irish bureaucrats such as the moderate lawyer Sir Thomas Cusack.[16]

circuit each quarter, and to name justices of the peace in each county, anticipated Elizabethan reforms by nearly a half century. See also *S.P. Hen VIII*, vol. 2, pp. 207–16.

10. Guy, *Star chamber*, pp. 5–6.   11. Wood, 'Castle chamber', 154.
12. Ellis, *Reform and revival*, p. 155.
13. Ellis, 'Henry VIII, rebellion and the rule of law', *Hist Jn*, xxiv (1981), 524–28. King's bench proceeded against the rebels in Co. Dublin, but did not execute all those brought to trial, suspending punishment while awaiting the decision of the crown. Ellis further claims that the bill of attainder in the parliament of 1536 was milder in scope than the expected ruthlessness toward traitors. Ibid., 516, 521–23.
14. Ellis, 'Thomas Cromwell and Ireland, 1532–40', *Hist Jn*, xxiii (1980), 510–19. A perusal of the State Papers for 1534–56 shows very little judicial work done in the Irish council, while instructions for St Leger and his council in 1550 were largely silent on matters of adjudication. See PRO, SP 60 and HL, Ellesmere MS 1700. For a fuller discussion of the origins of the castle chamber and Irish privy council, see Crawford, *Anglicizing*, pp. 174–84.
15. Bradshaw, *Irish constitutional revolution*, pp. 83, 88.
16. Ibid., pp. 90–93.

Bradshaw characterized the period after 1534 as an experiment in 'unitary sovereignty' designed to create in Ireland a microcosm of English government while avoiding the expense of conquest and offering a means of assimilation to Gaelic lords through surrender and regrant.[17] Though the leadership of Sir Anthony St Leger and Sir Thomas Cusack gave continuity to the 'reform era' of the mid-century until 1556, the judicial role of the privy council remained inchoate and under-utilized. In contrast, Ciaran Brady has argued that this period was primarily one of faction, corruption and Dublin-based assimilation which undercut the putative 'Irish constitutional revolution' theory favoured by Bradshaw.[18] The brief and cryptic mention of adjudication in the surviving council book for the St Leger era (1542–1556) indicates that the ordinances were not implemented in the post-Cromwellian interlude.[19] However, the judicial capacity of the privy council itself was evident from the land disputes among leading Irish peers and merchants. An order between the earl of Thomond and Donald O'Brien in 1554 preceded a 'Controversie betwixt Edward Galway of Corke and Andrew Leysagh of Limericke, concerninge the bridge in Limericke'.[20] Anticipating later adjudication involving foreign merchants, the table of the council book made note of an 'Order, well drawne, after the manner of chancerie, betwixt certain merchants of Chester and Gilliam Pippin of St Malous for a ship laden with seck taken by him'.[21] The theoretical star chamber jurisdiction over cases of riot and administrative malfeasance was not exercised by the Irish council and there is little to demonstrate either an institutional foundation or the structural carpentry of an enhanced conciliar tribunal. Brief references to petitions, submissions, concordats, recognizances and proclamations suggest that the executive functions of the viceroy and council were mixed untidily with aspects of adjudication. The famous reference to Gaelic legal tradition in 1543, 'Controversie referred to brehownes', also suggests the limits of the council as a venue for litigation in early Tudor Ireland. Brehons were probably used to support the common law system, rather than to rival it, in this period, and the council recognized that in Irish-speaking regions the brehons had more credibility and ease of access than the distant courts in Dublin or the infrequent appearance of assize judges. The court took note of the marital complexity of the Clanricarde earldom in 1544, citing the survival of his three wives at the time of the death of Ulick, the first earl.[22] By 1551, however,

17. Ibid., pp. 112–19, 122–24, 140–42.
18. Brady, *Chief governors*, pp. 25–30, 45–48.
19. BL, Add. MS 4792, ff. 117–24. See HMC, *Haliday MSS*, pp. 273–82. The 'table to the redd counsell booke' is nearly identical to a copy in TCD, MS 843, ff. 1–18.
20. HMC, *Haliday MSS*, p. 282.
21. Ibid. The continuous struggle over prise wines, involving the earl of Ormonde and towns of Waterford and Ross, claimed the attention of the council throughout the period.
22. HMC, *Haliday MSS*, pp. 275–78. The text anticipated the determination of the 'lawfull heire male' and noted the three wives of O'Carroll, Lynch and de Burgo clans. In 1548, the famous brehon legal family were referenced obliquely in the privy council register thus: 'The Dorans challenge Cloghgrenan'. Ibid., p. 279. The interaction between brehon law and prerogative

the council under St Leger confidently asserted this warning: 'Against the orderinge of causes by Brehoun law, but by arbitrators.'[23]

The extant records of the early Tudor privy council in Ireland, a pathless archival thicket, obscure the judicial activity of the board as a tribunal. However, the council book for the earl of Sussex, begun in 1556, provides fuller detail of the council's judicial work. Much of this was handled by delegation to other authorities, including the orders given on 10 August 1556 to Sir George Stanley, marshal of the army, to be general in Ulster. Judicial functions were delegated to the marshal, to wit:

> Item: We give to hym power and auctorytie to heare and determyne all manner of controversies betweene partye and partie the same not beyng matter of enherytance within Ulster for the said tyme ...
> Item: He shall cawse to be ponnyshed all those that shall comytt treasons, murders, felony, rape or any other crymynall offence as to the offences commytted in those cases shall appertayne for the saide tyme.[24]

The council in Ireland thus provided to its surrogate an extension of conciliar adjudication while also acknowledging that he should have the right to execute martial law as to him appeared convenient.[25]

In Febuary 1557, the council undertook to arbitrate a controversy between Shane O'Neill and the baron of Dungannon, requiring both of them to return all property taken since Shane's illness, and sending the lord primate and the baron of Lowth to Dundalk where they were to make the declaration and see to the execution of the council's order.[26] This effort to keep old adversaries at arm's length was plainly a stopgap measure, yet the full hearing of the case before a meeting of ten privy councillors indicates the intent of the government to require even the Ulster peers to honour its deliberations. An indenture made at Dublin on 24 July 1557 between the lord deputy and council and John and Walter Bremingham in Offaly demonstrated the complex interaction between policy-making and adjudication. The strategic citadel of Kannafad was essential for defence of the frontier of the Pale and Offaly, so money was committed for its strengthening to the Berminghams, who alleged ownership of the castle as it was on their estate. The council found that the proofs could not be heard and the cause determined at that time, yet the fortification was a critical element in crown policy, so they entered an indenture with the Berminghams for a three-year lease of the castle and bawn, the parties agreeing that this would not prejudice the claims of the queen or the Berminghams to title.[27] This indenture, apparently

---

justice, and the persistence of Irish marcher law, need fuller attention by a new generation of historians.

23. Ibid., p. 280; TCD, MS 843, f. 12.
24. RIA, MS 24 F. 17, ff. 8–8v: Articles 5 and 8 of the instructions.
25. Ibid.: Article 6 of the instructions. A similar commission was given to Andrew Brereton as general of Ulster on 15 Sept. 1556. Ibid., f. 13.
26. Ibid., ff. 41–41v.   27. Ibid., ff. 48–49.

pursuant to a legal claim, was made subject to the plantation of Leix and Offaly then under way, and illustrates the *ad hoc* equilibrium struck by the court between indifferent justice and critical military imperatives.

On rare occasions, the records of the Irish privy council detail much of the hearing and deliberation of the court as well as the orders taken in the case. Rarer still were questions involving international implications, but on 26 December 1556 the viceroy heard allegations from the town of Waterford surrounding a complex commercial transaction involving merchants of Flanders, Spain, France and Ireland. Francisco Dias, the factor and attorney for Spanish merchants, brought suit against the Flemish captain Henry Corneilson, for goods discharged in Waterford that were allegedly sold, alienated or conveyed to La Rochelle in France. The lord deputy, and presumably others on the council, heard allegations on both sides and found that Corneilson lacked authority or warrant to sell, bargain or give away the goods in question, requiring the latter to restore the goods to the mayor and bailiffs of Waterford, including any money or bills of debt received for them. And for the goods sent to La Rochelle, a dispute arose between Corneilson's factor there, James Donyll and James Salynger as to the sum of money received at the port from Waterford, based on documents received from the public notary. The court gave Corneilson one year to provide new evidence by certificate from La Rochelle, under the town seal, that the actual sums owed were less, as he claimed, than the amounts demanded by the agents there. The court required Dias to discharge Corneilson of his indemnity once the money was delivered to him, or else to place the money in question in the hands of the corporation of Waterford, pending 'order taken by us for delyvery of the same to the right owners as to justice appertaynethe'.[28] The fugitive Corneilson was finally required to yield his body to prison or provide surety for his due performance of the order, with a bond of £500 to answer for any further liabilty or claim that might yet come to light.[29] Dias was also required to defray costs on Corneilson's account, based on the original contract made in Flanders, in acknowledgment of the first lading of the goods and other reasonable and necessary charges undertaken by Corneilson as determined by the mayor and aldermen of Waterford.[30] While this interim order may not be taken as a harbinger of future star chamber proceedings, it clearly shows that judicial interventions by the council, however occasional they might be, were painstaking and in this case extensive as well. Nonetheless, the cause was taken up again in an order of council on 25 November 1559 in the next reign. Rehearsing the details of the proceeding and violations of the order of the court, the earl of Sussex gave order that Dias, on behalf of the Spanish merchants, should receive a third part of the value of the goods laden in Flanders. The council had met in Waterford on 1 February 1559 to give final order in the case and obtained the consent of both Dias and Corneilson. But the wily Fleming had in the interval secured his release on the bond of four men of

28. Ibid., f. 62v.   29. Ibid., ff. 61v–63.
30. Ibid.

Waterford and promptly sped away out of Ireland, so the viceroy ordered them to compensate Dias in the amount of 200 marks sterling. Dias was left to his own devices, to 'recover against the said Henrie, whersoever they shall finde his bodie or his goodes'.[31]

Interruptions and unsatisfactory compromises plagued the work of the council as a court, and many of its orders remained incomplete. Prior to the advent of the court of castle chamber, the council was compelled to address numerous suits in law that more properly belonged to another forum. One of the benefits of the initiation of the star chamber court was to refine more systematically the litigation that properly came before the council itself. Nonetheless, well into the next century, property disputes were routinely brought to the court and determined there. One such suit involved two members of the Pale establishment who were also military officials. Francis Agarde, the seneschal, obtained a lease of two manors in Co. Wexford by letters patent under the regime of Sir Anthony St Leger, but Anthony Colclogh had established a previous interest in the farms of these manors. Under the new regime of Seneschal Philip Isham, the lease of Colclogh had been called in and cancelled, so the latter brought suit and the Irish council sent the matter to the judges and others learned in the law. Their decisions were entered in the record book of the council, advancing the suit of Colclogh, so the council met on 16 May 1558. In favouring the cause of Colclogh, the council recognized the right of a lessee, Patrick Browne, who had obtained rights to sow the fallow land, and to build upon the premises of the manor of Rosgarland. The court concluded that Browne's lease upon the manor of Colclogh was valid and that he should pay rent to Philip Isham until the next Michaelmas, occupying the houses after Michaelmas and moving no tenants until the next May. The court declared they had arrived at a conclusion by 'indyfferente justice' with eight councillors in attendance.[32] The remarkable intervention of the highest tribunal in Ireland to determine cases of real property involving the rights of tertiary lessees is an indication of the state of unreformed judicial formulae. Though it would take a decade of relentless proposals from the powerful viceroys Sussex and Sydney, the eventual refinement of Ireland's judicial establishment provided greater clarity and efficiency to its superstructure. Real property litigation continued nonetheless to come before the conciliar court.

Frustrations with the under-developed court system in Ireland appeared in numerous orders of the council. In 1559 the lord justice and council gave orders to commissioners to take up the case of the baron of Upper Ossory and Edward Butler in a controversy between their men and estates in Co. Kilkenny. Both alleged numerous preys and outrages, including the killing of their men and disturbance of the peace. The council explained,

---

31. Ibid., f. 112. See also f. 72v for the case of Antwerp merchants against the mayor and town of Waterford in May 1558, in which the restitution of sequestered goods was ordered by the council.
32. Ibid., ff. 70–71v.

Forasmoche as due prouf and tryall is to be made in place or places whear the same ought and that we, for other occasions and impedimentes, cannot in person Repeyer to those borders to call before us all suche proufs as shall or may be produced for tryall of the trueth and certeintie on either side,[33]

then named eight commissioners to take depositions and determine the suit, giving orders on behalf of the council at a hearing in Rathkeale. Joining Lucas Nettervile and Nicholas White, both learned in the laws, to military officials such as Captains Nicholas Heron and Francis Cosby, the council explicitly required them to resolve the local efforts at intimidation which prevented men of either side from approaching the market at Kilkenny.[34] In 1560, anticipating a complaint heard throughout the period, Sussex and seventeen councillors met at Waterford to declare that

a greate number of billes, causes and complaints exhibited unto us and remytted by us to the ordre and determynacion of dyvers persons rest, by the negligence of them to whom the bills, causes and complaintes be remytted, utterly undetermyned.[35]

The council declared that anyone given a commission to order and determine any bill, cause or complaint should proceed expeditiously and certify the results to the sheriff or other official to see justice administered and executed. Failure to comply with this administrative streamlining of procedure might lead to forfeiture of a sum equal to that demanded by the successful party in the suit, according to the order of 1 August, and the sheriffs and 'chief person dwelling in that county' were further exhorted to full compliance with their respective obligations according to the order in the suit.[36] A similar case heard at Waterford by the lord lieutenant and council on 1 August 1560 manifested the complex roles of the council, being in turn a tribunal, board of arbitration, and chief executive. The endless disputes between the retainers of the earls of Ormonde and Desmond were described as unlawful assemblies needing grievous punishment by the council. Yet the peers were merely warned to abide previous orders and to submit to the arbitration of commissioners who were authorized to hear and determine all causes in controversy between the earls, their men and followers.[37]

33. Ibid., ff. 99–101.
34. Ibid. Dr Edwards has argued that the 'MacGiollapadraigs' offered only perfunctory collaboration while resisting the claims of English law and refusing to attend the sessions in Co. Kilkenny. He asserts that Sir Thomas Cusake, James Dowdall and John Synnott were merely facilitators of a 'Gaelic settlement' between Upper Ossory and Viscount Mountgarret, in 1559, deferring to the resolution of the brehon lawyers, the O'Dorans, who kept a famous school in the territory. Edwards made no mention of this Fitzpatrick acknowledgement of the superior jurisdiction of the council in a resolution of the same year. Edwards, 'Collaboration without anglicisation', pp. 86–87.
35. RIA, MS 24 F. 17, f. 134   36. Ibid., ff. 134–35.   37. Ibid., ff. 140–41.

Seventeen councillors sat at this hearing, testimony to the traditional handling of aristocratic conflict as a matter of provincial diplomacy rather than a novel aspect of common law adjudication

ARRESTED DEVELOPMENT: PROPOSALS FOR THE ERECTION OF A COURT OF CASTLE CHAMBER, 1560–1571

In his important essay on the crafting of Elizabethan policy toward Ireland, Ciaran Brady found the earl of Sussex both an aggressive promoter of administrative change and a conventional opportunist. Brady argues that the policy of anglicizing the government of Ireland became gradually more consistent, exclusive and comprehensive in its formulations. Concentrating on the military problems faced by the viceroy and his creation of the presidential councils as a means to confront the 'ubiquity of faction', Brady demonstrated the vigour and focus of Sussex's detailed plans for the reformation of Irish governance. He concluded,

> like St Leger, finally he [Sussex] understood that the best way of cutting through the old alignments was through the construction of an alternative political framework based upon a general, if gradual, acceptance of the procedures of English common law.[38]

The process of anglicization was addressed in a series of proposals to the crown between 1560 and 1562, described by Brady as a 'programmatic approach' that was so narrowly defined and delimited that Sussex was willing to alienate potential sources of support among the Palesmen and native Irish councillors.[39] Brady did not mention Sussex's simultaneous call for the creation of a new star chamber court. Nonetheless, the establishment of a prerogative jurisdiction that would both empower the Irish privy council with superintendence of the judicial apparatus of the common law while adding to conciliar oversight of a new category of offences was viewed by Sussex as an imperative. In his detailed report on the state of Ireland to the queen in 1562, this was what he argued:

> Great numbers of disorders and riots and taking of possession by force be daily committed and left unpunished, for that there is no place to hear and determine those matters but at the Council Board, which for the most part is occupied with other affairs of greater weight; and therefore it were necessary to have a like court of record established here by Parliament as the Star Chamber is in England, to order the like causes here.[40]

38. Brady, *Chief governors*, p. 75. 39. Ibid., p. 81.
40. *Cal. Carew MSS, 1515–1574*, pp. 342–43.

Since the crown rarely took up a matter of this weight without substantial correspondence and ministerial consideration, we may surmise that the operation of a star chamber jurisdiction in Ireland was under discussion from 1560. The report of Sir James Croft on 12 February 1561 blamed the disorders in Ireland on a lack of sufficient judges, calling for 'Graund scoles' to be erected in Ireland for the training of lawyers and maintaining that the extension of the common law through commissions and other means would gradually quell Irish disobedience.[41] At the same time, Sussex's government was under attack by a group of lawyers and law students in London who charged his government with arbitrary handling of the administration of cess.[42] The viceroy's extensive report on the state of Ireland in Lambeth MS 609 is undated. These ponderous rehearsals of policy initiatives and grave warnings of the disordered state of Ireland were often anticipated by exchanges of ideas between ministers. It is possible that the response of the queen, dated July 1562, may have occurred prior to the official report from Ireland. More likely, the viceroy's summary arrived in London prior to the queen's official response. While she gave a hearing to the lawyers in opposition to cess, and the foundations of Sussex's government were being shaken by shadow factions at court, Elizabeth gave her unqualified approval for a star chamber and called upon the lord lieutenant to move forward with its implementation. The first article of her reply to the 'state of Ireland' ordered that,

> where we understand that dyvers grete ryottes piriuryes and such lyke publick offences be often tymes committed within that our realme, ye punishment wherof wold be also notable for example. We have thought mete that by conference with our counsell there a place might be apoynted for ye oppen hearinge [and] determyning therof lyke to our Counsell chamber called sterr chamber at Westminster and the lyke authoritie and Jurisdiction might be devised for you our lieutenant or for ye deputy, is for our great counsell of our realme sittye [sic] in our counsell in ye sayd place called ye sterr chamber. The devise whereof we referr to be furder consydered by you and our Counsell there.[43]

Although the court of castle chamber received its first clerk by the appointment of Thomas Walshe on 5 October 1563, the commencement of its hearing of litigation was apparently suspended for another eight years until 1571. A series of three other clerks were named to the court in that period, but the formal erection of the star chamber jurisdiction had to await the commission of 1571.[44]

41. PRO, SP 63/3/42.
42. See my *Anglicizing*, pp. 384–87; Brady, *Chief governors*, pp. 101–07.
43. PRO, SP 63/6/101. If the Sussex report was given prior to July 1562, the order of the documents in *Cal. Carew MSS, 1515–74*, pp. 330 and 342–43 should be reversed. For a discussion, see my *Anglicizing*, p. 218.
44. Hughes, *Patentee officers*, p. 135. John Bathe (10 July 1565), Edward Waterhouse (1 February 1566) and John Harepenny (11 October 1569) succeeded Walshe. Ibid., pp. 8, 63, 136.

The decade 1562–71 saw the gradual destruction of the Sussex regime and a quarrelsome interval under the leadership of Sir Nicholas Arnold. Sussex had been confronted by agents of the Pale, including law students in residence at the inns of court, for his excessive charges in the administration of cess. The complaints were taken to the queen herself in 1562, complaints citing the 'lycentious lyving and disordre of the captaines and souldiors' in the Pale, and seeking immediate redress.[45] The master of the rolls, Sir John Parker, was accused by Sussex of leading a conspiracy against his government, Sussex claiming 'I know ther is one that went from place to place to gett mens handes unto a booke agaynst me'.[46] A group of Irish councillors wrote in support of the lord lieutenant against accusations of misgovernment by Arnold in October 1563, so when Arnold himself assumed the government, he found the incumbents truculent and himself isolated.[47] On 26 April 1565, Arnold wrote to Cecil that the queen

> needs a governour and counsaill here, as will rather bende themselfes to her best shrvice and welthe of the countrey then as sume of them nowe daily doo, to the Impungnyng or crossing of any thing I can doo or speake, how reasonable or necessarie so ever it maye seeme to the rest of the counsaill here, if it agree not with the former governementes and advertisementes into Englande ... so that no faulte can be amended as long as we that rest here of her Maties counsaill do stande at suche division.[48]

Further testimony of conciliar division came at the expense of Arnold's successor in a memorandum of 20 October 1566:

> Generally we have gatherid by many argumentes that though he [Sydney] have not so apparently as Sir N. Arnold, yet hath he directid the Cours of his government to be guydid by the counsellors rather of the birth of Irland then of England, which we neither can allow nor ever cowde heere good reason to allow.[49]

Not surprisingly, only one judicial action by the council was recorded in the Arnold governorship. On 13 July 1564, David Hay, esquire, and his son James, of Co. Wexford, were put at liberty by the lord chancellor and secretary of state after 25 weeks of imprisonment in Dublin Castle, giving bonds as security for their appearance if new evidence were laid against them before the next Michaelmas. The two men had been accused before the lord deputy and council in Dublin of

45. PRO, SP 63/6/23. The law students included the names of men who became leading Pale lawyers and critics of the regime, such as Henry Burnell.
46. BL, Add. MS 40,061, f. 446. On 26 Nov. 1562 Richard Netterville was interrogated before the Irish privy council regarding the accusations against Parker.
47. Bodl., Carte MS 58, f. 22.   48. PRO, SP 63/13/77.
49. PRO, SP 63/19/49.

felony and high treason on 13 January 1564, but no further evidence or accusation was made against them. The record made note of the procedure of the council, referring the hearings, examinings, discussion and deliberation of the matters to the judges and learned counsel. In the interim, the Hays alleged they had been robbed and spoiled of their goods in Co. Wexford by the rebels and traitors Edmund and Piers Butler, losing their goods and cattle and tenants. In the final order, the defendants were told to return the next Michaelmas session to present themselves before the lord deputy and council where their bonds would be cancelled if no further objections were made against them.[50] This quasi-judicial decree by the chancellor and secretary of state typified the council as a court, where charges were deliberated upon by an attenuated panel of judges and issues rarely proceeded to formal trial at law. It serves as further evidence of the need for regularization of the council's judicial work.

The council book is entirely silent for the year 1565, while Sir Henry Sydney laid out his plans for a new regime as lord deputy in Ireland.[51] No records were entered from 10 December 1564 to 20 January 1566. Brady discussed the contractual nature of Sydney's pre-departure arrangements in England, explaining his 'persistent eclecticism' in reference to the need for a hastily broadened yet 'fragile coalition' that was moved by different considerations in its preliminary support of the programme. Brady concentrated primarily on factional rivalries at court as an explanation of the energetic and ambitious reform launched by Sydney. He found the detailed and exhaustive compendium of instructions for Sydney merely a restatement of earlier positions taken by Sussex that had lapsed during the commission of inquiry and its aftermath.[52] Dr Canny, by contrast, argued that Sydney's programme was a 'new departure', emphasizing the importance of provincial presidencies and projects for colonization, and showing how military power would pave the way for an 'extension of English common law over a wider area, and eventually through the entire country'.[53] Canny explained that 'while it was acknowledged that only a military man could be an effective president at the outset, his principal function was defined as being an administrator of justice'.[54] By using lesser landowners who would become sheriffs and justices of the peace and also act as jurors, Sydney 'hoped to open the way for the extension of English common law', so each president was accompanied by two justices.[55] When, in February 1566, Sydney and the council issued instructions to the president of Munster, these were modelled on those of the council in the Marches of Wales, containing responsibility for the administration of justice; commissions of oyer and terminer and gaol delivery, having all the powers of an assize court; as well as martial law.[56] On 20 January, a note was inserted in the

50. RIA, MS 24 F. 17, ff. 194–94v. David Hay may have been a former privy councillor, having signed the council book in 1557. However, the council book was signed occasionally by officials who were not councillors, often depending on whether the venue was outside Dublin and the Pale.

51. HMC, *Haliday MSS*, p. 149. 52. Brady, *Chief governors*, pp. 115–17.

53. Canny, *Elizabethan conquest*, p. 48. 54. Ibid., p. 49.

55. Ibid., p. 50. 56. Ibid., p. 99.

council book attesting to the arrival of Sydney as lord deputy, noting that he took his oath of office in Christ Church on that day.[57]

Surprisingly, few have commented on the importance of the spring of 1566 as a formative stage in the judicial framework of Ireland. The vigorous approach of Sydney was demonstrated by a spate of letters to the queen and her ministers, and a series of related meetings of the Irish privy council. On 8 February 1566, Sydney met the council for the first time to deliberate on the use of gallowglasses for the queen's military force. On 20 February, the council met at St Sepulchres for an extraordinary run of business, after a long period of dormancy. Hearing three cases on that day, and another on the next, the council concluded its hearings there on 25 February. Anticipating by several decades the activism of Wentworth and other Stuart viceroys, Sydney heard numerous petitions and issued inter-locutory decrees, presumably acting with the assent of the council. After considering the complaints on both sides from Sir Barnaby Fitzpatrick, son of the baron of Upper Ossory, and his rival the chief of the O'Carrolls concerning riotous dispos-session of the castle of Ballaghmore and other property in contention, Sydney named as arbitrators the military veteran Francis Cosby and the gentleman John MacGilpatrick to hear and determine the controversies. Both sides were to put in pledges by 5 March, and the arbitrators were given one month to complete and publish their determination of the issues before them. And although Fitzpatrick was left in possession of the castle, the order declared that O'Carroll should have the right to declare further his claim to the property before the lord deputy and council and they in turn would issue further order and give judgement in the case.[58] The suit demonstrates Sydney's willingness to bring before the council matters that would normally have claimed the attention of a star chamber court, particularly the violent conflicts among provincial landowners. A similar order given to arbitrators on that day concerned alleged murders of the men of Sir Frances Herbert by Hugh MacShane, the order requiring the commissioners to certify their findings to the lord deputy and council before the last day of March.[59] The final case on that day dealt with taking a distress from Art O'Molloy in Offaly by the

---

57. HMC, *Haliday MSS*, p. 149; RIA, MS 24 F. 17, f. 209v. The use of a new secretary hand in the manuscript and the gap of thirteen months suggests the premonitory nature of this event.

58. RIA, MS 24 F. 17, ff. 210–10v. Dr Edwards does not mention this attempt at arbitration by the Irish privy council, asserting that Fitzpatrick 'co-operation with the extension of English common law was so slow it was almost imperceptible'. His discussion of the 1559 arbitration between the first baron and Viscount Mountgarret demonstrates the close involvement of three legal experts from the Irish council, including Sir Thomas Cusack, but he characterised the result as 'a Gaelic settlement' and the lawyers 'neutral mediators'. Another dispute between Fitzpatricks and Butlers in 1572 was settled, absent of crown participation, yet Edwards acknowledges that Lord Chancellor Gerrard and others pressured the baron of Upper Ossory to accept the formal shiring of his territory. Edwards, 'Collaboration without anglicization', pp. 86–88.

59. RIA, MS 24 F. 17, ff. 210v–11. A subsequent case heard at Arklow on 12 March found that MacShane mistook the order of the court, and he was allowed another week to put in his pledges. Ibid., f. 213.

captain of the queen's gallowglasses, Callagh MacTurelagh. Commissioners sent to review the evidence were ordered to make final resolution.[60]

Anticipating the progress of the lord deputy and council on the Leinster circuit, the final decree issued at St Sepulchres took up the matter of Sir Edmund Butler and Oliver Fitzgerald on 25 February 1566. Requiring each of them to make restitution for offences with which they were charged, and deferring a final resolution until the return of the viceroy to Dublin, the order declaimed,

> It is therefore consydered and ordered by us, the said lorde deputie, that those complaynntes so moved by the parties aforesaid one against the other, and before us depending; shall have contynuance in the same state as now they stand untill the fyrst day of the next terme, and then to be further herd consydered and ordered as justice shall requier.[61]

It was a week later, on 3 March 1566, that Sydney wrote to Cecil, recommending the success of the new star chamber court and calling for the formal commission and seal. Having spent much of the first month of office on matters that would normally have been heard in star chamber, Sydney made the establishment of this court a high priority, writing just before he left Dublin as follows:

> In the last government of my lord of Sussex here, A sterre chamber was by hym erected by the name of the Castell chamber, whereof by his lords short departur he sawe no greate effect followe. Nevertheless I finde yt a Court so necessary and of so great consequence here, as I must both allow and greately commend the erection and allso desier you that yt may be farder established by sending us hither the orders of the starre chamber, especially that which is to observid by the Clerke, and the order of the processes and the forme of the Seale therunto belonging togither with full auctority as the Clerke hath there for the accepting of recognizances, and cancelling of bandes, where of yf advertisement might come before the next terme, that Court shuld be fully established which being yet but in its infancy was worth to the Queene this last terme in ————* abought one hundreth poundes.[62]

Sydney made note at the time of the proliferation of cases before him, expressing his frustration with the judicial structure.[63] While it is apparent from later correspondence that the court of castle chamber had not been fully erected at this time, Sydney's appeal for support from London highlights the inchoate operation of the court within the work of the privy council in Ireland. The absence of formal routines of the court apparently did not prevent the clerk from taking related fees, though perhaps the estimate of £100 is based on judicial costs owing to the council acting as a tribunal.

---

60. Ibid., f. 211.
61. Ibid., f. 212v.
62. PRO, SP 63/16/110. *Blank in manuscript.
63. Canny, *Elizabethan conquest*, p. 54. Plate 5.

The first progress of the new lord deputy gave further evidence of his determination to use prerogative justice as an instrument to reform the country. At Arklow on 12 March 1566, Sydney heard two cases involving the O'Byrnes and O'Tooles of Co. Wicklow. A murder had been committed by Morrough McDowle against a kinsman, so the council appointed arbitrators to hear and determine the case, requiring Lucas O'Toole to provide bond for the good behaviour of the defendant.[64] At Kilkenny on 23 March 1566 the viceroy and council, after hearing complaints by the baron of Dunboyne against Piers Butler and Patrick Sherlock, deputed Sir Warham St Leger and the commissioners in Munster to complete the hearing and determining of the cause. Sydney noted that 'the short abode of us, the said lorde deputie, here and the conveniencie of tyme and place hath not served to the orderly fynisshing or deciding of those variaunces', but he required the principals to appear in Dublin on the first day of the next term 'to attend the further order of this bourde'.[65] Returning to Dublin, the viceroy undertook to hear the complaints of the earl of Desmond and Sir Morrice Fitzgerald of the Decies 'in the castell chamber there' on 9 April 1566. Appearing before the lord deputy and council, the two rivals from distant Kerry were required to return all prisoners and ransom taken during their recent conflict, and to attend the lord deputy at Youghal on his next visit to Co. Cork, allowing St Leger and the Munster commissioners to conduct the hearing of evidence there in the meantime. While this proceeding was certainly not a trial, the council anticipated a proper formal hearing at some later time, and, in doing so, asserted a judicial oversight that anticipated the advent of the castle chamber court in like cases.[66]

When Sydney's letter of 3 March was received in London, the queen's reply was affirmative. She wrote on 28 March 1566 to the lord deputy:

> Where you requyre to have some ordres sent you for the direction of yourself and our Counsell there in the heering and determining of the causes in that place which was erectid by our cosin of Sussex and named the Castell Chambre, to resemble our Sterre Chamber at Westminister; you shall have the same sent to you with speede, as if wynde and passage let not, may be with you before the next terme.[67]

Despite the promise of quick action and full compliance with his request, Sydney was ultimately disappointed. He wrote throughout the summer on at least three other occasions, but failed to receive the formal documents that had been so easily promised.[68] There is insufficient evidence to indicate why this hiatus occurred, but Sydney was undeterred. He continued to employ the council in hearings throughout the year, and on 3 May 1566 in Dundalk he considered two separate allegations against Richard, earl of Clanricarde. Teig MacWilliam O'Kelly charged

---

64. RIA, MS 24 F. 17, f. 213v.
65. Ibid., ff. 216–16v.
66. Ibid., ff. 215–15v.
67. *Sidney S.P.*, pp. 19–20.
68. *Cal. S.P. Ire., 1509–73*, pp. 303, 307, 309–10.

that the earl imprisoned his wife and eldest son during a confrontation over an estate. The court demanded that Clanricarde release Sabine, the wife of O'Kelly, and submit to arbitration of the archbishop of Tuam and the bishop of Clonfert, acting with the mayor of Galway.[69] The second hearing involved the complaint of Brian O'Kelly against the earl's son, Ulick Burke, for the murder of his son, Hugh O'Kelly. The court found that Ulick rescued a prey that had been taken by Hugh before he was killed, but that Ulick did not commit the murder with his own hands, though he was in the company of the malefactors (for the record, his father later apprehended the principal and had him executed). The court decided that the earl should return the prey to the father of the deceased, the complainant Brian O'Kelly, with other matters to be decided by the court when the lord deputy repaired into Connacht.[70]

Further evidence of the continuance of adjudication before the council is to be found in an unusually full deposition of ten witnesses at Naas, recorded in the Irish council book for 4 October 1566 by three commissioners deputed by the lord deputy and council, in regard to the estate of Cotlandstown, Co. Kildare.[71] The order of the council was given on 27 June 1566 at Kilmainham to some 26 deponents on the issue of whether the lands at Cotlandstown were subject to the cess, and a separate order to the three commissioners was given at Dublin on 26 August.[72] The deposition being read into the entry book at the commencement of Michaelmas term suggests the willingness of the council to take up the cause on behalf of a veteran, Sir Frances Herbert, and his son and heir, Nicholas, who brought the suit. Although the record is silent on the eventual disposition of the case, the council possessed the authority to change the terms of cess and was probably looking for justification to ease its burden on a loyal soldier and landowner.

If we follow Canny on the thrust of Sydney's government, it can be argued that Sydney now turned to the primary features of his regime, the implementation of provincial presidencies and colonies.[73] Also, he was preoccupied with the general hosting and the cess for the remainder of 1566 and may have turned away from this unpromising venture in the expansion of prerogative justice. He campaigned energetically through the summer against Shane O'Neill. It is clear, nonetheless, that Sydney was the primary champion of the court of castle chamber and surprising that the adroit Cecil did not engineer the final institutionalization of the court at this time. The spurt of conciliar adjudication in 1566 was not succeeded by fuller proceedings, and the council book has few entries between 15 June 1567 and 24 January 1570.[74] However, as Dr Kenny has shown, Sydney was also sympathetic to the new lease of Blackfriars to 25 lawyers for the King's Inns in January 1567. This lease of twenty-one years was issued to a cadre of mostly Old English officials, including Chief Justice Dillon, the master of the rolls, the chief baron and the three law officers.[75] This attention to the establishment of a

---

69. RIA, MS 24 F. 17, ff. 217–17v.   70. Ibid., ff. 218–18v.
71. Ibid., ff. 256–57.   72. Ibid., ff. 257v–58.
73. Canny, *Elizabethan conquest*, pp. 50–54, 99.   74. HMC, *Haliday MSS.*, pp. 200–01.
75. Kenny, *King's Inns*, pp. 53–58. Other lessees included Nicholas White, future master of the rolls;

judicial infrastructure was suspended in the latter stages of his administration. During much of 1568, Sydney was absent in England, where he negotiated the terms of his second stint as lord deputy, sought approval for the presidencies, lent his name in support of colonies, organized plans for a new parliament and attempted to reorganize Ulster after the death of Shane O'Neill. Faced with a revolt of the Butlers in 1569, Sydney staged an expensive military campaign. He was finally recalled in 1570 after pleading with Cecil for years to be replaced.[76]

Frustrated by the failure of his supporters in London to approve final implementation of the court of castle chamber, Sydney continued to use the Irish privy council as a tribunal. In 1568, the Devon adventurer Sir Peter Carew prosecuted his claim to lands in Co. Carlow and Co. Meath before the Irish council. Resting his argument on the strength of the queen's support and propounding an antiquarian thesis advanced by his client, John Hooker, for title to the Meath property, Carew brought suit against Sir Christopher Chyvers. The respected Chyvers appeared in council with eight lawyers to challenge the jurisdiction of the court, claiming that

> that court was no ordinary court for trial of lands, and therefore the Lord Deputy and Council were no competent judges; secondarily, that no person should be impleaded for any lands but by the order and course of the common law, and not otherwise.[77]

Rising to the challenge, Carew's English lawyer William Peryam argued the case for the authority of royal prerogative in any matter, citing precedent of like cases that had come before the lord deputy and council and chancery when suitors were 'driven to an extremity or wanting just trial'.[78] Chyvers was confronted with the opinion of the two chief justices and solicitor general who concluded that Carew could not obtain a fair trial at common law, so he pleaded for a settlement. The agreement accepted by Carew awarded him a small sum for the estate without a turbulent hearing. In contrast, Carew won a legal victory in his suit against the Cavanaghs of Co. Carlow for the barony of Idrone. The council rejected the claim offered by the Irish sept of prescriptive right by descent from the king of Leinster, Dermot MacMurrough, accepting instead Carew's tenuous genealogical connection

Edward Fitzsymon, a future serjeant at law; and James Stanyhurst, recorder of Dublin. By 1578, however, Sydney's attitude turned sour during the confrontation with some of these same lawyers over the cess. Owing to the machinations of Ormond in London, a new lease of Blackfriars to the earl, for his client Laurence Alford, was given in February 1578 at the height of the cess controversy. Ironically, the opposition leader Henry Burnell retained his chambers there until he was displaced in 1609. Ibid., pp. 65–66.

76. Brady, *Chief governors*, pp. 125–36. The council book records an extensive correspondence regarding the treason of the earl of Thomond and related problems in the new presidency of Connacht in 1570. HMC, *Haliday MSS*, pp. 201–17.

77. *Cal. Carew MSS, 1515–74*, p. c.   78. Ibid.

to the original barons. Sydney had departed Dublin, leaving the hearing to the lord chancellor and council on 7 December 1568.[79]

In the case of another English adventurer, the council imprisoned Thomas Stukeley, Sydney's erstwhile client, on a charge of high treason against the queen. At his appearance before the tribunal on 6 June 1569, Stukeley was ordered to remain close prisoner in Dublin Castle while awaiting his trial. However, after eighteen weeks of incarceration, neither his accuser nor any other man appeared to give evidence, while the estates of Stukeley were ravaged during the rebellion of the Butlers. On 11 October, the council agreed to free the defendant, accepting a £500 surety for his appearance at the next Hilary term.[80] Stukeley finally departed the country for service against the queen on the continent, but the trial demonstrated that the council heard cases against even its trusted captains.[81] In 1571, Sydney was still using the council as a court of record when the court of castle chamber had finally obtained its formal authorization (see below). On 17 February he met with eight councillors to hear the cause of John Horne, a merchant of Gloucester, against the mayor and town of Wexford. Horne charged that his ship was robbed of £90 sterling while anchored in the river at Wexford, and the master was murdered by inhabitants of the town. Castigating the commissioners who were deputed to prosecute the malefactors at Wexford, the council was offended by the negligence, concealment, partiality and dishonour of their work, which had ended without any indictment being preferred. The council required the commissioners to return to Wexford, empanel leading men of the town and country, and impose on them a cess in the amount of the robbery, £90, to fall most heavily on those held in suspicion of complicity in the offence, and to collect the sum for the use of the complainant prior to 20 May 1571. This draconian order of the council was meant to intensify the commissioners' search for the evildoers, since the order would be terminated once the offenders were arraigned. In defence of its prerogative order, the council explained:

> wee doe earnestly pray you, and for the honor of this state, specially require you to publishe and make openly knowen unto them in our behaulf (that we hold the fact so horrible, the doinge of it so detestable, the poore mens losses so lamentable, the consielment so crafty and the searche so negligent and the bolsteringe of it so stowte,) as we by oure discreacions do judge it more agreeable with reason, conscience and lawe and consequently more with the honor of this borde to make a president [i.e. precedent] of it in this sort as we have appoincted then by the sufference of it unredressed or unpunisshed.[82]

79. *Cal. pat. rolls Ire., Hen. VIII–Eliz.*, pp. 520–21. See also *Anglicizing*, pp. 197–98; Brady, *Chief governors*, pp. 278–79; Canny, *Elizabethan conquest*, p. 68.
80. RIA, MS 24 F. 17, ff. 319–19v.
81. Brady, *Chief governors*, pp. 121, 200, 273, 276, 278. Stukeley entered the service of the pope, and later led an expedition aimed for Ireland that was diverted to Morocco, where he was eventually killed in 1578. Lennon, *Sixteenth century Ireland*, p. 223.
82. RIA, MS 24 F. 17, f. 342v and see ff. 341v–43.

The council's order rehearsed the substance of the original commission, finding the members of it in default without naming them. Horne's factor in Wexford, Henry Smithe, was grievously wounded in the affray. In a similar order on 21 March 1570 to the mayor and corporation of Waterford, the council demanded their attendance in Dublin at the beginning of the next term to offer full testimony or forfeit their recognizance of £200.[83] The inception of the court of castle chamber was designed, in part, to alleviate the council from the burden of hearing cases of riot and affray.

The council maintained a vigilant scrutiny of relations between the Old English and Gaelic Irish communities, using its judicial mien to interpose a kind of domestic diplomacy between rivals. Recognizing that its orders would come under continuous pressure, the council referred to previous adjudication while settling accounts between warring neighbours. In the case of Sir Barnaby Fitzpatrick, baron of Upper Ossory, plaintiff, against Sir William O'Carroll regarding the murder of Melaghlan McMorrough and the stealing of ten stud mares, the council took up assorted old grievances at its meeting in Philipstown on 6 February 1570. O'Carroll charged Fitzpatrick with robberies and spoils committed by the baron's servants and followers, but two days later he acknowledged that he had disobeyed previous orders made in 1566 and 1563, and agreed to pay 200 kine to the queen and 200 kine to the lord deputy for those violations. Enjoining both litigants to keep the peace after the hearing of extensive complaints, the council said they

> shuld joyne and continew in unfained frendship, amitie and brotherlie love and serve togethers in any of her majesties affaires without quarelinge or grudginge one to the other and not revenge any disorder that shuld hapen betwen them before complaint first made to the lorde deputie or other governor.[84]

The council's order required the offending party to provide treble damages whenever one of their followers committed a robbery of cattle or other beasts, leaving to commissioners the further hearing of other allegations not proved at the council's deliberations. Francis Cosbie and Owny McHugh were ordered to hear and determine the remaining charges, defraying restitution already made by O'Carroll to the baron of Upper Ossory and concluding the adjudication before Easter.[85] Although Dr Edwards has recently claimed that Upper Ossory 'kept the crown's officials at bay until the late 1570s', maintaining their own Gaelic practices in law, his assertion that historians should substitute 'Gaelic survival strategies for English reform policies as the main focus point of investigation' needs to be tempered in view of the evident penetration of common law and viceregal arbitration in the territory throughout the Elizabethan period.[86]

---

83   Ibid., ff. 335v–36. The first order for their appearance before the council was made on 30 January 1570. Ibid., f. 330.   84. Ibid., f. 331.   85. Ibid., ff. 331–31v.
86. D. Edwards, 'Collaboration without anglicisation', pp. 87, 96. Edwards acknowledges that the

A contention between three septs of the Kinsellaghs in Co. Wexford against the farmer of the castle of Ferns, the constable Thomas Masterson, was resolved by the council in favour of the Irish suitors. Meeting at Leighlin on 16 May 1570, by deputation to the senior councillors Thomas Cusake and Francis Agarde, the council heard the Irishmen's claim that Masterson imposed on them a surcharge of 12 spars in addition to the 120 spars of bonaght due to the queen's gallow-glasses in the fort.[87] The two Irish-speaking councillors used the testimony of the brehon lawyers in the hearing and affirmed the rights of the Kinsellaghs, joining their testimony to that of Anthony Colclogh, the former constable of the castle, who also confirmed that the twelve spars of bonaght were assessed out of the sum of 120 spars due and not as a surcharge. Hugh O'Bolgir, an 'ancient man that some tyme in those countries was serjant to the said Colcloghe and leavied and receaved the said twelve score sparres',[88] agreed. On behalf of the council, the commissioners concluded that Masterson had no right to the additional 12 spars of bonaght, using a mixture of Gaelic Irish and official English testimony to find for Irish suitors. They explained their deliberation thus:

> We, therefore, for our better satisfaccion and knowledge of the truthe how the twelve sparrs ought to be answereed, called unto us certeine of the aunciente and gravest men of the Odorans, Bolgirs and others in those parties, and for that purpose examined them upon there solemn othe: Thei confessed and declared that McMoroghowe, from tyme to tyme had allowed unto him twelve sparrs out of the said six score ... and that the said twelve sparrs so now demaunded above the said six score sparrs is onelie by extorcion and ought not of right nor dutie to be paide.[89]

barons 'promised time and again to obey English law and to answer the royal writs', offering hospitality to crown officials and judges in order to preserve their freedom of action. Comparison with the aristocracy in the north of England and other estates far from the court would probably reveal strategems of a quite similar nature. Ibid., p. 87. See also S.G. Ellis, *The Pale and the Far North: government and society in two early Tudor borderlands* (Galway, 1988); and 'Crown, community and government in the English territories, 1450–1575', *Hist*, lxxi (1987), 187–204.

87. Spars were smaller than timbers, usually of hardwood and about six inches in thickness, useful in both construction and navigation. *OED.*

88. RIA, MS 24 F. 17, ff. 336–36v. See also N. Patterson, 'Gaelic law and the Tudor conquest of Ireland: the social background of the sixteenth century recensions of the pseudo-historical prologue to the Senchas mar', *IHS*, xxvii (1991), 193ff; and Edwards, 'Collaboration without anglicization', pp. 81, 87–91, who denies that the O'Dorans' accommodation of brehon law signified the achievement of anglicization in the territory.

89. RIA, MS 24 F. 17, ff. 336–36v. Cusake and Agarde signed for the council, acting on its behalf in this case, a clear example of the delegation of conciliar business and of the admixture of Gaelic and English legal practice.

CONCLUSION

Despite the hesitant and uncertain beginnings of the court of castle chamber in this period, it is clear that powerful men considered its establishment a benefit to the crown's government in Ireland. From Cromwell's Ordinances in 1534 to the ministrations of Sussex and Sydney, there is enough correspondence to suggest that the foundation of a star chamber court for Ireland was frequently under consideration. Multiple causes doomed the initial enterprise, including the turbulence of the mid-Tudor era in England; the military crises and factional disputes that interrupted Irish administrations and led to frequent commissions of inquiry; and the competing agendas of adventurers who sought to exploit the Irish situation for their own benefit, leading to an administrative stalemate in which the castle chamber court remained merely a totemic gesture in the architectural blueprint for Irish governance. The mid-Tudor privy council in Ireland struggled to maintain a judicial presence throughout the countryside without the regimen of assize and circuit courts or presidencies, so the inchoate court of castle chamber lacked the judicial network for a full-scale model of the English star chamber court. Nonetheless, the implementation of the court was urged relentlessly by Sussex and Sydney. As governors in the North of England and Wales, respectively, they understood the usefulness of a well-established provincial system of justice in relation to the central courts. When the castle chamber court was instituted at virtually the same time as the lords president and councils in Munster and Connacht, the interaction of these tribunals became a steadily growing source of litigation. While some writers have focused on the use of martial law and the lords president as military veterans, it is also clear that the chief justices of the presidency courts were active judges and sought to implement the foundation of common law jurisdictions.[90]

Sussex and Sydney, as chief promoters of the court of castle chamber, were typical soldier/statesmen in the Elizabethan mould, preferring the style of government in Kent and using the norms of justice with which they were familiar by establishing justices of the peace, sheriffs, assize judges and a network of reliable landowner élites. The radical departure they sought in Ireland was in fact merely a copy of the conservative shrieval pattern they inherited as great landowners in the south of England. Their efforts to implement English ways in Irish culture met with mixed success, and as judges they often deferred to commissions and legal experts. But their overriding confidence in the ministration of prerogative justice in Ireland stemmed from a concern to institutionalize the authority and integrity of crown governance, resting on a strong network of well-affected landowners rather than small and isolated garrisons. In this way, their inherent conservatism should be recognized as an important dimension of their reform proposals, so prominently discussed in the works of Brady, Canny and

90. Canny, *Elizabethan conquest*, pp. 97–100; D. Edwards, 'Ideology and experience', pp. 128, 133, 137, 142.

others. While both Sussex and Sydney were frustrated in the end by bureaucratic inertia, and the court of castle chamber was inaugurated in the next administration, they were instrumental in bringing it about. When Sydney and six other councillors signed the entry book for the last time on 22 March 1571, they unwittingly ended an era. For, in the next administration, conciliar records would be reformed and the new entry book of the court of castle chamber detailing the work of the Irish star chamber, would end in 1621.[91]

91. RIA, MS 24 F. 17, f. 343v is the last entry in the Irish privy council register begun by Sussex and calendared in HMC, *Haliday MSS*. BL., Add. MS 4792, ff. 136–44 contains the table of the Fitzwilliam council book, calendared in the Haliday MSS by John Gilbert, with entries that begin in 1571 and end in 1619 with the death of Lord Chancellor Thomas Jones, and referencing a tome of 445 original folios. Fitzwilliam authorized another council book in his second administration, begun in 1589 and ending with the Essex administration in 1599. The Haliday MSS table made from this document contains only two pages, though based upon an original manuscript, now lost, of 372 folios.

CHAPTER FIVE

The first years of the court of castle chamber, 1571 to 1579

[Citing the lawyers' arguments against cess] ... they should be drawn by her Maties Attorney into the nature of an informacon against them, and their procurers, and so in the castell chamber at a daie appoincted for the pourpose, in the prsence of yor L.[ordship] and the Councell and the rest of the LLs usinge to sitt in that Courte, to be exhibited againste them in as earneste and effectuall mannr as you can devise.

Privy council to Lord Deputy Sydney, 22 March 1578[1]

THE FIRST REGIME of Sir Henry Sydney came to an inglorious end in the spring of 1571. The ambitious viceroy had disappointed the queen by conducting a profligate campaign against the Butlers in 1569 after she had been assured of peace in Ireland upon the sudden death of Shane O'Neill late in 1567. The parliament of 1569–71 did not produce substantial new revenue, but instead witnessed a store of grievances against the incumbent governor. The powerful earl of Ormonde chafed at the leadership of Sydney, who sought to rein in the provincial autonomy of Ireland's peers. Colonization in Ulster proceeded despite Sydney's lukewarm approval, offending many without establishing the anticipated anglicization of the province. Adventurers like Sir Peter Carew harmed the reputation of the viceroy for even-handed justice, laying claim to the lands of settled Anglo-Irish leaders like Sir Christopher Chyvers. The long-delayed accounts of Fitzwilliam demonstrated the financial drain of ambitious reforming chief governors, in power since the tenure of Sussex in 1556. His nominee to become the first provincial president in Munster, Sir Warham St Leger, had been withdrawn by the queen, and his replacement was the ruthless military captain, Sir Humphrey Gilbert. The presidency of Connacht raised such violent opposition that the beleaguered Sir Edward Fyton called for the help of the viceroy in taming the Burkes and others. Sydney was recalled at his own request. And yet, the inauguration of the star chamber jurisdiction apparently went forward without him, suggesting that his impact on institutions of government was more positive than his legacy in other areas.

1. PRO, SP 63/60/51v.

ERRATIC BEGINNINGS: FITZWILLIAM'S COURT OF
CASTLE CHAMBER

While Sydney negotiated his release from the burdens of office, he was replaced by the veteran Sir William Fitzwilliam as lord justice, a man whose career as viceroy suggests nothing of the ambition or energy of his two predecessors. Fitzwilliam was by this time a forty-five-year-old senior official with a long record of service in financial administration, clouded by negative results in the latest accounts of his tenure as vice-treasurer. His was the classic caretaker administration, yet the new court of castle chamber was apparently launched during his first year in office. The reasons for this would appear to lie with Cecil's ministry and the ongoing support of both the previous viceroys for implementing the star chamber jurisdiction. We can confirm that one of these powerful Elizabethan courtiers made the case at Westminster for the erection of a prerogative court. The draft of the commission for a court of castle chamber was amended, refined and finally approved on 14 June 1571 by Sydney himself. His client, Edmund Tremayne, addressed the document to the queen's legal officers, who signed the draft at the end. In Sydney's words, 'As many leaves of thys booke as aperyth to be affyrmed or amyned by G. Gerrard & Tho Bromley attorney & solycitor generall I have redd and thynk the matter [in] the same conteyned reasonable & expedyent.'[2] Tremayne charged the Irish administration with laxity, saying the lawyers of Ireland 'do slenderlie see unto the Queenes profitts'.[3] He blamed the Irish judges for partiality, faulty record-keeping, ignoring statute law and failing to issue recognizances.[4] Eased by a thin film of bureaucratic momentum, and coupled with the arrival of peace on all frontiers in 1571, a commission with full powers to establish the court of castle chamber finally arrived in the summer of 1571. Cecil authorized the draft of the commission on 14 June 1571 after making note of it in his memorandum of 4 June, and the commission received the privy seal on 28 June. Defining the listed offences that the court was established to correct, the queen's order continued thus:

> For the better remedye whereof & to the intent that suche execrable & p[er]nicious evels & greffes shall not escape without just and dew correction & ponyshement we have thought mete to appoint that a p[ar]ticuler court for the hering & determynacion of thoes detestable enormyties faultes & offences shalbe holden within or castell of or cyttie of Dublin in that or raelme of Irland ... & that the same or court shalbe cauled & namyd the castell chamber of or said raelme of Irland.[5]

2. PRO, SP 63/32/166.   3. PRO, SP 63/32/182.
4. PRO, SP 63/32/186–87.
5. PRO, SP 63/32/162; *Cal. pat. rolls, 1569–72*, pp. 276–77; *Cal. S.P. Ire., 1509–73*, p. 449. On 10 July 1571 the privy council in England confirmed John Harepenny, clerk of the court of castle chamber, in his possession of a lease of tithes in Ireland, noting the absence of the lord deputy at that time. The

Sir William Fitzwilliam began his career as viceroy on 1 April 1571 without the customary fiscal bargaining that attended the start of his two predecessors' regimes in Ireland.[6] Instead of a long campaign of negotiation in the corridors of power in England, Fitzwilliam was left in charge of a discredited government with the authority of an interim lord justice. His regime as lord deputy did not begin until the end of the year, in December 1571, after others were considered for the post.[7] He quarrelled endlessly with the ineffective Sir Edward Fyton, the first lord president of Connacht, and much of his tenure was taken up with rebellions that Fyton had sparked in the western province. The council was called upon to hear the dispute between Fyton and the earl of Clanricarde in the spring of 1571, connected to the rebellion of the earl's sons in Connacht. The intrusion of the lord president into the traditional norms of Irish governance in the distant west had sparked unrest in Thomond which rapidly spread, and Clanricarde was accused of withholding his support for the provincial government. On 24 May 1571, Fitzwilliam wrote to Cecil that the council had summoned both Fyton and Clanricarde to Dublin where a trial of six days was held concerning the allegations against the earl. At that time, the council decided that the earl was needed in the province and his contumacy would be tolerated for reasons of expediency.[8] On 26 March 1572, however, the council held another full hearing of matters between the earl and the president, concluding that by the custom of the country he should be held responsible for his sons' rebellion, and committing him prisoner in Dublin Castle on the testimony of the bishops of Clonfert and Tuam.[9] The records of this trial demonstrate that Fyton had prepared two books of charges against the earl, supplemented on 22 July 1572 by accusations of treason which the lord president impudently withheld at the council meeting. On this occasion, Sir John Plunkett, chief justice of queen's bench, proclaimed that unless Fyton produced the evidence he may as well be dead, and Fyton was cautioned by the privy council in England to pursue 'pollitique proceedinges wth the said Earle' rather than to exacerbate conditions in the province. They continued:

tentative status of Fitzwilliam was implied in the conditional language of the award, noting that a subsequent commission might be needed to satisfy Harepenny. *Acts privy council, 1571–75*, p. 35 (letter of privy council to lord justice and lord chancellor of Ireland). A subsequent commission was solicited in 1581 by the lord deputy and council because the court apparently lacked full authority under a lord keeper in the absence of a lord chancellor. *Cal. pat. rolls, 1569–72*, pp. 276–77. See also Wood, 'Castle chamber', p. 155; 'Cal. Council book, 1581–86', *Anal Hib*, no. 24 (1967), p. 112.

6. PRO, SP 63/32/9–11v shows Sydney left Dublin on 25 March; Fitzwilliam took up office on 1 April 1571.

7. See *Anglicizing*, pp. 454–55; Fitzwilliam was a very active Irish councillor, but failed to reform the exchequer and had a debt to the crown of £7,000 by 1569. PRO, SP 63/25/15–16. Helen Walshe saw him as favouring coercive measures in religion, but doing little to enforce them. Walshe, 'Enforcing the Elizabethan settlement: the vicissitudes of Hugh Brady, bishop of Meath, 1563–84', *IHS*, xxvi (1989), 367.

8. PRO, SP 63/32/116–17, 112–13v, 124–25 ; BL, Add. MS 4792, f. 136; Brady, *Chief governors*, pp. 137–39.

9. Bodl., Carte MS 56, f. 69; Carte MS 57, ff. 513–14.

And by cause we finde by some of yor lres sente unto us that you Sr Ed
Fitton have in a gen[er]allitye pronounced that you have matter whearwth
to charge the said Earle, as an offender in treason wch being required to
utter in specialtye you have forborne, we cannot but merveyle of such a
mann[er] of proceedinge to give suche Cause to Charge a noble man of soe
good a Credyte as he hath byne and neyther to utter it to you the L.
Deputye nor to any other of yt Counsell nor yett to advertise her matie
thereof nor any of us of her Counsell.[10]

When the earl of Clanricarde submitted to the council on 6 August 1572 and
offered his full support in quelling the uprising, the lord president worsened the
affair by bringing forth an indictment of treason against him.[11] The council
explained in a letter of 24 September that 'for suspicion of unkindnesse emongest
oure selves generallie' they swore to each other's good will, noting that they had
decided to release Clanricarde for service in Connacht with assurances that he
would work cooperatively with Fyton.[12] By the end of the year, Fyton was recalled
from the presidency, though he continued to plague the earl with litigation, and
the council again heard the charges and rebuttals in a meeting of 9 May 1573 at
Dublin Castle. Fyton's charges amounted to 22 articles that the earl sought to
disprove, while the latter brought 54 claims against the president. At the conclusion of these deliberations, the council thought it best to postpone its decision
until the queen's instructions arrived, since any judgement against the earl would
incite a new uprising in the province.[13] Allegations of this sort, involving treason
and the alleged malfeasance of provincial officers usually came before the court of
castle chamber after 1575. Though Fyton was recalled as lord president in 1572,
returning to his estates in Cheshire, he was named as vice-treasurer in Ireland in
1573 and returned to engage in further conflict with the lord deputy. Fitzwilliam
was given no particular charge other than to govern economically and to lend his
support to the Ulster expeditions of Sir Thomas Smith and the earl of Essex,
another rival for power and influence in Ireland.[14] Notable for the contentiousness
of his regime in Ireland, it is not surprising that the council gave orders 'against
breons and breon law', followed by a more general proscription 'against bardes,
carroghs and rimors' in the abbreviated table to the council book.[15] With Sydney

---

10. BL, Add. MS 32,323, f. 28v; Bodl., Carte MS 57, f. 443. The rift between Fitzwilliam and Fyton
    also needed resolution, and the queen sought the lord chancellor and archbishop of Dublin to
    amend their controversies on the council.
11. PRO, SP 63/37/64–66, 66v–67.   12. PRO, SP 63/ 37/121–22.
13. PRO, SP 63/40/130–33; Fyton to Cecil, ibid., 63/40/95. When the two rivals were ordered to
    embrace at the council table, the matter apparently ended. Letters to Clanricarde from the
    council in October 1573 ordering him to see Athenry refortified made no mention of the trial.
    SP 63/43/77–78.
14. Hiram Morgan, 'The colonial venture of Sir Thomas Smith in Ulster, 1571–1575', *Hist Jn*,
    xxviii (1985), 261–78.
15. BL, Add. MS 4792, ff. 136–37; see HMC, *Haliday MSS*, pp 283–84. This undated reference

challenging the fiscal probity of his administration and offering to cut expenses in dramatic fashion if he were to return as lord deputy, Fitzwilliam's government was continuously under fire from rivals at court and in his own administration.[16]

The Black Council Book ended with the last entry of Sydney's administration on 22 March 1571 and a new council book was begun in April to mark the commencement of Fitzwilliam's regime.[17] This document, now missing, was chronicled as 'a table of the principall matters contained in the counsell booke which begun the first of Aprile 1571'.[18] The nearly simultaneous appearance of the entry book of the court of castle chamber may be demonstrated by reference to cases commenced as early as 29 November 1571.[19] The entry book begins with two undated references that dismissed a long list of defendants, and some fourteen pages are now missing from the document. On the vellum cover of the entry book the barely legible date of 1570 is scrolled, probably by the under-tasked clerk of castle chamber.[20] Owing to the tardy receipt of the commission in Ireland, the origin of the court must be placed in the government of Fitzwilliam, rather than in that of Sydney, though the latter laid the important groundwork for the court and apparently prepared the entry book itself during his administration.

A not unexpected period of transition occurred, during which some of the litigation normally heard before the council was delegated to the new star chamber jurisdiction, while other matters remained within the purview of the council itself. The earliest mention of a case before the castle chamber occurs by reference to a bill of riot filed on 29 November 1571 by John Plunket, gentleman, of Loughcrew, Co. Meath against a rival, Edmond Darcie of Jordanston, another gentleman, and others. Based on similar charges in the entry book, we assume the riot involved a larger controversy over land in Co. Meath. The case was dismissed on 7 November 1582 along with eighteen others, some undated.[21] Lord Justice Fitzwilliam and the

occurred before April 1573 and marks a contrast with Sydney's efforts to use brehon law in the resolution of cases involving the Gaelic Irish.

16. Brady, *Chief governors*, pp. 144–46.

17. The chronological table in HMC, *Haliday MSS* ends abruptly on p. 255, with folio 343v, an order of 22 March 1571, signed by Sydney and 6 others, for proper payment to pursuivants and messengers by Irish peers. The text of the Black Council Book concluded with the oath taken by councillors from the reign of Mary [a reference to 'all saints' was crossed out in the manuscript], and the Stuart clerk William Usher included his own oath of office, signing the document on 19 September 1609. Ware refers to the subsequent 'Council Book of Fitzwilliams' from 1571 to 1619 in his 'Chronicle of Ireland', BL, Add. MS 4813, f. 92.

18. It is tabled inadequately and the first 106 folios covered the entire four years of Fitzwilliam's government, showing very little adjudication at the council. BL, Add. MS 4792, ff. 136–44; HMC, *Haliday MSS*, pp. 282–84; the entire council book of 445 folios ends with the death of Thomas Jones, lord chancelllor, in 1619. See also 'Cal. Council book, 1581–86', *Anal Hib*, no. 24 (1967), 109.

19. BL, Add. MS 47,172, ff. 67–67v, where cases of long standing were dismissed in the government of Lord Deputy Grey, including another case of 30 November 1572, otherwise unreferenced in the entry book.

20. Ibid., ff. 1–3.   21. BL, Add. MS 47,172, f. 67.

council heard a case on 17 December 1571 between Sir Barnaby Fitzpatrick and the earl of Ormonde, alleging the earl's followers had committed sundry spoils and taking of cattle on the baron's estates in Ossory. Taking note of the imminent departure of Ormonde from Ireland, the council sent a commission of oyer and terminer to adjudicate all the complaints between litigants of either side at the borders of Kilkenny and Ossory. In the meantime, the council ordered that evidence of further 'preys, bodrages or stelthes' between the two countries should be 'tracked' to the owner of the land to which the track would lead, compelling the owner who could not otherwise avoid the onus of responsibility to make restitution to the party aggieved.[22] Fitzwilliam and Lord Chancellor Weston both signed the document, an example of conciliar adjudication during the transition to full implementation of the court of castle chamber. No mention of star chamber is made in the document, though it is clear that a full hearing of pleas and allegations on both sides had taken place before the council.[23]

Formal hearings before the council itself were rare in this period, though on 16 September 1572 they heard the confession of Walter Dormer to counterfeiting the hand of the lord deputy. The council in Ireland sat with nine members at St Sepulchre's in Dublin to hear the case, but no mention was made of castle chamber.[24] Two cases recorded in the first folios of the entry book merely listed the names of persons found guilty after indictment, indicating their respective fines and in some cases their social class and place of abode. In the first list, we see the names of several cottagers and other men of Co. Louth, particularly those of Termonfeckin, five miles from Drogheda. Only Patrick Plunkett was listed as a gentleman. The second list includes two women, several Plunketts, and concludes with the name of 'John, also sundrye of Patrick Plunketts howsehold men'. In this second list were persons who had 'confessed to be at the spoyle of the said shippe', including three other gentlemen. In the second list, only two placenames

---

22. Bodl., Carte MS 57, f. 194; and see W.N. Osborough, 'The Irish custom of tracts' in *Studies in Irish legal history* (Dublin, 1999), pp. 64–65, 68–70. This further insertion of conciliar authority in Ossory mitigates the claim of Edwards that the baron enjoyed practical independence of action while flouting the common law, though it remains of interest that the lawyers continued to sanction the Gaelic practice of 'tracking'. See Edwards, 'Collaboration without anglicization', pp. 88–89.

23. Bodl., Carte MS 57, f. 194. A similar delegation of formal hearing to a commission was reported within days of Sydney's departure, on 20 March 1570. The citizens of Dublin exhibited to the council a complaint against the mayor and the master and warders of the Trinity guild of Dublin, alleging injury from the guild's detention of certain privileges, franchises and commodities from the whole city. The council declared 'For that or leisure then wold not suffer us to heare the controversye betwene them', they deputed Agarde and three lawyers to hear and determine the cause. After days of hearings, they perused the charters and on 15 March gave an order upholding the complaint. Sydney affirmed on 20 March that the order had the authority of the government. Ibid., f. 622.

24. Ibid., f. 622v. Subsequent cases of counterfeiting the hand of the chief governor were recorded in the entry book of castle chamber court, particularly under Sir John Perrot, so it is clear that the council retained certain aspects of prerogative jurisdiction during and after this transition period. See below, Ch. 6 and BL, Add. MS 47,172, ff. 79–81v.

occurred although Baltra, on the coast of Co. Louth near Drogheda, is named in both lists and there were McMahons named in both lists. Lacking external evidence, it would appear that these cases were directly related since the names of the councillors who signed the entry book were identical in both documents; surnames and placenames recur in both of them; and the fines in both lists were very similar. No dates were given, but it would appear that the entries were devoted to settlement of a single case in which a ship was spoiled off the coast of Co. Louth, in 1571 or 1572.[25] Another case of riot involving Co. Meath, also dismissed in 1582, was brought by Thomas Darcie, gentleman, from Lugher, and other plaintiffs against Patrick Coyne from Lesmollen, along with other defendants, on 30 November 1572. Nothing more is known of the case, though it was still pending ten years later and many suits of this kind were ultimately settled at other venues or by arbitration without formal record in the entry book of the castle chamber court.[26]

One of the earliest cases heard before the court of castle chamber was not recorded in the entry book, though a digest of the suit may be found in the records of Trinity College Dublin. On 30 January 1573, the court heard a complaint by Dame Jenet Sarsfield, late wife to the former lord chancellor Sir Thomas Cusake, accusing Margaret Howth of a riot and forcible abduction in the 'taking aweye of the said Dame Jennett the fourth of October 1571'.[27] The widow Howth, of Corballyes in Co. Meath, was accused with others in the riot though none of the other names appear in the digest. However, the entry book makes note of the case when the clerk dismissed suits of long standing in 1582, citing other defendants including Richard Nugent and Frances Birmingham, gentleman, of 'the Corballie', Co. Meath, among them.[28] Typical of the laconic records of the court in this period, the account offers little beyond the final decree to explain the circumstances of the offence, the pleas or the rationale of the court. The defendant was convicted of consenting to the riot and forcible abduction of the plaintiff, and similar occurrences usually involved the transfer or inheritance of property, though it is not clear in this case. The absence of this decree from the entry book may be explained by the omission of some fourteen folio pages from the beginning of the document in the British Library, Additional Manuscripts 47,172.

The court of castle chamber frequently became embroiled in jurisdictional disputes that touched upon land, political rivalry and religion. On 25 February 1573, the lord deputy and council wrote to Perrot as lord president in Munster, asking him to determine title to the land of Sir Peter Carew, who had approached

25. BL, Add. MS 47,172, ff. 1–1v. Fitzwilliam signed the document, followed by Adam Loftus as lord keeper, the bishop of Meath and councillors Fyton, Lucas Dillon, White and Agarde.
26. Ibid., f. 67v.
27. TCD, MS 852, f 95v The court heard the case over a year later and found the said Margaret guilty of the alleged offence, ordering her to be held prisoner in Dublin Castle during pleasure and to pay a fine of £20 in addition to costs of court.
28. BL, Add. MS 47,172, ff. 69–69v, 74. The latter entry mentions Lady Cusake in her suit against Nugent.

the council itself for a final determination of his suit. Noting that the time was not apt for stirring up the Irishry, the council deferred to Perrot as more knowledgeable of the situation:

> wee resolved that the matter might better … be furthered by yor ls. discreete dealinge there … then if we, unskilful of thone, and lacking the comoditie of thother, should … either send for them hither or send comissioners thither …[29]

The president of Munster showed no such timidity in his approach to the law, demanding in 1573 that the privy council take up the matter of Perrot's alleged encroachment on the earl of Ormonde's liberty of Tipperary. Complaining that he had been charged in his absence with violation of his mandate, Perrot requested the Irish council to bring Ormonde's officers and lawyers before them. The council summoned John Ayleward, steward of the earl, to ask about the alleged encroachment, whereupon Ayleward put forth certain articles devised by Richard Shee, the earl's principal officer. Shee maintained that he had given Ayleward the articles on condition that he not prefer them without the advice of learned counsel, to which the latter claimed he did not prefer them and was never privy to Shee's intention.[30] This contretemps among the absent earl's household officers led the council to write to Cecil in an effort to clear the name of Perrot. Signed by nine of the councillors, the document shows that the council continued its involvement in disputes concerning provincial government, an important issue that became central to the role of the castle chamber court in the next decade.

Acting occasionally as an appellate court, the council heard the writ of appeal by a daughter of one Browne, on 20 April 1573. The daughter of Browne contested the pardon of Feagh McHugh O'Byrne and Brian McCahir Cavanagh for the murder of her father. The master of the rolls, Nicholas White, conducted the case for the plaintiff. However, the court refused to authenticate the writ of appeal or to revoke the queen's pardon, explaining that Irish rebelliousness would be aggravated by failing to honour the royal promise. After long consideration, the council further stated,

> it apperithe that it is no great derogacon to the due corse of Justice and lawe (the state of this government considerid) to deny unto the sayd Browne the Benefit of the lawe in this behalf. And Forasmuche also as it is apparaunt that the graunting of that writ wold renue a blooddie rebellion wch withe great travell we have appaysed, whereof were lyke to insue the shedding of muche innocent blood and the spoile of manie a good subiecte [the avoyding

---

29. PRO, SP 63/41/39. Writing again on 10 June 1573 to the queen and privy council, the Irish council justified their delay in the resolution of Carew's title, suggesting the queen award him lands in England to avoid 'the peril of stirre' in Munster. PRO, SP 63/41/37–37v, 41.

30. PRO, SP 63/40/140.

wherof is to be preferred farre before the privat interes[t] and comoditie of anie one subiecte] And so by undiscreet graunting the corse of Justice to one, we should do great iniustice to manie.[31]

The court under Fitzwilliam was still in its infancy, deliberating numerous cases of this sort in council without turning to the fledgeling star chamber tribunal. Nonetheless, the appellate nature of the court of castle chamber gradually became more pronounced after 1575. It is also clear from the surviving evidence that the entry book itself is not a sufficient or final record of the business of the court, particularly during this transitional period.

The notorious disharmony on the Irish privy council was once again incited by the irascible Sir Edward Fyton, who returned to Ireland as vice-treasurer in 1573. He retained nominal leadership of the council in Connacht as chief commissioner, and the Irish council on 9 May 1573 required that the commission serve as justices, using oyer and terminer in the province to govern by authority of the common law, but adding, 'or otherwies, by their Discrecons, as causes in equitie and conscience shoulde move them where the rules of the lawes shoulde be to[o] straight and harde'.[32] On 4 June 1573 a memorandum detailed the remarkable case of Fyton's solitary defiance of the Irish council. The verdict of a coroner's inquest in Dublin found that James Meede, a yeoman of Dublin, killed one Rowdon, a gentleman, 'se defendendo', for which the Irish council gave Meede the queen's pardon. A fiant was issued, signed by all the councillors and sent to James Ryan the clerk of the rolls to be given the great seal, but Fyton as vice-treasurer called upon the clerk to see the fiant and detained it in his possession, refusing to give it up. Ryan complained to the council and Fitzwilliam sent his private secretary, and later Chief Justice Plunkett, to demand the fiant be returned. Fyton refused to surrender the fiant of Meede's pardon, saying it was given heedlessly, so the council declared his resistance 'a dangerous contumacie, disobedience and contempte against the dignitie, credit and authoritie of this her maties state', and committed Fyton to prison in Dublin Castle, only Nicholas White dissenting.[33] On 5 June 1573, Fyton was released but then refused to sit at the council meetings at 9 in the morning and 4 in the afternoon, despite being urged by the viceroy to serve the queen in his office of vice-treasurer. On 12 June, the exasperated viceroy wrote to Cecil that he had sent Fyton to his charge in Connacht, since he refused to attend council meetings. But the matter did not end with Fyton's banishment. Letters from the queen on 28 and 29 June 1573 addressed the original pardon, stating that Fyton was correct to resist the awarding of a general pardon. The queen said, 'And in that respect we do Judge & esteme that our counsell there did you wrong to put you to any Imp[ri]sonment for doeng that wch every good counsellor ought to do.'[34] She charged the council itself with hasty deliberation in

31. Bodl., Carte MS 56, f. 65v.   32. Bodl., Carte MS 57, f. 616.
33. PRO, SP 63/41/52–52v; Bodl., Carte MS 56, ff. 44–44v.
34. PRO, SP 63/41/152–52v.

the case of a slaying of a gentleman, finding the jury's result corrupt, and the viceroy's issuance of a general pardon excessive when a particular pardon on the indictment would have been appropriate. Her admonition to the council was an extraordinary rebuke, setting forth policy and principle while establishing the conditions of conciliar conduct in this case. She concluded:

> Yet, as aperith, you the rest of or Counsell there have done as litle your duties to god & us that you wold put your hands to it [the pardon] As whatsoever our Deputie for the tyme should allow or do, you wold streight ronne into the same rashnes, and affirme whatsoever he wold will yow wt the subscripcon of your hands, what nede there then eny counsellers, if the Counsellers be but the handes and applauders of or Deputie, yow are put there to be grave & sage advisers, to temper such sodeyn affections either thone way or thother, of love or hatred, as may chaunce to our Deputie, being a man made of flesh and blood who lightly can not be without them, And to have regarde to god first, and then to our honor, and the saufetie & good government of our Realme. Sir Edward fitton semeth to us onely a good & true counseller, who seing so unreasonable a pardon, so unadvisedly graunted, made stay of it to bring it to or Deputie to be better advised of it, not resisting but requiring more mature consultacon. And for this do you all agree to put him to that shame, to comit him as a contempner. He contempned in deede disorder & rashnes but he honored us, requiring more deliberacon & regarde then was had to be had to iustice the wch is clere taken away by that rash & uniust pardon as may apere by the copie therof. He refuseth to sit wt you and he hath cause, for you are all (as aperith) rather folowers of the Deputies affections, then carefull of iustice or of our honor. You should all have done as he did in such rashe doings, and required the Deputie to stay, to take better advisement.[35]

By September 1573 both Fitzwilliam and Fyton were still complaining against one another, and despite the benign intervention of White in November, the pugnacious Fyton refused to go on a mission to Munster where his previous experience as president in Connacht might have made him a suitable candidate as commissioner for the Irish council.[36] The ongoing dispute at the council probably handicapped the formal establishment of the court of castle chamber, since the handling of a simple pardon had produced so much dissension and recrimination at the council board. Nonetheless, the first recorded meeting of the prerogative court in the entry book on 4 November 1573 found both Fitzwilliam and Fyton present at the adjudication of a riot. Two servants of Edward Cusack, gentleman,

---

35. PRO, SP 63/41/154–55v. The queen ended with this warning: 'Yf this had bene in our fathers tyme, who removed a deputy there for calling one of the Cownsell disssenting from hs opinio[n] churle, you may understand how it wold have been taken.' Ibid.

36. PRO, SP 63/42/188–88v.

were accused of riot based upon their depositions heard at the court and presented by John Bathe, solicitor general. The defendants, Danyell Roo and Patryck
Taylor, were found guilty, imprisoned in Dublin Castle and fined forty shillings
each for their offence.[37]

The court of castle chamber gained further momentum during 1574. The
tribunal heard seven cases, including six that alleged a riot and one for perjury.
Two actions in Hilary term were brought against defendants in Co. Dublin.
William Clynche sued Nicholas Russell and five of his kinsmen, who were found
guilty and imprisoned in Dublin Castle on 10 February. Their fines were left to
the discretion of the lord keeper.[38] Two days later, James Fitzgarret sued Edward
Fitzmorris of Co. Kildare, gentleman, and four of his clients, the court finding
'uppon the pleadinges deposycons & other matter' that they were guilty, fining
them £5 Irish, and requiring Fitzmorris to bring in the other defendants by the
first day of the next Easter term.[39] Based on the fuller details of subsequent cases,
we may surmise that these offences involved a form of trespass by agents of the
defendants on lands of the plaintiff, and that the defendants were found not only
guilty of riot but of an implied conspiracy to gain advantage over their neighbours
by recourse to violence. The third case was heard in the next term on 5 May on
a bill of riot brought by Richard Fynn and John Garrahall against Tybott Walshe
and other defendants. This case was dismissed, but nineteen days later the entry
book referred again to the suit, citing the original bill of 10 April 1573 that charged
fifteen defendants with riot, along with Walshe. In both entries, the court discharged
the defendants and permitted them to recover court costs at the discretion of the
lord keeper. Both of the orders were signed by Fitzwilliam, White and Chaloner.
Though the documents differ in wording, it would appear the two entries refer to
the same cause of action.[40] In addition, the viceroy was asked to confer with the
council on instructions from the queen sent on 18 April 1574 on behalf of John
Rowe of Killeston, Co. Carlow. Rowe complained of an apparent assault by the
English official Robert Harpool and his servants, alleging destruction of his
tenants' houses and goods, a charge that would routinely come before the court of
castle chamber in the next administration. Conciliar adjudication may have proceeded to the initial stages before an interim solution was reached, or arbitrators
sent to deal with the problems directly. In these circumstances, no decree would
be entered in the record book, so the work of the council as a court remains often
undetected apart from petitions and other correspondence of this sort.[41]

In another manifestation of archival disarray, the court found it necessary to
record two versions of the same action. On 29 April 1574, Sir Morris Fitzgerald
of Lecagh sued sixteen servants of Owny McHugh of Ballybrittas for riot, the
court finding for the plaintiff. And on 1 July the court returned to the issue,
demanding that McHugh bring in the other defendants or pay their fines before

37. BL, Add. MS 47,172, f. 2.   38. Ibid., f. 3.
39. Ibid., ff. 3v–4.   40. Ibid., ff. 4v, 5v.
41. Bodl., Carte MS 56, f. 590.

the first day of the next Hilary term, confirming the view that the court required patrons or masters of defendants who were sued before it to enforce the orders of the tribunal. McHugh was not sued in either case, but named in both orders and made responsible for their fines of 26s. 8d. Irish apiece.[42] Another cause of action from Easter term was filed on 26 June 1574 by Robert Skerret, merchant of Galway, against his kinsman, the priest Sir Clement Skerret, charging him with perjury. A writ was issued in June 1574, to which Sir Clement replied on 20 October 1574, with rejoinder and interrogatories following. However, for unexplained reasons, the process of attachment was delayed until 1582, by which time the plaintiff was made to appear in court. He there explained that the suit had been judged and ended long before, and this was confirmed by commissioners and learned counsel of the court of castle chamber, so the suit was finally dismissed on 31 October 1582.[43]

The court heard three cases in November 1574, including a third action brought by the tenacious John Garrahall, naming Thomas Walsh (probably kinsman to the earlier defendant Tybbot Walsh) as defendant along with some 27 others. On this occasion, his bill of riot heard at the court on 5 November also charged William Ashpoole of Kenleston, gentleman, based on a bill originally brought in October 1573 (his first and unsuccessful action was brought on 10 April 1573). The proceedings apparently involved a full hearing of witnesses and interrogatories before the lord deputy and five other councillors, whereupon the court found all the defendants guilty and fined them 40 shillings each, except for Ashpoole. As the only person of quality, Ashpoole was fined £20 Irish and required to bring in all the defendants within a fortnight or to pay their fines himself.[44] On 6 November, the court heard a similar cause of riot, brought by Edmond Butler of Callan, Co. Kilkenny against Thomas Roth and nineteen of his kinsmen. As the case involved leading men of the county as adversaries, it was not surprising that the attorney for the defendants, Thomas Brownell, pleaded the queen's pardon for these and all other offences. The formal language of the pardon, dated 7 July, was inscribed in the entry book and the case duly dismissed with the defendants paying court costs to the plaintiff.[45] Finally, on 3 November

---

42. BL., Add. MS 47,172, ff. 5, 6. The second order made note of two letters ordering him to bring in the defendants, and several days of respite to make good on the decree, allowing him another term in which to fulfil its requirements.

43. Ibid., f. 64. The entry book cannot be read as a chronological record of conciliar adjudication, and the lacunae suggest much greater judicial activity than immediately appears. An explanation for the hiatus during summer was given by Ware: 'This sommer by reason of the Plague, the Councell stayed not in the City, for it begun about the beginning of June and continued till the latter end of October.' BL., Add. MS 4813, f. 96: Ware's 'Chronicle of Ireland'.

44. BL., Add. MS 47, 172, ff. 7–7v.

45. Ibid., f. 8 . At this hearing eleven councillors signed the entry, including two peers, Baltinglas and Slane, indicating the importance of the matter. Edmond Butler of Callan was a successful protégé of Ormonde who had served the earl as agent in Tipperary before becoming attorney general of Ireland in 1582, and in 1583 second justice of queen's bench. He served on government commissions to Munster regularly after 1572. Edwards, *Ormond lordship*, p. 41.

1574, the court dismissed a case of perjury. Nicholas Ley, a merchant of Waterford, sued 24 defendants, including James Purcell, William Power and Sir William Holmes, but failed to prove his case in a hearing attended by Fitzwilliam and four other councillors. Making note of the pleadings, proofs and examinations held before the tribunal, the entry book omitted other details of the case. We might surmise that the 24 persons so named were members of a grand jury that made an unfounded accusation against Ley in Waterford, but the evidence for this is barely circumstantial.[46]

The ongoing dispute over the right to prise wines enjoyed by the earl of Ormonde was brought to the attention of the council, acting as a court, in 1573. In this case, its jurisdiction was apparently shared with the chancery, since numerous pleadings were filed in both courts. The earl claimed, through his attorney, that a French ship of St Malo, laden with Spanish wines, avoided payment of two tons of the wine to the earl, but the defendants and their Dublin counsel demurred, claiming that French merchants owed only 2s.6d. to the queen, time out of mind, and that the conciliar court lacked jurisdiction since action of recovery was available at common law. Humphrey Forthe, the earl's attorney, showed his commission from the crown before the court, demanding that the mayor and his officers seize the prise wines pending adjudication. However, the attorneys for the city were joined by petitioners from Drogheda, and the trial was delayed. After interrogatories were drawn and witnesses examined, the viceroy received the queen's letter from Hampton Court on 20 January 1573, ordering him to hear the case and end the matter speedily. The attorney general testified that his search of the records showed the grant of prise wines to the earl in 1372, followed by other grants, and demonstrating these rights by custom and prerogative law. Fitzwilliam and the Irish council then accepted the written opinions of the attorney and solicitor general of England, hearing the opinions of the Irish judges on the issue. The attorneys for Dublin and Drogheda argued that all merchant strangers were discharged from prise wines by a composition made under Edward I; that subsequent commissions allowed them to pay only two shillings for every ton of wine; and that the city of Dublin enjoyed an exemption according to a star chamber decree in England of 1528. However, the queen's counsel rejoined that the right to prise wines was a continuous part of the crown's ancient prerogative, and though some arrangements might be made to set them aside, these exceptions were made in England and did not apply to Ireland. Fitzwilliam and the council decided the case for the earl on 8 February 1574, ordering the Dublin officials to give assistance to the farmers and agents of Ormonde against all foreign merchants.[47] At this early stage of its development, the court of castle chamber was virtually indistinguishable from the council itself, and the instant case

46. BL., Add. MS 47, 172, f. 6v.
47. *Ormond deeds, 1547–84*, pp. 244–54. The order was signed by six privy councillors, and an inspeximus taken for Ormonde was subsequently attested by Sir Henry Sydney at Dublin on 1 March 1576.

provides an unusual glimpse into the pleadings and the symbiotic nature of the court, showing its limited autonomy in cases of this sort. On 4 February 1577, Lord Chancellor Gerrard duly noted the earlier council order in the entry book of the court of castle chamber, on a complaint by the earl that his victory remained a dead letter since he was compelled again to sue for his rights to the prise wines (see below).[48]

The erratic performance of the court of castle chamber under Fitzwilliam requires some further explanation. It is clear that his role in the establishment of the court was muted and that he did little more than superintend its work during his tenure as viceroy. The court took a more active role in 1574 according to the entry book, though it is also clear that the Irish privy council continued to hear causes that would eventually become the province of the castle chamber court. It is essential to remember that the court was in many respects identical to the council sitting as a tribunal, so the formal delineation of judicial boundaries between them did not preoccupy senior statesmen at the time. The most active legist in the castle chamber was not the viceroy but the lord chancellor, Sir William Gerrard. By contrast, his predecessor, the docile divine Sir Robert Weston, lacked the temperament as lord chancellor for judicial activism. The council at this time was also, as we have seen, the locus of protracted conflicts between Fitzwilliam and his nemesis, Fyton, so that pugnacious meetings of the executive did not set the tone for calm deliberation needed in the court. As a consequence, some of the castle chamber deliberations were signed by only three councillors, Fitzwilliam, Sir Nicholas White and Secretary John Chaloner. Fitzwilliam was confronted with rebellious provinces and a rival jurisdiction in Ulster, where the earl of Essex was given practical autonomy during his colonial adventure and Sir Thomas Smith gained more attention from the crown than the senior administration in Dublin. Fiscal mismanagement and questions of probity doomed the Fitzwilliam regime in 1575 and the viceroy was himself eager to be recalled, though Brady asserts that this in turn jeopardized Sydney's administration by forcing him into risky economies of scale.[49] For the second summer, a plague raged in the Pale so that no Trinity term was kept in Dublin in 1575.[50] The entry book of the court reveals a gap of some twenty months between the last case heard by Fitzwilliam in November 1574 and the first case under Sydney in August 1576. Meanwhile, in London, the proposals of Edmund Tremayne for fiscal retrenchment and

48. BL, Add. MS 47,172, ff. 17–19.
49. Brady, *Chief governors*, pp. 144–46; Ellis, *Tudor Ireland*, pp. 264–68; Canny, *Making Ireland British*, pp. 85, 121–22.
50. BL, Add. MS 4813, ff. 98v–99: Ware's 'Chronicle of Ireland'. At the end of Fitzwilliam's regime, on 21 February 1575, the attorney general and the serjeant at law received additional grants of land in recognition of their service in the court of castle chamber. Edward Fitzsymon, serjeant at law, held a grant of the Grange, while John Bathe, attorney general, received the estate of Drumcondra in Co. Dublin. *Fiants Ire., Eliz.*, nos. 2551, 2552. On 8 March 1575, the queen approved of the changes in office made by Fitzwilliam on the death of the former serjeant, Richard Fynglas, appointing Richard Belyng to be the new solicitor general. PRO, SP 63/50/4–4v.

implementation of common law principles were being aired, at the expense of the hapless Fitzwilliam.[51]

DISCORD AND INNOVATION: THE PROMISE OF SYDNEY'S COURT OF CASTLE CHAMBER

Sydney's return as lord deputy was widely rumoured throughout the year 1575, so at his arrival on 8 September expectations were high. The viceroy made numerous progresses to the troubled provinces at the end of the year, and did nothing to reanimate the dormant court of castle chamber.[52] Indeed, Sydney's use of prerogative justice on a progress through Limerick illustrated the yawning gap between the availability of star chamber jurisdiction and the appetite for litigation in Irish communities. Owney Molan complained through an Irish interpreter that Ulick Bren [O'Brien] had ravished her, and after this allegation Sydney asked the woman if her assailant had first proposed marriage to her. Sensing a rude contre-temps, Sydney smiled when the witness, Owney's mother, gave her evidence:

> Sir Henry bade the interpreter aske the Mother was she present when Ulick had to do with her daughter, the mother Answered that she was, the Interpreter asked her why she did not crye out beinge present at that time, the mother againe made Answer because the ogly Churle promised to marry my girl if she would let him have use of her body, and nowe the villain is married to another. To this Answer all the Court laughed and Sir Henry sayd he commended the man for Marrying of another, then he bade the Interpreter aske her, how many times he had served her soe, she replied allmost twenty times which caused more laughter then before.[53]

It was Sydney's purpose to resurrect the damaged presidency system, installing veteran officials in Munster and Connacht who could reestablish crown policy, treat effectively with leading peers like Desmond and Clanricarde and ultimately stabilize the unruly provinces through the maintenance of common law juris-dictions. Fitzwilliam had used commissions in each province after the departure of the presidents, and Sydney campaigned for the installation of Sir William Drury as lord president in Munster, culminating in the detailed instructions sent to him on 20 June 1576. Drury was named in separate letters of 30 January, and

51. HL, Ellesmere MS 1701, ff. 1–8: 'Discourse on the Government of Ireland,' 1573, by Edmund Tremayne, clerk of the privy council. The thrust of his proposals was to use English officials in all senior posts, and a deputy who was 'above all sincerelie inclyned to justice without Respect of all faction in this Realme or in that': f. 5.

52. Ellis, *Tudor Ireland*, pp. 268–74.

53. BL, Add. MS 4813, ff. 101–01v: Ware's 'Chronicle of Ireland'. Sydney called for the register to draw a copy of the testimony to carry it over to the queen and council to make them merry. Ibid.

the council was identified by name, including the earls of Ormonde and Desmond, municipal officials from Waterford, Limerick and Cork and the military veterans Henry Davells and William Apsley. Nicholas Walshe was named justice of the council of Munster with John Meagh of Cork second justice, and the president was required to meet with them in session to govern the province by terms of the common law. They were ordered to hold sessions of the court, use commissions of oyer and terminer and limit the function of martial law to cases of greatest extremity. In 33 articles, the council's instructions focused primarily on legal matters such as the issuing of process after legitimate complaint to the president, hearing of all offences (including official malfeasance by sheriffs and mayors), punishment of corrupt jurors (by use of the pillory or stocks), awarding of damages, fines and other assessments and keeping a formal register of orders, proclamations and decrees.[54]

The commencement of Sydney's second viceroyalty was significantly enhanced by naming his close associate in Wales, the experienced vice-president Sir William Gerrard, as lord chancellor in Ireland. Called to office in April 1576, Gerrard laid down the framework of important judicial innovations, including the expansion of the regular assizes. On 11 July 1576, Gerrard penned a note to Walsingham in England indicating his itinerary prior to the commencement of Michaelmas term on 29 September. He intended to hold sessions on 24 August in Dublin, following a circuit to Drogheda, Ardee, Trim, Mullingar, Philipstown, Maryborough, Kilkenny, Thomastown, Ross, Carlow and Naas. Returning to Dublin on 28 September, the lord chancellor made it clear that he would be an active and energetic force for the immediate extension of common law jurisdiction through-out the Pale. Gerrard was the most energetic judicial reformer of the Tudor period in Ireland, and his memoranda to English officials are replete with critiques and proposals for improvement. In November 1576, he explained to Cecil that he 'toke the hearing of all causes, all thoughe more aptlie apperteiginge to the other Cortes' due to the corruption and inefficiency of the Irish judicial establishment.[55] Finding the elderly chief justices superannuated by partial and partisan Old English Palesmen, he called for their replacement by English judges.[56] He sought the printing of key statutes in 1577 and his comprehensive report on the state of Ireland urged the implementation of a full shiring of the country, followed by regular assizes.[57]

The deputyship of Sir Henry Sydney in Ireland has occasioned recent writers to celebrate his intentions and to denigrate his accomplishments. Dr Brady has

---

54. BL, Add. MS 4786, ff. 43–51; BL, Cotton MSS Titus B XIII, ff. 215–22. The use of torture was expressly limited to extreme circumstances, a tacit acknowledgement of the brutality of previous regimes.

55. PRO, SP 63/56/105.

56. LPL, Carew MS 628, ff. 311v–14; also see 'Gerrard's report on the state of Ireland, 1577–78', ed. C. McNeill, *Anal Hib*, no.2 (1930), 93–291.

57. 'Gerrard's report', ed. McNeill, pp. 124, 185–87, 96. See also *Anglicizing*, pp. 245–46, 210–16; Brady, *Chief governors*, pp. 154–58.

offered an insightful review of the second Sydney administration, highlighting the cleverness of his package of reforms in circumstances of opportunistic desperation. The emphasis on trimming expenses for an impecunious sovereign brought Sydney back to power in Ireland, but laid the foundation for his undoing by a fusillade of complaints from the Pale élite.[58] Citing the unconstitutional basis for new levies, a composition for the irregular tax known as cess, or purveyance, Pale lawyers and peers joined in an unusual compact to defeat the viceroy by framing their opposition in principled legal terms. By appealing to the settled law of the realm, the leaders of the Pale community established a template of constitutional resistance that won a hearing in London, ruined the viceroyalty of Elizabeth's most competent chief governor, and laid the foundations for lawyerly opposition under the Stuarts. The continuity and coherence of this undercurrent of judicial resistance, from the law students of the 1560s complaining against the Sussex regime to the celebrated attacks on Wentworth by Patrick Darcy in the parliament of 1640–41, has yet to find its scholar. Sydney's attempts to impose a composition for the cess on an unwilling populace suggest both a maladroit lapse of his studied attention to Irish politics and a mood of utter desperation in the timing of his reform. In the end, he lost the support of his own lord chancellor. Despite Gerrard's long service with Sydney in Wales and his shared commitment to reform in Ireland, the veteran judge refused to back the chief governor and sniped at his efforts to finance the government by manipulating a nominal and occasional household tax into a permanent assessment.[59] Nonetheless, it can be shown that both Sydney and Gerrard worked together on reform of the judicial system and their cooperation forged the continuous operation of the court of castle chamber.

Sir Henry Sydney was a decisive and careful judge as well as a military leader. His campaign for the installation of the new prerogative court won acceptance in 1571, as we have seen, and his return to Ireland four years later witnessed a subsequent reinvigoration of the tribunal. The instructions from the queen, sent on 5 October 1575, required the viceroy to improve the administration of law and justice:

> her majesty is informed that dyvers of the mynisters of the law as well the Juges as others ar not void of parciall affections towardes their friendes, both in cases aperteyning to her matie and also depending betwixt subject and subject; wherin the Jusice of that Realme is much slandered.[60]

Sydney was enjoined to install sheriffs in new counties, to send commissions of oyer and terminer throughout the English shires, to publish the statutes and to

58. Brady, *Chief governors*, pp. 143–58. Brady viewed the proposals of 1575 as the 'classic programmatic approach', following the lead of Sussex, and characterized Sydney's plan as 'dangerous' in a 'forbidding atmosphere'. Ibid., pp. 143–46.
59. Ibid., pp. 155–58. See also *Anglicizing*, pp. 392–404.
60. PRO, SP 63/15/19v. Dr Edwards has argued that Ormonde's opposition to Sydney's intrusive government was soon abetted by Gerrard, who visited Kilkenny in 1577 and found there substantial 'local acceptance of the common law' after he held a general sessions in the county

add legal officers to the councils in Munster and Connacht.[61] During his attenuated regime, the lord deputy presided at no less than fourteen cases before the
court of castle chamber, despite bearing the responsibility for numerous martial
expeditions and other duties. The replacement in 1573 of the lacklustre dean of
St Patrick's, Dr Robert Weston, by the quarrelsome archbishop of Dublin, Adam
Loftus, as lord keeper did little to stimulate the business of the castle chamber
court. This arid interlude finally ended with the installation of Gerrard in 1576
and the renewal of litigation in the Irish star chamber. The continued blending of
conciliar and judicial responsibilities is indicated by the records of general
hostings and clerical accounts in the entry book of the court. From Candlemas
term in 1577 until Easter term in 1578, the court heard an average of four cases
each session. The clerk of the court, Robert Kendall, was upbraided for charging
the suitors excessive fees and required to moderate his assessments by levying
rates in Irish currency only.[62] After the departure of Sydney in the autumn of
1578, Gerrard continued to regularize the operations of the court under Lord
Justice Drury, hearing cases in each term until the outbreak of the Fitzmaurice
Rebellion in 1579. With the sudden death of Drury in 1579, the sickness and
frequent absence of the lord chancellor (Gerrard died in Chester early in 1581),
and the military imperatives occasioned by a widening rebellion in Munster, the first
stage of the court's existence came to an end. There were no hearings at the court of
castle chamber recorded in the entry book between July 1579 and March 1581.

    Consistent with the aims of both viceroy and chancellor, the first hearing at the
court of castle chamber under this regime involved disorders in the provinces. On
13 August 1576, Donald O'Dolan and Redmond O'Ferrall sued Sir William
O'Carroll for a riot in taking away their cattle, horses and goods. The defendant
justified his action, claimed the goods and cattle were the property of John Burke,
which was denied by the complainants. The court held for the plaintiffs, requiring
O'Carroll to restore the cattle at Loragh in Co. Tipperary by 31 August or pay a
penalty to the owners. O'Carroll was instructed to pay a bond of £500 to appear
before the lord deputy and council on the first day of the next term and to answer
for the riot and wounding of the plaintiff's tenants. Captains Collier and Strange
were ordered by commission from castle chamber to hear and examine witnesses
on both sides regarding the ownership of other cattle and goods yet in question.[63]
The second case heard by the lord chancellor on 28 August 1576 interrupted his
plans for itinerant justice. Gerrard signed the interlocutory decree on behalf of
the court, giving a series of orders in the controversy between the seneschal of the

    courthouse and witnessed the impact of Ormonde's reforms. Meanwhile, Ormonde campaigned
    against Sydney relentlessly at court. Edwards, *Ormond lordship*, pp. 221–24.

61. PRO, SP 63/15/19v–21.
62. BL, Add. MS 47,172, f. 23v. Kendall was assured that the marshal of the court would arrest
    anyone who was delinquent in payment of court costs, turning them over to the constable of
    Dublin Castle for incarceration until they satisfied the claim of the clerk. Ibid.
63. Ibid., ff. 13–13v.

liberties of Co. Wexford, Thomas Masterson, and Bryan McCahir McArt Cavanagh alleging riot, dispossession and other offences against each other. The entry described sundry complaints made before the lord deputy against the servants, followers and accomplices of each man, noting a series of books that were compiled from previous commissions with depositions in each cause of action.[64]

In giving his judgment, Gerrard demonstrated his intention to resolve disputes in a systematic and comprehensive manner. His orders in the case suspended further action, pending deliberations at the full court of castle chamber on the first day of the Michaelmas term, and requiring all principals and their followers to keep the peace in Co. Wexford and Co. Carlow. Allowing continuance in possession of the estates in question, Gerrard named a commission to hear all the allegations of robbery, murder or manslaughter within twelve days by examination of witnesses. Those followers identified as offenders and indicted were to be brought to the trial by their patrons, and any cattle found by the commissioners to be taken unlawfully were to be restored to their owners immediately. The complainants were ordered to give bond of £1,000 for their appearance at castle chamber in the next session, and Masterson enjoined not to use his authority by martial law to execute any of the followers of Cavanagh. Finally, Gerrard required the commission to hear all witnesses and proofs regarding the ownership of the lands in question and to certify the results before the lord deputy and council on the first day of the next term.[65] The extensive preliminary handling of this matter, in anticipation of a fuller hearing before the court of castle chamber, indicates the intention of the new regime to give full effect to common law institutions of governance, including the upbraiding of local officials who exceeded their instructions or exploited their advantage in questions of title to land. However, the entry book is barren of any further record of this case. Masterson was a veteran local official who may have reached an accommodation with the Cavanagh chief, or the commission may have been delayed and frustrated by their inability to conclude their work in thirty days, prior to the Michaelmas term. The disappearance of the case from the records may also be due to the fragility of Tudor record-keeping in Ireland. But the lack of an outcome demonstrates the nature of the problem facing Gerrard, when lawlessness in the provinces confronted the slow process of English legal tradition. Despite two entries that required a hearing in castle chamber in the next term, the record book contains no judicial action for Michaelmas 1576.[66]

---

64. BL, Add. MS 47,172, ff. 14–16. Gerrard occasionally acted alone in making interlocutory decrees, signing the entry book as lord chancellor on behalf of the full court.

65. Ibid.

66. Masterson later became notorious for his slaughter of the Cavanaghs in 1580, ambushing and killing some 60 of them. Brady alleged that he kept the area of north Wexford in 'a state of continual disorder'. Drury blamed Masterson for laying waste the country and even dismissed him from office in 1579, but he soon resumed his post only to disgrace it in the following year. Brady, *Chief governors*, pp. 203, 276. See also D. Edwards, 'Ideology and experience', pp. 130-43.

The largest number of cases heard in the court of castle chamber in this era involved allegations of riot, though the *casus belli* between litigants was often stated more indirectly in the text of the entry. The litigious seneschal of Co. Wexford, Thomas Masterson, sued certain inhabitants of the town of Ross on 15 November 1577, naming three defendants for the wounding of Andrew Codd, a member of his company. Sydney heard the case along with five other councillors and found the defendants guilty, fining them £20 Irish and sending another of the townsmen, John Bolgier, to be imprisoned in Wexford Castle for the wounding of Codd.[67] Though Masterson was competent to defeat and punish affrays of this sort, it is significant that he approached the castle chamber court for a remedy. Given his previous record as a litigant, it is possible that he wished to avoid the onus of partiality in defending a member of his own company. Sydney's willingness to provide judicial remedy is also notable and consistent with his favoured application of legal principles as a remedy for outbreaks of social violence. An earlier case, heard before Gerrard and two other councillors, involved a local dispute, with Matthew Talbot suing Henry Cusake and others for a riot in Dublin, to which Cusake confessed in court. The fine of £50 sterling together with an award to the plaintiff of £17 for costs and damages was a striking rebuke, though it was later reduced by the court.[67a] On 8 February 1577, Gerrard heard another case of riot, forcible entry and unlawful assembly in the suit of Justice Talbot against Nicholas Nugent, and others. Finding the sole witness an insufficient proof of the allegations, the court dismissed all defendants without further comment, though the case apparently involved two noted judges in Dublin, one of whom later became chief justice of common pleas.[68] Sydney later dismissed charges of riot against William Browne and his servants in Co. Wexford, wherein the plaintiff, George Isham, was wounded at Ross, noting the humble submission of the defendant and the great costs Browne was already forced to pay. Adding a fine of £13 6s.8d. Irish to Browne's charges, Sydney apparently accepted the judgement of an inferior court in satisfaction of the claims of Isham.[69] The court frequently undertook the defence of women who were abducted, as in the case of Thomazene, the 'pretenced' wife of John Pentine, a merchant of Dublin. Thomazene was allegedly taken away by Lawrence Taafe, gentleman, and others in Co. Louth. Despite the show of violence in this case, the court was forced to accept Taafe's plea of the queen's pardon on 23 October 1577, dismissing the defendant with a recognizance to appear in future to answer any other complaint made by Pentine or his wife.[70] The entry shows that the bill, answer and replication were read in open court, but the pardon, dated 12 October 1577, trumped the

67. BL, Add. MS 47, 172, ff. 24–24v.

67a. Ibid., f. 19v The trial occurred on 10 May 1577.

68. Ibid., f. 16v.

69. Ibid., f. 22. The case was heard on 13 November 1577. An earlier case of 13 May 1577 involved the widow Anstace Brown in a claim of riot against Aristotle Scurlocke of Rosslare, finally dismissed without determination at the court on 7 November 1582.

70. Ibid., f. 21v.

accusations of the complainant, with the court leaving the plaintiffs to other remedies based on further allegations that might arise from the matter in contention. All charges against Taafe were dismissed in the 1582 review of dormant cases long pending before the court of castle chamber. Taafe was there identified as a servant to Viscount Gormanston.[71]

The judicial energy of Gerrard as lord chancellor frequently engaged the court of castle chamber in comprehensive and detailed litigation. It was a special burden for the prerogative court to uphold and maintain the authority of inferior courts, particularly those in the provinces struggling for legitimacy. Further, the mandate for Sydney's government included the wholesale implementation of a common law infrastructure, and this in turn required the continuous attention of the court of castle chamber. Gerrard attempted in February 1577 to determine conclusively the longstanding complaints of the earl of Ormonde regarding the prise wines. Charges that the unloading of wines at Drogheda and Dublin without paying the prise wines to the factors of the earl were heard before Dr Weston in chancery, and before Fitzwilliam and the Irish privy council (sitting in castle chamber) on special orders from the queen. Pursuant to an order of the council affirming the rights of the earl to prise wines, a new complaint was made against David Collther, a foreigner, and William Barnwall of Dublin, who bought the wines from Collther. It was customary to allow the agents of the earl to board a vessel and to sequester two tons of prise wines, but Barnwall had brought the Rochelle wines to Dublin quayside. Sydney then ordered the mayor of Dublin to sequester the two tons of wine, and the lord chancellor and council took up the matter in a subsequent hearing. They found that the earl's claims were still valid, rejecting the allegations of the foreigner that a previous order in star chamber against the earl's father freed aliens from the payment of prise wines. The court called upon Patrick Gough, late mayor of Dublin, to deliver the wines to the earl's agent, but he alleged that he had already delivered the two tons to Walter Godwyn, craynor of the port of Dublin. Godwyn in turn confessed he had delivered one ton to Nicholas FitzSymons without license of the lord deputy and council or consent of the mayor. Godwyn was jailed for contempt of the court, required to deliver the one ton remaining, and compelled to present a sufficient pawn to Gough, in lieu of the second ton to be delivered to the earl's agent. Gerrard completed his review of the case with a further order to allow the earl's agent three days after the arrival of a vessel within which to come aboard and sequester the prise wines. Since the towns of Dublin and Drogheda had a bill in chancery for reversal of the said order, the earl was given until 10 May 1577 to answer the bill, and the order was suspended until his answer was received in chancery. Gerrard signed this lengthy decree alone, as lord chancellor, demonstrating the complex interplay of chancery and castle chamber jurisdictions.[72]

71. Ibid., f. 71.
72. Ibid., ff. 17–19. The 'craynor' was a port official who was responsible for delivery of goods from ship to dock, usually by means of a 'crane' or jib.

In a second example of the interdependence of the chancery and castle chamber courts, Sydney and the council dismissed a charge of perjury filed against William Conlon, James Ryan, Thomas Man and Matthew Duffe. They were sued in castle chamber by Sir Thomas Fitzwilliam of Merrion and John Finglas, feoffees of trust to Dame Alison FitzLyons of Porteston, Co. Dublin, for corrupt depositions made in chancery regarding the lease of Busserdstown and its appurtenances. The demise of Busserdstown for 21 years to Simon Luttrell had been adjudicated by the lord chancellor on behalf of Luttrell, based upon the words of Dame Alison spoken to Luttrell after the death of her husband, Roger Finglas (certainly a kinsman to the feoffee, John). The appeal from chancery to the castle chamber court, alleging perjured testimony of the four defendants, was rejected after a hearing by Sydney on 25 April 1578. Hearing from other witnesses who testified to the authenticity of the lease, the court of castle chamber dismissed the charge of perjury and taxed court costs to the plaintiffs.[73] In an earlier case of riot, involving two of the litigants in the case, Sydney and the court of castle chamber fined Dame Alison and Oliver FitzGerald, her accomplice in a riot, at a hearing on 26 November 1577. Since the plaintiffs included William Conlon, along with Simon Gascoine and Thomas Raighe, alleging riot, affray and other misdemeanours, we may assume that the contested estate in Busserdstown may have been the occasion for this dispute as well.[74] Lacking information on this point, it is nonetheless clear that the widow Dame Alison found small comfort in the protections of the law regarding her verbal commitments made on the death of her husband.

The court of castle chamber also upheld the validity of provincial courts. The newly established lord president of Munster, Sir William Drury, was instructed to hold sessions throughout the province as a means to establish the authority of the common law. Drury and the commissioners for Munster authorized three inquest juries in Kilkenny to make inquiry of all felonies and treasons. Several bills were offered by the commissioners to the juries in question charging Donyll McShane, John Rocheford, Donough O'Kelly and James Shortall with treason. The bills were supported by witnesses, and the defendants in the suits submitted publicly before the court and confessed their faults, but the first jury, of which Gerald Blanchefield, gentleman, was foreman, returned a verdict of *ignoramus*, after which the proceedings against the defendants were stopped. A second jury was summoned with a near kinsman, David Blanchefield, as foreman, but they also returned an *ignoramus* despite hearing evidence against both Rocheford and Shortall. Finally, a jury in the town of Kilkenny, with William Ragged, merchant, as foreman returned an *ignoramus* in the charges against Rocheford, along with O'Kelly and Shortall, whereupon all three juries were charged in the court of castle chamber with corrupt verdicts in contempt of their duty and contrary to their oaths. The lord deputy and the court found all the jurors in contempt, jailing three of them in Dublin and fining the rest. The sovereign of Kilkenny was also

---

73. Ibid., ff. 32v–33.   74. Ibid., ff. 25–25v.

ordered to make inquiry of whom among the jurors said 'he would sticke by yt' before he would find the bills against any of the defendants. Not surprisingly, the kinsmen of the defendants were prominent among the jurors, including another James Shortall, Robert Shortall, Leonard Shortall, Walter Shortall and Edmond Shortall.[75] This case illustrates the determination of the court to uphold the dignity and effectiveness of provincial tribunals, while accepting that local conflicts would be coloured by circumstances beyond the control of the prerogative court in Dublin.

The work of the privy council in Ireland was perforce mixed with the adjudication of the court of castle chamber, and in some cases the proclamations of the council were recorded in the entry book. On the occasion of the rebellion of Rory Oge O'More and the O'Connors in 1577, Sydney ordered a general hosting in the English Pale to suppress the insurrection and to defend the Pale itself. O'More burned Naas and Leighlinbridge in 1577, events followed by the brutal retaliation known as the massacre of Mullaghmast by Robert Hartpool and Francis Cosbie.[76] The court of castle chamber took up the matter of resistance to military preparations when the expected contribution of carts and carriages by the gentlemen of the Pale was refused by several baronies in Co. Meath and Co. Dublin. Citing defiance of the council and recalling an earlier proclamation amidst the general rebellion in the Pale, Sydney on 20 December 1577 required the defaulters to appear before the lord keeper in Dublin and give bonds for their appearance in castle chamber court the next Trinity term. On 20 January 1578, the defendants appeared and were given until 13 February to answer the full charges at the court. On that date, the lord deputy and five councillors found them guilty of 'greate Disobedience and Contempt' of the council's proclamation and fined each of them personally for failing to provide archers, horsemen, carriages and other logistical support at the general hosting.[77] The disordered state of the

75. Ibid., ff. 33v–35v. The case was heard on 8 May 1578 upon information from the attorney general, Thomas Snagge. Sydney had come to the Kilkenny assizes in 1577 to seek the prosecution of a Butler client, Ferrdoragh McEdmund Purcell, and the castle chamber indictments of the three Kilkenny juries, seen by Dr Edwards as an extension of his campaign against Butler exceptionality, were a mark of desperation rather than judicial oversight. Edwards, *Ormond lordship*, pp. 221, 224.

76. Ellis, *Tudor Ireland*, pp. 273–74. Dr Carey has recently claimed that ' Sidney endorsed the type of activities which culminated in this particular atrocity'. V. Carey, 'John Derricke's "Image of Irelande", Sir Henry Sidney and the massacre of Mullaghmast, 1578', *IHS*, xxxi (1999), 319. However, the Gaelic sources used by Carey were not written down until the early eighteenth century, he uses Derricke's lyrical assertions in a speculative manner and he acknowledges that 'official sources are virtually silent on this event'. Ibid. Abuses of martial law were not uncommon, but it is probably overreaching to state that 'Government-sponsored slaughter was a fact of the English colonial experience in Ireland from the 1570s onwards, and this policy contributed to a legacy of bitterness and hatred'. The impact of Mullaghmast on the 'lore' of 'an emerging Catholic nationalism' took place in the minds of Catholic emigrés on the continent, without doubt, but there is no evidence the event blunted resort to the common law, or typified the policy of Sir Henry Sydney. Ibid., pp. 324–26.

77. BL, Add. MS 47,172, ff. 29–31v. One leading defaulter, Robert Caddell of Dowston, was

Pale in 1577 may account for this disobedience of a conciliar order, since the campaign against the cess was then well under way.

Sydney' s second administration in Ireland was clouded by the controversy over a prerogative tax, the centrepiece of his reform and the mantle of his troubled regime. Campaigning for another opportunity to bridle Irish resistance to English rule, the enterprising Sydney used his considerable influence to obtain the viceroyalty and curb the profligate spending that had doomed the governments of his predecessors. The composition for cess, adumbrated in piecemeal fashion by others, would now be substituted for the irregular taxation in kind imposed at the will of the chief governor. In principle, this streamlining of revenue appealed to the queen and seemed to resolve the complaint of arbitrariness levelled against the viceroys by Pale landowners. However, resistance to the cess was already fairly widespread, and the notion of a general tax was entirely unwelcome to the Pale, since landowners in the five counties nearest Dublin were already forced to accept most of the burden of defence and taxation for the entire country. The administration of the cess was notoriously erratic and arbitrary, since the wealthiest could obtain exemptions while the cessors in each barony were frequently corrupt. Sydney's attempt to find an alternative began with bargaining for a composition in the autumn of 1575, followed by extensive negotiations that ended in the withdrawal of all exemptions by the viceroy in November 1576. Resistance was not confined to the 'country opposition' that quickly emerged, since Nicholas White and others on the council questioned the merit and timing of the proposal. The opposition became more organized, leading to a formal petition against the cess in December 1576, a move that was preceded by a lawsuit in Co. Meath against the chief governor and the Irish privy council.[78]

At a hearing before Lord Chancellor Gerrard on 21 May 1577, Christopher Barnewall of Ardstown in Co. Meath, foreman of the jury at an assize held in the previous autumn, was accused of presenting a bill against the lord deputy and council for the illegal imposing of cess. Despite the warning of the chief justice who presided at the assize, Barnewall had the clerk draw up an indictment against the wrongful and extortionate implementation of the cess. He was further accused of conspiring to send agents of the country to London to complain against the viceroy, and had another clerk write the inflammatory words that we have earlier noted: 'Trissilian in tyme of kinge Richard the seconde was put to deathe for misconstruinge the lawes.'[79] The rest of the jury were released because they were 'so simple as neither understoode theffect of the presentmente nor what the sayd Christopher ment thereby'.[80] But Barnewall was accused of meddling in matters

accused in castle chamber of riot in February 1577, possibly in relation to this case, though the charge was dismissed in 1582. Ibid., f. 68.

78. For a full discussion of the cess dispute see my *Anglicizing*, pp. 388–407; Brady, *Chief governors*, pp. 146–58.
79. BL, Add. MS 47,172, f. 20.
80. Ibid.

of state, challenging the royal prerogative, slandering the judge and sowing dissension among the people. Though similar in form to cases where the court addressed the corrupt verdicts of juries, this case appeared to expand the jurisdiction of the court during a heated political controversy. Gerrard committed Barnewall to ward until 14 June and then required him to confess and seek pardon before the court of castle chamber. He was fined £50 for the offence, which was framed in part as an abuse of the power of jury foreman, since he used the clerk of the court to insert in the record a reference to Tresillian without the privity of the rest of the jury.[81] Remarkably, the truculent Barnewall appeared again before the court on 5 May 1581 as foreman of another corrupt jury that refused to award the crown a wardship in Co. Meath from the estate of Richard Lynham.[82]

By the time Barnewall's case was heard in castle chamber, the representatives of the Pale had petitioned against the cess and all prerogative taxation in January 1577, an action which was followed by the departure of agents of the Pale to London in February.[83] The veteran lawyers Barnaby Scurlocke, Henry Burnell and Richard Netterville were deputed on behalf of scores of leading Palesmen to address the queen and privy council with their complaints against the coercive nature of the cess.[84] The privy council deferred hearing the petition of the Palesmen, and the queen wrote to the viceroy in harsh language on 14 May, charging the government with a timorous failure to defend the royal prerogative as a contempt to the dignity of the crown.[85] This reprimand nearly coincided with the castle chamber hearing that resulted in the fining of Barnewall on 21 May 1577. The petitioners had been incarcerated in January, with Gerrard examining them individually on the prerogative, and they continued to defy the government until June, alleging they were not condemning the royal prerogative itself.[86] It was finally determined to send Gerrard to London in person to counter the defence of the Pale's representatives. Once in England, Gerrard took an independent line, hoping for reasonable compromise with the agents of the Pale, but withdrawing his support for Sydney's ambitious schemes of composition.[87] Emboldened by the

---

81. Ibid., ff. 20–21.
82. Ibid., ff. 44v–45v. The confession of the jurors including Barnewall was accepted by the lord deputy and council on 11 May and their fines reduced. Barnewall was seen as the one who led and seduced the rest, but his fine was lowered from £100 to £20 by the court. Ibid., ff. 46–47v. In April 1581, Barnewall and other jurors were ordered to pay 100 marks in recognizance for their appearance before the council chamber on April 21 to answer charges against them.
83. *Cal. Carew MSS, 1575–88*, p. 73. The case was argued by Burnell, Barnewall and Scurlocke before the court of castle chamber on behalf of the Palesmen in Hilary term 1577.
84. PRO, SP 63/57/1–1v; 63/58/45–48. Netterville and Burnell had signed the 24 articles against the cess in 1562 as law students in London; Scurlocke had been attorney general under Mary and Elizabeth from 1554 to 1559.
85. PRO, SP 63/58/67; *Cal. Carew MSS, 1575–88*, pp. 78–79.
86. PRO, SP 63/58/139, 149v; 'Gerrard's report', ed. McNeill, pp. 107–08.
87. On 12 September 1577, the viceroy and council wrote on behalf of the composition scheme, defending it as a means to lessen the charges to the crown and explaining how they had

incremental successes of their campaign, the agents of the Pale continued their defence and were rewarded by a summons to Dublin followed by incarceration. November 1577 saw a flurry of activity with the Palesmen offering a new victualling agreement, Burnell renewing the campaign in London, and the queen offering Sydney her tentative approval for demanding that the petitioners submit to the cess for another year.

Elizabeth's letter to the lord deputy on 31 October 1577 called upon him to require the leading Palesmen who refused to subscribe to the cess to appear in the court of castle chamber on 31 January 1578. Letters were sent to Viscount Baltinglas, the leading aristocratic complainant, and three other peers, together with seventeen gentlemen. Baltinglas pleaded illness, but the others appeared as required, and the queen's letter was read to them in court, with other persuasions used to obtain their submission to the cess. Desiring time for deliberation, the court allowed them until two that afternoon, and the next day they offered a letter that the court refused as inadequate. The court authorized a meeting between the attorney general and representatives of the Pale, including Nicholas Nugent, the second baron, and Christopher Fleming, a leading lawyer. Though a submission was drawn up at this conference, Baron Delvin kept the document for two days and then resolutely refused to subscribe to it on behalf of himself and the others. After another meeting at which they refused to subscribe, the defendants were committed to Dublin Castle on 5 February, returning to the castle chamber court two days later to be fined. The peers were assessed £500 sterling, though this was later reduced to Irish money, and the majority of the gentry were fined 200 marks.[88] The record in the entry book merely rehearsed previous appearances at the court by the defendants in the case, and the court used the punishment as part of an interlocutory decree rather than a full hearing and determination of the cause. While it is unsurprising that the court of castle chamber would be central to the protracted dispute, the relatively economical use of the star chamber jurisdiction in the case lends support to the view of Sydney's regime as essentially temperate. Certainly the judicial style of the Wentworth government would have handled the case differently.

Though Sydney had enlisted his son Philip and his personal secretary Edward Waterhouse as agents for his cause in London, the spring of 1578 witnessed the defeat of his campaign for the composition. Dissent from within the council itself was broadening, with the defection of the unreliable Sir Edward Fyton, who refused to sign a letter from council alleging an increase in revenue. Fyton challenged Sydney directly on the composition scheme and claimed the government's expenses were indeed exceeding its revenue.[89] The queen and privy council called

proceeded lawfully in imposing it. PRO, SP 63/59/13–13v. Thirteen councillors signed the document, though Nicholas White was conspicuously absent.

88. BL, Add. MS 47,172, ff. 26v–28v. Among the defendants, Baron Howth, Sir Christopher Chyvers and Nicholas Nugent had other experience as litigants before the court.

89. PRO, SP 63/60/69–70.

for a compromise with the Palesmen and Sydney's recall was being rumoured in March. The privy council wrote to the viceroy on 1 June 1578 to call for a meeting with the agents of the Pale, and by 24 July a conference managed to patch up a temporary accord. This was accepted in September by the privy council, but expectations that the agreement would be extended were unfulfilled and the outcome was a smaller cess to begin on 1 November 1578. By that time, Sydney had left the country in disgrace.[90] His successor, Sir William Drury, promised relief, saying he would pay in hard cash for the essential purveyance. But temporary agreement, concluding on 29 May 1579 with a guaranteed money payment in return for a year of cess, was quickly scuttled by the not unexpected invasion of James Fitzmaurice in July. Sydney's second administration in Ireland witnessed a constitutional crisis, led by the 'conservative subversives' in an incipient opposition movement.[91] The timing of the lawyerly confrontation, with extensive and laboured historical arguments tendered in both London and Dublin, exhausted the Elizabethan government of Ireland on the eve of the Desmond Rebellion. It was ill-prepared to meet the military necessity of an insurrection that developed on three fronts and finally involved the recalcitrant and embittered Viscount Baltinglas, leader of the Pale opposition since 1577. The temporary government of Drury, however, sustained for nearly a year the momentum of the court of castle chamber.

Sir William Drury was a veteran military officer who was pressed into service when the deputyship of Sydney ended prematurely. Conscious of the limits of the lord justiceship, little was expected of him. Nonetheless, it was Drury's government, spurred on by the tenacity of Lord Chancellor Gerrard, that managed a final spasm of adjudication before the court of castle chamber prior to the Desmond Rebellion. After replacing Sydney in August 1578, the new lord justice sat with the lord chancellor in castle chamber court during Michaelmas term, determining the suit of Roger Dillon against John Rochforde and others in a case of riot. The court found that the misdemeanours relating to the affray consisted in breaking down a water course erected by Dillon in Balnedronny, Co. Meath to carry water to his grist mill. Based on testimony of witnesses read before the court, Rochforde was found guilty and fined £10 for the offence. Furthermore, he was ordered to cause his wife Ann Barnewall to appear in the court on the first day of the next Hilary term to be committed to ward for her offence and to be examined regarding the others who accompanied her in this riot.[92] The relatively minor offence in this case, and the inclusion of the defendant's spouse, suggests that Gerrard was proceeding with his campaign to broaden the jurisdiction and impact of the court. The harried lord chancellor explained to Cecil on 3 January 1579 that he could not take up the private suit of a Dr Hector, owing to the burden of work on public causes.[93] On 30 January 1579, the court dismissed a bill

---

90. See my *Anglicizing*, pp. 395–406.   91. Brady, *Chief governors*, pp. 146–58, 232–44.
92. BL, Add. MS 47,172, f. 36. The case was heard on 29 November 1578. Plate 6.
93. The plaintiff had been in suit against the earl of Desmond in Munster for over three years before proceeding next to the chancery, whereupon Gerrard sought to bring the matter before the lord

of riot preferred by Walter McHerbert FitzGeoffrey against James Moyle Nugent, gentleman, of Donore in Co. West Meath, and 27 other defendants. The plaintiff sued in castle chamber on 18 October 1577, but ten of the defendants obtained a royal pardon for their offences on 5 July 1578, which was read in court, and so ended the proceedings against them. The rest of the defendants not so pardoned were to be prosecuted in the next term.[94]

The campaign to widen the circle of common law jurisdiction was shepherded conscientiously by Gerrard, who complained to Burghley that tenants of the English gentlemen of the Pale 'lived like Iryshe cottyers beinge of no habilitye or accompt' and urging that more English judges and settlers be sent into Ireland.[95] He wrote to Walsingham in May 1579 to complain that the chief justice of queen's bench was aged and nearly blind, and the chief justice of common pleas had been too ill to take up his place for the past four years. When Sir Robert Dillon finally died in the summer, he recommended Nicholas Nugent as the new chief justice, saying of the irascible judge, 'Of anie man I knowe in this lande he ys the meeteste'.[96] Gerrard castigated Archbishop Adam Loftus, the lord keeper, for hearing and determining causes in chancery in the absence of the chancellor, prompting Loftus to defend his conduct to Burghley in February 1579. When the chancellor left for England, many suitors complained that their cases went unheard, so Loftus obtained a commission to hear causes 'according to the ancient formulas found in the rolls', noting that suitors who lost hope of a remedy at law would be less inclined to resort to courts of justice.[97] On 18 April 1579, Gerrard described to Walsingham his late journeys on judicial circuits and expressed satisfaction at the results.[98]

The lord justice continued the process of anglicizing Irish countries, travelling to the north in June 1579 where he met O'Reilly, knighted him, and prepared to create a new shire where all would agree to live under English laws. Gerrard had remained in the Pale, where he called upon the Palesmen to pay their debts and reconcile accounts before him.[99] Writing to Walsingham on 26 June 1579, Drury recalled that he established the new county, ordered O'Reilly to repair once each year to Dublin, and explained his objective thus: 'to kepe peace in that borders but also to be a meane to make those wild-headed people acquainted and more familier with their more Civile neighbeures and so to enure them with seinge and heringe of Civilitie, Lawe and iustice.'[100] On the same day, Drury and Gerrard heard a case of riot and unlawful assembly in the court of castle chamber that

justice and council. PRO, SP 63/65/8. Gerrard wrote to Walsingham on 22 January 1579 to confirm he had examined an Irishman who had travelled in Spain, but found nothing treasonable against him. PRO, SP 63/65/72.

94. Gerrard presided at this hearing, wherein the Latin formula of the pardon was read into the entry book. BL, Add. MS 47,172, f. 36v. See also *Fiants Ire., Eliz.*, no. 3355. Eight of the ten so pardoned were gentlemen of Co. Westmeath.

95. PRO, SP 63/65/8.   96. PRO, SP 63/67/47.
97. PRO, SP 63/71/127.   98. PRO, SP 63/66/144.
99. PRO, SP 63/66/18–19.   100. PRO, SP 63/67/21.

more nearly comported with the historic definition of an affray. John Fuller and Walter Foxe, merchants of Chester, sued Philip Lamport, Patrick Synnott and others of Co. Wexford for the spoiling of their ship. According to the testimony at court, some 200 persons gathered unlawfully at the sea shore after the wreck of the plaintiffs' ship, and broke up and spoiled their goods, then floating on the water and drifting to shore, with axes and hammers and harbills, 'not once helpinge the pore Compltes [complainants] to any parte of there goodes'.[101] To compound the offence, Lamporte was accused of being a leader of the company, refusing to aid the plaintiffs and later urging them to sign a bill to give him one half of all the goods taken. The court ordered Lamporte and Synnott to be imprisoned in Dublin Castle and to pay £100 fine for their offence, with the rest of the defendants dismissed in respect of their poverty. The sheriff and the seneschal of Co. Wexford were named among commissioners to take depositions in the county regarding the goods received by other defendants, to fine them each accordingly and to commit twelve of the ablest of them to ward in Wexford Castle until they entered bonds for payment of £40.[102]

When the court of castle chamber heard cases involving peers of the realm, the suits were commonly about property or estates. However, in the notorious case of Lord Howth, the court undertook matters involving the dissolute and rogueish behaviour of the baron in litigation that would today be termed domestic abuse, and worse. On 22 May 1579, the solicitor general charged Nicholas Terrell, servant to Sir Christopher St Lawrence, Lord Howth, with perjury. After testifying before Lord Chancellor Gerrard on his oath that he did not see Elizabeth Bermingham on the previous Saturday night, it appeared from the examination of Elizabeth and from his subsequent confession that he spoke with her, supped with her and was in her company at that time. The perjury itself was explained in a larger context:

> the defendant hath been a lewde and badd Instrumente to worke dissencone betweene the L of Howth and his wyffe, whoe resteth nowe separated, and a pryvie comforter and supporter of his saide master to lyeve louslie [loosely].[103]

101. BL, Add. MS 47,172, f. 40v.
102. BL, Add. MS 47,172, ff. 40v–41. The commission was to tax the persons mentioned in a schedule for the fine and costs of court, but no mention of reparation to the plaintiffs was made in the order. Defendants were required to promise not to repeat the offence, but to assist shipwrecked persons to recover their goods. This fond hope of the court was more a statement of principle than a realistic settlement on behalf of the plaintiffs. In a subsequent order taken by Lawrence Holinshed, clerk of the court, in 1582 the seneschal, Anthony Colclogh of Tintern, was discharged of his responsibility for collecting the fine of £100 from Lamporte and Synnot. Noting that the late sheriff of the county was required to give an account to Colclogh of what sums were received from them, the seneschal apparently excused his default at a hearing before the court. Ibid., f. 58. On 5 September 1581, the court had affirmed the fine against Lamport of £100 to be inserted in the original order of the court of 26 June 1579. Ibid., f. 48.
103. BL, Add. MS 47,172, f. 39.

For his offence, Terrell was condemned to prison, pilloried on the two next Saturdays with a paper on his head proclaiming 'For willful perjurie', and his ears nailed to the pillory for two hours each day. He was to be given a knife to cut his ear free, or he could pay a fine of £10 to avoid the nailing of his ears.[104] In the last case heard by the court under Drury's regime, the full account of Lord Howth's career of domestic abuse against his wife and family was aired in court, and duly entered in the record book.

After a long trial and extensive examinations of witnesses, including Lord Howth, the court ordered that he should be fined £500 and committed to prison for the beating of his wife and daughter. Witnesses testified that

> when the said wiffe sholde seme to myslike with his open filthie manner of Conversacion, of liffe with strange weomen and yearlye Chardge, which for the space of twelve yeares together she espied him to haunte after she had borne him fourtene children, then fallinge into furiouse passiones woulde usually beat her in such raginge and cruell sorte as not tollerable and that, Causles in such a rage, he cruellie stroke and bette her with a staffe.[105]

Howth alleged he was sick, and defended his beating as a brutal farewell to his wife should he die, returning to beat her again as she lay in bed recovering from her earlier wounds. The court recited in great detail the cruelty of his treatment, noting that he beat her with two sally rods until they were both worn to the stumps, so that she could not abide clothing next to her skin for many days thereafter. The record showed that 'by this his usuall hauntinge & kepinge of [w]hores his wiffe became soe hatefull to him as he Coulde not without strikinge and beatinge of her suffycientlie satisfie the Crueltie of his mynde', and he would beat his servants also if they brought her bread and drink of a better sort, since he kept her in a close chamber.[106] Though his wife was over 50 years old, he accused her of being over familiar with his butler, and beat the man with two sally rods until he nearly died. In the final allegation, Howth was convicted of abusing his thirteen-year-old daughter, Jane, who had gone into Dublin with his daughter Mary for two days without his consent. The baron demanded his servant Nicholas Terrell to pick up the girl while two other women stripped her naked so her father could beat her with sally rods 30 or 40 times. Two days later she fell sick of an ague, which brought with it the flux, so she died within twelve days of the beating, her father refusing to come to her side and instead 'removed her in the tyme of her sickness from her accustomed bed to a rawe Coulde place called a yeeldinge howse', then refusing to come from Dublin to see her buried.[107] Given the evidence of apparent manslaughter, the terrified spouse of Howth made an excuse to go to

---

104. Ibid.
106. Ibid.

105. Ibid., f. 41v.

107. Ibid., f. 42v. The 'yielding house' would have been a sanctuary for the dying, an early modern hospice.

her brother's house, where she remained for eighteen months, while the butler fled from the estate and others were all too terrified to make complaint to the court. On 8 July 1579, the court fined Howth £1,100 for beating his wife, £300 for beating his servant, and £500 for beating his daughter, stating 'he had worthelie deserved the paynes of death'.[108] The court concluded that he must further endow his wife with money and land to permit her to live and raise his children outside the baron's home, 'as ys reported he kepeth [them] at home without any nurture or educacion and therfore not to be suffered to remayne in his Custodie'.[109] The court of castle chamber thus achieved two core objectives, imposing royal justice on an unruly Irish baron who flouted the law, and asserting a right to litigate heinous moral offences that might have escaped punishment in an inferior jurisdiction.

In the summer of 1579, amidst the outcry against the cess and the determined efforts of Gerrard to implement common law jurisdiction throughout the Pale and the English counties, the attention of the lord justice and council was swiftly and dramatically shifted to distant Kerry. Sir James Fitzmaurice landed in Smerwick on 17 July and in the next few months the government in Dublin metamorphosed into a council of war. The queen wrote in August to order that 'thre or foure selected psons to be assigned out of her maties privie counsell, whereof the Lo. High Threr to be one, and they to be as a speaciall or private counsell for thiese warres'.[110] The burden of correspondence for the rest of the year is laden with preparations for war, and Gerrard's proposals for the installation of English judges and for the expansion of common law jurisdiction were stalled.[111] Drury had become ill during the summer and died in October 1579 at Waterford. His replacement was Sir William Pelham, another military veteran, whose government was immediately beset with crises arising from the multiple rebellions in the provinces. Desmond sacked Youghal in November 1579, and in the following year Baltinglas rebelled in Wicklow, nearest to Dublin itself. In these circumstances, the operation of the court of castle chamber was sporadic at best and the record of deliberations before it is absent entirely.

---

108. Ibid., 42v. In an earlier appearance before the Irish chancery court in 1571, Lord Chancellor Weston issued a recognizance to Lawrence Sutton to forbear the beating of his wife, Jennet Eustace. The order declared that he 'shall do no mannr of hurt to the said Jenett of her body other wyse then as a husband ought to do'. BL, Add. MS 19,837, f. 3. [Contains recognizances in the court of chancery, *temp.* Elizabeth.]

109. BL, Add. MS 47,172, f. 42v. Howth successfully sued to have the fines remitted in the next administration, stating that he had been imprisoned for 19 weeks, that he was penitent and sorry for his offences, and that the fine of £1,000 would ruin his estate. The court remitted that fine to £500 in accepting his plea for pity and commiseration. Ibid., ff. 59–60v, 62, dated 5 July 1582.

110. BL, Add. MS 32,323, ff. 187–87v.

111. PRO, SP 63/71/68.

CONCLUSION

The abbreviated first decade of the court of castle chamber witnessed an erratic functioning of the court and an incomplete transition from the judicial functions of the privy council in Ireland. We may surmise from the revised record-keeping of the central administration in 1571 that the new entry book was designed to formalize the work of the castle chamber court as distinct from the largely administrative acts of the privy council. And, despite the muted performance of the court in its first three years of operation, the adjudication proceeded according to the design of the original commission, with cases of riot, judicial administration, foreign merchants, the abduction of women, corrupt juries and appeals from inferior courts filling up much of the court's calendar. The spasmodic bursts of judicial energy at the court of castle chamber may be explained by changes in its leadership, since the court quickly took on the mantle of the incumbent chief governor and the lord chancellor. Whereas the caretaker administration of Fitzwilliam and the pious Dr Robert Weston as his lord chancellor ushered in a quarrelsome and distracted era for the court, the work of Sydney and Gerrard from 1576 to 1579 in castle chamber is intimately connected with reform proposals for both the administration of justice and the composition for the cess. Gerrard's determination to improve the performance of common law institutions made it possible for the court to sustain its judicial momentum despite the removal of Sydney as chief governor in mid-1578. However, the subsequent absences of the lord chancellor, the weakness of the lord justice, and the advent of rebellion in the provinces combined to halt adjudication before the court in 1579, and it entered a period of enforced dormancy. The vital role of Sydney in sponsoring the first court was paradoxically suspended in 1571 during his four-year absence from Ireland at the court in England. The distractions of the Fitzwilliam era were concentrated primarily on conflicts with his senior administrators, though the court functioned systematically for an entire year during 1574. And, while it is possible to see the court of castle chamber as the engine of judicial reform under the leadership of Gerrard, his brief tenure in office was punctuated by numerous other disputes including the constitutional crisis over the cess. That the court of castle chamber was employed so seldom in this controversy is itself remarkable, testimony to the cleverness of the lawyers for the Pale in circumventing the Irish star chamber and appealing directly to the crown. Nonetheless, taken on its own terms prior to the Desmond Rebellion that began in 1579, the reform era that began in 1571 was a remarkable attempt at the comprehensive dissemination of common law institutions, from the star chamber jurisdiction and the provincial presidencies to the shiring of counties and the re-energized assize courts under the dynamic leadership of Gerrard. Efforts to improve judicial rectitude and efficiency, as well as superintendence of the provincial administration, led the new court to broaden its impact and its mandate while formalizing its jurisdiction over subordinate tribunals.

CHAPTER SIX

An unsettled era in the court of castle chamber, 1579 to 1588

The judgment [in Castle Chamber, against the sheriff Henry Ealand] passed contrary to the opinion of the Lord Chancellor, Her Majesty's Chief Justice, the Treasurer, the Lord Bishop of Meath and others; and only in the will of the Lord Deputy and two or three Irish Councillors, the sentence of his fine and penalty was given. A course never heard of before in any court, and much less in Her Majesty's High Court of Star Chamber, which ought to be the lantern to all the rest; but this they huddled up in haste, having laid down their plot before, and were well assured that the said Eyland would be in town the next day to answer for himself, as indeed he was.

Sir Richard Bingham, lord president of Connacht,
to Burghley, 13 March 1588[1]

FROM THE DEPARTURE of Sydney in disgrace in 1578 until the arrival of Sir John Perrot as chief governor in 1584, a series of interim chief governors led the Dublin administration during the multiple crises of war and rebellion. Despite the turbulence of the war years and the frequent absences of the viceroy, the court of castle chamber continued to hear cases. This was due in part to the energies of the reforming lord chancellor, Sir William Gerrard, and his ambitious successor, Archbishop Adam Loftus. Gerrard was knighted by Lord Justice Pelham who arrived in the autumn of 1579, but the chancellor suffered a long illness and remained in England during much of the next year, struggling to return to Ireland in March 1580 while anticipating his recall. He returned to Chester in early 1581 where he finally died in March.[2] Two military figures in succession, Sir William Drury and Sir William Pelham, led the government as lords justices from 1578 until the arrival of the new lord deputy, Lord Grey de Wilton, in 1580. Both governed for less than a year, and only Drury participated in hearings of the court of castle chamber, signing the entry book and presiding over important cases of

---

1. *Cal. S.P. Ire., 1586–88*, p. 494. Bingham defended the sheriff of Roscommon, his ally, who was convicted of numerous extortions and murders in Connacht under Bingham's direction: 'but for the most of it that he is charged withal, I dare assure your Honour upon my credit, they shall be found matters of mere spite and malice, done of purpose to disgrace me withal, and to bring my government in question.' Ibid., p. 495.
2. PRO, SP 63/73/20. At the urging of the queen, he wrote to Walsingham to compare the expenses in relation to the cess under Sussex and under Sydney.

riot and the debauchery of Christopher, Lord Howth. From 8 July 1579 until the trial of a corrupt jury from Co. Meath on 5 May 1581, the entry book contains only one record of the court of castle chamber.[3] In the classic statement of the calm before the storm, the Irish privy council wrote in June 1579 to its parent body in Westminster, 'The whole pale in generall god be thanked is in verie good quiett and the borders thereof not much molested.'[4]

DORMANCY AND DESPOTISM: JUDICIAL EXTREMISM IN A TIME OF CRISIS, 1580 TO 1584

Lord Arthur Grey de Wilton brought an infusion of new troops to Ireland for the campaign in the late spring of 1580, but promptly demonstrated his ineptitude on 25 August by losing a famous battle in the mountain pass of Glenmalure, just forty miles from Dublin, to the Irish chief Feagh McHugh O'Byrne. Grey's massacre of the Spanish and Irish rebel troops locked into the fortified enclosure at Smerwick in November 1580 was followed by the uncovering of a new conspiracy, led by William Nugent, scion of a leading Pale family. Once again convinced of the need for severity, Grey authorized the imprisonment of leading gentry and lawyers, executing some of them on flimsy evidence, and eventually sanctioning the trial and execution of the newly installed chief justice of common pleas, Nicholas Nugent, in April 1582.[5] When Lord Grey became the new viceroy with full authority as lord deputy on 7 September 1580, he brought into the Irish government new faces and a new attitude, born of war and rebellion.[6] Sir Geoffrey Fenton replaced the aged veteran John Chaloner as secretary of state, and he wrote to the earl of Leicester on 8 September 1580 that Sir James of Desmond might be executed by the commissioners in Cork, 'being before araigned and condemned iudicially'.[7] He continued to note that Desmond had been deprived of his confederates but said, 'This Rebellion has a depe Roote and is incorporated into a greate parte of the principall members of this land.'[8] Accusing many leaders in the Pale of treason, he went on to suggest that Co. Kerry might be expropriated for the benefit of Leicester's faction at court and given as an

---

3. On 29 April 1580, the court dismissed the case of Frances Lovell of Co. Kilkenny against Lawrence Power and eight other defendants on the non-appearance of Lovell or his attorney. Lord Keeper Loftus and Hugh Brady, bishop of Meath, signed for the court, assessing court costs against the fugitive Lovell, since his indictment did not prove riot against the Powers, and there was no compelling interest of the queen at stake. BL, Add. MS 47,172, ff. 43v–44.

4. PRO, SP 63/72/20. The Pelham letter book for 1578–79 preserved in the Carew Manuscripts has no references to castle chamber litigation. LPL, Carew MS 597.

5. See Helen C. Walshe, 'The rebellion of William Nugent, 1581' in R.V. Comerford et al., eds., *Religion, conflict and coexistence in Ireland: essays presented to Mgr Patrick Corish* (Dublin, 1990), pp. 26–52.

6. Ellis, *Tudor Ireland*, p. 330. His patent was signed on 15 July.

7. PRO, SP 63/76/32.   8. Ibid.

estate to Sir Philip Sydney or the earl of Warwick.[9] A second new official, the vice-treasurer Sir Henry Wallop, claimed that the Munster Rebellion would have been put down if Baltinglas had not rebelled in the Pale. However, he argued the rebellion was a papist conspiracy and defended the New English ruthlessness:

> Suche as put into her Majesties heade that the fawlinge awaie of the people here proceadeth not so much through anie evill inclynations in theim, or corruptione of Religione, as by reasone of the harde dealinges of thenglishe towardes theim ... conceave not rightelie of the matter in so perswadinge.[10]

The aspiring clerk Lodowyck Bryskett wrote to Walsingham on 2 March 1580 to complain of the 'universall Disposicion of the people to Disobedience', and likened the state of Ireland to an old cloak, often mended, but now beyond repair and needing a replacement.[11] Even the moderate reformer Gerrard wrote in December 1580 of 'ye pride they were in to massacre us all of Englishe birthe'.[12] The veteran soldier William Stanley in a letter to Walsingham on 26 April 1581 agreed: 'For generallie they hate us in such sorte that they are the worse when they see us, and where extreme hatred is, there is no obedience to be loked for but by compulsion.'[13] While the council added new English servitors with a more strident view of Ireland, the elderly chief justices died in 1580 and 1581, leaving only the exchequer court with a veteran head magistrate, the pliant chief baron, Sir Lucas Dillon.

Adjudication at the court of castle chamber was largely suspended during the months of rebellion, though accusations before the Irish privy council were not in short supply. On 29 April 1580, the lord keeper and bishop of Meath met on behalf of the court to dismiss a charge of riot by Francis Lovell of Knocktopher, Co. Kilkenny against Laurence Power and his kinsmen. After several court days of hearings, the plaintiff refused to obey a summons for his appearance, so the attenuated court ruled on behalf of the defendants.[14] The council complained that the earl of Kildare did too little to defend the Pale in the absence of the lord deputy, hiring only Irish kerne to fight the rebels and permitting them to burn the archbishop of Dublin's town of Rathcoole, four miles from Dublin. They alleged those rebels proclaimed 'no slaughter shuld be made upon enie of the Irish but uppon the Englishe which inhabited there, which for the most parte were soldiers ... uppon whose pore families their furie chieflie lighted'.[15] The council had examined many in the Pale concerning the Baltinglas rebellion, but decided not to prosecute them for treason due to the risk of bringing others into the general conflict, saying they would try them at law when the viceroy returned to Dublin.[16]

---

9. Ibid.
10. Wallop to Walsingham, 9 Sept. 1580: PRO, SP 63/76/40–40v.
11. PRO, SP 63/81/12.   12. PRO, SP 63/79/16.
13. PRO, SP 63/82/154.   14. BL, Add. MS 47,172, ff. 43v–44.
15. PRO, SP 63/78/8.   16. PRO, SP 63/78/10.

Their examinations revealed that the conspiracy had been known a full year before the rebellion of Baltinglas, implicating many in the Pale.[17] As a result of these suspicions, when Grey returned from the massacre at Smerwick in late December 1580, he summoned a grand council of the Pale nobility, at which the earl of Kildare and Baron Delvin were called to account for their complicity in the insurrection. Charging Delvin first, the council proceeded thus:

> We separated him &, uppon deliverie to the whole councell of what hadd bene founde by examinacion [in] falsifying his declaracon, all the board universallie (the Earle of Kildare being one) ordered his commitment to the Castell to be further delte with: he [Delvin] thus committed, we charged the Earle with suche apparant matter as proved he certainlie knewe the viscount woulde breake out, and hadd assured inteligence of divers his principall councellors and partakers, and that notwithstandinge, havinge the vicomte after in his companye, hee rather guarded him from apprehension then assented or liked to have apprehended him.[18]

On 1 March 1581, Grey wrote to Walsingham to forward the examinations of Kildare by Loftus, mentioning Sydney's nemesis, Henry Burnell, as the earl's counsel at law and witness to the examinations.[19] On 2 February 1581, Sir Nicholas White wrote to Cecil that Ireland was desolated, adding that the legal terms were put off and 'all things give place to war'.[20]

The apparent suspension of judicial activity during the crisis of the rebellion was pointed out by the secretaries, Geoffrey Fenton and Edward Waterhouse, writing in March 1581 upon the death of Lord Chancellor Gerrard. In a letter to Walsingham on 13 March 1581, Fenton lamented this state of affairs:

17. Ibid.
18. PRO, SP 63/ 79/55.
19. PRO, SP 63/81/1. Dr Carey has recently written that Kildare's difficult balancing act as the Pale's leading magnate exposed him to accusations of treason and his arrest in December 1580. Though defending the Pale during the Baltinglas rebellion in the absence of the viceroy, Kildare had been forewarned of the rebellion itself and met Baltinglas himself only twelve days before he joined the fray. Kildare and his wife harboured three priests and facilitated their escape during the crisis itself. The court of castle chamber was not, however, involved in his examination prior to his departure for England in custody. He was finally released from the Tower on 18 June 1583, relying on the queen's mercy, but died in 1585 without returning to Ireland. V. Carey, *Surviving the Tudors: the 'wizard' earl of Kildare and English rule in Ireland, 1537–1586* (Dublin, 2002), pp. 206–13. Kildare was previously detained in England from 1575 to 1578 on an accusation by Fitzwilliam that he was using Gaelic bands to 'overawe' his rivals, including covert support of Irish rebels. His careful balancing act was viewed as a sinister plot by the inexperienced and jealous New English officials who replaced the veteran trimmers in the early 1580s. In the view of Carey, 'Kildare was a *politique* in matters of religion and far too committed to the survival of his house to contemplate outright rebellion'. Ibid., p. 218.
20. *Cal. S.P. Ire., 1574–85*, p. 285.

I am bold againe to Remember your honor how hurtfull yt maie bee to the service of Irelande to suffer a long vacacion of the Chauncellores place, for that both the generall Combustions maie take a daungeris skoape [scope] to enlardge and breake out further. And even the particular assistance of the governor and councell will assuredlie stand much weakened for want of such a gravetie.[21]

Fenton explained that the viceroy was engaged in military campaigns away from Dublin, and there was no chief magistrate in the Pale to govern in his absence. Noting that the most loyal councillors were also employed in the field, he warned,

so the Residue [i.e. remaining councillors] in whom, for theire unsowndnes, we dare leave no absolut interest to direct or Comaund, Maie yet bee used as Residencers to lye at Dublyn having there a L. Chauncellor to beare swaigh above them in all deliberacions and Councells.[22]

Fenton concluded that the vacancy was akin to weeding in the garden during a rebellion, or a physician that tended to the 'outward partes' of a patient without looking to the heart, urging the need for 'an estat and bodye of A councell left at hoame to Compownd causes Civill and Aunswer complaints in justice'.[23] Writing again to Walsingham on 22 March from Beaumaris in Anglesey, Fenton called for the renewal of a commission of the court of castle chamber.[24] This admonition repeated the earlier appeal of Waterhouse, writing on 20 March from Dublin for the commission of the star chamber in Ireland. Waterhouse explained:

his l[ordship] writeth that the imperfections of thold comission and the articles to be incertid in the newe are collectid by her majesties Counsell lernid here; yet finding that their notes were very inaptlie gatherid her[e] forbare to send eny but wissheth that the comission be in all pointes made like to that wch auctoriseth the Court of starr chamber in England ... [adding that] Their be many prisoners in this castell wherof some knowen conspirators & other whose lives the lawe cannot towch and yet are thought fin[e]able for their offense in the starr chamber, and because the L: Deputy would have some example made of such the next terme he wissheth the more expedicion in the return of the bearer.[25]

Noting that the queen preferred a trial at law of the Palesmen accused of treason, Fenton worried that the corruption and partiality of the judges might prevent a successful proceeding, explaining 'the ordenarie waie of triall will wante force to attainte either liefe or living'.[26]

21. PRO, SP 63/81/57.   22. Ibid.   23. Ibid.   24. PRO, SP 63/81/88.
25. PRO, SP 63/81/83. Waterhouse wrote in January 1581 to Walsingham to urge 'the severite of lawe to catch hold uppon the p[er]sons and livings of offenders'. PRO, SP 63/80/29.
26. PRO, SP 63/82/37. Fenton urged calling a parliament in which to attaint the traitors' lands and estates.

The death of Lord Chancellor Gerrard was anticipated by widespread concern, and the veteran lord keeper, Adam Loftus, archbishop of Dublin, assumed his place on 6 March 1581. At the same time, Lord Grey authorized the new council book on 1 March, titling it 'A Giornall for entry of dayly and ordinary acts of the counsell being noe matters of state'.[27] The first entry in the extant table recorded an order for the bishop of Waterford, Marmaduke Middleton, against the mayor and corporation of Waterford for £40, and exempting the causes of the church of Waterford from the mayor's jurisdiction. This case was later heard in July 1581 by the lord deputy and council at Ross, where a charge of sacrilege was brought by the mayor against the bishop. After hearing all parties, the council found for the bishop, charged the citizens 100 marks for court costs and sent a proclamation to the towns of Waterford announcing his acquittal of the slander.[28] The journal of the council contains 34 entries for March 1581, one of which refers to a

> Letter of lord deputy and council to the lords of the council in England for a new commission for the court of Star Chamber in Ireland, the court not being competent under a lord keeper in the absence of the chancellor and to enlarge it in other particulars.[29]

The now-missing council book begun in 1581 was complementary to the entry book of the court of castle chamber, but the records differed markedly in form and purpose. According to Dr Quinn, the 'journal' of the Irish council contained 359 separate entries, though some matter was included from earlier administration, running to 253 pages for its six years.[30] By contrast, the entry book of the court contains 43 cases over the same period (1581–89) in some 92 folios.[31] The discrepancy in the record reveals that the parallel judicial work of the Irish privy council in support of the court of castle chamber was continuous, routine and systematic. Recognizances entered in the journal of the privy council supported the court's adjudication, requiring the attendance of suitors and executing the judicial orders and interlocutory decrees of the court. However, it is also clear that the council continued to act as a tribunal apart from its separate existence as a star chamber court. The commission of the castle chamber court recognized a limited category of suits that might come before it, while the privy council in its own right continued to adjudicate on matters that fell beyond those judicial parameters. Quinn has argued that the journal, or minute book, of 1581 had no predecessor

27. BL, Add. MS 4792, ff. 132–34v. Grey signed the document at the top, and the table contains entries up to 14 November 1589.
28. PRO, SP 63/84/23; BL, Add. MS 4792, f. 134. Another entry copied certain words used by Baron Delvin to the lord deputy and council regarding his intention to go to England to reveal secret matters to the queen. Ibid. See also 'Cal. Council book, 1581–86,' ed. D.B. Quinn, *Anal Hib*, no. 24 (1967), 109.
29. Ibid., p. 114.   30. Ibid., p. 93.
31. BL, Add. MS 47,172, ff. 44v–90.

and that documents entered in this new council book had been merely filed prior to that time. He confirms the view that the council made it a practice, occasionally, to adjudicate between suitors, claiming that 'the proportion of the judicial work of the council transferred to the court of Castle Chamber was not large'.[32] Quinn further argued that the journal became the primary record of conciliar actions, leaving a more ceremonial function to the council register, or Black Book, begun in 1571.[33] More than half of the entries in the journal of the council were recognizances, and the frequent references to cases being dealt with in the ordinary process of law buttress the view that the council was operating in a judicial manner quite apart from its parallel existence as a court of castle chamber.[34]

Since there were practically no recorded acts of the castle chamber court in its entry book for two years, it is essential to trawl through the journal for evidence of the court's continued existence. Reference to a case involving Christopher Barnewall of Ardstown, heard in castle chamber court in May, was mentioned in connection with his appearance in council chamber on 21 April 1581.[35] On 11 April 1581, another recognizance of 100 marks was demanded of Gervaise Foster and Gervase Hussey, Co. Meath, for their appearance 'in the Starre Chamber' to answer charges.[36] On 18 June, during the Trinity term, the council book documented a recognizance of Nicholas Deverox, Richard Synnot, William Browne, Walter Synnot and Philip Lamport of Co. Wexford for their appearances at the next Michaelmas term before the lord deputy and council. This referred to a castle chamber case that was ultimately dismissed in June 1582 after the fines were duly paid.[37] In an apparent suit heard before the lord deputy and council on 8 April 1581, Anne Bath, a widow, was awarded £20 from the assignee of John Bath of Drumconrath [Drumcondra], and her 'long depending' suit for the abbey of Athlone under a nuncupative will of her husband was dismissed.[38] The journal records 24 entries for the month of April 1581, but only ten entries during May, the beginning of the legal term that heralded the presumed reestablishment of the court of castle chamber.[39]

On 5 May 1581, the court of castle chamber sat to hear the case of a corrupt jury in Co. Meath, finding the foreman, Christopher Barnewall of Ardstown (mentioned above), and Christopher Hussey, the alleged ringleader, guilty of perjury and fining them £100 each.[40] The case involved a commission composed of Robert Dillon, then second justice of common pleas, Richard Bealing, the

---

32. 'Cal. Council book, 1581–86,' p. 98.   33. Ibid., p. 105.
34. Ibid., p. 104.   35. Ibid., p. 114.
36. Ibid., p. 115. A similar recognizance on 26 April 1581 was demanded of Thomas Fitzgerald of Lackagh, Co. Kildare, for his appearance on the first day of the next term. Ibid., p. 116.
37. Ibid., p. 119; BL, Add. MS 47,172, ff. 57–57v.
38. 'Cal. Council book,' p. 115. The nuncupative will is an oral declaration by a testator in his last sickness before a sufficient number of witnesses which is afterwards reduced to writing. *Black's law dictionary*, p. 1218.
39. 'Cal. Council book,' pp. 113–18.   40. BL, Add. MS 47,172, f. 44v.

solicitor general, and Alexander Fitton, gentleman, of Bective with others to inquire into the escheats and wardships of Co. Meath on 30 March 1581. The commissioners called a jury before them to examine the estate of the deceased Richard Lynham, who was possessed of two parcels of land called Thomaston and Turyn, held by knight service *in capite* of the queen. Despite the evidence given to the jury, they found that the apparent wardship of Lynham's son, Thomas, was defeated by the will of his father, leaving the two estates to his wife, Katherine Handcock, as her jointure. The court found the jurors had not only ignored the testimony given them, but lacked either witnesses or testimony to reach their conclusion on behalf of the widow Lynham, using 'Corrupt affeccion without Respect of Conscience or feare of god'.[41] A pitiful confession of the jurors was then entered loose leaf into the entry book, acknowledging their fault and blaming others who instructed and informed them to find for the widow. Their plea for clemency was approved six days later, when the court mitigated their fines and released them from further punishment. The routine interest of the court in finding a lucrative wardship for the crown obliged the queen's attorneys to challenge jurors in cases of this sort.[42] Although several cases were clearly pending before the court, a memorandum in the journal of the council declared that on 15 May 1581 it was resolved that the next Trinity term should be adjourned, without explanation.[43] On the same day, Lord Delvin appeared before the lord deputy and council with a demand for liberty to go to the queen, where he would divulge secret information only for her ears.[44]

Though the law term in summer 1581 produced no work for the castle chamber, the lord deputy was in Wexford on 10 June to hear sessions there in person along with the vice-treasurer, the chief baron and Secretary Waterhouse. Grey reported that the sessions were well attended, noting that some were accused of conspiracy in the late rebellion and imprisoned pending trial.[45] Writing to the privy council in July, Grey revealed that his transactions had met with some resistance. Continuing the sessions at Ross, where he called a number of the principal gentlemen of Co. Wexford before him to answer charges of confederation with the rebels, Grey deplored their response, fretting sourly that

41. Ibid., f. 44v. The other jurors were all fined £50, jailed and forced to stand upon the pillory.
42. Ibid., ff. 47–47v. They were spared the pillory, their fines lowered to less than £10 in some cases, and they made recognizances for payment by 6 November 1581. No mention was made of the earlier castle chamber case against Barnewall in 1577, when he led the campaign against the cess as a foreman of the jury in Co. Meath, but the explicit accusation against him justified a heavier fine. Ibid., ff. 20–21. Both Hussey and Barnewall were mentioned in recognizances levied by order of the council on 12 February 1582, with the latter to appear before the council on ten days warning. 'Cal. Council book,' p. 125.
43. 'Cal. Council book,' p. 115.
44. Ibid, p. 119. The council took many recognizances for the appearance of suitors before them at the next Hilary term, but none referred to the court of castle chamber. Ibid., pp. 120–23.
45. PRO, SP 63/83/111. He also sought his revocation and voiced a protest against the sending of a general pardon from England.

the best of the whole shier Nicholas Deverox, who had publiquely confessed before mee and the whole assembly matter worthy deathe, I caused him to be arreigned and although the most pt of the iury heard his confession and the matter so plaine and evidente as yt could not be denied, yet soche was theire unsounde dealing as they did most affectedlye acquite him, a plaine evidence to me how corruptly all causes for the queen are handeled, in the absence of the governour, when in my presence so greate an abuse was offredd.[46]

Meanwhile, a recognizance was taken on 18 June 1581 from Philip Lamport, Richard Synnot and others, convicted of the riot in spoiling a ship off Co. Wexford. Without citing the castle chamber case heard under Drury in 1579, they were required to appear before the viceroy and council at the next Michaelmas term.[47] Other cases heard by the council included a complaint by Thomas Jones, dean of St Patrick's in Dublin, against the estate of Lord Chancellor Gerrard for the repair of the deanery. Gerrard had left £80 in his estate for the purpose, but the executor refused to pay the money. The order of the lord deputy and council allowed the dean to accept instead an equivalent sum due for payments made to the army by Gerrard.[48] At the end of July the viceroy left Dublin with most of the council, only Lord Chancellor Loftus and Secretary Waterhouse remaining in Dublin to arrange victualling. The two chief justices were sent into the Pale to conduct sessions, so the central courts were effectively inoperative during this season.[49]

The only case recorded in the entry book for Michaelmas term 1581 took place on 5 September, when the lord deputy and council signed an order repairing a defect in the previous decree against Philip Lamport and others of Co. Wexford. The ship of John Fuller and Walter Fox, Chester merchants, had been raided at the seashore in Co. Wexford by over 200 persons, and several leading gentry were made responsible for their fines. Lord Justice Drury and the court had left a blank in the original order which was duly amended, and the £100 fine was made payable at the next Hilary term.[50] Adjudication before the court accelerated in the next year under Grey, but his record is one of a caretaker government, showing little ingenuity, since the entries are more concerned with clerical matters of this sort than an expansion of the common law. Geoffrey Fenton wrote often to seek reform of the government, and recommended Sir Lucas Dillon as the next lord chancellor, or Archbishop Loftus, though he preferred 'a temporall lawyer' sent from England.[51] He demonstrated his concern with rebellion in every missive, suggesting that Kildare and Delvin be sent to England for trial, and casually recommended the rack for the interrogation of their associate, Thomas Meagh.[52]

46. PRO, SP 63/84/23. Deverox was earlier charged in the riot at the spoil of the ship near Ross, and signed a recognizance for appearance at Michaelmas term on 18 June 1581. 'Cal. Council book,' p. 119.

47. 'Cal. Council book,' p. 119.   48. Ibid., p. 123.

49. PRO, SP 63/84/125.   50. BL, Add. MS 47,172, f. 48.

51. PRO, SP 63/84/129.   52. Ibid.

At the end of the year, Fenton called for the sale of escheated and attainted lands of the Pale rebels to natives who affected English manner and speech.[53]

Perhaps desperate to win a verdict against the rebels, the council finally resorted to judicial intimidation. Word of this first came from Fenton, writing to Walsingham on 23 November 1581 in praise of the juries and noting the large number of trials that had convicted rebels of both high and low calling. His satirical commentary deserves reporting:

> The Jurors, by a secret power of god workinge in their consciences, proceade in the tryalls wth great uprightnes, esteming it a singuler acte of pyetie to their Countrey to weede owte suche Corrupte members, and by their extirpacion to assure the better their owne estates … [while] … the Judges and Jurors with others of the privey Councell sytting with them *tanquam amici curiae.*[54]

Fenton indicated that Irish jurors would proceed to find even against their own kinsmen, when confronted by members of the government as 'friends of the court' sitting amongst them. This practice encouraged the good sort to obey and terrified the malcontents according to Fenton, though he lamented that Kildare had not been charged with any crime and no direct evidence could enculpate him, despite the breadth of the conspiracy. The Irish council wrote on 11 December that they had spent much time arraigning members of the gentry accused in the two Pale conspiracies, hearing confessions and answers, and commending the work of juries who dealt honestly 'without my working under hand or secrett dealing'.[55] The lord deputy concluded:

> The Judges and Councell lerned in the lawes for her Matie with some of the privey Councell sitting wth them *tanquam amici curiae* have by reasons and p[re]monitions so cleared all scruples in the generall reporte and assistancye of people, that there are none which are not satisfied (yf justice orderlie and sincerelie ministered and the consciences of twelve men lawfullie chosen and of their owne kynred and neighborheade maie suffice to resolve them) that it was a iust and necessarie service to cutt of so manie rotten members by whom the mayne bodie of their Country was in daunger to perishe.[56]

Four years after the departure of Sydney, the crisis over the cess re-emerged in the spring of 1582 to bedevil the regime of Grey. The lord deputy had obtained

---

53. PRO, SP 63/87/162.   54. PRO, SP 63/86/242.
55. PRO, SP 63/87/93.
56. Ibid. The solitary voice of Nicholas White protested at the waste of the Pale, counting the number of rebels who were executed and noting the conflict on the council between viceroy and chancellor over the cess on a prostrate countryside. White to Cecil, 9 Dec. 1581, from Dublin: PRO, SP 63/87/56.

approval in Michaelmas term 1581 for a new cess on the Pale, despite the devastation that had occurred during the recent rebellion. Though an assembly of nobles and gentlemen concurred, one Patrick Bermingham, a gentleman of Corbally, Co. Meath vigorously dissented, breaking into the council chamber to challenge the cess and present a supplication in the name of the Pale inferring general discontent. At a later session in Navan, Bermingham contested the cess and disputed the authority of a commission including members of the Irish council.[57] In March 1582, Bermingham presented a petition from 46 men of Co. Meath to the Irish council, stating the country was unable to pay due to rampant poverty, and reaffirming the earlier petition of Burnell, Netterville and Scurlocke to the queen. Bermingham alleged the new viceroy broke precedent with the recent trend of avoiding the cess and claimed Grey was acting unlawfully.[58] In response, on 23 March, the council ordered him arrested for his disorders in 'stirring up [common] people to discontentment and so to procure them rashly to Complayne'.[59] Bermingham wrote to the queen on 4 April 1582 to protest at having been jailed, citing earlier letters of the queen that forbade the cess for the viceroy's household in 1578.[60] He brought his attorney to Dublin to present the petition, and the Irish council responded that they would be at sessions in Trim to hear any man who informed against the abuse of soldiers.[61] After the departure of Grey, the lords justices agreed to hear Bermingham again on 29 August at a council session, giving him until after the harvest season to present his proofs.[62] They finally relented in November, explaining to Walsingham that they had dealt with the Pale reasonably, forbearing to cess several baronies, blaming Bermingham for raising a clamour, and imposing cess during pleasure only. The weakness of their position was based on the universal distress, the evidently punitive nature of Grey's imposition of cess and the bitter legacy of Sydney's unfinished struggle to employ the deputy's prerogative right.[63] While the conflict did not involve the castle chamber court directly, the council was preoccupied with this new crisis during much of the year, and it fortified the impression of Grey's ruthlessness.[64]

Further evidence of alleged conspiracy within the government itself arose during the various trials of Pale leaders, culminating in the extraordinary censure and execution in April 1582 of the former chief justice of common pleas, Nicholas Nugent. The privy council travelled from Dublin to a special sessions at Trim, a venue chosen on the grounds that such a hearing would be more convenient to the jurors, though a treason trial was rarely heard outside the capital. The lord deputy named a special commission as assistants to the judges, including himself and others of the Irish privy council. Some of them sat on the bench, and the jury

57. PRO, SP 63/92/76.   58. PRO, SP 63/91/63v–64.
59 PRO, SP 63/92/80; 'Cal. Council book,' p. 127. The council noted the absence of any gentlemen
    from the petition, referring to petitioners as the 'meaner sort'.
60. PRO, SP 63/91/25   61 PRO, SP 63/91/76
62. PRO, SP 63/94/106.   63. PRO, SP 63/97/171.
64. PRO, SP 63/91/22, 42; 63/92/198.

duly convicted both Nicholas Nugent, uncle of the Pale conspiracy's leader, William Nugent, and a great Pale landowner, Edward Cusack, of high treason, based on the testimony of a single witness. John Cusack, a former malefactor and conspirator who may have been coopted by Nugent's rival, Sir Robert Dillon, was pardoned by the lord deputy after the hearing, despite many efforts to impugn his motives and doubts about his veracity during the trial. Cusack asserted that Nicholas knew about the rebellion in advance and encouraged William Nugent and others 'to spare no man's goods'.[65] The viceroy claimed that, while Nugent refused to confess in public, he acknowledged his treason privately to Waterhouse, so the lord deputy ordered his execution on the day following the trial. Grey justified his precipitate handling of the case, in part, by sending to Walsingham copies of Nugent's previous submission in the controversy over the cess, citing his attack on prerogative taxation as evidence of his conspiratorial record.[66] The reliable Fenton reported on 13 April 1582 that Nugent had been executed, and his lands escheated to the crown.[67] The involvement of the lord deputy and council in Nugent's trial besmirched the reputation of prerogative justice, even though the court of castle chamber was not formally engaged in the adjudication. Under attack from all sides by midsummer the lord deputy wrote on 11 July to dispute the claim that the Irish 'woulde lyve in quyett if they weere not provoked'.[68]

Grey was a transitional figure. Much of his work in the court of castle chamber was done by a clerk, and the majority of cases heard during his regime were either dismissed or merely follow-up orders pursuant to earlier orders and decrees. Grey had no ambition to reform the judicial system or the court, and he lacked a reform-minded lord chancellor to sponsor an activist judicial presence outside the Pale. Against a backdrop of rebellion and vengeance, Grey's work was often punitive in character. If his role were custodial rather than inventive, it is nonetheless clear that he managed to improve the records of the court and speed up the processes of conciliar adjudication. In February 1582, Lord Grey was an active judge, convening the court of castle chamber to fine a perjured jury which refused to convict Morris Fitzjames Fitzgerald of high treason for abetting the rebellion of Viscount Baltinglas. The case had been heard in Co. Kildare and in Dublin at queen's bench, after which the verdict of innocent was challenged by the queen's attorney. The castle chamber court heard the evidence, 'All which was verified unto the courte to be true both by the Judges that sat in Judgment and by some of the pryvie Counsell that sate there at the declaringe of the said cause.'[69] At a

65. H.C. Walshe, 'Rebellion of William Nugent', p. 42.
66. PRO, SP 63/91/49. See also *Cal. S.P. Ire., 1574–1585*, p. 128, for the submission of Nicholas Nugent and Christopher Fleming to the viceroy and Irish council for consenting to send letters against the cess; and p. 359 for the lord deputy's narrative of the trial and execution of Nicholas Nugent.
67. PRO, SP 63/91/77. He also explained that a *custodiam* attached to the land meant that little profit accrued to the queen. Ibid.
68. PRO, SP 63/94/33.
69. BL, Add. MS 47,172, ff. 49–49v. All jurors were fined £100.

second hearing on 9 February 1582, the court fined Richard Dorran of Co. Meath for perjury in giving false testimony regarding the parcel called Chapel Orchard, claimed by Michael Cusake, gentleman. Dorran deposed that the parcel of land was the inheritance of James Tankarde of Castleton, and that he died seised of the land, but the court found for Cusake, the tenant, who took the profits from the land according to testimony at court. Dorran was fined £5. The adjudication of this case at castle chamber demonstrates the potentially broad reach of the court, since the small amount of the fine and the provincial nature of the offence would not lead to such a case being normally tried there.[70]

The reforming energies of Laurence Holinshed, gentleman, and clerk of the court, were prominent in its deliberations throughout 1582. Holinshed determined that the records of castle chamber were so disordered that cases long pending, through the inattention of suitors and the evident torpor of clerical staff, were irreparably flawed and should be officially terminated by the court. Writing to the lord deputy, he made the position clear:

> That whear the bookes of actes and orders of the same Court ar nowe very imperfecte and far out of order, by reason the actes and orders hearetofore pronouncyd in Corte have not bene entered into the same before the next courte theare holden, after the day that they were pronouncede, but set downe most comonly in Lewse papers, and by that meane often cast aside and lost, and so not at all entered into the saide bookes, and the most parte also suche as wer entered, wer slightly drawen by the Clerke of the Corte or his men (being ignorant, etc.) and comonly not comdered [commanded, ordered] upon and pennyd by her maties Lernyd counsell. And so the canc[ellarius] moving the corte to order, the same therein not Inserted, those actes and orders have often tymes ben reversed, for want of dewe informacon geven unto the Cort of the cause where they were first ordered, to the great prejudyce as well of her matie and her good subyectes and to the great Incorraging of thoffender to remayne in their evell actions for want of terror and poneshement for their former offences.[71]

The punctilious Holinshed requested an order of the chief governor to require greater care from both learned counsel and clerical staff, entering the memorandum in the court's record for good measure, and signing the entry 'yor dayly orator'.[72]

After the lord deputy assented to Holinshed's reform of the court, a number of inactive suits were promptly terminated. Three cases were summarily dismissed in the Easter term of the court, based on earlier indictments that were found insufficient. On 3 May 1582, at a full hearing of the court, the case of Michael,

70. Ibid., f. 51.   71. Ibid., f. 52.
72. Ibid., f. 52v.

bishop of Ossory, against John Archer and others was dismissed after a hearing by commissioners of the court.[73] A bill of riot brought by Robert Adam, gentleman, of Portlecester in Co. Meath, originally entered on 5 February 1579, was dismissed by the court on 18 May 1582. The defendants included numerous Dubliners, such as Richard Copperan, an apothecary, Roger Tavernor, a trumpeter, and William Beaughe, merchant, but the entry failed to describe the nature of the offence. A likely explanation involving some commercial transaction that went awry in Dublin was not mentioned in the entry book, and the court merely awarded costs to its own officers.[74] On the same day, another bill of riot, filed by Joyce Adryan of Dublin, leatherdresser, against Thomas Dermot, a merchant of Dublin, was dismissed more than two years after it was initiated.[75] In June, Holinshed prompted the court to dismiss an order for Anthony Colclough, former sheriff of Co. Wexford, to give an account of sums collected from former defendants in the castle chamber case against Philip Lamport, Patrick Synnot and others. Colclough had failed to make his return as demanded by 20 May 1581, and was summoned to the court in June 1582, but it was then found that the commission was missing, Holinshed stating 'that hee could finde no sufficient matter to prove the same sett downe emongest the Recordes of the Corte, having made dilligent searche therein to that ende'.[76] The court discharged Colclough, since it appeared that he returned a certificate of his proceedings in the case as required, annexing a schedule of the sums received by him and his predecessor.[77]

In the next term, Holinshed returned to his housekeeping of court records. A suit against Thomas Waring and other defendants was dismissed when some sixteen of the co-defendants failed to appear after being served with process, and Waring was made responsible to prosecute them for their appearance at the next Michaelmas term.[78] In suits of this kind, the principal offender was made responsible for the others, and it is likely that they were his clients, or tenants. The court also heard an appeal of Lord Howth (mentioned above) to reduce his fine of £1,000 imposed by the court in 1579. Appearing before the court on 5 July, Howth detailed his imprisonment for 19 weeks, the crippling burden of the fine, and other payments that threatened 'thantiquitie of his howse'.[79] On the following day, the full court heard from Holinshed that the docket was clogged with pending cases and agreed to make orders for the streamlining of their adjudication. The clerk complained that

> there werr not so fewe as 30 or 40 causes presently depending therin ready at hearing, and farre greater number not so farre proceeded in, and though divers as well pls as defs were in towne yet did they not prosecute the same.

---

73. Nothing of the original information of riot was mentioned in the entry except the date of 2 September 1581. The court moved to dismiss, with costs to the clerk and officers. Ibid., f. 54.
74. Ibid., f. 56.   75. Ibid., f. 55.
76. Ibid., f. 56v.   77. Ibid., ff. 57–57v.
78. Ibid., f. 58.   79. Ibid., f. 62.

It is therfore ordered and decreed, for verie reasonable causes the same Court moving, that process of attachment be adwarded against suche of them, as well pls as defs as shall not have their causes determined this terme, returnable octabis michis next and then the parties severally to enter into recognizance to prosecute with effect. And lykewise ordered that suche as shall hereafter exhibitt bills in the same court, her matie beeing not merely pl therin, shall severally enter into recognizance to prosecute the same wth effect, ere the Clerke of the Court geve fourthe his warrant for proces to be made therupon. And further ordered that the said Clerk shalbe Attorney for all suche as nowe presentlye are playntiffs or that hereafter shalbe playntiffs in the same Cort.[80]

The unusually assertive clerk thus highlighted the problems of the court and entered them in the record, claiming the right to punish dilatory pleading and to move the suits currently pending in his role as effective attorney for the plaintiffs. Though the lord deputy departed in August, Holinshed continued his campaign in the next administration, prevailing upon the lords justices to discharge cases which had lain dormant in the records for many years.[81]

The Michaelmas term of 1582 witnessed a dramatic increase in the judicial business of the court of castle chamber, but the impact of this burst of energy was to revive old suits in order to end them. On 31 October, the new lord justice, Loftus, and others sat to hear the case of Robert Skirret, a merchant of Galway, against Sir Clement Skirret, a priest of Galway, in a bill of perjury. Finding that the original suit, filed in June 1574, had been long since adjudicated by commissioners of the court, the tribunal dismissed the plaintiff and then proceeded to strike others from the record. It is possible to read the frustration of the court and its officers in this judicial cleansing. They presided over some 21 orders, discharging litigation that had begun when the court was first instituted in 1571. Most were bills of riot filed between neighbours, and it is probable that the idle cases were resolved by other means, or other courts, in the intervening period. All the cases were handled in the same manner, with a perfunctory formula used by the clerk to indicate that the court 'for verie reasonable causes' discharged the litigants with costs and fees to be paid to its officers. Based on the testimony of Holinshed, the 'reasonable causes' were probably the inactive status of cases in which neither the government nor the plaintiff had any further interest. Thus, on 7 November 1582, the court of castle chamber dusted off its files and eliminated pleadings and half-finished adjudication that had accumulated over a decade.[82] By

---

80. Ibid., f. 63.
81. Ibid., ff. 63, 63v to 76.
82. Ibid., ff. 64–75v. The earliest case was heard in Co. Meath on 29 November 1571, and most of the cases involved riots in that county. Some of them were not dated in the entry book, and two cases involved either perjury or corruption. Sixteen cases in all were dismissed perfunctorily on that day.

the time Sir John Perrot arrived as the new viceroy in Ireland, the court had become nearly moribund. Despite the claims of Holinshed that some forty cases were pending, it is suggested by the entry book that few of these suits were likely to proceed to final adjudication. While the administrative work of the court continued on a regular basis, little was done to finalize its decrees, so it is not surprising that the entry book contains no litigation for 1583. In one case, heard on 9 November 1582, the plaintiff, Aristotle Scurlocke of Co. Wexford, received an award against his neighbour, Thomas Deverox, and a number of Deverox's servants, as well as another gentleman, Walter Butler. At a full hearing, which interrupted the administrative record-cleaning operation of Holinshed, the court determined that Deverox and his clients were guilty of riot against Scurlocke and fined them for the disturbance. The case involved a gentleman as plaintiff against the yeoman Deverox and it was first filed on 13 August 1581. The full court heard deliberations on the matter before entering its judgement, fining Deverox twenty nobles and imprisoning him for one month. Other defendants were to spend up to three months in jail.[83] Another record of 7 November 1582 showed Anstace Browne of Coddstown, Co. Wexford, had sued Aristotle Scurlocke of Rosslare in May 1577 for a riot.[84] This case was dismissed after lying dormant for five years, and it is possibly related to the judicial victory of Scurlocke obtained two days later against Deverox and Butler. It was not unusual to see familiar names in the entry book, as the court became a reliable tool in provincial quarrels over land and estates.

Lords Justices Loftus and Wallop joined in a caretaker administration for nearly two years, but despite their long experience they did nothing to reform the court of castle chamber. It is possible that Loftus preferred to hold hearings in his own chancery court, of which he was a jealous custodian. At this time the work of the courts was hampered by the absence of some recently deceased incumbents, as Fenton remarked in August 1582 in a letter to Walsingham: the chief justice and attorney general had both just died. Fenton called for their replacement by English magistrates. Doubting the 'partial and affectionate' record of the senior second justice, James Dowdall, Fenton went on to describe the ideal attorney general thus:

> I doe likewise wishe him to be such one as for his other sufficiencies and gravetie he might be of her high privy Councell heare, whereby would growe to the table no small Assistance for that the Number of thenglishe Councellors ys farre lese then that of the Irishe which in manie Deliberacions doth often tymes appeare to the prejudice and disadvauntaige of the service.[85]

It would be nearly three years before Elizabeth appointed Robert Gardiner to the queen's bench, with superintendence of the inferior courts and an increase in

---

83. Ibid., ff. 73–73v.   84. Ibid., ff. 66–66v.
85. Fenton to Walsingham, writing from Dublin on 6 August 1582: PRO, SP 63/94/182.

fees to support him in Ireland.[86] The ineffectiveness of senior magistrates in Ireland, due to their illness or advanced age, and the long intervals when their offices lay vacant, undermined the efforts of the ablest reformers such as Gerrard. During his long career in Ireland as bishop and judge, Adam Loftus did more to advance the cause of his family fortune than the administration of justice. In a letter to Walsingham on 7 March 1584, the lords justices reported that they ordered the examination of the accused traitor, Dr Hurley, who was captured as Catholic archbishop of Dublin and hence the prime sectarian rival of Loftus. The partisan lords justices commissioned Secretaries Fenton and Waterhouse to 'toast his feet against fire with hot boots', and recommended that he be executed by martial law since he disdained to confess his treason, Irish juries would refuse to convict him, and the best lawyers declared that since his treasonable acts had been committed 'in foreign parts, and the law not stretching so far in Ireland as it does in England', he could not be convicted at common law.[87] The court of castle chamber was not used in cases of treason at this period, and the interim lords justices apparently felt they lacked authority to proceed in a treason case without clear instruction, and acted only on receiving Walsingham's order to proceed with judicial torture.

The gap of nineteen months (November 1582 to August 1584) in the records of the court of castle chamber may be explained in a number of ways. First, the lack of a new lord deputy robbed the government of a clear mandate. Second, the parallel provincial authorities demanded both the attention and the resources of the crown, since the final act of the Desmond Rebellion was delayed until the death of the earl in Tralee on 11 November 1583. Thirdly, efforts at plantation in Munster absorbed the attention of reformers and attracted much litigation that was delegated to other courts. Fourthly, the outrages of Grey's regime may have tarnished the reputation of the prerogative court, particularly after the dubious trial and execution of Chief Justice Nugent in the wake of rebellion. Fifthly, both Loftus and Wallop were probably viewed by potential litigants as English partisans who would reject Irish suits and favour their own relatives. And finally, the rumoured arrival of a new viceroy caused the delay of suits in the hope of a more generous policy toward the Old English. Nonetheless, the lords justices continued to demand recognizances for the appearance of suitors, and issued decrees in numerous controversies. For example, on 15 December 1582, the court ordered recognizances in the case of John Lye of Co. Kildare against his brother, Emery, 'to stand to the award to be made by the lords justices and council in the suit pending between him and his brother' over a lease of the castle and lands of Ballina.[88] This decree was entered in the council book on 2 June 1583, the decree ittself being based on the queen's letter of 9 August 1582 to Emery Lye for the

86. BL, Cotton MS Titus B XIII, f. 390.
87. *Cal. S.P. Ire., 1574–85*, p. 498. The justices followed up with letters on 8 March and 14 April, containing further examinations and inquiring what to do with Hurley. Ibid., pp. 499, 506.
88. 'Cal. Council book,' p. 136.

lands in question. The lords justices awarded the benefit of the lease equally to the two brothers since they found that John had disbursed expenses for part of the journey in return for a joint lease, to which both had agreed prior to Emery's journey to London.[89]

The lords justices gave orders that allowed controversies to progress in other courts during the hiatus of work in castle chamber. On 9 February 1583, an 'order of lords justices and council' gave the wardship of Christopher Barnewall, son and heir to Robert Barnewall, to his famous kinsman, Sir Patrick Barnewall, knight, pending the final award between Lords Gormanston and Slane in the matter.[90] A suit by the earl of Ormonde claiming title to the lands of Upper Ossory was deferred in June 1583 until the following Michaelmas term by an order of the council, allowing the baron of Upper Ossory to file an answer in court.[91] In July, a recognizance of Thomas Fleming in Co. Meath referred to a hearing 'by the council table' regarding a distress of sixty cows taken by Lord Trimleston from Fleming's lands in lieu of a 'head rent' to be determined by the council.[92] In August 1583, the lords justices heard a number of cases in Dundalk, awarding a marriage portion to Dame Eleanor Neil, 'late wife to Hugh McGennis'. On 15 August, the decree stated:

> And we do hereby order that in respect she was his wife for 16 years and more, and hath children by her, the said Sir Hugh shall pay and deliver unto her the sum of £200 and 200 good beeves, one half at Michaelmas next the other half at Michaelmas 1584.[93]

Two days earlier, the lords justices required both McGennis and the baron of Dungannon, Hugh O'Neill, to pay a £1,000 recognizance and to abide by the award of the council in the matter then depending between McGennis and his 'late' wife.[94] Few details were offered in the records, though it is clear that O'Neill was acting in support of his kinswoman's marriage portion, whose long union with McGennis was apparently set aside, 'or some consideration to be left to her for her better support'.[95] In another case involving domestic conflict, the court ordered the lady of Lackagh to support her two daughters by Sir Maurice Fitzgerald. On 31 November 1583, Margaret and Katherine Fitzgerald complained against their mother, Dame Margaret Butler, wife of Sir Maurice, for negligence. They asserted

---

89. Ibid., p. 143. This very full entry shows the lords justices adjudicating upon matters that would otherwise have come before the chancery, since castle chamber rarely heard property questions *per se*.
90. Ibid., p. 137: 'The lords to try their title at law.'
91. Ibid., p. 141. The frequent appearance of the barons of Upper Ossory before the conciliar tribunal must be weighed against Dr Edwards's assertion that 'MacGiollapadraig participation in the extension of English law was, at best, limited'. Edwards, 'Collaboration without anglicization', p. 90.
92. 'Cal. Council book,' p. 144.
93. Ibid., p. 146.
94. Ibid., pp. 145–46.
95. Ibid.

that she had turned them out of doors and refused them preferment or maintenance, and being called before the council board she refused to give them anything but what the extremity of the law would enforce her to. Wherefore the lords justices and council called upon Edmond Butler, second justice of the queen's bench and Serjeant Fitzsymmons, the feoffees of the will of said Sir Maurice FitzGerald by which he left everything to his said wife, to declare his intent, and they reporting that he intended that his said daughters should be preferred, it was ordered by the said lords justices and council that the said Lady of Lackagh should pay her said daughters £400 a piece.[96]

The equity jurisdiction of prerogative justice was again apparent in an order of 28 January 1584 when the council board enjoined Alexander Clinton, husband of Elizabeth, from meddling with the rents contrary to the settlement made between them, saying of Alexander 'whose detestable life to the world appeareth'.[97] The influence of a prelate who became entrenched as lord chancellor and was frequently made lord justice may be seen in these decisions, pronouncing on moral offences that would more appropriately have come before the ecclesiastical courts in an earlier period.

In a remarkable lapse of judicial probity, the lords justices apparently presided over one of the last episodes of trial by combat under the Tudors. The episode itself called into question their commitment to the rule of law. Secretary Fenton wrote to the earls of Warwick and Leicester on 13 September 1583 that two of the O'Connors were brought before the council in Ireland to debate counter-charges regarding assault and the murder of their respective followers. Teige McGillapatrick O'Connor justified the slaying of Connor McCormack O'Connor's retainers because they were confederates of a notorious rebel, Cahill O'Connor, which Connor denied. When Teige challenged his kinsman to a battle, the lords justices allowed it, and the inner court of Dublin Castle was chosen as the venue at 9.00 the next morning. The two combatants appeared, donned their swords and targets, and proceeded to do battle in full view of the council as witnesses, including Fenton. Teige wounded Connor, seized his sword and after much wrestling pierced him several times in the torso and so weakened his rival that he finally managed to decapitate him. Giving the bloody prize to his assistants, he offered his sword to the earl of Leicester and sought his favour as a 'civil man'. Fenton reported the feudal anachronism in an astonished tone: 'I think the like hath not been seen at any time before.'[98] Although there was no adjudication and the court of castle chamber was not involved, the sordid event did nothing to enhance the reputation of the government for exemplary justice, and it can only be explained in terms of an opportunist strategy of *divide et impera.* The charges laid against Lord Deputy Perrot of favouring the Old English must be understood

---

96. Ibid., p. 152.   97. Ibid.
98. *Cal. Carew MSS, 1575–1588*, pp. 361–62.

in the context of this blatant manipulation of clan rivalry by the cynical lord chancellor and his henchmen.

THWARTED AMBITION: THE REFORM POLICIES OF SIR JOHN PERROT AS CHIEF GOVERNOR

Sir John Perrot sought the office of chief governor for many years and won the post in 1584 on the basis of a programme reminiscent of the activist style of Sydney and Sussex. According to Brady, Perrot was the 'apotheosis of the programmatic governor'.[99] Perrot had been the first lord president in Munster under the deputyship of Sydney in 1570. He was a celebrated campaigner, a relentless and aggressive general during the Fitzmaurice Rebellion, and after his retirement to England in 1573 he proffered numerous reform essays for the queen's government of Ireland. His combative temperament and physical gallantry were known to his friends and enemies alike. When he assumed the sword of state as lord deputy in June 1584, there were high expectations for his energetic style of leadership. He proceeded to make a series of progresses throughout the country and demanded submissions from Irish chiefs, requiring them to cooperate with the new judicial framework he put in place.[100] His aim was to make composition agreements in every province and he proposed to hold an early parliament to finalize accords reached with the representatives of Ulster. Beginning in the fall of 1584, Perrot worked with Pale lawyers to draw up bills for the parliament and he was consumed with legislative business during the first two years of his regime. The factions that emerged almost immediately within the council in Ireland were resonant in the parliamentary sessions, and the enemies of Perrot seized every opportunity to frustrate his aims there.[101] Though he implemented a grand scheme for the administration of justice, he was compelled to write again in late 1585

> to sende over a Cheife Justice of the English birth, such a one as for sufficiencie and integritie might be a light and an overseer to the rest to bringe

---

99. Brady, *Chief governors*, p. 293.

100. Sir James Perrott, *The chronicle of Ireland, 1584–1608*, ed. H. Wood (Dublin, 1933), pp. 25–27.

101. V. Treadwell, 'Sir John Perrot and the Irish parliament of 1585–6', *RIA Proc*, lxxxv (1985), sect. c, pp. 302–03, and see pp. 259–308 for a full discussion of the contentious legislature. In January 1586 Perrot wrote to his agent at court, defending his efforts to achieve agreement for the cess and complaining that two lawyers, Burnell and Netterville, had scoured his accounts and challenged even the 'pettie provicions of rushes and every like necessarie that muste be had in a house'. He concluded, 'It angres me to make this bibble babble accompt, fitter to be toulde to boyes then to anie that have witt or Judgement, and I think fowle scorne they sholde put me to it.' 'The Perrot papers,' ed. C. McNeill, *Anal Hib*, no. 12 (1943), pp. 44–45. A meeting of the grand council in 1586 to set down a formal composition for cess ended without an accord, the deputy saying 'I founde they had been so longe weined from the cesse as they coulde not well brooke to heare of it'. Ibid., p. 53.

the Courtes and course of justice there into better [condition], synce such as were then there were (for the most parte) either insufficient, corrupt in religion, or affectionat to theyr kindred and frendes.[102]

Perrot spent much of his first year in the provinces, signing indentures to keep the peace among feuding landowners and implementing common law procedures in the counties.[103] Writing to the privy council in September 1585, Perrot complained that the gentlemen of the Pale refused to take the oath of supremacy when he named them justices of the peace, escheators, feodaries and high constables. Though he preferred 'severe correction', he accepted the advice of the council and

> proceeded no further against them, but bound them to their appearance in this Star or Castle Chamber, meaning to punish them there by fine at discretion, sithe they are not to be touched sharply enough by any law yet provided. They began to bow, but having received some heart from their agents belike in England, they bear up their heads boldly again.[104]

The incumbent privy councillors who met Perrot on his arrival in summer 1584 had witnessed four different regimes since the retirement of Sydney in 1578, in pointed contrast to the stability of three long-experienced viceroys in the previous 22 years. The two lords justices, Loftus and Wallop, had been governing in a collective tribunate for two years since the recall of Grey as lord deputy. Members of the council were also a veteran crew, including the hard-bitten marshal of the army, Nicholas Bagenal, though two chief justices had not been effectively replaced and the operations of the courts were dormant for long periods at various stages of the Munster Rebellion. The trial and execution of Nicholas Nugent in 1582 tainted the reputation of the judiciary and the factions among councillors had become explicit and potentially dangerous. When Perrot arrived to take the symbol of office from the lord chancellor, he was seizing power from an entrenched member of the New English landed élite, who also happened to be archbishop of Dublin. Not surprisingly, when Perrot's ambitious programme for change commenced with the proposal to seize Loftus's deanery of St Patrick's as the core revenue of a new university in Dublin, the venerable cleric quarrelled, offered to resign, and formed an inchoate opposition group within the council itself. The Perrot scheme had also involved the conversion of St Patrick's into a much-needed courthouse and the canons' houses into inns for the judges.[105]

---

102. Perrott, *Chron. Ire., 1584–1608*, p. 38.
103. 'Cal. Council book,' pp. 154–64. He required that two high constables be chosen for every barony 'after the manner in England', along with petty constables and searchers. Ibid., p. 160.
104. 'Perrot papers', ed. McNeill, p. 28. Writing to Burghley, Perrot added that the recalcitrant gentlemen of the Pale were among the best families 'whereof most [were] young lawyers', noting the lords of the Pale and even the Irish chieftains in Ulster 'do gladly embrace' the oath of supremacy. Ibid., p. 29.
105. Perrott, *Chron. Ire., 1584–1608*, p. 48. Loftus's own allies, kindred and friends, having got leases

Writing to Burghley in August 1584, Perrot argued that Dublin had no need of two cathedral churches, and explained his proposal thus:

> First, where there is here no place for the law, save only an old hall in this castle (as I am sure your Lordship knoweth), and the same very dangerously over the munition and powder, where a desperate fellow by dropping down a match might haply mar all. This church, which is 'roomthie' and large, would very sufficiently serve the turn for all the several courts, though the law should be, as I hope in time by good government it may and shall be, far better frequented than it is.[106]

Perrot followed a policy of conciliation in religion and favoured a generous treatment of the Old English élite, among whom Lucas Dillon and Nicholas White were his primary supporters on the council. Yet, in October 1584, he wrote that the judges, lawyers and officers of the courts were corrupt in religion: 'there is a great nest discovered of massmongers, and amongst them divers gentlemen, whereof some lawyers in places of credit, merchants, ladies and gentlewomen of good sort, with whom I mean to take a fit time and to deal as shall be meet.'[107] In December 1585, he was commended by Walsingham for efforts to defend the Reformation, but required to excuse gentlemen of the Pale from taking the oath of uniformity. In praising Perrot's intentions, the secretary added he should have lived in Henry VIII's time, 'when Princes were resolute to persist ... but our age hath been given to other manner of proceedings, [so he] must be content to conform himself as other men do.'[108] But he finally alienated both Wallop and the important secretary of state, Sir Geoffrey Fenton, the latter of whom he jailed for a time over the issue of a personal debt. By the time Sir Robert Gardiner arrived

---

of the best of these livings, opposed this conversion to a university. Among them was the marshal, Nicholas Bagenal, allied by the marriage of his daughter to Loftus's son. Perrot responded angrily when the queen wrote to prevent the conversion of livings in Dublin to a new university. Ibid., p. 49. See *Cal. S.P. Ire., 1574–85*, p. 524 for Perrot's plan for converting St Patrick's into a courthouse and canons' houses into inns for the judges, with livings to be used to construct courts and colleges. The colleges were to be endowed with £1,000 annually. Perrot to Walsingham, 21 August 1584. Perrot wrote to Leicester in 1587 that St Patrick's was an estate used to enrich 'one man and few of his children and kin', lying waste and used for 'a fewe singing men', though it could employ ten masters and up to 200 scholars. 'Perrot papers,' ed. McNeill, p. 29. Morgan claims that a partial explanation for the conflict was a decision by law officers Calthorpe and Wilbraham to sue Loftus, bishop of Meath Thomas Jones, and other clergy for large sums in unpaid first fruits. H. Morgan, *Tyrone's rebellion: the outbreak of the Nine Years' War in Tudor Ireland* (London, 1993), p. 46.

106. 'Perrot papers,' ed. McNeill, p. 8. A year later Perrot described St Patrick's as 'superfluous', lying 'out of all recourse of people' in the suburbs of Dublin. Ibid., p. 18. He challenged Loftus to a conference on the use of the church and declaimed to Walsingham that 'The ungodly gain that this archbishop doth suck out of that church to pamper up himself, his children and friends, as well in that realm as in this, is so sweet as he cannot endure any man to look towards it'. Ibid., p. 23.

107. Ibid., p. 11.   108. *Cal S.P. Ire., 1574–85*, p. 588.

in 1586 to become the new chief justice of queen's bench, with a mandate to reform both courts and administration, Perrot's rivals at the centre of government were legion.[109]

Perrot's regime in Ireland was troubled by the charges of his adversaries, and many suitors presented their claims in England, hoping to evade the notoriously imperious machinations of the viceroy. The queen complained of the number of Irish suits brought before her, and she consistently remanded cases to Ireland for adjudication.[110] On 10 July 1586, the privy council wrote in favour of Richard Shee, the powerful agent of Ormonde in Kilkenny, who had been incarcerated in Dublin Castle by the viceroy, removed from the commission of peace, and forced to put in bonds without being charged with a particular offence. The crown condemned Perrot's judicial harassment of Shee, implying the issues concerned his inheritance rather than mismanagement of his office.[111] On 30 July 1587, the privy council reprimanded Perrot again for incarcerating Thomas Lee, gentleman, for disobeying an order of the viceroy made without consent of the council in the matter of the town and lands of Castletown Reban then in controversy. Lee was left in quiet possession of the premises while the suit was tried at law.[112] On the other hand, the privy council was equalled displeased with the maladroit handling of cases in chancery by Perrot's adversary, Archbishop Loftus. Writing at the end of December 1586, the council charged the lord chancellor with error in the hearing of a controversy between Thomas Colclough and Thomas Williams over the estate of Tintern, stating 'their Lordships thought good to praie his Lordship for the avoyding of suspicion to forbeare to proceed anie further to the hearing and ordering of the case'.[113]

Returning to the matter in January, the English privy council noted that the parties in suit agreed to be bound by the decision of arbitrators, ordering the chancellor to refer the conflict to their final determination without any further decree or order from chancery, 'not meaning hereby to bring into mistrust the said Lord Chaunncellour's upright dealinges in matters of justice.'[114]

The court of castle chamber under Perrot's regime was notable for periods of apparent inaction, punctuated by episodes of judicial fury. The total of nine cases

---

109. For a full discussion see Morgan, *Tyrone's rebellion*, ch. 3, pp. 29–53; Brady, *Chief governors*, pp. 291–300.

110. *Acts privy council, 1586–87*, p. 373.

111. *Acts privy council, 1586–87*, p. 180. Perrot quarrelled with Ormonde over extending the queen's writ into Kilkenny, overriding the earl's traditional independence of action through agents like Shee. See Morgan, *Tyrone's rebellion*, pp. 32–33. In October another privy council letter charged the viceroy to assure an indifferent hearing for two suitors of Co. Wexford.

112. *Acts privy council, 1586–87*, pp. 177–78.

113. *Acts privy council, 1586–87*, p. 269. Colclough was apparently married to one of Loftus's daughters, so his son-in-law was before the lord chancellor in a manifest conflict of interest for the senior judge. On 6 Dec. 1586 Perrot jailed Colclough and his wife after her husband uttered contemptuous speeches against the deputy and his wife tried to prevent his arrest. Morgan, *Tyrone's rebellion*, p. 45.

114. *Acts privy council, 1586*, pp. 290–291. Arbitrators included the two chief justices, the chief baron, the master of the rolls, Nicholas Walsh, and the attorney general, Richard Bealing.

digested in the entry book include only two actions during 1584, both of which resulted in dismissal. By contrast, the court heard seventeen cases in 1582 alone, after which a hiatus of nearly twenty months occurred. This judicial dormancy coincided with the lord justiceship of Loftus and Wallop, and it is possible that Loftus simply took most of the cases into chancery during this time. In contrast, the perambulating viceroy sent a warrant to the clerk of castle chamber from Limerick on 4 August 1584, ordering Holinshed to cease to trouble the defendants in a case of riot which had been heard and determined by Lucas Dillon and Geoffrey Fenton as arbitrators from the court. The mayor and bailiffs of Limerick had been charged with riot and the case was terminated by consent of all the parties, though Perrot's unilateral order to discharge the matter in the official entry book was a typical affront to the normal judicial process.[115] The second case of 23 November 1584 was signed by Perrot, White and Dean John Garvey, indicating that the viceroy was again proceeding without a full complement of judges. In the suit of John Walwyn against Dominick Browne, alderman, Roebuck French and other merchants of Galway, the charge of riot was dismissed upon request of the plaintiff. Walwyn pleaded 'that in respect he is not hable anie longer to attend the prosecutinge of the said cawse by reason of his povertie, which hath growen (as he alledged) by the greate chardge and xpences that he hath susteyned in the saide sute,' he wished to dismiss the suit and cancel all proceedings according to motions agreed upon with the defendants.[116] Perrot did not return to the castle chamber for another eighteen months, a period when he was heavily engaged with parliamentary affairs. The solicitor general, Sir Roger Wilbraham, wrote to Burghley in July 1586 to announce 'our new late reviving of our Star Chamber Court', wherein two bills against corrupt sheriffs were preferred.[117]

When Perrot returned to the work of the star chamber court, he continued to preside over an unusual number of dismissals. Normally, the entry book did not record actions that never reached the stage of final decree. On 23 June 1587, the baron of Delvin motioned for dismissal of his bill of information against Captain Greene and others, a matter which was duly entered in the court records.[118] And on 2 February 1588, the full court heard allegations of a riot in Co. Cork which were ultimately rejected. Exceptional detail was offered to prove the unruly behaviour of the defendants, Morris Fitzmorris McGerrot and Thomas Gangagh. It was alleged that they and others,

> in riotouse manner arraied, viz with Gunes, swordes, skulls, Targetts, Speares & other weapons Defensible aswell on horseback as on foote, came

---

115. BL, Add. MS 47,172, f. 76.   116. Ibid., ff. 77–78v.
117. *Cal. S.P. Ire., 1586–88*, pp. 97–98. Wilbraham noted the usefulness of castle chamber to poor complainants without fees. The Council Book of 1581–86 also ended on 29 January 1586, without explanation, in the middle of Perrot's regime. A subsequent 'breviat' of certain orders included matters taken up as late as July 1586. See 'Cal. Council book,' pp. 176–80.
118. BL, Add. MS 47,172, f. 81v.

to the Towne of Loghan in the countie of Cork aforesaide, and then and there finding the Complainantes pore people at plow, did (for most parte) for the space of three daies dailie resort to the said towne of Loghan, brusing, beating and evill intreating the said pore people by which meanes theie were so terified as some of them ar never like to recover without daunger of their lives. And in like manner riotouse sort forceablie took awaie owt of the complainantes plowe eight garrons and oxen and thorough this outrage did drive awaie into unknown and forraine places divers Tenauntes and plows whoe wold have thoroughlie inhabited the said towne of Loghan and whoe nowe for feare will not Nor dare come to the said Landes, by means whereof the said towne of Loghan is in manner merelie wast, to the Complaynantes damage of A hundred poundes.[119]

Nonetheless, the Perrot court found the matter not proven, saying that the defendants came to the town only as the law did permit and that they should be free from further vexatious suits. The plantation of Munster was probably at issue here, and the plaintiff was attempting to use the court of castle chamber as the venue to harass his neighbours, who, in turn, probably resisted his settlement. The details of the case were unusual for the court and exceptional to Perrot's government, as we shall see below.

At the end of his administration, Perrot's court of castle chamber gave orders in four cases in the space of seven months. A jury in Co. Kildare was accused of perjury in finding a verdict of not guilty in a murder case, contrary to the evidence presented to them. On 10 May 1587, twelve jurors were convicted for their part in a corrupt verdict, the substance of which was so flawed that the leading judges found the two prisoners, Patrick and Edmund Flatisburie, were released in error.[120] The jurors were fined ten shillings each on account of their poverty, another overture of conciliation by the Perrot regime. Nine days later, the court delivered another decree in a case of alleged riot involving two kinsmen, Irriell O'Ferrall, sheriff of Co. Longford, and Ross O'Ferrall, gentleman. The sheriff had ordered his men to apprehend Manus O'Rourke, who was under indictment for felony and treason, but was then a guest in the house of Ross O'Ferrall at the Christmas season in 1585. The sheriff's men were resisted and Manus escaped in the ensuing riot, but Ross alleged he was a faithful subject of the crown. The court found pernicious the example of resisting a lawful arrest, though the circumstances led the deputy to demand the right to mitigate their fines and imprisonment. In due course, the fines of £100 were reduced to £30 for Ross and twenty shillings each for the rest of the defendants.[121] In a case which blended the

119. Ibid., ff. 86v–87v. The town of Loghan was probably depopulated in this period, since there is no modern equivalent, but the plaintiff, William Power of Shangarry Castle near Ballycotton (about 12 miles west of Youghal) sued McGerrott of Churchton. The modern Churchtown is located about 3 miles west of Ballycotton and 5 miles east of Power Head.

120. BL, Add. MS 47, 172, ff. 83–83v.   121. Ibid., ff. 84–84v.

allegations of riot and dispossession of property, the court sided with the plaintiff, Robert Long, gentleman of Castletown Rebane, Co. Kildare, against the defendant, William Bowen. Long alleged that Bowen had entered his property with fourteen other defendants and driven away all the cattle of the town, assaulting the inhabitants who raised hue and cry against them, and wounding Long himself by running him through with a horseman's staff. Bowen, a gentleman of Ballimore, Co. Dublin, claimed the rights to the property by an interest he obtained from Walter St Michell for 14 years and alleged he came in peace to distrain cattle on his property for damages, intending to pursue his rights at common law. Nonetheless, the court was persuaded by the wounding of Long, though it had occurred in 1583, that a riot had occurred and it fined Bowen £20 for the offence, noting the absence of the other defendants at court.[122] The relatively mild punishments of the Perrot court and his refusal to join in the prosecution of recusancy were later taken as evidence of his disloyalty to the crown.

Sir John Perrot was not exceptional in his deep respect for personal honour, especially when his own name and dignity were at stake. Consequently, the long and arduous prosecution of Henry Bird, the case which ultimately compromised the deputy himself, must be examined in the light of Tudor dynastic concerns about 'gravitas'. Even more, any fraudulent use of the deputy's signature was, by extension, a derogation of sovereignty and an offence to the crown. The entry book contains many brief and enigmatic references, but those concerning points of honour were among the most detailed and painstaking diaries of conciliar litigation. On 23 June 1586, the court took up the matter of the forgery of Henry Bird, register of the court of ecclesiastical causes. Bird was accused of forging the signature of the chief governor in four separate letters, repeated verbatim in the entry book, by which the convicted priest, Sir Denis O'Roghan, was given the viceroy's special pardon and recommended to local officials who were ordered to grant him safe conduct through their territories. Similar counterfeit letters were sent to recommend the vicar David Dermott to serve in the diocese of Limerick. The court found Bird guilty of the forgery, and by extension, of disloyalty to the crown, usurping to himself the special trust committed to ecclesiastical commissioners and to the lord deputy.[123] The irregularities of the trial were later rehearsed by the enemies of Perrot in the next administration, claiming that the lord chancellor and others took exception to the sentence; that the offence was properly justiciable within the ecclesiastical court and not castle chamber; and that the proceedings were not in due form since they occurred the day after the end of term. The castle chamber court later reversed itself under Fitzwilliam, condemning Perrot and restoring the credit of Bird.[124] However, the questionable testimony of O'Roghan was used in both cases and tainted the validity of each prosecution. According to Morgan, Perrot's successor, Fitzwilliam, orchestrated

---

122. Ibid., ff. 85–85v. Ten councillors sat in judgement on the case, including the two chief justices, chief baron, lord chancellor and master of the rolls.

123. Ibid., ff. 79–81.   124. Ibid., ff. 90v–92.

the campaign against Sir John with the connivance of senior English councillors. On this issue, then, the court of castle chamber played a substantial role in the undoing of a powerful Elizabethan statesman. The English privy council wrote in September of 1590 to the lord chancellor in Ireland, ordering him to reinstate Henry and John Bird to the clerkship and reversing the 'hard sentence' in castle chamber ordered by Perrot.[125] The politicization of the court would not end with the Bird case.

Perrot was a champion of the reform known as the Composition of Connacht and he relied upon the government there to enforce its terms. He installed Sir Richard Bingham as lord president of the province and knighted him in Dublin in 1584. However, Bingham's notorious oppressions in Connacht led to an estrangement between them when Perrot chided him for excessive severity at an assizes in 1586 at which 70 persons were condemned to death. On 29 November 1586, the court of castle chamber heard the case of Henry Ealand, sheriff of Co. Roscommon and a henchman of Bingham's, who was accused by Theobald Dillon of committing many extortions, oppressions and murders during his tenure in office. Some 27 articles were set forth in the information by the attorney general, Charles Calthorpe, notably murders under colour of martial law.[126] Ealand did not appear in court for his defence, which was seen as a dishonour to the court, so the murder charges were remanded for trial in queen's bench and he was found guilty *in absentia* of the charges of official corruption. He was fined £500, sentenced to a year in prison and to stand on the pillory.[127] On the day of the trial, Sir Nicholas White wrote to Burghley condemning the depredations of Ealand: 'These be the men that makes Her Majesty's laws hateful to Her people, and have been too long borne withal.'[128]

Sir Richard Bingham complained bitterly to all his allies, justifying Ealand's absence at court by citing his own authority to excuse the sheriff until the end of sessions then being held at Roscommon. Bingham claimed he had the right to defer the case and sent a message to the viceroy explaining his need of Ealand against the felons and traitors then being arraigned before commissioners of the peace. Three days later, on a windy, snowy day in Trim, Bingham learned that the case had already been determined in Dublin against his lieutenant. He explained that the writ was false, the term was already closed and the other judges refused to join the deputy. Primarily, however, he argued that Ealand was merely following orders.[129] Bingham's

---

125. *Acts privy council, 1590*, pp. 379–80. See also pp. 438–39. Morgan, *Tyrone's rebellion*, pp. 55–59.
126. *Cal. S.P. Ire., 1586–88*, p. 496. These charges were not identified in castle chamber records, but in a complaint by Bingham subsequently. Ealand was accused of hanging Pes McCostulo for treason; hanging a common rebel named McManus who had been a guide to the Scots and had murdered a bailiff arrant [itinerant] who was taking up the queen's rent; hanging Thomas O'Conon for stealing a garron and other robberies; and taking money from landholders to make stocks, gibbets and penfolds in the shire.
127. BL, Add. MS 47,172, ff. 82–82v.
128. *Cal. S.P. Ire., 1586–88*, p. 207.
129. Bingham to Burghley, 13 March 1588: *Cal. S.P. Ire., 1586–88*, pp. 493–95. The lord president

challenge to the court included much of interest. He accused Perrot of deception by holding court from mid-afternoon until nearly eight o'clock at night out of term time, concluding the case without hearing the accused or his attorney, and rejecting the opinions of the chancellor, treasurer, chief justice and bishop of Meath. He alleged this course of action was a derogation of star chamber's role as the superior legal jurisdiction, 'which ought to be a lantern to all the rest'.[130] Over a year later, on 20 February 1587, the council board sat to hear an accusation by Theobald Dillon against Bingham for abusing his authority as governor in Connacht. Perrot was notably absent, and the case was heard by the chancellor, chief justice, and others outside the parameters of the court of castle chamber, despite its evident authority to hear cases of judicial malfeasance. Bingham was duly acquitted by this rump council which found the charges malicious. They concluded,

> we find that the said Theobald Dillon hath filed in proof in the substance of all such articles as concerned the said Sir Richard ... rather for vexation and for dislike he hath to his government there, than for any probable just cause or matter, not forbearing to insert in the same most of his causes grounded upon hearsay not proved, nor any way concerning the said Sir Richard.[131]

Finally, on 1 April 1588, the privy council wrote to Perrot and the council in Ireland that they wished to have the Ealand case reviewed. Citing Ealand's petition to them against the damaging sentence of the star chamber in Dublin, the council wrote that they did not wish to undermine the authority of the castle chamber, but sought re-examination of the cause when Ealand might be able to appear in his own defence and view the charges and records of the court. Since Ealand had been charged by Bingham with responsibility in the field and used this to excuse his absence, the English council prayed the council in Ireland to look into the matter with indifference, and if they found cause, to mitigate or revoke the sentence.[132] By 1594, Sir Richard Bingham's misgovernment of Connacht had become a *cause de guerre* and the archives are littered with his anxious defences of murder and mayhem throughout the province.[133]

explained that he sought the legal advice of the other commissioners, including the chief justice of Connacht, before determining he had the right by virtue of his office to stay the *sub poena ad respondendum* for the sheriff until the sessions at Roscommon were concluded. On the 16th Bingham learned that castle chamber had already proceeded against Ealand in his absence.

130. Ibid., p. 494.
131. Ibid., p. 267. Among other councillors were Perrot's enemy, Marshal Bagenal, John Garvey, the bishop of Kilmore, Secretary Fenton, and Treasurer Wallop.
132. *Acts privy council, 1588*, p. 10.
133. *Acts privy council, 1595–96*, p. 145; *1596–97*, p. 9. See also Canny, *Making Ireland British*, pp. 93–103, for an excellent discussion of the 'frontier' province and the extortionate machinations of the presidents. Bingham and his kinsmen seized property, abused local lords as well as their fellow officials and favoured their dependants, including Gaelic subalterns selected for office. Canny viewed the presidency as an 'exploitative military institution', detailing the intermarriage of English captains with Irish wives and the employment of mainly Irish troops in their bands.

Despite its cautious reservations concerning the dignity of the Irish court, the privy council of England twice overruled the court of castle chamber under Perrot. Both the Bird and Ealand actions led directly to the fall and disgrace of the former lord deputy. Sir Robert Gardiner accused the chief governor of using his sole arbitrary power to hear cases respecting leases and escheats, judging suits without respect to the law and making all justices of the peace and sheriffs 'without either wealth, freehold or knowledge, some not inhabiting within the shire'.[134] Lord Chancellor Loftus added his bilious pique to the clamour for Perrot's recall in May 1587, claiming that the lord deputy made grants of land without seeking conciliar approval, heard causes of action privately and remitted the queen's debts, passing concordatums and pardons which should be debated at the council table and saying he could order resolutions by his sole power without the use of the council.[135] In a separate letter of 1586, Loftus complained, 'It is an usual thing with my Lord Deputy to remove such causes as are begun in Chancery out of that Court, and to call the same before himself, to be ordered by him and his favourites of this Council.'[136] Loftus further claimed that persons committed for contempt in his court of chancery were released by the deputy on his authority without reference to the chancellor; that judgements in the queen's bench were overruled and causes removed from the venue. He reported that others overheard the lord deputy say he cared nothing for the council, terming them 'dunghill churles' and 'beggars', and the queen's chief justices but 'ten shilling knaves', and other reproaches.[137]

Charges against Perrot had reached a crisis within the council itself on 15 May 1587. Perrot sent for Chief Justice Gardiner, White, Fenton and Marshal Bagenal to examine one Patrick Cullen, an agent of O'Neill, who was going to England with complaints against the lord deputy in the form of letters to the queen. Perrot was then at his lodgings and retired to his bedchamber according to White's report, when Bagenal broke into the room and accused Perrot of attending the examination by the judges. Perrot had asked the marshal to await him in the great chamber, but the marshal sought to assure the matter was heard in full at the council chamber and not privately, to avoid charges of partisanship. Perrot then apparently went to Bagenal, touching him on the cheek and laying his hand on his shoulder, saying 'You defy me'. Other reports claimed that Perrot cudgeled the marshal and called him a drunken dotard, after Bagenal threatened him with his staff. On the following day, Bagenal wrote to defend his actions, saying he was

---

134. *Cal. S.P. Ire., 1586–88*, p. 219.
135. Ibid., pp. 351–52. White wrote on 29 November 1586 to Burghley that the state of Ireland was tranquil, except for the continual bickering between the viceroy and the chancellor. He said, 'for even yesterday at the committing of Dudley Bagenall, second son to the Marshal, for breaking the Lord Deputy's letters of commandment for his appearance to answer a poor man's complaint, and beating of the party that delivered them, the Lord Deputy and Chancellor squared in opinion touching his commitment. Many like bickerings happen often, wherewith I will not trouble your Honour by writing.' Ibid., pp. 206–07.
136. *Cal. S.P. Ire., 1586–88*, p. 211.   137. Ibid. p. 212.

assaulted and seeking an examination without the viceroy's presence.[138] Perrot argued that the council board had no role in the examination of Cullen, despite appearances of impropriety. While the castle chamber court was not involved, the incident does much to explain the poisoned relations that existed among the councillors, perhaps suggesting reasons why the court was under-utilized in the period.

CONCLUSION

The cases of Bird and Ealand show that the court of castle chamber was occasionally at the centre of major programmatic ambitions launched by energetic lords deputy who sought to expand the rule of law and the effective supervision of newly implemented courts and judges. However, when Perrot himself fell from power in 1588 and in the following year was accused of treason, the handling of these prickly defendants in castle chamber became the source of the powerful deputy's dénouement. As Wentworth was to learn a half century later, reckless authoritarian policies produced more enemies than friends. The politicization of cases before the court of castle chamber eventually had a boomerang effect on the protagonists. The departure of Perrot on 30 June 1588, some four months after the designation of his successor, did not lead at once to his disgrace and imprisonment. It took the schemes of Loftus and others for nearly two years to obtain the testimony and generate the momentum for Perrot's final defeat. Once again, the court of castle chamber proved to be the instrument of Perrot's undoing, and the new viceroy, Fitzwilliam, abetted this leveraging of the tribunal for political ends, despite his own earlier departure under a cloud of suspicion. And, while the earlier trial and execution of Chief Justice Nicholas Nugent left a bad odour in the reputation of the Irish privy council and the judiciary, the Fitzwilliam government proceeded to combine the disgrace of the previous viceroy with the discredit of his chief allies, the last remaining Old English councillors, Sir Nicholas White and Sir Lucas Dillon. The entwining of judicial functions between the council and the court had, not surprisingly, added a strong political undertone to the work of the court of castle chamber. The hand of the archbishop and lord chancellor, Adam Loftus, may be seen in all of this conniving and manoeuvring. His political victory over Perrot and his deft management of his ecclesiastical estates made him the most powerful lord chancellor in Elizabethan times. Yet he made no effort to reform the judiciary and the comprehensive implementation of Gerrard's common law proposals was allowed to lapse in the final decades of the Tudor century. When the Armada descended on England, and conspiracy was once again bruited in Ireland, the Dublin government was led by a local dynast and an ageing functionary.

138. *Cal. S.P. Ire.*, *1586–88*, pp. 353–55. It appears Bagenal's son Henry may have counterfeited a
    letter from O'Neill and was charged with being manipulated by the earl. Perrot had accused
    Cullen, a client of the Bagenals, of conspiring to defame him to the queen, after Henry Bagenal
    appeared at court to advance the Bagenal faction's plans for Ulster.

CHAPTER SEVEN

Social violence, corruption and war: the court of castle chamber, 1588 to 1603

> I am lately put in fear here by one that seemeth to know much of these causes at the Court, that there is an intention, notwithstanding that I have sent my absolute submission into England, and have made the same voluntarily in public court to the Lord Deputy here, ... that this, notwithstanding, I shall be called into the Star Chamber (here named the Castle Chamber), and for this cause to be fined, &c.
>
> Sir Charles Calthorpe, attorney general of Ireland,
> to Burghley, 19 September 1592[1]

THE RECALL OF Sir John Perrot in 1588, against the background of further allegations that he pushed and slapped the ageing military leader, Sir Nicholas Bagenal, does much to explain the selection of his successor. Sir William Fitzwilliam had long experience in Ireland, serving continuously from 1556 until 1575 including a previous term as lord deputy. Although the court of castle chamber was formally initiated during his first period in office, Fitzwilliam was not a notable reformer. At the age of 62, he was a senior official past his prime who had no particular agenda for change, but he was well known to leading Irish magnates with whom he might work in restoring cooperation among leading members of the council. Forgotten, perhaps, were his frequent clashes with other senior officials such as Sir Edward Fyton during a prior administration, and his grasping for financial reward. Fitzwilliam abetted the charges levied against his predecessor, Perrot, and did little to heal the rifts on the council in Ireland. Yet his steady employment of the court of castle chamber suggests a style of government markedly different from the one for which he has become known. Fitzwilliam supervised the work of the court on no less than 29 occasions from 12 June 1589 until his departure on 11 August 1594. In addition, other cases which came before the court under his leadership were continued under his successors, making him the most active Tudor viceroy in the history of the prerogative court. Was this a

---

1. *Cal. S.P. Ire., 1588–92*, pp. 588–89. Calthorpe was involved in the commission to investigate the now exonerated Henry Bird in a previous castle chamber dispute. His role in that inquiry brought him to the peril of star chamber indictment and nearly ruined his career.

new Fitzwilliam, a more ambitious viceroy who began to fashion the work of the court in a style befitting the reputation of the august star chamber? Or, was the court now coming to maturity as an autonomous institution of government which continued to hear cases independently of the viceroy, suits usually commenced at lower court levels or initiated by reforming attorneys acting for the government?

A RIOT OF LIGITATION: SUITS AND SUITORS AT THE COURT OF CASTLE CHAMBER, 1588–1597

Both Hiram Morgan and Ciaran Brady have faulted Fitzwilliam for allowing events in Ulster to fester with heedless neglect.[2] Yet, as Morgan has shown, the deputy's handling of the MacMahon lordship in the newly shired county of Monaghan was intended to clear the way for a more tractable legal establishment with improved supervision by the chief governor. When Sir Ross MacMahon died in the summer of 1589, the lordship was in dispute. Fitzwilliam initially preferred Sir Ross's brother, Hugh Roe, who came to Dublin seeking letters patent while his rival, Brian McHugh in the meantime seized power in Monaghan. When Hugh was unable to regain power, the deceitful Fitzwilliam charged him with treason for interfering with the course of justice, resisting the authority of the sheriff and other offences. The trial was to be held in Monaghan sessions by common law, but no information survives to indicate how the viceroy became involved. In September 1590, he sent the chief justice, Sir Robert Dillon, and the solicitor general, Sir Roger Wilbraham, to England to verify evidence against MacMahon. In October, the execution of Hugh Roe had taken place, threatening the Gaelic lords to confirm their letters patent and to abide by the terms of common law jurisdiction. Accusations of injustice were levied against Fitzwilliam over this matter, and the incident clouded the early years of his administration, along with the ongoing dispute over Perrot's regime.[3] In similar fashion, the lord deputy conspired to undo the renegade lord of West Breifne, Brian O'Rourke, who had defied an assortment of chief governors in his distant dominions of Co. Leitrim. Lord President Bingham occupied his territories in the spring of 1590, and in February 1591 O'Rourke fled to Scotland with the intention of hiring Scottish mercenaries. In Glasgow a month later he was arrested by the authority of King James on a request from London, and he was extradited on 1 April 1591 on a charge of treason. These charges, heard in queen's bench in London, were vigorously supported by Bingham and Fitzwilliam on evidence from Connacht,

---

2. C. Brady, 'Sixteenth century Ulster and the failure of Tudor reform' in C. Brady and M. O'Dowd, eds., *Ulster: an illustrated history* (London, 1989), pp. 95–100; H. Morgan, 'The nemesis of Fitzwilliam' in *Tyrone's rebellion*, pp. 61–64.

3. Morgan, *Tyrone's rebellion*, pp. 61–65. Direct judicial intervention by Fitzwilliam in the common law trial of Hugh Roe in Monaghan proved unnecessary, though suspicions remain about a possible bribe from the new chief, Brian, the use of soldiers on the jury and the manipulation of old grudges against Hugh Roe.

where O'Rourke had been accused of various crimes and was a leading opponent of the policies associated with anglicization. According to Morgan, O'Rourke had also been an ally of Perrot against Bingham, so the criminal charges contained political overtones during the concurrent trial and disgrace of the former chief governor. O'Rourke was hanged, drawn and quartered at Tyburn on 3 November 1591, a victim of the 'no-nonsense' policy of Fitzwilliam that led directly to the outbreak of the Nine Years War.[4]

Fitzwilliam's government was reactive and impulsive in many respects. But the court of castle chamber pursued a steady course during the six years of his administration, increasing its caseload and solidifying its role as a pillar among the anglicizing institutions of late Elizabethan Ireland. Among 29 cases taken up by the court from 1588 to 1594, Fitzwilliam presided at the majority of these hearings, many of which addressed matters of judicial structure and provincial administration. For example, the court fined a jury in November 1590 which had failed to convict Walter Browne of treason in his escape from the jail in Co. Wexford. Fitzwilliam was sitting in June 1591 at the trial of John Tuite, gentleman, who committed a riot against the undersheriff of West Meath, John Talbot, at Parcelston. Talbot was authorized by a 'wethermand' from the sheriff to distrain the sheep or cattle of the defendant in a bawn at Parcelston, when Tuite and his retainers appeared with swords, targets, sculls, poleaxes and halberts to regain his possessions. In the event, ten garrons were forcibly taken from the hapless undersheriff, who suffered in the riot little more than the indignity of having his cloak pulled off and trod in the mire.[5] This slight to royal authority earned the unwonted attention of the court, though the fine of £13 6s. 8d. was relatively minor. The court intervened in a similar case to support the undersheriff of Co. Cork, Walter Coppinger. In this case, the assailant was himself a prominent official, a justice of the peace, John FitzEdmondes, and his brother-in-law, Thomas Gangogh. Learning that Coppinger had taken a distress from Gangogh, FitzEdmondes called him to account on 14 April 1592, whereupon the undersheriff produced as his authority a green wax book from the court of exchequer. Judicially cornered,

> The said John FitzEdmondes, havinge the sayd grene waxe booke in his hande, in great Collor and fury dyd sweare with grevous oathes that there was nothinge but knavery, packinge and shiftinge Conteyned in the sayd booke And Called the sayd Copinger knave, vyllane and many other vyle names for takinge the sayd Distresse. And the sayd John FitzEdmondes, not Contented therewith, increasinge further in fury Caused his sayd servauntes before named to take the sayd Copingers dagger from hime, and then and theire the sayd John Fitz Edmondes & the sayd servauntes dyd assault and

4. H. Morgan, 'Extradition and treason-trial of a Gaelic lord: the case of Brian O'Rourke', *Ir Jur*, xxviii (1987), 285–301.
5. BL, Add. MS 47,172, f. 94. A wethermand was an order to keep and distrain sheep ('wether' is a male sheep), or cattle.

grevously beate the sayd Walter Coppinger And did keepe from hime the
sayd grene waxe booke, to the great hinderaunce of her maties service.[6]

The court fined the defendant £20 on 7 February 1593 and imprisoned him
during pleasure. Cases of this sort, which strove to systematize the judicial
administration and protect its local officials from harm, indicate that the court
under Fitzwilliam was intent on expanding its effectiveness throughout the
country, supporting provincial presidencies and courts and demanding respect for
law officers. The unruly behaviour of the defendants in the Coppinger case
underscored the need to maintain vigilance over the local officials themselves.

In a similar vein, Fitzwilliam's court frequently took up cases in which seditious words threatened the queen's peace. It may be reading history backwards to
see in these cases an atmosphere of tension which adumbrates overt acts of
rebellion. Such cases had been heard previously, but a noticeable increase in the
number of them before the court at this time may be taken as evidence of
Fitzwilliam's effort to crack down on sedition, in the aftermath of the Armada
and prior to the Tyrone Rebellion. On 16 June 1591, for example, Fitzwilliam was
presiding when John Delahide of Co. Dublin was convicted of treasonable words
for recalling that Perrot, the former lord deputy, then on trial for treason in
England, had called the queen a 'piskitchen'.[7] On the same day, the court convicted John Keaghan of Co. Kildare, a husbandman, who had called the queen
'barren' in the Irish tongue.[8] Thomas Brookes, a soldier from Dublin, spoke
contemptuously of the queen and her officials, for which the court punished him
in 1593, and in the same year Nicholas White of Maynam, Co. Kildare was fined
and imprisoned for slandering the queen, repeating the allegation that a crown
was being sought in Rome for O'Donnell to become king in Ireland.[9]

Chronic dishonour to royal authority extended to the office of chief governor,
of which Fitzwilliam was a jealous custodian. Consequently, the court heard a
number of cases in which viceregal power was challenged, even obliquely. On 30
June 1594, Fitzwilliam and the other judges convicted the bishop of Leighlin,
Richard Bird, who had challenged the subsheriff in Co. Carlow for taking up the
stipend of a schoolmaster on the authority of the lord deputy. Bird was incensed
that an adventurous teacher named Brocke had seized upon his church revenues
and declaimed that 'I do not allow yt: for my Lo Deputye shall have no more to do
in my Diocesse then I will have to do with his swourde, and I will comaunde him
and his swourde'.[10] After due apologies were tendered in court, the penitent

6. Ibid., f. 106. Gangogh had come to the attention of the court as defendant in the case of William
   Power of Shangarry in 1588, though charges against him were dismissed (see above). Ibid., ff.
   86v–87v.
7. Ibid., f. 95.   8. Ibid., f. 96.
9. Ibid., ff. 105, 111. Morgan has argued that this assertion was 'widely disseminated', based on
   rather slender evidence. Morgan, *Tyrone's rebellion*, p. 143.
10. BL, Add. MS 47,172, f. 113v.

bishop was fined £29 and imprisoned for eight days by the court; Fitzwilliam had presided.[11] In February 1594, Sir Thomas Moore, sheriff of King's County, was convicted of disloyal speeches for alleging that the viceroy had countermanded an order of the lord president of Connacht, Sir Richard Bingham, for the arrest of two malefactors.[12] And in 1591, the court convicted Edward White, clerk of the council in Connacht, for revealing secret information with which he was entrusted regarding the queen's letters for the Irish government.[13] Clearly, then, the court was prepared to insist on matters of honour and to demand that protocol be maintained as a condition of the spread of common law institutions throughout the realm.

In one of the most politically sensitive cases during his tenure of office, Fitzwilliam led the court in November 1590 in a reversal of its own sentence against Henry Bird, the convicted forger of Perrot's signature in the previous administration. Signed by Fitzwilliam, the entry declared that Perrot was in error for accepting the 'bare oath' of a condemned priest, Bird's only accuser. The court concluded that Bird was denied legal counsel, that his trial was conducted on a day when litigation was normally suspended, and that the English-born councillors took exception to the proceedings but were outnumbered by the unusual presence of Irish noblemen at the hearing. In a separate section of the entry, the court took cognizance of a confession by O'Roghan retracting his accusation with profuse apologies during his long imprisonment in England. The entry begins with a copy of the letter from the privy council in England requiring a review of the case, effectively demanding a resolution which would conform with its own actions in Perrot's treason trial then under way. This was the culmination of Fitzwilliam's campaign to discredit his predecessor and his fallen comrades on the council, Sir Nicholas White chief among them.[14] The future course of castle chamber proceedings against enemies of the viceroy was thus here foreshadowed: the Elizabethan court was certainly not immune to politicization of this sort.

Since the cause of the clerk, Henry Bird, was closely entwined with the fate of the stricken former viceroy, further political fallout was not unexpected. Perrot's

11. Ibid., f. 114 See also *Cal. S.P. Ire., 1592–96*, p. 202. After the appointment of three English judges to the vacant places on the bench, the queen ordered the castle chamber fine of the bishop of Leighlin appropriated to the use of the new judges. Ibid., p. 91. The bishop was also implicated in the suit over Nicholas White's estate at Dunbrody and called to testify in June 1593. Ibid., p. 107.

12. BL, Add. MS 47,172, f. 115.

13. Ibid., f. 97. Dr Canny has shown that White was the leading detractor of Malbie as president, who had dismissed him from his post. He was joined by Thomas Dillon, Anthony Fitton, Edward Mostion and Robert Damport in his critique of Malbie's regime, and Bingham suffered a similar attack from Captain Robert Fowle during his discredited tenure in Connacht. Canny, *Making Ireland British*, pp. 97–98.

14. BL, Add. 47, 172, ff. 90v–92. Perrot was also blamed for selling the vacant office of Bird to his own client, who placed unfit men in service at the ecclesiastical commission. The post was properly in the remit of the lord chancellor as chief of the commission. See also *Acts privy council, 1590*, pp. 379–80, 438–39.

loyal ally on the council, Sir Nicholas White, was arrested by Fitzwilliam in June 1590 and sent to the marshalsea in London two months later, despite his ill-health. In March 1591, he was interrogated in the Tower concerning Perrot's alleged misgovernment, and he was replaced by an Englishman as master of the rolls. He died while in prison in 1592, the same year that his fellow Irish-born councillor, Sir Lucas Dillon, also died. The attorney general, Charles Calthorpe, was threatened with suit in castle chamber for corruptly mishandling an examination of O'Roghan in March 1590, along with Judge Nicholas Walshe and six others.[15] Once Bird had been exonerated by the court of castle chamber on 30 November 1590, the lawyers Walshe and Calthorpe were exposed for alleged complicity in his original trial. Calthorpe wrote to Burghley on 18 February 1591 to explain he was not guilty of favouring Perrot, having refused to sign a petition in the latter's support, and seeking Burghley's protection.[16] However, a memorial for Irish causes penned by Fenton in May 1592 referred to the anticipated trial of Calthorpe, Walshe and Sir Edward Moore in the court of castle chamber, just as White and the bishop of Leighlin were tried in the English star chamber.[17] This interesting politicization of the judicial process, with the castle chamber court shadowing its parent tribunal in England, is a rare good example of the interconnectedness of the two benches. Finally, on 19 September 1592, Calthorpe wrote to Burghley to say he had been restored to office and spared the trial in castle chamber owing to the intervention of his patron, yet worrying 'that I was the last and dealt least of any of the eight Commissioners, and … have received more disgrace and hindrance than all the commissioners except two'.[18] Subsequent letters from Burghley and Fenton made note of the restoration of Calthorpe and the naming of Walshe to a new judgeship, though their reputations were incompletely salvaged.[19]

The legacy of Perrot's dispute with Sir Richard Bingham plagued the subsequent administration as well. After his defence of the rogue sheriff Henry Ealand was used to malign the government of Perrot, Bingham continued to suffer accusations of tyranny for his rough handling of the people of Connacht. In February 1588, he was accused of 'taking a juror by the beard and threatening to inflict on him the punishment of a traitor if he persisted in his opinion' in the case of Donogh O'Connor Sligo.[20] In a March 1589 petition of Ferdorough O'Kelly,

---

15. *Cal. S.P. Ire., 1588–92*, pp. 322, 485. Calthorpe and the solicitor general, Roger Wilbraham, had examined Bird in 1585. The six commissioners in 1590 were White, Walshe, Lucas Dillon, Edward Moore, and the bishops of Leighlin and Meath.

16. Ibid., p. 385.

17. Ibid., p. 485.

18. Ibid., pp. 588–89. He had been suspended from office despite his eight years of service, complaining that he was ruined by detractors in Ireland and his example would discourage others from service there.

19. Ibid., pp. 527, 518, 462. Walshe was first nominated by Fitzwilliam to succeed Dillon as chief baron, but Fenton wrote against the prospect of replacing Dillon with another Old English judge, without disparaging the deceased veteran. Ibid., p. 471.

20. *Cal. S.P. Ire., 1588–92*, p. 127.

gentleman, of Aughrim, the governor was blamed for a reign of terror that alienated the province, leading O'Kelly to flee, and asking for a protection from the commissioners to Connacht whence O'Kelly could be restored to favour.[21] And despite Fitzwilliam's vote of confidence forwarded to Burghley in May 1589, the viceroy sent an enclosed report detailing Bingham's misgovernment. He had resisted the visit of commissioners to investigate accusations against him in Athlone, violated a protection recently given to the Burkes, and allowed his soldiers to harass the townsmen of Galway. The respected Galway elder, Roebuck French, sued in castle chamber for damage to his townhouse when troops tried to force open the door and threw wood at the windows.[22]

On 27 July 1589, the privy council in England wrote to Fitzwilliam to order a trial of Bingham in Dublin before the whole council of Ireland, excepting Sir Robert Dillon and the bishop of Meath, whom Bingham challenged as partisan.[23] By September, Fitzwilliam was writing to Burghley that Bingham generated fear and contempt in Connacht, yet the problems of bringing his accusers to Dublin might forestall the trial itself. Once the trial had begun in November, lasting over a week with depositions from the Burkes and others, Bingham wrote to Burghley that he feared the enmity of the lord deputy. White explained that the Burkes' book of complaints, exhibited on 12 June and read at the council board on 8 November, contained numerous indictments of Bingham, but worried that the accusers would not come to Dublin and so undermine their case. Among the charges were Bingham's alleged violation of protections he had given. In one case, Thomas Roe Burke came into the town of Creagh under such a protection, but was confronted by the undersheriff John Carie, who sought to apprehend his servant. After taking the skene [a dagger or small sword] of Burke, the sheriff and his men wounded both Burke and his servant, Walter Oge, who later died. Bingham himself then came to Creagh and demanded the castle of Nenany from Thomas Burke's brother, Richard Oge, which was duly given to him. But when the stunned defenders at Nenany resisted his coming, Bingham allegedly returned to Creagh and had Richard executed by martial law, without trial and in spite of his protection.[24] Bingham excused his tyrannical behaviour, blaming the Burkes and noting the emergency of rebellion, while impugning the bishop of Meath for

21. Ibid., p. 137.
22. Ibid., pp. 173, 178, 180, 188. The Burkes complained of illegal dispossession of their estates by sheriffs and the hanging of men by martial law, but Bingham continued to resist any investigation from Dublin, saying he felt disgraced.
23. Ibid., pp. 223, 225. Numerous other exchanges led to the depositions being sent to Bingham, delaying the trial until his accusers could send in their complaints.
24. Ibid., pp. 262–64. Two brothers, Moyler and Tibott Burke, who were in ward as prisoners despite their coming to Bingham for protection, were hanged at Athlone and Roscommon, the second one seeing his brother hanged before him. Edmond Burke of Castlebar, an elderly chief who was 80 years old and had lost his leg two years before, was summoned and hanged at Togher in Co. Mayo without trial. Bingham had also executed without trial three young sons of the Burkes, ages 14, 9 and 7, despite their scholarly training and proficiency in English. Ibid., pp. 263–65.

being twenty days in Connacht without preaching a single sermon.[25] Despite the evil reputation of the governor, a resolution by the Irish council on 4 December 1589 acquitted Bingham of all the charges, stating simply, 'No witnesses were produced by the complainants and Sir Richard was acquitted.'[26] Bingham wrote to the English privy council that his reputation was cleared, though his government struggled to achieve legitimacy, and Fitzwilliam ended the matter unsatisfactorily when he concluded that the complainants' charges could not be proved since they were unable to travel to Dublin.[27] The Bingham hearings did not mention castle chamber specifically and, as there was no final judgment, the case did not appear in the entry book. However, the jurisdiction of the star chamber court over administrative malfeasance was well-established, and the use of the privy council in Ireland as a venue indicates, once again, the incomplete separation of the two institutions in the late Elizabethan period.

Most of the cases heard under Fitzwilliam's administration, however, followed the earlier pattern set by the court, in which riot was alleged as a means of gaining access to the tribunal. These cases provide insights into the cultural conflicts that lay below the surface of the Elizabethan Irish polity and which paralyzed anglicizing initiatives. For example, Viscount Mountgarret alleged that Donagh McCreagh with a band of men ambushed him in April 1591 as he crossed a moor to his house, wounding his servants and threatening to kill the viscount himself. One year later, they were fined in the court of castle chamber for a riot which went largely unexplained in the records of the court.[28] A more aggravated assault occurred the next year when the baron of Slane, Sir Thomas Fleming, was going through the high street of Dublin toward St Patrick's, having been summoned by the lord chancellor. He and six servants were set upon by Viscount Gormanston and some thirty followers in the high street near the market cross, an affront to patrician decorum as well as a violation of the queen's peace. The baron was struck and one of his servants badly wounded, for which the viscount paid a fine of £100 and endured imprisonment at the pleasure of the viceroy.[29] The court made mention of the official business on which the baron was engaged, coming to be examined before 'Commissioners upon Causes greatly ymporting her Maties service' at St Patrick's.[30] Another peer of the realm, the baron of Inchiquin, was accused of a riot on the quay of Dublin in 1593, in which Sir Tirlough O'Brien was accosted on his way to the council chamber. Inchiquin and divers others set upon O'Brien, wounding him in the head with rapiers and daggers, for which the baron subsequently apologized. The court fined him 100 marks a year later,

25. Ibid., p. 271.

26. Ibid., p. 274.

27. Ibid., pp. 281, 299. Again accused of tyranny in December 1595, Bingham suffered another commission of inquiry in the next year and sought a hearing in England or Dublin, complaining repeatedly of his enemies at court. *Cal. S.P. Ire., 1592–96*, pp. 439, 469, 471–72, 520, 533.

28. BL, Add. MS 47,172, f. 100.

29. Ibid., f. 109.

30. Ibid. The events occurred on 26 April 1592; the case was determined on 9 May 1593.

showing again its regard for the probity required of men who were summoned to do the queen's business.[31] Based on these accounts, one must assume the streets of Dublin were dangerous places which the court was obliged to referee in the absence of a modern police force. It is also clear that the court blended its own priorities with those of complainants, since many cases of riot involved enforcement of crown policy. For example, James Power was condemned for assaulting Nicholas Power with a cudgel on the bridge of Dublin in June 1594, and the court also took notice that, on another occasion, he forcibly took from a servant of Nicholas a writ or injunction which was to be delivered to the sheriff of Co. Cork.[32]

Nearly 65 per cent of the cases heard by the court under Fitzwilliam alleged riot, and many of them involved simmering feuds between neighbours, if the bare accounts of the entry book may yield to some interpretation. For example, Patrick Talbot, a gentleman of Co. Dublin, sued John Quatermas, husbandman, and his kinsmen, for a riot that occurred on 1 June 1590; three of them were accused of cutting turf on his moor of Garriston.[33] Quatermas was fined twenty shillings for this outrage. The court took cognizance of an apparent countersuit, based on a riot the following day, 2 June 1590, in which William Talbot was accused of procuring the services of five henchmen to go to the moor of Garriston where they beat and pummelled Quatermas. The entry book made no mention of revenge and found Talbot not guilty, though the rest were duly fined and imprisoned.[34] An unusual case of riot (mentioned above) involving an employer and his workers was brought by Joyce Adryan, a leatherdresser of Dublin, against eight tanners and two women, probably related to them. Adryan claimed they entered his house in December 1586 in riotous manner, took from him a dicker [ten hides] of leather and assaulted him and his wife Elizabeth, who then gave birth to a stillborn child. The court found three of the defendants guilty, fining and imprisoning them.[35] The entry book offers little to explain the events which led to these apparently heinous offences. When Mary Pentny, late wife of John Malone, alderman of Dublin, gave information against Richard Stevenson and others in an action of assault and riot, the court merely observed that she had been wounded and hurt by a blow from a club. Noting the unlawful assembly of five men at Kilmainham with clubs, swords, staves and other weapons, the court laconically proceeded to fine them without making any provision for the beleaguered widow.[36] In the abduction of Frances Pipho, on the other hand, the court found that the aggravated circumstances merited more measured sentencing. Robert Pipho, a gentleman of St Mary's in the suburbs of Dublin, alleged that Patrick Tipper, Edward Sutton and ten others had broken into his house some two hours before midnight on 15 February 1593, abducted his daughter Frances, and despoiled him of a chest of goods while he lay asleep. Retreating, the intruders allegedly locked the doors of his house to prevent Pipho from chasing after them. The court

31. Ibid., f. 118.
33. Ibid., f. 98.
35. Ibid., f. 90.
32. Ibid., f. 120.
34. Ibid., f. 99.
36. Ibid., f. 119.

concluded that Edward Sutton was the ringleader and fined him 100 marks. Determining that Tipper had been guilty of similar offences before, the tribunal fined him twenty marks. The disorderly conspirators were all imprisoned and made to pay costs of court.[37]

The underlying culture of violence so apparent in the records of Dublin was more than matched by evidence from the country at large in this unsettled period. On the other hand, as we have witnessed before, allegations of riot were customarily employed to gain the court's attention in real property disputes. The entry book reveals numerous cases where the tenants of landowners were dispossessed of a castle or grazing rights or woods to which their lords had laid claim. Thomas Dalton, gentleman of Co. Westmeath, claimed that Sir John Tirrell came to Castlegaddre with his retainers at night on 19 December 1587 to break the walls and assault his servants. Tirrell was duly fined and imprisoned in April 1592 for this episode in manifestly chronic feuding with his neighbour.[38] A similar allegation was made by Thomas Fitzgerald, gentleman, of Co. Longford against Theobald Dillon and five others who came to his domain of Rathbeg and expelled the plaintiffs from their houses, killed their sheep and lambs, and drove away forty cows. In October 1592, the court fined Dillon and the others, jailed them during pleasure and made them pay legal costs.[39] A more serious affair was related by Katherine Barrett of Ballencolly, Co. Cork. One Cormock McDermod of Blarney and some 200 others

> by waye of insurrectione most riotouslye, routeslye [i.e. in a rout] and unlaw-fullye assemblede, with force and armes, viz with swordes, targettes &c, did assaulte, assayle, invyrone [i.e. to encircle] and besiege Castlenyhinche in the saide Countye, menasinge and moste cruelly and wickedlye threatininge one Kryvan McMoroghe and others, the servauntes of the saide Katherin, then beinge within the saide Castell.[40]

The siege continued for two entire days, 8–9 September 1589, during which time the poor servants were threatened with their lives and no sustenance could reach them. The court fined McDermod £10 and imprisoned him in Dublin for 15 days, releasing the rest of the defendants after assessing court costs. Considering the danger to public peace, the court's response would appear helplessly irresolute. However, exagggerated allegations were often discounted in these actions which mixed riot and property claims together, and the case was heard some five years after the event.[41] The court heard two cases from Galway in 1593, both involving the noted French family as petitioners. Edmund French sued Thomas Nolan and others for breaking into his castle of Liskenan and expelling his wife Aunstace French; later, while Walter French sued members of the rival Lynch

37. Ibid., f. 116.   38. Ibid., f. 101.
39. Ibid., f. 103.   40. Ibid., f. 112.
41. Ibid.

family for assaulting him in his townhouse in Galway.[42] Hearings from the distant provinces became increasingly frequent as the court of castle chamber matured, and stalwart members of the Old English plutocracy sought advantage over their municipal rivals by recourse to the Irish star chamber.[43]

The court of castle chamber did not adjudicate real property actions *per se*, although many cases before the court involved landed estates in dispute. However, the parallel jurisdiction of the lord deputy and council was frequently called upon to settle questions of inheritance, title, possession and related matters. The primary impetus for this exceptional focus on land law before the council was the relentless petitioning of Irish suitors to the crown. The privy council in England heard as many as thirty Irish suits in a single day, forwarding to Dublin required action to be taken by the council there.[44] For example, on 26 May 1589, the privy council wrote to the Irish council to take up the matter of John Luttrell, servant of Lord Mordaunt, whose lands in Dunboyne were detained through alleged fraud. Due to the poverty of his family he could not seek remedy at common law, so the deputy and council were urged to use the 'equitie and indifferencie' of the conciliar tribunal in a hearing of his case.[45] In Co. Galway, Fardarough O'Kelly, gentleman, pursued two complaints to claim his inheritance against his kinsmen, Egenegh and Hugh O'Kelly, who had usurped his rent and seignories. Again, the privy council wrote on 2 June 1589 to require the Irish council to initiate proceedings against the two defendants, if the circumstances warranted it upon further examinations.[46] Most cases of this sort alleged the lack of a remedy at common law, whether owing to the poverty of the complainant, distance from the venue or partisanship of local juries. In similar fashion, a minor heir, William Gough of Co. Down, lodged a complaint against the marshal of Ireland, Nicholas Bagenal, that he had been dispossessed of his manor of Ardagh upon his father's death. Noting that Gough had obtained a decree of the council in Ireland confirmed by exchequer seal, the English privy council required the council in Ireland to compel specific performance of the agreement and to examine his evidence and writings since the young petitioner lacked the ability to sue at common law.[47]

The remarkable number of Irish cases before the privy council in England requires some explanation. Irish petitioners sought legal remedy in a wide variety of actions by commencing suit at the English council, in the knowledge that it

---

42. Ibid., ff. 108, 110. The defendants were all fined £10 for the incidents which had occurred in 1589 and 1590, respectively.

43. A recent essay by Dr Garnham attempted to assess, for the eighteenth century, the relative violence of Irish society, finding that 'intemperate and savage behaviour was probably far more common than in contemporary England': N. Garnham, 'How violent was eighteenth-century Ireland?', *IHS*, xxx (1997), 390.

44. *Acts privy council, 1591–92*, p. 551.   45. *Acts privy council, 1588–89*, p. 212.

46. Ibid., p. 234.

47. Ibid., pp. 252–53. Bagenal's refusal to rejoin after the petitioner's bill of replication in chancery was cited in the order as a means of chiding the venerable soldier, who of course also sat on the Irish council.

possessed equity jurisdiction when sitting as the star chamber. By claiming the uniqueness of their petition and seeking remedy in equity rather than at common law, the suitors gained the attention of the crown. A glut of these petitions swamped the calendar of the queen's senior councillors, amounting to some 20 per cent of their business at any given time. Many of the cases were substantially reported in the register of the council, with orders to communicate the outcome of arbitration or hearings in Ireland. In 1591, the privy council heard the allegation of Richard Bourke of Co. Limerick of a riotous assault by Theobald Butler, lord of Cahir, against his possession of the barony of Caherkenlisse, a manor in dispute between them. The Irish council was ordered to examine the titles and claims of both parties, hear depositions of witnesses and other proofs, and give their decision in equity.[48] Here the privy council undertook a full examination of the cause before sending its order to Ireland, without formally adjudicating on the matter itself. The role of the English authority would seem to be one of vetting complaints, filtering the substantive from the casual among Irish suits, and assuring access to royal justice. On 24 June 1592, the frustrated privy council wrote to forestall Irish suits by those who refused to take the oath of allegiance, denying them access to royal favour.[49]

Fitzwilliam presided over important changes in the judicial personality of the Irish bench, despite his evident lack of interest in reform. While others had clamoured for English-trained lawyers for a generation, Fitzwilliam was serendipitously handed the opportunity to replace key Old English judges through a series of calamities that befell them. Sir Nicholas White and Sir Lucas Dillon were disgraced in the aftermath of Perrot's regime, and both died in 1592. Sir Robert Dillon, chief justice of common pleas, came under suspicion and was charged with treason and disloyalty in the same year. His accusers included both kinsmen and partisans of his late predecessor, Nicholas Nugent, and the accusations were made by questionable witnesses including the jailed priest, Shane McCongawney, writing from '24 foot under the earth' weighted by leg irons and starving in the dungeon.[50] Dillon was accused of treason for betraying state intelligence to O'Rourke (who was later executed) in advance of a campaign against him by Bingham. The lord deputy and council heard charges made by Lords Delvin and Howth, as well as the former rebel, William Nugent, on 7 November 1592. A week later they also heard the critic of cess, Patrick Bermingham, in the council chamber and received the petition of Dillon's accusers on 15 November, while the tethered Shane McCongawney's testimony, though taken in Irish, apparently aroused no suspicion at the time.[51] The privy council authorized the hearing by the council board against Dillon in December 1592.[52] A commission of inquiry led by Loftus and Gardiner did nothing to clear Dillon's name, but the viceroy wrote to Burghley for him on 1 March 1593, arguing that he was a wise judge.[53]

48. *Acts privy council, 1591*, p. 113.
50. *Cal. S.P. Ire., 1592–96*, pp. 15–27.
52. *Acts privy council, 1592–93*, p. 153.

49. *Acts privy council, 1591–92*, p. 587.
51. Ibid.
53. *Cal. S.P. Ire., 1592–96*, p. 79.

On 25 June 1593, the English privy council heard verbal argument against Dillon, called upon the viceroy to gather the judges and learned counsel after receiving the proofs from London, and required the conciliar court to proceed with a full trial if the information were sufficient.[54] On the evidence, Dillon was removed from office and imprisoned in October 1593, yet his supporter, Lord Chancellor Loftus, declared him innocent of the charges on 22 November. Five days later, Dillon was named a commissioner of ecclesiastical causes, and he was restored to the council the following year. At no time was the court of castle chamber formally engaged in the trial, but the council board and its leading English members apparently drove much of the adjudication. Dillon was granted the mercy of the queen on 30 January 1594 and permitted to come to England, but his career as a judge was nearly in ruins. Nonetheless, on the death of his replacement, Sir William Weston, on 23 September 1594, Fenton wrote to Burghley that Dillon should be restored to office, and he regained the chief justiceship by patent on 15 March 1595, a rare exception to the elimination of loyal Old English councillors after 1592.[55] Despite efforts by Fitzwilliam on 26 February 1592 to rehabilitate the reputation of Nicholas Walshe, second justice of queen's bench, Walshe was not nominated as chief baron to succeed Sir Lucas Dillon.[56] Fenton wrote on 6 March 1592 against nominating a chief baron of Irish birth, noting the opportunity for partisan dealing in lawsuits through the custom of fosterage and extended kinship.[57]

The replacement of Irish judges by three Englishmen learned in the laws was approved by act of the English privy council in May 1593. Sir Anthony St Leger, whose family had strong connections to the Irish administration, became master of the rolls; Sir William Weston was nominated to succeed Dillon as chief justice of common pleas; and Sir Robert Napper was to become chief baron.[58] On 4 May 1593, the privy council added that all incumbent officers should join with the new appointees in taking the oath of obedience, and those who refused should be suspended or replaced for nonconformity.[59] The new English judges were fortified with a further injunction that empowered them to retain causes determinable

---

54. *Acts privy council, 1592–93*, p. 331. The Irish council was cautioned not to tolerate delay by Nugent and to question closely the proofs alleging treason.

55. *Cal. S.P. Ire., 1592–96*, p. 274. Fitzwilliam thanked Burghley for the queen's clemency and Burghley's favour in protecting Dillon. The embattled Dillon died in 1597.

56. *Cal. S.P. Ire., 1588–92*, p. 462.

57. Ibid., p. 471.

58. *Acts privy council, 1592–93*, pp. 187, 214. Their fees were to be augmented from the deanery of St Patrick's and other sources.

59. Ibid., p. 217. These orders were extended to sheriffs, escheators, feodaries, seneschals and others, while all wards were to be brought up in the English habit and religion. Fitzwilliam's regime made little use of castle chamber in the enforcement of religious uniformity, leaving it to the ecclesiastical commission of 27 November 1593. Registered in Dublin and signed by the viceroy, this order called for 21 men to reform and correct all errors of recusancy. The five leaders were to be English-born, including the newly arrived justices. The timing of the commission on the eve of rebellion made it a dead letter, though the concept anticipated the rigor of the Chichester regime. 'Harris Collectanea', ed. C. McNeill, in *Anal Hib*, no. 6 (1934), pp. 424–28.

in their courts, requiring the lord deputy and council to avoid channelling ligitation from the common law courts to the star chamber.[60] The determination of the new English judges to preserve the judicial autonomy of their courts against the prerogative justice of the council board and castle chamber may explain the lacunae in the conciliar court's records after the departure of Fitzwilliam as viceroy. Writing to Burghley on 30 January 1594, Fitzwilliam sought his revocation at the age of 69 while taking satisfaction that recourse to law was now commonplace: 'For every one that was amenable to law six years ago there be now six. Her Majesty's writs of all natures current throughout the realm. The hall is too little to hold the suitors.'[61]

When the elderly Fitzwilliam was replaced at the onset of the Nine Years' War in August 1594 by an experienced military veteran, Sir William Russell, it might be expected that the court of castle chamber would become dormant amidst the flurry of wartime preparations. In fact, however, the court continued to operate well into 1597. Russell himself misjudged the situation badly on his arrival in August, permitting the earl of Tyrone to offer his submission in Dublin and releasing him on assurance of his good government in Ulster. He summoned the judges in November for Michaelmas term and sat in star chamber for the first time on 12 November 1594, according to his journal.[62] In May 1595, Edmond Barrett of Ballencoly, co. Cork, sued his neighbours and kinsmen who, with sixty in their company, came to his castle with swords, guns, great sledges, skenes, stones and staves in a riotous assault. Some four years previously, Andrew Barrett and others had broken down the booley house and gates of the castle and expelled the plaintiff. Edmond had then sued out a writ of restitution from the vice-president of Munster, Sir Thomas Norris, but Sir Fynes O'Driscoll, sheriff of the county, refused to execute the writ until Edmond paid him two silver cups as pledge of £4. The castle chamber court fined the sheriff in January 1595 for his extortion, then taxed Andrew Barrett and the other defendants in the case.[63] When the court adjudicated local quarrels of long standing, the route to final resolution was often complicated by judicial detours and compounded by the misdeeds of provincial officials.[64]

60. *Acts privy council, 1592–93*, p. 219. St Leger wrote to Burghley on 29 August 1593 to say that the judges received their patents before the end of midsummer term and sat only three days in their courts before riding the circuits in summer. *Cal. S.P. Ire., 1592–96*, p. 144. Three years later he wrote to Sir Robert Cecil to complain that the fees of the English judges were to be paid from the castle chamber fine of the bishop of Leighlin, but were yet unsatisfied since he had died in August 1597. *Cal. S.P. Ire., 1596–97*, p. 370.

61. *Cal. S.P. Ire., 1592–96*, p. 201.   62. LPL, Carew MS 612, f. 9v.

63. BL, Add. MS 47,172, ff. 121, 124. The aggrieved Barrett had paid the bribe, only to find the sheriff contemptuously refusing to execute the writ. Russell's regime has been characterized by a want of discipline, and Morgan found him incompetent. See *Tyrone's rebellion*, p. 169.

64. Dr Canny has recently discussed the problems of local governance, noting the favouritism of presidents, the peculation of captains and the self-interested aggrandizement of those who perverted the English common law to serve private ends. Canny, *Making Ireland British*, p. 99.

The trend of the court at this time was to undertake cases of administrative malfeasance, punishing officials at every level for their excesses or lapses of judgement. Russell himself presided when the court punished Captain Thomas Plunkett for a riot and assault at the castle of Kilcolman in Co. Cork. William Power of Kylblane, gentleman, sued Plunkett and others for an ambush that occurred in February 1593, in which well-armed horsemen, hidden behind some cattle that Power was about to seize for damages, attacked Power and wounded his servants.[65] On 6 May 1597, Captain John Norris, the famous Elizabethan soldier, was found guilty of uttering slanderous words against the queen at Athlone the previous September and fined 500 marks with the loss of both his ears and life imprisonment.[66] On the same day, the humble jailer of Mullingar, Co. West Meath, the widow Jane Hopp, was convicted of allowing two convicted traitors among the Nugents to escape, despite the special charge of the justices to look carefully to their incarceration.[67] In a remarkable case of two officials battling one another, Charles Egerton, constable of Carrickfergus, was convicted of leading three assaults on Captain Rice Mansfield in and near the garrison town in April 1597. The intervention of the mayor prevented further interruption of her majesty's peace, and the court fined Egerton 100 marks for the unprovoked tumult.[68] On the other hand, on 14 May 1596, the court took up the case of John Clinton, gentleman, of Co. Louth who informed against his more powerful neighbour, Patrick Verdon, esquire, in a case of nocturnal grazing on his field of wheat. The unremarkable facts told of a village conspiracy and pastoral bullying that the court found time to hear some four years after the incident occurred:

> Memorandum ... the xvth and xvjth Daye of August 1592 in the night tyme Henry Verdon of Togher, gent, Edward Verdon, Allexander Verdon, Rorye McShee and Neale OFarrall, by the Dyreccon, Comaundement, procurement and setting on of Patricke Verdon of Clonemort, Esquire, That they the said Henrye and the rest before named Ryoutously with force and armes arrayed in war like manner and weaponed with Swordes and other weapons Defensible, Came the said xvth and xvjth Dayes of August 1592 by night to a parcell of land Conteyninge three acres neare the old Towne or hamblt [hamlet] of Dodstowne in the said County of Loothe, then sowen with wheate ready to be reaped and brought with them forty plowe horses or there abowte and upon the said Thre acres sowne with wheate, the said persons did kepe the said plowe horses the said xvth and xvjth Daies in the

---

65. BL, Add. MS 47,172, ff. 122–22v.
66. Ibid., f. 128. The penalty was moderated thereafter. See also 'Russell's journal' in LPL, Carew MS 612, f 111v.
67. BL, Add. MS 47,172, f. 129; also 'Russell's journal' f. 110v.
68. BL, Add. MS 47,172, f. 127; see also 'Russell's journal', f. 110v. Egerton took advantage of his lightly armed rival who was overseeing fortifications outside the town, leading six warders in the assault.

night tyme whearby the said Three acres wheatt was maliciously and in riotous manner eaten, trodden, broken downe & Consumed, to the great hinderaunce of the said John Clinton.[69]

Patrick Verdon was forced to pay twenty nobles, and to bear the costs of his henchmen if they were unable to pay the fines.[70]

Other evidence from Russell's journal of his viceroyalty in Ireland adds detail to the work of the council and the court. On 9 April 1595, for example, the deputy and council sat all day and gave judgement in the trial of Walter Reagh. He was condemned to be hanged alive in chains, and the next day that sentence was carried out, though the journal is silent on the crime for which he was convicted.[71] On 23 May, the deputy and council sat in the star chamber where Lord Reagh, probably a kinsman of Walter, was arraigned for receiving Redmond McFeagh, a proclaimed traitor. Lord Reagh had allowed him to depart and was subsequently tried by jury, found guilty of treason and condemned to be hanged, drawn and quartered.[72] This was not a castle chamber trial, since treason was not an offence dealt with there; hence the reference to star chamber was probably to the room in Dublin Castle where the court usually met. Finally, on 26 May, the wife of Feagh McHugh O'Byrne, Rose O'Toole, was arraigned by a jury, found guilty of treason and condemned to be burned.[73] The evidence for a scorched earth policy by Russell is clear from the details of his journal, in contrast to the settled law and laconic entries to be found in the entry book of the court of castle chamber.

Russell sat in council often for days at a time, shuttling back to camp and returning immediately to council chambers on his return to Dublin.[74] His journal showed that the viceroy sat with the council almost daily during December 1596, hearing appeals and giving orders in pending cases.[75] Many suitors sought the intervention of the crown, particularly those with the ear of the sovereign. The queen wrote in 1596 to Russell and the Irish council on behalf of Sir Charles O'Carroll of the country of Ely, who was accused of slaughtering members of the Cantwell sept. Despite the gravity of the charge, Elizabeth was concerned that a hearing in the liberty of Tipperary would have the effect of acknowledging that O'Carroll was subject to the authority of the Butlers and the earl of Ormonde. Consequently, she ordered an indifferent commission to examine this contention, suspending the trial until the issue of O'Carroll's lands could be adjudicated: 'wee have thought yt no Interruption of Justice to have theise two points well and speedely considered of and yet cannot refuse in Compasion of his Case.'[76] Russell was holding a council meeting in Galway in November 1595 when he first heard

---

69. BL, Add. MS 47,172, f. 126.   70. Ibid.

71. LPL, Carew MS 612, f. 17.   72. Ibid., f. 20.

73. Ibid., f. 20v.   74. Ibid., f. 19v.

75. Ibid., ff. 90–99.

76. Ibid., ff. 37–37v . See also *Cal. S.P. Ire., 1592–96*, pp. 474–75. O'Carroll complained that his lands and tenants were spoiled daily by the Butlers during his incarceration.

of this suit, and he was then engaged in another politically charged indictment in Connacht. Once again, the tyrannical Bingham was accused of multiple offences by his adversaries, the Burkes, and he defended his government in a series of letters to Burghley from December 1595 to May 1597.[77] Bingham sought a trial of the issues in England, challenging the neutrality of Russell and others on the Irish council, and pronouncing himself insulted by their inquiries. He continued to badger the privy council, though Russell and others wrote on his behalf, claiming that Fenton, Gardiner and John Norris were his enemies in Dublin. Finally, he left for England in September 1596, without licence, to defend his regime.[78] Meanwhile, he was replaced in Connacht by Norris, who reassured the chief gentlemen of their rights to try the cause against Bingham.[79] The council board was thus adroitly avoided when suits at law that caught the attention of the queen and privy council were managed from London, despite the queen's admonition of 5 July 1596 to try the case in Dublin before the council, without Fenton and Norris. Bingham had no confidence in the neutrality of the councillors at this stage despite the queen's decision that he had to confront his accusers.[80]

HIATUS: SPASMODIC ADJUDICATION AND MOUNTJOY'S JUDICIAL TEMPERANCE, 1597–1603

Nothing in the record of the court for these years would indicate that the country was about to enter the maelstrom of war and rebellion. Yet the sudden lapse of any judicial action by the court after 1597 until well into the next reign can only be explained by the unhingeing of Irish society at this time, the atmosphere of crisis including the billeting of troops in Dublin itself, and the utter mismanagement of the viceregal office. A succession of ineffective chief governors passed through Dublin Castle after the departure of Russell on 22 May 1597, from Thomas Lord Burgh to the tragic figure of the earl of Essex. Interim lords justices such as the judges Adam Loftus and Robert Gardiner did nothing to resurrect the court in this period, while military men like Thomas Norris and George Carey had a tenuous hold on office and remained in the field. The hiatus of seven years in the work of the court may also be explained by ineffective record-keeping, since one castle chamber case, omitted entirely in the entry book, has been located in the file of court records now at Trinity College Dublin. However, lacking other formal documentation for its judicial work, we must conclude that the court lay dormant, as did many other institutions of government, during the height of the Nine Years War.

77. *Cal. S.P. Ire., 1592–96*, pp. 439, 469, 520, 524, 533.
78. *Cal. S.P. Ire., 1596–97*, pp. 112, 128.
79. Ibid., p. 130. Under arrest following his unauthorized departure, Bingham survived the crisis and returned to Ireland in early 1599 as marshal, only to die there at the age of 70.
80. *Acts privy council, 1596–97*, pp. 9–10.

On the departure of Russell in May, another military veteran succeeded to the office of chief governor. Thomas Lord Burgh made no impression on the legal history of Ireland, and died in office less than five months later. The veteran commander Thomas Norris succeeded him briefly as lord justice, to be replaced by Lord Chancellor Loftus and Chief Justice Gardiner on 27 November 1597. They governed as a duumvirate for eighteen months and did little to restore judicial momentum. When the earl of Essex arrived in April 1599 for his ill-fated expedition to Ireland, the rebellion and other emergencies caused the legal terms to be suspended periodically over a period of some years, and Essex did nothing to reclaim either the integrity or the continuity of the judicial system. After another interim period when Loftus joined with George Carey as lord justice from 25 September 1599 to 27 February 1600, Lord Mountjoy began his important career as chief governor. By that time, however, the reputation and standing of the Irish courts had been shredded by division among the judges, long intervals between terms, and suits long delayed. While there were no cases before the court of castle chamber during this period, it is important to review the state of the judiciary in Ireland prior to the arrival of Mountjoy and to assess the damage done to its infrastructure.

The records of the government are strewn with references to military preparation during this period, punctuated by accusations of soldierly abuse and corruption, and practically silent on judicial matters. However, the president and council of Munster complained in November 1597 that causes were taken from its venue to Dublin, alleging that lawyers in Dublin sought to procure process out of the senior courts, forcing litigants to go to Dublin for redress at great cost to them, and procuring writs of *certiorari* from the lord chancellor after losing a case in the Munster court. Sir Thomas Norris argued that this proceeding brought the reputation of his court into contempt, and the English privy council admonished the lords justices to use moderation in hearing appeals from Munster, while reasserting the right to determine when justice required continuance of a suit.[81] Responding to Norris on 13 November 1597, the privy council added:

> So on the other side, for as moche as there are divers of that Concell men of learnynge and knowledge in the lawes, … wee doe wyshe that you also would have regard not to deale in maters of controversy and that are fytt to be decyded by course of lawe, only of your selfe, without the opynion and assystaunce of those of the Counsell that are learned in the lawes …[82]

Affirming the sense of corruption of justice in Munster, William Lyon, bishop of Cork, wrote to Lord Hunsdon in July 1596:

---

81. *Acts privy council, 1597–98*, pp. 109, 117. Though Norris was at the time lord justice himself, the letter was written pursuant to an earlier statement of this grievance.
82. Ibid., pp. 117–18.

It has been common within these three years and less for lawyers and petifoggers, when they were ready to go to the term, to go about and inquire who would have a pardon, and so they would gather 2, 30 or 20 names, and for twenty shillings or four nobles a piece they might have their pardons.[83]

The saga of William Saxey, chief justice of Munster, suggests further evidence of judicial corruption in the handling of cases before his court. On 12 February 1596, the lord justice and council wrote to condemn Saxey for departing from Ireland without licence, saying he was not qualified to be a judge and to keep him in England, 'and no more returned to his office, being a person that has incurred so general a "mislike"'.[84] Saxey had earlier written to Burghley to explain his actions in the treason trial of John FitzEdmund, after the Dublin government sent commissioners to examine his 'intemperate and undecent proceedings' against him. Saxey asked that the case be brought for trial in England, saying there was no justice in Munster and seeking the trial of James Goold, second justice of Munster, who was not to be trusted.[85] By 5 December 1598, Saxey found himself whingeing to Robert Cecil that he was now alone, without employment in justice or private practice, bitterly condemning the administration of justice in Ireland. He argued that recusants and mere soldiers claimed the right to administer nisi prius, gaol delivery and oyer and terminer; blamed the lord chancellor for failing to observe the laws of England; called upon chief judges to keep circuits three times each year and to avoid the removal of cases from Munster to Dublin. He asked for military retinues to accompany the justices and accused sheriffs of corruption, while declaring that the English, when at trial with Irish litigants, 'hath a cold suit' due to the partiality of juries. He recommended that Cecil 'hold in suspect their treacherous hearts, than trust too much to their counterfeit looks'.[86] Writing to Cecil again on 1 December 1599, Saxey declaimed,

> The ground of this hatred in the hearts of the country is that they could not enjoy the benefit of law and due administration of justice, which they do greatly affect, the jurisdiction whereof has been greedily sought for by martial men, and too easily granted unto them, whose insolency and ignorance have exercised oppression in place of justice.[87]

Though he returned to Ireland again with Essex in 1599 and took up his former role as chief justice in Munster, he deplored the situation he found there:

> But the course of justice is so interrupted, and the Judges are so contemned, that, for avoiding of further inconvenience, the session must be abruptly

83. *Cal. S.P. Ire., 1596–97*, p. 20.
84. Ibid., p. 230.
85. Ibid., p. 224.
86. *Cal. S.P. Ire., 1598–99*, pp. 394–97.
87. *Cal. S.P. Ire., 1599–1600*, pp. 285–86.

broken up, to the great disgrace of Her Highness's authority and the discontent of the country.[88]

The reports from Munster were uniformly critical, though not without partisanship. An anonymous 'history' of the province, written on behalf of Ormonde, alleged that Irish leaders were abused and mistreated by Thomas Norris despite the protections given by Ormonde. The writer characterized the English adventurers as

> traitors, murderers, thieves, coseners, conycatchers, shifting mates, runners away with other men's wives, some having two or three wives, persons divorced living loosely, bankrupts, carnal gospellers, Papists, Puritans, and Brownists.[89]

Even worse, argued the critic, there was rampant dissension among the English themselves:

> They could not be content to scrape from the Irishry, but one inveighing and suing the other, troubling the courts, and disquieting the country. The English gentlemen in Leix and Offally contended among themselves. In Munster they jarred one with another, so that the Mayor of Cork gave forth that most suits depending before him were between the Englishry.[90]

Though everyone, without rank or distinction, clamoured to be a justice of the peace there was a dearth of qualified judges. Commissioners of the peace were satirized by the critic thus:

> There was one in Munster, a great swearer, they called him Justice God's Wounds; another, killing of Irish cows [and] selling hides and tallow, they called him Justice Tripes; another, having no land, but a stock of money, hunting, and hawking, and gaming, and coming once a year, they called Justice When-ye-will. Such insufficiency there was in their service.[91]

Suits long pending were delayed for up to ten years in this period. In one case involving the sons of the disgraced Nicholas White, John Itchingham sued to obtain the estate of Dunbrody monastery though White had intended to bequeath it to his heirs. Itchingham petitioned the privy council in England, and on 10 June 1593 they ordered that the controversy should be dismissed from a hearing before

---

88. Saxey to privy council, 23 October 1599: ibid., p. 196. He came to Cork on 24 September and announced a general session of gaol delivery to be held in Cork, but was forced to adjourn it. He condemned Warham St Leger and others for presuming to hold trials instead of a proper judge.
89. *Cal. S.P. Ire., 1598–99*, p. 429.
90. Ibid. He further alleged that Norris favoured the Irish over the English, begrudging him because he would not accept their bribes. Ibid., p. 430.
91. Ibid., p. 430.

the Irish council, allowing the plaintiff to pursue his case at common law. As White was a former councillor, Itchingham preferred his case in England and demanded that the bishop of Leighlin be examined touching the confessions of White made before his death.[92] Five years later, the privy council wrote to the lords justices, citing their previous orders to form a commission of the leading judges in Ireland to hear and determine the controversy, based on legal advice of the chief justice and learned counsel in England. Itchingham complained that Andrew White had made over leases of the estates and tithes to Sir Thomas Colclogh, taken distresses by force, and brought actions against him at common law before Sir Nicholas Walshe, acting as judge of nisi prius in the county. The English privy council ordered Colclogh and White to forbear disturbing the land, to restore distresses, and to submit to the determination of the lords justices, Loftus and Gardiner. They further required that Walshe, who had recently become chief justice of common pleas on the death of Dillon, should be removed from the trial, or else to proceed only with the assistance of other judges, since Itchingham alleged he was compromised as the father-in-law of Colclogh and an ally of Nicholas White. The privy council micro-managed the case after expressing their frustration with the long delay, concluding,

> And in case any of the said parties, Itchingham or White, shall refuse to submitt himself to your judiciall sentence herein, wee praie you to take such order for redresse as in equitie and justice you shall thincke most convenient.[93]

In November 1598, the lords justices were ordered to make haste, even though the chief baron and master of the rolls were detained in England, preventing a speedy resolution of the Itchingham suit.[94] In February 1600, the privy council wrote to Gardiner, St Leger and Robert Napper, three English-born judges, to support the petition of Itchingham who now protested against the judgement of the late earl of Essex in favour of White and Colclogh. Noting that Itchingham was allegedly put out of possession of Dunbrody without any examination of the cause by the lord lieutenant, a commission was ordered to hear the case and, if he was removed without a hearing, to be restored and the case heard by the lords justices.[95] Itchingham's determination, the unsettled legal terms, military campaigning in the province of Munster and the disgrace of both White and Essex may have played a part in the privy council's reversal, but it was a remarkable intervention in the judicial process at a time when the council was certainly preoccupied with weightier matters.

---

92. *Cal. S.P. Ire., 1592–96*, p. 107. On 12 February 1593, the privy council authorized the sons of White, who had died in the Tower, to bring his body back to Ireland for burial. *Acts privy council, 1592–93*, p. 44.
93. *Acts privy council, 1598–99*, p. 227.
94. Ibid., p. 299. William Bathe, second justice of common pleas, and Thomas Dillon, chief justice of Connacht, were named in their places.
95. *Acts privy council, 1599–1600*, p. 121.

The impact of Lord Mountjoy on Ireland goes well beyond the military arena, where he was spectacularly successful. Although his judicial role in the court of castle chamber was attenuated, and the condition of the Irish courts at his arrival little improved despite occasional suggestions to the contrary, Mountjoy engaged in a vigorous and important dialogue preliminary to the reforms of the next reign. Prior to the lieutenancy of his predecessor, Essex, the Irish council wrote to Robert Cecil on 24 March 1599 requesting the immediate dispatch to Ireland of two leading judges, Sir Anthony St Leger, master of the rolls, and Sir Robert Napper, chief baron. The council anxiously awaited their colleagues:

> After a long discontinuance the terms begin to be revived. And the last Michaelmas term, it was a hindrance of the subjects' causes that these two judges were absent. But if their places should be destitute this term, it wold more discourage the subjects and do harm to the Queen's affairs . For your Honour may guess what will be the proceeding of those Courts, in the absence of the Chief Baron, who is to stand for Her Majesty's revenues in the Exchequer, and when the Chancery is destitute of the Master of the Rolls, who is the only lawyer in that Court.[96]

Mountjoy periodically analyzed the state of Ireland, proclaiming his belief that the country could become prosperous and resourceful. On 27 October 1600, he wrote to Cecil in defence of his new administration, charging his fellow councillors with defensive self-regard and deceit:

> Only some of them, that have gone long round in this kingdom like millhorses, may tell me the form of the circle they have trod in, but I protest I think no men are more deceived touching the true estate of this kingdom and nature of this war than they are.[97]

On 22 March 1601, he sent a discourse blaming the corrupt magistrates, weakness of counsel, private ends and dissension among the English for the revolt. Saying the council and clergy were often men who lived in Ireland because of previous troubles in England, he yet argued the provision of good magistrates would reform Ireland after the army had reduced all to obedience.[98] Mountjoy's opinion was shared by the veteran lord president of Munster, Sir George Carew. Writing to Robert Cecil on 30 August 1600 from Cork, Carew argued that Munster could not be conquered by the sword alone, '*opus labori*', and protested that all the treasure of England would be consumed in such a folly unless the administration

---

96. *Cal. S.P. Ire., 1598–99*, p. 495.
97. *Cal. S.P. Ire., 1600*, p. 516. Mountjoy added, 'most of them do only lie at defence to save themselvs harmless, some of them to entrap me, but none of them … from whom I receive any manner of assistance to make this war as it should be.' Ibid. Plate 8.
98. *Cal. S.P. Ire., 1600–01*, pp. 251–52.

were staffed by able judges and professional lawyers. He sought the presence of the young Geraldine claimant to the earldom of Desmond, then held in London, to forestall renewed rebellion by a Geraldine 'Robin Hood'.[99] On the other hand, the wily Meyler Magrath, archbishop of Cashel, wrote to Cecil in October of the same year to seek commissions of martial law in Munster 'which will induce more fear and terror upon that country people than the ordinary course of common law, being not now very current there'.[100] The redoubtable William Saxey had returned to Ireland as both chief justice of Munster and second justice of the queen's bench, and he was cited often as an example of corruption, holding a fee of £100 per annum for his second role, yet never attending the queen's bench during term and refusing to name a deputy. Sir George Carey complained that the able Sir Nicholas Walshe had been previously removed as chief justice of Munster and said, 'The Fathers of the law at Dublin are directly of opinion that it is against the law for one man [Saxey] to hold two such places.'[101]

Although Mountjoy did not make ordinary use of the court of castle chamber, he received numerous petitions seeking legal redress and he was compelled to countenance the grievances accumulated under his predecessors. In one such case, in September 1600, Mountjoy authorized the two chief justices, Secretary Fenton and the bishop of Meath to hear the causes between Sir Patrick Barnewall and Sir William Warren over a wardship, explaining that Barnewall had offered immediate payment of £350 and awarding the wardship to the Old English aristocrat. Warren protested to Cecil, and Mountjoy was compelled to justify his decision in the case.[102] Angered by another accusation from Sir Patrick Barnewall against him, Warren offended the viceroy and Mountjoy imprisoned him in Dublin Castle. On 1 May 1601, Mountjoy and the council of Ireland heard the charge of Thomas Bathe, a gentleman of Irish birth, who gave information against one William Udall. Bathe claimed that Udall spoke with traitors and favoured Tyrone, saying he wished the queen's army would be overthrown, as Bagenal's force was. Four days later, Captain Marmaduke Neilson added other charges against Udall, saying he favoured the king of Scots to rule all three kingdoms. The council brought all of them to a hearing at which Udall claimed to have knowledge of matters of great secrecy involving danger to the queen's person. He refused to make them known unless he were sent into England, though Mountjoy named a special commission to hear the alleged conspiracy.[103] On another occasion involving the estate of Clontarf, owned by Secretary Fenton, the council refused

99. *Cal. S.P. Ire., 1600*, p. 389.
100. Ibid., pp. 475–77.
101. Ibid., p. 411.
102. Ibid., p. 509. Warren's losing bid of £400 was to be paid over time, but the debate had simmered under Mountjoy's predecessor and probably involved larger issues. Interestingly, the deputy favoured Barnewall even though he was deputed at the time to represent the interests of the Pale in charges against the administration over the abuses of soldiers. Ibid., pp. 430, 509, 512.
103. *Cal. S.P. Ire., 1600–01*, p. 316. Udall was sent to England in the custody of Captain Fisher. Ibid., p. 329.

a hearing to his lessee, George King. Fenton brought an action of ejectment against King which was pending in December 1600, so King petitioned the viceroy to revoke the lawsuit and judge the matter at the council table. Fenton wrote to Cecil on 12 December to protest at the 'rude and high style' of the libellous King, who was alleged to be a retainer of Ormonde and a Catholic, and seeking to prevent the case from being heard in England.[104] The Irish council agreed to hear a case in June 1601 involving two crown officials in Galway who had quarrelled over the security of the town. Captain Henry Clare alleged that the mayor of Galway, Francis Martins, scandalized his reputation after Clare took the keys to the town gates from the custody of the mayor and delivered them to a Protestant alderman, Marcus Lynch, for safe keeping. Saying the mayor had allowed a known felon to escape from the town, Clare also asked to be considered as the next governor of Connacht in his letters to Cecil. The council in Ireland assented to an examination of the misdemeanours alleged against the mayor, but remanded other charges to a trial at law.[105]

It was the consistent position of Mountjoy as lord deputy that religious moderation was the correct policy. In this, he countered the long-held argument of the archbishop of Dublin, Lord Chancellor Loftus, whose unyielding and forceful conviction was not deterred by the arrival of a new chief governor. Loftus wrote to Whitgift in 1600 to defend the six-year lapse of the ecclesiastical commission, noting that he continued to perform his duties, though frustrated by the gentle handling of Catholic priests in Ireland under the forgotten Perrot regime. He protested that some provincial governors were instructed not to stir or meddle in religion, so they allowed dangerous priests and rebels to remain at large.[106] He continued,

> And albeit it may be said that now it is an unseasonable time, in this general tumult and rebellion, to deal in matters of religion, or in any course to work a reformation therein (as indeed we must confess in the remoter parts of this realm, and amongst the rebels, it is a bootless labour to be undertaken), yet in these civil cities and towns, as Dublin and Tredath [Drogheda], and in the Counties of Dublin and Meath, within twenty miles of this city of Dublin (where law hath free course, and is obeyed, and civility is planted), how dangerous a thing it is to let loose the rein, and to permit a general liberty, to the dishonour of God, the public breach of law, the daily increase of a number of rebels, being perverted and seduced by traitorous priests, without any curb or bridle.[107]

104. Ibid., p. 58. Fenton recalled his 22 years of service, and sought the arbitration of three judges in Ireland to be named by Mountjoy. The action of the viceroy and the entire council was to remit King to the trial at law, giving him one of the attorneys Fenton had been using as his counsel. Ibid.

105. Ibid., p. 399 . The mayor petitioned against the rowdy behaviour of soldiers in the town on 14 July 1600, asking the viceroy to examine the complaint and to compel the captain, one Harvey, to make restitution if found complicit in the spoil of goods. *Acts privy council, 1599–1600*, p. 503.

106. *Cal. S.P. Ire., 1600*, p. 78.   107. Ibid., pp. 79–80.

On the other hand, the queen made it very clear to the viceroy and council in her instructions of June 1600 that, despite the hearing of mass in Dublin itself,

> If hereby any person shall conceive that we are minded now to fall into any curious inquisition of men's consciences, or to use severity at this time, they do mistake our purpose; for, although in our own heart we are sorry to see that by the remissness hitherto this infection is so general, yet we hope you the Lord Deputy can use such a mean, although you rake not into their doings, yet not to suffer even under your nose in our principal seat [the] notorious exercise of such idolatry, and to suffer friaries to stand, when we have an army of 17,000 men to fight withal.[108]

Once he had obtained from Tyrone an agreement to suspend military operations, the viceroy made preparations to join the rest of the council in Dublin. After spending nearly three years in the field against a stubborn enemy, he was reluctant to commence a rigorous persecution of recusancy. Writing to Cecil on 20 January 1603 from Trim, Mountjoy explained:

> I hear that in my absence the Lord Chancellor and Council have imprisoned divers for religion, and amongst them six or seven Aldermen of Dublin. I am loth to contradict any of their proceedings in matters of religion, for fear I may be esteemed backward in a reformation, but I am persuaded that a violent course therein will do little good to win men's consciences; but howsoever, it is too soon to begin it; and it is most sure that it will breed a new war and, as I believe, make all the towns and nobility solicit Spanish aids ... I am of opinion that all religions do grow under persecution. It is truly good doctrine and example that must prevail. But whatsoever shall be thought best, it is fit for me to let you know that if this matter be not discreetly handled you must look for a new war, the which I am afraid too many would be glad of, but I beseech God deliver us from it.[109]

By the end of February Mountjoy had won his point. The viceroy and council wrote to the privy council to make note of the 'mild course' they would now pursue with recusants and to put off the resurrecting of a court of ecclesiastical commission, excusing their recent imprisonment of Dublin aldermen by noting they were released from jail in two days.[110]

Although Mountjoy steadily managed the administration in Dublin while conducting a war of attrition throughout the country, winning the confidence of the crown, he was not without his critics. Much of the resistance to his government,

108. Ibid., p. 274.
109. *Cal. S.P. Ire., 1601–03*, pp. 555–56.
110. Ibid., pp. 567–69. The letter added, 'It is true that we moved the Lord Deputy to revive that Commission, after so long time of discontinuance, not thereby to strive with her Majesty's

not surprisingly, focused on the depredations of the soldiers encamped near the loyal towns. Two of the leaders of an incipient opposition were Nicholas St Lawrence, Baron Howth, and Sir Patrick Barnewall, members of the Pale élite. In June 1600, they lodged a petition to the crown to be heard by the queen herself against abuses of the troops, alleging extortions, spoiling of estates and ravaging the countryside. In one case, a whole company of foot journeyed to Dublin to fetch one barrel of powder, pillaging along the way. The queen sent the petitioners back to Dublin to be heard before the deputy and council.[111] On 14 September 1600, Howth reported to Cecil that the viceroy had summoned him to present evidence before the Irish council, joining with other barons and gentlemen of the Pale. They told Mountjoy of beatings of poor people and other outrages, all filed in the office of clerk of the council, and the deputy responded that he had a zeal for justice and would see to making amends.[112] On 27 October, Mountjoy reported the meeting to Cecil, acknowledging the complaints but defending his own government since most of the incidents had occurred prior to his assuming office in Ireland.[113] He lauded Baron Howth but reproached the lawyer Rochford, 'with whom I never spake but at the Council board; but believe me Sir he is the veriest kindle-fire and rebellious-spirited man that ever I did hear speak'.[114]

Sir George Carew was quick to point out evidence of the lawyerly opposition from the vantage point of Munster. As lord president, Carew commended the earl of Thomond, and advocated the usefulness of the young earl of Desmond to calm troubled waters among the Geraldines, but he warned of a conspiracy among the Munster towns. On 16 December 1600, Carew wrote to the privy council that the towns enriched themselves during war at crown expense, supplying the rebels at counterfeit prices, while enjoying the protection and security of the queen's peace.[115] Carew added that the corporate towns had recently

> made choice of professed lawyers to be their magistrates, and such as before time were ringleaders of their corporations; namely in Cork, John Meade, a man known to your Lordships, and whom of late you have justly reproved;

subjects in matters of their conscience, but to see what we cold do in the re-edifying and reformation of their own churches and to win them to their outward obedience to come to the church as all good subjects ought to do by the laws … In the meantime we shall observe the directions which your lordships have prescribed for this Commission, and shall do so rather as a grace from ourselves than by your order, so that they may not take occasion to insult the more.' Ibid.

111. *Acts privy council, 1599–1600*, pp. 507–09. On 15 June 1600, Lord Dunsany and 17 other nobles signed a second petition to the crown, naming agents from every shire, and complaining that Mountjoy put off the hearing. *Cal. S.P. Ire., 1600*, pp. 236–37.

112. Ibid., pp. 428–29.

113. Ibid., pp. 513–19. The lord of Howth and Sir Patrick Barnewell were sent over before he came to Ireland, so the grievances were not made against his government, though Mountjoy had done much to reform the abuses they complained of. On 20 July, the queen had written to Mountjoy to give answer to the grievances and redress them if they were proved. Ibid., p. 326.

114. Ibid., p. 301.   115. *Cal. S.P. Ire., 1600–01*, pp. 64–66.

in Limerick, one Geffrey Galway, son unto the agent of that town, and now attending your Lordships, since whose coming from the Inns of Court the inhabitants thereof have run into all those disorders, wherewith your Lordships have been so often troubled, and hath been the special man that hath wrought their forbearing to come to the Church, which formerly they were accustomed to do ... [and] ... in Clonmell, one White, a lawyer also is Sovereign, but as much Romish as any of the rest.[116]

Carew ended his diatribe against the towns by charging them with using the complexities of the law to evade punishment for their offences, claiming they insisted on the technical interpretation of their charters to justify themselves. The paradoxical triumph of the common law in Ireland apparently eluded the earnest veteran lord president. But the fearless advocate Meade wrote directly to Sir John Popham, chief justice in England, in November 1600 to protest against the abuses of troops and martial law, claiming, 'the strict sincerity of the common law might be used' to reform the province.[117]

Carew himself was frequently at the centre of disputes that ultimately found their way to the council table, though not adjudicated before the court of castle chamber. For example, Donnell O'Sullivan sought the recovery of his title and inheritance in a letter to Carew of 2 May 1601, arguing that he was dispossessed of the lordships of Beare and Bantry by his uncle, Sir Owen O'Sullivan, who claimed rights as tanist to the estate. As Donnell was then but two years of age, he waited until his majority to sue before the privy council and was granted the castle of Bearhaven while he awaited a decision of the lord deputy and council to partition the rest of the inheritance. However, the commissioners sent into Munster neglected their duties, and gave a corrupt decision, forcing Donnell to sue again to the privy council. After his uncle died, the heirs disputed the estate and finally an arbitrator gave a judgement which all accepted. Donnell claimed that 'the times' were 'now reduced to some quiet' in Munster by the spring of 1601, and he sought the final abolition of the pretended custom of tanistry at law.[118] Carew also defended the interests of Henry Sherwood, a former adherent of John Norris and a retainer of Ormonde, who was sued before the council in Ireland in May 1601 for a debt to the Dublin merchant, Philip Conran, owed by his former master, Norris. Sherwood claimed he was now penniless, could not afford such a debt, and the viceroy and council recommended that the obligation be assumed by the executors of Norris's estate.[119]

---

116. Ibid., pp. 65–66. Carew added that Edward Gough in Waterford was more tractable, 'yet savouring of the law'; while the sovereign of Kinsale was also brought up at the inns of court. Only Youghal and Kilmallock were viewed as loyal, Carew noting the garrisons permanently in residence there.
117. Ibid., p. 20.
118. Ibid., pp. 309–10.
119. Ibid., pp. 343, 345, 427.

The lone castle chamber case which survives from Mountjoy's tenure of four years involved bribery and corruption in a judge. On 19 November 1602, the court heard an unusual case in which Patrick Sedgrave, second baron in the court of exchequer, was accused of conspiring with two others to enrich himself at the expense of the crown. An inquest jury was held before his court to inquire into the queen's right to certain lands in Donshoghlin, Co. Meath, which had belonged to John Delahide. When Delahide was attainted for treason, Richard Read pretended title to the land and Sedgrave corruptly engaged with him to obtain a parcel of the land, in return for support of his claim of title. Read then engaged with another conspirator, David Russell, to make a bond of £100 for and to the use of Sedgrave for title to the parcel in question. All three men were found by depositions in court to be guilty of bribery and corruption, upon which evidence the court of castle chamber proceeded to sentence Sedgrave to pay a fine of £1,000 to the exchequer, to be deprived of his office and jailed during pleasure.[120] The case was also encumbered by the claim of Richard Cooke, chancellor of the exchequer, who stood to gain from the lease of Donshoghlin for 21 years, paying to the crown £20 per annum. The court found that Sedgrave had offered Cooke £1,000 to forbear discovery of the deception, but in fact it appeared that the involvement of the exchequer official on behalf of the crown was both prejudicial to Sedgrave and probably a conflict of interest. Nonetheless, after the castle chamber decree, Cooke had difficulty in prosecuting his case, so the Irish council wrote to favour his suit for a fee farm of the reversion of Donshoghlin and other suits.[121]

CONCLUSION

The judicial history of Ireland during the period from the Armada to the end of Elizabeth's reign is surprising in certain respects. The council and the court of castle chamber remained intensely politicized during the Fitzwilliam era, yet they continued to function systematically until his departure in 1594, determining at least 29 suits in castle chamber alone. Thereafter, the government was run by a series of military men, though Russell and Mountjoy proved reasonably active as judges. In the intervals, Lord Chancellor Loftus, acting twice as interim lord justice, did nothing to revive castle chamber and became preoccupied in defending himself against charges that he employed the court of chancery to favour the ambitions of his large brood of children. Despite the international implications of the Nine Years War, there were practically no cases involving foreigners. And though the court of castle chamber was suspended in its operation after 1597 until the end of the reign, the council functioned in other ways to maintain a judicial presence independent of the formal operation of the prerogative court. The council received petitions, heard suitors and deliberated

---

120. TCD, MS 852, f. 81.   121. LPL, Carew MS 615, f. 506.

upon numerous cases. What is more, it began to act more frequently as a satellite branch office of the senior privy council in England, to which numerous petitions were remitted from Ireland. When Mountjoy assumed office in 1600, charges of corruption were rife against the judiciary as well as the military, and the viceroy spent much of his political capital fending off accusations that ricocheted toward him from the failed policies of his predecessors. While Mountjoy campaigned successfully on the battlefield, his lawyerly critics petitioned the crown relentlessly against the abuses of the troops and established the foundation for a constitutional opposition movement in the next reign. The election of numerous lawyers to municipal posts throughout the leading Munster towns after 1600 foreshadowed judicial conflicts under the first Stuart viceroys. The recourse to lawful processes in the expectation of redress, even during the worst military crisis of the reign, demonstrates the durability and attractiveness of the rule of law at the end of the Tudor regime.

CHAPTER EIGHT

Chichester's campaign of judicial aggression: the court of castle chamber, 1603 to 1615

> We sent for them [Dublin aldermen] againe & then bounde them to appeare in the Castell Chamber at the first sitinge thereof this terme, which by reason of the infection was adiourned to Crastino Martini, in which meane time, peceavinge no conformitie in them, we advised to send severall Mandates under the greate seale to sixteen of the best of them, ... This course we thought fittest to hold with them, that thereby we might then rayse it hier [and] draw them to that outward obedience required: or the better convince them in the Castell Chamber of many greate contemptes yf they did disobeye.
>
> Council in Ireland to English privy council, 5 December 1605[1]

MOUNTJOY RECEIVED TYRONE'S formal surrender at Mellifont on 30 March 1603, six days after the death of Elizabeth I, a fact he withheld from the earl. Within a matter of days, upon receiving the news of James I's accession to the throne, the towns in Munster used the occasion to assert their corporate liberties, challenging the authority of the troops stationed in and near them after years of oppressions and continuous friction during the Nine Years War. The city of Cork was notably truculent, refusing to accept the governance of the council of Munster and delaying the proclamation of James I as king. In this spirit of independence, they refused to provide relief for the troops in the fort of Haleboling [Hawlboline], commandeered provisions and imprisoned two local officials. The recorder, William Meade, refused to allow troops into the city and justified his actions on the basis of the uncertainties surrounding the accession, while protesting loyalty to the crown. City aldermen were suspicious of the military, led by Lord President Charles Wilmot, and did not trust Irish mercenaries, noting that Wilmot had ordered all Englishmen out of the city. Nonetheless, when Mountjoy appeared at the head of an army, the Munster towns negotiated a rapid retreat. After threatening Waterford with siege, he was given the keys of the city of Cork on 10 May 1603 when he appeared at the city gates. While the mayor, Thomas Sarsfield,

---

1. TCD, MS 672, f. 22v. Chichester and the council prepared an extensive defence of their proceedings on the 'Mandates' against the Dublin aldermen for recusancy: 'we thought fitt to censure only 9 of the cheife of them, bothe by reason of the shortnes of the time, as also that theyre correction might worke somewhat with the rest who were not yett censured.' Ibid., f. 23.

made a quick submission, the recorder who had impudently told Wilmot that he no longer had authority in Munster after the death of the queen, refused to concede. Meade was taken into custody and charged with treason, though he had become a celebrity in Cork and it was nearly impossible to find a jury that would indict him.[2]

AN UNSETTLED INHERITANCE: POST-WAR IRELAND, 1603–05

Though Mountjoy left Ireland for the last time in May 1603, the Irish council continued his policies, keeping Meade in prison in Dublin Castle after he was indicted at a special sessions in Youghal. In December, Meade put himself upon the country, using 35 peremptory challenges against any potential jurors who were of English birth. The chief justice of common pleas, Sir Nicholas Walshe, was unable to prevail upon jurors to conclude a verdict of treason and the commission ended unsuccessfully.[3] More than a year after the events at Cork, the court of castle chamber proceeded to indict the jury for falsely acquitting Meade in his trial for treason. Citing precedents in the castle chamber court wherein juries were punished by fine for an *ignoramus* and for false verdicts, they laid out the six charges against Meade. He was held responsible for the riotous assembly at Cork, contradicting the power of the king, withholding possession of the king's fort of Skyddyes Castle, demolishing the fort of Haleboling, and contributing to the malicious killing of three Englishmen.[4] The jurors explained that they knew in their private consciences that Meade had no intent to commit treason. The court, however, 'Consydering that both his wordes and accons [actions], Wherby the intent of mans harte is Discovered, did prove and argue the Contrary', found the jurors guilty of wilful and manifest perjury. The foreman of the jury was fined 1,000 marks and the rest £500 apiece, and they were all forced to wear papers on their heads declaring their offence, both at the four courts then being held in Drogheda, and at the next general sessions in the city of Cork.[5] By this time, Meade had escaped to the continent where he campaigned for the rights of Irish Catholics and published a tract in 1611 arguing that the penal laws of 1560 had expired on the death of the late queen. The battle-hardened lord president of Munster, Sir Henry Brouncker, inaugurated a strenuous anti-recusant campaign in August 1604, which not only proclaimed the removal of all Jesuits and seminary priests, but threatened to eliminate the royal charters of nonconforming corporate towns.[6]

2. *Cal. S.P. Ire., 1603–06*, pp. 50–55; and Pawlisch, *Conquest*, pp. 103–05, 122.
3. The council in Dublin regarded his conviction as unlikely and recommended he be sent for trial into England. *Cal. S.P. Ire., 1603–06*, p. 65.
4. Ibid., p. 119. Previous trials in castle chamber were cited from 1578, 1581 and 1590, indicating the importance of the entry book and perhaps the existence of a larger archive, now lost.
5. BL, Add. MS 47,172, ff. 130–32.
6. Pawlisch, *Conquest*, pp. 104–10, 198.

On his departure for England in May 1603, the lord deputy selected as his replacement a veteran soldier, George Carey, to be lord justice. When Mountjoy became earl of Devonshire and lord lieutenant, his successor was named in turn lord deputy. But Carey made little mark on either the government or the court of castle chamber. He wrote to Cecil in the spring of 1603 to call for a new chief justice and master of the rolls, noting that neither the central courts nor the semi-annual assizes had been properly kept.[7] A year later, Carey wrote again to say that the sickness in Dublin caused the adjournment of Easter term, and announced that the midsummer term would be held in Drogheda. At that time, the court of castle chamber was prepared to hear the case of the recorder of Cork and the jurors who acquitted him, calling the clerk of the council of Munster, Sir Richard Boyle, to testify against them, *viva voce*.[8] By the time of the only notable castle chamber trial in this period, Carey had been replaced by interim lords justices while negotiations for a new chief governor were under way.

On 18 September 1603, Sir John Davies of the Middle Temple was granted the office of solicitor-general by the king, and Davies quickly became the most reliable source of information on the Irish courts. Writing to Cecil from Dublin on 1 December 1603, he remarked:

> for as soon as he had seen and observed the courts of justice (for the term did then continue), he saw so many causes depending, and such good forms of proceeding, as he was much comforted; for the people of this island (as it is observed of all northern nations), if they suffer injustice, either in deed or in their own opinion, resort presently to the sword to right themselves, being impatient of the delays that are found in the ordinary process of law; but being over assubjected, and their swords over-mastered, they appeal as willingly to the scales of justice and become the most litigious of all other.[9]

A memorial from 1604, probably penned by Davies, called for the banishment of lawyers from pleading at the bar or at the council table unless they frequented the established church, and requiring all judges, sheriffs, mayors, justices of the peace, recorders and other officials to take the oath of supremacy. The author sought the calendaring of crown records in a timely manner; demanded that departing officials be prevented from taking documents away; and called for staffing of the principal courts by three judges who would keep semi-annual circuits throughout the whole kingdom. He forecast the end of Irish customs such as the arming of servants, and called for free schools, jails and 'bridewells' in every county, along with a clerk of the peace and a *custos rotulorum*.[10] When Davies began his long

---

7. *Cal. S.P. Ire., 1603–06*, pp. 122–23.   8. Ibid., pp. 162–63.

9. Ibid., pp. 88, 111–12. Davies had arrived in Ireland on 20 November 1603. He explained laconically that the Dublin courts had lately been suspended due to sickness and famine, noting the success of Chief Baron Pelham on circuit the previous summer in Donegal.

10. Ibid., pp. 134–37.

career in Ireland, he became the tireless instrument of judicial reform. In February 1604, he explained to Cecil that the courts were not held in Dublin due to the plague, and in March called for more speedy trials and another judge in the principal courts, citing the need for the administration of justice on a routine basis as a means to prevent future rebellion.[11] He went on assize circuit in April 1604 with the chief baron and found in all seven shires 'many civil and substantial gentlemen and freeholders, who understood and dispatched their business in every way as well as justices of peace or jurors do in England'.[12]

In February 1605, Sir Arthur Chichester began a remarkably durable tenure of eleven years, during which he worked to create for the court of castle chamber a new role in government. Upon his arrival, the new viceroy was occupied with strengthening the Irish judiciary, since many posts were vacant and the elderly lord chancellor, Archbishop Adam Loftus, was very weak and decrepit. Sir John Davies pointedly recommended the next chancellor should be grounded in the policy and law of England, not grammar or Latin or moral philosophy. Davies wrote to Cecil that Chichester had been troubled with swarms of suitors on his arrival in Dublin, following which he had gone on commission to Ulster.[13] Typical of the unsettled quarrelsomeness in the early days of Chichester's regime was his first case held in the court of castle chamber on 4 February 1605. A controversy 'long dependinge in this honorable Courte' between Samuel Mollynex, marshal of the court of castle chamber, as plaintiff, and Tristram Caleston, constable of Dublin Castle, concerned the right to take custody of prisoners who were committed by the court. After reviewing the patents of office presented by the contending officials and their counsel, the assembled judges of all the central courts found the matter 'doubtfull', and proceeded to arbitration. The court determined that all peers of the realm, councillors of state, Gaelic lords, judges and barons of the central courts, justices of the peace, sheriffs, mayors, knights and deans of cathedral churches should be given in custody to the defendant in the case, the constable of Dublin Castle. All others were to be remanded to the custody of the marshal, Samuel Mollynex, who thereby lost most of the potential revenue of his office since his residual right to fines and the maintenance of wealthy prisoners were thereby alienated to his rival.[14]

---

11. Ibid., pp. 142, 154.
12. Ibid., p. 158. Davies admired the English gentry then governing locally in Leix and Offaly, but excepted Co. Carlow for the unrest between O'Byrnes and Kavanaghs who scorned English governance. Ibid., p. 159.
13. Ibid., p. 261, McCavitt, *Chichester*, p. 115.
14. BL, Add. MS 47,172, f. 133. The entry book did not reveal the reasoning of the court, and the order reserved the rights of the marshal of the four courts, as well as the privilege of the court itself, to remand prisoners to any official of its choosing.

RECUSANCY, REPRISAL AND REACTION, 1605–15

The touchstone of Chichester's Irish policy was a crusade against recusancy, one which aggressively outpaced the studied moderation which James I clearly preferred. Writing to the new viceroy when he was appointed on 16 October 1604, James urged Chichester to consult crown policy on matters of true religion and justice, with the caveat, 'and yet in all these things to proceed with that moderation that may stand with the safety of that kingdom.'[15] Acting upon the authority of a royal proclamation, in which James I explicitly disavowed any intent to change the religion of Ireland or to tolerate Catholic practices, Chichester began a strategy of official harassment against leading recusants in Dublin. This had, in fact, been prefigured by Davies prior to his arrival. Writing to Cecil on 8 December 1604, he discussed the refusal of the mayor of Dublin to take the oath of supremacy. Owing to the plague then raging in Dublin, the mayor took the oath before his predecessor and aldermen, in the absence of English officials from the exchequer. Thereafter, he refused to take the oath before the chancellor and chief baron, delaying his decision until he could consult with a priest named Dr Chaloner, so he was dismissed and replaced by another mayor who duly took the oath.[16] A proclamation was authorized at a meeting of the lord deputy and council at Howth on 16 October 1605, which required all subjects to repair to parish churches and hear divine service on the authority of the Elizabethan statute of uniformity, which they now ordered to be published verbatim.[17] Although this proclamation was reissued in Dublin on 24 October 1605 by the Irish council, some variance from the wording of the original text led to a second proclamation issued under the great seal on 16 and 17 November. This policy, dubbed the 'Mandates campaign', was inaugurated by Davies, who issued mandates to leading aldermen on 13 November.[18] By the middle of November, the viceroy had lost patience with the temerity of the Dublin aldermen, and a conciliar decree explicitly laid down that the citizens must attend Christ Church cathedral in Dublin along with the mayor, and there present themselves to the lord deputy and council on the next Sunday. Following their expected refusal, the council made numerous exhortations to them, including the offer of a disputation with learned divines on the subject of their disobedience, all of which were refused with the same deliberate phrasing, that their consciences would not allow it.[19]

15. *Cal. S.P. Ire.,1603–06*, p. 206. See McCavitt, *Chichester*, p. 111, who argues James made a stronger case for the advancement of Protestantism. Plate 9.

16. *Cal. S.P. Ire., 1603–06*, p. 212.

17. BL, Carte MS 61, f. 211. Despite the ecclesiastical import of the proclamation, the only bishop in attendance was Thomas Jones, bishop of Meath. The others were Chichester, St Leger, Walsh, Fenton, Lambert and Ley. Pawlisch views these Mandates as part of a larger strategy which commenced in Munster with the full support of the English privy council. Pawlisch, *Conquest*, p. 110.

18. Steele, *Tudor and Stuart proclamations*, ii, 17 (no. 183). See also Pawlisch, *Conquest*, p. 47.

19. BL, Add. MS 47,172, ff. 137–40; McCavitt, *Chichester*, pp. 116–17.

The chosen instrument of the new Protestantizing campaign was the court of castle chamber. On 22 November, Chichester brought the nine accused recusants before the castle chamber for failing to attend the service at Christ Church cathedral, citing both statutory law and the royal prerogative as his authority. The entry book first published the entire proclamation, denying liberty of conscience or toleration of religion and commanding all loyal subjects to attend divine service in their parish churches every Sunday according to the liturgy mandated by the late Queen Elizabeth. The court fined six of the aldermen £100 and deprived them of office. The judges fined an additional three citizens £50 and expelled from the country one Phillip Basset, being of English birth and a 'principal perswader' of the others to recusancy.[20] The court claimed that three aldermen and one sheriff began to conform and attended divine service, but the nobles and gentlemen of the Pale organized an opposition which soon became widely supported. A petition was drafted by some elder statesmen and presented by younger sons, including Sir James Dillon, eldest son of Sir Lucas, the compliant chief baron of the exchequer.[21] On 27 November 1605, a similar case was heard at castle chamber, resulting in the fine, imprisonment and deprivation of four more leading Dublin aldermen for refusing to attend divine service.[22] Dr Colm Lennon has shown that Elizabethan policy, in contrast, favoured religious peace, and very few of the Dublin aldermen were harassed for their non-attendance at Protestant service prior to 1603. The coercive policies of Chichester were viewed at the time as part of an orchestrated crown attempt to gain greater control of the political and economic liberties of the Dublin corporation. Throughout the campaign, the Dublin recusants maintained their confidence in lawful opposition.[23]

Sir John Davies's speech to the court of castle chamber in 1605 provides an unusual glimpse of the court in action. Davies argued

> that the cause should bee handled with a little more sollemnity bycause both the assembly of people & the emportation of the business was exceeding great, & being desirous withall to Justifie the proceeding itself by cause Exception had been taken against it.[24]

Claiming that his oration would be

> a defence of his maties roiall prerogative & of our proceeding in this cause, rather then an accusation of these persons to their contempt & disobe-

---

20. BL, Add. MS 47,172, ff. 137–40. At this meeting, the judges were in the minority (4 to 9 councillors); Thomas Jones (the new lord chancellor), James Ley (chief justice), Edmund Pelham (chief baron) and Anthony St Leger (master of the rolls). Chichester, Richard Wingfield (marshal of the army), Henry Harrington and Garret Moore represented the military contingent, and Secretary Fenton, then at least 65 years in age, balanced the rest.

21. TCD, MS 672, ff. 23v–24; *Cal. S.P. Ire., 1603–06*, p. 362.

22. BL, Add. MS 47,172, f. 141.   23. Lennon, *Lords of Dublin*, pp. 170–71.

24. Bodl., Carte MS 61, f. 148.

dience, ... albeit for the most part it bee needlesse or rather unfitt in Reason of state, for an absolute prince to make apologies or render reasons to his subjects of such extraordinary comandmentes as he shalbe pleased to publish upon occasion for the better government of his people (for though the Right prerogative, in poynt of interest, may many tymes fall to argument & disputation, as in particular of wardships & escheates and the like, the prerogative roiall, in poynt of government, is so high & transcendent as it may not be called in question & debated by subjects), yet in this caus wee do assure ourselves that it stands with his maties pleaure that all his subjectes should be satisfied that his proclamations & roiall mandates whereby you ar comanded to come to church ar grounded uppon good Reason, uppon good examples & especially uppon the good & ancient lawes under which we ar all borne.[25]

Davies cited precedents from Edward I, Edward III, Richard II, Henry IV, and all the Tudor sovereigns to demonstrate his case: 'So as it is evident by all our books & Records that or ancient lawes do give unto or king only the supreme power & Jurisdiction in matters Ecclesiasticall.'[26] Later, Davies wrote confidently to Cecil that the gentlemen of the Pale were loathe to risk their good estates and lands in a protracted conflict, but, if they held out, that 'the Court of Star Chamber, if the power and jurisdiction of it should be maintained and used as it was begun, would prove the best school to teach the people obedience that ever was erected in that kingdom'.[27]

The battle over the Mandates was soon joined. Sir Patrick Barnewall, a respected and talented lawyer and scion of an important family of Old English officials, led the recusant opposition which quickly formed in the aftermath of the castle chamber decision. Barnewall had been previously engaged as agent for the Pale during Mountjoy's administration, when he was sent to London along with Lord Howth, to complain against the extortions of soldiers.[28] The first manifestation of opposition to the Mandates was a petition signed by most of the Catholic nobles and gentry of the Pale and sent to Chichester in November 1605. This petition stressed the constitutional illegitimacy of using castle chamber as a 'spiritual consistory', which was against both law and precedent according to the weight of legal opinion in Dublin, while proclaiming the steadfast allegiance of the nobility and inhabitants of the English Pale who now suffered undeserved imputations of disloyalty. Prominent among the signatories were Lords Gormanston, Delvin and Trimleston, as well as Barnewall and the two lawyers from the campaign against cess under Sydney, Henry Burnell and Richard

25. Ibid, f.148v.
26. Ibid., ff. 151–51v.. He continued, noting that common law affirmed statutory law on the subject, going back to the Norman Conquest of England. See Pawlisch, *Conquest*, pp. 112–15.
27. *Cal. S.P. Ire., 1603–06*, p. 371.
28. *Cal. S.P. Ire., 1600*, pp. 513–19, 236, 326. Barnewall quarrelled with Sir William Warren over a wardship for which he offered £350 in the same year, and the cause was referred to a commission from the Irish council. Ibid., pp. 73–74, 430.

Netterville, both now septuagenarians.[29] On 8 December 1605, Lord Gormanston and other nobles wrote to Cecil, to protest at their imprisonment and fine in castle chamber, noting the violence done to their property in execution of the fines.[30] Barnewall wrote to Salisbury from prison on 16 December, claiming he revised the original petition to Chichester to avoid giving offence, yet now found his property damaged by ruthless serjeants-at-arms. He expressed concern that the arbitrariness of Chief Justice James Ley, who withheld from men impleaded in his court of king's bench a copy of their indictments, would lead to the scandal of injustice and lay the foundations of some future rebellion.[31]

In response to the vigorous opposition of the Pale, which they may well have anticipated, the lord deputy and Irish council wrote to the privy council in England on 5 December to justify their proceedings in castle chamber. Claiming that all fines were devoted to the repair of churches and the relief of poor scholars in college, the beleaguered council described their adversaries as 'busy-bodies' who were now contriving to send an agent to London.[32] Chichester followed up with a private letter to Salisbury two days later, in which he again defended his actions and proposed to extend the campaign throughout the countryside, sending letters to the provincial presidents and claiming, bravely,

> which notwithstanding, if his government be countenanced and supported in its endeavours, these heats will soon be qualified, and the kingdom, in this point, much reformed; which is the mark they shoot at, no way dreading this opposition or practice, so long as they have means to hold and draw this poor remnant of an army together.[33]

Sir John Davies added his voice to the pious disclaimers, telling Cecil that the court of castle chamber had done good work according to both law and precedent, excusing the resort to a prerogative court as warrantable by the common laws of Ireland.[34]

29. *Cal. S.P. Ire., 1603–06*, pp. 362, 365. With over 60 signatories and names like Luttrell, Stanyhurst, Plunkett, Russell and Fitzwilliam, this petition was plainly a defiance by the majority of loyal Old English families who had traditionally found a place in the Dublin administration under Elizabeth. The petition was received in England on 19 December 1605. A later petition to Cecil in London expressed outrage at the severity of penalties for not going to church, as if it had been for outrageous contempt or dangerous riot. See also Lennon, *Lords of Dublin*, p. 182.
30. *Cal. S.P. Ire., 1603–06*, p. 365. Lords Trimleston, Howth and Killeen joined Gormanston in the petition, a copy of which was sent also to the earl of Devonshire.
31. Ibid., pp. 373–74.
32. TCD, MS 672, f. 24; *Cal. S.P. Ire., 1603–06*, pp. 355–58.
33. *Cal. S.P. Ire., 1603–06*, p. 360. On 9 December he wrote again to explain that he had examined the petitioners separately and found that the originators of the plot were Barnewall, Netterville and Burnell who had met with Lord Gormanston at the lodgings of Lord Louth. Ibid., p. 367.
34. Ibid., p. 370. Davies famously added his judgement that the Pale gentry lacked the will to fight, feared for their lands, and had no 'man of spirit or greatness among them'. Ibid., p. 371.

At an early stage in the campaign it became clear that the sanctimonious intensity of the Irish lord deputy and solicitor-general on these matters was not shared by the leading councillors in England. The privy council wrote to Chichester on 24 January 1606 to express their concern. Considering how lately the Irish people nearly lapsed into general revolt, and how apt they might be to follow this road again, the English councillors cautioned:

> and when they observe that a main alteration in religon is not suddenly to be obtained by forcing against the current, but gaining by little and little, as opportunity may be taken, they are moved to bethink themselves how it may best be effected. To grant any toleration of that superstitous and seditious religion were greatly offensive to any meaning of His Majesty, were dangerous to the State and repugnant to good conscience. On the other side, to enter directly on a compulsory course, while the multitude swayeth on the contrary part, might more weaken the cause by taking the foil (if it should not thoroughly prevail) than bring present advantage. They advise a temperate course between both extremes, neither yielding any hope of toleration of their superstition, nor startling the multitude by any general or rigorous compulsion ... Admonition, persuasion, and instruction should be first tried before severity of law and justice be used.[35]

Despite the evident circumspection in these instructions, however, Chichester's Protestantizing campaign moved forward aggressively. During the next winter term, the court of castle chamber on 26 January 1606 found two more aldermen and a Dublin merchant guilty of violating the proclamation against recusancy.[36] And on 7 February 1606, the court acted swiftly to void deeds which were made out to the donees of five recusants who were attempting to avoid payment of their fines. They were accused of a conspiracy to

> make and forge fraudulent and false deeds with oute Dates of all there severall goods and Chattells, real and personall, quicke and Deade, above grounde and under grounde, unto the said severall Donees, therby to Defeate and overthrowe his maties right and intreste of Severall fynes ymposed uppon the said Severall Donors in his Maties high Courte of Castell Chamber.[37]

The court debated the matter an entire day, concluding that the deeds were fraudulent and voiding them, an action which went well beyond the customary jurisdiction of the prerogative tribunal to demand enforcement of its original decree. In the opinion of Davies, 'The Star Chamber would prove a good school-

---

35. Ibid., pp. 389–90. The privy councillors further urged the release of all the lords and gentlemen of the Pale, except for Barnewall who was bound for London as their agent.

36. BL, Add. MS 47,172, f. 141.   37. Ibid., f. 143.

house to teach that people obedience, if the authortity of that Court were upholden and used as it had been of late; and for the public justice in other courts, it began to have a good formal course.'[38] To place the predicament of Chichester in perspective, it should be noted that his attempt to require Sir John Everard, second justice of king's bench, to conform was met with strong resistance, and he was forced to retain the recusant judge for lack of a suitable replacement in February 1606.[39] The court heard another case against three Dublin aldermen on 16 May 1606, fining them as before.[40] Finally, in a case heard on 2 July 1606, two Dublin bakers were found in violation of the new ecclesiastical policy.[41] No further actions against recusants occurred in 1606 at castle chamber. The reason for the suspension of the policy in the summer of 1606 was to allow the crown's legal experts to review judicial precedents for the mandates. Nonetheless, the assize judges, led by the irrepressible Davies, continued to badger nonconformists throughout the realm. On 12 November 1606, Davies wrote to England that a session at New Ross, Co. Wexford, was held to examine an outrage when some 200 recusants came to the church two or three times each year 'to make a superstitious offering at the place where the high altar [formerly] stood', disturbing the minister during his sermon and interrupting the celebration of the communion. Davies was encouraged that over 300 civil petitions or bills were presented to the court, many native Irish being plaintiffs, but he noted they had to threaten the grand jury of Wexford with penalties in star chamber before they would present recusants for their outrage in the church. He intended to present the sovereign of New Ross for trial in castle chamber next term, and, in passing, noted that one prisoner was condemned to be executed for burning the Protestant vicar's house, though it was out of malice for his person rather than hatred of his religion.[42]

Although Patrick Barnewall was fined and imprisoned for his role in the opposition to the mandates, he remained confident of his position. A concerted effort to provide resources for his expected trip to London outraged Chichester. Archbishop of Dublin and lord chancellor, Thomas Jones, wrote in March 1606 to defend Chief Justice Ley against the calumnies of Barnewall, saying the latter had been examined before the lord deputy and council on charges that he had scandalized the court of chancery, though in the end his meaning was to accuse the court of castle chamber of tyranny.[43] On 7 March, the viceroy wrote in similar vein to explain that Barnewall had challenged the castle chamber's right to hear the case, claiming that a statutory enforcement of the proclamation was sufficient and that adjudicating the violation before the castle chamber was against the law.

38. Ibid., ff. 143–43v. A prior trial by jury of the fraudulent deeds was reported by Davies, who justified the subsequent pleading in castle chamber because the jurors had exonerated the donors. *Cal. S.P. Ire., 1603–06*, p. 401. The court suspended sentence against all the defendants, donors and donees, until the next term, and released all but two of them.

39. *Cal. S.P. Ire.,1603–06*, pp. 400–01; Ball, *Judges in Ireland*, i, 227. Chichester had knighted Everard in 1605 and employed him in assize circuits until he resigned voluntarily in 1607.

40. BL, Add. MS 47,172, f. 144.   41. Ibid., f. 145.

42. *Cal. S.P. Ire., 1606–08*, p. 15.   43. *Cal. S.P. Ire., 1603–06*, p. 411.

Chichester defended his proceedings against the accusation of tyrannical and illegal usurpations, saying he would soon enlarge Barnewall from confinement to allow him to make his journey to England. After proceedings in the previous term against Richard Netterville, Henry Burnell and Edward Nugent in castle chamber, the viceroy ordered them to enter new recognizances in order to be released from prison, which they refused in anticipation of Barnewall's successful mission to England.[44] At another meeting on 7 March 1606, Barnewall behaved brusquely toward the viceroy and lord chancellor, telling the viceroy his speech was 'without probability of lykelyhood', and calling on the chief justice to cease his carping.[45]

In late April, with Barnewall still in Ireland preparing his case, Chichester and the council wrote to England of their concerns, finding Barnewell a ringleader of opposition who dealt in a spirit of mischief, a stubborn and wilful adversary who refused to submit, and one who outraged the Irish council when he told them he would not answer their interrogatories. The seventh of these probed into the legal basis for Barnewall's challenge:

> Did all the learned in the laws in Ireland affirm that the fining of the aldermen and others in the Star Chamber was contrary to the law? What are their names that so affirmed, and to whom did they affirm the same; and when did you confer with them thereof? Were their opinions delivered before or after the sentence in the Star Chamber?[46]

Whether Barnewall genuinely represented an inchoate Old English opposition party is difficult to ascertain. However, he claimed to be acting on behalf of a clear interest group for the good of the kingdom, promising to effect a toleration of religion according to his enemies at court.[47] The consequence was that the court of castle chamber ceased its prosecutions for recusancy, Ley's court of king's bench was empty of litigants and men deferred their proceedings at law in anticipation of Barnewall's sojourn.[48]

Writing to the privy council on 29 May 1606, Chichester and the Irish council explained that they had put off their intention to renew prosecutions in castle chamber against recusants of Dublin who had been respited in the last term, partly in hope that by conferring with them they might conform. They also maligned the reputation of Barnewall who was seen to encourage the obstinacy of other recusants.[49] Plainly, the mandates campaign had been suspended while all sides awaited the outcome of the Barnewall mission to England. It is in this spirit of querulous petitioning that we must envisage the fearsome court of castle

---

44. Ibid., p. 415–16.
45. TCD, MS 672, ff. 32–32v. Here we see further examples of the ongoing pleadings before the castle chamber which went unremarked in the entry book. See also Pawlisch, *Conquest*, p. 111.
46. *Cal. S.P. Ire., 1603–06*, p. 449.
47. Ibid., p. 447.
48. Ibid., p. 451.   49. Ibid., pp. 485–86.

chamber under its ruthless viceroy, timidly retreating from the brink of political disaster while they awaited the probing inquiries sure to come from England. Not for the first time, nor the last, would an ambitious chief governor find himself confronted with constitutional defences in Ireland which undermined a programme of action for which neither institutions nor men were prepared. Though Barnewall was placed in the Tower, the privy council in England later wrote to Chichester to assure the petitioner's pending lawsuits were not prejudiced during his internment. On 3 July 1606, they wrote again to the viceroy, seeking more information on the laws and precedents used to justify the novel course taken in castle chamber against the recusants to compel them to come to church. Chichester continued to plead his case from a distance, while complaining that he had lost the confidence of the crown and council in England.[50] He did not suspend his anti-recusant policy entirely, examining the priest Shane O'Conan on 14 June before a small sub-committee of the council and questioning his loyalty.[51] No further prosecutions occurred in 1606 against the recusants, and Barnewall remained six months in the Tower. Far from a victory for the reckless viceroy, this hiatus gave the appearance of tacit withdrawal of support for his mandates campaign. The viceroy and council wrote to the privy council on 1 December 1606 to justify their proceedings, noting that people in Ireland were encouraged by Barnewall's apparent success in England.[52] On the last day of 1606, the privy council responded with a definitive pronouncement of the English judges, saying the proceedings in castle chamber were deemed to be lawful, and exonerating Chief Justice Ley from any imputation of arbitrary or improper behaviour in his court. On the other hand, the English councillors recommended Barnewall to the viceroy, saying he would now return to Ireland to offer his submission and finding him not culpable of acting as agent for the Pale community.[53]

During the Hilary term, on 4 February 1607, Chichester again returned to the mandates policy, fining two aldermen of Drogheda along with three others in the court of castle chamber according to the now familiar, even ritualized, formula in the entry book.[54] Writing to Salisbury on 20 February, the lord deputy temporized on his ecclesiastical policy, claiming he had made willing converts of many to the Protestant faith, though he had brought to trial no less than 34 men of Drogheda. Chichester avowed he had now set a temperate course with recusants, and would gladly leave management of that business to the clergy and the penal laws. In the same letter, he declared that his admonition to the lord president of Munster to

50. Ibid., p. 509.
51. TCD, MS 567, ff. 31–32. The interrogators, Ley, Lambert, Fenton and the viceroy, heard the priest confess his loyalty to both king and pope, noting he had departed Ireland some 67 years previously for colleges in France, Spain and Italy.
52. *Cal. S.P. Ire., 1606–08*, p. 41; McCavitt, *Chichester*, pp. 120–22; S.R. Gardiner, 'James I and the recusants', *N&Q, 2nd series*, vol. 10 (1860), pp. 80–85.
53. *Cal. S.P. Ire., 1606–08*, p. 49–50.
54. BL, Add. MS 47,172, f. 146. In the spring of 1607 Chichester travelled to Drogheda where some 200 persons were compelled to attend Protestant services. McCavitt, *Chichester*, p. 123.

proceed cautiously with the recusants had fallen on deaf ears, and seemed to agree with the notorious Brouncker that the multitude would go to Protestant services only if they perceived force might be used against them.[55] On 29 April 1607, the court of castle chamber fined two men of Dublin, including the son of Lord Howth, for recusancy, ending the enforcement of the mandates campaign in castle chamber for that year. Meanwhile, the redoubtable Sir Patrick Barnewall had returned to Dublin. A priest in Waterford admitted that the entire city had taken up money to support the charges of Barnewall's mission to London and he was regarded as a hero to many, and an affront to the lord deputy.[56] Chichester wrote to Salisbury that Barnewall came to him within five days of his return, but refused to submit to the chief governor, impudently claiming he would seek justice only from England. When Chichester charged him with bringing too many men in his retinue in a threatening manner, the lord of Turvey responded that he always brought six servants into Dublin, and complained directly to Salisbury in a letter of 19 May 1607.[57]

In his fine treatment of the Chichester regime in Ireland, John McCavitt has claimed that the viceroy's strategy 'was to use prerogative powers to underpin a campaign of "coercion", while simultaneously embarking on a programme of "persuasive" measures to ensure that conformity was followed by genuine conversion'.[58] Aiming to anglicize the country by first imposing religious uniformity, Chichester relied upon his own long soldierly experience in Ireland during the rebellion and showed a comprehensive distrust of Catholic spokesmen, regardless of their protestations of loyalty.[59] On the other hand, he began an inquisition into church property through which to finance the appointments of new ministers; proposed the establishment of schools and the printing of religious texts in Gaelic; and commenced to rectify clerical abuses in Armagh and unsettled areas of the north of Ireland.[60] Despite heated opposition, Chichester was apparently prepared to take the risk of open rebellion 'by indulging in a perilous game of brinksmanship in order to break recusant recalcitrance once and for all'.[61] After eight months of strenuous resistance, the lord deputy was prompted by the English privy council to reduce their fines and release the imprisoned officials on recognizance by 19 July 1606.[62] The coherent framework and lawyerly caution of

---

55. *Cal. S.P. Ire., 1606–08*, pp. 112–13; McCavitt, *Chichester*, pp. 120–24.

56. *Cal. S.P. Ire., 1606–08*, p. 117. The town of Waterford paid £32 to support his cause there.

57. Ibid., p. 149. Chichester allowed him to remain close prisoner in his own house after 28 March. Ibid. An informant claiming to know of communications between the earl of Tyrone and Barnewall in 1608 at Louvain was dismissed as not credible, though he claimed that the obstreperous lawyer stood ready to lead a conspiracy to bring munitions to Ireland on behalf of foreign princes to defend Tyrone. Ibid., p. 420.

58. McCavitt, *Chichester*, p. 111.   59. Ibid., p. 113.

60. Ibid., pp. 114–15; TCD, MS 672, f. 23v.

61. McCavitt, *Chichester*, p. 117. McCavitt's research demonstrated that thirteen of Dublin's twenty-four aldermen were incarcerated during this period, and some £1,145 was raised from twenty-seven recusant leaders during Michaelmas term 1606. Ibid., p. 124. Fines in castle chamber totalling £1,780 and 1,100 marks were meted out.

62. Lennon, *Lords of Dublin*, p. 180.

their defence was managed in secret by the head of the Jesuit mission in Dublin, Christopher Holywood, as well as agents of the Pale such as Barnewall. By the spring of 1607, when the policy was largely abandoned, the Dublin patriciate had survived financial duress and political intimidation to emerge with a stronger sense of the connectedness of religious principle and municipal liberties. At the end of Chichester's regime, as Lennon has well said, 'Catholicism was a rallying point for the preservation of a valued communal heritage by 1613.'[63] Yet, he added, 'Nevertheless the response of the urban leaders to the assertion of state control in political and economic as well as ecclesiastical matters was shaped within the traditional mode of constitutional and legal procedure up to 1613 and beyond.'[64]

It is difficult to sustain the argument made by Hans Pawlisch that the mandates campaign 'was designed as the necessary prelude to the mass conversion of colonial society' which enjoyed the full support of the English privy council, and which made obsolete the *de facto* toleration of Catholicism in the towns and the Pale.[65] To paraphrase James Bond, they were 'shaken, but did not stir'. On the other hand, McCavitt has demonstrated that Chichester's resolve set the stage for an accelerated ecclesiastical policy in the municipalities which, in turn, animated Old English opposition and awakened foreboding in London.[66] He concluded, 'The Mandates campaign represented a dynamic attempt to transmute radically the religious configuration of Ireland. The Reformation flag had finally been unfurled, only to be rather hastily hauled down as a result of the nervousness of the king and the London administration.'[67] Pawlisch's claim that the mandates campaign exemplified a new policy of judge-made law overstates the finality and durability of the constitutional conflict in 1605–07. Pawlisch argued that Davies, from his selective archival researches, constructed a 'coherent body of pre-Reformation legal principles derived from "popish judges" to establish the Court of Castle Chamber's jurisdiction over the mandates in 1605'.[68] Yet this defence of prerogative justice was met by the challenge of the Pale lawyers, and it became moribund when the crown denied its full support in 1607. After a suspension of five years, the clamour surrounding the reinvigoration of Chichester's anti-recusancy policy in the parliament of 1613–15 demonstrated the continuing strength of statutory principles in resistance to the assertions of prerogative law.[69]

Although crown officials declared the mandates policy was legal, it was brought to a sudden conclusion in the summer of 1607 due to the atmosphere of crisis surrounding the flight of the earls of Tyrone and Tyrconnell from Ireland. McCavitt has argued that the mandates campaign precipitated the departure of these former rebels, owing to the 'spasm of suspicion and conspiracy' attending Chichester's persecution of recusants.[70] It is important to remember that seething

63. Lennon, *Lords of Dublin*, p. 217.
64. Ibid., p. 190.
65. Pawlisch, *Conquest*, p. 120.
66. McCavitt, *Chichester*, pp. 125–28.
67. Ibid., pp. 126–27.
68. Pawlisch, *Conquest*, p. 113.
69. Ibid., pp. 46–47, 110–15. Far from being humiliated, Patrick Barnewall continued to sue for his legal rights in the aftermath of the mandates policy.
70. McCavitt, *Chichester*, p. 129.

Catholic resentment led to extensive litigation and constitutional challenges in the period, rather than violent opposition. More remarkable than Barnewall's famous warning to the crown about the inevitability of an expected rebellion was the long interval of civil peace which occurred at virtually the same time as the Thirty Years War on the continent.[71] The hardened enmity between Barnewall and the viceroy punctuated regular correspondence throughout the spring of 1607 after Barnewall's return to Ireland, until the crises surrounding the flight of Tyrone from Ulster overshadowed the intramural divisions within the Pale.[72] Despite the atmosphere of confrontation, however, two Dublin aldermen in April 1607 obtained the permission of the municipality to petition castle chamber for a portion of the fines paid by citizens of the city according to terms of the ancient charters.[73] The role of the court of castle chamber at the centre of a storm of controversy is instructive. Although several final decrees were ordered, many hearings were quasi-legal attempts to bully the opposition, to censure agents of the Pale for violating proclamations and to enforce mutable conciliar policy rather than the set body of prerogative law. The court's reputation for tyranny is thus based more on its inquisitorial extra-legal use of interrogatories, for instance, than on routine adjudication. In the absence of a court of high commission, ecclesiastical policy devolved to the court under Chichester and, to a degree, his immediate successors. It is difficult to avoid the conclusion that Sir Arthur Chichester crafted a new policy of brutal intimidation which did serious harm to the image of royal government and facilitated the gradual triumph of the Catholic Counter-Reformation in Ireland. There is a risk, however, in seeing these positions at the early stages of James's reign as having become crystallized and entrenched. Of the 57 cases determined in the entry book of the court of castle chamber during Chichester's long tenure in office, some 22 involved litigation against recusants, less than 40 per cent of the total.[74]

Although, in McCavitt's view, the lord deputy moderated the policy of full-scale evangelization after the London authorities withdrew support in 1607, Chichester presided over a remarkable recusancy case in June 1608 – one we have already encountered – in which the court was used as a bludgeon to outrage loyal Catholics. The vicar of Balrothery, Co. Dublin, Thomas Meredith, brought a case against James Barnewell and others over incidents occuring at the funeral of Barnewell's mother, it being alleged against them that they had behaved in a 'superstitious and idolatrous fashion' after attending divine service. The vicar apparently sought to intervene, after which a riot ensued in which he was assaulted so 'that his nose and mouth gushed Forth with Bloud', the Book of Common Prayer was trod underfoot, and his pregnant wife was thrown to the

---

71. Ibid., pp. 129–48. Despite the ferocity of legal battles and heated opposition in parliaments, Ireland was at peace from 1603 until 1641. The Thirty Years War convulsed the rest of Europe from 1618 until 1648.

72. *Cal. S.P. Ire., 1606–08*, pp. 41–43, 49, 129, 149.

73. *Anc. rec. Dublin*, ii, 472–73.   74. BL, Add. MS 47,172, ff. 133–211.

ground. Barnewell was fined and imprisoned by the court, and the record betrays no concern for the grieving son which would mitigate the £100 penalty.[75] On 29 May 1611, the court imprisoned and pilloried Symon Paulee for publishing in the Dublin shop of John Franckton, printer, the seditious rumour that the king had proclaimed a toleration of religion in England.[76] For the most part, however, Chichester tempered his campaign against the recusants after 1607, at least in castle chamber prosecutions. He aggressively pursued his goal of erecting Protestant plantations in Ulster and elsewhere, warily deferring for four years the time when he might return to the judicial intimidation of native Catholics.[77] The privy council wrote to Chichester on 20 August 1611 to caution him against extremism in the matter of the oath of supremacy, requiring that judicial officers swear only an oath of supremacy and not the more rigorous oath of allegiance. Citing the kings prudence, they explained,

> But for the oath of allegiance, his will is that it be suspended, first, because in matter of oath thereof ought to be greater caution; secondly, because His Majesty may receive dishonour when it is pressed and declined, and it may be doubted if it can be legally punished.[78]

From 1612 to 1615 Chichester's court of castle chamber once again systematically challenged the liberties of the provincial towns, convicting jurors in many Irish counties for refusing to indict recusants at the assizes. Together with the prosecution of Catholics who harboured or gave sanctuary to 'popish priests', the work of the court was largely taken up with penalizing the majority population for their religious practices. Following a predictable pattern and ritualizing the documentation of each case in the entry book, the court after 1612 returned to the punitive measures which characterized the first mandates campaign and eagerly went beyond them. A judicial model was fashioned wherein Protestant clergy formally presented to the general sessions in the tholsell of Dublin the names of recusants who refused to attend divine service. In the first case heard in castle chamber on 8 May 1612, six Dublin merchants were accused of refusing to join their fellow jurors in presenting recusants before the mayor, recorder and sheriff of the city. Upon separate examination of each juror in the court of castle chamber, they all refused to make true presentment of the accused recusants, for which they were each fined 100 marks English and imprisoned during pleasure.[79] Returning to the issue in Michaelmas term, the court heard three such cases on

---

75. Ibid., f. 151.

76. Ibid., f. 171. Paulee claimed to have seen letters patent to this effect in Yorkshire, in which certain sums of money could be paid to obtain toleration. For this he was whipped from the Castle Bridge to the Newgate and had both ears nailed to the pillory.

77. McCavitt, *Chichester*, pp. 169–73.

78. *Cal. S.P. Ire., 1611–14*, p. 96. The viceroy was urged to 'temper the execution with moderation', noting 'instruction should precede constraint'.

79. BL, Add. MS 47,172, f. 186.

25 November 1612. In the first, fifteen jurors from Mullingar in Co. West Meath were each fined 100 marks or more for refusing to present recusants who were accused of refusing to attend Protestant service. In the second case, another fourteen jurors from Cashel, in Cross Tipperary [the ecclesiastical jurisdiction of the ancient division of Tipperary], were found to have ignored the evidence of the local curate regarding non-attendance at church, and were fined between £30 and £40 English. Finally, another four jurors at Trim in Co. Meath were fined £20 for the same offence. In the latter instance, the curate was known to have identified over 100 persons as recusants, and the court duly noted that eleven of the original jurors agreed to make presentment after a conference with the assize judges.[80] By the end of the year 1612, it was clear that Chichester was prepared for another onslaught against religious pluralism.

This ironhanded policy had the effect of polarizing the religious communities in early Stuart Ireland, and it should be seen against the background of preparations for the hotly contested parliament of 1613–15. At the end of 1612, an outraged populace was horrified by the executions of two leading Catholic clergymen, one being Bishop O'Devany, the octogenarian head of the diocese of Down and Connor. The Pale gentry protested to the crown and raised the spectre of an orchestrated opposition prior to the next year's parliament. Chichester responded with the creation of forty Protestant boroughs from newly settled towns, largely in Ulster, with which to pack the house of commons. The expectation of drastic new penal laws formed the heated atmosphere in which the court of castle chamber went about its work in 1613.[81] On 10 February 1613, the council in Ireland wrote to justify its efforts in imposing the oath of supremacy in provincial towns, pursuant to the crown's letters of the previous September. Letters were sent to all the corporate towns in Michaelmas term 1612 to inform them of the requirement to make choice of none but persons conformable in religion, but the council now reported 'gross disobedience' of the law in Wexford, Limerick and Cork and other towns where there were no magistrates willing to take the oath. Detailing numerous evasions and supposing these refusals to be part of a priest-led conspiracy, the council detained a group of recusant officials in Dublin, while they awaited further instructions.[82] On 7 May, the court heard two more cases of fifteen jurors who refused to present recusants in Clonmel, Co. Tipperary.[83] One week later, the castle chamber court convicted four men who refused to join their fellow jurors in condemning robbers in Cork, citing reasons of conscience.[84] It was not, therefore, surprising that the opening of parliament

80. Ibid., ff. 191, 192, 193.   81. McCavitt, *Chichester*, pp. 175–82.
82. TCD, MS 746, ff. 36–36v.
83. BL, Add. MS 47,172, ff. 195, 196. Edwards's view that the Butler territories had been singled out for special treatment may exaggerate the handling of these cases, in view of the more comprehensive nature of Chichester's persecution. He argues that the campaign's effect was to polarize the two sectarian communities, strain the loyalty of the Old English and prepare the way for civil war in Kilkenny. Edwards, 'Poisoned chalice', pp. 65–67.
84. BL, Add. MS 47, 172, f. 197. McCavitt viewed this resumption of harassment in terms of a new

was the scene of constitutional jousting in which the gravity of the occasion was mocked by rivals who wrestled for the right to occupy the speaker's chair, symbolizing neutral and dispassionate sensibility. Sir John Everard, the recusant judge who had retired in 1607 from king's bench, was seated as the Catholic claimant while the Protestant majority were taking a division of the house. Returning from the adjacent corridor, the government forces seized upon the notoriously over-weight attorney general, Sir John Davies, and placed him in the lap of the respected former judge. The ensuing tussle was reported in the gravest tones by partisans of both sides, and the parliament was interrupted by a boycott of recusant members, some of whom later travelled to England to contend against the viceroy in the king's presence.[85]

On 17 May 1613, the viceroy received a petition of the recusant lords of Ireland in protest at their exclusion from the council which proposed legislation, claiming that a grand council was needed to transmit bills to the king. This was signed by ten of Chichester's leading opponents from the mandates campaign, including Viscount Gormanston and Lord Louth.[86] On 26 May, Sir Robert Jacob wrote to England that the Irish lawyers did more harm than the priests all combined in opposing the crown's work, electing burgesses and knights to the parliament from the city of Dublin who were 'seditious schismatiques'.[87] Although the petitioners fully intended to place their claims before the king himself in England, Chichester addressed their complaints on 15 June 1613 in a systematic defence of prerogative justice. The first allegation, that causes between party and party were properly determinable only in the ordinary courts of law and not at the council table, challenged the amplitude and flexibility of conciliar justice. The viceroy confidently explained that

> Some petitions are preferred at Council table, which are fitter for other courts, but their nature does not appear till the same are read at the board, and then they are commonly dismissed to the proper court, unless the petitioners are very poor, or mere Irish dwelling in remote parts, or if the petitions are exhibited during vacation time, when the courts of law are not open.[88]

The second complaint dealt with the intimidation of juries, it being maintained that in criminal trials the jurors were often threatened by king's counsel with

---

severity, explaining that Chichester had troops on standby to contend with opposition. He concluded, 'His conduct in Castle Chamber, it is worth stressing, was entirely consistent with his high-risk strategy of grasping the nettle of recusancy, something which his superiors in London were not prepared to endorse and would have been horrified to learn that he had been practising.' McCavitt, *Chichester*, p. 183.

85. McCavitt, *Chichester*, pp. 183–84; TCD, MS 746, f. 47v.
86. *Cal. S.P. Ire., 1611–14*, p. 342.
87. Ibid., p. 350. Jacob reported that the corrupt sheriffs of Dublin were bound over to castle chamber for their part in the disputed election and committed to prison for five days.
88. Ibid., p. 373. See also Bodl., Carte MS 61, f. 66.

punishment in the court of castle chamber so that jurors might convict an innocent man, sometimes accused out of malice, since they feared imprisonment, loss of their ears and goods. The lord deputy answered that recusant jurors were misled by their priests, and seldom found against their neighbours in criminal trials despite the weight of the evidence, so they had been censured in the star chamber court. In addition, there was the case where jurors refused to find for the king when an inquest showed the crown's right to an estate: here, for returning a presentment of *ignoramus* after the king's counsel advised them to reconsider the evidence, they rightly faced contempt charges in the court of castle chamber, though that court was not generally the proper venue for hearings in real property cases. Citing the opinion of the chief baron that jurors should always find according to their evidence unless they could show precise knowledge to the contrary, Chichester held fast to his view that the star chamber court was the proper instrument to impose uniform judicial rectitude on truculent jurors in such cases.[89] The third complaint alleged that assize judges had bound over to the castle chamber court jurors who refused to present notorious recusants, on the testimony of their ministers, and that the jurors on trial were allowed no representation or counsel. Chichester defended the policy, which he had inaugurated, claiming that jurors now agreed to present accused recusants and denying the practice had caused many to refuse to serve on juries.[90] The thrust of the petition dealt with legal contrivances that were burdensome and offensive to the Catholic community, particularly those which threatened their rights to land. But the tenth 'disorder' challenged again the exclusion of recusant lawyers practising in the courts, depriving the crown of native expertise and judgement as well as those learned in the Irish language who could understand the testimony of witnesses speaking only in Irish. Chichester's retort explained that three loyal Irish judges currently held office in the central courts and others who conformed would be welcome there, yet not so indifferent as the justices who came out of England. He averred that all Catholic lawyers were permitted to plead and provide legal advice, and all gentlemen of ability were made justices of the peace.[91]

---

89. *Cal. S.P. Ire., 1611–14*, p. 374. A finding of '*ignoramus*' by a grand jury occurs when they refuse effectively to confirm an indictment.

90. Ibid. Restoration England witnessed the abandonment of the practice of punishing jurors who did not return a verdict desired by the government.

91. *Cal. S.P. Ire., 1611–14*, p. 377. Disorder 15 protested against the giving of licences for aqua vitae and for tanning leather to only a few, even though others could make it with profit, so the monopoly hurt people without helping the king. Chichester replied: 'Making aqua vitae is restrained, because it wastes corn, breeds drunkenness, and enrages the minds of the people, and therefore it is hurtful to the commonwealth, and a trade not fit to be so generally used as they would have it.' Ibid., p. 378. Of the nineteen disorders in the complaint, most condemned Chichester's misgovernment in the handling of wardships, liveries, custodiams, process from exchequer, taking excessive fees, fining of jurors, and escheated lands. The eighteenth disorder alleged that the fines of 12*d.* for refusing to attend divine service were not used for the relief of the poor, as promised. Chichester responded that the actual fines levied amounted to only £15 during the past year in Dublin alone since 'most of them preferred to come to church than pay the fine'. Ibid., p. 380.

PLATES

1. Counties in Ireland in 1613. Based on Map of Ireland, counties 1542–1613 in *A new history of Ireland*, vol. ix (Oxford University Press, 1984), p. 41.

The counties of Ireland were 'largely stabilized' by 1613 according to K.W. Nicholls, who made the original map (from which this is derived) for volume IX of the *New history of Ireland*. However, the cartographical evidence of conventional English shires belied the conditions under which they were governed. The five counties nearest the Pale in Dublin were settled well before the end of the sixteenth century, despite the raids of Irish septs from the Wicklow mountains. Medieval counties such as Cork, Wexford, Limerick and Waterford, together with midland counties planted in the mid-Tudor period (King's and Queen's), plus Carlow, Kilkenny, and Tipperary were well-established though subject to the domination of regional powers like the earl of Ormonde. In the far west, much of Galway was a relatively stable bastion of Old English influence, though the erection of counties Mayo, Sligo, Roscommon and Clare in 1570 was only gradually attended by the expansion of English administration until the early seventeenth century. The distant county of Donegal did not come under English governance until after the flight of the earls in 1607, despite the shiring of Donegal in 1585. Similarly, the shiring of other Ulster counties in 1570 (Armagh, Down, Antrim, Longford) and 1583–91 (Leitrim, Cavan, Monaghan, Fermanagh, Tyrone) did little to establish effective English control at that time. After the plantation of Ulster in 1609, and the final addition of Londonderry in 1613, the counties of Ireland were served by sheriffs and assize courts on a regular rotation, though Catholic officeholders would be intimidated by several administrations until the Graces of 1628. Ephemeral counties like Ferns and Desmond, created in the late sixteenth century, lapsed quickly into more traditional entities (Wicklow and Kerry), while the county of Cross Tipperary merged with its secular neighbour in 1621. The principal towns are identified as points of reference for the narrative.

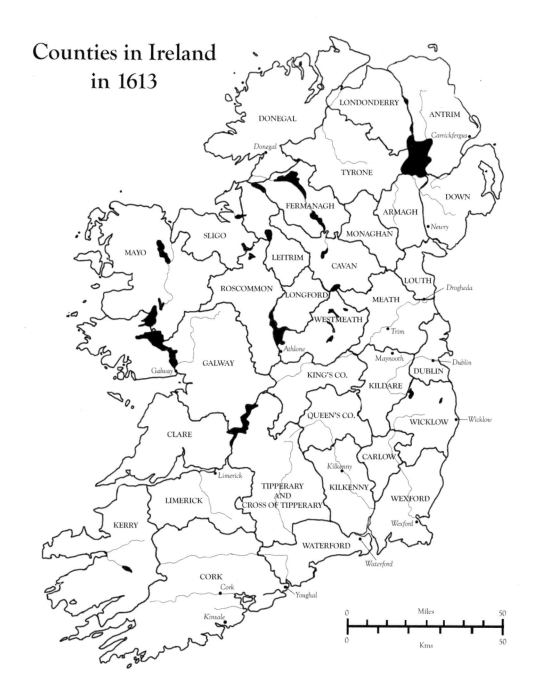

Counties in Ireland
in 1613

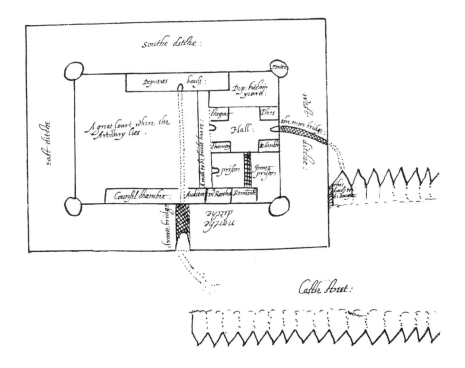

2. The anonymously executed plan of Dublin Castle was discovered by Dr J. Bowlby in a collection of maps by Richard Bartlett, cartographer of Mountjoy, featuring the topography of Ulster and its forts and waterways. Dr Hayes-McCoy placed the drawing of the plan in 1609 based on external evidence. The court of castle chamber would have met in the room of the 'Counsel chamber' above the gatehouse (not shown) and facing the drawbridge. Note the placing of the Four Courts in the Great Hall (until they were removed to Christ Church cathedral about 1610), a scheme which followed the practice in Westminster and which also allowed prisoners to appear before the judges from their adjacent rooms. The location of the 'Deputies house' about 100 yards across the 'great Court' from the 'Counsel chamber' gave the Dublin Castle complex an intimacy that reveals much about the character of early modern administration in Ireland. Unexecuted plans called for a new wall separating the 'Deputies house' from the gaol, and a 'house to be bought' which obstructed ingress to the 'new bridge', leading to the postern gate. This illustration is from G.A. Hayes-McCoy (ed.), *Ulster and other Irish maps, c.1600*, Irish Manuscripts Commission (Dublin, 1964), p. 31.

3. Rathfarnham, the estate of Adam Loftus, archbishop of Dublin, was confiscated from Viscount Baltinglas after his rebellion in 1583 and acquired by Loftus. He built the castle as a fortified manor house, with walls five feet thick to protect against the raids of the O'Byrnes and O'Tooles from the Wicklow mountains. Loopholes for gun emplacement remain in the contemporary house, along with the Elizabethan windows and the Long Gallery. A medieval castle dating from the twelfth century pre-dated the Elizabethan house. Loftus raised his 20 children in the present structure and was succeeded in 1605 by his eldest son, Sir Dudley Loftus, as owner of Rathfarnham. Dudley married Anne, daughter of the marshal of Ireland, Henry Bagenal. His eldest son, another Sir Adam Loftus who was born at Rathfarnham in 1589, inherited the estate and served the interests of Wentworth during the 1630s as master of the rolls. He was among those accused of illegally removing Mountnorris and Viscount Ely, and appeared in 1649 as a petitioner who was owed £4,128 as a result of the suspension of his office. His eldest son Arthur Loftus, later Viscount Lisburne, married Dorothy Boyle, daughter of the earl of Cork, in 1624. Photograph: National Library of Ireland, R 11,551.

4. Drimnagh Castle was the manor of the ancient Barnewall family in Dublin, built of local grey limestone in the thirteenth century by one of the earliest descendants. It possesses a Great Hall with beamed ceiling and minstrels gallery, an undercroft, a tall battlemented tower and an original moat. The seventeenth-century garden was probably laid out for Sir Adam Loftus after he purchased the estate from Marcus Barnewall in 1604, though he was forced to defend his possession at law on several occasions. Drimnagh was the Dublin residence of Loftus until he departed Ireland in disgrace in September 1639, after sixteen months of imprisonment in Dublin Castle. It is probable that his eldest son, Robert, also lived in Drimnagh Castle with his wife Francis Rushe, giving rise to the famous dispute over the Rushe marriage settlement. Another Barnewall estate, Roebuck Castle, was built in the fifteenth century and became the chief property of several Irish judges in the Tudor period. Roebuck Castle is currently on the campus of University College Dublin and, appropriately, serves as the headquarters of the law school. Photograph: Amanda Wilton.

5. Portrait of Sir Henry Sydney by Arnold van Brounckhorst, National Portrait Gallery, London, reg. no. 1902. Sir Henry Sydney (1529–1586) was a powerful Elizabethan courtier and statesman who became lord president in the marches of Wales and lord deputy in Ireland. Educated at court with Prince Edward, Sydney campaigned for office and favour from Penshurst Place, his Kentish estate near London. Knighted in 1550 and made a gentleman of the privy chamber, he married Mary, daughter of John Dudley, duke of Northumberland in 1551. He arrived in Ireland for the first time in 1556 in the train of his brother-in-law, the earl of Sussex, who had married his sister, Frances Sydney. At the age of only 27, Sydney became vice treasurer in Ireland, serving twice as lord justice until he returned in 1560 to become lord president in the marches of Wales in the new reign. He campaigned for the office of lord deputy in Ireland, receiving his first appointment there in 1565, and he became the chief sponsor of the new Irish court of castle chamber. Sydney was responsible for shiring Irish counties in the midlands, establishing the new presidencies in Munster and Connacht, and for rebuilding Dublin Castle with a new house for the chief governor. He was an active judge despite his numerous military campaigns and in his second administration (1575–78) he brought the reforming magistrate, Sir William Gerrard, from Wales to be lord chancellor. Sydney's portrait by, or after, Arnold van Brounckhorst, was painted in 1573 when Sydney was 44 years of age, showing him with the chain as a symbol of his office, an ermine stole emblematic of his status as privy councillor in England, and the seal of the knighthood of the Garter. He was a moderate in religion despite Puritan leanings and his earnest demeanour belies a witty and ironic sense of humour. Sydney was recalled in 1578 at the height of the cess controversy in the Pale, yet he became a trusted privy councillor in Elizabeth's inner circle until his death in 1586. The importance of his family in the English literary Renaissance included his son, Philip, who died suddenly in the Netherlands in 1586, and his daughter Mary, who became countess of Pembroke and was a patron of Ben Jonson.

An͂° dn͂i 1573.
Ætatis svæ 44.

6. Portrait of Sir William Drury by an unknown artist, National Portrait Gallery, London, reg. no. 1911. Drury was a military veteran who came to Ireland in 1576 at the age of 49, after serving as governor at Berwick. He was educated at Gonville, Cambridge and served in France and Scotland, helping to put down the Northern Rebellion in 1569. He was a client of the earl of Sussex, who had become lord president of the council in the North after returning from Ireland, and he was engaged in Scottish politics and diplomacy since his first mission to Edinburgh in 1559. Drury replaced Sydney as lord deputy in 1578 when the crisis of the cess was brewing in the Pale and the Desmond Rebellion was breaking out in Munster. He was forced to govern in the midst of widespread insurrection, yet he managed to lead the court of castle chamber in several trials and worked with Gerrard to plan the reform of the judiciary. His untimely death in 1579 at Waterford threw the administration of Ireland into some disarray, followed by the death of Gerrard two years later. The portrait of Drury shows a man of about 50 years, wearing a suit of armour; his Spartan demeanour, piercing gaze and troubled expression reflect the seriousness of his predicament.

7. Adam Loftus (1533–1605) dominated the Elizabethan Church of Ireland and served as lord chancellor for over two decades, yet he has been described as ineffective and self-serving. Educated at Trinity College, Cambridge, he came to Ireland as chaplain to Lord Deputy Thomas Radcliffe, Baron Fitzwalter, in 1560. He was consecrated archbishop of Armagh in 1563, but he resided in Dublin and in 1566 became archbishop of Dublin with his see at St Patrick's cathedral. He quarrelled with the bishop of Meath, and later with Lord Deputy Perrot, over establishing a new university by endowing it with the proceeds of the deanery of St Patrick's. As leader of the court of high commission in Ireland from 1567, Loftus put his orthodox stamp on the edge of church reform, yet he was resisted by more moderate voices on that tribunal. He campaigned for the office of lord chancellor in 1567 on the death of Robert Weston, and again in 1581 when Sir William Gerrard died in England. Finally appointed to this coveted post in that year, Loftus employed the chancery to enrich his large family of twenty children, earning a partisan reputation. He was appointed to the Irish privy council in 1563 and thus served on the court of castle chamber from its inception, though he also participated in questionable extra-judicial practices such as the treason trial at Trim of Nicholas Nugent, chief justice of common pleas, in 1582 and the torture and execution of Dermot O'Hurley, Catholic archbishop of Cashel, in 1583–84. At the time, he was serving as lord justice with Sir Henry Wallop, and he also served in that role in 1597–99 and 1599–1600. He was instrumental in the downfall of Lord Deputy Perrot in 1588, and connived at his trial for treason in 1592, but in the same year he was named first provost of the new university which became Trinity College Dublin. Loftus also levied charges against the veteran Old English councillors Lucas Dillon and Nicholas White, and both died in disfavour in 1593, while he continued to demand uncompromising enforcement of the Reformation. Reprimanded by Mountjoy for excessive and unstatesmanlike zeal, Loftus died in 1605 during the agitated politics of the new reign. The anonymous portrait (reproduced by courtesy of Trinity College Dublin), painted when Loftus was about 50, shows him with the symbols of office as lord chancellor, including the red chair and the curtain which concealed the court's deliberations from those of other courts in Dublin Castle. The angular Loftus wears the black robes of a chief judge, including a fashionable white ruff and black felt hat. He carries the red and gold purse, which contained the matrix of the Great Seal of Ireland and was emblazoned with the royal seal, symbolising the chancery court.

8. Sir Charles Blount (1563–1606), Lord Mountjoy and earl of Devonshire, was the second son of Baron Mountjoy and a successful soldier and courtier before coming to Ireland. He was educated at Oxford, attended Clifford's Inn in London, and studied at the Middle Temple in 1579, then aged about 16. He sought a military career and served with Sir John Norris in the Low Countries in 1585, where Leicester knighted him in 1587. However, Elizabeth preferred his company at court, and he became governor of Portsmouth in 1594 when he succeeded to the title of Baron Mountjoy. He was made Knight of the Garter in 1597 and managed to retain the friendship of both Sir Robert Cecil and the earl of Essex in the stormy period of the Tyrone Rebellion. Succeeding Essex as lord deputy in 1600, Mountjoy prosecuted a war of attrition against Tyrone, cleverly outwitting the Spanish invaders at Kinsale in 1601 and concealing from Tyrone the death of Elizabeth I when he orchestrated the Treaty of Mellifont in 1603. He managed the transition to the new reign by intimidating the rebellious Munster towns and cautioned against an aggressive Protestantizing campaign before retiring as earl of Devonshire to London, where he died prematurely in 1606. Known as a 'comely' and well-mannered statesman, he kept as a lover the wife of Lord Rich and had six children with Penelope Rich, finally losing his suit to marry her after she divorced her husband in 1605. The miniature portrait by Nicholas Hilliard shows Mountjoy, aged about 35, dressed as an Elizabethan courtier with a confident gaze, the lace collar and other accoutrements of the court taking precedence over the military insignia of his career as an officer. This illustration is published by permission of the Trustees of the Carew Pole family trusts; photograph: Photographic Survey, Courtauld Institute of Art, London.

9. Sir Arthur Chichester (1563–1625) was a trusted military captain with little civilian administrative experience who became chief governor of Ireland in the wake of the Nine Years War. He brought to the task an ambition to reform the Irish polity on an English model, implementing a common law regime in frontier outposts, finishing the creation of Irish counties, demanding full compliance with the strictures of the Protestant Reformation, re-establishing the King's Inns and ultimately presiding over the plantation of Ulster after the flight of the earls of Tyrone and Tyrconnel. Chichester's regime was the longest of any viceroy in this period and he weathered the controversies engendered by his draconian Mandates policy to become a leading privy councillor in England, ennobled as Baron Chichester of Carrickfergus. He worked closely with the attorney general, Sir John Davies, to implement common law protocols in places like Monaghan and Cavan in 1605, and he demanded from the Dublin aldermen full compliance with the 'mandate' to attend divine service. Chichester was educated at Exeter College, Oxford, though he did not graduate, and his military career included service against the Armada (1588), the last voyage of Drake (1595), and the siege of Amiens (1597) prior to his service in Ireland under Essex (1599). Mountjoy and others cautioned against his ruthless style of government, and Chichester withdrew from his stormy confrontations after 1607, but he set the style of a relentless Protestantizing administration that governed after him until at least the retirement of his successor, Oliver St John, in 1622. The impressive marble monument in Carrickfergus church was probably imported, showing the pious Chichester kneeling at prayer with his wife. He had married in 1605 the twice-widowed Lettice Perrot, daughter of the former lord deputy, and their only child died in infancy. The church of St Nicholas is located quite near the site of Chichester's stately baroque manor house, Joymount, dedicated to his predecessor in office and a testimony to his new-found wealth and power. He became the largest landholder in Ulster as a result of the plantation in 1609. He died in England in 1625. This photograph © Crown copyright; reproduced with the permission of Her Majesty's Stationery Office.

10. Archbishop Thomas Jones (?1550–1619) was a client of the first Adam Loftus, arriving in Dublin after graduating from Christ's College, Cambridge as BA (1570) and MA (1573). He was named chancellor of St Patrick's and was promoted to dean in 1582, finally becoming archbishop of Armagh in 1584, and bishop of Meath in the next year. Jones served faithfully as a privy councillor and judge at castle chamber for 35 years, becoming lord chancellor and archbishop of Dublin himself on the death of Loftus in 1605. Jones served until his death in 1619 and he was the last ecclesiastic lord chancellor in Ireland until the penultimate Restoration chancellor, Archbishop Michael Boyle. He became embroiled in numerous controversies as bishop, landowner and magistrate, yet he served as lord justice on two occasions and was speaker of the house of lords in the parliament of 1613–15. His grandiose monument in St Patrick's cathedral shows the archbishop kneeling in prayer in the upper tier, and his son, Roger, Viscount Ranelagh, recumbent in knight's regalia. The monument is an ironic testament to his success as a dynast, incorporating references to his wife, the sister of Loftus's wife, and his rival, Garret, Viscount Moore of Drogheda, whose daughter had married Roger in 1609 after a legal contretemps. Photograph: Davison and Associates Ltd.

11. Sir Henry Cary, Viscount Falkland (1575–1633), was a notable failure as lord deputy of Ireland. Educated at Exeter College, Oxford, he entered Gray's Inn in 1590 and probably served in Ireland under Essex, where he was knighted in Dublin in 1599. He was later privileged as gentleman of the bedchamber to James I, and he became comptroller of the household in 1617 when he was also made privy councillor. He was MP for Hertfordshire in 1614 and was raised to the Scottish peerage as Viscount Falkland in 1620. Falkland won appointment as lord deputy in Ireland in 1622 with the help of Buckingham, after a scathing review of his predecessor's regime that resulted in creation of an Irish committee of the privy council, circumscribing the authority of the chief governor. He came to Ireland with his wife Elizabeth, but she converted to Roman Catholicism and returned to England in 1625, disgracing her husband who, in turn, repudiated her publicly. Falkland quarrelled ceaselessly with adversaries in both England and Ireland, including his own son, Lucius, and he was the target of the Irish opposition movement which penned the 'Graces' in 1628, demanding concessions for Catholics and Old English landowners. He was removed in 1629 and died in England in 1633. The portrait, an engraving done by G.P. Harding after a portrait in oils by Paul van Somer (National Gallery of Ireland, cat. no. 10807), shows the young Falkland as a courtier with silk waistcoat and jaunty hat, velvet gloves, silk stockings and ribboned shoes. The studied pose conceals his sword in the thick folds of his elegant cape, a marked contrast to the menacing posture of his predecessors in office.

12. Richard Boyle, earl of Cork (1566–1643), was an Elizabethan adventurer who built a fortune in Munster after the Desmond Rebellion and became one of the most successful politicians of the age. He was educated at Corpus Christi, Cambridge and the Middle Temple before coming to Ireland in 1588. His vast personal fortune was accumulated as escheator of concealed lands after the Munster Rebellion, capped by the purchase of Sir Walter Raleigh's holdings and his marriage to the daughter of his ally, Geoffrey Fenton, the powerful secretary of state. His children married into the Buckingham and Howard families in England, and he became Baron Youghal in 1616 and earl of Cork in 1620. Boyle became lord justice along with Loftus, Viscount Ely, from 1629 to 33. His baroque monument in St Patrick's cathedral was placed behind the altar in 1632, and this grandiose over-reaching was reviled by his successor, Viscount Wentworth, who demanded that the tomb be removed to a less exalted position near the church entrance, where it now stands. Cork was later indicted at the court of castle chamber for the illegal impropriation of church lands in Youghal, and Wentworth exacted from him a punitive fine before terminating the suit. The large monument in St Patrick's to his wife Katherine Fenton contains a pastiche of New English élites, from Robert Weston, Katherine's grandfather and lord chancellor, to her mother Alice and father Geoffrey Fenton, the secretary of state for over 20 years. Cork was sworn in as a privy councillor in England in July 1640 and testified against the fallen Wentworth in November. Photograph: Davison and Associates Ltd.

13. Sir Adam Loftus, Viscount Ely, was a nephew of the venerable archbishop of Dublin. He was educated at Jesus College, Cambridge, receiving the BA in 1586 and MA in 1589, and then attended Thavies Inn and Lincoln's Inn before venturing to Dublin in 1592 at the age of about 24 to become prebendary of St Patrick's cathedral. By 1598 he had become master in chancery and in 1612 won appointment as judge of the admiralty court. Loftus received his knighthood from Lord Deputy Carey in 1604 and was named to the Irish privy council in 1609. His stormy career involved disputes over property with the earl of Thomond, the earl of Cork, Viscount Falkland, and Wentworth. He became lord chancellor in 1619 at the age of 51, when this portrait was painted, and he was made Viscount Ely three years later, serving as lord justice with Cork from 1629 to 1633. A vigorous defender of the chancery court, he was accused of corruption and arbitrariness in his judicial decisions and was suspended, imprisoned, and removed from office in 1638–39. Seen here in his black judicial robes, he is clutching a sealed document and the tasselled purse which was a symbol of the court. Though vindicated by parliament in 1641, he was not restored to office, lost most of his Irish lands, and died in England in 1643. Artist unknown; National Gallery of Ireland, cat. no. 410.

14. Sir Thomas Wentworth, Viscount Wentworth and later earl of Strafford (1593–1641), arrived in Ireland in 1633 after campaigning for office as a Caroline courtier. He was educated at St John's College, Cambridge and the Middle Temple, and he was knighted in 1611 at the age of only 19 years. Three years later the precocious Wentworth was MP for Yorkshire and became a baronet, spending the next fourteen years as a parliamentary adversary of crown policies. Wentworth aligned himself with the king in 1628 when he was made lord president of the council in the North and privy councillor, earning the trust of Archbishop Laud and becoming a critic of the viceroy of Ireland, Viscount Falkland, and his successors. Wentworth's stormy tenure in Ireland lasted only seven years, but he ruined the careers of his most prominent adversaries, including Viscount Mountnorris, the vice treasurer, and Lord Chancellor Loftus. He alienated the landowning élite, threatening many with outright dispossession, and he used both the castle chamber and the privy council in Ireland to intimidate opponents. His portrait in the style of van Dyke shows Wentworth about 1633, dressed in a fashionable suit of armour with his hand resting on the hilt of a sword. His relentless gaze matched his vigorous application of royal authority, while one hand rests upon his cane, a symbol of the gout with which he was afflicted. Though he was promoted by Charles I to lord lieutenant of Ireland in 1640, he was impeached by parliament later that year and executed for treason in 1641. This portrait by an unknown artist is reproduced by permission of the National Portrait Gallery, London, reg. no. 2960.

Earl of Strafford.

15. Extract from Court of Castle Chamber entry book of orders and decrees, 1571–1621. British Library, Add. MS 47172, f. 160.

Memorandum wheare Gerald Earle of Kildare, by ... his ...
Attorney Exhibited informacion into the most honnoble Courte of Castle
Chamber, against Dame Mabell Dowtesse Dowager of Kildare, wieffe
to Gerald late Earle of Kildare & Robert Digbie knight the Lady Lettice
wieffe to the said & Robert Digbie and Walter Bennett and Roger
Bradley servantes to the said Dame Mabell, that shee the said Dame
Mabell, havinge an earnest desire and intention to advance the ...
of her owne Bodie and namely the said Ladie Lettice, secretly and ...
corruptly conspired and practized with the said Bennett and Bradley
together with the said & Robert Digbie and the said Dame Lettice, That
they the said & Robert Digbie and Dame Lettice, to disinheritt the said
Gerald the Complainante of all the landes tenementes and hereditamentes ...
conteyned in a Deed of ffeoffmente bearinge date the xviith of September
anno octavo of the late Quenes maiesties Raigne, did of Newe ...
and Collusion agree together that the said & Robert Digbie and Dame
Lettice should exhibite a Bill in this honnoble Courte against
the said Dame Mabell surmisinge the said deed of ffeoffmente to be
forged, and that the said Dame Mabell knowinge thereof did publishe
the same, and by the said Dame Mabell faint pleadinge or volluntary ...
Confession thereof contrary to her owne Consciens, the said deed of ...
ffeoffment might be disproved defaced and overthrowen, and
Consequently the Complainantes estate defeated; To which Bill
of Complainte the defendantes made severall answere and the ...
Cause proceedinge to repliçacion rejoinder and witnesses examined
on either syde and vowall daies of hearinge of the said Cause.
And this day Appointed for the hearinge of the said Cause, at
a fforasmuche
as uppon full hearinge and deliberate disinursinge of the said Cause, yt
Appeared unto this honnoble Courte that the said ... sufficient Cause ...
Conteined thereof were grounded us upon euery suche Cause ...
and no sufficient matter adduced by the plaintiff to ...
the said defendantes for the Causes alleadged in the said Bill, yt
is therefore ordered adiudged and decreed by this honnoble Courte
that the said defendantes and euer of them are and shall from ...
henceforth be dismissed acquitted and discharged from Anrther ...
examynacion syute or trouble whatsoever Concerninge the said ...
Bill ... geven at the ... Courte of Castle Chamber the ...
day of ffebruary 1608 in the ... yere of ... Raigne
of England ffraunce and Ireland the ... of Scotland the ...
... and ffortieth /

present
The Lo: Deputie
The Lo: Chancelor
The Lo: ...
Mr Treasurer
The Lo: Cheiff Iustice ...

The Lo: Iugtmann
& Alanlosten
& Tho: ...

16. Extract from Court of Castle Chamber precedent book. Trinity College Dublin, MS 852, f. 81.

Mr [Attorney generall] ... oretenus informes the Court ag[ainst] Patrick Sedgrave Esquire second Baron of her Ma[jes]ties Court of Exchequer, Richard Read and David Russell for that the said Patrick Sedgrave contrary to his oath and trust reposed in him as a Judge in the said Court of Exchequer, uppon an Inquest of Inquirye returned before him, then to enquire whether her Ma[jes]tie had right to certaine landes in Duckestoun in the Countie of Meath sometime belonging to John d'Lahise late attainted of treason, and by reason of the said attainder now belonging to her Ma[jes]tie, respecting the said Richard Read pretended title, did sinisterly compact with the said Read to have a great of the said landes then in question assured unto him and his heirs to support and countenance the said Read his pretended title ag[ainst] her Ma[jes]tie in the rest, and to that end caused the said Richard Read to assist a bond of one hundred poundes unto the said David Russell for and to the use and behoofe of the said Patrick Sedgrave, as by view of the said bond thereof read in Court and severall other depositions did Manifestly appeare, uppon proofe whereof and of the bribery and corruption comitted by the said Patrick Sedgrave, whereunto the said Read was a partie in giving, and the said Russell an actor and broker of the said bribery and corruption. It was therefore uppon the xix day of November 1602, adjudged and decreed that the said Patrick Sedgrave should be deprived and dismissed of his said office of second Baron, and of all other offices and authorities which he now holdeth under her Ma[jes]tie, and shall pay for a fine to her Ma[jes]ties use one thousand poundes in her Ma[jes]ties Court of Exchequer, and to be imprisoned during the Lo[rd] deputies pleasure. And the said Read to pay for his offence twoe hundred poundes, and likewise imprisoned. And the said Russell for his offence (being out of the terme) to pay three hundred poundes. And to be likewise imprisoned during the Lo[rd] deputies pleasure.

Mr that sam[e] Attorney generall informing the Court oretenus ag[ainst] Robert Travers Esquire for that the said Robert Travers being Officiall to the late Lo[rd Bishop] of Meath, in his life tyme, and as vicar generall after his decease sede vacante, had informeaunth himselfe in his said place by receiving of bribes and extorting severall somes of mony from her Ma[jes]ties subiects. And the said Robert having bene examined by the said Mr Attorney, and his examinacions read, in Court the said Travers had confessed that he had received ... for leaving out John warren who was excommunicate for recusancie out of the writt de excommunicato Capiendo, and that the said warren afterwardes being departed this life, the said Travers would not suffer him to buried before he had received fifty shillings for a licence, And further confesseth, that one henrie Corie being in prison in ...

At this stage, James I attempted to placate the rival factions by a proclamation of 26 July 1613, in which he officially accepted the petition of the aggrieved legislators, while condemning their disorderly proceedings, and ordered them to await his return from royal progress in the countryside.[92] The king was particularly outraged by the testimony of William Talbot, a leading lawyer, who maintained the legality of deposing kings in some circumstances. Talbot was fined £10,000 and committed to the Tower.[93] James wrote to Chichester on 8 September 1613 to explain that he had ordered a commission of inquiry to Ireland to investigate the charges in order to induce the petitioners to rely on royal compassion rather than on any resort to arms.[94] In the autumn, the king made up his mind to support the beleaguered viceroy. Acting on the advice of Sir Francis Bacon and Sir Henry Hobart that the oath of allegiance was lawful, if insensitively administered, James proceeded to require in a proclamation of 7 October that those learned in the laws and other councillors at law or officers in crown courts, including advocates or pleaders at the bar, and mayors and local officials must be required to take the oath of supremacy.[95] The king assured Chichester that the commission of inquiry was designed to mollify the recusant opposition and to expose the latent disloyalty inherent in their posturing, but the viceroy was irritated that his policies were to be scrutinized officially, and felt betrayed. The commission was authorized in November to examine abuses in the parliament and the country, citing the writs of election, undue practices of sheriffs, oppressions by the soldiers, the new plantation of Wexford and the state of religion. The operation of the court of castle chamber was not mentioned in its remit.[96]

The determined lord deputy did not move further prosecutions of recusancy in castle chamber that year, though on 24 November he and the council wrote to the council in England that they had imprisoned Sir James Gough, who returned from England and made the claim that the king would now offer clemency and toleration to the recusants.[97] According to Gough, the delegation from the Irish parliament, which included Lord Gormanston, Viscount Roche, Patrick Hussey and himself, met with the king in the presence of his leading expert on Irish

---

92. Ibid., pp. 386–88; Steele, *Tudor & Stuart proclamations*, ii, 21 (no. 210).
93. McCavitt, *Chichester*, p. 187.
94. *Cal. S.P. Ire., 1611–14*, p. 421. James explained to Chichester that his motive was 'to induce them by some formal way of satisfaction on all occasions of grievance rather to address themselves to the sovereign by way of humble petition and to expect relief from him, than after the old fashion of that country to run upon every occasion of discontent to the bog and wood and seek their remedy that way'. Some twenty commissioners went to Ireland, including the judges Sir Humphrey Winch and Sir Richard Wilbraham, reporting their proceedings on 15 October. Ibid., pp. 426, 436.
95. Ibid., p. 424. See also *Acts privy council, 1613–14*, pp. 223–25, 255–56, and McCavitt, *Chichester*, pp. 187–88.
96. *Cal. S.P. Ire., 1611–14*, p. 436. Commissioners included the secondary figures Sir Humphrey Winch, judge of common pleas, and Sir Roger Wilbraham, master of requests, both former magistrates in Ireland, and others.
97. Ibid., p. 456.

affairs, Sir Humphrey May. Gough initially reported in careful language that the king would not impose on the consciences of priests and other recusants so long as they did not compass rebellion or conspiracy. He declared on numerous occasions that

> I am asured yt his Matie did not nor do he conceave the execution of his lawes established to be the extorting or forceing of mens consciences but yt it is his will and pleasure to have the lawes executed in that behalf everywhere ... But yt his subiectes should be compelled by violence or other unlawfull meanes to resorte to the protestant Churches I thincke it not his pleasure nor that they shold be compelled by opparission [oppression] and undue infliction of punishment to acknowledge the use of the sacrament contrary to their Conscience.[98]

Chichester examined Gough on the matter on 20 November, and required him to acknowledge that he omitted the king's insistence on obedience and honour to all crown officials, adding 'that [the] king wold not have us to be soe emboldened from the meeting as either for every light occasion hereafter appealed from this state to his majestie'.[99]

The year 1614 brought further uncertainty, as the viceroy and the recusant leaders vied for the king's favour, using arguments that ranged from veiled threat to constitutional technicality. Chichester was invited by the crown to come to London, where he defended his policies. Recusant leaders were imprisoned for a time, but the king listened with some sympathy to their charges against Chichester's government. By the end of summer 1614, the king had temporized long enough, sent the Pale leaders back to Ireland, and provided the lord deputy with enough authority to implement a scaled-down version of his parliamentary platform.[100] On 5 June 1615, the king instructed Chichester to return with full authority to penalize municipal officials who refused the oath of supremacy. They were to be censured at the council table or in the castle chamber, and if they persisted in electing recusants, the viceroy was ordered to seize the liberties of offending corporations.[101] Writing to the attorney-general of Ireland, Lord Chancellor Ellesmere and Francis Bacon declared that if a mayor or other chief officer of a corporate town exercised his office before taking the oath of supremacy, in contempt of the law, he was punishable in the castle chamber there, citing the authority of 2 Elizabeth on uniformity of religion. Further, the chief legal officers

98. TCD, MS 567, f. 29v, and see ff. 27–29.
99. Ibid. On 4 January, the king wrote to approve Chichester's handling of Gough. *Cal. S.P. Ire., 1611–14*, p. 462.
100. McCavitt, *Chichester*, pp. 190–98. On 20 April 1614, James's speech to the petitioners in London, with Chichester in attendance, upbraided them for 'causeless expostulations' and found their proceedings to have been 'rude, disorderly, inexcusable, and worthy of severe punishment': *Cal. S.P. Ire., 1611–14*, pp. 474–75.
101. Ibid., p. 484.

in England made clear that mayors and other local officials were bound by the statute, though not chosen immediately by the crown, and that those cities or towns which elected them without regard to their recusancy might have their charters questioned on that point. Having made clear the legal basis for the actions of castle chamber, however, they went on:

> Notwithstanding, for the tyme to come our advice is, that severall Comissions for ministring the oath bee Directed to the presidentes in the provinces, and to the BBs [bishops] & other cheife officers there, And likewise to the BBs and some of the privie Councell within the Pale, to remayne Dormant with them, and to bee executed from tyme to tyme as occasion shall arise.[102]

In fact, the campaign in castle chamber against the recusants went forward even without the presence of the viceroy, since the court on 20 May 1614 found seven jurors of Co. Monaghan guilty of failure to present recusants.[103] Once Chichester returned to Ireland, the policy was resumed in earnest in November 1614 when three juries from Co. Longford and Co. Louth were condemned for refusing to present recusants.[104]

Chichester was preoccupied in 1615 with the management of a difficult parliament, which was complicated by rumours of an Ulster conspiracy centring on the return of Tyrone. This placed the recusants in a compromising position and they responded with a subsidy bill that was passed without obtaining concessions on religious freedom. Chichester prosecuted no less than five juries (from Counties Meath, Kildare, Wexford, Kilkenny and Carlow) for refusing to present recusants during two legal terms of 1615 (May and November).[105] In May 1615, the court of castle chamber took the unusual step of reinforcing the jurisdiction of the senior court, condemning a king's bench jury which had acquitted nine men of Navan, Co. Meath, for hearing mass with a multitude of other men and women in the town. The fine of £3 each was unusually mild for a case of this sort, held during parliamentary sessions in the capital at a time of enormous tension.[106] McCavitt has argued that the achievement of the parliamentary session was, in the end, a qualified victory for the viceroy, since he obtained the subsidy without yielding on the hard-line anti-recusancy policies, authorized by the crown in extra-parliamentary orders that did not require statutory enactment. Proclamations were issued banishing priests and prohibiting the education of children abroad, while Catholic lawyers were excluded from practising at the bar

102. Bodl., Carte MS 61, f. 83.
103. BL, Add. MS 47,172, f. 200.
104. Ibid., ff. 202, 203, 204. Among the jurors in Co. Longford were two members of parliament, Connell and John Ferrall. McCavitt, *Chichester*, p. 198.
105. BL, Add. MS 47,172, ff. 207, 208, 209. See also McCavitt, *Chichester*, p. 204. The two MPs for Co. Meath, John Warren and Patrick Begg, were fined as jurors in this new campaign. McCavitt, *Chichester*, p. 198.
106. BL, Add. MS 47,172, f. 207.

and justices of the peace were required to take the oath of supremacy.[107] Not surprisingly, Sir John Denham, chief justice of king's bench, wrote on 13 June 1615 that 'the courts of justice have small resort unto them,' during the time of parliament when men withheld prosecution of suits pending a more favourable atmosphere.[108] On 20 August 1615, the viceroy wrote to the privy council that resistance to anti-recusancy policies was widespread, justices of the peace had refused the oath, and there was no one to serve in their role. He stated that Co. Meath was 'universally popish' except for a dozen English gentry, yet over 300 recusants go to Protestant service, terrified by their priests and hounded by their officials.[109] By 17 October, the king was advising the viceroy to dissolve parliament since the remaining bills could be given effect 'in a course of prerogative, either by Act of Council or by Proclamation'.[110] When Chichester retired from Ireland at the king's invitation in December 1615, his long campaign against recusancy was still at full throttle. Yet, in the end, his opportunistic evangelism was more of a *cause de guerre* than a carefully calibrated scheme to win the Irish people to the Protestant religion.

ANGLICIZING THE JUDICIAL SYSTEM, 1605–1615

More than half of the cases before the court of castle chamber under the Chichester regime addressed secular concerns, despite his near obsession with recusancy. The court sustained the Elizabethan policy of punishing the malfeasance of local and provincial officials. On 6 February 1605, the lord deputy presided over the hearing in castle chamber at which Oliver Scurlocke, recently sheriff of Co. Donegal, was convicted of extortion. The renegade sheriff had been tried at the assize court in Donegal and found guilty of demanding money from households for keeping nightly watch and for grazing their cattle on the mountains. The assize judges, including Sir John Davies, remanded the case to the viceregal court for condign punishment, perhaps in view of the recent shiring of Donegal in the aftermath of war and rebellion.[111] Another miscreant sheriff, John Barry of Co. Cork, was convicted in 1605 of riot and corruption in assisting the designs of Brien McOwen to take possession of the town and castle of Dromynyn. McOwen had failed to obtain a writ of restitution from the assize court in Youghal, but persisted in his claim and won the support of the chief justice of Munster, William Saxey, who sent the writ to Barry. The plaintiff, Cahir O'Callaghan, then procured from the court of king's bench a writ of *supersedeas* to stay the writ of restitution and

107. McCavitt, *Chichester*, pp. 206, 207, 228.
108. *Cal. S.P. Ire., 1615–25*, p. 67.
109. TCD, MS 746, f. 96v.
110. *Cal. S.P. Ire.,1615–25*, pp. 93–94. The king ordered the obsolete statutes of Kilkenny and other laws prohibiting commerce between English and Irish to be suspended until the next parliament when they could be repealed.
111. BL, Add. MS 47,172, f. 134.

delivered this to Barry, who nevertheless gathered a force of 200 well-armed men, disobeyed the writ of *supersedeas*, and took forcible possession by breaking down the doors of the castle at midnight. Such riotous behaviour in a public official brought down the wrath of the viceroy and court of castle chamber, and a heavy fine of £200 was demanded of the principals.[112] On the other hand, the court also found it necessary to reinforce the power of local officials when they were threatened or compromised. On 31 January 1612, the court fined and imprisoned James Barnwell and his wife for 'rescuing' a distress that had been levied against their estate of Brymore in Co. Dublin by the sheriff, Robert Talbott, on the authority of a writ of seizure from the court of exchequer.[113]

As the gradual anglicization of the judicial system deepened and spread into the provinces, the court required stricter observance of procedural rules and proprieties. In one case, John Condon of Co. Cork, sued James Sherlocke of Co. Tipperary in 1608 for forging a roll of attainder in order to divest him of his rightful inheritance. For claiming falsely that the plaintiff's father had been convicted of treason during the Fitzmaurice rebellion in 1570, Sherlocke was fined £100, forced to stand on the pillory, have his nose slit and seared and his ears cut off, after which he was jailed during pleasure. This notably cruel punishment was imposed in Waterford, perhaps as a signal to the community that legal documents could not be manipulated to the advantage of opportunist litigants.[114] On 23 November 1610, the court indicted leading aldermen and lawyers of Galway for hearing a case of murder in their municipal jurisdiction which should have been prosecuted in Dublin as high treason. Walter French, a lawyer and principal counsellor to the mayor and aldermen, was fined £200 for his role, viewed by the court as a derogation of the king's authority and possibly also a form of collusion to avoid the ultimate penalty of attainder.[115] Finally, on 25 November 1614, the court fined the former sheriff of Co. Wexford for reprieving a prisoner who had been condemned to die by the assize judges. Sheriff John Allen confessed that he reprieved the prisoner for six days without any warrant to do so, and he was fined £20 for his act of clemency.[116]

The establishment of clear title to property was a preoccupation of the early Stuart courts, particularly in view of the unsettled land disputes arising from war, rebellion and plantation. The court of castle chamber did not take up issues arising directly from the plantations in Ulster and elsewhere, yet the litigation before the court frequently dealt with contested title. In a case of very long standing and extraordinary political implications – again one we have already introduced – the earl of Kildare was sued at common law in 1602 for rights and estates owed to the female heir of his predecessor, Lady Lettice Fitzgerald, wife

---

112. Ibid., ff. 135–37. Brian McOwen was also fined £200 for his part in attempting to corrupt justice by preferring the writ at the assize court in the name of a notorious rebel who had been slain two years previously. The questionable behaviour of Judge Saxey went unnoticed by the court.

113. Ibid., f. 183.

114. Ibid., f. 150.

115. Ibid., f. 170.

116. Ibid., f. 205.

of Sir Robert Digby. The case finally came to the attention of the court of castle chamber on 11 November 1607 in several days of hearings. With Chichester presiding, the judges heard that the attorney for the dowager countess of Kildare, Lady Mabel, had improperly endorsed the deed of the late earl by a forgery which disinherited Lady Lettice. The agent was the septuagenarian Henry Burnell, the well-known Pale lawyer with important credentials as an adversary of crown policies since the cess controversy. Burnell had been sought by Lady Mabel for his advice, and he explained that the deed was defective, though he could repair it with later endorsements in regard to livery and attornment. He was censured on 3 February 1609 and fined 500 marks for authoring the forgery, although the merits of the case were left to be tried at common law.[117] The tenacity of the Digbys had become notorious in both London and Dublin, with the councils in both kingdoms attempting to avoid making a final judgement.[118] Chichester and the Irish council wrote to the privy council in England on 21 December 1607 that the hearing lasted the entire previous term, 'humbly wishing them to move His Majesty to take this cause into his own hands, and to stay them from going to sentence.'[119] After the castle chamber's interlocutory decree resolved nothing of substance, the privy council wrote on 20 March 1608 to Chichester, asking him to attempt some arbitration of their troubles and voiding their previous order to sequester Kildare's estates in the event of the death of the dowager Countess Mabel.[120] Chichester responded that the suit remained in hearings before the castle chamber 'for the most part of these last two terms without intermission, every Star-chamber day'.[121] In the autumn of 1610, Countess Mabel died and the litigants tried to seize her lands, for which they were in turn censured by the privy council.[122] The earl of Kildare complained for a year at the disgrace to his honour and at the impoverishment of his estate, and was to die suddenly at Maynooth in February 1612 after feeling a pain in his stomach.[123] Once again, the dispute over the estate was left to arbitrators to compound their differences, leaving the countess Elizabeth in a weakened position with her young son now the king's ward.[124]

In similar fashion, the court heard testimony regarding the title of the earl of Clanricarde on 10 November 1610 when Richard Burke, the earl, preferred a bill in castle chamber against his own brothers for falsely accusing him of illegitimacy and of conspiracy to have them killed. During eighteen months of litigation, including a commission to take depositions regarding the marriage of his parents,

---

117. Ibid., ff. 154–59v.
118. A countersuit by the earl against the Digbys and their witnesses for conspiring to disinherit him was dismissed on the same day at castle chamber. Ibid., f. 160. See also Treadwell, *Buckingham and Ireland*, pp. 116–18.
119. *Cal. S.P. Ire., 1606–08*, pp. 361–63.   120. Ibid., p. 442.
121. Ibid., p. 470. An offhand remark of Chichester about the clogging of castle chamber jurisprudence with elaborate pleas and counterpleas is important, if faint, evidence of the regular business of the star chamber in Ireland.
122. *Cal. S.P. Ire., 1608–10*, p. 524.   123. *Cal. S.P. Ire., 1611–14*, p. 245.
124. Ibid., p. 470.

Ulick and Honora Burke, and the birth of the incumbent earl six years later, exceedingly detailed genealogy of the earl was read into the record of the court. Chichester and the other judges concluded on 31 May 1612, after full debate in open court, 'that the said Sir Thomas Boorke, knight, is guiltye of the untrue, unnaturall, scandalous and malitious reportes and Speeches aforesaid', tending to the reproach and scandal of the earldom.[125] They did not take up the further charge that Sir Thomas intended to become earl of Clanricarde at the first hint of rebellion, but they fined him £1,000 and imprisoned him during pleasure.[126] In the same vein, Anne, the wife of Sir Edward Blayney, sued in castle chamber on 29 May 1611 to defeat the claim of a bastard son of her former husband, George Blunt, to his estate (in preference to their legitimate daughter, Elizabeth Blunt). This attempt to exploit the court for personal advantage implicated Maurice, bishop of Killaloe, in a case of unintended forgery, since he was the unwilling instrument of a conspiracy to determine the legitimacy of Christopher, the son of Sieve ny Carroll by George Blunt. Using the bishop's declaration of legitimacy, the conspirators published their claim to the estate in April 1611 at Louth. In its decree of 27 November 1611 the court mitigated its censure and fine, citing the 'natural affection' of the mother for her son, but demanding that the illegally procured instrument be 'quite Dissanulled, Damned, Cancelled & defaced as undulie, unlawfully and Corruptlie made, and to be reputed of noe value or force'.[127] Attorney-general Davies took note of the case in his lengthy discussion of the common law of Ireland, finding that the right of the crown to take up ecclesiastical cases in common law courts was undoubted. Since the case involved fraudulent dealings, it was properly handled by the court of castle chamber, and the bishop erred in taking depositions without any suit being commenced, or writ moving him to act, in the temporal courts.[128] Although the court had no jurisdiction in property cases, a remarkable number of real property actions found their way to the prerogative tribunal, and the court generally offered a judicial remedy. In the case of John Deverox, a gentleman of Co. Wexford, the court was informed by the attorney-general, Davies, that Deverox had filed suit in chancery on behalf of 'A Clamorous and poore woman named Margret Bowton, als Browne' who claimed spurious title to the town and lands of Ballinor then held by copy of court roll by Nicholas Turner. On 19 May 1609, the court of castle chamber found Deverox guilty of champerty for having covenanted with Browne to defeat the good title of Turner and then convey half the property to himself.[129]

---

125. BL, Add. MS 47,172. f. 177.   126. Ibid., ff. 172–77v.   127. Ibid., f. 179.

128. Sir John Davies, *A report of cases and matters in law resolved and adjudged in the king's courts in Ireland* (Dublin, 1762), pp. 139–42. Davies further noted that the bishop acted privately, in collusion with his kinswoman, Sieve ny Carroll, and without customary notification of his peers, '*convocatis convocandis*', thus compromising the jurisdiction of his court. And, while matrimonial questions were properly the charge of church courts, testamentary questions lay with the temporal courts, and the crown could move the case in either venue, as it governed both.

129. BL, Add. MS 47,172, f. 161. Turner's estate was founded on 'beinge seised in his Demeasne as

Delicate points of honour were contrived by the prodigious egos of many peers and gentry of the Stuart period, in Ireland as well as in England. As Dr Kelly has shown in his treatment of duelling, the public reputation of a gentleman had to be 'free of stain or slight' so the man of honour was compelled to defend it with his life.[130] This was no less true of institutions, so the court took great offence when John Cage, a Dublin merchant, accused Sir Edward Brabazon, privy councillor, 'in manifest scorn and contempt' of taking for himself the goods of one Lawrence Clearck on pretence of seizing them for the crown. Compounding this slander, Cage refused to doff his hat in deference to Brabazon, saying he owed him no respect and that he kept as servants men who were as good as the complainant. When told by the mayor he had the right to complain to the lord deputy and council against Brabazon, the feisty merchant said he would have no remedy there and would be laughed at for his labours. Cage's defence of the vanished Clearck, who had fled for debt, was seen, during the hearing on 11 February 1614, as a dangerous and malicious sedition which compromised the reputation of the crown itself.[131]

One of the most striking cases before the court of castle chamber took place on 15 June 1610, involving two elder sons of the Pale élite, participants in an affray in Dublin. The case involved riot, honour, treason and politics, and yet lacks the gravity of other deliberations owing to the bizarre behaviour of one of the protagonists, Sir Christopher St Lawrence, who became the 10th Baron Howth in 1607. St Lawrence was a soldier of fortune who had fought bravely in the Nine Years War and had recently returned from campaigns in Europe. After his travels, he claimed to have knowledge of numerous conspiracies involving Irish leaders who were in league with the recently expatriate earl of Tyrone.[132] One of these men was Sir Garret Moore, a wealthy landowner and Irish privy councillor, who had entertained Tyrone at Mellifont on the eve of his flight to the continent. Lord Howth accused Moore of treason on 11 September 1608, but refused to detail the evidence at several hearings, both in England and Ireland, claiming the viceroy and council were hostile to him.[133] Moore was incarcerated and paid large bonds for his security, but was freed after enduring an interrogation by Davies, Ley and St Leger which allowed him to parry with counter-charges against the baron.[134]

---

of fee by Coppie of Courte Roule, accordinge to ye Custome of the Manner of Ballinore.' Though Deverox was fined £40, the woman was not punished by the court.

130. J. Kelly, *'That damn'd thing called honour': duelling in Ireland 1570–1860* (Cork, 1995), p. 12.

131. BL, Add. MS 47,172, ff. 198–99.

132. McCavitt, *Chichester*, pp. 86, 124, 130–31, 136.

133. *Cal. S.P. Ire., 1608–10*, pp. 24, 113, 137; G.E.C., *Peerage*; *DNB*.

134. *Cal. S.P. Ire., 1608–10*, pp. 164–66. Moore claimed in March 1609 that Howth had maligned the king for reversing his promise of a regiment in the Low Countries, recalling that the baron had been removed as governor of Monaghan for malicious speeches and for wrongly hanging a poor Englishman. He had threatened at the time to 'murder the whole council in the council chamber if they offered then to have stay of him'. Moore was created baron in 1615 and Viscount Moore of Drogheda in 1621. Ibid.

Over a year later, the son-in-law of Moore, Sir Roger Jones, eldest son of the lord chancellor and archbishop of Dublin, Thomas Jones, insulted Howth and a row ensued. On 8 November 1609, Howth claimed that Sir Roger Jones attempted to murder his ally, the son of the late chief justice of common pleas, who was forced to escape to the lodging of Chief Justice Winch.[135] Sixteen days later the celebrated contretemps occurred in the streets of Dublin which led to the castle chamber trial.

Reportedly, Baron Howth came to the tennis court on St Thomas Street where Sir Roger Jones was wont to spend much time, bringing in train some ten or more servants and armed with a cudgel. Words were exchanged and Jones drew his sword, outnumbered and surprised. Howth was supported by his servants, Jones broke his sword in the affray, and his elderly aide, Simon Barnewell, was slain trying to protect him. Jones was then taken and cried out he would be murdered, when Howth intervened, demanding, 'will you now call me coward?' Jones replied he never called him coward, only a valiant man among cowards, which Howth understood was just the same. Jones refused to take back the insult, and Howth struck him on the face with his rapier, calling him but a boy and releasing him. The lord deputy heard of this immediately and ordered the mayor to take Howth and his retainers into custody, and in the following months competing accounts embellished the story to the advantage of both sides.[136] When the case finally reached the attention of castle chamber on 15 June 1610, the issue was no longer the murder itself, but a point of law raised in the court of king's bench in giving instruction to the jury. The twelve jurors were empanelled before Chief Justice Sir Humphrey Winch during the previous Easter term to hear evidence in the trial of eight defendants for the murder of Simon Barnewell in November 1610. The jurors were instructed that, if the eight persons were aiding and abetting in the quarrel and affray, 'that then as many of the said persons at the Barr as drew theire swordes and tooke parte with the said Lo of Howth were guyltie of the fellonious killinge of the said Simon Barnwell.'[137] The jurors proceeded to give a verdict of acquittal for the eight defendants, noting that 'yt was not proved unto them who yt was in Certaine and by name that did kill the said Simon Barnwell'.[138] The court of castle chamber found the jurors guilty of a misdemeanour in bringing their verdict against the evidence and refusing to accept the point of law, fining and imprisoning them after public humiliation at the pillory.[139] The wily

---

135. Ibid., p. 320. The heir of former Chief Justice Robert Dillon was accosted by the son of Garrett Moore, in the company of Jones and others, who then tried to break down the door of Winch's house in Dublin, according to Howth's letter to Salisbury. The prominence of Jones was assured by the close connection of his father and father-in-law with the viceroy, who knighted him and awarded him 1,000 acres in the Wexford plantation. Sir Roger was MP in the Irish parliament of 1613, and later became Baron Jones and Viscount Ranelagh. *DNB*; McCavitt, *Chichester*, pp. 66, 82. For Lord Chancellor and Archbishop Thomas Jones, see Plate 10.

136. *Cal. S.P. Ire., 1608–10*, pp. 320–21, 391, 427; Kelly, *Duelling*, p. 14.

137. BL, Add. MS 47,172, f. 166.   138. Ibid.

139. Ibid., f. 167.

Lord Howth was not indicted with his fellows, and he subsequently took his case once again to England without licence, burdening Salisbury and the privy council with ceaseless allegations. The castle chamber trial was employed with little effect in this case, and the simmering dispute remained unreconciled for years between the protagonists, demonstrating the court's genuine concern for the dignity of the judicial process, while revealing the limits to which its jurisdiction would reach.

The court traditionally undertook numerous cases in which jurors were fined and imprisoned for their refusal to find guilty verdicts according to their evidence. This wielding of prerogative law in castle chamber was justified in several ways. First, the court understood its role to be superintendent of the process by which common law institutions were implemented systematically throughout the country. Deliberations in jury trials were theoretically sacrosanct in common law, but there is abundant evidence in English legal practice for subsequent judicial review when jurors appeared to determine cases without the impartiality required of them. Second, the court took upon itself the correction of administrative malfeasance and the jury system was viewed as an instrument of crown policy. Finally, the Chichester regime sought to bring uniformity of judicial outcomes to Ireland, offering common law predictability instead of the familiar, but idiosyncratic, standard of the village or the sept. In concept, the synchronization of the judicial process would provide an impartial hearing to everyone in Ireland. In practice, however, the system favoured English-trained lawyers and landholders and offered the viceroy a wedge through which to drive his new policies and settlements. On 14 November 1610, the court heard a case in which the jury foreman in the court of king's bench reported a verdict of manslaughter, though the jurors had found a verdict of murder. Cahir O'Toole was fined £100 and pilloried with the loss of both his ears, and the other jurors were fined and imprisoned, for giving a false verdict in the murder trial of Arte McBrien O'Byrne.[140]

Most of the cases in which juries were condemned in castle chamber involved hearings in the provinces. The court heard one such case on 21 November 1610, in which the defendant, Edmund Duff, was acquitted by the jury on a charge of relieving a notorious traitor, Terlaghe Gallchowe, in Co. West Meath. Two justices of assize heard the case at Mullingar and remanded the jurors for trial in castle chamber on the charge of refusing to convict Duff according to the weight of the evidence. The court of castle chamber found all the jurors guilty and fined them, singling out one James Dyce as the ringleader, and dismissing their defence with an obscure reference to 'alleadginge vaine excuses which this Court did not allowe of, but absolutlie reiecte'.[141] In a case heard before Chief Baron Methwold and Judge Lowther on assize circuit in Cork, four jurors refused to join their fellows in returning a verdict in the robbery trial of Con McCahir. As a result of their

---

140. Ibid., f. 168. The notorious rivalry of O'Tooles and O'Byrnes in Co. Wicklow provided an interesting, if unreported, scenario for the trial itself, involving the murder of another O'Byrne. Castle chamber took up the case only four days after the hearing in king's bench.

141. Ibid., f. 169. Another case with similar results was heard on 6 May 1612 in Carlow. Ibid., f. 184.

decision, the accused was acquitted of robbing Thomas Andrews, and the court of castle chamber was unable to change their minds, despite the threat of fine and imprisonment.[142] On 5 May 1615, the court was strangely circumspect on the trial of Geoffrey Keating, perhaps the same secular priest who became famous for his manuscript histories and Catholic devotional works written in Irish during this period. He was arraigned before the assize judges in Maryborough on charges of treason for relieving Piers Keating (probably a relation), accused of the murder of the crown official Henry Davells. The court was faced with the obduracy of the entire jury of twelve men, finding them guilty but reducing their fines to the token amount of £3 apiece.[143] Chichester detailed the case in correspondence to the privy council dated 3 February 1613, noting that Davells received an insult from Keating, who in turn charged Davells with cutting off the finger of his brother. The viceroy had sent two justices of the peace to Queen's Co. to keep the peace, but an affray was begun when Sir Thomas Loftus delivered a verbal challenge to Davells, who rose up from his sick bed and came into Carlow town with his sword drawn. Davells was killed by Piers Keating with two bullets from a fowling piece. Keating was still at large, and the sheriff was unable to get a jury to indict Loftus until the next Hilary term. The viceroy concluded, 'Nor for myne own part, I will do nothing therein in favour or disfavour of either partie, but as it shall become me in ye direct course of Law, without any respect of persons.'[144]

In another instance, faced with the stubborn resistance of four jurors in the assizes at Limavady, including two O'Cahans, the assize judges were unable to get a verdict of treason in August 1609 against numerous supporters of O'Cahan in Co. Coleraine. The jurors were subsequently fined in November in castle chamber.[145] No mention was made in the court's record of the simultaneous plantation of Ulster, the dispossession and imprisonment of Donal O'Cahan, nor of O'Cahan's legal challenge to the primacy of Tyrone in the Dublin courts in 1605.[146] Pursuant to his plans for plantation in Co. Wexford, Chichester used the

142. Ibid., f. 197.   143. Ibid., f. 206.

144. TCD, MS 746, f. 35v and see ff. 34–35v.

145. BL, Add. MS 47, 172, ff. 163–63v. Donal O'Cahan had been arrested along with other Ulster lords for complicity in the 1608 rebellion of Sir Cahir O'Doherty, beginning in February. After the flight of the earls of Tyrone and Tyrconnell in September 1607, the restless province was further disturbed by widespread confiscations of the lands of lesser Ulster lords and by 1609 the chiefs themselves, including O'Cahan, rested in the Tower of London to end their days as 'unconvicted prisoners'. The verdict of treason was thus part of a comprehensive effort to disinherit a generation of the native Ulster landowning élite. See Canny, *Making Ireland British*, pp. 184–90. The assizes were led by Davies and Chief Justice Winch, charging the defendants with rebellion and with relieving rebels, based on the testimony of three principal witnesses. The four stubborn jurors were sent to Dublin, interrogated and then fined £100 each, pilloried and jailed for their offences. BL, Add. MS 47, 172, ff. 163–63v. See also F.W. Harris, 'The rebellion of Sir Cahir O'Doherty and its legal aftermath', *Ir Jur*, xv (1980), 298; R. Gillespie, *Conspiracy: Ulster plots and plotters in 1615* (Belfast, 1987).

146. Such disembodied entries in the record book, shorn of the essential context of the case and its political implications, cautions the reader to be circumspect in appraising the court. O'Cahan

court of castle chamber to intimidate jurors who refused to find crown title to lands in January 1612. Five jurors refused to join the rest in a quasi-judicial commission appointed by the viceroy to find crown title to lands in Wexford, after which they were summoned to the court of exchequer to explain their obduracy. The court of castle chamber fined and imprisoned them for contempt of the court of exchequer, in a dubious manoeuvre. However, the court was not frequently called upon to intervene directly in property disputes of this sort.[147] Importantly, Walter Sinnott, kinsman of one of the convicted jurors, had taken the leading role in opposition to the Wexford plantation and was elected member of the Irish parliament in the following year.[148] The right of star chamber to fine jurors for corrupt verdicts was well-established in this period according to the records of the English court, and that right passed to king's bench in 1641 until its 'tyrannical example' was formally abolished in 1670.[149]

Traditionally, the court of castle chamber heard a majority of cases of riot in its efforts to bring civility to an unruly society. Under Chichester, the cases of riot before the court were fewer in number, only eleven decisions rendered in seven years. Some of the cases involved genuine disorder and violence, amounting to an affray, while others found their way to the court by the route of vexatious litigation, since the allegations were primarily of dispossession and destruction of property. On 6 February 1607, the court sat to adjudicate the suit of Henry Bennett, a gentleman of Co. Wexford, against John Deverox, his sons and sixteen others for a riot committed on 12 December 1604. The defendants were accused of coming armed to his castle of Dunbarde Island with swords, pikes and guns, taking possession of the castle and its goods, and throwing his wife down the stairs. Deverox and the others were further accused of compounding their offence by taking the corn and other provisions for their horses. Deverox, as the prime offender, was fined, imprisoned and made to restore the value of his goods to the plaintiff as a condition of his release.[150] Feuding of this sort was fairly commonplace in areas

---

had been urged by Davies to pursue legal claims to part of the Tyrone patrimony in spite of the earl's acknowledged overlordship in his Ulster dominions. By manipulating the claims of lesser lords, Davies and Jacob hoped to secure a portion of all deeded property to the crown. See Canny, *Making Ireland British*, pp. 182, 185.

147. BL, Add. MS 47, 172, f. 182. The jurors empanelled at Wexford before the commission, led by the bishop of Ferns, were asked to inquire into crown title to the lands of the Morroghs and Kynsalies. Upon their refusal, they were summoned to Dublin and declared before the chief baron that it was against their conscience to find for the crown.

148. The jurors included Edmond Sinnott, Walter Bryan, James Butler and Edmond and Thomas Codd, all members of the Old English élite who were subject to dispossession. They were represented in London by the lawyer, Henry Walsh, before the commissioners for Irish causes. McCavitt, *Chichester*, pp. 162–68.

149. J.H. Baker, 'Criminal courts and procedure at common law, 1550–1800' in J.S. Cockburn, ed., *Crime in England 1550–1800* (Princeton, 1977), p. 24.

150. BL, Add. MS 47, 172, f. 147. Marion Bennett, as the wounded party, may have claimed the particular attention of the court in this case some two years after the events. Deverox fell afoul of the law again in the case of champerty (see above).

newly settled by Chichester's plantations, but some riots were aggravated by more ancient quarrels. Sir Richard Bingham had been a belligerent Elizabethan lord president of Connacht, where he established his family and fought endlessly with the traditional lords of the region, the Burkes of Mayo. In May 1612, the court of castle chamber heard an information by the plaintiff, Sir John Bingham, against Sir Theobold Burke and his sons who, with their retainers, assaulted the tenants of Bingham and destroyed their small houses. The Burkes succeeded in ruining the village which surrounded Bingham's home of Castle Barry in 1606, raising the issue of why it took Bingham six years for the suit to be resolved in castle chamber. The senior Burke was fined for his part and imprisoned in Dublin Castle on 20 May.[151]

The court was especially concerned with riot when it interfered with the administration of justice. In some cases, it compelled its own officers to obey the law. For example, on 22 November 1611, the court heard the case of Captain Richard Tyrrell of Co. Cavan and his servants, who assaulted Caher McPhillip and expelled him from his property. The offence occurred in September 1607 when Tyrrell was justice of the peace, and it was clear from the language of the court that he had abused the powers of his office. After entering Mc Phillip's lands,

> And havinge gotten the possession thereof, [he] gave divers threateninge and terrible wordes to one Bryan Mc Caher, tennant of the said lande, and ryotously entered into his howse, And said the said Tyrrell would kill him if he woulde not avoyde the possession of his howse and landes: which he refusinge, the saide Capten Tyrrell, beinge a Justice of Peace for the said countie of Cavan, and the said other deftes did then and there ryotously and unlawfully beate and wounde the said Bryan Mc Caher whereby the said Bryan and the reste of the tennantes dwellinge upon the said lande weare enforced to forsake the saide landes.[152]

Tyrrell was imprisoned and fined £20 for the offence. On the other hand, the court was willing to extend its purview to protect the work of commissioners who laboured to seek out concealed lands in advance of a plantation scheme. On 20 November 1612, the court heard a case involving the escheator and surveyor-general of Co. Dublin who held a commission in Bray, Co. Wicklow in February 1611. Sir William Parsons and other officials, along with several lawyers, heard a panel of witnesses before a jury empanelled for the purpose when the volatile Sir Richard Graham and his sons appeared at the courthouse. Having assembled some forty followers, armed with swords, daggers and pikes, the Grahams marched into the courthouse,

151. Ibid., f. 185. The rest of the defendants had already been punished in separate trials at inferior courts. The aim of the castle chamber decree was probably to hold the Irish chief publicly responsible for the affray.
152. Ibid., ff. 178–78v.

and did then & there openly and publiquely before the said Comissioners & Jury geve very reprochefull scandelous and threateninge speeches before the said Comission & Jury against the Credite of the said witnesses Calleing them [a] Company of Garran stealers & Rebelles, with many other Disdainfull and hatefull speeches and alsoe uttered verie foule & threateninge speeches to the said Peter Delahyde that he would pull his bearde from his face and would make the hayer of the Crowne of his head fall to his nose. And not contented therwith the said Thomas Greame the xvjth daie of February followeinge with diverse other of that Riotouse Company meeteinge with one of the said witnesses did riotousely and maliciousely beate batter & bruse him & after Drewe their swordes upon Charles Valentyne, gent, beinge one that attended his maties service in that Comission for rebukeinge the said Thomas Greame for streyking the said witnes.[153]

For their affront to public decorum and royal justice, Sir Richard and Thomas Graham were fined £10 and imprisoned in Dublin Castle.[154] The relatively mild punishment may be explained by the heightened anxiety of landowners confronted with the possibility of dispossession in the interests of the crown.

Some litigants were frequently sued before the court of castle chamber in cases of riot involving property disputes. John Deverox, of Wexford, as we have seen, was one such defendant. Another was John Wolverston, a gentleman of Kylpoole, Co. Wicklow. Wolverston and others were sued in June 1612 by Denys Byrne, a merchant of Dublin, for driving away thirty cows from his lands of Ballenepark in Co. Wicklow, thus depriving Byrne's tenants of their livelihood. It is not unlikely that Wolverston claimed this property as his own, but the court fined him £10 and imprisoned him in Dublin Castle for his offence.[155] The aggressiveness of Wolverston led him to the attention of the court once again in the same year, since he was sued by Dermot McGylpatrick of Co. Wicklow for a riot committed in July 1612. The court heard the case on 13 November, finding Wolverston and his allies guilty of riot and trespass. The evidence showed that

the said John Woolverston, Edmond Mc Cavenagh & Morrogh McShane in riotouse and unlawefull maner did not onely beate & evill intreate the said Hugh Moyle and the reste but alsoe forceably did take from the said persons all the Garrans & harrowes from the said Dermot McGylpatrickes servants and ledde them of[f] from the said Lande to a parcell of the said John Woolverstons owne lande and there in riotouse & unlawefull manner Cutt in peeces all the harroweinge harnes and tooke and ledde away with them all the Garrans.[156]

153. Ibid., ff. 189–90. Parsons was a principal beneficiary of numerous plantations and became an outspoken advocate of plantations in Wexford as the head of the new court of wards after 1622. See McCavitt, *Chichester*, pp. 161–68; Canny, *Making Ireland British*, pp. 259–61.
154. BL, Add. MS 47, 172 f.190.   155. Ibid., f. 187.   156. Ibid., f. 188.

Despite this evidence of recidivism, Wolverston was fined only £5 and his accomplices 40s. and 20s. each for their offences.[157] The temperate measures of the court must be understood in terms of the actual harm done to men of low social position who were not themselves litigants before the court.

Allegations of riot were frequently made in connection with physical damage to property, and in some cases these amounted to vexatious suits. The court of castle chamber heard these grievances in order to take cognizance of issues of public order, to increase the court's profitability from fines and to provide allies of the leading councillors with access to crown justice. On 24 April 1607, the court fined and imprisoned David Power, gentleman, of Co. Cork, who with some forty retainers dispossessed the plaintiffs of their cows, sheep and swine. The court made particular note of the cruel assaulting of three husbandmen, lessees of the freehold from Edmond and Thomas FitzJohn Gerald, who were probably financially responsible for bringing the action in castle chamber.[158] On 22 November 1609, the court heard the case of Brien O'Brien, gentleman, of Co. Limerick who alleged that his two weirs in the River Shannon were destroyed by a company of men from the corporation of Limerick which was just down river from his weirs.[159] Two of the leading aldermen of Limerick, along with the recorder, John Sarsfield, joined other gentlemen and merchants in destroying the weir, shooting rifles in the air to discourage any who would oppose them. The leader of this troupe was Arthur Sexten, a gentleman of Limerick, who was found guilty of the riot and compelled to pay a fine of £200. Importantly, the court made note that the corporation of Limerick would be liable for the fine if Sexten were unable to pay it.[160] Probably, the city was attempting something in the order of flood control, an early modern example of urban planning that lacked important dimensions of civility and due process. Perhaps the most unremarkable riot in the entry book was recorded when Walter French, a powerful attorney and landowner of Galway, sued his neighbours in 1613 for grazing four score cows and oxen on his lands in Chapel Hamlet and Cowlrahan, claiming they 'Riottously and forceably kept uppon the said Land the said Cattle for Divers Dayes'.[161] On the other hand, the potential for genuine social violence continued to gain the attention of the court, especially when wilful and premeditated mayhem was apparently the intent. On 31 January 1610, the court heard the case of James Edwards and his wife Jennet, of Co. Dublin, who complained that three years previously they were forcibly dispossessed of their house, their eight children were thrown out and their goods destroyed. The eight defendants were convicted and forced to pay restitution to Edwards who, at the time, was lying sick in his 'naked bed'.[162]

157. Ibid. In 1617 Wolverston was again in court, this time as plaintiff, for a tumult which occurred in October 1614 (see below). By that time, the turbulent landowner had become a crown official.
158. Ibid., f. 149. The husbandmen, Dermott McTeige, Towhill O'Maly and Teige O'Hanrahan were tenants of the Fitzjohn Geralds at Ballymacahell in Co. Cork.
159. Ibid., f. 164.	160. Ibid.
161. Ibid., f. 194. They were fined £10 each. French had appeared before castle chamber in 1610 (see above) on a charge of malfeasance in the murder trial at Galway of a traitor.
162. Ibid., f. 165. Only three of the defendants answered the pleadings and they were fined,

CONCLUSION

Chichester's use of the court of castle chamber was remarkable in several ways. His defiance of the norms of the Pale community was egregious and inflammatory. The Mandates policy was his alone, finding but a patina of support from the crown and government in London. Chichester and Davies authored the innovative use of the court of castle chamber as a 'spiritual consistory', defending its judicial rigor due to the absence of a court of high commission, and on the basis of the alleged risk of Catholic conspiracy against the crown's government after the Nine Years War. Chichester encountered spirited resistance to his anti-recusant policies and he was compelled to moderate some of his positions as a result. Among the most prominent casualties of the anti-recusant policies of Chichester were the loyal Palesmen and the urban patriciate of Dublin, who refused aldermanic service in the years of crisis, 1605–06 and 1612–13.[163] In addition, his management of the plantation policy and its related land disputes was taken up in quasi-judicial venues apart from castle chamber, though he profited personally from various machinations and was scorned by some for his implacable severity. Nonetheless, he professed concern for the dispossessed and offered to arbitrate in numerous property quarrels. Draconian ruthlessness marked the path of his career, yet he confidently appealed to the crown and to judicial precedent with uneven success. His supervision of the judicial system was adroit, since he expanded the assize circuits rapidly and effectively, brought action in castle chamber against evildoers among the local officials, and staffed the central courts with a full complement of judges. As a consequence, the resort to courts of law was seen as a remarkable achievement of his tenure of office. Writing at the beginning of the regime, Davies reviewed for Cecil the energetic work of the viceroy on assizes throughout the Ulster counties of Monaghan, Fermanagh and Cavan.[164] In Cavan, the lord deputy met a poor Irish town full of suitors, both accusers and accused, where he empanelled a jury and began to assure the people that their property rights would be safeguarded.[165] His is perhaps the best documented period of the court of castle chamber, and the records demonstrate the importance of the court, acting both in its purely judicial role and in its secondary function as the instrument of policy. At the end of his administration, the combative viceroy was defending the record of his parliament and maintaining constant pressure on recusant juries through suits in castle chamber. His successors were unable to sustain the vigorous justification of his policies, though they made no attempt to reverse them.

On the departure of Chichester, there was ample momentum for the lords justices to use the court of castle chamber as a weapon against recusancy, yet the

---

imprisoned and forced to pay costs of court. Nothing else is known about these apparent neighbours, Nicholas Begg, Robert Corbally and Peter Erward, the presumed ringleaders.
163. Lennon, *Lords of Dublin*, p. 184, and see his chapter, 'Recusancy and the defence of privilege'.
164. TCD, MS 842, ff. 113–27.   165. Ibid., f. 126.

records demonstrate an equally lively resistance to this relentless campaign. The recent failure of the Irish parliament and the commission of inquiry did nothing to reinforce the lame duck status of the two veteran judges who took up the reins of government. The new administration of Chichester's follower, Oliver St John, was long expected and the court soon entered a new phase of politicized manoeuvring under the strong influence of the favourite, the duke of Buckingham. The effective boundaries of the St John regime took the form of two sceptical commissions of inquiry, from that of 1613 to the second in 1622, both of them occasioned by the quarrelsome resistance of lawyers and their aristocratic supporters in the Pale. While it may have been the inspiration of Davies rather than the chief governors in this case that lay behind the continuance of determined prosecutions, it is also clear that the use of vexatious suits, the dogged obstinacy of jurors, and the crown's reluctance to employ coercion resulted in a kind of judicial stalemate. The monotonous regularity of crown pleadings on the issue of recusancy soon became formulaic. By the middle decades of the reign, a turgid litany had been substituted for any record of the pleading, evidence or circumstances of the trial. After the names were read into the entry book, a simple rhetorical device followed which led to fine, imprisonment and expulsion from office. In many cases, these fines were followed by a 'reducement' which routinely mitigated their effect. This apparent acknowledgement of the pointlessness of litigation left the court with a genuinely offensive policy in which it no longer fully believed. After the initial salvo and a few other invectives designed to excuse the policy of judicial intimidation, the court no longer resorted to ingenious defences of its actions. Among the purposes of its existence at this time was the mandate to increase crown revenue; hence, the court was content to impose fines as a way of meeting this secondary obligation, refusing either to abandon the policy itself or to pursue it to the next level of inquisitorial brutality. Despite its reputation for harsh intimidation, the Irish star chamber court made little headway against recusancy and its efforts to resolve suits over title to land served only to delay further adjudication by adding to its complexity.

CHAPTER NINE

Petitions, inquiries and Graces: the court of castle chamber under attack, 1615 to 1629

> That witnesses examined upon oath at sessions and assizes, or by Commis-
> sioners, be no longer bound over to the Castle Chamber without apparent cause
> of perjury or subornation, and, if so, not without having a right to claim treble
> damages from a sufficient relator if they shalbe dismissed on hearing.
>
> Requests to the crown on behalf of the subjects of Ireland, 24 May 1628[1]

The withdrawal of Chichester in 1615 after the protracted battles with an unruly
parliament left the government of Ireland in the hands of two veteran judges.
Chichester was under fire from the recusants, the target of a petition to the crown
and subject to a commission of inquiry into his government. On 28 November
1614, Oliver St John wrote to Secretary Winwood that the work of parliament was
slow, noting that the Catholic leader Sir John Everard offered a petition in the
house of commons to restore recusant lawyers to their practice and to suspend the
penalties for non-attendance at church.[2] A similar message was sent to Winwood
by Sir John Denham, chief justice of king's bench in June 1615: 'Touching the
civil government, [he] confesses that by reason of the privileges of Parliament, the
extent whereof can hardly be limited, the courts of justice have small resort unto
them, yet they have been the principal means of continuing the happy peace they
now possess.'[3] When Chichester was finally recalled on 27 November 1615, the
government was placed in the hands of Chief Justice Denham and the sexa-
genarian lord chancellor and archbishop of Dublin, Thomas Jones. Included
among the instructions sent in December 1615 was this admonition:

> They shall often seriously advise with the Council about the state of affairs
> of that kingdom and not spend time in idle and petty businesses, such as are
> unfit to be brought to that board, but are to be referred to such of the
> ordinary courts of justice as the same shall properly belong to, or to the
> judges in their circuits.[4]

1. *Cal. S.P. Ire., 1625–32*, p. 336. 2. *Cal. S.P. Ire., 1611–14*, pp. 526–27.
3. *Cal. S.P. Ire., 1615–25*, p. 67.
4. Ibid., p. 102, and see pp. 101–05 for instructions to the new government. Plate 10 (Jones).

During nearly eight months in office, the lords justices gave orders in ten cases now found in the entry book of the court of castle chamber. They continued to prosecute jurors for refusing to present recusants in Co. Westmeath and Co. Longford; and they fined officials for executing their offices without taking the oath of supremacy in Kilkenny, Thomastown, Kilmallock, Inistioge, Cork, Limerick, Waterford, Clonmel, Dublin, Drogheda and Dundalk.[5] The momentum of the court which had been sustained under Chichester did not slacken under his temporary replacements, despite the recent petitions against his heavy-handed dealing with Catholic dissenters. On the other hand, the large number of defendants from towns all over the country indicates that the policy was having little effect. Officials such as the late mayor of Kilkenny, Lucas Shea, and the late portreeve of Inistioge, James Dulan, were indicted before the court, fined and imprisoned.[6] Yet the wily recusant leaders, undaunted, mounted a campaign of legal harassment against their New English adversaries which brought them before the lords justices in the castle chamber. On 10 May 1616, the petition of Edmond Sexten of Limerick was heard in which the former mayor of Limerick, William Haly, and twenty co-defendants, including five aldermen, were accused of conspiring to keep the complainant in continual suits at law. Sexten alleged that the defendants met together in May 1615 to plan vexatious suits which would prevent him from growing to such wealth that he might purchase lands and tenements in and around Limerick to the value of £1,000. The suit alleged that the defendants

> did then and there wickedly, malyceously and unlawfully Combyne and Conspire amongst themselves by any means whatsoever to Disturbe and brynge the said Edmond Sexten into suyte of law for Certayne tenementes lyeinge in the suburbes of the said Cittie of Lymericke.[7]

In August of that year, led by the then mayor, Haly, the defendants allegedly assembled in riotous manner to interrupt the carpenters employed by Sexten on his estate, the former abbey of St Maryhouse in Limerick, after which they, '[in]

5. BL, Add. MS 47,172, ff. 214–17, 219, 221. One suit fined the mayor and two sheriffs of Kilkenny; another fined the portreeves and sovereigns of Thomastown, Kilmallock, Gowran and Inistioge; while a third fined the mayors of Cork, Limerick, Waterford, and Clonmel. The last suit fined the sheriffs of Dublin and Drogheda, and the bailiff of Dundalk. The effect of this high-handed stringency was to strip local governments of their elected officials, throwing the machinery of government into confusion without providing an orderly transition. Eleven of the loyal towns were thus alienated by a policy which had not been shown to work.
6. Ibid. Other officials fined for taking up office without swearing the oath were Patrick Dobbyn, sovereign of Thomastown, Gearod Verden, sovereign of Kilmallock, and William Nash, portreeve of Gawran.
7. Ibid., f. 220. The allegation of conspiracy was coupled with the accusation of riot to attract the jurisdiction of the star chamber court, though the substance of Sexten's charge was an inadequately concealed suit over real property.

lyke foreceable and outrageous manner did dispoyle breake and plucke downe to the ground the mayne tymber of the house the said Edmond Sexten had then lately sett uppe and erected uppon the said tenementes.'[8] In finding Haly and other defendants guilty, the court apparently held once again that mere property damage, without inflicting harm to a person, was sufficient to prove a charge of riot. The case of riot, mixed with conspiracy and mischievous suits at law, gives evidence of the tenacity and pluck of recusant officials who were apparently far from awed by the threat of a suit in star chamber. The orchestration of a lawful adversary movement among skilful townsmen during the early Stuart period merits further study.

The Munster towns had provided ample substance for similar prosecutions in castle chamber from the beginning of the reign, and Cork was evidently a source of recusant opposition to government religious policy. John Coppinger, the mayor of Cork, and Patricke Croninge, one of the sheriffs of the city, were fined for executing their offices without taking the oath of supremacy on 8 May 1616.[9] The powerful local family of Coppingers was led by the wealthy merchant, Walter Coppinger, a former mayor of Cork and lately possessed of a large landed estate. Walter and Richard Coppinger, his brother, were among the defendants charged in a petition before castle chamber in February 1616. Thomas Crooke and James Salmon of Baltimore, a town newly planted with English tenants of Crooke, had sued the Coppingers in 1613 for preferring unjust and malicious indictments against them at quarter sessions in Co. Cork, including one for high treason against Crooke himself.[10] Alleging various riots and other offences in order to gain the attention of the court, Crooke protested against the Coppingers' effort to 'subplant' his new English tenants by judicial harassment, an interesting twist on the traditional view of English interlopers manipulating the common law for their advantage. The Coppingers and O'Driscoll were found guilty of one riot that occurred on 1 July 1611, but other charges were dismissed.[11] Walter Coppinger himself had built his impressive Jacobean mansion house near Ross Carbery around 1612, planning to

---

8. Ibid., f. 220v. The Limerick aldermen included William Stritch, a former mayor himself, Domynick Roche, Piers Creagh, Domynicke Creagh and Edmond Fox. Castle chamber found Haly guilty of leading the conspiracy, along with eighteen others, but acquitted Stritch as no evidence was produced to show he was present at the alleged riot. Sexten claimed these officials had been 'armed in warlyke and hostile manner with swordds, head peeces, gunnes, staves and other weapons ' during their attack on his 'buyldynges begune'. Ibid.

9. Ibid., f. 219. Symon Fannynge, mayor of Limerick, John Skiddy, mayor of Waterford, and Bennet White, mayor of Clonmel, were found guilty of the same offence, fined and sentenced. Coppinger and Fanning were fined £30 English; Skiddy and White £20 English; while Sheriff Cronynge was fined only £10 Irish.

10. Ibid., f. 212. The Coppingers were joined by Donogh O'Driscoll and Edmond Power and others as defendants in the case, which was continued from Trinity term in 1613 until Hilary term 1615. Richard Coppinger and O'Driscoll were found guilty of the 'malyceous and uniust indictmentes' against Crooke and his English tenants.

11. Ibid., ff. 212–12v. The Coppingers were fined £20 each for their multiple offences.

add a model village, so the dispute was more nearly one between rival agents for change, in this case a well-established Cork merchant of Danish origins.[12]

Despite their successful prosecution in castle chamber, Crooke, Salmon, John Winthrop and Sir John Skinner joined in a petition to the privy council in England against Coppinger in April 1618, in which they despaired of a remedy in the Irish courts for protection of their newly purchased lands in the barony of Carbery, where they became Coppinger's neighbours. Claiming that Coppinger had worked for ten years to prevent their plantation of colonies of English people, towns and religion, and citing the support of the lord president and the lord deputy, the petitioners claimed that Coppinger had unlawfully got possession of many lands belonging to the crown and the church. They concluded,

> Whereupon the said Coppinger and divers of his confederates have been censured in the Star chamber there, for procuring multitudes of indictments of treasons, felonies, riots, and other crimes to be found against the said English inhabitants upon some feigned surmises and corrupt oaths, with practices by popish juries, and for committing bloody riots upon them to weary them from those parts. Notwithstanding all which discoveries and punishments, the said Coppinger, continuing his malicious and covetous desire to supplant the said plantationers and get their possessions, has by very many forgeries, champerties, maintainers and other like corrupt and unlawful courses, (for which he is yet uncensured,) gotten several pretended titles to all their lands; under colour whereof he continues these unjust vexations to their excessive damage, and many of their undoings.[13]

On 29 November 1619, the lord deputy and council sent to the privy council in England a petition from the redoubtable Coppinger, claiming on behalf of the freeholders of Kerrycurrihy, Co. Cork, that Dominick Sarsfield had misused his office of chief justice to procure a rent from every ploughland to himself and his heirs. St John presided over a full meeting of thirteen councillors in the absence of Sarsfield, showing that the council itself was unwilling to adjudicate on matters involving a fellow member.[14] Coppinger demonstrated his ability to exploit the

12. Terence Reeves-Smyth, *Irish castles* (Belfast, 1995), pp. 24–25. Coppinger's Court is today a picturesque ruin which preserves large Jacobean chimneys, a long hall 68 feet across and over 300 mullioned windows. It is located about 25 miles from Baltimore.

13. *Cal. S.P. Ire., 1611–25*, p. 191. The petitioners sought a commission to take depositions and a summons for Coppinger to appear before the English privy council itself. Crook and Salmon were joined by John Winthrop and Thomas Notte and other gentlemen adventurers in the purchase of lands in Carbery with the aim of erecting English towns and planting colonies of English people to settle the 'true religion' in Co. Cork. Ibid., pp. 190–91.

14. Ibid., p. 268. In subsequent petitions to the crown in 1626 and 1630, Crooke continued to complain against Coppinger until Charles I ordered a hearing in the English star chamber, saying, 'We desire, seeing how our Court of Castle Chamber was lately divided on this question, to have it tried before us and our Privy Council in our Court of Star Chamber.' *Cal. S.P. Ire., 1647–60, Addenda, 1625–60*, pp. 82, 163.

judicial system throughout his long career. He was part of an understudied element of early modern Irish society: loyal, Catholic, an adroit litigant and former municipal official who became both landowner and successful businessman.

In May 1616, the lords justices found themselves implicated in the web of intrigue which the surveyor, William Parsons, and Edward Fisher had built in Co. Wexford, based on letters patent as undertakers for the complainants' lands. A petition from Redmond McDamore and others to the English privy council protested against the commission of defective titles, claiming that the judges of assize in 1609 assured them of clear title based on their surrender to the crown and alleging the intimidation of jurors from Wexford who were brought to Dublin, examined by the poll, and 'for their intractability were then presently committed to the Marshalsea, and often censured in the Star Chamber, without allowance of counsel'.[15] The petitioners alleged the council of Ireland refused their complaint, permitted Parsons and Fisher to take possession of the land by force and complained they had been ruined by counter-suits after being dispossessed.[16] In similar fashion to the machinations of Walter Coppinger, the English adventurer Sir William Parsons took the benefit of vexatious pleadings, questionable suits and partisan manipulations of his office to amass a great estate. Involved in the plantations of Ulster, Leitrim, Longford and Wexford, Parsons had succeeded his uncle, Sir Geoffrey Fenton, as surveyor-general in 1602. He became a notoriously unscrupulous master of the new court of wards in 1622 and was made an Irish councillor in 1623. Though he was made a baronet and became lord justice in 1640, Parsons retired to England in 1648 amid accusations that he did much to stimulate the Irish rebellion.[17]

The lords justices extended the persecution of recusants, indicting a senior member of the peerage for concealing a Jesuit and hearing mass in his Dublin house. On 25 April 1616, they explained the matter to the privy council in England:

> On Wednesday the 24th instant (being a day for causes depending in His Majesty's Court of Castle Chamber) called the Lord of Incequyn before themselves, and sundry privy councillors of this State, and most of the judges, and laid to his charge the breach and contempt of His Majesty's three procla-

---

15. *Cal. S.P. Ire., 1615–25*, pp. 124–26. The petition detailed a long history of suits in Co. Wexford in which jurors steadfastly refused to find for the crown, despite the empanelling of gentlemen sympathetic to the undertakers such as Sir Lawrence Esmond. The jurors were brought to Dublin and examined in the court of exchequer, but they steadfastly affirmed the rights of the petitioners and some were then fined in the star chamber. At last, other jurors were employed who found title for the crown, and Parsons sued an English bill in exchequer against the petitioners to gain possession of their estates. Ibid.

16. Ibid. Collectors from all counties produced a total of £8,168 13s. 9d. from all the courts, including justices of assize, in the previous Lent circuit of 1616. On 18 June a memorandum of judicial fines indicated the castle chamber had collected a good part of the £807 4s. 0d. levied during the past year. Ibid., p. 127.

17. *DNB*. See also Canny, *Making Ireland British*, pp. 249–55, 259–61.

mations published against the receiving and relieving of Jesuits, &c. by his entertainment of one Nicholas Nugent, a Jesuit, in his house in September last, hearing of his masses and wilful retaining of him for 20 days.[18]

The lords justices found that Inchiquin had been imprisoned and fined previously for the same offence,[19] so they jailed him in Dublin Castle and fined him £100 Irish for his contempt of the court.[20] In the following spring, the court heard a petition from the attorney-general against Walter Cregg of Mount Rosse in Scotland, who was accused of bringing Nugent, along with another priest named William Malone, to Inchekatherine on the River Shannon at the request of Anthony Arthur, a merchant from Limerick. Cregg had been in Lisbon loading salt for transport to Limerick, and he apparently conspired with Arthur to return to Ireland with the priests.[21] The information was strangely silent on the fate of the merchant himself, or the priests, but this was evidently an effort to follow up on the Inchiquin prosecution.

A CROWDED CALENDAR: THE FORCEFUL PROSECUTIONS OF ST JOHN'S COURT, 1616–1622

The lords justices delivered the sword of state to Oliver St John as the new lord deputy on 15 July 1616. St John had been master of the ordnance since 1605 and sought the viceregal office during the final three years of the Chichester regime. His mother Elizabeth Blount was a kinswoman of Mountjoy, and St John enjoyed the favour of the last Elizabethan lord deputy, who knighted him in 1601 before the siege of Kinsale. Though a soldier of fortune who had fled the country after killing George Best in a duel in 1584, St John possessed legal training. In fact, he graduated B.A. from Oxford in 1578 and was admitted to Lincoln's Inn in 1580. As the most trusted adviser of Chichester, he was closely involved in the plantation of Ulster, received 1500 acres in Co. Armagh and served as courier to the court where he explained Irish business to the king in 1614. Through his family connections with the rapidly ascending favourite, St John received Buckingham's support as lord deputy-elect in April 1616 and thereafter worked closely with his patron to establish in Ireland a powerful Villiers clientele. As St John's niece, Barbara, was married to Sir Edward Villiers in 1612, the vast estates of the childless lord deputy in England and Ireland were willed to his great-nephew, William Villiers, after St John was created Viscount Grandison in 1621.

18. *Cal. S.P. Ire., 1615–25*, p. 122.
19. BL, Add. MS 47,172, f. 213.
20. The document was signed by eight judges and attorneys, including Dominick Sarsfield, William Methwold, Francis Aungier, Christopher Sibthorp, John Blennerhasset, and Gerard Lowther. Inchiquin confessed to the offence, acknowledging that Nugent had said mass at his manor house several times with the servants and his wife present.
21. BL, Add. MS 47,172, f. 218.

He found posts for the reliable Henry Holcroft as his secretary in 1616 and for Thomas Stockdale as clerk of castle chamber in 1618.[22]

After 1615 the court of castle chamber under Lord Deputy St John hewed to the policy set out by Chichester. Despite the fact that both viceroys were under the strong influence of the duke of Buckingham, as Treadwell has now amply demonstrated, the entry book and other records show a consistent pattern of litigation that owed more to the inspiration of Chichester than to the king's favourite.[23] The prosecution of recusancy, for example, continued apace with the castle chamber hearing 43 cases involving recusants, out of the 57 total cases conducted under St John from 1616 to 1620. Of those suits, 32 decrees found jurors guilty of failing to prosecute their neighbours as recusants; in another five cases Catholics were sued for harbouring Jesuit priests, or for transporting Jesuits or their books and letters from Lisbon; and in another five cases prominent local officials were tried for executing their offices without taking the oath of supremacy. Other cases heard in castle chamber under the St John government included indictments for riot and assault, for abduction of women, for fraudulent deeds and counterfeiting the viceroy's signature. On Chichester's departure in November 1615, a spate of thirteen cases against recusancy were held in fourteen days, and in the next year sixteen cases were heard in May (8) and November (8) against recusants. It is difficult to avoid the conclusion that the court of castle chamber had become an engine of religious reform under both Chichester and St John, yet the pattern of litigation suggests that the policy was not working. Indeed, one defendant was pilloried in addition to his fine, the court noting that he had previously been prosecuted for recusancy and had promised to attend church regularly. The tedious monotony of these perfunctory decrees in the record book of the court belies the atmosphere of tension during a time when English planters and officials were undermining the security of tenure of all property owners in Ireland. An uneasy civil peace was being frayed by contentious litigation at the court of castle chamber and elsewhere. Yet, despite the schemes of opportunist viceroys eager to compel religious uniformity, the period was notable for the absence of violent conflict. After 1618, prosecutions for recusancy fell off dramatically and the caseload of the court was severely diminished.

In its deliberations of 11 July 1617 over the charter of Waterford, the English privy council advised circumspection on recusancy issues. While urging the punishment of truculent local officials and castle chamber prosecution of those who harboured priests, the council wrote to the lord deputy and council in Ireland, advising them to temporize with persons of quality and 'winke at' the admission of recusants as local officials as long as they were competent in other ways.[24]

The privy council temporized on numerous issues in their missive, requiring the viceroy to imprison two lawyers, Wadden and Butler, who had assisted the

---

22. V. Treadwell, *Buckingham and Ireland*, pp. 48–50. St John had four nieces married to Buckingham clients, including Sir Allen Apsley.

23. Ibid.   24. *Acts privy council, 1616–17*, pp. 311–14.

Waterford corporation; to challenge the city's charter and prevent the mayor from sitting on proceedings related to the liberties of Waterford; and to prosecute the city for defects under the great seal of Ireland.[25] However, the councillors preferred to keep the priests under guard in a castle located in a lake, as opposed to a castle chamber hearing, interning them in a manner 'nor yet … soe hard and meane, as to give cause of noate or scandall by extremytie'.[26] Worrying that the local officials who endorsed the Reformation would lack credibility since they were chosen from the 'meaner sort', the English privy council sought to proceed against some of the leaders while advising the viceroy to 'abide tyme' in efforts to promote the Reformation.[27]

In the first case heard under the leadership of St John, the recitation of familiar formulae was used to describe the routine interrogation of recusant officials for executing their offices without taking the oath of supremacy. Named as defendants in the action were the mayors of Waterford, Kilkenny, Limerick and Fethard, as well as sheriffs and bailiffs from the Munster towns. They were fined according to their ability to pay and sentenced to jail during pleasure of the lord deputy on 13 November 1616.[28] Two days later, the court heard the case of Nicholas Fitzwilliams, esquire, of Co. Dublin who was convicted of harbouring Patrick Duffe, a priest whom he had known for seven years. The two were apprehended by the warrant of the viceroy in Dublin city after the defendant 'openlye at noone day broght the said Patrick Duffe in his Company from Burdmegan to the Cittie of Dublin to the view of soe many as would have ann eye uppon him'.[29] The viceroy and the court were outraged at the brazen exposure of the priest and the frequent resort of the lord of Howth and other gentlemen to his house.[30] The wave of recusancy cases in the Michaelmas term of 1616 under St John continued in the succeeding year at a less hectic pace. Attempting to refine the bludgeon of peremptory sentencing, the court heard evidence against a grand jury in Kilkenny and employed three different punishments on those who refused to present recusants for failure to attend divine service. The judges found nine were poor and ignorant men who submitted to the mercy of the court and fined them £10 apiece, citing John Stafford for his promise that he would faithfully attend church and remitting both his £20 fine and imprisonment in the hope that he would produce a certificate of his attendance at the court by the next Michaelmas term. By contrast, the court fined Patrick Roche £100 for his contemptuous misdemeanour before the court itself during proceedings and sentenced him to wear a paper on his head before each of the four courts, and at the next assizes in Co. Wexford, declaring the

25. Ibid. They also advised finding an alternate means of governing Waterford once its charter had been dissolved lawfully.
26. Ibid., pp. 313–14.
27. Ibid., p. 314. Lamely adding that the children of recusant leaders should be brought up in Protestant schools under the watchful eye of the lord deputy, the privy council left the government of Ireland without a clear sense of direction.
28. BL, Add. MS 47,172, f. 222.   29. Ibid., f. 223.
30. Ibid.

nature of his offence.[31] Five days later, on 28 May, the court again expressed outrage at the boldness of the defendant, William Baggott, a merchant of Dublin, for harbouring a priest during the past four years. Stating the case more explicitly and drawing out carefully the dire political consequences of the offence, the court declared in its sentence,

> for that his said fault was greatlie augmented by the Circumstances of tyme and place, as in respect of tyme the Preist was harboured in the Parlyament tyme, that he might be ready to advise and consult with or to direct (accordinge to his Capacite) such of the Romanistes as were specyally Interested in the publique afaires, how they might any way either hinder the good indeavoures of the well Disposed or promote the evill motives of the evill affected and turbulent spirites, and in respect of place, the house was made a kynd of Church standing in the most frequent street of the Cittie and wholie Dedicated to superstition and the highest Idolatrie.[32]

The court of castle chamber interpreted its role as the enemy of sedition. Consequently, a number of cases were described at length when the welfare of the Irish polity was in danger. On 15 May 1618, for example, a priest named David Verdon was sentenced for maliciously defaming the archbishop of Canterbury. Verdon had circulated a rumour among witnesses from Drogheda in Co. Meath that George Abbot, the archbishop in England, was placed in the Tower for claiming that the king was a foreigner who usurped the throne and that the king sought a Spanish match for the heir in order to overthrow the English. The sentence of imprisonment and a fine of £500 was augmented by the pillory, where he was to lose both his ears.[33] On the other hand, the trial of Richard Nugent and his wife Elinor, was a poignant reminder of the tragic implications for ordinary families of the rough policy of James's government. Nugent and James Brown, merchants of Dublin, had received letters from the imprisoned Nicholas Nugent, a Jesuit priest formerly sentenced in castle chamber, and probably a kinsman, as well as several letters from the Irish colleges in Spain and Portugal. Elinor Nugent was specially convicted of sending eleven shillings in gold to her son, John, at the Irish College in Lisbon, which, along with other letters and payments, Brown proposed to convey during Easter term to Portugal. Richard Bolton, the solicitor-general, demonstrated before the court

---

31. Ibid., ff. 246–46v. Dr Edwards has argued that castle chamber served a coherent policy to disempower the newly installed Catholic earl of Ormonde in Kilkenny by threatening his clients with fine and punishment after 1614. After five different mayors were forced to resign in 1616, the grand jury was fined and leading landowners were threatened with forfeiture owing to defective titles. Edwards, *Ormond lordship*, pp. 274–79.
32. BL, Add. MS 47, 172, ff. 247–47v.   33. Ibid., f. 270.

how dangerous and insufferable yt ys in subiectes to have intercourse by letters and intelligence with, or to supplie moneys unto, the professed enemies (to the religion and gouvernment established) reciding beyond the Seas, in the Nurseries of seditious spiritts, who are there instructed and doe begin, both to learn and practize howe to sowe sedition in the mindes of ill affected subiectes.[34]

Having made their point, the court proceeded to reduce the fines on all three defendants, in respect of their poverty, to £5 Irish. Although tiresomely arbitrary and paranoid, the court managed to appreciate the tenderness of a mother sending money to a son away at college, silently acknowledging the many occasions of the sort which went undetected by officials who were complicit in the act.[35] On 23 May 1620, the lord deputy sat along with seven judges to hear the case of Patrick Plunkett who was charged with receiving a barrel of books and pictures from priests in foreign jurisdictions. In strong language, the court accused Plunkett of seeking 'to infect the myndes of his maties subiectes with supersticon, and … with malignant thoughtes of treason and rebellion'.[36]

The court of castle chamber under St John supervised the entire infrastructure of judicial administration, taking up petty causes in order to reprimand corrupt officials and intervening to upbraid renegade jurors who had refused to follow the evidence. For example, the court heard a case in 1617 on an information from the attorney-general, Sir John Davies, against twelve gentlemen empanelled as jurors at the assizes in Galway on 29 August. In the murder of Henry Sprat, a gentleman late of Killdyney in Co. Galway, the jurors acquitted James Evers of the murder and absolved Ann James of conspiracy. All the jurors were fined for giving a verdict against the evidence, according to their ability to pay.[37] On 24 April 1618, the court admonished the subsidy collectors from the barony of Ballinacor in Co. Wicklow for taking the second payment in sterling instead of Irish money, contrary to their instructions. On a petition from Redmond McFeagh O'Byrne against Luke Toole and Theobold Archbold, the court found that these local officials had exceeded their directions and extorted additional money from the complainant and others. They were imprisoned, fined and compelled to make restitution after acknowledging their offence at the next assizes in Wicklow.[38] The glut of petitions and pleadings before the court occasioned a brief entry on 10 June 1618, when the exasperated judges dismissed a cross-suit filed by two Limerick merchants against one another which they had secretly agreed between themselves not to prosecute, without informing the court. William Stritch, alderman, and Dominick White, merchant, were held in contempt of the court for conspiring to defraud its officials of their fees and sustaining their fraudulent

34. Ibid., f. 272v.   35. Ibid.
36. Ibid., f. 278. The court reduced the fine of Plunkett owing to his great poverty, but again affirmed the close link between recusancy and rebellion.
37. Ibid., f. 248.   38. Ibid., f. 263.

prosecutions, contrary to instructions of the court.[39] The close connection between assizes and the castle chamber was made evident in a suit which was initiated by the viceroy himself on 17 November 1619 against Gilbert Butler, sheriff of Co. Tipperary. At the assizes held in Clonmel before the chief baron and Sir John Blennerhasset, the sheriff had been instructed to carry out a death sentence upon a notorious rebel (unnamed in the suit), but he instead reprieved the prisoner in hope of gaining his pardon. The star chamber court, with Chief Baron William Methwold sitting among its four judges and giving testimony against the sheriff, accepted his confession and reduced his fine out of compassion for his mean estate, yet their judgement gives weight to the vital connection between local enforcement and formal proceedings. They began,

> Howbeyt forasmuch as his offence in shew proceeded from too high a presumption, but especially for that the Due execution of the law is the life & soule of the law, so as without yt noe Comon welth can subsist and bee, and for that also if such offences should escape unpunished, and chiefly when the offenders are men of emmynent note, from whome the lower rankes are ever apt to take example, and encouragement to doe the like, yf not worse.[40]

In 1620, the court heard a charge of embracery and maintenance which bore witness to the fragility of the jury system. With the lord deputy presiding over seven days of hearings and offering testimony to the frequency of the problem in Irish courts, the complainant, David Fitzgibbon, charged seven defendants with perjury and subornation of perjury. Hearing the case upon an ejectment from a trial at king's bench, the court acquitted four of the defendants before hearing the accusation that Gibbon FitzMorris conspired to bribe several jurors and potential witnesses in his case pending against Fitzgibbon in Co. Meath. Using Donogh O'Grady and Nicholas Freeman as his agents and solicitors, FitzMorris tried to bribe Francis Fytton of Co. Limerick and solicited many freeholders prior to the trial on his behalf, some of whom later confessed their involvement. The court offered an extensive rationale prior to fining and imprisoning the defendants:

> Uppon which evident and demonstrative proffes the Court was pleased to proceed to censure, and knowing that the offences of periury, subornacon of periury, Champertye, mayntenance and embracery are exceeding frequent in this kingdome, as the principall Judges yea the Lo Deputy hymself, knew and did testifye, that yf such offences soe comon, soe pernicious and soe pestilent, as that having already infected divers members of this politick body, yf they be not cauterized in tyme, may peirce into, and thoroughly infect the whole body, for as good lawes and the due execucon of

---

39. Ibid., f. 271.
40. Ibid., f. 275. The precarious balance struck by Chief Baron Methwold as both judge and accuser in the case escaped the attention of the punctilious magistrates.

them are the mayne supporters of all well governed comon wealthes, soe the neglect to take fitt opportunytyes to chastize delinquentes and transgressors of the law, may (by the ympunyty and freedome of punishment in some) give occasion, incouragement and boldnes to others, exorbitatntly to run ryott into all manner of mischeifes, for prevencon whereof, and to Terrifye all, that will take example from the executing hand of Justice.[41]

The court heard charges of counterfeiting and forgery, causes ordinarily adjudicated in other venues, in order to establish a clear and forceful expectation of financial probity that was punctuated by the threat of punishment in star chamber. In a case involving the wife and daughter of a deceased gentleman from Carrickfergus, John Dalway, the court found for the complainant, Margaret Dobb, against the widow, Jane Dalway and her son by another marriage, James Walsh. The widow Dalway conspired in 1615 to defraud her daughter of the inheritance by sending a letter purporting to be from her husband to John Bennis, a Dublin alderman, with instructions to deliver a trunk of Dalway's in his custody to James Walsh. Using this ruse, the defendants were accused of altering the feoffment that entitled Margaret Dobb to certain lands, and the court found them guilty of a forgery. The information was placed before the court on 15 November 1616 and final judgment was rendered on 11 February 1617, when the court sentenced the widow and son to a fine of £10 and left the validity of the feoffment to trial at common law. Evidently, the court felt strongly that such a perversion of trusted agreements merited strong punishment, even though castle chamber was theoretically not involved in property litigation.[42] In 1619, John Jones was censured, pilloried and imprisoned by the court for a counterfeit of the lord deputy's hand to a deed which was shown in court. Noting that all warrants passed by the royal prerogative 'may be termed a sacred hand', the court banished Jones from Ireland after the end of his sentence.[43] In similar fashion, the court punished John Geshell for counterfeiting the viceroy's signature to a protection in order to prevent arrest or suit from his creditors, fining him £40.[44]

In the first full year of his administration, St John took cognizance of an information in castle chamber brought by John Wolverston, a justice of the peace in Co. Wicklow, against Nicholas and William Walsh for an assault against a public official. The language of the case demonstrates an acute concern for the dignified management of judicial sessions, especially when commissions of the peace were delegated to local officials at a distance from the central courts. On 7 October 1615, Nicholas Walsh attempted to provoke Wolverston to fight by using contemptuous words, after which his brother William 'gave him the lie' when he was

41. Ibid., ff. 276–77.
42. Ibid., ff. 261–61v.
43. Ibid., f. 273.
44. Ibid., f. 274. Geshell was imprisoned during pleasure and made to stand on the pillory after acknowledging his offences in all the four courts in Dublin.

leaving the courthouse itself and going to his home. On the same night, the contentious ruffians came to the house of Wolverston where Nicholas demeaned his birth, claiming the Walshes were more honourable gentry (unlike the Wolverstons who claimed only on the mother's side). The next day Nicholas Walsh struck Wolverston in front of the sessions house and drew his dagger, threatening to use his sword against him. The star chamber court provided extensive detail in the record book to justify its hearing of the cause, commending Wolverston for showing restraint and keeping the peace. The affront to public justice aggravated the assault, as well as the dishonour to members of the gentry of Ireland, so the judges proceeded to fine and imprison the Walsh brothers, demanding they appear at the next sessions in Wicklow to acknowledge their offences and express sorrow at their 'follye and Rashnes'.[45] The court also accused William Walsh of challenging Wolverston to fight, 'well knowynge the said John Woulverston to be then one of his maties Justices of the peace for the said County.'[46]

Sir Oliver St John possessed both legal training and, by 1620, ample judicial experience as a councillor and viceroy. The last two cases which were recorded in the entry book of the court of castle chamber give evidence of the ongoing scrutiny of the court in cases of aggravated assault which threatened not only breach of the peace, but derogation of the honour of high office and the expectation of aristocratic demeanour. On 23 June 1621, the lord deputy presided at the court, along with ten other judges, to hear the extraordinary case of Sir Christopher Draycott who had spat in the face of Sir Francis Roe, the mayor of Drogheda, cudgelling his wife in her own house and striking his servants. The court made particular note of the indignity to public office, citing Draycott for assaulting the mayor's macebearer in the street and subsequently throwing his 70-year-old jailer down fourteen steps. The impenitent Draycott further calumniated his adversary, 'calling [him] a base knight, a scurvey knight, and a shitten pockye knight, and that as he was Sir Francis Roe, he cared no more for hym then he cared for the Roe of a hearing, and as he was maior of Drogheda he cared no more for him then he cared for a turd.'[47] In its extensive recording of details of the case, the court was moved to declare its high purposes in this lowly matter. Draycott's attorney pleaded that he was drunk at the time, he had no prior offence and he was a younger brother 'whose estate ys litle and uncerteyne'.[48] But the

---

45. Ibid., f.235. Wolverston had a reputation for violence. In 1612, he was twice convicted for riot against his neighbours in Co. Wicklow, driving away 30 cows in one case, then beating the servants of his rival and leading off their garrons. Ibid., ff. 187, 188, and see above, pp. 318–19. The fact he was selected as justice of the peace five years later may be testimony to the conditions of the rough frontier at Dublin's back door, and the lack of suitable gentry of English birth. For the Tudor background, now see C. Maginn, *'Civilizing' Gaelic Leinster: the extension of Tudor rule in the O'Byrne and O'Toole lordships* (Dublin, 2005). The silence of the court on Wolverston's earlier recidivism as defendant is redolent of the separate treatment of other multiple litigants such as Walter Coppinger.

46. Ibid., f. 235.   47. Ibid., f. 279v.

48. Ibid.

judges returned to the principles governing its decision to hear the case, saying that a gentleman of good descent should never degenerate so far in his behaviour, and affirming repeatedly the importance of Roe as the crown's servant, protected by the royal mantle, which was undermined by the scandalous treatment of Draycott. For his punishment, Draycott was fined £520, imprisoned in Dublin Castle during pleasure, and made to kneel before Sir Francis and Lady Roe in Drogheda to ask their forgiveness.[49]

Seven days after the Draycott hearing, St John presided over another egregious violation of the king's peace. On 30 June 1621, the court censured Martyn Plunkett, Edward Plunkett and Matthew Bath for abducting Margaret Cusack to be married to Martyn against her will, as a means of gaining her lands and livelihood. Fining Martyn £500 and the others £200 each, the court duly noted the statutory basis for the suit and debated over several court days whether the case should properly be tried at king's bench in the next term. No mention was made of the outcome of the intended marriage, nor the harm which might have come to the woman herself while she was kidnapped for four days. But the court was determined to exercise jurisdiction in the matter since it was apparently not uncommon:

> Howbeit uppon mature consyderacon of the nature of the offence and the native disposition of this country in like cases, but especially in respect of his Maties strong inclination to clemencye and mercy in sparing the lives of his subiectes, and in lieu of their lives to inflict pecuniary and corporall punishmentes which power derived from his majestie was now here invested in the person of the Lo Deputie, who, openly declaring himself to be the true servant of soe mercifull a master and Soveraigne, did deliver his judgment and soe did determine that this cause should now receive a finall Censure in the Court.[50]

Once again, prerogative justice had an appellate, or prior, jurisdiction over pleadings which were seen to have political, or even symbolic, implications.

Under St John, the commissioners for Irish causes heard numerous petitions seeking English-based arbitration in causes long pending. In 1619, for example, the Irish experts heard a petition from Sir Thomas Fitzwilliams against a decree of the late lord chancellor. Sir Thomas protested that the award of £520 granted to Christopher Fitzwilliams was originally charged to his estate by his father, who was only tenant for life and who altered terms of the bequest during the petitioner's minority to favour the defendant, against the terms set forth by his grandfather. The commissioners remanded the case for mediation to the lord deputy, the new lord chancellor, the two chief justices and the master of the rolls, to hear the parties and their counsel and offer to reconcile them, or to certify the privy council on the matters in evidence.[51] Cases before the court of chancery

49. Ibid., ff. 279–80.   50. Ibid., f. 281.   51. *Cal. S.P. Ire., 1615–25*, p. 579.

were commonly reviewed by the powerful commissioners, just as were the petitions appealing decrees of the court of castle chamber. The removal of cases from Irish jurisdiction was certain to cause long delays and the near inevitability that resulted of having to seek further evidence from Ireland usually requiring the continued involvement of the original Irish court of record. In this way, all litigation became vexatious, regardless of the merits of the case or the original intent of the complainant.

In his study of the puissant influence of the duke of Buckingham on Ireland, Victor Treadwell asserted the importance of 'reconstructing the Irish social pyramid' during the viceroyalties of St John and Falkland.[52] The covert aim of this '"British" social engineering' was to establish a new ascendancy in Ireland which was British and Protestant, using a 'massive but discriminating distribution of honours'.[53] The role of the court of castle chamber in this process was peripheral, but it is important to bear in mind how the intensely litigious process of transformation within the Irish nobility bore the stamp of parallel jurisdictions in England and Ireland. The lord deputy and council received numerous petitions on behalf of the claimants to several noble titles and estates, and the entire period 1616 to 1629 was littered with failed strategems and ploys designed to finalize legitimate inheritance and to parry the legal thrusts of rivals, their counsel and their patrons. The tortuous route to security of title for the embattled senior earldom of Kildare demonstrates the genealogical hazards awaiting the historian in this complex era. From the death of the eleventh earl of Kildare in the Tower of London in 1585 to the marriage of the sixteenth earl in 1630 with the widowed daughter of the earl of Cork, who happened to be a lord justice of Ireland at the time, the estates and titles of the earldom were continually in litigation. The death in 1580 of the eleventh earl's eldest son left three women with claims on the estate: his widow, the dowager Countess Mabel; his son Lord Offaly's widow, Lady Katherine, daughter of Francis Knollys; and his granddaughter, Lady Lettice. Succession to the earldom had passed after 1585 to the younger sons of the eleventh earl, Henry and William, who both died without heirs in 1597 and 1599, respectively. In the latter year, Gerald Fitzgerald, a cousin born in England, laid his claim to the title and estates of the earldom.[54]

The stalwart Lady Lettice, who had married Sir Robert Digby of Warwickshire in England, began to assert her right to the title of baroness of Offaly in 1599. The countess dowager, meanwhile, assserted that the new earl of Kildare had broken into her jointure house at Maynooth and taken evidence crucial to the claim of her granddaughter. Digby had become a member of the privy council in Ireland and a justice of the peace for Co. Kildare, while the embattled earl appointed Richard Hadsor, a Middle Temple lawyer and Secretary Cecil's adviser on Irish affairs, as his London agent. As early as 1602, Lady Lettice and her husband filed a complaint in the court of castle chamber against Gerald, the new

---

52. Treadwell, *Buckingham*, pp. 103–24.   53. Ibid., p. 107.
54. G.E.C., *Peerage*, 'Kildare'.

earl of Kildare, the countess dowager and her attorney Henry Burnell, charging them with fraudulently altering the will of the eleventh earl. The petitioners claimed that Lady Lettice was the heir general of the Kildare estate and that the original deed of 7 September 1566 had been altered by Henry Burnell and his agents to disinherit her, giving the countess dowager, Lady Mabel, a jointure in the estate with reversion to Gerald, the fourteenth earl. On the death of her husband in 1585, the bill alleged, the Lady Mabel consulted Henry Burnell about the legal status of the lands and tenements of the estate and Burnell advised her that he should insert into the testament a deed of entail to the heirs male of the deceased earl, which he then forged. Years later, Burnell again asked to see the deed for her jointure when they were at Maynooth, and with the consent of the countess dowager added a certificate of execution by livery and atornment, together with the names of witnesses who were long since dead. The incumbent earl of Kildare subsequently published the deed and proceeded to take other evidence from the house of Maynooth which would have supported the claim of Lady Lettice. The extensive reporting of the case in the record book shows a keen interest in the outcome, though careful to demonstrate the innocence of the countess dowager. Many witnesses were heard before the court and several days spent in hearing proofs and allegations after the pleading began on 11 November 1607. The court determined to leave the validity of the deed to be tried by a jury at common law, despite the serious misgivings raised in regard to its alteration by Burnell and others.[55]

Turning finally to the issue of the forgery itself, and reciting in excruciating detail the depositions of several witnesses to the seven endorsements on the back of the deed, the court proceeded to its final determination on 3 February 1609. The court required that the seven endorsements on the deed 'shalbe Damned and never geven in Evidence to prove any Execution of any Estate to be Passed Accordingly in or by the said deed of feoffment'.[56] This interlocutory decree in a property dispute was certainly an unusual exercise of its prerogative authority by the court, showing once again its interest in the final disposition of the earldom and its estates. However, the final order blamed only Burnell for the forged endorsements and fined him 500 marks, discharging the countess and the earl and other defendants owing to the clumsy manner in which the original bill was drawn. Stating that Burnell was guilty of 'a very great faulte deservinge Seveare punishmente in A Counsellor at Lawe', the court resisted the temptation to severity.[57] The fragility of the fourteenth earl's claim was weakened by his sudden death in 1612, only seven weeks after the birth of a son. The wardship of this successor was seized by his two Protestant uncles, but his Catholic mother struggled valiantly to have custody of the boy, who died in 1620 at the age of nine. Another child heir, George Fitzgerald, son of the fourteenth earl's brother, was

55. BL, Add. MS 47,172, f. 156.   56. Ibid., f. 157v.
57. Ibid., f. 159.

raised in England and sent to Oxford where his destiny was sealed by the intervention of the ambitious earl of Cork. The estate, by this time, had suffered from the claims of three rival jointures for over thirty years. Dame Lettice was awarded the manor of Geashill in King's County and confirmed in her possession of the manors of Portlester, Woodstock and Athy until 1632. Although her husband died in 1618, the tenacious Fitzgerald heiress established her son, Robert, as Baron Digby of Geashill in 1624 and retained her title of Baroness Offaly until her death in 1658.[58]

The correspondence of the era is taken up with similar allegations and threats of litigation in both London and Dublin on behalf of numerous claimants to noble title. Dr Treadwell has amply illustrated the tribulations of the Catholic successor to the earldom of Ormonde, Sir Walter Butler. The judicial harassment of the new earl of Ormonde commenced in 1614 when he assumed the title from the loyal Protestant incumbent, the Elizabethan champion of Old English privileges, Thomas Butler. In November 1616, the court of castle chamber had to remit a fine imposed on the sheriff of Tipperary for failing to take the oath of supremacy, owing to the fact that the Ormonde liberty had never before been subject to crown jurisdiction.[59] And on 19 November 1619 the court censured the high sheriff of Tipperary, Gilbert Butler, for reprieving a condemned prisoner, despite his conviction and sentence by the assize judges in Clonmel. In words which challenged the Ormonde liberty obliquely, the court found that Butler acted out of 'self presumption of his Aone authoritie (grounde uppon a false principall)', but reduced his fine from £40 to £10 after he confessed that he acted out of 'meere ignorance'.[60] St John proceeded thereafter to appoint loyal sheriffs and by 1621 Ormonde had lost the ancient rights to the liberty of Tipperary by judicial order, along with the hard-won customs of the prise wines. Ormonde's chief rival was Richard Preston, Lord Dingwall, who had married Elizabeth Butler, daughter of Earl Thomas and widow of the previous heir, Viscount Tulleophelim. The Dingwalls contested the inheritance of Ormonde for five years, eventually receiving 21 manors and threatening to fracture the estate. Ormonde spent six years in the Fleet in London (1619–1625) while refusing to accept the award of much of his inheritance to his rival, who became earl of Desmond in 1619. While the estate was at risk during ten years of litigation, the new earl of Ormonde fought off numerous challenges to his impressive estates. Accepting a compromise in 1625 which led to his release, Ormonde exploited the

58. Treadwell, *Buckingham*, pp. 114–21. The earl of Cork arranged for his widowed daughter, Sarah, to marry Baron Digby in 1626. See also *Cal. S.P. Ire., 1615–25*, p. 139, directing the viceroy to stay further proceedings in the case.

59. *Cal. S.P. Ire., 1615–25*, p. 122. The lords justices wrote in April 1616 to inform the privy council that they had called in the judges of Ireland to consider the county palatine of Tipperary and concluded the new earl had no just claim to it. See also V.T.H. Delany, 'The palatinate court of the liberty of Tipperary', *AJLH*, v (1961), 95; and *Cal. Carew MSS, 1603–24*, pp. 328–29.

60. BL, Add. MS 47, 172, f. 275.

tentative diplomatic conditions in the new reign to resume legal challenges for his liberty of Tipperary and other estates. These property disputes were generally tried in other courts, but the ongoing subordination of aristocratic titles in Ireland to the Buckingham connection was a distinctive feature of the St John administration in other ways as well.[61]

Another dispute over noble inheritance threatened to ruin the estate of a young heir, raised in the Protestant religion and trained at Trinity College in Dublin. The young Edmond, Lord Burke of Castle Connell, claimed that his uncle, Theobald Burke, Lord Brittas, had squandered his estates during his minority and laid claim to the castle and manor of Castle Connell, including all its lands and hereditaments.[62] In 1618, the lord deputy and council demanded that Brittas convey the title to his nephew.[63] Brittas was imprisoned for seven months, and in December 1619 petitioned the privy council for his release, promising to relinquish his claims to his nephew's estate. The Irish lawyers, including Richard Hadsor, reviewed the petition and drafted a release to be signed by each claimant, but in 1620 the proposal was challenged by Castle Connell and his agent in England, prolonging the endless dispute with his uncle.[64] The court of castle chamber adjudicated in numerous cases where noble title and estates were at issue, thus functioning as an intermediate tribunal when petitions were returned from the privy council in Westminster.[65]

Commissions of inquiry usually heralded the end of an Irish administration, disgracing the chief governor and tarnishing the reputation of the Irish privy council. The Irish commission of 1622 was designed to provide a systematic review of the government of Ireland, initiated by Cranfield for both financial and political reasons. Following the model of the earlier commission of 1613 which immediately preceded the removal of Chichester as viceroy, it was understood that St John would be compromised by revelations of corruption and his departure was a foregone conclusion. However, St John, as the recently ennobled Viscount Grandison, was provided with an orderly exit strategy since he was included on the quorum of the commission itself and his patron, Buckingham, asserted repeatedly that he was in high favour with the king. The instructions for the commission consisted of detailed factual questions concerning the entire spectrum of

61. Treadwell, *Buckingham*, pp. 121–30. See also Edwards, 'Poisoned chalice', pp. 64–68. Edwards has shown that the viceroy undermined traditional authority in Kilkenny, selecting the Dingwalls' senior servant in Ireland, Henry Staines, as the new sheriff of Co. Kilkenny in 1618. Earl Walter was summoned before the English star chamber in November 1618 for refusing to accept the crown's partition of the estate, and in June 1619 he was committed to the Fleet while juries in Kilkenny proceeded to hear inquisitions into the earl's estate. Edwards, *Ormond lordship*, pp. 278–82.

62. *Cal. S.P. Ire., 1615–25*, p. 169. The original feoffment was dated 24 February 1608 entailing the lands in farm to Brittas, but the wardship and profits were granted to Laurence, Lord Esmond, in May 1618 by the lord deputy. Ibid., pp. 193, 197.

63. Ibid., pp. 219–20.   64. Ibid., pp. 241–12, 249, 257, 264, 270, 281–82, 286.

65. *Cal. S.P. Ire., 1625–32*, p. 242.

government, including the courts of law. Among the commissioners was the Irish-speaking Old English lawyer, Richard Hadsor. His observations on the conduct of the judicial establishment are embedded in the findings of the commission. Hasty preparations in December 1621 for the coming of the commission proved unnecessary, since the members only arrived after many delays in early April. They often met in tandem with the privy council in Ireland, setting aside Wednesdays for examination of the courts of justice. A dispute over enrolling the terms of the commission was ended on 25 April when Grandison received his warrant of recall, and he left for England on 4 May 1622. Exposing his vulnerability to censure, Grandison at once set about securing the private papers left for his successor in Ireland. On 18 June, the king rebuked the commissioners for invading the privacy of Grandison's personal papers and the former viceroy escaped the formidable critique which seemed to await him.[66]

Included in the instructions of 20 March 1622 was the injunction 'To inquire into the courts of justice, and whether any causes are unduly drawn from the courts to the Council table, and what is fit to be done'.[67] Working with two other professional lawyers, Sir William Jones, judge of common pleas, and Thomas Crewe, Hadsor managed to complete the first and only certificate from the commission which was drawn independently of politicians in London, sending a review of the courts of justice to the privy council while the commission itself was still in Ireland.[68] The certificate of the commissioners in June 1622 was signed in England by former Irish judges including James Ley, Humphrey Winch, John Denham and John Davies. Having surveyed abundant grievances against the administration of public justice, the commissioners offered numerous regulations limiting the discretion of judges in cases where judgement had been rendered. They were ordered not to stay execution on any pretence or supposition of equity; not to restore possession except by warrant; and not to ride on assize circuits in the countries of their birth or habitation. Lords president were ordered not to reprieve prisoners who had been condemned and not to hold pleas of replevin.[69] The critique was reviewed in England, given the approval of the privy council, and published in Dublin that summer as 'His majesty's directions for ordering and settling the courts within his kingdom of Ireland'.[70]

66. Treadwell, *Buckingham*, pp. 192–93, 199–200.
67. *Cal. S.P. Ire.,1615–25*, p. 347.
68. The rest of the commissioners named in March were: Adam Loftus, lord chancellor; Christopher, archbishop of Armagh; Oliver, Viscount Grandison, lord deputy; Charles, Viscount Wilmot, president of Connacht; Toby, Lord Caulfield, master of the ordnance; Sir Dudley Norton, secretary of state; Francis Blundell, baronet; Sir William Parsons, surveyor-general; Sir Dudley Digges; Sir John Jephson; Sir Thomas Penruddock; Sir James Perrot; Sir Thomas Phelps; Sir Nathaniel Rich; Sir Henry Bourchier; Theodore Price; Thomas Crewe; and Hadsor.
69. *Cal. S.P. Ire., 1615–1625*, p. 354.
70. V. Treadwell, 'Richard Hadsor', pp. 317–32; Hand & Treadwell, eds., 'Directions for the courts', pp. 185ff; TCD, MS 853, ff. 45–149v, where the 46 clauses are detailed. Though much of the text concerned affairs at the council table, the court of castle chamber was not mentioned specifically.

Based upon the king's private instruction 'rather to use clemency and grace than strictness and severity', the commissioners finished their work in a discreet manner and omitted any indictment of individuals or their behaviour.[71] By October 1622, most of the commissioners were anxious to return to England, prompted by the expectation of reward and the competition for honours at court. In addition, the contest for power between the reforming lord treasurer, Cranfield, the earl of Middlesex and the powerful royal favourite, Buckingham, compromised the Irish commission. Its members were recalled individually and its work silenced on key issues during the autumn of 1622 at the insistence of Buckingham, whose minions were threatened by revelations of the commissioners. In spite of the manifestly high expectations for the work of the commission of 1622, sweeping changes in the Irish administration, coupled with the indictment of corrupt officials, were not forthcoming. Nonetheless, the reforms which the commission inaugurated were important, though often based upon recommendations of long standing, including the establishment of the Irish court of wards in December 1622.[72] In addition, the English privy council proceeded to add an institutional remedy for the corruption in Irish administration by establishing a standing commission for Irish affairs.

This executive committee was designed to meet once every week to continue the review of the 1622 commission's findings, to vet all projects and proposals and grants of bounty, and to report to the privy council its recommendations. Founded on 9 May 1623, the new commission thus obtained substantial intermediate authority over Irish governance, though it also decelerated further the achingly familiar delays on petitions and counter-claims which have been discussed above.[73] Richard Hadsor was added to the commission in May 1625, thus adding his valuable expertise on Irish law to that of his former colleagues on the 1622 commission, William Jones, Nathaniel Rich and Thomas Crewe. The new commission had opportunity to scrutinize the proposals submitted from the gentlemen of the Pale during negotiations which led to the Graces in 1628. On 23 June 1624, the commission offered their opinions on grievances from the landholders of the English Pale. The signatories to this document included three former viceroys, Grandison, Carew, and Chichester, as well as the legists James Ley and William Jones. Since the committee members in this case were each party to the policies which were being criticized, the noncommittal response of the group was not unexpected. Article five of the grievances addressed the practice of the court of castle chamber thus:

> Complaint of the course in the castle chamber, where if any one defendant be censured, no one of the rest (though they be acquitted) shall have any costs, many being often inserted in a bill and those of the nearest in

71. Treadwell, 'Hadsor', p. 321.
72. Ibid., p. 322, and see Treadwell, *Buckingham*, pp. 204–11.
73. Treadwell, 'Hadsor', p. 323.

friendship or alliance to the principal defendant, who at the time of the riot were perhaps 20 miles off from that place, and therefore it were fit to meet with this malice by allowing cost to the acquitted.[74]

The laconic response of the commissioners that 'the course of the Star chamber of England be observed there', was typical of their calculated Fabian tactics, leaving to others the technical refinements of policy while trusting in the lapse of time to blunt the edge of inchoate opposition.[75]

POWERFUL RIVALS AND SHACKLED GOVERNANCE: THE COURT UNDER FALKLAND, 1622–1629

The commission to investigate causes in Ireland was given a complex mandate, including the review of Irish finances. The duke of Buckingham sought a smooth transition by which executive power would be shifted from Lord Deputy St John, by now Viscount Grandison, to his expected replacement, Henry Cary, Viscount Falkland, without compromising the reputation or perquisites of office enjoyed by the incumbent.[76] The penurious Falkland was thus ushered into the viceregal office by the unusually powerful commissioners, who were burdened with comprehensive instructions for their oversight of Irish government. When they returned to England, however, having cut short their proposed scrutiny, Falkland discovered that a new layer of authority had been added to Irish government. Aside from the important Villiers group suffused throughout the Irish administration, a new privy council committee for Irish affairs was established in Westminster, composed of veteran bureaucrats such as Grandison, Sir James Ley, Chichester, Hadsor and Sir Humphrey May.[77] Although the privy council in Westminster was staffed by Irish experts for decades, including both William and Robert Cecil as principal secretaries, the establishment of a complementary and parallel commission of legal scholars to advise the executive committee on Irish matters was a significant refinement. Apart from the manning of this board with Buckingham supporters, it is vital to see the important role of this committee in the governance of Ireland. A turning-point had apparently been reached in 1622 when the king's council demanded full, and sometimes prior, knowledge of Irish affairs before the lord deputy and council could take action. This indicates the extent to which Irish government had become polarized by contending factions, yet the attempt at micro-management by the privy council ended in frustration.

The Falkland administration was uniquely conditioned and circumscribed. The lord deputy was inaugurated at a time of undue scrutiny by the 1622 commission of inquiry and his government was often circumvented by appeals to the

74. *Cal. S.P. Ire., 1615–25*, p. 507.   75. Ibid.
76. Treadwell, *Buckingham*, pp. 192–93.   77. Ibid., pp. 259–60.

new commissioners for Irish causes.[78] Significantly, the new court of wards was also set up at this time, though it did nothing, technically, to alter the caseload of the court of castle chamber.[79] He was unable to pursue an independent course of action owing to the authority of his powerful patron, the duke of Buckingham, and his policies were seen as partisan in view of his client status at court. His mismanagement of the parliament of 1626 suggested that he was overmatched in the office of chief governor, and he complained frequently that his work was undermined by others. In the matter of Sir Edmund Blanchfield, for example, Sir Piers Crosbie petitioned the privy council against Falkland in April 1626 for bungling the case of a murder committed by Blanchfield's brother. One Purcell had wounded Sir Edmund in the face, after which Leonard Blanchfield killed Purcell and fled the kingdom. Falkland summoned Sir Edmund to Dublin Castle, imprisoned him and took possession of his estates.[80] The viceroy vindicated himself to the king on 17 May 1626, explaining that his actions were taken at the behest of the widow of Purcell and that Blanchfield would have a fair trial in king's bench. In September, he wrote to Secretary Conway to seek satisfaction against Crosbie, labelling him an informer, and advising that the king should not let England become 'an asylum for those who have committed foul crimes in Ireland'.[81] Later, writing to the privy council on 4 June 1626, Falkland explained that he had called the chief justices, the chief baron and Sir Christopher Sibthorpe to settle a dispute between Sir Thomas Fitzwilliams and his younger brethren, but at their meeting feared they had no power to settle the matter owing to a restraint on interference published under the royal signature. Falkland's decision to suspend proceedings gives some evidence of judicial paralysis during his tenure of office, often punctuated by partisan backstabbing and personal rancour.[82] Educated at Oxford, a soldier, courtier and politician, Falkland was ill-suited to become chief governor since he was easily offended and financially enfeebled. His wife, Elizabeth, made a notorious conversion to Catholicism that led to her return to England in 1625, though his son and heir, Lucius Cary, was educated at Trinity College Dublin in 1622.[83]

At the accession of Charles I, Falkland and the council in Ireland wrote on 15 April 1625,

78. Treadwell, 'Hadsor', pp. 323–25.
79. V. Treadwell, 'The Irish court of wards under James I', *IHS*, xii (1960), 1 at 19–21.
80. *Cal. S.P. Ire., 1625–32*, p. 109. Crosbie intimated that Blanchfield's arrest was prompted by a corrupt interest in his property by 'some person of power in Ireland' and moved the privy council to void the transfer of property until a fair trial could be held before jurors. The privy council wrote to Falkland to require him to be careful of 'the covetous humours of men to pursue the lives of our subjects in cases where the law submits favourable interpretations'. Ibid.
81. Ibid., pp. 123, 155. Falkland asserted Blanchfield was guilty of murder, though he had not yet been tried.
82. Ibid., p. 129.
83. *DNB*. See also A. Clarke, *The Graces* (Dublin, 1966), p. 7, where Falkland is described as 'Ireland's harassed, bitter and endlessly complaining lord deputy'. Plate 9.

The Star Chamber which sat by Commission from England is determined [i.e. terminated] by the death of the late King. They request that a new Commission may be sent, and that promptly, as time [for the new term] is approaching. If winds delay it they will presume to renew the Commission under the Great Seal there.[84]

A month later, Falkland wrote that a copy of the commission for the castle chamber had been received with instructions to revise or amend it as desired and return it without delay.[85] He then explained that a commission in Dublin had been issued to allow the court to operate during the Trinity term, but sought the royal charter as soon as possible. Meanwhile, Falkland wrote to Conway on 31 May 1625 that one Lewis, a merchant who bribed the customer of Limerick to amend the docket of a ship's lading, was censured before the court of castle chamber for a false confession.[86] Despite the viceroy's efforts to obtain a new charter promptly, the formal document was not signed until 1 October 1625. Citing his father's appointment of the court in August 1603, the king declared that,

> finding the same Courte to be of verie necessary and good use for the advancement of publicke Justice, the suppressing of greate Malefactors, releving our quieter subiectes and retayning all sortes in peace and due obedience of the lawe, [we] have resolved to continue the same Courte.[87]

The judges of the court were explicitly to incorporate the two chief justices, the chief baron, the master of the rolls and the secretary of state, while the viceroy, the chancellor, the treasurer or vice-treasurer were always to be one among the quorum of at least four judges.[88] The court was ordered to hold its hearings in each of the four ordinary terms 'from tyme to tyme two Dayes in every weeke of the said Termes'.[89] The viceroy was empowered to act on behalf of the king, '[to] have in our behalfe the full and whole power of Cheife head and principall Justicer and Determiner and shalbe our Cheife head and principall Judg in and of all such matters and causes as shalbe in the same Court propounded Debated or controversed.'[90] No mention was made of the court's activist prosecution of recusancy throughout the previous reign, nor was any basis offered for the determination of title to land or honour.

---

84. *Cal. S.P. Ire., 1625–32*, p. 4.   85. Ibid., p. 10.
86. Ibid., pp. 13–14.
87. TCD, MS 852, f. 74. The charter listed maintenances, embraceries, confederacies, alliances, false banding and taking of money by common jurors, untrue demeaning of sheriffs, riots, routs, unlawful assemblies, forcible entries and other disorders.
88. Ibid., f. 74v.
89. The charter identified Wednesday and Friday as court days, allowing the judges to meet as convenient, and authorizing them to call as associates on the court as many of the lords spiritual and temporal, judges and privy councillors as they found useful. Ibid.
90. Ibid., f. 76.

The last case in the entry book of the court of castle chamber was adjudicated in 1620, but fragments taken from an official record book that probably succeeded it (now missing) offer tantalizingly incomplete and sporadic evidence of the court's activity under Grandison and Falkland. It is evident that the castle chamber was reauthorized in the full expectation that it would continue as a central pillar of prerogative government. The brother of Buckingham, Sir Edward Villiers, lord president of Munster, wrote in March 1626 that he undertook many hearings on commission, noting that Sir Laurence Parsons had been censured for misdemeanours in the Irish star chamber, a fact that dishonoured his office in the admiralty court.[91] Under Falkland, the court continued to hear cases of riot involving underlying property disputes. On 1 June 1627, the court censured Sir Valentine Browne, baronet, for taking a distress in the night from the land of Dermot McCarty's mother-in-law, whose tenants thereafter abandoned the cultivation of the land for three years. It appeared to the court that Browne, with ten or more men, used violent force in seizing fifty cows and beating the tenants who sought to retrieve them. Browne protested that he had already compensated the tenants by an order of the assize judges, but the court fined him £200 for the riot and for dispossession of the jointure of the plaintiff's mother-in-law.[92] The tender sensitivity of the court to scandal was outraged on several occasions under Falkland. In 1628, an Englishman named Richard Browne, gentleman, was convicted of passing rumours in Carlingford to the effect that the duke of Buckingham had been committed to the Tower of London for sending a basin and ewer to the king of Spain – an episode we have earlier discussed. For his temerity, Browne was fined £1,000, jailed and pilloried by the court.[93] And in the same year, Thomas Velden, gentleman, of Co. Meath was convicted of malicious speeches against the deputy himself. Velden cited previous viceroys who had been hanged for exceeding their instructions, after protesting against the viceroy's cessing of four troops on his estates. Velden did not help his case by saying the troops themselves should be hanged.[94]

The commission for Irish causes reviewed petitions which were originally sent to the privy council in England. The impact of this new threshold of government

91. *Cal. S.P. Ire., 1625–32*, p. 107. The charges against Parsons were not identified and there is no independent evidence on this cause of action. On 17 October 1627, the king returned to Falkland the petition of William Bromfield and Captain Thomas Butler who were being sued in castle chamber. He neglected to mention the nature of the offences, and there is no direct confirmation of this adjudication. Ibid., p. 275.

92. TCD, MS 852, f. 97. Not unimportant was the subsequent vacancy of the tenants from the land for up to three years, contributing to the damages alleged by McCarty.

93. Ibid., f. 99. Browne had been drinking at a tavern with two retainers of Sir Marmaduke Whitchurch, who reported the affair. For his offence, Browne was sentenced to be pilloried, whipped through the streets of Dublin, his ears cut off, and made to acknowledge his offence in each of the four courts.

94. Ibid., f. 99v. One soldier apparently aggravated the intemperate landowner, saying that even if the soldiers committed an offence for which they should be hanged, the viceroy had the power to pardon them before he left office.

was to limit the power of the viceroy and the court of castle chamber, since petitions normally received by the chief governor and adjudicated in Dublin Castle were now initiated across the Irish sea. A number of causes dealt with the powerful and wealthy Richard Boyle, earl of Cork, whose many business interests led to mountains of litigation.[95] For example, on 14 May 1626, a petition of John Fitzgerald and his wife, Ellis, asked for relief in the matter of a lease of the town and lands of Shean, Co. Waterford, made by the earl in 1605 to Ellis and her late husband. They alleged the earl had obtained the estate in trust before her second marriage and now had expelled their cattle and forced them to become his tenants. The petition to the privy council was referred to commissioners for Irish causes. They, in turn, remanded the issue to the lord chancellor of Ireland for arbitration, to be followed by trial in the Irish chancery if the parties could not be reconciled.[96] On 7 July 1625, the commissioners granted the petition of Lady Raleigh against the earl, who refused to answer her writ of dower in ordinary court, referring the matter to the lord deputy and council and ordering that Cork be compelled to appear and plead at that venue.[97]

The cumbersome interdependence of judicial venues was never more apparent than in Cork's suit against Sir William Power over the settling of meres on their estates of Broghill, Rathgogan and Kilbolane. The earl petitioned the president and council of Munster on 29 January 1623 to order a commission and award of the meres and bounds of their lands, which was confirmed by order of the earl of Thomond, lord president of Munster, in October 1623. On 5 March 1624, the council in Ireland required Power to appear to answer for slanderous words spoken against the earl, and, not surprisingly, the board found in favour of their fellow councillor, censuring Power and confining him in Dublin Castle. In September 1624, Cork learned that Power had appealed to Secretary Conway in England, and the earl then promised Falkland that he would reconcile with his adversary by arbitration. Falkland wrote to Conway in November, explaining that he

> was himself of Conway's opinion, and uttered it at the Council table when his [Power's] cause was there argued and he censured; but the whole bent of the board running upon the contrary basis, he wanted confidence to stick to his own single opinion.[98]

95. Cork had come to Ireland in 1588 as an adventurer, took up several official positions in Munster and enriched himself from the lapsed estates of wealthy Munster landowners. He married the only daughter of the powerful secretary of state, Sir Geoffrey Fenton, in 1603 and was knighted in Dublin the same year. Three years later he became a councillor in the Munster presidency court and in 1613 won the office of privy councillor in Dublin. He became Baron Youghal in 1616 and earl of Cork in 1620. *The Lismore papers*, ed. A.B. Grosart (London, 1886), ii, 106. See also N. Canny, *The upstart earl: a study of the social and mental worlds of Richard Boyle, first earl of Cork, 1566 to 1643* (Cambridge, 1982).

96. *Cal. S.P. Ire., 1625–32*, pp. 120, 128.   97. Ibid., p. 22.

98. *Cal. S.P. Ire., 1615–25*, p. 544. Falkland had written to Cork in July to propose a pacification with Power, who by this time had confessed his error and craved pardon of the council and the earl in the castle chamber. Ibid., pp. 400, 434, 470, 524, 544–45.

Ultimately, Cork revived his suit against Power in 1630 during his tenure as lord justice, had him arrested in England, and moved for dismissal of Power's suit in the court of castle chamber on grounds of his absence at the Easter term of the court.[99]

In the lengthy suit of Henry Wright and Richard Blacknall against the earl over their lease of his ironworks, the petitioners sought relief from the powerful nobleman's manipulation of legal proceedings. On 21 June 1627, the commissioners for Irish causes learned that Cork obtained letters from the king staying all suits in Ireland against him, after which he began prosecution of the petitioners at common law. They called upon a select committee of Irish councillors to act as referees in the matter, recommending the stay of all prosecutions there, pending a report to the king. This important case demonstrates the use of supplementary legal proceedings to protect the interest of ordinary men against members of the council in Ireland who were generally active members of the court of castle chamber.[100] The king wrote to Falkland on 10 July 1627 to stay all common law proceedings against Wright and Blacknall until the deputy and the Irish council returned their certificate to the crown, a matter subsequently left to the master of the rolls in commission. Cork had Blacknall arrested for debt in January 1628, claiming that the stay of his suits did not extend to prosecution for debt, since the petitioners did not appear in Michaelmas for trial in chancery. But Falkland reproved Cork for arresting Blacknall, and ordered the mayor of Youghal to release him. Although both the king and the commissioners demanded that the petitioners be restored to their 'nailhouse' in February 1628, based on the legitimacy of their 21-year lease, both men again petitioned against Cork on 22 February, citing his threats to 'bring them to their knees'.[101]

The glut of petitions coming from Ireland included the trivial as well as the important. On 17 May 1626, for example, the commissioners acted on a petition of Sir Jasper Herbert who complained against a chancery decree in Ireland that forced him to break down a bank to allow water to run into his neighbour's estate, thus ruining his mill. They advised the neighbour to bring an action in chancery, or else to allow Herbert to repair his wall, thus settling one issue by initiating another.[102] These peremptory decrees did little to resolve Irish litigation, simply adding another layer of judicial scrutiny and legal fees to the burden of the harried complainant. In the following week, however, the commissioners demanded that the lord deputy and council take up the petition of the widowed Catherine Codd on behalf of her daughter against the bishop of Leighlin, spurring them to prompt

---

99. *Cal. S.P. Ire., 1625–32*, p. 554. Power wrote to Lord Dorchester to raise the old issue, saying his case was finally dismissed and Lord Justice Loftus feared offending Cork and so allowed it.

100. Ibid., p. 243. The petitioners had leased a nail-making house from Cork that employed 32 men, in addition to the ironworks in question.

101. Ibid., pp. 243, 255, 272, 306, 310, 314. The case proceeded endlessly without final resolution for decades, but never came to the castle chamber because Cork was a principal judge as well as party to the suit.

102. Ibid., p. 124.

action in a case long delayed over the estate of Codd.[103] In July 1626, the commissioners took up fourteen petitions of individuals in Ireland, referring most to the lord deputy and council or to the Irish courts.[104] A series of petitions from the mayor, sheriffs and citizens of Dublin and Waterford was referred to commissioners for Irish causes in December 1626 over the payment of 3*d.* gage money for each barrel on casks, a levy which violated the terms of the cities' charters. This apparent increase in levies sanctioned by the Irish government was challenged by the commissioners thus:

> We have considered their protest and, finding it against the law, think that the Deputy, Chief Judges and the rest of the Irish Council should be ordered to certify how these exactions are made and to what use they are put, and if there be really no warrant, the taking of the 3*d.* a barrel should be suspended till your Lordships' pleasure is further known.[105]

In a rare instance, to mitigate the severity of the court of castle chamber, the commissioners responded to a petition of Christopher Draycott, who, as we have seen, had been fined £500 for an assault on the mayor of Drogheda and his wife in 1621. Noting that the fine still stood, and could not be remitted except by special letter from the king, they recommended the fine be reduced, despite the affront to the dignity of a public official.[106] The extreme litigiousness of Irish society at this time was perhaps testimony to the firm settlement of common law institutions, but the inauguration of the commissioners quickly produced a series of caveats. In 1626, a memorial to Secretary Conway noted how Irish business was delayed by frequent petitions to England, and on 9 December 1628 the earl of Marlborough wrote to the commissioners to resolve the multitude of petitions against the earl of Cork and others who had been troubling the privy council.[107] In an earlier letter of 1626 to Conway, John Cusack of Dublin prayed for a star chamber bill to release him from prison to pursue his suit for the estate of Sir Thomas Cusack, the former lord chancellor of Ireland.[108]

---

103. Ibid., p. 127. On the same date commissioners called upon the deputy and council to compel the earl of Londonderry to pay his debts or remand the case of two Devon petitioners to Irish courts. Ibid.

104. Ibid., pp. 138–39.

105. Ibid., pp. 182,184. A letter of May 1632 from the privy council demanded that the new Lord Deputy Wentworth and the council in Ireland take final action TCD, MS 843, pp. 142–44.

106. *Cal. S.P. Ire., 1625–32*, p. 298.

107. Ibid., pp. 191, 412. Blame was specially laid at the foot of Irish commissioners in England, causing poverty and discontent among the petitioners. Ibid., p. 412.

108. Ibid., p. 152. Cusack, an Old English Catholic educated in France, appealed to the English courts for relief and asserted the primacy of the English judiciary, arguing that 'the decisions of all Irish institutions were subject to review by whatever bodies in England were nominated to that purpose by the monarch, who was the ultimate arbiter on Irish affairs'. Canny, *Making Ireland British*, p. 409.

Clearly, the lord deputy was looking over his shoulder when acting in his judicial capacity, and the work of the court of castle chamber was apparently being siphoned off to special commissions at this time. In addition, Falkland complained on 22 March 1627 to the privy council that local juries refused to indict accused rebels. Citing the unrest in seven northern counties, he grumbled, 'The common law is deluded by the subtilitie of this people who will not find a bille of indictment, be the evidence never so pregnant, not fearing the penalty of the Star Chamber.'[109] A more indirect affront to the judicial competence of the regime was offered by the powerful earl of Antrim in August 1627. Sir Richard Bolton, chief baron of the exchequer, and Samuel Mayart had gone as judges of assize to Antrim where they ordered the sheriff to find garrons for the lord deputy, but the earl of Antrim forbade him to take them from his lands, and threatened to beat him. When the sheriff arrested an accused felon, the earl took the prisoner away. He was known to put bailiffs in the stocks for trying to execute writs in the county, fining in his own court those who sued in the sheriff's venue.[110] In February 1628, the commissioners for Irish causes intervened on behalf of Sir Walter Coppinger, who petitioned for final acquittal of charges brought against him by Sir Allen Apsley in 1625. However, on 26 May, the king wrote to Falkland, ordering the lord deputy to alter a decree of acquittal in the court of castle chamber into a censure against Coppinger, a highly unusual affront to the star chamber court.[111] Apsley was a client of Buckingham and a kinsman of Grandison, which may explain the preferred treatment he initially received.[112] But a subsequent royal letter of 21 November 1628 confirmed the original decree of castle chamber, acquitting the defendant, without comment. The power of the crown to alter judgements of the prerogative court on subsequent petition may have caused the lord deputy to limit his use of the court, since litigation initiated by the viceroy appears to have diminished under Falkland's administration. On the other hand, the chief governor and the Irish privy council were empowered to hear all suits between

---

109. *Cal. S.P. Ire., 1625–32*, p. 220.

110. Sir Robert Heath in England advised that the earl should be punished in star chamber, but no process was sued against him for his arch independence. Ibid., pp. 277–78. See also Ohlmeyer, *Civil war and restoration*, pp. 68–91.

111. *Cal. S.P. Ire., 1625–32*, pp. 312, 341. No independent confirmation of the castle chamber case has been found in records of the court.

112. Ibid., p. 405. Apsley had married Lucy St John, Grandison's niece. He had been commissioner for victuals in Munster during the Nine Years War and obtained a manor in Co. Cork in 1620. Treadwell, *Buckingham*, p. 50. The case involved Coppinger's eligibility for a royal pardon in the suit brought by Apsley at castle chamber, despite the fact that he did not originally plead pardon. The viceroy and five judges voted to censure Coppinger, but seven other judges voted to acquit him, citing the pardon of the last parliament. The clerk entered an acquittal based on the majority opinion, which was challenged by Apsley. Humphrey May and the Irish committee found that the judges decided on the merits, not on the pardon itself, and sought to uphold the 'honour of the court' in confirming the original decision. *Cal. S.P. Ire., 1647–60, addenda, 1625–60*, pp. 123–25.

undertakers in the plantation of Ulster in 1628, an apparent expansion of the judicial duties of the council which did not involve the court of castle chamber.[113]

In a dispute reminiscent of the quarrels between Sir John Perrot and his lord chancellor, Falkland warred continuously with the incumbent chancellor, Adam Loftus, Viscount Ely. The lord deputy sought advantage for the prerogative court over its rival equity jurisdiction in a series of clashes which ended, paradoxically, in a royal decree favouring the chancellor and demanding trial of his accusers in the court of castle chamber. On 22 October 1624, Falkland wrote to Loftus to reassert his demand that the chancellor sign the fiant for tanning in Carlow and for a licence to Sir Samuel Smith to make *aqua vitae*, stating that Loftus had signed a similar one in the previous administration of Grandison. The viceroy commanded Loftus to obey his warrant, arguing that only the king might countermand his orders. Six days later, he asked whether the chancellor wanted Falkland for his enemy.[114] The lord chancellor responded on 25 October that the fiant for tanning was not warranted by law, nor by statute, nor by the king's letters, praying the chief governor to take the advice of the judges who would review the documents. He rejoined,

> Great as is the Deputy's power, yet never did he perceive it to be so great as that it might require obedience without limitation. Further, if the sole command of the seal be in his Lordship's power, vain and needless is the place of a Chancellor.[115]

On 24 November 1624, Secretary Conway referred the matter to former lords deputy, Chichester and Grandison, assisted by two judges, without prejudice to the office of either man.[116] In 1626, a formal review by five English judges found the lord chancellor in contempt for challenging the viceroy's determination in the licence for Smith and for committing the licensee to prison, noting that the original patentee, one John Miagh, was disabled from holding the licence due to a prior conviction at law.[117] In attempting to resolve the matter, the king wrote to the lord deputy and council on 16 May 1626, after taking the advice of Chichester and Grandison, assisted by Richard Weston and Humphrey May. Declaring that the chancellor should respect the role of the viceroy, he added,

> That if the Chancellor refuses the seal to a grant on a question of state, you may appeal to the Council, and if they assent to its being given and he still

---

113. *Cal. S.P. Ire., 1625–32*, pp. 349–50. According to this instrument, the deputy and four or more councillors could accept surrenders and regrants, delimit parishes from escheated lands and pass grants by letters patent.

114. *Cal. S.P. Ire., 1615–25*, pp. 532, 540.

115. Ibid., p. 533.

116. *Cal. S.P. Ire., 1625–32*, p. 547.

117. Ibid., pp. 188–90. The judges and attorneys addressed the questions whether the lord chancellor should obey orders of the viceroy, and whether he could revive in equity jurisdiction a patent legally extinct.

refuses, he may appeal to us; but this at his peril, if our interests suffer any prejudice in the meantime. [And] That if he refuse it on a question of law, the appeal be put to the judges, and then if the Chancellor still objects, to us. [And] That in the event of a refusal of the Lord Chancellor to send judges on the circuits desired by the Lord Deputy, the appeal shall be to the Council, whose decision shall be final.[118]

After the embattled lord chancellor responded in detail to 18 accusations, the king wrote on 4 August 1628 to the lord deputy and council, clearing the lord chancellor of all charges, restoring him to full favour and ordering 'that the people who brought against Lord Loftus the charges of which he has recently cleared himself, to the satisfaction of the King and Council, [shall] be proceeded against in the High Court of Castle Chamber'.[119] After enduring the humiliating suspension from his office by Falkland, the tenacious servitor returned to his post in triumph, though he was finally undone under the next administration.

The reputation of the lord deputy was jealously guarded against attack, and Falkland enjoyed the support of the star chamber in England on occasions when his judgements were challenged at law. After spending much of his administration defending himself against the depredations of his enemies, Falkland sued in the English star chamber Sir Arthur Savage, Lord Mountnorris, Philip Bushin and others for defamation and slander. Bushin had accused the viceroy and Chief Justice Sarsfield of taking his father's life and estates, and he was encouraged by Savage and Mountnorris to petition the parliament and the duke of Buckingham for recovery and damages.[120] The justices in star chamber gave their solemn judgements for Falkland, citing his sobriety and care in making sure the goods of Bushin were sequestered, and fining Savage and Bushin for defamation and calumny against the lord deputy. Viscount Wentworth, sitting in judgement by virtue of his office as lord president of the Council in the North, adumbrated the tenor of his subsequent administration in Ireland:

---

118. Ibid., pp. 121–22. On 7 April 1627, the king was compelled to write to the viceroy again regarding a charge by the earl of Cork, alleging that the lord chancellor was prejudiced in questions at issue in chancery involving the earl's daughter. Ibid., p. 223. A more cautious lord chancellor told Dublin merchants that they could not proceed in equity against the customs house officers in March 1626 because he would not act against the lord deputy. Ibid., p. 104.

119. Ibid., pp. 373, 379. Loftus had been called to London in June 1627 to answer charges of corruption, and Falkland accused him of working behind the scenes with the advocates of the Graces during that year. No castle chamber litigation pursuant to this order of the king has been found in records of the court.

120. The original case was heard in 1625 before Sarsfield as judge on a charge of murder against Bushin. He was accused of throwing a trencher at his wife, Grace, killing her and later slaying a servant who witnessed the event. Bushin deposed that his wife died in his arms with bloody flux during the night, and that the false accusation was made in order to win his property, worth £2,000. *Cal. S.P. Ire., 1633–47*, p. 26.

Factions betweene persons of quallity in yt Realme I doe conceive to bee the cheif cause of many disorders raigning there. The king by that meanes is deceived in execucon of Justice, when his Ministers doe bandy one against another. And though the bedd be changed yet doth the disease as yet continewe. Heere I finde a poore Innocent man condempned to dye an ygnominious death, a Deputy slaundered, his Maties Justice traduced.[121]

Turning to the handling of the original trial, the judges were uniformly offended by the behaviour of Chief Justice Sarsfield. Sir Nicholas Hide, chief justice of king's bench, declaimed:

certainly I cannot comende the proceeding of the Lo: Sarsfield for if the Jury will not finde according to their evidence, the court may discharge them & ympanell newe, but not examyne them by the pole, and, in Liew of them that did disagree, to place others with the former. It was a good advise of a Chancellor in this Realme to a Judge, yor duty is (said hee) to open the Jurors Eyes, but not to leade them by the Nose.[122]

The case offers a rare opportunity to witness the involvement of the senior star chamber court in Irish judicial proceedings.

On the other hand, in the contentious matter of the plantation of Co. Wicklow, Falkland was upbraided for mishandling the trial of Phelim McFeagh O'Byrne. Phelim petitioned the privy council in England, claiming the judges and juries in his case were corrupt and citing each of them by name. He charged Sir Henry Bealing with intimidating witnesses and said Lord Esmond and other undertakers had corrupted the judicial process, despite his good title to land, received from the sovereigns Elizabeth I and James I. The petition took exception to the commissioners in the case, noting they failed to take depositions from Esmond and Sir William Parsons, who were directly involved in the plantation, concluding that the commissioners 'savor of malice' and perjury. Although Phelim and his sons were lodged in the prison of Dublin Castle, Falkland saw in the petition a direct challenge to his own government. He soon found himself the target of a commission of inquiry which included his adversary, the lord chancellor, and he proceeded to challenge both their findings and their establishment as a derogation of his authority. The viceroy argued

that by this Late Comission legall proceedings are discountenanced, that shold cutt off criminalls being brought to the Civile Justice; Rebellions

---

121. TCD, MS 843, p. 418.
122. Ibid., pp. 417–18, 425. On 20 November 1633, the star chamber case against the corrupt officials ended in the imprisonment and deprivation of Sarsfield with £7,000 in penalties, along with the corrupt sheriff, Beling, and the foreman of the jury. *Cal. S.P. Ire., 1633–47*, pp. 26–31.

wilbe growne to an unsupportable greatnesse ... [and] The Judge will be in Danger to become corrupt.[123]

In April 1629, the besieged Falkland was informed of his impending recall and his venomous rejoinder to the king blamed his enemies, including Phelim McFeagh O'Byrne, Sir Arthur Savage, the lord chancellor and the commissioners who impugned his administration.[124]

The religious policy of Falkland's administration manifested an abrupt about face, reflected in the relatively few prosecutions of recusancy in the court of castle chamber. Whereas Chichester and St John used the court as a cudgel with which to pound away at the hard stone of Counter-Reformation Catholicism, Falkland practically abandoned the inquisition during the protracted diplomacy of the Spanish Match, invented by his patron, Buckingham. On 9 January 1624, the viceroy wrote to Secretary Conway that the Catholic nobility and gentry near Dublin were making subscriptions for the collection of money to send a delegation to the king, reflecting their confidence in the impending betrothal. Instancing the election of recusant magistrates, sovereigns and mayors in the cities of Ireland, Falkland promised to remain silent and bide his time during the sensitive negotiations, choosing reliably Protestant gentry in places near Dublin and closely supervising the rest. Indicating his contempt for 'their conceit of a general toleration', Falkland promised to impose the oath of supremacy once it became clear that the king supported it:

> For then it would be important for His Majesty to secure himself of their fidelity by the oath the law requires to be taken of them, which they would certainly refuse, and so become liable to the Star Chamber, where good fines might be imposed upon the refusal, which could well be borne, they being of the best and ablest men in every corporation, and without question such who were the worst affected to His Majesty's state.[125]

After receiving Conway's letter of clarification, Falkland wrote on 24 January that he would now proceed to execute two books of rules to govern the church and banish all titular bishops and priests, while imposing the oaths of allegiance and supremacy.[126] Months later, however, the chief governor was again on the defensive. On 23 October 1624, the lord deputy and council wrote to the privy council in England to seek their advice. Explaining that they had suspended the execution of two of the articles for the government of the church, they now found that most towns in

---

123. TCD, MS 843, f. 154v and see ff. 151–55, 167.
124. *Cal. S.P. Ire., 1625–32*, pp. 445, 449. The council wrote to the king on Falkland's behalf, assuring him of the rule of English law and noting Sir Francis Annesley, Viscount Mountnorris, was now brought to suit in the star chamber of Ireland. Falkland's letter of 24 March blamed Annesley and Wilmot for his troubles with Phelim McFeagh. Ibid., p. 443.
125. *Cal. S.P. Ire., 1615–25*, p. 455.
126. Ibid., pp. 458–59.

Munster had elected recusant officers, believing there would now be no proceeding upon statute against them. The viceroy and council sought new directions on whether to accept an oath of allegiance as a sufficient alternative to the oath of supremacy.[127] Again, on 23 August 1625, Falkland told Conway that the election of magistrates for Michaelmas term was imminent and that many in Galway promoted recusant leaders who were worthy and loyal, saying: 'I confess that the papists in this county are men of the best estates, and govern best when they hold offices of trust. But the "constitution of this time" makes it dangerous to trust them.'[128] After two decades of relentless prosecution of recusants in the court of castle chamber under his predecessors, the Falkland regime cynically chose religious moderation out of a concern to avoid political recriminations.

Nonetheless, while Falkland felt constrained to limit his prosecutions for recusancy during the initial stages of his regime, fearing to be at cross purposes with the king, he was applauded in 1627 for the egregious use of torture on an unlucky priest. Writing on 30 May 1627, Conway conveyed the king's support after the lord deputy put the priest to the rack, promising to send from England orders on the legality of the rack's use:

> in this and all cases which reach to that high degree of treason and treasonable matter you might with boldness and without any shadow of doubt execute the utmost of the law not only for putting to the rack but even to take away that man's life or as many others as shall be found guilty of treason of so high a nature.[129]

The king himself wrote to Falkland on 12 May 1627 to require that the attorney and chancellor for the archbishop of Armagh be sued in castle chamber for misdemeanours in the fraudulent concealment of a lapsed church living.[130] By 1629, the viceroy proceeded more resolutely against the intrusion of Jesuits into the realm, promising on 2 April that the council would 'endeavour to square our proceeding with the laws and statutes of the kingdom', and to move against papal jurisdictions, erection of colleges, and unlawful meetings by proclamation:

> The judges are considering at our request the points of a [court of] High Commission on the lines laid down in the statute of 2 Eliz., and we shall also use the machinery of the Star Chamber and the Exchequer in order to strike at the Papists and their property. We will meantime not touch the secular priests nor the abused laity, except by the proclamation; but we hope to reform them.[131]

127. Ibid., p. 538.
128. *Cal. S.P. Ire., 1625–33*, p. 31.
129. Ibid., p. 238.
130. Ibid., p. 235.
131. Exposing the depths of their cynicism, the council sent a proclamation forbidding the exercise of all foreign jurisdictions, ending with this admonition: 'A drawn sword is essential in the treatment of these matters.' Ibid., pp. 444–45.

Three days after the proclamation in Dublin, Falkland reported to the privy council that papists had left Dublin, their houses locked up, protesting they were only humble poor souls.[132] The king wrote to Falkland on 1 July 1629 that the lands of the bishopric of Killala had been much decayed, the tenants paying no rents and the buildings fallen into ruin. The viceroy was enjoined to repair parish houses, begin the markets and fairs and to prevent 'petifogging prosecutors' from suing prelates and clergy in the star chamber 'unless there be a respectable number of people *bonae famae* to sign the bill against them'.[133] Apparently, the recusants saw the court of castle chamber as a double-edged sword which might benefit them through the legal harassment of their adversaries, including the very clergy sent to reform them.

Under Falkland, the exponential growth of suits over titles and estates in Ireland continued apace. With the advent of the court of wards in 1622, many of these issues were now to be resolved in the new tribunal. However, since the senior members of the aristocracy were now continuously engaged in litigation on various issues, the lord deputy and council often took cognizance of the suits when inferior courts might be overwhelmed or intimidated. On 13 November 1624, the lord deputy and council wrote to the lord president of Munster, acting on a complaint by Walter Browne, gentleman, against his adversary in Co. Limerick, Sir Thomas Standish. Their dispute concerned a dam made by Browne on the river Cawer that Standish, a member of the council of Munster, treated as a nuisance and wished to remove. When Browne refused, Standish had him pilloried on the streets of Limerick, despite the fact that a previous decision by the grand jury returned an *ignoramus* to Standish's suit on the matter. The viceroy and council ordered the president of Munster to arbitrate, obliging Standish to forebear taking any action to destroy the dam. Falkland here used the council in a preliminary fashion to address a potential star chamber issue, that of malfeasance by a local official.[134] The council in Munster was ordered to require the appearance of the two adversaries and the Irish council demanded to know the basis for Standish's intimidation of Browne. Their testimony before the provincial council was reported by the earl of Cork on 17 January 1625.[135]

Falkland and the council undertook numerous suits on points of honour touching the Irish peerage, most of which also turned on matters of property in dispute. On 20 June 1627, nine years after the initial suit, Falkland wrote to Buckingham in favour of Lord Burke of Castleconnell who wished to serve as a

132. Ibid., p. 446.
133. Ibid., p. 458.
134. Chatsworth, Lismore MSS, vol. 15, item 114 and see item 133. On 1 January 1625, Standish wrote to the earl of Cork, grousing that Browne and two of his brothers came with their swords to his chamber, where he was lying lame with gout, and demanded to see the order of the viceroy and council, saying he would 'have me to Dublin' for alleged offences. Ibid., item 133. The lord president responded on 17 January 1625 that they had heard the complainants, verifying the account of Browne.
135. Ibid., vol. 16, item 21v.

soldier since he was too poor to be a baron. Castleconnell petitioned the king for redress on 8 December 1627, charging that his uncle, Lord Burke of Brittas, had weakened his estate while he was a minor and seeking the restoration of both his property in Co. Limerick and a pension of £100. After referring the case to commissioners for Irish causes, the king cited the statute *Quia emptores* and ordered the restoration of his estate without further molestation from the court of wards. The council in Ireland was ordered to take advice and make the young Burke a grant of £100 a year in free socage.[136] On the following day, the deputy and council issued a proclamation to resolve a dispute between Lords Blayney and Balfour involving the unpaid execution of a marriage portion promised to Balfour on behalf of Blayney's daughter. Citing the king's wish to settle differences between subjects of high rank, the council ordered Blayney to pay in total £1,500 within two years time, and for Balfour, on payment of £1,000, to set apart land to the value of £300 to be held in trust to the use of Lady Balfour, Blayney's daughter, and to cancel and burn publicly all previous documents relating to the disputed jointure.[137] The ascending career of Dominick Sarsfield, chief justice of common pleas, who was honoured with a new title, Viscount Kinsale, led to a suit in castle chamber in 1626. Sarsfield alleged he had exclusive right to the title against the claim of John, Lord Courcy, averring on 18 June,

> I made a complaint to the Star Chamber here, where I cannot draw the Courcies without cart-ropes ... [and] I pray that if Viscount Courcy cannot prove this title he may receive censure in the Star Chamber.[138]

A counter-claim by Courcy was made in the same month to the privy council in England by his son, referring to Sarsfield as the 'son of a mean Cork merchant' who had procured a *quo warranto* writ and sued him in castle chamber. Courcy prayed that the suit be continued in England before the earl marshal, and the commissioners for Irish causes agreed, inviting Sarsfield to join suit there and demanding all similar suits in Ireland to cease. In the next month, Sarsfield's suit to have precedence over the chief justice of king's bench, owing to his title of nobility, was resolved by the privy council in favour of the senior judge, except when they met as councillors of state or accompanied the lord deputy to church.[139]

The court of castle chamber under Falkland continued its vigilance regarding the maintenance of judicial probity in the Irish courts. Reaching effectively as far as Co. Mayo, the court in February 1627 condemned Thomas Nolan and his son, James, for conspiracy, subornation of jurors and perjury in their attempt to frame the petitioner, Michael Cormack, gentleman. The Nolans had plotted to suborn

---

136. *Cal. S.P. Ire., 1625–32*, pp. 242, 291. See above, p. 339, for the original dispute.
137. Ibid., p. 291. Two years later, Falkland wrote to the king on behalf of Blayney, citing his impoverishment brought about by this suit and seeking a pension for him which was recommended by the commissioners. Ibid., p. 420.
138. Ibid., p. 133. See above, p. 73, for an account of Sarsfield's dénouement.
139. Ibid., pp. 139–40, 143. The king wrote to the viceroy in 1627 favouring the suit of Courcy, sinking the claim of Sarsfield to his coveted title. Ibid., p. 234.

two witnesses, Thomas McHubert and Feudoragh McCormack, to swear to an indictment of Cormack for treason in relieving a pirate, Captain Burke, with powder, bullets and victuals. The court fined the Nolans £1,000 each, taxing the corrupt witnesses £500 each, and nailing their ears to the pillory in both Dublin and Co. Mayo at the next assizes.[140] On 23 January 1626, the court censured Nicholas Woulfe of Kilcolman, Co. Kildare, a gentleman who had conspired to subvert two jurors in a capital case involving four prisoners. The bailiff, Edward Bell, charged with the safe keeping of the jurors, was induced to drink with Woulfe at a tavern, where the defendant won the opportunity to speak with the jurors in the night. Concerning the evidence in the case, Woulfe offered his opinion to the jurors that no man should ever be condemned upon the testimony of 'one notorious malefactor'. For this treacherous embracery, Woulfe was fined £50 and imprisoned during pleasure, based on his attempt to prejudice the jurors' impartiality.[141] Toward the end of his administration, Falkland was engaged in a suit involving the estate of Phelim McFeagh O'Toole against the Grahams, who sought his lands in Co. Wicklow. Depositions reported from the trial in 1628 purported to show that the sheriff, Sir Henry Belling (or Bealing), manipulated the evidence of Irish witnesses, bribing some with clothes and offers of land and money, and detaining them in order to obtain confessions and testimony against O'Toole.[142] Bealing offered to interpret for Donell Nensellagh, who had been held eleven weeks in restraint, since the deponent neither spoke nor understood English.[143] The plantation of Wicklow and the close examination of 35 witnesses in the case showed that official intimidation of witnesses often accompanied legal proceedings, though there is little to indicate that this adjudication was prosecuted at the court of castle chamber.

The parlous state of Irish finances and the diplomatic risks undertaken by Charles I and Buckingham led to negotiations with the Old English delegates on behalf of the Catholic landowners in Ireland. Although opposed by Protestant officials and glumly supported by the viceroy, 'The Graces', as they were called,

---

140. TCD, MS 852, ff. 82v–83.

141. Ibid., f. 88v.

142. TCD, MS 672, ff. 197–209v. The document referred to a castle chamber case in which depositions were taken before the lord chancellor, chief justice, archbishop of Dublin and Sir Arthur Savage for the court. Deponents claimed that their husbands were imprisoned and then bribed to accuse Phelim; threatened with hanging, burning and the rack; and imprisoned in leg and neck irons to induce a false accusation. Another testified that a convicted felon, Lysagh Duffe McMelaghin, was seen in Dublin 'very fatt in flesh & well cloathed' owing to the viceroy's reward 'for accuseinge Phelim McPheagh and his sons for the releeving of Morrogh Baccogh', even though he confessed that 'he could not accuse them justly with any thing, but belyed them to save his owne life'. Ibid., f. 203.

143. Ibid., f. 198. Another deponent, Rose Ny Cnogher, refused to indict O''Toole, despite threats to burn her, while Owny O'Byrne lied under oath to avoid being hanged and racked a fourth time during his examination. Ibid., f. 207.

represented a significant compromise on many legal issues for the Falkland administration. The lord deputy himself undertook negotiations with delegates from the Old English aristocracy commencing in 1626, employing the promise of relaxed penal laws against recusancy in return for an annual subsidy. The Great Assembly of April 1627, summoned by Falkland, won momentum for the calling of a parliament as part of the bargain.[144] A delegation to the king obtained a formal audience in March 1628, and on 14 May some 51 articles received royal approval in return for an annual subsidy of £40,000 sterling. The Graces allowed the replacement of a forthright oath of allegiance for the testamentary oath of supremacy as a condition of suing one's livery or other grants from the Irish court of wards, and the burden of proof in disputed land titles was now shifted from the incumbent to the claimant.[145] Despite the incompetence of Falkland in calling a parliament for which the essential statutory preconditions under Poynings' Law were not sent to England, the Graces were seen as fully embodied in law. The parliament of 1628 was postponed indefinitely and a protest meeting in Dublin objected to the imposition of a subsidy and an enlargement of the army without statutory foundation. When Falkland left Ireland in 1629, the Graces were partially implemented and the subsidy was reduced along with the army. A tentative beginning promised many rewards, and among them were a series of important judicial refinements, the burden of which was to resolve a number of ongoing disputes in the council and the castle chamber.[146]

Among the first articles in the Graces were several which engaged the lord deputy and council in the management of trade and commerce, including a final resolution of the sale of *aqua vitae*, tanning of leather and charging of customs duties by the clerk of the market. The regulation of the court of wards, summoning of juries, handling of assize courts and appeals to England were standardized, and the imposition of fees by sheriffs and others was harnessed to customary practices in England. In article 15, the king expanded the framework of all litigation when he announced,

> That all Natives that have ben or shalbe Students in the Inns of court in England for five yeares or more be indifferently and freely admitted by the judges in Ireland to practise there, takeinge onely this oath of allegiance.[147]

The constitutional import of that clause was profound, since the loyal opposition could lay claim to its first major success using lawful means. The exclusion of Catholics from the practice of law, based on their refusal to take the oath of

144. Clarke, *The Graces*, pp. 8–13.
145. Ibid., pp. 14–16.
146. Ibid., pp. 16–26; *Cal. S.P. Ire., 1625–32*, p. 156; Treadwell, *Buckingham*, pp. 277–99. Treadwell emphasizes the interlocking features of the Petition of Right, the Graces and the sudden death of Buckingham in 1628 which crystallized, then vaporized, the royal inclination to negotiate.
147. TCD, MS 672, f. 193.

supremacy, had been a Chichester-era penal rubric that was not regularly administered until 1613. Thereafter, numerous English officials questioned the merit of the policy, since Catholic petitioners were less likely to sue in court, causing profits to decline, and depriving younger sons of Pale families of a likely profession. The practising attorneys after 1613 lamented that few could speak Irish, but Catholic students such as Patrick Darcy continued to enter the inns of court during the period. The carefully crafted legal protests against Wentworth's government in the 1640s were a direct result of the readmission to practice of recusant lawyers.[148]

The intent of the Graces was nowhere more manifest than in circumscribing the work of the court of castle chamber. Article 43 confirmed that,

> No witness between party and party at sessions or assizes, or before any commissioners whatsoever are to be bound over to the Castle Chamber; and if information be put in against any such, then a relator to be named, who shall be thought sufficient to answer a recompence to the party informed against according to the award of the Court, if sufficient ground shall not appear in the information.[149]

In an effort to encourage more responsible government, the king allowed that

> Order shalbe given to the lo: deputie and Councell that whensoever any gentleman of qualitie shall exhibit any publique greevance, they shall give them favorable hereinge & redressse and shall give encouragement and Countenance to any such as shall modestly represent unto them misgovernment and abuses of the country where they are resident.[150]

Although castle chamber was not specially mentioned, the latter article plainly exhorted the court to provide access to judicial remedy in cases of official misconduct, a role which it had performed since its inception. In an oblique reference to castle chamber, article 31 ordered, 'No judges or commissioners shall bind over any jurors to any court whatsoever, unless it be for very apparent suspicion of corruption or partiality.'[151] The annotated draft of article 31 mentioned castle chamber specifically, adding that at least one judge should be a native speaker of Irish since many subjects at the bar could not be understood without interpreters.[152] On 20 June 1628, the lord deputy and council sent an order to the master of the rolls, requiring chancery to allow native Irish lawyers to plead in crown courts after taking the oath of allegiance.[153] Aidan Clarke has suggested that the majority of the Graces were observed, though abuses by the soldiers continued and a protest against them was lodged at a meeting of the Old English

148. Kenny, 'Exclusion of Catholics', pp. 344–49.
149. Clarke, *Old English*, p. 251.
150. TCD, MS 672, f. 192v.
151. Clarke, *Old English*, p. 248.
152. *Cal. S.P. Ire., 1625–32*, pp. 334–35.
153. Ibid., p. 353.

at Dublin in November 1628.[154] When Falkland left office in 1629, a tentative threshold had been constructed in the judicial establishment which promised a more even-handed treatment of all litigants under the close supervision of the lord deputy and council. The disappointment of these hopes under the new regime of Lords Justices Cork and the newly ennobled lord chancellor, Viscount Ely, was reversed when Wentworth sought the confirmation of the Graces in return for the promise of a subsidy. Though it is possible to view these protracted negotiations with the scepticism of hindsight, the near triumph of Old English interests as expressed in the Graces was a measure of success for the rule of law during a long period of civil peace (1626–1634), ending in bitter resentment with the collapse of Wentworth's parliament.[155]

CONCLUSION

The court of castle chamber under Falkland attracted a notoriety out of all proportion to the body of evidence which it has left for modern scholars. His administration was ushered in during the commission of inquiry of 1622 which explicitly called for limits on the judicial reach of the star chamber court. While quarrelling among themselves, the councillors faced another critique of prerogative justice at the hands of negotiators for the Graces in 1626. On his departure in 1629, Falkland left a legacy of vindictive recriminations which continued well into the succeeding administration.[156] The court of castle chamber was navigating a judicial course steadily throughout the rough seas of Falkland's tenure, and the court was reauthorized with full powers at the accession of Charles I in 1625. However, the frequent petitions to Westminster undermined the authority of both the lord deputy and the court, extending litigation which might otherwise have been formally concluded in Ireland. Falkland summoned all his resources to protect the prerogatives of the viceroy, but his bitter disputes with the lord chancellor and others diminished the stature of both the man and the office. Nonetheless, when he left Ireland in 1629 with professed reluctance, Falkland continued to serve at the court and to offer advice on Irish affairs just as his predecessors had done since the departure of Chichester in 1615.

154. Clarke, *Old English*, pp. 56–59.
155. Ibid., pp. 75–89; Clarke, *The Graces*, pp. 21–25.
156. In June 1630, Lord Wilmot wrote to Dorchester in favour of Sir Arthur Savage, who was 'vexatiously summoned to England to answer a bill in the Star Chamber' by the malice of Falkland. Wilmot charged Falkland with partisan vengeance, noting he had pursued Savage in the past, and accusing him of using his new post as privy councillor to pursue his old enemies in Ireland. *Cal. S.P. Ire., 1625–32*, p. 545.

CHAPTER TEN

The menace of judicial despotism: the court of castle chamber, 1629 to 1641

> The Lords and Commons have just come to us to ask why the Courts of
> Chancery, Star Chamber and Wards are not sitting. We said that the impeach-
> ment of the Judges prevented it. Many members do not like this delay.
>
> Lords Justices to Secretary Vane, 7 June 1641[1]

ONLY PORTIONS NOW survive of the judicial record for the regime of the two lords
justices, the earl of Cork and Adam Loftus, Viscount Ely, lord chancellor of Ireland.
Their tenure in office has been overshadowed by the authoritarian Wentworth who
succeeded them and nearly ruined both their careers. What is more, events in
England after the assassination of Buckingham and the Petition of Right drew away
the attention of the privy council in this important era, leaving the Dublin officials
to carry on without a clear mandate. Therefore, the court of castle chamber in this
period reflects an interesting preoccupation with the interstices of government itself,
the management of public affairs from Dublin and the insistence upon a heightened
judicial rectitude. Many of the cases deal with the minutiae of lawsuits, alleging
wrongful litigation which sought to exploit the courts of law for the partisan
advantage of the complainant. For example, in February 1629, Edward Fitzgerald of
Dublin sued Sir William Bishop, the former mayor, and John Nolan, esquire, for
wrongful prosecution in the court of king's bench, where Fitzgerald had been
acquitted of conspiring to murder Nolan. Bishop heard the original case as mayor
and imprisoned Fitzgerald on suspicion of attempted murder and robbery, holding
him without bail. The vindictive Fitzgerald subsequently prosecuted Nolan in castle
chamber for perjury and false accusation, and the court found for the plaintiff,
imprisoning Nolan and fining him £200.[2]

PROSECUTING MISCONDUCT: THE COURT UNDER LORDS JUSTICES CORK AND LOFTUS, 1629–33

The readiness to support a public official who was accused of maladministration
became the hallmark of the court during the Cork-Loftus lord justiceship. In

---

1. *Cal. S.P. Ire., 1633–47*, p. 298.
2. TCD, MS 852, f. 83. The mayor was found not guilty despite charges of malfeasance in office.

another case, the court heard a bill alleging that Christopher Kirovan, a merchant of Galway, plotted the disgrace of a justice of the peace for Co. Roscommon, one Josias Lambert. Kirovan had obtained a writ of *supersedeas* from the vice-president of Connacht to stay an action by Lambert at quarter sessions against his tenants. After summoning the tenants upon recognizances, Lambert viewed the *supersedeas* and properly dismissed them. Kirovan, however, alleged that Lambert illegally voided the *supersedeas* and jailed his tenants, so that Lambert was in turn detained and fined by the presidency court. The court of castle chamber determined that the writ of *supersedeas* issued from the presidency of Connacht was followed correctly by the justice of the peace, and on 8 February 1631 convicted Kirovan of conspiring to disgrace a public official.[3] The court of castle chamber expressed here its key function as the summit of a judicial super-structure in Ireland which could sort out competing jurisdictions and counter-claims at law. The court was acutely conscious of its duty to assist provincial officials, such as the sheriff of Co. Roscommon, who was beaten back to Athlone from the castle of Moyvanan by Robert Nugent in a hail of great stones and hot water. Nugent was convicted of riot and making false claims against the plaintiff, Christopher Jones, in castle chamber and other courts in 1632.[4]

The court of castle chamber under the two rival Irish peers, who were by this time wealthy and powerful landowners as well as crown officials, maintained a lively and crowded judicial calendar. Many of the suits dealt with simmering contentions that arose in the provinces and could not be remedied elsewhere. Some of them had their origin in the castle chamber court itself. For example, when Thomas Nolan of Ballinrobe, Co Mayo and his son James were censured in castle chamber on 7 February 1627, they were to be sent back to Mayo after their punishment in Dublin, to be pilloried before the assize court there prior to returning to the dungeon in Dublin Castle. The subsheriff of Co. Meath, Garret Archbold, allowed James to escape from his custody, and the sheriff of the county, Patrick Sedgrave, alleged Archbold had no authority from him, claiming the sheriff of Co. Dublin, Lamorack Nottingham, was responsible for the escape of Nolan. At a hearing on 17 June 1629, the court of castle chamber sat to hear testimony on the shrieval authority for Nolan, finding that Sedgrave had indeed given Archbold the green wax book as symbol of office, and making the errant sheriff responsible for the burden of Nolan's castle chamber fine.[5] Another sheriff was accused of extortion in his corrupt mishandling of a jury trial, when a titular priest named James Ronow was being sued for debt and the jury found no just contract or due payment. The sheriff, James McCarton, then threatened the jurors, and they duly found the contract valid, after which the sheriff granted executions against the goods of the priest and others, penalizing the jurors three

---

3. Ibid., f. 83v. The court ordered Kirovan to pay £100 damages to Lambert in addition to his fine.
4. Ibid., f. 83v.
5. Ibid., f. 84v. Archbold's responsibility was not addressed by the court, though the original suitor, Michael Cormack, was awarded damages from Sedgrave on behalf of the escaped James Nolan.

shillings each for fines due to him. The court found the sheriff guilty of extortion and fined him £200, ordered him to the pillory in Dublin and in Downpatrick, stating his offence was hardly less than high treason.[6]

The abiding peevishness of the two lords justices was occasionally aggravated by the temperamental behaviour of their associates on the court. On 3 February 1629, for example, the chief baron, Viscount Kilmallock and Viscount Mountnorris, the vice-treasurer, agreed upon a censure and fine in the case of Edward Fitzgerald against John Nolan on a charge of assault and attempted murder (cited above). Nolan was fined £200 by agreement with the lord chancellor and the earl of Cork, sitting privately, despite the preference of Lord Aungier for a lower fine, and imprisonment without the pillory. Lord Chancellor Loftus arbitrarily reduced the sentence, omitting the pillory from Nolan's censure and changing the terms of the court's action, but Cork challenged him and offered the testimony of others, after which the senior judge abruptly walked out of the castle chamber. The case, as recalled by Cork in his journal, was not entered in the record book, and it demonstrates that the collaborative nature of castle chamber decisions sometimes made it impossible to reach a judgement.[7] On another occasion, Cork obtained a promise from his fellow lord justice and rival on 2 April 1630 to recuse himself from the earl's pending cases in chancery, Loftus undertaking to have them heard and ordered by four judges who would in turn send their opinions independently to the lord keeper of the seal for a final decree.[8] Later, the earl found Lord Mountnorris's speeches in castle chamber impertinent and worthy of censure, since he loudly rejected the imputation that his accounts were in arrears in a debate on 25 June 1630. Mountnorris rejected a petition lodged against him seeking investigation into his accounts, and the chancellor refused to sign a certificate of inquiry on the request of Cork, detaining the document in his possession.[9] Conciliar wrangling over the issue of Mountnorris's payment to his captains continued well into November of that year, the chancellor siding with the vice-treasurer, and castle chamber was so frequently interrupted that the court obtained a reputation in Dublin for its ill-will.[10] Earlier, Mountnorris was accused of giving offence to the earl of Cork, and thus to the crown, in the court of castle chamber, when he loudly condemned the defendant, Patrick O'Mulvaney, on 5 February 1630. O'Mulvaney was convicted for slandering members of the Irish nobility and scandalizing others, for which he was whipped and pilloried, humbled before each of the four courts, and placed in life imprisonment. Mountnorris complained to the privy council in England that he followed the orders and direction of the viceroy, keeping his silence when necessary as he 'endured the displeasure of some governors under which he still suffers'.[11]

6. Ibid., f. 86v.
7. Chatsworth, Lismore papers, Letter book of earl of Cork, p. 16. Loftus responded to the charge of Cork by wagering that only two judges sought the pillory, to which Cork demurred, asking the attorneys for their testimony in the matter.
8. Ibid., p. 22. 9. Ibid., p. 40. 10. Ibid., pp. 45, 49, 51, 63.
11. TCD, MS 843, ff. 427–49. He blamed his enemies, including Falkland, for the allegation, noting

The court of castle chamber heard two countersuits on 28 April 1630, in which the complainants were both found guilty of riot and assault emerging from outrages committed against each other in Co. Tipperary. In the first case, Alexander Power sued David Walshe and eight of his kinsmen for marching against the town and land of Bally McRedmond. Walshe demanded that Power come forth from the house, based on his claim of a lease from the rightful owner, Thomas, Baron Cahir. The bill said Walshe threatened to set fire to the house, and then blocked up the doors and windows. The defendant allegedly laid waste to the property for three days, denying Power meat and drink, alleging further that he

> went into the backside of one Richard O ffinose, one of the pltes tenantes in the said towne, and ther spoyled him [of] two or three hives of Bees, cut his plowharness all to peeces, and espiying a maide servant of the said Richarde coming towarde his howse with a paile of milke uppon her head, and another with a pack of woll, he threw the said milke to the ground and spilt yt, and threw the woll into the Ryver of Annor [Nore].[12]

When Power complained to the mayor of Clonmel, that official sought the presence of Walshe, who refused to attend him, then threatened to cut off his hand if he tried to relieve the imprisoned Power or open the door of the house at Bally McRedmond. The court determined that Walshe and his kinsmen were guilty and fined them for their disorders.[13] In the second case, Walshe sued Power and 17 kinsmen for accosting him in the town of Clonmel, then raiding his house in Bally McRedmond at midnight. Power wounded both Walshe and his servants with deep cuts from a sword, barricading them in the house, and threatening them thus:

> crying out to the said complt that he should lye there till he did eate his owne excremente, the said Alexander comaunding the rest to charg their guns and shute att such of the pltes servantes as they should see about the howse, and to sett fier uppon the said howse, and burne yt about them.[14]

The court found it necessary to keep the well-armed gentry from resorting to violence over contested property rights, making no mention of a previous trial at law over the lease from Baron Cahir, and finding Power guilty of the riot as alleged.[15]

The court often heard petitions on behalf of female suitors, employing the original concept of offering an equity forum to litigants who were unable to sue at common law. In one case, James Cusack wrote to Lord Dorchester on 24 August 1631 that his sister had suffered an outrage at the hands of Christopher Terrell

---

the charge was not made until 12 July of that year. This case was not reported in the principal archives of the court. Ibid., ff. 436–40.

12. TCD, MS 852, f. 97v.   13. Ibid.

14. Ibid., f. 98.   15. Ibid.

and some accomplices. Terrell endeavoured to carry away the woman, saying he would marry her or 'outrage her', and causing her to fall from her horse so that she 'lay growling' on the ground and was sick long after.[16] The woman refused marriage and instead sued Terrell in the court of castle chamber, though no other record of the suit appears in the extant archives.[17] On the other hand, the court found the widow Jane Hamilton guilty of a forgery when she was accused by her husband's brother of changing the will on his deathbed to permit her to act as the sole executor of the estate, this all happening despite his weak protest and contrary to his formerly expressed wishes. Finding that she had erased important sections of the original document, excising the name of John Hamilton, the plaintiff, and then seeking to have the will proved in the consistory court of Armagh, the castle chamber court fined the widow £200 and imprisoned her.[18] Aside from the evident property implications, the court may have addressed circumstances involving recusancy and wardship, though the record is silent on these matters.

Adding to its increased involvement in Irish litigation through standing committees, the government in England took cognizance of Irish suits in the English star chamber court. In an oblique reference to a case not recorded in castle chamber records, the king intervened in another suit of Sir Allen Apsley against Sir Walter Coppinger. Apsley alleged that Coppinger had assaulted Gennet Grant, striking out one of her teeth, and abused Ellen O'Driscoll, throwing her over a cliff into the sea. Ordering Sir Walter to appear in England and all further cases between Coppinger and his tenants to be stayed, the king observed that the court of castle chamber was 'divided' on the question and sought trial in the English star chamber court.[19] On 9 June 1630, Lord Wilmot wrote to Dorchester on behalf of Sir Arthur Savage, who was sued by the former lord deputy, Falkland, along with others. He contended that any summons to the English star chamber was not answerable in Ireland unless issued by the king himself–a dubious claim–concluding that Savage now has 'a pursuivant following him about' and suffers the indignity of having people think he is charged with treason.[20] He further argued that Savage would have to make an expensive journey, citing previous hostile encounters with Falkland in Ireland.[21] In similar vein, Sir William Power

---

16. *Cal. S.P. Ire.*, *1625–32*, p. 628. 17. Ibid. 18. TCD, MS 852, f. 87v.

19. *Cal. S.P. Ire.*, *1647–60, addenda, 1625–60*, p. 163. Apsley and Coppinger were continually at law over the plantations in Co. Cork and this collateral action was further evidence of the exploitation of castle chamber for the advantage of malicious suitors. Grant was alleged to be a poor relative of Coppinger, while O'Driscoll was wife to David Barry, a client of Apsley. Coppinger, as we have already seen, had been a frequent suitor at castle chamber since late in the reign of Elizabeth I.

20. *Cal. S.P. Ire.*, *1625–32*, p. 545. Wilmot cited the opinion of the 'best counsellors' in Ireland and a previous instance in the time of Chichester when such a summons was withstood. However, it would appear that the English star chamber could summon both witnesses and defendants from Ireland without separate action on the part of the crown. See, for example, the case of Perrot in the 1590s, requiring the presence and testimony of Nicholas White.

21. Ibid. A subsequent petition by Falkland to the king, citing an order of star chamber against

wrote to Dorchester on 5 July 1630 against the harassment of Cork in a case over five years old, accusing the lord justice of abusing his power. Though the case concerning the young earl of Kildare had been settled in the court of wards, Cork now revived the suit after he became lord justice and obtained an interest in the Kildare estate. He had Power arrested in England, then moved the dismissal of Power's suit against him in castle chamber, since Power could not attend the court by the first sitting of the next Easter term.[22] On the other hand, the judicial relationship between English and Irish courts was occasionally manipulated by suitors to the disadvantage of the lords justices themselves. On 12 February 1632, Chancellor Loftus wrote that his enemy, Lord Ranelagh, tried to get suitors in his court to appeal to the English privy council, stating, 'He threatened in the Council Chamber lately to have me called before you.'[23] Finally, the star chamber suit in England against the London planters for their failure to carry out the terms of their undertaking in Ulster exercised many Irish witnesses, but did not claim the attention of the court of castle chamber. It is, however, another example of how the senior courts of the Irish judicial system were frequently circumvented in this period. And it does much to explain the remorseless determination of Wentworth to reestablish the rights and privileges of viceregal government in 1633.[24]

Although the court of castle chamber has been the target of obloquy for centuries, based on its inquisitorial procedures as a prerogative court, Lords Justices Cork and Loftus found that there were severe practical limitations to the enforcement of unpopular policies. On 20 March 1633, the council in Ireland wrote to explain their actions in relation to a tumult in the streets of Dublin. The council had observed that popish clergy were frequenting the houses of Dublin recusants, erecting altars and saying public masses, so they ordered the arrest of two friars who were saying mass on 26 December 1632, a day calculated perhaps to offend the majority of worshippers. With the archbishop of Dublin, the mayor, sheriff and recorder of the city, who were all Protestants, a small company of the garrison marched to the mass house and arrested the two friars. This provocation on the day after Christmas produced a spontaneous riot by a

> great number of people of mean Condicon who, without regard to the emynencie of their persons or places, fell resolutely uppon them, forced the

Savage and Philip Bushin, sought the crown's favour to send letters to the lords justices to execute payment of £3,000 in damages from Savage to Falkland. *Cal. S.P. Ire., 1647–60*, p. 174.

22. *Cal. S. P. Ire., 1625–32*, p. 554. Power claimed that Chancellor Loftus feared to offend the earl of Cork, so declined to favour his suit despite letters from the king himself to offer a fair hearing.
23. Ibid., p. 646.
24. Ibid., pp. 630–31. In September 1631, Sir Thomas Phillips wrote that the Londoners were much alarmed at their star chamber suit, though witnesses against them were difficult to find since most people on the plantation were agents or farmers from Dublin. See Canny, *Making Ireland British*, pp. 213–30, 264, 297. For a good account of the star chamber suit against the London companies, see T.W. Moody, *The Londonderry plantation, 1609–41: the city of London and the plantation of Ulster* (Belfast, 1938).

two fryers from them, and pursued the Archbpp, the mayor and the rest into the street, casting stones atte them in great nombers to the apparent hazzard of their lyves.[25]

After the escape of the public officials into a house in Skinner Row, the councillors rescued them and proceeded to issue a proclamation commanding all persons to return to their houses, gathering the next day to prosecute the malefactors. However, most of the rioters were apprentices, women, country people and of the 'meanest sort' who were difficult to apprehend. The council imprisoned leading recusants for their failure to support the archbishop in his official duties, seized ten houses which had been used as sanctuary for priests, and imprisoned others to make an example to the town. Nonetheless, the council feared a repetition of the sudden fray and clearly expressed alarm at the mismanagement of the affair. This scene of municipal mayhem, fired by the scornful policy of the chief governors during the Christmas season in Dublin, illustrates that popular resistance to arbitrary decrees made it difficult to impose tyrannical rule.[26] Despite the manifest precedents for its use against recusancy and riot, however, the court of castle chamber was not employed in this instance.

AN INSTRUMENT OF ABSOLUTISM: THE COURT UNDER WENTWORTH, 1633–1639

Sir Thomas Wentworth made lengthy preparations for his viceregal government in Ireland, and his anticipated arrival left the lords justices with a lame duck status that did nothing to augment their authority. Prior to his arrival in Dublin, the English privy council remanded a case of very long standing for final adjudication by the new lord deputy and council in Ireland. When the issue of the right of customs in Dublin was first taken up in 1626 by the commission for Irish causes, the case was referred to attorneys general in Ireland and England to establish the right of the crown. Two merchant traders from outside Ireland, Peter Weibrant and John Bullard, had petitioned the English privy council against a decree in the Irish exchequer chamber favouring the city of Dublin for payment of 3*d.* in the

---

25. Chatsworth, Lismore papers, Letter book of earl of Cork, p. 29. The lords justices had aggravated conditions by ordering the suppression of all religious houses, including the destruction of St Patrick's Purgatory on Lough Derg, Co. Donegal, in September 1632.

26. Ibid. See also *Cal. S.P. Ire., 1625–32*, p. 504. Wilmot wrote that the lords justices faced a mob of 3,000 strong, who stoned the mayor and primate, and that 17 priest houses had been established in the past four months. Critics of the government had written anonymously in 1630 to complain that the lords justices continued to persecute recusants despite the crown's revocation of the proclamation banishing priests. They noted that assize judges were ordered to present recusants for not attending church and jurors who refused were bound over to the council table or star chamber and fined up to £20, a maverick continuation of Chichester's policy. *Cal. S.P. Ire., 1647–60*, p. 161.

pound as customs, and the lords justices were required in 1631 to defer the taking of the customs, pending a final decision by the privy council in England. Suspending judgement until the arrival of Wentworth, the English councillors on 3 May 1632 required a full hearing of the case by the lord deputy and council, adding that they should 'settle a Course by act of state for the prevention of all undue and unfitt Retaylinge of the said merchantes strangers borne out of his Maties dominions'.[27] The lords justices were snubbed in favour of the new viceroy, despite the relatively low profile of the case at the council board. Evidently, the privy council expected Wentworth to move with celerity to settle pending adjudication, knowing the temper of the man they were sending to Ireland, since he was one of their own.

Before his departure for Ireland, and during extensive negotiations surrounding his assumption of the chief governorship, Wentworth made the calculated decision to support Old English grievances against the incumbent government. The lords justices had pursued a more active anti-Catholic policy and alienated the Old English by refusing to move forward with a confirmation of the Graces.[28] Wentworth exploited the divisions within Ireland by supporting continued payment of the subsidy in advance of a proposed parliament which would offer statutory confirmation of the Graces. Upon his arrival in 1633, the new lord deputy committed himself to a parliament which would confirm the legislative foundation of a regular subsidy and place his government on a sound financial basis. The cunning Wentworth employed the deceitful ruse of dividing parliament into two sessions, the first of which was exclusively devoted to financing the government. A second session would, in theory, address the grievances of the Old English. While both houses proceeded with legislation in July 1634 to undergird the Wentworth administration financially, committees were named to examine the election returns and to review each article of the Graces. As a harbinger of things to come, the court of castle chamber on 11 June 1634 prosecuted and censured a Dublin sheriff, a merchant of the city named Christopher Brice, who was discharged from office for 'mutinously' subverting the execution of the writ of election for the city. Wentworth accused him of acting on the advice of priests to secure the election of Catholic members, and to refuse to cooperate in his examination at the council board and in open court. Wentworth quashed the original election and engineered the choice of the serjeant at law, Catelyn, debarring Brice in perpetuity from holding office in Dublin. Brice was fined £700 for his offences.[29] Although parliament expectantly prepared the grievances in the form of legislation to be presented at the next session, Wentworth used the recess in August to critique their proposals. He adjudged seven articles relating to the court of wards, the army and royal title to land as

27. TCD, MS 843, p. 143 and see pp. 140–43.
28. Ford, *Reformation in Ireland*, p. 213.
29. *The earl of Strafforde's letters and dispatches*, ed. W. Knowler, 2 vols. (Dublin, 1740), i, 270; *Anc. rec. Dublin*, iii, 291. Plate 14.

contrary to the interests of the crown and denied them outright. The others, he declared, with only four exceptions, were to be implemented by administrative action through the privy council in Ireland and hence did not require statutory authorization. This discretionary amplitude provided the viceroy with substantial independence, and he explained to the committee that he would not recommend to the king any Graces which prejudiced royal interests. By April 1635, the Old English outrage at this betrayal of their cause was silenced by the closing of the parliament. This first taste of Wentworth's duplicity heralded future conflict. But the Old English were not uniformly targeted for another campaign against heterodoxy.[30]

The famously extra-legal machinations of Wentworth as lord deputy of Ireland were prefigured in his multiple star chamber cases in England. At the senior court, Wentworth commenced an action in 1632 against his Yorkshire neighbour, David Foulis for 'scandalous words', alleging that the defendant accused the lord president of the Council in the North of taking double payment from Foulis for his honour of knighthood. The impertinent Foulis was fined £3,000 by the court and his lands were attached for payment in 1634.[31] From 1636 to 1639 Wentworth was engaged in a protracted suit against his former ally, Sir Piers Crosbie, over words spoken which dishonoured the viceroy. The star chamber decree of 22 May 1639 demonstrated the problems which the hot-tempered Wentworth created for himself. The viceroy was accused of striking Captain Robert Esmond several times with his cane which caused the man's death within three days, an outcome, supported by numerous witnesses for the defence, that inspired criticism of the chief governor and derisory statements by Crosbie and others. Esmond had been ordered to take some goods for the viceroy on his barque, but he demurred, saying it was fully laden. Esmond was then brought before the lord deputy, who committed him to prison for this offence, where he died. Despite ample testimony to the fact that Wentworth cudgelled Esmond during their contretemps, the star chamber court agreed with the lord deputy, citing other witnesses who claimed he merely shook the cane over the head of Esmond, without striking him, and accepting the view that he died of old wounds, aggravated by consumption.[32] Crosbie and Lawrence, Lord Esmond, kinsman of the deceased, were convicted of spreading false and scandalous reports of the events and encouraging Margery Turner, widow of the deceased, to complain to the king. The attorney, Marcus Cheevers, when asked about the incident, asserted that 'it was a greater offence in the Lord Depty than in a private man'.[33]

30. Clarke, *Old English*, pp. 87–89, and see pp. 65–89; Kearney, *Strafford*, ch. 7.
31. WWM STR P, 24–25, items 428–32.
32. Ibid., item 474, ff. 1–10.
33. Crosbie and Esmond were fined £4,000 and £3,000 respectively, in recognition of their senior positions as councillors, while Cheevers was fined £1,000 and made to participate in the collective payment of £5,000 damages to the viceroy. Ibid., ff. 2, 9–10; A. Clarke, 'Sir Piers Crosby, 1590–1646: Wentworth's "tawney ribbon"', *IHS*, xxvi (1988), 142–48.

Wentworth's employment of star chamber suits in his own interest, coupled with his experience as a member of that court, suggests that he would become an active litigant and judge in Ireland.

The court of castle chamber under Wentworth has been viewed as an instrument by which the governor could terrify his opposition. However, the new lord deputy quickly found that the Irish councillors were reluctant to support his early initiatives, so he approached the king to have his own secretary, Sir George Radcliffe, sworn of the Irish council:

> Finally, I find so little Help at the Council Table here, having only the Master of the Rolls [Christopher Wandesford] there that I can be confident of; as I must become an humble Suitor to his Majesty, that I may have a letter for swearing Mr Radcliffe of this Council, there being many of them already at this Board, almost beneath him as far in Estate, as they are in Parts and Understanding, to serve his Majesty.[34]

Wentworth employed the court as a threat to his adversaries, intimidating Lord Wilmot through bills in castle chamber and in exchequer so that he would agree to transfer his interest in the castle of Athlone to the crown. Wilmot appealed to England directly, seeking to avoid suit in castle chamber, and Wentworth responded by heaping new accusations on the defiant lord president of Connacht.[35] Finally, it should be noted that, despite his own frequent manipulation of judicial venues, Wentworth was strongly contemptuous of legal proceedings when they deviated from the course he had set out for them. In 1638, he confided to Secretary Coke his belief that provost marshals in each of the four provinces had more effect than justices of the peace, concluding,

> Besides, the bad minded Irish are better contained, held in more Fear and better Duty by one Provost Marshal, and the Terror of his executing Martial Law upon them than by twenty others, be they Justices of Peace or Justices of Assize, a Truth as clear in Experience as any can be.[36]

In fact, the celebrated cases in which the lord deputy wielded his power rarely involved a full and formal trial in the prerogative court. For example, the threat of a heavy fine and imprisonment levied against the former lord justice, the wealthy earl of Cork, was accompanied by delays and brokered counter-offers which culminated in the humiliating capitulation of the earl prior to a full hearing of his cause. The records are very full of preliminary depositions leading to the trial. At

---

34. *Strafforde's letters*, i, 100. A few cases adjudicated in castle chamber are noted in passing by Knowler, such as the trial of the cooper and quartermaster in 1633 who robbed mariners of their victuals. Wentworth wrote to Coke that both were sued in the 'star chamber here' by the attorney-general so their examples would serve to admonish such 'villainy'. Ibid., i, p. 152.

35. Ibid., i, 399–400, 495–96; ii, p. 22.   36. Ibid., ii, 197.

issue was the earl's fraudulent possession of the college of Youghal, an ecclesiastical endowment which yielded a handsome profit but outraged his enemies. An information against him was presented at the court of castle chamber on 17 November 1634 by the attorney-general, William Rives. The charge detailed how the earl gained possession of the premises during unsettled times of war and rebellion at the end of Elizabeth's reign and exploited the income for his own purposes, depriving the church of its foundation by a fraudulently devised conveyance to a proxy. The attorney-general sought a full trial on the forged deed, the earl's withholding of evidence and his violation of an act of state issued in 1615 against unreasonable leases made by the clergy of their livings.[37] The earl was summoned to appear before the court of castle chamber in Michaelmas term by warrant from the lord deputy on 22 September 1634, but Cork submitted an affidavit that his evidence was 'in the country', that is, at his dwelling in Lismore, and thus not available to him for trial.[38] After numerous delays, the deeds were delivered into the court on 20 March 1635, showing the manner in which the earl obtained a grant of the college of Youghal. But Cork alleged that the lord deputy lost his patience with this process and intervened in the case on the issue of abrogating an act of state. Cork protested that the act of state had no validity, as it was promulgated in the previous reign by a chief governor now deceased, to which Wentworth reportedly gave his famous reply: 'I will make you and all others in this kingdome know that any Act of State made or to be made, shalbe as byndeing to the subiectes of Ireland as any Act of Parliament can be.'[39] By the summer of 1635 the earl's attorneys were bargaining for more time in order to examine the depositions in the case and trying to change the venue of the trial to an ecclesiastical jurisdiction.

The substance of the case against the earl of Cork was not, in the end, a matter of the impropriations of the church livings from the college of Youghal. Wentworth was offended that the earl had made a loan to the crown of some £15,000 for which he soon demanded repayment, and the viceroy was determined

37. WWM STR P, 24–25, item 437, ff. 1–29. The information is a rare example of pleading before the court of castle chamber, containing the form of the plea as well as substantial argument. Cork was accused of plotting to 'disappropriate' the estate of some £700 in value from its divine purpose, noting that the college of Youghal held a number of vicarages, parsonages and other spiritual estates. The drawing of a conveyance in Secretary Fenton's house and concealing the matter by proxy settlement on Sir Lawrence Parsons was seen as evidence of conspiracy to defraud the crown, and the decision by the warden and fellows to sue the earl for dispossession in 1627 led to further bargaining. The information was signed by Anthony Stoughton, clerk of the court of castle chamber, along with the senior law officers, Nathaniel Catelyn, William Ryves and Edward Bolton. See also Chatsworth, Lismore papers, vol. 18, item 29.

38. Chatsworth, Lismore papers, vol. 18, item 42. This information was registered by Stoughton on 29 November 1634. Examinations of the earl of Cork and the bishops of Waterford and Cork were then ordered. Ibid., items 60, 61. In March 1635, the original lists of deeds were brought into the court, including a deed of 1605 signed by Boyle, conveying the college to him by grant from Lawrence Parsons and signed by the bishop of Cork. Ibid., item 67.

39. Chatsworth, Lismore papers, vol. 18, item 72.

to have that sum back from the earl. Compounding the threat of trial in castle chamber, the lord deputy demanded a fine to avoid litigation, saying he would deprive Cork of office and imprison him in Dublin Castle. Cork protested to the viceroy that 'I did not Deserve to be brought into the Castlechamber for soe good and charitable a worke'.[40] However, he learned from the primate of Ireland that

> the Lo Deputy told him that he did hope I would disobey his commaund and not deliver upp my wrytings, which yf I did he would … commit me to the Castle of Dublin and not enlarge me untill I had paid as great a fyne to his Matie as the Colledge of Yoghall was worth.[41]

The earl, after months of delay and intimations of peril from his friends on the council, finally agreed to pay the fine in May 1636.[42] Meeting his old rival, Lord Chancellor Loftus, on the way to court in early May, Cork heard that many on the council believed he was innocent of the charges, but Loftus warned, 'it was very necessary for me to be exceeding carefull of my self for that it was not my cause but my judges I was to feare.'[43] On 24 January 1640, the king wrote to the lord deputy, by then earl of Strafford, to inform him that the earl had paid his fine and now sought a grant to his heir, Lord Dungarvan, of an estate in fee simple in the new college house of Youghal. The king commanded, 'We also desire you to free him from the claims of people who have trespassed on the lands, and strike out the suit against him in the Castle Chamber and take it off the file.'[44] It had occurred to many silent witnesses that the intimidation of the wealthiest man in Ireland was a show trial, held in star chamber instead of the appropriate ecclesiastical court at the behest of the chief governor. Using the court to threaten adversaries was a novel perversion of its mandate, made worse by the fact that no formal trial of the evidence was ever held.

40. Ibid.
41. Ibid., item 134. He added, 'And yf I would condiscend to give the king thirty thowsand pounds he would be my frennd and the suite in Castle Chamber should be withdrawne, otherwise he would prosecute me without any further delay'. Ibid. Speaking directly with the viceroy on 25 April 1635 before lunch in the withdrawing chamber, Cork argued 'that I conceaved the proper Court for Determining thereof was not in the Castle Chamber, but in the Court Christian'. Ibid.
42. Ibid., items 133, 134. Cork employed his son, Lord Dungarvan, in the negotiations with Radcliffe and others, and received Lord Ranelagh as emissary from the viceroy. The legal machinations of the viceroy himself were not above suspicion. The Byzantine manner in which he accumulated vast estates in Co. Wicklow through his agents and proxies, at the expense of the O'Byrnes and others, was hardly a model of judicial impartiality. See Kearney, *Strafford in Ireland*, pp. 174–84.
43. Chatsworth, Lismore papers, vol. 18, item 134. On 2 June 1636, Cork related a subsequent encounter with Wentworth, who came to his house in Dublin prior to leaving 'with the tide' and asked him to sign a petition to the king for a new grant of the college of Youghal. Cork demurred, saying he had not seen it before, but the viceroy, 'standing with one legg within his study doore, and the other without,' pressed him and said he should trust his good word and sign it without delay, which he did. Ibid.
44. *Cal. S.P. Ire., 1633–47*, p. 233.

The litigious viceroy destroyed the career and reputation of another of the most senior Irish councillors shortly after his arrival in Dublin, though the court of castle chamber was involved only indirectly. In December 1635, Wentworth held a council of war at which the court-martial of the vice-treasurer and treasurer-at-war in Ireland, Lord Mountnorris, was convicted of insolence and sentenced to hang. This extraordinary quasi-judicial event was inspired by an apparently innocent mishap. One of the servants in the presence chamber moved a footstool on which the gout-ridden leg of the lord deputy was resting. The volcanic temper of Wentworth again got the best of him, and he beat the servant in full view of Mountnorris and others. The veteran councillor

> publiquely and in a scornefull, contemptuous manner answered, 'Perhaps it was done in revenge of that publique affront which my lord Deputy had done him formerly. But he had a Brother that would not take such a revenge.'[45]

Sir Francis Annesley had been principal secretary in Ireland from 1618 until he was made vice-treasurer and raised to the peerage as Lord Mountnorris in 1628. He was involved in the downfall of Falkland as lord deputy, and Wentworth found him unreliable, corrupt and vain. The viceroy determined to crush Mountnorris in 1635, initiating an inquiry into his dishonesty as vice-treasurer and obtaining an order from the privy council against him as early as May 1634. Although Mountnorris did not suffer the ultimate penalty, he was deprived and imprisoned for insulting the vanity and dignity of the lord deputy.[46] A petition to the crown, sent by Lady Mountnorris from Dublin on 28 April 1636, alleged that Wentworth sentenced her husband to death by court-martial, acting both as accuser and judge. Further, her complaint alleged,

> He was then arraigned this month of April before the Star Chamber, and Lady Mountnorris could not procure for him the right of being represented by counsel. The Deputy was in the court in person when he was tried, and ordered the accusations to be read out by the Attorney-General, which was done in a reproachful way. This was done before there was any proof of the accusations laid to his charge in the Star Chamber. On April 11 he was committed to the Tower.[47]

45. Chatsworth, Lismore papers, vol. 18, item 107. Wentworth explained his use of the council of war against Mountnorris, basing it upon 'inciteing a revenge ... which his Matie in his said lres [letters] Declares to be an offence much unbeseeming the gravity of a privy Councellour to us the Lord Deputie and the Dutie of a Captaine to his Generall and not to be suffered in any well governed Army'. Ibid. Those who signed the order included the military officials John Borlase, Charles Coote, Faith Fortescue, Arthur Blundell, Lawrence Esmond and Lord Ranelagh. Few of them were privy councillors or members of the court of castle chamber. Ibid.

46. *DNB*, 'Annesley, Sir Francis'.

47. *Cal. S.P. Ire., 1633–47*, pp. 128, 131. A further petition from Mountnorris in March 1637 complained that he had been prisoner in Dublin Castle for fourteen months, despite the king's

Wentworth's management of the Cork and Mountnorris cases outside the parameters of the star chamber jurisdiction demonstrates his cavalier disregard for precedent and protocol.

In unusual circumstances, the lord deputy took it upon himself to instruct local juries in their duties to the crown. Pursuant to his ambitious plans for plantation in Connacht, Wentworth travelled to Boyle in Co. Roscommon on 9 July 1635, and there began a series of judicial intimidations by which jurors were compelled to find for the king's title to the province. Again at Ballinrobe and at Sligo, Wentworth 'bullied and threatened his way to a favourable verdict'.[48] Arriving in Co. Galway for his final triumph, the lord deputy took up residence in Portumna, along with four companies of soldiers, at the new palatial residence of the powerful earl of Clanricarde. Martin Darcy, the sheriff, had empanelled a jury of his own choosing, and Wentworth examined each of them singly, interrogating them in regard to the king's title, which they partially refused to affirm.[49] Wentworth then proceeded to bind over the jurors to appear in the court of castle chamber, fined Darcy £1,000 and charged David Meade with corruption for testifying to the authenticity of titles entered by the defence, adding his name to the list of offenders to be tried in castle chamber. Just as a defence of the jurors was about to be mounted by Patrick Darcy and other lawyers in London, the old earl of Clanricarde died in England in November 1635, leaving Wentworth in command of the occasion. On 27 May 1636, the Galway jurors came to trial at the council board, 'for a wilful refusal to find the title of his Majesty to the whole county of Galway contrary to their evidence'.[50] Again the jurors were examined separately,

interventions. Ibid., p. 152. Wentworth wrote on 6 January 1638 that Mountnorris had left for England, 'wondrously humbled as much as Chaucer's friar'. Ibid., p. 178. No evidence of a subsequent 'star chamber' trial has been uncovered, so Lady Mountnorris was probably mistaking the *ad hoc* council of war for a castle chamber trial.

48. Clarke, *Old English*, p. 93. Wentworth wrote to Coke, 'I resolved to have Persons of such Means as might answer the King a round fine in the Castle Chamber in Casse they should prevaricate, who, ... [for] ... that Reason would be more fearful to tread shamefully and impudently aside from the Truth, than such as had less, or nothing to lose.' *Strafforde's letters*, i, 442. He continued, 'I desired them first to descend into their own Consciences, take them to Counsel, and there they should find the Evidence for the Crown clear and conclusive; next to beware how they appeared resolved or obstinate against so manifest a Truth, or how they let slip forth of their Hands the Means to weave themselves into the Royal Thoughts and Care of his Majesty thorough a chearful and ready Acknowledgement of his Right, and a due and full Submission thereunto'. Ibid., p. 443.

49. In one account, 'The Jury Delivered theire verdict according to theire Evidence and refused to find more then was contained in the said offices taken soe longe agoe & spoke by one of them [i.e. foreman of the jury] by agreement of all according to the usuall manner. And yet the lo: Depty examined every one of the jury apart whether he was for the kings title or agt it. Whereat two of the Jury said they would have found the title if the rest had found it'. TCD, MS 672, f. 242.

50. Clarke, *Old English*, pp. 101–02, citing Bodl., Carte MSS, i, ff. 139–52; Kearney, *Strafford in Ireland*, pp. 95ff. Both Kearney and Clarke cite the castle chamber case based upon surviving correspondence, but no record of the adjudication itself has been found. Again, lacking the entry book for this period, it is difficult to say whether a formal adjudication took place. Wentworth

and the court found that they were guilty of disobeying the proclamation calling upon them to acknowledge the royal title, compounded by their subsequent efforts to petition the king directly by sending agents to England. In addition, the sheriff was found guilty of partiality in the selection of them (one, Ambrose O'Madden, was illiterate). The court found for the prosecution, ordering a new inquisition, and fining each of the jurors the ruinous sum of £4,000, imprisoning them along with the sheriff. When the king gave Wentworth his full support, the resistance collapsed.[51] On 9 December 1636, the jurors submitted to Wentworth at the council board and their fines were thereupon reduced, after which they were to acknowledge at the court of castle chamber the justice of the prosecution against them. In April 1637, the assizes in Galway found the king's title to the county and town of Galway. Wentworth's manipulation of the legal system undermined confidence in the prerogative court at an early stage in his regime through his 'occasions of organized intimidation'.[52] The lack of a substantial record of the trial at castle chamber suggests that Wentworth may have managed this judicial victory within the privy council in Dublin, which included a cohort of military officials who were customarily absent from the court.

Considering the earlier record of the court of castle chamber in pursuing recusancy, the Wentworth court was initially silent on this issue. In December 1633, Wentworth wrote to Laud, assuring him that he would administer the church with a strong hand, and adding,

> It was in my Mind to trounce a Bishop or two in the Castle-Chamber, who have aliened since, and contrary to the Act of State made twenty Years agone, to prevent such fraudulent Sales [of diocesan property], being of Opinion one Example in this Kind would do infinite Good in this Kingdom.[53]

held the inquisition in Portumna's great hall, where his soldiers were placed in threatening manner. His troops slaughtered the deer in Clanricarde's park and grazed their horses in his meadows with impunity, so the impression of merciless vandalism did little to win the admiration of local observers. M. McMahon, *Portumna Castle and its lords* (Nenagh, 1983), pp. 12–13.

51. Secretary Coke wrote to approve of Wentworth's proceeding in the court of castle chamber against the sheriff, the jury and the agents of Co. Galway, including one Richard Burke who tried to intervene in the jury's deliberation by plucking a juror by the sleeve. *Stafforde's letters*, i, 464–65. Wentworth then fined the agents and their confederates 'which are neither few, nor of low condition', adding that, though the jurors put in their findings to the exchequer, they continued to protest in England against their fines. Ibid., i, 493–94; ii, 14.

52. Clarke, *Old English*, p. 93 and see pp. 93–103; Kearney, *Strafford in Ireland*, pp. 97–99. Legal machinations in England by the earl of Clanricarde stymied progress, but fear of the arbitrariness in prerogative courts spread widely among the Old English after 1637. On 9 February 1637, Wentworth received a petition on behalf of the Galway jurors from over 100 gentlemen of Galway, asking the viceroy to take account of the frailty of their judgement in failing to acknowledge crown title to Co. Galway. *Cal. S.P. Ire., 1633–47*, p. 149. Richard Martin sought to be restored to his practice after being suspended during the Galway contest, having subsequently admitted his transgression and encouraged all men in Galway to submit to the crown. Wentworth agreed, saying he had borne his chastisement well. *Stafforde's letters*, ii, 98.

53. *Stafforde's letters*, i, 173. Wentworth added he would punish the buyers as well as the sellers of

Wentworth was admonished by the king in June 1635 to proclaim an act of state enjoining all bishops to administer an oath against simony and to punish those guilty of this sin in the court of castle chamber or the court of high commission.[54] The viceroy attacked the earl of Cork for impropriations of church livings from the college of Youghal, and compelled him to remove his grandiose marble tomb in St Patrick's cathedral, Dublin from the high altar to a side aisle.[55] But these were political contests which occurred in the arena of a corrupted Erastian church. For the most part, Wentworth permitted a *de facto* religious toleration among majority Catholics while gradually establishing a firm foundation for church orthodoxy, including the infusion of Laudian clergy in the episcopacy and the establishment of the court of high commission.[56] On occasion, the viceroy took umbrage at the persistence of Catholic practices that came to the attention of the castle chamber. Writing to Coke on 31 January 1634, he mentioned that the proofs read in the court of castle chamber contained, along with testimony on the matter of subornation, an oath, taken before a priest upon the altar and sacrament, that what the deponent had sworn was true. The unrepentant counsel urged this testimony to be therefore conclusive. Wentworth seized the opportunity to condemn such oaths made and sworn in the court of castle chamber, whereupon he was told it was an ordinary practice to legitimize sworn testimony. The viceroy found the oaths a high misdemeanour, and ordered the courts and judges to refuse to accept testimony so derived, and the king's attorney to prefer an information against any priest or party to suit who engaged in the procurement of such oaths, so priests could no longer interest themselves in the king's courts 'extrajudicially'.[57]

The subsequent work of the new prerogative court of high commission was designed primarily to shore up the indiscipline of the established church rather than to harass nonconformists. Laud and Wentworth agreed to defer the foundation of the tribunal until after the outcome of the parliament was known in April 1635, but an act of state required that, in the interim, proceedings should commence in castle chamber against clergy accused of simony. The membership of the commission included the lord deputy and selected members of the Irish privy council along with 23 clergymen. It was designed to work in tandem with the court of castle chamber, so there was no need to replicate the membership

---

ecclesiastical lands, reforming the alienations and other transgressions of the bishops and citing 'Reason of State' as well as religion in his rationale. The bishops of Cashel, Down, Clonfert, Killaloe, Limerick and others were summoned before the council board. Ibid., pp. 171–73.

54. *Cal. S.P. Ire., 1633–47*, p. 106.

55. V. Jackson, *St. Patrick's cathedral* (Irish Heritage Series) (Dublin, n.d.), pp. 9–10. The ungainly baroque memorial to his beloved wife, Katherine, included Boyle's children; his wife's grandfather, a former dean of the cathedral and lord chancellor, Dr Robert Weston; and his father-in-law, the secretary of state under two sovereigns, Sir Geoffrey Fenton. The bulky monument of several tons was erected in 1632, during the lord justiceship of the earl of Cork, and was, in some respects, also a symbol of his own political power, so Wentworth saw a need to strike it down. Plate 12.

56. Kearney, *Strafford in Ireland*, pp. 111–20.   57. *Strafforde's letters*, i, 202.

entirely on the new court. Despite its tyrannical reputation, only four of the 21 surviving case records involved nonconformity, while eight of them concerned the details of clerical income and property rights. Dr McCafferty has concluded,

> It [high commission] ran alongside the other prerogative tribunals as part of an interlocking system at the centre of which lay a chief governor pursuing a coordinated programme for church and state. The court of High Commission was, in many ways, a perfect miniature of the workings and assumptions of Wentworth's viceroyalty.[58]

As an instrument of Absolutism, the court provided a quirkily oblique and highly selective forum through which to impose conformity. In comparison with the court of castle chamber's intemperate pursuit of recusants under Chichester, the court of high commission under Wentworth was a surprisingly muted voice.[59]

Since the court of high commission was not formally established by letters patent until 11 February 1636, the court of castle chamber continued to deal with cases involving ecclesiastical matters. On 18 November 1635, the court heard testimony which provided evidence of a rival jurisdiction in Ireland, that is, a disciplined and hierarchically structured system of church courts operating entirely outside the ambit of the Protestant establishment, and owing its allegiance to the pope in Rome. In an extensive memorandum by the clerk of castle chamber, William Stoughton, the orders of the court revealed the operation of this covert ecclesiastical tribunal. Three prominent Dubliners, Nicholas Stephens, an alderman; Robert Lalor, a merchant; and Patrick Brangan, a priest; were imprisoned in Dublin Castle for spreading a letter obtained from Cardinal Barberini of the college of cardinals in Rome concerning the exercise of an outlawed foreign juris-diction. The letter to Thomas Fleming, titular archbishop of Dublin, authorized the titular bishop of Meath to expel from the diocese of Dublin one Paul Harris, another priest, for resorting to temporal courts in a dispute with Brangan. The dispute began when Brangan allegedly detained a book from Harris, a fellow priest, and Harris sued him in the civil court for wrongful dispossession. For his peremptory departure from the parochial remedies available to him, Brangan complained to Fleming, who banished Harris from the diocese of Dublin.[60] Harris refused to obey the titular archbishop, who then pronounced sentence of excommunication against all who heard mass from Harris. As this method of coercion also failed, the letter from Barberini was obtained from Rome, which was evidently ignored by the titular bishop of Meath, leaving the frustrated Brangan to take matters into his own hands. He translated the letter from Italian into English and proceeded to publish the missive in his Dublin parish, thus, in effect,

---

58. J. McCafferty, 'Bramhall and reconstruction of the Church of Ireland, 1633–41', Ph.D. disser-tation, Cambridge University, ch. 3. The author wishes to thank Dr McCafferty for permission to view his important new research prior to publication.

59. Ford, *Protestant reformation*, pp. 268–74.   60. WWM STR P, 24–25, item 460, ff. 1–9.

executing the sentence of the congregation of cardinals, and violating the injunction against any foreign jurisdiction. The sentence of castle chamber expressed outrage at this bold challenge to the governance of the official church, amounting to high treason and deserving the full extremity of the law. Brangan was imprisoned for life and fined £3,000 as he was the principal offender, though if he were pardoned by the king he must depart, and give bond never to return again. Stephens, 'whose turbulent spirit in matters of this nature hath bin well knowne to the Court' was fined £500 and imprisoned during pleasure, while Lalor received the same punishment.[61] Remarkably, the court seemed to countenance the existence of this rival and parallel judicial apparatus and made no further reference to Harris or his ecclesiastical superiors. The case demonstrates that a recusant ecclesiastical structure thrived in Dublin despite official efforts to prejudice its survival, yet the Catholic hierarchy was hardly a monolithic presence, suffering as it did from internal disputes and factions which were exacerbated by the heavy fines levied against its members.

Despite the establishment of a new ecclesiastical tribunal designed to complement the prerogative decisions of the court of castle chamber, the Irish privy council continued to hear some cases on appeal which would appear to require the attention of the high commission. For example, a petition of Bartholomew Bey and William Bridges claimed the possession of two gardens and 'backsides' by virtue of a lease from the dean and chapter of St Patrick's cathedral. They sought the protection of the deputy's court against vexatious suits and writs launched by one John Williams, and the viceroy accepted their petition in September 1637 for a hearing at the council.[62] Similarly, a petition of William Griffin, a curate in Co. Meath, laid claim to the tithes of his parish, including the tenth part of all turf cut upon the land of the great Ardrumes in his district. Griffin alleged that the farmers and tenants refused to pay during two years, saying they were forbidden to do so by the landlords, Patrick and Hugh Hussey of Galtrim, so Griffin sued in the consistory court of the diocese of Meath and proved his case. The defendants, nonetheless, now commenced a suit against him in the court of common pleas to stay the sentence of the consistory court, and Griffin appealed against this 'tedious, troublesome and chardgeable' counter-suit to the viceroy.[63] The case presents an overview of the judicial system and its interlocking parts, showing that the council itself remained poised to handle ecclesiastical disputes, particularly when a senior common law tribunal was apparently being manipulated to overturn the decree of a provincial church court. Contests over jurisdiction threatened

---

61. Ibid. The court took up the ecclesiastical litigation for numerous reasons, including the present danger of having such a strong Catholic hierarchy in Dublin itself. Indirectly addressing the question of its jurisdiction, the castle chamber decree cited the sentence from Rome against Harris, 'Which was sufficient to cause all men of the Romish Religion to forbeare his Company, *the said sentence of Exile beeinge a merely temporall punishment*, and as it was in this case used beeing alsoe a new found device never before heard of or practised in any of his Maties dominions when Popery was at the highest'. Ibid., f. 8 [italics mine].

62. BL, Harleian MS 430, f. 258.   63. Ibid., f. 269.

costly delay in the court system, and the conciliar courts were quite prepared to intervene to prevent the egregious use of secular power and influence against a poor clergyman. The record does not show the religious leanings of the parties to the dispute, though it is highly likely that the Protestant incumbent was resisted in his efforts to lay claim to traditional sources of income for his living. In a case heard in castle chamber on 26 January 1637 against Edmond Sexton, the younger, and his mother, Joan, the attorney-general maintained that Edmond Sexton, the elder, an alderman of Limerick, had been denied access to Protestant ministers on his deathbed. For tempting the late Sexton, senior, out of the Protestant religion, his son was fined £1,000 and his wife £5,000, and both were forced to stand in the pillory at the next assizes, confess their crimes in open court and apologize to the ministers they offended with their 'high impiety'.[64] The unstated reason for using castle chamber in this case in preference to high commission was probably the need to expose the temerity of these evidently devoted recusants. On 15 June 1641, the king received a petition of the widow, Joan Sexton, seeking the discharge of her sentence in castle chamber and the fines against her two young children, citing the 'corporal punishment of great infamy' which they had endured.[65]

The preponderance of the evidence for arbitrary judicial decrees by the court of castle chamber is taken from the regime of Wentworth and his notoriously arbitrary treatment of his adversaries. However, in the absence of an entry book for the period 1633 to 1640, the record of the court must be compiled from extraneous sources, including the apologia of Wentworth himself in copious records from the Wentworth Woodhouse Muniments. Petition books to the lord deputy survive for several years, during which the governor is revealed as an assiduous, if peremptory, judge and arbiter. From the partial and partisan records of his tenure of office, Wentworth emerges as a complex figure, determined to impose his will on powerful adversaries such as the earl of Cork, while offering judicial remedies to men and women of limited means. For example, on 6 October 1633, a petition of Mary McCoghlan, widow of Sir John McCoghlan, sued to recover goods and lands seized from her by Terrence Coghlan. The petitioner asked for a warrant to the sheriff of Co. Galway to maintain her possession until the case was resolved by course of law. The clerk duly entered Wentworth's decision thus: 'Let this petition bee delivered to the Court of the Councell where wee require to present it unto us at the boarde where wee will take theise requests into further consideracon.'[66] A similar appeal for equity was made by the widow Amy Duffe in July 1637 to recover the use of her house in Dublin, noting that she

---

64. *Cal. S.P. Ire., 1633–47*, pp. 227–28. The case was reported in a memorandum of 22 November 1639, perhaps as a guide to the new lord deputy, Wandesford.

65. Ibid., p. 304. A castle chamber sentence of £100 in a perjury case held on 10 July 1639 was also noted in June 1641, omitting names of the defendants, perhaps to furnish evidence of how the court was being used in an arbitrary manner at a time when its employment was under severe attack. Ibid., p. 306.

66. BL, Harleian MS 4297, f. 129v.

had been the victim of vexatious suits and lax enforcement of the decrees of local courts. She sued to require a resident in her house, Catherine Stronge, alias Whitte, to allow her to use her own rooms or to let them to others, claiming that Stronge had been sued successfully for abusing the widow Duffe and denying her access to her premises. Wentworth listened with some care to the pleadings of the humblest petitioners, including a number of women, and considered the council board, or castle chamber, an appropriate venue for appeals to enforce prior decrees in local jurisdictions, in this instance the aldermen of Dublin.[67] In February 1637, castle chamber agreed to hear charges of abducting the daughter-in-law of John O'Carroll, one Elizabeth Clancy, who was seized by Conly Geoghegan and apparently married to him. Geoghegan and his confederates were accused of

> plottinge & Conspiringe to convey Elizabeth Clancy the plts daughter in Lawe from the custodie of Mr Parry to whome she was sequestred by the Consistery Court of Dublin and for forciblie and riotouslie conveighinge her away and for sendinge her into the Country in mans apparell [i.e. dressed like a man].[68]

Responding to another petition by a smitten mother in a disputed wardship, Wentworth employed the long reach of the conciliar court to review an action by the court of high commission. Alison Gernon petitioned the viceroy on 20 September 1637, alleging that her only daughter Anne, by her first husband, Edward Ball, had been detained by the terms of a custodial agreement obtained by her late husband's trustee, one Barry, an alderman of Dublin. By terms of the wardship, her daughter was to be given in custody to Barry, along with an allowance of £5 per annum until her age 10, and £10 per annum until she married. However, the petitioner alleged that Barry never sought custody of Anne until she was over six years old, when her new husband Roger Gernon tried to obtain the return of lands detained by Barry under terms of the agreement. Barry then demanded custody of the daughter, who refused to go with him, whereupon he sued in the court of high commission and obtained an order for the mother not to come near her daughter, along with a fine of £60. Gernon petitioned from the Marshalsea prison, where she was sent for being unable to pay the fine along with her husband, 'by reason whereof their Children are like to perish and sterve'.[69] The woman claimed that her friends would assist her to pay the fine, but she sought the favour of the viceroy to reverse the court's decision:

> yor supplt is willing to undergoe such further Censure as shalbee imposed by that honorable Court, if shee shall hereafter be found troublesome or

67. BL, Harleian MS 430, f. 14. A prior tenant, James Ryan, vexed her with suit although she recovered her use of the premises by the 'Arbitrement of Merchantes', probably a quasi-judicial venue available to poor petitioners. Ibid.
68. WWM STR P, 24–25, item 411. The folio was endorsed 'Castle Chamber: Two cawses appointed to bee heard on Wednesday the 15th of February 1636/7'.
69. BL, Harleian MS 430, f. 145v.

offensive by any frequent or undecent visiting her said Daughter, either in the Custody of Mr. Barry or any other, which yor supplicant will not by any meanes oppose.[70]

Wentworth laconically admitted the petitioner to the venue of the council table to consider whether the poor woman and her husband should be set free on security, claiming the 'impossibility of performance of the said Order'.[71] The conciliar court was manifestly the last resort for cases of poor petitioners, aggrieved widows, and those whose censure in other courts was deemed excessive. The attractiveness of the tribunal for female complainants is thus easily explained. Whether their petitions received a fair hearing and just ordering is a question on which the archives are largely silent.

In another petition presented to the viceroy on 12 July 1637, we learn a great deal about the interdependence of prerogative jurisdictions. Robert Nugent and Edward Kolly were defendants in a prior action in 1632, in which they were censured and fined by the court of castle chamber in the amount of £390 on the complaint of Christopher Jones. Three years later, on 17 April 1635, Nugent and Kolly preferred a bill in castle chamber against Jones and his witnesses for subornation in the original case (details of which were omitted in the petition).[72] Nugent was ordered by the court to put up £300 as security in case the claim should be dismissed. The process of the court was thereafter ignored by three of the witnesses until one Donogh Fihilly was brought in to the Marshalsea of the court by the sergeant, but Fihilly refused to answer the petitioners' bill. Although the excruciatingly slow process of the court was duly observed, Nugent was abruptly jailed for non-payment of the security. He protested:

> And whereof dyvers writtes of habeas Corpus were by orders of the Councell Table and Courte of Starrchamber graunted to your peticoner for those two yeares last past to enable your peticoners & prosecucon and that hee might bee at liberty to follow ye said cause. Soe it is, rt honorable, that ye said Christopher Jones, most canteously and of purpose to hinder your petr proceedings in his said cause, hath procured an order this last Tearme to put your Peticoners into a dungeon for none payment of ye said Damadge if not paid within 20ty daies, though ye said Jones receives the profittes of the said Kollys Landes yearely untill the said costs and damadge bee paide, by a former order of the said Courte, and that ye D[efendant] Jones ever since the said order hath rec 'd the A[foresaid] profitts.[73]

---

70. Ibid.
71. Ibid., f. 146. In June 1638, the widow Jennett Plunkett sought the intervention of the deputy to preserve her former husband's estate against James White, her new husband, who now dispossessed her. NAI, MS M 2448, p. 22.
72. BL, Harleian MS 430, f. 57.   73. Ibid.

Nugent further alleged he lacked the ability to pay the £300, having a wife and eight children living with friends in the country, and not able to maintain himself in the prison of Dublin Castle but through the charity of friends. The frustrated Nugent finally appealed for a writ of *habeas corpus* to allow him liberty until the next term to prosecute his case, or else to refer the petition to the master of the rolls or to Sir George Radcliffe who would 'upon sight of ye order of the Councell board & Castle Chamber' recommend further action in the case.[74] As an example of slow process, judicial harassment and the burden of litigation before the conciliar courts, the case is a model of its type. Wentworth perfunctorily admitted the petition for consideration at the council table.

On the same day, in a crowded judicial calendar, the lord deputy heard the petition of John Bunbury, seeking the return of a prisoner to Co. Wexford to face trial at the assizes. The petitioner asserted that Turlogh Ultagh was indicted for treason for releasing rebels in Wexford, forfeited a recognizance to the crown of £100, and remained at large until his recent incarceration in Dublin Castle. He also complained against one Francis Allen, who had encouraged Ultagh to void his recognizance, and, owing to the 'multiplicacon of hearings and causes there depending', and the nearness of the assizes in Wexford, the petitioner sought the immediate return of the prisoner for trial at the next assizes.[75] In all, the viceroy heard some 37 petitions on this day, 12 July 1637, indicating the extent of litigation, in its various guises, then before the prerogative court. On the petition of David Hoberts who had been imprisoned for 18 days on a charge of debt by John Philips, burgomaster of Maryborough, trial in castle chamber was sought, owing to the poverty of the petitioner. He charged Sir Walter Crosby, Thomas Beard, Thomas Lawrence, another burgess, and Dennis Byrne, marshal, with subornation, confederacy and other injuries, pleading,

> out of your knowne and noted goodnes to men distrest and opprest with iniuryes to give yor most poore petitioner leave to impleade the above delinquentes in his Maties most high Courte of Castle Chamber in forma Pauperis, yor honor most favorably [a]signeinge unto your supplicant such Councell as yorr Lops most grave wisdome shall seeme most expedient.[76]

In another petition to Wentworth, the minor child of John Woodward of Sligo, deceased, sued in 1632 to have her third part of the estate secured against the

74. Ibid., f. 57v. Nugent also mentioned that Jones put in a cross bill to the court in an effort to hinder the prosecution without being required to put up similar security. Absent the entry book of the court, these fragments of castle chamber adjudication demonstrate its continuous operation and broad purview. The lack of judicial finality is also a hallmark of the court.
75. Ibid., f. 61. Bunbury was probably a sheriff, since he described chasing Ultagh from county to county and apprehending him in 'remote parts'. He rehearsed a previous petition to the viceroy of 22 June regarding the dispute with Allen, who had in turn sought advantage against the justices of the peace and the deputy clerk of the crown in Co. Wexford. Ibid.
76. Ibid., f. 61v. Hoberts claimed he was not worth five pence due to the vile imprisonment he suffered through subornation of the defendants.

depredations of her stepmother, Elinor, recently re-married. Elizabeth Woodward sued on behalf of 'all distressed persons and fatherlesse children' to protect her rights.[77] Wentworth agreed to move the matter in castle chamber. In an earlier case of 19 June 1635 the court of castle chamber had censured the mayor of Dublin, Sir James Carroll, for violating Wentworth's decree allowing the poor of the city to purchase coal at reasonable rates. The viceroy had declined to take up coal at the 'king's rate' and directed that it be sold reasonably to the poor. But the mayor, who was also clerk of the market in Dublin, rated the coal at twice the normal rate of eight shillings per ton, pocketing the difference for himself. Carroll alleged ignorance of the proclamation in his defence before the court, but he was duly convicted, discharged from office, imprisoned during Wentworth's pleasure and fined £1,000 sterling.[78]

Some of the Absolutist tendencies of Wentworth's government were linked to his 'bluenose' inclinations in religion, along with his strategic plans for a Protestant reedification of Irish society. Using a conciliar act of state that was signed by 18 councillors on 9 February 1636, Wentworth proclaimed that no tavern, inn or alehouse in Dublin would henceforth be allowed to house, admit or receive any fellows, students or scholars of Trinity College. The act cited examples of tippling and riotous disorders, gambling and pawning their goods, to the moral undoing of the youth who were intended to be the foundation of an exemplary new Irish social order. Requiring the proctor of the university, with the authority and approval of the provost, to enter and search houses of ill repute, the lord deputy aimed to harness the resources of the university to those of the council in an effort to punish transgressors of the act, and called upon the mayor to proclaim its contents in the city and suburbs of Dublin.[79] In due course, two offenders were tried before the prerogative court led by Wentworth, pursuant to the act. One Daniel Weld, a student of Trinity College, and Elizabeth Jones, a widow, were questioned on 29 May 1638 in Dublin Castle and charged with violating the act of state. It was alleged that Weld had gone to the dwelling of Jones at ten in the evening, knowing that ale or beer was sold on the premises, and that the watch discovered him there in the company of Jones some five hours later where 'it may well be conceived that they intended lewdness and Folly therein'.[80] The court rejected Weld's plea of ignorance of the act of state, noting that he had

---

77. Ibid., f. 12.
78. Steele, *Tudor & Stuart proclamations*, ii, 34: A Proclamation concerning Coales that none from henceforth be taken up at the Kings Rates, 16 Jan. 1633/4. *Anc rec. Dublin*, iii, 306–08. This fragment of the castle chamber records is another example of the dispersed archive under Wentworth, suggesting the court was highly active during his tenure. Carroll was examined by Serjeant Catelyn, Secretary Mainwaring and Solicitor-General Edward Bolton; Catelyn and Bolton argued the case before the viceroy and court.
79. J.W. Stubbs, *The history of the University of Dublin from its foundation to the end of the present century* (London,1889), Appendix, pp. 406–08. The author wishes to thank Professor Nial Osborough of the Faculty of Law, University College Dublin, for this citation.
80. Ibid., p. 408.

confessed to being at the house before, and also that he might have chosen to go to his father's house that night after he was locked out of the gates of the university. The court fined Weld £40, imprisoned him during pleasure, and left his further punishment to the provost of the college, referring to Trinity as 'the Place where the children of all sorts of people of this Kingdom are seasoned and fitted for the service of the Church and Commonwealth, in which respect we are desirous of keeping that fountain clear'.[81] The widow Jones was fined and pilloried, and further required to acknowledge her offence publicly at the college, leaving terms of her humiliation to the provost.[82]

The petition books for 1638 and 1639 also contain hundreds of these requests for arbitration, judicial intervention or final determination. The viceroy commissioned local officials to take depositions, remanded any ecclesiastical issues to the hearing of John Bramhall, bishop of Derry, and in many cases promised to consider the questions in fuller detail 'at the council board', a reference to the judicial companion of the court of castle chamber. On 21 May 1634, the lord deputy promised a hearing to Charles Mulloy of King's County, who was wrongfully dispossessed of his ancient inheritance at the plantation there 'by reason of ye petitioners father beeing but an illiterate man and knew not how to make his right knowne to the Com[mission]ers assigned'.[83] On 6 June 1638, the viceroy ordered a petition brought to the council table wherein it was claimed that the high sheriff of Co. Meath, Lawrence Dowdall, had exceeded his instructions and damaged the plaintiff's garrons and cattle in executing a warrant from the chancery. Nicholas Kent had won his suit against Christopher Dugenan in 1637, but the sheriff had negligently refused to execute the warrant for six months, at which time Kent assigned some of those goods to satisfy a debt to Neil Dugenan. The sheriff was apparently told to seize the cattle and garrons to the value of £22, but took only £12 worth of cattle from Dugenan before proceeding to take some £50 of cattle from the petitioner. The livelihood of Kent was at stake in this case, but the courts seemed oblivious to the problem of executing precisely a warrant of debt which had to be taken in kind from the fields of Co. Meath.[84] On 13 July 1638, the lord deputy agreed to consider an allegation of riot, normally heard at the court of castle chamber. Richard FitzHarrris, a squire of Co. Wexford, complained that Cahir O'Ryan and Hugh Duffe O'Doyle, lately servants to Sir Morgan Cavanagh, had become rebels, joining the proclaimed traitor Brian Oge Cavanagh. Protesting against various outrages that occurred both day and night, and seeking peace and quiet in their domains, FitzHarris demanded that Sir Morgan bring in his former servants to answer for their depredations. The plantation of Wexford and its attendant disruptions to security of tenure probably lay behind this charge.[85]

81. Ibid., p. 409.
82. Ibid. The court of castle chamber was not cited in the entry, but the accused were 'questioned at this Board for the breach of an act of Council made by this Board'. This may also have been an example of the ongoing exercise of prerogative adjudication animated by Wentworth's high-handedness.
83. BL, Harleian MS 4297, f. 157v.   84. NAI, MS 2448, p. 29.
85. Ibid., p. 109.

The court of castle chamber issued a decree on 23 February 1638, ordering Thomas Lestrange to pay £10,000 as a fine for malicious libel against Sir Arthur Blundell. The odd survival of this fragment demonstrates that the court was operating continuously, requiring the defendant to confess his crime publicly in the four courts in Dublin and at assizes to be held in King's County. He was removed from the commission of the peace, imprisoned during pleasure and made to pay 1,000 marks to the relator in the case.[86] A month later, Edmund Wale petitioned the king over the conduct of Richard Wall, alleging that Wall had him fined unjustly in castle chamber in a dispute over his land, after which Wale went abroad and his enemies ruined his house and took away his timber for their use.[87] These oblique references to actions at castle chamber provide occasional glimpses of a busy court, occupied in the ordinary work of judicial hearings and subject, like all the other courts, to continuous review of its decisions by higher authorities. On 10 May 1638, Wentworth gave an order in the complex action between Lord Conway as plaintiff and Sir Hercules Langford and Arthur Langford, awarding possession of the lands of Camlin and Killultagh to the plaintiff, and requiring the defendant to forestall any plans to use or to waste the lands in question until trial at common law. He added that Arthur Langford should be tried in castle chamber by information of the attorney-general for his corruption of due process in the execution of commissions regarding those lands. Both litigants claimed the right to hold courts leet and baron in the territory, and the viceroy held for the plaintiff on that issue, demonstrating the long reach of royal justice and its tolerance of autonomous tribunals of feudal origin.[88] The marginal role of castle chamber in the case suggests that the court provided a complementary jurisdiction for property litigation when the accused exploited pleadings or pre-trial manoeuvring for his or her advantage. In summary, evidence for the decrees of the court, in the absence of the entry book for Wentworth's regime, offers an odd mix of the mundane and the 'show trial', leaving the researcher with only a patchy record from which to recreate the profile of the Caroline court.

The petition books of Wentworth's regime, though largely devoid of castle chamber records, furnish substantial detail on the pleadings before prerogative courts in anticipation of a full hearing. In one such case, the petitioner was authorized to proceed at the council table by an order of 5 October 1638. Nicholas Bridges of Co. Kildare had sued Nicholas Woolfe of Oldcourt, Co. Kildare for several misdemeanours and the case was initially referred to Judge Cressy for his opinion. He recommended the case be heard at council table, where an order to proceed in castle chamber was given, showing both the interdependence of the two courts and the cognizance of a judicial boundary between them. Bridges petitioned the judges of assize for Co. Kildare, who named commissioners to view and perambulate the meres and bounds of land between the two litigants, finally issuing a commission from the chancery to enclose the lands in question. Though

---

86. *Cal. S.P. Ire., 1633–47*, p. 183.   87. Ibid., p. 184.
88. Ibid., p. 190.

Woolfe refused to share the costs, the petitioner proceeded with the enclosure along with his servants, and, on 22 September 1638,

> the sd Woolfe ... came unto yor sup[plican]t and unknowne to yor pet[itione]r stroake yor suplt to the ground wth a hazell plant neere 6 foote long, & 4 inches thick, & being downe the sd Woolfe againe violently stroake yor suplt 2 stroakes more wth the sd staffe, intending noe less then to have murthered yor petr if he had not bene prevented by those that were inclosing the sd meare.[89]

The aggrieved Bridges further alleged that Woolfe had previously wounded two pigs belonging to his servant, Thomas O'Dallany, and thereafter beat the servant and 'bound him & two of his sonnes to the peace'.[90] Bridges concluded by seeking the intervention of the conciliar court to require Woolfe to share the costs of enclosure, desist in his malicious wounding of the petitioner and his servants, and cease to vex them by making false allegations of breach of the peace.[91] The extensive reporting of details in the petition and the prior litigation of the issue at numerous venues laid claim to the attention of the viceroy, and the allegation of assault would normally require a hearing in the court of castle chamber. The case also demonstrates how adversaries combined judicial intimidation with physical resistance in promoting their claims.

The court of castle chamber was silently acknowledged as the appropriate venue for cases of riot and official malfeasance that frequently appear in the Wentworth petition books, the court being rarely mentioned by name. For example, on 2 August 1638, one Edward Morris petitioned the lord deputy for redress after an assault by William Hudleston and one of his journeymen saddlers, who seized him by the hair and stabbed the complainant in the head. Morris sought an attachment against the defendants 'they being men of noe residency (by wch meanes he is not able to have his present remedy at Comon law)', and Wentworth ordered the parties to appear 'before us', that is, at a hearing of the council board, presumably acting as the court of castle chamber.[92] The chief governor referred a case explicitly to castle chamber on 12 September 1638, noting that a bill had been presented at that court two years previously by the petitioner, William, earl of Meath against Thomas, Viscount Merryon. The frustrated nobleman, citing many delays caused by his adversary, asked for an immediate examination of his witnesses, who were residents of Scotland and likely to leave the kingdom before the date of trial.[93]

Cases of riot occasionally rose to the level of genuine public danger. In a petition involving the dignity of the crown at a tavern in Wexford, the lord deputy required the parties to appear before the council table to explain their roles in an

89. NAI, MS M 2448, pp. 451–53.   90. Ibid.

91. The urgency of his claim was intensified by his deposition that enclosing the meres and lands 'cannot by reason of a bogg be done in winter tyme'. Ibid.

92. Ibid., p. 321.   93. Ibid., p. 439.

affray. On 26 August 1638, two members of the Wexford garrison – Abraham Bell and John Blankship – went looking for another of their company and encountered two bailiffs of the town – Matthew Paie, an innkeeper, and John Codd – who verbally abused them, maintaining

> there were better souldiers there then any of theire Company & bidd them gett them gone like Roagues, To wch the said Souldiers answering that they knew noe Roague that wore his Mates Cloath, and that the said Bailiffes might answere the sd wordes, thereupon the said Paie & Codd (beeing ill affected as it seeme to the sd foote Company & being the baliffes and officers of the sd towne, & sworne & respectively bound by the Dutie of their places to performe & kepe his Mates peace), Contrarie thereunto in most violent manner wthout any other cause given them then as aforesd, made an assault upon the two souldiers & by the assistance of their Confederates then present did throw the sd Bell Downe a paire of staires betwene sixtene & xxtie steppes and then by the sd Bell lyeing in a great amazement the sd Paie then gott the sword of the sd Bell & gave the sd Bell therewith one great wound on the head 5 inches long, by reason whereof & of the bruises gotten in the sd fall Downe the staires the sd Bell became & laie senceles a good spate all besmeered in his owne blood & was in greate Dispaire of his life.[94]

The wounded man was carried to the surgeon after he was refused a room at the tavern, and the next day the lieutenant complained of the bailiffs to the mayor of Wexford.[95] When the mayor, who was a justice of the peace there, refused to examine the bailiffs separately or to examine Blankship, the partner of the wounded soldier, the lieutenant petitioned the viceroy to hear the case.[96] The account indicates the underlying atmosphere of tension in urban society in this period of Irish history, when public officials were at odds with one another and municipal confrontations might have dire consequences. The substantial detail of the petition supports the view that Wentworth took matters of local administration very seriously.[97]

Adam Loftus, Viscount Ely, was a powerful lord chancellor and resolute adversary, yet he too became a victim of the wrath of Wentworth. Loftus had been judge of the admiralty court in 1612 and served on the council in Ireland from

94. Ibid., pp. 511–12.
95. The wounded Bell cried out that he was murdered, leading the assailants to reply that 'it was but a scratche & others bidding cut off his head'. The petitioners noted it was a 'romane taverne', which did much to explain the acrimony of the assault. Ibid.
96. Ibid., ff. 511–14.
97. In 1637, Wentworth heard the petition of John Warren, a citizen of Dublin, who charged two notorious blackguards with assaulting a woman in the streets of Dublin after attempting to force her to come alone with them. Wentworth ordered the two accused men to appear 'before us' to answer the complaint. BL, Harleian MS 430, f. 13.

1609, finally obtaining the coveted role of lord chancellor in 1619 on the death of his predecessor, Thomas Jones, archbishop of Dublin. Loftus served as lord justice of Ireland on three occasions, and became Viscount Ely in 1622. He shared with his rival, the earl of Cork, the interim government from 1629 to the arrival of Wentworth in 1633 and, as we have seen, he quarrelled with Lord Deputy Falkland in the previous regime when he was temporarily deprived of the great seal. Having amassed great personal wealth, Viscount Ely in 1621 arranged the marriage of his eldest son, Robert, to Eleanor, daughter of Sir Francis Rushe, and the couple apparently lived in the chancellor's household until 1637. Another daughter, Anne Rushe, married Sir George Wentworth, brother of the lord deputy, an ominous connection indeed. In 1636, Sir John Gifford, half brother of the Rushe sisters, sued the lord chancellor for specific performance of a verbal promise to settle upon Robert Loftus and Eleanor and their children an estate of over £1,200 a year in land.[98] In March of that year a second petition against the chancellor was sent to the crown by Wentworth's brother, George, husband to Eleanor's sister.

The strange case was complicated by the colossal stature of the lord chancellor as defendant, so the king ordered the cause to be heard by the lord deputy and council. Although not formally a suit before the court of castle chamber, the trial illustrates the employment of prerogative jurisdiction by Wentworth on behalf of the sister of his brother's wife. Loftus complained that the petition was improperly drawn and that the testimony of a single witness was accepted to a verbal agreement made nearly twenty years before to Sir Francis Rushe, who had died in 1629. Nonetheless, the lawsuit was deemed a point of honour by the viceroy and Loftus's delaying tactics produced a sharp rejoinder. A decree of the lord deputy and council was issued on 1 February 1638, requiring specific performance by the lord chancellor of a valid contract, upon the petition of Gifford but without the participation of Robert Loftus, the eldest son and putative claimant.[99] A crown letter of 16 March 1638 was prepared for the lord deputy and council, noting the

---

98. *DNB*; Ball, *Judges in Ireland*, pp. 326–27; *Cal. S.P. Ire., 1633–47*, p. 180; Marsh's Library, MS Z.3.2.6, pp. 313–17. Gifford first petitioned the lord deputy, who forwarded the allegations to the crown. The king ordered the lord deputy and council 'to hear and determine said cause for the honour of the family'. Marsh's Lib., MS Z.3.2.6, p. 313. The allegations claimed, among other things, that Loftus promised a marriage portion of £1,750, the manor of Monasterevan in Co. Kildare, and a jointure of £300 to Lady Loftus, with other consideration to follow. HMC, *rep. 9, pt. 2*, app., pp. 303–06 (*Drogheda MSS*). Plate 13.

99. Marsh's Lib, MS Z.3.2.6, items 113, 114, pp. 313, 316. Loftus repeatedly asserted that his son was never privy to the lawsuit and did not consent to it. The council board heard the case, using the same formulae that applied in litigation before the court of castle chamber, taking up three days of hearings after the replication, rejoinder and examination of witnesses. The council found Chancellor Loftus in breach of contract to his eldest son, ordering him to perform the agreement, pay arrears of £200 a year with damages until he departed his residence in the chancellor's house, along with £2,000 for yearly maintenance of Robert and Eleanor. Wentworth signed the order along with thirteen other councillors including the judges Shurley, Parsons, Lowther, Bolton and Wandesford. HMC, *Drogheda MSS*, pp. 305–06.

delays of the lord chancellor in depositing money pursuant to the decree against him, and authorizing sequestration of his land and other profits until the sum of £3,342 8s. 9d. was secured. The truculence of Viscount Ely was duly noted by the committee for Irish affairs, so the king, on petition from Gifford, called for the lord chancellor to be made close prisoner, since he refused to provide the grounds for his appeal and dishonoured the viceroy by his demeanour. The letter concluded that the lord deputy and council should proceed against the chancellor by information in castle chamber if he continued his obstinacy.[100] Although aged about 70 years at this time, Loftus was compelled to kneel before the lord deputy and was committed to prison in Dublin Castle, where his health deteriorated quickly. In April 1638, the lord chancellor denied the allegations put to him before the viceroy and the council of Ireland, such as refusing to kneel before the lord deputy at his entrance to the council board. He was ordered to give up the great seal on 20 April 1638 and incarcerated again for his refusal, with the signatures of sixteen councillors appended to that of Wentworth.[101]

The prostrate lord chancellor was subsequently hounded by the archbishop of Dublin in May 1638 for his wrongful possession of the archdeaconry of Glendalough, having sought to surrender it without the privity of the archbishop. Viscount Ely appealed to the king, while the archbishop sought the intervention of the lord deputy and council whose handling of the matter was, he claimed, 'perfectly fair'.[102] The following month Samuel Powell, clerk of the council, joined in the pursuit, lodging a petition against the chancellor for his mishandling of an equity case; in this, he claimed that his son, Edward Loftus, had taken one third of an estate to himself, with Powell never securing his share. Powell argued that he was appointed trustee of the estate of a Dr Metcalf, but the chancellor had threatened the judge who was to award the trusteeship and sought to arrange the transfer of the case to chancery. Based on a pretended will that left his own son, Edward Loftus, as executor, the chancellor allegedly forced Powell to accept a third of the estate.[103] In October 1638, Wentworth went to great lengths to justify the council's order against Loftus, claiming that the entire board supported his view that the chancellor had disgraced his office by 'universal irregularities', disordered the whole frame of justice and undermined all the courts of judicature in the kingdom.[104] At the end of the year, Wentworth and the council reported that the stubborn chancellor remained in confinement, having submitted publicly,

100. WWM STR P, 24–25, item 475, ff. 1–2. In November 1639, the king dismissed the appeal of Loftus against the decree of the lord deputy and council. *Cal. S.P. Ire., 1633–47*, p. 227.

101. *Cal. S.P. Ire., 1633–47*, pp. 184–87; WWM STR P, 24–25, item 476. See also *Strafforde's letters*, ii, 160–61. The great seal was temporarily held in commission by the lord deputy and council.

102. *Cal. S.P. Ire., 1633–47*, p. 189. The archbishop wrote to the archbishop of Canterbury for assistance, complaining the chancellor lacked clear title and was not in canonical orders.

103. Ibid., p. 192.

104. *Strafforde's letters*, ii, 227–28. Dame Sara Loftus, Viscountess Ely, petitioned the viceroy and council to allow her daughter and a doctor to visit the imprisoned nobleman while he lay sick, or let him be removed to his own house. WWM STR P, 24–25, item 476.

yet continuing to defy elements of the crown order against him. Saying he had 'notably trifled with us', the council pointed out that Loftus's strategy was to use the confinement as a tool to cite the oppression of his person and estate, bringing the council itself into contempt.[105] It should be noted, in passing, that Wentworth pursued others who engaged in administrative malpractice, such as Lord Balfour. On 12 May 1634, Wentworth wrote to Secretary Coke that Balfour should be proceeded against in castle chamber, requesting that he be sent over to Ireland for that purpose to answer for many outrages committed while he was riding the assize circuit:

> Believe me, I do not think there is such another Tyrant in the King's Dominions, who, utterly drunk with the Vice of Violence, hath with unequal and staggering Paces trod down his Majesty's People on every side.[106]

The pattern of judicial persecution by Wentworth and his allies distorted the organ of prerogative justice into a vehicle for oppression and an instrument of despotism. Subsequent accusations of malfeasance did little to excuse the trifling nature of the original complaint against the lord chancellor, especially when seen against the background of previous mistreatment of his fellow councillors.

After sixteen months of stubborn resistance, Loftus submitted to the conditions of the viceroy and left for England without licence on 9 September 1639 to make his appeal to the crown.[107] On 19 November 1639, the privy council, sitting in the king's presence at Whitehall, heard his appeal against the Irish council's order and rejected it, after 'mature deliberation', finding the original order of the council board just and equal. Though not a castle chamber decision, it was a case that would normally have fallen within the purview of the prerogative court instead of its sister, the executive committee.[108] Upon losing this stage of the battle, Viscount Ely was deprived as chancellor in 1639 and remained in England until he died in 1643. The pyrrhic victory of Ely in his declining years was finalized in an order passed on 3 May 1642 in the house of lords at Westminster, voiding the decree of the Irish council of 1638 and restoring the payments and conveyances made pursuant to the decree. Ely had petitioned the commons in 1641, seeking trial of his cause in the English house of lords, and naming the Irish councillors as defendants.[109] On 9 September, the lords granted his petition for a hearing in November, requiring the attendance of all the defendants or their counsel. The weakened councillors demurred:

105. *Strafforde's letters*, ii, 259.
106. Ibid., i, 245. A subsequent letter protested against the pardon sought by Balfour in England for outrages committed in his Irish jurisdiction. Ibid., i, 270.
107. Ibid., ii, 387.   108. Ibid., ii, 389.
109. Marsh's Lib, MS Z.3.2.6, p. 316. The councillors were Robert, Lord Dillon; Sir Adam Loftus; Sir George Shurley; Sir William Parsons; Sir Gerard Lowther; Sir Richard Bolton; Sir John Borlase; Sir Philip Mainwaring; Sir Charles Coote; Sir George Radcliffe and Sir Robert Meredith, adding Sir George Wentworth, Sir Paul Davys and Sir John Gifford as co-defendants.

And wee offer to the consideracion of their Lordships whether or noe this cause, though there were noe other power of judicature in the Governour and councell, was not a matter of State, consideringe that it was a matter of Equitie and wherein the complaynant could have noe reliefe but in Equitie, and that even against him whoe [as Chancellor] then was the sole Judge of Equitie in his Majestie's Courte of Chancery, and hee soe previledged as hee could be sued in noe other Court, and it was a fayler of justice if there were noe remedy to be hadd in Equitie, even against that Judge.[110]

Nonetheless, acting on the advice of the commons, the lords in November 1641 granted all Loftus's requests, declaring the proceedings against him illegal and ordering them cancelled and annulled.[111] By that time, of course, Sir Robert Loftus had died, Strafford had been executed, and the civil war ruined the inheritance which Ely had built up over a lifetime.[112] Reversal of the conciliar decree by the parliament in England was a constitutional contrivance, perhaps, but the complete voiding of its terms was a triumph for the aged Viscount Ely, whose fines and estates were now restored to him. The circumstances of the Loftus case formed article 8 of the impeachment of Wentworth as earl of Strafford in the Long Parliament. In the long history of the Irish conciliar court, the impeachment and attainder of Strafford by English statute provided a definitive termination to the work of castle chamber.

Recent reappraisals of the government of Wentworth have confirmed the view that his administration was both arbitrary and despotic. Ciaran Brady has argued that Wentworth ushered in the boldest experiment in viceregal government, using the model of his predecessor Sir John Perrot to fashion a crown authority which was ruthless, expedient and profitable, without regard to the dangerous political combinations he encountered there.[113] Nicholas Canny deems the Wentworth period by no means exceptional but rather as extending the inquisitorial policies of Chichester and Davies from earlier in the century. Canny explains that 'normal constitutional relations between the English monarch and his Irish Catholic subjects were developed only during the years 1622–29', and this only because of unusual diplomatic circumstances, an expedient cloak with which to conceal the

---

110. HMC, *Drogheda MSS*, p. 312.
111. Ibid., p. 317. The accused councillors justified their hearing of the matter in council, citing previous cases in the 'hearing and determining causes between party and party' involving lands, mortgages, rents, debts, distresses, patentees, annuities, estates and inheritances since Henry VIII. HMC, *Drogheda MSS*, p. 311.
112. WWM STR P, 24–25, item 477.
113. C. Brady, 'England's defence and Ireland's reform: the dilemma of the Irish viceroyalty, 1541–1641' in J.S. Morrill and B. Bradshaw, eds., *The British problem, c.1534–1707: state formation in the Atlantic archipelago* (London, 1996), pp. 89–92; 99–103; 113–17. Brady overstates the role of the court of castle chamber in the recovery of church lands for the crown, and his conclusion that 'the fluid and fissiparous states of Ireland could never be fitted into the complex conceptual structure of the multiple British monarchy' is too facile. Ibid., p. 116.

'programmatic' policy of plantation which dominated Stuart Irish politics.[114] Canny is correct, of course, in assessing the Wentworth administration as one of imperious action and devious manipulation, driven by an overt plantation policy. However, it is important to position his endeavours within a framework of constitutional boundaries and legal parameters. In the first place, Canny concedes that Wentworth was unable to follow through with the full implementation of colonies throughout Ireland due to the Scottish crises of 1638. Canny places undue emphasis on secret letters to his confidants and private investigations which reveal the extent of his ultimate purposes.[115] The presumption that Wentworth was familiar with Spenser's writings does not conclusively demonstrate a linear pattern from the putative 'Elizabethan conquest' to the tentative Caroline expropriations.[116] Furthermore, policy was not systematic in the period 1603 to 1642. It was subject to frequent interruption and to the partisan infiltration of high court politics and local corruption. Far from recommending 'the drastic course' which Canny defines as the single overarching purpose of all governments from the mid-sixteenth century, most Stuart viceroys were hounded by critics in Ireland, sceptics in England, fiscal retrenchment and fears of a return to war and rebellion. Jane Ohlmeyer has recently demonstrated that the obstreperous viceroy carried on internecine warfare at court against the powerful young earl of Antrim, who had married Buckingham's widow in 1637, a political battle which cost the chief governor years of legal wrangling and much political capital. Antrim was denied preferment and titles by Wentworth, finally moving to Ireland in 1639 where he maintained a strong Ulster presence to rival the centralizing power of the viceroy.[117]

While they continued to work out the terms of plantation in every province, the viceroys also maintained a vigilance over Irish jurisprudence which provided access to the courts and to the crown. The constitutional norms which were gradually extended to all parts of the kingdom were arguably more successful than the arrested development of colonial settlements. As Canny has stated, both James I and Charles I were reluctant to pursue confrontational and aggressive postures in Ireland, so Wentworth remains the absolutist exception to constitutional rule.[118] Although joined by powerful interests at court, from Buckingham and the

---

114. N. Canny, 'The attempted anglicisation of Ireland in the seventeenth century: an exemplar of "British History"' in J.S. Morrill, ed., *The political world of Thomas Wentworth, earl of Strafford, 1621–1641* (Cambridge, 1996), pp. 168–69; Canny, *Making Ireland British*, pp. 275–78.

115. Canny, 'Anglicisation', pp. 179–80; *Making Ireland British*, pp. 276, 279.

116. Canny, 'Anglicisation', pp. 182–84; *Making Ireland British*, pp. 281–88. Canny assumes that Wentworth's policy was influenced by contemporary theories, derived from surviving texts from his papers, but the determination of government direction was set by the lord deputy and council, acting upon advice from London, so the full extent of political dialogue concerning Irish policy in this period must be reexamined to assess the role of other statesmen and their subordinates.

117. J. Ohlmeyer, *Antrim*, pp. 68–91. Wentworth consumed two years in negotiation to deny Antrim an allowance of £200 from his wife's dower out of manors and estates in Queen's Co. Ibid., p. 68.

118. Canny, 'Anglicisation', pp. 184–85. He concluded that both Catholic landowners and veteran

earl of Carlisle to the 'impecunious fortune hunter' Robert Maxwell, earl of Nithesdale, Wentworth's policies were not uniformly embraced in London.[119] Crown administrators, from the chief secretaries to the Irish committees of the privy council to the commissions for Irish affairs, were acutely aware of the disputes on Irish issues, and sought to provide systematic channels through which the endless flood of petitions could move more rationally. The argument that 'British history is constitutional history', which Canny rejects, is strongly supported by the events of the concluding years of the court of castle chamber. J.P. Cooper has asserted the importance of common law restraints on arbitrary power generally:

> Given a prolonged period without Parliament, the king might have suc-
> ceeded in moulding the ambiguous inheritance of the common law to suit
> his own purposes, but immediately it was still genuinely an inheritance
> which gave both common interests and arguments to the dominant part of
> his subjects.[120]

Some earlier writers have contended that Wentworth used the court of castle chamber in novel ways, incorporating the tribunal into a systematic pattern of Absolutist rule. Hugh Kearney revised the earlier treatment of Standish O'Grady, an apologist for Straffordian government. The O'Grady interpretation claimed that Wentworth respected the impartiality of the law, campaigned against the entrenched corruption of Irish officials and favoured the suits of lesser men against their more powerful neighbours. He argued for an arbitrary judicial boundary which, in practice, did not exist: 'The Council Board in Ireland corre-sponded closely to the Star Chamber in England and should not be, in any way, confused with the Castle Chamber, which was a personal court of the Deputy and had far less power.'[121] O'Grady's conclusion was based on the highly idiosyncratic use of the executive by Wentworth and ignored the commissions and charters establishing the court of castle chamber. The privy council and the court did indeed have practically identical membership and the two bodies met in the same venue in Dublin Castle, usually on the same afternoon. Nonetheless, O'Grady averred that the castle chamber was a truncated hybrid: 'It was no part of Royal policy to give the Deputy's personal Court anything like the powers of the Irish

English servitors were deceived by Wentworth, who worked to install an entirely new English Protestant landowning élite. *Making Ireland British*, p. 300.

119. Canny, *Making Ireland British*, p. 299.

120. J.P. Cooper, *Land, men and beliefs: studies in early modern history*, ed. G.E. Aylmer and J.S. Morrill (London, 1983), p. 108. Cooper described the symbolic shape of Wentworth's arbitrary rule in his pretentiously grandiose construction of Jigginstown House, the foundations of which near Naas, Co. Kildare may still be seen. At a cost of £22,000, the finished house would have been the largest residence Ireland had ever seen, with a length of some 390 feet punctuated by fine windows. Ibid., pp. 165–66.

121. S. O'Grady, *Strafford and Ireland; the history of his viceroyalty with an account of his trial*, 2 vols. (Dublin, 1923), i, 27.

Council or of the English Star Chamber.'[122] O'Grady discerned in Wentworth's agenda a determination to oppose common law prevarication which the viceroy saw as a great vested interest, subject to partisan manipulation:

> This rising class [of common lawyers] was hostile to the Council Board and the Castle Chamber, to the Dispensing power of the Prerogative, to the claim of the Executive to interpret Law according to the exigencies of a case instead of in accordance with inferences from Statutes, judicial decisions and case law.[123]

An example of the closeting of prerogative justice occurred when Wentworth ordered the chancery to accept a bargain which he brokered, favouring his client Sir Philip Perceval. In a hearing on 27 February 1638 before the deputy, Sir Adam Loftus, vice-treasurer, the chief justice of common pleas and the chief baron of the exchequer, Perceval and Lord Brabazon petitioned the deputy for specific performance of a lease from Calcott Chambre. The deputy ordered a bill in chancery to require the defendants to submit to his order on behalf of his close friend, Perceval.[124]

Hugh Kearney's treatment of castle chamber under Wentworth differs in that he saw the court as a useful instrument against the pretensions of New English colonists and other litigants who suffered exorbitant fines.[125] Instead of an efficient model of royal compassion, Kearney described castle chamber 'as a system more suitable for catching the guilty than saving the innocent and certainly it is hard to deny its inquisitorial character'.[126] Wresting control of the membership of the court by expelling Mountnorris and staffing it with his cohorts, Wentworth proceeded after 1636 to quash opposition to his policies in Galway and Wicklow. Kearney summarized the work of the court thus:

> Here indeed was the classic example of the way in which reluctance to carry out the wishes of the administration could be regarded by the lord deputy as falling under the heading of those crimes which Castle Chamber was competent to deal with. Since he himself controlled the court, the verdict could be predicted in advance ... The Court of Castle Chamber was thus only a court in theory; in practice, it was an instrument at the full disposal

---

122. Ibid., p. 31. O'Grady claimed the castle chamber offered 'simple, drastic and cheap justice' in an equitable manner to poor petitioners under Wentworth. Ibid., p. 69.

123. Ibid., p. 70. Wentworth tried to cut legal fees while bolstering the prerogative, citing the castle chamber as the king's venue for judicial discretion on matters of public policy, based on equity and expediency over the strict letter of the law.

124. WWM STR P, 24–25, item 418, ff. 1–4.

125. Kearney, *Strafford in Ireland*, p. xviii. His off-handed comparison of Wentworth with Sydney, calling Strafford 'a latter day Elizabethan', conflates the intricacies of the two periods and unduly exaggerates the power of Sydney as viceroy.

126. Ibid., p. 70.

of the lord deputy, particularly after the fall of Mountnorris in 1635. It ceased to be used against the recusants as a body and was in the main directed at those who ventured to oppose in any way the policies of the lord deputy ... The Court of Castle Chamber lay at the heart of Wentworth's administration, making the rule of Thorough possible. It became the instrument of a despotism as severe as that of Richelieu in providing an arbitrary sanction for every act and organ of the administration.[127]

Another insight which Kearney brought to his discussion of crown government was the orchestration of senior prerogative courts under Wentworth to achieve Absolutist objectives. In both the court of wards and the commission for defective titles, staffed by senior judges such as William Parsons, Gerard Lowther and Richard Bolton, the aim was to provide firm title to those requesting it. However, Wentworth manipulated the tribunals so that their membership was identical to that of castle chamber, and, together with the court of high commission, the machinery of justice was now harnessed to a single administrative purpose.[128] The question for historians is now whether this situation was distinctive to the years of 'Personal Rule' in Ireland. In fact, the gradual institutionalization of viceregal power through the establishment of senior courts simply crystallized the authority of the chief governor in matters where he traditionally exercised the prerogative. It may be argued that the regular functioning of these courts demanded a more circumspect use of royal power than the more arbitrary, if more occasional, flexing of political muscle by the lord deputy, acting alone. Moreover, as John McCafferty has explained, Wentworth employed his loyal satraps such as John Bramhall, bishop of Derry, in the court of high commission and thus his actual presence was not required for the normal functioning of the crown's judicial role.[129]

The 'show trial' aspect of the Wentworth regime has highlighted his Procrustean arbitrariness and his autocratic treatment of senior officials in the government of Ireland, but Wentworth was not alone in pursuing Absolutist measures. He successfully imposed a 'close oligarchy' of his minions who dominated legal as well as administrative machinery and worked long hours under the tutelage, if not the presence, of the lord deputy. Further, Wentworth had obtained a proclamation of 1635 prohibiting anyone from leaving Ireland without permission of the lord deputy, stifling challenges to his work before the privy council in England.

---

127. Ibid., pp. 73–74. 128. Ibid., pp. 76–84.

129. J. McCafferty, 'Bramhall and reconstruction of the Church of Ireland', ch. 3, pp. 3–6, 7–9. Laud sought the inclusion of all the council and judges and bishops in making the commission, but left open the possibility of hearing causes in England that 'may appear too strong for that court, or in any great respect be fit to be heard here'. Ibid., p. 3. Prior to the final establishment of the commission, the court of castle chamber, as we have seen, proceeded against clerics accused of simony according to an act of state. Ibid., p. 4. McCafferty concluded that, 'Whereas in Castle Chamber Wentworth worked to establish complete control by excluding almost all of those not of his party, this ecclesiastical tribunal was, especially in its clerical members, more of a mixed bag'. Ibid., p. 7.

Kearney concluded: 'From 1635 therefore there was no appeal from the rule of the Court of Castle Chamber and other organs of Wentworth's government.'[130] Dr Barnes has identified an interesting parallel for star chamber of the 1630s when the number of cases in England fell, owing in part to the clogging of judicial arteries by 'celebrity cases' and the increasing number of priority prosecutions by the attorney-general, forcing ordinary suits to the sidelines. The trial of the city of London in star chamber for its mishandling of the Londonderry plantation consumed all of Hilary term 1635 and ten more days in vacation.[131]

DÉNOUEMENT: THE COURT OF CASTLE CHAMBER AND THE END OF ABSOLUTISM, 1638–1642

Absolutism, however, proved to be an elusive goal for the Irish administration of the second Stuart king. A powerful government in the hands of a determined pasha was undermined by the febrile uncertainties of Charles I, revealing the cracks and fissures just below the surface of his policy of Thorough. Wentworth himself was called to England in 1638 to assist the king in preparing for war against the Scots, and in his absence the government ceased its aggressive campaign for the implementation of threatening policies on land and title in the provinces. The disturbed conditions of British politics from 1638 until 1640 resulted in the suspension of an Absolutist rigour, a fact which compels us to conclude that the policy obtained only temporary success while generating opposition from all corners of the realm. The implementation of Absolutism was arrested and incomplete after 1638 and operated only fitfully under a caretaker administration. The antagonistic government of Wentworth thus raised the profile of an intrusive and expansionist regime to a new summit of visibility, while at the same time exposing its vulnerability to a host of potential adversaries. Kearney's view that Wentworth, who became earl of Strafford in 1640, was a heroic failure rests on the premise that he alienated everyone, uniting Ireland in the paradoxical fashion of forging multiple layers of dissent into a common thrust against an outsider who refused to work with any interests represented in the Irish polity itself. By relying wholly on the king and a coterie of supporters who were equally alien to the matrix of Irish politics, Wentworth forfeited the support he might have gained from a more subtle interweaving of crown policy with Irish interests. Absolutism in Ireland was an inappropriate and, in the end, shallow veneer which contrived to impose a comprehensive resolution of problems which were regional, complex and historically intractable. On the other hand, the policy of Thorough generated a strong constitutional response, led by an array of experienced lawyers working through parliamentary and judicial avenues to overthrow the expedient and arbitrary mechanisms of the lord deputy. Unfortunately, this legalist

---

130. Kearney, *Strafford in Ireland*, p. 84.   131. Barnes, 'Slow process', p. 334.

opposition was, in its turn, overwhelmed by the seismic shifts which rapidly plunged the Atlantic archipelago into revolution and civil war. Ireland prior to 1641 may be seen as a crucible of antagonistic constitutional doctrines hanging in the balance, both of which enjoyed fitful and limited success.[132] It is possible to re-imagine pre-revolutionary Ireland as a tangle of possibilities, from royal despotism to loyal opposition, rather than as a road to civil war.

After 1638 the lord deputy of Ireland was burdened by the unforeseen dénouement of the policy of Thorough. Wentworth advised the crown on confrontation with the Scots Presbyterians, and in 1639 offered to provide an Irish army of 8,000 troops to crush Scots resistance, a ploy which intensified opposition in England. He was in London in May 1639 to prosecute his star chamber trial against Sir Piers Crosbie and others, and by September he became the king's informal chief adviser, urging resort to loans from the privy council and the calling of a parliament. Distracted as he was from events in Ireland, Wentworth no longer provided his idiosyncratic leadership to the court of castle chamber or the privy council in Ireland. He was created earl of Strafford in 1640 and made lord lieutenant of Ireland, the first since Mountjoy to hold that office. He visited Ireland for the last time in March 1640 to manage the subsidy from a pliant Irish parliament, leaving affairs in the hands of his relative, Christopher Wandesford, as lord justice. By June 1640, however, the parliament had recovered its equilibrium and opposition to the viceroy united, at least temporarily, the rival clusters of Protestant New English and Catholic Old English members. While Strafford was in England, the Irish commons challenged his manipulation of parliamentary boroughs, seeking writs for seven Old English boroughs excluded from the parliamentary election. They offered a modest subsidy while complaining of the plantation in Connacht and plans for an army in Ulster.[133] Before adjourning, the committee of grievances petitioned the lord deputy and council for the withdrawal of an act of state regarding tracts and the suspension of penal laws against plowing by the tail, burning corn in the straw and pulling the wool from living sheep. During the summer of 1640, the council issued an order to sheriffs in Ulster, based on the petition, requiring British freeholders in those counties to

---

132. Dr Russell has challenged the notion of a loyal opposition, stating that every stripe of political opinion strove to speak on behalf of the crown, and he argues there was no Absolutist regime because no one claimed the king could make law independently. Since there was no overarching 'struggle for sovereignty', early Stuart politics must be viewed on its own terms. C. Russell, *Unrevolutionary England*, pp. xiv–xvi.

133. Clarke, *Old English*, pp. 126–131. Members turned initially to petitions on personal matters and in June the 'act against carnal knowledge of women children [i.e. girls]' received its third reading. TCD, MS 615, f. 5. On 9 June 1640, 'Lord Caulfield moved that until the Subsidies were paid a Suspencon should be of all penall [laws] in point of Execution: [the] Lord Chancellor declares that this house have not power to make any Law, nor to order in those already made, but may petition the Lord Deputy and Counsell which the Comittee of grievances may do'. Ibid., f. 10. See also B. McGrath, 'Parliament men and the confederate association', in M. Ó Siochrú, ed., *Kingdoms in crisis*, pp. 90ff.

assemble at the next assizes in a 'grand panel' and to consider the petition, returning their votes to the council. On 29 September 1640, the council, acting on the wishes of the freeholders, proceeded to annul the act of state, prevent frivolous lawsuits by bailiffs and informers and suspend the penal laws. Citing the legal foundation for the penal laws, the council nonetheless declared that 'wee so much desire the satisfaction of these petitioners and the Ease of his Majesties subjects as wee will provide that those Lawes be for a time so moderatly pursued as that none of the poorer sort be questioned thereupon'.[134]

While Strafford turned his attention to pressing military matters in England, urging the king to take aggressive action, the Irish parliament met in October 1640 to take up grievances against his regime by setting up a committee of 35 members, including some of his own clients. By 22 October, the commons had recovered their nerve, challenging a suit before the lord deputy and council which involved the right of the deposed former lord chancellor, Adam Loftus, Viscount Ely, to sit as a member of the parliament.[135] When articles of impeachment were introduced against Strafford in the English house of commons in November 1640, over half of the 28 articles impugned his actions as lord deputy of Ireland. His legion of enemies came forward to castigate the viceroy, and the Irish parliament sent sixteen specific grievances against him to England. A deputation of thirteen members was received by a committee of the whole house of commons in December.[136] On 22 November 1640, the king and privy council resolved that a committee, including the earl of Cork, should attend the lord lieutenant to receive his advice on the grievances sent from the Irish parliament to the crown.[137] The 28 articles impugning the administration of Strafford contained accusations of high-handedness and tyranny, dating from his tenure as president of the Council in the North. For example, it was alleged that he told the justices of the peace on 31 August 1632 in York, before all the people there assembled, 'that some of the Justices were all for the law and nothing would please them but Lawe, But they should finde that the kings little finger should be heavier then the lynes of the Lawe'.[138] In similar vein, the new lord deputy had declaimed on 30 September 1634 before the peers and gentry as well as the leading citizens of Dublin

> that Ireland was a Conquered Nation, & that the king might doe with them
> what hee pleased, And speakeing of the Charters of former kings made to

---

134. TCD, MS 615, ff. 12–14. The petitioners charged that sheriffs, bailiffs and informers made too many presentments at the assizes, sometimes 40 or 50 accusations, yet informers never appeared at trial, so that the accused still had to pay fines to the court and the king, without having any resolution of the cause.

135. TCD, MS 615, ff. 21–22. The lords seized the moment to take up the issue before a committee of privileges and thus denied any jurisdiction of the matter to the council of Ireland.

136. Kearney, *Strafford*, pp. 191–204; Clarke, *Old English*, pp. 133–37. No documentation exists for the apparent collaboration of the English and Irish committees charged with the investigation. Clarke, *Old English*, p. 133.

137. *Cal. S.P. Ire., 1633–47*, p. 247.   138. TCD, MS 867, f. 298.

that Cittie Hee further then said that their Charters were nothing worth and did binde the king noe further then hee pleased.[139]

Strafford was specifically denounced for using the court of castle chamber to humble the earl of Cork in his suit over the college of Youghal, and for violating legal process in the trial and sentencing of Viscount Mountnorris in a council of war. His handling of the case against Viscount Ely as lord chancellor was pointedly identified as an abuse of his authority, as well as his imprisonment and dispossession of the earl of Kildare.[140] The catalogue of Strafford's offences included suits at the council table, such as the petition of Thomas Hibbot, who sued Dame Mary Hibbot, a widow, for an estate in land. Strafford recommended the petition to the council, but

> the most parte of the Councell gave their vote and opinion of [i.e. for] the said Ladie. But the said Earle, finding fault therewith, caused an order to be entred against the said ladie and threatened her that if shee refused to submitt thereto, hee would imprison her and fine her five hundred poundes.[141]

The article alleged Dame Hibbot was thereby compelled to relinquish her estate, which was conveyed to Sir Robert Meredith for the use of Strafford himself.[142] Accusations of personal enrichment and corruption of the judicial process were intertwined throughout the grievances against the viceroy.[143] The impeachment of Strafford thus accelerated the momentum which was initiated by the commons' grievances of 1640. The third of those articles alleged 'the proceedings in Civill Causes att councell Board [are] contrary to the Law and great Charter [and] not lymited to any certeyne tyme or season'.[144] The council itself was also condemned for voiding letters patent of the king's subjects on the basis of private opinions at the council board, without using evictions sanctioned by legal process.[145]

Under the leadership of John Pym, the English house of commons had gathered a mountain of evidence against Strafford, culminating in Pym's speech

---

139. Ibid., f. 299.
140. TCD, MS 867, ff. 299–303. Strafford compelled Kildare to surrender his title to the manor of Castle Leigh in Queen's Co. after a period of incarceration. In 1638, Thomas, Lord Dillon, was deprived of lands and tenements in Cos. Mayo and Roscommon by a contrived opinion of 'procured judges'. Strafford drew up the 'case of tenures upon defective titles' and, without trial by jury or other legal process, acting solely on the basis of the judges' opinion, took possession of the land in question. Ibid., f. 302.
141. TCD, MS 867, f. 303v.   142. Ibid.
143. Dr Kearney has demonstrated that Wentworth's plans for his own profit were as grandiose as his vision for royal government. His plan for Jigginstown House in Naas, never completed, was larger than both Hatfield and Longleat. He purchased 24,000 acres in Co. Wicklow, including the estate of the Grahams at Cosha, where he built a country estate. He obtained Shillelagh for a hunting park nearby and renamed his manor 'Fairview', accumulating 34,000 acres of land in only five years. Kearney, *Strafford*, pp. 173–84.
144. TCD, MS 867, f. 29.   145. Ibid., f. 30v.

of 10 November 1640 which demanded the arrest and imprisonment of Strafford on a charge of high treason.[146] By 25 November, the articles in support of the accusation were published by the commons, showing that

> Strafford hath Trayterously endeavoured to subvert the fundamentall Lawes and government of the Realmes of England and Ireland and instead thereof to introduce an arbitrary and tirannicall government against lawe, which hee hath declared by trayterous words, councells and accons.[147]

He was further accused of enriching himself unlawfully, encouraging papists so he might use their dependence on himself against his enemies, stirring enmity between the subjects of England and Scotland, prohibiting men of quality from departing the kingdom without his licence and hindering their access to the crown, and taking excessive legal fees, customs and subsidies. Of the sixteen grievances sent from Ireland, three dealt specifically with prerogative justice. The Irish commons attacked Strafford for his

> arbitrary decision of all civil causes and controversies by paper petitions before the Lord Lievetenant and lord deputy and infinite other Judicatories upon references from them derived in the nature of all accions determinable at the Comon law, not limited to a certain tyme, cause, reason or thing whatsoever. And the consequence of such proceedings ... [that] the subject looseth the benefit of his writ of error, bill of Reversall, vouchers and other legall and iust advantages and the ordinary course and Courtes of Justice are declined.[148]

The other prerogative courts experienced an equal hammering, especially the recently established court of high commission. The petition alleged 'The proceedings of the said Court [are] in many causes without legall warrant, And yet soe supported as prohibitions have not been obteyned, though legally sought for, And the excessive fees exacted by the Ministers thereof'.[149] Without naming the court of castle chamber, the commons used the charge of extra-judicial and tyrannical government as the basis for the incarceration of Wentworth. Pym declared: 'The Earle of Strafford hath not been bredd in the studie and practice of the lawe, and having strong lusts and passions to incite him and lesse knowledge to restraine might more easilie be transported from the Rule.'[150] He charged Sir George Radcliffe with corruption and wilful suspension of his reason and judgement, since he was better trained in the law and of a more moderate temper.[151] At the end of November, news arrived in Ireland of the arrest of Strafford and his client, Radcliffe, and the removal of restrictions on travel to

146. Ibid., f. 1.   147. Ibid., f. 4v.
148. Ibid., ff. 29–29v; TCD, MS 541, ff. 83–83v.   149. TCD, MS 541, f. 85.
150. TCD, MS 867, f. 68.   151. Ibid., f. 68v.

England. During January and February 1641, Radcliffe defended his actions and those of the council in Ireland, saying it was always a court of justice, now used to protect the authority of the church and the planters.[152]

The sudden collapse of Wentworth's government compromised that of his successors and demonstrated the inherent fragility of the prerogative courts. Tainted by the arbitrary handling of its cases under the previous administration, the court of castle chamber came under attack by the enemies of the viceroy. Yet, while the court of wards and the court of high commission were inundated by the torrent of vituperation and quickly eliminated by statute, the court of castle chamber survived the disparagement and censure to reemerge after the Restoration in a series of halting improvisations designed to resurrect crown authority in Ireland.[153]

Though the disgraced Viscount Ely was formally replaced as lord chancellor and a renewed commission for the court arrived on 29 November 1639, few trials were recorded and castle chamber was beset by its critics. The justices aggravated their circumstance when a defendant, Sir John Fitzgerald of Inishmore, was sued by Patrick, lord of Kerry and Lynogh, and his wife, Lady Honora, for a scandal (the details of which were not recorded). Fitzgerald had been elected member of parliament for Inistioge on 11 November 1640, replacing the Wentworth client, Sir Robert Loftus, who had died suddenly. When the castle chamber decree was rendered on 2 December, Fitzgerald was sentenced to heavy fines and imprisonment, but he pleaded parliamentary immunity from prosecution. Castle chamber rejected his plea and sentenced Fitzgerald to pay damages of £5,000 to the lord of Kerry, and a fine of £10,000 to the crown, tokens of further judicial harassment. Rather ominously, the new lord deputy, Wentworth's client, Christopher Wandesford, died the following day. The house of commons had been prorogued for the holiday and resumed its session on 25 January, hearing the case of Fitzgerald's claimed immunity and seeking a conference with the lords. On 18 February 1641, the commons determined in his favour, admitting Fitzgerald as member, freeing him from the Marshalsea and setting aside his fines.[154] The commons rejected the arguments of the court that Fitzgerald was a non-resident of the borough, that his election was in error, and that he enjoyed no parliamentary privilege while the house was not in session. In doing so, the parliament asserted a practical superiority over the court of castle chamber that the justices were in no position to dispute.

The history of the court concluded with a paradoxical notoriety that no longer matched either its pretensions or its power as a tribunal. Upon the death of Wandesford, the grasping Sir William Parsons, master of the court of wards,

---

152. *Cal. S.P. Ire.*, *1633–47*, pp. 253, 257. Radcliffe wrote 22 pages of legal defence on 9 January to which the committee replied a month later.

153. The 'ritual erasure' of the court of high commission, including the control of nonconformity, was accomplished by August 1641. J. McCafferty, 'Bramhall and reconstruction of the Church of Ireland', ch. 3, pp. 13–16. McCafferty views high commission as an important symbol of both episcopal rule and the 'abuse of prerogative powers by the Lord Lieutenant'. Ibid., p. 13.

154. *Cal. S.P. Ire.*, *1633–47*, p. 228; *Commons' jn. Ire.*, i, 320, 325–28, 331, 349–52; Edwards, 'Poisoned chalice', p. 79.

became lord justice. At the age of 70, Parsons was still a strong advocate of plantations throughout Ireland, from which he had obtained numerous estates and interests. He was soon joined as lord justice by Sir John Borlase, master of the ordnance. Borlase was another Wentworth client, a veteran soldier with no judicial experience, who offered little guidance to the prerogative court of castle chamber.[155]

The definitive legal test of Absolutism in Ireland began in February 1641 when the Galway lawyer, Patrick Darcy, led a systematic protest against the arbitrariness of Strafford's regime. On 13 February, the Irish commons appointed a committee to review a series of questions about the legality of the government, including specific charges levelled against the court of castle chamber. On 16 February, the Queries, as they were called, were adopted by the commons as 'a calculated policy of rendering impossible a repetition of the events of the recent past by establishing an agreed delimitation of the competence of the executive government'.[156] On 27 February, a large committee of the commons proceeded to write articles of impeachment against the lord chancellor, Sir Richard Bolton; the chief justice of common pleas, Sir Gerald Lowther; John Bramhall, bishop of Derry; and Sir George Radcliffe. Bolton, elevated to lord chancellor after the disgrace of Loftus, had been recorder of Dublin, solicitor-general, attorney-general to the court of wards and chief baron of the exchequer since 1625. His partiality to Wentworth caused him to be included in articles of impeachment for treason in 1641, shortly after he became lord chancellor, even though he was speaker of the Irish house of lords. In the following month, Strafford was put on trial in the house of lords in England where he defended his actions vigorously. The parliamentarary advocate, John Pym, adroitly manipulated the commons into a full hearing on the tyranny of Strafford in April 1641 so that the impeachment trial was superseded by a bill of attainder, accusing Strafford of treason. Pym employed many witnesses from Ireland, including Strafford's enemies Mountnorris, Cork, Roebuck Lynch and Charles Wilmot. This proceeding was rapidly concluded on 21 April, after which the lords approved the act of attainder on 8 May and sent it to the king for the royal signature, requiring the execution of Charles I's closest personal adviser. Signed by the king on 10 May 1641, the act of attainder was duly enforced the following day when Strafford was executed on Tower Hill.[157]

---

155. Lord Dillon of Kilkenny West was briefly named lord justice after the death of Wandesford on 3 December; Borlase replaced Dillon on 30 December in subsequent instructions. *Cal. S.P. Ire., 1633–47*, pp. 247–48. Wentworth's proposal of the Protestant earl of Ormond, James Butler, as the new lord deputy in late 1640 was vigorously attacked by his enemies both in England and Ireland. Edwards has argued that Ormond fatally compromised his position in Kilkenny itself by aligning himself with the meteoric chief governor and his cronies in Dublin. Edwards, 'Poisoned chalice', pp. 80–81.

156. Clarke, *Old English*, p. 142. See also his recent essay, 'Patrick Darcy and the constitutional relationship between Ireland and Britain', in J. Ohlmeyer, ed., *Political thought in seventeenth century Ireland* (Cambridge, 2000), pp. 35–49.

157. Kearney, *Strafford*, pp. 207–11.

The destiny of the court of castle chamber, along with the fate of its members, now lay in the hands of two ambitious legislatures, ready to parlay their newly won freedom of action into a permanent foundation for parliamentary rule. On 13 February 1641, Patrick Darcy and others launched the systematic inquiry into Absolutist misrule in Ireland with the initiation of a committee in the Irish house of commons. This group examined charges against Strafford's regime, as we have seen, in the form of questions, or 'Queries', which attacked the legality of specific executive decisions and undermined the constitutional basis for prerogative justice itself. Adopted by the commons on 16 February, the Queries were sent to the lords with a request to demand of the judges an immediate answer, while reassuring the cowed executive with a disavowal of any punitive action based on their findings.[158] Kearney saw in the Queries an important constitutional advance, similar in form and substance to the challenge by the English parliament against Thorough. He concluded: 'In the form of the Queries and the character of the individual clauses may be seen the hand of the common lawyer. The legal element in the Irish opposition was as important as in its English counterpart.'[159] The delay of the Irish judges prompted the commons to submit the Queries to the English parliament for a ruling on the points of law, but the instructions to the committee now broached the difficult legal subject of the crown's position in Irish government. Darcy would later claim, in his speech of June 1641, that 'Ireland is annexed to the crown of England, and governed by the laws of England'.[160] Clarke summarized the argument in this way:

> This assertion of Irish legislative independence was associated with a willingness to recognize the authority of the English parliament in other spheres: recourse to that parliament, for instance , was a remedy given by law to the king's subjects in Ireland, just as they also had legal recourse to the king's bench of England. Being governed by 'one law' in short involved the right to use the machinery for the administration of that law in England … In short, the English and Irish legislative systems were co-ordinate, while their judicial systems interlocked.[161]

Darcy's meaning was that Ireland was annexed to the crown of England, not to the government of England, making appeals directly to the crown a legitimate means of circumventing a chief governor.[162] Clarke summarized: 'It was not the relationship of the Irish and English parliaments which was at issue, but the relationship of the executive government to the law.'[163]

---

158. Clarke, *Old English*, pp. 141–42.
159. Kearney, *Strafford*, p. 211.
160. P. Darcy, *An argument delivered … by the express order of the house of commons in the parliament of Ireland* (Dublin, 1764), p. 108, quoted in Clarke, *Old English*, p. 146.
161. Clarke, *Old English*, p. 146. The corollary to this lay in an acceptance of discretionary prerogative powers of the crown when parliament was not in session. Ibid., p. 147.
162. Ibid., p. 148.   163. Ibid., p. 149.

The Queries stated in a substantial preamble that the people of Ireland were free, loyal and dutiful subjects, bound by the common law of England and by statutes of force in Ireland, who now sued to regain their birthright as citizens. The second of the Queries addressed the power of the viceroy over the judges of Ireland, questioning whether he had the authority to hinder or delay the suit of any subject, judgement of any court or enforcement of any judicial decree by act of state, proclamation, writ, letter or direction under the privy seal or privy signet. The third interrogatory was the vital one for the continued existence of the conciliar court. Darcy and his lieutenants attempted here to place the burden of proof on the crown to demonstrate the legal basis for the expansion of prerogative government. They asked,

> Whether the kings majesty privy counsell, either with the cheif governor or Governors of this kingdom or without him or them, bee a place of Judicature by the comon Lawes, and wherein causes between party and party for debts, Trespasse, accompts, portion or Tytle of lands or any of them, and which of them, may be heard and determined [there], and of what civill causes they have Jurisdiction, and by what law and of what force is their order or Decree in such Cases or any of them.[164]

The fourth Query asked the same question 'of the chief Governor [acting] alone,' suggesting that Strafford arrogated to himself the judicial power of the council board, acting *in loco regis*, as it were.[165] Demanding next to know the legal authority for grants of monopoly, the articles then challenged the right of the lord deputy and council to fine, imprison, pillory or mutilate those who violated the regulation of monopolies. These questions placed the Irish judges in a hopeless quandary, since the lord lieutenant was now impeached, the lord deputy had recently died, the lords justices were personally compromised and the judges themselves sat on the very tribunals which were now under attack.

At the very heart of prerogative rule lay the force of proclamation, by which the viceroy and the council in Ireland made law in the absence of parliament. This constitutional innovation had been launched under the Tudors and was usually termed an 'act of state'. It was generally acknowledged a satisfactory and practical tool of executive power, but the parliament now confronted its practitioners. The seventh Query raised this point:

> Of what force is an Act of State or proclamation in this kingdom to bynd the Lybertyes, goods, possessions or Inheritance of the Natives thereof, whether they or any of them can alter the Comon Law or the infringers of [th]ym loose their goods, chattles or leases; or forfeit the same by infringing any such act of state, proclamation or both, and what punishment doe the

sworne judges of the Law, that are privy Counsellors, Incurr that voate for such acts and Execution thereof.[166]

Since the judges to whom the Queries were remanded for consideration were the very common law magistrates mentioned in the article, it is little wonder that the entire corpus of interrogatives was finally sent, unabridged, on to the parliament in England. After questioning the arbitrary use of martial law in time of peace, the ninth Query asked 'Whether voluntary Oathe taken freely before [articulators] for affirmance or Disaffirmance of any thing, or for the true performance of anything, bee punishable in the Castle chamber or any other Court and why and wherefore'.[167] The next article raised another objection against the inquisitorial practices of the conciliar court, in both its guises, showing that the dissenters' perception of the council's judicial powers was that they were practically merged. The tenth article asked:

> Why and by what Law or by what Rule of pollicy is It that none is admitted to reducement of fines or other penaltye in the Castle Chamber, or Councell Table untill they confess the Offences for which he is Censured when as Revera [revealed?] they might be Innocent thereof, though subord[inate] proofes or scircumst[ance] might induce the Censure.[168]

The parliament showed in the tenth inquiry that it wished to examine conciliar jurisprudence in detail, circumscribing its ancillary powers and curbing the opportunity for coercive measures.

The targeting of castle chamber by the Queries is a remarkable, even modern, example of legislative reform posing as interrogation. In the tradition of commissions of inquiry sent to examine the putative corruption of disgraced chief governors, the articles expanded the parameters of review to include the constitutional basis for executive actions of many kinds. They accused judges of king's bench and other courts of denying the copies of an indictment of felony or treason to the parties accused. They demanded the right to appeal directly to the king for redress of grievances, and asked whether a proclamation of treason could be levied against one who steals a sheep or commits other felonies 'and, after, flyeth courts of justice or lyeth in woods or mountains upon his keeping'.[169] Three of the Queries form the core of the challenge to the work of castle chamber. Without claiming that the court was inherently illegitimate, the articles found that the tribunal had become a rogue carnivore, tearing ruthlessly at the social fabric and undermining the faith and trust of the king's subjects in his law. Recalling the censures of the Chichester regime in spirit, they scrupled:

---

166. Ibid., f. 18.
168. Ibid.

167. Ibid.
169. Ibid., f. 19.

15. By what Law are Jurors that give verdict according their Conscience and are the sole Judges of the fact, Censured in the Castle Chamber in great fines and some times Pillor[i]ed with Loss of eares and boared through the tongue and marked some time in fore head with a hott iron and other like infamous punishment.

16. By what Law are men Censureable in the Castle Chamber with the mutilation of members or any other brand of Infamy, and in what Causes and what punishment in each Case there is due without respect of the quality of the person or persons.

17. Whether, in the Censures in the Castle Chamber, regard be to be had to the words of the great Charter Salvo convenemento &c.[170]

The final article challenged the right of judges to take four pence in the pound by way of fine in cases of defective title, noting that the judges condemned the voiding of such patents 'in an extra Judiciall way'.[171] The Queries passed a third reading in the house of lords and proceeded to committee on 23 February 1641. The lords added an appeal to the king against Strafford, citing his great disservice to the peers, raising sundry persons of mean position to serve in great offices. The petitioners sought restoration to places of favour and trust in the management of crown affairs in Ireland.[172] On the same day, the lords justices and council wrote to Sir Henry Vane, secretary of state in England, that the lord chancellor and chief justice of common pleas and the vice-treasurer could not be spared to testify in England. Citing their many legal duties, including that of speaker in the house of lords, the council in Ireland also explained that neither the court of castle chamber nor the commission to remedy defective titles could sit in their absence.[173]

Simultaneous with the demands for constitutional limits on prerogative power, the Irish parliament commenced the impeachment of senior judges in the administration. On 27 February 1641, Lord Chancellor Bolton, Bishop Bramhall, Chief Justice Gerard Lowther and Sir George Radcliffe were accused of high treason, and the commons sought their sequestration from 'places of judicature and from the council board'.[174] The lords received this petition and dissolved into a grand committee to consider how to proceed, noting the late impeachment of Strafford in England and determining to follow the precedent set there in treason trials. The portentous quarrel took on high constitutional principles, including the right of the Irish parliament to proceed by impeachment. Lord Chancellor Bolton remained as speaker during the dispute, though his tenure of office and his potential replacement were at the core of the argument. Despite the inconclusive

---

170. Ibid. The star chamber in England was under similar attack at this point and on the verge of extinction, which may explain the defiant tone of the parliamentary inquisitors.

171. Ibid., f. 21.   172. Ibid., f. 22.

173. *Cal. S.P. Ire., 1633–47*, pp. 258–59.

174. TCD, MS 615, f. 22. See also J. McCafferty, '"To follow the late precedents of England": the Irish impeachment proceedings of 1641', in D.S. Greer and N.M. Dawson, eds., *Mysteries and solutions in Irish legal history* (Dublin, 2001), pp. 61–69.

nature of the dispute in the lords, the articles of impeachment were written into the journal of the commons on 4 March, charging Bolton, Bramhall, Lowther, and Radcliffe with treason for their arbitrary and tyrannical government. In a letter to Secretary Vane on 8 March 1641, the lords justices and council explained that the four officials had been indicted for treason in the commons, and the lords took recognizances from the lord chancellor, noting the absence of the bishop of Derry and the chief justice. The commons demanded that the officials be dismissed, and sought bonds of £20,000 for their appearance, but the council tried to delay, seeking the advice of law officers of the crown. Finally, the council met in the afternoon to declare that only the king had the right to remove members from the privy council in Ireland, though Bolton and Lowther were told to come to council meetings only by special request. The enfeebled councillors complained to Vane that both the lord chancellor and chief justice were needed on the board, yet they appeared willing to suspend their attendance.[175] In this constitutional maelstrom, the suspension of the legal terms and the dormancy of the court of castle chamber are easily explained. On 10 March 1641, Lord Chancellor Bolton responded that Poynings's Law afforded no right of the Irish parliament to proceed by impeachment, adding that the charges were too general and produced no evidence against him.[176]

After interminable debates, parliament was prorogued to 11 May 1641 and the king ordered the proceedings to be discontinued unless precedents were found to authorize a trial by the Irish house of lords. This, in turn, led the opposition to intensify its search for a new legitimacy, grounded upon legal principles and wedded to its inherent rights, descended from its maternal parent, the legislature in England.[177] Since the leading judge on the court of castle chamber, Lord Chancellor Bolton, was himself facing articles of impeachment, along with Chief Justice Lowther, close parliamentary scrutiny of prerogative justice apparently discouraged the court from hearing new causes after 1639. As Dr McCafferty has recently explained, the conjunction of the Irish impeachment process with that of Strafford in England was vital, so the slender evidence produced in the charges, coupled with the sudden execution of the lord lieutenant, left the proceedings in Dublin on very doubtful foundations.[178] Nonetheless, the Irish committee of the privy council, writing on 11 May 1641, replied to the Queries by simply restating the judicial boundaries which delineated the star chamber in England and required castle chamber to conform to them, while condemning the 'extra-judicial determination of grievances by paper petitions' as an illegal excess by the chief governor. The presidency courts were also held to the limits of equity jurisdiction, though it added 'The High Commission Court should not be suspended but totally dissolved'.[179]

175. *Cal. S.P. Ire., 1633–47*, p. 259.
176. TCD, MS 615, f. 25.
177. Clarke, *Old English*, pp. 143–44.
178. J. McCafferty, 'Irish impeachment', pp. 51–52, 63–65.
179. *Cal. S.P. Ire., 1633–47*, p. 284. Presidency courts were also limited to equity jurisdiction

Writing to Secretary Vane on 18 May 1641, the lords justices revealed that they had tried to get the parliament to allow Bolton to remain as speaker of the house of lords, but the upper chamber demanded another. Sir William Ryves, second justice of king's bench, was then accepted, with the prior approval of the crown. The lords then sent word that they believed Bolton and Lowther should be imprisoned, but the lords justices answered that it would then be impossible to hold the court of castle chamber or the court of wards, in which Lowther was also attorney of the court. On 12 May, the commons sought from the lords an answer to the Queries which the judges were to review.[180] The commons apparently planned a public demonstration against the indicted officials, so the lords justices summoned both houses to the presence chamber and read the letters of the king insisting that the officials remain free on bail. The sceptical parliament demanded authentic copies of the letters, which were duly given, and the bishop of Derry was given leave to go to his house, and from thence abroad. The lords justices feared the intent of parliament to proceed 'capitally' against the two judges and the bishop, explaining they doubted the validity of precedent for this, and seeking advice from England.[181] They explained in a letter of 7 June 1641 that representatives of the lords and commons had come to complain that the courts of chancery, castle chamber and wards were not sitting, to which the chief governors declared that the impeachment against the judges prevented the courts from normal operations.[182] Indirect evidence of this came from the king's order to Viscount Ranelagh, lord president of Connacht, for a commission to try a case against Henry Dillon, who had published scandalous speeches against a peer and the state at Athlone the previous May.[183] The court of castle chamber would have been the normal venue for this accusation.

In the crisis of the spring of 1641, led by two aged veterans of the second rank in Irish administration, the government was badly shaken and the courts ceased to function. After much delay and royal prevarication, the accusations of high treason against the chancellor and others were dismissed on 22 June 1642 and orders were given to restore them to their positions in parliament, to their offices and credit.[184] By that time, however, the constitutional dismantling of the

according to their commissions. Two days later the committee recommended that a statute be enacted to prevent the chief governor and council taking jurisdiction of personal, real or mixed actions at law. Ibid., p. 286.

180. Ibid., p. 288.   181. Ibid.

182. Ibid., pp. 298–300. The commons declared 'That the Court of Castle Chamber did not sit this term, the court of Chancery only once, and the court of Wards very seldom'. The commons denied responsibility for the courts' dormancy. Ibid., p. 300.

183. Ibid., p. 301. The king ordered the new lord lieutenant, the earl of Leicester, to proceed with this commission, but he never arrived in Ireland so it was a dead letter. On 4 July, the king wrote to the lords justices 'Ordering that, in spite of the verdict given in their favour by a corrupt jury, proceedings shall be instituted in the Court of Castle Chamber against Teig O'Connor Sligo and his friends, who … forcibly entered the Manor house of Sligo, which, with half of its lands, should have escheated to the king by the attainder of the earl of Strafford'. Ibid., p. 312.

184. TCD, MS 615, f. 26.

government of Ireland resulted in the quiet death of the court of castle chamber. Sir Adam Loftus explained in a letter to Vane of 14 June 1641 that the parliament had descended to partisan wrangling over matters of religion, concluding 'At my coming over I found a strange state of things, the officers and council overawed by Parliament'.[185] After the execution of Strafford in May, Charles I proceeded to address the Irish grievances by his own authority, rather than that of parliament. Sitting with twelve members of the privy council on 16 July 1641, the king ordered the secretary of state, Dudley Carleton, to enter the royal answers in the register of the council and to prepare letters to be given to the Irish parliament. In answer to the grievance against paper petitions decided before the chief governor alone, or by the council board, the royal response was routine:

> Answer. Matter of patents and plantations, which are to be treated as matters of State, must be determined by the Lord Deputy and Council publicly at the Council Board, and not otherwise. Questions of title between party and party grown after these patents granted are within the jurisdiction of the ordinary Law Courts.[186]

Similarly, the royal decree demanded that the court of castle chamber be regulated on English models in relation to its treatment of jurors, accepting the substance of the grievance in principle:

> Grievance. An Act should be passed forbidding any juror to be bound to the Castle Chamber or to be there in any sort questioned excepting corruption be proved against them. Juries shall not be compelled to respect the evidence of notoriously bad characters.[187]

Five days later, Lord Justice Parsons wrote that the Queries were again being debated in parliament, despite the cautious replies of the Irish judges. It was plain, Parsons continued, that parliament wished to interpose its own judgement, which amounted to a derogation of the king's prerogative and the powers of the council and the courts.[188] The king wrote to the new speaker of the house of lords in the Irish parliament on 10 August 1641, seeking to calm the waters. He indicated that he would be more willing to hearken to their other demands if they would proceed tenderly with the indicted officials, Bolton, Bramhall and Lowther, noting their physical infirmities and the need for royal compassion.[189]

---

185. *Cal. S.P. Ire., 1633–47*, p. 302.
186. Ibid., p. 318.
187. Ibid., p. 320.
188. Ibid., p. 323. McCafferty has argued that the impeachment process lost its credibility when Bolton protested its illegality in the spring, but the commons pressed on during the summer. They set up a committee to draw up formal charges and asked permission from the lords justices for review of all conciliar records since 1633. McCafferty, 'Irish impeachment', p. 65.
189. *Cal. S.P. Ire., 1633–47*, p. 332.

When the Irish judges finally presented their opinions on the Queries in August 1641, their guarded phrasing added little to the corpus of evidence. On some matters they refused to rule at all, such as the prerogative and commissions to the chief governor and star chamber. The judges began with numerous demurrers, explaining that many judges might differ on the key points and declining to bind future judges by their answers. They further explained that the people of Ireland were subject to the laws of England, but that many Irish laws differed, such as that which required forfeiture of all property to the crown if a man were killed while in rebellion in Ireland. They averred that acts of state or proclamations could not override the common law, but were useful and, when not given *ultra vires*, violators were punishable in courts of law. They affirmed that jurors which gave their verdict clearly against the weight of evidence have been and ought to be censured by the castle chamber. In a possible reference to recusancy cases, the judges asserted,

> The taking and giving of voluntary oaths may be illegal, as the king alone, the fountain of justice is empowered to give them. Persons doing these things may be tried by the common law, or in bad cases by the Castle Chamber.[190]

Implicit in their reasoning is the assumption that the court of castle chamber stood as a senior jurisdiction where the power and validity of royal authority could be upheld by principal judges acting in concert with the executive power.

Neither of the lords justices had the stature to maintain the judicial presence of the court in the face of unrelenting hostility, so the tribunal became the focus of reprisal and reversal of its judgements. Henry Stewart and James Gray had refused to take the 'Black Oath', an oath of allegiance demanded of Scots resident in Ireland during the Bishops' War of 1639. Sitting in judgement of their case at castle chamber on 7 September 1639 were Sir William Parsons, Sir Richard Bolton, Sir Gerard Lowther, Sir Adam Loftus, Sir George Radcliffe, Sir Robert Meredith, and the bishops of Derry and of Cork. With Bolton now the lord keeper and Bramhall having seized the initiative in demanding religious orthodoxy, Strafford's *provocateurs* in court enforced an aggressive and risky policy in the absence of the lord deputy.[191] Though Stewart defended the Scots covenant as a loyal oath to the king, the attorney-general argued that his refusal to swear the king's oath amounted to high treason, saying the authority of the king was received immediately from God.[192] The court sentenced Stewart, his wife and daughters, along with Gray to life imprisonment and fined them £13,000, proceeding to draw up extents against their estate for raising the money for the fine. After 18 months in prison, Stewart petitioned the English house of lords to have his judgement reversed.[193]

---

190. Ibid., pp. 334–35.
191. *Cal. S.P. Ire., 1633–47*, pp. 222–23. Bolton was made lord chancellor by order of the king on 6 December 1639. Ibid., p. 228.
192. Ibid., p. 222.
193. Marsh's Lib., MS Z.3.2.6, item 117, p. 329. The petition alleged that Stewart refused 'to take

The council in Ireland responded to Stewart's petition on 30 July 1641 with a singularly defensive counter-plea, alleging that they could not be spared to defend themselves against a suit in London during the sitting of the Irish parliament, and defending the original decision based on a valid order which had been sought by loyal Scots and approved by the king himself. They advanced an important doctrine, justifying the work of the council and the court of castle chamber as lying beyond the reach of malicious recriminations, since the validity of all judicial decrees in Ireland was at stake. Appealing to the privy council, the lords justices and councillors wrote:

> It would be dangerous to admit the doctrine contained in the petition, for, if it were admitted, people would be afraid to become Privy Councillors, lest they should be liabel to damages for not understanding a case so fully as God might have enabled them to do. The error in practice was bringing such suits before, and trying them in, the Castle Chamber; but this is an error which has been made continuously for a century. To cast doubt upon all legal practice in the kingdom at this moment would be a most dangerous thing ... [adding] The decisions of the Board and of the Castle Chamber Court are closely united, and depend one upon the other. Their credit stands together. If the credit of the Castle Chamber is impugned, so is that of the Council. We hope, therefore, that the matter may be allowed to drop.[194]

After much delay, the house of lords proceeded with sanction against the eight named councillors on 9 September 1642, finding their original decree in the Irish star chamber unjust and illegal. They were required to pay damages of £1,500 to Stewart and £400 to Gray.[195] The constitutional import of the case raises numerous questions about the independent authority of castle chamber, but the final decree occurred in the context of what may be deemed revolutionary justice, and thus may not reflect routine appellate jurisdiction of the English parliament over the Irish court.

On 19 August 1641, Thomas Tempest, attorney-general for Ireland, wrote to Lord Littleton that the judges were absent on circuit and unable to advise the lords in parliament on matters of law. Explaining that the lords claimed a right to hear writs of error to reverse actions taken by the council in Ireland, Tempest worried that 'The Judges are unpopular, and it is difficult to maintain the King's authority'.[196] The dormancy of the court had important consequences for clients

---

an unlawfull oath in Ireland which was contrived by the earl of Strafford' to be imposed upon Scots then resident in Ireland. Ibid.

194. *Cal. S.P. Ire., 1633–47*, p. 326.   195. Marsh's Lib., MS Z.3.2.6, item 117, p. 329.

196. *Cal. S.P. Ire., 1633–47*, p. 333. A list of fees for the auditor general of the government of the confederation of Kilkenny included a table showing £0 0s. 6d. for copies of pleadings and depositions in both castle chamber and chancery. The statement of 1647 suggests the continued existence of the skeletal structure of the court, mentioning the work of the philizer of castle chamber and the nominal sealing of writs for castle chamber and the cursitor's office. Ibid., p. 752.

of the late earl of Strafford. Sir Philip Perceval, his personal secretary, had bought the manor and lands of Teig O'Connor Sligo, the elder, in trust for Strafford and Radcliffe, half of which the king had now granted by escheat to three petitioners, Joshua Carpenter, George Carr and Guilford Slingsby. On 4 July 1641, Charles I wrote to the lords justices to order that the younger Teig O'Connor Sligo and his friends should be tried in the court of castle chamber for having forcibly entered the manor house of Sligo to contest the grant of the crown.[197] Undoing the work of the Strafford regime was proceeding at a rapid pace, though the king was apparently unaware of the dormancy of the Irish star chamber. On 16 July 1641, Charles had granted to the Irish committee a second series of concessions, suspending the court of high commission and closely regulating the court of wards and the court of castle chamber.[198] However, the government proceeded to adjourn parliament on 7 August in order to forestall any further deterioration in its position. And the Old English opposition, never more than a substantial minority in parliament, began to see the unwieldy combination with majority Protestants weaken their constitutional stance, one which depended more on the prerogative and less on the legislature, 'still only an occasional partner in the business of government'.[199]

On 22 October 1641, the rebellion in Ulster by Phelim O'Neill and the arrest of conspirators in Dublin by the lords justices created a military emergency which made the return of normal judicial routine impossible. Within a few days, the proclamation of rebellion was succeeded by the proroguing of parliament and suspension of the legal terms until the new year.[200] On 27 October, the council in Ireland officially adjourned the Michaelmas sessions until the next Hilary term, citing the unrest that required all men to remain in their habitations rather than travel to Dublin for the legal terms. Pending matters in all courts, including castle chamber, were to have continuance, and all monies due and payable were to be collected on pain of contempt of the courts.[201] Fighting quickly drew into the conflict all the Irish counties, and outrageous military excesses widened the gap between adversaries and made negotiations more difficult, although every side in the deepening civil war claimed to be fighting for the crown. However, Dr Canny has shown that there were some who 'wished to retain some middle ground after the hostilities commenced'.[202] Meanwhile, the lords justices and council, who

---

197. Ibid., p. 312. The king also condemned the 'verdict given in their (O'Connor Sligo's) favour by a corrupt jury', though he did not order the jury held accountable in star chamber. The escheated lands represented the moiety of the estate allegedly owned by the attainted earl of Strafford. No record of this trial has been discovered to date and it is highly unlikely that proceedings were commenced, despite the order of the king to the lords justices.

198. Ibid., pp. 317–22 at pp. 319 and 320; Clarke, *Old English*, p. 149.

199. Clarke, *Old English*, p. 151.   200. *Cal. S.P. Ire., 1633–47*, p. 342.

201. *Corporation book of Youghal*, ed. R. Caulfield (Guildford, 1878), pp. 212–13.

202. Canny, *Making Ireland British*, p. 366. He has shown that some Catholic landowners tried to remain aloof, while Protestants like the earl of Cork attempted to preserve the possessions of his Irish tenants. See his ch. 8 for a thorough study of the 1641 depositions and the sectarian

were also under indictment in the house of commons for a corrupt verdict rendered in the case of Chancellor Loftus, penned an extensive memorandum on 22 October 1641 to excuse their actions. The nine clauses contained important disclaimers that reflected on the judicial capacity of the council board. The councillors argued,

> First it hath bin ofte declared by some whoe of late did sitt in cheife heere, and indeede soe farre as it was taken heere for graunted, that the Privy Councellors heere are not judges at the Boord, but that the judgement is solely in the Deputie or Cheife Governour, as representing the King's person, and that all the Privy Councellors are only asistants to him; which being soe, it then follows necessarily that, uppon any misjudgement there, those whoe only asssist thereat, and have not in them the judicature, cannnot be lyable to question for any judgements that is not theirs, but annother's.[203]

This disingenuous avoidance was followed by another excuse:

> wee conceive (under favour) that, by the lawes of the land, noe Judges or Councellors are to be lyable to damages for any erronious judgements, noe corrupcion appearing therein. And wee conceive his Lordshipp can lay noe corrupcion to the charge of those whoe assisted in that judgement. And wee, of the members of the Boord whoe assisted in that hearing doe professe that wee had no corrupt or synister end in that business towards his Lordshipp.[204]

The desperate officials alleged that members of the council would suffer loss of esteem and prejudice against their endeavours on behalf of the crown if they were to be sued for doing their duties, and concluded that Loftus had other remedies at law. They further argued that Loftus himself was privy to similar proceedings as both chancellor and lord justice:

> the Lord Loftus, a person whoe hadd the honour to sitt at this Boord soe long as hee did, and serving his Majesty in soe emynent a condicion as his chauncellor, and whoo could not but well knowe the custome and practise of the Boord, did in all that tyme assist in Councell with the Deputies and Councell in hearings of such nature as hee nowe labours to render extrajudicial.[205]

---

violence that disturbed nearly every community in Ireland. Though unexpected, Canny argues that the frustrations of the Irish Catholic community since 1603 culminated in a frenzy of lawlessness 'once the political mould had been broken'. Ibid., pp. 460, 550.

203. HMC, *Drogheda MSS*, p. 314.
204. Ibid., p. 315.
205. Ibid. The officers sought dismissal of Loftus's suit and pardon from the lords of parliament, excusing the delay of their letter, sent on 13 November, by reason of the late rebellion in Ireland. Ibid.

On 3 May 1642, the house of lords heard the case and reversed the verdict of the council in Ireland against Loftus, awarding him damages and restoring his estates to him.[206]

The defection of the Old English of the Pale from the government in December 1641 was followed in June 1642 by establishment of a rival, and parallel, government at Kilkenny which muddied the problems of jurisdiction and allegiance.[207] The outbreak of rebellion suspended all forms of political negotiations on the Queries and other constitutional protests, and the profound confusion of the lords justices in the face of multiple threats to royal authority magnified the impression of administrative meltdown. Dr Clarke has explained that the 'essential conservatism' of the Old English as rebels from late 1641 was a reflection of their more consistent and vigorously pressed constitutionalism during the period from the articulation of the Graces to the Queries of 1641.[208] Far from inevitable, the rebellion must be seen as part of the political breakdown which commenced in 1638 throughout the British Isles, and hence as a reciprocally 'British' event. Indeed, Dr Gillespie has argued that events in Ulster in 1641 were unexpected, after years of accommodation between native and settler, including intermarriage, landholding, giving of bonds and routine hospitality among neighbours.[209] Against the established legacy of lawful protest, parliamentary negotiation and the judicial threat of impeachment, resort to violence was exceptional. As Clarke has said:

> it seems clear that the character of the outbreak was determined less by the obvious long-standing grievances of the Irish than by the particular circumstances of the year 1641 itself, and that the nature of the Old English reaction to it was determined partly by this almost accidental character which it had assumed, and partly by recent political experience, with which it neatly dovetailed.[210]

---

206. Ibid., p. 316. The feoffees of the estate were made to reconvey all the properties to Loftus and his heirs, but Loftus's successor, Edward, was forced to sue for nonperformance of the agreement. In 1662, he pursued his claim by petition to the duke of Ormonde as lord lieutenant, against the heir of his deceased brother, Robert, one Dacre Barrett. The latter petitioned the crown in 1673 and received a hearing in the next year, but his remedies came to an end in 1678 when parliament reconfirmed the original decree on behalf of Chancellor Loftus in 1642. Ibid., pp. 317–18, 322, 327–28. See HMC, *Var. Coll. 3* (1904), pp. 158–255 for a full account of the legal manoeuvring on both sides from 1642 to 1678.
207. See M. Ó Siochrú, ed., *Kingdoms in crisis: Ireland in the 1640s* [essays in honour of Donal Cregan] (Dublin, 2001), for a thorough study of the rival jurisdictions.
208. Clarke, *Old English*, p. 228.
209. R. Gillespie, 'Destabilizing Ulster, 1641–2' in B. MacCuarta, ed., *Ulster 1641: aspects of the Rising* (Belfast, 1993), pp. 110–111. Gillespie argued that the superstructure of common law was perhaps fragile and shallow, in the end giving way under the pressure of bad harvests, economic weakness, the presence of a standing army, and Scots resistance to the persecutions beginning in 1638.
210. Clarke, *Old English*, p. 220.

CONCLUSION

The court of castle chamber was at the heart of the disturbed politics of Ireland from October 1629 when Cork and Loftus became lords justices, until October 1641 when the rebellion broke out in Ulster and Leinster. It is therefore nearly impossible to separate the judicial operation of the court from its political matrix. The rival lords justices in 1629 were accused of partisanship and corruption and their work was often undermined by appeals to the crown. Furthermore, the court heard cases of affront to public order and indignity to crown officials that certainly captured the attention of Wentworth as he made plans to become chief governor in 1633. The lord deputy charted a new course for Ireland, using the court of castle chamber as an instrument of arbitrary rule after he deceived the parliament in 1634 and thereafter sought to govern by act of state, in contravention of the Graces and constitutional norms. Though he compiled a lengthy and important series of castle chamber decrees for his use as chief governor, the records of the court are entirely missing for his regime and must be pieced together from fragments in the state papers and from highly partisan accounts. Nonetheless, the petition books from his period in office show a concern for systematic adjudication of grievances at the highest level, and Wentworth signed thousands of documents that called his attention to the humblest request. His employment of the court of castle chamber as the instrument of tyranny is somewhat exaggerated, since he used the court-martial against Mountnorris, and sat alone in arbitrary judgement against the Galway jury. He threatened Cork with a castle chamber suit, but the matter was resolved prior to formal adjudication. Wentworth's exploitation of prerogative justice operated for only five years (1633–38) prior to the outbreak of war with the Scots, and the constitutional crises which he precipitated in Ireland overwhelmed both the courts and his own administration. The sudden withdrawal of Wentworth from the government and the coherent attacks on his policies by the parliaments of both England and Ireland led to the dénouement of the court of castle chamber and a long period of desuetude after 1641. The death knell of the court was quietly inserted in a proclamation of the Irish privy council made on 27 October 1641, when the Michaelmas term was adjourned until the next year, with all matters in the courts of chancery, wards and castle chamber to have continuance.[211] Though mentioned infrequently during the period of war and rebellion, there is no evidence of new adjudication before the court beyond 1641 and the suspension of its business silently became permanent.

---

211. *Corporation book of Youghal*, ed. Caulfield, pp. 212–13. The Irish council expressed its fear of a 'concourse of people' coming to Dublin from all over the kingdom, imperilling the government and reducing its defences, while promising that all payments due to the crown must continue to be paid.

The court in quiet disrepute

EVIDENCE FOR THE CONTINUED operation of the court of castle chamber after 1641 is extremely thin. Its royal prerogative doubtful, the privy council nonetheless continued to operate as the executive arm of a government in turmoil and rebellion. On 23 January 1641, the lords justices and council gave order for the continued operation of the mills at Kilmainham in order to provide corn for the army. Noting that the mills were in bad repair due to the neglect of the miller, Francis Macavey, who was in open rebellion against the king, the council took the mills into their responsibility. The order required that Sir John Temple, master of the rolls and privy councillor, should receive the mills and place them in the hands of a competent miller. The incumbent lessee from Macavey should be compensated from profits of the restored mill by Temple, after repairs were duly made, with any further profits reserved to the king's use.[1] In a subsequent report on the matter made in 1643 by the council, Temple was accused of corruption, having used the miller's interest for himself, defrauded the king of his profit, and keeping much corn from the army's use. After Macavey had been outlawed for treason in the previous Hilary term, the rent of £200 owed by his tenant to the crown was concealed by Temple, who was called to account for profiteering.[2] This case demonstrates an ongoing role for the council, acting as a court, in the punishment of maladministration, the traditional role of the castle chamber. It would suggest that the court of castle chamber, now subsumed within the council, continued to function sporadically according to traditions that pre-dated its foundation in 1571 under Elizabeth I. However, since the evidence does not show that a trial was held, it is difficult to state that this function was inherently judicial in nature, and the record seems to indicate that the council was proceeding by executive authority.

In 1647, the judge of the general judicature for the Leinster committee, working under the auspices of the Confederation of Kilkenny, ordered the auditor-general to pay certain judges and civil pensioners for work done. This brief notation, as we have already had occasion to observe, called for fees to be paid 'for copies of all sorts of pleadings and depositions as well in the Castle Chamber as in Chancery'.[3] Mentioning the work of the philizer and cursitor in

1. *Cal. S.P. Ire., 1633–47*, p. 382. This order was signed by Temple himself, along with Lords Justices Borlase and Parsons, and Councillors Loftus and Robert Meredith.
2. Ibid. Temple had purchased a legal interest in the mill itself in the interim, on a grant from the king which concealed the previous actions of the council in Ireland.
3. Ibid., p. 752.

both chancery and castle chamber, the order set down the fees to be levied for certificates and writs out of those courts. However, there is no evidence that the court of castle chamber continued to function as a tribunal in this period, and references of this sort might be interpreted to mean simply the venue located in Dublin Castle, long used for the tribunal. The supreme council of the Confederation of Kilkenny combined administrative, executive and judicial functions. The council acted as the final court of appeal, hearing cases in criminal jurisdiction, and attempting to govern through an emasculated version of the justices of oyer and terminer in the provinces.[4]

At the Restoration, while the reinstatement of the court of castle chamber was being debated in the corridors of Whitehall, its officials were guaranteed payment of their sinecures. In 1666, the civil list for the Irish court of star chamber named Sir George Lane as clerk, to be paid £10 per annum, along with George Rutledge, marshal of the court, who also received £10 as his fee.[5] Three years later, Secretary Arlington inserted in the king's civil list another reference to the fees of these two superannuated functionaries, demanding that their fees be paid along with those of the puisne justices, despite the report of a committee recommending retrenchment of the Irish bureaucracy.[6]

From the work of Dr Barnard on Cromwellian Ireland, we learn that law reform was inspired by resentment against the payment of exorbitant fees in common law tribunals, the power of lawyers and archaic judicial usages, rather than allegations of tyranny by the central courts.[7] The Catholic clergy in 1649 requested the reintroduction of assizes, quarter sessions and conventional judicial means for the redress of grievances.[8] However, the law reforms of the Cromwellian period witnessed experiments such as commissioners for justice in Leinster and the other provinces, pursuing an *ad hoc* strategy of judicial intervention. Over time, they employed experienced former judges and the justices of the peace gradually regained their local authority by 1655.[9] The complete restoration of the legal system with the revival of the four courts in 1655 was not matched by the restoration of the court of castle chamber or other prerogative tribunals, despite the intent to bring back the system of 1641.[10] Chancery was reestablished in 1656, and the aim of returning to the traditional courts of justice – thereby improving access to legal remedy – embraced the fundamental principles of the common law.

General suspicion attached to veteran judges such as Sir Gerard Lowther, yet few qualified men would leave England for an Irish post, so genuine reform was

4. Michael Ó Siochrú, *Confederate Ireland, 1642–49: a constitutional and political analysis* (Dublin, 1999), pp. 49–50, 207, 218. No attempt to revive the court of castle chamber was made by the Kilkenny government.
5. *Cal. S.P. Ire., 1666–69*, p. 74.   6. Ibid., p. 728.
7. T.C. Barnard, *Cromwellian Ireland: English government and reform in Ireland, 1649–1660* (Oxford, 1975), p. 256. Barnard asserted, 'War, and the rival political authorities in Ireland, dislocated the legal network between 1641 and 1649.' Ibid.
8. Ibid.   9. Ibid., p. 257.
10. Ibid., p. 259.

thwarted, despite ambitions to elevate the practice, and thus the quality, of the Irish legal system.[11] In the latter stages of the Protectorate, the council itself was described by Henry Cromwell to Secretary Thurloe on 9 September 1657 as hopelessly deadlocked, 'a meere faction of three against three', implying that any concerted action as a prerogative court was beyond their abilities.[12]

With the Restoration in 1660, the four courts resumed normal operations after a hiatus of some months, but the court of castle chamber itself remained moribund. Parliamentary efforts to revive it were adumbrated in correspondence from 1661 to 1669. In May 1663, for example, the new lord lieutenant, the earl of Ormonde, and the Irish council wrote from Dublin to Secretary Bennett that, among other bills being sent for approval in advance of the meeting of the house of commons, a bill 'for punishing several officers in the King's Court of Castle Chamber' was to be transmitted.[13] And although a second letter of 9 September 1663 referred to approval of the bill,[14] the lord lieutenant wrote to Bennett in November that all the bills in question would have to be deferred. The bill for renewal of the court of castle chamber, along with bills regulating the customs and for confirmation of marriages, waited while the Act of Settlement was being prepared for parliament. Judging that none of the bills would pass into law if the alterations then under consideration for the Act of Settlement were made chargeable to the country, such as payment of soldiers and adventurers, the viceroy made plain that any tendentious legislation would have difficult sailing in the Irish parliament of the Restoration.[15] Meanwhile, the king was beset with lawsuits seeking to overturn decrees of the court dating from the tenure of the late earl of Strafford. In May 1662, Lord Athenry and Sir John Bourke petitioned the crown to have set aside the remainder of the fine imposed by castle chamber on the Galway jury that refused, in spite of Strafford's threats, to find title for the crown in the celebrated case heard before the lord deputy at Portumna. Alleging that most of the fine had been paid, and that Charles I had remitted the remainder, the petitioners claimed that process had lately been issued against heirs of the jurymen for payment of the remaining fine. The king wrote on behalf of the heirs to require that the fines be remitted, as his father had arranged, thus undoing the work of castle chamber some seventeen years after the original jury was empanelled in Co. Galway.[16]

Tantalizing fragments of information from the reign of James II and later suggest that the court of castle chamber maintained a phantom presence in the archives long after it ceased to function as a tribunal. For example, instructions for

---

11. Ibid.

12. *Thurloe state papers*, vi, 505–06. Thanks are due to Professor Osborough for this reference.

13. *Cal. S.P. Ire., 1663–65*, p. 81.   14. Ibid., p. 261.

15. Ibid., p. 289.

16. *Cal. S.P. Ire., 1660–62*, p. 540. A similar suit to the king by the new earl of Cork requested that lands in Dublin, alienated to the estate of the earl of Strafford, be restored to the heirs of Cork. Ibid., p. 327.

the lords justices in Ireland sent on 27 March 1685 called for the reestablishment of the court: 'Whereas of late there has been a discontinuance of the Court of Castle Chamber, you shall take the matter into your serious consideration and see that it be restored and made use of according to law.'[17] This admonition was repeated in the instructions for Henry Hyde, second earl of Clarendon,who was sent as lord lieutenant to Ireland in October 1685.[18] Whether this was occasioned by a perceived need to deal with seditious libel on the accession of James II, as suggested by Professor Osborough in private correspondence with this author, the court apparently remained dormant throughout the period in question. In 1688, Lord Deputy Tyrconnell brought allegations of corruption against his personal secretary, Thomas Sheridan, leading to a private hearing on the matter by a committee of four judges, with Lord Chancellor Fitton presiding. This *ad hoc* treatment of semi-official misfeasance would probably have been heard in the court of castle chamber during its heyday, so perhaps we can accept this irregular proceeding as further evidence of the court's demise under the later Stuarts.[19]

Subsequent references to the court of castle chamber in Ireland are few, and often lack historical accuracy. However, the general concept of a star chamber jurisdiction and its tyrannical manipulations of prerogative law, were embedded in judicial dialogue. For example, in a case of 1784, John FitzGibbon, the then attorney-general brought a motion to attach the high sheriff of Co. Dublin, one Reily, for illegally summoning a meeting of freeholders to press for parliamentary reform. One of the judges took the opportunity to remark that, although '17 Car. I took away Star Chamber' it was thereafter accepted that 'any crime previous to that Act punishable in Star Chamber' was 'now punishable in King's Bench'. It is clear from the text that the Irish judge was referring to the statutory abolition of the English court, perhaps inferring that the Irish court was included in this general proscription.[20] Opponents of Sunday golf at Portrush in Co. Antrim protested in a case of 1923, seeking the intervention of the chancery division of the Northern Ireland high court, and basing their lawsuit on the Sunday Observance Act of 1695. Judge Wilson declined to take up the case, arguing that to do so would once more 'set in motion the criminal jurisdiction of the Star Chamber'.[21] Gratuitous references to an Absolutist style of star chamber proceeding are abundant even in contemporary sources. In one case of 1992, *Goodman International* v. *Mr. Justice Hamilton*, it was argued that the act of 17 Charles I, c. 10 (1640) abolishing star chamber in England reflected 'an abhorrence of inquisitorial process of justice and compulsory self incrimination'.[22]

17. *Cal. S.P. Dom., 1685*, pp. 110–14. I wish to acknowledge, with thanks, for this and subsequent citations, the researches of Professor Osborough in the modern archives.

18. Ibid., p. 397.

19. The judges' report is printed in *Anal Hib*, no. 1 (1930), pp. 46ff, and the matter is discussed by John Miller in 'Thomas Sheridan (1646–1712) and his "Narrative"', *IHS*, xx (1976), 105. See also J. Miller, 'The earl of Tyrconnell and James II's Irish policy 1685–88', *Hist Jn*, xx (1977), 803.

20. *The King* v. *Reily*, Ir Term Rep 204, 225.   21. *Watt* v. *McLoughlin* [1923] 1 IR 112, 120.

22. [1992] 2 IR 542, 574. Counsel mistakenly referred to the legislation as an act of 6 Charles I.

Ironically, the meek and apologetic defensiveness of the Irish privy council during the impeachment proceedings of 1640 and after did little to mitigate the reputation of a court feared as a symbol of private malice and public pugnacity under Wentworth. Despite occasional references to an Irish star chamber after 1641, there is no evidence that it continued to function as a court.[23] Following the Restoration, the court was viewed as part of the Absolutist superstructure of the early Stuart viceroys such as Chichester and Wentworth, who exploited the tribunal to achieve their own policy ends, alienating the majority of Irish subjects in the process. Lacking a death warrant, the court of castle chamber experienced an end that suited its ambiguous and uncertain beginning. The undoing of Sydney and Wentworth as chief governors was prophetic for the subsequent dismantling of their prerogative tribunal, demonstrating that, in practice, the exalted reputation of Absolutist rule in Ireland was grounded in a fragile connection to king and court. And the opposition movements to both regimes made the most of common law resistance to conciliar jurisprudence, charging that the Irish star chamber was a menacing exception to the rule of law. Ironically, the growing resort to adjudication, and to constitutional objections to the operation of the prerogative courts, was a sign of the vitality and success of common law principles in Ireland and proved the court's undoing.

Changes to the legal system during the land agitation of the 1880s, it also merits recording, drew condemnation from opponents of the government on the grounds that these changes introduced 'star chamber' procedures. Specially targeted was the provision for free-ranging criminal inquiries entrusted to magistrates under the terms of section 1 of the Criminal Law and Procedure (Ireland) Act 1887. See, for example, Timothy Harrington, *A diary of coercion being a list of cases tried under the Criminal Law and Procedure Act*, 3 parts (Dublin, 1888–90), passim.

23. The recent volume edited by Jane Ohlmeyer on Irish constitutional history after 1640 contains no references to the court from that period, apart from Dr Clarke's discussion of the Queries. J. Ohlmeyer, ed., *Irish political thought in the seventeenth century* (Dublin, 2000).

The entry book of orders and decrees of the court of castle chamber, 1571–1621

The names of those psons as Wear founde gylti [by] Indytement. viz
Barnabe Comiske of Tarmonfekin   xiij s iiij d str
Willm Maglassan   X [i.e. crossed out, not 'ten']
David Kernan de eadem, cott[ager] vj s. viij d. str
Patrick Omelaghlen xxvjs. viij d. str
Collo Okyllie de eadem, cott[ager] vj s viij d. str
Thoms Goodman xiij s viij d. str
John Merneghan de eadem vjs viij d. str
Neill Omolegan ijs vj d ster
Melaghlen boy McCraner ij s vjd. str
Patricke McGillero de ead[em], cott[ager] x s. str
John Cosvaghan   X [crossed out]
Patricke Cosvaghan vi s viij d str
John Crille de eadem, Cottyer xxiij s viij d. str
John Doyne of Kilclogher, cottier iijs vjd str
Patricke McIlawe de Cruston [blank]
Cahill McGawre de Kilclogher vj s viij d str
Meghell Durnan de Baltra vjs viijd str
Wm McGenett of Tarmonfekon   xxvj s viij d str
Patricke McGuire [of] Callistone   vj s viijd str
Gilduff Omiry[?] de eadem xxvj s viij d str
Richard Keran de eadem xlvj s iiij d str
Thoms McKamie [of] Castlecow xiiij s iiij d str
Patricke Comiske of Almerton
Dowle OFegan of Tarmonfekin   X [crossed out]
Patricke Plunkett de eadem, gent xx li str
Patricke Helie Jun[ior] de eadem xxvj s viij d str
John Staffe[? 'S' crossed out in MS, hence: Taffe] de eadem vjs viij d str
John McNewry de eadem x li
Collo O Boyle de Almerton xvj s viij d str
Donough McGillane de Baltray
Edward Delinge of Tarmonfekin
Neill McKrill de Kilclogher   [all crossed out with single large 'X']
Conoher McDermott de eadem
Thomas McMahon de Baltra
Neill McGrogan of Termonfekin xiij s iiij d str
Laghlen Gormeyle de Kilclogher xiij s iiij d str
Willm Hire de eadem ij s vj d str

[original signatures of court] WFitswylliam, Adam Dublin custos sigilli, H Miden, Edw Fyton, Lucas Dillon, N Whyte, Francis Agarde[1]

1. BL, Add. MS 47,172, f. 1. There is no date in manuscript. Another series of pagination begins on f. 1 as page 17, which continues in series with pages 18, 19 and so on through p. 60. This suggests that there are missing

The names of such personnes as in there severall answers have confesssed to be at the spoyle of the said shippe [no explanation of the litigation or why fines occur at castle chamber], viz

Turlogh McNemy[?] xxvj s viij d str
Owen O McKame xxvj s viiij d str
Walter Plunkett xxvj s viij d str
John Raylie vij s viij d str
Edward Plunkett, gent xl li str
John Manninge, gent vj li vj s viij d str
Henry Morgan v li str
Joane Eny McMahon X [crossed out]
Patricke McCartan xiij s iiij d str
Peyre Manninge xxvj s iiij d str
Thomas McCartan of Bewly xxvj s viij d
Bele Mando, wieff to George Fitzjohn of Baltra, gent x li str
Patrick Welshagh xj s viij d
John Duffe vj s viij d
Turlaghe McQuorte xiijs iiij d
Patrick Muldane X
John Roderar   X
Manus Toyle [amount in MS blotted out]
Henrye Brodergan xiij s iiij d
Conor Hagan xiij s iiij d
Richard McKahill xxfj s viiij d
Turlogh Smyth   x li str
Patricke Lidde xxvj s viij d
Lawrence More, gent   vj li xiij s iiij d
Henry Quyn [blank]
Brian ODowde x li str
Patrick McKardell, horseman X
Robert Morgan iiij li
Patricke Quin iiij li
William Quyn xxvj s viij d.
Cowle McEnlue [blank]
Simon Brere xiij s iiij d
Donogh McLayne [blank]
Richarde Whyte [blank]
Walter Butterley xiij s iiij d
John McMahon de [?blank] X
Neill Rudde   X
John Connor ij s vj d
James Brim x li str
Thomas Dornam vj s viij d
Edmond Ronowe vj s viij d
Thomas Ronowe
Mighel Dornam
Patricke McCowrte
Cristofer Fitzjohn
John, also sundrye of Patrick Plunketts howsehold men.

cases which might have been entered for the earlier period, including up to 16 pages of text. However, these cases have not been found and no reference is made elsewhere to the existence of a missing text. Abundant references to the haphazard methods of record-keeping by the clerks of the court suggest that these and other documents may represent sizeable lacunae in the archival record. See below, ff. 67–67v, for references to cases in castle chamber of 1571 and 1572. Termonfeckin is in Co. Louth, the seat of the Protestant archbishop of Armagh until 1613, and Clogherhead (?Kilclogher) is a fishing village on the coast. Patrick Plunkett, gentleman, is the only person of substance named among mostly cottagers. Plunkett is also identified in the next case, but the names are otherwise entirely different.

[original signatures:] WFytswilliam, Adam Dublin custos sigillli, H Miden, Edw Fyton, Lucas Dillon, N White, Francis Agard.[2]

Itm where John Bathe esquyer her maties Solycytor of Lawes brought a bill of Ryott in this her maties honourable Court of Castlechamber against Danyell Roo and Patryck Taylor late servant[s] to Edward Cusack, gent, and others as by the said bill more at large doth and may appeare. And for as much as uppon the hearing of the said matter before us the L Deputy and Counsell in the said Court of Castlechamber whose names hereunder are wrytten, it appeared unto us by ther deposycons that the said Danyell Roo & Paricke Taylor were gyltye of the Ryott mencyoned in the said bill. It is therefore ordered and adjudged by us the said L Deputy and Counsell whose names are hereunder subscrybed to this order, that they shall pay to the quenes matie uses fortye shillinges a pece as a fyne, and also shall yeld ther bodyes prysoners to the castle of Dublin there to remayne till they shalbe dyscharged from thence by us. Geven at her maties castle of Dublin the fourth day of November 1573.

[signatures] WFytswylliam, Adam Dublin, H Miden, Tho Slane, Ed Fyton, Jo Plunkett, Lucas Dillon.[3]

Itm where Willm Clynche of the C [Ms. torn] Castle brought a bill of Ryott in this her maties honorable Courte of Castlechamber against Nicholas Russell, John Russell, Patryck Russell, Thomas Russell, Nicholas Russell Fitzthomas and John Kynsley, as by the said bill more at large doth and may appeare. And for as much as upon hearing of the said matter before us the L Deputie and counsell in the said Court of Castlechamber whose names hereunder are wrytten, it appeared unto us by there deposycons & other meanes that the said Nych[ol]as, John, Patrycke, Thomas, Nycholas Russell FytzThomas and John were gylty of the sayd Ryott mencyoned in the said bill. It is therefore by ys the said L Deputie and Counsell whose names are hereunder wrytten, ordered and adjudged that [blank] shalbe adwarded to the [?sheriff; MS torn] of the Countye of Dublin for ther app[re]he[nd]ing against the fyrst day of the next Easter [term; MS torn] whereby they may be comytted to her maties Castle of Dublin, there to remayne for [to] receyve punisshement as this said honourable Court shall thincke meete. And also to pay such Coste as shalbe taxed by the Right hon[or]able the L Kep[er] of the Great Seale of this [realm; MS torn]. Given at her maties court of Castlech[amber] the tenth of February 1574.
[signed] WFytswilliam, Roland Baltynglas, H Miden, Tho Slane, Edw Fyton, Jo Plunkett, Lucas Dillon.[4]

Idm where James Fitzgarrot of Damaston in the Countye of Dublin brought a bill of Ryott in this her highnes Court of Castlechamber against Edward Fitzmorrise of Blackhall in the Countye of Kyldare, gent, John Fitzmorrisse, Edmond Keating, James Reynold, Meylor More and Thomas Wogan as by the said bill more at large doth and may appeare. And for as much as upon the hearing of the said matter before us the L Deputye & Counsell in the said Court of Castlechamber whose names ar hereunto wrytten it appeared unto us uppon the pleadinges, deposycons & other matter that the said Edward Fitzmorrisse, John Fitzmorrise, Edmond Keating, James Reynold, Meylor More and Thomas Wogan were gyltie of the said Ryott mencyoned in the said bill. It is therefore by us the said L Deputy & Counsell, whose names are hereunder wrytten, ordered, decreed and adiudged that the said Edward Fitzmorrisse shall pay or cause to be pd to the Clarke of this Court to her maties use at or at thys syde the last day of the next trynyte terme the some of fyve poundes Lawful money of Ireland. And the said Edward shall entr int[o] bond of Recognizaunce of one hundreth markes for to

2. f. 1v. Manuscript has no date. Alternate pagination continues as page 18; another foliation, probably later, begins f. 71 without explanation. Patrick Plunkett, gentleman, is named in case above, and the only two placenames, Baltra and Bewly, are also named above. Along with Kilclogher, perhaps modern Clogherhead, these were villages in Co Louth. Names of the judges in these two cases are identical, possibly indicating the two actions were heard at the same time and were integrally related.
3. f. 2.   4. f. 3.

bring in or cause to be brought in unto this Court the bodyes of the said John, Edmond, James, Meylor & Thomas & every of them at or at thys syde the fyrst day of the next Eastr terme to stand to such order as this said court shall adjudge. And shall yeld & pay to the said playntiffe all such costes and charges as shalbe taxed by the Right honourable the L kep[er] of the greate seale of this said Realme. Geven at her matie Court of Castlechamber the xijth daye of Februarye 1574.
[signed]W Fitzwylliam, N White, John Chaloner.[5]

Idm where a bill of Ryott was exhybyted in this most honourable Court by Richard Fynn and John Garrahall against Tybbott Walshe and others as by the same upon the phylaces remayning doth and may appear. For as much as uppon the reading of the pleadings, controversye & deposycons it cold not appeare to the Right honorable Sir William Fitzwyllyams, knight, L Deputy of this her highnes Realme of Ireland & the rest of her maties counsell in the sayde most honourable Court that the sayd Tybbott & the rest of the defendants did comytt any ryott in manner & forme as in the said bill was alledged. It was therfore ordered by the said L Deputy and those whose names are hereunto subscrybed that the said Tybbot & the rest of the sayd defendauntes shalbe dyscharged & recover such charges as the right honorable the L kep[er] shall taxe. Yeoven at her maties Court of Castlechamber the fyft day of May 1574.
[signed] W Fitzwylliam, N White, John Chaloner.[6]

Item where Sir Morrisshe Fitzgarold of Lecaghe, knight, brought a bill of ryott in this honorable Court of Castlechamber against Morroghe McTyrlaghe McHugh, Hugh McTyrlaghe McHughe, Caher Reagh McEdmond Carraghe, Owne McPhelyn Ryoughe, Leysaghe McOwney McTyrlaghe, Phelim McBreyne, Owne McEdmond, Moyle McJames, Edmond McDonell oge McAltyem, Donogh O Kelly McShane, Donoghe McTegg, McDonoghe OKelly, Gerrott McShane McDonell, Moyle OKelly, Donell Bane McShane, McMuroghe Duff, Owen Boye McOwen, [and] Rorye OCassye, servants to Owney McHughe of Ballybryttas, with divers other who did not appear. Forasmuche as it appeared evydently upon the pleadinges & depossycons that the forenamed defendaunts with such others as were in their company comytted the Ryott in manner & forme as the said bill purporteth. It is therefore ordred by the Ryght honorable the L Deputye and counsell whose names hereafter ensue that every of the forenamed def shall paye to her matie xxvj s viij d currant money of Irland for a fyne, and also a letter to the sayd Owney for brining in of them into this Court by the fyrst of the next trynytye terme. And also that they shall pay to the sayd pl such costes as shalbe taxed by the Ryght honourable the L Keper. Yeoven at her maties Court of Castlechamber the xxviiii [xxix]th day of Aprill 1574.
[signed] W Fitzwylliam, N White, John Chaloner.[7]

Idm where a bill of Ryott was exhibited in this most honorable Court of Castlechamber by John Garrahall the tenth of Aprill 1573 against Tybbott Walshe and fyfteene [others] as by the same doth and may appear. For as much as upon the Reading of the pleadinge and deposycons It cold not appeare to the Right honorable the L Deputy and the rest of her maties counsell whose names are hereunder wrytten that ether the said Tybbott or any other of the defendaunts spy[ci]fied in the said bill dyd comytt any ryott as the said bill purporteth. It is therfore ordered that the said def shalbe dysmyssed from the sayd Court & receveth such costes & charges as shalbe taxed by the Right honorable the L Kep[er] of the Great Seale. Yeoven at her maties Court of Castlechamber the xxiiijth day of May 1574.
[signed] W Fitzwilliam, N White, John Chaloner.[8]

5. ff. 3v–4.
6. f. 4v. See below ff. 7–7v for another case involving Garrahall as plaintiff.
7. f. 5.
8. f. 5v. See above f. 4v for nearly identical case nineteen days earlier, in which Garrahall was the only plaintiff and no date was given of the original trial. This was probably a subsequent record-keeping correction of the original case. See below ff. 7–7v for another case in which Garrahall appears as plaintiff.

Where order was taken in this most honorable Court of Castlechamber at the sute of Sir Morrysshe Fitzgarold of Lecagh, knight, against Morroughe McTyrrelaghe McHughe and dyvers others, servauntes to Owney McHughe of BallyBrittas, gent, as by the said order bearing date the xxviijth of April, 1574, signed with the hand of the Right honorable Sr Wm Fitzwilliams, knight, L Deputye, & other of the Counsell. Wherein it was ordered yt the said Owney shold bring into this said Court the psons named in the said order for the accomplysshing thereof. And for as much as he had two several Letters to lyke effect from the said Court & severall dayes of respyte for bringing in the said psons acording the said order the psons mencyoned in the same. It is therefore ordered that the said Owney shall pay all such fyne & fynes as is taxed (at or befor the fyrst day of hillary terme next) upon ev[er]y of them. Also such costes to the pty pl[aintiff] as shalbe taxed by the L Kep[er] of the greate seale. Yeoven at her maties said Court the fyrst day of Julye 1574.

[signed] W Fytzwylliam, Adam Dublin, custos sig, Jo Plunkett, Lucas Dillon, N White, John Chaloner.[9]

Memorandum whereas James Purcell, Edmond McTheobald, alias Tibbot, William Poer McWalter, Thomas Purcell, David Hobbeg, Conor Flynne, Dermot O Flynne, Shane McThomas Poer, Richard Jordan, William McMorishe, Thomas Pheolan, Thomas Boy McMorish O Dowan, Morishe McEdmund Brenaghe, Shane McMorishe, Shane Moele McWilliam Poer, Richard Kealichan, Edmund McThomas Poer, Edmund McDonill O Flynne, Nicholas Poer, Shane O Morisee, William McMorisee, Shane McTeig, Morraghe O Sheaster and Sir William Holmes were sued in this most honourable Court of Castlechamber by Nicholas Ley of Waterford, merchant, in a cause of perjurie. For as muche as the parties defendants according to his allegation in his bill and the rest of his pleadings p[roo]fes and examinacons in the courte against the said Def[endant]s by him proponed could not in that said cause of periurie be found giltie. It is therfore ordered yt the right honourable Sir Willm FitzWillms, knight, L Deputie of thes her maties realme of Irland and the rest of hir maties privie counsell in that her said realme in that said Courte assembled for the deciding of that cause whose names hereafter ensue, ordred and decreed that the forenamed def[endant]s shalbe acquited from the said action of periurie and dismissed from the said courte with suche costes and chardges as shalbe taxed to them in that behalf by the most reverend father in god Adam, L Archbishop of Dublin, L Keper of her maties great seale in this realme. Geven at her maties said Courte of Castlechamber the third of November 1574.

[signed] W Fytzwylliam, H Medensis, Lucas Dillon, N White, John Chaloner.[10]

Idm where John Garrahall, pl, brought a bill of ryott in this most honorable Court of Castlechamber against Willm Ashepoole of Kenleston, gent, Edmond McSyrmourghe, Tegg McDonell, Richard Asshepoole, Dermott McDonell, Hugh McMourghe Glasse, Thomas Walche, Hugh Cullon, Thomas Moyle, Donogh Kelly, Rychard McDonoghe, James McGarrott, Tyrrelaghe Englysshe, Shane Reaghe, Shane McWilliam, Shane Kearde, Donell Boye, Patryck Duffe, William McTybbott, Hughe Fynne, Dermott Tressye, Hughe McTegg Duffe, Thomas Rowe, Dermott More, Hubbert Duffe, Edmond Carraghe, Hugh McPadyn and others def[endants], as by the said bill and several ther ?rate [i.e. pleadings] annexed, bearing Date the seventh day of October 1573, Doth and maye more playnely appeare. In which sayd matter p[ar]tes dyscended to an yssue, interrogatoryes Drawen, witnesses produced for the tryall of the said Ryott publysshed and heard at Large in the said Court. And for as muche as it appeared evydently uppon the debating of the said matter to the right honorable Sir William Fitzwilliams, knight, L Deputie of this her maties Realme of Irland & the rest of her maties counsell then & there in the said Court whose names are hereunto subscrybed that the defendautntes above named were gyltye of the sayd ryott in manner and forme as in the bill is set fourthe. It is therefore ordered, decreed, and adjudged by the said L Deputie and Counsell whose names are hereunder wrytten that the said Wm Ashepoole shall pay to the quenes matie for a fyne the some of twentye poundes current money of Ireland, and every of the rest of the defendauntes Fortye

9. f. 6. See above fol. 5 for earlier case, commanding defendant to bring in some seventeen of his servants, convicted of a riot, to appear in court by the first of Trinity term. He was subsequently forced to pay their fines of xxvj *s.* viij *d.* Irish for each person, and costs of court.
10. f. 6v.

shillinges of lyke money. And it is further ordered, decreed and adiudged that the sayd Wm shall bring in the sayd def and every of them into this court for ther imprysonment within fo[rt]night after the date of this sayd order. And also it is likewise ordered that so many of the defendauntes as shall not be founde or able to pay such fyne or fynes as is taxed uppon them that the sayd Willm shalbe aunswearble for the sayd fyne or fynes. Yeoven at her maties Court of Castle Chamber the fyft day of November 1574.

[signed] W Fytzwilliam, H Miden, Lucas Dillon, N White, John Chaloner.[11]

Idm where a bill of Ryott was exhibited in this most honorable Court of Castlechamber by Edmonde Butler of Callan in the Countye of Kylkennye and Walter Archer the younger the xxvth of Januarye 1573 against Thomas Rothe FitzRobert, John Roth FitzRobert, Lawrence Archer, Patryck Ragged, Walter Roth Fitzrobert, Lawrence Archer, Patryck Martyn Archer, James Garrott, James Roth FitzRobert, Willm Langlen, Thomas Langlen, Willm Comerford, John Roth Fitz Davyd, Walter Marshall Fitz Robert, Thomas Raghter, Richard Ragged Fitz Patryck, Edmond Purcell, Elysus Shethe, Mahowne Donell, Tegge O'Bryen, Davyd Kyrryne, Patryck Kellye, William McEdmond, Mallage Roddyne, John Fitz John, Patrick Ro O'Kelly, Henry Droughe, Thomas Seix, Nycholas Ragged Fitz Patrycke,Thomas Walshe,William Marshall, John Garrott, Richard Kathewill, Robert Murfye, Walter Coursye, Nicholas Donyll FitzThomas, Nicholas Keoghe, Padyn Roth, Davyd Hanraghane, Patryck Fossard, Richard Flemyng, Mallache Clery, Donoghe O'Martyne, William O'Martyne, Walter Ragged, Patrick Brenaghe, Mortaghe Cormycke, Thomas Beerye, Thomyne Owre and Dyvers others as by the said bill and psonall answers doth and may appeare in which said matter the ptyes descended to an yssue, witnesses of the ptyes pleynetyffe examyned & publysshed, Day of hearing graunted, at which day the sayde def pleaded the quenes maties pardon word for word as hereafter followeth. Thereunto the sayd Thomas Roth Fitz Robert, John Rothe Fitz Robert, Lawrence Archer, James Garrett the rest of the def by ther Attourney Thomas Brownell doth say that of the Ryot, Rowte, unlawfull assembly and all other offences conteyned in the bill or informacon supposed to have been commytted by them or any of them contrary to her maties peace they nor any of them ought not to be impeached nether ought any iudgement for the sayde offence or any of them be gyven against the said def or any of them for they and every of them by ther said Attorney doth saye that long tyme after the said Ryott Rout unlawfull assembly and all other p[re]misses supposed to have byn commytted by them, and sythenes [since] the last contynuance of this sute or soveraigne lady the quenes matie that now is by her lettres patent sealed with her greate seale of Ireland of her speciall grace & mere mocon hath pardoned & released to them & to every of them severally all manner of Ryote, Rowte, mysprysons, conseirace [conspiracy], confederace, supportinge oppressyons, trespasses, contemptes, extorcons, unlawful uttering of wordes and all other misleharges [?misdemeanors] crymes and offences by them or any of them before the xxvijth day of June in the xvjth yere of her maties Raigne don or comytted and all maner indytements, condempnacons, Judgementes, execucons against them or any of them to be graunted or gyven by reason of the p[re]misses or of any of the same as by the said letters patentes dated at Dublin the vijth day of July in the xvjth yeare of her maties Raigne showed in this court more at large may appeare the tennor of which Letters patentes hereafter doth ensue. Elizabeth dei gra Angl France & Irland Regnia fidei defensor etc. [hereafter ensues a formal pardon in Latin, reciting the names of defendants as above, and adding the following names: Willm Hanraghan, Patricio Conreyne Nevers, John Loghname, Denis Kyrwane, Thome Nolan, Edo Mounsell, Morgano Coltane, Willo Learyse, Jacobo Nolan, cotters, Henry Dolsen, Morgano Craghe, Patricio Doneyng, Walter Newer, Willm FitzDemos(?), Patricio Brenaghe, alias Walshe Taylor, Oweno McDonogh, medice, Robt Joyne, clerico, Walter Archer, Junior, Edw Shortall de Kilkenny, per de generoso, Donoughe Moy, John Convey, Gerott Cogly Masens, Patricio Roo, Bowchers, Willo Lang, Thome Dullany, Thome Ragged, John Dullany, Thome Byary Smythes, Peter Joynor, Denis Drygan, Donaldo Oge, John Fitz Phillipp, yeoman, Donogh Nolen, Willo Marten, glovers, Thome Boughome, alias Owre, yeoman, Robt Power, glover, Thome Dowlery, John Murphy, Rico Mondy, Clement Walshe, merc, Edo Brenane, Shewmaker, John Harrold, Malage Vonane, John Vonane, yeoman, Willo Neyle, Bowcher, Jacobo Brytt, John Neyle,

11. ff. 7–7v. See above for two earlier entries wherein Garrahall was plaintiff in actions of riot during 1574. It is likely this was another pleading of the same cause of action, although over 27 defendants were named in this case, whereas some 15 were cited in the earlier entries.

Ph[ilip]o Cloell] apud Dublin vij die July Anno regni usi xvj of the which her maties gracyous letters patentes of pardon the said def and every of them prayeth allowaunce & by everie of the same to be by this honorable Court of the premisses dysmissed which accordingly was graunted and the sayd def dysmissed from this Courte. Provyded yet nevertheless that they shall pay to the said pl such costes and charges as shalbe taxed by the L Kep[er] of the greate seale. And such fees & duties to the Clarke of this Courte & other offycers as in lyke cases or by lawe is dewe. Yeoven at her matie Court of Castlechamber the xijth day of November 1574.

[signatures] WFytswylliam, Roland Baltinglas, T Amriachan, H Miden, Tho Slane, Edw Fyton, Jo Plunket, Lucas Dillon, John Chaloner, N White, J Garvey.[12]

Apud Dublin xiij die Augusti 1576 Regni Regine Elizabethe xviijo. For the matter in controversie betwixte Donalde O Dolane and Redmond O Ferrall, complainantes, and Sir Wm O Kerroll, knyght, defdt. Forasmoche as the saied Sir William hath confessed the taking awaye of Nombers of kyne from the posession of the complainantes, alleging the same to be the goodes of John Bourke. Forasmoche as the complainantes deposed upon the holie Evangelist that the same kyne so taken awaye weare the severall goodes of the saied compl and ther tenantes and no parte of the goodes or Catteles of the saied Bourke, and have also deposed that the saied Severall kyne, horses and garrons as are subscribed weare taken from eyther of them. Therefore and for that the saied Defendants hathe shewed no Leafull or Sufficient Cause for takinge of the same awaye and that the pore tennantes of the saied complts for want of the same Cattell are greatlie dystressed. It is by the L Deputie ordered that the saied Sir Wm O Kerroll shall bringe or Cause to be brought all and singuler the Cattell Subscrybed, beinge the verie same Cattel taken awaye and no other, to Loraghe in Ormonde, in the Countie of Tipperarie, the last of this August, and ther and then the same Cattell and evrie of them to delyver unto the said comp[lainants] or souche as they shall sende for them. And shall alsoe at the same tyme restore to the compl and ther tenantes the appearell and pannes Subscrybed. And it is furder ordered that the said Sir William O Kerroll shall paie to the said Complainantes for everie houre that he shalll faile to delyver at the Saied Daye twentie shillinges str. And for the Matter of Ryote, woundinge and hurtinge dyvers of the tenantes of the complainants, the same is referred to be harde and ordered in the Castell Chamber. The said Sir William O Kerroll to be bownde in Land of Recognizance of vc ^{li} [£500] for his apparence the first of the nexte tearme before the L Deputie and Counsell or the L Chancellor and counsaile in the saied Courte for proceadinge in the saied Ryott, and so appearinge, not to departe without lycence. And farder it is ordered that a comyssion shalbe dyrected oute of the saied Court of Castell chamber to Captaine Collyer and Captaine Strange to examyne souche wytnesses as the Compl shall bringe before them, as well to prove what other yonge Cattell was taken from them and ther tenantes, which nowe they knowe not, and the valewe of the same, as allso that all the same Catell weare the proper goodes of the same Compl and ther tenantes. And farder to examyne souche witnesses as the defendant shall bring to prove the same Cattell to be the goodes of John Bourke. [no signatures]

[underwritten:] The number of kyne, horses and apparel taken from Donald: lxxxxvj kine; iiij caples; j colt. Nine pannes and the apparel of lxxxiiij tenants. Such as is taken from Redmonde O Ferrall: lxxxxix kyne, ij garrans, ij horses.[13]

By the L chauncellor assisted wth others of her Maties previe counsell whoes names are hear unto subscrybed in her Maties Castell Chamber of Dubline the xxviij of August 1576.

Whereas sondrie grevous complaintes have ben exhibited unto the right honorable the L Deputie of this Realme, as well in generall clayme of the whole countie of Wexford, as in particular in bills by Thomas Masterson, esquier, Seneschall of the Lyberties of that countie and Bryan McCayher McArte Cavenaghe, eche of them against the other, and the servantes, followers and complices of eche of them, as for whom they are holden to answeare, as well for the supposed wrongfull occupienge or disturbinge of the rightfull occupacon, Mainrante [mainrent] and possession of certen landes and tenementes in that Countie claymed and Challenged by the saied Bryan McCagher as his enheritance and freeholde by sondrie dyscentes frome his auncestors and claymed by the saied

Thomas Masterson by force of a lease for tearme of yeares to hime as syned by Rychard Synote of Ballibrenan in that Countie, Esquier, and to him the saied Richard demysed and graunted for yeares yet to come by the Quenes Matie, as allso for dyvers Manslaughters, Robberies, Spoiles, Ryotes and dysturbances of her maties peace on eyther parte complayned of to have ben commytted in that quarrell, and otherwyse of malicious and propensed purpose by them or their saied sarvantes, followers or complices as for whome they are holden to aunswere whoes names and factes beinge on eyther Syde particularlie obiected in wryting are in a scedule to this order annexed conteyned. Whearbie it apperethe as some of the saied factes have ben of either partie confessed, so dyvers of them denyed, all thoughe by former Commyssion either partie hath in sorte by some one or more witnesses proved the same as by the saied particular bookes annexed more playnelie appearethe. For the whiche severall Causes, aswell touchinge the Landes aforesaid as the saied severall wrongs, it is at this tyme ordered that for the quiet of the countie and preserving of her Maties peace untill farder order shalbe taken to Wheather of them in right of the land in controvesie doe belong, that either of them for themselves and their servantes, followers and complices, aswell alreadie confessed and knowne as allso whiche hearafter shalbe proved and knowne, to be souche as they are holden to aunswere for shall for and duringe the meane tyme and untill farder order be taken well and trewlie kepe her maties peace everie of them against the other, and that neither of them shall procure or abett anie other to the breache thereof, neither that they or anie of them or anie ther followers shall in the meane tyme commyt anie spoyle, praye or fellonyous offences the one upon the other or anie ther folloers or anie thinhabitants in the countie of Wexford or countie of Caterlaghe. And it [is] farder ordered in avoydinge of all occasions of the breakinge thereof that the saied Landes and tenementes in controversie shall for the meane tyme and untill farder order be taken remayne and be peaceable and quietlie in the severall Manurance, holdinges and possessions of everie of those which nowe have the same in manurance, holdings and possession, Without dysturbance of thadverse partie or of anie in ther name or by ther procurement. And as towchinge the severall Spoyles, Roberies, Murthers or Manslaughters wherewith everie of them have partyculerlie chardged thother and wherewith anie prosecution for the countie of Wexford hath Chardged the saied Bryan or Wherewith the saied Bryan hath Chardged the saied Countie Commytted sithence the last aryvall of the L Deputie into this realme of Irland, It is ordered that a commyssion withe the Scedule inclosed containinge everie of the saied wronges shalbe addressed to the persons subscribed, willing and commaunding them with convenient speade withe in xij dayes after the receipte of the saied commyssion to examine all souche Witnesses as either of the saied parties for themselves and ther followers shall bring before them proofe as well of the trothe of ther saied allegacons wherein the one of them have particulerlie chardged the other, or for or against the countie of Wexford and Caterlaghe by either of them Suggested, as allso for the better manifestacon of the trothe. Whether the persons in another scedule inclosed [in] whiche either of them have chardged thothers to be ther folowers, and by everie of them uppon ther othes denyed bye ther follwowers, in trothe or not. And it is farder ordered that if anie of the folloers or anie of them be indicted for anie of the offences aforesaid that everie of them shall at the next sessions not onelie bring thither the same person and persons, Leavinge him ther to Receave tryall, but allso rest answearable at all tymes for souche offences as they or anie of them shall Comite on and besyde the bringinge in of the bodies of ther saied followers to be answerable to Lawe. And it is farder ordered that the saied Commyssions within six dayes after thexecucon of the saied Commyssion shall so take order as all the Cattell dewlie proved before them by either of the said parties to be spoyled or taken shalbe restored to the right honors [owners] imedyatlie. And it is farder ordered that eyther of thes saied parties shall appeare again before the Lord Deputie, or in his absence the L Chauncellor, and counsell in the Courte of Castellchamber the first daye of the next tearme, then and ther to answeare ther Severall offences and to abyde such order as the Councell shall take for the same, and uppon ther apparance not to Departe withoute Lycence of the saied L Chauncellor and Councell. And for the better performance of this order, It is farder ordered that either of the saied parties, with sufficient sureties withe hime souche as the L Chauncellor and councell shall allowe of, shall enter into bandes to the Queenes matie in the some of one thowsande poundes for the dew performance of this order, and the saied comyssions to certyfie ther proceedings to the saied Court of Castellchamber the saied first daye of the saide tearme. And it is farder ordered that if the said Seneschall shall in the meane tyme of the said daye take the saied Bryan or anie of his followers for anie felonious offences, all thoughe the same be apparente to the saied Seneschall, that yet the saied Seneschall shall commyt and send hime or them so taken to the Gayole, ther by Lawe to receave ther Tryall, and not to execute anie of them by auctoritie of his Lawe Marshall. And it is

farder ordered that wheare the saied Thomas Masterson allegeth that he is in possession of the Landes and tenementes in a scedule annexed and subscribed by his name, And wheare the said Bryan Mc Cayher Lyckwise alleagethe that he is and hathe ben in possession of dyvers parcells of the saied Landes conteined in a Scedule and allso Subscribed Withe his name, that the saied Commyssions shall have auctoritie to examine all souche witnesses as either of them shall bringe before them in p[roo]fe of ther allegacons, and all souche proffs as either of them shall bringe to prove anie excepcons as either of them shall obiecte against the saied wittnesses, and the same deposicions to certifie the saied daye to thintent the saied L deputie and Councell maye therein take order not onelie to settell the possession accordinge to Justice, but allso to punishe souche of them as shalbe fownde by entringe into the possession contrarie to this order [to be]Infringers of this order.
Willm Gerrard, cancellarius.[14]

In the matter in varyence dependinge before the L Chauncelor and Cownsell in her highnes Courte of Castellchamber betwixte the Justice Talbote, pl, and Nicolas Nugent and others, defende[nts], beinge openlie harde and debated. Forasmoche as it is not thoughte to anie thre of the Cownsell of the saied Courte that the Wittnes on the pte of the saied complaynante doe sufficientlie p[ro]ve the contentes of thinformacon as the same Cownsell maye theruppon take order to convince [?convict]the defendants of any souche Riotte, forcyble entrie or unlawfull assemblye as in the same bill is surmysed. Therfore the Defende[nt] and everie of them are for the same matter dysmyssed oute of the saied Courte. Geven at her Maties Castell of Dubline [the] viijth daye of Februarie Ao dom 1577.
[signed] W Gerrard, Jo Plunket, [another indistinct].[15]

Wheras uppon complainte heartofore exhibited by the ryght honorable Thomas erle of Ormonde against certen strangers forthe unlading of certen wynes aswell within the Porte of Drogheda as allso within the porte of Dubline. The pryse wynes supposed to be dew to the saied erle not paied and ther severall answeares made to the said complainte and the longe debatinge of the matter beenge desended to hearinge before the late Lorde Chauncellor Doctor Weston in the Courte of Chancerie, and after [Weston] before Sir William Fitzwilliams and others of her highnes privie counsell within this Realme of Ireland by vertue of ltres dyrected from the Quenes Matie to the saied L deputie to call the same Matter before hyme and to heare and order the same. Severall orders weare taken against the severall straungers Whearbie the same strangers were ordered to paie to the saied Earle and his assignes the Pryse Wines within the saied order dew for the wynes brought into the saied Portes by the same straungers, and allso by the same order all strangers whoe shoulde at anie tyme after bringe unto either of the saied Portes of Dublin or Drogheda anie Wynes Weare ordered to paie to the saied Earle and his assignes pryse wynes as uppon syghte of the saied orders openlie showed in Courte more plainlie appeareth. And wheare after uppon Complainte made to the right honorable Sir Henrie Sydney nowe Lorde Deputie of this Relme that certen wynes weare broughte in by one Davide Colltherte, a straunger, and that William Barnewall bought the same wynes, and before the said Earle or his agente could make seisure caused the same to be brought to the keye of Dubline, requyringe in accomplyshment of the saied order to have delyverie of so moche of the saied wynes as shoulde be dew for price wynes. Whearuppon the saied Deputie graunted severall lttres to the mayor of the Cittie then beinge, to seise into his handes as sequestered ij tones of the saied wynes dew to the saied Erle for the prise wynes of the saied wynes so brought into the saied portes and unladen, And wheare petition hath ben made to the saied deputie that now is on the erles behalf for deliverie of the saied ij tones of wynes so sequestered to the saied erles assignes, Whearbie he myght have full execucon of the saied order, and that the saied Lorde Deputie hath referred the consideracon and order of the matter to us the Lorde Chauncellor and Counsell to be harde and determyned. And wheareas upon the hearinge and debatinge of the same matter it appeareth that the saied several orders so taken as is aforesaied remaine in full force And oughte to have ther perfecting untill by order the same be avoided, and that the saied Earle is untill that tyme to have the benefit thereof, and that it cannot be denyed but that thos weare the wynes of strangers Whoe, the order standing in force, ought to pay price wynes, and nothinge alleaged in stay of the execucon of the saied

14. ff. 14–16.   15. f. 16v.

order but that the wynes were unladen before seisure and that strangers ought to paie no pryse wynes, neither had paied anie, and that in discharge of strangers of paiement of prise wynes order had ben taken uppon lyke [occasion] against thearle of Ormonde his father in the Starchamber. Which allegacons the saied L Chauncellor and Councell waye not as materyall or of anie force to staie the execucon of the saied later orders beinge with souche delyberacon as is aforesaied set downe and ordered. Therfore the saied L Chauncellor and Councell called Patericke Goughe, late mayor of Dubline, who had the sequestracon of the wynes meaning to have chardged hyme with deliverie of the said ij tones sequestered to the Earle his agente accordinge to the effecte and in accomplishment of the saied order. And forasmoche as the saide Goughe in Open Court declared that at the tyme of the sequestracon he was mayor of the Cittie and delyvered the same as mayor to Walter Godwyne, crayn[or] of the said porte, to kepe in sequestracon accordinge to the dyrection of the saied ltres, and that the Crayner being sent for in open court confessed he so receved the same wynes, and beinge willed to deliver the same to the said earles agent, acknowledged that he had delivered one tone of the saied wynes to Nicholas FitzSymons withoute lycense of the Lorde Deputie and Counsell or consent of the saied Goughe. Therefore the saied Craynor is for his contempte comytted to the Castell of Dubline, ther to remayne untill he have delyvered that one tone remayninge, and allso a sufficiente Pawne in lieu of the other to the saied Goughe, the Earle his agent to remayne wth hyme the space of fyfty dayes and if defaulte of paiement be made to the saied Goughe of eyght poundes for the saied tone taxed by the Lorde Chauncellor and counsell as an indyfferent pryse for the saied wyne, confessed to be Rochell Wynes [i.e. from La Rochelle], then the saied Pawne to be by the saied Goughe praysed [appraised] and solde and therewith to make satisfaction to the saied Earle, and the overplus to restore to the Crayner. And it is farder ordered that if anie stranger shall bringe in at anie tyme hearafter and duringe souche tyme as the saied order shall stande in force anie wynes at or to anie of the aforesaied portes, that no person shall presume to take to Land anie of the aforesaied wynes by the spate of three daies, within which tyme the saied Earle his factor, agent or assygnes shall and maye come aborde anie souche vessell and ther accordinge to the Comon usadge Seale and make souche pryse wynes as shalbe dew to the earle for the same Wynes so brought into the saied porte and the same take and receave withoute interruption. And wheare they of the townes of Dublin and Drogheda have exhibited a bill against the saied Earle for the Reversal of the saied order, It is ordered that the saied Earle shall send his aunsweare to the same bill into the courte of Chauncerie at or before the tenthe of Maye. And if he faile by that tyme to send in the same answeare, then the saied Earle after that and until souche tyme as he shall so send in the saied answeare, to take no benefite by this order for execucon of the former orders. Yeoven at her maties castell of Dublin the fourthe daye of Februarie Ao 1577.
Willm Gerrard, canc.[16]

Wheare for the matter in variaunce betweene Matthew Talbote, Compl, and Henry Cusake and others, def, For a riote, affray and other misdemenors affyrmed to be Committed within the Cyttie of Dublin, And forasmoche as uppon the hearinge and debatinge thereof in open courte yt manifestlye appeared by suffycient proffs of wittnessses then redd before the right honorable the L Chauncelor of this her Maties Reallme of Ireland and other of her highnes Pryvie counsell then and there beinge in the sayde Courte, that the sayd Henry Cusake was giltye of the said Riotte Comytted in sort as in the saied Bill was alledged, wch uppon the hearinge with humble submission the said Henry Confessed. It is therefore ordered, decreed and adiudged by us the sayd L Chauncelor and counsell whose names are hereunder subscribed that the sayd Henry Cusake shall for his sayd offence be Comitted to Warde, there to remayne for the space of viij dayes for his imprysonment, and untyll he shall content and paye to her maties use the some of L li [£50] starlinge for his fyne, and untill he satisfye and paye to the pl the some of xvij li iiij s viij d ster for his Costes and damadges. Given at her maties Courte of Castellchamber the xth daye of Maye 1577.
[signed] Wm Gerrard, Adam Dublin, Lucas Dillon.[17]

Where Christopher Barnewall of Arrdestowne in the Countie of Meethe gent, beinge chardged that he latelie imparted amongest others to enquire for and on the behalf of the Quenes matie before her

highnes Chiefe Justice and sworne forman of the sayd Jurie beinge chardged to enquire for and on her maties behalf of suche matters as comenlie are geven in chardge, practised and devised howe he might touche and sclaunder the L deputie and Counsell for theire proceadinge with ymponinge of Cesse for the vyttlinge of the Soldiers and maintenance of the L deputies house, and which shewe of an inditement to further the practise of dyvers of the Countrye, then prepared to travell to England with Complaint to the Quenes Matie for the said matter of Cesse offred in Courte imperfecte noates to the sayd Cheife Justyce without consent of the jurie to indite the sayd L deputie and Counsell and that notwithstandinge warninge geven to him by the sayd Cheife Justyce, to beware how he should meddle with the states, yet having a Clerke assigned to him to wryte the presentment he Caused the sayd Clerke to drawe an inditement against the sayd L deputie and Consell for that they wrongefullie and extorcionslie had Contrarie to Lawe imponed the sayd Cesse, and not so satisfied caused another symple Clerke, to wryte under the sayd presentment, this sentence <Trissillian in tyme of kinge Richard the seconde was put to deathe for misconstruinge the lawes> and after came againe to the Barr offringe to have presented the same to the Chief Justyce by whose perswacon [persuasion] then crossed out the same. Uppon an other practise whereof beinge at severall tymes examined, hathe Confessed to the same alledginge that the other Jurors agreed to all Conteined in the sayd presentment savinge the Cause touchinge Trissillian which he invented of himself, not makinge the rest of the Jurie pryvie to the same. Forasmuche as upon the examination of the rest of the Jurie yt apperethe that the dyvers of them weare so simple as neither understoode theffect of the presentmente nor what the sayd Christopher ment thereby, savinge that as they alleadged he sayd yt was a matter for the wealthe of the Countrye, and that the presompteous dealinge to touche the state, and namelie in a cause onelie concerninge the service of her matie which he can in no wise aunswere but rather practised of will to sowe discention, sclaunder the magistrate and hinder her matie of that which to her Roiall prerogative belongethe, worthie of severe ponishement. Therefore it is ordered and adiudged by us the sayde L Chauncellor and Councell Subscribed that the sayd Christopher Barnwall shalbe Committed to warde there to remayne untill the xiiijthe of June next and then to be brought to the Castell chamber then and there openlie to Confesse his lewde and arrogant attempt to deale or meddle in Causes appteninge to the estate and humblye to reqyre the L deputie and councell of pardon & forgiveness & to make a lyke knowledge & Confession of his willfull incertinge of the Clause Concarninge howe Tresillian was put to deathe for misconstruinge the lawes, and wherefore he allowed with out makinge eny of the Jurie previe thereunto should so arrogantlie deliver upp the same to the Courte to remaine of recorde & to desyre those whom he ment to touche by the same of forgyveness, and after to returne to warde, there to remaine untill he shall paye to the quenes matie use the some of fifte poundes starlinge for his ffyne [crossed out in MS: and for the chardge of this Courte yeaven at her matie castellchamber the xxith of May 1577]
[signature] Willm Gerrard canc [lord chancellor][18]

Wheare for the matter in variaunce betweene John Pentnye of this cittie of Dublin merchaunt and Thomazene his wief pl and Lawrence Taaffe gent, Def, for the takinge awaie of the saied Thomazene from Dromiskene in the Countie of Lowthe and other misdemeanors affirmed to be committed by the saied def against the saied Thomazene. Forasmoche as the saied def came this daie unto the courte before us the L deputie and Counsell and there shewed forthe her maties gracious pardon dated at Droghedae the xijthe of October, in the seventeenthe yeare of [her] highnes Reigne, Whereuppon the Bill [aunsweare] and replicacon touchinge the saied matter was redd in open Courte, and then by us agreed that the saied Courte Coulde holde no further pley touchinge that Cause by reason the def was acquited by the saied pardon for the offences complained of as aforesaied. It is therefore ordered by us the saied L Deputie and counsell whose names are hereunder Subscribed that the saied def shalbe for this matter dismissed And doe also order, that he shall enter [withe sureties] into bondes of Recognizaunce to appeare and aunsweare, to any Complaint or Complaintes that the saiede Pentine and Thomaszene or either of them shall exhibite against them either before us the saied L deputie or any other her maties Courte or Courtes, touchinge this matter Complained of here in this Courte, as aforesaied [and doe also observe obey and performe all suche orders or decrees as shalbe taken therein either by us the saied L Deputie and Counsell or by eny

18. ff. 20–20v.

other Competent iudge before whom the saied matter shalbe Complained of as aforesaied]. Geven at her maties Courte of Castellchamber the xxiijth of October 1577.[19]

HSydney
Wheare uppon the informacon exhibited into this honorable Courte in the behalf of George Isshame of the Countie of Wexforde gent, against William Browne of Ballrancane in the saied Countie, gent, Waltere Browne, his brother, John Rocheffourde of Balletubberraghe, Nicholas Prendercast and Phillippe Roche of Tamon, in the Countie aforesaied, for a Riote, affraye and other misdemeanors by them Committed at Rosse uppon the saied George Isshame, wherein he was sore hurte and wounded as more at large in the saied informacon dothe and maye appeare. To whiche informacon the saied William Browne hathe made aunsweare and consideringe withe himself that yf he shoulde stand to iustice him self and the rest of the defendantes touchinge that matter and the same to be proved against him, should deserve the less favoure and therfore hathe made his humble submision withe his hand to the same in manner and forme followinge, To the right honorable the L deputie, William Browne of Balrancane in the Countie of Wexford esquire in most humble wiese beeng right penitent for evry his misdemeanors dothe submitt him self unto your honors Determinacon, whatsoever for and concerninge, a Riote informed against him before yor L and her maties Counsell in her highenes Courte of Castellchamber in the behalf of George Isshame of Brianstowne in the Countie aforesaied, wherein he protestethe eny his offence to proceed of noe contempte or prepensed malice whiche he humblie beseochethe yor L to consider, affirminge the same hereby to stand to and abide your honorable determinacon in the premisses aswell for him self as also for all and singuler his servauntes comprised in the informacon of the Riote aforesaied, most humblie beseching yor good L of yor accustomed goodnes, and Clemencie not onelie to accept this his humble submission but also to see the servauntes aforesaid discharged of the said Riote, your simpl bearing and satisffieng what so ever your L shall determine of or adward against him and them in that behalf and he according his most bounden duetie shall daielie praie for the prosperous preservacon of yor honorable estate longe to continue, uppon perusing of which submission, wei[ghi]nge the greate some of money that the saied Willm Browne is appoincted and ordered to paie to the saied George Ishame in consideracon and recompense of the greate hurtes and woundes he received in that ffraye and also the greate Loss and hinderaunce the saied Browne hathe otherwiese sustained, we have thought good that the saied Wiliam Browne and the rest of the defendantes for that matter shalbe dismissed fourthe of the saied Courte without any Further pleadinge in the same. And doe also order decree and adiudge, that the saied William Browne shall paye to the queenes matie as a Fyne for him self and the rest of the defendants the some of xiij li vj s. viij d. Irysh and shall also satisfie and paie to the handes of Robert Kendall, Clerk of the same Court suche Costs and Chardges as shalbe taxed for the presentinge of that matter by the most Reverent father in god Adam L archeBusshope of Dublin L keepere of her maties great seale of this reallme, Geven at her maties sayd Courte of Castellchamber the xiijth of November 1577.
[signatures]: T Armachan, Adam Dublin, H Miden, J Garvey[20]

HSydney [signature] By the L Deputie and Counsell.
Wheare uppon motion made before us in her maties highe Courte of Castellchamber against Robert Kendall her maties Clerke now beenge of the same Courte, For takinge and receyvinge of Fees whiche were suggested to be excessyve and the saied Clerke beeinge thereon in open Courte called to aunsweare, and iustifienge the takinge of the fees then in question to be none other then suche as for the most parte in former tymes by others the Clerkes of the saied Courte have beene receyved and taken and the same warranted also by order certified out of the Reallme of England under her maties greate seale of that Reallme. Yet neverthles wee we[igh]inge the disabilitie of a nomber of the sewtors followinge theyre Cauwses and sewtes in the saied Courte to be suche as yf some quallificacon of the rattes and Fees so formerlye ordered should not by us be sett downe and taxed in certaintie to avoyde the dislyke of the Complained excessyvenes, The same moughte in tyme growe

19. ff. 21–21v. The case was reported twice in the entry book, and the second entry contained some additional language which is here incorporated in brackets. The two entries are substantially identical.
20. f. 22. In margin: 'The sayd fyne is payd to the hands of Tho Say.'

to be overburdensome to those sewtors and ptyes sewed. It ys by us therefore considered, concluded, ordered and agreed in respectes the Fees Formerly taken and received either by the saied Clerke or eny other Officere or minister of that Courte accordinge to the order of the saied taxe certified owte of the Realme of England weare of Currant money of England That nowe ere From henceforthe the Fees hereafter to growe dewe to the saide Clerke or any other the saiede officeres or ministers shalbe received and taken onelye in Currant money of Ireland For all manner of writinge entries and Coppies of what nature or kynde soever they be of mencioned and Comprised in the saied Order and Certificate from England, that as the taxes and rates there are menconed to be of sterlnge monie of England as ys receyved in the sterchamber there so here the saied fees and rates shalbe of money Irishe and not of higher rates, And Forasmoche as yt was at the same tyme Complained by the saiede Clerke and Officers of the saied Courte on theire partes unto us that the sondrye the sewtors neglect and refuse to paye and satisfie unto them after theire travaille taken suche Fees as grewe duewe to them hethertoe, For that they have no aucthoritie to staie them that so doe refuse till they have payed theyre Fees and other dewtyes. For reformacon whereof wee the L Deputye and Counsell whose names are hereunto Subscribed Consideringe yt as matter meete that the saied Clerke and the other Offycers and ministers of the saide Courte should not be defrauded of theyre saiede dewtyes and Fees uppon whiche they are to lyve and be mainetained and attende theire servyces to her matie, Doo herebye furder order and aucthorise the marshall of the saied Courte uppon warrant from the saide Clerke to arest and staie all suche person or persons as are alredye or heareafter shalbe so indebted and refuse to paye theyre ffees as aforesaied growen in arryre or heareafter to growe duewe in eny wise, and he or they so staied or arested to be delivered and committed to the Constable or viceconstable of her maties Castell of Dublyne, ther to remayne till they have paied or satisfied the same. Geven at her maties Courte of Castellchamber the xiijthe of November 1577.
[signatures] T Armach, Adam Dublin, HMiden, Henry Colley, Jo Plunket, J Garvey, John Chaloner.[21]

Wheare for the matter in variaunce between Thomas M[aste]rson, esquire, Shenishall of her maties libertie in the Countie of Wexforde, pl, and John Archere, Thomas Hide, Robert Leonur [Leonarde] and the rest of the inhabitauntes of the towne of Rosse in the saied Countie, def, for a Riote, afraie and other misdemeanors affirmed to be committed by the saied def uppon the saied Compl and one Andrewe Codd and the rest of the saied compl[ainants] companie, in whiche saied matter the parties on bouthe sides discended to an yssue, interrogatoreies drawen, wittnesses produced and examined for the triall of the saied riote and misdemeanors, and the same publisshed and harde at large. And forasmoche as uppon the hearinge and debating thereof in open Courte yt manifestlie appeared by sufficient proffe of wittnesses then redd before the right honorable Henry Sydney, knight of the most noble order, L Deputie generall of this her maties Realme of Ireland, and other of her highnes privie counsell then and there beenge in the saied Courte, that the saied John Archere, Thomas Hide, Robert Leonarde and the rest of the inhabitauntes aforesaide was gilte of the saied Riote and other misdemeanores Comitted in sorte as in the saied Bill or informacon was alleged. It ys therefore ordered, decreed and adiuged by us the saied L Deputie and Counsell whose names are hereunder subscribed that one John Bolgiere, one of the inhabitauntes of the saied towne, for the hurtinge and wounding of the saied Andrew Codd, shalbe forthwith [by the] sufferaigne of the saied towne safelie sent and delivered to the constable of her maties Castell of Wexforde to remaine as prisoner in the saied Castell till the further pleasure of the saied L Deputie be knowen for his enlargement. And that also the saied John Archere, Thomas Hide, Robert Leonarde and the rest of the inhabitauntes aforesaied shall paie to the Quenes matie for a fyne the some of twenty poundys Irysh and shall also satisfie and paye to the handes of Robert Kendall, Clerke of the same Courte, to the use of the Compl, such Costes and chardges as shalbe taxed in that behalf by the most Reverent father in God, Adam, L Archebusshope of Dublin, L Keper of her Maties greate seale in this Reallme. Yeaven at her maties saied Courte of Castellchamber the xvthe of November 1577.
[signed] H Sydney, Adam Dublin, Jo Plunket, H Miden, Lucas Dillon, J Garvey.[22]

21. ff. 22–22v.
22. ff. 24–24v. In left margin, using a different hand: 'The fyne mencioned in this order and the costes taxed by the L Archebusshope of Dublin is payed to the hands of Thomas Say, Deputie to Robert Kendall.'

[signed] H Sydney By the L Deputie and counsell

Wheare for the matter in variaunce betwene Simon Gascoine, Thomas Raighe and Willam Conton, Compltes, and Dame Alson FitzLyons, Olyver FitzGarald, and others, def, for a Riote, affraie and other misdemeanors affirmed to be committed by the saied defendantes. And forasmoche as uppon the hearinge and debatinge thereof in open Courte yt manifestlie appeared by sufficient proffes, witnesses on the pl[aintiff]es behalf then redd before the right [honorable] Sir Henry Sydney, of the most noble order, knight, L Deputie generall of this her maties Reallme of Ireland and other of her highnes privie counsell then and ther beenge in the saied Courte that the sayd Dame Allson FitzLyons and Olyver FitzGerald wth the rest of the defendantes was giltie of the sayd riote and misdemeanors committed in sort as in the sayd bill was alledged. It ys therefore ordered, decreed and adiuged by us the sayde L Deputie and Counsell whose names are hereunto subscribed that the sayd Olivere FitzGarralde shall for his saied offence be committed to her maties Castell of Dublin, there to remayne for the space of ten daies for his imprisonment, and untill he shall content and paie to her maties use the some of xiij ^li^ vj s viij d for a ffyne cessed uppon him and the saied Dame Allson and the rest of the defendantes, and untill he satisfie and paie to the handes of Robert Kendall, Clerke of this Courte, such costes and chardges as shalbe taxed by the most Reverent Father in god, Adam L Archebusshope of Dublin, L Keepere of her maties greate Seale of this Reallme. Yeaven at her maties saied Courte of Castellchamber the xxvijth of November 1577.[23]

By the L Deputie and Counsell

Where for the better suppression and the extirpation of tharchetraytors Rore Oge OMore and the Connors, and others of their adherentes and accomplishes, wch daylye anoyethe and spoyleth her maties good Subiectes in sondry partes of this Reallme, especially within the Inglishe Pale. It was thought meete and agreed upon here by us the sayd L Deputie and /Councell that a general hosting should be proclaimed for forty two days to begin the [blank] of [blank] last past and to end the [blank] of [blank] next following, wch proclamation was made and proclaimed according the order and custome heretofore used, by wch proclamacon aswell the gentillmen of the Country was warned to attend and aunswere that service as both by custom and their tenures they are bounden to all generall hostinges ...[24]

H Sydney By the L Deputy and Councell

Wheare the Queenes most excellent matie by her highnes ltres under her mates Pryvie Signet, bearinge date the last of October 1577, hathe signified unto us the sayed L Deputye the whole discourse of her mates doenge and proceedinge touchinge the grieves and Complaintes of her highnes subiectes of the Pale, preferred by there Solicitors as instrumentes of other principall personages remaininge in this reallme touchinge the Cesse by them alleadged to be contrary to Lawe and Justice, wherein her highnes hathe not onely signified her resolucon and iudgement touchinge the same, But also Commaunded us to Call before us, aswell all suche of the nobilytie as weare at the last assemblye for the Cesse last agreed uppon and dyd refuse to subscribe unto the same, as also all other principall persons that weare before by us comytted for ympugning of the sayd Cesse, accordinge to w[hi]ch her mate Commaundment wee addressed o[u]r lres to the vycount of Baltinglas, the Barron of Delven, the Barron of Howthe, the Barron of Trymeleston, Sir Olyver Plunckett, knight, Sir Thomas Nugent, knight, Sir Willam Sarsfield, knight, Sir Christopher Chievers, knight, Nichas Nugent, second Barron, Patrycke Nangyll, Richard Sett [?or Missett; part crossed out in MS], Sir Patrycke Hussey, knight, George Plonckett, Thomas Nugent, Lavallie Nugent, James Nugent, Xpofer Fleming, Willam Talbott, John Netterville, Edward Pluncket, [and] Patrycke Berminghame to appeare before us the last of January last past in her mates high Courte of Castellchamber, at whch daie and place excuse was made in the behalf of the sayd vycount of Baltinglasse that, by reason of his sycknes, he could not then personallye appeare, and yet was one of the principall personages

---

23. ff. 25–25v. See below for another appearance of Dame Alison FitzLyons as defendant in a property dispute, ff. 32v–33.

24. f. 26. No date or signature following this formula, excerpted from council book. This is evidence of the close alignment of conciliar and court jurisdictions in Ireland when compared with that of star chamber and privy council in England.

formerlie dyd ympugne the sayd Cesse, and was for the same emongest others formerlye Comitted, and the rest dyd there appere before us the sayd L Deputye and Councell, uppon whose apparaunce her highnes sayd l[ett]re was soundry tymes publickly redd unto them, and her mates pleasure therein Contained throughlie delyvered and sette forthe, wth many requests and persuacons in open Courte made unto them by us the sayd L Deputye and Councell, not onely to subscribe to a submission and acknowledgment of there fault, But also in writinge to allowe of her highnes sayd prerogatyve of Cesse, and of the Custome used in that behalf, acordinge to the tennor of her mates sayd lres. At which tyme they desyred respect [?respite] to annsweare, whiche was gyven them tyll two of the Clocke in the afternoon of the same daye, at which howre they appeared and prayed further daye, whereuppon tyme was gyven them, till the next morowe in the afternoone at wch tyme they agayne appeared and delyvered a writinge wch they termed a submision, neither contayninge matter of submission nor absolute allowaunce of her mates sayd prerogatyve of cesse, wch was for that Cause reiected, and then they made request to have the Coppye of her mates sayd letter and also Conferrence wth her highnes Attorney generall for the drawinge of there submission, according to the tennor of her mates lres, wch requeste weare graunted. Whereuppon the sayd Barron of Delven, Nicholas Nugent, second Barron of the Eschequere, John Newterville and Christopher Fleminge, learned in the lawes, dyd Conferr wth the sayd Attorney in wch Conference a submision withe myelde and qualified wordes and termes, Consonant and agreeng to her mates resolucon sett downe in her highnes sayd lres, was drawen and delivered to the sayd Barron of Delven, uppon his request to be farther advised of, whch he kept in his handes allmost twoe dayes and in the ende redelyvered the same to the sayd Attorney, agayne with resolute aunsweare for him self and the rest that, they woulde not subscribe to the same, but to make some shewe of obedyence they the sayd LL[ords] knightes and gentillmen uppon there next apparaunce tendered unto us another writinge, wch they also termed a submission, not satisfieinge her mates sayd lres in substaunce for her highnes sayd prerogatyve to be certaine and of antequitye, but Comprisinge matter of incertantye, Dought and open evasions, eftsones to bringe her mates saied prerogative into question and to move and Continewe thereby disloyall argumentes and doughte of her highnes saide prerogatyve, and by no meanes woulde agree to the same absolutely. And after longe debating of that matter and many persuacons eftsones used unto them to subscribe to the submission so drawen by the sayde Attorney uppon Conference as aforesaied, and after soundrye treatyes with them to that ende, aswell publickly as privatlie, pynctlye[?], severallye and appartlye, they nevertheles, (except Barnabe Scurloke, Christopher Fleminge and John Missett) expresslye and obstinatlye refused to subscribe. Wheareuppon yt was thought meete by us the sayd L Deputy and Councell, perceyvinge there Contynuell willfullnes [in] said disobedyence, to put in execution against them her mates sayd sentence and iudgement, and them the fyfte of February followinge Comytted prisonners to her mates Castell of Dublin where they presentlye remayne. And for that there disobedience and contempt was still Contyneweng, as yet yt ys, they weare the seventh daye of February next by the Constable of the sayd Castell broght to the Barr in the sayde Courte of Castellchamber before us the sayd L Deputye and others of her mates Councell, whom wee Called to have there advise, accordinge theffect of her highnes sayde lre whose names are hereunto subscribed, wheare for there Contynual disobedience and Contempte they weare severallye fyned, as heareafter followethe, viz:

Uppon the sayd vycount of Baltinglas v C li ['ster' is crossed out in MS..]
Uppon the sayd Barron of Delven v C li
Uppon the sayd Barron of Howth   v C li
Uppon the sayd Barron of Trimleston CCC li
Uppon the sayd Sir Patricke Hussey knight CC markes
Uppon the said Sir Oliver Pluncket knight CC markes
Uppon the saied Sr Thomas Nugent knight CC markes
Uppon the saied Sir William Sarsfield knight CC markes
Uppon the saied Sir Xpofer Chevers night CC markes
Uppn the saied Nicholas Nugent second B[aron]   CC markes
Uppon the sayd Patryck Nangill xl li
Uppon the sayd Edward Plonckett xl li
Uppon the sayde George Plonckett C li
Uppon the sayde Thomas Nugent CC markes
Uppon the sayde Lavallie Nugent   xx li
Uppon the sayd James Nugent xl li

Uppon the sayd Wiliam Talbott   C li
Upon the sayd John Newtervile   lxxv li
Uppon the sayd Patrick Birmingham   xl li

Geven at her mates sayd Courte of Castellchamber the sayde seventh daye of February 1578. And further wheare wee the sayd L Deputie upon perusinge of the sayd order before the same was signed, weyinge the severall fynes above written to be contrary to our meaninge, the somes beeing as yt was sett downe [in] starlinge, thought good with the advise of the sayd Councell to myttigate the same from starlinge to Irishe, and so the same to be payed, and not otherwise. And also forasmoche as the sayd L vycount of Balltinglas hathe sent his excuse that by reason of his sycknes he was not able to travell to appeare as the rest have done, as by us the sayd L Deputie he was Comaunded, wee doe therefore hereby order with thadvise aforesayd that Robart Kendall, Clerke of the sayd Courte of Castellchamber, shall forthwith repayre to the sayd Vycount of Balltinglas with the sayd submission so denyed by the rest, fyned as aforesaied, and the same to offer to his L to subscribe accordinge her maties pleasure signified by her sayd lres. Which yf he shall refuse to doe, and the same refusall Certified unto us by the sayd Kendall that thereuppon It ys ordered that his L shall paye as a fyne for his disobedyence and Contempt, the some of fyve houndreth poundes Irishe.
[signed] H Sydney, Adam Dublin, Edw Fiton, John Chaloner.[25]

By the L Deputye and Councell   H Sydney

Wheare for the better suppression and thexterpacon of the arche traytors Rory Oge OMore and the Connors and others of there adherentes and accomplisshes which dayelye anoyeth and spoieleth her mates good Subiectes in soundrye partes of this Realme, especiallye within that Inglishe pale, It was thought meete and agreed uppon here by us, the sayd L Deputye and Counsell, that a generall hostinge should be proclaimed for fortye twoe dayes to begynne the [blank] of [blank] last past, and to ende the [blank] of [blank] next followinge, wch proclamacon was made and proclaymed, acordinge the order and Custome heretofore used, by wch proclamacon aswell the gentyllmen of the Countrye was warned to attend and annsweare that service as bothe by Custome and there tenures they are bounde to all generall hostinges, as also all others of the Countrye to be redy with there Cartes and Carriadges for the same as heretofore they have beene accustomed, in whiche sayd service wee the saied L Deputie with soundrye other of the Counsell yssued forthe in person to that Jorney so farr as Kylkenny and in o[u]r Journey thether wee Caused a muster to be made of all suche gentyllmen and others that was bounde and ought to have served with there severall nombers Duringe that generall hostinge, in which muster there was soundrye defaltes made aswell in the Baronyes of Duleeke, Skryne, Deece, and Moyferragh, beeng in the Countie of Meethe, as also the Barony of Ballrothery within the County of Dublyn, whch defalte beeng Certified unto us the sayd L Deputye, subscribed by Olivere Bamford Deputye to the Clerke of the Check, we sent the same certificate inclosed in or lres Dated at Athye the xxth of December 1577 to or very good L tharchebusshpe of Dublyn, and the rest ioyned in Comission with his L to take Care for the safgard of thenglishe Pale in or absence, desyringe his L to take order that those who had made defalt as aforesayde might be by him and the rest of the Comissioners sent forthwith to appeare before them, and uppon there apparaunce, to be Chardged for there defaltes and so bondes to be taken of them for there apparaunce in the Court of Castellchamber the Firste daye of the next Terme following, to thend that Fynall order mought be taken for there Fynes and other ponisshement, according the qualitye of there faltes. Uppon receipt of which lres the sayd L Archebusshope and the rest of the Comissioners addressed there Commissions to the sheriffes of the sayd Countyes of Meethe and Dublin to Commaunde and warne all those persons nominated in the sayd certificate forthwith to appeare before them. Whereuppon some of them dyd accordinglye appeare and entred into bondes to make there apparaunce, the xxixth of January last in her mates sayd Courte of Castellchamber, where they with the greatest nomber of the rest dyd appeare before us, the sayd L Deputye and Counsell, at which tyme they weare severallye articuled withall touching ther sayd Defaltes and had further daye gyven them to annsweare and appeare againe till the xiijth of February followinge, at wch daye the greatest nomber of them dyd appeare and could shewe no suffycient matter to dischardge suche Defaltes as

25. ff. 26v to 28v. The fines were originally listed in sterling, then each fine had word 'ster' crossed out in MS.

of right they were then chardged withall, wherefore yt was then adiudged by us the sayd L Deputye and Counsell, whose names are hereunto subscribed, that they and every of them had used therein greate Disobedience and Contempt, for the wch there disobedience and Contempt they weare severally fyned as heareafter followethe, viz:

Uppn Robert Caddell of Doweston, gent, for xxvi dayes defalt, adiuged and taxed at xviij ster per diem } xxxix s str [26]

Uppon the Plounckettes for xxiij horssmen the defaltes whereof are adiuged Duringe the whole tyme of the hostinge, and taxed at iijs str per die every horssman } Clj li iiij s str

Uppon Olyvere Darcye of Acarne [?] gent for the defalt of one archer on horssback adiuged During the whole tyme of the hostinge taxed at xviij str per diem } Lxiij s str [in margin: 'Duleek']

Uppon Aim Fitzimmons, Richard Stanihurst [another name crossed out; ? John Brewerton] for the defalt of one archere on horssbacke, adiudged Duringe the whole tyme of the hostinge taxed at xviij ster per diem } Lxiij s ster. Divided among Fitzsimmons, Stanihurst and Brewerton [margin: Ballrothry]

Uppon Michell Sarsfield of Sarsfeildston, gent, for the defalt of xvj dayes for one archere ahorsback, taxed as before } xxiij s ster [margin: Duleek]

Uppon Thomas Fynglas of Wespleston, gent, for the defalt of one archere on horsback adiuged Duringe the whole tyme of the hostinge taxed at xviij d ster per diem } Lxiij s str [margin : Balrothery]

Uppon Peter Traves of Ballecoye, gent, for the defalt of two archers on horsback During the whole tyme of the hostinge at xviij d per diem } vj li vj s ster [margine: 'Ballrothery, respited until furder viewe of the book be taken']

Uppon Christopher Fagane of the Cyttye of Dublyn, merchaunt, for the lady Barnwall, late wiefe to Sir Xpofer Barnwell, for the defalt of one archere on horssback adiuged duringe the whole generall hostinge, taxed at xviij d per diem } Lxiij s str [margin: Duleek]

Upon Waltere Fitzsimons of Ballmadvoghe, gent for the defalt of one archere on horsback during the whole tyme of the hostinge, but the Cariage not answeare[d], the same taxed as foresaied } Lxiij s ster [margin: Ballrothery]

Uppon Robert Rathe of Colpe, gent, for the defalt of one archere on horsback duringe the whole tyme of the hostinge taxed at xviij s per diem} Lxiij s str [margin: Duleek]

Uppon John Feild of Painston, gent, for the defalt of one archere on horsbback duringe the whole tyme and taxed as aforesaied } Lxiij s str [margin: Duleek]

Uppon Robart Preston of the Ynche, gent, for the defalt of one archere on horsback duringe the whole tyme and taxed as aforesayd } Lxiij s stre [margin Duleek]

Uppon Thomas Talbott of Dardeston, gent, for the defalt of two archers on horsback during the whole tyme and taxed as aforesaied } vj li vj s str [margin: 'Duleek, respited til the book be furder Considered']

Uppon John Hamlyng of Smitheston, gent, for the defalt of one archere on horsback duringe the whole tyme and taxed as aforsayd } Lxiij s str [margin: Duleek]

---

26. Later note in MS: 'This fine paid to Michaell Kettlewell the viijth of February, as appeared by his acquitance.' In left margin: 'B Skryne', i.e. Barony of Skryne. Nearly identical entries for each of succeeding defendants.

Uppon the saied Xpofer Fagane for the saied Lady Barnwall for the defalt of fyve archers on horsback Duringe the whole tyme and taxed as aforesaied } xv li xv s str [margin: Ballrothry]

Uppon Christofer Fleming of Dyrpatrick, gent, for the defalt of one archere on horsback, during the whole tyme taxed as aforesaied } Lxiij s str [margin: Deece and Moieferagh]

Uppon Henry Dueke, gent, for the defalt of one archere on horsback Charged uppon Richarde Croste of Castellior [?his] Dame [query: surrogate for female respondent] during the whole tyme taxed as aforesayd } Lxiij s str [margin: Deece and Moifenragh]

Uppon the Heyre of Bathe of Landeston [interlineation: 'viz Nicholas Bathe'] for the defalt of one archere on horsbacke during the whole tyme taxed as aforesayd } Lxiij s str [margin: Ballrothry]

Uppon Jenyco Goldinge of Typpersoule, gent, for the defalt of one archere on horsback during the whole tyme taxed as aforesayd } Lxiij s str [margin: Ballrothery]

Geven in her mates sayd court of Castell chamber the xiijth of February 1578.
[signed:] Adam Dublin, Edw Fiton, Lucas Dillon, John Chaloner.[27]

H Sydney   By the L Deputy and Councell
Memorandum whereas Sir Thomas Fitzwilliams of Meryonge, knight, and John Finglas of Tobersoule, gent, feoffeees of trust unto Dame Alson FitzLyons of Porteston, in the towne of Bussardiston in the Countie of Dublin, hath by ther informacon exhibited into this most honorable Court of Castle Chamber before us, the L Deputie and Counsell, impeched one Willm Conton, James Ryan, Thomas Man and Matthew Duffe of periurie, viz: in affirminge by there deposicon taken by the examinator of the Chancery upon sute latelie depending betwixt the sayd Sir Thomas and John Finglas against one Simon Luttrell of Busserdston aforesaid before the right honorable the L Chauncellor in the Chancerye, concernynge the saied towne of Busserdstowne, that the saied Dame Alson dyd lett and Demyse by wordes uttred in those presens the sayd Towne of Busserdston wth thappartenaunces unto the said Simon Luttell in the harvest next after the death of Roger Finglas, late husband unto the said Dame Alson, for terme of xxjtie yeres. And for as much as the witnesses produced by the said Sir Thomas and John Finglas to averr and prove the said periurie by them assigned could not prove the said periurie but suche persons and proffe as was produced to that grewe by no manner as [?perjurie] and subbornacon as it appeared very manifestlie it could not tend sufficientlie to prove the sayd periurie, by the saied Sr Thomas and John Finglas surmised to attaynt the Def thereof. And for that the said demise for twenty and one yeares of the saied towne of Busserdston proved by the said Defendauntes in Chancerye, hathe bene there confirmed by the decree of the right honor[able] the L Chauncellor, and also that by other witnesses of the Defendauntes parte, it is sufficientlie before us here in this most honorable court affirmed that the said def have truly deposed in affirmacyon of the said demyse in the Chancerye as aforesaid, therefore it is ordered by us the saied L Deputie and counsell yt the saied Defendauntes shalbe Dismist of the saied periurye, and that the plaintiffes shall pay or cause to be payde to Robert Kendall or his deputy, clerk of the said Court, to the Defend[ante]s use such costs and chardges as shalbe taxed by the right most reverend father in god, Adam, L Archebusshope of Dublin, L Kep[er] of her maties greate seale in this Realme. Yeoven at her maties saied Courte of Castle Chamber the xxvth of Aprill 1578.
[signed] T Armachen, Adam Dublin.[28]

H Sydney   By the lord deputy and Counsell
Memorandum wheare Thomas Snagge, Esquyre, her maties Attorney generall within the Realme of Ireland, exhibyted informacon before the Ryghte honorable the L Deputye and Counsell in her

27. ff. 29 to 31v. Fol. 32 contains only marginal note: 'iijd qd xvi die Aprilis 1578 Robert [Kendall, clerk of court of castle chamber].'
28. ff. 32v–33.

maties court of Castellchamber that at a cessions holden at Kilkenny the viijth day of February in this present xxth yeare of her maties raigne before the right honorable Sir William Drewry, knight, L Presydent of Mounster, and others her maties commissioners in that behalf aucthorised, three severall inquests of the countye and towne of Kilkennye weare sworne and chardge geven everie of them to enquyre of all fellonies, treaons and other offences within that shyre, after whiche chardge then was delyvered unto the enquest of gent[tlemen], wherof Gerald Blancheffield was forman, three severall bills to be enquired, of the one as concerning Donyll McShane and other touching John Rocheford, the third concerning Donough O Kelly and James Shortall, purporting severall treasons to have been by them severallie commytted. And albeyt that the contentes of these Bills were sufficientlie proved before the saied Commissioners by oathe of soundrie witnesses and the Commissioners handes sett to the Bills testifying the same, with a furder note whoe they weare that proved the same uppon there oathes, and withall the saied Donyll McShane, John Rocheford, Donogh Oge and James Shortall, before the delyverie upp of the saied bills and before the saied enquest weare dischardged, submitted themselves publicklye in the face of the Courte, confessing their fault, the which confession was likewise tolde the saied Jurie, that notwithstandinge most contempteously would not fynde the saied Bills, but retorned ignoramus against their owne express knowledge by the meanes aforesaid, and so disloyallie and undewtifullie concealed the Contentes thereof, whereby the proceedinge according to the Cours of Lawe against those persons was stopped. And likewise the second Jurie, whereof James Blanchefield was forman, havinge delivered unto them the saied Bill concerning Donogh Og O Kelly and James Shortall, and the Jurie of the towne of Kilkenny, whereof one Ragged was forman, receivinge the same Bill and the Bill concerning Rocheford, having likewise ministered the testimonies aforesaide proving the contentes of the saied Bills, would not find the saied Bills nor none of them but in like manner retorned ignoramus, and so bothe last recyted Juries contempteouslye, in favor of the saied malefactors and contrarie to ther oathe and chardge, disloyallie and undewtifullie concealed the contents also of the saied Bills. Whereunto the saied severall Juries beeing called to aunsweare in this her Maties Courte of Castell Chamber exhibited their severall aunsweares, wheareuppon the matter publickly debated before the saied L Deputie and Counsell in her maties saied Court of Castell Chamber by her maties learned counsell and the Counsell of the saied severall Juries most manifestlie appeared by the testimonie of dyvers her maties commissioners then present that the contents of the saied informacon against the said severall Juries was trewe, and that the said severall Juries had mistred [?ministered] and opened unto them the instructions, proffes and testimonies contained in the saied informacon with other cyrcumstaunces, whereby the Contentes of the saied severall Bills was manifestlie proved trewe unto the saied Juries. Wherefore and for that nothing materiall was either shewed or proved by the saied severall juries nor anie of them for the dischardge of there saied contempt and concealementes. It is therefore ordered, adiudged and decreed by the saied right honorable L Deputye and others of her maties pryvie counsell then presente in the saied Courte of Castellchamber, whose names are hereunder subscribed, that Thomas Cantwell, Thomas Denn and Robert Shortall, beenge three of the Graunde [Jury] and for the Jurie whereof Gerald Blanchefield was forman, beenge then present in Courte, shall be committed to her maties Castell of Dublin, there to remaine at the will and pleasure of the saied L Deputye, and withall that the saied Thomas Cantwell, Thomas Den and Robert Shortall, as also everie one of the saied severall juries hereafter particularlie named, there heyres, executors and assignes, shall satisfie and pay unto her matie, her heyres and successors, soch some and somes of money for there severall fynes as particularlie ys laied and sett uppon the polls of everie of them. And shall also satisfie and paie to the handes of Robert Kendall, Clerke of the same Court, or to his deputie such costes and chardges as shalbe taxed in that behalf by the most reverend father in god, Adam, L Archebusshoppe of Dublin, L Keper of her maties greate seale in this Reallme. And yt is furder ordered that a commission be Derected to the Sufferaigne of Kylkennie to make diligent inquirie whoe of the saied severall Juries uttered and saied, before the bills aforesaid weare gyven uppe to the commissioners, that he would sticke by yt before he would fynde the saied Bills or anie of them. Yeaven at her maties saied Court of Castell Chamber the viijth of Maye 1578.

[first jury, with note in left margin as follows: 'This jury is dischardged by order of the L Deputy and Counsell in her maties Court of Castell Chamber as far [as] doe appeareth in the opate {MS unclear: ?opinate, i.e. record} of actes of the sayd Cort for the fyne of xxiiij [lib] yrishe sed uppon them.'

Fines for each person crossed out in MS.]
Uppon Gerald Blanchfielde of Blanchfieldston, gent
Uppon Thomas Cantwell of Cantwellston, gent
Uppon Thomas Den of Grenane, gent
Uppon James Shortall of Ballilorean, gent
Uppon Robert Switche of Glasshecra, gent
Uppon Robert Bremaghe of Ballimbruge
Uppon Gerald FitzGerald of the Burnechurche
Uppon Robert Shortall of Kilferaghe, gent
Uppon Patricke Sentleger of Tullighambeage
Uppon Piers FitzGerald of Gloslingiston, gent
Uppon Patrick Purcell of Lismeane, gent
Uppon Henrie Quensford of Ballmackawe, gent
Uppon David Howlinge of Kilrey, gent

[second jury]
Uppon David Blanchefield of Howlingston, gent xx s
Uppon John Payne of Ballinbolly, freeholder xx s
Uppon Maurice Archedeakon of Kylmorie, gent xx s
Uppon Richard Power of Powersodd, gent
Uppon Archdeakon of Archdeekeston, gent
Uppon Edmond Shortall of Clorane, gent
Uppon John Brenagh of Ballihaurie, freeholder
Uppon John Fretewan of Castelliffee, gent
Uppon Oliver Fanninge of Croane, gent
Uppon William Wale of Tulleweyne, gent
Uppon Leonarde Shortall of Kildermagh, gent
Uppon Thomas Barron of Clone, gent
Uppon Edmond O Kyane of the Pellagh, gent
Uppon Walter Shortall of Forstalston, gent
Uppon Thomas Bremeaghe of Ballihomyne, gent

[third jury]
Uppon Willm Ragged of Kilkenny, mrchaunt
Uppon Ric Savage of Kilkenny, Burgess
Uppon Wm Seixe of Kilkenny, Burgesse
Uppon Edmond Donill of Kilkenny, merchaunt
Uppon Willm Archere of Kilkenny, mcht
Uppon Godfrey Rothe Fitzwm of Kilkenny, mrcht
Uppon Redmond Purcell of Kilkenny, mcht
Uppon Maurice Kiocue [?Keogh], mcht
Uppon David Dobene of Kilkenny, mrcht
Uppon Wm Reminghame of Kilkenny, shoemaker
Uppon Wm Prendercast of Kilkenny, shoemaker
Uppon Patricke Brenaghe of Kilkenny, tailor
Uppon Walter Ragged of Kilkenny, shoemaker
Uppon Willm Clerie of Kilkenny, shoemaker

[signed] T Armagh, Adam Dublin.[29]

W Drury   By the L Justice and Counsell
M[em]er[andum] where for the matter in variaunce betweene Roger Dillon, pl, and John Rochforde
and others, deftes, for a Riott, route and other misdemenors affirmed to be committed in braking
downe of Certayne work made by the saied Roger to conveie a water course to a griste mille in

29. ff. 33v–35v.

Balnedronny in the Countie of Meathe. Forasmoche as uppon the hearinge and debatinge thereof in open Courte, it manifestlie appeered by sufficient profe of witnesses then redd before the right honorable the L Justice, the L Chauncellor and others of her maties pryvie councell then and there beenge in the saied Courte that the saied John Rocheforde and the rest of the deftes mencioned in the bill were giltie of the saied riot and misdemeanor Comitted in sorte as in the saied bill was alleadged. It is therfore ordered, decreed and adiudged by us the saied L Justice, L Chauncellor and Counsaile whose names are hereunder subscribed, that the saied John Rocheforde shall for his saied offence be committed to warde, there to remayne untill he shall contente and paie to her maties use the some of ten poundes for this fine and to the pl[aintiff]es the some of [blank] for the costs of courte. And furder it is alsoe ordered that the saied John Rocheford shall cause his wife Ann Barnewall to appeare in this Courte the first daie of the next Hillarie tearme that she may be committed to warde for the offence by her committed in this cause. And alsoe ordered that her maties Solicitor shall examine the saied John Rocheforde uppon his Booke othe whoe were the persons, and howe manye whoe were in company of his wife at the committinge of the Riott, to thende they maye receave such punishment for examples sake at suche time and place in the Countrie where the offence was Comitteed as by us the saied L Justice & Counsaile shalbe thought mete. Yeaven at her maties saied Courte of Castell Chamber the xxixth of November 1578.
[signed] W Gerrard, H Miden, Edw Fyton, John Chaloner.[30]

By the L Justice and Counsell
Md where a byll of Ryott was exhibited in this moste honnorable Courte of Castellchamber by Walter McHarbarde FitzGeffreye the xviijth of October 1577 Agaynste James Moylle Newgent of Donnowre in the County of Westmeathe, gent, Richard Newgente of the same, Sonne and heyre to the sayde James, Edwarde Ledwiche of Ballenelake, Edmonde Wallshe of Colaine, Walter McThebbott of Unaside, Chrystopher Ledwyche of Lake, Garrott Newgente FitzPatrycke, Teige Boye McEvene of Ballefurte, Cownley O Rourke, McEdmonde O Rourke, Owin Roe of the Grandge, John McGarrotte, Richarde O Rourke, Wyllm Boye O Rourke, Hobbert Ledwyche of Regemine, Thomas Wallshe, McWalter Reaghe, Thomas McSardorghe of Arglas, Richard McSardorghe of Arglas, Edmonde Oge of Colingne, Nicholas Daltonne of the Capp, Carberye McLaghlen of Trahasspycke, Malaghlen McLaghlen of the same, Donoghe Bane McDermot, Richarde Ledwyche of Balleharin, Owin McHue of Donowre, Connor O Dowd of Ballifarren, Thomas O Kerevane of the same, and Arte McGarre of the same, as by the sayde Bill more at lardge dothe and may appeare. And after bothe partyes proceadinge in pleadinge, The sayde Richarde Newgent of Donowre in the County of Westmethe, gent, Walter Dalamare de Manysfyelde in the sayde Countie, gent, Edmonde Ledwyche of Lecarricke in the sayd Countye, gent, Edmonde Wallshe of Collane in the sayde County, gent, Thomas Dalamare of Connolaghe in the same Countie, gent, Nicholas Daltonne of the Porte in the same Countye, gent, Edmonde Dalamare of Culloine in the same county, gent, Carberi McClaghlein of Rathpyckes of the same husband[man], and Melaghlin McClaghlin of the same county, husband[man], In there proper persons saythe as to the unlawfull assemblye, Ryotte, Route and other tresspaces supposed in the sayde Byll, the Courte noe further in tryall therof to proceade, for the Quenes mooste excellente matie of her aboundant grace and mere mocyon have by her letters patente reddye to be shewed beringe date the fyfte Daye of Julij in the xxth yeare of her maties Raigne, amonge other thinges after the sayde offences Comytted, hathe pardoned them and every of them of the sayde offences, the tenor of which lettters patentes ensuethe, [Latin formula, ending fol. 38].
Therefor the sayde Richarde, Walter, Edmonde, Edmonde, Thomas, McNicholas, John, Edmonde, Carbery and Melaghlen prayethe of the sayd Riott, rout, unlawfull assemblye and all other trespaces in the sayde Byll conteyned, to be dischardged and dismyssed. Whereupon the ryghte honnorable Willm Gerrarde L Chauncelor and other of her maties pryvy Counsell whos names are herunto subscybed, uppon mature deliberacon had of the premyses, hathe ordered and Decreed that the sayd Richarde, Walter, Edmonde, Edmonde, Thomas, Nicholas, John, Edmonde, Carbery and Melaghlin and every of them, of the sayd Ryott, unlawfulll assemblye and other the offences conteyned in the Byll, shalbe Dischardged and frome henceforthe thereof Dysmyssed, and the matter to be prosecuted

30. f. 36.

agaynst the rest of the def that are not pardoned. Geven at her mates sayde Courte of Castellchamber the xxxth of Januarij a[nn]o 1578.[31]

M[em]er[andum] where Richarde Beallinge her maties solicitor at Lawes within this her heighnes Reallme of Irlande exhibited Informacone before the ryght honnorable the L Justice and Counsell in her maties courte of Castell chamber in the behalf of her highnes, how one Nicholas Terrell, servante to Sir Christopher, L of Howthe, the day of [blank] in the xxjth yeare of her maties Raigne, beying examyned before Wyllame Gerrard, Esquier, L Chauncellor of the sayde Reallme uppon his corporall othe, whether he sawe Elizabeth Brymingham the Saturday at nighte next before his sayd examynacon did utterlie deny that he sawe her the same nighte, wher in trothe yt playnelie appeared, as well by the examynacone of Elizabeth Bremyngham as by his owne Confessione in Courte, and not denyed by his Answere, that he was sente from the sayd L of Howth his master of purpose to convey her from thence, and the same night spake with her, suppped with her and was that nyght in her companie at several tymes. For as moche as uppon debatyng of the Cause yt playnelie appeared that the defendant hath been a lewde and badd instrumente to worke dissencone betweene the L of Howthe and his wyffe, whoe resteth nowe separated, and a pryvie comforter and supporter of his saide master to lyeve louslie [i.e. live loosely] and did of verie wyll and purpose wyllfully periure hym self, supposing thereby to have shadowed thapprehendinge of the sayd Elizabethe in that he knewe not wher she was to be founde, and that suche wyllfull periuryes are of small accompte in this, and that therfore It is therefore ordered by the L Chauncellor and Counell, whose names are hereunder subscrybed, that the sayd Nicolas Terrell shall presentlie be commytted as prysoner to her maties Castell of Dublin there to remayne and that upone Saturdaye, beeinge the xxxtie of this present monthe, to be broughte by the Constable of the sayde Castell to the Sheriffe of this Cittie of Dublin and the Sheriffe to take the same to sett hyme at tyme of the clocke in the forenone of the same daye, and putting his head throughe one of the holes of the Pillarie to fyx uppon his heade in greate letters to be wrytten, for wyllfull periurye. And allso to nayle his righte eare to the Pillarye and to Delyvere him a knyffe with the same to Cutt or otherwyse to tear of[f] the same, and after there remayned by the space of towe howres to be retorned agayne to the constable, and to remayne in the Castell untyll Saturdaye after, and then to be lyckwyse the same daye at the Lycke howre sett uppon the Pillorie to Contynue for lycke spate, and to have in lycke sorte the Lyfte eare naylled and after he hathe ther remayned towe howres to be returned into the Castell. Neverthelesse yf the sayde Nicholas shall paye for a fyne to the Quenes Maties use the some of x ^{li} at or before the tyme he is appoynted to receive the naylling of his righte eare, then that parte of the punyshement to be spared. And lyckwyse if he paye the lyke some of x ^{li} for a lyke fyne, at or before the tyme appointed for his leyfte eare to be naylled, to have in lyke sorte that parte of the punyshemente sparede, and after to be in lyke sort retorned to the sayd Castell, there to remayne as prysoner tyll furder order be taken for his enlardgement and untyll he have payde the some of [blank] for Costes of courte. Geven at her maties sayd Courte of Castellchamber the xxijth of Maij a[nn]o 1579.[32]

W Drury   By the L Justice and Counsell

Whereas uppon Complaincte exhibited in this honorable Courte by John Fuller and Water Foxe of the Cittie of Chestare, marchauntes, pl against Phillip Lamporte, Patrick Synnott and others of the Countie of Wexforde, yt playnly and manifestlie appered uppon examynacon of the same as well by the examynacons of some of the saide parties as also by the deposicons of some others, that there was gathered and unlawfully assembled together to the number of towe hundred personnes by some deposicons and by some other a lesse number to the Sea shore within a short tyme afer the Shipwracke and losse in the saide Complainte specefied made and there, some with hardilles [?hurdles] and other Carriage and some others with axes and hamers breakinge, spoylinge and carryinge a waye suche parte of the saide shippe and others the goodes of the saide complaynantes flotinge uppon the water as came to the saide shore and that they the saide persones seeking by rapin [rapine] and praye to make spoyle and havocke of the broken partes of the shippe and goodes did take and carry a weye the same every one suche share as he Coulde gett, not once helpinge the pore

31. ff. 36v to 38v.   32. ff. 39–40.

Compltes to any parte of there goodes or to theire use to preserve the same. And forasmoche alsoe as yt appered by the examynacons and deposicons aforesaide that the saide Complaynantes beinge owners of the saide Shippe and goodes and presentlie there seinge the same spoyles and taking a waye before there faces, coulde not by reason of the terror and feare they were dreven unto in respecte of the great multitude and nomber there then assembled together withstande the spoylinge of them and although complayninge and movinge them to the saide Lamporte one of the deftes and the principall of that disordered companey after he had taken divers parcelles of the goodes to his owne howse, yet coulde they have not restitucon of that nor redresse of the rest of there wronges, but most gredelie urged them to singe [sign] a bill wherby to gyve to him thone halfe of all there good[s] takin and begotten to be holpen to the reste wich in riotus disordered and unlawfull manyer of spoyle of all vesselles and personnes soe caste a waye in those partes where the Costes are daungerouse or so usuall[?] as convenient to be prevented and met with. Therfore it is ordered by the Right honorable the L Justice and Counsell whose names are hereunto subscribed that the saide Phillipp Lamporte and Patricke Synnot now apperinge be comytted as prisoners to her maties Castell of Dublin there to remayne untill furder order by the saide L Justice and counsell shalbe taken for there inlardgement and alsoe untill there by pade unto the Queenes maties use the some of one hundrethe powndes for there fine & for the fine of all the other defs convicted by the order for the offences aforesaide and alsoe the some of [blank, line crossed out in MS]. And whereas in respecte of the povertie of divers others in like sorte complayned of and apperinge for savinge of there Chardges were licensed to departe, offringe to abide what order shold be taken with the saide towe defendantes who they chosed to abide and answere the saide Complaintes. It is therefore further ordered by the saide L Justice and Counsell that a comyssion be dyrected to the Seneschall, the Sheriffe George Dormer and Walter Roche or eny towe of them whereof the saide Dormer to be one to call before them as well all such personnes as hath appered as also all those who are nomynated in the scedull annexe[d] to the saide Commyssion and callinge before them the saide personnes to trye out by all the wayes and meanes they can the nomber of the others soe assembled and whate goodes they receaved and theruppon to taxe uppon every of them towardes the payment of the saide fyne of suche some and somes as they shall fynde by the quantitie and qualitie of there offence and the abilytie of the personnes Convenient and to commytte twelve of the ableste of them to her maties Castell of Wexforde there to remaine by the space of three dayes and untill they and every of them have entered into sufficient boundes to her maties use in the some of fortie poundes that they shall not onlye paie such some or somes of money as shalbe by the saide Comyssioners taxed uppon them and the reste mencyoned in the saide scedule and uppon evry of them for the payment of the fyne and Costes aforesaide, but alsoe that they shall not hereafter at any tyme uppon any suche licke chaunce happenninge repayre in suche dysordered manner to the saide shore for any other purpose but to helpe and presarve the goodes of any personnes soe wrecked and Comynge alande to the use and behowfe of the saide owners. Yeaven at her maties Castell of Dublin the xxvith daye of June 1579.
[signatures] Wm Gerrard, Ad Dublin, N Bagenall, JGarvey, Lucas Dillon [last name crossed out in MS].[33]

[signed] W Drury   By the L Justice and Counsel.
Whereas the matter informed of to the L Justice and others her maties Counsell in her maties high Courte of Castellchamber against the L Baron of Howthe uppon the informacion caused the examynacon of the saide Barron uppon Interogatories and uppon the sighte of certaine witnesses deposed hath had full debatinge and hearinge, forasmuche as yt manifestlie appe[re]the, as well by the Confession of the saide L of Howthe as otherwise that he often tymes used to beat his wiffe noe lawfull Cawse declared, but as maye well be gathered by good presumpcions, when the saide wiffe sholde seme to myslike with his open filthie manner of Conversacion, of liffe with strange weomen and yearlye Chardge, which for the space of twelve yeares together she espied him to haunte after she had borne him fourtene children, then fallinge into furiouse passiones woulde usually beat her in such raginge and cruell sorte as not tollerable and that Causles [i.e. without cause] in such a rage he cruellie stroke and bette her with a statfe. The firste beatinge Complayned and enformed of in this

33. f. 40v. See f.1v for a list of persons who confessed to being at the spoil of a ship in Co. Louth. This case was heard under the deputyship of Fitzwilliam, but the entry book records only the names of the accused without reference to a trial, or date.

Courte as forced she kepte her bedde by the space of one fortnight, noe Cawse geven as by his answer maye appere, but for that he so sick as he alledgeth as readie to departe life, perceyvinge her to Sownde [?] wolde bestowe those stroackes for a farewell shoulde he die, in which mynde Continuinge as appeareth as well by the declaracion of his wiffe sworne in open Courte. Uppon the debatinge of the Cawse, as otherwise partlie by his owne Confession, that She was well recovered of the former strokes he repayred to the Chamber where She laie, and findinge his former cruell beatinge had not sufficientlie aswaged that his passionate and Cruell mynde and humor, of furiouse Distraught passion did moste bylye [i.e. with bile] to be recyted settinge a parte all modestie, shamefastnes and humayne regarde eftesones with towe sallye roddes ready before hande provided for satisfaccion of his unshamefaste meaninge, Eftesones upon the naked and bare fleshe beate her untill eyther of those roddes, thone after thother, were bothe worne to the stompes, of which Cruell beatinge (noe Cawse alledged by hime self) She laie as by testimonye sufficient appeared many dayes not hable to abide the skyn takin a waye any Clothe to touche her. The seconde manner of beatinge his saide wiffe & in the saide informacion Contayned: And for that yt alsoe appeared that by this his usuall hauntinge & kepinge of hores, his wiffe became soe hatefull to him as he Coulde not without strikinge and beatinge of her suffycientlie satisfie the Crueltie of his mynde, soe Coulde he not digeste that any of his servantes or followeres shoulde owe to her the dutie of a servant and therfore perceyvinge that his Butler had geven to her some bread and drinke of a better sorte and in more ample proporcion then was by hym assigned to be geven and allowed to her, beinge seperated from his Company bede and table and kepte in a Close chamber prisoner like in moste Cruell and tyrranicall sorte, he toke the saide pore man his Butler, strypped him cleane naked, tyed him to a poste or Cheare [chair] and soe saked beett him, firste with two sallie roddes one after the other and after with surseigle [?MS not clear] in suche sorte as the pore man was greatly endaungered of his life, alledgynge noe Cawse soe to abuse the pore man his servaunte but that he sawe him and his wiffe over famylier, the Ladye his wiffe beenge of thadge of fiftie and odd yeares and havinge borne to him children, known to all the Contrye to be an honest Chaste Ladye never suspected of suche Cryme, wherby might well be gathered the hatred towardes his saide wiffe to be such as not satisfied with the Cruell manner of beatinge of her as a foresaide but alsoe by slaunderinge of her to heape more infamy to her person. The thirde offence Contayned in the saide enformacion and for that also lastlye yt moste plainely appeared by the testymonye of wytnesses, as well by his servant Tyrrell as others, that he sente the saide Tyrrell to Dublin to brynge home one of his daughters Called Jane, a gyrle of thortene yeares of adge or thear aboutes Whoe, as he saide, went from his howse with his daughter Marye to Dublin towne dayes before against his will, and uppon her retorne, havinge provided like sallie roddes as accustomed, Caused the saide Tyrrell to pluck uppe the simple terefied & feared gyrle uppon his back whoe takinge either of her handes aboute his neck for holde her and Causinge one or tow women standinge by to unstrippe her Clothes and houlde her legge did in such shamefull unnaturall and mercylis sorte beate her, gevinge her as Comon reporte gave owtt three skore strokes but affyrmed by Tyrrell to be thertye or fortye, [so] as the saide girle then well (the beatinge excepted) by that Cruell manner of strikinge fell that night, as some depose, the daye after as others depose, But within two dayes after as all the wytnesses affyrme, sore sick of an ague which broght with it the flyxe [flux] as within tenne or twelve dayes after she died. Of whose lief he had soe small regarde, althoughe he the father and she the Childe, as durynge her lyinge sick removed her in the tyme of her sickness from her accustomed bed to a rawe Coulde place called a yeeldinge howse, and untill her deathe he never once eyther sawe her or sent to her to see howe she did, the pore gyrle kepte and Comforted all the tyme of her sicknes by poore neighbors, neyther upon the understandinge of her deathe, beinge at Dublin and never further of [off] duringe her sicknes, woulde not him self repayre home to see her buried. And although Comon brute gave owte that the strockes of his Cruell beatinges appeared uppon her [at] the tyme of her wyndinge afer her deathe and at the tyme of her death, of which strokes the univerall brute & Comon reporte was she died, yet caused he not any to falsefye the same brute to take vewe of her bodye before she was buried, but mainteaninge [?MS not clear] uppon knowledge of her deathe, willed the same Tyrrell whoe brought him worde therof to gett home and burye her. By and throughe which manner of most tyrrannycall usinge of him self over those his wiffe, servauntes and Chylde, the wiffe for sevegard [safeguard] of her lief, with feigned excuse to fetche money from her brother, Conveyed her self to her brothers howse where she hathe remayned a yeare and a half, his Butler fledd not daringe to Complaine, and his naturall Childe broght to her untymely grave, worthie for examples sake of all severe & Condigne puinishment to terrefie by his example all of like Callinge, and other inferiors, to beware to comytt such like disorders [and] Cruell

out radge to eny. Therfore and for that, the other seacreat Causes knowen to the L Justice and counsell and not fitt to be remembred in this order, which Comon fame and not Causeles hath manifested to sturre him to the hate of wiffe, Childe and servant and all other his good and honest ffrendes who frendly & privatlie openinge his faulte have wished his reforme & have occasioned him by that tolleracion and stayinge from any Complainte in hope of amendment, and for livinge without Correction to sinck into a deper encrease of his Cruell behavior, wicked and licenciouse life. Therefore yt is by the saide L Justice and Counsell ordred that the saide L of Howthe be Comytted to the Queenes maties Castell of Dublin, there to remayne untill he have Contented and paide to the Queenes matie the some of one thowsande poundes for a fyne, that is to saye for the first beatinge of his wiffe one hundreth poundes, the second beatinge of her beinge stryped naked three hundreth poundes, and the beatinge of his saide poore servante as aforesaide one hundreth poundes, and lastlie for his unnaturall, unmercyfull and vile beatinge of his saide daughter, of which beatinge hadd she died as was proved she did of the ague which that beatinge wrought her unto, he had worthelie deserved the paynes of death, the some of five hundreth poundes, and untill he shall enter into good and sufficient bondes and assurance to observe and kepe the Queenes maties peace against his wiffe, children and famylie, and untill he shall enter into like bondes to give and allowe to his saide wiffe towardes her findinge such porcion of lande and livinge to finde her self with and bringe upp her children, Whoe as ys reported he kepeth at home wihout any nurture or educacion and therfore not to be suffered to remayne in his Custodie, as the saide L Justice and Counsell shall set downe by order uppon the booke remayninge before them for that purpose. Yeaven in her maties saide Courte of Castell chamber the viijth daie of Julye 1579.
[signatures] WGerrard, Ad Dublin, N Bagenall, Lucas Dillon, N Malbie, John Chaloner, J Garvey.[34]

Wheras uppon informacon or complaynt made into this honorable Courte of Castell Chamber by Fraunces Lovell of Knocktoffer in the Countie of Kylkenny, gent, against Lawrence Power of the same, gent, Adam Power, Geffrey Power, Walter Power, James Power, David Power, David Nollan, Rychard Roe Brenaghe and Harrye Nollan, deftes, for A ryote supposed by them to be comytted uppon the said Fraunces Lovell, as by the said byll answere [and] personall Answeres doth and may appeare. In wch said matter the parties descended to an yssue, witnes on bothe parties examyned and published, and severall daies of heringe graunted and appointed, and soundry proces adwarded and executed aswell uppon the said Fraunces Lovell as uppon dyvers of the deftes, ad audiec iudicum. Wch Fraunces refused styll to appear, either by hym self or by his atturney to present the cause, and for that the said Adam Power, Walter Power, James Power, Walter Power, James Power and Harrye O Nollan appeared and the matter on their behalf by their learned counsell moved in Courte before the most reverent father in god Adam L Archebusshoppe of Dublin, L keper of her mates great seale in this Realme, and others of her mates privie Counsell, who referred the same to be considered by her highnes sergiannt and atturnie to understand, uppon the perusing of the pleadinges and deposicions, if any matter might be found to benefitt her matie and to make reporte therof to their LL the next Courte day following, being fryday, this xxixth of this instant monnethe of Aprell. At which day the said Sargiaunt and atturney declared in oppen Curte before their LL that they could fynde no matter or proffe to make for her highnes, saving the deposicons of the said Fraunces Lovell and one of his men wch proffe was thought not sufficient to prove the Riot. It ys therfore ordred and decreed by the said L keper and the rest of the LL and others of her mates pryvie Counsell in that said assembly for the decyding of that cause, and others whose names here after ensue, that all the forenamed deftes shalbe acquited from the said action comenced agaynst them and dysmyssed from the said Courte with their Costes. And also ordred that the said Fraunces Lovell shall pay furthwith to the Clearke of the said Courte suche fees Costes and chardges as shalbe taxed to the said deftes and the said Clearke in that behalf by the ryght honorable the said L keper. Geven at her mates said Courte of Castell Chamber the said xxixth day of Aprell 1580.
[signed] Ad Dublin, custos sig, H Miden.[35]

34. ff. 41v–43.   35. ff. 43v to 44.

Ld Grey   By the L Deputie and Counsell.

Md where Thoms Dillon of Dublin, gent, exhibited on her Maties behalf Informacon befor the Right honorable the L Deputie and Counsell of this realme in her highnes honorable Court of Castlechamber that Robert Dillon, Esquier, S[e]c[on]de Justice of her Maties Courte of Comon Pleas wthin the said Realme, Richard Belinge, gent, her maties Solicitor within the said Realme, and Alexander Fitton of the Bectife, gent, wth dyvers others being aucthorised by vertue of a commission to them directed, satte to enquyre for her maties escheates and wardshipppes within the Countie of Meth and Donboyne within the said Countie of Meth the xxx daye of Marche 1581. Wheare the said daye and yeare upon a mandate by the said Robert Dillon and Richarde Belinge the Jurators undernamed appered before the said Commiss[ion]ers and herd there Charge geven them accordinge the effecte and meaninge of the said Commission and in especially what landes or hereditaments eyther in possession or use the late decessed Richard Lynham of Adamston, gent, had at the tyme of his deathe within the said Countie of Methe, of whom the same was holden and by what Tenures. And for her matie it was geven in evidence to the said Jurye emongest other thinges that the said Richard Lynham was seised as in estate of Inheritance the day of his death being the xxviijth of August 1580 of two parcells of land within the said Countie of Methe called Thomaston and Turyn wch the said Richard Lynham helde of her Matie by knight service in capite of her Royall person and that Thomas Lynam was sonne and heyre to the said Richard Lynam and within age. And for as mouche as the said Jurors, notwithstandinge the said evidence geven on her Maties behalfe, as befor havenge neyther wytnesses nor testimony produced before them, nor any dewe or just knowledge emongest them soever contrary to the said evidence geven them, beinge as it should seme caried away wth some Corrupt affeccion without Respect of Conscience or feare of god, gave in ther verdict falsely and uniustly that the said Richard did leave by will to Katheryne Handcocke, his wyfe, Turyne and Thomaston and xltie acres in Laraghcon as her Joytor [Jointure] wth a condicon to Redeme them. It is therfor uppon the severall hearinges and debatinge at large of the said matter in the said Courte of Castle chamber, wayinge and only consideringe the circumstance of every parte thereof, ordered, adiudged and decreed by us the L. Deputie and others of her maties privie Counsell then present whose names are hereunder subscribed that the said Jurors for there heynous and grevous offence to god besides the great perilous evell and dangerous example to others hereafter yf the same shuld Remayne uncorrected that for there false and untrewe verdicte geven they and every of them shalbe presently Committed to Warde, there to Remayne during the said L Deputies pleasure, and lickwyse it is ordered by the said L Deputie and counsell that they and any of them for their said periurye shall pay to her maties use such severall some[s] as appeareth hereunder uppon every of there polls [i.e. heads], that is to say, upon Xpofer Barnewall one hundreth poundes. In this respecte because the said Barnewall was forman of the said Jurye and by whose mouthes they all spake and upon Xpofer Hussey one other hundreth poundes, for that it appared he was the Ringe leader of the said Jurye and by whose untrue Informacon they were caried away, and the Rest of the Jurye in fiftie poundes every of them. And it is further orderedd that the said Jurye shall stande upon the pillorye for the periurie with papers on there heades during the said L Deputies pleasure. Geven at her maties courte of Castlechamber the vth of Maye 1581.

Xpofer Barnewall of Arrotston £100
Xpofer Hussey of the ?Aheardrons £100
Gerald Foster of Kilcregie £50
Patricke Phepo of Roan £50
Simon Roe of Waringston £50
Maurishe Ley of Clanrosse £50
Xpofer Torran of Moyglane £50
John Eustace of Lescartan £50
Richard Pentyney of Cabbrighe £50
Patrick Ley of Clonrose £50
Richard Sale of Saleston £50
[signatures] A Dublin, cust sig, H Wallop, Lucas Dillon, N White, Nicholas Nugent, J Garvey, Ed Waterhouse.[36]

36. ff. 44v to 45v.

In most humble wise sheweth unto your honor the poore infortunate and simple Jurors nowe condempnede of p[erjury: MS torn], whoe weare lede and seduced by others whoe are not unknown to your L, through mere ignorance, and weare instructed and informede by them that if [they: MS torn] did not as they have done that they should doo uniustlie and untrulie, which nowe thei understand to be untrue, to ther utter undoinge. Therefore they acknowledging ther faulte doo most humblie beseche yor honor to pardone and release ther periurie and fine unto them they are adiudgede, and the rather for the conscider[ation] aforesaide and that your honorable L will of your clemencie and goodnes have remorse and pittie of [the] povertie and miserable estate of your poor suppliants and they shall dailie pray, etc.

[signed]

Gerald Forster	Richard Penteney
Symon Row	Morrishe Lee
Christopher Barnewall	Richard Delasale
Patrick Pheypo	Patricke Ley
Crystofer Hussey	John Eustace.[37]

[text of petition by jurors (above, fol.46) is copied exactly at top of following order]

[signed] L Gray　　　　　　　　　　　　　　　　　　By the L Deputie and Counsell

Upon wch humble submission so by them reade and delivered unto us, weying and consideringe they do confesse that the said periurie so by them Committed was Rather through the perswacon of others whoe induced and ledd them thereunto then of ther owne willful doinge, and wayinge also the disabilitie and greate povertie of the said parties to be farre unhable to pay the whole somes of these fynes by our order taxed upon them: We have Condescendid and agreed for Causes aforesaid and other Consideracons us movinge to have Commiseracon and Remorse, not only for there dischardge from ther punishment of the pillory, but also to mittigate ther said fynes. It is therfore ordered by us the said L Deputie and others of the privie counsell whose names are hereunder subscribed that the said Jurours that so have made submission shalbe released from there said punishment of the pillorie and also ther severall fynes to be mittigated in manner and forme following, viz: Xpofer Barnewall to xx ˡⁱ str, Xpofer Hussey, xx ˡⁱ str, John Ewstace, xx ˡⁱ str, Maurice Ley, x ˡⁱ str, Patrick Pepoe, x ˡⁱ str, Richard De La Sale, xiij ˡⁱ vj s viij d str, Simon Row, 100 s str, Xpofer Torran, iiij ˡⁱ str, Patrick Ley x ˡⁱ str, Richard Penteney, v ˡⁱ str, Gerald Foster, x ˡⁱ. And also further ordered that they and every of them shall enter into severall bandes of Recognisance wth sufficient suerties for the payment of theire severall somes to thandes of Edward Waterhouse, esquier, Receavor of her maties Casualties, or to his deputie in that office, to her heighnes use at or by the vjth day of November next ensewinge the date hereof. Yeven at her maties Castell of Dublin the xjth of May 1581.

[signed] Ad Dublin, H Wallop, N White, Lucas Dillon, J Garvey, Ed Waterhouse.[38]

Ld Gray　　　　　　　　　　　　　　　　　　By the L Deputie and Counsell

Where upon Complainte exhibited unto this honorable Courte of Castle Chamber by John Fuller and Walter Fox of Chester, merchauntes, pl, against Phillip Lamport & others of the Countie of Wexforde, in the tyme of Sir William Drurye, knight, late Ld Justice of this Realme, for an outrage Committed by the saide Lamporte and the rest of the def. It was agreed by the said L Justice & Counsell ther psent in Courte that the said Lamporte and the said deftes should paye as a fyne to her maties use the some of one hundreth poundes and an order thereof entered and signed by the said Ld Justice and certen of the Counsell leaving a blanke for the some as by the same ordre dated the xxvjth of June 1579 appeareth. Which fyne being made doubtfull by Reason of the said blanke was nowe brought in question befor us by the Clerke of the Courte for his discharge and therin advouched by the right honorable the Ld Kep[er] and others of her hyghness pryvie counsell, that the said fyne of an hundreth poundes was fully adiudged and agreed upon in open courte and appointed to be taxed and levied upon the said Lamporte and the rest of the deftes to her maties use. It is therfore ordered and agreed by us the L Deputie & Counsell whose names are hereunto

---

37. f. 46. This petition inserted loosely into entry book, although foliation continues sequentially.
38. ff. 47–47v.

subscribed that the said £100 fyne so adiudged and agreed upon as aforesaid shalbe sett downe & written into the said blanke and so to be answered and paied by the deftes to her highness use by the second retorne of hillary terme, yf the said def in the meane tyme do not showe good matter of Cause before us the said L Deputie, Ld Chauncellor or Ld Keper and Counsell in discharge of the same. Yeven at her maties Castell of Dublin the first of September 1581.

[signed] Lucas Dillon, H Wallop, N Bagenall, Nychol Malbie, Ed Waterhous.[39]

L Grey   By the L Deputie and Counsell

Md where Xpofer Fleminge, the Quenes maties attorney generall at lawes, exhibited informacon before the Right honorable the L Deputie and Counsell in her highnes Court of Castle Chamber, howe the xxvijth day of Januarie in the yeare of the Reigne of our Soveraigne ladye the quenes matie the xxiiijth, Twelve men of the Countie of Kildare and Dublin (whose names are underwritten) were sworn upon the holy Evangelist befor her matie in her Chief Place within this Realme to trie and fynde whether Morishe FitzJames als FitzGeralde of Osbaston in the said Countie of Kildare was giltie of heigh Treason, whereof he was indyted, That is to say, the mainteyninge, helpinge and Comfortinge of James Eustace, late vicomte of Baltinglasse, Thomas Rocheforde, Oliver Ewstace and others in the Rebellion against her matie, which xij men, contrary to very apparante, manifest and playne matter delivered them, aswell by the Judges as by the Quenes learned counsell, by presompcons, good Testimonie and apparante proofe, did fynde the said Morishe FitzJames not giltie of the said treason, but giltie of mispricon. By which verdite the said twelve men Committed playne and manifest periurye, example so perilous and dangerous in every comon wealthe as, yf severe punishement do not followe, thereof great harme and danger will ensue. Wherefor the said attorney prayed thordre of this honorable Courte, whereunto the said twelve men answered that they made a true Othe and were not periured in maner as thenforacon is alleged, and after the matter being herd in open Courte and very effectually debated, It manifestly appeared that the said Jury had given them in Evidence, aswel by strong and vehement presompcons as by proofe, testimonie and other sufficient matter that the said Morishe was giltie of the said Treason, All which was verified unto the courte to be true, both by the Judges that sat in Judgment and by some of the pryvie counsell that sate there at the declaringe of the said cause. Wherefore it is ordered and adjudged by the Right honorable the L Deputie and others of the pryvie Counsell, Judges of the said Courte, whose names ensueth that every of the said Jury shall pay unto her matie for a fyne for their shameful periurie a hundreth poundes, and such of the said Jurie whose landes and goodes as will not amount to satisfie the sayd fyne of £100, there variete of payment to be supplied by the Residewe Jurors of best habilitie and Chiefest doers in procuringe and leading the simpler sorte, over and above the £100 on themselves assessed. [Crossed out in MS: 'And it is further ordered that the said Jurie shall stand upon the pillorye for there said willful periurie with papers on there heades during the said L Deputies pleasure'.] Yeven at her maties courte of Castle Chamber the vjth of Februarie 1582.

[signed] H Wallop, N Bagenall, Robert Dillon, Lucas Dillon, N White, Ed Waterhous, Geffrey Fenton.[40]

[no date; text in different hand, refers to jurors in above case]
John White of Chaynelly [?Chapelizod], soldier
John Barnewall of Barymore
Willm Lock of Colmanstone
Patrick Tallon of the Meston
Robte Tyrrell of Powerstone
James Golding of Tobbersowle
Richard Jacob of Ballycullan

39. f. 48. See Quinn, ed., 'Cal. Council book', p. 119 for recognizance of Lamport and four other defendants, dated 18 June 1581, to appear before the lord deputy and council the first day of the next Michaelmas term. See above, f. 40v, for initial hearing of the case before the court of castle chamber, dated 26 June 1579. Also see below, ff. 56v–57, for enforcement of order by two sheriffs in Co. Wexford.
40. ff. 49–49v.

Nycholas Den of Tassagarde
Richard Sedgrave of Baranstown
Patrick Bellewe of Raynoldstown
Walter Crey of Thomastown
Patrick Saunders of the Newetowne.[41]

[signature] L A Grey.   By the L Deputie and Counsell.
Md where Michell Cusake of Ratheholron in the Countie of Meth, gent, hath by informacon exhibited unto her moste honorable Courte of Castle Chamber befor us the L Deputie and Counsell impeched one Richard Dorran of Dorranston within the said Countie, freholder, viz that he deposed and affirmed that a parcel of grounde Called Chaple Orcharde was thinheritaunce of James Tankarde father to Patrick Tankarde of Castleton and that he used ocupied and toke the proffittes therof all his lyfe tyme, and died seysed therof, to which informacon the def by his answere mainteyned his deposicon to be true. For as muche as upon the hyringe & debatinge therof in Open Courte it manifestly appeared by sufficient proofe and witnesses then Redd in Courte, that the said Tankarde did not dye seysed of the said parcell of grownde Called Chaple Orchard, but that the saide Michell his tennante used the same, and that he also toke & Receaved the proffittes therof from tyme to tyme. It is therfor upon the severall hyringe and debatinge at large of the same matter in the said Courte of Castle Chamber, wayinge and dewly Consideringe the Circumstance of every parte therof, Ordered, adiudged and decreed by us the L Deputie and others of her maties privie Counsell then present whose names are under written that the said Richard Dorran for his heynous periurie Committed by his untrue deposicon shalbe Comitted to warde there to Remayne duringe the L Deputies pleasure. And further the said Richard shall pay to her maties use fyve poundes Curr[ent] money for his fyne, and shall also paye for Costes and Charges of the Courte as shalbe adiudged by the L Chauncellor. Geven at her maties Courte of Castle Chamber the ixth of Februarie 1582.
[signatures:] HWallop, N Bagenall, Robert Dillon, Lucas Dillon, N White, Ed Waterhous, Geffray Fenton.[42]

To the right honorable Sir Arthur Grey, knight of the most noble order of the garter, Lo Greye of Wilton, Lo Deputy generall of the Realme of Ireland.
Most humbly beseching, sheweth unto your L yor dayly orator, Laurence Hollyneshed, Clerke of her maties Corte of castell chamber, That whear the bookes of actes and orders of the same Court ar nowe very imperfecte and far out of order, by reason the actes and orders hearetofore pronouncyd in Corte have not bene entered into the same before the next courte theare holden, after the day that they were pronouncede, but set downe most comonly in Lewse papers, and by that meane often cast aside and lost, and so not at all entered into the saide bookes, and the most parte also suche as wer entered, wer slightly drawen by the Clerke of the Corte or his men (being ignorant, etc.) and comonly not comdered [?commandered, ordered] upon and pennyd by her maties Lernyd counsell. And so the canc[ellarius] moving the corte to order, the same therein not Inserted, those actes and orders have often tymes ben reversed, for want of dewe informacon geven unto the Cort of the cause where they were first ordered, to the great prejudyce as well of her matie and her good subyectes and to the great Incorraging of thoffender to remayne in their evell actions for want of terror and poneshement for their former offences. May it therefore please yor good L to dyrect yor lres to her maties lerned [counsel] reamyning [MS torn; remaining] and eavery of them thearebye carefully and consyderately thearein to deale, So as the clarke bringinge to them any acte orr order, drawen uppon any acte or order heretofore pronounced and yet not entred into the bookes or hearafter to be pronouncede, they do accordinglye wth suche expedicon correcte and per[fec]tly forme for the best advauntage of her matie and her good subyectes as the Clarke may have suffycyent tyme theareuppon to enter the same into the bookes of the Court before the next cort then to be holden, and yor said orator will dayly pray, etc.
[signed] Laurence Hollinshedde.

41. f. 50. See Quinn, ed., 'Cal. Council book', for apparent reference. 'Recognizance of John White of Chapelizod and ten [?eleven] others, all tenants of the queen, in £40 each to appear in the Castle Chamber on Tuesday next if then called upon, if not at the first sitting of that court in Easter term next.' (p. 124)
42. ff. 51–51v.

If racoth [MS unclear: ?it please] your L, lres to be dyrected to her maties lernyde counsell and eavery of them, requyring thereby considerately to pen all soche actes and orders alredy pronounced in the said Cort and not entered into the bokes of actes and orders thereof [text repeats the substance of memorandum, above].

Graunted, for yt it is enformed y[t] surli hathe been ever ye order of that courte.
[signed] A Grey.[43]

Termino Pascha 1582	Frydaye the iijth of Maye 1582
[judges listed]	
The L Depute	Baron Dillon
Mr Threr	Mr of the Rolles
Mr Marshall	Mr Waterhous
Justice Plunkett	Mr Secretarye Fenton
Justice Dillon	

Wheare an informacon of Ryott was exhibited in this honorable Courte the Second daye of September in the yeare of our Lorde 1581 by the Reverend father in God Michall [MS not clear], by gods providence Bisshopp of Ossorie pl: against John Archer and othere Defts as by the same informacon remayning upon the Philace of the saide Courte dothe and maye at lardge appeare. Uppon hearinge of the matter by us her maties Counsell, Commissioners and assistauntes of her highnes saide Courte, yt is ordered and adiudged for good Cawses the Courte moving that the same matter and parties bee Dismissed and dischardged out of this Courte paying onely all manner of Fees due to the Clearke and officeres of the same Courte.[44]

Termino Pascha 1582	Frydaye the xviijth of Maye
Present: The L: Chauncellor	The Mr of ye Rolls
Mr Threr	Mr Waterhous
Justice Dillon	Mr Secretary Fenton
Mr Chiefe Baron	The Deane of Christchurche

Where Joyce Adryan of Dublin, Letherdresser, exhibited a bill of Ryot into this honorable Courte of Castell Chamber the xxxth daye of Januarie 1580, againste Thomas Dermott of the same Citie, m[er]chaunt, bothe parties apparing in Courte this daye, it was there ordered and adiudged, for verie reasonable cawses the Corte moving, that the saide pties and their cawse sholde bee dismissed out of the said Courte without paying Costs the one of them to thother, or otherwise save costs and fees of Corte to bee dewe to thofficers of the same and either of them fyve shillinges to bee brought into the same Corte to bee by order of the same distributed to the poore. Dated at the said Corte of Castell chamber Friday the xviijth of Maye 1582 as aforesaid.[45]

Termino Paschae 1582	Frydaye the viijth of Maye
[judges listed]	
The L Chauncelor	The Mr of the Rolles
Mr Threr	Mr Waterhouse
Justice Dillon	Mr Secretary Fenton
The chief Baron	The deane of Christchurche

43. ff. 52–53v. The memorandum from the clerk is inserted laterally into the entry book, loose leaf, and the response is based on a digest of it, to which the lord deputy gave informal assent. It is suggestive of a larger burden of work for the court which was never entered or recorded by the clerical staff. Fols. 52v–53 are blank.
44. f. 54. The names of the judges are listed here, rather than signed, and the clerical reorganization of records is manifest.
45. f. 55. Note in margin scribbled by Holinshed identifies litigants and discusses fine. Fol. 55v is blank.

Where Robte Adame of Portlecester in the Countie of Methe gent exhibited a bill of Ryot in this honorable Courte of Castell Chamber the vth of Februarye 1579 against Theobald Dillon, Thomas Plunkett, William Hamon, Christofer Noland, William Goghe, Alexander Barnewell, Thomas Fielde, John Giggens, John Sarsfeld, Nicholas Fyan, Roger Roache, John Usher, Thomas Byrne, Nicholas Weston, Nicholas Borran, Thomas Barry, Edward Bulger, Stephen Borran, Walter Duff, Gerrat Nugent, Henry Cormock and William Betaughe of the Citie of Dublin merchauntes, Richard Copperan of the same Citie, Appoticary, and Roger Tavernor of the same Citie, Trumpettor are by [the] bill remaynyng upon the Philace of the saide Courte dothe and maye appeare. The same matter being moved this daye in Corte was for verie reasonable cawses the Corte moving dismissed, and ordered that neither partye shold paye eny costes to the other or otherwise, save only [Ms torn] to bee due to the officers of the same Corte. Dated the saide xviijth of Maye as abovesaid.[46]

Termino Trinitatis 1582
[judges listed]
The L Chauncelor
Justice Dillon
The Chief Baron

Fryday the xxijth of June

Sir Nicholas Malbye
The Mr of the Rolls
Mr Waterhouse

Where Lawrence Hollinshed gent, Clerke of this Courte, informed the same this daye that a Commission of Rebellion had before that tyme viz the xxth of Maye 1581 beene awarded out of this Corte and directed to Anthonie Colcloughe of Tynterne in the Countie of Wexforde Esquire, then Shreve of that Countie, and otheres retournable xv Srd [?September] michis [Michaelmas] nowe Last past and then nott retourned accordingly nore at eny tyme since. Whereupon the saide Colcloughe being present in Courte this daye alleaged that in suche Comission made to him delyvered, the contrary whereof was nott then, neither by the same Clerke nor by eny other proved, the Clerke alledging for his excuse that the matter passed in the tyme when Robte Kendall, gent, nowe deceased was Clerke of the Corte, and that hee could finde no sufficient matter to prove the same sett downe emongest the Recordes of the Corte, having made dilligent searche therein to that ende. It was therefore ordered and adiudged by the same Corte that the saide Colcloughe sholde for that matter bee dischardged and dismised out of the Courte. Dated Frydaye the xxivth of June 1581 as aforesaid.[47]

Where Lawrence Hollinshed gent Clerke of this Courte informed the same this daye, that a commission of dedimus potestatem had before that tyme dated the xviith daye of Julye 1581 beene awarded out of this Corte and directed to Anthonie Colclough [of Tynterne in the Countie of Wexforde, Esquire, then Shreve of that Countie and otheres] returnable crastino animarum [i.e. November 3] then next followinge, whereby he was not onelie aucthorised but also streatlye chardged and comaunded fourthe with to call before hym one Walter Synnot, late Sherief of the said Contye of Wexford, willing and requyring hym to deliver unto the said Colclough a perfect accompt in wryting what some or sommes of money he, or any by his appoyntement, had receved of Phillippe Lamport, Patricke Synnot and others, upon whome £100 fine and £iij vj s. viii d. Costs had before that tyme ben ymposed by this honorable court and with all to shewe unto the said Colclough the truthe how and in what sorte he had or cold dischardge hymself of suche some or somes of money as he had alredye receved and what remeyned of that alredie receved in his handes to deliver to her maties use unto the handes of the sayed Colclough, and further to doe divers other thinges menconed in the said Comission and certyfye in to this honorable Corte crastino animarum then next ensewinge his procedinges therin, which he had not don accordingly. Whereupon the said Colclough beinge present in court that daye required a sight of the said forme [of] Comission which the Clerke of the court by order of the same courte delivered unto him accordingly. Whereupon the sayed Colclough was ordered to retorne the same ageyne the next court daye following, being this present daye, togeather with suche returne and certificate of his former procedyinges as he wolde stand unto, which

46. f. 56.
47. f. 56v. See above, f. 40v for original case, f. 48 for adjustment of fine, and below, f. 57 for enforcement in Co. Wexford.

he performed accordinglie as appeareth by a scedule to the same Commission anexed by hym returned, together with the same Comyssion into this Courte this daye and Delivered to thandes of the Clerke of the Court by order thereof. Wherupon for causes and consideracons the court moving it is adiudged and ordered that the said Colclough sholde for that matter be discharged and dismised out of the Courte. Dated the xviith of July as aforesaid.[48]

Thursdaye Vto Julij 1582
[judges listed]
The L Chancelor   The Mr of the Rolls
The busshop of Meath   The deane of Christchurche
Mr Threr   Mr. Waterhowse
Mr. Justice Dillon   Mr. Secretary Fenton
Mr. Chiefe Baron

Wheras a subpena was awarded ageynst Thomas Waring and others the defs returnable this daye, wheruppon the sayed Thomas Waring being served therwith appered accordingly, and John Berford, Elizabeth Talbot, Calpe [?MS not clear] horsboye, John Conan, Walter McLaghlyn, Willm Lawlesse, Willm OHoyne, Patricke OHoyne, John Glasse, Nicholas Dillon, Bryne OMeloy, Manus OMaltally, Patrick Evers, Donaugh Lonnyne and Tayle McEvard being also defs and served with the like proces by Denys Jurdan, the Sherieffs clerke, Tuesdaye last have not appered accordingly. It was thereupon ordered and adiudged by the same Corte for verie reasonable causes the saeme moving that the sayd matter be dismyssed and the sayed Waryng to be bound in x ˡⁱ to prosecute with effect and ageynst the said names. Proces of attachment awarded ageynst the sayd Manus OMaltally to apper agayne quiadens sci Michis [Michaelmas] next.[49]

Termino Trinitatis 1582   Wednesdaye the xxviith of June
[judges listed]
The L Deputie   Sir Nicholas Malbye
The L Chancellor   The Mr of the Rolles
Mr Threr   Mr Waterhouse
Mr Justice Dillon
Mr Chief Baron

The Baron of Howthe beeinge served with process of Subpena appeared thereupon this daye where it was ordered uppon hearing of the matter that the Fyne of a Thowsand poundes beefore that tyme imposed uppon him by the same Corte sholde bee mitigated and reduced to the Some of fyve hundreth poundes. Dated the xxvijth of June as aforesaid.[50]

Termino trinitatis 1582   Thursdaye vte Juliu 1582
[judges listed]
The L Chaunclor   The Mr of the Rolls
The Busshop of Meathe   The Deane of Christchurch
Mr. Threr   Mr Waterhowse
Mr. Justice Dillon   Mr. Secretary Fenton
Mr. Chief Baron

48. ff. 57–57v. See above for the case in question involving Philip Lamport and others, fined for an affray at a shipwreck, dated 26 June 1579 [fol. 40v].
49. f. 58. Case not recorded in Lomas edition of court records. Waring was made responsible for other defendants, OMaltally was sought by process of attachment, no bill or indictment was mentioned and the sheriff's clerk was not identified by county. Fol. 58v is blank.
50. f. 59. See the original case against Lord Howth above, ff. 41v–43, dated 8 July 1579. Another case originally cited in manuscript was subsequently crossed out. The effect was: 'Patricke Kimanynge pl, Elizabeth Talbot of Kilmarchton and others def. This matter beying this day moved in Corte was for reasonable causes the same

Where Christopher St. Lawrence L. Baron of Howthe was in the tyme of the government of Sir William Drewrye, knight, then L Justice of this realme condemned in a fyne of one thowsande poundes to bee paide unto the Queenes Matie by the said L Baron of Howthe for certein offences by him comitted, ar by thorder therof remayning of recorde in the saide Courte of Castell Chamber more att lardge appeareth. And the saide L Baron beeng called into the saide Corte to shewe cawse why hee shold nott satisfye and paye the saide some of m th li. unto her matie according to the saide order, made humble Peticon unto the right honorable the L Deputie and the rest of the privie Counsell then sitting in the saide Courte whoese names are subscribed, declaring unto them howe hee had alreadie beene punished for the saide facte by imprisonment by the space of xix teene weekes to his intollerable chardge and hinderaunce. Hee declared also how the payment of so great a some wolde bee the quite overthrowe and undoing of him and his howse. And last howe hee was verie penitent and sorye for the saide cawse, humblie beseeching their honors to have pittie and comiseracon uppon him and thantiquitie of his howse and to reduce and qualify the saied fine uppon the Consideracone aforesaid as to theire grave wisdome shold seeme good. Whose request and peticon beeing duely and advisedly considered uppon by the saide Court: It was ordered and decreed that the saide fyne of one thowsand poundes sholde bee qualified and brought downe to the some of fyve hundred poundes. Dated the vth of Julye 1582: as aforesaid.[51]

Thursdaye vto Julij 1582.
Present: the L Chancelor, the Mr of the Rolls, the Busshop of Meath, the deane of Chri[st]church, Mr Threr, Mr Waterhowse, Mr Justice Dillon, Mr Secretary Fenton, Mr Chief Baron.
Whereas Lawrence Hollynshed, clerke of this court, informed the same this daye that there werr not so fewe as 30 or 40 causes presently depending therin ready at hearing, and farre greater number not so farre proceeded in, and though divers as well pls as defs were in towne yet did they not prosecute the same. It is therfore ordered and decreed, for verie reasonable causes the same Court moving, that process of attachment be adwarded against suche of them, as well pls as defs as shall not have their causes determined this terme, returnable octabis michis next and then the parties severally to enter into recognizance to prosecute with effect. And lykewise ordered that suche as shall hereafter exhibitt bills in the same court, her matie beeing not merely pl therin, shall severally enter into recognizance to prosecute the same wth effect, ere the Clerke of the Court geve fourthe his warrant for proces to be made therupon. And further ordered that the said Clerk shalbe Attorney for all suche as nowe presentlye are playntiffs or that hereafter shalbe playntiffs in the same Cort.[52]

Wednesday the last of October 1582.
[Present:] The L Justice Lofthowse, Mr Waterhowse, Justice Dillon, Secreatary Fenton, the Mr of the Rolls, Justice Dowdale.
Where one Robert Skeiret of Galvey, marchaunt, exhibited a bill of periurie in this honnorable court of Castle Chamber the xxvjth of June 1574 against one Sir Clement Skirret, priest. Whereupon a writt of S:q was adwarded, returnable the xxviijth of the same moneth. Whereunto the said Sir Clement appered and answered the xxth of October then next following. Whereunto the said [plaintiff] Replied the xxvjth of October then next following. Whereunto the sayd Sir Clement reioyned and thereupon Interrogatories being mynistered on the behalfe of ether partie, witnesses were theruppon examined accordinglie. Forasmuche as proces of attachemente was the last Trinitie terme awarded and delivered to the mayor and Baylives of Galvey aforesayd to attache the said Robert and Clement, retornable xv° sci michis last, who by vertue therof attached the bodie of the said Robert, who thereupon appered and the said Clement being returned non est inventus appered

movyng dismyssed, paying fees due to thofficers of the same.' f. 59. Fols. 59v–60 are blank except for note: 'The L of Howth order for reducing his fyne of m li to v li.' f. 60.
51. ff. 62–62v. A note at left margin editorializes: 'Just some and somes.' Folios 61–61v are blank, while fol. 60v includes the following memorandum, in rough hand: 'Wher Christofer St Lawrens L baron of Howthe was in the tyme of the govermt of Sir Willm Drury knight Justice of the realme condemned in a fyne of one thowsande poundes to bee paide unto the Queenes Matie by the said L Baron of Howthe for certain offences by him comitted ...' See above, ff. 41v–43 for original action, dated 8 July 1579.
52. f. 63.

not, the sayd Robert Skerret informeing the Court this day that the matter was aiudged long tyme synce, whiche some of the commissioners of the sayd Court and some of her maties lerned Counsell affirmed to be true. It was therefore and for other most reasonable causes the court moving, ordered that the said parties and matter be dismissed out of this court, paying the fees due to the officers of the same. Dated the last of October 1582 as is above written.[53]

Wednesdaie the last of October 1582. The L Justice Lofthouse, Mr Waterhowse, Justice Dillon, Secreatary Fenton, the Mr of the Rolls, Justice Dowdale, present.
[text in margin, crossed out: 'Patrick Manning, pl, Elizabeth Talbott, def.']
[Formula A (our italics)] *This matter beinge moved in court this daye is ordered to bee dismissed.*[54]

Wednesday the vijth of November 1582.
[Present:] The L Justice Lofthowse, The L Justice Walloppe, Therle of Thomond, The barron of Howthe, Justice Dillon, The Mr of the Rols, Mr Secreatarye Fenton [crossed out in MS: Justice Dowdall].
Where Willm Butler of Rosse in the Countie of Wexford, marchaunt, exhibited a bill of Riot in this honorable Court of Castle Chamber against Walter Deverox of Battalston in the said countie, gent, and others as by his bill remaynyng uppon the philaces of the said Court doth and maye appere. The same matter being moved this day in Corte was for verie reasonable causes the Court moving dismissed and dischardged out of this Court, paying all manner of fees due to the clerke and officers of the same court.[55]

[See formula A, fol. 65, used in following entries, wherein the same date and judges are repeated, litigants and causes of action recited, and matters long depending at court dismissed and discharged, with fees paid to the court officials.]
Where Anstace Browne of Coddestowne in the Countie of Wexford, widdow, exhibited a bill of Riot in this honorable Court of Castle Chamber against Aristotle Scurlocke of Roslare in the said Countie, gent, and others ... [case dismissed].[56]

[See formula, above] Where Anstace Browne of Coddestowne in the Countie of Wexford, widdow, exhibited a bill of Riot ... [identical matter to case above, adding] ... the xiijth of Maie 1577 ...[57]

[See formula, above] Where John Plunket of Logh Crewe in the countie of Meath, gent, exhibited a bill of Riot in this honorable Court of Castle Chamber the xxixth of November 1571 against Edmond Darcie of Jordanston in the said countie, gent, and others ... [case dismissed].[58]

[See formula, above] Where Thomas Darcie of Lugher in the countie of Methe, gent, and others exhibited a bill of Riot in this honorable Court of Castle Chamber the xxxth of November 1572 against Patrick Coyne of Lesmollen in the said countie and others ... [case dismissed].[59]

[See formula, above] Where Thomas Snagge, Esquier, hier Maties Attorney generall att Lawes exhibited a bill of Riot in this honorable Court of Castle Chamber the vijth day of Februarie 1577 against Robert Caddell of Dowston in the countie of Meth, gent, and others ... [case dismissed].[60]

[See formula, above] Where Simon Luttrell of Luttrellston in the Countie of Meath, Esquire, exhibited a bill of Riot in this honorable court of Castle Chamber [no date] against John Harforde of Doonboyne in the said countie, housband[man], and others ... [case dismissed].[61]

53. f. 64.   54. f. 65.
55. f. 65v.   56. f. 66.
57. f. 66v.   58. f. 67.
59. f. 67v.   60. f. 68.
61. f. 68v.

[See formula, above] Where Dame Jennet Sarsfield, late wiffe to Sir Thomas Cusake, knyght, exhibited a bil of Riot in this honorable court of Castle Chamber [no date] against Richard Nugent and others ... [case dismissed].[62]

[See formula, above] Where Dame Jennet Sarsfield, late wiffe to Sir Thomas Cusake, knyght, exhibited a bill of Riot in this honorable court of Castle Chamber [no date] against Fraunces Byrmyngham of the Corballie, co Meath, gent, and others ... [case dismissed].[63]

[See formula, above] Where Robert Phipole of Holliwood in the countie of Dublin, gent, exhibited a bill of Riot in this honorable Court of Castle Chamber against William Eustace and others ... [case dismissed].[64]

[See formula, above] Where Richard Bealinge her highnes [solicitor general] at lawes exhibited a bill of Riot in this honorable court of Castle Chamber against Nicholas Tirrell, sarvant to Sir Xpofer, L of Howth ... [case dismissed].[65]

[See formula, above] Where John Pentennie of the citye of Dublin, merchant, and Thomazene, his wyfe, exhibited a bill of Riot in this honorable Court of Castle Chamber against Lawrence Taffe, sarvant to the L vicount of Gormanstowne and others ... [case dismissed].[66]

[See formula, above] Where her maties Attorney Generall at Lawes exhibited an Informacon in this honorable Court against Peter Eaylward, mayor of Waterford, and others ... [case dismissed].[67]

[See formula, above] Where Stephen Mountney of Dublin, gent, exhibited a bill of Ryote in this honorable Court of Castle Chamber the xxiijth daye of June 1579 against Edward Brabazon of Thomas Court, Esquire, and others ... [case dismissed].[68]

[See formula, above] Where Hugh O Rayelye [of] Dromlomane in the Countie of Cavan, knyght, and others exhibited a bill of Riot in this honorable court of Castle Chamber [no date] against Iryeall O Ferall of Mornye in the County of Longford, gent, and others ... [case dismissed].[69]

Wednesdaie vijth of November 1582
Present: The L Justice Lofthowse, Justice Dillon, The L Justice Walloppe, The master of the Rolles, The earle of Thomond, Secretary Fenton, The Barron of Howthe
Where Aristotle Scurlocke of Ballynore in the countye of Wexford, gent, exhibited a bill of ryot in this most honorable court of castle chamber the xijth daye of August 1581? [last digit missing in MS] against Thomas Deveroxe of Litle Killyan in the said countye, yeoman, Walter Butler of Butleriston, gent, James Browne of Lynseston, horseman, Thomas Whithey and Richard Whithey, servante unto the said Thomas Deveroxe, as by the same remayning upon the philaces of this court, Dothe and maye more at large apeare. For asmuche as upon the deliberat hearing of the matter before us the LL Justices of the realme of Ireland and other her maties commyssioners of the sayde court of castlechamber and assistances of her maties nobilitie, clergie, privy counsell and Justices of her

62. f. 69.   63. f. 69v.
64. f. 70.
65. f. 70v. See above, ff. 39–40 for original case, dated 22 May 1579.
66. f. 71. See above, f. 21 for original case, dated 23 October 1577.
67. f. 71v.   68. f. 72.
69. f. 72v.

courtes there present, whose names are hereunto sett downe. It apeared evidently by certen deposicions in open court Deliberatly red and considered upon there this daye that all the said Defendantes were guilty of the said ryot in mannor and forme as the said Scurlockes bill purportid. It is ordered and adiudged by us the said LL Justices and the rest whose names hereafter ensewe That the said Thomas Deveroxe one of the said Defendantes shall paye to her maties use for a fyne the some of twenty nobles and shall indure imprisonment in her maties castle of Dublin by the space of one monethe. And the said Walter Browne an other of the said Defendantes to paye for a fyne to her maties use the some of fyve poundes and indure imprisonment by the space of twoe monethes. And that everye one of the rest of the Defendantes mencioned in the said informacon shall paye for a fyne to her maties use everye one of them fourety shillinges, and indure and abyde imprisonment every one of them by the space of three monethes. And that processe be awardid to every one of the said Defendantes presently to yeald theire bodies prisoners to the said castle of Dublin there to remayne prisoners without baile or mainprise as aforesaid untill further order be taken by this said court touching their inlargment and that they the said Defendantes and every one of them shall paye to the said plentyfe for his costes in this suyte expendid suche somes of money as the right honorable the L chancelor of this realme of Ireland shall taxe and assesse. Yoeven at her maties said court of castle chamber Frydaye the ixth of November 1582 and in the yeare of the raigne of our Soveraigne Ladie Queene Elizabeth the xxiiijth.[70]

[See formula A, fol. 65] Where the Ladie Cusacke [Dame Jenet Sarsfield] late wife [to Thomas Cusake] exhibited a bill of Riot in this honorable court of Castle Chamber [no date] against Richard Nugent and others ... [case dismissed].[71]

[See formula, above] Where Richard Belinge, her maties solicitor at lawe exhibited a bill of ryot in this honorable court of Castle Chamber [no date] against James Shortall and others ... [case dismissed].[72]

[See formula, above] Where Christofer Fleminge, her maties Attorney Generall at Lawes, exhibited a bill of periurie in her highnes behalfe against Anthony Peppard and others of the Jurie in her majesties Courte of Castell Chamber ... [case dismissed].[73]

[Endorsed:] To or Wellbeloved Hollingshed, Clar[k] of the Castle Chamber within the Castell of Dublin.
By the [L Deputie; MS torn]
Whearas John Strich, late maior of Lymerik, Piers [MS torn: and] Arthur, then baileffs of the same, Richard White, [?MS torn] Fanning, Jourdan Roche, Daniell Arthur and others of the same wear accused by Captein Richard [MS torn: of] a Riot supposed to be committed by them at Lym[erick] and intred in the Castell Chamber within her [maties castell: MS torn] of Dublin. Referred by us to be taken upp and [MS torn] the said parties by Sr Lucas Dillon, knight, and [MS torn: Edward] Fynton, Esquier, who by consent of the said par[ties] and defendants ended and ordered the same. Th[at] theis are to will and comaund you to surcease for calling uppon the said parties or any of them [MS torn] to proceade any farther in that sute so that they and [any of] them be troubled hereafter for that matter and in yor book that they arr Dischardged of the [blank], this shalbe yt sufficient warrant in that be[half]. Yeaven at ther maties cittie of Lymerik the iiijth of August 1584.[74]

---

70. ff. 73–73v. Note different dates for document: enrolled 7 November, and decree issued later, 9 November 1582.
71. f. 74.
72. f. 74v.
73. f. 75. Note manuscript is torn at spine, and original pagination is out of sequence, missing some five pages, or two folios. A memo. of dismissed cases alludes to the foregoing, and folio 75v is blank. There is an interval of two years and the pagination ends at 75v which is also page 163.
74. f. 76. Document entered loose leaf, damaged at the edge, apparently an order from Lord Deputy Perrot to the clerk to cease troubling the litigants in a cause already settled by commission from the court.

J Perot   xxiiij Die Novembris 1584
By the L Deputy & Counsell
Memorand Where informacon was exhibited in this honorable Court by John Walwyn against
Dominicke Browne of Galway, Alderman, Jeffrey Browne, Alexander French, Robucke French
Fitzmich[ael]as and others of the same, merchauntes, for a Ryott supposed to be done by them
against the said Walwyn, which hath longe contynued sute here. And forasmuch as the said Walwyn
hath made humble request and sute unto us the L deputie and Counsell, that in respect he is not
hable anie longer to attend the prosecutinge of the said cawse by reason of his povertie, which hath
growen (as he alledged) by the greate chardge and xpences that he hath susteyned in the saide sute,
And also for that he and the said defendants by there Agent here are of there owne mocyons agreed
no further to deale in the said cawse but that the same might be Dismist by ther consaynte out of this
honorable Court. It is therefore ordred by us the said L Depute and Counsell whose names are
hereunder subscrybed that the said matter shalbe dismist, and the severall pleadinges proceaded
therein, and Recognizances acknowledged by the Defendantes, be withdrawne and Cancelled, the said
parties payinge such fees to the Clerke of the Courte, as are growne dew and unpayde.
[signatures] N White, J Garvey.[75]

By the Lo Deputie & Counsell
Md Wher Charles Calthroppe and Roger Wilbraham the Q Mates Attorney and Solicitor generall at
lawes exhibited enformacon before the right honorable the Lo Deputie and Councell in hir highnes
Court of Castle chamber, howe aboute the moneth of June 1585 and in the xxviith yeare of hir maties
raigne one Henrye Byrd, Register to the highe Commissioners in causes ecclesiasticall within this
Realme of Irland, of ane insolent corupt and disloyall minde, without regard of allegeance to hir
matie or the state heerof this hir highnes Realme and without direction from anie, did write in the Lo
deputies name diverse warrantes, preceptes and straight comaundementes of severall natures, some
purportinge generall protections and pardons for all causes to one Sir Denis ORohan, priest, other
some for attachinge severall persons, And allso warrantes giving absoluton and generall aucthoritye
to hir maties subiectes to take Recognizances of such hir highnes people as the said Sir Denis shold
present unto them. And after the writinge of those preceptes and warrantes did counterfeit and sett
in forginge maner the Lo Deputies hand, which passed forth and was spredd amongest her maties
Subiectes as the Acte and deed of the said Lo Deputie which were forged, written & counterfeyted
by the said Byrde, with more large & dangerous woordes then ever his Lo used, or entended, or might
with warrantize passe to anie, which seemed to be don with a moste malicious intent and dangerous
for his Lo[rdship] yf they in tyme had not bin found oute. And the said Henrie Byrde escaping
unespyed and uncontrowled, for the foresaid disloyalties to hir matie and the State heer in this hir
highnes Realme did likewise of alike presumptuous minde, only by pretence he was Register to highe
commisioners, make and signe with his owne hand in his owne name publicke and generall ltres
testimoniall aucthorizinge by the same one David Dermott to be publicke minister of divine service
and Sacramentes and denouncinge himself by his said Ltres to be a protector to the said David
Dermott against all personnes. Wherby moste insolently and disloyally the said Henrie hath usurped
and prowdlye assured to himself muche more then the absolute aucthoritie upon specyall trust
comitted to her maties honorable Comissioners in causes ecclesiasticall, and the peculier Aucthoritie
& Jurisdiction of all Archbushoppes and Bushoppes of this Realme might by anie warantize passe or
grant, as by the said severall warrantes and commissioners made, and counterfeyted both in the Lo
Deputies name, and allso passed forth under the hand and subscription of the said Henry Byrde,
being here verbatim expressed more plainely apeereth, viz:

[here is copied into the entry book, in the same hand, several letters in evidence of the charge,
allegedly composed by Byrd, pretending to write as chief governor]

75. f. 77. Note the interval of two years, November 1582 to November 1584, in formal adjudication by the court
of castle chamber is not explained. Two or three leaves are missing, probably cut out of entry book at binding;
the hand is slightly different in the second entry; and f. 77 is signed by the judges rather than presence noted
by the clerk. Folio 78 is an identical copy of f. 77 above, following an empty folio, not numbered. Folio 78v has
spare entry as follows, without text: 'Thoms Nugent of Moyrauh[?], pl, Tyrlaghe Donell and Edmond Donell,
Def.'

'Perrott   By the Lo Deputie
We greet yo well: Forasmuch as this bearer, Sir Denys Orohan, priest havinge bin apprehended and comitted to prison of alonge tyme for severyall causes aswell spirituall as temporall, repugnant to hir highnes lawes, hath nowe recanted from the erronyous religion of Papistry, which he professed, as under his hand writinge may appear. And havinge submitted himself unto hir maties Statutes & ordinances hath sworne to hir supremacye, with promise hensforth to become a trewe and loyall Subiect. These are to give yo to understand, that we have frely pardoned, forgiven and sett free the said Sr Denys from all misdeameanors and badd actions whatsoever by him heretofore comitted uppon hope of his good services and better conformitye. And have allso lycensed him to travayle about his affayres throughout this owre Reame of Ireland willinge and comandinge ye and every of yo within this said Realme of Ireland to whom in case it may apertaigne to suffer & permitt the said Sir Denys to passe and repasse throughout yor citties, townes and Contreyes without any molestacons trobles or arreastes, he behavinge himself like a dutiful Subiecte, unles ye shall receave specyall direction from us, or any of our Councell for the same. Wherof yo may not faile as yo shall answere the contrary at yor extreeme perilles. And this shalbe yor warrant. Given at the Castle of Dublin the xxvijth of June 1585.'

'To all & singuler maiors, Sheriffes & Soveraignes, Bailiffes, Seneshalls, Constables, Captaines, Portrives, hedlowwes [?headboroughs, parish officials], Searchers, Comptrolers & all others hir maties officers & loving subiectes to whom it shall apertaigne.
Perrott   By the Lo Deputy
These are in hir maties name straightlye to charge and comaund yo to aprehend and attache the bodies of those priestes undernamed, and them to send in safe maner unto us to be dealt withall touchinge suche maters as shalbe obiected against them wherof yo may not faile as yo shalbe answerable to the contrarie at yor perills. And this shalbe yor warrant for the same. Given at Dublin this xxviijth of June 1585.
To the Seneschal of the countie of Wexford or to the Shereffe of the same or to the Sheriffe of the countie Typerarye. The priestes names: Sir Teige OHeylan, priest, Sir Willm Clere, priest, Morgan FitzEdmond of the abbey Inishelenaught, Sir Dermott McCragh, Doctor, Edmond Ley, Sir Caribre O Creghane of Killibane in the countie of Kilkennye.'

'Perrott   By the Lo Deputie
Forasmuch as this bearer, Sir Denys Oroghan, priest, for some good services done to hir matie stand in bodely feare of loesinge his lief by diverse and sundry personss within this realme of Irland. These are to will and require yo and allso to aucthorize yo to bynd every suche person who he shall uppon his corporall othe present unto you in sufficyent bandes and Recognizances that neither they, nor anie of them shall misuse, hurt or endanger the said Sr Denys of his lief, for any cause whatsoever. And that yf he shall offend anie person, the matter to be delivered to some of aucthority wherby he may be answerable to lawe accordinge the quality of the cause. Wherof yo may not faile uppon yor further perill. And this shalbe yor warrant. Given at Dublin this xxxth of June 1585.'

'To all maiors Sheriffes Seneshalls, Justices of peace and all other hir maties officers of aucthority:
Unto all men to whom these shall apertaigne: let it be knowen that I Henry Byrd, principall Register to hir maties highe Commissioners for causes ecclesiasticall throughout Irland, and allso Register to the Court of Faculties in Irland, having perused the tytles of Davyd Dermott vicar of Killofrai, and beinge well acquainted of his upright lief, and good behaviours in hir maties lawes, have alowed the said Davyd Dermott to serve within this Dioces of Lymericke or in anie other place of hir highnes Domynions, & so far forth as the said Davyd shall behave himself well and iustlie in his doinges & charges I doe promise by these presentes to be his defendor, frend and protector. In wittnes I have subscribed my name the xxth of Aprill 1585.

Henry Byrde, Register.'

[Transcript of trial record continues] Upon declaracon of all which, the said Birde beinge at barr, having put in his answere to the enformacon aforesaid, and beinge examined upon his personall Interrogatories, And having learned councell alowed him by the said Lo deputie to defend his causes, cold not deny the writinge of those warrantes with his owne hand, but counterfeytinge the Lo deputies hand to those warrantes which he with his owne hand did wright he utterlie denyed. Wheruppon many presumptions were laid downe by hir maties said Attorney and Solicitor to insynuat [insinuate] the Court to take knowledge of his said counterfeytinge which tended both to a private benefite to himself, & to increase his owne Lucre and gaine, And allso warrantes not pertinent to be passed from the Lo Deputie for anie suche matter but only by the high Commissioners aucthorized for those cawses. And yf anie such warrantes had passed from his Lo: the same shold have bin written and don by the clarke of the Councell hir maties officer apointed for those causes or his Lordships Secretarye. Besides diverse conferences and speches proved to have bin betweene the said Bird and the said Sir Denis which by implicacon tended to the matter, and full proof of the informacon proponed against him. And afterwards the said Sir Denys was brought in facie Curie to confront the said Birde, who protested and vowed to god that the said Byrd did both write the warrantes, and allso did counterfeyt the Lo Deputies hand unto them, himself beinge by in his chamber at St. Pattrickes, At which tyme the said Byrde caused the said Sir Denys to swear upon his booke othe, to kepe his councell for the forgerye. And allso the said Sir Denys being condempned to dye was by the Lord Deputie offred pardon for his lief, yf he could counterfeit the libe[l, i.e written statement] hand, which by no meanes he could doe. Whereuppon the matter being longe debated by hir maties learned Councell, and the Councell of the other side, the said Byrd was by the Court found giltye aswell in the forging of the Lo Deputies hand as of the writing of the said warrant. Wherfore it is adiudged & ordered that the said Byrd shall stand upon the Pillory in some publicke place, and shall abide one yeares imprisonment for his offences and misdemeanors used in all the premisses above written.   Termino trinitatis die Junij, 1585.[76]

Wheras the Baron of Delvin exhibited a Bill of information into this ho[norable] Court against Oney Moley, alias Captayne Greene, George Fitz Peeter, James Curran, Con Duffe OMoley, Richard Nugent Fitzpeter, and George Swayne. Upon the motion and petition of the sayd Baron and other Causes moving them theyrunto, yt was thought good to the sayd Court and the Queenes learned Councell to dismisse the sayd matter out of this Court, the parties paying such fees as are due to the officers of the sayd Court. Given at hcr maties Court of Castle Chamber the 23 of June 1587 and the 29 yere of her maties Raigne.[77]

By the lo Deputie and Counsell xxix die November 1585 A[nn]o Regni Dne Mie Eliz & Picesimo nono.
Whereas Charles Calthroppe, her maties Attourney Generall, by the Relacon of Theobald Dillon, gentillman, on the behalf of her matie Exhibited Informacon unto this ho[norable] Courte of Castell Chamber That Henry Ealand late Shrieffe of the Countie of Rosscomon, had duringe his saide office of Shrievealtie there Comytted & donne dyvers & sondery extorcons, wronges, forces, bryberies, oppressions and Iniuries, agaynst many her Maties trewe & faithfull subiectes within the saide Countie of Rosscomon, Accordinge as is particularlie sett forthe in Twentie & seaven Ar[tic]les of Complaynte, mentyoned in the saide Informacon, Contrary to her highnes lawes and ordinances, and to the great damage and Iniuryous oppression of her highnes saide faithefull subiectes, And to the daungerous example of other lyke evill disposed officers. Whereunto the saide Ealand made Annswer, and after the cause orderlie proceeded to replicacon, and Reioynder, and wittnesses examined on the behalf of the Quenes matie, Proces ad audiendo Iudicin, was served uppon the Deffendaunte, as appeareth by affidavit, to have appeared to Justiffie himself at this daie in open Courte. But the saide Deffendant Contemptuously made Defaulte, Whereupon the Courte proceeded to the hearinge of the cause. And the Bill, Aunsere and replicacon, beinge openly redd, and the wyttnesses produced for her matie to prove every one of the said seaven & twenty Articles in the Informacon, beinge lykewyse redd and inforced by her maties lerned Counsell. Forasmoche as it appearethe unto this most ho[norable] courte, uppon full and deliberat hearinge of the Cause, that the greatest parte of the saide seaven and Twentie ar[ti]cles are suficiently proved agaynst the said Ealand, And that the same offences arc most odious, Abhominable, and pernicyouws in example. It is therefore by the Lord

---

76. ff. 79–81. Note Perrot sat in judgment on the case, and exceptional level of evidentiary detail entered in record book.
77. f. 81v. Note this entry is on verso of previous folio, entered in a different hand, some two years later than the Byrd case. The clerks apparently made these entries of dismissal in an informal, even haphazard manner.

Deputie and Counsell the lordes of the Spiritualty and of the nobilitie and her maties learned Judges, And by the whole Courte This daye ordered, adiudged and Decreed, That the matters in the first and second ar[tic]les of the Informacon, wherein the Deft is ympeached, for murtheringe some of good creditt unlawfully by cooller of marshall lawe, shalbe Dismysst out of this ho[norable] Courte, and prosecuted in her maties benche [i.e. kings bench] where properly it is to be determyned. And for the rest of the offences, proved agaynst the Deft It is lykewise further ordered and adiudged by this moste Ho: Courte: That the saide Henry Ealand shall pay to [her] matie for a Fyne the some of Fyve hundrethe poundes current money of England. And to be ymprisoned by the space of one whole yere and until he have received tryall in the kinges benche of the said supposed offences, Comytted to that Court. And it is moreover ordered That the said Henry Ealand shall make restitucon of all rewardes, giftes, brybes & extorcons proved this day against him to be by him, his officers & servauntes unlawfully exacted or taken from any her maties good subiectes. And lastlie the said Henry Ealand shall stand in some markett place in markett tyme in some towne in the said County of Rosscomon with a paper uppon his head Declaringe the quallitie of his offences.[78]

By the Lo Deputie and Councell 10 of Maie 1587.
Present: The Lo Deputie, Sir Henry Wallop, knight, the Lo Chauncelor, The Chief Justice Gardener, The Byshop of Killmore, The Chief Justice Dillon, The Byshop of Ossorie, The Chiefe Baron, The Byshop of [blank in MS], The Mr of the Rowles.
Where Jesse Smythes, her Maties Solicitor generall, exhibited information into this honorable Court of Castle Chamber within this her Maties Realme of Ireland that wheras Patricke Flatisburie of Johnston in the Countie of Kildare, gent, were indited before her matie in hear highnes Chiefe Place in good and due forme of lawe, as by record of the same inditement maie more lardgly appeare for the killing of one Hugh Burn, late of Baronrath, her maties faithfull and liege subiect, the sayd Patricke and Edmund upon their severall araignments pleaded severally therunto not guiltie and for their severall trialls put them upon the Countrie. Wherupon and as for due proces for a Jurie of gent and freeholders twelve men were elected, tried and sworne for triall of the Issue, the names of which xij ensueth, viz: Edward Misset, Bartholomewe Long, Willm Rochford, Patricke White, John Shurlocke, John Fitzgerald, Thomas Brimicham, Oliver Wogan, Maurice Westy, Thomas Wogan, Patricke Saunders and Gerrott Fitzphillip. Who after manifest evidences and credible witnesses produced and effectually delivered them by her maties learned Councell against the said notorious malefactors for proving the said Patricke and Edmund to be guiltie of the fellonie aforesaid, yet neverthelesse the said Jurors, of a corrupt and willfull disposition, not regarding their oth and contrarie to their evidences in that behalfe, did find that the sayd Edmund and Patricke nor eyther of them were guiltie of the felonie aforesayd, by which their verditt they comitted willfull and apparent periurie to the dangerous example of Juries in lyke causes of triall and to the mischievous incouradgment of all other notorious heynous malefactours. Wherunto the said Jurors made their answere alleaging divers and manifold presumptions in excuse of the said periurie, and upon Bill, answere and replication the matter was divers several dayes heard and debated at large by her highnes learned Councell, and the defendantes learned Councell in the Terme of Hilarie last. And for difficulties appearing in the verdict, the verdict was comitted to her highnes Chief Justices of her Bench, and Common Place to consider whether the said defendantes had comitted wilfull periurie by their said verdict or not, who declared this daye in open Court that the[y] thought the Jurors had comitted (in a sort) periurie agaynst their consciences and the truth of the evidence, yet ought not by that verdict the prisoners to have been discharged, so as thearby the qualitie of their periurie ys not of so heynous nature as the bill purporteth. Yt ys therfore ordered, adiudged and decreed by us the Lo Deputie and others of her maties privie Councell with lo: spirituall and temporall that everie of the said Jurors in regard of their povertie shall paie unto her matie for a fine the some of tenne shillings str apeece.[79]

---

78. f. 82. This case forms part of the long struggle between Lord Deputy Perrot and his adversary, Richard Bingham, lord president of Connacht, whose client was Ealand.
79. f. 83. The defendants were apparently brothers, Patrick and Edmund Flatisburie, though only Patrick was named in the first sentence of the information, and they were tried in a single hearing.

By the LoDeputie and Councell 19 May 1587.
Present in Court: The Lo Deputie, Sir Henrie Wallop, The Lo Chauncelor, Sir Robert Dillon, the Lo of Upper Ossorie, the Chief Baron, the Byshop of Killmore, Sir Nicholas White, the Byshop of Ossorie.

Where Irriall Offerall, gent, being Sheryffe of the Countie of Longford, exhibited information into this honorable Court that Rosse Offerall, gent, of the same Countie, about Christ tyde in ano 1585 had in his companie at his house one Manus McShane O Rwarke,wherof the said Irriell having intelligence, sent his officer with divers others accompanying him to the said Rosse Offeralls howse to apprehend the said Manus for felonie and Treason, wherof also he gave the said Rosse advertisment at his first meeting them together, and that he the said Rosse (accompanied with divers other ill disposed persons, not dulie regarding her maties officers) not only denied his assistance to apprehend the sayd Manus, but allso made such violent resistance and riott that he the sayd Manus escaped, contrarie to her highnes lawes and ordinances, to the grievous hurte of her maties sayd officer and other her faithfull subiectes, and to the most daungerous example of all ill dysposed persons. Wherunto the sayd Rosse Offerall made answer and pleaded that the sayd Manus McShane O Rwarke was a dutiful and faythefull subiect and ameanable to lawe. Wherupon the cause orderly proceeding to replication and reioynder and thexamination of witnesses on both partes, upon Fridaie the 19 of Maie 1587 and the 29 yeare of her maties Raigne, the bill, answere, replication, reioynder and the depositions of witnesses on both partes being openly red, and the matter beinge heard and debated at large betweene her maties learned Councell and the Defendantes learned Councell, forasmuch as yt manifestie appeared to the right ho: the lo: deputie and the rest of the Commissioners then sitting that the matter and substance alleaged in the information was sufficiently proved agaynst the defendauntes and weighing allso that the same their offence ys most dangerous in practize and pernitious in example. Yt ys therfore ordered, adiudged and decreed by us the said Lo Deputie and Councell that the said Rosse Offerall for that he was principall in the action and a leader of the rest to that violent attempt shall paye to her maiestie for a fine the some of one hundreth poundes and indure Imprisonment in her maties Castle of Dublin and that the rest of the said Defendantes shall paye to her maiestie for a Fine as hereafter followeth, and indure lykewyse imprisonment in the Countie gaole of Longford, provided that as well the mitigation of all their fines and the lymitation of the tyme for their imprisonment be wholie referred to the said Lo Deputies pleasure. Yt ys allso further ordered and decreed that the said Defendantes shall paye or cause to be payd to the handes of Anthony Stoughton or his Deputie Clerke of the Castle Chamber to the plaintiffes use all such costes and charges as shallbe taxed by the right hon: the Lo Chauncelor of this her maties Realme of Ireland, and shall further paye unto the Clerke and other officers of the sayd Court all such fees as shalbe due by acrie [?account]. Geven at her maiesties Court of Castle Chamber the said yere above written.

The names and fines of every the defendantes mentioned in the information. Rosse Offerall of Aghehaltan 40s; Hubert McDonogh Merscall 40s, Cahill McDonogh Merscall 40s, Willm McDonogh Merscall 40s, Richard McRorie 40s, Teige McCryawane 40s, Gillernowe Duffe McCryawne 40s, Willm McMorough FitzJames 40s, Teig Bane Mc Cryawne 40s, Gerald Offerall 40s, Cahill McCryawnie 40s, Cowghor McCryawne 40s, Meale FitzEdmond 40s, Rory McCormocke FitzJames 40s, Patricke McCryawne 40s.[80]

By the Lo Deputie and Counsell the 30 of July 1587.

Present:	
The Lo Deputie	The Earle of Thomond
The Lo Chauncelor	The Chief Baron
The Primate of Armagh	The Mr of the Rowles
The Byshop of Meath	Sir Thomas Le Strange
The two chief justices	

Where Robert Longe of Castletowne Rebane in the Countie of Kildare, gent, exhibited a Bill of Information into this honorable Court of Castle Chamber that wheareas he quietly from tyme to

---

80. ff. 84 84v. Note at bottom of f. 84: 'This fyne of one hundred poundes layd downe uppon Rosse Oferall is by warraunt of the L Depty remytted to xxx li and the fynes layd downe uppon the rest of the deftes remytted to xx s, which warrant remayneth with me Anthony Stoughten, Clerke of the Court of [MS torn: Castle Chamber].'

tyme manuring the ferme and using the pastures of the sayd Castletowne, one Willm Bowen of Ballimore in the Countie of Dublin, gent, wth others whose names are underwritten, in most riotous and all most rebellious manner upon the 20th daye of Januarie 1583 did repayre unto the sayd Castletowne and did thence take and drive away all the kine of the sayd towne, and yet not therwith content did allso wth a most malicious and murthering intent, assault such of her maties subiectes as pursued them with hewe and crie and them did beate and wound, and amongest others did runne the sayd Long through the Bodie wth an horsemans staffe upon which wound he was lyke rather to perish then recover. Wherunto the sayd Willm Bowen alone made answeare and pleaded therunto as well an interest he had gotten for tearme of 14 yeares in the sayd landes, tenementes and hereditamentes of the sayd Castletowne from Walter St Michell, as allso that he (advised by his learned Councell) repayred to the lands of the sayd Castletowne wth one in companie, in peaceable manner, and Distrayned such catle as he there found [?seeking] damadges fer the same to the end that the matter might be tried and ended by course of her maties lawes. Wherupon the cause orderly proceding to replication, reioynder and examination of witnesses in both partes, upon Friday the 30th of July 1587 and the 29 yere of her maties Rayne, the Bill, Annsweare, Replication, Reioynder and the depositions of witnesses on both partes being openly read and the matter being openly heard and debated at large betweene her maties learned Councell and the Defendantes learned Councell. Forasmuch as yt manifeslie appeared to the right ho: Sir John Perrott, knight, Lo: Deputie and the rest of the Commissioners then sitting that the Riott and hurt of the sayd Long alledged in the information was sufficientlie proved agaynst the Defendant and weighing allso that the sayd Bowens offence was most dangerous as well in respect of the complainantes hurt, as allso for example yf yt should remayn unpunished. Yt is therfore ordered, adiudged and decreed by us the said L Deputie and Councell that the said Willm Bowen for his notorious offence shall indure imprysonment in her maties castle of Dublin during the said Lo Deputies pleasure, shall paye to her Maie for a fine the some of twenty poundes ster and shall pay allso to the handes of Anthony Stoughton or his Deputie, clerke of the sayd Court, to the use of the Complaynant all such Costes and Charges as shalbe taxed by the lo Chauncelor of this her maties realme of Ireland and shall fur[ther] pay to the Clerke and other officers of the sayd Courte all such fees as shalbe due unto them or any of them by account [?MS unclear]. Yt is also further ordered and decreed that the rest of the defendauntes shall likewise make their answeare. Given at her maties Court of Castle chamber the daye and yere above written. The names of the rest mentioned in the Bill. Willm Davell, Gerrott Offar, Owen McGerrott, George Hetherington, Gerrott Fleming, Walter Wald, Edmund Offar, Derby Kely, Tege O Dolan, Patrick McRorie, Donogh O Crony, Donnell Duffe McMeache, Morogh O Newe.[81]

Termino Hillary 1587. By the L Deputie and counsell, the seconde of Februarie 1587.
Willm Power, pl, Thomas Gangagh and others, Defts.
Present: The Lorde Deputie, The L Chancelor, Cheif Justice Gardener, Sir Robert Dillon, Sir Lucas Dillon, Sir Nicholas Whyte, Justice Welch.
Where Willm Power of Shangarrie in the Countie of Cork, gent, exhibited a bill in hir maiesties high Cort of Castell Chamber against Morrishe Og Fitzmorrishe McGerrott of Churchton, Thomas Gangaghe of Carrickottie and divers others, defendants, whose names in the said Bill and the actes and records of this honorable Court be specified and conteined. That theie the said Defendauntes about the xvth of Maie in the xxvijth year of her Maties Raigne in riotouse manner arraied, viz with Gunes, swordes, skulls, Targetts, Speares & other weapons Defensible aswell on horseback as on foote, came to the Towne of Loghan in the countie of Cork aforesaide, and then and there finding the Complainantes pore people at plow, did (for most parte) for the space of three daies dailie resort to the said towne of Loghan, brusing, beating and evill intreating the said pore people by which meanes theie were so terified as some of them ar never like to recover without daunger of their lives. And in like manner riotouse sort forceablie took awaie owt of the complainantes plowe eight garrons and oxen and thorough this outrage did drive awaie into unknown and forraine places divers Tenauntes and plows whoe wold have thoroughlie inhabited the said towne of Loghan and whoe nowe for feare will not Nor dare come to the said Landes, by means whereof the said towne of Loghan is in manner merelie wast, to the Complaynantes damage of A hundred poundes as by the said pretensed bill

81. ff. 85–85v.

remayning in this honorable Cort amongest other Records doeth and maie at lardg appeare. Whereunto the Defendauntes answered and the Cause proceading to replicacon, reioinder, examinacon of witnesses on ether part and this day assigned to be finally heard. Forsomuch as uppon the full hearinge & deliberat discussing of the supposed Complt before the L Deputie and others her maties Commissioners of the honorable Cort of Castlechamber aforesaid whose names be subscribed yt evidentlie appeared by certen Deposicons and other exhibits in Cort publiquelie redd and maturelie considered uppon, that the said supposed Bill and the contents thereof wer untrue, grounded without iust cause and noe proof sufficient in Lawe was produced or in Cort exhibited, by which the said Defendaunts everie or any one of them might be justlie convict[ed] for or uppon the supposed Riott or anie other misdemeanors in the said pretensed bill conteyned. Nor that the said Defendauntes cam not into the said Loghan in anie other manner and sort then the Lawes of this Land did and doeth tolerat and permitt and was and is lawfull for them to doe. Yt was and is therefore the daie and year aforesaid ordered, adiudged and finally decreed by us the Lord Deputie and Councell aforesaid that the suppposed Bill of Complaint wth the substance and matter in the same conteyned be false and untrue, and that the said Morrish Oge FitzMorrish McGerrott of Churchton, Thomas Gangaghe of Carickottie with the rest of the Defendaunts all and everie one of them ar and shall from hensforth be dismissed, freed, acquitted and Clerlie discharged from further vexacon, impeticon, sute travaile or troble whatsoever concerning the said Bill or any matter, clause or sentence in the same conteyned.[82]

Ultimo die Januarij 1588.
Wheare her Maties Serieant, Attorney and Solicitor exhibited Information into this honorable Courte of castle chamber with in this her hieghnes Realme of Irland That Alexaunder Plunckett of the Bawne in the Countye of Looth, gent, Bearing a moste disloyall harte unto the sacred Matie of the Quenes moste Royall person and malygnyng the happy goverment and blessed prosperitie of her Maties Domynions of England and Irland, And endevoryng by sedecyous Speaches and false Rumores to disturbe the quiett peace of this her Maties realme, hath in march last in the Churche yeard of Monnfyeldstowne in the Countie aforesayd dyvulged and publyshed amongest dyveres her Maties good and faythfull Subiectes in this Realme those detestable sedycious and rebellious Rumores And Counterfayt newes, viz: That within two yeares of this springe or this springe tyme yt self The Spanyardes would retorne into Irland agayne to conquer Irland, And that all the Irishe men would Joyne with the Spayniardes agaynst the Quenes Matie. And after they had Conquered Ireland the Spanyardes with the forces of Irland wold goe into England, And there Crowne a kinge And dryve the Quenes Matie to flyght out of the Realme. By which his sedycyous speaches malycyously blowen abroad the saied Plunckett hathe disloyally practysed (yf it were possible) to strycke a terror and causeles feare into the hertes of all her Maties lovinge and loyall subiectes of this land, And to anymate and ymbolden suche disloyall persons as seeke by ther trayterouse practyces dayly to impeach the Quiett estate and Peaceable governmente of this realme. Upon declaration of all which, the sayed Plunckett being called to Answere Could not deny the same. Besydes towe wyttnesses Sworne in Court who affirmed to have hard hime speake the wordes in the place aforesaid. Whereuppon this day yt is adiudged and ordered by the right honorable the lord Debite & councell that the sayed Pluncket shall stand on the pyllory at the lo Debuties pleasure within the Cittye of Dublyn one houre on a markett day with his eares nayled on to the pillorye. And frome thence to be had to Ardy or some other place within the Countie of Looth wheare there in like sorte to stand one the pillory, one of his eares to be cut of. And from thence to be brought to the Castle of Dublyn there to remayne in prison duringe the lorde deputies pleasure. And his land (yf any he have) to be sased [seised] to the Quenes Maties use duringe his life.[83]

Wheare Joyce Adryan of Dublyn, Letherdresser, hath exibyted a bill of Ryott in her Maties highe Courte of Castle Chamber agaynst Nycholas Nolan, Thoms Eustace, Willm Spryngan, Patrycke Creyffe, Patrycke Bath, Nycholas Course, John Lewisse, Patricke Doyne of Dublyn, Tanneres, &

82. ff. 86v–87v. Fols. 88–88v are blank.
83. Ibid. ff. 89–89v.

Alson Keaddy and Katherin Whyte of the same. That they the sayed Defendantes the xxth day of December 1586 in the xxviijth yeare of her Maties raigne in Ryotouse manner arrayed, viz: with halbardes, Swordes, and other weapons defensyble in the parishe of Saynt Katherynes in the subburbes of the Cittie of Dublyn. And then and there in most Ryotouse sorte did assault, beate and greavously hurt the sayed Joyce and Elizabeth, his wyeffe, deceased, by whiche misdemenors she was inforst to beare a dead borne child then and there, with like force and misdemenors toke from the sayd Joyce a dicker [i.e. ten, usually hides] of tanned lether paie foure poundes ster. Whereunto the defendantes answere, And the cause proceadinge to replycation, reioynder, examynacion of witnesses on eyther parte, And this daye assigned to be herd. For asmuche as uppon full hearinge and delyberate discusyng of the sayed Cause yt manyfestly appeared to the right honorable the L Chauncelor and the rest of the Judges then syttyng, that the Ryott was Comytted by three of the sayed Defendantes, viz: Nycholas Course, Nycholas Nolan and John Lewisse. Yt is therefore ordered, adiudged and decreed by the sayed L Chauncelor and Judges that the sayed Nycholas Course, Nycholas Nolan and John Lewisse shall pay to her Matie for a fyne eyther of them fyve markes and indure imprisonmente in her Maties Castle of Dublyn duringe pleasure. The rest of the Defendantes to be dismyssed, payinge the Costes of the Courte. Gyven at her Maties Courte of Castle Chamber the xith day of June 1589.

Present: The L chauncelor, Mr Justis Gardner, Sir Nycholas Whyte, Mr Justys Walshe.[83a]

[signed] WFytswilliam
Wheras we have receaved lettres from the right honorable the lls of her maties privie Counsell, the tenor wherof ensueth. After our harty Comendacons unto your Lo and the rest. Wheras Henry Birde that hath served ther to his brother for deputy, John Birde, as Register for the Ecclesiasticall Comission, hath made humble suite unto us to be relieved and acquitted of a Sentence given in the Castell Chamber there against him Wher he was Condempned uppon the bare oath of Sir Denis ORoghan, Preist, to have Counterfeyted the hand of Sir John Perrott then Lo Deputy of that Realme, the said Preist [sic] being then a Condempned person. And dothe further Informe us that there was an extrordinarie Course of proceedinge held against him, sith in that the same sentence was given the day after the tearme, beinge a daie onely appointed for orders. Wher not onely the said Sir John Perrott was present in person, but others of the Irishe Nobillitie Called thither of purpose that were not acquainted with the former proceedinges in that Cause. And nevertheless as well the L Chauncellor as others of the Counsell did discent and take exception from and to the said Sentence, and that divers of the rest gave not their Judgmentes but their Censures onely what punishment wer fitt and that Condicionallie if that accusacon and deposicon were true as well alledged, and that also that day he was barred to have his learned Counsell. Consideringe this Course of Proceedinge (if it be true as we are enformed) and that the said Sir Denis hath sithence that tyme and doth nowe also retracte his former accusacon of the said Birde he gave [alleging he] Counterfeyted the hand of the said Sir John Perrott to those warrantes, and doth Clere him altogether of that Cryme, We are not onely induced verelie to believe the said Birde was Innocent of the facte and forgerie for which he was then condempned, but are moved to pray yor Lo and the rest (the Credite of the younge man beeinge so greatly and uniustly blemished to perpetuall defamacon) that you will Cause this matter againe to be Considered of by that Courte. And seeinge his onely acuser doth acquite and dischardge him of the forgerie wherwith he hath Chardged him and that the Cause of proceedinges (if it were such as we are enformed) was not orderlie and auctenticall as it ought to have been, that you will Consider of some Course howe that Sentence, uppon better Informacon and more due Consideracon of the Cause, may be repealed and reversed, And the Innocence of the younge man pronounced for the reparacon of his fame and good name, beinge a mater bothe of equitie and Conscience. Moreover whereas John Birde, brother to this supli[cant], beinge Register of the Eccliasticall Commission and receavor and Collector of the fynes accrewing by that comission, his said Offices were taken from him by Sir John Perrott, partlie for the factes supposed to be Comitted by his brother Henry, and the same bestowed on some of the servauntes of the said Sir John Perrott who have made sale of those offices (as we are Informed) to persons lesse fitt to execute the same, on whose behalf lettres have beene written also by us heretofore for his enioyinge of the saide offices. We are to pray yor Lo. and the rest because the bestowinge of those roomes and places doth properlie belonge to the Lord Chauncellor,

as Cheef of the ecclesiasticall Comission. And for that the facte of one Brother (though he had been faultie) ought not to preiudice the other, that the said John Byrde may be restored to his foresaid Offices with the ffees appertayning to the same, in such sorte as before tyme he did enioye the same notwithstandinge any graunte made sithence of the same. And Henry Birde permitted to exercise the said Offices as deputy to his brother. So prayinge your Lo and the rest that you will take order in this Cause accordinge to this our direccon, wee bid you hartily fare well.

From the Courte of Otelandes this 24th of August 1590. Yor Lo: rt [right] very lovinge frendes the Lo: Archb. of Canter, the Lo Chauncellor, The Lo Threr, the Lo Admirall, the Lo Chamberlaine, the Lo Cobham, the Lo Bukhurst, Mr. Secretarie Wallie [Walsingham], Mr. Fortescue, Mr. Waade, Clerke of the Councell. And for accomplishment of theire l[ordshi]ps pleasures signyfied by their said Lettres the said Henry Birde hath in the beginninge of This terme preferred his humble peticon in writinge in this most honorable Courte and withall hath produced before us the Retractacon of the said Sir Denis under his owne hand writings (who was the onely accuser and wittnes against him) the tennor whereof is as followeth.

To all xpen [?Christian] people to whom these presentes shall Come, greetinge. Knowe yee that Sir Denis O Roghan, Preist, nowe prisoner in the gatehouse of Westmynster in London, havinge in the governement of Sir John Perrott, late Lo Deputy of Ireland, uniustly accused one Henry Birde of Dublin, gent, Deputy Reg[iste]r to the high Commissioners for to have Counterfeyted or forged the hand writinge of the said Sir John Perrott unto three severall warrauntes for the which uppon my only accusacon he was wrongfully Condempned, to his great defamacon and hinderance, whose manyfest wronges by me don him beinge often prickes to my guilty Conscience and I hartely repentinge me of the same. In parte satisfaccon for the saide wronges and hurtes hereby don to the younge man And for the better Restitucon of his former Credit by me blemyshed, I have and doe not only most humbly uppon my knees of my harte and body aske forgevenes of the said Henry Birde before god and the world, but also in signe of my true penitencie and sorowe I do hereby voluntarely acknowledge to the generall notice of all men that I have falsly accused the said Birde, and that he nether forged the hand of the said Sir John Perrott (as he was uniustly Chardged) nether was he privie or Accessary to the same. In witnesse that this is a true Confession I have written the same with my owne hand and therunto subscribed my name the xxviijth of August 1590. In the xxxij yeare of her maties raigne. By me Denis O Roghan. In the presentes of those persons whose names are underwritten, Morrice Pickeringe, Edward Reynoldes, Humfrey Walsingham.

Wheruppon we have entred into examynacon of the said Sentence in this booke mentoned and perusinge the proceedinges therein do fynde it was gven the xxiijth of June Ano 1586, in the xxviijth yeare of her maties Raigne, being the day after Trinity Tearme, and that the said Sir Denis (then a Condempned man) was the onely wittnesse that testefied the said supposed forgery to have ben comitted by the said Henry Birde. And havinge had daily Conferences in this Cause, wee are nowe perswaded to thinke by reason of the preistes said retractacon & other wise that the said Henry Bird is altogether Innocent of the said forgery (Accordinge as the lls of her mates privie Councell in England have declared their opinions in theire said l[ett]res). And therfore we do nowe pronounce and publishe that in or opinions the said Henry Birde was falslie and uniustly accused of the said forgerie and that he is altogether Innocent and guiltlesse therof. And we order that the said Sentence for the supposed forgerie shall not be put in any farther execucon. But that he shalbe sett free from all punishment Inflickted ther in against him. And that the said sentence shall not be preiudiciall or of any efficacie in lawe or other wise to blemishe his good name or to disable him in any Courte or Cause what soever. But that he shalbe ever herafter reputed and esteemed of honest demeanor and as a faithfull and true subiecte to her matie, the supposed forgery in the said sentence notwithstandinge. Yeoven in her maties Courte of Castelll Chamber the vith day of November 1590. [signed] Ad Dublin, canc, Milerus [Ar] Cassel[ens]is, Tho Midensis, Robert Dillon, Lucas Dillon, George Carewe, Nicholas Walshe, G Bourchire[84]

Where Roger Wilbraham, her maties solycitor generall, exhibited informacon into this most honorable Court of Castle Chamber within this her highnes Realme of Irland That, Where as Walter Browne, late of Newbane in the County of Wexford, gent, was indicted for that he beinge Comited

---

84. ff. 90v–92. See above, ff. 79–81 for the castle chamber prosecution of Henry Bird under Lord Deputy Perrot. Fol. 92v is blank.

by George Isham then sheriff of the said County to her maties Gayle and Castle of Wexford for suspicon of treason, that is to say for abettinge and aydinge traitorously Cahier Eglan als Caher McBrien Cavanagh, then a notoriouse traitor and Rebbel, and beinge so in prison and in her maties gayle for suspicon of the treason aforesaid the xxiiijth day of Apriell in the xxviijth yeare of her maties raigne, traiterously and willfully escaped out of the said gayle. Wherupon the said Walter Browne in July 1589 beinge araigned in the said County of Wexford before her maties Justices of gayle delivery for that County pleaded not gylty and put him self uppon trial of the Contry, and after many Challandges allowed and all due Ceremonyes of Lawe observed, xij men were sworne for tryall of the Issue the names of which xij men ensueth. viz. Walter Synnott of Ferraldston, Martin Codd of Castlstowne, Thomas Whitt of Litle Killean, Patricke Butler of Butlerstowne, Roberte Prendercast of the ?Gurgius, Phillip Roch of the Newbane, Stephen Synnott of Ballarell, Nicholas Bore of the Growtowne, Walter Pierse of Ballele, John Codde of Ballyele [Ballylee?], Ferganauyne McMocierty of Assconsin and John Hore of the Michwoodd, who afer manifest evidences and Credible wittnesses produced and effectually Delivered unto them in open Cessions to enquire betwene the Quenes matie and the said Browne, Whether the said Browne was gilty of the said escape accordinge to the said endictment or not, and after theire oath taken the evidence was explaned and made Perspicouse [perspicuous] to the said Jurors by divers her matie Commissioners provinge fully the said Walter to be gilty of the escape aforesaid. All this notwithstandinge the said Jurors, of a Corupte and willfull disposicons, not regardinge theire oathe towardes god nor their duty to her matie, and contrary to theire evidence in that behalf, did fynde the said Walter Browne was not gilty of the escape aforesaid, by which theire verdicte they Comitted willfull and apparant periury to the daungerouse example of all Jurors in like Case of triall, and to the mischeifouse incuradgment of all other notoriouse malefactors. Wherunto the said Jurors made aunswer alledging some weake presumptions in excuse of their said periury, and uppon bill, aunser, replicacon and reioinder the matter was heard and debated at lardge by her maties learned Councell, and the learned Councell of the deffes. Wheruppon it is this day adiudged, ordered and decreed by the right honorable the L Deputy and the rest of the iudges and Councell then sittinge that all the said deffes (Phillip Roch of Newebane onely excepted) shalbe ymprisoned duringe the L Deputies pleasure, stand on the Pillory in some markett day in the Citty of Dublin and likwise in the towne of Wexford, and shall also pay unto her matie for a fyne eche of them the some of tenn poundes . Geven in her matis Court of Castell Chamber the xxth daye of November 1590.[85]

Where Charles Calthropp, esquier, her Mates Attorney generall exhibited information into this most honorable Courte by the relacion of John Talbott, undersheriffe of the Countie of Westmethe, that the saide undersheriffe the xxiijth day of May was at Parcelston in the same Countie as a true and faithfull subiecte beinge in god and her Mates peace, and John Tuite of the Somaghe in the saide Countye, gent, with diverse others the saide day and yeare, in riotouse manner did assemble themselves together araied with divers kinde of weapons, viz swordes, knyves, targettes, sculles, pollaxes and halbartes as well on horsebacke as on foote at Parcelston aforesaid and then and there in most Riotouse, outragious, forceable and warlike manner did enter into the Bawne of Parcelston aforesaide and there did assaulte the saide undersheriffe and him did evell intreat with pulling of his Cloake, throwinge and treadinge the same under foote in the myre, halinge him and tearinge his other apparell, takinge perforce from him out of the saide Bawne ten Garrons of the goodes and Cattell of the said John Tuite which the saide undersheriff, by vertue of A wethermand [an order to keep or distrain the sheep, or cattle] directed to him in that behalfe from Edwarde Nugent, high sheriffe of the saide Countie, did take and keepe in the saide Bawne accordinge to the direction and authoritie aforesaide, and put him in perill and feare of his life, Contrarie to her maties peace and contrarie to diverse actes heretofore intended and provided in that behalfe. Wherunto the Defendantes aunswered and the Cause proceadinge to replication, reioynder and witnesses examyned and this day assigned to be harde. Forasmuch as uppon full hearinge and deliberatelie dicussinge of the saide Cause it manifestlie appeared to the right ho[norable] the Lo: Deputy and the rest of the Judges and Counsaile then sittinge that the Riott was Comitted by the deffes in manner as in the informacon is handed downe, it is therefore ordered, adiudged and decreed by the saide Lo deputie, Judges and

85. ff. 93–93v. Entry was not signed, judgement recited facts of case rather than accepting presumption of jury's perjury.

Counsell that the saide defendantes, John Tuite aswell for himselfe as for the rest of his men then in action, shall paie to her matie for a fine the some of thirtene poundes, Six shillinges, eight pence Currnt money of Englande, indure imprisonment the space of twentie daies, and also to make present satisfaction unto the plt of all suche Chardges as shalbe taxed by the right ho: the Lo: Chauncelor on his behalfe. Geven at her maties Courte of Castell Chamber the xith day of June 1591.[86]

Where Roger Wylbraham, Esquire, her matis solycytor of this her highnes Realme of Ireland, exhibited informacon into this most honorable Court of Castle Chamber that one John Delahid of Bellantree in the county of [blank], gent, nothinge regardinge his duty of alleageaunce nor bearinge that reverence nor honor to the sacred name of the Queenes most excelent matie as in duty of a loyall subiete he ought, hath in assemblies in [blank] Last at Donboyne in the County of Dublyn published theis speeches not out [?publicly] meete to be remembered, viz That if Sir John Perrott had not Called her matie Pischyechyne [piskitchen] he had bene enlardged longe ere this. And the said Delahyde beinge called to aunswer his said undutifull and most vyle speeches against her Royall matie Could not denay but that he had spocken and uttered the same as in the information is layde downe, albeit he was Offered by the L Deputy and others the Judges that if he Could bringe forth any aucthor for the same, he shold receave favor in the punishment for the said undutifull speeches, yet he either Could not or would not bringe forth any aucthor for the said speeches, Whereuppon the Court proceedinge to Judgment, it was this day ordered, adiudged and decreed by the right honorable the L Deputy and the rest of the Judges and Councell then syttinge that the said Delahyde shall stand three marcket dayes on the Pillory, one day in the next markette towne nearest adioyninge to his Dwellinge place, one other markett day in Tryme or Drogheda and the third day in the Citty of Dublyn whear one of his eares shalbe nayled to the Pillory, not to be unloosed untill it be Cutt of[f] or himself Doe teare it of[f], and that he shall forfeyt the one half of his goodes to her matie and endure ymprysonment the L Deputies pleasure. Yeoven at her maties Court of Castle Chamber the xvith day of June 1591.[87]

Where Roger Wilbraham, Esquire, her maties solicytor of this her highnes Relme of Ireland, exhibited informacon into this most honorable Court of Castle Chamber that one John Keaghan of Carnalway in the County of Kildare, husbandman, Contrary to his duty of Alleageance to the Queenes most excellent matie and Contrary to the obedience of a Dutifull subiett to his soveraigne prynce, the xiijth day of March last at Carnallway aforesaid, of a most Corrupt Disposicon malycyously uttered and spake very detestable and most disloyall speeches of her sacred matie, Callinge and termynge her highnes Bauryne [barren], done in Irishe, the whiche are not otherwyese Convenient for the hatefullness of the wordes to be published. The which his said vyle, detestable and malycyouse speeches were apparauntly proved to proceed out of the said Keaghans mouthe by three severall wittnesses, wheruppon the Cause proceadinge to iudgment yt was this day ordered, adiudged and decreed by the right honorable the L Deputy, Judges and Councell then sitting that the said Keaghan shall stand three markett dayes on the pillory in this Citty of Dublin, the last day both his eares nayled to the Pillory and Cutt of[f], whipped throughout the Citty, forfeit all his goodes to her matie, and endure Imprisonment the L Deputies pleasure. Yeoven at her maties court of Castle Chamber the xvith day of June 1591.[88]

Where Edward FitzSymons her maties serieaunt at lawes within this her highnes Realme of Ireland exhibited informacon into this most honorable Court of Castle Chamber that one Edward White, Clarke of the Councell within the Province of Conaught, beinge specyally sent for to appeare before the Right honorable the L Deputy and Councell to be examyned uppon many weighty Causes greatly ymportinge her maties service, and uppon his apparaunce was told by the said L Deputy and Councell, and so chardged uppon his duty of alleageaunce and uppon his Corporall oath, not to disclose to any person any parte of the matter wherof he shold be examyned without lycence or pryvite of the L Deputy and Councell wch the said White undertook, and theruppon was examyned before the L Deputy and others of her highnes privy Councell of this Realme aucthorised in that behalf Uppon Certayne Artcles and Interrogatories sent hether from her maties most honorable privy Councell of England necessary for her mates service. Neverthelesse, the said White, Litell regarding his said othe or his duty to the advauncement of her maties service, most disloyally and as a periured man did discover the secreasy of the said deposicon to divers [persons] by messadges, speeches and letres. And the said White beinge Called to aunswer Cold not deny any parte of the said informacon and Confessed he wrytt one letre, well knowen to the L Deputy and divers of the Councell heere, to Contayne a Discourse of his said Deposicon. Wheruppon the Cause proceadinge to Judgment yt was this day ordered, adiudged and decreed that the said Edward White shall pay unto her matie for a fyne the some of twenty poundes and endure ymprisonment [during] the L Deputies pleasure. Geoven at her maties Court of Castle Chamber the xvith day of June 1591.[89]

Md where Patricke Talbot of Garriston in the County of Dublin, gent, exhibited a bill of Ryot in hir maties high Cort of Castell Chamber against John Quatermas of the Newton, George Quatermas of the same, Symon Ryan, Thomas Quatermas, Richard Quatermas of Prynatston, James Magwyre[?], John Magwyre[?] of the Newton, Willm Corrolan, John Heele of Garriston, Richard Quatermas of the Newnynges, Walter Pyper of the Grallagh, Donogh Snallen of the Holywood and Teig Reagh of the Newton aforesayd. That they the sayd Defendauntes the first day of June in the xxxijth yere of hir maties Raigne, by procurement of the sayd John Quatermas, came unto the moore of Garriston all in Riotous and warlike in armor arayed, Came unto the moore of Garriston aforsayd and the same Day and yeare Riotously and wrongfully did enter into the sayd Patricke sayd place and playne in the sayd moore, and then and there in like mannor did Riotously and wrongfully Cutt and make Turffe in and upon the sayd place and playne. Wherunto the Deffs aunswerred and the Cause proceedinge to Replicacon, Reioynder and Surreplicacon and witnesses examined on either parte and this Daye appoynted to be hard. Forasmuch as upon full hearinge and deliberate discussinge of the sayd Cause, yt manifestly appeared to the Right honorable the Lo: Deputy and the rest of the Judges then sitting that the Ryott was Committed by Three of the Deffs, vz. John Quatermas, George Quatermas and Richard Quatermas of the Newton. Yt is therfore ordered, Judged and Decreede by the sayd Lo: Deputy and Judges That the sayd John Quatermas shall paye to hir maty for a fyne xxs ster: and the sayd George and Richard eyther of them x s. ster: and indure ymprisonment [during] the Lo Deputyes pleasure, the rest of the Deffs to be dismissed, payinge the Costs of the Court. Geven at hir maties court of Castell Chamber the xxvjth day of November 1591.[90]

Md where John Quatermas of Garrestonne in the County of Dublyn, husbandman, exhibited a bill of Riott in her maties high Court of Castell Chamber against Thomas Coursy, Richard Maken, John Cheevers, Edmond Younge, Willm Dillon, and Willyam Talbott, esquire. That they the sayd defendtes the seconde daye of June in the xxxijth yeare of her maties Raigne by the procurement of the sayd Willm Talbott Came unto the moore of Garrestonne all in Riotousse and warlike mannor arayed, and the same Day and yeare aforsaid and at the place aforsaid did assault, beate, and evill entreate the sayd John Quatermas and put him in feare of his liffe. Whereunto the Defendtes aunswered and the Cause proceadinge to Replicacon, Reioynder and witnesses examyned on either parte, and this Daye appoynted for the hearinge therof. Forasmuch as upon full hearinge and Deliberate Discussinge of the sayd Cause, yt manifestly appeared to the Right honorable the Lo Deputye and the rest of the Judges then syttinge, That the Riott was Committed by all the Defendantes, savinge the sayd Willm Talbott. Yt is therfore ordered, adiudged and decreed That the sayd Defendantes shall paye unto her maty for a fyne The some of sixe poundes viz: Thomas Coursy forty shill[ing]es; The other Foure, Twenty Shillinges each of them apeece And endure ymprisonment till the next Wedsdaye. The sayd Willm Talbott to be Dismissed, payinge the Costes of the Court. Geven at her mates Court of Castell Chamber, the xxviijth of January 1592.[91]

89. f. 97. Fol. 97v is blank.   90. f. 98.
91. f. 99. See above, f. 98, for John Quatermas as principal defendant in a case of riot involving the cutting of turf
    on 1 June 1590, for which he was found guilty. On the following day, 2 June, he was apparently assaulted in the
    same moor by men in the employ of a relative of the original plaintiff, Patrick Talbot, although the alleged

Md where Edmonde, Lo vicount Montgarret, exhibited A bill of Riott in her maties high Courte of Castell Chamber against Donagh McCreagh, John McDonnell, Donogh FitzJohn, and Divers other, that they the sayde Donogh, John & Donogh, and the rest named in the bill the xxith of Aprill 1591, having of prepenced malice Conspired to murder and kill the sayd Edmonde, Lorde vicount, Rebelliously and most unlawfully assembled themselves togither being all arayed in warlike manner with swordes, Skeaves, Scules, Targettes and sondry other weapons, secretly Conveyed themselves to a moore thorough which the sayd Lo: vicount shoulde passe on his waye from Contrileagh towardes his owne houwse, and there the sayd persons abovenamed, with the rest, remayned in ambush untill the sayd Lo. vicount rydinge very neare unto them, they sodenly started fourth, and in most riotousse and Rebellious manner assaulted the sayd lo: vicount and his servauntes, throwinge many Dartes and speares at them, and with drawne swordes furyously Ranne upon the sayd Lo: vicount, and with there Dartes and speares wounded divers of the sayd Lo : vicount, his men and horses, and put himself in greate Daunger of his liefe. Whereupon three of the defendauntes, viz Donogh McCreagh, John McDonyll and Donagh FitzJohn aunswered and the Cause proceadinge to Replicacon, Reioynder, and witnesses examyned on either parte and this day appoynted for hearinge thereof. Forasmuch as upon full hearinge and deliberate discussinge of the saide Cause, yt manifestly appeared to the right honorable the Lo: Deputie and the rest of the Judges then sittinge that the Riott was Comitted aswell by the sayd Donogh MCreagh, John McDonyll and Donogh FitzJohn as the rest named in the bill. Yt is therfore ordered, adiudged and Decreed that the sayd Donogh McCreagh and John McDonyll shall pay unto her matie for a fyne each of them six poundes, thirtene shillinges & foure pence, and the said Donogh FitzJohn in respect that he is sonne to the sayd John McDonyll and to be Comaunded by his father shall pay but fortie shillinges, and also that the sayd Defendantes herein named shall make present satisfaccon unto the pls of all such Charges as shalbe taxed by the right honorable the Lord Chauncellor in his behalf. Geven at her maties Courte of Castell Chamber the xxjth Daye of Aprill 1592.[92]

Memorandum: where Thomas Dalton of Imp[er], pl, in the Countie of Westmeith, gent, exhibited a bill of Riott in her maties high court of Castle Chamber against Sir John Tirrell, knight, Walter Tuite and others that they the sayd Defendantes, the xixth daye of Decembe 1587, in warlike manner arayed came to Castlegaddre aboute the fallinge of the night of the sayd Daye and then & there most forcibly, Riotously & willfully did breake the walles of the Complaynauntes sayd Castle in foure places, Wherein with like force & Riotouse manner they entred & dyd assault Willm Warren & Pyers Dalton, the Complts servauntes. Wherunto the Defdantes aunswered & the Cause proceedinge to yssue and this Daye assigned to be harde & forasmuch as upon full hearinge and Deliberate Discussinge of the sayd Cause it manifestly appeared to the right ho: the Lo: Deputye and the rest of the Judges then sittinge that the Riott was Comitted by the sayd Defendants. And for that the sayd Sir John Tirrell & Walter Tuyte were the principalle in the action and that the rest of the Defendt were Servauntes and followers of the sayd Sir John Tirrell. Yt is therfore ordered, adiudged and Decreed That ye sayd Sir John Tirrell shall pay unto her maty for a fyne six poundes, thirtene shillinges, and the rest of the Defendauntes for the respecte aforesayd shalbe Dismisste. And also the sayd Sir John Tirrell & Walter Tuyte shall make present satisfaccon unto the plt of all such Charges as shalbe Taxed by the right honorable the Lo Chauncellor on the pltes behalf. Yeven at her maties Courte of Castle Chamber the xxjth daye of Aprill 1592.[93]

Memorande[m] that wheare Roger Wilbrham, esquire, her maties Solicitor generall, exhibited informacon into this most honorable Courte of Castle Chamber That Donogh McCarye of St. Michaells in the Countie of Longford, vicar, Comitted willfull and manifest periurye. And the sayd Donogh McCarye beinge Called to aunswere the sayd periurye Could not Denaye the same but

instigator, William Talbott, was found not guilty. The hearings were some two months apart, but clearly involved the same incident over two days.
92. f. 100.
93. f. 101. Note the delay of nearly five years between incident and trial.

openly in courte Confessed the same, whereupon it was this Daye ordered, adiudged and Decreed by the right honorable the Lo Deputie and Judges then sittinge, That the sayd Donogh McCarye shall for his sayd willfull and manifest periury paye unto her matie for a fyne the some of Twentie poundes and to be Comitted to prison untill he have satisfied and paye the same. And also enter into bande of Recognisaunce with suerties to appeare at the next generall Cessions holden at Longford in the Countie of Longford before her maties Comissioners there, and from thence not [to] Depart without Licence of the sayd Comissioners. And further if the sayd Donogh McCarye doe not satisfie and paye the fyne of xx li imposted upon him as aforsaid within the space of one half yeare after his Judgment, That then the sayd Donogh McCarye to be put upon the pillarye and both his eares nayld to the same and soe Cutt of[f]. Yeoven at her maties Court of Castle Chamber the fifte daye of Maye 1592.[94]

Me: Wheare Thomas Fitz Gerrald of Rathbegge in the County of Longford, gent, Bryan McMelaghlyn, Terlagh McGawran and Hugh O Killen of Rathbeg aforsayde exhibited a bill of Riott in her maties high Court of Castell Chamber, against Theobald Dillon, John Talbott, Patricke Dwigenan, Edmond Dillon, John Fitznich[ol]as, and others. That they the sayd Theobold, John, Patricke and the rest named in the bill the vth daye of Aprill 1587, in warlike manner arayed, In Riotous manner Came to the sayd Rathbegg and there with force entered into the pltes howses, thrust them and there familyes out of Doores, and did kill there sheape & Lambes and did likwise forcibly take and Drive away the nomber of forty Cowes. Whereunto the Defendauntes aunswered, and the Cause proceedinge to Replicacon, Reioyndor and witnesses examyned on either parte And this daye appoynted for the hearinge thereof. Forasmuch as upon full hearinge and deliberate discussinge of the sayd Cause it manifestly appeared to the right ho[norable] the Lo: Deputy and the rest of the Judges then sittinge that the Ryot was Comytted by the sayd Theobold Dillon, John Talbot, Patricke Dwigenan, Edmonde Dillon and John Fitznich[ol]as in manner and forme aforesayd. It is therefore ordered, adiudged and Decreed by the sayd Lo Deputy & Judges That the sayd Theobold Dillon shall pay unto her Maty for A fyne the some of six poundes, thirten shillinges and foure pence, and the sayd John Talbot, Patricke Dwigenan, Edmond Dillon and John Fitznicholas shall each of them also paye to her maty, the some of forty shillinges, endure ymprisonement the Lo: Deputyes pleasure, and also shall paye to the plts all such Charges as shalbe Taxed by the Right honorable the Lo: Chaunccellor on theire behalfes. The rest of the Defendauntes named in the bill to be dismissed. Geven at her maties Court of Castell Chamber the xxvijth day of October 1592.[95]

Me: where Donogh McCormocke, als McDonogh of Kyntwicke in the County of Corke, esqr, exhibited a bill of Ryot in her mates high Court of Castell Chamber against Teig McOwen, Owen McTeig, Cormocke McTeig, Donogh McTeig of Dryshane in the County of Corke aforsayd, with Dyvers others, That they the sayd Defendauntes the Last of March 1591 Came with force and armes to the Townes and landes of Dromscokan, Gortnegowny and Killeclonbarry in the County aforsayd, in Riotous and warlike manner arrayed, and from the sayd Landes did expulse the sayd Donogh McCormocke and manured the sayd Landes. Wherunto the Deffs aunswered and the Cause proceedinge to Replicacon, Reioynder and witnesses examined on either parte and this Daye appoynted to be hard. Forasmuch as upon full hearing & deliberat discussinge of the sayd Cause yt manifestly appeared to the right Ho: the Lo: Deputy & the rest of the Judges then syttinge that the Riott was Comitted by the sayd Teig McOwen, Owen McTeig, Cormock McTeig and Donogh McTeig in manner and forme aforesayd. Yt is therefore ordered, adiudged & Decreed by the sayd Lo Deputy & Judges that the sayd Teig McOwen, beinge the principall leader of the rest, shall pay unto her matie for a fyne The some of six poundes, Thirtene shillinges & foure pence. The other Three of the Deffs, viz Owen McTeig, Cormocke McTeig and Donogh McTeig shall pay likwyse to her maty for a fyne each of them Twenty shillinges a peece, and also the sayd Teig McOwen to endure ymprisonement untill he have payd the sayd severall fynes with all such Costes and Charges of the Court as shalbe Taxed by the Right ho: the Lo: Chauncelor on the pltes behalf. Geven at her maties Court of Castell Chamber the xxiiijth of November 1592.[96]

94. f. 102. No details of the perjury are recorded.
95. f. 103. Note interval of over five years between incident and trial. Fol. 103v is blank.
96. f. 104.

Me[morandum] wheare Charles Calthropp and Roger Wilbraham, esquires, her maties Attourney and Solicitor, exhibited informacon into this most honorable Courte of Castell Chamber against one Thomas Brookes, late of Dublyn, Souldier, who not regardinge his Duety and alleageaunce nor bearinge that Reverend respect towardes the Quenes most excelent matie as in Duety he ought, very disloyally, Contemptuously and Sediciously published most wicked & Detestable wordes, viz that he Cared not for her maty, the mayor of Dublin nor any other maiestrate [magistrate] her highnes had in Ireland. Addinge further that her ma[jest]ty watch were the Quenes geese, And the sayd Brookes, beinge brought to aunswere Could not denay but he had uttered part of the sayd wordes, The rest was proved by sufficient witnesses. Whereupon the Court proceedinge to Judgment, It was then ordered, adiudged and Decreed by the Right ho: the Lo: Deputye and Councell then syttinge, that the sayd Thomas Brookes shall Remayne in prison tyll the next market Daye, And on the same Daye to be sett on the pillory with A paper about his heade, Conteyning the sayd Disloyall & Contemptuousse speaches as before is Rehearsed, And shall also endure ymprisonement the Lord Deputies pleasure. Geven at her maties Court of castell Chamber, the vith of February 1593.[97]

Me: wheare Roger Wilbraham, esquior, her maties Solicitor generall, enformed in this most honorable Court of Castell Chamber That John Fitz Edmondes of Clone in the County of Corke, esquire, one of her maties Commissioners for the Peace in the sayd County, havinge intelligence that one Walter Copinger, undershrieffe of the sayd County, had taken a Distresse from one Thomas Gangogh, brother in Lawe to the sayd John Fitz Edmondes the xiijth of Aprill 1592. The sayd John FitzEdmondes beinge in his owne howse at Corke accompanied with foure of his servauntes, viz Morrice Browne, Garret Barry, John Sleny & Morryce Powre, the sayd John FitzEdmondes sent for the sayd Walter Copinger to Repaire unto hime to shewe by what Aucthority he had taken the sayd Distressse. The said Copinger presently repayred unto the said John FitzEdmondes, And delivered unto hime A grene waxe boke, under the Seale of her Maties Exchequor of this Realme of Irelande. The said John FitzEdmondes havinge the sayd grene waxe booke in his hande in great Collor and fury dyd sweare with grevous oathes that there was nothinge but knavery, packinge and shiftinge Conteyned in the sayd booke And Called the sayd Copinger knave, vyllane and many other vyle names for takinge the sayd Distresse. And the sayd John FitzEdmondes not Contented therewith increasinge further in fury Caused his sayd servauntes before named to take the sayd Copingers dagger from hime, and then and theire the sayd John Fitz Edmondes & the sayd servauntes dyd assault and grevously beate the sayd Walter Coppinger And did keepe from hime the sayd grene waxe booke, to the great hinderaunce of her maties service. Which his sayd Contempt, Ryot and misdemenor was proved in the most part by sufficient witnesses examined before the Lo: Deputy & Councell, and by his l[ordshi]ps and Councells Comission, as allso by the sayd Copinger viva voce in Court. Whereupon the Court proceedinge to Judgment, the learned Councell of the sayd John FitzEdmonde & himeself beinge hard at large, was this daye ordered, adiudged & Decreed by the Right honorable the Lo: Deputye & this most honorable Court That the sayd John FitzEdmondes shall for his sayd Ryott and misdeamenor pay unto her matie for A fyne the some of xx li And endure ymprisonement at the Lo: Deputies pleasure. Yeaven at her maties Court of castell Chamber the vijth of February 1593.[98]

Me wheare Andrewe Russell, Guyden [guidon, an official] unto Capten Christopher Carliell, exhibited A bill of Ryott in her maties high Court of Castell chamber against John Dalway & others that they the sayd Defendauntes unlawfully assembled themselves togither the xiijth daye of Aprill [and] with sounde of Drom in riotous and Rebellous sorte Came upon the Land of the Ilande [island] McGuy and there forcibly Rescued and dyd take away from the sayd Russell a distresse of two hundred and Twenty Cowes and two garrans Contrary to her maties peace and lawes. Whereunto the Defendant Dalwaye aunswered and the Cause proceedinge to the Replicacon, Reioyndor and witnesses examined on either parte and this Day appoynted to be harde. Forasmuch as upon full hearinge and deliberate discussinge of the sayd Cause, yt manifestly appeared unto the Right honorable the Lo Deputy and the rest of the Judges then sitting that the Ryott was Committed by the sayd Dalwaye in manner and forme aforesayd. It is therfore ordered, adiudged and Decreed by the sayd Lo: Deputy & Judges That the sayd John Dalwaye shall pay unto her maty for A fyne The some of Three poundes sixe shillinges and eight pence, endure ymprisonment the Lord Deputies pleasure, And shall also paye all such Costes and Charges of the Court as shalbe Taxed by the Right honorable the Lo Chauncellor on the pltes behalf. Gyven at her maties Court of Castell Chamber the ixth of February 1593.[99]

Me wheare Edmonde French of Galwaye, merchaunt, exhibited A byll of Ryot against Thomas Nolan of Galway, gent, and others that they the xiith Daye of June in the xxxijth yere of her maties Raigne in warlike manner arrayed Came unto the Castell of Liskenenan in the Countie of Galwaye And thereunto with force and violence dyd Ryotously breake upp the Doores and entreys of the same Castell, and then and there dyd forcibly and Ryotously put out Anstaunce French and others out of the sayd Castell and Ryfled & spoyled A greate Deale of the goodes of the sayd Edmond French. Whereunto the sayd Thomas Nolan aunswered and the matter beinge at yssue and this Daye appoynted to be harde. Forasmuch as upon full hearinge & Deliberat Discussinge of the sayd Cause yt manifestly appeared unto the Right honorable the Lo: Deputy and the rest of the Judges then sittinge that the Ryott was Comitted by the sayd Thomas Nolan in manner & forme aforsayd. Yt is therfore ordered Adiudged and Decreed by the sayd Lo: Deputy and Judges That the sayd Thomas Nolan shall pay unto her matie for a fyne The some of Tenn poundes, endure ymprisonement [during] the Lo Deputies pleasure, And shall also paye all such Costes & Charges of the Courte as shalbe Taxed by the Right honorable the Lo: chauncellor on the pltes behalf. Gyven at her maties Court of Castell Chamber the vijth of February 1593.[100]

Me wheare Sir Thomas Flemynge, knight, Lo: Barron of Slane, exhibited informacon into this honorable Courte of Castell Chamber against Christopher Prestone, Lo: vicount of Gormanston, Christopher Pluncket, Willm Fitzwilliam and divers others. That he the Lo: Barron of Slane beinge sent for by the Right honorable the Lord Chauncellor and others, her maties Commisioners, to make his present Repayre to Dublin to be examined before the said Commissioners upon Causes greatly ymportinge her Maties service, And the said Lo: Barron of Slane goeinge thorough the high streete of Dublin with five or sixe of his ordinarye Servauntes towardes St. Patrickes Churche wheare the said Commissioners were the xxvjth of Aprill 1592. In the said high streete neare the said market Crosse The said Lo: vicount of Gormanston with the nomber of Thirtye persons or there aboute did meete the said Lo: Barron of Slane and then and theire, with force and armes in most Riotous sort, did assault the said Lo: Barron of Slane and gave hime divers blowes, and in the said assault Bartholmewe Laughn one of the Lo Barron of Slanes servauntes was sore wounded and in greate perill of his lyffe. Whereunto the said Lo: vicount of Gormanstone and the rest of the Defendauntes made Aunswer and the Cause proceedinge to Replicacon, Reioyndor and witnesses examyned on either parte and this day appoynted to be harde. Forasmuch as upon full hearinge & deliberate discussinge of the said Casue yt manifestly appeared to the right honorable the Lo: Deputy and councell then sittinge that the Ryot was Comitted by the said Lo vicomte and his said Company. Yt is therfore ordered, adiudged and decreed by the said Lo: Deputie and the reste That the said Lo: vicount of Gormanston aswell for himeself and the rest of his Company, Defendauntes, shall paye unto her maty for a fyne the some of one hundred poundes, and the said Lo: vicount restrayned of his libertie [during] the Lo: Deputies pleasure. Yeoven at her maties Court of Castell Chamber the ixth day of Maye 1593.[101]

Memorandum wheare Walter French of Galwey, gent, exhibited a bill of Ryotte in her maties Court of Castell Chamber against James Linche FitzAmbrose, Walter French FitzNicholas, Stephen Linche FitzJames and others of the saide Towne of Galwey, that they the saide Deffendantes unlawfully assembled them selves together the thirde day of Aprill 1589 in riotouse sorte, came to a

99. f. 107.   100. f. 108. Fol. 108v is blank.
101. f. 109. Fol. 109v is blank.

howse or tenement of the saide Walter Frenche in the saide town of Galwey and entrede forceblie into the saide howse uppon the said Walter, beinge theire in God and her maties peace, and him did riotouslye assaulte, beate and evill intreate, with divers other mysdemeanors, contrary to her maties lawes. Wherunto the saide Deffendauntes made answeare and the Cause proceedinge to Replicacon, Reioyndor and witnesses examyned on either parte and this day appoynted to be harde. Forasmuch as upon full hearinge & deliberate discussinge of the said Cause yt manifestly appeared to the right honorable the Lo: Deputy and councell then sittinge that the saide riott was comyted by the Deffendantes. And for that also it appeared unto the Court that the saide James Linche FitzAmbrose and Walter Frenche FitzNicholas were the principall actores. It is therfore ordered, adiudged & decreed that the saide James Lynch FitzAmbrose and the saide Walter French FitzNicholas shall pay unto her matie for a fyne each of them tenne poundes, endure imprisonment two monthes, and shall also make present satisfaccion unto the plentife all such chardges as shalbe taxed by the Lo. Chancellor. The rest of the deffendantes to be dismyssed, paieinge the Costes of the courte to the Clearke and other Offycers. Yeoven at her maties Courte of Castle Chamber the xxiijth day of November 1593.[102]

Memorandum that Roger Wylbraham, esquier, her maiesties Solicytor generall within this Relme of Irelande, enformed to this moste honorable Courte of Castell Chamber againste Nicholas White of Maynam in the Countye of Kyldare that he the saide Nicholas had trayterouslie publyshede that there was a prophecie in Irelande that ODonell shoulde be kinge in Irelande, and that theire was an oulde Crowne of the kynges of Irelande in Rome, and that the Catholicke Bushoppes of this Lande did write to Rome for that Crowne and to advaunce their Religion, of wiche his disloiall & rebellious speeches he coulde not bringe forthe his pretended Author, althoughe upon his examination before the right honorable the Lo: Deputy & Councell he confessed the saide traiterous speeches in effect. Therfore her maties Sollicitor humbly prayed deserved punyshement to be inflicted uppon the saide Whyte for his trayterous & sedicious speeches. Wheruppon yt was this daie ordrede, adiudged & Decreed by the right honorable the Lo: Chancellor and the rest of the Judges then sittinge that the saied Nicholas White shall stande one the pilorye within the Cittie of Dublin thre markett dayes with a paper on his hede conteynynge his disloiall and undutifull speeches. The firste day one of his eares nayled to the pillorye & that eare cutt of, the seconde day the other eare nayled and the eare cutt of, last of all to be whipped on a market day throughe the Citty, and afterwardes to remayne in prysone duringe the Lo: Deputies plesure. Yeoven at her maties Courte of Castell Chamber the xxviijthe daye of November 1593.[103]

Memorandum wheare Katherin Barrett of Ballencolly in the Countye of Corke exhibited informacione into this moste honorable Court of Castell Chamber, that the viijth daye of September 1589 one Cormocke McDermode of Blarnye in the saide County of Corcke, Esquier, Donogh McTeige McCormocke, Bryen McDowell, with divers others to the number of two hundrede persons, the saide daye and yeare in warelicke manner by waye of insurrectione most riotouslye, routeslye [i.e. in a rout] and unlawfullye assemblede, with force and armes, viz with swordes, targettes &c, did assaulte, assayle, invyrone [i.e. to encircle] and besiege Castlenyhinche in the saide Countye, menasinge and moste cruelly and wickedlye threatininge one Kryvan McMoroghe and others, the servauntes of the saide Katherin, then beinge within the saide Castell. And that he the said Cormocke with the rest of the saide Ryotters wolde have entrede into the saide Castle violently and forceably, and threatenede to cutt of the heades of the sayde Kryvane and the reste of the Companye within the saide Castle yf they woulde not yelde the same, and theire saide assaulte and seige in warelicke and moste undutifull manner the saide Cormocke McDermode and the reste of his accomplices did unditufullye [sic] and riotouslye contynue the saide viijth day of September and the whole ixth day followinge of the same moneth, not sufferinge the Companye within the saide Castle to yssue forthe nor any other to have egresse unto them for theire vict[ua]linge and other lawfull assayes. Wherunto

102. f. 110. Note inverval of four years from incident to trial.
103. f. 111. Note the first mention of a Roman Catholic conspiracy in records of the court, in conjunction with the severest penalty imposed on a defendant, occurring on the eve of the Tyrone Rebellion.

the saide Cormocke and the reste made aunsweare and the Cause procedinge to Replicacon, Reioyndor and witnesses examyned on either parte and this day appoynted to be harde. Forasmuch as upon full hearinge & deliberate discussinge of the said Cause yt manifestly appeared to the right honorable the Lo: Chauncellor and councell then sittinge that the saide ryotte and unlawfull assembly was comytted by the saide Defendauntes, and for that also yt appearede unto the Courte that the saide Cormocke Macke Dermode was the principall Actor & the other Defendauntes at the saide Cormocks comaundement. Yt is therfore ordred, adiudged and decreede by the saide Lo: Chauncellor and Judges that the saide Cormocke McDermode shall paye unto her maty for a fyne the some of tenn poundes, and endure ymprisonment in her maiesties Castle of Dublyne the space of xv dayes, and shall also make present satisfaccione unto the plte all such Charges as shalbe taxed by the Lo: Chauncellor on his behalfe, the reste of the Defendauntes to be dismysedd, paieinge the fees of the Court to the clearke and other Officeres. Yevin at her maties Courte of Castell Chamber the xxvth daye of Januarye 1594.[104]

Memorandum the laste terme Roger Wylbraham, Esquier, her matis Solicitor exhibited an informacione in writinge into this moste honorable Courte of Castle chamber that Richarde Berd, Bushope of Leighline, the eleventhe daye of September 1593 at oulde Leighlyne in the Countye of Catherlaughe, shewinge him self discontente that one Brocke, a scolem[aster] at Maribroghe, had twentye poundes per Annum of the Dioces of the saide Bushopricke, which scolemaster and lymytacone of stipende was erected by the right honnorable the Lo: Deputy and Counsell by the aucthoritie of the late Statutes in that Case provided, and in prouffe of the saide Bushopps discontentment therin the said Bushoppe in publique audience then saide that the saide Brocke shoulde not have the saide stipende unles he woulde kepe schole at Catherlaughe or oulde Leighlyne, and the saide Lo. Bushope required further to know who had taken upp the saide stypende out of his Diocese for the laste yeare, to whom Mr Batho, brother in lawe to the saide Bushope and his stewarde, aunswearede that the subsherif had taken yt upp for the laste yeare. The Bushoppe then askede him by what auctoritie did the subsheriffe take yt upp. Batho aunsweared that he sawe the Lo: Deputyes warraunte for yt and that he did allow yt, but, sayde the Bushoppe, thoughe yo do allowe yt I do not allow yt: for my Lo Deputye shall have no more to do in my Diocesse then I will have to do with his swoorde, and I will comaunde him and his swoorde. To which informacione of disloiall speeches the saide Lo Bushoppe the firste daye of this Terme aunswerede by writinge, utterly denyenge that ever he spake any such undutifull or disloyall speaches, and this daye called into Courte by solemn attestacons denyede the saide speaches & protestinge his humble loialtie saide that, admyttinge them spoken, yet they were not ment of the swoerde of estate, & might in some sence be spoken without offence in respect of his spirituall iurisdiccione. Wheruppon the Court proceadinge to iudgement yt appearede by the oathe of two wytnesses examyned before the Lorde Deputy and Counsell that the saide Bushoppe spoke the wordes in the informacione, to one of which saide wytnesses there was no exceptione taken. But to the other, the Bushope saide that he was a crymynous preeste in his diocese & deprived by him & upon that malyce falslie accused him, and that provinge by one wytnes alone he ought not by law to be convynced [i.e. convicted]. And her maties Sollicitor enforced the credyte & sufficiencie of the wytnesse by many reasons, that the said Bushope coulde not in any dutifull sence affirme that he might comaunde the roiall swoorde. Forasmuch as the Courte is perswadede that some unadvised & undutifull speches were used by the saide Lo Bushoppe, althoe without entent of disloialtie, Therfore it is ordrede and adiudged by the Courte that the saide Bushope shall paye unto her maty for a fyne the some of twentye poundes and endure ymprisonment for eight dayes. Geoven at her maties courte of Castell Chamber the xxxth daye of January 1594.[105]

Memorandum wheare Charles Calthorpe and Roger Wylbraham, Esquiers, her maties Attorney and Sollycitor generall within this Realme of Irelande, have by speeche enformede this most honnorable Court that Sir Thoms Moore of Crogham in the Kinges County, knight, in an open and great asemblye or metinge of Dyvers gentlemen and inhabitauntes of that Countye at a parle hill [a parley

---

104. f. 112. Note the interval of over four years between incident and trial.
105. f. 113v–14. Fols. 113, 114v are blank.

hill, place for speaking to men of county] called Ballybirne in the saide Countye, had spoken and uttrede againste the nowe Lo: Deputye and in disgrace of his Lps governement undutifull speeches, viz, that the saide Sir Thomas had receavede dyrection by lres from Sir Richard Binghame, knight, chief Comysioner of the province of Conaught and Thomounde, to apprehend two mightie men for greate matters of that Countye callede OFallons, which dyrectione he made knowen to his Lpe, and then and theire saide that he was restraynede from thexecution therof by dyrectione of the Lo: Deputye, And the said Sir Thomas beinge this daye callede to answeare the saide undutifull speches which tendide to the Dishonor of his Lps governement, and for that the sayde speaches were provede by two sufficient wytnesses againste whose Credites no excepcons coulde be taken. Wheruppon the Courte procedinge to iudgement, yt was this day ordred, adiudgede and Decreede that the saide Sir Thomas More openly in Courte make his submyssione, confessinge his unadvisednes and rashnes therin, which submyssione he then and theire made, as also to make the licke submyssione unto the Lo: Deputye and his persone, & to paye to her maty for a fyne the some of tenn poundes, and shall also be comyttede to prysone whensoever the saide Courte shall comaunde him, duringe the Lo: Deputyes pleasure, which ymprysonment is respytede and deferrede in Consideracione that the saide Sir Thomas Moore ys Sheriffe of the saide Countye and for that tyme to be employed in her maties servyce. Yeovin at her maties Courte of Castell Chamber the vijth day of February 1593/4.[106]

Memorandum wheare Robert Piphoe of St Mary in the suburbes of Dublin, gent, exhibitede Informacione into this moste honnorable Court of Castell Chamber that the xvth daye of February 1593 one Edwarde Sutton, gent, Patricke Tipper, Lawrens Sutton, with dyvers others to the nomber of twelve persons, came to the saide Robert Piphoe his howse at St Mary Abbey aforsaide by night tyme betweene ten and eleven of the Clocke, the saide Robert beinge in his bedd aslepe, the saide Edwarde Sutton, Patryke Typper, Lawrens Sutton and the reste moste disorderlye, ryotuslye in warelicke manner with theire weapons drawen did enter into the saide Robert Pyphoe his howse and from thence, the tyme and yearre aforsaide, did forcebly, ryotuslye and maliciouslye procure and carrye away with them one Frances Pyphoe, Daughter unto the saide Robert, and did also take away with them one Cheste of the saide Roberte goodes, and when they hadd gotten awaye the saide Frauncys and the saide Cheste, they locked the Doores of his howse uppon him wherby the sayde Robert was not able to prosecute the saide Edwarde Sutton and the reste out of his howse. Wherunto the saide Edwarde Sutton, Patryke Typper and Lawrens Sutton, thre of the Defendaunts made Answeare and the Cause proceadinge to Replicatione, Reioynder and wytnesses examynede one either parte and that day the Cause appoyntede to be hearde. Forasmuche as uppon full hearinge and deliberate discusinge of the saide Cause yt manifestlye appeared to the Courte that the sayde Ryotte, unlawfull asemblye and mysdemeanore was comytted by the saide Edwarde Sutton, Patryke Typper, Lawrence Sutton and the reste in the informacon mencionede. Yt is herfore ordrede, adiudgede and decrede that the saide Edwarde Sutton, being the cheiffe and principall actor and leader of ye reste of the Defendauntes, shall paye unto her matie for a fyne the some of one hundrede markes and endure ymprisonment the Lo Deputies pleasure. And the said Patrike Typper, in respecte of this offence and some licke offence before tyme comytted, shall paye unto her matie for a fyne the some of twentye markes and the saide Lawrens Sutton to paye also to her matie for a fyne the some of tenn poundes. The reste of the defendaunts in asmuche as they never aunsweared the informacione are respitede. And also ordrede that the saide Edward Sutton, Patryke Typper & Lawrens Sutton shall paye unto the plte all such Costes of Courte as shall be taxede by the honnorable the Lo: Chauncellor one his behalf. Yeovin at her maties Courte of Castle Chamber the xxiiijthe daye of Aprill 1594.[107]

Md wheare Thomas Flemynge of Bealgoly in the County of Corke, gent, exhibited informacione into this moste honnorable Courte of Castle Chamber that, the xxth day of Aprill 1593, one Phillipp Roche FitzPhillipp of Kynesale, merchant, Edmonde Oge McIdegane, James FitzEdmonde of Imokelly, gent, Edmonde McMoryshe, Dowlegh Roch of Keanelie, gent, Davy FitzThomas Roch, Richard FitzThomas Roche, Thomas Sherlock, Davy OConnell, Owen ODowdy, Shane OCarrane and John Regge of the saide Countye of Corke, with dyvers others, unlawfully assembled themselves

together in warelicke manner furnyshed with swords, targettes, halbertes & other weapons
defencibles, routeslie and ryotuslye did enter uppon xxtie acres of lande called Ballendelure, percell
of Bealgoly in the saide Countye of Corke, beinge his ancient inheritance, and upponn the saide xxtie
acres the saide persons did ryotuslie cutt downe fowere Carres of woode their growinge and carriede
awaie the same. Wherunto the saide Phillip Roch and the rest of the said Defendantes made answeare
and the Cause proceedinge to Replicacon, Reioynder and witnesses examyned on either parte and this
day appoynted to be harde. Forasmuch as upon full hearinge & deliberate discussinge of the said Cause
yt manifestly apeared to the right honorable the Lo: Deputy and councell then sittinge that the ryott
was comytted by the sayde Phillip Roch Fitz Phillip, Edmonde Oge McIdegaine and the rest before
named in maner and forme as in the informcon is set downe. It is therfore ordred, adiudgede and
decreede by the saide Courte that the saide Phillip Roche Fitz Phillipppe shall paye unto her maiestie
for a fyne the some of fyve pounds, endure ymprisonment the Lo Deputies pleasure, and shall also paie
unto the pl all such Costes of Courte as shall be taxed by the right honnorable the Lo Chauncellor one
his behalf. The reste of the Defendauntes before named shall also paie unto her maty for a fyne each of
them twenty shillings. Yeoven at her maties Court of castle Chamber the thirde of May 1594.[108]

Wheare Arthur Cary, Esq, hir matie Serieant, enformed this daye in Court against the Lo: Baron of
Inchequin that he, the iiijth day of June in the xxxvth yeare of hir maties raigne, accompanyed with
Thomas Caddell of the Malle, gent, with dyvers others unknowne persons, armed with swordes,
daggers, Rapyeres and gauntlettes, did meete Sir Tirlaughe OBryen, knight, on the key of Dublin
the iiijth day of June aforsaide, who was then repairinge to the Councell Chamber, which Sir
Tirlaugh havinge no weappon about him but a small Dagger, the saide Baron, not regardinge the
preservacione of hir maties peace, with dyvers otheres did then and theire in most furious maner
draw theire Rapyers and daggers and grevouslie wounded the saide Sir Tirlaughe in the heade and
put him in Despaire of his lyf. Wheruppon the saide Baron beinge this day called into the Court
made answeare humblie submitting himself to the iudgement of the saide Courte, and acknowledginge his unadvised act. It is therfore ordered, adiudged and decreed by the right honnorable the
Lo: Chancellor and the rest of the Judges then sittinge in Court, that the saide Lo: Baron shall pay
for a fyne to her maiestie the some of one hundrethe markes, the one moitie [half] theirof to be paide
before his enlargement, and to put in good securetie for answearinge the rest, and to remain in prison
in hir mates Castell of Dublin duringe the plesure of the Court. Yeovin at hir mates Courte of Castle
Chamber the viijth of June 1594.[109]

Memorandum wheare Mary Pentny, widdo, late wief to John Malone of Dublin, alderman,
Deceased, exhibited informacione into this most honorable Courte of Castell Chaamber that, the
eightenthe Daye of January 1594, one Richard Stevensone, John Chambers, Henry Mann, Leighlyne
Byrne, Patrike Brangan of Kylmaineame in the Countye of Dublin with divers others unlawfully
assembled them selves together in warelicke manner with Clubbes, Swords, staves, and other
weappons at Kilmaineame aforsaid and in riotus maner the saide persons did assault the saide Mary
Pentny and the said Richard Stevensone did wounde and hurte the saide Mary with a blow of a Clubb
on the heade. Wherunto the saide Richarde Stevensone and the rest of the saide Defendaunts made
answeare, and the Cause proceadinge to Replicacon, Reioynder and witnesses examyned on either parte
and this day appoynted to be harde. Forasmuch as upon full hearinge & deliberate discussinge of the said
Cause yt manifestly apeared to the right honorable the Lo: Chancellor and councell then sittinge that the
riott was comytted by the saide Richard Stevensone John Chambers, Henry Mann, Leighlin Byrne and
Patrik Brangan in maner & forme as in the informacione is set Downe. Yt is therfore ordered, adiudged
and decreed by the right honnorable the Lo Chancellor and the rest of the Judges then settinge that the
saide Richard Stevensone shall paye unto her maty for a fyne the some of fyve poundes. The other fower
defendant[s] ech of them to paye twentye shillinges apece, to be comytted to prisone till the next Courte
day, and to paie all such Costs of Courte as shallbe taxed by the right honnorable the Lo: Chancellor.
Yeoven at hir maties Courte of Castle Chamber the xijth of June 1594.[110]

108. f. 117.   109. f. 118.
110. f. 119.

Wheare Charles Calthropp, Esquire, hir maties attorny generall, enformed this day in Court against James Poer that he, the eleventh of June 1594 in the xxxvjth yeare of hir maties raigne, uppon the bridge of the cittie of Dublin, did assault Nicholas Poer then and there in riotous manner did strike and beate the said Nicholas with a Cudgell or trunchion, and the saide attorney generall lickwise enformed that the saide James Power did at another tyme forceblye take from the saide Nicholas Powers servant a writt or Iniunction, which writt was to be delivered to the sherif of the Countye of [blank in Ms], and the saide James Power beinge called to answeare could not denye any part of the saide Informacione. Wheruppon yt is ordred, adiudged and decreed by the right honnorable the Lo Chancellor and the rest of the Judges then settinge that the said James Power shall paye to her matie for a fyne the some of twentye pounds and endure imprisonment [during] the Lo: Chauncellors pleasure. Geovin at hir maties Court of Castell Chamber the xijth June 1594.[111]

Memorand wheare Edmonde Barrett of Mogellye in the Countye of Corke, gent, the xxiiijth of November 1592, exhibited informacion into this moste honnorable Courte of Castle Chamber that Andrew Barrett with divers others, beinge indicted of a forcebile entrie and deteyner of the Castle and Baron[y] of Ballencolly in the saide County of Corcke. Wheruppon the sayde Edmonde Barrett had a wrytt of restitucion of Sir Thoms Norrys, knight, vicepresident of Mounster and others her maties Justices of peace in the saide Countye, which beinge delivered to Sir Fynes ODryscoll, knight, the Sheriffe of the Countye, he extorcionsllye refucede to restore the Informe[r, i.e. plaintiff] accordinge the saide wrytt, till he was dryven to delyver him two sylver Cuppes in pledge of fower poundes sterlinge, which beinge paide the saide Sir Fynes most canteouslye [i.e. canting, using language of thieves] did nevertheles omytt the execution of the saide writt. Wheruppon the saide Sir Fynes was called to aunsweare and the Cause proceadide to hearinge and witnesses examyned on either parte and this day appoynted to be harde. Forasmuch as upon full hearinge & deliberate discussinge of the said Cause yt manifestly apeared to the right honorable the Lo: Chancellor and councell then sittinge that the said Sir Fynes ODriscoll was guiltie of the extorcion in the informacion set Downe. Yt is therfore this daye ordered, adiudged & Decreede by the right honnorable the Lo: Chauncellor and the rest of the Judges then sittinge that the saide Sir Fynes shall paye unto her matie for a fyne the some of ten poundes, endure ymprisonment [during] the Lo: Chauncellors pleaure, And shall also paie unto the plte all such Costes of Courte as shalbe taxed by the Lo: Chauncellor on his behalf. Yeoven at her maties Courte of Castle chamber the xxixth day of Januarye 1595.[112]

Md. Wheare Willm Poer of Kylblane in the Countye of Corcke, gent, exhibited Informacion into this moste honnorable Courte of Castle Chamber, that one Capten Thomas Plunkett, Richarde Plunkett, Thomas Plunket and others that they the saide Defendantes, the xxjthe Daye of Februarye 1593 at Kylcolman in the Countye aforsaide, in warelicke manner with Swords, Gonnyes, pykes, horsemens staves, Targettes, hedpeeces and other offenceve weappones did assemble together and theire the saide Defendauntes contynuede together for the space of two or thre Dayes in Ambyshe, placinge all their Cattell and so many of their tenaintes and neighbors as they coulde gett neare theire saide Ambushe as a trayne to Drawe the saide Wyllm Poer thether with intent to murther him. And the saide Wyllm Poer passinge throughe the saide Lande of Kylcolman aforsaide, sawe the saide Catle pasturinge thereuppon which the saide Wyllm intendede to Destrayne for Damadges sezaunt [seized, seizeable]. Wheruppon the saide Capteine Plunkett with other his Accomplices beinge assembled together as is aforsaide, sodeinlie arose out of theire saide place of Ambushe, rescuede the saide Cattell, and not theirewith content, but moste Riotouslie did assaulte, beate, wounde and evill intreate the saide Wyllm Poer, Garott Sutton, John FitzWyllm and Maymed one Richard Poer. Wheruppon the saide Capteine, Thomas Plunkett, Richard Plunkett, Chr[ist]offer FitzAlexander Plunkett, Mahowne OGowne, Gilipatrike Moore & Gilpatrik Gowne made Aunsweare and the Cawse procedide to Replicacion, Reioinder, and wytnesses examynyede. Forasmuche as uppon full hearinge and Deliberat Discussinge of the Cawse yt manifestly appered to the right honnorable the Lo: Deputy and the reste of the Judges then syttinge that the Ryott was comytted by the saide Defendauntes and evry of them in manner and forme as in the informacion is set Downe. Yt is therfore this Daye orderede adiudgede and Decreede by the saide Courte, that the saide Capteine Thomas Plunkett shall paye to her matie for a fyne the some of twentye poundes, the saide Richard Plunkett tenn poundes, the saide Chr[ist]offer FitzAlexander Plunket, tenn poundes, Gylpatrike OGowne, Mahowne OGowne and Gilpatrike Moore shall also paie ech of them thre poundes, six shillinges, eight pence, [and] endure ymprisonment [during] the Lo Deputy pleasure. And shall also paye unto the plentiff all such Costes of Courte as shalbe taxed on his behalf by the right honnorable the Lo Chauncelor. Yeovin at her matie Courte of Castle Chamber the last Daye of Januarye 1595.[113]

Memorandum wheare Edmonde Barrett of Ballencoly in the Countye of Corcke, gent, exhibited informacione in this moste honnorable Courte of Castle Chamber that about July 1591 one Andrew Barrett, Willm Barrett, Meoris [Maurice] Osowlevan [OSullivan] with Dyvers others, to the nomber of lx persons, the xviijth Daye of July aforsaide at Ballinecollye aforsaide, did rowtouslie assemble them selves together, and with force and armes, viz withe Swordes, Gonnes, great sledges or hammers, skeynes, stones and Staves, one Bolie howse then and theyre standinge unto the gate of the said Castle did remove, and then and theire the iron grate and parte of the wall of the saide Castle by the saide gate did riotuslye with a great hamer breake, and into the saide Castle, towne and Landes did expulse the saide Edmonde Barrett and did also levie a great Crye to the Disturbance of her maties subiectes, and to the grevous Damadge of the saide Edmonde. Wherunto the saide Andrew Barrett, Willm Barrett and Meorys OSwyllevan, thre of the Defendauntes, made Aunsweare and the Cawse procedide to Replicacion, Reioinder, and wytnesses examynyede. Forasmuche as uppon full hearinge and Deliberat Discussinge of the Cawse yt manifestly appered to the right honnorable the Lo: Deputy and the reste of the Judges then syttinge that the saide Ryott was comytted by the saide Andrew, Wyllm, Meorys and the rest in the byll specefiede in manner as in the saide byll is Declared. Yt is therfore orderede, adiudged and Decreede by the saide Lo Deputy and Judges then sittinge that the saide Andrew Barrett shall paye unto her matie for a fyne the some of twentye poundes, the saide Willm Barrett fyve poundes and the saide Meorys OSowlevan thre poundes, six shillinges, eight pence, endure ymprisonment the Lo Deputyes pleasure. And shall also make present satisfaccion unto the plte all such Charges as shalbe taxed by the right honnorable the Lo Chauncellor in his behalf. Yeovin at her maties Courte of castle Chamber the xxiijth of May 1595.[114]

Memorandum wheare John Clinton in the County of Looth, gentelman, exhibited Informacon into this honorable Courte of Castell Chamber that the xvth and xvjth Daye of August 1592 in the night tyme Henry Verdon of Togher, gent, Edward Verdon, Allexander Verdon, Rorye McShee and Neale OFarrall, by the Dyreccon, Comaundement, procurement and settinge on of Patricke Verdon of Clonemort, Esquire, That they the said Henrye and the rest before named Ryoutously with force and armes arrayed in warlike manner and weaponed with Swordes and other weapons Defensible Came, the said xvth and xvjth Dayes of August 1592 by night, to a parcell of land Conteyninge three acres neare the old Towne or hamblt [hamlet] of Dodstowne in the said County of Loothe, then sowen with wheate ready to be reaped and brought with them forty plowe horses or there abowte and upon the said Thre acres sowne with wheate, the said persons did kepe the said plowe horses the said xvth and xvjth Daies in the night tyme whearby the said Three acres wheatt was maliciously and in riotous manner eaten, trodden, broken downe & Consumed, to the great hinderaunce of the said John Clinton. Whereunto the Defendauntes made Aunswere and were examined upon personall Interrogatories and therupon the pl John Clinton Joyned yssue and this day the Cause appoynted to be hard. Forasmuche as uppon full hearinge and Deliberat Discussinge of the Cawse yt manifestye appeared to the Cort by the Confession of all the Defendauntes aswell in there Aunswear as in there examinacons upon personall Interrogatories that the Ryott was comitted in manner and forme as before is said & by the Comaundement Direccon and setting on of the said Patricke Verdon, beinge the principall procurer of the said Ryot. [He] shall pay unto her majtie for A fyne the some of Twenty nobles, the said Henry Verdon fyve poundes, the said Edward Verdon, fyve poundes, Allexander Verdon fyve poundes and the said Rory McShye and Neale OFarrall each of them fortye shillinges, endure ymprisonement duringe the pleasure of the Cort and shall also make present satisfaccon to

113. ff.122–22v. Fols. 123–23v are blank.   114. ff. 124–24v. Fols. 125–25v are blank.

the plaintiffe of all suche Costes of Cort As shalbe taxed by the Right honorable the Lo Chauncellor on his behalf. And it is further ordered that if the said Neale OFarrall and Rory McShye be not of abillity to Answere the fyne ymposed upon each of them, That then the said Patricke Verdon, there maister, shall answere and paye the same. Yeoven in her maties Cort of Castell Chamber the xiiijth daye of May 1596.[115]

Memorandum this Daye her maties learned Councell enformed to this most honnorable Courte by the relacion of Capteine Ryce Mannfyelde, Esquier, That Charles Egerton, Counstable of her maties Castle of Carigfergus and Governor of her maties forces there residinge, the xviijth day of August 1596, and in the xxxviijth yeare of her highnes raigne, did upon a prepencede [i.e. premeditated] malyce the saide day of purpose croste the highe wayes uppon the saide Mannfeylde, beinge then about her maties service in oversight of a fortificacion in the saide towne. And so the saide Charles Egerton with two warders in his Companye percevinge the saide Ryce Mannsfeylde to be in the feyldes about thre quarters of a myle from the saide towne, having but one in his Companye and both weapponed but verie barlie [i.e. barely weaponed], the saide Charles Egerton with two of her maties warders of the saide Castle, the saide Egerton armed with a Gauntlett and oher warelicke weappones, and then without occasion given by the saide Capteyne assaulted the saide Capteine and wounded his lyeftenant that was with him and presentlie after the saide firste assaulte theire came to ayde the saide Egerton six or vij warders more, who againe assaulted the saide Mannsfyelde by the instigacion of the saide Egerton, uppon which freshe assaulte a great tumulte and outcrye was raysed in the saide towne of Carrigfergus, wheare her maties guarrison laye for the Defence of the saide Towne, and the said Mr Egerton, not content with the former asaultes, beganne againe to assawlte the saide Mannsfeylde within the saide towne before the maior and the rest of that towne, by which severall assaultes and riotous mysdemeanors of the saide Egerton and his associates theire was licklie to growe great perill to all her maties Guarrison theire and utter confusion to the saide towne had yt not bene pacefied and stayed by the saide Maior and some well affected in that town. To which enformacion the saide Charles Egerton with his Councell aunsweared in his excuse alleadginge he was not guiltie of the saide informacion. Wheareupon the Courte proceadid to iudgement, and uppon deliberat hearinge and Discussinge of the Cawse, the wytnesses on both sides beinge readde and hearde at large, and her maties learned Councell as also the Councell of the saide Egerton havinge Debated the matter and circumstances on both sides, the saide Egerton was founde guiltie of the saide informacion in manner and forme as the same ys laide downe Whearsoever consideringe his great owtrage and mysdemeanor to the evill example and daunger of all the Guarison theire. Yt is adiudged ordered and Decreede by this moste honnorable Courte, that the saide Charles Egerton shall paye to her maiestie for a fyne the shome [sum] of one Cth [100] markes, and endiure ymprisonment [during] the Lo Deputies pleasure. Yeovin in her maties Courte of Castle Chamber the xvth Day of Aprill 1597.[116]

Md this daie her maties learned councell enformed to this moste honourable courte that John Norries, als Capten Norries, contrarye to his Dutye had spoken at Athlone in September last moste slaunderous, false and devious wordes against the Quenes moste excellent Maiestie, wch moste false and slaunderous wordes were manyfestlie proved by fower severall wytnesses to have been uttered and spoken by the saied John Norreys. And the saide John Norrys haveing been prysoner ever sithence in the Castell of Dublin for that offence was called this day to the Barr and the matter being obiected against him, stoode only uppon the denyall thereof. Whereuppon the matter having bene examined before the councell and proved as aforesaide, And the Courte proceding to iudgement and uppon deliberat hearinge and Discussinge of the Cawse, the wytnesses on both sides beinge readde and hearde at large, and her maties learned Councell as also the Councell of the saide Norreys havinge Debated the matter and circumstances on both sides, the said John Norreys, for his great offence and mysdemeanor, shall paie to her matie for a fyne the some of fyve hundred markes, stand uppon the pyllorye on a markett daye, both his eares to be cutt of, and to remayne in pryson during his lyeffe. Yeovin at her maties Courte of Castle Chamber the vjth daye of May 1597.[117]

115. ff. 126–26v. Note interval of nearly four years from event to decree of court.   116. ff. 127–27v.
117. f. 128. Norris was the general of forces in Ulster, a rival of the lord deputy, and brother of Sir Thomas Norris (see above). Fol. 128v is blank.

Memorandum this daie her maties learned Councell enformed to this moste honnorable Courte that Jane Hopp, wydoe, being at the Barr, having the [custody] of her maties Geole at Molyngare in the countye of Westmeathe, to whch Jayle ther were comytted emongest others two notorious and knowen traytores of the Sept of the Newgentes. And at a generall Cessions last holden at Molingare the Justices of Assize, findinge that the escaping of the saide two Newgents would breede great danger to the quiet of those borders, gave speciall chardge unto the said Jane Hopp, [who] neithe[r] regardinge the Comaundement of the saide Justices nor the care she ought to have hadd for the saffekepinge of all prysoners comytted to her Chardge, she negligentlie and carelesslye sufferde them to escape, Wherby great trouble and gar'boyle [i.e. disturbance, tumult] is likelie to happen in that Countie by the escape of so daungerous traytors, humblie praieinge that her offence might be punyshed most severe in example of all other Jaylors by whose usuall and negligent escapes great enormities hath growen to this comon wealthe. Wheareuppon this Daye [the matter having bene examined before the councell and proved as aforesaide, And the Courte proceding to iudgement and uppon deliberat hearinge and Discussinge of the Cawse, the wytnesses on both sides beinge readde and hearde at large, and her maties learned Councell havinge Debated the matter and circumstances on both sides] that for the same escape the said Jane Hopp shall paie to her matie for a fyne the some of two hundred poundes and suffer ymprisonment during the Lo Deputyes pleasure. Yeovin in her maties Courte of Castle Chamber the vjth day of May 1597.[118]

Wheare Sir John Davies, knight, his Maties Solyctor generall within this Relame of Irland, made informacon ore tenus in this most honorable Court of Castell Chamber That Willm Miagh, late recorder of the Cyttie of Corke, being indicted of soundry heynous treasons Consisting partly in Contradictinge his maties tytle to the Crowne of this realme, And partely in levying warr agaynst his Matie within this kyngdome, was in December last arraygned uppon the sayd indyctment before specyall Comissioners at Youghall in the County of Corke And therunto pleaded not gylty and for this tryall put hime self upon the Countrey. Whearuppon dyvers pryncypall gentlemen and free holders of the sayd County of Corcke being ympaneled for that tryall, and peremptory Challenge being made by the sayd Miagh of all that were of Englyshe byrth, at last for tryall of the sayd issue twelve were sworne whose names ensue, videlicet, 1 Rychard FytzDavid Barry Oge of Robertstowne, Esquier, 2 Thomas FytzJohn Gerrald of Rostelane, gent, 3 William Power of Shangarrye, gent 4 Gregory Lombard of Buttevant, gent 5 David Nagle of Moneaminny, gent, 6 Miles Roche of Kyleaghe, gent, 7 Donell O Donovan als O Donovan of Castle Donovan, gent, 8 John Ronane of Youghall, gent, 9 Nicholas Galwane of the same, merchant, 10 Moen McShihne of Kylletworagh, gent, 11 Wyllm Hodnet of Ballywody, gent, 12 and Donell Moell McCowty of Fyall, gent. To those Jurors his matie Attorney of the province of Mounster gave evydence agaynst the sayd Miagh, Wherby yt was fully and Dyrectly proved by Dyvers wytnesses of good valewe and Creadyt, That the sayd Miagh, having notice of the Death of the late Queene Elizabeth and of the proclayminge of his maties tytle that nowe ys, aswell by lettres from the Councell of State heare Dyrected to the Cyttye of Corke, amonge others, as also by pointed proclamacons sent with the sayd Ltres, Wherof the said Miagh tooke Coppies. Notwithstandinge he the sayd Miagh, being Desyred to asiste dyvers others of his maties Subiectes in proclayminge his maties tytle in the sayd Cytty of Corcke, did not only refuse so to doe But did also prohibytt and forbyd the said proclamacon to be made. And speach being moved to the sayd Miagh of the kynges Matie that nowe ys, the said Myagh affyrmed he knewe notinge [nothing]. And after that when proclamacon of his matie tytle was made within the said Cyttye the said Myagh absented hime self purposely & malycyously, to thend he might not heare the sayd proclamacon. Moreover yt was clearely and manyfestly proved that the sayd Myagh, having Contradicted the proclayming of the kynges Maties tytle as aforesaid, did cause a place called Skyddyes Castle wherin his maties stoare of Mynytion layd to be taken by force, and having seysed uppon his maties munytion and victuals would not suffer any parte therof to be yssued toward the relieffe of his maties Army resyding neare the Cyttye, But did spend and use parte of his maties munytion agaynst the sayd Armye. And lastly that the said Myagh did cause a forte of his Maties

---

118. f. 129. The husband of Hopp had been the previous jailer. Note this is the final case for the late Elizabethan period, a time of warfare and confusion in the Dublin government. A hiatus of some seven years ensues until the next case in the reign of James I in June 1604.

newly buylt on the South syde of the said Cytty of Corcke to be demolyshed and broken Downe, affirmyng the same to be his owte? and that he would Justyfye yt. These Actes being apparantly and dyrectly proved agaynst the said Myagh, Sir Nycholas Walshe, knight, Chieffe Justyce of the comon plees, And others of the Judges of this Realme whoe satt in Comission for that servyce did delyver their opynions to the sayd Jurors that the sayd Actes so proved agaynst the said Myagh were high treason, And that yt was so resolved uppon a Conference had at Dublyn by all the Judges of this realme. And therupon they dyrected the sayd Jury to fynd the sayd Myagh gyltie of the said treasons accordingly. Notwithstanding the sayd Jurors, Contrary to their oath, Contrary to their obydence, and Contrary to the Dyrectyon of the Judges, did wyllfully and wyckedly acquytt the sayd Myagh and by their verdyct found hime not gyltie. This informacon being made by his maties sayd Solycytor was proved by the sayd Lycitor [i.e. lictor, officer of magistrate] in this honorable Courte in every poynt to be trewe aswell by shewing forth the deposytyons of the sayd wytnesses under the handes of the reverent father in god the Lo Bushoppe of Meath, the sayd Sir Nycholas Walshe and Sir Anthony Sent Leager, knighte, being three of his maties pryvie Councell in this kyngedome, as also by the testymony viva voce of the sayd Sir Nicholas Walshe and others of the sayd wytnesses whoe weare now present in this honorable Courte. Wherunto the sayd Jurors appearinge in this honorable Courte and having Learned Councell assigned unto them and being hard at large did by them selves and their Councell make no other aunswer in efect but that, notwithstanding the sayd evydence were geven agaynst the said Myagh, yet they in their pryvate Conscience knew that the sayd Myagh had no intent to Comytt any treason, but shewed not any probable reason of their pretended knowledge nor any matter of argument that moght move or induce their conscience to acquytt the said Myagh of the sayd treasons, Consydering that both his wordes and accons, Wherby the intent of mans harte is Discovered, did prove and argue the Contrary. Wherby yt appeared to this honorable Courte that the sayd Jurors had in acquyttal of the sayd Myagh Comytted manyfest and wylfull periury in Contempt of Almyghty god, the kinges Matye and the symbolyke Justyce of this realme, to the evyll example of other Jurors and to the encouradgment of malefactors. And therefore yt is this daye ordered, adiudged and decreed by the right honorable the lord deputye and the rest whose names are underwrytten, sytting in the sayd honorable Court of Castle Chamber at Drogheda, that the sayd Defendantes shalbe ymprysoned duryng the Lo Deputyes pleasure, the foreman of the sayd Jurye, Rychard FytzDavy Barryoge, to paye for a fyne to his matie use one thousand markes. And all the rest to paye to his maties use each of them fyve hundred poundes a peece. And that they shall weare papers upon there heads declaryng their sayd offence in the face of the foure Courtes holden this trynitye terme at Drogheda. And shall lyekwyese weare the lyke papers at the next generall cessions to be holden at the Cyttye of Corke in the sayd province of Mounster. Yeven in his maties courte of Castle Chamber the xvth day of June 1604.
Being present: The Lo: Deputy, The Lo: Chauncellor, The Lo: Prymate, The Lo Bushopp of Meath, The Lo: Coursey, Sir Nicholas Walshe, Sir Edmond Pelham, Sir George Bourcher, Sir Oliver Lambert, Sir Frauncis Stafford, Sir Rychard Cooke, Sir James Fullerton, Justice Everard, Justyce Comerford.[119]

Md Wheare Controversye hath ben long dependinge in this honorable Courte betwene Samuell Mollynex, Marshall of this Courte, plt, And Trystram Caleston, counstable of his maties Castle of Dublyn, Defendt, both of them Clayminge the Custody of such prysoners as shall at any tyme be Comytted by order of this Courte, Which Controversye so dependinge was referred by this Courte to Sir James Lea, knight, Chieffe Justis of his maties Chieffe benche, and Sir Edmond Pelham, knight, Chieffe Baron of his highnes Courte of Exchequer, to take a viewe of both their patentes and to certyffy unto this Corte their opynion in whome the right was, Whoe Calinge to their asystance Sir Nycholas Walshe, knight, Chieffe Justice of his Maties Courte of Comon plees. Wheruppon the sayd Judges Cauling before them the said plt and defendt, the 4th day of February 1605 and in the yeare of the raigne of our soveraigne lorde James, Kinge of England, France and Ireland the seconde, and of Scotland the xxvijth. And having seene and perused both their patentes and fully harde the parties and their Councell and their allegacons, And fynding the matter in Controversye betwene them

119. ff. 130–32. Note first case of James I's reign, involving challenge to the legitimacy of the succession, heard in Drogheda by an unusually large court.

Concernyng the Custodye of prysoners Comytted by this honorable Courte to be very doubtfull, Wee thought fytt to move the parties to a quiett and arbytrable ende. Whoe by our dyreccon gave their Consent to this Course followinge, viz, That all Barons and persons precedent unto barons, Counselors of estate, Justices of the benches, Barons of the exchequier, Lordes of Iryshe Countreys, Shryeves of Counties, Mayors, knightes, Deanes of Cathedrall Churches, and Justices of peace, heareafter to be Comytted by this honorable Court, shalbe in the Custodye of the Counstable of the said Corte. And that all other persons heareafter to be Comytted by this honorable Courte shalbe in the Custody of the marshall, which wee thinke to be very Convenyent and ffyt to be ordred to Contynewe for ever. All which wee leave to the censure of this honorable Courte, provyded that this order shall not extend to the preiudyce of the marshall of the foure Courtes. And provyded also that yt shalbe at lybertye for this honorable Courte to Comytt any prysoner by expresse wordes to any officer whatsover, uppon Which certyffycate of the sayd Judges ys on this day ordred, adiudged and decreed by this honorable Cort that the same shall Contynewe accordingly. Present: The Lo Chauncelor, The Bushopp of Meath, Sir James Lea, Chieffe Justys of the Chieffe bench, Sir Nycholas Walshe, Cheiffe Justys of the Comon plees, Sir Edmond Pelham, Chief Baron of the exchequier, Sir George Bourcher, Sir Richard Cooke, Sir Gerrot More.[120]

Termio Hillarii Sexto die Febrarij 1605 Die Veneris
Me Wheäras dyvers Complaynts were preferred before Sir Edmond Pelham, knight, Chieffe Baron of his maties Court of exchequier, and Sir John Davyes, knight, his maties Solycitor, Justices of Assysse at A cessyons of Gayle Delyverye holden In the Countye of Donegall, agaynst Olyver Scurlocke, late shrieffe of that Countye, for many offences, extorcons and mysdemeanors Comytted and don by the sayd late shrieffe within the said Countye in the tyme of his shryvaltye, viz that Contrary to lawe he Caused proclamacon to be published in the said Countye that every house hold, for want of keping watch every night, should paye to the said Shrieffe foure shillynges for their Default. Also made Lyke proclamacon that whosoever should feade his Cattle on the montaynes should paie hime ten shillynges each household, and that each Glybbe [glebe, or cultivated land] should paie hime syxe pence with dyvers and soundry other extorcons, offences and mysdemeanors. And that upon examynacon therof the said offences was manyfestly proved by many wytnesses, wheäruppon the said Justices of Gayle Delyvery did bynd over the said Scurlocke to appeare in his maties Courte of Castle Chamber, there to appeare the first Courte daye sytting of the sayd Courte this hillary terme. Wheäre appearinge, the said Sir John Davys informed ore tenus agaynst the said Scurlocke of his said offences before the Lo Deputye and others the Judges then sytting. Uppon hearynge of which Informacon, the Causes alleadged Could not be denyed by the said Scurlocke but [he] Confessed the greatest parte of the said accusacons and submytted himeself to the mercye and favor of the Courte. Wheäruppon the Courte proceadinge to sentence yt is this daye ordered, adiudged and decreed by the Corte that the said Scurlock shall paye unto his matie for fyne one hundred markes, Comytted prysoner to the Castle of Dublin Duryng the Lo: Deputyes pleasure, attend the Comissioners that next shall hold cessyons in the said Countye, and there before them in the cessyons tyme upon his knees shall aske his matie forgevenes for the sayd offences, And lyekewyse to acknowledge the same to the whole Countrey. Dated the vjth daye of February 1605.
Present: The Lo Deputy, The Lo Chauncelor, The Lo vicount Roche, The Bushoppe of Meath, The Lo Coursey, The Lo Bourke, Sir James Ley, Sir Nicholas Walshe, Sir Edmond Pelham, Sir George Boucher, Sir Gerrott More, Sir Rychard Cooke.[121]

Termino Trinitatis 1606
Memorand Wheäre Cahir OCallaghan of Dromynyne in the countie of Corck, gent, exhibited informacion into his maties Court of Castle Chamber against John Barrie, Esquier, late Sheriffe of the County of Corck, Brien McOwen of Castlemore & Conoghor O Callaghan, als O Callaghan of Clonemynes in the said County, gent, Conteyning severall foule practizes & misdemeanors of Divers

---

120. f. 133. Note the internal administration of court is recorded along with entries and decrees, using principal judges to arbitrate protocols among lesser officials.
121. ff. 134–34v.

natures Comytted by the said Brien McOwen in practizing to gayne an uniust & wrongfull possession of the Towne landes and Castle of Dromynyn in the said County of Corck, as alsoe an unlawfull assemblie, outradge and manifest Ryott Comytted by the said John Barrie then Sheriffe by collor of his office, the said Brien McOwen, Conoghor O Callaghan als OCallaghan, and many others. The misdemeanors and practizes used by the said Brien McOwen consisting in these poyntes, viz that he the said Brien McOwen prefered a Bill of Indictment of forceable Entrie at an Assizes holden at Youghall in the said County of Corke in the name of Owny McRowrie O Mory, one of the chiefest notoryous & knowen traytors that hath bene in this kingdome, who was notoriouslie knowen to be slaine in action of Rebellion two yearres before the said Byll of Indictment was preferred. And the Byll beinge found by the Jurie And the said Briens practize Discovered to the Comissioners and Justices of Asizes then holding Assizes at Youghall aforesaid, the said Justices and Comissioners then gave speciall Direction to the Clearke of the Crowne of the said County to make stay of yssueing any writt of Restitucon uppon the said Byll untill further Consideracon wer had thereof, And a Caveat entred for the same in the Court Book, And the said Cessions Dissolved. The said Bryen McOwen fayling of his purpose and all the said Comissioners and Justices (saving Justice Saxey, then Chief Justice of the Province of Mounster) being Departed the Towne of Youghall, The said Brien practized againe with the said Chieff Justice that A writt of Restitucon might yssue to the said Sheriffe to Deliver unto him the posession of the said Castle and landes of Dromynyn, which writt was graunted by the said Justice & Deliverdd unto the said Sheriff, which being knowen to the Complaynant Cahir OCallaghane that, contrarie to the Caveat entred and Contrarie to the Commissions & Justices meaning, the writt was graunted by the said Chief Justice. He procured his maties writt of supersedeas, out of [his] maties Chief place for the stay of the execucon of the said writt of restitucon And Delivered the same to the said John Barry then Sheriff one whole daie before the said writt of Restitucon. Nevertheless, the said Sherriff being led with Corrupt Desire to geeve sattisfaction to the said Brien McOwen refused to obey his maties said writt of supersedeas, and afterwardes the said Sheriff accompanied with the said Brien McOwen, Conogher OCallaghane & others, to the nombre of 200 persons all armed and weaponed, some with peeces with match [?in Cork] to the nombre of 60, some others with pykes to the nombre of 40 persons, others with halberdes Swordes Targettes headpeeces, Bernignes [?] and other weapons, as also scaling Ladders, axes and other instruments, came to the said Castle after the receipt of his maties writt of supsed[eas] and at xij of the Clock in the night tyme assaulted the said Castle of Dromynyn, sett upp their scaling Laddrs, hewed in peeces the Doors of the said Castle, entred therinto & violentlie thrust out of the said Castle the Compltes [complainant's] servantes which kept the same, and took from thence goodes & Chattles to the value of 60 s ster[ling] from the pls & his tenantes. Wherunto the said John Barry & Bryen Mc Owen and Conoghor O Callaghan made aunswer and the cause proceading to Replicacon Reioynder and witnesses examyned on eyther party And this day appoynted to be heard. Forasmuch as upon full hearing and deliberat discussing and debating of the cause ... [formula] ... proved by many witnesses aswell the severall practizes & misdemeanors Comitted by the said Brien McOwen in wrongfuly and indirectlie seeking to gayne an unlawfull possession, as also the misdemeanor, unlawfull assemblie and Riott Comytted by the said John Barry, Brien McOwen, Conoghor OCallaghan and all the rest. Yt is therfore this day ordered, adiudged and decreed by the Court that the said John Barry for his severall misdemeanors, contemptes & offences in disobeyinge thexecucion of his maties wrytt of supersedeas and saying he would first execute the writt of Restitucon being contermanded by the said writt of supersedeas, as also for gathering so great a multitude of Armedd men unlawfully to comytt so great and manifest an outradge, misdemeanor and Riott, that for the said offences he shall pay to his maty for A fyne the som of two hondred poundes, except he shall bring certificate that he hath bene formerly fyned in his mates chief place in one hondred poundes & shall paye the same, that then the said C s [i.e. £100] to be alowed out of the fyne nowe ymposed upon him, otherwise the said fyne of two hondred poundes to stand and himself to be sent for by Comaundement from this Court or any other comissioners appoynted in his Lps absence. The said Bryen McOwen, for his severall offences, viz for preferring A Byll of Indictement of forceable entry in the name of a notorious and knowen Traytor knowen to be slayne in Rebellion two yeares at the least before the preferring of the said Byll as also after a Caveat was entred by the Comaundement and Direction of the said Commissioners and Justices of Assize that no writt of Restitucon should ysue upon the verdict of the said Byll in regard aforesaid By practize with the then Cheiffe Justice of Mounster the said Bryen Mc Owen obteyned a writt of Restitucon contrarie to the Directions of the said Justices and the Caveat entred that no such writt shold be graunted, by which his practize and procuring the said writt he caused the said Sheriffe and others to Comytt A great Ryott, outrage and misdemeanor. For which his severall offences he shall pay to his matie for a fyne the some of two hondred poundes, be comytted prisoner to his maties Castle of Dublin Dureng the L Deputies pleasure and yt he shall make sattisfaction unto the Complaynant for all suche forceable entrie into the said Castle & expulsion of the servantes of the pl by the said Sherriffe and his Company, and also for all the Damadges by the pl and his tenantes sustayned by the meanes of the said wrongfull entry and expulsion as shalbe proved upon examinacon therof uppon Comission from this court. And shall also make present sattisfaction unto the pl of all such chardges and costes of court as shalbe taxed by the right honorable the Lo Chauncellor in his behalf. And that the said Conogher shall also pay for his offence, being one of the princypall setters on of the said outradge, misdemeanor and Riott, the some of one hundred poundes and to be sent for by Comaundement from this court for his present apparaunce before Lo: Deputy and Councell or any other Commissioners appoynted in his Lps absence. And also that so many of the Defendantes as the said Bryen hath by his Band of Recognizaunce undertaken for their apparaunce in this Court the next Michaelmas Tearme. Dated at Cary hospitall the xxvijth day of June 1605.[122]

Anno James [MS torn at right edge]
Memorandum wheare his matis learned Councell this prese[nt] [MS torn] informacon ore Tenus in this most honnorable Courte of Castle [MS torn] against John Elliott, John Shelton, Thomas Pluncket, Robert [MS torn], Walter Sedgrave, Edmond Purcell of the Cittie of Dublin, Ale [MS torn; ?Alexander], Thomas Carroll, Edmond Mallone of the same Cittie, merchaunt [MS torn], Phillip Bassett of the same, gent, To this effecte, (viz) That [MS torn] the kings most excellent matie by a late Publicke proclamacon [MS torn] his hand at his Maties pallas [palace] of Westminster the Fourth daye of [MS torn] the thirde yeare of his highnes Raigne of Greate Brittayne [MS torn] and Ireland followinge in lre verba,

Whearas wee are informed [MS torn] our Subiectes in that our Realme of Ireland have since the deathe [MS torn] of our deare Sister Quene Elizabeth been much abusede by an outrai[geous? MS torn] Suggestion and reporte insinuated and spreade amonge them to the efecte That wee for our parte have a purpose or inclination [?to offer; MS torn] libertie of Conscience and tolleration of religion unto our said Su[bjects? MS torn] in that kingdom Contrarie to the expresse lawes and Statuts en[forced? MS torn] in that Realme and Contrarie to that uniformitie of Religion [MS torn] hath ever beene Constantly profesed by us and universally used and observed [MS torn] in our other dominons and Countries. By whiche false Rumors there is [?not; MS torn] onely a secrett imputation caste uppon us, as if wee weare more remiss or less carefull in the Government of the Church of Ireland then In those other Churches Whearof we have the Supream Chardge, b[?ut] alsoe divers of our Subiects in that kingdome are hartened and encouradged to contynewe in there Superstition and Recusancy and such [?MS torn] Jesuites, Seminarie Priests and other Priests and Bishops ordayned by foraigne Aucthoritie as did Secretly before lurke in soundrie partes of that Realme Doe now more boldly and presumptuously showe and Declare them selves in the use and excersise of there functions [?MS torn, not clear] and [MS torn] Contempte of us, our Lawes and Religion. We have therfore [MS torn; thought?] meete to Declare and publishe [MS torn] unto [MS torn] Raigne Sp [MS torn] that our Realme of Irland, That wee have Just cause to be highly displeased with the said reporte and Rumor and which the authours [MS torn] & spreaders therof, Soe are wee resolved never to doe any such [?acte; MS torn] as may confirme the hopes of any creature that they [MS torn] all eaver[?] have from us any tolleracon to excercise any other Religion then that which is agreable to gods worde and [MS torn] established by the Lawes of our Realme. In which Consideration wee doe now the rather by this publicke acte of owrs declare to our subiects our resolution, And doe herby straightly admonishe and Comaund them of that Realme, that they and eavery of them doe from hencefourth duly resorte and com to there Severall parishe Churches or Chappels to heare devine Service and Sermons every Sunday and holydaye accordinge to the tenour and intente of our said Lawes and Statutes uppon the paines and penalties contained therin. Which wee will have from hencefoorth duly put in execution.

And whearas wee are advertised that a greate number of Jesuites, Semynary Prieste and other Prieste made by foraigne authoritie doe raunge up and downe in that our kingdome and doe not onely

---

122. ff. 135–35v. Bryen McOwen apparently signed the order in entry book.

seduce our people there to embrace there superstitious cerremonies but doe malitiously endeavor to alienate the hartes of our Subiects from us, by insinuatinge and breeding a distaste in them both of our Religion and Cyvill government, takinge uppon them the orderinge and decidinge of causes both before and after they have receaved Judgements in our Courtes of recorde. Wee doe therefore declare, publishe and proclayme that it is our Royall will and comaundment that all Jesuites, Semynarye Priests and all other Priests what soever made and ordayned by any authoritie derived or pretended to be Derived from the Sea of Rome shall before the tenth day of December next ensewinge the date hereof departe out of that our said kingdome of Ireland. And that no Jesuite, Semenarie Prieste or other Prieste ordayned by foraignie authoritie as aforesaide shall from and after the said tenth daye of December repaire, com or retorne unto that our kingdome uppon our high displeasure and indignation, and uppon such further paine and penaltieas maye Justly be inflicted uppon them by the lawes and Statutes of that our Realme, And uppon the like paine wee doe expresly forbyde all and every of our Subiects within that our kingdome to receave or relieve any such Jesuite, Seminary Priest or other Prieste which after the said Tenth daye of December shall remayne or abyde in that our Realme or retorne or com unto the same or any part therof, contrarie to the intente of this proclamacon. And wee doe further declare publishe and Comaund that if any suche Jesuite, Semynarie Prieste or other Prieste shall willfully Contynue or abyde in that our kingdome of Irland after the said tenth daye of December or shall voluntarily repaire or retorne into the said kingdome or any parte therof, or if any of our said Subiectes shall receave or relieve any of the said Jesuits or Priests in Contempte of this our proclamation, Then all and every our Governors Shereffes, Justices of Peace, Soveraignes, Portrevs, Constables and all other our loyall Subiects in that kingdome shall use their best Diligence and endevor to aprehend the bodye and bodyes of all and every Jesuites, Semynarye Priests and other Priests ordayned by foraigne authoritie as aforesaid. And ye body and bodyes of all and every theire receaver or receavers and them and every of them to Comite to som safe and streight Prison, to thende our livetennt or Deputie for the tyme beinge, with the advise of our Councell of that Realme, maye take such order for theire punishment as shall seeme fitte in his or their Dicreacon. Provided alwaies that if any of the said Jesuits, Semynary Priests or other priests what soever, shall before the said tenth daye of December or when Tenn dayes after his or theire repaire or retorne into that our kingdome of Ireland, Submytt them selves before our liuetennt, Deputie or other Governor of that kingdome for the tyme beinge, or other Governor of any province, or before any of our privie Councell in that Realme, and shall thereuppon conforme them selves and repaire to the Church Duely and orderly acordinge to the intente of our said Lawes, it shall and maye be lawfull for all and every such Jesuits, Syminarie Priests and other Priest what soever that shall soe submitt or Conforme them selves, to Continue and abyde in that kingdome, or to repaire and retorne into the same and to have and enioye of the benifitt of our Lawes and Royall protection in as free and Ample manner as any of our good and Loyall Subiectes, soe longe as they or any of them shall continue in there said Conformytie.

By which said proclamacon his highnes did admonysh and straightly Comaunde all his subiectes in this Realme that they and every of them should from thencefourth duely reorte and com to theire severall parishe Churches and Chappells to heare devyne Service and Sermons every Sonnday and holly dayes accordinge to the lawes and Stattuts of this kingdome. Notwithstandinge, they the severall persons before named, havinge notice of the said proclamacon being Published in two places within the said Cittie of Dublin, did after the publicacon therof Contemptuously Disobey his maties Comaundment sett forth in the said proclamacon, utterly refusinge to repaire to theire parishe Churches or to any Cathedrall Church in the said Cittiee according to the tennor and entent of the said proclamacon and the Lawes and Statues in that behalf made. Wheareuppon they the said severall persons weare called before his Maties privie Councell in this kingdom and weare by them in mylde and temperat manner required eftsones to yealde ther obedience to his maties said proclamacon, or to render some good reason to the Contrary, they the said severall persons before named wolde not yelde any other reason of theire disobedyence but that theire Conscience would not permitte them to obey the said proclamacon and testyfied the same under theire hands before his Maties said privie councell. And wheras in regarde of some materyall varyance found betwene the prynted Coppies of the statute and the orygynall recorde or roll made in the seconde yeare of the Late Quene Elizabeth for the unyformitie of Comon praier, whearby it is enacted that all his Maties Subiectes in this Realme shall endevor them selves to repaire to theire severall parish Churches or Chappells accustomed, yt was thought mete to publyshe a true transcripte or exemplificacon of the same originall recorde under the greate Seale of this Realme. Whearuppon the said recorde or rolle beinge transcripted and exemplyfied under the great Seale of this Realme, was publyckly proclaymed in the said Cittie of Dublin in the perclose [enclosure] wherof was conteyned,

This doe wee the Lorde Depute and Councell in his Maties name declare and publishe to be the true transcripte or Coppie of the very oryginall recorde of the said acte, worde for worde, as it is to be founde and sene in the Roles of the Chauncery as aforesaid. And therefore wee doe in the name of the kings moste excelent Matie expresly and straightly Chardg and Comaunde all and every of his maties Subiects within this Realme upon every Sonday and other Daies ordeyned and used to be kepte as holly daies to report and repaire to there severall parishe Churches or Chappells and then and there to abyde soberly and orderly duringe the tyme of comon praier, preachinge or other service of God. And further to observe and obaye all and every the clauses and Articles of the said Acte accordinge to the tennor and true meaninge of the same, not onely uppon the penalties therin Contyned but also uppon the paine of his maties high displeasure and indignacon, and suche further punyshmentes as may Lawfully be inflicted uppon the willfull contempners of his Maties Royall Comaundementes, proclamacons and prerogative. Geven at his maties Castell of Dublin the xxiiijth daye of October in the thirde yeare of his highnes Raigne of Greate Brittayne Fraunce and ireland.

Which second proclamacon the said severall persons did also disobeye and Contempne by theire like obstynate recusancye as aforesaid. And wheras also his Matie by his highnes Severall Writtes or mandates under the greate Seale, bearinge date the xjth and xiijth of November 1605, did Chardge and Comaunde every of the before named persons in the faith and alleageaunce by which they and every of them were bound unto his matie and by his highnes authoritie and prerogative Royall, all excuses and delayes sett aparte, upon the next Sounday after sight therof, And so uppon every sondaye and other dayes ordayned and used to be kepte as holly daies, that they and every of them Resorte and repaire to their parishe Churches or Chappells accutomed and then and there to abyde soberly and orderly duringe the tyme of comon praier, preachinge or other service of god there to be used accordinge to the Lawes and statutes of this his highnes kingdome of Ireland. Or ells from tyme to tyme that they and every of them to give theire personall attendaunce uppon the mayor of the said Cittie of Dublin for the tyme being at such tyme as he shall uppon the same dayes repaire to the Cathedrall church comonly caled Christe Church within that said citie to heare devyne service and sermons And ther and then to present and showe them selves before his maties deputie generall or Councell, there to contynewe Duringe such service and Sermons Whearof they and every of them weare required not to fayle uppon paine of his maties high displeasure and indignacon and of such further punishmentes as might be inflicted uppon Contempne[r]s of his highnes Lawes, Stattuts proclamacons and Royall prerogative. Which severall writts or mandates weare delyvered unto the saide severall persons before named, and yet they and every of them in Contempte of his Maties said Comaundement and prerogative Royall did utterly refuse and forbeare to repaire to any Church or Chappell uppon the Sonday next followinge the receipte therof, or to the said Cathedrall Church accordinge to the tennor of the said severall writts or mandates. Uppon all which matters thei the said severall persons, beinge bounde to appeere in this honnorable Courte, After many godly exhortations and perswasions used by the Courte to withdrawe them from theire perverse disloyall oppynions to the due obedyence of his matie his lawes and Royall prerogative, and after divers offers made unto them of conference with learned devines for there better satisfacon, And contemptuously denyinge to obey his matie proclamacons and mandates aforesaid, they presistinge stil in there obstinacy, afirmed that they wolde not repaire to any devine service or Sermon ordayned accordinge to the Lawes of this Realme and utterly refused all Conference, aledginge further that they had byne breede in the Romishe Religon and that it is againste there Conscience to goe to the Church to heire Service or Sermon. Uppon which there owne Confession and willfull obstinancy the courte proceedinge to sentence and Judgment. Yt is this daye ordered, adiudged and decred by this honnorable Courte that for there said Contempte and willfull obstinancy and disobedyence, The said John Elliott, John Shelton, Thomas Plunckett, Robert Kennedy, Edmond Malone and Walter Sedgrave shall paie every of them for a fyne the some of one hundred powndes sterlinge, to be levyed uppon there bodyes, Landes, goods and Chattells, the Moytie wherof to be Converted to the repairinge of decayed Churches and to other Charitable uses at the disposicon of the Lo Deputie and Councell, thother Moytie to be paide into his Maties Coffers, and that all and every of the said persons shalbe Comytted prisoners to his highnes Castell of Dublin, theire to remayne duringe the Lo Deputies pleasure. And to be put from all Magistracy or office what soever within this Cittie or ells wheare in this kingdome untill they & every of them shall Conforme them selves and take the oathe of Supremacye. And that the said Thomas Carroll, Edmond Purcell and Phillipe Basette to paie eache of them for a fyne fyftie pownds of like monney to be likwise levied upoon there bodyes, Landes, goods and Chattells, and to be disposed as aforesaid and ymprisoned in his maties said Castell duringe the lo Deputies pleasure and putt from all Magistracy or office within this Cittie or ells wheare in this kingdome untill they or every of them shall conforme them selves and take the oathe of Supremecye. And that the said Phillipe Bassett, beinge of Englishe Birth and a principall perswader of others to recusancy, within thirtie dayes afer this present day shal retire and withdrawe him selfe or be sent into England, there to remaine and be governed by the Lawes and Statuts under which he was borne, without retorninge in to this Realme. Dated the xxijth day of November 1605.[123]

Memorand wheare his maties learned councell this present daie made informacon ore tenus in this most honnorable Courte of Castell Chamber against James Bellewe, Nicholas Stephens, William Turner, Richard Ashe of the Cittie of Dublin, merchauntes, and Fraunces Marshall of the said Cittie, gent. That they and every of them hadd comitted many disloyall, willfull and disobediente contemptes against his matie his lawes and severall stattutes proclamacons and other special Comaundment under his maties greate seale of this Realme. Wherby they and every of them weare straightly Chardged and Comaunded uppon theire duties of allegiance and by his highnes prerogative Royall that they and every of them shoulde repaire to there severall Churches or Chappells to heare devine Service and Sermons. [Formula B (our italics)] *Wheanuppon they and every of them weare called to aunswere there said contemptes and disobedience, [but] woulde make no other aunswer but that there Consciences lede them to the Contrary, And that they and every of them did utterly refuse to goe to the Church to heare any service or Sermon. Uppon there owne confession and willfull obstinacy the Courte procedinge to sentence, Yt was this daye orderede, adiudged and Decrede by this honnorable Courte that for there said Contempts and willfull obstinancy and disobedience* The said James Bellewe, Nicholas Stephens, William Turner and Richard Ashe shall paie every of them for a fyne the Some of one hundrede poundes sterlinge, [formula C (our italics)] *to be levied upoon there bodies, Landes, goods and Chatteles, the moytie thereof to be converted to the repaireinge of decaied Churches and to other Charitable uses at the disposission of the Lo Deputie and Councell, thother moytie to be paide into his Maties Coffers.* And that all and every of the said persons shalbe comitted prisoners to his highnes Castell of Dublin, there to remaine duringe the Lo Deputies plesure, [formula D (our italics)] *And to be put from all magistracy or office what soever within this Cittie or ells wheare in this kingdome untill they or evry of them shall conforme them selves and take the othe of Supremacy.* And that the said Fraunces Marshall to paie for a fyne fiftie poundes of like money to [be] levied uppon his bodie, landes, goodes and Chattells and to be disposed of as aforesaid, And ymprisoned in his Maties said Castell duringe the Lo Deputies pleasure, and putt from all magistracy or office within this cittie or ells wheare in this kingdome untill he shall conforme himself and take the oathe of Supremacy. Dated the xxvijth of November 1605.[124]

Memorand wheare his Maties learned Councell this present day made informacone ore Tenus in this moste honnorable Courte of Castell Chamber againste Phillipe Conran, Patricke Browne of the Cittie of Dublin, Aldermen, and John Goodinge of the same, marchaunt, that they and every of them had comitted manij Disloyall willfull and Disobedient Contemptes against his matie his lawes and severall stattutes, proclamacons and other spetiall Comaundments under his Maties greate Seale of this Realme. Whearby they and every of them weare straightlie Chardged & comaunded uppon there duties of allegance and by his highnes prerogative Royall that they and everij of them shoulde repaire to there severall parishe Churches or Chappells. [See formula B above, ff. 137–140] The said Phillipe Conran shall paie for A fyne the some of two hundred markes sterlinge to be levied of his body, Landes, goodes and Chattells, the moytie thereof to be converted to the repaireinge of decaied Churches and to other Charitable uses at the disposision of the Lo Deputie and councell, thother moytie to be paide into his Maties Coffers. And that the said Patricke Browne and John Goodinge shall also paie every of them one hundred poundes sterlinge to be levyed likewise of their bodyes, Landes, goods & Chattells and comitted prisoners to his maties said Castell During the Lo Deputies

123. ff. 137–40. First case to condemn recusants comprehensively, using language of royal prerogative, and employing legal sanctions against Roman Catholic leaders of the city of Dublin.
124. f. 141.

pleasure, and to be put from all magistracij or office whatsoever within this cittie or ells wheare in this kingdome. And also to be removed from the said Castell to some other of his maties Castells or fortes within this kingdom as before except in the meane tyme they and every of them shall Conform them selves and take the oath of Supremacye. Dated at Cary Hospitall the xxixth Daie of January 1606.[125]

Memorand wheare his Maties learned Councell this present day made informacon ore Tenus in this moste honnorable courte of Castell Chamber againste Walter Sedgrave, John Shelton, Robert Kennedy, Thomas Plunckett, and Edmond Maloane, Donors, And Nicholas Weston, Richard Usher, John Galtringe and John Forster, Donees, That they the said severall donors and donees had compacted and consulted together to make and forge fraudulent and false deeds with oute Dates of all there severall goods and Chattells, real and personall, quicke and Deade, above grounde and under grounde, unto the said severall Donees, therby to Defeate and overthrowe his maties right and intreste of Severall fynes ymposed upon the said Severall Donors in his Maties high Courte of Castell Chamber. For theire manyfest Contemptes and wilfull disobedyence unto his highnes Lawes and Stattuts of this Realme and divers proclamacons and other speciall Comaundmentes under his highnes greate seale of the same, that they and every of them should by a Daye in the said comaundmente prefixed repaire to theire parishe Churches. Uppon which informacon thei the said Defendauntes and every of them were callede to aunswer for there said false and fraudulent forged deeds, and beinge allowed lerned Councell to speake for them, nether theire Councell nor them selves could make anij other aunswer or Defence for theire said misdemeanors, But that thei did the same uppon good consciences for the payment of their Debts And for the mayntenance of them selves, theire wyves and Children. Uppon theire severall aunswers the said Fraudelent false mattere was at Lardg Debated, aswell by his maties learned Councell at lawe as the Councell of the said Defendauntes. Uppon hearinge wherof, yt manifestly appeared by manie circumstances, and examynacon of the Donees them selves and not much deined [sic; denied], by the Councell of the Defendauntes. Wheruppon the Courte procedinge to sentence and Judgment, yt is this day ordered, adiudged and Decrede by this honnorable courte that the said deedes of Walter Sedgrave, John Shelton, Roberte Kennedij and Thomas Plunkette are all faulse, fraudelente and forged deedes, and of no force or effecte in Lawe eyther to barr his matie of his fyne or any other person what soever for any claime of any debte or demaunde due from any of the said Donors, but shalbe utterly frustrate and voyde to all intentes and purposes, nor shall from hencforthe be shewed or allowed in anij his maties Courtes of recorde, or other courte whatsoever. And that the said Edmond Maloanes deed made to the said Richard Usher shall not barr his matie of the fyne ymposed upon the said Maloane nor shalbe of any valydytie or force in anij Courte of recorde or otherwise but only against the said Edmond to the said Richard Usher for the performaunce of xxx [li] by the yeare for a Joynture to his daughter maryed to the said Maloane. And that for the severall punishmentes of the said Donors and donees for theire misdemeanors and offences Comytted in forginge the said fraudulente and false Deedes to barr and overthrowe his maties right to the said fynes, the Courte hath thought fitte (the Daye beinge spente in Debatinge of this matter) to tollerate the gevinge of sentence thereof untill the firste courte day of the nexte terme. And such of the Defendauntes that weare formerly Comytted to retorne to the same place from whence they came. And for those that were not comitted, beinge Nicholas Weston and John Galtrie, nowe to be comitted to the marshall of this Courte, there to remaine Duringe the Lo Deputies pleasure. And also that the said Deedes shall remaine in the Custodie of the Clerke of the Courte untill other order shalbe taken. Dated at Carie Hospitall this vijth of Feber[uary] 1605.[126]

Memorand wheare his mates learned councell this present daie made informacon ore tenus in his most honnorable courte of Castell Chamber againste James Jans, Mathewe Handcocke and Michaell Chamberlyn of the cittie of Dublin, Aldermen, that they and every of them had comijtted many Disloyall wilfull and disobediente contemptes against his matie his Lawes and severall stattutes,

---

125. f. 142. Note the use of formulaic expressions in this and future recusancy cases, citing the rationale and punishment almost exactly as in the second case, f. 141.
126. ff. 143–43v. This was the only attempt to employ conveyancing of estate in order to avoid the effect of a castle chamber sentence.

proclamacons and other speciall comaundtes under his maties greate seale of this Realme. Whearby they and every of them were straightlie chardged and Comaunded uppon their duties of allegance and by his highnes prerogative Royall, that they and every of them shoulde repaire to there severall parish churches or Chappells to heare devine service and Sermones. [See formula B, f. 141.] The said James Jans and Mathewe Handcocke shall paie eache of them for a fyne the some of two hundred markes sterlinge [see formula C, f. 141] And that the said Michaell Chamberlyn shall also paie for a fyne the some of one hundred poundes sterlinge to be levied likewise uppon his body Landes, goods and Chattells and comytted prisoner to the marshall of the Courte Duringe the Lo Deputies pleasure [formula D, f. 141] except in the meane tyme theij and every of them shall conforme them selves and take the oath of Supremacy. Dated at Carij hospitall the xvjth Daie of May 1606.[127]

Memorand wheare his maties learned Councell this presente daye made informacon ore Tenus in this moste honnorable Courte of Castell Chamber againste James Browne and Patricke Englishe of the Cittie of Dublin, Bakers, that they and each of them had comytted manij Disloyall willfull and Disobedyente contemptes againste his matie his Lawes and severall stattutes, proclamacons and other speciall Comaundmentes, whearby they weare straightlie chardged & comaunded uppon there duties of allegyance and by his highnes prerogatie Royall that thej and eache of them should repaire to there severall parishe Churches or Chappells to heare devine service and Sermones [see formula B, f. 141] Yt was this daie ordered, adiudged and decred by this honnorable courte that for there said contempte and willfull obstinacy and disobedience, The said James Browne and Patricke Englishe shall paie eache of them for a fyne the some of fortie poundes sterlinge to be levied uppon there bodyes, Landes, goodes and Chattels [see formula C, f. 141.] Dat[ed] at Cary hospitall the ij° Daie of July 1606.[128]

Memorandum where his maties learned Councell this present daie informed this honnorable Courte of Castell Chamber againste George Devonishe and John Dowde, late Sheriffe of the Citty of Dublin, Thomas Fleminge and Stephen Duffe of the Towne of Droheda, Aldermen, and Andrewe Hamlen of the said Towne, merchante, That they and everie of them had Comitted many Disloyall willfull and Disobedient contempte[s] againste his maties Lawes and severall Statutes, proclimacons and other speciall mandates under his maties greate Seale of this Realme, wherby they and everie of them were straighty chardged and Commanded [see formula B, f. 141] It was this daie ordered, adiudged and Decreed by this honorable Court, that for their said severall contemptes and willfull obstinacy and disobedience, The said George Devonishe shall pay unto his matie for a Fine the some of two hundred markes, the said John Dowde one hundred poundes, The said Thomas Fleminge one hundred poundes, The said Stephen Duffe two hundred markes, And the said Andrewe Hamlin one hundred markes. And forasmuch as the said George Devonishe and John Dowde have ben formerly comitted by the Mayor and Brethren of this Cytty for some Contemptes and Disobedience donn by them against the Lawes and ordinances of the said Citty, the Court hath thought fitt to Comitt them to the Custodie and sauffekeepinge of the nowe Sheriffes of the said Citty untill the Lo Deputies pleasure be futher knowen for the Removing of them to any other prison his lp shall thincke meete. And that the said Thomas Fleminge, Stephen Duffe and Andrew Hamlen shalbe Comitted prisoners to his Maties Castell of the said Citty of Dublin, there to remaine during the Lord Depupties pleasure. Dated at his Maties Court of Castell chamber the fourth day of February 1607.[129]

Memorand wheare Henry Bennett of Dunbarde Iland in the County of Wexford, gent, Exhibited informacon into this honnorable Courte of Castell chamber that, on the xijth Day of December 1604, one John Deverox of the Dypps in the said County, esquer, Phillipp Deverox, Nycholas Deverox, Edmond Sinnott, Phillipp Synnott, Cosnegh ODoyran and Thomas Echomore, with Divers others to the number of xvj persons at the least, the said Daie and yeere in warlike manner most Riotously, routously and unlawfully with force and Armes, viz with Swordes, pikes, gunnes and other weapons, Assembled themselves togeather, haveinge in ther Company A pyper, Came to the Castell of

---

127. f. 144. 128. f. 145.
129. f. 146. Fol. 146v is blank.

Dunbardes Ilande aforesaid, Beinge then in the quete [quiet] and peacable possession of the said Henry Bennett, and then and there the said John Deverox, Phillipp Deverox, Nycholas Deverox, Edmond Synnott, Phillip Synnott, Cosneghe ODoyran, Thoms Echomore with the rest Riotously and Routously entered into the said castell and then and ther most Riotously and Routously did assault beate and evill entreat Maryon Bennett, wiffe unto the said Henry Bennett, and with force and violens the said John Deverox Caused the said Maryon Bennett to be dragged out of the said Castle and threwe hir Downe a payre of stayres, therby puttinge her in greate Daunger of her liffe, to the terror of the inhabitantes neare adioyninge, and not Content ther with the said John Deverox and the rest tooke into ther possession all the goodes, Corne and other provision within the said Castle, Convertinge the same to their owne use, and the said John Deverox Caused a great Rike [i.e. rick, or stack] of Corne of the said Henry Bennettes goodes beinge within the Bawne of the said Castell and the same Carryed into the said Castle and did give a great part therof unto their horses and the rest Converted to their owne use. Wherunto the said John Deverox, Phillip Deverox, Nicholas Deverox, Edmund Synnott, Phillip Synnott, Cosnegh O Doyran and Thomas Echomore made Answer, And the Cause proceedinge to Replicacon, Reioynder and wittnesses examyned on either part And the said Cause this Day appoynted to be heard. Forasmuch as upon ful hearinge and Delyberate Discusinge of the same it manyfestly appeared to the Courte that all matters and circumstances Conteyned in the Bill was proved by many wittnesses wherunto The Deffendant could take no excepcons, it is therfore ordered adiudged and Decreed by this honnorable Courte that the said John Deverox as the principall plotter and setter on of all the rest, beinge most of them either his sonnes or servantes, shal pay for himself to his Matie for a ffine the some of one hundred poundes and Comitted prisoner to his maties Castell of Dublin During the Lo Deputies pleasure, and that he shall also pay unto his matie for A fine the some of twenty poundes for each of the persons before named, viz for Phillipp Deverox, twenty poundes, Nicholas Deverox, twenty poundes, Edmond Synnott, twentie poundes, Phillipp Synnott, twenty poundes, Conseghe O Doyran, twenty poundes, and Thomas Echomore, twenty poundes. And it is furhter ordered by this Court that he shall pay unto the said Henry Bennett for his goodes, Corne and Damadges sustained by the said forcible entry and expulsion the some of forty poundes before he shalbe released out of prison. Dated at his maties Courte of Castle chamber the vjth day of February 1606.[130]

The Deffendants appearinge uppon Band of Recognisance, his Maiesties Learned Concell ore tenus informed this Courte that the said Deffendants and every of them had Comitted many Disloyall wylfull and disobediente Contempts against his Maiestie his Lawes and severall Statutes, proclamacons and other Specyall Comandments [see formula B, f. 141] It was this Daie ordered, adiudged and Decreed by this honnorable Courte that for ther said Contempts, wilfll obstinacy and Disobedience the said Xpofer Wyrrall, shall paie his Maiestie for a ffine the some [of] one hundred pounds Currante money in England [see formula C] And that the said Charles St. Lawrence, als Howth [kin of baron Howth?] and John Blackney shall alsoe paie each of them the some of one hundred markes of like money, be comitted prisoners to his Maties Castell of Dublin duringe the Lo Deputies pleasure, And like wise to be put from all Magistracy or office within the towne of Drogheda or els where in this kingdome. Dated at his Maties Courte of Castell Chamber the xxix Daie of Aprill 1607.[131]

Memorandum wheare Dermott McTeige, Towhill OMaly and Teige OHanrehan of Ballymaccahell in the Countie of Corcke, husbandmen, Exhibited informacon into this most honnorable Courte of Castle Chamber, That on the vijth Daie of Marche 1604 they beinge quiettly and peaceably grasinge and Depasturinge with their beasts and Cattele upon the land of Balligarran and Ballygoganij in the said County of Corcke by licence of Edmond FitzJohn Gerald and Thomas FitzJohn Gerald whose free hold and inheritance the said land is, one David Power of Shangary in the said County, gent, Phillipp Hoare, Patricke Hoare with many others to the number of forty persons [on] the said Daie and yeere, in warlike manner most Ryotously, Routously and unlawfully with force and armes, viz with swoardes, pykes, Clubes and other weapons asembled them selves togeather at Ballyngarron and

---

130. ff. 147–47v.   131. ff. 148. Fol. 148v is blank.

Ballyngogany aforesaid, and then and ther the said David Power, Phillippe Hoare, Patricke Hoare and the rest forcebly, routously and Riotously did take, lead and Cary away from the said Landes of Ballygarran and Ballyngogan all the Cowes, Sheepe and Swyne then Depasturinge uppon the said Land, and alsoe most Routtously and Riotously did beat batter and Cruelly wounde the said Dermot McTeige, Towhill OMaly and Teige OHanrehan and others. Wher proceedinge to Replicacon and wittnesses Examyned on the p[l]aintiffs parte, And this Daie appointed to be heard. Forasmuch as uppon full hearinge of the Cause It manyfestly appeared to the Courte by severall wittnesses that the Riott was Comitted in manner and forme as in the inforrmacon is laid Downe and the Deffendante haveinge examyned no witnesses to Disprove the same, It is therfore ordered, adiuged and Decreed by this Courte that the said David Power, beinge the principall setter on of all the rest of the Deffendants, shall paie to his maiestie for a Fine the some of twenty poundes Englishe, to be Comitted to prison Duringe the Lo Deputies pleasure. And for that the rest of the Deffendants were servauntes and tenants to the said David Power and at his Comaundment, And that none of them had made answere for any thinge apearinge to the Courte, It is ordered that they shalbe Dismissed. Dated at his maiestys Courte of Castle Chamber the xxiiijth Aprill 1607.[132]

Memorandum wheare John Condon, als McMancke, of Carygygenry in the County of Corcke, gent, exhibited informacon into this honnorable Courte of Castle Chamber Against James Sherlocke FitzPiers of Carrigneshury in the Countie of Tipperary, gent, for Forginge and Publyshinge A Supposed Rolle of Attainder against Richard Conndon, als McManck, Father unto the said John Condon, of highe Treason which Rol did purport that the said Richard Condon was, in And uppon the Seventh Day of July in the xijth yeare of the Raigne of our late Soveraigne Ladie Queene Elyzabeth, at the Guyldhall of the Cittie of Waterford in the Countie of Waterford before the then Maior of Waterford and Nicholas Walshe, Esqr, then Seconnd Justice of the Provence of Mounster, indycted of highe Treason, viz for the releevinge of James FitzMoris FitzGerrald, als James of Desmond, knight, knowinge him to be in actuall rebellion, and that the said Richard Condon was uppon the said indictement arayned and pleaded therunto not guyltie and for his triall put him selfe uppon the Countrey, and that Another Jury found the said Richard guyltie of the said Treason, Whereuppon Judgment of Death for highe treason past Against the said Richard Condon as the said Roll imported, By which pretext of the said forged and false Attaynder and Publyshinge therof the said John Condon was like to be Disinherited of Divers Castles, Landes and Tenementes in the said Countie of Corcke. Uppon which informacon the said James Sherlocke appeared and made Aunswer unto the said informacon and the Cause proceedinge to replicacon, reioynder and wyttnesses examined on either parte, And this Day the Cause appointed to be heard. For as much as uppon full hearing and Deliberate Discussinge therof yt manifestly Appeared to the Courte that the said roll of Attaynder was false, Counterfeyte and forged and that the said Sherlocke had published the same knowinge the said Roll to be forged and no true Roll of Attainder. It is therfore ordered, adiudged and Decreed by this honnorable Courte that the said James Sherlocke for his wicked and notorious offence shall pay to his matie for a fine the some of one hundred poundes, to stand on the Pillory in the Cittie of Waterford on A markett day with his eares nayled therunto untill he teare them of [off], his nose to be slytte and seared, and to be imprisoned duringe the Lord Deputies pleasure. And that for somuch of the said Subposed Roll as shall any way conteine the Attainder of the said Richard Conndon shall for ever henceforth be utterly voyd and of no effecte in Lawe or otherwise to preiudice the said John Condon, sonn and heire to the said Richard, and so to be entred uppon the said Roll of Attainder, and also that the said James Sherlocke shall pay to the plaintiff such Costs of Courte as shalbe Taxed by the right honnorable the Lo Chauncellor on his behalfe. Geven at his maties Court of Castle chamber the xxth day of Aprill 1608 and in the Sixte yeere of his maties raigne of England, Fraunce and Irland and of Scotland the one and Fortiethe.[133]

Memorandum wheare Thomas Meredythe, Clearke, vicare of the parishe of Ballrotherie in the countie of Dublin, Exhibited Informacon into this most honnorable Court of Castle Chamber

132. f. 149. Note the last two cases are out of chronological order by five days, indicating clerical practice of bunching case to be recorded. Fol. 149v is blank.
133. ff. 150–50v.

Against James Barnewell, Richard Bellew, Willm Stoakes, John Wogan, Roberte Barnewell, Nicholas Phillippes and Willm Kenan and Divers others to the nomber of tow hundred persons beinge Ryottously, Routously and unlawfully assembled together at Balrothery aforesaid the First Day of November 1607, beinge Sonday and all sainctes Day, in the Fyfth yeare of the kinges Maties Raigne of England, Fraunce and Irland and of Scotland the one and fortyethe. At which Day and time the said Thomas Meredith was prepared and Attendinge at the said Church aswell to saie Divyne Service Accordinge to the Lawes and Statuts of this Realme of Irland as also to Burie the Dead Corps of the said James Barnewall his mother whoe was then to be brought to the said Churche to be Buried, and beinge so prepared the said James Barnewall, Nicholas Bellewe, William Stoakes and the rest, havenge before hand determined and resolved to Bury the said Corps Afer A Superstycous and Idolatrous fashion and not Accordinge to the kinges Maiesties iniuncons [injunctions] and ordinances in that behalf provided, The said James Barnewell, Nicholas Bellewe, Willm Stoakes and the rest of that Company the said day most Riotously, rowtously and forcibly entred into the said Churche of Ballrothery and then and there, in most mallicyous and Dispightfull [despiteful] meanes, dyd Asaulte, Beate, wound and evell intreate the said Thomas Meredith, puld [pulled] Away A greate parte of his Beard, buffeted him on the face that his nose and mouth gushed Forth with Bloud, and not therwith Contented Did Strike the Booke of Comon Praier out of his hand and trode yt under their Feete, and Spurnd yt with thire feete in most scornfull and Disdainefull Manner, interruptinge the said vicarr to say Divine service, in manifest Contempt of the word of god and his maties good and holsome Lawes. And Also the said James Barnewell in very malycous sorte did then and there beate the said vicars wieffe and throw her to the ground, beinge greate with Child. To which said informacon the said James Barnewell, Nicholas Bellewe, Wiliam Stoakes, Nicholas Phillipps, Robert Barnewell, Willm Kenan and John Wogan made Aunswer and the Cause proceedinge to replicacon, Reioinder and wittnesses examined on either parte, and this Day the Cause appointed to be hard. And the same beinge at large hard and Debated by the Learned Councell as well on the part of the pl as of the Deffendants, uppon full hearinge and Delibrate Discussinge of the said Cause yt manifestly appeared to the Courte by soundry wittnesses and some of there owne Confessions that the said James Barnewell, Nicholas Bellewe and Willm Stoakes had Comitted and don all the said Assaultes, Beatinges, Contemptes and other misdemeanors in the informacon Laid Downe. Yt is therfore ordred, adiudged and Decreed by this honnorable Courte that the said James Barnewell for his offence shall paie unto his matie for A Fyne the some of one hundred Poundes ster money of England, And shall also paie unto the plaintiffe twentie poundes sterlinge Englishe money for his Damadges besydes such Costes of Courte as shalbe Taxed by the right honnorable the Lo Chancellor on the pltes behalfe, Comitted to the Castle of Dublin here to remaine duringe the kings pleasure. The said Nicholas Bellew also to paie to his maiestie for A Fyne the some of one hundred poundes ster like money, Comitted to the marshall of this Courte here to remaine Duringe the kinges plesure. And the said Stoakes to paie unto his maiestie for a Fyne Twentie poundes ster and Comitted to the said marshall Duringe the kinges pleasure And for asmuch as there was no pregnante proofe against the said Roberte Barnewell, Nicholas Phillips, John Wogan and Willm Kenane to Convynce [i.e. convict] them or any of them of the said Severall offenses, the Courte hath thought fitt to dismisse them, payeng the fees to the Clearke and other officers of the Court. Dated the first day of June 1608 in the sixth yeere of his Maties Raigne of England, France And Irland and of Scotland the one and Fortyeth.[134]

Memorandum wheare Moriertaghe McMorrough, Gerrott Scullicke and Morroghe ODoyle exhibited informacon into this most honnorable Courte of Castle Chamber, against John Sinnott, Walter Sinnott, Edward Sinnott, Gerald Sinnott and Gerrald McOwen That they the said John Sinnot, Walter Sinnott and the rest, the xiijth Day of Maie in the Fourthe yeere of his Maties Raigne of England, fraunce and Irland, by the Combynacon, Comaundment and procurment of Sir Willm Sinnott, knight, the said persons the Day and yeere aforesaid Riottously, rowtously and unlawfully Assembled them selves together at Ballinraghe in the Countie of Wexford and then and there ryottously and unlawfully Did take uppon the Landes of Ballinraghe aforesaid the nomber of Five Cowes and twoe garrons beinge then in the quiete possession of the said Moriertaghe McMorroghe

134. ff. 151–52. Fol. 152v is blank.

From the said Landes of Ballinraghe with other oppressions and misdemeanors in the said informacon Layd Downe against the said Sir Willm Sinnott, John Sinnott and the rest. To which Informacon the said Sir Wilm Sinnott, Walter Sinnott, Edward Sinnott and John Sinnott made Aunswer, and the Cause proceedinge to yssue and wittnesses Examined on both partes and this Day appointed to be hard. And forasmuch as uppon full hearinge and Delibrate Discussinge of the said Cause by the Censure of the greater Nomber then Sittinge in Courte, the said Sir Willm Sinnott and all the rest were acquitted of the subposed Ryott. But for the opresion and misdemeanor yt manifestly appeared to the Courte that the said Sir Willm Sinnott and John Sinnott were guyltie of that parte of the informacon. It is therfore ordered, adiudged and Decreed by this honnorable Courte that Sir Wilm Sinnott and the said John Sinnott shall paie unto his matie for A Fine each of them the some of twentie poundes apeece, and endure ymprisonment duringe the kinges pleasure. And for that ther was no pregnant proofe produced against the said Walter Sinnott, Edward Sinnott, Gerrald Sinnott and Gerrald McOwen to Convynce them or anie of them eyther of the Riott oppression or misdemeanor, It is thought fitt by the courte they shalbe Dismissed, paieinge the fees Due to the officers of the Courte. Dated At his maties Courte of Castle Chamber the Eight day of June 1608 and in the sixt yeere of his maties raigne of England, Fraunce and Irland and of Scotland the one and fortyethe.[135]

Memorandum qd Termno Sci Mich[aelm]is Anno Domini 1602 Sir Robert Digby, knight, and the Ladie Lettice, his wieff, Exhibited there Bill of Complainte into this honnorable Courte of Castle Chamber, Against Garrett, now Earle of Kildare, Dame Mable, Countesse Dowager of Kildare, Somtime wieffe to Garret, Late Earle of Kildare, and Henry Burnell, Esqr, Deffendantes, and therby shewed that wheras Garrett, Late Earle of Kildare, was seised in his demeane as of fee of and in the Barrony of Ophaley and of divers honnores, Landes and hereditamentes within this Realme of Ireland, The which of right Descended or ought to Descend to the said Ladie Lettice, one of the complainantes, from the said Late Earle, shee beinge his Cosen and next heire, viz the Daughter and heire to the Lord Gerald, Eldest sonn and heire of the said Earle Garrett, being both deade. And therin Further Suggested, that the saide Dame Mable, understandinge that the said Lady Lettice was her Late Maties warde and not knowinge the danger of Lawe, Nor how the said Late Earle her husband had provided for hir selffe and hir Children, Called for the said Henry Burnell, one other of the Deffendants and others of hir La[dyshi]p Counsell and Freindes, About the Tenth of November in the xxvijth yeere of the Late Queenes Raigne, And demaunded of them what was Best to be don for hir and hir Childrens Advouncmente. Wheruppon the said Henry Burnell Advised her that shee shold procure A mandamus to be sued out of the Chauncery and Directed to the Escheator to find an office to enquire after the Death of the said Late Earle, hir husband, what Landes and Tenementes and of what Estate he the said Late Earle died seised of, And that for the Advauncment of the yssue marshalle of the said Earle Garrett and Disinheritinge of the Ladie Lettice one of the Complainants should record, finde and inserte into the said office one deede of Intaile to the heires male of the said Earle Garrett with some remainder over, which shold fully aunswer all there said Devise and practise, and prevent all advantages that might ensue to the Late Queene by the wardshipp of the said Ladie Lettice, which deed shold importe to be made and Executed by the said Late Earle, the Seaventh Day of September in the Eight yeere of the said Late Queenes Raigne. By which deed all the honnors, mannors and hereditamentes which were the said Late Earles shold seeme to be Conveyed to Sir Christopher Barnewall and others, feoffyes named in the said Bill and there heires for ever, To Certaine intentes Expressed in the said Bill. Which deed was then forged Contrived and made by the said Henry Burnell, or by some other by his Counsell and Direction, and if not then forged yet did the said Countesse by the advise of the said Henry publishe the same, and they did publishe or Caused the same to be published and recorded in the said office, knowinge the same to be forged and Contrived for the Disinheritinge of the said Lady Lettice, the Complaynante, and Defeatinge of the saide Late Queene of the wardshipp of the said Ladie Lettice. In which Bill the said Complainantes did insert many resons and argumentes to prove the said Suposed deed to be Forged and Further Suggested in and by the said Bill that, long After the Deathe of the said Late Earle, The said Henry Burnell in the then Mansion howse of the said Ladie Mabell, Countesse Dowager aforesaid,

135. ff. 153–53v.

perswaded the said Ladie Mabell to lett him see the said deed that shee had for her Jointure to Add some thinges to yt that shold be for the Better Strengthening of the same, for that if yt should remaine as yt then was yt would Easely be Avoyded by the heire generall if yt be Called in question. For that uppon the said Deed ther was noe due execution Certified of Liverie and seisin Seallinge and Deliveringe nor Atturnemente of Tenantes which he said he intended to sett Downe and make perfecte. Wherupon the said Lady Mabell not knowinge nor Suspectinge the unlawfullnes of such practizes nor the mischyeffes that might ensue such fraudulent devises, But relyinge Confidently uppon the Creditt of the said Burnell, whome shee Supposed to be A man of Sound Conscience & Counsell, was Easely Seduced to Deliver the said deed unto him. And after the said Henry Burnell Endorsed or Caused to be Endorsed and added uppon the said Deed the Testimony and names of wittnesses longe before that tyme deade, Testifieing the execution of Estates by Liverie and Atturnemente, and afterwardes falsely and wickedly Engrossed or Caused to be Engrosed the same deed and all the wittnesses names soe newly Endorsed in A skine of parchmente, and Annexed the same to the said office and Inquisicon soe formerly formed and remayninge in the Excheqr. And they further Complained by the said Bill that the said Henry Burnell Animated, encoraged and Counselled the right honnorable Gerald FitzGerald, now Earle of Kildare, to make Claime and title to the reversions and remainder of all the said honnors, mannors and hereditamentes (by the Lymittacons in the said Deed) and that the said now Earle, by the Advise of the said Henry Burnell, at Divers times within two yeeres Last past hath published the said Deed knowing yt to be forged, and that the said now Earle with the noomber of Twentie persons, his followers, entred Riottously the house of Maynooth and there tooke away all the Evidences of the Earldome under Coullor of the said Deed, which of right belongeth to the said Lady Lettice then her late maiesties warde, as by the said Bill more at large may appeare. Unto which Bill of Complainte the said Deffendantes made there severall annswers and maintained the said deed bearing date Septimo Septembris Anno Octavo of the Late Queens Maiesties Raigne to be A trew deed and not forged, and used many Evidencementes, Resons and Argumentes soe to prove the same, and the said Henry Burnell and the said Now Earle did denie the misdemeanor wherwith they were Charged in and by the said Bill. The said Countesse Confessed in her said Aunswer that shee being told that the saide deed was defective both for hir selffe and hir Children, she procured the said Henry Burnell to Com unto hir, to whome shee told that shee understood that the said deed was defective, wherunto the said Burnell Answered that yt was not of his drawinge, Neverthelesse he would looke uppon yt. Which beinge by him Accordingly perused the said Henry Burnell as shee remembreth Acknowledged the said deed to be defective, But said as shee remembreth that those defectes might be Supplied by Endorsmentes uppon the deed, where uppon shee delivered the said deed to Walter Foster, her Steward, to be hollpen in those omissions at theire pleasures, shee being then Iynocante [innocent] of any thoght of harme or guyle therin, and shortly after shee receaved the said deed againe from the said Foster as yt is now, with the Endorsmentes and Addicons to bee seene uppon the Backe of the said deed, the Contentes wherof shee neyther then nor now knoweth. After which Annswer soe made they were severally Examined uppon personall Interrogatories, and the Cause beinge at yssue Both the Complaynantes and deffendantes proceeded to the Examinacons of many wittnesses on both sydes, which were published and the Cause brought to hearinge in this honnorable Court the eleaventh day of November 1607, The which Day and Divers other Dayes being spent in hearinge of the proffes and allegacons of either syde. After Longe and mature delyberacon and Consideration of the said proofes and allegacons, This honnorable Courte thought fitt to Leave the vallyditie or unvalyditie of the Body of the said deed dated Septimo Septembris Octavo Elizabethe to be tried by A Sufficiente Jury at the Common Law, and neither to impeach or Approve the Bodie of the said deed by thier Censure, and therfore this Courte findes no Cause to Censure the Earle, the Countesse or Mr Burnell for publishinge the Bodie and Contentes of the said deed, as knowinge the same to be a false or a forged deed. But for that yt doth plainly appeare unto this Courte by the Aunswers of the said Lady Mabell, one of the Deffendantes, made unto personall Interrogatories that her said Steward Foster, After the death of the Earle, her said Late husband, Told her he thoght her deed of Jointure was Defective, and wished her to send for the said Henry Burnell to be advised by him, which shee did Accordingly, and shewed him the said deed, and that After he had seene the said deede, he said yt was defective (yett to be amended) then shee Desired him to Amend yt (if in good sorte yt might be Don) and that he said he wold doe his best Endeavor to Amend yt, if shee would lett him have yt, and that then shee delivered the said deed to Walter Foster, to be Caried with the said Burnell to be Amended. Wheruppon Immediatly they went together into A Chamber in the howse of Maynooth, And that

Anone after one of them (whom shee thincketh to be Foster) Came to her and Demanded if shee Could, Remember what servantes were about the Late Lord her husband, about the eight yeere of Queene Elizabethes Raigne, And then shortly After the said Deed was Delivered to her againe with thinges written & Endorsed uppon the Backe of yt, which were not ther before when shee Delivered the same to the said Foster, and that Foster said yt was written and don by Buckler, But by whose Direction shee knoweth not, But yt was told her as much was donn to the said writtinge as Mr. Burnell thought fitt to be don, and that then the said Foster wyshed her to use yt soe as yt might be Slubered [glossed or daubed over so as to conceal: *OED*] wherby the said Endorsementes newly written might not be Discerned from the other. Shee also Confesseth that Bradley was in the Gallery at all that Conference, which Bradley in his Deposyconnes Concureth and agreeth in all thinges with the Confession of the said Lady Mabell, that he was present in the Gallery at Mainouth when Mr Burnell Came to the Countesse and did heere there Conference, and that Burnell affirmed to the Countesse that all the Contentes of the Body of the said deed was good, But yt wanted sondry Endorsmentes and Addicons of names, and other thinges Necessary for the perfectinge of the said deede, in soe muche as yf yt were not Amended yt would not only overthrowe hyr owne Estate (But her Sonnes alsoe) if yt were shewed in Any Courte, if there were any there, that would take advantage for the Queene in the behalf of the heire, which was not hir Sonn (But her Eldest Sonnes Daughter in England, whoe was But younge and fallen to be warde), The said Countesse Lamented and asked how shee and they shold doe then, To which Speaches Burnell Annswered, that yt was not soe defective But yt might Easely be Amended, soe that yt were performed with Secresy, and Mr Burnell promised to doe his best Endeavor to amend the said deed. The said Countesse then referred the same to Mr. Burnell and Foster to doe what they thought Expedient, and that Burnell and Foster so departed and went out of the Gallery together into the Comptrollers Chamber, and that soone After Foster Came upp into the Gallery and Demanded of the countesse if shee Could remember what servantes did serve the Earle her husband about the Eight yeare of the Queenes Raigne, and that Afterwardes he the said Bradley the deponente resorted to the Comptrollers Chamber and there found Buckler, Fosters servante, alone, and saw the deed lyeinge with the Backe upwardes, and found Certaine Lynes of the first Endorsment of the said deed to be put out, to the Number of Fower Lynes as he remembreth, he asked Buckler how he Came by the said deed, whoe told him tht his Mr, [master] to wytt Foster, had delivered yt to him, and had sworne him to Secresy, A good while after, he sawe the deed had many Endorsmentes added by Buckler which were not there before and saith that to that particuler Endorsment, which Conserned the Landes in Meath, he saw were Added those woordes in A small Differringe hand from the other, viz (in the name of all the Landes in the Countie of Meathe), and that Burnell soone after Comynge into the Chamber where these thinges were adoeinge found faulte with the Letter, R: in this woord Kildare. The [said] Bradley alsoe Deposethe that Foster Demanded of Burnell if he might not Joine many Liverie and seisenes in Divers Counties together in one Endorsmente, and that Burnell aunswered he might soe doe if he left out the Kinges Countie. He Further alsoe Deposeth that Shergoldes writtinge of his name to the Attornamente, which is to be seene upon the Intente of the said feoffmente written by Shergoule, was don by the Direction of the said Foster, havinge the Advise of Mr. Burnell, whoe soe advised in the hearinge of the said Bradley in the greate Arbore of the Gardene of Mainouth. And for that alsoe yt plainly Appeareth, by the Confession of the said Henry Burnell in his Examinacone to personall Interrogatories, that the said Foster told him the said Birnell, that there wanted some Endorsmentes of Liverie and seisin, and other perfections uppon that deed, and asked him what he thoght therof, whoe Answered that they wer not hurtfull if they Could be proved. Then Foster Asked him if yt were hurtfull to Add such Endorsmentes, Burnell answered if he Could finde by Examinacons any such perfections were observed he thought he might Enter them soe uppon the deed without offence, and alsoe for that yt appeared by the view and perusall of all the Seaven Severall Endorsmentes uppon the deed of feoffmente and Intente herunto Annexed that all the said Endorsmentes were either Added and Endorsed or allowed since the death of the said Earle, According to the before recyted Deposycons and Confesiones, which is not for the most parte Contradicted by the Deffendants themselves. Therfore This honnorable Courte This presente third day of Februarij Adiudged, ordred and decreed that all the said Endorsmentes both uppon the deede and uppon the Intente, beinge Seaven in Nomber, shalbe Damned and never geven in Evidence to prove any Execution of any Estate to be Passed Accordingly in or by the said deed of feoffment. And for that allsoe yt Appeareth to this honnorable Courte by the Confession of the said Countesse and Deposycons of Bradley, that the said Henry Burnell was sent for, to amend the defectes of the said deede, and that he said they might be Amended if yt were performed with Secresy, and promised to doe his best Endeavor to Amend the same, yf the Countesse wojld Lett him have the deed, and that shee delivered the deed to Foster to be Caried with Burnell to be Amended, and that they wente both together into the Comptrollers Chamber, where the Deed was left and amended, and that yt was told the Countesse that so much was don uppon the said deed as Mr Burnell had thought fitt to be donn, and For that yt doth appeare unto this Courte that the said Countesse did not trust or relye uppon any other counsellor save only uppon Mr Burnell, who as yt Appeareth by Bradly his Deposicons did peruse and see the new writtinges and Endorsmentes don by Buckler, and Answeres the Question of Foster for the addition of Liverie in Severall Counties in An Indorsmente. And that he the said Burnell advised Shergold to Subscribe his name to the Indorsmente of his Attornamente. For these and other good Causes this Courte are of oppinion that those new Endorseents upon the Backe side of the deed of feoffment, and uppon the Intente were written by the Advise and direction of the said Burnell, geven to the said Foster, Mr of the said Buckler, who directed his said servante Accordinge to Mr Burnells advise, or by Burnells advise Immediatly geven to Buckler. And therfore this Courte doe Adiudge the said Henry Burnell to be gyltie of Counseling, advisinge and Causinge to be Endorsed and Added the said additions and Indorsmentes Wherwith he is Charged in and by the said Bill, And therfore doe impose uppon him the said Henry Burnell the Sume of 500 markes to his Matis use for his said offence and his Body to be in prison duringe the Lord Deputies pleasure. And wheras the said Burnell doth Confesse that he Advised the Countesse to Cause the said deed to be found in the office, Afer the Deathe of the said Earle, In which office or Inquisicon the said deed and Intente with all the new Endorsmentes are inserted verbatim, which he then knew to be newly added, which this Courte Doth Accounte to be a very great faulte deservinge Seveare punishmente in A Counsellor at Lawe, yet because the offence is not Sufficiently Laid Downe in the said Bill for this Courte to Censure the said Henry Burnell for the said offence, This Courte doth forbeare to proceed to Censure him for that particular. And thoughe the Lady Mabell the Countesse was told her deed was deffective, and that shee delivered the same to be Amended, and that shee doth Confesse shee Receaved the same Amended, yett because shee is not Charged in and by the said Bill That shee did knowe what was added to the said Deed nor the offence Comitted by such addytions, But rather is Excused of that offence by the said Bill, This Courte ffindeth noe Cause to Censure the said Countesse for her said offence, Neither to Censure the said Earle of Kildare for the Supposed Riott wherof he is Accused In and by the said Bill. And therfore this Courte doth acquitte and Discharge them both of the said tow last offences. Yeoven at his maiesties Courte of Castell Chamber the said third day of February 1608. And in the Sixth yeere of his highnes Raigne of England Fraunce and Ireland, and of Scotland the two and fortieth.

Present: The Lo Deputie, The Lord Chauncellor, Master Thresarer, The Lord Chieff Justice Winche, The Lord Justice Walshe, Sir Adame Loftus, Sir Richard Cooke [crossed out in MS: Lord viscount Roche, Lord Barron of Dellvine].[136]

Memorandum where Gerald, Earle of Kildare, by Meyler Fay, his Attorney, Exhibited informacon into this most honnorable Court of Castle Chamber, against Dame Mabell, Countesse Dowager of Kildare, wieff to Gerald, late Erle of Kildare, Sir Robert Digbie, knight, the Lady Lettice, wieffe to the said Sir Robert Digbie, and Peeter Bennett and John Bradley, servantes to the said Dame Mabell, that shee the said Dame Mabell, havinge an earnest desire and intention to advance the issue of her owne Bodie and namely the said Ladie Lettice, Secretly and Corruptly Conspired and practized with the said Bennett and Bradley, together with the said Sir Robert Digby and the said Dame Lettice, That they the said Sir Robert Digbie and Dame Lettice to disinheritt the said Gerald the Complainante of all the landes tenementes and hereditamentes Conteyned in a deed of feoffmente bearinge date Septimo Septembris anno Octavo of the Late Queenes Maiesties Raigne, did of Covin [i.e. conspiracy: *OED*] and Collusyon agree together that the said Sir Robert Digbie and dame Lettice shold exhibit a Bill in this honnorable Courte against the said Dame Mabell, furninshinge the said deed of feoffment to be forged, and that the said Dame Mable, knowinge therof did publishe the same, and by the said Dame Mabells fainte pleadinges or voluntary Confession therof, Contrary to her owne Conscience, the said deed of feoffment might be Discredyted, Defaced and overthrowen, And

Consequently the Complainantes estate Defeated. To which bill of Complainte the deffendantes made severall annswers and the Cause proceedinge to replicacon, reioinder and wittnesses Examined on either parte and Severall Daies of hearinge of the said Cause And this day Appointed for the Censuring the same. Forasmuch as uppon full hearinge and delibrate discussinge of the said Cause yt appeared unto this honnorable Courte that the said bill and Contentes therof were grounded without eny Just Cause, and no Sufficient prooffes produced by the plaintiff to Convince the said deffendantes for the Causes Alleadged in the said Bill, yt is therfore ordred, adiudged and decreed by this honnorable Courte that the said deffendante and everie of them are and shall from hencforth be dismissed, acquitted and discharged from further vexacon suyte or trouble what soever Concerninge the said Bill. Yeoven at hir maties Courte of Castle Chamber the third day of February 1609 in the Sixth yeere of his maties Raigne of England, Fraunce and Ireland and of Scotland the tow and fortieth.
Present: The Lo Deputie, The Lo Chauncellor, Mr Thresaurer, The Lo Chieff Justice Winch, The Lo Justice Walsh, Sir Rich. Cooke.[137]

Memorandum wheareas Sir John Davies, knight, his maties Attorney general, exhibited informacon into this Most honrable Courte of castle Chamber, by the relacon of Nicholas Turner of Wexford in the Countie of Wexford, gent, that he the said Nicholas Turner, beinge seised in his Demeasne as of fee by Coppie of Courte Roule, accordinge to ye Custome of the Manner [manor] of Ballinore in the said Countie of Wexford, of the Towne and Landes of Churchtowne within the said Manner, one John Deverox of the Dippes in the said Countie of Wexford, gentl[man], forgetting the feare of god his Dutie to the kings Matie and willfully violating his highnes Lawes and statutes, of A Coveteouse and ungodly manior, having hard of A Clamorous and poore woman named Margret Bowton, als Browne, to have some old clayme unto the said towne and landes, Champerteously and Covetously Combyned his ill indevor to her yll tytle, and agreed, Compounded and Covenanted with hir Champerteously for and in Consideracon shee should passe the Moytie of the said Towne and Landes unto him, to followe and prosecute hir Clayme, title and interest, being Contrary to Divers Lawes and statutes made and provided against Champertie. Notwithstandinge, the said John Deverox at his owne proper Costs and Charges upheld and prosecuted the said suyte against the said Nicholas Turner in his maties high Courte of Chancery in this kingdom of Ireland, uppon a speciall Covenant agreed, Concluded and past betweene the said John Deverox and the said Margrett OBowton that the said John Deverox should have the moytie of the said towne in Demaund yf yt should be recovered. To which informacon the said John Deverox made aunswer, and the Cause proceedinge to replicacon, reioinder and wittnessses examined on either parte and this Day appointed to be hard. Forasmuch as uppon full hearinge and Deliberate Discussinge of the Cause yt manifestly appeared unto the Courte aswell by soundry wittnesses as also by a band of the said John Deverox shewed openly in Courte of the agreement made in Manner as aforesaid, that the said John Deverox was gyltie of the said Champertie in the informacon sett forth. Yt is therfore this Day ordred and adiudged and Decreed by this honnorable Courte that the said John Deverox for his said offence shall pay to hir Matie for a fine the some of Fortie poundes, endure imprisonment the Lo Deputies pleasure, and shall alsoe pay unto the plte all such Costes of Courte as shalbe Taxed by the right honnorable the Lo Chauncellor on his behalf. Dated at his maties Courte of Castle Chamber the xixth day of May 1609 and the vijth yeere of his Maties raigne of England, Fraunce and Ireland and of Scotland the xlijth.[138]

Memorandum where his Maties learned Councell this presente Day made informacon ore Tenus in the most honnorable Corte of Castle Chamber againste Bryen McReddy, Neyle McTyrlagh OCahan, Bryen Modder OCahan, and Hugh OMergy, fowre of the Twelve Jurors that were ympaneled at the laste Assize holden at Lemevaddy in the Countye of Colrane, the xviijth daye of Auguste 1609, for the tryall of Dyvers the Clenlojkynes, Gylleegrome OMullyne, James OMully, Gylleduffe OKelly, Tyrlagh OKelly, Donogh Keethe OMullyne and Donogh Backaugh OMullyne, which said persons

---

137. f. 160. Plate 15. See above case of *Digby* v. *Dame Mabel*, involving the fraudulent deed of Henry Burnell.
138. ff. 161–61v. Fols. 162–62v are blank.

were Indicted and arraigned at the said Cessyons in the said Countye of Colrane the said xviijth day of Auguste befor Sir Humfrey Wynch, knight, Lo: Chyeffe Justice of Yrelande, and Sir John Davies, knight, his Maties Attorney general within the said Realme, Justices of Assize for the said County of Colrane, for severall greate and heynous treasons Commytted in the said Countye of Colrane by them the said Clenlojkyns and the Reste. Uppon which theire severall Arraignementes many wyttnesses were produced which did manyfestly and dyrectly prove all the treasones the said parties were chardged withall. Nevertheless, the said Bryen McReddy, Neile McTyrlaugh OCahan, Bryen Modder OCahan, Hugh OMergy with the reste of theire followers, Jurors, most Corruptly [and] Contrary to theire Dyrecte evydence, did acquytte the said traytors. Whereupon the said Justices of Assize bounde the said Bryann McReddy, Neyle McTyrlagh O Cahan, Bryen Modder OCahan and Hugh OMergye, Fowre of the Twelve Jurors to appear in this Corte to aunswere theire said mysdemeanor. Which said persones after they had appeared by the dyreccon of this Courte were examyned by his Maties seriante at lawes, uppon which theire examynacons they and every of them Confessed that there were Three wyttnesses which gave Dyrecte evydence that the said Clenlojkyns were in actuall Rebellyon. They alsoe Confessed that uppon Tharaignment of the said Gyllegrone OMullyn, Dyvers wyttnesses did dyrectly prove the Treasones he was chardged withall, then lykewyse Confessed that there were three wyttnesses that proved dyrectly that Gylleduffe OKelly and Tyrlagh OKelly did releeve Donogh McCowye Oge OCahan and Terry OCahan, the said Donogh and Terry OCahan beinge in acton of Rebellyon. And further Confessed that Rory McBryen McCojkyne and Cormocke McCoskye gave dyrecte evidence that Donogh Keethe OMullyn and Donogh Backagh O Mullyn were both in accon of Rebellyon. Yett the said Bryen McReddy, Neile McTyrlagh OCahan, Bryan Modder OCahan and Hugh OMergye Confesste and acknowledged they acqytted the said Traytors, Dyrectly Contrary to theire evydence, alleadgeinge vayne and slender excuses to Color and myttigate theire saide offences which this Corte did not allowe of, but absolutely reiecte. And therefore, upon theire owne Confession then Redd in Courte, yt is ordered, adiudged and Decreed by this honorrable Courte that the said Bryen McReddy, Nele McTyrlagh OCahan, Bryen Modder OCahan and Hugh O Mergye for theire said offences shall paye ech of them to his Maty for a fyne the some of an hundred poundes le peece and be ymprysoned Dureinge the lo: Deputyes pleasure, and shall alsoe stand and be nayled on the Pyllory on some Markett daye in this Cyty of Dublyn with papers on theire heades Declareinge theire said offence, and that they shall alsoe stande on the Pyllory at the nexte generall assizes to be holden in the Countye where they Comytted the said periurye, at the place where the said Assize shalbe holden in the said Countye and with a like paper on theire heades Declareinge theire said offences, and that one of the Eares of each of them shalbe Cutt of the same day they shall stande on the Pyllory in the Cyttye of Dublin. Dated at his Maties Corte of Castle Chamber the xvijth day of November 1609, In the seaventh yeare of his Maties Raigne of Englande, Fraunce and Irelande, and of Scottlande the xliijth.[139]

Memorandum wheare Bryen OBryen of Carygogownell in the Countie of Lymericke, gent, exhibyted informacon into this most honorable Courte of Castle Chamber that wheare he was quietly seised and possessed of the mannor of Carigogownell aforesaid with the appurtenances and two weares in the Ryver of Shanen in the said Countie as parcell and belonging to the said Mannor, and the proffytts of the said weares he and his Auncestors from tyme to tyme did take and receave to theire owne uses and behooffe, without the let or Disturbance or interruupcon of any person or persons whatsoever. Nevertheles, on the xxiij of Aprill 1604, Nicholas Bourke of the Cittie of Limericke, Aldermann, Wyllm Stritch of the said Cittie, Alderman, John Sarsfield, Recorder of the said Cittie, Arthure Sexten of the same, gent, Willm Arthur FitzJohn of the said Cittie, merchant, Morysh OHenery, John ONea Laughlen [ne scoule?] Mahowne OCastyll, Richard ODonogh and Walter ODonoghe of the said Cittie, yeoman, with Divers others to the number of fourscore persons or therabouts, in warlike or rather rebellyous Manner, all Armed with Gunnes, pykes, Swoordes, halbardes and Divers other weapons, marched from the said Cittie of Limericke unto Ballinoe, parcell of the said Mannor of Carriggogownell where one of the said weares was buylte, and then and there the said Arthure Sexten, being Capten and leader of all the rest of the said Riotouse and Disorderly Company, he the said Arthure and the rest did most riotously, wrongfully and malyciously breake, pull downe and utterly deface the said weare, Discharginge peeces with bulletts against any that should come to resyst them in their Riotouse and Malyciouse outrage and mysdemeanor. Wherunto the said Arthure Sexten. one of the Defendants, made aunswer and beinge examyned uppon personall interogatories, Confessed the greatest parte of the informacon to be true. Nevertheles, wytnesses were examined onn either parte and this Daie the Cause appointed to be hard for somuch as Concerned the said Arthure Sexten. For asmuch as uppon full hearing and Deliberate Discussinge of the said Cause yt manifestly appeared to this Courte aswel by his owne Confession as by many Pregnant and apparrant wytnesses that the said Riott was Comytted by the said Arthure Sexten and the rest of his said Riotouse Company. It is therefore ordered, adiudged and decreed by this honnorable Courte that the said Arthure Sexten for his said offence shall paie to his matie for a fyne the some of two hundred poundes and to be Imprisoned during the Lo Deputies pleasure. And if the said Arthure Sexten be not of Abyllytie to paie the said fine, then the Corporacon of Limericke to Satisfie and paie the said fine to his Maiesties use. Dated the xxijth Daie of November 1609 and in the vijth yeare of the Raigne of or Soveraigne Lord king James and of Scotland the xliijth.[140]

Memorandum wheare James Edwardes of Clomethan in the County of Dublyn, fermor, [and] Jennett his wiffe exhibited informacon into this most honnorable Courte of Castle Chamber That, the xxiijth day of June 1607, one Nicholas Begg of Boranstone in the County of Dublyn, Marlewe Begge of the same, Roberte Corbally of Notstowne, Peter Herward of Clomethan, John Knowd, Richard Sennett, Thomas Kelly and Thomas Herny, with Divers others unknowen, the xxiijth dai of June aforesaid, did Ryotously, Routously and unlawfully assemble them selves together at Clomethan as aforesaid and then and there forceably entred into the said James Edwarde his house, the said James then lyinge very sycke in his naked bed, which said persons forceably and violently hirled the said James Edward out of his bed and Dragged hyme out of his said house by the heeles and layd hime in the streate. And presently after, forceably and vyolently thruste out the said Jennett and eight chyldren out of the said house, and did alsoe Cast all the goodes and householde stuffe of the said James Edward and threwe yt out of the house and broke and spoyled the same, and after so doinge kept the possesion of the said house forceably and violently from the said Edward. Wheareunto the said Nicholas Begge, Roberte Corbally and Peter Herward, three of the Defene[dan]tes, made Aunswer and the Cause proceadinge to Replicacon, Reioynder and wytnesses examyned on eyther parte and this daj appoynted to be herd. Forasmuch as uppon full hearinge and delyberate discussinge of the said Cause yt manyfestly appeared to this Court that the said Ryott, Rout forceable entry and Misdemeanor was Comytted and don by the said Nicholas Begge, Roberte Corbally and Peter Herward & the reste of the persons named in the bill in manner as in the said bill is declared. Yt is herefore ordered, adiudged and Decreede by this honnorable Courte that the said Nicholas Begge shall paye to his matie for a fyne the some of thirty three poundes, sixe shillinges, eight pence Currant money in England, Roberte Corbally to pay fyfteene poundes lyke money and Peter Herwarde to paye ten poundes lyke money, to be ymprisoned durynge the Lo Deputies pleasure, and to pay unto the playntyffe twenty markes lyke englishe money for ther Damages susteyned, and all such Costes of Courte as shalbe taxed by the right honnorable the Lo Chauncellor on the plts behalfe. Dated at his Matie Courte of Castle Chamber the last daije of January 1610 and in the seventh yeare of his maties Raigne of England, Fraunce and Ireland and of Scotland the xliith.[141]

Memorandum wheare his maties learned Councell this present Daie ore tenus made informacon into this most honnorable Courte of Castle chamber against Christopher FitzWilliams, Nycholas McConnell, Richard Nugente, Michaell Sedgrave, John More, Thomas Deyce, Jamees Byrne, Richard Eustace, John Byrkett, Simon Maloane, Thomas Garland and John White of the Cittie of Dublin whoe were Impanelled for the triall of John Drake, Richard Ferall, Edward Ivers, John Plunckett, Edward Plunckett, George als Jerdie Greane, John Cruce and John Chamaberlaine, which said persons were indicted and Arraygned in his maties Chieffe Bench before Sir Humphrey Wynch, knight, lo Chieff Justice of Irland, Sir Domynick Sarsfyeld, knight, and Christopher Sibthorpe, esquier, Justices of the said bench in Easter Tearme last in the eight yeare of the kinges Maties raigne of England, France and Irland and of Scotland the xliijth for the fellonious killinge of Simon Barnwell, gent, the 24th daie of November last past. Uppon which araygnment, many examinacons of wittnesses taken by the Right honnorable the lo Deputie and others of the Counsell were produced and reade unto them which did manyfestly and directly prove that the said Simon Barnwell was killed by sond[ry] of those persons who tooke parte with the lo of Howth in An assaulte and affray made uppon Sir Roger Joanes, knight, and that the said eight persons Arraygned at the barr were aydinge and abetting unto the said Lo of Howth in the said quarrell and affray, and that they were directed by the Lo Chieff Justice and thother Judges for matter of Lawe that if any one who tooke parte with the said Lo of Howth in the said affray did kill the said Simon Barnwell, that then as many of the said persons at the Barr as drew theire swordes and tooke parte with the said Lo of Howth were guyltie of the fellonious killinge of the said Simon Barnwell. Notwithstandinge, the said Christopher FitzWiliams and the rest of the said Jurors, Contraray to their said evidence and the Direction of the Courte, did acquitt the said John Drake and all the rest. Wheruppon his Maties said Judges bound all the said Jurors to appeare in this Courte to aunswer theire said mysdemeanor, which said persons after they had appeared by the direction of the Courte were examined by his Maties Serieant at Lawes, uppon which theire examinacons they all Confessed everie parte of the evidence that was then geven and that the same was inforced unto them by the kinges Councell, and tenn of them did likwise Confes the said Direction of the Judges for the matter in Lawe, excusinge theire acquitinge of the said John Dracke and thother person for that yt was not proved unto them who yt was in Certaine and by name that did kill the said Simon Barnwell. Wheruppon the Evidence formerlie geven unto the said Jurij at the barr of his maties Chieff place and Confessed by them was now openly read in Courte. Uppon Reading wherof yt appeared to be manifest and Directe that some of those who tooke parte and drew there swordes on the Lo of Howthes parte against Sir Roger Joanes did kill the said Simon Barnwell, takinge parte and standing in Defense of the said Sir Roger Joanes. Whearuppon this honnorable Courte, gravely and advisedly consideringe that the said Jurors Could not pretend Ignorance, either for the matter in facte which was most plainly and Directly proved unto them that the said Simon Barnwell was killed in the Defence off Sir Roger Joanes by some of the Lo of Howthes parte, and being Directed by the Judges for matter in Lawe that if any one of the Lo of Howthes parte did kill him, that then all the rest that tooke with the said Lo of Howth were guiltie therof, they ought to have geven faith and Creditt unto the said Judges who are aswell sworne to deliver trew Lawe unto them as they were to Deliver A trew verditt. And for that their Ignorance of the Lawe in such a Case we maie excuse the offence of the said Jurors and therfore they receave greate favor by the Direction of the said Judges, Soe as the periury and partiallitie of the said Jurors was without all collour of excuse. Wherfore for the Just punishment of the said offenders and for the Admonishinge of others not to Comitt the Like haynous misdemeanor heerafter, It is ordered, adiudged and Decreed by this honnorable Courte that the said Christopher Fitz Williams, Nicholas McConnell, Richard Nugent, Michell Sedgrave, John More, Thomas Deyne, James Birne, Richard Eustace, John Birkett, Simon Maloane, Thomas Garland and John White each of them shall paie unto his maiestie for a fine the some of one hundred markes le peece, endure Imprisonment at the Lo Deputies pleasure, And shall stand in some publicke place within this Cittie of Dublin with paperes on their heddes Declaringe theire said offence. Dated at his Maiesties Courte of Castle Chamber the xvth daie of June 1610 and in the eight yeere of his Maties Raigne of England, France and Irland and of Scotland the fortieth three.[142]

Memorandum whear his Maiestis Learned Councell this present xiiij daie of November 1610 made informacon ore Tenus in his Most honnorable Courte of Castle Chamber against Cahire Toole, Terrellagh McDonoghe, Gerald McDonogh, Hubbert Archbold, Wylliam McFary Oge, Morrogh McCallowe, Mellaghlyn Duff, Cahire McMorishe, James Byrne, Edward Archbold, James McPhelyme and Dermod McPhellyme that were ympanelled in his Maties Chieff place, the xth Daie of November 1610, for the triall of Arte McBrien OByrne whoe was indicted and Arraygned in his Matis said Chieff place the said xth daie of November before Sir Humfrey Winche, knight, lord Chieff Justice of Ireland, Sir Dominicke Sarsfyeld, knight, and Christopher Sibthorp, esquier, Justices of the said Chieff place, for the malicous and wilfull Murthering of Donell Reoghe OByrne.

142. ff. 166–67.

Uppon which Arraygnment of the said Arte McBrien OByrne many wittneses were produced which did manifestly and Directlie prove the said wilfull murtheringe of the said Donell Reoghe OBirne by the said Arte McBriene OBirne. Nevertheless the said Cahire Toole, Terrelagh McDonoghe, Gerrald McDonoghe and the rest of there fellow Jurors before named, most Corruptlie and Contrary to theire Directe Evidence, did Acquitt the said Arte McBrien OByrne. Wheruppon the said Justices of his maties Chieff place Bound the said Cahire and the rest of the Jurors aforesaid to appeare in this Courte to Annswer theire misdemeanors, which said persons were severally examined by Sir Robert Jacob, knight, his maties Solycyter. Uppon which theire examinacons they and everie of them Confessed the said evidence to be Delivered to them in Courte, yet the said Cahire Toole and the rest Confest and acknowledged they acquitted the said Arte McBrien OBirne, Directlie Contrary to their evidence, alleadging vaine excuses which this Courte did not allow of, But absolutlie reiecte. And therfore, uppon theire owne Confession being read in Courte, yt is therfore this Daie ordered, adiudged and decreed by this honnorable Courte that nyne of the said Defendants, viz Terrlaghe McDonogh, Gerrald McDonoghe, Hubbert Archbold, Willm McFary Oge, Morroghe McCallowe, Mellaghlin Duff, Cahire McMoris, James Birne and Dermot McPhellem shall paie each of them to his matie for a fine the some of fortie poundes, to weare papers on theire heades Declaring theire offence, and ymprisonment Duringe the lord Deputies pleasure. Cahyre Toole, one other of the Deffendants, whoe after he and the rest of the Deffendants had agreed to deliver upp theire verdycte for wilfull murther, and appointed by the rest of his fellowes to saie for them, pronounced theire verdycte to be but Manslaughter, and for his said offence yt is ordered and Decreed that he shall paie to his Maiestie for a fine the some of one hundred poundes, to be sett in the pillory with both his eares nayled and Cutt off, weare paper Declaring his offence, and imprisonment During the lo deputies pleasure. And for Edward Archbold and James McPhellyme whoe were Consentinge to the said false verdycte pronounced by the said Cahire, either of them, to paie to his Matie for a fine the some of one hundred markes a peece, to be sett in the pillory and one of theire eares to be nailed therunto and Cutt off, weare papers Declaring theire offences, and imprisonment during the lo Deputies pleasure. Dated at his Maties Court of Castle chamber the said xiiijth daie of November 1610 and in the eight yeare of his maties raigne of England, France and Ireland, and of Scotland the fortieth fower.[143]

Memorandum wheare his Maiesties learned Councell this present xxjth Daie of November 1610 made informacon into this most honnorable Court of Castle Chamber against James Dice, William Terrell, Edmound Cousen, William Moore, William Ledwych, Piers Delamare, Gerrot Nugent, Owen OCuffie, Thomas Uryell, Richard Terrell, Thomas Dardise and Henrie Dalton, xij Jurors that were ympanelled at the last assizes holden at Molengar in the Countie of Westmeath, the vijth Daie of August 1610, for the tryall of Edmound Duff for the trayterous Rescuinge of one Terlaghe Gallchowe a notoryous traytor, which said Edmond Duff for the said rescues was indicted and araigned at the said Cessions in the said Countie of Westmeath the said vijth daie of November before Sir John Blenerhassett, knight, and John Beere, esquier, Justices of assize for the said Countie of Westmeath. Uppon which his Arraignment manie wittnesses were produced which did Manifestlie and Directlie prove the said Trayterous rescues the said Edmound Duff was Charged withall. Neverthelesse, the said James Dice, William Terrell, Edmound Cusen William More and the rest of theire fellowes Jurors before named, most Corruptlie Contrarie to theire Directe evidence, did acquitt the said Edmound Duff. Wheruppon the said Justices of assize bound the said James Dice, William Terrell, Edmound Cousen, William More and the rest of the Jurors aforesaid to appeare in this Courte to answere theire misdemeanor, which said persons after they had appeared by Direction of thi court were examined by the examinators of this Courte.

Uppon wich theire examinacons they and everie of them Confessed all the said evidence to be Delivered unto them in Court, yet the said James Dyce, William Terrell, Edmond Cousen, William More and the rest Confest and acknowlwedged they acquitted the said Edmound Duff, Directlie Contrary to their Evidence, alleadginge vaine excuses which this Court did not allowe of, but absolutlie reiecte. And therfore uppon theire owne Confession being Reade in Courte, yt is ordered, adiudged and Decreed by this honorable Courte, that the said James Dyce, being the leader of all the rest of his fellowes to acquitt the said Edmound Duff of the said trayterous rescues, shall paie unto

143. ff. 168–68v.

his Maiestie for a fine the some of fortie poundes, ymprisonment Duringe the lo Deputies pleasure, all the rest each of them to paie to his Maiestie for a fine twentie poundes le peece, and ymprisonment duringe the lo Deputies pleasure. Dated at his Maties Court of Castle Chamber the said xxjth Daie of November 1610 and in the eight yeere of his Matie raigne of England, Fraunce and Ireland and of Scotland the fortieth fower.[144]

Memoradum where Sir John Davys, knight, his Maties Attorney generall within this Realme of Irelande, exhibited informacon into this most honorable Courte of Castle Chamber against Stephen Kyrwan, late Mayor of Gallway, Walter French, learned in the Lawes, Vallentyne Blake of the saide Towne, Allderman, and James Oge Darcy, one of the Bayliffes of the saide Towne, for attempting to houlde Plea of matters towching and apperteyning to his matie his Crowne and dignity without sufficient Warrant soe to doe from his Matie or from some of his highnes Progenytor. And whereas one John Griffyn a Solicitor under the leading of Sir Thomas Rotherham, knight, haveing willfully murdered one Andrew Blake of the saide Towne of Gallway, marchant, in his owne howse the xvth day of July 1610, And the saide John Griffyn being founde guiltie of the saide willfull murther by a Jury of xij men of the saide Towne, ympanyled and sworne by the Coroner of the saide Towne of Gallwaye, the saide Stephen Kyrwan, then mayor, Walter Frenche, Valentyne Blake, James Oge Darcy one of the Bayliffes, with divers others of the Alldermen of the saide Towne on the xxjth daie of the saide moneth of July next following, without Warrant or authoritie, proceeded to the tryall of the saide John Gryffyn for the fellonious killing and murthering of the saide Andrewe Blake. Uppon which tryall the saide John Griffyn was fownde guiltie of the fellonious killing and murthering the saide Andrewe Blake, where the saide John Griffyns tryall showlde and ought to have bene for highe Treason. For which their proceedinge without warrant or authoritie, being called into this Courte by his Matie saide Attorney to answere the saide contempte and misdemeanor, the Cause proceeded to Replicacon, Reioynder and wittnesses examyned on eyther parte and the Cause this daie appoynted to be harde. And forasmuch as uppon full heareing and deliberate discussing of the saide Cause yt manifestlie appeered unto this courte, that they hadde noe warrant or authoritie to proceede uppon the tryall of the saide John Griffyn in manner as aforesaide and thereby have comitted a greate Contempt and misdemeanor. It ys therefore ordered, adiudged and decreede by this honorable Courte that the sayde Walter Frenche, being a principall Councellor and advisor for the comitting of the saide contempt and misdemeanor shall paie unto his matie for a fyne the some of twoe hundreth powndes, ymprisonment dureing the Lo Deputyes pleasure. The saide James Darcy to paye likewise to his matie for a ffyne the som of fortye powndes, and ymprisonment during the Lo Deputyes pleasure. The saide Valentyne Blake for that there appeered noe sufficient proofe to finde him guiltie of the saide misdemanor yt is thought fitt by this Courtt that he be dismissed from any further trouble. And for the said Stephen Kyrwyn his death hath freed him. Dated at his maties Courte of Castle chamber the xxiijth day of November 1610 and in the eight yeere of his maties raigne of Englande, Fraunce and Ireland and of Scottlande the fortyeth fower.[145]

Memorandum where Sir John Davys, knight, his maties Attorney generall within this Realme of Ireland, ore tenus made Informacon in this most honorable Courte of Castle chamber against one Symon Paulee who, not regarding his Duty and allegyaunce nor beareing that Reverend respect towardes the kinges most Excellent Matie (as in Duty he ought), very disloyally, Contemtuosly, falsly and sediciously published in the Shoppe of John Francton in the Citie of Dublin, Printer, before Dyvers persons these false, malicious, sedycious and slanderous wordes following: viz: That he sawe the kinges Letters Pattent in a Towne called Northallerton in Yorkeshire brought thither by a Scotishman for a tolleracon of Religion without controwlement for the kinges Lyfe, the Queenes lyfe and the lyfe of the prynce. And that certeyne Soms of mony was to be geven for the saide tolleracon. Which false, Sedycious, wicked & slanderous speeches the saide Paulee, being examined before the right honorable the Lorde Deputy and Councell, confessed the same besydes fowre severall witneses being present when the saide Paulee uttered and published the saide words, being likewise examyned, directlie proved that he spake the saide words in the shoppe of John Francton, Prynter. Whereuppon the courte proceeding to sentence yt is ordered, adiudged and decreed by this Courte that the saide Symon Paulee shalbe presently comitted to the grate in the Castle of Dublin, there to remayne prysoner till the next market Day and then to be whipt from the Castle bridge to the Newgate, and then brought bck to be sett on the Pillory, his eares nayled and a paper on his head declareing his offence. And shall during his standing in the Pillory publickly acknowledge his offence and then to retorne to the grate, there to remayne prisoner during the Lo Deputyes pleasure. Yeven at his mates Courte of Castle chamber the xxixth Daie of Maye 1611 and in the nynth yere of the raigne of our Soveraigne Lorde Kinge James of England, Fraunce and Ireland and of Scotland the xliiijth.[146]

Memoradum where the Right honnorable Richard, Earle of Clanrickard, Lo President of the province of Conaght, and one of his Maties privie counsell of this Realme, the Tenth day of November in the seventh yeare of his highnes Raigne of England, France and Ireland and of Scotland the xliijth, preferred a bill of Complaincte unto his highnes in this his highe Courte of Cstle chamber against Sir Thomas Boorke of Bealanesloe [Ballinasloe] in the Countye of Galway, knighte, John Boorke of Downsandell in the Countie afforesaid, Esqier, and Thomas Lichefeild, gent, Declareinge that where kinge Henrye the Eight (of famous memorie) by his highnes Lres pattentes bearinge date the firste daye of Julye in the fyve and thirtyth yeare of his Raigne did Creat[e] Ullicke Boorke (then called McWilliam) The Compl[ainan]ts greate grandfather, Earle of Clanrickard and Barron of Dunkellyn. And by the said Lres pattentes granted to him, the said Ullicke, the state, tytle, honnor & dignitie of Earle of Clanrickard and Barron of Dunkellyn To have & to hould to him the said Ullicke and the heires males of his boddie Lawfullye begotten. And for the better supportacon and maintenance of his said state, tytle, honnor and dignitie, the said kinge Henrye the Eighte by the said Lres pattentes did graunte unto the said Ullicke, Earle of Clanrickard, and his said heires males, divers and sundrie Castles, Lordships, Manors, Landes, Tenements and herreditaments. And that the said Ullicke beinge by vertue of the Lres pattentes aforesaid invested in the said state, tytle and honnor, and seised of the said Castles Lordships, Townes, Landes, Tenements and hereditaments graunted unto him by the Lres pattentes aforesaid the said Ullicke died seised therof, wherby the said tytle of honor and all and singuler the Landes, Tenements, and hereditaments aforesaid discended to Richard, the Complainants grandfather, as sonne and heire male of the boddie of the said Ullicke. By vertue whereof the saide Richard all his liefe tyme enioyed both the said Tytle of honor and all and singuler the Landes, Tenements and hereditamentes aforesaid and dyed therof seysed. After and by whose death the said tytle of honor and all other landes, Tenements and hereditaments aforesaid discended to Ullick Boorke, the Compltes father, as sonn and heire male of the boddie of the said Riccard. And the said Complte did lykewise set forth in his said bill that the said Ullicke Boorke (the Complte father), in the lief tyme of the said Riccard, Earle of Clanrickard (the Compltes graundfather), viz aboute the xxvthe daie of November in the yeare of our Lo God 1564, did publicklye marrie and take to wief (accordinge to the Lawes of hollye Church) Honora Boork, daughter to John Boorke of Clochroucke in the Countye of Galway aforesaid, esquier, in the parishe Church of Athenrye in the countye aforeaid, and that after the said marriadge soe solemnized the said Ullicke had yssue upon the boddie of the said Lady Honora a sonn called Riccard Boorke, and afterwardes a daughter Called Marye Boorke, both which Children soone after their birthes died, and that afterwardes, viz fyve or sixe yeares after the said marriadge, the said Ullicke had yssue upon the boddye of the said Lady Honora, Riccard (the nowe Earle of Clanrickard, Complt). And that afterwarde the said Ullicke (the Compltes father) dyed aboute eight yeares before the exhibittinge of the said Bill of Complainte, after and by whose death the name, state, style and honor of Earle of Clanrickard and Barron of Dunkellyn and all and singuler the Castles, Lordships, Manors, Landes, Tenements and hereditaments aforesaid discended and Came (as of right they oght to discend & come) to the said Complte as the lawfull son and heire male of the boddie of the said Ullicke. By force wherof the said complt did assume and take upon him the said state, tytle, honor and dignitie of Earle of Clanrickard and Barron of Dunkellyn and entered into all and singuler the said Castles, Lordships, Manors, Landes Tenementes and hereditamentes and was ever since the death of his said father quietlye and peaceablye seised therof as of his lawfull inheritance, takeinge the yssues &

146. ff. 171–71v.

proffittes therof to his owne use, as lawfull was for him to doe. And that the said Complte, aboute foure yeares before the exhibittinge of the said Bill of Complt, had yssue Ullicke Boorke, comonlye called Barron of Dunkellyn, upon the boddye of the La[dy] Fraunces, his wief. And that, the premisses notwithstanding, the said Sir Thomas Boorke (beinge but second Brother to the said Complt), knowing all and singuler the premisses to be true, not haveinge the feare of God before his eies, nor regardinge his highnes iust and honnorable Lawes against unlawfull Conspiracies & Combinacons and against scandalls & seditious Rumors tendinge to the dishonor of the Peeres and other Chief Officers of this kingdome, did wickedlye, fraudelouslye & Contemptuouslye at divers and sundrye tymes & places Conspire and Combyne himself with the said John Boorke (an other brother of the said Complt) and with the said Thomas Lichefeild and divers other personnes, unlawfullye to disinherite the said Complt [and] his said sonn and heire apparant both of the said tytle of honor and of all and singuler the Castells, Lordships, Manors, Landes, Tenements and hereditamentes aforesaid. And that, to that end the said Sir Thomas Boorke, John Boorke and Thoms Lichfeild, after divers Consultacons had betwene them selves, did wickedlye and seditiouslye resolve and conclude that, aswell by speeches and reportes as by Lettres and messadges to divers gent of Accompte in the said province of Connaght and to some other great persons of Chief and eminent place in this kingdome, they the said Sir Thomas Boorke, John Boorke and Thomas Lichfield should give out, publishe and declare that the said Complt was not the lawfull sonn & heire of the said Ullicke, late Earle of Clanrickard, but that the said Complt was borne by the said Lady Honora before anie lawfull mariadge had betwene the said Ullick, late Earle, & the said Lady Honora, and soe that the said Complt was a bastard by the lawes of this Realme. After which seditious and scandalous speeches soe spred abroade by the said Sir Thomas Boorke, John Boorke and Thomas Lichfeild, they the said Sir Thoms Boorke, John Boorke and Thomas Lichfeild did malitiulye conclude and resolve that upon the first stirr or popular comocon that should happen within the said province of Connaght, the said Sir Thomas Boorke shold declare himself to be the lawfull sonn and heire male of the said Ullicke and should lykewise take upon himself to be Earle of Clanrickard and Barron of Dunkellyn, and should then enter into all and singuler the Castles, Lordships, Mannors, Landes, Tenements and hereditaments. And the said Complt did lykewise set forth by his said Bill that, accordinge to the moste wicked and seditious resolucon aforesaid, the said Sir Thoms Boorke, John Boorke & Thoms Lichfeild, not haveinge the feare of god before their eyes nor yet regardinge the lawes and statutes of this kingdome against seditious and slaunderous speeches and Rumors tendinge to the dishonor & defamacon of the peeres and other Chief Officers of this Realme, did at divers & sundrie tymes and places falselye and slaunderouslye give out, publishe and declare aswell by speeches & Lres as otherwise that the said Complt was not the lawfull son and heire of the said Ullicke (late Earle of Clanrickard) but that the said Complt was a bastard, borne by the said Honora to the said Ullicke (late Earle) before anie Lawfull marriadge had betwene them the said Ulicke and Honora. And that the said Sir Thomas Boorke was the true inheritor of the honor and lands aforesaid, and that the said Complt did plott and practise the death and distruction of the said Sir Thomas Boorke, all which scandalous & slanderous speeches were alleadged by the said Complt in his said Bill of Complt to be most manifest and shameless untruthes, given out and published by the said Sir Thomas Boorke, John Boorke and Thomas Lichfeild, falslye, slaunderouslye, malitiouslye & seditiouslye tendinge to the great dishonor of the said Compltes name, blood and honor, and to the disinherison [sic] both of himself and of his said sonn and heire apparant, and of his posteritie for ever. In Consideracon wherof and because the said wicked conspiracies and combinacons and the said scandelous & reprochfull speeches weare directlye Contrarie to divers and sundrie of his highnes lawes and statutes of this kingdome, and for avoydinge of evill example which might be given to others, the said Complt humblye prayed the ordinarie processe of the said Courte to be awarded against the said Sir Thomas Boorke, John Boorke and Thomas Lichfeild to answere to the premisses, and that such punishment might be inflicted upon them as the qualitie of thier said offence deserved as by the said Bill of Complte more at large appeareth. Wherupon the ordinarie processe of this Courte yssued and was served upon the said Sir Thoms Lichfeild because he could not be found, beinge then departed the kingedome, by vertue of which process the said Sir Thomas Boorke and John Boorke appeared and made severall answers to the said Bill of complt wherby they denyed all & singuler the Combinacons, Conspiracies, scandelous Rumors and speeches aforesaid in such maner as by their said severall answers maie appeare. Wherupon yssue beinge Joyned accordinge to the ordinarie Course of this courte both parties did exhibite thier Interrogatories to be ministred to such witnesses as should be examined in the said Cause, for examinacon of which witnes A Comission did yssue by consent of both the said parties to William, Lord Arch bishopp of Tuam, Sir John Everard, knight, Abell Walshe, precher and Henry Linche of Galway, Counsellor at lawe, or to anie three of them, to examine upon their oathes all such witnesses as on eyther side sould be produced upon the said Interrogatories anexed to the Comission afforesaid, and the examinacons of the said witnessses soe to be taken to returne into this Courte at A certaine daie in Easter Tearme then next followinge the date of the said Comission. Accordinge to which comission divers witnesses beinge produced by eyther of the said parties were dulye examined and thier examinacons returned into this courte and afterwardes the said examinacons beinge published by order of the said Courte and a daie of heareinge appointed in this present Trinitie Tearme, the said Complt and the said Sir Thoms Boorke and John Boorke appeared in proper personnnes in this Courte this present day, beinge the laste daye of May in the nynth yeare of his highnes Raigne of England, France and Ireland and of Scotland the xliiijth. At which tyme and place the said Cause beinge publicquelye and solemlye heard and debated by the learned Counsell of both parties in open Courte before the Comissioners aucthorised to heare sentence and decree all Causes examinable in this Courte, viz before the Right honnorable Sir Arthure Chichester, knight, Lo Deputye of this Realme of Ireland, Thomas, Lo Archbishop of Dublin, primate & Metropolitan of Ireland & Lo Chauncellor of the same, William, Lo Archbishopp of Tuam, David Lo Viscount de Roche of Fermoye, comonlye called the Lo Roche, Richard, Lo Barron of Delvin, Sir Thomas Ridgwaye, knight, his highnes vicetrer and Threr at warres within this kingdome of Ireland and one of his highnes privie Counsellors of the same kingdome, Sir Richard Wingfeild, knight, marshall of his maties armie and one of his highnes privie counsell, Sir Nicholas Walshe, knight, Lo Chief Justice of his highnes Courte of Comon pleas and one of his highnes said privie Counsell, Sir John Denhame, knight, Lo Chief Barron of his highnes Cort of Exchequer and one of his highnes said privie Counsell, Sir Frances Angier, knight, master of the Rowles and one of his highnes said privie Counsell, Sir Oliver St Johnes, knight, mr of the Ordinance and one of his highnes privie Counsell, Sir Richard Morrison, knight, vice President of the province of Mounster and one of his highnes said privie Counsel, Sir Richard Cooke, knight, his highnes principall Secretarie of estate within the said kingdome and Sir Adam Loftus, knight, one of his highnes said privie Counsell, before whome sittinge in this Courte to heare and decree the said Cause, yt was moste manifestlye and pregnantlye proved by such and soe manie notable Circumstances, demonstracons and Causes of knowledge as a matter of facte cannot possiblie be proved more evidentlye, fully & plainlye by the depositions of Twelve or thirtene good and Lawfull witnesses, most of them beinge persons of good estate and qualitie, all which were present and eye witnesses that the said Ullicke, late Earle of Clanrickard ,was publicquelye, solemlye & Lawfullye marryed to the said La Honora Boorke in the parishe Church of Athenrye aforesaid, in the Countie of Galwey aforesaid, in the presence of the said witnesses and of one hundred persons more about fyve or sixe and fortye yeares then paste. And yt was lykewise as apparantlye, evidentlye & manifestlye proved by all the said witnesses that aboute two yeares after the said mariadge the said Ullicke had noe Children by the said Lady Honora and that afterwardes the said Ullicke had yssue first upon the boddye of the said Lady Honora a son Called Richard Boorke and after a daughter called Marye Boorke, and that both the said Children (soone after their birthes) died. And some of the said Witnesses did lykewise depose that after the birth of the said two Children the said Lady Honora had another Child borne dead before the bearth of the said Complainant. It was alsoe most plainlye, fullye, undoubtedlye and Clearlye proved by the depositions of all the foresaid Twelve or thirtene witnesses that the said Ullicke, Late Earle of Clanrickard, had yssue upon the boddie of the said Lady Honora the Complt, Richard, now Earle of Clanrickard, sixe yeares or theraboutes after the said marriadge soe solemnized as aforesaid. And yt was lykewise well and substantiallye proved both by the Depositions of severall good and substantiall witnesses and by the said Sir Thomas Boorkes fainte denialles, amountinge to implyed confessions, aswell in his answere to the said Bill as in his examinacons upon personall Interrogatories, and by a Clayme made by him the said Sir Thomas Boorke and entred of Record in the Courte of Comon pleas to a fyne levyed by the said Complt of all the Landes, Tenementes & hereditamentes descended to him, the said Complt, from his said father & other his Auncestors, by which Claime the said Sir Thoams Boorke pretended right and tytle to all the Landes, Tenementes and hereditamentes descended to the said Complynant, and alsoe by A missive ltre written by the said Sir Thomas Boorke his owne hand and sent to the said Right honorable Sir Arthure Chichester, knight, then and nowe Lo Deputye of this Realme of Ireland, in which lre the said Sir Thomas Boorke did cast a doubte of the Compltes legittimacie and did insinuate the said Complt to be a Bastard and directlye affirmed that the said Complt did plott and practise the death and destruction of the said Sir Thomas Boorke with an earneste offer in the said Ltre to verrifie and prove whatsoever he had written in the said Lre, which offer induced the Lo Deputie to shewe forth the said Lre for that yt concerned a man of soe high a Ranke and qualitie as the Complt is and in soe high a nature, and that the suppossinge therof might in tyme to come not onelye preiudice the estate of the said Complt and his posteritie, but alsoe indaunger and drawe into perill the publique quiet and government of this Realme. Upon publique heareinge of which Lre (read in open Court) The said Sir Thomas Boorke acknowledged the same to be his owne Acte and hand wrytinge, wherby and by other apparant proves and pregnant and violent presumptions yt plainlye appeared that the said Sir Thomas Boorke did divers and sundrey tymes declare, publishe and give out the malitious scandalous & reprochfull speeches aforesaid against the Legittimacie of the said Complte And that the said Sir Thomas Boorke did lykewise declare, publishe and give out that the said Complt did plott & practise the death & distruction of him the said Sir Thomas Boorke as aforesaid. All which wicked and malitious speeches appearinge to be most false, scandalous, unnaturall & ungodlye were apparantly proved to have bene impiouslye and falselye published & divulged by the said Sir Thomas Boorke wherby he did not onelye entend to dishonor and traduce the said Complt, beinge his eldeste Brother, but alsoe to deprave and scandalise the deceased Earle and Countesse (beinge his owne naturall parentes), who lyved and died both vertuouslye before god and in greate honor and reputacon in the world. Uppon deliberate and due Consideracon of all which matters the said right honorable the Lo Deputye and all the reste of his Assotiates aforesaid and Assistance did publishe, pronounce and declare, and doe hereby decree, sentence, pronounce, declare and adiudge, that the said Ullicke, late Earle of Clanrickard, was undoubtedly lawfullye, solemlye and publicquelye marryed in the face of holye Church to the said Lady Honora aboute seven and fortye yeares sithence at and in the place and in the presence of the persons aforemenconed and that the said Complt was borne to the said Ullicke by the said Lady Honora aboute sixe yeares after the said marriadge soe solemnized as aforesaid, and that consequentlye the said Richard, nowe Earle of Clanrickard (the Complt), is the lawfull and undoubted son and heire male of the said Ullick, late Earle of Clanrickard. And further, the said Righte honorable the Lo Deputye and the rest of his said assotiates and assistantes did with lyke uniforme consent pronounce declare and adiudge and doe hereby decree, sentence, pronounce, declare and adiudge that the said Sir Thomas Boorke, knight, is guiltye of the untrue, unnaturall, scandalous and malitious reportes and Speeches aforesaid, viz that he the said Sir Thomas Boorke did most falselye, unnaturally & wickedlye publishe declare and give oute that the said Richard, nowe Earle of Clanrickiard, was not the lawfull sonn and heire of the said Ulicke, late Earle of Clanrickard, but that he the said nowe Earle was A Bastard borne before anie marriadge had or solemnized betwene the said Ullicke, late Earle, and the said Lady Honora. And that he the said Sir Thomas Boorke did with lyke falsitie and malice unlawfullye publishe, declare and give out that the said Complt did plott and seeke the death and destruction of the said Sir Thomas Boorke, for which false scandalous and ungodlye speeches, obloquies and aspercons of and against the Complt tendinge to the reproche & scandall both of his person and government, the said Right honorable the Lo Deputye and all the rest of his said assotiates and assistantes doe hereby order, adiudge, sentence and decree that the said Sir Thomas Boorke, knight, for his Offences and misdemeanors shall paie for a fyne to his Matie the some of One Thowsand poundes. And that he the said Sir Thomas shalbe comitted to the Custodie of the Constable of the Castle of Dublin, there to remaine dureinge the said Right honorable the Lo Deputies pleasure. And as concerninge the unlawfull conspiracie and Combinacon alleadged in the said Bill of Complte to be made by the said Sir Thomas Boorke, John Boorke and Thomas Lichfeild, although ther were some proofe & stronge presumptions induceinge the private Consciences of the said Lo Deputie and the rest to thinke that the said Defendantes did enter into the said unlawfull Conspiracies and Combinacons, yet because the Courte did not Conceive that ther was soe apparant and full proofe therof as they might ground A Censure thereof, the said Right honorable the Lo Deputye and the reste did acquite and dischardge the said Sir Thomas Boorke and the said John Boorke and Thomas Lichfeild therof. And lastlye for that the said proofe did not retche [reach] to Convince the said John Boorke of the said slanderous speeches toucheinge the said Compltes illegittimacie nor to the supposed practise of the death and destruction of the said Sir Thomas Boorke, Therfore the said Right honorable the Lo Deputie & the reste have dismissed the said John Boorke therof. Given at his maties Courte of Castle Chamber the last daie of Maie 1611 and in the nynth yeare of the Raigne of our soveraigne Lord Kinge James of England, Fraunce and Irland and of Scotland the xliiijth.

Present: The Lo Deputye, The Lo Chauncellor, The Lo Archbishopp of Tuam, The Lo Viscount Fermoy, The Lo Barron of Delvin, Mr Trer, Mr Marshall, The Lo Justice Walshe, The Lo Chief Barron, The Mr of the Rowles, The Master of the Ordinance, Sir Richard Morrison, Sir Richard Cooke, Sir Adam Loftes.[147]

Memorandum where Sir John Davyes, knighte, his maties Attorney generall within this Realme of Ireland, the fowre and twentiethe day of November Anno dom 1609, exhibited an Informacon into this honorable Courte of Castle Chamber againste Capten Richard Tyrrell of Drumlaghan in the countie of Cavan, Hughe OReartie, Feriagh OHanlie & Willm McDonnell, all servauntes or followers to the said Capten Tyrrell. In which Informacon his maties said Attorney amongste other thinges chardged the said Capten Tyrrell and the saide other Deftes That by the settinge on and procurement of the said Capten Tyrrell They did all of theym togither with the said Tyrrell in and upon the seaconde day of September in the yeere of our Lorde god 1607 att Killibadricke in the said Countie of Cavan ryotously, rowtously and forcibly enter into the Landes of one Caher Mc Phillipp of Killibadricke aforesaid. And havinge gotten the possession thereof gave divers threateninge and terrible wordes to one Bryan McCaher, tennant of the said lande, and ryotously enterd into his howse. And said the said Tyrrell would kill him if he woulde not avoyde the possession of his howse and landes. Which he refusinge, the saide Capten Tyrrell, beinge a Justice of Peace for the said countie of Cavan, and the said other deftes did then and there ryotously and unlawfully beate and wounde the said Bryan McCaher whereby the said Bryan and the reste of the tennantes dwellinge upon the said lande weare enforced to forsake the saide landes. To which bill the said Capten Tyrrell made answere and the cause proceedinge to replicacon and witnesses examined on the pltes parte and this day appointed to be hearde. Forasmuch as upon ful hearinge and deliberate discussinge of the cause, It manifestlie apeared to this Courte That the said ryott, forcible entry and misdemeanor was comitted and done by the said Richarde Tyrrell and thother persons named in the bill in manner and forme as in the bill ys alleadged. It ys therefore ordered, adiudged and decreed by this honorable Courte that the said Capten Richard Tyrrell shall paye to his matie for a fyne the some of xx[li] and to paye all such costes of courte as shalbe taxed by the righte honorable the Lorde Chancelor. Dated att his maties Courte of Castle chamber the 22th day of November 1611 and in the nynthe yeere of his maties Raigne of England, Fraunce and Irelande and of Scotland the xlvth.[148]

Memorandum where Sir Edward Blaine, knight, Dame Anne his wyfe, late wiefe of George Blunt, Esquier, deceased, and Elizabeth Blunt, sole daughter and heire of the said George Blunt, lawfullie begotten uppon the Body of the said Dame Anne, the twentie nynthe day of May one thousand six hundred and eleven, exhibited their Bill of Complaynt into this honorable Courte of Castle Chamber against Morrice, Lorde Bishoppe of Killalowe, Seive Ny Carroll, Christopher Blunt, otherwise called Christopher Carroll, and dyvers other defendantes. In which Bill of Complaynt they the said Complaynantes alleaged the said Christopher Blunt, als Carroll, to be the Bastard sonne of the saide George Blunt, begotten unlawfullie on the body of the said Seive Ny Carroll, and soe to have bene reputed amongst all people that knewe him from the daie of his Birth to this present daye, and chardged the said defendantes, Seive Ny Carroll and Christopher Blunt, als Carroll, that they showlde procure one Richard White, James Cromell, Robert Culame and Dermode OMullvihill to take theire corporall oathes before the saide Lo Bishoppe that the sayde George Blunt and Seive Ny Carroll were, in the lyfe tyme of the saide George, lawfullie maryed togither, with which Complott, the saide Bishoppe being acquainted, agreed to take their examinacons according to the request of the saide Christopher and Seive Ny Carroll. According to which practyse and Combinacon the saide Richard White, James Cromell, Robert Culam and Dermode Mulvihill not being called by anie Citacon by the procurement of the saide Seive Ny Carroll and with the advise and direccon of the sayd Lo Bishoppe did uppon the tenth day of Marche then last past repayre to Ennishe in the County of Clare where the saide Lo Bishoppe then was and then and there he the saide Lo Bishoppe of Killalowe, not haveing any writt directed unto him from any of his maties temporal Courtes or Judges aucthorising him soe to doe, and allsoe well knowing the saide Christopher Blunt to be a Bastarde,

147. ff. 172–77. Fol. 177v is blank.   148. ff. 178–78v.

did unlawfullie examyne the saide Richarde White, James Cromell, Robert Cullam and Dermode OMullvihill uppon their corporall oathes what they did knowe or had harde touching the mariage or contract supposed to be made betweene the saide George Blunt and Seive Ny Carroll. Whereuppon the saide Richard White, and Dermode OMullvihill did corruptlie depose then and there before the saide Lo Bishoppe that the saide Geoge Blunt and Seive Ny Carroll at Clare aforesaide about twentie six yeares then last past were contracted and maryed in the presence of them the saide Richard and Dermod and others. And the saide Robert Cullam and James Cromell did likewise depose that the saide George Blunt did in his lyfe tyme confesse unto them that he was maryed to the saide Seive Ny Carroll, which deposycons being then and there reduced into writing, the saide Lo Bishoppe did then and there cause the same to be transcripted and engrosed in parchement in Forme of a Pu[b]lique Instrument or exemplificacon, To which transcript, exemplificacon or Instrument the saide Lo Bishoppe did then and there putt his hande and Seale and delivered the same instrument to the saide Christopher. Whoe afterwardes, about the first day of Aprill then last past, did publishe the same at Mellefont in the countie of Lowth and at divers other places and tymes and thereby still gveth out that he is the lawfull Sonne and heire of the saide George Blunt. To which Bill the saide Lo Bishoppe of Killalowe, Seive Ny Carroll and James Cromell made their answere, and thereuppon ioyned yssue and is this daye appointed to be heard. For as much as upon full hearing and deliberat discussing of the Cause itt manifestlie appeared to the Right honorable the Lo Deputie and the rest of the Commissioners in this honorable Courte that the saide Deposycons of the saide Fowre wittnesses were unduelie taken by the said Lo Bishoppe by the procurement of the saide Seive Ny Carroll, and that the Coppie of the saide Deposycons were caused to be engrossed into publique Instrument and signed with the hande and Seale of him the saide Lo Bishoppe and by him the saide Lo Bishoppe delivered to the said Christofer in manner and forme as in the Bill is alleadged. And for as much allsoe as this honorable Courte conceaveth that the misdemeanor of the saide Seive Ny Carroll was by reason of the natural affeccon she bare to her saide Bastarde Sonne chrystofer, And likewise in regarde the saide Lo Bishoppe hath before this honorable Courte acknowledged his error and misdemeanor and is repentantlie sorrowfull for the same, and allsoe hath by a letter written to the Right honorable the Lo Deputie humblie craved pardon for his Error, the tenor of which letter heare ensueth:

To the Right honorable the Lo Deputy of Ireland: Right honorable, my humble duty rememberred to your Lordship. Whereas I am brought in Suite in his maties highe Courte of Castle chamber by Sir Edward Blany, knight, and Dame Anne, his wief, for takeing thexaminacon of certeyne wittnesses in the behalf of Seive Ny Carroll And reduceing their deposycons into paper. Wherein I acknowledge my Eror for not observeing a Legall Course in examining the said wittnesses. Therfore I am humbly to crave your honorable Lordship to be pleased this tyme to remitt my Error and negligence for which I shall for ever rest [thankful]. And I humbly desyre the said examinacons unduly taken may be Cancelled by order of this Courte [in] Dublin the xxijth of November 1611. Yor honorable Lordships humblie to comaunde, Maurit [Maurice] Lord [Bishop of Killaloe].

Which being considered by this honorable Courte, allthough both their offences be great and worthie of seveare and exemplary punichment yet the reasons aforesaide doe somwhat mittigate the rigor of their Censure and move them to Clemencie in inflicting a small punishment for a great offence. It is therefore ordered, adiudged and decreed by the Right honorable the Lord Deputie and the rest of the Comissioners of this honorable Courte That the saide Deede, Instrument or exemplificacon soe signed by the saide Bishoppe as aforesaide shalbe quite Dissanulled, Damned, Cancelled & defaced as undulie, unlawfully and Corruptlie made, and to be reputed of noe value or force. And that the saide Maurice, Lo Bishop of Killalowe, shall paye to the kinges matie for a fine the some of an hundred Markes ster. And to be ymprisoned during the Lo Deputyes pleasure And to pay all such Costes of courte as shalbe taxed by the Right honorable the Lord Chauncellor. And that the saide Seive Ny Carroll shall paie to the kinges matie for a fine the some of fowrtie pownds sterling and to be ymprisoned untill she bring in or Cause to be brought into this honnorable Courte the saide Instrument or Writing to be cancelled, according to the Censure of this honorable courte. Dated at his Maties Courte of Castle chamber the xxvijth of November 1611 And in the nynth yeare of his highnes Raigne of England, Fraunce and Ireland and of Scottland the fyve and fortieth.[149]

---

149. ff. 179–81. Fol. 181v is blank.

Md: where his maties learned Concell ore tenus this xxixth of Januarij 1611 made information in this most honnorable Court of Castle Chamber against Walter Bryan, Edmond Synnott, Edmond Codd, James Butler, and Thomas Codd, five of the Jurij ympannelled at Wexforde to enquire for our soveraigne lord the kinges maiestie touching his highnes tytle to the lands of the Morroghes and Kynsalies in the said Countie of Wexford before the Lo Bushopp of Fearnes and others, Comissioners appointed in that behalf. Uppon which inquiry all the said Jurie, except the said Walter Bryan, Edmond Synnott, Edmond Codd, James Butler and Thomas Codd weare resolved to fynd his maiesties title to all the said landes then given in Charge, but the said Walter Bryan, Edmond Synnott, Edmond Codd, James Butler and Thomas Codd, out of a malycious and Corrupt Disposicion, not regarding their Duty to his matie nor the pregnant and apparrant evidence then given unto them and the rest of theire fellow Jurrors, absolutly refused to Joine with their fellowes to fynde for his maiestie. And after being Called into his maties Courte of exchecquer before the lo Chieffe Barron and others, Comissioners appointed in that behalf, to render an accompt their Reasons whye they refused to Joine with the rest of their fellow Jurrors Could make no other annswere but that thier Conscience would not suffer them to Joine with the rest uppon the evidence given them to fynde for his maiestie. Whereuppon the Courte proceedinge to censure [it] was this day ordered, adiudged and decreed that the said Walter Brian, Edmond Synnott, Edmond Codd, James Butler and Thomas Codd for thier manyfest Contempt and misdemeanor shall pay each of them to his maiestie for a fyne the some of thirty powndes english and ymprisonment During the lo Deputies pleasure. Dated at his maties Courte of Castle Chamber the said xxixth Day of Januarij 1612 and in the ixth yeare of his maties raigne of England, Fraunce and Ireland and of Scotland the xlvth.[150]

Memorandum wheras Robert Talbott of Temple oge in the County of Dublin, Esquier, Late Shiriffe of the Countie of Dublin, exhibited informacon into this honnorable courte of Castle Chamber against James Barnwell of Brymore in the Countie of Dublin, Elyzabeth his wyffe, Nicholas Connor, Thomas Rusell and Divers others for the rescueing and forceably taking of a Distres [which] the said Robert Talbott, being then Shiriffe of the said County of Dublin, had taken of the goodes and Chattells of the said James Barnwell upon the Landes of Brymore aforesaid by vertue of his maties wrytt of seysure for the taking the said Distresse out of his Maties Courte of Exchequier. Whereunto the said James Barnwell, Elizabeth his wyffe, Nicholas Connor and Thomas Russell made answer and the Cause proceeding to replicacon, reioynder and wyttneses examined one the pltes partes, the Deffendantes in theire owne Default Loosing the benefitt of theire wyttnesses, and the Cause this day apointed to be hard. Forasmuch as upon full hearing and Delyberat Discursing of the said Cause yt manifestly appeared to this Courte by many wittnesses and partely Confessed upon theire examinacons upon personnall inter[rogatories?] that the said James Barnwell, Elizabeth Barnwell, Nicholas Connor, Thomas Russell and the rest of the persons did forceably and violently Rescue, take and Cary away the said Distres from the said Robert Talbott and his Company being then in his possession. Yt is therefore ordered, adiudged and Decreed by this Courte that the said James Barnwell and Elizabeth his wyffe shall paie to his Matie for a fine the somme of one hundred pounds Currant English mony, and imprisonment during the Lord Deputies pleasure. The said Nicholas Connor and Thomas Russell to pay each of them tenn poundes apeece like englishe mony and ymprisoned during the lord deputies pleasure. Dated at his maties Courte of Castle chamber the Last Day of Januarij 1612 And in the ixth yeare of his maties Raigne of England, Fraunce and Ireland and of Scotland the xlvth.[151]

Memorandum where his maties Learned Councell this presente vjth daie of May 1612 made Informacon ore tenus in this moste honorable Courte of Castle Chamber against Edmond Bourne of Williamstone, Edmond Bourne of Porte Rushin, James Archebolde, Phillippe Walshe, Edmond Walshe, James Cooke, Thomas Eustace and Walter Grace and others that were ympannelled & sworne at a generall Assizes and Geale Delivery holden at Catherlogh the xxvth Daie of February laste before Sir John Blenerhasset, knight, and John Beare, esquier, then Justice of Assize, for the triall of Donell OMackyn whoe was then indicted and araigned of Treason for Reeleevinge of Teig

Boy Donogh OShea and Walter Deverox, knowen to be notoriouse Rebells and Traytors. Upon which araignment of the said Donell OMackyn, witnesses were produced which did manifestely and Directely proove the Releevinge of the said Rebells and Traytors by the said Donell OMackyn severall tymes. Neverthelesse, the said Edmond Bourne & Edmond Bourne, James Archebolde and the reste of the said Jurors before named, moste Corruputely and Contrary to their directe evidence, did acquite the said Donell OMackyn. Wherupon they the said Justices bounde the said James Archebolde and the reste of the Jurors afforesaid to appear in this honorable Courte to answer the misdemeanor, which said persons were severally examined before his Maties Seriante and solicitor, upon which their examinacons they and every of them confessed the said evidence to be Delivered unto them in Courte upon the araignemente of the said Donell O Mackyn. Yet the said James Archebolde and the reste Confessed & acknowledged they acquited the said Donell OMackyn directely Contrary to their evidence, alledginge vaine excuses which this Courte did not allowe of, but absolutely reiecte. And therefore upon their owne Confession beinge read in Courte yt is this daie ordered, adiudged & decreed by this most honorable Courte thtat the said Edmond Bourne of Williamston and Edmond Bourne of Porte Rushyn, in respecte they were the principall leaders and inducers to draw thother defendants to Comitte the misdemeanors layed to their Charge, are Censured by this Courte to paye unto his matie eache of them the some of fortie poundes Englishe for a fyne. And the other sixe, viz James Archbolde, Phillippe Walshe, Edmond Walshe, James Cooke, Thomas Eustace & Walter Grace shall eche of them pay to his matie for a fyne the some of twentie poundes Englishe and all of them to be ymprisoned Duringe the Lord Deputies pleasure. Dated at his maties Courte of Castell Chamber the vjth daie of May 1612 and in the tenth yeare of his maties Raigne of England, Fraunce and Ireland and of Scotlande the xlvth.[152]

Memorandum where Sir John Bynghame of Clonegashell in the county of Mayo, knight, exhibited Informacon into this moste honorable Courte of Castle Chamber against Sir Theobolde Bourke, knight, Myles Bourke, his sonne and heire, Cosney McEgan, Edmond McPhylpin and diverse others, riotouslely, Routousely and unlawefully beinge assembled on the xvjth daie of Auguste in the thyrde yeare of his maties Raigne of England, Fraunce and Irelande, came to Castle Barry in the said county of Mayo, beinge in the peaceable and quiet possession of the said Sir John Bynghame, knight, and then & there violently & forceablie the said Sir Theobolde Bourke & the reste pulled Downe to the grounde Diverse small houses and Cottages, wounde and beate the poore tenantes there inhabitinge, and Drove them from the possession of the said landes. To which informacon the said Sir Theobolde Bourke, knight, Myles Bourke, Cosney McEgan, Edmond McPhillipyn and the reste made answer to the Informacon, and the Cause proceedinge to Replicacon, Reioynder and witnesses examined on either parte and this Daie the Cause finally hearde & determined. Forasmuch as yt manifestely appeared to this Courte by the testimonie of many witnesses that the said Sir Theobolde Bourke, Myles Bourke, Cosney McEgan, Edmond McPhilpyn and the reste of the said Sir Theoboldes Company had Comitted the said Riotouse, routouse and unlawefull outerages, Riottes and many other misdemeanors layed downe in the said Informacon, and for that the said Sir Theobolde Bourke had the Comaunde of all the reste of the Defendantes and at the Comittinge of the Riotte they attended on him, as alsoe for that the said Defendants were formerly punished for the said offence. Yt is therefore ordered, adiudged and Decreed by this honorable Courte that the said Sir Theobolde Bourke shall paie unto his matie for a fyne the some of fortie poundes and ymprisonmente Duringe the Lo Deputies pleasure. And the reste of the Defendantes to be freed of anie fyne or ymprisonmente. Dated at his Maties courte of castle Chamber the xxth daye of May 1612 and on the tenth yere of his maties Raigne of Englande, Fraunce & Ireland & of Scotlande the xlvth.[153]

Memorandum where his maties Learned Counsell this presente viijth Daie of May 1612 ore tenus made informacon in this moste honorable Courte of Castle Chamber against Peeter Larkyn, Edward Eustace, Martyn Foster, James Garlande, Patricke Cleere & Xpofer Whyte of the Citie of Dublin, merchants, that were amongest others ympannelled at a generall Cessions holden in the Tolsell of the Citie of Dublin the [blank] Daie of [blank] 161[?] before the mayor, Recorder & Sheriffe of the said

---

Citie for the true presentinge of all such Recusantes as did willfully & obstinately refuse to Come to thier severall parishe Churches to heare divine service accordinge to his maties lawes & statutes of this kingdome. And the said Peter Larkyn, Edward Eustace, Martyn Foster, James Garlande, Patricke Cleere and Xpofer Whyte with ten other persons of the said Citie of Dublin beinge sworne before the said Mayor, Recorder and Sheriffe to make true presentemente of all such Recusantes accordinge to such evidence as then should be geven unto them. Wherupon the ministers & Clearkes of Dublin were produced to deliver unto the said Jury in open Courte the names of all the Recusantes within their severall parishes in writinge that did obstinately and willfully refuse to Come to the Churche to heare devyne service upon the Sabothe Daye and other holy dayes, to which they were all severaly sworne before the said Jury that all the said persons soe named did not Come to their severall parishe Churches at any tyme to heare Divine service accordinge to the said lawes and statutes. Neverthelesse, the said Jury obstinately & willfully refused to presente the said Recusants or any one of them. Wherupon all the said Jury were severally examined by the said Recorder The Reason why they refused to make presentemente accordinge to thier evidence geven them, but the said Peter Larkyn, Edward Eustace, Martyn Foster, James Garlande, Patricke Cleere & Xpofer Whyte obstinately and willfully refused to ioyne with their fellowe Jurors in the same. Which said persons beinge questioned with all by this Courte Whye they refused to ioyne with their fellowe Jurors alledged vayne & idle excuses which this Courte did not allowe of, but absolutely reiected. Yt is therefore ordered, adiudged and Decreed by this moste honorable Courte for their said Contempte & willfull obstinacy in refuseinge to ioyne with the reste of their fellowe Jurors That the said Peter Larkyn, Edward Eustace, Martyn Foster, James Garlande, Patricke Cleere and Xpofer Whyte shall paye to his matie for a fyne eche of them the some of one hundred markes englishe a peece and ymprisonement Duringe the Lorde Deputies pleasure. Dated at his maties Courte of Castell Chamber the viijth daie of May 1612 and in the tenthe yeare of his maties Raigne of Englande, Fraunce and Irlande and of Scotlande the xlvth.[154]

Memorandum where Denys Byrne of the Citie of Dublin, merchante, exhibited Informacon in this honorable Courte of Castle Chamber against John Woolverston of Kylpoole in the county of Wyckelowe, gent, Edmond McCavenagh, Donogh OBroe, Edmond ODoran and Patricke Neveagh and divers others, beinge Riottouslely, routousely and unlawefully assembled the xvijth daie of Marche in the eight yeare of his Maties Raigne of Englande, Fraunce and Irelande, Came to the Towne and landes of Ballyneparke in the County of Wyckelowe, beinge the proper Inheritance of the said Denys Byrne and his Auncestors and in his quiet possesion, and then & there the said John Woolverston, Edmond McCavenagh and the reste before named and diverse others unknowen, riottousely, routousely & unlawefully did dryve and take away from the said Landes of Balleneparke the nomber of thyrtie Cowes, beinge the onely meanes and sustenance the poore tenants of the said Towne of Ballyneparke had to releeve themselfes. To which Informacon the said John Woolverston, Edmond McCavenagh, Donogh OBroe, Edmond ODoran and Patricke Neveagh made answer and the Cause proceedinge to Replicacon, Reioynder & witnesses examined on either parte and the Cause this Daie appointed to be hearde. Forasmuch as upon the full hearinge & deliberate discussinge of the said Cause yt manifestly appe[are]d to this Courte by the proofe of many witnesses that the said thyrtie Cowes were wrongefully taken and that by meanes therof diverse of the poore tenantes were in danger to be starved. Yt is therefore ordered, adiudged and decreed by this honorable Courte that the said John Woolverston shall pay to his matie for a fyne the some of tenne poundes harpes and the said Edmond McCavenagh, Donogh OBroe, Edmond ODoran & Patricke Neveagh shall eche of them paie fyve poundes harpes and all of them to be ymprisoned Duringe the Lorde Deputies pleasure. Dated at his maties Courte of Castle Chamber the xixth Daie of June 1612 and in the tenthe yeare of his maties Raigne of Englande, Fraunce and Irelande and of Scotlande the xlvth.[155]

Memorandum where Dermot McGylpatricke of Kylmacurragh in the county of Wyckelowe, gent, exhibited informacon in this most honorable Courte of Castle Chamber against John Woolverston of Kylpoole in the county of Wyckelowe, gent, Redmond McCavenagh, Morrough McShane and divers others that they the said John Woolverston, Edmond McCavenagh, Morrough McShane & the reste the tenthe daie of Julie in the ninthe yeare of the Raigne of our Soveraigne Lorde Kinge James of Englande, Fraunce & Ireland Came to the towne & Landes of Kylmacurragh and there finding diverse of the servantes of the said Dermot McGylpatricke, viz Hugh Moyle, Hugh McWiliam and James McDermot harroweinge a peece of the said Landes, beinge the said Dermottes lawefull Inheritance, the said John Woolverston, Edmond McCavenagh & Morrogh McShane, in riotouse and unlawefull maner, did not onely beate & evill intreate the said Hugh Moyle and the reste but alsoe forceably did take from the said persons all the Garrans & harrowes from the said Dermot McGylpatrickes servants and ledde them of[f] from the said Lande to a parcell of the said John Woolverstons owne lande, and there in riotouse & unlawefull manner Cutt in peeces all the harroweinge harnes and tooke and ledde away with them all the Garrans. To which Informacon the said John Woolverston, Edmond McCavenagh, Morogh McShane and the reste made answer And the Cause proceedinge to Replicacon, Reioynder & witnesses examined on either parte and the Cause this Daie appointed to be hearde. Forasmuch as upon full heareinge and Deliberate Discussinge of the Cause yt manifestely apperred by the testimony of diverse witnesses that the said John Woolverston, Edmond McCavenagh and Morrogh McShane were giltie of the misdemeanor in manner as in the informacon is layed downe. Yt is therefore ordered, aiudged and Decreed by this honorable Courte That the said John Woolverston shall paye to his matie for a fyne the some of fyve poundes Englishe, the said Edmond McCavenagh fortie shillinges englishe and the said Morrogh McShane twentie shillinges englishe, and all of them to be ymprisoned Duringe the Lorde Deputies pleasure. Dated at his Maties Courte of Castle Chamber the xiijth Daie of November 1612 and in the tenth yeare of his Maties Raigne of Englande, Fraunce & Irelande and of Scotlande the xlvjth.[156]

Memorandum where Sir John Davis, knight, his maties Attorney generall, exhibited Informacon in this most honorable Courte of Castle Chamber That where there issued a Comission under the great Seale of Irelande Directed to Nicholas Kenny, Esquier, his Maties Escheator within the province of Leynster, William Parsons, esquier, Surveyor generall of all his Maties Landes within the Realme of Irelande, Christopher Flattesbury, esquier, learned in the lawes, and William Crowe, Esqier, pregnitory [i.e. questioner] of his Maties Courte of Comen pleas in Irelande, or any two of them, Comissioners appointed to enquire what Landes tenements & hereditamentes were concealed and wrongefully withholden from his matie within the Countrey & territory of Imale in the County of Wyckelowe, which Comission by vertue of their said Comission directed their Warrant to the Sherif of the said County to geve warninge unto the gentlemen and freeholders of the said County to apper at the Towne of Bray in the said county of Wyckelowe on the xvth Daye of February in the eight yeare of his Maties Raigne of Englande, Fraunce & Irelande and of Scotlande the xliijth. At which daie and place the said Comissioners and the said gentlemen & freeholders did meete and the said Comissioners then & there satte in the execucon of their said Comission and haveinge called a Jury of the said gentlemen & freeholders & sworne them to enquire what landes, tenementes & hereditamentes were Concealed & wrongefully withholden from his Matie as alsoe of other matters concerninge his maties service, and Peter Delahyde, Esqier, Learned in the Lawes, beinge then appointed & ready to set forthe his Maties title to the saide Landes before the said Jury and many witnesses then & there produced to prove his maties title, aswell to the said Landes as for other matters conceringes [his] maties service, ready to Deliver their knowelage before the said Comissioners & Jury, Sir Richard Greame, knight, Thomas Greame, Marcus Greame, George Greame and diverse others, to the nomber of forty persons, haveinge a purpose & resolucon before hande to Crosse all proceedeinges of the said Comissioners in performance of the kinges Maties service, and alsoe to discouradge & discountenance aswell the said Learned Counsell produced to be there to sett forthe his Maties Right and title to the said concealed Landes, and alsoe all such witnesses as were produced to prove his maties said title. The said Sir Richard Greame, Thomas Greame, Marcus Greame, George Greame and the reste accordinge to their purpose & resolucon assembled themselfes togeither at Bray afforesaid the xvth Daie of Februrary in the year afforesaid in riotouse, routouse and warlicke maner, armed with swordes, daggers, peykes and other warlicke weapons, marched forward to the place where the Comissioners were then sittinge executinge his

156. ff. 188–88v. Note second appearance of Woolverston as defendant in property disputes in Co. Wicklow.

maties Comission, to the terror of the said Comissioners and other his Maties subiectes, and did then & there openly and publiquely before the said Comissioners & Jury geve very reprochefull, scandelous and threateninge speeches before the said Comission & Jury against the Credite of the said witnesses, Calleing them Company of Garran stealers & Rebelles, with many other Disdainfull and hatefull speeches and alsoe uttered verie foule & threateninge speeches to the said Peter Delahyde, that he would pull his bearde from his face and would make the hayer of the Crowne of his head fall to his nose. And not contented therwith, the said Thomas Greame the xvjth daie of February followeinge, with diverse other of that Riotouse Company, meeteinge with one of the said witnesses did riotousely and malicioiusely beate, batter & bruse him & after Drewe their swordes upon Charles Valentyne, gent, beinge one that attended his maties service in that Comission for rebukeinge the said Thomas Greame for streyking the said witnes. To which Informacon the said Sir Richard Greame, Thomas Greame & many of the reste made answer and the Cause proceedinge to Replicacon, Reioynder and witnesses on either parte examined and this Daye the Cause appointed to be hearde. Forasmuch as upon full heareinge & deliberate Discussinge of the Cause yt manifestely appeared by many witnesses that the said Sir Richard Greame and Thomas Greame Comitted the said misdemeanor in manner & forme as it is layed Downe in the Informacon. Yt is therefore ordered, adiudged and decreed by this most honorable Courte That the said Sir Richard Greame and Thomas Greame shall pay unto his matie for a fyne eache of them the some of tenne poundes a peece and ymprisonemente duringe the Lorde Deputies pleasure. Dated at his maties Courte of Castle Chamber the xxth daie of November 1612 and in the tenthe yeare of his maties Raigne of Englande, Fraunce and Irelande and of Scotlande the xlvjth.[157]

Memorandum where his Mates learned Counsell this prsente xxvth Daie of November 1612 ore tenus made Informacon in this moste honorable Courte of Castle Chamber against James Terrell of Castleloste, James Fitz Gerralde of Laghragh, Richard Terrell of Robinson, Hugh McEoghegan of Castleton, Olyver Tuyte of Sonogh, Richard Dalton of Malmaghan, William Gouldinge of Bealanston, Barnarde ODally of Kylkleagh, Wiliam FitzGerralde of Preiston, Olyver Tuyte of Ballybroughe, Redmond Dalton of ?Noghorad, Edmond OBrenan of Adamston, William Terrell of Ballynegall, Richard Nangle of Ballacrocky and James Browne of Ranaghan that were ympannelled and sworne of a Grande Jury at a generall Cessions holden at Mollyngar in the County of Westmeathe the xxjth of Auguste 1612 before Sir William Methwolde, knight, Lorde Cheef Barron of his Matie Courte of Exchequer in Irelande and Daniell Pecke, esquire, Justice of Assize for the said County for make[ing] true presentement of all such Recusants as willfully and obstinately refused to come to their severall parishe Churches to heare Divine service according to his Maties Lawes & statutes of his kingedome. Upon fower severall papers signed with the name of the said Daniell Pecke, one of the said Justice of Assize, testified by the oathe of fower severall persons, viz Thomas Kerly, James Byran, John Mentforde & Thomas Lyslee, that all the said persons nominated in the said severall papers did absente them selfes from hearinge divine service upon the Sabothe Daies and other holy daies in their severall parishe Churches accordinge to the said lawes and statutes, [formula E (our italics)] *in manifeste Contempte of their Duetie to his Matie and his highenes Lawes. Nevertheless, the said Jury willfully and obstinately refused to presente the said Recusantes or any one of them. And the said Jury beinge examined by John Beare, Esquire, his Maties Sergeant at lawes, by the appointement of this Courte they all confessed soe much as they were Charged with all upon the Informacon of his Maties learned Councell. And beinge asked the reasons why they soe refused to make presentement accordinge to their evidence, alledged vayne & idle excuses which this Courte did not allowe of but absolutely reiecte. Wherupon yt is ordered, adiudged and Decreed by this most honorable Courte for their said Contempte, Willfull obstinacy and misdemeanor in refusinge to make presentement accordinge to there evidence,* That the said James Terrell, beinge foreman of the said Jury, shall paye to his Matie for a

---

157. ff. 189–90. Postscript in different hand follows: 'John Hill for statte, Bee itt knowne unto all men by this present that I, Richard Hall of the Citty of Dublin, marchaunt, doth acknowleg my selfe to owe and to be justly Indebted unto William Jones of the same ye full and just Some of ten poundes star[ling], due to bee paide to the said Richard Hall the 14th of July 1634. [signed] Arthur Hall, Willm Usher, John Hill, Richard Right.' This shows the entry book was in use among conciliar records well after the final text written in 1620. Folio 190v is blank.

fyne the sume of one hundred poundes Englishe. And all the reste, viz James Fitz Gerralde, Richard Terrell, Hugh McEoghegan, Olyver Tuyte, Richard Dalton, William Gouldinge, Barnarde ODally, William FitzGerrolde, Olyver Tuyte, Redmond Dalton, Edmond OBrenan, William Terrell, Richard Nangle and James Browne shall likewise paie to his Matie for a fyne eache of them one hundred markes le peece like Englishe money and ymprisonemente duringe the Lorde Deputies pleasure. Dated at his Maties Courte of Castle Chamber the xxvth daie of November 1612 and in the tenthe yeare of his Maties Raigne of Englande, France & Irelande & of Scotlande the xlvjth.[158]

Memorandum where his Maties learned Councell this present xxvth Daie of November 1612 ore tenus made Informacon in this most honorable Courte of Castle Chamber against Edmond Butler of Cloghicullyn, Thomas Laffan of Greastowne, Thomas Butler of Garryarde, Peter Comyn of Kylbraigh, Jeffrey Mockeler of Ballynatten, Walter Prendergast of Freghans, Peter Stapleton of ?Garan Pyckard, Thomas Stapleton of Leanston, Donnell Oge Ohycky of Ballyconegan, James Butler of Drysseg, Beollagh McEgan of Shesherogh Kelly, William McEnchro of Cashell and Thomas Creagh of Cashell in the county of Crosse Typ[er]ary that were ympannelled & sworne of a Grande Jury at a generall Cessions holden at Cashel in the said County the vijth Daie of Julie 1611 before Sir Nicholas Walshe, knight, Lorde Cheef Justice of his Maties Courte of Comen Pleas, and John Beere, Esquire, his Maties Seriant at Lawes within the Realme of Irelande, Justice of Assize within the said Coun[ty], to make true presentemente of all such Recusants as willfully & obstinately refused to Come to their parishe Churche upon the Sabothe Daies & other holly daies to heare Divine service accordinge to his Maties lawes & statutes of this kingedome. Whereupon the names of soe many persons as did absente themselfes from their parishe Church on the said Daies to heare Divine service accordinge to the said lawes & statutes were Delivered unto the said Jury under the hande writinge of Christopher Flangan, Curate of the parishe Church of St Johnes in Cashell, and testified by the said Christofer Flangan before the said John Beere, and the same Certified by the said John Beere unto the said Jury that all the said persons did absente themselfes from their said parishe Churche on the Sabbothe Daies and other holy Daies accordinge to the said lawes and statutes, [see formula E, fol. 191] ... the said Edmond Butler and Jeffrey Mockeler, beinge the principall leaders and inducers of the reste, shall paie to his Matie for a fyne eache of them the sume of fortie poundes Englishe a peece, and the reste, viz Thomas Laffan, Thomas Butler, Peter Comyn, Walter Prendergaste, Peter Stapleton, Thomas Stapleton, Donell Oge OHycky, James Butler, Beolagh McEgan, William McEnchro and Thomas Creagh shall likewise paie to his Matie for a fyne eache of them thyrtie poundes le peece like Englishe money and all of them to be ymprisoned duringe the lorde deputies pleasure. Dated at his Maties Courte of Castle Chamber the xxvth daie of November 1612 and in the tenthe yeare of his Maties Raigne of Englande, France and Irelande and of Scotlande the xlvjth.[159]

Memorandum where his maties learned Councell this presente xxvth Daie of November 1612 ore tenus made Informacon in this moste honorable Courte of Castle Chamber against Robert Plunket of Posickeston, Gerrald Cruice of Bryttas, Richard Balfe of Cregge, and Gerralde Lynce of Kylmorre in the county of Meathe that were amongest others ympanelled at a generall Cessions holden at Tryme in the said County the xjth Daie of Auguste 1612 before Sir William Methwolde, knight, Lorde Cheef Barron of his Maties Courte of Exchequer in Irelande, and Daniell Pecke, Esquire, Justice of Assize for that County, to make true presentemente of all such Recusantes as willfully & obstinately refused to come to their severall parishe Churches upon the sabothe Daies and other holy daies to heare Divine service accordinge to his Maties lawes & statutes of this kingdome and the said Robert Plunket, Gerralde Cruice, Richard Balfe and Gerralde Lynce with ten other persons of the said County beinge sworne before the said Lorde Cheef Baron and Daniell Pecke to make true presentemente of all suche Recusantes accordinge to suche evidence as then should be geven unto them. Wherupon Myles Pemerton, Curate of the parishes of Clone & Castleryckard in the said

158. f. 191. Italicized phrasing is used below as a formula in similar cases, rehearsed by the clerk for ease of record-keeping and devoid of any references to particular cases or litigants.
159. f. 192.

County, Delivered the names of one hundered persons at the leaste within the said two parishes in writinge under his hande unto the said Daniell Pecke, one of the said Justices, & testified the same by oathe that not any one of the said persons did resorte to their parishe Churches on the Sabothe Daies or other holly daies to heare Divine service accordinge to the said lawes & statutes, which names in writinge the said Daniell Pecke did under his hande Certifie to the said Jury. Nevertheless, the said Jury willfully & obstinately refused to presente the said Recusantes or any of them. Wherupon all the said Jury were severally examined by the said Justice the Reasons why they refused to make presentement accordinge to their evidence geven them upon which their examinacon eleven of the said Jurors were agreed to make presentement accordinge to their evidence geven them. But the said Robert Plunket, Gerralde Cruice, Richard Balfe & Gerralde Lynce willfully and obstinately refused to ioyne in the same. Which said persons beinge by the appointemente of this Courte firste examined by John Beere, Esquier, his Mates seriante at lawes and after questioned withall by this Courte could alledge nothinge in their excuse but that they knewe not soe much as the reste of the said Jury did. Wherupon the Courte proceedinge to Censure yt was ordered adiudged and Decreed by this honorable Courte That the said Robert Plunket, Gerralde Cruice, Richard Balfe and Gerralde Lynce shall eache of them paye to his Matie for a fyne the sume of Twentie poundes Englishe a peece and ymprisonmente duringe the Lorde Deputies pleasure. Dated at his Maies Courte of Castle Chamber the xxvth Daie of November 1612 in the tenthe yeare of his maties Raigne of Englande, France & Irelande and of Scotlande the xlvjth.[160]

Memorandum where Walter French of the towne of Galway, esquier, exhibited information into this most honnorable Court of Castle chamber that, on the xvijth Daye of October 1611 and in the ixth yeare of his Maties raigne of England, Fraunce and Ireland and of Scotland the xlvth, that Domynick Browne of the said Towne, marchant, Ambrose Bodkyne of the same, merchant, Richard Oge Bourcke, Gilly Duffe OCullene, Neale McClanchye, Melaghlyn McGillernowe and Teige O Molcloghye, being Ryotously, Routously and unlawfully assembled the Daye and yeare aforesaid, came to a wast [?i.e wasteland], Chappell, Hamlett and Lands called and knowne by the name of Cowlrahan in the Countie of Galway, and being soe assembled, came uppon the said Lands of Cowlrahan being in the plantiffs quiet and peaceable possession and did enter uppon the said Landes and Did put uppon the same foure score Cowes and oxen of the said Domynick Brownes and there Riottously and forceably kept uppon the said Land the said Cattle for Divers Dayes together in Ryottouse and forceable manner, and many other misdemeanors the said Domynick Browne and the rest of the said Riottouse personnes Comitted. Uppon which information the said Domynick Brown and the rest weare called to annswere and the cause proceeding to replycation, reioinder and wittnesses examened on either parte and the Cause this Daye appointed to be heard. For asmuch as uppon full hearing and Delyberatte Discussinge of the Cause yt manyfestly appeared unto this court that the said Domynick Browne and all the rest of the Defendantes Comitted the Ryott and misdemenaor thej weare Chardged withall. Yt is therefore ordered, adiudged and decreed by this honnorable Court that the said Domynick Browne, being the principall offendor, shall pay to his matie for a fyne the some of one hundred powndes and Imprysonment During the lo Deputies pleasure. The said Ambrose Bodkyn, Rickard Oge Bourck, Gilly Duffe OCullenan, Neale McClanchye, Melaghlin McCullernowe and Teige OMolcloghye shall lickwise paye unto his matie for a fyne each of them ten poundes a peece and Imprisonment Duryng the Lo Deputies pleasure. Dated at his maties Court of Castle Chamber the last Day of Aprill 1613 in the xjth yeare of his Maties Raigne of England, Fraunce and Ireland and of Scotland the xlvjth.[161]

Memorandum where his maties learned Councell this present vijth day of Maye 1613 ore tenus made information in this most honnorable Court of Castle Chamber against James Braye, William Brenock, Waler OMulryan and Thomas White of the Towne of Clonmell in the County of the liberty of Tipperarye that weare amongst others ympanelled and sworne at a generall Cessions holden at the said Towne of Clonmell in the said County the xxijth Day of February 1612 before Sir William Methwold, knight, lord Chiefe Barron of his maties Court of Exchecquer and Garrald

160. f. 193.   161. f. 194.

Loather, esquier, one of the Justices of his highnes Court of Comon Pleas, Justice of assize for the said County, to make true presentment of all such Recusantes as willfully and obstinately refused to Repaire to their severall parish Churches to heare Devyne service according to his maties lawes and statutes of this kingdome. Whereuppon a list of all the names of the inhabitantes of the Towne of Clonmell was sent unto them by the said Justices of assize, Testified by the oath of the Mynister of the parishe before them, that all the personnes therein mencioned weare recusants and had not repaired to their parish Church sithence the last former Cessions holden for that County. Nevertheles, the said Jurie, Contrary to their evidence, willfully and obstinatly refused to present the said recusantes or any of them, and being examined by the said Justice the Reasons whye they soe refused uppon which examenation the whole Jurie savinge the said Braye, Brenock, OMulryan and White weare agreed to make presentment according to their evidence given them. But the said Braye, Brenock, OMulryan and White willfully and obstinately refused to Joine with the rest of their felow jurors, which said personnes being by the appointment of this Court examined by John Beare, Esquier, his maties sergeant at lawes and after questioned withall by this Courte Could aleadge nothing for their excuse but that yt was against their Conscience. Whereuppon the Courte proceedinge to Censure yt was ordered, adiudged and Decreede by this honnorable Court that the said James Braye, Wiliam Brenock, Walter OMulryan and Thomas White shall pay to his matie for a fyne each of them the some of fortie powndes english apeece and Imprisonment During the Lo Deputies pleasure. Dated at Dublin the said vijth day of Maye 1613 and the eleventh yeare of his maties Raigne of England, Fraunce and Ireland and of Scotland the xlvjth.[162]

Memorandum where this present vijth Day of May 1613 his maties learned Councell ore tenus made information in this most honnorable court of Castle Chamber against Pierce Butler of Knockgrafond, Richard Purcell of Loghmoy, John Tobin of Killagh, John Purcell of Aghboye, John Keating of Nicholstowne, Cahir OMulryan of Kilnecappagh, John Fanynge of Farrynory, Rowry OKenedy of Ballynecloghy, Richard Wall of Magyenstowne, Phillip English of Boulraganran, Phillipp Hackett of Sherrifestown, and Phillip Travers of Kyedragh in the County of the liberty of Tipperarye that weare ympaneled and sworne of a grand Jury at a generall Cessions holden at Clonmell in the County of the liberty of Tipperarye the xxijth day of February viz before Sir Wylliam Methwold, knight, Chiefe Barron of his maiesties Court of exchecquer, and Garrald Loather, esquier, one of his maiesties Justice of his highnes Court of Comon Pleas, Justice of Assize for the said County, to make true presentment of all such Recusantes as wilfully and obstinatly refused to repaire to their parish Churches to heare Devyne service according to his maties Lawes and statutes of this kingdom. [Upon fower severall papers] signed by one Dybsall, a minister, that Divers of the parishioners of Lisronagh in the said County had not repaired to their parish Churches sithence the last former generall Cessiones holden for that County … [see formula E, f. 191] … the said Pierce Butler, Richard Purcell and John Tobin shall pay to his maiestie for a fyne ech of them two hundred powndes english a peece and ymprisonment during the lo Deputyes pleasure, and the rest, viz John Purcell, John Keating, Cahir OMulryan, John Fanyng, Rorye OKenedye, Richard Wall, Phillipp English, Phillip Hackett and Phillipp Travers shall paye to his matie for a fyne each of them the sume of fortye powndes english a peace and ymprisonment during the lo Deputies pleasure. Dated the said vijth day of Maye 1613 and in the xjth yeare of his maties Raigne of England, Fraunce and Irland and of Scotland the xlvjth.

Memorandum where his maties learned Councell this present xiiijth day of Maye 1613 ore tenus made information into this most honnorable Court of Castle Chamber against Calaghan McCroghor OCalaghan of Clonyne, Donnell McTeige Carte of Dysert, Owen McDonogh of BallyMcMuragh and Donnell McDonnogh Sassynagh of Twonagh in the county of Cork that weare amongst others ympanelled and sworn at a generall Cessions holden at Corcke the [blank] of [blank] before Sir William Methwoold, knight, Lo Chief Barron of his maties Court of exchecquer, and Garald Loather, esqr, one of the Justices of his highnes Court of Comon pleas, Justice of Assize for that County, uppon the tryall of Con McCahir then indicted and araigned fo the Robbyng of Thomas

162. f. 195.

Andrewe. Uppon which tryall all the said Jurors except the said Callaghan McConnor OCallaghan, Donnell McTeige Carty, Owen McDonough and Donell McDonnogh Sassynagh weare agreed to fynd the said Con McCahir guilty of the said Robbery. Nevertheles the said O Callaghan, Donell McTeige Carty, Owen McDonogh and Donell McDonogh Sassynagh most obstinatly and willfully refused to ioyne with their fellowe Jurors to fynde the said Con McCahir guilty of the said Robbery, and beinge examyned aswel by his maties learned Councell by the appointment of this court as alsoe by this Court the Reasons whye they refused to ioyne with their fellowe Jurors had noe excuse or any answere to make but that yt was against their Conscience. Where uppon the Courte proceeding to censure [it] was ordered, adiudged & decreed that the said Callaghan McConnor OCallaghan, Donell McTeige Carty, Owen McDonnogh and Donnell McDonogh Sassaynagh shall paj to his matie for a fyne each of them the some of fortie powndes a peece and ymprisonment during the lo Deputies pleasure dated at his maties Court of Castle Chamber the said xiiijth day of May 1613 and in the xjth yeare of his maties raigne of England, Fraunce and Ireland and of Scotland the xlvjth.[163]

Memorandum where Sir Edward Brabazon, knight, one of his maties privije Councell within this kingdome of Ireland exhibited information into this most honnorable Court of Castle Chamber against John Cage of the Cittie of Dublin, marchant, that notwithstanding the said Cage well knowing the said Sir Edward Brabazon to be a privie Councellor in this kingdome, not having the feare of god before his eyes nor yet regarding his maiesties lawes and statues of force in this kingdome against the Telling, publishing or conterfeyting of any false newes and tales, whereby Discord or matter of Discord or slander might growe betweene his matie and his lyege people or the greate men of this Realme, and against the Conterfeytes of horryble and false lyes of prelattes, Dukes, Earles, Barrons and other nobles and greate men of the Realme, and alsoe of the Chauncellor, Treasourer, Clearke of the privye seale, Steward of the kinges house, Justice of those benches and thother, and of other greate officers of the realme, of thinges which by the said prelates, lords, nobles and officers aforesaid weare never spoken, touched nor thought, to the slander of the said prelates lords and officers, whereof Discord or any slander might aryse within this Realme, nor yet regarding of a privy Councellor whereunto the said Sir Edward Brabazon was by his maiestie called unto; Butt, in manyfest scorne and contempt of the same, the thirtieth day of Januarij in the tenth yeare of his maiesties raigne of England, Fraunce and Ireland, and sithence his maiesties generall pardon at Dublin in the Countie of the Cittie of Dublin, the said John Cage did most maliciously, falselie, scandalouslie and contemptouslye in the prsence of Divers of his maiesties faythfull subiects, Chardge the said Sir Edward Brabazon to his face that hee, the said Sir Edward Brabazon, did seeke greedyly, unlawfully and covetously to gaine to himselfe the goodes of one Lawrence Clearck, whoe was then flede for Debt, which the said Cage then aleaged was more then the said Sir Edward Brabazon could doe by lawe. And said further that the said Sir Edward, perceaving the same, did invite the lord Chauncellor to his house of purpose to make good a seizure that the said Cage did falsly affirme that the said Sir Edward had made of the said goods. And the said Cage did then and there, in contemptouse and scorneful manner, putt on his hatte before the said Sir Edward Brabazon, that hee did not owe him any respect, and the said Cage said further that hee did keepe as good men as the said Sir Edward Brabazon was, and the said John Cage afterwards (that is to say the last day of Januarij in the said tenth yeare of his maiesties Raigne of England, Fraunce and Irland), Continuying his said malicious and ungodly purpose falslye [and] maliciously to traduce and scandalize the said Sir Edward Brabazon, and of purpose to make the said Sir Edward hatefull both to his matie and generally to all his highnes subiects in this kingdome of Ireland, at Dublin in the Countie of the said Citie of Dublin in the hearing of Sir James Carroll, knight, mayor of the said Cittie, and of Sir James Hamelton, knight, one of his maties privije Councell in this kingdome, did againe falsfly, maliciouselye and slanderouslye publish and speacke of the said Sir Edward Brabazon these wordes following, viz that the said Sir Edward Brabazon had staied and seized certaine goodes of one Lawrence Clearck, beinge fled for Debt as a fugitive, but had don it to his owne use, and that hee had made a coulor or pretence to seize the said goodes for the king but wold gaine the same to himself greedyly and Covetouslie, which was more then hee Could Doe by lawe. And that the said Sir Edward, fynding that his owne warrant was not good and that hee had comitted such an error as hee

163. f. 197. Fol. 197v is blank.

cold not Aunswer, did seeke to thrust it uppon the lord Chauncellor, and that the said Sir Edward had invited his lordship to his howse of purpose to make good what the said Sir Edward had don therin. And the said Cage did then and there further likewise affirme that hee respected not the said Sir Edward Brabazon, and then said John Cage did alsoe further publish, affirme and saye in the presence of the said mayor and Sir James Hamelton and of Divers others that hee had kept as good gentlemen for his men as the said Sir Edward Brabazon then was. And further did publish, affirme and saye in the presence of the said mayor and Sir James Hamelton and divers others that the said Sir Edwrd Brabazon was neither a worthy knight nor a worthye gentleman, and that it was greate pittye hee or the like of him should be suffered to live in a kingdome. And the said Cage then being tould by the said mayor that his speeches weare very unfitt to be spoken of one of his maties privij Councell, and that yf the said Sir Edward Brabazon had don him wronge hee might have complained to the Lord Deputy and Councell, the said Cage aunswered that hee shold have had much Remedy there, hee should have ben Laughed at for his labour. To which information the said Cage made aunswere and wittnesses exameined on eyther parte and the cause this Day apointed to be heard for as much as uppon full hearing and Deliberate Discussing of the cause it manyfestly appeared unto the court by the Deposicions of divers substantiall wittnesses that the said Cage had published, affirmed and spoken all the said scandalous, malicious and Contempttouse speeches against the said Sir Edward Brabazon, in manner and forme according as in the said information is laied downe. It is therefore ordered, adiudged and Decreed by this honnorable Court that the said John Cage for his said offence and misdemeanor shall pay to his maiestie for a fyne the some of two hundred pownds english, ymprisonment during the lo Deputies pleasure, and shall alsoe make publique submision in this Court aswell to the said Sir Edward Brabazon, acknowledging his offence and misdemenor committed against him, as alsoe his offence Comitted against the lord Chauncellor and the lord Deputie and state in this kingdome. Dated at his maiesties Court of Castle chamber the eleventh Day of February 1613 and in the eleventh yeare of his maties raigne of England, Fraunce and Ireland and of Scotland the xlvijth.[164]

Memorandum where his maties Learned Councell ore tenus made information in this his maties most honnorable Courte of Castle Chamber against Thomas Gernon, James McMahowne, Hugh Oge ODuffye, Con McHugh McMahowne, Con McRoarye McMahowne, John McCollo McMaghowne and James Flemyng of the Countie of Monoghane that weare amongst others ympanelled and sworne at a generall Cesiones holden in the said Countie of Monoghan the xvjth Day of March 1613 before Sir Willm Methwold, knight, Lo Chieffe Barron of his maties Courte of eschequier, and Wyllm Sparke, esquier, one of the Justices of his maties Chieffe place, Justices of Assize for the said Countie, to make true presentment of all such Recusantes as willfully and obstinatly refused to repaire to their severall parish Churches to heare Devyne service according to his maties lawes and statutes of this kingdom. Whereupon a lyst of names weare Delivered unto the said Jurors of soundry inhabitantes within the said Countye by the said Justices and Testifyed by the oath of the mynisters of the severall parishes within the said Countie that all the personnes in the said lyst mencioned were recusants, absenting themselves from their parish Churches. Nevertheles the said Jurie, Contrary to their evidence, wilfully and obstintly refused to present the said Recusants or any of them … [see formula E, f. 191] [therefore it was ordered] and Decreed by this honorable Court that the said Thomas Gernon, being the pryncypall leader and inducer of the rest of the said Jury not to present the said recusants, shall pay to his matie for A fyne the some of twentie poundes english money. All the rest, viz James McMaghowne, Hugh Oge ODuffy, Con McHugh McMaghowne, Con McRorye McMaghowne, John McCollo McMaghowne and James Flemynge shall each of them pay to his matie for a fyne the some of five powndes ir[ish] and all of them ymprisonment durng the lls Justices pleasure. Dated at his maties Courte of Castle Chamber the xxth Day of May 1614 and in the xijth yeare of his maties Raigne of England, France and Ireland and of Scotland the xlvijth.[165]

Md where Edmond Conyain of Conyainstowne in the County of Wycklowe, gent, made information into this most honnorable Courte of Castle Chamber that, on the xxvjthe Daye of May 1612 in the

---

xth yeare of his maties raigne of England, France and Ireland, and of Scotland the xlvth, Cahir McMorogh Byrne of Kilcolman, gentlman, Donough Oge OCullen of the same, Callough McEdmond Oge OByrne of the same, Teige OByrne, Bryen McDonnough and Divers others Ryotousle and Disorderly persones being unlawfully assembled together came to our parcell of land of Conyainstowne aforesaid where one Donell Duffe and Wyllm Roe, servantes to the said Edmond Conyain, weare plowing, and then and there the said Cahir and the rest of the said Ryotouse Company forceably put the said Donell Duffe and Willm Roe from the plowing the said land and threatened them that yf they should offer to plowe the said land any more they should be well beaten. And not there with Content, the said Cahir and the rest came to the said Landes the xxvijth Day of the said Moneth and used the like force and threatnyng to the said Duffe and Roe which were plowing the said land and put them from plowing againe, and not therewith content the said Cahir and the rest of his said Company came uppon the said land the viijth Daye of June in the yeare aforesaid of purpose to Disturbe the said plowemen that were then plowing uppon the said land, which viijth Day the said Edmond Conyan was then uppon the said land, and hearing the said Cahir Comaunde some of the said Ryotouse Company to goe stopp the guying? of the said plowe, the said Conyan forbad them soe to Doe. Whereuppon the said Cahir went to the said Edmond Conyan and tooke hold of him and pluckt away his Cloake from him and wrapt the same about his lefte arme and presently drewe his sworde and assaulted the said Edmond and wounded him in his left Arme. And in the tyme of the said Cahir his assault, the said Donnogh Oge O Cullen and Callough McEdmond Boye O Byrne struke the said Edmond Conyan behinde on his back. Uppon which Information the said Cahir and the Rest were Called to aunswere and wittnesses examyned and the Cause this Day appoynted to be heard. Forasmuch as uppon full hearing and Discussing the cause yt appeared unto this Court by many Deposityons that the said Cahir and the rest had Comitted the said Ryotte and Misdemeanor in manner and forme as it is layed Downe in the informacon. Yt is therefore ordered, adiudged and decreed by this most honnorable court that the said Cahir McMorrough O Byrne shall pay to his matie for a fyne the some of ten poundes, the said Donogh Oge OCullen and Callough McEdmond Oge OByrne each of them five powndes apeece, and the said Bryen McDonnough five markes, and ymprysonment during the lls Justices pleasure. Dated at his maties Court of Castle Chamber the third day of June 1614 in the xijth yeare of his maties raigne of England, France and Ireland and of Scotland the xlvijth.[166]

Memorandum wheare his maties learned Councell ore tenus made informacon in this most honnorable Court of Castle Chamber against Gerald OFerrall, Edmond OFerrall, Conell OFerrall of Tyrilicken, Donell OFerrall of Bealclare, Murogh OFerrall, John OFerrall, Teige McCommicke, Edmond McComicke, Terlagh OFerall, Edmonde OFerrall, Gerrald OFerrall of Gurtamoylan, Hubart OFerrall, Charles OFerrall, James OFerrall, Patricke McKedaugh, Donell OFerrall and Rory McTerlaugh of the County of Longford That were ympaneld and sworne at a generall cessyons holden in the said County the xxviijth day of August 1614 before Christopher Sybthorpe and Willm Sparke, esquiers, two of the Justices of his Mate Chieffe bench, Justices of assize for the said County of Longford, to make true presentment of all recusantes as willfully and obstynatly Refused to repayre to their severall parishe Churches uppon the saboath dayes and other holy Dayes to heare Devyne service accordinge to his maties lawes and Statutes of this kingdome, [see formula E, f. 191] ... for their offence they shojld each pay a fine of xx li a peece and imprisonment during the lord deputies pleasure. Dated at his maties Court of Castle Chamber xvjth day of November 1614 and in the xijth yeare of the kinges maties raigne of England, Fraunce and Ireland and of Scotland the xlviijth.[167]

Memorandum wheare his maties learned Councell ore tenus made informacon in this most honnorable Courte of Castle Chamber agaynst Willm OFerrall, Lysaugh OFerrall and Edmond Nugent of the County of Longford that were amongst others ympannelled and sworne at a generall cessyons holden in the said County the xxviijth day of August 1614 before Christopher Sybthorpe and Willm Sparke, esquiers, two of the Justices of his Maties Cheiffe bench, Justices of assize for the

166. f. 201.   167. f. 202.

said County of Longford, to make true presentment of all such recusantes as willfully and obstinately refused to repayre to their parishe Churches uppon the saboath daye and other holy dayes to heare devyne service according to the lawes and Statutes of this kingdome, [see formula E, f. 191] Wheruppon the said Jury were severally examined by the said Justices the Reasons why they refused to make presentment accordinge to their evydence geven them. Uppon which their examynacons, eleven of the said Jury Confesed they were agreed to make presentment accordinge to their evydence, but the said Willm OFerrall, Lysaugh OFerrall, and Edmond Nugent willfully and obstinately refused to ioyne in the same, and beinge examyned by his maties sergeant at lawes by order of this Court the reasons why they refused to Joyne with their fellow Jurors, as alsoe questyoned withall by this Court uppon hearinge the Cause, Could make noe other aunsweare [or] excuse but that it was against their Conscience, and the said Edmond Nugent further said that what he did was well don. Wheruppon the Court proceadinge to censure yt was ordered, adiudged and Decreed by this honnorable Courte that the said Willm OFerrall and Lysaugh OFerrall shall pay to his matie for a fyne each of them the some of twenty poundes a peec, and ymprisonment duringe the Lord Deputyes pleasure. And that the said Edmond Nugent for his Contemptues and insolent speeches in the face of the Court shall pay to his Matie for a fyne the some of forty poundes, and Comytted Close prisoner Duringe the Lo Deputies pleasure. Dated at his maties Court of Castle Chamber the xvjth day of November 1614 and in the xijth yeare of his maties raigne of England, France and Ireland and Scotland.[168]

Memorandum wheare his maties learned Councell ore tenus made informacon in this most honnorable Courte of Castle Chamber against Richard Rath, Edward Hollywood, James Taaffe, Thomas Taaffe, Allexander Pluncket, Roger Chamberlayne and Christopher White of the County of Looth that were amongst others ympanneled and sworne at a generall sessyon holden in the said County the fyfte of August 1614 before Wyllm Methwoold, knight, Cheiffe Barron of his maties Courte of exchequier and Sir John Ellyot, knight, one of the Barrons of the said exchequier, to make true presentment of all such recusants as willfully and obstinately refused to repayre to their severall parishe Churches uppon sondayes and other holy dayes to heare Devyne service according to the lawes and statutes of this kingdome, [see formula E, f. 191] Whereuppon the whole Jury beinge severally examined by the said Justices the Reasons why they refused to make presentment accordinge to their evydence geven them uppon which examynacons nyne of the said Jury confessed they were agreed to make presentment accordinge to their evydence, but the sayd Richard Rath, Edward Hollywood, James Taafe, Thomas Taafe, Allexander Pluncket, Roger Chamberlayne and Christopher White willflly and obstynately refused to Joyne in the same and beinge examyned by his maties sergeant at lawes by order of this Courte the reasons why they refused to Joyne with thier fellow Jurors, as alsoe beinge questyoned by this Courte whye they would not Joyne with their fellowes haveinge such pregnant and apparrant evydence, Could make noe other answer or excuse but that it was against their Conscience. Wheruppon the Courte proceedinge to censure yt is ordered, adiudged and Decreed by this honnorable Courte that the said Richard Rath and all the above named pesons shall paye each of them to his matie for a fyne the some of forty poundes and ymnprisonment duringe the Lord Deputies pleasure. Dated at his maties Courte of Castle Chamber the xviijth daye of November 1614 and in the xijth yeare of his maties raigne of England, France and Ireland and of Scotland the xlviijth.[169]

Memorandum wheare his maties learned Councell ore tenus made informacon in this most honnorable Courte of Castle Chamber against John Allen, late high sheriffe of the County of Wexford, that he beinge specially Comanded by the Justices of Asize at a generall cessyons holden in the said County this last sommer assizes 1614 to execute a prisoner then Condempned to Dye without any intermission or delaye of tyme, nevertheles the said John Allen, contrarye to the speciall charge geven, of his owne voluntarye Disposytion Did reprive the said prisoner the space of six Dayes after the Comaundement geven him, haveynge no warrant for the same. And beinge Called to Annswer his said Contempt and misdemeanor, [he] Could not Deny the repryvinge of the said

---

168. f. 203. Fol. 203v is blank.   169. f. 204. Fol. 204v is blank.

prisoner. Wheruppon the Court proceedinge to censure yt is ordered, adiudged and decreed by this honnorable Courte that the said John Allen shall pay to his matie for a fyne the some of twenty poundes and ymprisonment duringe the Lo Deputyes pleasure. Dated at his maties Court of Castle Chamber the xxvth day of November 1614 in the xijth yeare of his maties raigne of England, France and Ireland and of Scotland the xlviijth.[170]

Memorandum wheare his matie learned Councell made Inform[ation] ore tenus in this most honnorable Court of Castle Chamber against Henry Breerton, Barnaby FitzPatricke, esquiers, John Moore, Walter FitzGerrald, Hugh Dempsie, Theobald Butler, Walter Grace, Allexander Donell, Patricke Forstall, Donell McNeale, Donell FitzPatricke and Roger Dongon that were ympannelled and sworne at a generall Cessions and Geale Delivery holden att Marriborogh in the Queenes County the [blank] daye of 161[blank] before [blank] then Justice of Assize for the triall of Geffery Keating, then indicted and arraigned of Treason for the trayterouse Releavinge of Piers Keatinge, a notorious traytor, for the wilfull Murtheringe of Henry Davells, esquier, his maties loyall and fathfull subiect. Uppon which arraignment of the said Geffery Keatinge, three severall witnesses were produced which did manifestly and directly prove in open Court that the said Geffery Keatinge had releived the said Piers Keatinge. Nevertheles the said Henry Breerton, Barnaby FitzPatricke, John Moore and the rest of the afornamed Jurors, most Corruptly and Contrary to their Direct evydence, did acquit the said Geffery Keatinge of the said treason. Wheruppon the said Justices of Assize bound over all the said Jurors to appeare in this honnorable Court of Castle Chamber to annswer their Contempt and misdemeanor, which said persons were severally examyned by his maties sergeant at law and uppon their examynacon Confessed the materiall Contentes of their evidence to be true, which was then shewed againe to them in writinge. Upon which confession the Court proceeded [to] Censure and theruppon it was this day ordered, adiudged [and decreed] by this most honnorable Courte that the said Henry Breerton, Barnaby FitzPatricke, John Moore, Walter FitzGerrald, Hugh Dempsie, Theobald Butler, Walter Grace, Allexander Donell, Patricke Forstall, Donell McNeale, Donell FitzPatricke and Roger Dongan shall pay unto his matie for a fyne accordinge to the Reducement each of them the some of three poundes le peece, and ymprisonment Duringe the lo Deputyes pleasure. Dated at his maties Court of castle Chamber the fift day of May 1615 and in the xijth yeare of his maties Raigne of England, Fraunce and Ireland and of Scotland the xlviijth.[171]

Memorand wheare Informacon was exhibited into his maties most honorable Court of Castle Chamber by Sir Robert Jacob, knight, his maties Soliciter, against Walter Barnwell, Edward Pentney, Willm Betagh, Thomas Plunckett, Christopher Barnwell, Patricke Barnwell, Edward Flemynge, John Flemynge, David Russell, Peter Dyllon, Thomas Pluncket and Henry Crompe that they beinge ympannelled and sworne uppon the tryall of a travers in his maties Cheife bench wihin the County of the Cittie of Dublin between the kinges matie and John Darcy, John Warrynge, Robert Everard, Edmond Mannynge, Willm Delahide, Patricke Begg, James Cusacke, Richard Read, Thomas Read and Thomas Neterville of the County of Meath, beinge Indicted for hearinge a Masse at the Navan in the said County of Meath the xxviijth day of July in the nynth yeare of his maties raigne of England, Fraunce and Ireland. Uppon tryall of which travers many witnesses were produced in open Court proveing manifestly and apparantly that all the said personnes with a multitude of other personns, both men and women, to bee present and at the hearinge of the said masse in the said towne of Navan the day and yeare aforesaid, and sayd and Celebrated by one Richard Mysset, a Popish Priest. Neverthe[le]sse, the said Walter Barnwell, Edwrd Pentney, Willm Betagh and the rest of the said Jury, Contrary to direct evydence given them, did Corruptly and unlawfully acquit the said John Darcy, John Warrynge, Robert Everard, Edmond Mannynge, Willm Delahide, Patricke Bege, James Cusacke, Richard Read, Thomas Read and Thomas Netervil of hearinge the said Masse, wherin they and everey of them Comitted most wilfull and Corrupt periurye and Mysdemeanor. Wheruppon the Court proceedinge to Censure yt was this Day ordered, adiudged and Decreed by this honnorable Court that the said Walter Barnwell, Edward Pentney, Wilm Betagh, Thomas

170. f. 205. Fol. 205v is blank. The prisoner in question was unnamed and the charge not identified.
171. f. 206.

Plunckett, Christopher Barnwell, Patricke Barnwell, Edward Flemynge, John Flemynge, Davyd Russell, Peter Dyllon, Thoms Plunckete and Henry Crompe shall each of them paye to his matie for a fyne the some of three poundes a peece, and ymprisonment durynge the lo Deputyes pleasure. Dated at his maties Court of Castle Chamber the vth day of May 1615 in the xiijth yeare of his maties Raigne of England, France and Ireland and of Scotland the xlviijth.[172]

Memorand wheare his maties learned Councell ore tenus made Informacon in thes most honnorable Court of Castle Chamber against Patricke Aylmer, Nicholas Conway, Allexander Eustace, Nicholas Woulfe, Gerrald Wesley, Patricke Sanders, Thomas Ash Fites[Fitz]Edward and Garrald FitzGarrald of the County of Kildare that were amongst others ympannelled and sworne att a generall Cessions holden in the said County the nynteenth day of August 1615 before William Methwoold, knight, Cheife Barron of his maties Court of Exchequier, and Peter Palmer, esquier, one of the Justices of his highnes Court of Common pleas, Justices of Assize for the said County to make true presentment of all such Recusantes as willfully and obst[in]ately refused to repaire to their severall parish Churches upon Sondayes and other holy dayes to heare Divyne service accordinge to the lawes and statutes of this kingdome. Wheruppon there was Delyvred unto the said Jury a lyst of names in writinge [see formula E, f. 191] Wheruppon the whole Jury beinge severally examyned by the said Justices the Reasons why they refused to make presentment accordinge to their evydence given them, uppon which examynacones the rest of the Jury Confessed they were agreed to make presentment accordinge to their evidence. But the said Patrick Aylmer, Nicholas Conway, Allexander Eustace, Nicholas Woulfe, Gerrald Wesley, Patricke Sanders, Thomas Ash FitzEdward and Garrald Fitz Garrald willfully and obstinatly refused to joyne in the same and beinge examyned by his maties Sergeant at law by order of this court the reasons why they refused to Joyne with their fellowes, haveinge such pregnant and apparrant evidence, As allsoe beinge questioned by this Court why they refused to Joyne with their fellow Jurors, Could make noe other aunswer or excuse but that it was against thier Conscience. Wherupon the Court proceeding to Censure [see formula E, f. 191, citing fine of five pounds Irish, Gerrald Wesley fined forty shillings Irish] Dated at his maties Court of Castle Chamber the fifteenth Day of November 1615 and in the thirteenth yeare of his maties Raigne of England, Fraunce and Ireland and of Scotland the fortie nyne.[173]

Memorandum wheare his maties learned Councell ore tenus made Informacon in this most hon[ora]ble Courte of Castle Chamber against Rowland Rowceter, John Walsh, John Roch, Donell McFardaraigh, Domaigh McMoriertagh, Stephen Synnot, Mathew Furlonge, Oliver Keatinge, Jesper Codd, Teige McMoriertagh and Thomas Scurlocke of the County of Wexford that were Ympanelled and sworne at a generall Cessions holden in the said County the second day of August 1615 before Sir William Methwould, knight, Cheife Barron of his Maties Court of exchequier, and Peter Palmer, esquier, one of the Justices of his highnes Court of Common Pleas, Justices of Assize for the said Countie of Wexford, to make true presentment of all Recusant as wilfully and obstinatly refused to repaire to their severall parishe Churches upon the saboath Daye [see formula E, f. 191, with order to fine each of the jurors] twentye nobles ster a peece accordinge to the reducement, and imprisonment durynge the Lo Deputyes pleasure. Dated at his maties Court of Castle Chamber the xvijth day of November 1615 and in the xiijth yeare of his maties Raigne of England, Fraunce and Ireland and of Scotland the nyne and fortieth.[174]

Memorandum that wheare his maties learned Councell ore tenus made Informacon in this most honnorable Court of Castle Chamber against Edmond Ragged of the Cittie of Kilkenny, Nicholas Archer of the same, Walter Cleere of the same, Richard Purcell of Cellerstowne , Thomas Treyne of the Cittie of Kilkenny, Daniell Martin of the same, Patricke Macky of the same, Donnogh OBrohe of the same, John Sprice of the same, John Ronan of the same, William ODullochoute of the same, James Donan of the same, John Ragged of the same, and Edmond OTehan of the same that wear

172. f. 207. 173. f. 208.
174. f. 209.

Impannelled and sworne at a generall Cessions holden in the said Cittie of Kilkenny the xixth Day of August 1615 before Sir William Methwould, knight, Cheife Barron in his maties Court of Exchequier, and Peter Palmer, esquier, one of the Justices of his highnes Court of Common pleas, Justices of Assize for the said Countie of the Cittie of Kilkenny to make true presentment of all recusantes as wilfully and obstinatly refused to repaire to their severall parish Churches upon the sabooth Dayes [see formula E, f. 191, jurors each fined four marks Irish]. Dated at his maties Court of Castell Chamber the xvijth Day of November 1615 and in the xiijth yeare of his maties Raigne of England, Fraunce and Ireland and of Scotland the nyne and fortieth.[175]

Memorandum wheare his maties learned Councell ore tenus made Informacon in this most honnorable Court of Castle Chamber against James Purcell, Teige McCahire, Gerrald McCahir, Xpofer Everson, Terrence OLeyne, Robert Goarst, Hugh Fagan, Donald McHugh of the Countie of Catherlagh that were amongst others Impannelled and sworne at a generall Cessions holden in the said Countie the tenth day of August 1615 before Sir William Methwould, knight, Cheife Barron of his maties Court of Exchequier, and Peter Palmer, esquier, one of the Justices of his maties Court of Common pleas, Justices of Assize for the said County, to make true presentment of all such recusants as willfully and obstinately refused to repaire to their severall parish churches uppon Sondaies and other holy daies [see formula E, f. 191]. Upon which examinacons the rest of the Jury Confessed they were agreed to make presentment according to their evidence, but the said James Purcell, Teige McCahir, Gerrald McCahir, Xpofer Everson, Terrence OLeyne, Robert Goarst, Hugh Fagan and Donald McHugh wilfully and obstinately refused to Joyne in the same, and beinge examyned by his maties Sergeant at law by order of this court the reasons why they refused to Joyne with thier fellow Jurors, as allsoe beinge questioned by this Court why they wold not Joyne with their fellowes haveinge soe pregnant and apparrant evydence, Could make noe other answer or excuse but that it was against their Conscience. Wherupon the Court proceedinge to Censure It is ordered, adiudged and Decreed that the said James Purcell and all the above named persons shall each of them pay to his matie for a fyne accordinge to the reducement the Somme of five poundes Irish a peece and Imprisonment Duringe the lo Deputies pleasure. Dated at his maties Court of Castle Chamber the xxijth Day of November 1615 and in the xiiijth yeare of his maties Raigne of England, Fraunce and Ireland and of Scotland the nyne and fortieth.[176]

Memorandum wheare Informacon hath beene exhibited into this most honnorable Court of Castle Chamber by Thomas Crooke and James Salmon of Baltymore in the County of Corke, pltes, against Walter Coppinger, Richard Coppinger his brother, Donogh ODriscoll, Edmond Power and many others of the said County, Deffendantes, for many and sondry offences and misdemeanors supposed to be Comytted by the said Walter Coppinger, Richard Coppinger, Donnogh ODriscol, Edmond Power, Thomas Beckworth, Aulife? Croane and John Brenagh, Indevouringe to subplant the said Thomas Crooke and James Salmon and all other the said Thomas Crookes English tennauntes, Inhabitantes at Baltymore. And for preferrnge of severall uniust and malyceouse Indictmentes against the said Thoms Crooke and a great nomber of his English tennauntes And theise for one Indictment preferred against the said Thomas Crooke of high Treason at a quarter Cessions of the peace for the said County of Corke, without any Cause or Coulor of Cause. Alsoe for severall Ryottes and many other misdemeaores and offences alleadged by the said Informacon to have been donn and Comytted by the said Walter Coppinger, Richard Coppinger, Donnogh ODriscoll, Edmond Power and the rest before named against the said Thomas Crooke and his English tennauntes, Inhabitinge and newly setled and planted at Baltymore aforesaid. Wherunto the said Walter Coppinger, Richard Coppinger, Donnogh ODriscoll, Edmond Power and the rest of the said Deffendauntes were by order of this Court Called to aunswer the said Informacon, and the Cause proceedinge to Replicacon, Reioynder and witnesses examyned on eyther parte and many Dayes apoynted for hearinge the said Cause, which hearinge had Contynuaunce from Trynitie terme 1613 to this present Hillary Terme 1615, and uppon the fynall hearinge therof yt appeared unto this honnorable Court by Depositions of severall witnesses that the said Walter Coppinger, Richard Copinger and Donnogh ODriscoll were

175. f. 210.   176. f. 211.

guiltye of Comyttinge of one Ryott uppon the said Thomas Crookes tennauntes at Baltymore the first day of July 1611. It allsoe appeared unto this honnorable Court by the Depositions of many witnesses as alsoe by the severall Bills of Indictmentes shewed in Court uppon hearinge of the Cause that the said Richard Coppinger and Donnogh ODriscoll were guilty of the malyceous preferringe of the said uniust Indictmentes, and the said Richard Coppinger, for that said Indictment of Treason without Cause or Coulor of Cause soe to Doe, and Dyvers other lyke malyceous and uniust Indictmentes against the said Thomas Crooke his English tennauntes Inhabiting att Baltymore, falcely and uniustly. For which thier severall offences and misdemeanors the said Walter Coppinger is Censured by this honnorable Court to pay to his matie for a fyne the some of twenty poundes english for the Ryot proved against him to be Committed the said first day of July 1611, and to be Comytted Durying the Lord Deputyes pleasure. The said Richard Coppinger Censured to pay to his matie for a fyne twentie pound english aswell for beinge an actor at the Comyttinge of the said Ryott, as alsoe for preferringe soe many malyceous and uniust Indictmentes against the said Thomas Crooke and his English tennauntes, and especially for the said Indictment for Treason and to be Comytted Duringe the lo Deputyes pleasure. The said Donnogh ODriscoll is lykwise Censured to pay to his matie for a fyne the Somme of twentie markes english aswell for beinge an actor at the Committinge of the Ryot the said first Day of July at Balltymore, as allsoe for the preferringe of the said malyceous and uniust Indictmentes against the said Thomas and his said tennauntes, and to be Comitted Duringe the Lord Deputies pleasure. And of the other misdemeanors Chardged uppon the said Walter Copinger, Richard Coppinger and Donogh ODriscoll the Court doth acquite and Dischardge for want of sufficient proofe against them or any of them. And for all the rest of the Deffendauntes noo sufficient proofe beinge against them for any the offences alleaged in the Informacon, they are acquited, dischardged and dismissed for any further trouble touchinge the same. Dated at his maties Court of Castle Chamber the seventh day of February 1615 and in the thirteenth yeare of his maties Raigne of England, Fraunce and Ireland and of Scotland the nyne and fortieth.[177]

Memorandum wheare his Maties Solyciter generall ore tenus made Informacon in this most honnorable Court of Castle Chamber against the lo Barron of Inchiquyn, that he the said lo Barron about [blank] of [blank] received into his l[ordshi]ps house one Nicholas Nugent, a Jesuyt, and relyeved, Comforted and harboured him in his owne Dwellinge house for the space of xviij or xxtie dayes, in which tyme the said Nicholas Nugent said and Celebrated the service of the masse in the said Lo Barrons house severall tymes, his Lo[rdship and] his Lady with many of his servauntes beinge present and hearinge the said Masse, Wherin he the said Lo Barron had Comytted a high and great Contempt against his matie who hath by his severall procla[ma]cons pupblyshed his pryncly pleasure, exhibitinge and straightly forbiddyng all his highnes subiectes what soever that they shall not att any tyme receave into their houses or relieve or harbour any Jesuyt semynary priest or any Popish priest, uppon payne of his maties high Displeasure and Indignacon. To which Informacon the said Lo Barron of Inchyquyn was Called into this honnorable Court to Aunswer his said Contempt, and beinge examyned, as allsoe former examynacons taken by his maties sollicyter, Confessed that he had receaved the said Nicholas Nugent and kept and releyved him in his house the space of fourteen Dayes or therabouts and that he had said masse in his house Durynge his aboad [abode] there. Uppon which his owne Confession the Courte proceedinge to Censure, yt was ordered, adiudged and Decreed by this honnorable Courte that the said Lo Barron of Inchyquyn shall pay to his matie for a fyne accordinge to the Reducement the some of one hundred poundes Irish, and ymprisonment Duringe the lls Justices pleasure. Dated at his Maties Cort of Castle chamber the xxiiijth day of Aprill 1616 and in the fourteenth yeare of his Maties Raigne of England, Fraunce and Ireland and of Scotland the nyne and fortieth.[178]

Memorandum wheare his maties sollycyter generall this present day made Informacon ore tenus in this most honorable Court of Castle Chamber against Wylliam White, William Fitz Garrald, Garrald Dillon, Edmond Dalton, James Dillon and James Dalton that were ympanelled and sworne of a grand Jury at A generall Cessyons holden at Mollyngar in the County of Westmeath the xxvijth day

---

of February 1615 before Sir John Blenerhasset, knight, one of the Barrons of his maties Court of Exchequer, and William Sparke, esquier, one of the Justices of his highnes Court of Cheife bench, Justices of Assize for the said County, to make true presentment of all such recusantes as wilfully and obstinatly refused to repayre to their parish Churches to heare Devyne service accordinge to his mates lawes and Statutes in this kingdome, [see formula E, f. 191] uppon which their Confession the said William White, William FitzGarrald, Garrald Dillon, Edmond Dalton, James Dillon and James Dalton were Censured by this honnorable Court each of them to pay to his matie for a fyne the some of tenn poundes harpes a peece accordinge to the Reducement, and ymprisonment Durynge the lls Justices pleasure. Dated at his mateis Court of Castle Chamber the xxvj day of Aprill 1616 and in the xiiijth yeare of his maties Raigne of England, Fraunce and Irland and of Scotland the xlixth.[179]

Memorandum wheare his maties Sollyceter generall this present day made Informacon ore tenus in this most honnorable Court of Castle Chamber against Connocke OFerrall, Lysaugh OFerrall, Donnogh McRichard, James McHubert OFarrell, Garret McRowry, Owen McKagan, [and] Brian McMelaughlin That weare ympannelled and sworne of A Grand Jury at a Generall Cessiones holden att [blank] in the County of Longford the fourth day of March 1615 before Sir John Blenerhasset, knight, one of the Barrons of his maties Court of exchequer, and Willm Sparke, esquier, one of the Justices of his highnes Court of Cheife bench, Justyces of Assize for the said County, to make true presentment of all such recusantes as willfully and obstinatlye refused to repayere to their parish Churches to heare devyne service [see formula E, f. 191]. Uppon which their Confession the said Connocke OFarrell and James McHubert OFarrell, for that uppon their examynacons before his matie said sollyciter did say that if they were to passe in the lyke Jury againe they would doe noe otherwise then they had donn before, were Censured by this honnorable Corut to pay to his matie a fyne accordinge to the reducement the some of xxty markes english a peece. The said Lysagh OFarrell, Donnogh McRichard, Garret McRory, Owen McKagan and Bryen McMellaghlyn Censured to pay for a fyne accordinge to the reducement each of them the some of tenn poundes harpes a peece and all of them ymprisonment durynge the lls Justices pleasure. Dated att his maties Court of Castle Chamber the xxvjth Day of Aprill 1616 and in the xiiijth yeare of his maties Raigne of England, Fraunce and Ireland and of Scotland the xlixth.[180]

Memorandum where his mates solliceter Generall ore tenus made Informacon in this most honnorable Court of Castle Chamber against Lucas Shea, late mayor of the Cittie of Kilkenny, and Adam Bryver and Willm Murphey, late Sheriffes of the said Cittie, that the said Lucas Shea beinge elected and Chosen mayor of the said Cittie of Kilkeny and the said Adam Bryver and Willm Murphey beinge sherifes of the said Cittie, executed their said offices of Mayoryltie and sherifes in the said Cittie before they had taken the oath of Supremacy, which by the lawes and statutes of this realme they ought to have donn. And the said Deffendauntes beinge severally Called to Aunswer Confessed that they and every of them had executed their said severall offices from the feast of St. Michaell tharchangell in the yeare of our lord god 1614 untill the xvijth of March followinge and that they nor any of them had taken the oath of Supremacy before nor att any tyme since they tooke uppon them the execucon of their severall offices. Uppon which their owne Confession they were by the Court Censured to have Comytted a high Contempt against his matie and the lawes and Statutes of this realme. For which their severall Contemptes the said Lucas Shea is Censured to pay to his matie for a fyne the some of fortie markes Currant english money and ymprisonment Durynge the lls Justice pleasure. And the said Adam Bryver and Willm Murphey each of them to pay the some of twenty markes english money and ymprisonment duryng the lls Justices pleasure. Dated at his maties Court of Castle Chamber the first day of May 1616 and in the xiiijth yeare of his maties Raigne of England, Fraunce and Ireland and of Scotland the xlixth.[181]

Memorandum wheare his maties solliceter Generall ore tenus made Informacon in this most honnorable Court of Castle Chamber against Patricke Dobbyn, late Soveraigne of Thomastowne,

179. f. 214.
181. f. 216.

180. f. 215.

George Verden, late Soveraigne of Killmallocke, Willm Nash, late portrive of Gawran, and James Dulan, late Portrive of Inystyoge, that the said Patricke Dobbyn beinge elected and chosen Soveraigne of the said Thomastowne, George Verden, Soveraigne of the said Killmallocke, Willm Nash, Portrive of the said towne of Gawran and James Dulan, Portrive of the said towne of Inystyoge executed their said severall offices of Soveraigntie and Portrives in the severall townes before they had taken the oath of Supremacy, which by the lawes and Statutes of this realme they ought to have donn. And the said Deffendauntes beinge severally Called to answer, Confessed that they and every of them had executed their said severall offices from the feast of St. Michaell the Archangell in the yeare of our lord god 1615 untill the xvijth of March followinge and that they nor any of them had taken the oath of Supremacy before nor at any tyme synce they tooke uppon them the execucon of their severall offices. Uppon which their owne Confession they were by the Court Censured to have Comytted a high Contempt against his matie and the lawes and Statutes of this Realme for which their severall Contemptes the said Patricke Dobbyn, George Verden, Willm Nash and James Dulan are Censured to pay to his matie for a fyne the some of twenty markes english money a peece and ymprisonment durynge the lls Justices pleasure. Dated at his maties Court of Castle Chamber the first day of May 1616 and in the xiiijth yeare of his maties Raigne of England, Fraunce and Ireland and of Scotland the xlixth.[182]

Memorandum wheare his Maties Sollicyter generall made Informacon ore tenus in this most honnorable Court of Castle Chamber against Walter Cregg of Mount Rosse in Scotland that the said Walter Cregge, beinge att Lysborne [Lisbon] in Spayn [Portugal merged with Spanish monarchy from 1581] and theire fraighted with salt to transporte the same into Ireland to the Cittie of Lymericke, Contrary to his Duty to his matie and Contrary to severall proclamacons Published in this kingdome that noe person whatsoever beinge his highnes borne subiect shold bringe into this kingdome any Jesuyt, Semynary Priest or any other Popish priest whatsoever. Notwithstanding, the said Walter Cregg at the request of one Anthony Arthur of Lymericke, merchaunt, brought with him into this kingdome one Nicholas Nugent, a knowen Jesuyt, and one Willm Maloane, a priest, and landed them at Inchekatheryn within the River of Shannon. And beinge Called into this Court to Annswer the said Informacon, Confessed openly in Court that he brought with him in his barque from Lysborne the said Nicholas Nugent and Willm Maloane at the desire and request of the said Anthony Arthur and landed them at Inchekatheryn aforesaid. Uppon which Confession he was Censured by this honnorable Court to pay to his matie for a fyne according to the Reducement the Somme of tenn poundes Irish and ymprisonment duryng the lls Justice pleasure. Dated at his maties Court of Castle Chamber the third day of May 1616 and in the fourteenth yeare of his maties Raigne of England, Fraunce and Ireland and of Scotland the nyne and fortieth.[183]

Memorandum wheare his maties Sollycitor generall made Informacon ore tenus in this most honnorable Court of Castle Chamber against John Coppinger, mayor of the Cittie [of] Corke, Symon Fannynge, Mayor of the Cittie of Lymericke, John Skiddy, mayor of the Cittie of Waterford, Bennet White, Mayhor of the Cittie of Clonmell, and Patricke Cronynge, one of the sherrifes of the said Cittie of Corcke, that they the said severall mayors and the said sherife executed their severall offices as mayores and sherife in the said Citties before they or any of them had taken the oath of supremacy, which by the lawes and statutes of this realme they and every of them ought to have donn. [Formula F (*our italics*)] *And the said Deffendauntes and every of them being Called to Answer their severall Contemptes Confessed that they and every of them had executed their severall offices ever since they were Chosen officers and that they nor any of them had taken the oath of supremacy before nor att any tyme synce they tooke uppon them the execucon of their severall offices.* Uppon which their owne Confession, the said John Coppinger and Symon Fannynge were Censured to pay to his matie for a fyne according to the Reducement each of them the some of thirtie poundes english. The said John Skyddy and Bennett White to pay to his maties for a fyne according to the reducement each of them the some of twenty poundes english a peece. The said Patricke Cronynge is lykewise Censured to pay

---

182. f. 217.
183. f. 218. Nugent was earlier involved in saying mass at the house of Lord Inchiquin, see fol. 213, above.

to his matie for a fyne accordinge to the reducement the some of tenn poundes Irish, and all of them Imprisonment duryng the lls Justices pleasure. Dated at his maties Court of Castle Camber the eight day of May 1616 and in the fourteenth yeare of his maties Raigne of England, Fraunce and Ireland and of Scotland the nyne and fortieth.[184]

Memorandum wheare Edmond Sexten of the Cittie of Lymericke, esquier, exhibited Informacon into this moste honnorable Courte of Castle Chamber that whear the said Edmond Sexten was quietly seised in his Demeasne as of fee of and in the late Abbey or Monestery Called St. Maryhouse in the Cittie of Lymericke, and of and in all landes, tenementes & hereditamentes therunto belongeinge, and the yssues and proffittes therof hath from tyme to tyme taken and Converted to his owne use and behoofe without the Interrupcon or Disturbance of any person or persons whatsoever. Nevertheles Willm Haly, Domynicke Roch, Piers Creagh, Domynicke Creagh, Edmond Fox, William Stritch of the said Cittie of Lymericke, aldermen, Walter White FitzNicholas, Robert White, Thomas White, George Richford, George Sexten, Willm Mahowne, James Stackpoll, Willm Creagh FitzMartyn, Thomas Mulrony, Phillip Ronan, Stephen Woulfe, Piers Oge Creagh, Richard Gallway and Stephen White FitzEdmond of the said Cittie of Lymericke, merchauntes, and Dyvers other of the Inhabitantes of the said Cittie of Lymericke, merchauntes, and Dyvers other of the Inhabitantes of the said Cittye wickedly and malyceously, envyenge and malignynge his estate and haveinge an ungodly purpose to diseize [disseisin] and Disinherite the said Edmond Sexten of parcell of the possessions of the said Abbey, did in and uppon the twelth Day of May in the xijth yeare of his matie Raigne of England, Fraunce and Ireland and of Scotland the seven and fortieth, and at dyvers tymes synce, at the City of Lymericke aforesaid Routeouslye and unlawfully assemble themselves together and then and there did wickedly, malyceously and unlawfully propound amongst themselves that if the[y] kept not the said Edmond Sexten in Contynuall suyte of law he would grow to such wealth as that he would purchase landes and tenementes within the County and Cittie of Lymericke worth a thousand poundes per annum. And theruppon did then and there wickedly, malyceously and unlawfully Combyne and Conspire amongst themselves by any means whatsoever to Disturbe and brynge the said Edmond Sexten into suyte of law for Certayne tenementes lyeinge in the suburbes of the said Cittie of Lymericke, parcell of the said late abbey or Monestery called St Maryhouse, and alsoe beinge parcell of the said Edmond Sexten his Inheritance. And for the Accomplishment and execucon of which wicked proposition, Combynacon and Conspiracy they the said Willm Haly, beinge then Mayor of the sayd Cittie of Lymericke, Piers Creagh, Domynicke Creagh, Domynicke Roch and the rest of the before named persons dyd afterwarde, that is to say the fourth day of August in the said xijth yeare of his maties raigne of England, Fraunce and Ireland and of Scotland the xlviijth, Routeously and unlawfullye assemble themselves together at Lymericke aforesaid and then and there wickedly, malyceously and unlawfully did Consult, Conspire and resolve amongst themselves Ryotously, Routeously and in warlyke manner to goe unto the said Edmond Sexten said tenementes in the said suburbes to Interrupt, Disturbe and Dryve away Certayne Carpenters and workemen the said Edmond Sexten had there ymployed about his buyldinge to thend they might brynge the said Edmond into suyte of law. Accordinge to which wicked Conspiracy and resolucon they the said Willm Haly, Piers Creagh, Domynicke Creagh and the aforenamed Ryotous persons beinge armed in warlyke and hostile manner with swordds, head peeces, gunnes, staves and other weapons offensive and deffensive did in and uppon the said fourth day of August in the xijth yeres of his maties raigne of England, Fraunce and Ireland and of Scotland the xlviijth and then and there in Ryotous, Routeous and Rebellyous manner did repayre and Come to the said Edmond Sextens sayd tenementes in the suburbes of the said Cittie and then and there Ryotouslye, Routeously and foreceably did Interrupt Disturbe and Dryve away the said Edmond Sextens said Carpenters and workmen to the overthrow of the said Edmonds buyldynges begune and Intended in and uppon the said tenements. And the said Willm Haly, Pearas Creagh, Domynicke Roch, Domynicke Creagh and the rest of the said Ryotous persons before named, beinge not satisfyed with the said outrages and misdemeanors and beinge armed as aforesaid, afterwardes, that is to say in and uppon the eight day of August in the year aforesaid, in manyfestacon and execucon of their said malyceous Conspiracyes and resolucons aforesaid at Lymericke aforesaid, Ryotously, Routeously and [in] lyke foreceable and

184. f. 219.

outrageous manner did dispoyle, breake and plucke downe to the ground the mayne tymber of the house the said Edmond Sexten had then lately sett uppe and erected uppon the said tenementes. To which Informacon the said Willm Hally and all the said persons made Answer and the Cause proceedinge to Replycacon, Reioynder and witnesses examyned on eyther parte. And this day the Cause beinge hard yt manyfestly appeared unto this most honnorable Court by the testymony of many witnesses that the said Willm Haly and all the rest before named, except Willm Stritch, were guyltye of Comyttynge of the severall Ryottes, outrages and mysde[me]anores in the Informacon specyfied. It is therfore ordered, adiudged and Decreed by this honnorable Court that the said Willm Haly, the pryncipall leader of all the rest and beinge then Mayor of the said Cittie of Lymericke, shall pay to his matie for a fyne the some of twenty poundes english. And thother Deffendauntes beinge eighteene in nomber shall pay to his matie for a fyne each of them the some of tenn poundes english a peece, and ymprisonment durynge the lls Justices pleasure. The said Willm Stritch to be acquitted and Dismissed, noe proofe beinge produced against him that he was present at the Comyttynge of the said Ryott and misdemeanors. Dated at his maties Court of Castle Chamber the tenth day of May 1616 and in the xiiijth yeare of his maties raigne of England, Fraunce and Ireland and of Scotland the nyne and fortieth.[185]

Memorandum wheare his matie Solliciter generall made Informacon ore tenus in this honnorable Court of Castle Chamber against Thomas Orpye and Walter Usher, late sherifes of the Cittie of Dublin, against Stephen White and Thomas Groome, late sherrifes of the towne of Drogheda, and against James Dowdall, late one of the Balyffes [in] the towne of Dondalke, that they the said severall Sherifes and Balyfes had executed their severall offices as Sherifes and Baylyfe in the said Cittie and Towne before they or any of them had taken the oath of Supremacy which by the Lawes and Statutes of this Realme they and every of them ought to have donn. [See formula F, f. 219] ... the said Thomas Orpye was Censured by this honnorable Court to pay to his matie for a fyne according to the Reducemente the some of fortie poundes english. The said Walter Usher to pay to his matie for a fyne acordinge to the Reducement the some of one hundred markes english, and the said Stephen White, Thomas Groame and James Dowdall were lykewise Censured to pay to his matie for a fyne accordinge to the reducement each of them the some of twentie markes english a peece, and all of them Imprisonment durynge the lls Justice pleasure. Dated at his maties Court of Castle Chamber the seventh day of June 1616 and in the fourteenth year of his maties Raigne of England, Fraunce and Irland and of Scotland the nyne and fortieth.[186]

Memorandum whear his maties Attorney generall ore tenus made Informacon in this most honnorable Court of Castle Chamber against Allexander Cuffe, late mayor of the Cittie of Waterford, John Rooth FitzPiers, late mayor of the Cittie of Kilkenny, Christopher Creagh, late mayor of the Cittie of Lymericke, Patricke White, late sherrife of the Cittie of Waterford, Lewes Bryen, late sherrife of the Cittie of Kilkenny, Piers Bray, late Baylife of Clonmell, and Patricke Gerard, late Soveraigne of the towne of Fetherd, that they the said severall Mayors, Sherifes, Baylife and Soveraigne had executed their severall offices as Mayors, Sherrifes, Baylife and Soveraigne in the said Citties and Townes before they or any of them had taken the oath of Supremacy, which by the Lawes and Statutes of this realme they and every of them ought to have Donn. [See formula F, f. 219] Uppon which their owne Confession the said Alexander Cuffe, Christopher Creagh and Patricke White were Censured to pay to his matie for a fyne accordinge to the Reducement each of them the some of fortie pounds english a peece. The said John Rooth FitzPiers is lykewise Censured to pay to his matie for a fyne accordinge to the reducement the some of fiftie pounds english. The said Lewes Bryen is lykewise censured to pay to his matie for a fyne accordinge to the reducement the some of twentie pounds english. And the said Patrick Bray and Patricke Everard are lykewise censured to pay to his matie for a fyne accordinge to the reducement the some of tenn pounds english, and all of them Imprisonment duryng the Lord Deputies pleasure. Dated at his maties Court of Castle Chamber the

185. ff. 220–20v.
186. f. 221. Formula in use for neglecting to take oath of supremacy is similar to that in use for jurors who refused to convict defendants of recusancy in spite of the evidence before them.

thirteenth day of November 1616 and in the fourteenth yeare of his maties raigne of England, Fraunce and Ireland and of Scotland the fiftieth.[187]

Memorandum wheare uppon Informacon ore tenus of Sir John Davies, knight, his maties Attorney generall, in this most honnorable Court of Castle Chamber against Nicholas FitsWillms of Burdmagan in the County of Dublin, esquier, That he the said Nicholas FitsWilliams, well knowinge that sondry proclamacons in this kingdome have beene made in his maties name for the banishment of Jesuytes, Semynary Priest, Fryers and Popish Priestes out of this kingdome that hath beene made and ordayned by forrayne Authoretie. And allsoe by the said proclamacons all his maties true and loyall subiectes have been expressly prohibited and forbidden to Cherrish, Comforte or releeve any such Jesuyte, Semynary Priestes, Fryers and any other Popish Priestes made and ordayned by forrayne Authoretie uppon payne of his maties indignacon and high displeasure, and uppon payne of such further punishment as might Justlie be Inflicted uppon the Contemners of his maties royall prerogatives and Comandmentes. Nevertheless the said Nicholas FitzWilliams, in high Contempt of his matie and the sondry proclamacons made in his highnes name, in the begynnynge of October last 1616 and at dyvers other tymes, receaved into his house at Burdmegan aforesaid one Patricke Duffe, a Popish Priest, very well knowne to the said Nicholas Fits Williams to be a Popish Priest made and ordeyned by forrayne Authoretie, which Patrick Duffe the said Nicholas FitsWilliams did not onely Cherish, Comfort and releive in his owne house But allsoe openlye at noone day broght the said Patricke Duffe in his Company from Burdmegan to the Cittie of Dublin, to the view of soe many as would have ann eye uppon him. And the next day after the said Nicholas FitsWilliams and the said Patricke Duffe Came to Dublyn the said Patricke Duffe Came to the said Nicholas FitsWilliams lodginge at the house of the widdow Gernon in Dublin, in which house the [said] Patrick Duffe was apprehended by the right honnorable the Lord Deputies warrant in the presence of the said Nicholas Fitswilliams. And the said Nicholas FitsWilliams beinge Called to Annswer his high Contempt to his matie and his highnes said proclamacons, and being examyned by order of this Court by his matie said Attorney as allsoe openly in Court Confessed that he had knowen the said Patricke Duffe those seven yeares and allsoe knew him to be a Popish Priest made by forrayne Authhoretie and that he hath been in his house with the Lord of Hoath and Dyvers other gentlemen sondry tymes. And allsoe Confessed that the said Patricke Duffe Came in his Company from Burdmegan to the Cittie of Dublin at noone day at the begynnynge of October last, and that the said Patricke Duffe Came the next Day after his Comeinge to his lodginge in the after noone and there the said Patricke Duffe was apprehended by his lordships warrant. Uppon which his owne Confession and for that the said Nicholas FitsWilliams Could then make noe reasonable excuse of his said manifest Contempt the Court proceeded to Censure. Wherupopon it was ordered, adiudged and Decreed by this honnorable Court that the said Nicholas FitzWilliams for his manifest and high Contempt and misdemeanor shall pay to his matie for a fyne accordinge to the Reducement the some of forty poundes english, and Imprisonment durynge the Lo Deputies pleasure. Dated at his maties Court of Castle Chamber the fifeenth day of November 1616 and in the fourteenth yeare of his maties Raigne of England, Fraunce and Ireland and of Scotland the fiftieth.[188]

Memorandum wheare his maties Attorney Generall made Informacon in this most honnorable Court of Castle Chamber ore tenus against Willm OMara, sherrife of the County of Tipperary, that notwithstandinge his maties lawes and Statutes of this Realme and severall proclamacons prohibitinge all personnes whatsoever within this kingdome to take uppon him or them any magistracy or office under his matie before they had first taken the oath of supremacy. Nevertheles, the said Willm OMara, Contrary to the said lawes, Statutes, [and] proclamacons, tooke uppon him the execucon of the office of Sherife of the Countie and liberty of Tipperary before he had taken the oath of Supremacy. His maties said Attorney further enformed this honnorable Court that the said Willm OMara beinge sherrife of the said County at the last Lent Assizes held in the said County, Dyvers prisoners were Comytted to his Charge and saufe keepinge them in prison untill they and every of them had payd the severall fynes that were ymposed on them by the Justices of Assizes then

---

187. f. 222.   188. f. 223.

there. Nevertheles, the said Willm OMara, Contrary to the Charge given him by the said Justices, he sett them all at lybertie the next Day after the said Justices had ended their Cessions, of his owne pleasure, not Answerynge the fynes Due to his matie. And forasmuch as it appeared unto the Court that the Sherrife of the said Countie hath been nomynated and appoynted by the Earles of Ormond in former tymes and none of them have had the oath of Supremacy offered unto them, yt hath pleased thes honnorable court to remytt the said first offence. And for thother offences in settinge those prisoners at lybertie without any Authorety before they had payd their fynes, It is ordered, adiudged and Decreed by this honnorable Court that he the said Willm OMara shall pay to his matie for a fyne accordinge to the Reducement the some of twenty poundes English, and Imprisonment Durynge the Lord Deputyes pleasure. Dated at his maties Court of Castle Chamber the twentieth day of November 1616 and in the fourteenth yeare of his maties Raigne of England, Fraunce and Ireland and of Scotland the fiftieth.[189]

Memorandum wheare his maties Sollyceter generall ore tenus made Informacon in this most honnorable Court of Castle chamber against Nicholas Laffan of the Slane, Jasper Synnott of Ballymore, Balthazer Codd of Garrylegh, Richard Lewes of the Nagge, Walter Rowceter of Slavoy, John Sutton of Ballysepp, Callowe McWilliam of Conlartan, Thomas Maloane of Garreniske and Rowland Rowceter of Tomcedilly that were Impannelled and sworne of a grand jury at a generall Cessions holden for the County of Wexford the [blank] of [blank] 1616 at [blank] before Sir Willm Methwould, knight, Cheife Barron of his maties Court of exchequer, and Sir John Elliott, knight, third Barron of his maties said Court of exchequer, Justices of Assize for the said County, to make true presentment of all such recusantes as willfully and obstinately refused to repayre to their parish Churches to heare Dyvyne service [see formula E, f. 191] ... the said Nicholas Laffan, Jasper Synnott, Balthazer Codd, Richard Lewes, Walter Rowceter, John Sutton, Callowe McWilliam, Thomas Maloane and Rowland Rowceter shall paie to his Matie for a fyne eache of them twenty poundes English a peece, and ymprisonemente duringe the Lorde Deputies pleasure. Dated at his maties Courte of Castle Chamber the twentieth daie of November 1616 and in the fourteenth yeare of his maties Raigne of England, Fraunce and Ireland and of Scotland the fiftieth.[190]

Memorandum whear his maties Atorney generall thes present day made Informacon ore tenus in this most honnorable Court of Castle Chamber against Edmond Brenan of Adamstowne, John Hopp of Ledwichstowne, Thomas Magoghegan of Comynstowne, Richard Ledwich of Mollingar, Patricke Frayne of Telegeigh, Robert FitsSymons of Fowre and Nicholas Dalton of Ballybogg That were Impannelled and sworne [on] a Grand Jury at a generall Cessions holden at Mollyngar in the County of Westmeath the First Day of Augut 1616 before Sir Domynicke Sarsfield, knight, Cheife Judge of his maties Court of Common Pleas, and Willm Sparke, esquier, one of the Justices of his maties Court of Cheife Bench, Justices of Assize for the said Countie, to make true presentment of all such Recusantes as wilfully and obstinately refused to Repayre to their parish Churches to heare Devyne service accordinge to his maties Lawes and statutes in this kingdome, [see formula E, f. 191] ... the said Edmond Brenan, John Hopp, Thomas Magoghegan, Richard Ledwich, Patricke Frayne, Robert FitsSymons and Nicholas Dalton shall paie to his Matie for a fyne eache of them twenty poundes English a peece, and ymprisonemente duringe the Lorde Deputies pleasure. Dated at his maties Court of Castle Chamber the twentieth Day of November 1616 and in the fourteenth year of his maties Raigne of England, Fraunce and Ireland and of Scotland the fiftieth.[191]

Memorandum whear his maties Sergeant at law made Informacon ore tenus in this most honnorable Court of Castle Chamber against Christopher Shea of the Cittie of Kilkenny, John Rooth FitsEdwards of the same, John Honygham of the same, Symon Seise of the same, Robert Brenagh of the same, Donell ODulany of the same, John Howyn of the same, Nicholas Wery of the same, John Raggett of the same, and James Dobbyn of the same That were Impannelled and sworne of a Grand

189. f. 224. 190. f. 225. Fol. 225v is blank.
191. f. 226.

Jury at a generall Cessions holden at the said Cittie of Kilkenny the nynth Day of August 1616 Before Sir William Methwold, knight, Cheife Barron of his maties Court of exchequer, and Sir John Ellyott, knight, third Barron of his maties said Court of Exchequer, Justices of Assize for the said Cyttye, To make true presentment of all such Recusantes as willfully and obstinatlie refused to repayre to their parish Churches to hear Dyvyne service accordinge to his maties Lawes and Statutes of this kingdome ... [see formula E, f. 191] Uppon which their owne Confession the said Christopher Shea, John Rooth FitsEdward and John Honyghan were Censured to pay to his matie for a fyne accordinge to the Reducement each of them the some of five pounds english a peece. The said Symon Seise, Robert Brenagh, Donell ODulany, John Howyn, Nicholas Wery, John Raggett and James Dobbyn lykewise Censured to pay to his matie for a fyne accordinge to the reducement the some of forty shillings english a peece, and all of them Imprisonment duryng the Lord Deputies pleasure. Dated at his maties Court of Castle Chamber the twentieth Day of November 1616 and in the fourteenth year of his maties Raigne of England, Fraunce and Ireland and of Scotland the fiftieth.[192]

Memorandum wheare his maties Attorney generall made Informacon ore tenus in this most honnorable Court of Castle Chamber against Willm Byrne of Oldtowne, Willm Barry of Miltowne and Davyd McJefferye of Ballycanrygam That were Impannelled and sworne of a grand Jury at a Generall Cessions holden at Catherlogh in the County of Catherlogh the nynteenth Day of August 1616 Before Sir William Methwould, knight, Cheife Barron of his maties Court of exchequer, and Sir John Ellyot, knight, third Barron of his maties said Court of exchequer, Justices of Assize for the said County, To make true presentment of all such recusantes as wilfully and obstinately refused to repayre to their parish Churches to heare Dyvyne servyce accordinge to his maties lawes and Statutes in this kingdome [see formula E, f. 191] Uppon which their owne Confession the said Willm Byrne, Willm Barry and Davyd McJefferye were Censured to pay to his matie for a fyne accordinge to the Reducement each of them the some of twentye pounds english a peece, and all of them Imprisonment duryng the Lord Deputies pleasure. Dated at his maties Court of Castle Chamber the two and twentieth day of November 1616 and in the fourteenth yeare of his maties rayne of England, Fraunce and Ireland and of Scotland the fiftieth.[193]

Memorandum wheare his maties Sergeant at law made Informacon ore tenus in this most honnorable Court of Castle Chamber against James Dalton of Ballynecrany, Olyver Grace of Ballyhiggen, Richard Purcell of Lysmayne, Richard Butler of Vantsestowne, Danyell Oge OHonoghen of Coalcashell, Piers ORyan of Stackally, Robert Walsh of Ballynecrolly, Edmond Dobbyn of Lysnetane, Thomas Purcell of GarryDuffe and Nicholas Archdeacon of Cloughela that were Ympannelled and sworne of a Grand Jury at a generall Cessions holden for the Countie of Kilkenny at [blank] the twelth [*sic*] Day of August 1616 before Sir Willm Methwould, knight, Cheife Barron of his maties Court of Exchequer, and Sir John Ellyott, knight, third Barron of his maties said Court of excquer [*sic*], Justices of Assize for the said County, To make true presentment of all such recusantes as willfully and obstinately refused to repayre to their parish Churches to heare Dyvyne service accordinge to the Lawes and Statutes of this kingdome, [see formula E, f.191] Uppon which their owne Confession the said James Dalton, Olyver Grace, Richard Purcell, Richard Butler, Danyell Oge OHonoghen and Pierce ORyan were Censured to pay to his matie for a fyne accordinge to the Reducement each of them the some of tenn pounds english a peece. The said Robert Walsh, Edmond Dobbyn, Thomas Purcell and Nicholas Archdeacon lykewise Censured to pay to his matie for a fyne accordinge to the reducement the some of twentye pounds english a peece, and all of them Imprisonment duryng the Lord Deputies pleasure. Dated at his maties Court of Castle Chamber the two and twentieth Day of November 1616 and in the fourteenth yeare of his maties Raigne of England, Fraunce and Ireland and of Scotland the fiftieth.[194]

Memorandum wheare his maties Sergeant at law made Informacon ore tenus in this most honnorable Court of Castle Chamber against James Eustace, Gilbert Sutton of Ardrasse, Morrice FitsGarrald

192. f. 227. 193. f. 228.
194. f. 229.

of Killrush, Edmond Wesley of Narrogh, Meyler Fay of Herbertstowne, Henry Stanyhurst of Kiloone, Peter FitzGarrald of Bealan and John FitsGarrald that were Impannelled and sworne of a grand Jury at a generall Cessions holden for the County of Kildare at the Naas the three and twentieth Day of August 1616 before Sir Willm Methwould, knight, Cheife Barron of his mates Court of exchequer, and Sir John Elyott, knight, third Barron of his maties said Court of excquer [sic], Justices of Assize for the said County to make true presentment of all such recusantes as willfully and obstinately refused to repayre to their parish Churches to heare Dyvyne service according to the lawes and Statutes of this kingdome, [see formula E, f. 191] Uppon which their owne Confession the said James Eustace, Gilbert Sutton, Morrice Fitzgarrald, Edmond Wesley, Meyler Fay, Henry Stanihurst, Peter FitsGarrald and John FitsGarrald were Censured to pay to his matie for a fyne according to the Reducement each of them the some of twentie pounds english a peece, and all of them Imprisonment duryng the Lord Deputies pleasure. Dated at his maties Court of Castle Chamber the two and twentieth day of November 1616 and in the fourteenth yeare of his maties raigne of England, Fraunce and Ireland and of Scotland the fiftieth.[195]

Memorandum wheare his maties Attorney generall made Informacon ore tenus in this most honnorable Court of Castle chamber against Phillip McDonell McCragh of Montayne Castle, Donell McThomas McCragh of Banfowne, Walter Manfield of Ballenemultenagh, Thibbot FitsJohn of Cloneigh, John Power of Garranmellane, Richard Power of Clondonell, William Wale of Cowlenemicke, James Butler of Creghamnagh, Morrice Power of Ballyscanlan and Morrice Power of Ballynebannagh that were Impannelled and sworne of a grand jury at a generall cessions holden for the County of Waterford the [blank] day of [blank] 1616 at [blank] before Sir John Blenerhasset, knight, one of the Barrons of his maties Court of excquer, and Richard Bolton, esquier, Justices of Assize for the said County, to make true presentment of all such recusantes as wilfully and obstinatlie refused to repayre to their parish Churches to hear Dyvyne service according to his maties lawes and Statutes in this kingdome, [see formula E, f. 191] Uppon which their owne Confession the said Phillip McDonell McCragh, Donell McThomas McCragh, Walter Manfield, Thibbot FitsJohn, John Power, Richard Power, William Wale, James Butler, Morrice Power and Morrice Power were Censured to pay to his matie for a fyne according to the Reducement each of them the some of twentie pounds english a peece, and all of them Imprisonment duryng the Lord Deputies pleasure. Dated at his maties Court of Castle Chamber the xxijth day of November 1616 and in the xiiijth yeare of his maties raigne of England, Fraunce and Ireland and of Scotland the fiftieth.[196]

Memorandum wheare his maties Sollyciter Generall ore tenus made Informacon in this most honorable Court of Castle Chamber against William Mansell of Cattellyastowne, Rory OKennedy of Killeny, Geffry Mockler of Mocklerstowne, Nicholas Saure of Sawrestowne, John OMeagher of Clonekenny and Edmond Comyn of Tullaghmayne that were Impannelled and sworne of a Grand Jury att a Generall Cesions holden for the County of the Cyttie of Tipperary the [blank] of [blank] 1616 at Clonmell before Sir John Blenerhasset, knight, one of the Barrons of his maties Court of Exchequer, and Richard Bolton, esquier, Justice of Assize for the said County, to make true presentment of all such recusantes as willfully and obstinatly refused to repayre to their parish Churches to heare Dyvyne service according to his maties lawes and statutes in this kingdome, [see formula E, f. 191] Uppon which their owne Confession the said William Mansell, Rory OKennedy, Geffry Mockler, Nicholas Saure, John OMeagher and Edmond Comyn were Censured to pay to his matie for a fyne according to the Reducement each of them the some of twentie pounds english a peece, and all of them Imprisonment duryng the Lord Deputies pleasure. Dated at his maties Court of Castle Chamber the two and twentieth day of November 1616 and in the fourteenth yeare of his maties raigne of England Fraunce and Ireland and of Scotland the fiftieth.[197]

Memorandum wheare his maties Attorney generall ore tenus made Informacon in this most honnorable Court of Castle Chamber against Thomas Butler of Moretowne, Thomas Stapleton of

195. f. 230. 196. f. 231.
197. f. 232.

Lynestowne and John ODwyer of Dendrumyn that were Impannelled and sworne of a grand Jury at a Generall Cessions holden for the County of Crosse Tipperary at Cashell the [blank] day of [blank] 1616 Before Sir John Blenerhasset, knight, one of the Barrons of his maties Court of exchequer, and Richard Bolton, esquier, Justices of Assize for the said County, to make true presentment of all such recusantes as wilfully and obstinately refused to repayre to their parish Churches to heare Dyvyne service accordinge to his maties lawes and Statutes in this kingdome, [see formula E, f. 191] Uppon which their owne Confession the said Thomas Butler and Thomas Stapleton were Censured to pay to his matie for a fyne accordinge to the Reducement each of them the some of twentie pounds english a peece, and the said John ODwyer was lykewise censured to pay to his matie for a fyne the some of fifteene pounds english, and all of them Imprisonment duryng the Lord Deputies pleasure. Dated at his maties Court of Castle Chamber the two and twentieth day of November 1616 and in the fourteenth year of his maties raigne of England, Fraunce and Ireland and of Scotland the fiftieth.[198]

Memorandum wheare his Maties Solyciter generall ore tenus made Informacon in this most honnorable Court of Castle Chamber against Symon White, late Soveraigne of New Rosse, Mighell Archer, late Sherrife of the Cittie of Kilkenny and Thomas Aysh, late Portrive of the Naas, that they the said Soveraigne, Sherrife and Portrive had executed their severall offices of Soveraigne, Sherrrife and Portrive in the said Cittie and townes before they or any of them had taken the oath of Supremacy which by the Lawes and Statutes of this Realme they and every of them ought to have Donn. And the said Deffendantes and every of them beinge Called to Answer their severall Contemptes Confesed that they and every of them had executed their several offices ever synce they were Chosen officers and that they nor any of them had taken the oath of Supremacy before nor at any tyme synce they tooke uppon them thexecucon of their severall offices. Uppon which their owne Confession the said Symon White, Mighell Archer and Thomas Aysh were Censured by this honnorable Court to pay to his matie for a fyne accordinge to the reducement each of them the some of tenn poundes English a peece and all of them Imprisonment Durynge the Lo Deputys pleasure. Dated at his maties Court of Castle [Chamber the] xxvijth Day of November 1616 and in the fourteenth yeare of his maties raigne of England, Fraunce and Ireland and of Scotland the fiftieth.[199]

Memorandum whear John Woulverston of Wicklow in the County of Wicklow, esquie[r], beinge one of his maties Justices of the peace within the said County, Exhibited Informacon in this moste honnorable Court of Castle Chamber against Nicholas Walsh of Galtowne in the said County gent, and William Walsh of Donbarr in the said County, gent, that the said Nicholas and William Walsh, disrespectinge the said John Woulverston and Contemnyng his personn and his maties Authority Comytted unto him by his highnes Comyssion of a Justice of the peace in the said Countye of Wicklow, the said Nicholas Walsh and William Walsh on the seventh day of October in the xijth yeare of his maties raigne of England, Fraunce and Ireland and of Scotland the seven and fortieth unlawfully Combyned and Conspired at Wycklow aforesaid to abuse the said John Woulverston, beinge then one of his maties Justices of the peace in the said County of Wicklow, first with Contemptuous and Disgracefull wordes and speeches, therby to Incense and provoucke the said John Woulverston to fight with them and to assault and stryke the said John Woulverston. And afterwards the said seventh Day, the said John Woulverston Comeynge from the Court house Where then the quarter Cessions of the peace was held in Wicklow aforesaid, and goeinge towarde his owne house the said William Walsh mett with him. Uppon which meetynge the said William Walsh Chardged said John Woulverston that he has used some speeches which the said John Woulverston denyed to have spoken. Wheruppon the said William Walsh gave him the Lye and Challenged him to the field to fight with him, the said William well knowynge the said John Woulverston to be then one of his maties Justices of the peace for the said County. And soone after the said seventh day at night, the said Nicholas Walsh followed the said John Woulverston to his house wheare the said Nicholas renewed the former Disgracefull wordes and speeches with Comparisons of the Dyfference betweene the Walshes and the Woulverstons bloud and byrth Uppon which quarrellynge and Disgracefull wordes the said John Woulverston Desyred the said Nicholas Walsh to leav his house, which he did.

198. f. 233. 199. f. 234.

And the next day beinge the eight day of the said month of October, the said John Woulverston goeinge to the Cessyons house to performe his Duty to his maty in the execucon of his office, the said Nicholas Walsh mett him neare the Cesions house Dore and Demanded of the said John Woulverston whether he would make good the wordes that he had spoken in his owne house the night before, whoe Answered he would. The said Nicholas Answered that he lyed in those wordes and presently gave the said John Woulverston a box on the eare and withall drew his Dagger on him and the Dagger beinge taken from [him] by the standers by, the said Nicholas Walsh offered to Draw his sword, to the Contempt of his matie and of his highnes Authorety Comyttted to the said John Woulverston by his highnes Comyssyon of the peace. To which said Informacon the said Nicholas Walsh and William Walsh made Aunswer and the Cause proceedinge to Replycacon, Reioynder and witnesses examyned on either parte and published and this Day the Cause appoynted to be hard. And forasmuch as upon full and Delyberate hearinge and Discussinge of the Cause yt mayfestly appeared to this honnorable Court by the Deposycons of sondry witnesses that the said William Walsh uppon the said seventh day of October meetynge the said John Woulverston Comeynge from the Cessyons house where he had sitt uppon the Bench exercyseinge his office of a Justice of the peace, without any Just provocacon gave the said John Woulverston the lye and challenged him to fight with him neere the Cessyons Dore, which was a Contentious misdemeanor to a Justice of the peace whoe should have had reverence and respect from the said William Walsh, especialy at that tyme and place. And allsoe it was manifestly proved that the said Nicholas Walsh the same night went to the house of the said John Woulverston where he first demanded of the said John Woulverston what had happenned betwixt him and the said William Walsh, whoe Annswered that the Churle had much abused him. Wherunto the said Nicholas Walsh sayd that the Walshes were better then the Woulverstons and that the said Woulverston was noe gent but by the mother syde. And the next Day as the said John Woulverston was goeinge to the Cessyons house the said Nicholas Walsh mett him neere the Cesyons house Dore where Dyvers of the gentlemen and freeholders of the County were walkeinge and thother Justices sittinge within in the Cessyons house holdinge Cessions, and there the said Nicholas Walsh uppon Repetycon of what passed betweene them the night before gave the said John Woulverston a blow on the eare with his fist and then Drew his Dagger and stabbed at the said John Woulverston, which Dagger beinge taken from him the said Nicholas Walsh offered to draw his sword but was hyndered therin by the Company [i.e. bystanders]. Wherby ther was a great tumult and uproare in the place and much harme lyke to have ensewed if the said John Woulverston had not Comaunded his servauntes and perswaded his frendes to be quiet and to keepe his maties peace. Which this honnorable Court Doth adiudge to be an outrageous and exorbytant misdemeanor, aswell in regard of the personn soe stroken and abused as of the tyme and place where the same outrage was Comytted, the said John Woulverston and thother Justices of the Peace of the said County beinge then assembled and holdinge Cessyon to admynister Justice unto the Countie and to punish all breachers of the peace. Soe as the same was not ann offence onely against the said John Woulverston but allsoe against his matie and his highnes Authorety and Justice Comytted unto the said John Woulverston and thother Justice of the peace by his highnes Comyssion and wherby great bloodshed and slaughter of many his maties good and faithfull subiectes might have ensewed if the said John Woulverston, with great temperaunce and Discrecon, had pacefied and prevented the same. It is therfore ordered, adiudged and Decreed by this honnorable Court that the said William Walsh for his said Contencious offence and misdemeanor to a Justice of the peace in the tyme of a quarter Cessyons shall satisfie and pay to his matie for a fyne accordinge to the Reducement the some of fyve poundes english and that the said Nicholas Walsh for his said outrageous offence in strykeinge a Justice of the peace at the Cessions Dore as he was goeinge to execute his office and in the view of the Countrye, and for Drawinge his weapons in soe publycke an assembly, shall pay unto his matie for a fyne accordinge to the Reducement the some of tenn poundes English, and that both of them for their said offence shalbe Comytted to Prison there to remayne Durynge the Lord Deputye pleasure. And for that the said offences were publycke and Comytted in Contempt of Magistracye and Justice and that the Inhabitantes of the said County of Wicklow may take notyce what a Judgment and opynion this honnorable Court hath of the same and how tender and Carefull they are that all Reverence and Respect should be given to such as are placed in Authorety and have admynistracon of Justice under his maiestie, And that all men may feare to offer any Indignitie or abuse unto Justice and Magistrates hearafter, It is further ordered that the said Nicholas Walsh and William Walsh, before they be Inlarged out of prison, shall fynd suertyes to appeare at the next generall Cessyones to be holden for the said County of Wicklow and not to Departe without the lycence of the Justice of Assize. And that the said Justice of Assize shall Cause this Decree to be publyckly read in the hearinge of the Countrye and in the presence of the said Nicholas Walshe and William Walsh, after the readinge wherof the said Nicholas Walsh and William Walsh shall publycklie and Distinctly Confesse and acknowledge their said offences and acknowledge their Censure for the same to be Just, and that they are sorie for thier follye and Rashnes in Comyttynge thereof. Dated at his matie Court of Castle Chamber the xxiiijth Day of January 1617 and in the kinges maties Raigne of England, Fraunce and Ireland the xiiijth and of Scotland the fifteeth.[200]

Memorandum where in his maties Learned Councell ore tenus made informacion in this Most honnorable Courte of Castle chamber against Symon Malone and Walter Locke, late shreves of the Citty of Dublin, and James Archdecon, late Portriffe of Inistioge in the County of Kilkenny, that the said Shreves and Portriffe had executed their said severall offices before they or any of them had taken the oathe of Supuremacy as by the Lawes & statutes of this Realme they and every of them ought to have Donn. And the said Defendant being severally called to answere, Confessed that they and everie of them had executed their severall places & offices and that they nor any of them had taken the oath of Supremacie before nor att any tyme since they took upon them the said severall offfices. Uppon which their owne Confession the said Symon Maloane and Walter Locke was Censured by this honnorable Courte to pay to his matie for a fyne according to the reducement each of them the some of forty poundes english a peece and imprisonment in the Marshalsey During the lo deputies pleasure. Dated att his maties Courte of Castle chamber the xxixth day of January 1617 And in the xiiijth yeare of his maties raigne of England, Fraunce and Ireland and of Scotland the fiftieth.[201]

Memorandum where Donogh McThomas of Roskeagh in the County of Wicklowe, gent, exhibited an informacon in this Most honnorable Courte of Castle Chamber that on the fifteenth Day of September in the xiiijth yeare of the kinges Maties raigne of England, Fraunce & Ireland and of Scotland the nyne & fortieth, Edmond Conyan of Conyanstowne, John Boy McMorrogh, Patrick Ballagh, Patrick McHugh, Owen McHugh, Conell McDonogh with divers others Riotouse and disordered persons, being unlawfully asembled on the saboth day, came to the landes of Kilnemanaghbegg in the said County of Wicklowe, being the Landes and possessions of the said Conogh McThomas, and brought with them the number of one hundred Cowes of the said Edmond Conyan and his tenantes of purpose to consume, eate and Destroy the grasse growing uppon the said Landes of Kilnemanaghbegg. Which the said Thomas perceiving, without other in his company, went to Distraine the said Cattle damage fesance and offering to Drive the said Cowes to have impounded them for the trespasse they had comitted, the said Edmond Conyan, armed with a sword, and the person[s] before named with a great number of other riotouse persons, forceably rescued the said Cowes and kepte them with like force all the same day, till milking tyme. Uppon which Informacon the said Edmond Conyan and the persons before mentioned were called to answere and witnesses on either parte examined, and the case this Day appointed to be heard. For as much as uppon full hearing and deliberatt Discusing of the cause it appeared to this honnorable Courte by the Deposicon of severall witneses that the said Edmond Conyan and the aforenamed person[s] and divers other in their company Comitted the said Ryotouse misdemeanor in manner and forme as laid downe in the Informacon & on the saboth Day. It is therfore ordered, adiudged and decreed by this honnorable Courte that the said Edmond Conyan shall pay unto his matie for a fyne for himself & the other five persons before named according to the reducement the some of tenn poundes Englishe, and all of them imprisoned During the Lord Deputies pleasure. Dated att his Maties Courte of Castle Chamber the last day of January 1616 and in the fourtenth yeare of his Maties Raigne of England, Fraunce and Ireland and of Scotland the fifteeth.[202]

---

200. ff. 235–36v. Note Woolverston appeared as defendant before castle chamber in two previous actions, ff. 186–87.

201. f. 237.   202. ff. 238–38v.

Memorandum wheare his maties Attorney Generall ore tenus made Informacon in this most honnorable court of Castle Chamber against Nicholas Devourox, late mayor of the Towne of Wexford, that he the said Nicholas Deveroux had executed the said office of Mayoraltie before he had taken the oath of Supremacy as by the lawes and Statutes of this realme he ought to have donn. And the said Defendant beinge Called to Annswer his said Contempt Confessed that he had executed the said Place and office And that he had not taken the oath of supremacy before nor at any [time] since he tooke uppon hm the execucion of the said office. Uppon which his owne Confession, the said Nicholas Deveroux was Censured by this honnorable Court to pay to his matie for a fyne accordinge to the Reducement the some of fiftie poundes English, and Imprisonment Duringe the Lo Deputyes pleasure. Dated at his maties court of Castle Chamber the fourteenth Day of May 1617 and in the fifteenth year of his maties raigne of England, Fraunce and Ireland and of Scotland the fiftieth.[203]

Memorandum whearas the said Thomas Flemmynge and Edmond Garret at the last assizes holden for the Countie of Corcke, beinge Impanelled uppon a pettie jurie for the tryall of Tibbott Roch FitsJohn for the wilfull murderinge of John Og ne Moyle. Forasmuch as by ther owne Confesion uppon their voluntarie oathes, read openlie this day in court, It appeared that they had heard all the evydence openly Delyvered at the assizes both by witnesses examyned viva voce, and by Deposicons taken in writinge by the lo President of Mounster and Sir Domynicke Sarsfield, knight, Lo Cheife Justice of the Common Pleas, and by the said Lo Sarsfield in open Court avouched soe to have beene taken. And that the same Deposicons in writinge, were allsoe read privately amongst them selves who were of that Jurye (all which the said Defendauntes the last Court Day in face of this Court, had wilfully, peremtorilie and Impudently Denyed). Uppon which testimonies and proofes, the rest of that Jury by the evydence of the said Deposicon did Conceave pregnant and sufficient matter leadinge them to have given a verdict that the said Tibbot Roch FitsJohn was guiltie of the murderinge of the said John Og Ne Moyle. All which notwithstandinge, these two onely, viz Thomas Flemynge of Bealgoly and Edmond Garret of Garretstowne in the said County, gent, out of a Corrupt Conscience by willfull breakinge their oathes in not agreeinge with the rest of their fellow Jurors to fynd a verdict according to their evydence, and out of an high and manifest Contempt of the kinges matie and of his lawes, uppon a resolved purpose (soe much as in them laye) not onelye to prevent the ordenary Course of Justice, and allsoe to have served the rest of that Jury if that mischeife had not Carefully byn prevented by the Judges. And for that, (for the better satisfaccon of the Court) not only his matie Attorney generall did lay open the same and effect of all the Deposicons Delyvered as aforesaid at the said Assizes, but Dyvers of the same Deposicons were allsoe read openly in this Court wherby it evydently appeared, and the Court was therin satisfied, that the said Tibbot Roch FitsJohn, out of a propenced and inveterate mallice, Did with his owne handes wilfully murther the said John Og Ne Moyle. Yt hath therfore been thought fit by this Court and by the same thies day accordinglie is adiudged and Censured that (as well for the prevention of the lyke Disobedience in others, as allsoe for the Condigne punishment of the said Thomas Flemynge and Edmond Garret, for that they have soe wilfully and presumptuously transgresed against God, against the kinge, against their owne Consciences, against publique Justice and Directly against their evydence) each of them by way of fyne shall pay unto his matie according to the reducement the some of twentie poundes english a peece, and besides shalbe Comitted to prison and shalbe set on the pillory on the most frequent marquet Day in the weeke, beinge Saturday, from eight to eleven of the Clocke in the forenoone. And then and ther shall wear papers on their heades with an Inscripcon breifely expressinge their offences, and shall lykewise not only be brought to present themselves in every of the foure Court[s] hear at Dublin this Terme (at the Judges their sittinges) with lyke papers

203. f. 239. Note insertion of a clerical record dating from Restoration period, to wit: 'My Lords, Capt Jacob Knolles haveing sarved as an officer in Iarland [*sic*] under my Command, Carrying him selfe very well, I recomend to your Lordshipps that he may bee setteled in some military Imployment in that Kingdome, I Reamaine,

    Yor Lordships very affectio[nate] friend & Servtt
        Albemarle   Cork ye 27 Jan 1661.'

This note indicates ongoing use of entry book well after the last case entered in 1620. This draft document appears on fol. 239v.

on their heades, and there publiquely acknowledge their offences, and from thence shalbe retorned to the prisons from whence they shalbe taken, there to remayne until it shall please the Lo Deputy to remove or release them. And lastly that they, the said Thomas Flemynge and Edmond Garret, and each of them for ever hearafter, shalbe Disabled from bearinge any office in the Comon wealth, to be Impannelled uppon any Jury, to be accepted for witnesses, or to give testimonie in any Cause whatsoever. Dated at his maties Court of Castle Chamber the sixteenth Day of May 1617 and in the fifteenth year of his maties raigne of England, Fraunce and Ireland and of Scotland the fiftieth.[204]

Memorandum wheare his maties learned Councell ore tenus made Informacon in this most honnorable Court of Castle Chamber against Christopher Taaffe of Braganstowne, John Taaffe of Stephenston, Lawrence Sedgrave of the Graunge, Christofer White of Ballugg, Patricke Clinton of Irishton, and Alexander Pluncket of the Bawne, all of the County of Louth, that were amongst others Impannelled and sworne of a Grand Jury at a Generall Sessions holden in the said County of Louth the seventeenth Day of March 1616 at the towne of Dondalke before Gerrald Lowther, esquier, one of the Judges of his maties Court of Common Pleas, and Sir John Davis, knight, his maties Attorney Generall, Justices of Assize for the said County, to make true presentment of all such recusantes as wilfully and obstinately refused to repayre to their parish Churches uppon sondayes and other holly dayes to hear Dyvyne service accordinge to the lawes and statutes of this kingdome, [see formula E, f. 191] Whereuppon the said Jury beinge severally examyned by the said Justices the reasons why they refused to make presentment accordinge to their evydence, uppon which examynacons the rest of the Jury Confesed they were agreed to make presentment accordinge to their evydence, but the said Christopher Taaffe, John Taaffe, Lawrence Sedgrave, Christopher White, Patricke Clynton and Alexander Pluncket wilfully and [obstinatly] refused to Joyne in the same. And beinge examyned by the said Gerrald Lowther, esquier, by order of this Court the reasons why they refused to Joyne with their fellow Jurors, as all soe beinge questioned by this Court why they wold not Joyne with their felowes haveinge soe pregnant and apparrant evydence, Could make noe other excuse but that it was against thier Conscience. Wheruppon the Court proceedinge to Censure yt was this day ordered, adiudged and Decreed by this honnorable Court that the said Christopher Taaffe, Lawrence Sedgrave, John Taaffe, Allexander Pluncket, Christofer White and Patricke Clynton shall each of them pay unto his matie a fyne accordinge to the reducement the some of twenty poundes English a peece and all of them Imprisonment Durynge the Lo Deputyes pleasure. Dated at his maties Court of Castle Chamber the xxith day of May 1617 and in the fifteent yeare of his maties raigne of England, Fraunce and Ireland and of Scotland the fiftieth.[205]

Memorandum wheare his maties learned Councell ore tenus made Informacon in this most honnorable Court of Castle Chamber against John Magenisse of Corogh in the County of Downe that was amongst others Impannelled and sworne of a Grand Jury at a Generall Sessions holden at Downe in the said County of Downe the one and twentieth day of March 1616 (before Gerrald Lowther, esquier, one of the Justices of his maties Court of comon Pleas and Sir John Davies, knight, his maties Attorney generall, Justices of Assize for the said County to make true presentment of all such recusants as wilfully and obstinatly [refuse] to repayre to their parish Churches uppon Sondayes and other hollydayes to hear Dyvyne service, [see formula E, f. 191] ... but the said John Magenisse wilfully and obstinatly refused to Joyne in the same [verdict]; And he beinge examined by his mates Sergeant at law by order of this Court the reasons why he refused to Joyne with his fellow Jurors, As allsoe beinge quetioned by this Court why he would [not] Joyne with his fellowes in prsentinge the said recusantes, haveinge soe pregnant and apparrant evydence, Could make noe other Defence or Annswer, but that it was against his Conscience. Wheruppon the Court proceedinge to Censure yt was this day ordered, adiudged and Decreed by this honnorable Court that the said John Magenisse shall pay unto his matie a fyne accordinge to the reducement the some of twenty poundes English

204. ff. 240–40v. 'The kinges matie, plte [vs] Thomas Flemynge and Edmond Garret, Defendauntes' cited in left margin, in different hand. Note the sense of outrage, wherein the court intensified punishment for rogue jurors in a murder case, using exemplary punishment and banishing them from judicial system therafter.
205. ff. 241–41v.

and Imprisonment Durynge the Lo Deputyes pleasure. Dated at his maties Court of Castle Chamber the xxjth day of May 1617 and in the fifteenth yeare of his maties raigne of England, Fraunce and Ireland and of Scotland the fiftieth.[206]

Memorand[um] whear his maties learned Councll ore tenus made Informacon in this most honnorable Court of Castle Chamber against Morough Offarrell of Cashelbegg, Edmond McConnoucke of Faslongort, Thomas McTeige OFarrell of Sannagh, Donnogh McGarret of Shanclony, John Oge OFarrell of Aghaffyn, Richard McDonough of Corre and Shane Quyn of Lissechuill, all in the County of Longford that were amongst others Impannelled and sworne of a Grand Jury at a Generall Sessions holden at Ardaugh in the said County of Longford the fyve and twentieth Day of March 1617 before Sir Fraunces Aunger, knight, mr of the Rolles and Sir Robert Oglethorp, knight, one of the Barrones of his matis court of exchequer, Justices of Assize for the said County, to make true presentment of all such rescusantes as wilfully and obstinately refused to repayre to their parish Churches uppon Sondayes [formula G (our italics)] *and other hollydayes to hear divyne service according to the lawes and Statutes of this kingdome. Wheruppon a list of names in writinge were delyvered unto the said Jury testified by the oathes of the severall mynisters of the severall parish Churches within the said Countye that all the personnes named in the said List were recusantes and refused to repayre to their parish Churches acording the said Statutes. Nevertheles, the said Jury wilfully and obstinately refused to presentment [sic] according to theire evydence the said recusants or any of them. Wheruppon the said Jury beinge severally examyned by the said Justice the reasons why they refused to make presentment according to their evydence given them, uppon wch examynacon the rest of the Jury confessed that they were agreed to make presentment according to their evydence. But the said Morrogh OFarrell, Edmond McConnoucke Thomas McTeige OFarrell, Donnogh McGarret, John Oge OFarell, Richard McDonnogh and Shane Quyne wilfully and obstinatelye refused to Joyne in the same. And they beinge examyned by his mate Attorney Generall by order of this Court the reason why they refused to Joyne with their fellow Jurores in presenting of the said recusantes, as allsoe beinge questioned by this Court why they would not Joyne with their fellowes haveinge soe pregnant and apparrant evydence could made noe other defence or Annswer but that it was against their Conscience.* Wherruppon the Court proceedinge to Censure It was this Day ordered, adiudged and Decreed by this honnorable Court that the said Morrogh Offarrell, Edmond McConnoucke Thomas McTeige OFarrell, Donnogh McGarret, John Oge OFarell, Richard McDonnogh and Shane Quyn shall each of them pay unto his matie for a fyne acordinge to the reducement the some of tenn poundes english le peece, and all of them Imprisonment Durynge the Lo Deputyes [pleasure]. Dated at his maties Court of Castle Chamber the xxjth Day of May 1617 and in the fifteenth yeare of his maties raigne of England, Fraunce and Ireland and of Scotland the fiftieth.[207]

Memorandum whear his maties learned Councell ore tenus made Informacon in this most honnorable Court of Castle Chamber against Teige O Connor of Cryve, Owen McNeyle McSwyne [Sweeney] De Carrowcashell, Mulrone McDonnogh of Clonnetemackine, Thomas Greene of Cowlesheagh, Dermot McGrany of Ballederanye all of the County of Sligo that were amongst others Impannelled and sworne of a Grand Jury at a Generall Sessions holden at Sligo in the said County of Sligo the fourth day of Aprill 1617 before Sir Fraunces Aungier, knight, Mr of the Rolles, and Sir Robert Oglethorp, knight, one of the Barrons of his mateis Court of exchequier, Justices of Assize for the said County, to make true presentment of all such recusants as willfully and obstinately refused to repayre to their parish Churches uppon sondayes … [see formula G, f. 243] Wherruppon the Court proceedinge to Censure It was this Day ordered, adiudged and Decreed by this honnorable Court that the said Teige O Connor and Owen McNeyle McSwyne shall each of them pay unto his matie for a fyne acordinge to the reducement the some of twentie poundes english le peece, and Mulrone McDonnogh, Dermot McGrany and Thomas Greene shall each of them pay unto his matie for a fyne acordinge to the reducement the some of fiftie poundes english le peece, all of them Imprisonment Durynge the Lo Deputyes pleasure. But forasmuch as the said Thomas Greene, Dermott McGrany and Mulrone McDonnogh have entred into bond before the Lo Chauncellor for

206. f. 242.   207. ff. 243–43v.

their repayringe to church accordinge the lawes & statutes of this kingdome, It is therfore ordered that their said fynes shalbe remitted. Dated at his maties Court of Castle Chamber the one and twentieth Day of May 1617 and in the fifteenth yeare of his maties raigne of England, Fraunce and Ireland and of Scotland the fiftyeth.[208]

Memorandum wheare his maties learned Councell ore tenus made Informacon in this most honnorable Court of Castle Chamber against Nicholas Whittie of Batlestowne, Hamond Stafford of Ballyconnor and John McKerhoe of Ballyellis in the County of Wexford that were amongst others Impannelled and sworne of a Grand Jury at a Generall Sessions holden at Wexford in the County of Wexford the eleventh Day of March 1616 before Sir William Methwould, knight, Cheife Barron of his maties Court of exchequer, and Peter Palmer, esquier, one of the Justices of his maties Court of Common pleas, Justice of Assize for the said County, to make true presentment of all such recusantes as wilfully and obstinately refused to repayre to their parish churches upon Sondayes [see formula G, f. 243] Wherruppon the Court proceedinge to Censure It was this Day ordered, adiudged and Decreed by this honnorable Court that the said Nicholas Whittie shall pay unto his matie for a fyne acordinge to the reducement the some of fiftie poundes english. And the said Hamond Stafford shall pay unto his matie for a fyne acordinge to the reducement the some of five and twentie poundes english, and the said John McKerhoe shall pay unto his matie for a fyne acordinge to the reducement the some of tenn poundes english, all of them Imprisonment Durynge the Lo Deputyes pleasure. Dated at his maties Court of Castle Chamber the xxith day of May Anno Domini 1617 and in the fifteenth year of his maties raigne of England, Fraunce and Ireland and of Scotland the fiftieth.[209]

Memorandum wheras his maties Seriant at law ore tenus made Informacon in this most honnorable Court of Castle chamber against Richard Rooth FitsEdward, John Mouney, Thomas Stringer, John Donnoghoe, Danyell Martyn, John Flemynge, John Hue, James Troy and John Neale that they at the last Generall Sessions holden for the County of the Cittie of Kilkenny were Impannelled and sworne uppon a Grand Jurye in the said Cittie to make true presentment of all such recusantes as wilfully and obstinatlie refused to repayre to their parish Churches to heare Dyvyne service ... [see formula G, f. 243] ... and beinge demaunded by the Court a reason of their refusall would yeald noe other then that they were poore and Ignorant men, wherby evydently appeared that they, by breakeinge thier oathes, had wilfuly transgressed against the lawes. Yet for that they willinglie submitted themselves to the mercie of this Court, It is therfore ordered, adiudged and Decreed that the said Richard Rooth FitsEdward shall pay unto his matie for a fyne the some of twenty poundes english, and the said John Mouney, Thomas Stringer, John Donnoghoe, Danyell Martyne, John Flemynge, John Hue, James Troy and John Neale were lykewise Censured to pay to his matie for a afyne accordinge to the Reducment each of them the some of tenn poundes Irish a peece, and all of them Imprisonment Duringe the Lo Deputyes pleasure. And whear as his matie Attorney generall made lyke Informacon against Patricke Roch and John Stafford, beinge two of the Grand Jury at the last Assizes houlden for the Countie of Wexford, that they in lyke Case had broken their oathes and wilfuly against the law and their owne Conscience had offended, never thinkeinge how others before them in lyke Case had offended and been punished. For asmuch as the said Patricke Roch, besides the wilfull breakinge of his oath as a Grand Juror, had alsoe broken faith with this honnorable Court and Contemptuously misdemeaned himself this Day in open face of the Court, It is therfore this Day allsoe ordered, adiudged and Censured that the said Patricke Roch by way of fyne shall pay unto the kinges matie the some [of] 100 ᵗⁱ poundes sterling, and shall to morrow wear a paper on his head with a breife Inscripcon of his said offences in every of the foure Court[s] while the Judges are sittinge, and then and ther shall make submission and acknowledg his offences, and at the next Comeinge generall Assizes to be houlden for the said Countie of Wexford, he the said Patricke Roch shall lykwise weare a paper on his head with the lyke Inscripcon at the tyme of the Judges their sittinge in Court, and then and there shall acknowledg his said offences, And shalbe Comitted to prison Duringe the Lo Deputyes pleasure. And further, albeit the said John Stafford had greeveously offended by breakinge his oath as a Grand Juror, for asmuch as he did assure the Court that he hath ever Come to

208. f. 244.   209. f. 245.

Church and ever will Doe, pretendinge that his great error proceeded of meere Ignorance as never haveinge byn of any Jury before and hath faithfully promissed the Court to reforme his error at the said next Assizes to be houlden for the County of Wexford, and is to enter Recognisaunce of 100^{li} to performe the same, the Court therfore adiudged and Censured that the said John Stafford shall by way of fyne pay unto his matie the some of twentie poundes sterlinge, but with this Condicon that if he shall bringe authentique Certificate into this Court at the next Michaelmas Terme that he hath amended his error and performed his promissed service and Dutie, that then this twentie pounde fyne shalbe remitted unto him, and in hope therof his Imprisonment for the present is remitted. Dated at his maiesties Court of Castle Chamber the three and twentieth Day of May 1617 and in the fifteenth yeare of his maties raigne of England, Fraunce and Irland and of Scotland the fiftieth.[210]

Memorandum whear his maties Attorney Generall ore tenus made Informacon in thes most honnorable Court of Castle Chamber against William Baggott of the Cittie of Dublin, merchaunt, that he was most apparently guiltie of breakinge the kinges lawes and wilfully, obstinately and presumptuously Disobayinge the kinges Edictes and proclamacons whearby his matie by his Imperiall Comaundment hath straitly Charged and strictlie forbidden all his loyall subiectes from any Conference or Conversacon with Popish preistes and Jhesuites [*sic*], yet this bould Defendaunt, Contrary to his knowledge, Contrary to his Dutie of Alleageance, and Contrary to both godes law and mans law, Dared to entertayne Popish priestes and Jhesuites the publique knowne [i.e. publicly known to be Jesuits] and Inwardly the professed and practiseinge enymies against the kinge, against his Crowne and against the glorious Gospell of the said Christ now professed in the most places, and by the greatest parte (by oddes) of all his subiectes. Now forasmuch as the said Defendaunt (by order and authorite of this Court) beinge examyned by his maties said Attorney Generall hath voluntarilye Confessed and by his Confessions read openly in Court hath Clearly, manifestlie and directly declared that from Michaelmas 1613 to this present month of May 1617 he hath entertayned in his house one [blank] knowinge him to be romishe priest, and yet for Conscience sake would never Discover him, and for that the said Preist was taken in his house by the extraordenary vigelancie and Care of the Lo Chauncellor at such tyme as he was readie to goe to say his Masse, as did appear by the Alter ready drest with all other ordinarye appendances and accoustrementes prepared for the celebracon of that Detestable and Divelish Idolatrie, and for that his said fault was greatlie augmented by the Circumstances of tyme and place, as in respect of tyme the Preist was harboured in the Parlyament tyme, that he might be ready to advise and consult with or to direct (accordinge to his Capacite) such of the Romanistes as were specyally Interested in the publique afaires, how they might any way either hinder the good indeavoures of the well Disposed or promote the evill motives of the evill affected and turbulent spirites. And in respect of place, the house was made a kynd of Church standinge in the most frequent street of the Cittie and wholie Dedicated to superstition and the highest Idolatrie. And lastly for asmuch as he openlye in Court Denyed that all the foresaid tyme of neere foure yeares he never had Conversacon with the said Preist or at any tyme went to his masses and service, out of which Denyall may necesarily be Collected, or Demonstratively concluded, that he was either a manifest notorious and most Impudent lyar, if he did goe, or a very neer Atheist if in soe longe tyme he would never goe wher he supposed the name of God was Called uppon and Jhesus Christ in his true naturall body, though Invisible, was elevated and adored. It is therfore this Day ordered, adiudged and Decreed by this honnorable Court that the said William Baggott shall pay unto his matie for a fyne accordinge the Reducement the some of xx ^{li} english and Imprisonment Durynge the Lo Deputyes pleasure. Dated at his maties Court of Castle Chamber the eight and twentieth day of May 1617 and in the fifteenth year of his maties raigne of England, Fraunce and Ireland and of Scotland the fiftieth.[211]

Memorandum wheare uppon Informacon exhibited into this most honnorable Court of Castle Chamber by Sir John Davis, knight, his maties attorney generall, against John Moore of the Bryce in the County of Galway, esquier, Feagh Bourke of Downsman in the said County, esquier, Teige ODaly of Killymore in the said County, gent, Nicholas Hamynge of Old Castle in the said County, gent,

210. ff. 246–46v.   211. ff. 247–47v.

William Oge Lally of Ballenebanby in the said County, gent, Fardarragh McRickard of the Moate in the said County, gent, Thomas OManyn of the Crose in the said County, gent, John Spensfield of Castlegard in the said County, gent, William Roe Bourke of Ballenduffe in the said County, gent, Lawrence Bodkyn of Farhgar in the said County, gent, Morris McEdward of Bally McGuard and Teige OFlaghertie of Kilbride in the said County, gent, that were Impannelled and sworne at Generall Assizes houlden at the late Dissolved Abbey of St. Fraunces neare the Towne of Galway in the said County of Galway the xxixth day of August in the fourteenth yeare of his maties Raigne of England, Fraunce and Irland and of Scotland the fiftieth for the tryall of James Evers, late of Killmurry in the County of Galway aforesaid, and Ann Janes of Oghill in the said County, whoe were Indicted and arraigned before Sir Fraunces Aungier, knight, Mr of the Rolles in Ireland, and Sir Robert Oglethorpe, knight, one of the Barrons of his maties Court of exchequer, Justices of Assize for the said County of Galway, the said xxixth day of August for the malycious and wilfull Murtheringe of Henry Sprat, late of Killdyny in the said County of Galway, gent. Uppon which arraignment of the said James Evers and Ann Janes many witnesses were produced before the said Judges and Jury in open Court which did manifestly and Directly prove that the said James Evers dyd most malyciously and wilfully murther the said Henry Spratt and that the said Ann Janes was the plotter and procurer of the said James Evers to Comytt the said wilfull murther. Nevertheles the said John Moore, Feogh Bourke, Teige ODaly and the rest before named of his fellow Jurors did most Corruptly and Contrary to direct, manifest and apparent evydence acquitt the said James Evers and Ann Janes of the said Malycious and wilfull murthering of the said Henry Spratt. Uppon which Corrupt and wilfull Periury, Contempt and misdemeanor the said John More, Feagh [Bourke], Teige ODaly and the rest of the said Jurors were bound by the said Justice to Annswer their said Contempt and offence in this honnorable Court. Wheare uppon full hearinge and Delyberate Discusssinge of the said Cause it manifestleye appeared unto this most honnorable Court that the said John Moore, Feagh Bourke, Teige ODaly and all the rest of the said Jurors had Comitted Corrupt and Wilfull Periury, A manyfest Contempt and misdemeanor against his matie and his highnes lawes and Statutes in this kingdome. For which thier said Contempt and offence It is this Day ordered, adiudged and Decreed by this honnorable Court that the said John More shall pay unto his matie for a fyne according the Reducement the some of two hundred markes english. The said Feagh Bourke and Teige ODaly to pay to his matie for a fyne according the reducement each of them the some of one hundred poundes english le peece. The said Fardararagh McRiccard and Nicholas Hammynge to pay to his matie for a fyne acording the Reducement the some of fiftie poundes English a peece. The said William Roe Bourke and William Oge Lally to pay to his matie for a fyne acordinge the Reducement each of them the some of thirtie poundes english a peece, and the said Lawerence Bodkyne to pay to his matie for a fyne the some of fortie poundes english.[212]

Memorandum wheras Walter Archer, esquier, ore tenus made Informacon in this most honnorable Court of Castle Chamber against Richard Wale, John McKeogh, Owen Boy McKeogh and James Glynn of the County of Crosse Tipperary that were amongst others Impannelled and sworne uppon a Grand Jury at a Generall Assizes houlden at Cashell in the said County of Crosse Tipperary the [blank] day of [blank] 1617 before Sir John Blenerhasset, knight, one of the Barrons of his mates Court of exchequer, and William Sparke, esqr, one of the Judges of his maties Court of Cheife Bench, Justice of Assize for the said County, to make true presentment of all such Recusants as wilfully and obstinatly refused to repayre to their parish Churches uppon sondayes ... [see formula G, f. 243] but the said Richard Wale, John Mc Keogh and Owen Boy McKeogh and James Glynn wilfully and obstinately refused to Joyne in the same. Wheruppon the Court proceeded to Censure and it was this day ordered, aiudged and Decreed by this honnorable Court that the said Richard Wale, John McKeogh, Owen Boy McDeogh and James Glynn shall pay each of them to his matie for a fyne the some of five poundes le peece and Imprisonment Durynge the Lo Deputyes pleasure. And shall goe to the foure Courtes this present Trynitie Terme at the tyme of the Judges sitting in Court with papers on their heades with an Informacon of thier offence and their acknowledge their offence

---

212. ff. 248–48v. Customary formal dating for castle chamber trial omitted at the end of entry, though original trial held on 29 August 1617. Four jurors not mentioned in fine, i.e. Thomas O Manyn, John Spensfield, Morris McEdward and Teige OFlaghertie.

openly, and lykwise shall at the next Generall Assizes in the Court of Crosse Tipperary appeare before the Judges there in the tyme of their sittinge in Court with lyke papers on their heades and with lyke acknowledgment of their offence. But in regard of their povertie it hath pleased the right honnorable the Lo Deputy to remytt the said fyne of five poundes. Dated at his maties Court of Castle Chamber the fourth day of July 1617 and in the fifteenth yeare of his maties Raigne of England, France and Ireland and of Scotland the fiftieth.[213]

Memorand wheras Walter Archer, esquier, ore tenus made Informacon in this most honnorable Court of Castle Chamber against Edmond Ohedyne, Phillip English, Piers Comyn and John Mother of the County of the lybertie of Tipperary that were amongst others Impanelled and sworne uppon a Grand Jury at a General Sessions houlden at [blank] in the said County of the lybertie of Tipperary the [blank] day of [blank] 1617 before Sir John Blenerhasset, knight, one of the Barrons of his maties Court of exchequer, and Willm Sparke, esquier, one of the Judges of his mates Court of Cheife place, Justices of Assizes for the said County, to make true presentment of all such Recusantes as wilfully and obstinately refused to repayre to their parish Churches uppon sondayes ... [see formula G, f. 243, imposing fine of five marks on each defendant] Which fyne hath beene lessened in regard of the service the said personnes had donn in Causing to be apprehended a notorious Murtherer. Dated at his mateis Court of Cstle Chamber the fourth day of July 1617 and in the fifteenth yeare of his maties raigne of England, Fraunce and Ireland and of Scotland the fiftieth.[214]

Memorandum whereas his matie learned Councell ore tenus made Informacon in this most honnorable Court of Castle Chamber against John Roch FitzJohn of the Cittie of Corcke, merchaunt, John Colman of the same, merchaunt, and Edmond Coppinger of the same, merchaunt, that were amongst others Impannelled and sworne uppon a grand Jury at a generall Sesions houlden at the Cittie of Corke in the County of the Cittie of Corke the xxiijth day of September 1617 before Sir William Methwold, knight, Cheife Barron of his maties Court of exchequer, and Sir John Blenerhasset, knight, one of the Barrons of his maties said Court of excequer [*sic*], Justices of Assize for the said County, to make true presentment of all such Recusantes as willfully and obstinately refused to repayre to thier parish Churches to heare dyvine service uppon sondayes ... [see formula G, f. 243, with fines of twenty pounds English imposed on each defendant] Dated at his maties Court of Castle Chamber the seventh Day of November 1617 and in the fifteenth yeare of his maties Raigne of England, Fraunce and Ireland and of Scotland the one and fiftieth.[215]

Memorandum wheras his matie learned Councell ore tenus made Informacon in this moste honorable Court of Castle Chamber against Boetius McEgan of Sesseraghkell in County Crosse Tipperary that were amongst others impannelled and sworne uppon a Grand Jury at a Generall Sessions houlden at Cashell in the said County of Crosse Tipperary the tenth Day of September 1617 before Sir Willm Methwold, knight, Cheife Barron of his maties Court of excequer [*sic*], and Sir John Blenerhasset, knight, one of the Barrons of his maties said Court of excequer, Justices of Assize for the said County, to make true presentment of all such recusantes as wilfully and obstinatly refused to repayre to their parish Churches uppon sondayes ... [see formula G, f. 243 with fine of ten pounds English imposed on defendant]. Dated at his maties Court of Castle Chamber the seventh day of November 1617 and in the fifteenth yeare of his maties Raigne of England, Fraunce & Ireland and of Scotland the fiftieth.[216]

Memorandum wheras his maties learned Councell ore tenus made Informacon in this most honnorable Court of Castle Chamber against Nicholas Power of Downhill, Walter Power of Kilballykelty and William Power [of the same, interlineation] and Nicholas Power of Whitstowne, Rowland Power of Carduffe, Jeffrey Power of Fedane, Teige Bryan of Ballyknocke and Nicholas

213. ff. 249–49v.
215. f. 251.

214. f. 250.
216. f. 252.

Power of Georgestowne that were amongst others Impannelled and sworne uppon a Grand Jury at a Generall Sessions houlden at [blank] in the County of Waterford the [blank] day of [blank] 1617 before Sir Willm Methwold, knight, Cheife Barron of his maties Court of excequer, and Sir John Blenerhasset, knight, one of the Barrons of his maties said Court, Justices of Assize for the said County, to make true presentment of al such Recusatnes as wilfully and obstinatly refused to repayre to their parish Churches upon sondayes ... [see formula G, f. 243] Uppon which their owne Confession the said Nicholas Power of Downhill, Walter Power of Kilballykelty and William Power [of the same] and Nicholas Power of Whitstowne were Censured to pay to his matie for a fyne accordinge to the Reducement each of them the some of thirtie pounds english a peece. The said Rowland Power of Carduffe, Jeffrey Power of Fedane, Teige Bryan of Ballyknocke and Nicholas Power of Georgestowne lykewise Censured to pay to his matie for a fyne accordinge to the reducement the some of twentie pounds english a peece, and all of them Imprisonment duryng the Lord Deputies pleasure. Dated at his maties Court of Castle Chamber the twelfth day of November 1617 and in the fifteenth year of his maties Raigne of England, France and Ireland and of Scotland the one and fiftieth.[217]

Memorandum wheras his maties learned councell ore tenus made Informacon in this most honorable Court of Castle Chamber against Peirs Butler FitzWalter of Nodstowne, Piers Hacket of Ballytrasny, John OKennedy of Lackine, John Keatinge of Nicholstowne, Teige OMulryan of Lysnesilly, Rory OKennedy of Ballynecloghie, James Marnell of Lysnemrocke and Edmond OHedyne of Moynard in the county of Tipperary that were amonst others Impannelled and sworne upon a Grand Jury at a Generall Sessions houlden at Clonmell in the said County of Tipperarye the seventeenth day of September 1617 before Sir William Methwold, knight, Cheife Barron of his maties Court of exchequer, and Sir John Blenerhasset, knight, Justice of Assizes for the said County, to make true presentment of all such Recusantes ... [see formula G, f. 243] Uppon which their owne Confession the said Peirs Butler FitzWalter of Nodstowne, Piers Hacket of Ballytrasny, John OKennedy of Lackine were Censured to pay to his matie for a fyne accordinge to the Reducement each of them the some of thirtie pounds english a peece. The said John Keatinge of Nicholstowne, Teige OMulryan of Lysnesilly, Rory OKennedy of Ballynecloghie, James Marnell of Lysnemrocke and Edmond OHedyne of Moynard lykewise Censured to pay to his matie for a fyne accordinge to the reducement the some of twentie pounds english a peece, and all of them Imprisonment duryng the Lord Deputies pleasure. Dated at his maties Court of Castle chamber the twelfth Day of November 1617 and in the fifteenth year of his maties Raigne of England, Fraunce and Ireland and of Scotland the one and fiftieth.[218]

Memorandum wheras his maties learned Councell ore tenus made Informacon in this most honorable Court of Castle Chamber against Robert Rooth of the Cittie of Kilkenny, esquier, Walter Dowlinge of the same and Richard Troy of the same, gent, that were amongst other Impannelled and sworne uppon a grand Jury at a Generall Sessions houlden at Kilkenny in the County of the Cittie of Kilkenny befor Sir Willm Jones, knight, Cheife Jutice of his maties Court of Cheife [Place] and Garrald Lowther, esquier, one of the Judges of his maties Court of Comon Pleas, Justices of Assize for the said County, to make true presentment of all such Recusants ... [see formula G, f. 243] Uppon which their owne Confession the said Robert Rooth was Censured to pay to his matie for a fyne accordinge to the Reducement the some of fortie pounds english. The said Richard Troy and Walter Dowlinge lykewise Censured to pay to his matie for a fyne accordinge to the reducement the some of tenn pounds english a peece, and all of them Imprisonment duryng the Lord Deputies pleasure. Dated at his maties Court of [Castle] Chamber the xijth day of November 1617 and in the fifteenth yeare of his maties Raigne of England, Fraunce and Ireland and of Scotland the one and fiftieth.[219]

Memorandum where his maties learned Councell ore tenus made Informacon in this most honnorable Court of Castle Chamber against Bryan Oge Magrory Magenis of Killwarly in the

217. f. 253.
218. ff. 254–54v.
219. ff. 255–55v.

County of Downe that were amongst others Impannelled and sworne uppon a Grand Jury [at] a Generall Sessions houlden at Dromore for the County of Downe the seventh day of October 1617 before Sir Domynicke Sarsfield, knight, Cheife Justice of his maties Court of Comon pleas, and [blank] Brereton, esquier, his maties Sergeant at Law, Justices of Assize for the said County, to make true presentment of all such Recusantes ... [see formula G, f. 243, with fine of twentie pounds English imposed on defendant] Dated at his maties Court of Castle Chamber the twelfth day of November 1617 and in the fifteenth yeare of his maties Raigne of England, Fraunce and Ireland and of Scotland the one and fiftieth.[220]

Memorandum whearas his maties learned Councell ore tenus made Informacon in this most honorable Court of Castle Chamber against Connell OFarrell of Tynnelicke, Lysagh McJames of Killsrow and Edmond Reogh OFerrall of Ryne in the County of Longford that were Impannelled and sworne uppon a Grand Jury at Generall Sessions houlden for the said Countie the last day of July 1617 before Sir Fraunces Aungier, knight, Mr of the Rolles of the Chauncery, and Sir Robert Oglethorp, knight, one of the Barrons of his maties Court of exchequer, Justice of Assize for the said County, to make true presentment of all such Recusantes as wilfully and obstinately refused to repaire to their parish churhces ... [see formula G, f. 243] Uppon which their owne Confession the said Connell OFarrell was Censured to pay to his matie for a fyne according to the Reducement the some of twentie pounds english. The said Edmond OFarrell lykewise Censured to pay to his matie for a fyne accordinge to the reducement the some of tenn pounds english a peece, and the said Lysagh McJames lykewise censured to pay to his matie for a fyne accordinge to the reducement the some of threescore pounds english and all of them Imprisonment duryng the Lord Deputies pleasure. Dated at his maties Court of Castle Chamber the xijth day of November 1617 and in the fiteenth yeare of his maties raigne of England, Fraunce and Ireland and of Scotland the one and fiftieth.[221]

Memorandum where his matie learned Councell ore tenus made Informacon in this most honnorable Court of Castle Chamber against Walter Talbott of Ballyconill and Thomas Flemynge of Cabragh in the County of Cavan that were amongst others Impannelled and sworne uppon a Grand Jury at a Generall Sessions houlden at Cavan in the County of Cavan aforesaid the thirteenth day of August 1617 before Christopher Sibthorp, esquier, one of the Judges of his maties Court of Cheife place, and Sir John Davies, knight, his maties Attorney generall, Justices of Assizes for the said County, to make true presentment of al such recusantes ... [see formula G, f. 243, with fines of threescore pounds English imposed on each defendant] Dated at his maties Court of Castle Chamber the xijth day of November 1617 and in the fifteenth yeare of his maties raigne of England, Fraunce & Ireland and of Scotland the one and fiftieth.[222]

Memorandum whearas his maties learned Councell ore tenus made Informacon in this most honnorable Court of Castle Chamber against Rosse McGoghegan of Moycassell and Garrald Terrell of Pacekilbride in the County of Westmeath that were amongst others Impannelled and sworne uppon a Grand Jury at a Generall Sessions holden at [blank] the eleventh of September 1617 before Sir Fraunces Aungier, knight, Mr of the Rolles of the Chauncery in Ireland, and Sir Robert Oglethorpe, knight, one of the Barrons of his maties Court of excheqr, Justices of Assize for the said County of Westmeath, to make true presentment of all such recusantes ... [see formula G, f. 243, with fines of twentie pounds English imposed on each defendant] ... and before they be enlarged shall acknowledge & Confesse their offence under their handes. Dated at his maties Court of Castle Chamber the nynteenth day of November 1617 and in the fifteenth year of his maties raigne of England, Fraunce & Ireland & of Scotland the one and fiftieth.[223]

Memorandum wheras his maties learned Councell ore tenus made Informacon in this most honnorable Court of Castle Chamber against Donnell Oge ORoryke of [blank] in the County of

220. f. 256.
222. ff. 258–58v.
221. ff. 257–57v.
223. f. 259.

Leytrym that were amongst others Impannelled and sworne uppon a Grand Jury at a Generall Sessions houlden for the said County the [blank] day of [blank] 1617 before Sir Fraunces Aungier, knight, Mr of the rolles in Ireland, and Sir Robert Oglethorp, knight, one of the Barrons of his maties Court of exchequer, Justices of Assize for the said County, to make true presentment of all such recusants … [see formula G, f. 243, with fine of ten pounds English imposed on defendant] Dated at his maties Court of Castle Chamber the xxvjth day of November 1617 and in the fifteenth yeare of his maties raigne of England, Fraunce and Ireland and of Scotland the one and fiftieth.[224]

Memorandum wheras John Dobb, gentleman, and Margaret, his wife, of the Cittie of Dublin exhibited Informacon into this most honnorable Court of Castle Chamber the fifteenth day of November 1616 against Jane Dalway, widdow, and James Walsh, her sonn, that they the said Jane Dalway and James Walsh in the year of our lo[rd] god 1615 in Dublin in the County of the Cittie of Dublyn did plott Combyne and Conspire with Dyvers other personnes as yett unknowne to yor matie said subiect by Corrupt and unlawfull meanes to gett into the said Jane Dalwayes handes aswell the last will and Testament of John Dalway, late of Carrygfargus, esquier, Deceased, as allsoe all Lres Patentes, exemplyficacons of all Lres Patentes, Deedes, Wrytinges and evydence Concernynge the landes of the said John Dalway which descended to the said Margaret Dobb as sole Daughter and heire of the said John Dalway, together with a Draght of a feoffment of all the said Landes. And to that end it was Conceaved and resolved by and betweene the said Jane Dalway and the said James Walsh and other the unknowne personnes that the said James Walsh shold Conterfeite and forge or procure some other bad personn to Counterfaite and forge a lre in the name of the said John Dalway, beinge then Dead, to be Directed unto John Bennis of Dublin, alderman, falsly signifieinge unto the said John Bennis that the said John Dalway had given order to the said James Walsh to receive a truncke wherin the said writinges were Contayned, which trouncke was in the Custodye and keepinge of the said John Bennis. By which false and forged lre the said trouncke with all the said former writinges therin Conteyned were by the said John Bennis Delyvered to the said James Walsh. And it was further Concluded and resolved betweene the said Jane Dalway and the said James Walsh and the rest of the Conspirators as yet unknowne that if the said James shold gett the said Truncke into his handes that some or one of them should breake upp the said Trouncke wherin the said writinge were Contayned and take into their handes aswell the said last will and testament of the said John Dalway, as allsoe all other the evydence and writinges Contayned in the said Trouncke. And that theruppon they the said Jane and James, or some or one of them the said Conspirators, shold Cancell or otherwise subpresse the said last will and Testament and the rest of the said wrytinges and evydence which shold anywayes entytle the said Margaret unto the said Landes or any parte of [them]. And that to make the said Draught of a feoffment to seeme and to be taken for a perfect feoffment, the said Jane Dalway and James Walsh or some other by their procurement should forge and Counterfaite sondry Indorsmentes uppon the said writinge or Draught of a feoffment as the Acte and deed of the said John Dalway as allsoe that Lyvery and seisen was theruppon made in the severall Counties where the landes Contayned in the said feoffment did lye and the severall tenements of the said lande did allsoe Atorne unto the said supposed feoffment. To which Informacon the said Jane Dalway and James Walsh made Aunswer and witnesses examyned on either parte and the Cause this Day appoynted for hearinge. And for as much as upon the hearinge of the Cause it appeared unto this honnorable Court by the Confession of the said Jane Dalway that shee procured the lre to the said John Bennis to be written in the name of her husband John Dalway and subscribed his name therunto for the Delyvery of the said Truncke of writinge to the said James Walsh her sonn, and that uppon the said lre the said Trunke was Delyvered to the said James Walsh, whoe also Confessed that, after he had received the same, opened it and perused the wrytinge and evydence that were Contayned in the same. Uppon which their owne Confession It is this Day ordered, adiudged and Decreed by this most honnorable Court that the said Jane Dalway and James Walsh for their said severall offences shall each of them pay unto his matie for a fyne accordinge the Reducement the some of tenn poundes English a peece and Imprisonment Durynge the lord Deputies pleasure. And for the validitie of the said feoffment the Court hath though[t] fitt to leave it to the tryall of the law. Dated at his matie Court of Castle Chamber the eleventh Day of February 1617 and in the fifteenth yeare of his maties raigne of England, Fraunce and Ireland and of Scotland the one and fiftieth.[225]

224. f. 260.   225. ff. 261–61v.

Memorandum where his maties Attorney Generall ore tenus made Informacon in this most honorable Court of Castle Chamber against Marten Skerrett of Galway, merchaunt, That he the said Martyn Skerret, beinge at Lisbone in Portingall [Portugal], mett with one Richard Carrene, otherwise named John Wooldlocke, a fryer in Lysbone aforesaid, and that the said Marten Skerrett and the said Richard Carrone shortly after their meetinge Imbarqued themselves in a Shipp that was bound for Galway. And the said Martyn Skerret uppon his examynacon Confessed that he suspected that the said Richard Carrone was a fryer and, albeit the said Skirret thought him to be a fryer, Nevertheles the said Skirret uppon their landinge at Galway Conveyed the said Richard Carrone to an English mans house without the West gate of Galway and the said Martyn Skirret beinge Called into this Court to Answer the said Informacon openly in Court Confessed soe much as formerly uppon his examynacon before his maties said Attorney he had Declared. Upon which his Confession he was Censured by this most honnorable Court to pay to his matie for a fyne according to the reducement the some of tenn poundes English and Imprisonment Durynge the Lo Deputyes pleasure. Dated at his maties Court of castle Chamber the xjth Day of Februarij 1618 and in the fiteenth yeare of his maties Raigne of England, Fraunce and Ireland and of Scotland the one and fiftieth.[226]

Memorandum wheras Redmond McFeogh OByrne of Keilyvanagh in the County of Wicklowe, esquier, exhibited Informacon into this most honnorable Court of Castle Chamber against Luke Toole of Castellkavan, Theobold Archbold of Mallinteige in the said County of Wicklow, gent, and Dyvers others the servauntes and followers of the said Luke and Theobald, that they the said Luke and Theobald beinge appoynted Collectors for the Collectinge and receiveinge of the second payment of the subsidy graunted unto his matie within the Barrony of Ballenecorr in the said County of Wicklow, out of their Corrupt affeccon and pryvate gayne to themselves, not regardinge their Duty to the kinges matie nor the trust reposed in them for the Collectinge of the said second payment, did forceably, Corruptly and unlawfuly extorte, take, Levy and extorte from Dyvers the Inhabitantes of the said Barrony of Ballenecor that were assessed to pay the said second payment in Irish money and noe more. The said Luke and Theobald did exact and extort from the said Inhabitantes of the said Barrony sterlinge English money for Irish money, and not Content therwith did exacte and extort from many of the Inhabitantes of the said Barrony Dyvers and sondry somes of money that were not assessed to pay any subsidy money at all. And the said Luke Toole and Theobald Archbold beinge Called into this Court to Annswer their severall extorcons and misdemeanors Confessed the same but made excuses that they were ignorant whether they were to receive Irish or ster[ling], albeit it was manifestly proved in Court uppon hearinge of the Cause that the said Luke and Theobald had warnynge given them that they were to receive but Irish money for the said second payment. And for asmuch as it appeared to this most honnorable Court aswell by the testimony of many witnesses that did manifestly prove the said unlawfull exaccons and extorcons, as allsoe [by] their owne Confession, It is therfore this day ordered, adiudged and decreed by this most honnorable court that the said Luke OToole shall pay unto his matie for a fyne according the Reducement the some of thirtie poundes Ir[ish] and that the said Theobald Archbold shall pay unto his matie for a fyne according the reducement the some of twentie poundes Ir[ish] and both of them Imprisonment Durynge the Lo Deputyes pleasure. And before they be enlarged shall enter into bond to acknowledge their offence publyckly at the next Generall Assizes to be houlden for the County of Wicklow. And alsoe that the said Luke Toole and Theobald Archbold shall make present restitucon unto the Inhabitantes of the said Barrony of Ballynecor of the surplisadge [surplus] of all such money as they have wrongfully received. And for asmuch as their was noe proofe made by witneses or otherwise against the rest of the Defendantes but that they were the servauntes and followers of the said Luke and Theobald, the Court hath thought fitt that they be Dismissed from any further trouble touchinge the same. Dated at his maties Court of Castle chamber the xxiiijth day of Aprill 1618 and in the sixteenth yeare of his maties raigne of England, Fraunce and Irland and of Scotland the one and fiftieth.[227]

---

226. f. 262.   227. f. 263.

Memorandum wheras his maties learned councell ore tenus made Informacon in this moste honnorable Court of Castle Chamber against Melaghlen McGranell McLoghlin of Clonneshenagh and Owen ORorcke of Cashell in the County of Leytryme that were amoungst others Impannelled and sworne uppon a Grand Jury at a Generall Sessions houlden at [blank] in the said County of Leytrym the [blank] day of [blank] 161[blank] before Sir Fraunces Aungier, knight, Mr of the Rolles in Ireland, and Sir Robert Oglethorpe, knight, one of the Barrons of his Maties Court of Exchequer, Justices of Assize for the said County, to make true presentment of all such Recusantes as wilfully and obstinatly refused to repayre to their parish Churches uppon sondayes ... [see formula G, f. 243] Wheruppon the Court proceeded to Censure and it was this day ordered, adiudged and decreed by this honnorable Court that the said Owen ORorcke shall pay unto his matie for a fyne the some of thirtie poundes Irish and Imprisonment Durynge the Lo Deputyes pleasure. And before he be enlarged shall acknowledge his offence under his hand in writing and enter into bond to acknowledge the same publicklye at the next Generall Assize to be houlden for the said County of Leytryme at the tyme of the Judges sitting in Court. And for asmuch as the said Melaghlen McGranell had beene formerly Censured in this Court for the lyke offence and entred into bond before the Lo Chauncellor for his Duly repayreinge to Church accordinge the lawes and Statutes of this kingdome, Wheruppon his said fyne was remitted. It was therfore this day lykewise ordered, adiudged and Decreed by this honnnorable Court that the said Melaghlen McGranell his bond shall be estreated and that he shall stand on the Pillory with a paper on his head expressinge his offence and Imprisonment durynge the Lo Deputyes pleasure and before he be enlarged shall acknowledge and Confesse his offence under his hand in writinge and enter into bond to acknowledge and Confesse the same publicklye the next Generall Assizes to be houlden for the said County of Leytryme at the tyme of the Judges sitting in Court. Dated at his maties Court of Castle Chamber the xxixth day of Aprill 1618 and in the sixteenth year of his maties raigne of England, Fraunce and Irland and of Scotland the one and fiftieth.[228]

Memorandum whear his matie learned Councell ore tenus made Informacon in this most honnorable Court of Castle chamber against Martyne Flemynge of the towne of Drogheda, merchaunt, Patricke Conny of the same, merchaunt, Nicholas Hamblyn of the same, merchaunt, Patricke Field of the same, merchaunt, and William Flemynge of the same, merchaunt, that were amongst others Impannelled and sworne uppon a Grand Jury at a Generall Sessions houlden at Drogheda in the County of the towne of Drogheda the xviijth day of February 1617 before Sir Domynicke Sarsfield, knight, Cheife Justice of his maties Court of Comon Pleas, and William Sparke, esquier, one of the judges of his maties Cort of Chiefe Place, Justices of Assize for the said County, to make true presentment of all such recusantes ... [see formula G, f. 243] the said Martyne Flemynge shall pay unto his matie for a fyne, beinge a Ringleader of all the rest, the some of one hundred markes Irish, and the said Patricke Conny, Nicholas Hamblyn, Patricke Field & Willam Flemynge were lykewise Censured to pay to his matie for a fyne the some of thirtie poundes Irish a peece, and all of them Imprisonment during the lo Deputyes pleasure. And that before they be enlarged shall each of them acknowledge their offence under their handes in writinge and enter into bond to acknowledge the same publickly at the next Generall Assizes to be houlden for the said towne of Drogheda at the tyme of the Judges sittinge in Court. Dated at his maties Court of Castle Chamber the xxixth day of Aprill 1618 and in the sixteenth of his maties raine of England, Fraunce and Ireland and of Scotland the one and fiftieth.[229]

Memorandum wheras his maties learned Councell ore tenus made Informacon in this most honnorable Court of Castle chamber against William Ash of the Cittie of Dublin, merchaunt, that he the said William Ash, Contrary to his Duty and Contrary to severall proclamacons in this kingdome made against Releiveinge, Comfortinge, abettinge and entertayning of Popish priestes, Jesuites and Semynaries, Nevertheles the said William Ashe, out of his Corrupt and Disloyall affeccon to his matie and the State of this kingdome, did relieve Comfort, Abett & maintayne one James Guyne, a priest, knowing him to be a popish priest ordayned by forraine Authoritie. And the

228. ff. 264–64v.   229. f. 265.

said Defendant, beinge examyned by Sir John Davies, knight, his maties Attorney Generall and Sir Robert Jacob, knight, his maties solliciter Generall by order of this Court, Confessed that the said James Guyne was Dyvers Dayes and tymes in his Company and did severall tymes releive him with meat, drinke and money and did lykewise provide for him a barque for his transportacon beyond the Seas wherin the said William Ashe himselfe was purposed to acompany him. Uppon which his owne Confession It was this Day ordered, adiudged and Decreed by this honnorable Court that the said Wiliam Ashe for his said Contempt shall pay unto his matie for a fyne accordinge the reducement the some of tenn poundes engl[ish] and Imprisonment duryng the Lo Deputyes pleasure. Dated at his maties Court of Castle Chamber the sixt Day of May 1618 and in the sixteenth year of his maties raigne of England, Fraunce and Ireland and of Scotland the one and fiftieth.[230]

Memorandum wheras his maties learned Councell ore tenus made Informacon in this most honnorable Court of Castle Chamber against William Sweetman of Castleleise, William Sweetman of Kilkrosse and William Drylinge of Kilbereghan in the County of Kilkenny that were amongst others Impannelled and sworne uppon a Grand Jury at a Generall Sessions houlden at [blank] in the said County of Kilkenny the thirteenth Day of March 1618 before Sir William Joanes, knight, Cheife Justice of his maties Court of Cheife Place, and Gerrald Lowther, esquier, one of the Judges of his maties Court of Comon Pleas, Justices of Assize for the said County, to make true presentment of all such recusantes ... [see formula G, f. 243, with fines of one hundred pounds Irish imposed on each defendant and acknowledgement of their offences] ... under thier hande in writinge ... Dated at his maties court of Castle Chamber the sixt Day of May 1618 and in the sixteenth yeare of his maties raigne of England, Fraunce & Ireland and of Scotland the one and fiftieth.[231]

Memorandum wher his maties learned Councell ore tenus made Informacon in this most honnorable court of Castle Chamber against Piers Comyn, James Butler, Theobald Butler, Richard Prendergast, William Butler and Thomas Butler of the County of the lybertie of Tipperary that were amongst others Impannelled and sworne upupon a Grand Jury at a Generall Sessions houlden at [blank] in the said County of the libertie of Tipperary the [blank] day of [blank] of 161[blank] before Sir William Methwold, knight, Cheif Barron of his maties Court of Exchequer, and Sir John Blenerhasset, knight, one of the Barrons of his maties said Court of Exchequer, Justices of Assize for the said County, to make true presentment of all such recusantes ... [see formula G, f. 243, with fines of fifty pounds sterling imposed on each defendant and release only after acknowledgement of their offences at the next assizes in Tipperary] Dated at his maties Court of Castle Chamber the eighth day of May 1618 and in the sixteenth yeare of his maties raigne of England, France & Ireland and of Scotland the one and fiftieth.[232]

Memorandum wher his maties learned Councell ore tenus made Informacon in this most honnorable Court of Castle Chamber against Nicholas Boyton, Redmond Hacket and Richard Butler that were amongst others Impannelled and sworne uppon a Grand Jury at a Generall Sessions houlden at Cashel in the County of Crosse Tipperaray the [blank] day of [blank] 161[blank] before Sir Willm Methwould, knight, Cheife Barron of his maties said Court of exchequer, and Sir John Blenerhasset, knight, one of the Barrons of his maties said Court of exchequer, Justices of Assize for the said County, to make true presentment of all such recusantes ... [see formula G, f. 243] Wheruppon the Court proceeded to Censure and it was this day ordered, adiudged and Decreed by this honnorable Court that the said Nicholas Boyton, beinge Ringleader of all the rest, shall pay to his matie for a fyne the some of one hundred markes ster & Imprisonment Durynge the Lo Deputyes pleasure. And before he be enlardged shall acknowledge his offence under his hand in writinge and enter into bond publickly to acknowledge the same at the next Generall Assizes to be houlden for the said County of Crosse Tipperary at the tyme of the Judges sittinge in Cort, and shall also at the tyme of the said Assizes in open Court the Judges then sittinge wear a paper on his head with a breife Inscripcon therin expressinge his offence. And it was lykewise ordered, adiudged and decreed by this honnorable Court that the said Redmond Hacket and Richard Butler shall each of them pay unto his matie for a fyne the some of fiftie pounds ster a peece and both of them Imprisonment Durynge the Lo Deputyes pleasure and before they be enlarged shall each of them acknowledge their ofence under their handes in writinge and enter into bond to acknowledge the same publykly at the next Generall Assizes to be holden for the said County of Crosse Tipperary at the tyme of the Judges then sittinge in court. Dated at his maties Court of Castle Chamber the eight day of May 1618 and in the sixteenth yeare of his maties raigne of England, Fraunce & Ireland and of Scotland the one and fiftieth.[233]

Memorandum wheras Sir John Davis, knight, his maties Attorney Generall, exhibited Informacon into this most honnorable Court of Castle Chamber against David Verdon, Clarke [i.e. clergyman], whoe Confeseth him selfe to be a Popish Preist that he the said David Verdon Contrary to sondry lawes and Statutes in force in this kingdome, bearinge great mallice and envy to the personn and religion of George, now Lo Archbishopp of Canterbury, beinge a great Prelate and one of his maties most honorable privie Councell in England, on or about the month of Jannuary last past 1618, Did of his owne head and wicked Invencon malyciously and Diabolycally Devyse and Contryve a moste horrible and false Lye of and uppon the said Lo Archbishopp, theffect wherof was, viz that the said Lo Archb of Canterbury was Lately before Comitted to the tower in England for two Artycles of Treason, first for sayinge it was not fitt that a forrener should be kinge of England seeinge there was an heire apparent to the Royall bloud within the said kingdome, secondly for affirmynge that the kinges matie did seeke purposely to match with the kinge of Spayne in marriadge to Ruyne and overthrow the English. And the said David Verdon haveinge soe malyciously and wickedly Devysed and Contryved the said false and horrible Lye afterwardes, viz uppon the tenth day of February 1618 at Stedalte in the County of Meath, and at Dyvers other tymes and places in the hearinge of Marcus Draycott of Stedalt aforesaid, gent, and of Richard Dillon of Proudstowne in the said County of Meath, gent, and of Dyvers other the kinges maties subieces of this Realme advisedly, Contemptuously and with a malyciouse purpose to defame and Dishonnor the said Lo Archbishopp did utter and publish for newes the said false and horrible lye before menconed and expressed. To which Informacon the said David Verdon was by his maties writt of subpena Called into this Court to make Annswer therunto. Uppon which his Annswer, as allsoe uppon his examynacon uppon personall Inter[rogatory], Confessed that he did report and publish to the said Marcus Draycott and the said Richard Dillon at Stedalt aforesaid the said horrible false and forged Lye before Recyted. Wheruppon this Court proceedinge to Censure It is this Day ordered, adiudged and Decreed by this honnorable court that the said David Verdon for his said offence shall pay to his matie for a fyne the some of five hundred poundes sterling and shall uppon some markett day be sett uppon the Pillory with a paper on his head expressinge his offence and both his eares nayled to the same and afterwarde both his eares to be Cutt of, and shall alsoe remayne prisoner in his maties Castle of Dublin Durynge the Lo Deputyes pleasure. Dated at his maties Court of Castle Chamber the fifteenth day of May 1618 and in the sixteenth year of his maties raigne of England, Fraunce and Ireland and of Scotland the one and fiftieth.[234]

Memorandum wheras Willm Stritch of the Cittie of Lymericke, Alderman, and Domynicke White of the said Cittie, merchaunt, exhibited Grosse Bias thone against the other, which Bills were proceeded in to Annswer and examynacons uppon personall Inter[rogation], and afterwards the said plte surceased and left from any further prosecucon of their said suites and Compounded betweene themselves without lycence of the Court Contrary to the orders layd Downe in the said Court. And the said Domynicke White beinge Called into the Court to Annswer the said Contempt Confessed that the said Stritch and him selfe had given their Consent not to prosecute their Causes any further in the Court. And forasmuch as the Court fyndinge the Causes were not great in Difference betweene them It was therfore ordered and Decreed by the Court that the said William Stritch and Domynicke White for thier Contempt shall pay to his matie for a fyne the some of fiftie shillinges ster a peece and both the Causes to be Clearly dismissed and Dischardged out of the Court, payinge the fees due to the officers of the Court. Dated at his maties court of Castle Chamber the tenth Day of June 1618

233. f. 269.   234. f. 270.

and in the sixteenth yeare of his maties raigne of England, Fraunce and Ireland and of Scotland the one and fiftieth.[235]

Memorandum That wheras Sir Richard Bolton, knt, his Maties Sollicitor generall did ore tenus inform this most honorable Court of Castle Chamber that Richard Nugent of the Cittie of Dublin, merchant, Elinor Nugent his wife, and James Brown of Dublin, merchant, had receaved divers and sondrie leters from divers and sondrie persons in this kingdome which were taken in the custodie of the sayd James Browne by Sir Lawrence Esmond, knight, one of his Maties privie Councell heere and by him sent to the L Deputie, all which letters were brought into the Court and acknowledged to have bin receaved as followeth. The sayd Richard Nugent and Elinor his wife confesed under their handes in writing and (their confessions beeing openly read in Court) were by them freely acknowleged to be true, viz that they had receaved one letter from Nicholas Nugent, a Jhesuite, beeinge a prisoner in his Maties Castle of Dublin which they sent to the sayd James Browne. And Richard Nugent further confessed that him self had receaved one other letter from Phelim Kearnan directed to his brother Thomas Kearnan, a student in the Irish howse or College at Civill [i.e. Seville] in Spaign, and that himself also wrote one letter to Mychaell Carmicke, merchant, abiding at Lysbone in Portugall, and one other letter to John Nugent, his sone, then abiding (as he thought) in the Irish College at Lysbone. And the sayd Elinor confesed that shee had sent eleven shilling in gould to the sayd John, her sonne. All which letters and money the sayd James Brown, both under his hand and publiquely in Court, confessed to have receaved from the sayd Richard and Elinor. And the sayd Brown further confessed that he had receaved divers other letters, As one from William Brown, a preist, with twentie shillinges in money to be delivered to the Provost of the sayd College in Lysbone, two other letters from Edward Brangan, servant to Mr Devenish [and] two other from Robert Morgan of Arcloe [Arklow]. All which leters and money the sayd Brown confessed to have receaved as aforesayd with a purpose and intention to have delivered the same at the Irish College in Lysbone, soe soone as hee shold arive there, hee having purposed (about Easter last) to have made a voyage thither. Now forasmuch as some of the sayd letters, beeing openly read in Court, did conteigne both matter of sedition and also of publique slander of the Justice of this kingdome and most wicked scandall to the established religion professed by his Matie and all his most loyall and most faythfull subiectes, As terming the professors therof heretiques. And for that his Maties sayd Sollicitor shewed at large howe unlawfull yt ys in yt self and how preiudiciall yt maybe to the State and safetie of the comon wealth for any persons to receave and conveigh away letters whatsoever from any of his Maties prisoners (without first acquainting the publique Magistrat with the contentes) especially from a Jhesuit, being a Prisoner and a known and professed enemie to the true religion, and iust gouvernment established. The said Sollicitor also further shewed how dangerous and in sufferable yt ys in subiectes to have intercourse by letters and intelligence with, or to supplie moneys unto, the professed enemies (to the religion and gouvernment established) reciding beyond the Seas in the Nurseries of seditious spiritts who and [sic: are] there instructed and doe begin, both to learn and practize howe to sowe sedition in the mindes of ill affected subiectes and also, yf opportunitie should serve, to incite and stirr them upp to open rebellion. In consideration wherof and for a prevention to others to doe the like, the sayd Sollicitor humbly moved the Court to proceed to censure. Wheruppon the Court did order, adiudge, censure and decree that the said Richard Nugent for him self and his wife should pay unto his Matie by way of fine the some [of] twentie poundes, which some by warrant under the L Deputies hand, bearing Date the 13 of May 1619, was reduced (in respect of their povertie) to five poundes Irish. And that the said James Browne should pay unto his matie by way of fine the some of fortie poundes. Which some (reguard and compassion being had of his extreme povertie) by warrant under the L Deputies hand, bearing Date the 26 of May 1619, was likewise reduced to five pounds Irish. Soe as they did presently paye thier severall reducementes into his Maties receipt. And the sayd Richard Nugent and James Brown were ordered censured and adiudged to be comitted to prison there to remain during the L Deputies pleasure. Dated at his maties high Court of Castle Chamber the 23 Day of Aprill 1619 and in the seventeenth yeare of his maties raigne of England, France and Ireland and of Scotland the two and fiftieth.[236]

---

235. f. 271.
236. ff. 272–72v. Note how this case is used as an example to others, implicitly acknowledging the likelihood of similar situations in families throughout the kingdom, though diminishing the fine under these circumstances.

Memorandum that wheras Sir Richard Bolton, knight, his Maties Sollicitor generall, did ore tenus inform the Court that John Jones, standing at the barre, had contrefaicted a deed in parchment with teste and seale unto yt openly shewed in Court and had delivered yt in lieu of the true deed, of a wicked purpose to Deceave. And that hee had also contrefaicted the L Deputies hand to a warrant which was likewise openly showed to the view of all the Judges of the Court, and both the sayd contrefaictinge confessed by the sayd John Jones to bee true. Now for that the sayd Solicitor enferred that the L Deputies hand was the warrant wherby all his Maties lands, pardons, protections and all other grantes whatsoever depending upon and warranted by his Maties prerogative royaull are passed within this kingdome, and in that respect may be termed a sacred hand. The Court therfore ordered, adiudged, censured and decreed that the sayd John Jones shuld bee sett on the pillory of Dublin the next marquett Day with a paper on his head briefely notifying his offences, and that from the pillorie with the same paper on his head hee shold bee carried into every of the fower Courtes (while the Judges sate) and there acknowledge his offences, and from the Courtes to be carried to the prison where he remayned uppon an exequetion. And lastly that when he hath freed him self from the exequetion he ys then to be banished out of this his Maties kingdome of Ireland. Dated at his Maties high Court of Castle Chamber the 26 of Aprill 1619 and in the seventeenth yeare of his Maties happie raigne of England, France and Ireland and of Scotland the two and fifteth.[237]

Memorandum that wheras Sir Richard Bolton, knight, his maties Sollicitor generall, ore tenus informed the court that John Geshell, standing at the barre, had contrefaicted the L Deputies hand alone to one manuscript of a protection for him self, wherby he might freely passe wheresoever hee would within this kingdome, without the arrests, troubles, or molestations of any his creditors during the tyme limited in the same contrefaict protection. And where the sayd Sollicitor further informed the court, that the sayd John Geshell hath also contrefaicted the L Deputies and the L chief Barons handes to an other manuscript, both which baring open he showed in Court, and by him the said John Geshell openly confessed to be truly his own dooing. Now for that yt was enferred by the sayd Sollicitor that the contrefaicting of a protection was an offence of a verie high condition, as usurping and intruding uppon the highest point and most speciall prerogative of his Maties imperiall power and therfor to be punished with the infliction of a much more grievous scourge then many other offences. Howbeyt in respect of the said Geshell his free acknowledgement of his sayd offences, making publique attestation of his grief for the same by his shedding of teares and faythfuly promising never to attempt to doe the like again, The Court therfore being moved to comiserat his poore and lamentable estate yf his eares should be nayled to the pillorie, and conceaving hope of his true repentance for his sayd high offences, did order, adiudge, censure and decree that the sayd John Geshell should only bee sett on the pillorie of Dublin the next marquet day with a paper on his head briefly Declaring his offences and that, with the same paper on his head, he should be carried from the Pillorie into everie of the fower Court[s], while the Judges are sitting, and in every of them acknowledge his offences. And further that the sayd John Geshell, shall by way of fine, pay unto his Matie the some of fortie pounds and lastly that he shalbe comitted to prison, there to remain during the L Deputies pleasure. Dated at his Maties high Court of Castle Chamber the fowerth day of June 1619 and in the seventeenth yeare of his Maties raigne of England, France and Ireland and of Scotland the two and fyfteth.[238]

Present: The Lord Chancellor, The Lo Sarsfeild, The Lo chief Baron, the Mr of the Rowles.
Memorandum that whereas Gilbert Butler, Esquire, according to the Comaundment of the Lo Deputy, hath this Day appeared in Court to answere such Matters as on his Maties behalf should be obiected against him. Now forasmuch as the Lo cheif Baron being one of the Judges of the last Assizes holden at Clonmell for the County of Tipperary was best acquainted with the offence Comitted by the Deft, his Lordship was required by the Court to make relation thereof. Who in open Cort averred that one [blank in MS], a notorious rebell being indicted of [blank] and thereuppon putt uppon triall of his life, by a lawfull Jury was by the said Jury found guiltie, and was accordingly Condemned to suffer Death for the same. And his lordshp also further ordered that before his and

---

237. f. 273.   238. f. 274.

his Brother Judge (Sir John Blenerhassett. knight) their Departures out of Clonmell, they gave Comaundment to the said Gilbert Butler (as being then high Sherief of the said County of Tipperary) to see the said Condemned prisoner to be presently exequeted. Yet notwithstanding the said Gilbert Butler, out of a self presumption of his Aone [i.e. own] authoritie (grounde uppon a false principall) Did reprive the said Condemned prisoner, in Desire and hope to have gotten his pardon. All which the said Gilbert Butler could not but confesse to bee true, and thereupppon humblie acknowledging his greate Error, Comitted of meere ignorance, hee humblie besought the pardon and Comiseration of the Cort for his said offence. Howbeyt, forasmuch as his offence in shew proceeded from too high a presumption, but especially for that the Due execution of the law is the life & soule of the law, so as without yt noe Comon welth can subsist and bee, and for that also if such offences should escape unpunished, and cheifly when the offenders are men of emmynent note, from whome the lower rankes are ever apt to take example and encouragement to doe the like, yf not worse, yt is therfore this day ordered, adiudged and decreed by the Court, and that in due regard had aswell of the defendants free acknowledgment and repentance of his offence, as also in a Compassionable respect of his present meane estate, that he the said Gilbert Butler shall by way of fyne for his offence pay unto his Matie the some of forty poundes currant mony of and in England, reduced to xli ster [interlineation], and shalbe comitted to the Marshalsye [prison] there to remayne dureing the Lo Deputyes pleasure. Dated at his Maties high Court of Castle chamber the Seaventeenth day of November 1619 and in the Seavententh yeare of his maties Raigne of England, France & Ireland and of Scotland the three and fiftyeth.[239]

Present: The Lo Deputye, The Lo Chancellor, Mr. vicethrer, The Lo Sarsfeild, The Lo Cheif Baron, The Mr of the Rowles.

Memorandum that whereas David FitzGibbon exhibiting his bill into this high Court against Gibbon FitzMorris, Gerald FitzMorris, Donnogh OGrady, Nicholas Freeman, John OGrady, Cormock OHeys and Edmond Schoole, defendants in generall for periury, subornacon of periurye practises, and ymbracery, and upon full and deliberate heareing of this cause, begone on the tenth day of this Moneth of May when the pltes Councell was only heard, and ended and determyned this present day. Now forasmuch as no probable proof was brought to convict John OGrady or Gerrald FitzMorris of all or any of the Crymes charged on them in the pltes bill, and for that no sufficient prooffe was made of the periurye wherwithall Cormack OHeis and Edmond Scoole were charged to have comitted uppon a tryall at the kinges bench barr uppon an eiectment, the Court therfore acquitted the said Gerrald FitzMorris, John OGrady, Cormack OHeis and Edmond Scoole and every of them of the Crymes and the punishment due for them, yf they had bene convicted. But forasmuch as uppon evident and demonstrative prooffe by thexamynacon taken of sondry Esquires and gent of good worth in the said County of Meath, yt doth appeare to the Court the Gibbon FitzMorris was the setter on and principall mover, abetter, assistant and maynteyner of Donnogh OGrady and Nicholas Freeman to be sollicitors and agentes for hym to make, embrace, and labour (by promyses and offer of rewardes) with as many as they could ymagine, yf they were not of the Jury that they should speake withall and intreat those of the Jury to befreind the defendantes upon the tryall and passing of the verdict, and yf they were of the Jury then to give their furtherance that the verdict might passe for the defendantes. And first Donnogh OGrady, knowing that Frauncis Fitton, esquire, (though dwelling in the County of Lymerick, yet by reason of his allyance in the County of Meath) the said Donnogh OGrady first offered the said Frauncis one hundred poundes soe as he would procure his freindes in Meath to befreind Gibbon FitzMorris in a suite depending betwixt hym and David FitzGibbyn, and was to be tryed by a Jury of the County of Meath, which offer the [said] Frauncis utterly refusing, and Donnogh OGrady thereuppon apprehending that Frauncis Fytton might happily wish well to the plt and his cause, and fearing that the said Frauncis his presence yf he should goe into the County of Meath might give some furtherance and countenance to the plts suite, he the said Donnogh therfore at a second tyme offered the said Frauncis the some of forty poundes soe as yf he would not befreind the defendante, he should not oppose them but remayne a newter [i.e. neutral]. And then for that yt was more then sufficiently proved by the oaths of worthy gent that the said Nicholas Freeman, at the request and for good consideracon made and better promysed, before

239. f. 275.

the ympannelling of the Jury at Trime, came in Company with the said Gibbon FitzMorris into the County of Meath, where by the space of seaven or eight weekes togither he continued and dayly went from one gent to another and from one freehoulder to another, solliciting them first in generall to the end that yf they were of the Jury to be freindes to the defendantes cause, and yf they were not themselves of the Jury, then to move those of the Jury to further what they could that the verdict should be given for the defendante. Then in particular as may appeare by the deposicon of Mr William Dillon that the said Freeman comeing to his house and lodging with hym, the said Freeman tould hym that he had byne with Mr Aylmer, but found hym very cold. Whereuppon afterwardes, when the Jury came to be sworne, excepcons were taken against Mr. Aylmer, then the said Freeman tould Mr Dillon, that he had byne with Anthony Alleyn (who was afterwards of the Jury and did not feare hym). And Mr Dillon further deposed that after the verdict was given, meeting with Nicholas Beetagh, one of the Jury, in the street of Dublin tould the said Beetagh that he, with others being present at the tryall, marvayled that the Jury gave their verdict against the plt. Whereunto Nicholas Beetagh answered that he was sorye that he was of that Jury, and that yf he had knowne as much as he then did, he would rather have byne fyned for non appearance, then have byne of the Jury by reason of the yll caryage which he had observed in that busines. Uppon which evident and demonstrative proffes the Court was pleased to proceed to censure, and knowing that the offences of periury, subornacon of periury, Champertye, mayntenance and embracery are exceeding frequent in this kingdome, as the principall Judges, yea the Lo Deputy hymself, knew and did testifye, that yf such offences soe comon, soe pernicious and soe pestilent as that having already infected divers members of this politick body, yf they be not cauterized in tyme, may peirce into, and throughly infect the whole body, for as good lawes and the due execucon of them are the mayne supporters of all well governed comon wealthes, soe the neglect to take fitt opportunytyes to chastize delinquentes and transgressors of the law may (by the ympunyty and freedome of punishment in some) give occasion, incouragement, and boldnes to others, exorbitantly to run ryott into all manner of mischeifes. For prevencon whereof, and to Terrifye all that will take example from the executing hand of Justice, The Court hath therfore this day ordered, adiudged, Censured and decreed, first that the said Gibbon Fitz Morris (for his offence & being the first mover, the instigator and anymator of the said Donnogh OGrady and Nicholas Freeman to sollicite and embrace Jurors and Jury men partially to favor and abett any cause whatsoever, either right or wrong) shall pay unto his Matie by way of fyne for his said offence the some of one hundred poundes ster, and shalbe comtted to prison, there to remayne dureing the Lo Deputyes pleasure. And then that Donnogh OGrady (for his offering of bribes, and rewards to procure a gent of worth or any other, either to be partial or in a cause for the tryall of what sute soever, depending in any Court of Justice) shall by way of fyne for his offence pay unto his Matie the some of three score poundes ster and be ymprisoned dureing the Lo deputyes pleasure. And thirdly that Nicholas Freeman, as being a more generall Sollicitor for Gibbon Fitz Morris and practizeing with and imbraceing many more then Connogh OGrady (yet with great comisseracon of his poverty), the Court hath also ordered, adiudged, censured and decreed that the said Nicholas Freeman for his offence shall by way of fyne pay unto his Matie the some of Twenty poundes ster, to be ymprisoned dureing the Lo Deputyes pleasure, to be sett on the pillory at Dublin on two severall marquett dayes with a paper on his head declareing his offence, and that in terme tyme while the foure Courtes are sitting shall from the pillory be brought each day into every of the foure Courtes with the paper on his head. And lastly, in as much as neither periury nor subornacon of periury was proved against any of the defendantes, the Court therfore thought fitt and soe did order and adiudge that the former severall censures passed uppon the said Gibbon FitzMorris, Donnogh OGrady and Nicholas Freeman, nothwithstanding the verdict given at the kinges bench barre in the Cause controverted betwixt the said David FitzGibbon and the defendante, shall remayne without blemysh in righte full creditt and efficacye. Dated at his Maties high Court of Castlechamber the seavententh day of May 1620 And in the Eighteenth yeare of his Maties Raigne of England, Fraunce and Ireland and of Scotland the Three and fiftyeth.[240]

---

240. ff. 276–77. Note the role of castle chamber in the review of judicial administration at every level, incorporating legal theory in its accusation of corrupting the process of adjudication.

Presente: The Lord Deputy, The Lord Chauncellor, The Lo Prymat, The Lo Bp of Fernes, The Lo Bp of Dromore, The Lo Sarsfeilde, The Lo Cheiff Baron, The Mr of the Rowles.

Memorandum that whereas Pattrick Plunckett appeareing in Court, his Maties Attorney generall fully openyng the nature of his offence and his examynacons being read in Court and confessed by himself to be true, whereby yt appeared that he had received a barrell of bookes and pictures from the handes and by the procurement of Romysh preists and Jesuites beyond the Seas, notoriously knowne to be most malignant opposites to his Maties happy government and the true religion which his highnes and all his faythfull subiectes professe, and who seeke by all possible endeavours to withdraw his Maties Subiectes from the true Christian fayth to the Romish supersticon and from their due obedience to their lawfull Soveraigne unto all manner of disloyaltye and stronge rebellion yf they cold, as might manifestly appeare by their finding out so fitt a messenger to bring, and (yf he had not byne prevented) to have dispersed soe many bookes and superstitious pictures by the pictures and some of the bookes to infect the myndes of his Maties subiectes with supersticon, and other bookes, and namely the Analectes, to season the affections with malignant thoughtes of treason and rebellion. Now forasmuch as the said Patrick Plunkett could not but know that his insolent bouldnes (yf it come to light) should not escape without punishment, The Court therfore hath this day ordered, adiudged, Censured and decreed, but with great Comisseracon of his poverty, that he the said Patrick Plunkett for his said offence shall by way of fyne pay unto his Matie the some of forty poundes ster, and shalbe comitted to prison there to remayne dureing the Lo Deputyes pleasure. Dated at his Maties high Court of Castle Chamber the xxiijth day of May in the eightenth yeare of his Maties Raigne of England, Fraunce & Ireland & of Scotland the three and fiftyeth.[241]

Present: The Lo Deputye, The Lo Chancellor, The Lo Bp of Ossory, The Lo Bp of Downe, The vice Threr, The threr at Warres, Sir George Shurley, knight, L Cheife Justice of his Maties Court of Kinges Bench, The Lo Sarsfeild, The Lo Cheiff Baron, The Mr of the Rooles.

Memorandum that the Contentes of Christopher Draycott, gent, his bill and the sondry outrageious misdemeanors, Contemptes of publique Justice and scandalizing of Sir Francis Roe, knight, being a publique Magistrate, maior of Drogheda, a principall port towne of this his Maties kingdome of Ireland, and in particular by spitting in the face of Sir Francis Roe, knight, divers tymes, by striking of the Lady Roe, wife to the said Sir Francis, a great blow on her face in her owne house, when she came only to pacifye him, by striking the said Sir Frauncis, his porter, with a naked sword crosse his shoulders, by often strikeing of John Greenhaugh, a gent, that served the said Sir Francis, who hearing of the porters being hurt, came downe only to save the porter from the further outrage of the said Christopher, by strikeing the said Maiors Macebearer in the street, by strikeing of Bartholomew Brett, whome the said Maior (of speciall favor notwithstanding his former miscariages) permitted to be his guardian, to the end to have prevented his ymprisonment. And after that the said Christopher Draycott (for his aforesaid unsufferable misdemeanors) was comitted to prison, and remayning there awhile, espying the marshal of the prison, John Neale (a man of seaventy yeares of age) offering to goe to shutt the prison dore, the said Christopher speedily following him ast [asked] hym what authority he had to keep him there, but the said Marschall, comaunding him in the kinges Maties name to stay, he the said Christopher thereuppon toke the said Marschall by the shoulders and violently threw him downe the stayres 14 stepps and thereby soe greivously hurt and bruised him that he was inforced to keep his bedd a moneth after and more and hardly escaped with his loife. And not content therewith, the said Christopher (the next day) sayd that he was sory that he had not broken the Marschalls neck. And lastly to accumulat and consumat the greivousnes of his Misdemeanors the said Christopher used most vile, reviling, scandalous, and opprobrious speeches to the said Sir Francis, not only derogatorie to the honorr of his knighthood, but also the disparagement and contempt of his present Magistracy, as in calling [him] a base knight, a scurvey knight, and a shitten pockye knight, and that as he was Sir Francis Roe, he cared no more for hym then he cared for the Roe of a hearing [i.e. herring's roe], and as he was maior of Drogheda he cared no more for him then he cared for a turd. Now the Contentes of the bill being thus layd open, the defendantes Councell were moved to say what they could, to mayntayne the defendante answere to the pltes bill, which the

241. f. 278. The Analects refers to *Analecta sacra nova et mira de rebus catholicorum in Hibernia pro fide et religione gestis*, by David Rothe, later Catholic archbishop of Ossory. See HMC, *Egmont MSS*, vol. 1, p. 58. See note by Mrs Lomas.

defendantes Councell wayving and alleadging no other excuse then Dronkennes at that tyme and that the defendt had not byne knowne to have comitted the like outrage before, humbly submitted the cause to the favourable Censure of the Court. Howbeyt his Maties sollicitor moved to have the defendantes answeare read, which was done. Whereuppon the said Sollicitor generall humbly prayed that thexamynacons taken to prove the severall misdemeanors alleadged in the bill might be read, which being read did more then sufficiently prove all and every of them and more then were sett downe in the bill, to the greife of the Court and all the hearers, that a gent of good discent shold soe much degenerate from the true cariage of gentrye. Thereuppon the said Sollicitor, shewing at large and enformyng the heynousnes of the severall misdemeanors and offences comitted by the defendant, not only in fastning soe unworthy ymputacons uppon soe worthy a person in himself, for his virtue, valor and many good services, bravely performed in the service of his soveraigne, but also for vilifying of him, as haveing the place of his Maties Lieutenant within the libertyes of Drogheda and as being a cheife member in his Maties politique body, thereby undermyning both the Creditt and authority of the subordinat magistracy and in yt tending to overthrow and supplant the root and to drye upp the fountayne and spring head of Justice, without due admynistracon whereof in the Soveraigne by comaunding, and in his mynisters by exequuting, no Comon wealth can subsist and bee. The said Sollicitor therfore humbly besoght the Court to proceed to censure. Whereuppon, though yt was well knowne that the defendant was a younger brother whose estate ys litle and uncerteyne, and in that respect might be thought the more to be favoured, yet forasmuch as true Justice must be blind in the proportioning of punishmentes according to the quality of the offences, and not of the persons, and that others of what rancke soever may learne by example and punishment of this delinquent not to emboulden themselves to comitt the like outrages, The Court therfore hath this day ordered, adiudged, censured and decreed that the said Christopher Draycott (for his afore recited manyfould and most exorbitant offences) and outragious misdemeanors shall pay unto his matie by way of a fyne the some of five hundred poundes ster, and shall pay unto the aforesaid John Nele by way of satisfaccon for his greivous hurtes the some of Twenty pound ster. And shalbe comitted to the Castle of Dublin there to remayne untill the said some of five hundred poundes ster to the kinges Matie and twenty poundes ster to the said John Neale be paide. And yt is further also ordered, adiudged, censured and decreed for righting in part of the said Sir Frauncis and Lady Roe [i.e. to rehabilitate their social standing] that he, the said Christopher Draycott, (at the next generall Sessions to be houlden at Drogheda) shalbe sent thither and then and there in the Sessions house, in the face of the Countrye, the Judges sitting, shall uppon his knees openly and freely confesse all and every of his aforesaid vile, opprobrious and scandalous speaches, that they were very unworthylie put uppon him both as he was a worthy knight and as he was an eminent Magistrate in that place. And at the same tyme in the same place and after the same manner on his knees, shall also submitt himself to the Lady Roe, and ask her forgivenes for his inhumane and barbarous strikeing of a Lady of her worth and dignitye. And shall pay unto Sir Francis Roe his agent, John Greenhaugh, gent, such coste as shalbe taxed by the Lo Chauncellor. And in case that Sir Francis Roe, now sick, shall depart this life before that tyme, then shall the acknowledgment (of the offences done to a publique magistrate of that towne) be made to the Maior that then shall be in like manner as yf the present Maior had byne there in person. And yt is further ordered that the said Christopher Draycott shall put in good security before the Lo chauncellor that, being for the tyme released from out of the Castle of Dublin, and having done and performed what afore is sett downe for him to doe and performe in manner and forme as before is sett downe and prescribed, that then the said Christopher shall make his undelayed retorne to Dublin, and render himself prisoner to the Castle of Dublin as before, there to remayne as aforesaid, and soe much longer as to the Lo Deputy his honorable pleasure shalbe thought fitt. Dated at his Maties high Court of Castlechamber the xxiijth day of June in the Eighteenth yeare of his Maties Raigne of England, Fraunce and Ireland and of Scotland the Three and fiftyeth.[242]

Present: The Lo Deputy, The Lo Chancellor, The Lo Primate, Mr Vice Threr, The Threr at Warres, The Lo Chief Justice, The Lo Sarsfield, The Lo Chief Baron, The Mr of the Roules, Sir Thomas Roper, Sir Francis Annesley.
Memorandum that whereas the last Court day the learned Judges in the law were of opynion that Martyn Plunkett, Edward Plunkett and Mathew Bath were rather to be tryed at the Kinges Bench

242. ff. 279–80. Extraordinary detail reported in multiple accusations of assault, defaming public official, dishonour of gentleman. The 'shitten pockye' insult was a common term of intense reprobation and dislike (*OED*).

for fellonye then to be censured in this Court for their riotous Conspiracy and barbarous Cariage in the exequetion of their wicked purpose by useing inhumane violence in carrying away Margarett Cusack to be married to the said Martyn Plunkett against her will. Yt was then thought fytt by the Lo Deputy being psent, and soe ordered that the Chief Justices of the Kinges Bench and Comon pleas, the lo chief baron & master of the Roles should every of them deliberately consider of a stuatute (enacted in 3 k. H. 7.) made for prevention of such mischiefs as might arise by the exorbitant desires of gent and others in attempting the taking away of women endowed with good lands or livelihood, whither the defendtes be w[ith]in the compass of that statute or not, and were assigned to deliver their opynions from this court day. Now the said Judges according in the point that the defendtes violence in the taking the plt away and forcibly keeping her in their possession three or foure dayes together as was manifestly proved the last court day, were of opynion that they were properly to be tryed in the Kinges Bench for [the term] following. Howbeit uppon mature consyderacon of the nature of the offence and the native disposition of this Country in like cases, but especially in respect of his Maties strong inclination to clemencye and mercy in sparing the lives of his subiectes, and in liew of their lives to inflict pecuniary and corporall punishmentes, which power derived from his majestie was now here invested in the person of the Lo Deputie who, openly declaring himself to be the true servant of soe mercifull a master and Soveraigne, did deliver his judgment and soe did determine that this cause shoujld now receive a finall Censure in the Court. Whereuppon the Court, ryght well knowing the Comunyty and frequency of this offence in this kingdome, and esteeming withall that the sendarer [sense: to communicate a symbolic message] the punishment is that lighteth uppon some delinquents in this kind may deter many others from committing the like outragious offences, hath this day ordered, censured and adiudged and decreed that Martyn Plunkett, out of a disordinat, filthey and coveteous desire, by evill, inhumane and barbarous violence to ymprove and advance his owne private fortunes by the pltes meanes of livelyhood, as being the first and principall [MS torn: mover?] of so great a transgression, shall pay unto his matie by way of fyne for his offense the some of fyve hundred pounds ster, shall stand uppon the pillory of Dublin on a markett day dureing the markett tyme with a paper on his head briefly declaring his offence, shalbe bound to his good behavior for three years next ensuying and shalbe commytted to the castle of Dublin, there to remayne during the Lo Deputyes pleasure. And the Court hath also ordered, censured, adiudged and decreed that Edward Plunkett and Matthew Bath, for being assistantes, coadiutors and fellow actors in the effecting of soe wicked a purpose, shall each of them by way of fyne for their severall offences pay unto his matie two hundred pounds ster le peece, shall likewise stand uppon the pillorye with papers on their heads briefly declaring their offences, shalbe bound to their good behavior for those three yeares next ensuing, and shalbe committed to the Castle of Dublin, there to remayne during the Lo Deputies pleasure. Dated at his Maties High Court of Castlechamber the xxxth day of June in the eighteenth yeare of his Maties raigne of England, Fraunce & Ireland and of Scotland the three and Fiftyeth.[243]

Fiat lre de Sir P versus W R de Kilkenny ad comparendum Cora d[omi]na Regina et concilio suo in Camera Castelli sive Camera sua stellata in Castro Dubllin xv Michis per x ad solvendum ad maneris Robartis Kendall Clereci Dice curie ad usum denariois legali monet anglie pro fine eos taxat in curia prej Dat secundo die Sept 1578
Fiat lre de S P versus W R de Kilkenny ad comparendum cora dua Regina et consilio suo in camera Castelli sive Camera sua stellata in Castro Dublin xv Michis per x ad solvendum ad manus Robarti Kendall Clereci Dice curie undecem? libras et sept folios legali monet hibirne per mi fis? expensis curie perei taxata Dat secundo die Sept 1578.[244]

243. f. 281. This is the last full entry recorded in the manuscript. Fol. 282 is blank, while fol. 282v has an unsigned memorandum, to wit: '14th of May 1660 A note of whatt money I doe owe to Mr William Latties of ye Citty of Dublinge.'
244. f. 283v. Fol. 283 is blank. This note in Latin refers to an earlier clerical account in which the clerk, Robert Kendall, took up a fine for work in castle chamber. Fol. 284 includes many incomplete scribbled clerical drafts, including: 'Be it knowen unto all men by theise presentes that I Thomas McTeige of the Citie of Dublin, gentellman, Doe owe and stand indebted unto …' Fol. 285 is loose and fol. 286 forms part of the original binding in vellum.
For an abridged edition of the entry book which preserves the sense of the court's decision and a list of most litigants, see the calendar written by Mrs Sophie C. Lomas in *Haliday MSS, Manuscripts of the earl of Egmont* (H.M.C., 1905), vol. 1, part I, pp. 1–60.

The Irish star chamber trials, 1621–1632

The entry book of the court of castle chamber remains the only substantial text which was clearly produced by and for the court and its officials. Nevertheless, despite its abrupt termination in 1620, there is substantial evidence for an ongoing archive of the court. The records are mentioned often, the clerks were appointed continuously until at least 1641 and the work of the court formed the core of parliamentary disputation for over a decade under Charles I. It is curious, then, that these important original documents have apparently disappeared. The entry book which forms the text of Appendix One was completed, bound and later appropriated by Sir Philip Perceval, one of the court officials. No subsequent entry book has been discovered, although the writs and decrees of the court must have been abundant. They are cited often in the correspondence of Richard Boyle, earl of Cork and Thomas Wentworth, earl of Strafford, among others. Consequently, it is necessary to reconstruct from surviving documents the work of the later Jacobean and Caroline courts.

Fortunately, an extensive manuscript copy of castle chamber activity was made for the use of the court, apparently under the newly appointed lord deputy, Thomas Wentworth. This bound volume is found in the manuscripts collection of Trinity College Dublin, MS 852. Titled 'Star Chamber Tryals &c'. The compilation includes copies of a petition to the king from John Elliot, the forms for issuing writs and other requirements for holding a parliament, and verbatim copies of castle chamber cases. In addition, the volume contains the formal decree of Charles I authorizing the continuance of the court, the writs, fines and other judicial formalities appropriate to a star chamber jurisdiction, and other pertinent information for the use of the new chief governor. Despite this apparent purpose, the volume fails to reveal its provenance. There is no evidence of a validating authority and the copies are written in several distinctive hands. Additional manuscripts in the possession of Trinity College contain matter regarding the castle chamber and the privy council in Ireland from this period, so it is possible that a collection of documents for the use of the government in Dublin was compiled from disparate sources at about this time. And, while most of the copies appear to be taken from the original, verbatim, it is difficult to know how the clerks may have edited the texts for the use of readers.

The narratives which follow have been selected from the manuscript to provide additional information about the court, based on its original records. The cases were organized according to subject categories and some of them were fully reported in Appendix One, above. Most of the cases reported here are thus dated from 1620 or later, since the decrees which are omitted have been fully transcribed from the entry book. This digest of entries was thus intended to show the Caroline court and the chief governor how adjudication proceeded before the tribunal. The folios are neither sequential nor chronological. Due to the arrangement of the text by subject entry, and the probability that many other cases were unreported in this compendium, an editorial decision was made to follow the logic of the manuscript itself. It is important to remember that this document must be seen as a fragment, taken from the original record, edited for the use of the court and arranged arbitrarily to provide an overall impression of the practice of the tribunal before the coming of Wentworth. Ironically, the painstaking transcription was used by the latter more as a point of departure than as a foundation for the meting out of crown justice. As we shall see, the later Caroline court was to become a more arbitrary instrument of executive partisanship than it had been previously.

Bribery and Corrupcon in a Judg.
Me[morandum] That her Matie [attorney] ore tenus informed the Court agt Patrick Sedgrave, Esquier, second Baron of her Mate Court of Exchequer, Richard Read and David Russell, for that the said Patrick Sedgrave, contrary to his oath and trust reposed in him as a Judg in the said Court of Exchecquer, uppon an Inquest of Inquirye retorned before him ther to enquire whether her Matie had right to certaine landes in Donshoghlin in the Countie of Meath, sometyme belonging to John De Lahide, late attainted of treason, and by reason of the said attainder now belonging to her Matie, wherunto the said Richard Read pretended title, did sinisterly compact with the said Read to have a parcell of the said Lande then in question assured unto him and his heires, [in return, he] to support and countenance the said Read his pretended title agt her Matie in the rest, and to that ende procured the said Richard Reade to perfect a bond of one hundred poundes unto the said David Russell, for and to the use and behoofe of the said Patrick Sedgrave, as by viewe of the said bond shewed & read in Court And severall other deposicons did Manifestly appeare. Uppon proofe wherof, and of the bribery and corrupcon comitted by the said Patrick Sedgrave, wherunto the said Read was a partie in giving, and the said Russell an Actor and Broker of the said bribery and corruption, It was therfore uppon the xixthe Day of November 1602, Censured and Decreed that the said Patrick Sedgrave should be deprived and dismissed of his said office of second Baron, and of all other offices and authorities which he now houldeth under her Matie, and shall paie for a fine to her Matie use one thowsand pounds in her Matie Court of Exchecquer, and to be imprisoned during the Lo Deputies pleasure. And the said Read to paie for his offence two hundred poundes and likewise imprisoned. And the said Russell for his offence (being one of the Jurie) to pay thre hundred poundes, And to be lykewise imprisoned during the Lo Deputies pleasure.[1]

Briberie and extorcon in a Bishops officiall.
Md that Mr Attorney generall informing the Court ore tenus agt Robert Travers, Esquire, for that the said Robert Travers being Officiall to the late Lo Bp of Meath in his liefe tyme, and as vicar generall after his Decease, sede vacante, had misdemeaned himselfe in his said place by receiving of bribes and extorting severall somes of money from his maties subiectes. And the said Robert, having

1. TCD, MS 852, f. 81. This case occurred during the putative hiatus in the court record from 1597 to 1604, showing that the entry book itself is at best a spotty account of the caseload and determinations of the castle chamber. There is no explanation for the arrangement of categories, which do not follow a chronological order nor an apparent structure based on the gravity of the offences. Fol. 81 begins the copies of court records, all in the same hand, and summarized briefly in the margin. See Plate 16.

beene examined by the said Mr Attorney and his examinacons read in Court, the said Travers had confessed that he had recieved x^{li} for leaving one John Warren, who was excommunicate for Recusancie, out of the writt de excommunicate Capiendo, and that the said Warren afterwardes being departed this liefe, the said Travers woud not suffer him to [be] buried before he had received fifty shillings for a license. And further confesseth that one Henrie Gorie, being in prison in the Sheriffe Custody being arrested uppon the writt De Excommunicate capiendo, the said Travers for xv^{li} gave Direccons for his enlargment. And one Patrick Halfpenny for tenne poundes was lykewise discharged. And severall somes of money of divers other[s] for Discharging them out of the writt De Excommunicato Capiendo. And of Divers other being questioned for having their Children Christened by Popishe Preste. And for Clandestine Mariage, for their Discharg, And of Divers others being suspected of Adultrye to forbeare Inquisicon or prosecucon. Uppon which confession of his The Court uppon the 16th of November 1621 ordered, Censured & Decreed that the said Robt Travers should paie unto his Matie by way of fyne, for his said offences the some of three hundred poundes. And should be removed and disabled from the execution of all manner of Jurisdiccon or office in any of the Eccl[es]iasticall Courtes within this kingdome, And shold be committed to prison during the Lo Deputies pleasure.[2]

Champertie and mainetennance.
Md that a bill being exhib[it]ed by John More, Esquire, agt Sir John Bourke, Walter Oge McJames McMorris, David Bourke and others for Champertie, maynetennance, misleading [and] inveighing of Jurors and Commissioners, and other misdemeanors And this cause being fullie heard uppon the vjth daye of May 1621. It plainely appeared unto the Court that Sir John Bourk had misdemeaned himselfe, not only agt Jurors but allsoe agt Commissioners. And that the said Sir John Bourk and the said Walter Oge McJames McMorris were both of them guilty of Champertie for that Sir John, by contract betweene himselfe and the said Walter Oge, he the said Sir John shold have halfe the land which should be gotten by his charge expended in the prosecucon and mainetenance of the suite for recovery of such lands as the said Walter Oge had right unto. And that the said Walter Oge was likewise guiltie of Champertie for that he contracted to give halfe the land unto Sir John Bourk that shoud be recovered by his meanes and mainetenance of that suite. And the said David Bourke found guiltie of a great and presumpteous misdemeanor for that he, understanding that an Inquest was impannelled concerning Sir John Bourk, came riding post hast in a tempestuous night and knowing wher the said Jurie and Inquest was kept in a roome by one of the Sheriffe Baylieffe[s] chanting uppon their evidence in the night tyme, the said David Bourk, notwithstanding he was charged by the Bayliffe in the kinges name not to enter the roome, hee nevertheless violently thrust into the Roome and privatly conferred with one of the Jurie. The Court therfore uppon the said xjth day of May 1621 Censured, adiudged and Decreed that the said Sir John Bourke shold [pay] unto his Matie by waie of fyne for his said offences the some of three hundred pounds ster. And Walter Oge McJames McMorris for his offence shold paye unto his Matie by way of fine the some of twenty poundes ster. And David Bourke for his offence shold pay unto his matie by way of fine for his offence the some of one hundred poundes ster, And all three to be comitted to Prison during the Lord Deputies pleasure. And for the rest of the Defendtes noe proofe being made agt them to convict them or any of them of any the misdemeanors layed to there chardg in the bill, they were dismissed without Costes.[3]

Conspiracie subornacon and periurie.
Md that Michaell Cormack of Inver in the Countie of Mayo, gent, exhibited a bill agt Thomas Nolan, Esquire, James Nolan, his sonne, Thomas McHubert and Feudoraghe McCormack therby setting fourth that the said Thomas Nolan and James Nolan had conspired and labored to suborne wittnesses to sweare to a bill of Indictment to accuse Michaell Cormacke of treason in releiving Captaine Bourke, als Truse, a Piratt, and proclaymed t[r]aytor with powder, Bullettes, lead, munition and victualls and to that purpose had suborned the said Thomas McHubert and Feudoragh McCormack to swere to the said bill of Indictment and had labored to suborne manie others to ioyne with the said Thomas and Feudoraghe by offering great rewardes to sweare the said bill. Which

2. TCD, MS 852, ff. 81–81v. Folios hereafter abbreviated as ff. 81–81v.
3. ff. 81v–82. Fol. 82 case of 21 May 1577 is found in entry book.

Indictment being (att an Assizes houlden for the county of Mayo) prosecuted by the said James Nolan for the offences abovesaid, the said Thomas McHubert and Feudoraghe McCormack did sweare the contentes of the said bill to be true, And by reason of the said conspiracie, subornacon and periurie the said Michaell was in Danger of the loss of his liefe, goodes and Landes and Defamacon of his person and posteritie for ever. And uppon full hearing of this cause the Councell being fullie heared on both sides it plainely appeared unto the Court that the said Thomas Nolan and James Nolan were guilty of the said conspiracy and subornacon, and the said Thomas McHubert and Ferdoraghe McCormacke guiltie of periury, the said Ferdoragh having confessed his periurie in his answer. The Court therfore upon the 6th Day of Februarie 1627 adiudg[ed], Censured and Decreed that the said Thomas Nolan and James Nolan shold paie unto his Matie by way of fyne for their offences the some of one thowsand pounds ster a peece, and thre hundred pounds ster Damages to the said Michaell Cormack. And the said Thomas McHubert and Ferdoraghe McCormack shold paye unto his Matie by way of fyne for their offences the some of five hundred poundes ster a peece, and all of them comitted to the Marshall of the Courte. And that all fower of them shold upon the next Markett Day in Dublin be sett uppon the Pillory in Dublin with papers on their heades Declaring their offences, And the said Thomas Nolan and James Nolan to have each of them one of their Eares cutt of, And the said Thomas McHubert and Ferdoragh McCormack shall have each of them one of their fares nayled to the Pillorie and to teare them out with their owne force and from thence all of them to be carried with the said papers on their heades to the fower Courtes, the Judges sitting, and att barr of each Court upon their knees acknowledg their offences. And agt the next Assizes to be houlden for the County of Mayo to be conveyed thether, and att the said Assizes to be sett uppon the Pillory with the like papers on their heads, and the said Thomas and James Nolan to have their other Eares cutt of, and the said Thomas McHubert and Ferdoraghe McCormacke to have their other eares nayled to the Pillory and to pull them of with their owne force and from thence to be carried to the Sessions howse with the like papers on their heades and at the Barr upon their knees (the judges sitting) acknowledg their offences, and shall then be conveyed againe to Dublin where the said Thomas Nolan and James Nolan shalbe comitted During the Lo Deputies pleasure. And the said Thomas McHubert and Ferdoraghe McCormack to be comitted for three yeares absolute and afterwardes during the Lord Deputies pleasure.[4]

Conspiracie and periurie.
Md that Edward Fitzgerrald of the Citty of Dublin, gent, exhibited a bill agt Sir William Bishop, knt, late Maior of the said Citty, John Nolan, Esquire, and Divers others therby setting fourth that the said Defendts had maliciously combyned and plotted together how to Disgrace and mischeife the said Edward by charging and accusing him that he should have combyned and conspired most unhumanly with one John Quin of the said Citty, merchant, to kill and murther the said John Nolan and to robb and steale his goodes out of his howse in the high streate. According to which combinacon the said John Nolan caused the sayd Edward to be apprehended and brought before the said Sir William Bishop, then Maior of the said Citty, was by him examined and comitted to prison and ther remayned without bayle or maineprise close prisoner for a long tyme, (althoughe he offered good bayle to answer the accon [action]) untill he procured his maties writt of Corpus cum causa out of his Mates Court of Cheife place, where he was tryed. And being to be tryed uppon an Indictment for the said attempt of murther and robbery, the sayd John Nolan swore the contentes of the bill of Indictment to be true, wheruppon the grand Jurie found the bill and by the pettie Jury was legally acquited. And this cause being fully heard by the Counsel on both sides, it plainely appeared unto the court that the sayd John Nolan was guilty not only of a foule, wicked and malicious practice in falcely accusing the plt of the said combinacon and attempt of murther and robbery of him, the said John Nolan, but allsoe of periurie in swearing to the said bill of Indictmt. It was therfore uppon the fifthe Daye of February 1629 Censured and Decreed that the said John Nolan shall paie unto his Matie by way of fyne for his said offence the some of two hundred poundes ster, and paie unto the plt one hundred markes ster Damages, and should be sett uppon the Pillory in Dublin one markett Daye that terme with a paper on his head Declaring his offence, and shalbe imprisoned During the Lo Justices pleasure. And for the rest of the Defendts nothing being proved to convince them of any of the offences layed to their charg, they are therfor Dismissed.[5]

4. ff. 82v–83.   5. f. 83.

Conspiracy.

Md that Josias Lambert, Esquire, exhibited a bill into the Court agt Xpofer Kirovan of the Towne of Gallway, merchant, therby setting fourth that the said Josias Lambert, being one of his Maties Justices of the peace for the Countie of Roscommon, had bound over Divers of the tennants of the said Xpofer to appeare att the next Quarter Sessions to answer to such thinges as on his Maties behalfe should be alleadged agt them, and that the said Kerovan att his owne Coste and charge obtayned a supersedias from the vice president of the Province of Connoughe to stay the sayd bonde not to be returned to the Quarter Sessions, but the said Recognizances were sent by the said Josias Lambert his man before the said Supersedias was shewed unto him, and att the said Quarter Sessions the said persons being called, appeared, and shewing the said supersedias were Dischargied. Yet notwithstanding, the said Kirovan went to the Court of Presidencie and ther made affidavit that, in contempt of the said Supersedias the said Josias Lambert had caused one of his said tennantes so bound over to be comitted, uppon which afft [affidavit] att his owne coste and charge he obtayned a warrant Directed to the Sariante att Armes for the apprehencon of the said Josias Lambert, and being apprehended and brought to the said Presidencie Court was fined in fortie poundes and Comitted. And this cause being fully heard by the Councell on both sides, it plainely appeared unto the Court that the said Kirovans tenant was not committed and therfor the affidavit was falce. The Court therfore conceives yt as plott & practice of the said Kirovan to Disgrace the said Mr Lambert. Uppon the 8the of Febr 1631 Censured the said Kirovan to pay unto his Matie by way of fyne for his said offence, the some of one hundred pounds ster, And to paie unto the said Josias Lambert forty pounds Damages and to be committed During the Lord Justices pleasure.[6]

Conspiracy and 2 Ryottes.

Md that Xpofer Jones of Athloane in the County of Westmeathe, merchant, exhibited a bill agt Robert Nugent, Edmund Kelly, Farrall McKigan, John McNemar[ra], John OHanyn, Donogh McNemarra, and Div[er]s others, therby setting fourth that the said Robert Nugent and Edmund Kelly had combyned and conspired together to stirr up Divers suite agt the said Xpofer Jones, aswell in his Maties high Court of Castle Chamber as in other his Maties Courtes of Justice, to charg the said Xpofer with many crimes and offences, and labouring to suborne wittnesses to prove the said accusacons. And that the said Xpofer Jones having obtayned his Maties writt of Iniunction Directed to the Sheriff of the County of Roscomon to putt the said Christopher in possession of the Castle, towne and landes of Moyvanan in the said County, being then in controversie betweene the said Xpofer and the said Nugent, and the said Sheriffe coming to Moyvanan aforesaid to putt in execution his Maties said writt of Iniunction, but the said Nugent having notice of his coming procured the rest of the Defendantes with himselfe to make good the said Castle agt the Sheriffe and would not suffer him to enter to give possession to the said Xpofer according the tenor of the said Iniunction. And the said Sheriffe, coming two daies after with greater force to execute his said writt, was resisted by the said Defendantes by throwing great stones from the top of the Castle, and whot [sic] water out of the windowes, soe as the said Sheriffe seing himselfe in Danger Departed, with out executing his writt, and Dispersed his companie, which when the said Defendantes espied they issued out of the Castle all armed, and followed some of the said Sheriffes company that were going towardes Atheloane, and overtaking them greivously assaulted them and beate them and wounded one of them that he was in Danger therby to loose his liefe and carried one of them as a prisoner before the vicepresident who Discharged him. And this cause being fullie heard by the Councell on both sides on the 13th of June 1632 the said Defendantes were found guiltie of the said misdemeanors and therfore ordered, Censured and Decreed that the said Robt Nugent shall paie unto his Matie by way of fyne for his offence the some of thre hundred poundes ster, And the said Edmund Kelly two hundred pounds ster, And the said Robert and Edmund to paye to the plt two hundred pounds ster Damages. And the said Farrall McEgan, John McNemarra, John O Hony[n] and Donnogh McNemarra to paie unto his Matie the some of one hundred markes ster a peece, and all of them to be commited during the Lo Justices pleasure. And the said Robert Nugent the next markett Daie to be sett uppon the Pillory in Dublin with a paper on his head Declaring his offence and from thence to be carried to the fower Courts with the same paper on his head, and att the barr of each Court, the

6. f. 83v.

Judges sitting, uppon his knees acknowledg his offence. And agt the next Assizes to be houlden for the countie of Roscomon to be sent from Sheriff to Sheriffe thether, wher he is to be brought to the Barr (the Judges sitting) with the lyke paper on his head, and uppon his knees acknowledg his offence, and then to be sent back from Sheriffe to Sheriffe till he be comitted to his Maties Castle of Dublin, ther to remayne until he have paid his Matie said 400^li, the pltes said 200^li Damage besides Costes of Court, and bring in the bodyes of the said Farrall McEgan, John McNemarra, John O Hanyn and Donoghe McNemarra to answer the said Censure. And afterwardes During the Lo Justices pleasures &c The rest of the Defendantes nothing being proved against them are Dismissed.[7]

A counterplea betweene two Sheriffe about the escape of James Nolan.

Md that Thomas Nolan of Ballinrobe in the Countie of Mayo, Esquier, and James Nolan, his sonne, were Censured in his Maties Court of Castle Chamber the vith Daie of Febr 1627 att the prosecution of Michaell Cormack of Inver in the said County of Mayo, gent, in the some of one thowsand pounds ster a peece, and to stand uppon the Pillory in Dublin with papers on their heades Declaring their offences and to have each of them one of their Eares cutt of, And agt the next Assizes to be houlden for the County of Mayo to be sent thether to stand likewise uppon the Pillory and to have their other Eares cutt of, and acknowledg their offences, and to be returned back to the Marshall of the Court, with him to remayne During the Lo Deputies pleasure, and to paie unto the said Michaell the some of thre hundred pounds ster Damages and thirty poundes ster costes. Now the said James Nolan, having stood uppon the Pillorie in Dublin and had one of his Eares cutt of And went to the fower Courts and acknowledged his offence uppon his knees, And being sent by warrt to be conveyed from Sheriffe to Sheriffe into the County of Mayo to receive ther the rest of his punishment according to the said Censure, was Deliver[ed] by the Sheriffe of Dublin [city] to Lamorack Nottingham, Esquire, highe Sheriffe of the Countie of Dublin to be sent as aforesaid, who Delivered him to one Garrett Archbold, pretended Subsheriffe to Patricke Sedgrave, Esquire, high Sheriff of the County of Meath, who carried him the said James as farr as Tirrells p[l]ace, and there willfully lett him escape. Wheruppon both the said Sheriffes were summoned to appeare in Court, to answer the said escape, and appearing the sayd Patrick Sedgrave denied that the said Archbold was his Subsheriffe or had anie power from him to execute anie such office. But the said Nottingham averred that he was his Subsheriffe, wheruppon wittnesses were examined to prove their allegacons on each side, and the cause being fully heard by the Councells on each side, uppon the 17th of June 1629, yt plainely appeared unto the Court, that the sayd Garrett Archbold was Subsheriffe to the said Sedgrave, in yt he had received the Greenwax bookes, had executed writtes by the appoyntment of the said Sedgrave, and had given bondes with surety for Discharging of the sayd office. The Court therfore adiudged and Decreed that the said Patrick Sedgrave should paye unto his Matie the fine of the said James Nolan which was according to the reducement five hundred markes ster, to pay Michaell Cormack the thre hundred and thirty pounds ster Costes and Damages, And to paye the said Lamorack Nottingham such Costes as he hath beene att in the prosecucon of this cause.[8]

Extorcon in a Sheriffe.

Md that his Maties learned Councell ore tenus informed that Peirce Pretherye, Esquier, high Sheriff of the Countie of Downe had taken and seized into his Custodie the goodes of one Donoghe McBrian, accused (but not convicted) of fellony, and that the said Sheriffe had securety tendred him for the fourthcoming of the said goodes to his Maties use if the said Donogh should be convict[ed] of fellonie, the said Sheriffe notwithstanding Detayned the said Donoghes goodes in his owne handes. All which appearing to be true by the said Sheriffe his owne confession, The Court therfore uppon the xiijth of June 1621 Adiuged, Censured and Decreed that the said Sheriffe should paye

---

7. ff. 83v–84.
8. f. 84v. See castle chamber case involving Nolan above, f. 83, and on f. 81 a case involving a Patrick Sedgrave and rights to land in Co Meath in 1602, wherein he was deprived of office for corruption and bribery as a judge in the exchequer. Whether he was the same person, appearing twenty-five years later as high sheriff in Co. Meath is not known. Folios 85–86 contain four cases which were previously recorded in the entry book, prior to 1620.

unto his Matie by way of fyne for his said extorcon the some of one hundred poundes ster and shalbe committed to prison during the Lo Deputies pleasure.[9]

Extorcon in a Sheriff.

Md that a bill being preferred by Michaell Cormack of Inver in the Countie of Mayo, gent, [against] Gregorie Nolan, Esquire, late high Sheriffe of the said Countie of Mayo, for manie exorbitant extorcons by him comitted in the tyme of his Sheriffalty as uppon full proofe by manie wittneses att the hearing of this cause appeared. The Courte therfore uppon the 7th Day of Februarie 1626, in Comisseracon of the said Gregory his weake estate (his Father being living), adiudged, Censured and Decreed that he shall paie unto his matie by way of fine for his offence the some of one hundred markes ster, and be committed During the Lord deputies pleasure.[10]

Extorcon and other misdemeanors in a Sheriffe.

Md that Mr Sariant Cattlin, his Maties second Sariant att law, att the relation of Rorie Oge McGennis exhibited an Informacon agt James McCarton, late Sheriffe of the Countie of Downe, therby seting fourthe that the said James houlding a Countie Courte att Downe in June 1629 Did enter Divers accons [actions], thirtie in number, agt Divers of his Maties subiects (att the suite of one James a Ronow, clayming to be titulary preist of the parishe of Aynehelt in the said Countye, by power from the Pope) for severall somes of money in recompence of tithes, due to the said Ronow, being their preist as aforesaid, to which accons the Defendante pleaded and issue ioyned, a Jurie was impannelled and sworne for triall of the accons wherof the said Relator was foreman. And uppon hearing the evidence the Jurors perceived the said pleas were not grounded uppon anie iust contract or debt due by the lawes, did altogether refuse to trie the said issues, wherupon the said Sheriffe threatened the said Jurors to commit them unless they would finde for the plt, the said preist. Wheruppon, the said Jurors having fasted Divers Daies and fearfull of comitting, found the said issues for the said preist, uppon which verdictes soe found the said Sheriffe graunted out executions agt the goods and Chattels of the said persons for levying the same, and extortionously tooke of some of them thre shillinges or thre shillinges sixpence, as fees due unto him without shewing anie cause how the same should be due. And uppon full hearing of this cause, it plainely appeared unto the Court, that the [said] James McCarton was guiltye of all the misdemeanors layed to his charge by the said Informacon. The Court therfore uppon the xith day of November 1631 Censured and Decreed that the said James McCarton shall paie unto his Matie by way of fine for his said offences (being not inferior to anie except high treason) the some of two hundred poundes ster, and shall sitt uppon the Pillory in Dublin one markett Daie, and be carried to Downepatricke there to stand uppon the Pillorie another markett Daie, and be imprisoned During the Lord Justices pleasure, and before he be enlargged shall find suerty for his good behavior. And the bond of 300[li] taken of him and his suerty for his personall apparance att the hearing of this cause, and being called, appered not, is to be estreated.[11]

Forgerie of a will.

Md that John Hamelton, Esquire, exhibited a bill agt Jane Hamelton, widowe relict of William Hamelton, Esquire, late Deceased, therby setting fourth that the said William Hamelton being sick, and Divers of his freinds being att his howse Desired to make his will, which being written according to his Directions, was publickly read unto him in the presence of the Defendant and others and then signed by the said William and given to the said Defendant to keepe, in which will he had appointed the plt and Defendant to be his executors. And that the Defendant had afterward a little before the said William his Death caused a Codicell to be Drawne according to her owne Dictating, Desiring her husband to signe the same, [but] he refusing, wishing her to lett it alone till his brother the Lo of

9. f. 86.
10. f. 86v. Note Michael Cormack of Inver was also litigant in castle chamber against Thomas and James Nolan, probably kinsmen of Gregory Nolan, in a case heard 6 Feb. 1627. A clerical error may explain why the cases were heard a year and one day apart before the court.
11. f. 86v. Fols. 87–87v contain four cases which were fully reported in the entry book on matters involving forgery of the chief governor's hand.

Claniboye came, but she being soe urgent, and himselfe soe weake, and Desiring to be att rest, agt his will (as is supposed) signed the same, and presently after Departed this liefe. And yt after his Death the said Jane Hamelton had rased [i.e. erased] many Lynes out of the said will, and altered the sence of it in many places, and putt out the name of John Hamelton from being an executor, and left her selfe sole Executrixe, and being soe forged and rased preferred the same to be proved with the said Codicell in the Prerogative Court of Armaghe, as the true will and Codicell of the said William and so rased and altered by his Directions in his liefe time. And this cause being fullie heard uppon the second of May 1632, It plainely appeared unto the Court that the said Hamelton was guilty of the rasing and altering the said will and unlawfullie to gett her said husband to signe the said Codicell soe neare his Death. The Court therfore Censured and Decreed that the said Jane Hamelton for her said offences shall paie unto his Matie the some of two hundred pounds ster and should be committed during the Lo Justices pleasure, and that the said will shalbe and stand in the same state and force in Lawe as when it was first made by the said William Hamelton att the signing therof, and the said Codicell to be Dambe [i.e. damned, voided].[12]

Embracery.

Md that his Matie Solliciter generall ore tenus informed the Court against Deran McBran, Tirlagh Leagh, Teig McShane and John McMorrough Birne that the said Deran McBran, being Mother to a prisoner in the Gaole who was uppon his triall for treason, procured Teig McShane to write a lre in Teig Oge OBirne his name unto John McMorroghe Birne, being one of the Jurie for triall of the said prisoner, by the said John McMorroghe to have Labored the rest of the Jurie to acquite the said prisoner. And that the said Turlaghe being acquainted with the contentes of the said lre did convey the said lre to John McMoraghe when the Jurie were chanting uppon their evidence. And the said John McMoraghe having received the said lre Did communicate the same to the rest of the Jurie, to the ende they shoud have consented to the acquitall of the said prisoner, but could not prevayle. All which being confest uppon their severall examinacons, The Court uppon the 22th of November 1620 Censured and decreed that the said Deran McBran shall for her offence paie unto his Matie by way of fine for her offence the some of forty [pounds] ster, Tirlaghe Leaghe for his offence forty poundes ster, Teig McShane one hundred pounds ster and John McMorroughe Birne the some of one hundred pounds ster, for their severall offences. And that all of them shall the next markett daye be sett uppon the Pillorie in Dublin with papers on their heades declaring their offences, and from thence with the same papers on their heades be carried to the four Courtes, the Judges sitting, and att the barr of each Court acknowledg their ofences, and thence to be carried to prison there to remaine During the Lo Deputies pleasure. And att the next generall Sessions to be houlden for the Countie of Wickloe they should likewise be pillored and with like papers on their heades be carried into the Sessions howse, the Judge sitting, and ther in like manner acknowledg their Offence.[13]

Embracery.

Md that Nicholas Woulfe of Killcolman in the Countie of Kildare, gent, being informed agt by Mr Attorney generall ore tenus that the said Nicholas had confessed uppon his examination that hee, meeting with one Edward Bell, one of the Bayliffe[s] appoynted for keeping of a pettie Jurie impannelled for triall of iiii prisoners uppon Liefe and Death, and the said Edward complayning that he had fasted all that Daye, the said Nicholas tould him that he would give him some drinck att the next howse, and drincking together the said Woulfe insinuated soe far that he gott oportunity to speake with two of the Jurie in the night time and uppon conference betweene them, they asked the said Woulfe his opinion concerning the evidence that was given agt the prisoners, wherunto the said Nicholas answered that yf he were one of the Jurie he would never condempne anie man uppon the testimonie of anie one notorious malefactor, for that he had heard that noe man ought to be condemned without the testimony of one or two honest men. Uppon which confession of his, the Court uppon the 23th of Januarie 1626, ordered, Censured and Decreed that the said Nicholaus for

---

12. f. 87v.
13. f. 88. There is no record of this case in the entry book, since the last case documented there was on 30 June 1620.

his said offence shall paie unto his Matie by way of fine the some of fifty pounds ster & be imprisoned during the Lo Deputies pleasure.[14]

Misdemeanors in Gouldsmithes.

Md that his Maties Solliciter generall informed the Court ore tenus against Frauncis Browne and Barnaby Ratcliffe, Gouldsmithes, they having beene first examined by Mr Solliciter, The said Francis Browne had confessed that [he] had made a spoone then shewed unto him to have in it but halfe an ounce and a shilling worth of ster silver, and that he sould the said spoone waying one ounce and the waight of six pence for five shillinges twooe pence ster. And the said Barnaby Ratcliffe likewise confessed that he had not only made another spoone but nine more allsoe and sould them to one Alice Willson, being under the value of ster sillver by two pence in the ounce, and further confessed that he had often wrought sillver worse then that ster, alleadging that the bringers of the sillver would have yt soe. Uppon which confessions the Court the 15 of November 1622 Censured and Decreed that the said Francis Browne and Barnaby Ratcliffe shall pay unto his matie by way of fine for their offences the some of tenne pounds le pece. And shalbe sett upon the Pillory in Dublin the two next markett Dayes with papers on their heade Declaring there offences, and from thence to be carried eache markett day with some papers on their heades to the fower courtes, the Judges sitting, and to be comitted during the Lo Deputies pleasure.[15]

Misdemeanor in stealing Custome.

Md that Mr Attorney generall informed the Court ore tenus against George Clerck of the Cittie of Dublin, merchant, the said Georg having beene examined by Mr Attorney, confessed that he had brought into the harbor of Dublin in the Barque of one Bennett of Kilbree a Trunck and a truss of his merchandize and goodes, he valewing the goodes in the trunck att tenne poundes, and the goodes in the truss att xx ⁱⁱ ster, which said trunck and truss betwixt [blank] and eleven of the clocke in the night he tooke out of the said Bennettes Barque, lying att the Custome howse key [quay], and putt them aboard one Henrie Andrew his Barque, lying att the wood key, and from the said Barque conveyed them a shore without entring them with the officers of the Custome howse, or paying any Custome for the same. Uppon which confession the Court upon the 26 Daye of November 1623 Censured and Decreed that the sayd Georg Clercke shall paie unto his Matie by way of fine for his said offence, the some of one hundred pounds ster, and be comitted During the Lord Deputies pleasure.[16]

Periurie in making a falce affidavit.

Md that Willm Bryan of Killmacenrry in the Countie of Corck, gent, exhibyted a bill agt Edmund Wale of Downeanally in the said County, gent, therby setting fourth that a suit being depending in his maties high Courte of Chauncerie betweene Robt Wale of Downeanally aforesaid, plt, and Richard Wale and the now Complt, Defdt, in which suit the said Robert Wale obtayned his Maties writt of Iniunction against the said Richard and the Compt, therby enioyning them to permitt and suffer the said Robert to enioye the said Landes or otherwise to appeare in the said Court to shew cause to the contrary. Theruppon the said Edmund Wale shewing the said Iniunction to the plt and wrapping the labell wheron the Seale wax [was] fixed about his owne finger and offered to snatch yt from the plt while he was reading of yt, tore of[f] the seale and afterwardes coming to Dublin before Thomas Carie, Esquire, one of the Masters of the said Court and there made an affidavit that he had served the said Iniunction uppon the plt Willm O Bryan and att the time of the serving the said Iniunction the said William did offer to beate him, and that the said William tore the said Iniunction

---

14. f. 88v. Fols. 88v to 92v contain 18 cases which were fully reported in the entry book, dealing mainly with recusancy, publishing counterfeit news, harbouring priests, executing office without taking the oath of supremacy, reprieving a prisoner without warrant and allowing a prisoner to escape.

15. f. 93.

16. f. 93. Fols. 93 to 94 contain three more cases recorded fully in the entry book charging abuse of public officials and perjury in making a false affidavit.

most contempteously and said he cared not for anie Iniunction that should issue by the Lord Angier or the high Court of Chancerye. Uppon which afft [affidavit] process issued agt the said William, and being attached, was uppon his apparance committed to the Marshalsie of the fower Courts for his said contempt, till he had cleard himselfe of the same. And uppon full hearing of this cause, uppon the 30 of Aprill 1630 It plainly & manifestly appeared unto the Court by the testimony of many wittneses and heard all the passages betweene the plt and Defendt, that the said Defendt in swearing the said affidavit had willfully periured himselfe. Wheruppon the Court Censured and Decreed that the said Edmund Wale shall paie unto his Matie by way of fine for his said offence the some of one hundred poundes ster and xx^li str Damage to the plt, shalbe sett uppon the Pillory att the next Assizes to be houlden for the County of Corcke, and ther to have his eares nayld, And afterwardes imprisoned During the Lo Justices pleasure.[17]

A Ryott in taking a Distress in the night.
Md that Dermott McCartie exhibited a bill agt Sir Valentine Browne, Baronett, John Roe, als Rose, and Divers others therby setting fourth that the said Sir Valentine with the number of tenne or twelve in his companie in the night tyme, all armed, tooke by way of Distress from the pltes tenantes for arrerage of a certaine porcon of rente payable to his Matie with other landes belonging to the Defendt, the number of 50 or 60 Cowes and other Cattell. And the said plte in following the said Sir Valentine to have their Cattell againe weare grevouslie beaten but their Cattle notwithstanding were driven away by the said Sir Valentine and his companie and that the said tenantes left the said Landes for two or thre yeares afterwardes to the plte great damage. To which the Defendtes Councell alleaged that the Defdt Sir Valentine by an order made by the next coming Judge of Assizes had made full restitucon to all the said plte tenantes as by their acquittances produced and read in Courte appeared. But the Court, in regard of the riotous taking the said Distress in the night from the lande in his Mothers the plte wyves possession, beinge parte of her ioynture, and beating of the tenantes and causing the land to ly wast as aforesaid, uppon the first of June 1627 Censured and Decreed that the said Valentine Browne should paie unto his Matie by way of fine for his said offences the some of 200 ^li ster, and one hundred pounds ster Damages to the plt, And be imprisoned During the Lo Deputies pleasure. Nothing being proved agt the said Rose, [he] is acquited.[18]

A Ryott by making a forcible entrie into landes and imprisoning the plte in their howses.
Md that Alexander Power of Powerstowne in the County of Tipp[er]arie, gent, exhibited a bill agt David Walshe, John Walsh, Nicholas Walsh, Edmund Daniell, Wiliam Wale, Patrick Walsh, Davy FitzJohn, Phillip McTeig and Thomas Hacker and Divers others, therby setting fourth that Thomas, Lord Barron of Cahir, was seized in his Demesne as of Fee of an estate of inheritance in the Towne and Lande of Bally McRedmond in the said County, which estate the said Lord Barron morgaged unto the plt for 240^li ster. And having sealed the said deed of morgage with his feoffee, and the tenantes to the Complt the said David Walshe pretending title to the same, assembled all the rest of the Defendtes to him and in riotous manner, being all armed in warlicke manner, marched to the said towne of Bally McRedmond and came to a howse where one Wm Power and Teig McKnogher were left to keepe the possession, the said David and his companie willed the said Wm and Teig to come fourthe of the said howse that he might enter, or elce he would sett fier on the howse. But they refusing, he the said David and the rest of his companie caused the Dores and windowes of the said howse to be blocked upp with timber wood and stones and there kept a strong guard for thre Dayes and thre nightes to keepe them from anie meate or drincke. During which tyme the said David with some of the said Ryotours went into the backside of one Richard OFinose, one of the pltes tenantes in the said towne, and ther spoyled him two or three hives of Bees, cut his plowharness all to peeces, and espying a maide servant of the said Richarde coming towarde his howse with a paile of milke

---

17. ff. 94–94v. Fols. 94 to 97 contain nine more cases reported fully in the entry book charging perjury against a public official, a jury and a vicar; riotous abduction of women; and public affrays involving a burial and a dispute between peers of the realm.
18. f. 97. Note the case synthesizes riotous violence, the rights of women, fields laying waste three years after frightening tenants away as justification for amending a previous settlement of the suit at local level.

uppon her head, and another with a pack of woll, he threw the said milke to the ground and spilt yt, and threw the woll into the Ryver of Annor [?Nore]. And the Compt complayning to the then Mayor of Clonmell of the said force and prayed him to remove the same, wheruppon the said Mayor wrote to the said David to come to him, but the said David refused soe to doe, saying he would not leave the place for his warr[an]t nor for the Lo Presidens neither. Wheruppon the said Maior with the Complt and divers others in their company went to the said BallyMcRedmund to remove the said force, and to releive the said Wm and Teig with meate and Drincke which they carried with them. And coming to the place wher the said Riotous companie weare, the said Mayor offered to open the dore of the howse wher the said William and Teig were, but the said David and his companie said that yf the said mayor or anie of his company offered to open the said Dore, they wold cutt of their handes, and therupon forcibly tooke the meate and drinck soe brought to releive the said Wm and Teig, cutt yt in peeces and gave yt [to] dogges and swyne to be eaten, and spilt the beare upon the ground. Wheruppon the Mayor seing such violence, Departed and went away. And this cause being fullye heard by the Councell on both sides, and all the said Misdemeanors fully proved, the Court upon the 28 daie of Aprill 1630 Censured and Decreed that the said David Walshe should paie for a fine to his Matie for his said offence one hundred poundes ster, John Walsh 40^{li} ster, And Nicholas Walsh, Edmund Daniell, William Wale, Patrick Walsh, David Fitz John, Phillip McTeig & Thomas Hackett xx^{li} ster a peece, and all of them be comitted during the Lo Justices pleasure.[19]

Ryott for forcible entrie.
Md that David Walshe of Rothconan in the County of Tipperarie, Esquire, exhibited a bill agt Alexander Power of Powerstowne in the said County, gent, Robert Power, Teig McConner, James Power FitzDavid, William Sutton, William Tobin, Conner McDermod, Richard Mara, Arte OToghill, Dermod OSpellane, Will McConnor, William OMeagher, Robert Nogle, Richard Finosie, William OLyne, Teig OShannaghan, Morrice Nogle, Donnell McMelaghlin, and divers others, therby setting fourth that the said David Walshe having a lease from the right honorable Thomas Lord Barron of Cahir of the towne and landes of Bally McRedmond in the said County for the terme of 21 yeares, beginning the xth of Jannuarie 1627, and being possessed accordingly the said Alexander having an uniust Desire to Dispossed [*sic*] the Complt therof, Did on the xvjth of Maye in the 4th yeare of his Maties raigne att the markett Cross att Clonmell before a multitude of people (after giving the ly to the Complt) Did in threatning and reviling manner saye to the plt that before twenty howers were att an ende he wold make the plt come out of Bally McRedmond, and the next day having assembled his companie all the persons abovesaid, being all armed, Did in a Riotous, Routous and rebellous manner betweene 11 and 12 of the Clocke in the night march into the Towne of Bally McRedmond, taking in their companie one William Power and Teig McOnogher, wher the said Riotous persons having first broken Downe some of the wales and Dores of the howse wherin the said David and his servantes weare in bed, and then furiouslie pulled the said David out of his bed, and dragd him in his shirt out of dores, and cruelly wounded him in the head with a sword, and one cruell wound in the lower part of his back with a sword in length 4 inches and in depthe 4 inches, and that one William Wale, a servant of the plte, coming to defend and assist his said Master was grevouslie wounded with the sworde of the said Riotous persons, having receaved fower Dangerous hurtes in the head, one wherof was six inches long, and six broade. And afterwardes the said riotous companie retorned neare to the gate of the said Towne where the said Alexander reprehended the rest of the companie for leaving the plt alive, and said in Irishe theis wordes, viz lett us returne and kill all that are in the howse, for it [is] a like to kill one as to kill all, or wordes to that effect. Wheruppon they all retorned to the said howse, and finding the Dore fast boulted in the howse where the said David was, they gathered together Divers peeces of timber, stumps of trees and other peeces of wood, and therwith blocked up the said dore, crying out to the said complt that he should lye there till he did eate his owne excremente, the said Alexander comaunding the rest to charg their guns and shute att such of the pltes servantes as they should see about the howse, and to sett fier uppon the said howse, and burne yt about them. And this cause being fullie heard with the cross bill [i.e. the previous case, reversing pl and def] the 28 of Aprill 1630 and all the charges aforesaid being proved. The Court Censured and Decreed that the said Alexander should paie to his Matie for a fine five

19. f. 97v.

hundred poundes ster and one hundred poundes ster Damages to the plt. And the said Robt Power, Teig McConnor, Willliam Tobin, Richard OMeara, Art OTohill, Dermod OSpellane and Teig OShannaghan should paie his matie for a fine one hundred pounds ster a peece, and all of them comitted during the Lo Jutices pleasure. And nothing proved agt the rest, they are dismissed.[20]

Scandall agt the Duke of Buckingham.
Md that his Maties Attorney generall informed the court ore tenus agt Richard Browne of Bromyeard in Herefordshire in England, gent, standing att the barr, who having beene examined by Mr Attorney and his examinacon read, had confessed that himselfe with one Harding, coming out of England together and travelling towardes the north of Ireland uppon Shrove sundaye in the afternone, came to Carlingford to the howse of one Griffin, a walsh man [i.e. Welsh], and there meeting with two of Sir Marmaduke WhitChurch his men who after they had dranck a while together asked the said Browne what newes in England to whome the said Browne answeres (being in drinck) that the Duke of Buckingham was committed to the Tower of London, and for his cause of knowledg said he saw him looking out of his Chamber windowe and said that the voyces of the people in England was that the said Duke was comitted for sending a Bason and Ewre [basin and ewer] to the King of Spaine esteemed to be worth 30,000[li] and that yt was Discovered by a falling out betweene the said Duke and some other noble man in England, and that the matter being examined by Sir Randall Crew yt was proved that the said Duke had sent the said Bason & Ewre as aforesaid. And further confessed that the said Harding did soe confidently reporte the same to him that he reported it as confidently that he saw the Duke in the Tower himselfe. All which being confessed as abovesaid The Court therfore uppon the 18th of June 1628 Censured and Decreed that the said Richard Browne should paye unto his Matie for a fine 1,000[li] ster, be sett upon the Pillory in Dublin the fower next markett Dayes with a paper on his head declaring his offence, and after pilloring to be carryed to the fower Courtes and att each barr uppon his knees to acknowledg his offence, and to be whipt through Dublin every of the said dayes and the last daie whilst he is upon the Pillory to have both his eares cutt of, and comitted to the Castle of Dublin During the Lo Deputies pleasure.[21]

Scandall agt the Lord Fawlkland Lo Deputie.
Md that his Maties Attorney generall exhibited an informacon agt Thomas Welden of Raffin in the County of Meath, gent, therby setting fourthe that the said Thomas Velden had spoken malicious, reprochfull and scandalous speeches agt the Lo Deputie for 4 of the Lo Deputies Troope being Cessed uppon him in June 1627 by vertue of his Lo[rdshi]ps warrant. The said Velden tould the said Trowpers, that all the Lo Deputies Troupe should be hanged for cessing uppon the Countrie soe soone as his Lo[rdshi]p had left the sword [i.e. vacated his office], wherunto one of the Troupers answered that if they had comitted any such offence as Deserved Death, his Lo:p had power to pardon them before he left the sword, to which the said Velden replyed that the Lord Deputye might doe well to looke to himselfe, for that he had seen a Lord Deputie hanged before that tyme, intymating therby that the said Deputye, for Directing his warrant for the Cess acording his Maties speciall instruccon and commaunde, ought to suffer Deathe. And this cause being fully heard uppon the 4th of February 1628, and the said malicious speeches fully proved, The Court Censured and decreed that the said Velden for his offence shold paie unto his Matie for his offence, by way of fine, two hundred poundes ster, and be committed during the Lo Depties pleasure, and come to the fower courtes, the Judge sitting, and att the barr of each Court acknowledg his offence uppon his knees. And shall make the lyke acknowledgment att the next Assizes to be houlden for the countie of Meathe.[22]

---

20. f. 98. Note this case is a counter suit, one of the few recorded in this period. See the original suit by Power, f. 97v above, heard on the same day and involving a disputed title to land held of the baron of Cahir. Fols. 98v to 99 contain four cases recorded fully in the entry book charging scandalous speeches against the queen and the archbishop of Canterbury

21. f. 99.   22. f. 99v.

Scandale agt the Earle of Westmeathe.

Md that his Matie Sollisciter generall informed the Court ore tenus agt Humphrie Walshe, the said Humphrie having beene examined by order of Court and being read. The said Humphrie had confessed that as he was travelling a yeare since from the markett of Ould Castle towarde his owne dwelling in the County of Cavan, he mett by chance in the high way with a Scottish boye, about 12 or 14 yeares of age, whome he never saw before nor since, which boye then tould him that if the plott of the Irish had held, then the Earle of Westmeathe should have beene king of Ireland. And about three weekes after, the said Walshe meeting with one Benedick Cottman and others and they asking him what newes, he answered them that it was reported that the Earle of Westmeath should be king of Ireland. Upon which confession after Mr Sollisciter had att larg sett fourth the heynousnes of his offence, The Court upon the 4 of February 1624 Censured and Decreed that the said Humphrie Walshe should paie unto his Matie for a fine 500^{li} ster, and be comitted to the Castle of Dublin during the Lord Deputies pleasure, should be sett upon the Pillory in Dublin the next market Daye with a paper on his head Declaring his offence, to have one of his eares nayld to the Pillorye, and after to be carried to the 4 Courts with the same paper on his head and att the barr of each Court, the Judge sitting, acknowledge his offence. And agte [against] the next Assizes to be houlden for the county of Cavan wher the said wordes weare spoken, to be sent thether and to be sett uppon the Pillory with the like paper on his head and have his other eare nayld and to be carryed to the Court, the Judge sitting, and ther lykewise to acknowledg his offence, and then to be committed to prison againe During the Lo Deputies pleasure.[23]

23. f. 99v. This ends the digest of castle chamber entries, with nothing to indicate the provenance or authority for it. Fol. 100 contains a form for Thomas Preston to be created Ulster King of Arms in Ireland in the presence chamber at castle chamber in Dublin, dated 1 November 1633. Fol. 138 contains information for use of the clerks in castle chamber, including fines, writs and the authority for deputies. The document ends on fol. 153 without further explanation of its author or intent. Wentworth had arrived in Ireland in July 1633, but he spent over a year planning for his administration and the document may have been prepared between the summer of 1632 and his arrival. Preparations for the Irish parliament of 1634 were adumbrated in several memoranda in fols. 1 to 73, citing usage in England for election of a speaker, use of proxies, writs for creation of a peer, proclamations, writs of election, and numerous other parliamentary technicalities.

Royal commission of the court of castle chamber, 1625

The authorization of the court of castle chamber was independently and formally proclaimed by order of the crown in each reign. While the Elizabethan court was created in a series of hesitant steps culminating in a partially autonomous tribunal, the subsequent history of the court was more well-defined. The court under James I did not operate until 1604, amidst a number of uncertainties regarding the establishment of the new reign. However, the Caroline court was re-authorized without hesitation and the full text of this document appears below. It was copied verbatim into TCD, MS 852, along with the digest of castle chamber cases made for the new lord deputy in 1632. In addition, a number of other protocols taken from the court of star chamber in Westminster are listed for the use of the officials in Ireland. These give formal evidence of the manner in which castle chamber proceedings were authorized and enacted.

Castle Chamber.
Charles, by the grace of God king of England, Scotland, Fraunce and Ireland, Defender of the faith &c, To our right trustie and right welbeloved the Lo Deputie, Lietenante, Justice or Justices of our Realme of Ireland and Chauncellor or keeper of our greate Seale there, now being and that hereafter shalbe, our Lord Threr of the same Realme, now being and that hereafter shalbe, our vicetrer of the same Realme now being and that hereafter shalbe, The Lord cheife Justice of our high bench in that our Realme now being and that hereafter shalbe, The cheife Justice of our Comon please in the same Realme, now being and that hereafter for the time being shalbe, The cheife Baron of our Exchecquer there that now is and that hereafter for the time shalbe, The Master of the Rolles of our Chauncerie in the same Realme that now is and for the time shalbe and our Secretarie and Secretaries of state of our said Realme now being and that for the time shalbe, greeting. Wheras our most Deare and Royall father king James of blessed memorie im[me]diatly after his access to the Imperiall Crowne of this kingdome, taking into his princely consideracon the particuler estate of the said Realme of Ireland did finde that by unlawfull mainetenances, Inbrac[er]ies, confederacies, alliances, falce bandinge and takinge of money by the comon Jurors of that Realme, and allso by untrue demeaninge of Sheriffe in making of Pannells and other untrue retornes, and by Riottes, routes u[n]lawfull assemblies, forcible entries and other like hatefull Disorders, misdemeanors, contempte, Defaulte and offences [against] the pollicie and good rules of that Realme was then well neare subverted, and for not punishing of theis inconveniences and by occation of the premises nothing or verie Little was or might be there found by inquiry, wherby the Lawes of that Realme in execution did and could doe little or noe effect, but there ensewed encrease of murthers, periuries and un[blank] of the subiectes of that Realme and loss of their landes and goodes, to the greate hinderance of the service of our said deare father and displeasure of Allmightie god. For the better remedye wherof and to the intente that such execrable and pernicious evills, contemptes and greifes should not escape with iust and due correction and punishment: Our said Deare father did thinck meete and by his speciall Comission and lres patentes under the great Seale of England bearing date att hampton Courte the tenth day of

August in the first yeare of his raigne of England did appointe that a particuler Court for the hearing and Determining of theis detestable enormities, faults and offences shold be houlden within the Castle of the cittie of Dublin in that Realme of Ireland or in such other place where the ordinary termes should be kept in that Realme, And that the same Courte should be called and named the Castle Chamber of the Realme of Ireland. Wee well approving of that honorable and provident institucon of our said most Deare and Royall father, finding the same Courte to be of verie necessary and good use for the advancement of publicke Justice, the suppressing of greate Malefactors, releving our quieter subiectes and retayning all sortes in peace and due obedience of the lawe, have resolved to continue the same Courte. And by thes presentes doe ordaine, constitute and appoint that the said high Court of Castle Chamber in our said Realme of Ireland shall have continuance for hearing and Determining of all causes and matters and in such manner and forme of prosecution and proceedings as in and by these presente is particularly sett downe and declared. Know ye therfore that wee, reposing speciall trust and confidence in yor wisdoms, Judgmente, Integrities and Circumspections, and conceiving the like hope and assurance of such as by our appointment shall succeed you in the said offices & places of Charg and gover[n]ment which you hould under us in that kingdome of Ireland, Have constituted and appointed and by theis presente doe appoint and constitute you and such as shall from time to time execute the foremenco[n]ed offices which you now hould, or anie fower or more of you or them (wherof the said Lord Deputie, Liewtenant, Justice or justices of our Realme of Ireland, The Lo: Chauncellor or keeper of our said great Seale, The Lo: Threr or vicetrer to be one) our Comissioners and Justices of our said Court of Castle Chamber, together with such as by authority of this Comission shalbe associated unto you in the four ordinary termes to be houlden within that our Realme from tyme to tyme, two Dayes in every weeke of the said Termes, That is [to] saie Wensday and Fridaye, or any other daies and tymes when you or any two of you (wherof the said Lord Deputie, Livetenant, Justice or Justices, Lord Chauncellor or Keeper of the great Seale, our Lo Threr or vicetrer to be one) shall thincke meet and convenient to hould and keepe the foresaid Court of [Castle] Chamber, and to proceed therin according to the forme hereafter expressed. And further wee doe give full power and authority to the Lo Deputie, Liuetennant, Justice or Justices, Lo Chauncellor or keeper of our said great Seale, our Lo Threr and vice Threr of our said Realme and to everie of them for the tyme being and which shalbe present att any time of sitting in the said Court, to call and associat unto him or them and unto the rest of our Comissioners then present such and so many of the Lords spirituall and temporall and such of our privy Councell or Justices of anie of our Benches within our said Realme of Ireland as they or anie of them as above is said authorized for the time being shall thincke meete to sitt or ioyne with him or them, and with the rest of our Comissioners then present in the hearing and determining of such causes and matters as in our said Court shalbe heard or determined. And further by theis presente wee give unto you, or anie fower of you for the tyme being (wherof the said Lo Deputie, Liuetenant, Justice or Justices, Lo Chancellor or keeper of our said great Seale, our Lo Threr or vicetrer to be one) together with such of the said Lord Chauncellors and Justices or such a Competent number of them or anie of them as then shalbe called and present to sitt with you as aforesaid full power and authority to receive heare and determyne all and all manner of Bills, Complainte, Suplicacons and Informacons to be made, preferred, exhibited or sett fourth in our said Court of Castle Chamber touching and concerning any Riottes, Routs, Forcible entries, unlawfull assemblies, Deceipte, periuries, forgeries, Defaulte, falcities, misdemeanors of Sheriffe and other officers, Contempte, Disorders, misdemeanors and offences comitted or hereafter to be comitted within our said Realme of Ireland, and all dependentes and Incidentes upon the same, in such like manner, sorte, forme and qualitie to all intentes as such like offences are or heretofore have beene used to be received, heard, ordered or determined in the Court of Starr Chamber within our Realme of England. And doe allsoe by theis presentes give full power and authoritie unto you, or four of you (wherof the said Lo: deputie, Leiutenant, Justice or justices, Lo: Chauncellor or keeper of our said great Seale, Our Lo: Threr or vicetrer to be one) to awarde all ordinarie process as well uppon all the said Bills which be or hereafter shalbe exhibited for anie the causes or offences aforesaid, as allso uppon all and singuler Contemptes to be done or comitted in anie of the said matters in like manner and forme as is used in our Court of Starr Chamber within our Realme of England, the manner and forme wherof wee have hereunto caused to be annexed. And wee doe allsoe by theis presentes give unto you or anie four or more of you (wherof the said Lo: deputie, Lieutennant, Justice or Justices, Lo: Chauncellor or keeper of our said great Seale, or Lo: Threr or vicetrer to be one as before) full power and authoritie together with anie such yor associates as afore is said, or the more number of you and them, to call and comaund before you into the said

Courte by all meanes and wayes that shalbe thought expedient, all and singuler the misdoers and offenders that shall so be complayned uppon and to proceed to the execution, Discussion and Determinacon of the said Disorders, offences and enormityes in such and the same manner and order as in our said Court of the Star Chamber here in England is used. And such as you shall finde to be in fault, to punishe by fines to our use, Imprisonment and otherwise after their demerit, and according to your Discrecons. And allso to tax and assess to our use amerciamentes, fines and penalties for Default to be made by non apparances, Departures from the Court without licence or other Defaultes or Disobediences of the Sheriffs or other persons and whatt soever to be comitted within that Court, or ag[ains]t the authoritie of the same. And for the levying therof to award process in the like manner and forme as is used for the having or obtayning of anie our Debtes or Duties within our said Realme of England and the same to be to the use of us our heires and Successors and to be accompted for in such manner and forme and sorte as other the perquisittes or forfeytures of other our Courtes within our said Realme of England be or shalbe accompted for. And wheras it tendethe much to the quiett and good Goverment of that Realme that all enormous offences, especiallie oppressions, extorcons, periuries, subornacon of periuries, Riottes, maintenance and Champertie comitted by anie person or persons of what qualitie, condicon or degree soever be duly prosecuted and severelie punished by Censure in our said Court of Castle Chamber, wee doe hereby straightlie charg and comaund you our said Comissioners and Justices to take especiall care to see the same performed accordingly. And that noe suite, being once comenced in our said Court, be dischargied or compounded without licence to be given in open courte and entred in the booke of orders of that Court uppon a resonable fine to be assessed unto us for the same and payable by the partie that shall sue fourth the said licence. And wee further will and comaund that if anie plte [plaintiff] in that Court will not proceed in his suite, our Attorney generall for that kingdome shall and may prosecute the same on our behalfe, And that the plte be fined per false clamore [i.e. for false clamouring, or claim]. And that noe fine once sett in our said Court of Castle Chamber be afterwordes reduced, qualified, mittigated or installed but in open Court uppon the last sitting daie of the Terme wherin they shalbe imposed, or in the Terme after att the furthest. And in that qualificacon, mittigacon or reducement you our said Comissioners to have a speciall respect to our Revenue, And if noe mittigacon, qualificacon or reducement be made within that tyme, the fines to stand as they were first pronounced or imposed. And that all fines be within tenne Daies after the ende of the terme next ensewing that terme wherin they were first imposed [be] estreated into our Exchecquer. And such bondes Duly Certified thether as shalbe taken for payment of any the fyne or fynes aforesaid. And that the first remembrancer of our said Exchecquer doe theruppon send out such process for levying thereof as is therin prescribed and agreable to the forme of that Courte, wherby wee may be the more spedily answered of all casuall Revenue of that kinde. And wee doe by theis presente, by authority of our Royall Prerogative, graunt and declare that all Judgmentes, taxacons, Decrees and orders that shalbe given, made and taken by you or any four of you (wherof the said Lord Deputie, Lieutenant, Justice or Justices, Lord Chancellor or keeper of the great Seale, our Lo: Threr or vicetrer to be one, together with anie yor associates so to be assembled as aforesaid) shalbe of the like and same force, validity, strengthe and effect ag[ains]t the partie or parties as any the Judgmentes, taxacons, Decres and orders given, made or taken in the court of Starr Chamber with[in] our Realme of England arr or ought to be. And allso wee doe will and order by theis presentes that the Lo: Deputie, Leiutennant, Justice or Justices of our said Realme of Ireland for the tyme being shall and may from time to time att his and their will and pleasure come in his or their person or persons into our said Court of Castle chamber and During or their presence in the same shall have in our behalfe the full and whole power of Cheife head and principall Justicer and Determiner and shalbe our Cheife head and principall Judg in and of all such matters and causes as shalbe in the same Courte propounded, Debated or controversed, any thing, cause or matter in theis our ltres of Comission to the contrary in any wise notwithstanding. And therfore wee doe by the tenore hereof will and commaund you that you and every of you shall withall earnest Deligence two Dayes in the weeke in the fower terme tymes of the yeare as is aforesaid give yor attendance in and about the due and full execution of the premisses in manner and forme aforesaid. And wee doe allsoe give in straight charg and commaundment to all and singuler our faithfull subiectes to whome it shall in everie manner appertaine, of what estate, Degree, Condicon, calling or office so ever he or they shalbe or presently be, that they shalbe obedient, answerable and Dutifull unto you and to such finall orders and Judgmentes as touching the premisses shalbe from tyme to tyme taken and had by you as shall appertayne, and they and everie of them will eschew our high Indignacon and will answer for the contrarie att their extreme perills. In wittnes wherof wee have caused theis our ltres to be made patentes. Wittnes our selfe att Foxley, the first daie of October in the first yeare of our Raigne.[1]

A note of all causes which the most honorable Court of Starr chamber att Westminster doth from tyme to tyme heare and Determine, together with the manner and forme of the proceeding in the same causes aswell by process as otherwise.

First the Court Doth heare and determine all such causes as the same is authorized unto by the Statute made in Anno tertio of king Henry the Seventh, viz all Ryottes, all unlawfull assemblies, all unlawfull retayners & mainetenances, imbraceries of Jurors, untrue demeanors of Sheriffes in making of pannells and falce retornes, and taking of money by Jurors, and allsoe by comon use the Court doth Deale with periuries of Jurors uppon acquitall of fellons, with willfull periurie of wittnesses, with fordging of deeds and writinges, with fordging of slanderous bills, lettres or privie tokens to slander or deceive any man, with great extorcons of Sheriffes and other Officers, and with manie other misdemeanors as they shall fall out in their severall kindes.[2]

The Lord Chancellor of England, or the Lord keeper of the great Seale for the time being, The Lord Threr of England and the Lord privy Seale, or two of them, one Bishopp, one temporall Lord of the Kinges most honorable Councell, and the two Cheife Justices of the Kinges Bench and Comon Pleas, or other two Justices in their absence, by authority of the same statute Doe sitt to heare and Determine all the said Causes and so doth all other Lordes and councellors to his Matie, and the rest of the Judges of both the Benches somtymes sitt with them likewise the Daie after the end of the terme, and the causes are orderly prosecuted in the same Court in such sorte as followethe.[3]

The partie greved must make his bill of Complaint in parchment signed by a learned man contayning such matters as lieth within the Jurisdiccon of the court. And theruppon the clerke of the Courte is to make out a warrant for process to be made and sealed under the great Seale to call upp as many offendors as shalbe thought requisite to answer the same matter, and when the Defendant[s] Doe appeare, the Clerke of the Court is to record their apparances, albeit the Councell be not present therat, and soe uppon putting in the Defendante answer, which the Clerke of the court Doth receive by oath, the same Defendante[s] are to be examined uppon Interrogatories severally, If the plainte doe require the same, which Interrogatories are to be broght in within thre or fower daies or theraboutes, or elce the Defendant to be licensed to depart and to answer by an Attorney. And if the Defendant Doe not answer in convenient tyme, or if after they have answered they Doe Depart before they have beene examined, then an Attachment passeth if the plt will soe require it by the order of the court, to call them againe.

After the Deft hath answered and is examined or licensed to departe for want of Interrogatories in the plte Default, then the plt is to reply to the Defte answer by the first Day of sitting the Court the next terme after that the Defendte have answered & bene examined as before, unless they be att full issue uppon the bill and answer, which if he doe not then the Defendantes are to be Dismissed with their costes uppon motion to be made by them to the Courte for the same, which Costs are to [be] taxed by the Lo Chauncellor of England or the Lord keeper of the great Seale for the tyme being. But if the plt Doe Replie in convenient tyme alledging some new matter in his Replicacon, then he is to call the Deft by process to reioyne, if he refuse to reioyne gratis, and soe to grow to issue

1. TCD, MS 852, ff. 74–76. At the end of document the clerk has inserted 'per ipsum Regem. Edmondes [clerk who transcribed document].'
2. f. 76v. The succeeding folios describe in detail the form and manner of proceeding at the star chamber court in Westminster, in the same clerk's hand as that which transcribed the proclamation of Charles I, above. This is an evident continuation of the protocols made for the use of the new lord deputy, Wentworth, about 1632, and containing the exact procedural basis of castle chamber transactions. It is important to note that the star chamber practice comprehends the identical charges so often made in castle chamber against recusants wherein jurors can be accused of perjury, witnesses indicted for false accounts and slander against public officials is prosecuted. The wide presumptive latitude of the court and the basis for arbitrary proceeding were thus enshrined in prerogative justice well before the coming of Wentworth to Ireland.
3. Note the discrepancy in membership of the two courts, wherein the castle chamber normally contained the chief governor and the core of the Irish privy council meeting at the time. Star chamber thus lacked the blending of executive and judicial officers which distinguished the personnel of its Irish satellite. By the time of the Caroline court, military officers had normally ceased to function in this judicial capacity.

and theruppon both the parties are to produce and bring their wittnesses in to the Court to be examined by the Clerk of the court, or elce they are to ioyne in a Comission to be awarded out of the Court to certaine indifferent gent[lemen] by the nominacon of both parties for the examinacon of their wittnesses uppon such Interrogatories as both the parties shall minister before the same Comissioners. Wherin if either partie shall refuse to ioyne, then the other side is to have a Comission alone if he shall require yt.

Uppon retorne of the same Comission and full examinacon of wittneses on both sides publicacon is to be graunted, and then uppon the hearing of the same matter uppon the bookes published the Court is to proceed to order and Judgment therof, and the partie convict[ed] or found guiltie uppon hearing of the cause is to be by order of the Court comitted to ward and make fine, according to the greatnes of the offence, and costes to be allowed uppon the Defendte that be found guilty. And likewise Costes to be awarded to the Defendte if the plt prove not his matter, which Costes are to be taxed by the Lord Chauncellor or Lo Keeper as before. And upon the hearing of the matter in open Court the youngest Councellor Doth first begin to Declare and shew his opinyon and Judgment and if the Court Doe not all agree uppon order and Judgment, then the more number to take place and the order to goe that waye.

A note touching such fees as be due to the Clerck of the Courte.
Imprimis for every warrant that he maketh for proces except Comissions
and dedimus protatems   ij s
For every warrant for Comission and Dedimus potestatem   ij s vj d
For apparance of everie person   xij d
For takeing of every affidavit   ij d
For the Dismission of every partie.   ij s
For the Admittance of everie one to Attorney   ij s
For smale orders to be entred in the Booke   j s
For the Drawing and entrie of everie ther order and Decree and somtimes
more as it is in lengthe iij s iiij d
For examining every partie and wittness   ij s
For everie Recognizance taken of anie partie in the Court   iiij s
For Coppies made by the Clerck of the Court of Bills, Answers, Replicacons,
Reioynders, Depo[s]icons of wittnesses and other Recordes for everie
sheete, wherin is usuallie contayned fifteene lynes   xij d
For everie twentie shilinges costes taxed by the Courte   xij d.[4]

4. ff. 77v–78. Latin abbreviations and formulas follow [ff. 78v–8ov] for affidavits, subpoenas, writs, commissions, interrogatories endorsed 'per Consilium' or 'coram Consilio', or the council bench, i.e. castle chamber.

Petitions and cases relating to the court of castle chamber under Wentworth

The records for the court of castle chamber during the tenure of Thomas Wentworth as chief governor are largely missing. Ironically, despite his formidable reputation as a litigator and judge, and even after going to great lengths to establish a substantial record of cases precedent for his use in the court, only fragments of its adjudication remain. Nevertheless, some of the most partisan and heated judicial encounters of the early modern period occurred during Wentworth's regime, involving members of the privy council of Ireland as defendants. The reputation of the later earl of Strafford for legal chicanery and unconstitutional excess dates from this important period, so it is essential to reconstruct from surviving documents a profile of his diverse and at times contradictory record as a magistrate. Using a variety of sources, we may distinguish the use of the court as a political weapon under Wentworth and compare his manipulation of the tribunal with that of his predecessors.

The texts which are transcribed below were presumably copied from the original entry book(s) which are now lost, but they also include copies of original petitions made to the lord deputy. These petition books for the years 1633–35, 1637–39 and 1638 are invaluable. They show the close involvement of the lord deputy at the initial stages of litigation, his authority to determine the appropriate venue of suits at law and his intent to govern by a high level of personal attention to allegations of injustice or inequity. On the other hand, the letters and papers of Wentworth and the earl of Cork show the private rancour and personal agenda of contestants who were not merely Irish councillors but Caroline courtiers in England. From earlier evidence, we can see that both men were experienced petitioners at law and that they were engaged in litigation almost continuously during the 1630s. Therefore, it is possible to overstate the high stakes gamble which they apparently undertook in battling each other in castle chamber. On the other hand, the celebrated dénouement of the petulant earl of Strafford is directly related to his arbitrary management of the government of Ireland, not least of all his treatment of rivals in courts of law. In sum, we may say that the fragmentary record offered here is eloquent of a far more substantial body of litigation before the court of castle chamber than that which has presently come to light.

A letter book for the years 1633 to 1635 contains petitions to the lord deputy which were then re-directed to appropriate venues. Although the volume was titled 'Orders for the Ecclesiastical Commission in Ireland 1633–1634', the text contains many references which were purely secular, including a number directed thus: 'Let this petition bee presented unto us at our first and next sitting at the Councell table and there the same shall bee taken into Consideracon and such order given thereupon as shall bee answerable to the instruccon given by his late matie for the settlement of the Ulster plantacon.'[1] The burden of cases were referred to Dr Bramhall, bishop of Derry, but many were taken up at the council table for final resolution if no composition between the parties could be arranged. Interim awards and conditions were assessed, apparently by the chief governor and others acting in a judicial capacity, pending the determination of the case. The petitions were each handled with careful attention to the details of the case, showing the lord deputy as a fulcrum or catalyst for subsequent adjudication and hearing charges from throughout the realm. The volume demonstrates the close working relationship of prerogative courts which were putatively distinct, that is, the castle chamber, the ecclesiastical commission and the committee for plantation affairs. Indeed, one might argue the case for a pragmatic merging of these courts with the inherent judicial capacity of the Irish privy council, especially during the four legal terms. This blending of capacities is suggested in the following order: 'Let this petition bee delivered to the Court of the Councell to bee presented unto us at the boarde where wee will take the requests thereof into their Consideracon.'[2]

On 22 April 1634 the chief governor ordered a petition from one Mary Gatten, widow, to be taken up and considered before the council sitting as a court. The plaintiff alleged she took a farm of three score acres of plantation land in King's County, being a proportion of one Morrice Simon, who promised the plaintiff a lease for term of years, upon which land the plaintiff bestowed great cost in trenching and draining the same, it being

a meere bogge not worth 40 sh paine, before the perfecon of which Lease the said Morrice dyed. Whereby the said Land came unto one John Groin, the surveyor, who perfected articles to your suppl sonne to make a Lease of the premisses for five Lives, but before the said Lease cold bee perfected the said Groin sould the whole propercon unto one Morgan Higgeins and William Higgins, both natives of this kingdome, who notwithstanding the Charge disbursed as aforesaid and the Cost of planting of an Orchard on the said land, will not permitt ye supplicant neither to enioy her Lease parcell at 4^{li} per annum nor permitt ye petitioners sone to have the benefitt of the said articles for Lives at 6^{li} the yeare, but most unconscionably and uniustly threatneth to put ye petiioner out of the possession of the premisses at May day next, unless ye petitioner dubble his rent reserved as aforesaid. Which ye suplicant humbly prayeth your lordship to take into favorable Consideracon and in regard ye petioner is an aged Lame woman who for these 20 yeares together hath given entertainement to all the Lord[s], Knights and Gent that travell betwixt this Cittie and Conaght that yo honor will bee pleased to take such Course as yo honor shall think fitt …[3]

---

1. BL, Harleian MS 4297, f. 170v. The petition showed that an Irish tenant in Co. Tyrone refused to move from plantation lands of an undertaker, Sir William Parsons, who was an official of the court itself. The volume concludes with orders regarding the state of the church and schools in Ireland for 1623, and instructions for the new lord lieutenant in July 1669 (f. 178).
2. BL, Harleian MS 4297, f. 138v. The case involved land in the new plantation of Co. Leitrim, by a petitioner who 'beeing ignorant' entrusted an English agent with his lands who converted them to his own use.
3. Ibid., f. 157.

Another view of Wentworth as judge casts doubt on his impartial demeanour when involved in cases of political import. The papers of Richard Boyle, earl of Cork, demonstrate the interaction of political and judicial influences during the course of litigation. When the earl was accused of illegally impropriating tithes from the college of Youghal, an ecclesiastical foundation which was in his care, the lord deputy threatened him with an enormous fine, out of all proportion to the nature of his offence. The case demonstrates as well the protracted course of litigation, in which we see from the perspective of a defendant the bounty of legal responses demanded by the court. Even though Cork was an experienced petitioner and a former lord justice, he was overwhelmed by the cascade of paperwork and the threats of punishment in a court of which he was a member of long standing. The Boyle correspondence which is transcribed below helps us to see how the court of castle chamber worked by informal means as well as by open hearings to achieve its ends.

A warrant by Lord Deputy Wentworth was issued on 22 September 1634 to William Stoughton, clerk of the court of castle chamber, to issue letters missive to the earl of Cork, 'requiring his lordship to apeare in his Maties high court of Castlechamber and answere an informacon there to bee exhibited against him by his Maties Atorney on his Maties bihalf, returnable the first sitting Day in the said Court of Castlechamber the next terme. Where you may not faile. And for soe doeing this shalbe your warrant.'[4] In the Wentworth Muniments preserved at Sheffield, a full transcription of the attorney's information in castle chamber is extant, giving the patient reader a rare glimpse of the burden of charges made in this highly politicized case. A substantial excerpt from this document appears below, dated 17 November 1634.

To the Kings most excellent matie in his highness Court of Castlechamber. In most humble manner informeth your most excellent Matie, Sir William Rives, knight, your Maties Atturney generall for and on the behalfe of your Matie, That whereas some of your most Royall predecessors in theire Zeale unto gods Church and for the reformacon of this your Maties Kingdome did erect a Colledge, or at the least gave Licence that there should be a Colledge erected and founded in or neere Youghall in the Countye of Corke within the Province of Monster, and for the better Rule and Govermt thereof did Constitute and appointe that there shoud be in the said Colledge a warden & eight fellowes, or collegieners, and eight Choristers and that Such as shold be Chosen Fellowes of the said Coledge shold be men without exception, both for theire life and learning fitt to preach godes holy word in the said towne and parish of Youghall and other adioyneing parishes, and to performe such other dutyes as to the Care of soules doth apertaine. And that the said warden and fellowes might the better attend and dischardge theire said Injunction, divers of your maties most Royall predecessors and many others well disposed persons by theire Licence did endowe the said Colledge, being erected as aforesaid with Lardge and great possesions, and in particular did appropriat unto the warden and fellowes of the said Colledge and theire Succesors for ever twelve Parsonages which then had and yett have the Cure of soules annexed unto them, a great number of presentative vicarages, and severall other spirituall possesions which at this present are worth to be yearely att seaven or eight hundread poundes ster at a moderate and easye rent, by meanes whereof Religion and Learning whilst the said Colledge did subsist did flourish in theat parte of the Kingdome, the Cure of soules was dischardged

4. Chatsworth, Lismore MSS, vol. 18, item 29. This warrant was signed by Wentworth, to appear in the next Michaelmas term. In October, the commissioners were named to take the information, three for the court and three for the earl of Cork.

by the said warden and fellowes, and much good did thereby redound to the Kingdome in generall. But your said Att[orney] doth informe your most excellent Matie that about three or foure and thirtie yeares Since, when by reason of the warres and troublesome tymes which untill then did Long continue in this Kingdome, the said Colledge was abandoned and noe such care taken thereof as was [done] uppon the first foundacon, the right honorable Richard, Earl of Corke, did gaine an estate for yeares or otherwise of and in the premises or in some parte thereof, and haveing by collour thereof gotten into the possession of the said Colledge, and of all the Landes, Rectoryes, tythes and other hereditamentes thereunto belonginge, and perceiveing how easye a matter it was in those tymes to make a prey thereof, the said Earle of Corke did plott and devise how to disappropriate the same from that pious life for which at first it was destinated and to gaine the same unto himselfe and his heires. And to that end and purpoose and the better to effect what he had formerly propounded unto himselfe, the said Richard, Earle of Corke, soone afer his entrye unto the possession of the premisses, did soe farr worke and prevaile with the reverent father in god, Richard Bryte, now Bishop of Corke, a neere Kinsman of the said Earle who then was and yett is warden of the said Colledge, that by his meanes the comon Seale of the said Colledge and all the Charges and evidences Concerning the said Coledge and the possessions thereof which were in the Custodye of the said fellowes or some or one of them were about seaven and twenty yeares since taken from the Custody of such of the said fellowes in whose Keepeinge the said seale and evidences then were and the said seale and evidences were, uppon soche pretences best Knowen unto the said Earle and warden, delivered unto the said Earle to be Kept in trust for the safety and prservacon of them, and the said Earle, for some ends of his owne best knowen unto him selfe, hath ever since detained and kept the said Seale and evidences from the said Warden and fellowes. And albeit the said Earle hath beene often requested by the said warden and fellowes to deliver the said Seale and evidences yett the said Earle in manifest breack of the said trust, hath and doth still detaine the same. And yor said Atturney doth further informe or most excellent Matie that the said Earle, haveinge by this meanes gotten the said Seale and evidence into his possession and haveing them but some short interest or terme for yeares in the premises or in some parte thereof, the said Earle did further practise and devise by fraud and circumvencon to gaine a further Interest therein, and haveing found by experience how easye itt was to worke uppon the said warden his Kinsman the said Earle did deale with the said warden to repaire to Dublin, whoe Comeing thither according to the said Earles appoointment, the said Earle procured him to goe with him to Sir Gefferye Fentones house, to whose daughter the said Earle was maryed, and haveing prepared aforehand a Conveyance ready drawen and ingrossed in parchment, purporting a graunt from the said warden and fellowes eyther for a Long Terme for yearres or in fee farme of all the possessions of the said Colleges, the said Earle did then and there, in a most undue and unlawfull manner with much importunitye and Solicitacon, Circumvent and procure the said warden to subscribe unto the said conveyance which was drawen as aforesaid in the name of the said warden and fellowes without theire direction, privity or allowance, protesting that if the fellowes would nott Joyne in the graunt that then he wojld yeld it upp againe, and the better to coullour this his hard practise and in hope that if the same were discovered it should take the lesse hould uppon himselfe the said conveyance was made to and in the name of Sir Lawrence Parsons, Knight, deceased, by yett in confidence and trust and to and for the use of the said Earle. And the said Earle haveing by this meanes procured the said warden to subscribe unto the said conveyance and haveing the said Conveyance Seale in his Custody as aforesaid, the said Earle as your said Atturney is informed did uniustly, fraudulently and Contrary to his said former protestacons putt or cause to be putt the said Seale without the privitye or Consent of the said warden or any of the then felowes unto the said Conveyance, and soe did forge the said deede by putting the said Seale in manner aforesaid thereunto contrary to your Maties Lawes and Statutes of force in this yor Kingdome. And the said Earle, feareing that his practise might come to Light if he the said Earle should make eyther a sudden or totall seisure of all the posessions of the said Colledge, the said Earle did permitt his said Kinsman to Continue the name of warden in some two or three to beare the name or names of fellowes in the said Colledge and did allow unto the said warden and fellowes four smale meanes out of the rentes of the said Colledge, but yett soe as the said Earle would nott aquitt the said warden or any of the said fellowes to Lodge or dwell within the said Colledge, but turning them out of the Doores did wholy possesse himselfe thereof and used the same for a dwelling howse. And the said Earle to gaine himselfe the further thereinto did turne away the auncient Bayliffe or Collector formerly imployed by the said warden and fellowes for the levying and Collecting of the rentes and revenues of the said Colledge, and did ymploy onne of [his] owne meniall srvantes in the said office, and when any of the fellowes of the said Colledg dyed or their places became voyde, the said Earle did hinder and oppose as much as lay in him the chusing of any new fellowes in theire place soe as in the end the number of the said fellowes by the said devises were reduced unto some fiev, and uppon the matter the said Earle became Warden, fellowes and Choristers of the said Colledge. And your said Atturney doth further informe your most excellent Matie that the said Earle haveing by this tyme tasted the sweetness of the said possessions and fearing that the succeeding warden and fellowes might Question and avoyde the said Conveyance which he had gained as aforesaid, did further practise how he might overthrow the very foundacon of the said Colledg and gaine the posession thereof unto himselfe by a title paramount. And to that purpose the said Earle haveing gained as aforesaid the evidences and writeings which did Concerne eyther the first foundacon of the said Colledg or the generall endowmentes thereof, the said Earle began to prey thereinto with Eagles eyes, and being in formedd by some Counsell as ill disposed towardes the said colledg as himselfe that the said Colledg was not well founded, or if the said evidences were suppressed that then the fundacon cold not be proved, and that by suppressing the said evidences a good title might be made unto yor matie most Royall father for all the possessions of the said colledg, the said Earle did most Sacrylegioiusly and indirectly, contrary to the first trust which was reposed in him, Cause all the possesions of the said Colledg to be passed uppon a generall letter procured by Sr James Hallerter, knight, or some other as his assignees from or said Father for the paseing of Concealed Landes, never expressing that there was any purpose to passe the possessions of the said Colledge uppon the said Letter, for that he did well know that your most royall father who was the fountaine and favourer of Learning would never have given his consent (if that his said matie had beene truely enformed) that the said possesions should have bin pased away from the said colledg unto any Lay or Sacrylegious handes, and the said Landes being past uppon the said letter, the said Earle according his former Compact and agreement did for som triflinge and poore Consideracon procure an assignement to be made thereof in his owne name, or in the name of some other in Confidence and trust to and for his use, and the same was carryed soe Close and in such a secrett manner as very few had notice thereof. And yor said Atturney doth further enforme your most excellent matie that the said warden and such other said fellowes as the said Earle did allowe and permitt to Continue fellowes of the said Colledg viz the Reverend father in god Michaell, Lord Bipp of Waterford and Lismore, Robert Doberne, Deane of Lismore, and John Lancaster, Clerke, all fellowes of the said Colledge, haveing some notice given unto them of the said wicked practise and devises and considering which themselves what wronge they were like to doe unto posterity if that they did sufer such undue Courses to be taken in theire tyme, and to passe in silence to the disinheritance of the said Colledge, the said warden and fellowes did first Sollicitt the said Earle to deliver unto them the said Seale and evidence Concerning the said Colledge which were Comitted to his Keepeing and which the said Earle had soe long detained from them, but being putt of by dilatory answers and excuses that the said seale and evidences were at his howse at Youghall the said warden and fellowes began to enter into a more serious confederacon of the state of ye said Colledg and haveing considered the severall wages and Courses which the said Earle had taken to gaine uppon the said Colledg, the said warden and fellowes did in the moneth of Aprill which was in the year 1627 enter into a mutuall Covenant that they would putt the said Richard, Earl of Corke, into suite for the premises and feareing least the said Richard Earle of Corke might, after his wanted and usuall manner, inveagle and worke uppon them by diverting them from this their pious and godly resolucon the said warden and fellowes did take a solemne oath uppon the holly evangelist that neyther they nor any of then wold make any composicon or agreement with the said Richard Earle of Corke for or concerning the premisses without the Consent and full agreement of the fellowes and warden testifyed under the handes and seales of them and every of them as by an Instrument in writeing made to that purpose. [The agreement was then read into the information of the text, along with subsequent letters exchanged with the earl, leading to the accusation made before the court, arguing] ... and that likewise Condigne punishment may be inflicted uppon the said Earle and the said Richard, Bp of Corke and Michaeall, Bp of Waterford, which may deterr others from Committing the like enormitous offence and that a Course may be taken for the restoreing of the said Colledg unto all the meane profittes of the premises which soe long have beene soe uniustly detained by the said Earle, and Your said Attorney doth further informe yor most excellent matie that whereas by an Act of State established in this kingdome in the year of our lord God one thowsand six hundred and fifteene by direccons from yor most royall father for the good of the church, divers and severall provisions have bin made against unreasonable and unconscionable Leases made by the Clergye of this Kingdome, it is provided amongst divers other things in and by the said act that noe parson or vicar of any church putative should make any Lease or grant of any lande, tenementes, hereditaments or profitts whatsoever belonging to theire parsonage or vicarage for any longer tyme then dureing theire severall incumbences in and upon the said parsonages and vicarages ... [accusing the earl of knowingly violating this act of state, and demanding that he] bring in evidences to court at a certaine day and to depose before the lord depty and council in the court of castle chamber then and there to answer the premises and to abide all such further censure and judgement as to the said lord deputy and counsell shalbe thought fitt to be inflicted uppon them.[5]

On 29 November the earl made appearance in court to give affidavit that 'The said Richard earle of Corke beinge present in Court hath this Day made faith that his writings & Evidences are in the Countrye, without sight whereof hee cannot make answeare unto the Informacon exhibited into this Court against him'.[6] On 4 February 1635, the attorney general, William Ryves, gave the two bishops of Cork and of Waterford additional time to respond to the extensive information given in court by Cork and his agents. On 4 March 1635 the attorney general charged Cork with wrongly withholding lands, deeds and conveyances concerning the college of Youghal, demanded the deeds and conveyances be brought into the court and ordered two senior officials to examine them. In February 1635 the earl wrote to explain his actions as a work of charity on behalf of a former employee, blaming Dr Bramhall for interfering in a cause against him, and complaining that the lord deputy exceeded his authority. An interesting exchange occurred in which the concept of an act of state was debated between them, in the course of defending his presumed benevolence.

And therefore did hope that I did not Deserve to be brought into the Castlechamber for soe good and charitable a worke, his Lopp answered me that by my soe doing I had infringed the Act of State. I told his Lopp how the poore Minister being runne in Debt was clapt in prison, and kept in a Dungeon in bolts amongst theeves & traytors and his wyfe and children by wants ready to perish. And that the Lo Bpp seeming sensible of the poore Ministers sufferings had by his lres interceeded effectually with me to ioyne in a lease' to assist the minister, and his wife was sent to the earl from Kerry over the mountains to plead her case, so the earl signed the lease without consideration. 'But his lordshipp told me that my Charity wold be noe excuse for the breakinge of the Act of State. I replyed to his Lopp that that Act of State was never proclaymed nor any publique notice given of it in the country where I lived, neither had I ever heard of any such untill the Bill was preferred agt me. He told me ignorance shold give no excuse for me, Then I told his Lopp that since the Bill was preferred agt me I had enqired after that Act of State & found that it had never been proclaymed and that it was voide in it selfe, in reguard that it was made in King James tyme who was dead, and in the tyme of the governement of the lord Grandison lo Deputie who was likewise deceased, and soe of no force. His lopp replyed unto me, Sir, as great as you are, I will make you and all others in this kingdome know that any Act of State, made or to be made, shalbe as byndeing to the subiectes of Ireland as any Act of Parliament can be, with many other menacing words to that effect.[7]

On 20 March 1635 the earl of Cork was confronted in court, and he made the following transcript of that occasion.

5. Sheffield City Library, WWM STR P, 24–25, item 437, ff. 1–29. 'Copia vera Anth Stoughton, Morrice Eustace, Nath Catelin, Willm Ryves, Edward Bolton.' The original document was evidently signed by the court officials and copied for the use of the lord deputy.
6. Ibid., vol. 18, item 42.
7. Ibid., vol. 18, item 72.

This day my L Deputy comaunded [me] to attend [MS torn] of the Lordes, Judges and Comissioners in the Court of Castle chamber, yt being firste rumored thoroughout the Cyttie, that the Vincente Gookines cause should be handled there at this meeting, wich opynon induced a great confluence of the better sorte of the people to thronge thither, my self amoungste the rest of the Judges of the Court (being by the pursevant this very morning, without any premonicon or notice of the cause, lykewise warned to atttend his Lo[rdshi]p). And when the Court was sett his Mates Attorney generall taxed me with delaying the putting in of my answer to his informacon (which in itself was moste untrew) Then he moved further that notwithstanding a former order of the Cort I had not brought into the Court thancient evidences and seale belonging to the Colledge of Yoghall (which order was made the last Daie of the Laste Tearm, since which day the Court never satt). Wheruppon in tymely obedience I this day had the said ancient wrytinge and seale in a boxe by themselves, and the deed made to Sir Lawrence Parsons of the said Coledge, and the whole possessions therof in another Boxe ready in Court in another Boxe and I was ordered delivered them up in Court uppon oath, there publicquely ministered unto me by the L Chauncellor, Then Mr Attorney, further moved that the owld lease of the Colledge made to Sir Thomas Norris (never moved for in Court before nor menconed in any former order of Court) might also be by me produced, which I also promised this night to deliver up to thofficer to be by him coppied and thoriginal to be brought back unto me againe. Then Mr Attorney moved that Dermott Dingle, one other of the Defendantes, in regard of his age and disability to travell, might for expediting the cause have a dedimus potest[atem] graunted to some solvent gentlemen in the Country to receave his answer & examinacon ...[8]

In June 1635 the earl requested additional time, since his witnesses were dispersed in England, Munster and Connacht, while some were impotent and unable to travel. Commissioners were then named, to report in October after examining the witnesses in England and elsewhere. The record is silent on the case until the following spring, but the earl suggested that efforts were made to compose an agreement with him to accept a large fine in lieu of proceeding with his cause in castle chamber. On 23 April 1636 Cork received a visit from the primate of Ireland who reported the lord deputy's intent to fine and imprison him if he were to be found guilty. 'And yf I would condiscend to give the king thirty thowsand pounds he would be my frennd and the suite in Castle Chamber shold be withdrawne, otherwise he wold prosecute me without any further delay, for he would see an end of it before he went into England.'[9] On 25 April the lord deputy offered an open debate on the matter before proceeding to trial, but Cork refused, arguing 'that I conceaved the proper Court for Determining thereof was not in the Castle Chamber, but in the Court Christian'. The lord deputy on that occasion declined to pursue the matter, although they had spent five hours of the morning on the subject, and two days later they discussed his case privately for another two hours on the walls of Dublin Castle. Wentworth sought the intercession of Lord Ranelagh and offered a compromise wherein Cork would pay £15,000 fine to the crown and lose the rights to parsonage and tithes from the college of Youghal. By early May 1636 the earl of Cork was prepared for his trial, spending long hours with his counsel and solicitor. On 2 May the lord chancellor came to him to say that 'it was very necessary for me to be exceeding carefull of my self for that it was not my cause but my judges I was to feare'.

8. Ibid., vol. 3, f. 69. This volume contains the journal of the earl, and its entries should be seen as a diary of his work.
9. Ibid., vol. 18, item 133.

Apparently, the earl of Cork was persuaded by his friends and colleagues in the privy council to relent, avoiding the threat of fine, imprisonment and loss of office were he to proceed to trial of his cause. On 5 May the lord deputy sent for the earl and asked if he had paid the fine of £5,000 into the exchequer and security for the rest. Cork replied he needed more time, but the deputy argued he had as much in store houses. Cork remembered his exchange with Wentworth as follows. 'I prayed him to consider well, whether in iustice he could impose soe great a fyne upon me, Whereunto he replyed, Gods wound Sir, When the last Parliament in England brake upp yow lent the King fifteen thowsand pounds, And afterward in a very uncivill unmannerly manner you pressed his Matie to repay it yow, Whereupon I reserved before I came out of England to fetch it back againe from yow, by one meanes or other, And now I have goten what I desired, you and I wilbe frends hereafter.'[10] On 30 May 1636 the lord deputy signed an order for Cork to pay the fine of £15,000 by prior agreement, including £5,000 already paid, £5,000 before 24 June and the rest at midsummer day. The use of castle chamber to intimidate enemies and rivals of the chief governor was increased under Wentworth and became a major complaint of the parliament against prerogative justice in 1640 and after.[11]

Another book of petitions to Lord Deputy Wentworth from 1637 to 1639 is preserved in Harleian MS 630 in the British Library. Again, the records demonstrate a preliminary written pleading, presumably by counsel, before the chief governor. Wentworth signed most of these documents himself, directing in many cases that the defendant 'is required to appeare forthwith before us to answer this complaynt'.[12] While this suggests the employment of a conciliar jurisdiction, the court of castle chamber is not always mentioned as the court of record. Nevertheless, the formal appeal to the lord deputy and the decision to hear cases 'at the Councell table', citing allegations such as riot and maladministration of judicial officers which properly belonged to the venue of castle chamber, suggest that the court was busy with adjudication which was initially presented to the chief governor for resolution. Some of these cases cite castle chamber directly and give evidence for its work in the later Caroline period. Three of these texts are cited below.

The peticon of Robert Nugent shewinge that about some five yeares last past ye petr and one Edward Kolly were justly Censured in his maties high Courte of Castle Chamber in 240^{li} costs & damadges and fyned to his Matie in 150^{li} by one Christopher Jones, prosecutor of ye said cause, for which censure your peticoners on the 17th day of Aprill 1635 preferred this bill in the said courte agst the said Jones and his wittnesses in the said cause for subornacon, and that all the proces of ye said courte were sent aft[er] three of the said wittneses whoe stand in contempt thereof, untill that aboute three moneths past Donnogh Fihilly, one of ye said three, was brought in by the serieant and beinge ever since in the Marshalsie of ye said Courte refuseth to answere yor petitioner said bil. And your peticon before hee was admitted to exhibit his bil agt the said Jones and the said wittnesses did

10. Ibid., vol. 18, item 133.
11. Ibid., vol. 18, item 133. Cork later had the satisfaction of reporting Strafford's trial in parliament in 1640 and his own recovery of estates. Ibid., vol. 21, item 91.
12. BL, Harleian MS 630, f. 14.

put in sufficient security in 300^{li}, as may appear by the order and certificate thereof annexed, in case they shold be dismissed. And whereof dyvers writtes of habeas Corpus were by orders of the Councell Table and Courte of Starrchamber graunted to your peticoner for those two yeares last past to enable your peticoners & prosecucon and that hee might bee at liberty to follow ye said cause. Soe it is rt honorable that ye said Christopher Jones, most canteously [slyly, by trickery] and of purpose to hinder your petr proceedings in his said cause, hath procured an order this last Tearme to put your Peticoners into a dungeon for none payment of ye said Damadge if not paid within 20^{ty} daies, though ye said Jones receives the profittes of the said Kollys Landes yearely untill the said costs and damage bee paide by a former order of the said Courte and that ye D[ef] Jones ever since the said order hath rec'd the A[foresaid?] profitts. And your petr is able to prove and ready to depose that hee is not able to pay the said costs, hee haveinge a wife and eight children liveinge of a Charge upon theire freindes in ye Country (hee not able to maintaine himselfe here in ye Castle of Dublin but through the charity of his freinds and acquaintances). And whereas ye said Jones hath exhibited a crosse bill of purpose to hinder yor petitioner from prosecutinge his said bill without putinge in of any security for payment of costs & damadges, your petr most humbly prayeth that yor Lp would bee pleased by a hab[eas] Corpus to direct your peticoner [to have] liberty untill ye next Tearme to prosecute such of the said Defendants as are not as yett brought in, or to referr the Consideracon of this peticon unto the honorable the Mr of the Rolls or Sir George Radcliffe, knt, to certifie your Lp what thej upon sight of ye order of the Councell board & Castle Chamber doe in their opinions conceive fitt to bee done to enable yor petr to prosecute the said cause, which otherwise by reason of his strict durance hee might bee forced to relinquish. And etc.

D[ublin] C[astle] 12 July 1637. Lett this Peticon bee presented at ye Councell Table & there ye same may be taken into consideracon and such answere given thereunto as shalbee fitt.[13]

The petition of David Roberts, showing that the 'supplicant hath lately suffered a most uniust, disgracefull and vile imprisonment as ever true subiect suffered and yt upon pretence of Debt for the space of 18 Dayes at ye suite of one John Phillips, now burgomaster of Maryburrowgh, as alsoe by the illegal subornacon and Combinacon of Sir Walter Crosby, Barr[onet], and one Thomas Beard, senior, his uncle, together with the affeccious [affected, dissembling?] Confederacy of Thomas Lawrence, Burgesse, and Dennis Birne, marshall. Now soe it is, right honorable, that your poore peticoner is soe disable and poverisht by his Longe iuspencine [MS unclear: iust [suit?] pending?] and disgracefull relacon to ye said Crosbyes that hee is not worth five pence at his present in the world. May yor honors therefore bee graciously pleased, out of your knowne and noted goodnes to men distrest and opprest with iniuryes, to give yor most poore petitioner leave to impleade the above delinquentes in his Maties most high Courte of Castle Chamber in forma Pauperis, yor honor most favorably [as]signeinge unto your supplicant such Councell as yorr Lo[rdshi]ps most grave wisdome shall seeme most expedient ...

D.C. 12 July 1639, Lett this matter bee moved in the Courte of Castle Chamber and there the Same may bee taken into Consideracon and surcharge were given thereunto as shalbee fitt.[14]

The petition of John Dobb, Marshall of his maties high Court of Castle Chamber. Most humbly shewth that the last Tearme it pleased your honors fo impose a fine of 10 ^{li} upon yor supplicant for not appeareing and quietting some sudden noyse & rumor which was then made in the said Court of Castlechamber by some indiscreete & Disorderdd persons. Now so it is, right honorable, that yor petitioner (being then very sick & so hath since Continuedd not able to stir out of his chamber) Did in regard of your honors personne that Day in court appoint Divers of his servantes to attend in and aboute the said Courte, which accordingly was peaceably & quietly kept & attended untill at last Some of your honors guard at the doore, entering into the said Courte, tooke of [off] the hatte from of the heade of Divers people, Notwithstanding they were Desired by yor supplicants servantes to forbeare. Whereupon some of the said severall persons looking to regaine theire hattes made this sudden noyse which by reason of the great throng & multitude of people then in & aboute the said

13 Ibid., f. 57. Note the petitioner shows that his case was in litigation for five years in castle chamber, with numerous counter pleas and cross bills which demonstrate the wide circumference of the court's attention and the extent of adjudication which went beyond the final acts and decrees of the court.

14. Ibid., f. 61v.

Court yor supplicants said servantes could not so suddenly appease the same, but afterwardes & ever since as yor supplicants hopeth the same hath beene quietly & peaceably kept by yor supplicantes servantes, yor supplicant (by reason of his said sicknes being not able to attend himselfe). May it please yor honors to give order that the said fine be struck out & wholy remitted …
D.C. This petition be presented unto us at the Councell table where the same shalbe taken into or further Consideracon.[15]

The Wentworth Woodhouse muniments preserved in the Sheffield City Library contain a number of castle chamber documents, the survival of which appears serendipitous. The papers of Thomas Wentworth, earl of Strafford, demonstrate his litigious nature in many ways. A star chamber case against David Foulis, dating from his tenure as lord president of the council in the North, is extensively recorded, ending in a fine of £3,000 to the earl as plaintiff. Another star chamber case against Sir Piers Crosbie resulted in extensive charges and pleas over five years, during the time Wentworth was chief governor in Ireland.[16] However, the only castle chamber decree which was fully reported concerned a dispute between priests in Dublin, a matter in which Wentworth was not directly concerned. The text is transcribed fully below.

Memorandum that Nicholas Stephens of the Cittie of Dublin, Alderman, Robert Lalor of the same, marchant, and Patricke Brangane of the same, Priest, all prisoners in his Maties Castle of Dublyn, havinge ben examined by directions of the Right honorable the Lord Deputy toching the spreadinge and divulginge of a Letter obteyned from Cardinall Antoine Barbarini by order of the Congregacon of Cardinals de fide in propaganda in Roome, which letter was directed to Thomas Fleminge, the Titular Archbishop of Dublin, and concerneth the exercise of forrayne Jurisdiction within this his highnes kingdome of Ireland The Tenner whereof followeth in haec verba, Most Illustrious and Reverend Lord as ar heere. It is written unto the Bp of Meath that he Comaund the same Paul Harris to departe forthwith from yor Dioces, otherwise to give order by authorritie of the same congregacon to the faythfull people that none shall receave from him the holy sacramentes nor heare his mass. And that some scandall arise not by meanes of this order, your Lopp may give unto the said Bp when he receaveth the inclosed such advertisements and Informacons as you shall thincke fitting for prevencon thereof. To Conclude I offer and Comend my selfe to your Lordshipp, yor most affectionat as brother, Cardinale Antoine Barbarini, Roome, 13 December one thousand six hundred thirty and fowre. Francis Ingeby, Secretary. The said Nicholas Stephens, havinge upon his examynacons taken and this day read in Court (he beeinge present and acknowledgeinge the same), confessed that he received a copie of that same letter from one Whitside and gave it to one Thomas Taylor. Wherfor the said Robert Lalor likewise havinge upon his examiniacons read in court (himself beeinge present and acknowledginge the same), confessed that he receaved a coppie of the said letter from the said Patricke Brangane, and that he gave it to his mistres. And the said Patricke Brangan upon his examinacons read in Court himselfe beeinge present and acknowledginge the same, confessed that he sawe the originall of the said Letter in Italian in the handes of the said Titular Arch[bishop] of Dublin to whome it was directed from Roome by the Cardinall Barbarini with a letter inclosed to the Titular Bp of Meath, he alsoe confessed that he translated it out of Italian into English and gave a coppie therof to Robert Lalor, which Lalor wrote out with his owne hand And that the originall remaines in the handes of the said Titular Archbishop of Dublin. Uppon readinge of all which examinacons the same beeinge acknowledged by everie of the said parties respectivly, Mr Attorney gennerall on his Maties behalfe havinge opened unto ye Court the heynousnes of the offences

---

15. Ibid., 69v. No date is given in manuscript, though the context and other cases suggests mid-July 1639. The Dobb case reveals much about the temper of the court and its judicial demeanour in the presence of a multitude of litigants. Fols. 50v to 68 include many petitions involving 37 cases in which the lord deputy deployed agents such as sheriffs to take depositions and otherwise defer hearing the cause.
16. WWM STR P, 24–25, items 428–32, 461–74.

whereof the said parties weare by thiere owne confesions under theire hands respectively guilty, Humblie praied the Right Ho[nora]ble the Lord Deputy and Court to proceede unto the Censure of the said parties (Ore tenus), they now standinge at the Barr. Whereupon the Court takeinge into grave and serious consideracon the greatnes of theire offences, And whereas it hath bin manifested and notoriously knowne unto the state heere, and to the whole Country that a forrayne quarrell or difference beween the said Brangan and the said Paul Harrys did originally arise, for that the said Paul Harrys had converted the said Brangan before a temporall Judge of this kingdome for detayneinge of a booke from the said Paul Harrys and that thereupon the said Brangan had complained unto the said Tittular Archbpp of Dublin and procured him to Comaund the said Paul Harrys to departe out of his pretended diocese of Dublin and soe to banish him, and because the said Paul Harrys refused to obey him therin, he the said Tittular Archbpp denounced the Sentence of excommunicacon against all such as should resort to the said Paul Harrys to heare his Masse, and when those courses against the said Paul Harris did not take such effect as was expected, Meanes was made unto Roome unto the Congregacon of Cardinals de propaganda fide there, and from thence were obteyned the said Letters from the said Cardinal Barbarini, governor of the said Congregacon unto the said Titular Archbp of Dublin & to the titular Bp of Meath whereby the said Tittular Bp of Meath was required to proceed against the said Paul Harrys as is in the fore recited Letter expressed as by the verie Letter it selfe directed to the said Tiittular Bp of Meath now produced in court did appear. Howbeit the said Tittular Bp of Meath refused to medle therin, or to have any thinge to doe therewith, and therefore the said Brangan translated the said Letter directed to the said tittular Archbp out of Italian into English and undertooke the publishinge and notifyeinge thereof, and did publish the same as in his examinacon is expressed, supposinge it should take as good effect in the myndes of the people as if the said Tittular Bp of Meath himself had done that which he was required as aforsaid, for that all people might thereby fully understand that the said Paul Harris was required by the said congregacon of Cardinalls to departe out of the diocese of Dublin, or if he did not, that none ought to resort unto him to receave the sacramentes or heare his Masse and soe the publicacon of the said Letter aforerecited in the said examinacon was not only the publicacon but in substance & effect the execucon of the sentence of the said Congregacon of Cardinals, Whoe tooke uppon them to banish and Comaunde the kings subiectes out of the diocese of Dublin. And for that it is manyfest that the excercise of all forrayne Jurisdiccon uppon any of his Maties subiectes residinge within this his dominions and the puttinge in execucon any sentence decreed under such forrayne Jurisdiccon is to the high derogacon of his Maties Royall power and dignity and hath bin adiudged in all ages to bee in extreme usurpacon uppon the Imperial Crowne of theise Kingdomes, and the fautors and maintainers of such foreigne usurped authority by bringinge any bulls of excommunicacon or other decrees from the pope into the kingdome have bin adiudged and declared to bee traitors and suffer as traitors if the extremity of the Lawe should bee extended against them, and in the mildest Censure to suffer Ymprisonment and confiscacon of goodes. And for that the translacon of the said Sentence of Exile out of Italian into English by the said Brangan and spreadinge & deliveringe coppies thereof which is confessed by him and the rest of ye defendeantes is within the direct wordes of the statute which previnteth all houldinge and standinge with such forrayne pretended authority to sett forth the same, and is in a manner a verie execucon of the said Sentence by notefyeinge to the Country heare Said Paul Harrys was sentenced at Roome to bee exiled out of the diocese of Dublin, Which was sufficient to cause all men of the Romish Religion to forbeare his Company, the said sentence of Exile beeinge a merely temporall punishment, and as it was in this case used beeing alsoe a new found device never before heard of or practised in any of his Maties dominions when Popery was at the highest. And for yt it appered unto the Court that the said Brangan hath bin a greater and deep offender then the rest, as beeinge the originall stirrer upp of this busines, And that he for his parte had done as much as the Titular Bishopp of Meath could have don in ye publishinge of the said Sentence, The Court hath this day ordered, Adiudged, Censured and decreed yt the said Brangan shall for his offence pay unto his Matie by way of fine the some of Thre thousand poundes ster and shalbe ymprisoned during his life. Whereof if his Matie shalbe pleaseed to graunt him a pardon that then before he bee enlarged he shall enter into bonds with good suertyes to departe this kingdome and never to returne againe. And yt is Further ordered, adiudged, Censured and decreed that the said Nicholas Stephens, whose turbulent spirit in matters of this nature hath bin well knowne to the Court, shall for his offence in givinge a coppie of the said Letter to an other, to the end to spread the same abroad, pay unto his Maty by way of fine the some of five hundred poundes ster and shalbe ymprisoned duringe the Lo Deputies pleasure, and yt before he bee enlarged he shall enter into bondes with good suerties for the good behavior duringe his Life. And lastly It is ordered, adiudged, Censured & decreed yt the said Robert Lalor shall pay unto his Mty by way of fine for his offence the some of five hundred poundes ster and shalbe ymprisoned duringe ye Lord Deputies pleasure. Given at his Maties said Court of Castlechamber the eighteenth day of November in the Elleaventh yeare of the raigne of our Soveraigne Lord Charles by the grace of God kinge of England, Scotland Fraunce & Ireland, defender of the fayth etc. Anno que dom 1635. Wm Stoughton, dep Cler[k], Cas[tle] Camer[a] Castelli.[17]

A third petition book to Lord Deputy Wentworth rests in the National Archives in Dublin, titled 'Petitions and Decisions in Irish Law Courts 1638'. This leather bound manuscript contains copies of the original petitions in a consistent formula, running to 616 pages of text. In customary fashion, the chief governor offered preliminary solutions by agreement, to be followed by arbitration if possible, and finally an appearance in court as a last recourse. The burden of these documents deal with real property issues and many supplicants plead their impoverishment as a reason for seeking the intervention of the lord deputy. The court of castle chamber is seldom mentioned, but the admonition to 'appear forthwith before us to answer this complaint' is a common formula, suggesting prerogative justice was available at the council table for most of these litigants. A petition of Edward Morris on 2 August 1638, for example, contains matter plainly within the ambit of the castle chamber's authority. Morris alleged that he

was affronted in most scandalous speeches not fitting to be repeated by one Wm Hudleston who, not being thereby contented, in a most Barbarous manner assaulted yor pet[itione]r and for his better assistance Ruth? Grandy, the said Hudlestons mrs, and one Thomas Pickerin, one of her Jorneymen sadlers, seized upon yor petr pulling him by the hayre of the head, and afterwards stabbed yor petr in the head in 3 severall places eyther with a knife or other weapon, by which meanes yor poore petr lyeth under the Chyrurgions hands to his great Cost and utter undoeing. May it therefore please yor honor in tender Comiseracon of the premisses to graunt an attachment agt the said Hudleston and Pickerin, they being men of noe residency (by wch meanes he is not able to have his present remedy at Comon law), And that the said Mrs Grandy may be compelled to put in good security to answere yor petr allegations wch he is able to prove by siufficient witnesses.[18]

Two further petitions were heard by the lord deputy at his new residence in Co. Wicklow, Cosha, involving cases previously heard in castle chamber. In the first instance, William, earl of Meath alleged

that yor pet[itione]r aboute two yeares past, exhibited a bill in his Maties Courte of Castle Chamber agt Thomas, lord Viscount of Merryon and others, to wch bill, after longe delaye, Ea[ch] defte Answered. Right ho[nora]ble soe it is that, through the defendte severall delayes, noe Comission isssued for Examining of witnesses in this Cause, in soemuch that some of yor petr witnesses are nowe going for England and some more of them are Scotch men dwelling in Scotland but nowe all of

17. WWM STR P, 24–25, item 460, ff. 1–9. A brief schedule of parties and charges to be heard in castle chamber on 15 February 1637 involved the abduction of Elizabeth Clancy, a ward and daughter in law of John O'Carroll, esquire, against Conly Geoghegane, who apparently married her by force. The charge read: 'For plotting & Conspiringe to convey Elizabeth Clancy, the plts daughter in Lawe, from the custodie of Mr Parry, to whome she was sequestred by the Consistery Court of Dublin, and for forciblie and riotouslie conveighinge her away and for sendinge her into the Country in mans apparell.' Ibid., item 411.
18. NAI, MS 2448, p. 321. The incident in question occurred only four days previously, surely a record for the doughty castle chamber jurisdiction. The parties were, again, required forthwith to appear 'before us', presumably at the council table, where castle chamber also met as a court.

them are to bee found in this Kingdome. Therefore yor petr humble request is that yor Lor[dshi]p willbe pleased to give direccon to the Examinator of the sd Courte for the speedy Examining of yor petr sd witnesses, otherwise they will not be found in convenient tyme, to his Maties hindrance, and yor petr greate delay and damadge.

Cashaw, 12 Sept 1638. Wee referr this matter unto the Courte of Castle Chamber to bee taken into consideracon if there bee cause.[19]

In a subsequent petition of October 1638, Nicholas Bridges of Tullaghgory, Co. Kildare, sued his neighbour Nicholas Woolfe of Oldcourt for several misdemeanours in relation to a contested piece of land. The case was first referred to Justice Cressy, whose recommendation was presented at the council table, and thereafter the case was remanded to castle chamber. An interim order was obtained by Bridges from the judges of assize in Co. Kildare, who named commissioners for viewing and perambulating the lands in question. However, when the complainant went to enclose the said lands with his servants, and after five days of work, on 22 September 1638

the sd Woolfe as yor suplt was seeing his servant goeing forward in the sd inclosure came unto yor suplt and, unknowne to yor petr, stroake yor suplt to the ground wth a hazell plant neere 6 foote long & 4 inches thick, & being downe the sd Woolfe againe violently stroake yor suplt 2 stroakes more wth the sd staffe, intending noe less then to have murthered yor petr if he had not bene prevented by those that were inclosing the sd meare. The same day the sd Woolfe out of a malitious minde & intent went to sweare the peace agt yor suplt & 21 one psones more, & since will not permitt the said worke to goe forward, Notwthstanding the Ditch was made according the boundes & Meares laid forth by the said Comissioners, as appe[re]th by a Certificate also ready to be shewne. Besides the sd Woolfe to shewe his inveterate malice towardes yor supplt & those that belong unto him, aboute 8 of Aug last, haveing wounded two pigges of the goodes of Thomas O Dallany, a servt of yor Petrs, that theire intralles [entrails] came forth of theire side and backe, did violently beate the said Thomas for demanding of them & after bound him & two of his sonnes to the peace. Forasmuch as yor suplt & the Inhabitantes of the sd Towne of Tullaghgory have suffered great wrong & prejudice by the sd Woolfe his long & continewed malice towardes them undeserved, And for that he may not persist in those abusieve waies whereby further to wound & ympoverish yor suplt & his tenntes, yor Petr humbly prayeth yor Lp to be pleased to require the sd Wolfe & give order that he, yor supplt & his servantes, wthout further lett, may inclose the sd meares & landes wch cannot by reason of a bogg be done in winter tyme, & that the sd Woolfe may beare halfe charge thereof according the proclamacon in that behalfe provided. That yor Lp wilbee alsoe pleased to give order that the sd Woolfe be bound to the good behaviour or that yor Lp will inflict such Condigne punishment on the sd Woolfe for Contemning his Mates Proclamacon & for his abuseing yor suplt & wrongfully bynding of the said tennts to the peace as to yor Lp shalbe thought fitt.

Dublin Castle, 5 Octo[ber] 1638. Lett this Petr be presented att the Councell Table, & there the same may bee taken into Consideracon & such Answere given therunto as shalbee fitt.[20]

A final petition alleging violence and assault involved the crown's soldiers in a common affray, tainted by the slanderous tone of the combatants in an atmosphere of tension. The charge was levied by Sir Arthur Loftus, whose foot company was garrisoned in the town of Wexford, and on whose behalf Abraham Bell and John Blinkship [Blankenship?] went to the tavern of Mathew Paie to seek others of their company. As they were asked by the publican and one John Codd,

19. Ibid., p. 439. No cause of action was mentioned in this fragmentary note, though long delays were common in castle chamber adjudication.
20. Ibid., pp. 451–53.

a bailiff of the town,whom they sought, the soldiers engaged in the following
conversation:

and thereupon the sd Baliffes said unto the Souldiers that there were better souldiers there then any
of theire Company & bidd them gett them gone like Roagues. To wch the said Souldiers answering
that they knew noe Roague that wore his Mates Cloath, and that the said Baliffes might answere the
sd wordes, thereupon the said Paie & Codd (beeing ill affected as it seeme to the sd foote Company)
& being the baliffes and officers of the sd towne, & sworne & respectively bound by the Dutie of their
places to performe & keepe his Mates peace, Contrarie thereunto in most violent manner wthout any
other cause given them then as aforesd, made an assault upon the two souldiers & by the assistance
of their Confederates then present did throw the sd Bell Downe a paire of? sene staires betwene
sixtene & xxtie steppes, and then by the sd Bell lyeing in a great amazement the sd Paie then gott the
sword of the sd Bell & gave the sd Bell therewith one great wound on the head 5 inches long by
reason whereof & of the bruises gotten in the sd fall Downe the staires the sd Bell became & laie
senceles a good spate, all besmeered in his owne blood, & was in greate Dispaire of his life, and hath
ever since languished thereof. Upon swearing whereof the Chirurgion was and still is of opinion that
his skull is perished and the wounds mortall, or verie little hope of recoverie thereof, his inward
bruises being alsoe very Daungerous, And the said Bell after a little recovering his sences cried out
that he was Murthered and thereupon the said Blaikshipp endeavoured to goe help him. Whereupon
the sd Coddd haveing gott & Drawne the sword of the said Blankeshipp did hould the point thereof
to the said Blakeship breast, threatning him that if hee should stirr hee would runn him thorow
therewith, and that he would give him as much as Bell had if he held not his tounge [*sic*]. Yett the sd
Blakeshipp escapeing Downe the staires, his sword being taken from him by the sd Confederates, he
the sd Blakeshipp findeing the sd Bell in Imminent Danger of Death caried him upp the staires to
the intent to have his hurts searched & dressed and then fetched the Chirurgien of the Company for
that purpose, whoe comeing & being aboute searching of his woundes & hurtes of the sd Bell, the
said Confederates in great skorne ?slentched the sd hurts, some of them saying it was but a scratche
& others bidding cut of[f] his head & in respect of the Danger of the wounds wch might be encreased
by carying him into the aire, the Chirurgion Desired the sd Paie to afford the sd Bell a lodgeing there
that night, it beeing a roman Taverne, wch the sd Paie peremptorily refused to doe & protested he
would throwe him downe the staires and cause him to be caryed out wth Porters if the Chirurgion &
the sd Blankship would not carry him away wch thereupon they wer enforced to doe. Of wch
passages James Rochford, yor petr Leiftent, haveing bene enformed did the next day severall times
repaire to the house of Patrick Turner, then Maior of the sd Towne, to enforme him of the same but
he was still Denyed to yor petr Leiftent to bed within, although the sd Maior and the sd Baliffes were
then in the sd house together. And shortly after came altogether out of the same house towards the
Markett place, of whch the sd Leiftent haveing notice did meete them theire & acquainted the sd
Maior wth the said passages & desired an examinacon of the matter might be taken before him of
both parties ... the Maior then being a Justice of peace there ... [21]

The court then took cognizance of the mayor's default in refusing to hear
information on the breach of peace and failing to correct his errant bailiffs' violent
assault. The mayor had examined the bailiffs jointly instead of separately, allowing
them to compare their testimonies, and refused to take examination of Blank
[en]ship and others despite the protestations of the lieutenant. The final
allegations bringing the case to the attention of castle chamber were misfeasance
in office by the bailiffs and mayor of the town, which 'might have bredd a greate
mutanie & uproare amongst the soldiers if it had not bene prevented by the Civill
care & disretion of the sd Leiftenant'. In his order of 11 October 1638, the lord
deputy agreed to take up the petition at the council table and to call the parties

21. Ibid., pp. 511–14.

complained of to make their answer.[22] While the case was reported extensively in the archive and evidently contained allegations which were normally brought before castle chamber, there was no explicit mention of that court in the text. This omission permits us to assume that much of the work of castle chamber was subsumed within the conciliar jurisdiction more generally under Wentworth and his predecessors.

After Wentworth departed Ireland in 1639 to attend on the king, his pugnacious methods had damaged the reputation of the Irish court of star chamber. The arbitrary manner and officious meddling of his Absolutist style was particularly notable in the handling of a highly political case, that of Henry Stewart and James Gray. When the defendants, two Ulster Scotsmen, were ordered by decree of the lord deputy and council to take the oath of supremacy, they refused for reasons of conscience. In 1639 they were tried in castle chamber for treason, fined £13,000 and imprisoned for life. This exceptionally harsh treatment was imposed by leading justices including Sir William Parsons, Sir Richard Bolton, Sir Gerard Lowther, Sir Adam Loftus, the bishop of Derry, the bishop of Cork, Sir George Radcliffe and Sir Robert Meredith among others, acting without the presence of the lord deputy. Stewart and his wife and daughters were imprisoned for 18 months, along with Gray, until they sought relief from the Long Parliament in England. In a remarkable parliamentary reversal of the judicial decree, an order of the House of Lords dated 9 September 1642 declared that the original sentence against Stewart and Gray in castle chamber was unjust and illegal; that the judges in the case, named above, should pay damages to Stewart and his family of £1,500 and to Gray and his heirs £400. The judges were called to appear in their own defence on 3 June 1642, an order which they subsequently resisted pitifully. The Stewart case and its aftermath represent the final adjudication of the court of castle chamber for which any substantial record has been found to date.[23] Opposition to the court was already building and its activities were probably circumscribed by the political turmoil and uncertainties of 1639 and 1640.

---

22. Ibid.
23. Marsh's Library, Dublin, MS Z.3.2.6, item 117, p. 329; item 116, p. 327. This collection of documents consists of copies of formal orders by the Lords and other courts, often without date, as well as petitions to earlier councils in Ireland.

Bibliography

MANUSCRIPT SOURCES

Armagh Public Library

    Notes and observations (1629–1640) of Sir Richard Bolton, lord chancellor

Bodleian Library, Oxford
  Carte MSS
55–59, 131	Papers of Sir William Fitzwilliam, 1556–1594
61	Petitions and responses on the Mandates, 1604–05
62	Letter book of Sir Arthur Chichester

  Rawlinson MSS
D 657	Report of Sir William Gerrard, lord chancellor, 1577
C 98	Instructions to Sir William Drury as lord justice

  Tanner MSS
458	Papers of Sir George Carew

British Library, London
  Additional MSS
4763	Tables to sixteenth century Irish council books
4783	Extracts from the Sidney papers
4785	Letters to Elizabeth I from lords deputy of Ireland
4786	Letters from Irish council; instructions to provincial councils
4792	Tables to Irish council books, 1543–1600
4801	Letters of various sovereigns to Irish council, 1547–1603
4813	Chronicle of Ireland, 1559–1590, from works of James Ware
4819	Instructions to Irish council, 1556–1663
19,837	Recognizances in the court of chancery, from *c.* 1558 to 1634
32,323	Orders of the privy council, Elizabethan period
47,172	Entry book of records and decrees, court of castle chamber, 1571–1620

  Cotton MSS
Titus B XII, XIII	Instructions and documents of Irish council, 1556–1565

  Harleian MSS
35	Letters and papers of Irish council, 1560–86
430	Petition book of Sir Thomas Wentworth, 1637–39
697	Council Book of Munster, 1601–40
4297	Petition book of Sir Thomas Wentworth, 1633–35

Huntington Library, San Marino, California
Ellesmere MS 1700	Instructions to Sir Anthony St Leger, 1550
Ellesmere MS 1701	Discourse on government of Ireland by Edmund Tremayne, clerk of the Irish council
Ellesmere MSS 1702, 1707, 1711	Extracts from the Burghley papers
Ellesmere MS 1731	Discourse on government of Ireland by Sir Thomas Lee

Lambeth Palace Library
    Carew MSS 597   Letter book of Sir William Pelham
                600   Instructions from council for Tremayne
                605   Life of Sir Peter Carew; letters to Sir George Carew
                609   Report of the earl of Sussex on state of Ireland
                611   Proceedings against the lord deputy and council
                612   The journal of Lord Deputy Sir William Russell, 1594–97
                615   Letters of Sir George Carew, president of Munster
                619   Letters on the cess controversy
                628   Tables of council books, 1543–1605; Sir William Gerrard's
                           report on law officers; instructions to council in Ireland

Public Record Office, London
    State Papers Ireland
            SP 31, vol. 1   Transcripts of Carte papers, Bodleian Lib.
            SP 60, 1532–47   State papers of Henry VIII
            SP 62, 1553–58   State papers of Mary
            SP 63, 1558–1603 State papers of Elizabeth I
            SP 64, vols. 1–3 maps of Ireland, 1588–1625

National Archives, Dublin
    Lodge Manuscripts   Extracts of patent rolls of Ireland, 1506–1603
                         Patentee officers and offices in Ireland
                         Records of chancery rolls, vol. 1, 1509–1603
    MS 2445   Letter book of Sir Arthur Chichester
    MS 2448   Petition book of Sir Thomas Wentworth, 1638
    MS 2532   Extracts from Irish council books, 1548–95

Marsh's Library, Dublin
    MS Z 3.2.6   Petitions relating to chief governors St John, Falkland and
                         Wentworth

Chatsworth House
    Lismore Manuscripts
        MS 78   Letter books of the earl of Cork, 1629–33
        Vols. 15–18, 21 Letters of the earl of Cork, 1611–1641

Royal Irish Academy, Dublin
    MS 24 F. 17   Irish council book for 1556–1571

Sheffield City Library
    Wentworth Woodhouse Muniments
    Strafford Papers 24–25 Letter books and legal papers of Sir Thomas
                            Wentworth, earl of Strafford

Trinity College Library, Dublin
    MS 541   Speeches in Irish parliament 1640; grievances against
                         administration of Wentworth
    MS 567   Cases against recusants in Irish council
    MS 580   Irish council letters on prerogative
    MS 581   Interrogations of lawyers against the cess; expeditions of
                         Sir William Russell
    MS 615   Notes on the Irish parliament, 1639–42, including text of the
                         Queries

MS 649	Star chamber procedures in England
MS 651	Sir John Davies's defence of prerogative justice
MS 672	Proceedings of Sir Arthur Chichester in castle chamber on Mandates; depositions, instructions and grievances: from Falkland to Wentworth
MS 721	English star chamber cases, treatises
MS 722	Treatise on star chamber in England
MS 745	Sidney State Papers, 1565–70
MS 746	Correspondence of Sir Arthur Chichester, 1612–14, on recusancy, parliamentary opposition
MS 802	Ordinances for the court of star chamber
MS 808	Charles I civil list, commission of defective titles
MS 842	Sir John Davies on assizes; trial of Nicholas Nugent, 1582
MS 843	Tables of the Irish council books; star chamber cases; defence of the Mandates
MS 845	Letters and papers of Irish council
MS 852	Charles I commission authorizing court of castle chamber, 1625; procedures of court, including fees; digest of cases from entry books of court of castle chamber, 1577 to 1632
MS 853	Charles I orders for settling the courts
MS 867	Impeachment of Strafford in English parliament, 1640

PRINTED SOURCES

'Additional Sidney state papers, 1566–1570', ed. D.B. Quinn, *Anal Hib*, no. 26 (1970), 91.

Annals of Connacht. ed. A.M. Freeman. Dublin, 1944.

'The annals of Dudley Loftus', ed. N. White, *Anal Hib*, no. 10 (1941), 225.

The annals of Loch Cé. A chronicle of Irish affairs from AD 1014 to AD 1590., ed. W. Hennessy. 2 vols. Dublin, 1939.

A bibliography of royal proclamations of the Tudor and Stuart sovereigns, 1485–1714, ed. R. Steele. vols. 5–6 of Bibliotheca Lindesiana. Oxford, 1910.

Blake family records 1300–1600., ed. M.J. Blake. London, 1902.

Black, H.C. *Black's law dictionary*. 4th ed. St. Paul, MN, 1951.

Borlase, J. *History of the rebellion, 1641–1660*. London, 1680.

Burke's genealogical and heraldic history of the peerage, baronetage and knightage, ed. P. Townend. 104th ed. London, 1967.

Calendar of the ancient records of Dublin. Vols. 2–3, ed. J.T. Gilbert. Dublin, 1891.

'Calendar of the Harris manuscripts (now in the National Library of Ireland)', ed. C. McNeill, *Anal Hib*, no. 6 (1934), 248.

'Calendar of the Irish council book 1581–1586', ed. D.B. Quinn, *Anal Hib*, no. 24 (1967), 91.

Calendar of the patent and close rolls of chancery in Ireland, of the reigns of Henry VIII, Edward VI, Mary and Elizabeth, James I and Charles I. 3 vols., ed. J. Morrin. Dublin, 1861–62.

Calendar of Ormonde deeds, ed. E. Curtis. vols. 5–6 (1584–1603). Dublin, 1941.

'A calendar of salved chancery proceedings concerning Co. Louth', ed. K.W. Nicholls, *Louth Arch Soc Jn*, xviii (1972), 112.

A collection of the state papers of John Thurloe, esq., secretary to the council of state and the two Protectors, Oliver and Richard Cromwell. 7 vols. London, 1742.

The complete peerage of England, Scotland, Ireland, Great Britain and the United Kingdom. ed. G.E. Cokayne, rev. by V. Gibbs. London, 1910.

Composition book of Connacht, ed. A. Freeman. Irish Manuscripts Commission. Dublin, 1936.

The council book of the corporation of the city of Cork, ed. R. Caulfield. Guildford, 1876.

The council book of the corporation of Kinsale, ed. R. Caulfield. Guildford, 1879.

The council book of the corporation of Youghal, ed. R. Caulfield. Guildford, 1878.

Davies, J. *A report of cases and matters in law resolved and adjudged in the king's courts in Ireland*. Dublin 1762.

——, *A discovery of the true causes why Ireland was never entirely subdued* (1612), ed. J.P Myers (Wash., DC, 1988).

Desiderata curiosa Hibernica: or a select collection of state papers during the reigns of Elizabeth, James I and Charles I. 2 vols., ed. J. Lodge. Dublin, 1772.

The dictionary of national biography, ed. L. Stephen and S. Lee. 21vols. Oxford, 1917.

Dymmok, J. *A treatise of Ireland*, ed. by Richard Butler for Irish Archaeologicial Society. Dublin, 1842.

The earl of Strafforde's letters and dispatches, ed. W. Knowler. 2 vols. London, 1739.

Donovan, B.C., and Edwards, D. *British sources for Irish history, 1485–1641, a guide to manuscripts in local and specialised repositories in England, Scotland and Wales*. Irish Manuscripts Commission. Dublin, 1997.

The first chapter act book of Christ Church cathedral, Dublin, 1574–1634, ed. R. Gillespie. Dublin, 1997.

'The Fitzwilliam manuscripts at Milton', ed. C. McNeill, *Anal Hib*, no. 4 (1932), 287.

Facsimiles of national manuscripts of Ireland. Vol. iv, sec. 1. London, 1882.

Great Britain. Historical Manuscripts Commission. *Calendar of the manuscripts of the marquis of Salisbury preserved at Hatfield House*.

—— *The manuscripts of Charles Haliday, esq., of Dublin. Acts of the privy council in Ireland, 1556–71*.

—— *The manuscripts of the marquess of Ormonde, formerly at Kilkenny Castle*. 3 vols.

—— *Report on the manuscripts of the earl of Egmont*. vol. 1. Entry book of orders or decrees of the court of castle chamber, Dublin. Ed. by Sophie C. Lomas

—— *Report on the manuscripts of Lord De L'Isle and Dudley preserved at Penshurst Place*. vols. 1–2.

—— *9th Rep*, Appendix ii, Report on the manuscripts of the marquis of Drogheda.

—— *12th Rep*, Appendix, part ii, Report on the manuscripts of the earl of Cowper.

Great Britain. Privy Council. *Acts of the privy council of England*. new ser. vols. 7–31 Elizabeth I.

——. James I (1603–25).

——. Charles I (1625–41).

Great Britain. Public Record Office. *Calendar of the Carew manuscripts preserved in the archiepiscopal library at Lambeth, 1575–1624*, ed. J.S. Brewer. London, 1869.

—— *Calendar of the patent rolls preserved in the Public Record Office. Elizabeth I*. vols. 1–2, 4–5. HMSO, 1966.

—— *Calendar of state papers, domestic, James II*.

—— *Calendar of state papers, Ireland. Henry VIII, Edward VI, Mary, Elizabeth I, James I, Charles I, Charles II (1669–70: Addenda)*.

Great Britain. Record Commission. *Liber munerum publicorum Hiberniae ab anno 1152 usque ad 1827: or the establishment of Ireland*, ed. R . Lascelles. 2 vols. London, 1852.

'Harris Collectanea', ed. C. McNeill, *Anal Hib*, no. 6 (1934), 424.

'Henry Sidney's memoir of his government of Ireland', *Ulster Arch Soc Jn*, iii (1855), 91.

'His majesty's directions for ordering and settling the courts within his kingdom of Ireland', ed. G.J. Hand and V. Treadwell, *Anal Hib*, no. 26 (1970), 177.

Ireland (Eire). Irish Manuscripts Commission. Sir William Herbert. *Croftus sive de Hibernia liber*, ed. and trans. A. Keaveney and J.A. Madden. Dublin, 1992.

—— *The Dignitas Decani of St. Patrick's cathedral*, ed. N.B. White. Dublin, 1957.

——. *Sidney State Papers, 1565–1570*, ed. T. O'Laidhin. Dublin, 1962.

—— *The Walsingham letter book, or register of Ireland, 1578–79*, ed. J. Hogan, N. McNeill, P. O'Farrell. Dublin, 1959.

Ireland. Public Record Office. *Reports of the Deputy Keeper of the Public Records of Ireland. 9th to 13th reps*.

—— *Calendar to fiants in the reigns of Edward VI, Mary and Elizabeth*.

Ireland under Elizabeth and James I, ed. H. Morley. London, 1890.

The Irish fiants of the Tudor Sovereigns. 4 vols., ed. K.W. Nicholls. Dublin, 1994.

The Irish statute staple books, 1596–1687, ed. J. Ohlmeyer and E. Ó Ciardha. Dublin, 1998.

Irish Free State. Irish Manuscripts Commission. *Calendar of Ormonde deeds, 1172–1603.* vol. 5. ed. E. Curtis.

—— *The chronicle of Ireland, 1584–1608, by Sir James Perrott*, ed. H. Wood.

—— *The Irish patent rolls of James I.* Dublin, 1966.

—— *The O'Doyne Manuscript*, ed. K.W. Nicholls. Dublin, 1983.

—— *The Tanner letters*, ed. C. McNeill. Dublin, 1943.

Irish history from contemporary sources, 1509–1610, ed. C. Maxwell. London, 1923.

Journals of the Irish House of Commons, 1613–66. Dublin, 1796.

Journals of the Irish House of Lords, 1634–98. Dublin, 1779.

The Lismore papers [of the earl of Cork], ed. A. B. Grosart. 2 series. 10 vols. London, 1886–88.

'A manor court in seventeenth century Ireland', ed. R. Gillespie, *Ir Econ Soc Hist*, xxv (1998), 81.

Monck Mason, William. *The history and antiquities of the collegiate and cathedral church of St. Patrick near Dublin, from its foundation in 1190 to the year 1819.* Dublin, 1820.

Patent rolls of chancery in Ireland in the reign of James I. Vol. 1, ed. J.C. Erck. Dublin, 1846.

'Patrick Darcy, an argument', ed. C.E.J. Caldicott. *Camden miscellany, xxxi*, Camden Soc. 4th series, vol. 44. London, 1992.

'The Perrot papers', ed. C. McNeill, *Anal Hib*, no. 12 (1943) 1.

The Rawdon papers. Ed. E. Berwick. London, 1819.

'Records of the Irish court of chancery: a preliminary report for 1627–34', ed. J. Ohlmeyer in D.S. Greer and N.M. Dawson, eds., *Mysteries and solutions in Irish legal history.* Dublin, 2001.

'Report on the State of Ireland by Lord Chancellor Gerrard', ed. C. McNeill, *Anal Hib*, no. 2 (1930), 93.

'Rowland White's "Discors Touching Ireland", c. 1569', ed. N. Canny, *IHS*, xx (1976), 439.

'Rowland White's "The Dysorders of the Irisshery", 1571', ed. N. Canny, *Studia Hibernica*, xix (1980), 147.

Rushworth, J., ed. *Historical collections of private passages of state, 1618–48.* 6 vols. London, 1682–1701.

'Some documents on Irish law and custom in the sixteenth century', ed. K.W. Nicholls, *Anal Hib*, no. 26 (1970), 103.

Spenser, Edmund. *A view of the present state of Ireland*, ed. W.L. Renwick. Oxford, 1970.

Tudor royal proclamations, ed. P.L. Hughes and J.F. Larkin. 3 vols. New Haven, 1964–69.

'A viceroy's vindication: Sir Henry Sidney's memoir of service in Ireland, 1556–1578,' ed. C. Brady. Cork, 2002.

The whole works of Sir James Ware, ed. W. Harris. 3 vols. Dublin, 1739.

MONOGRAPHS

Andrews, K.R., Canny, N.P. and Hair, P.E.H., eds. *The westward enterprise: English activities in Ireland, the Atlantic and America, 1480–1650.* Liverpool, 1978.

Aylmer, G.E. *The king's servants: the civil service of Charles I, 1625–1642.* London, 1961.

Bagwell, R. *Ireland under the Tudors.* 3 vols. London, 1890–95.

—— *Ireland under the Stuarts.* 3 vols. London, 1895–97.

Baker, J. *The legal profession and the common law: historical essays.* London, 1985.

—— *Legal records and the historian.* London, 1978.

—— *An introduction to English legal history.* London, 1979.

Ball, F.E. *The judges in Ireland, 1121–1921.* 2 vols. London, 1926.

Barnard, T.C. *Cromwellian Ireland: English government and reform in Ireland, 1649–1660.* Oxford, 1975.

—— and J. Fenlon, eds. *The dukes of Ormonde, 1610–1745*. Woodbridge, 2000.

Bartlett, T. and K. Jeffery, eds. *The Cambridge military history of Ireland*. Cambridge, 1995.

Beckett, J.C. *The making of modern Ireland, 1603–1922*. London, 1966.

—— *The Anglo-Irish tradition*. Ithaca, NY, 1976.

Bellamy, J. *Crime and public order in England in the late middle ages*. London, 1973.

Bindoff, S.T. , Hurstfield, J., and Williams, C.H., eds. *Elizabethan government and society: essays presented to Sir John Neale*. London, 1961.

Blatcher, M. *The court of king's bench, 1450–1550: a study in self-help*. London, 1978.

Braddick, M.J. *State formation in early modern England, 1550–1700*. Cambridge, 2000.

Bradshaw, B. *The Irish constitutional revolution of the sixteenth century*. Cambridge, 1974.

Brady, C. *The chief governors: the rise and fall of reform government in Tudor Ireland, 1536–1588*. Cambridge, 1994.

—— *Interpreting Irish history: the debate on historical revisionism, 1938–1994*. Dublin, 1994.

—— and Gillespie, R., eds., *Natives and newcomers: essays on the making of Irish colonial society, 1534–1641*. Dublin, 1986.

——, O'Dowd, M. and Walker, B., eds. *Ulster: an illustrated history*. London, 1989.

Brooks, C.W. *Pettyfoggers and vipers of the commonwealth: the 'lower branch' of the legal profession in early modern England*. Cambridge, 1986.

Brooks, F.W. *The Council of the North*. London, 1953.

Bryson, W.H. *The equity side of the exchequer: its jurisdiction, administration, procedures and records*. Cambridge, 1975.

Butler, W.T.F. *Confiscation in Irish history*. Dublin, 1917.

Canny, N. *The Elizabethan conquest of Ireland: a pattern established, 1565–1576*. New York, 1976.

——, *The formation of the Old English elite in Ireland*. Dublin, 1975.

——. *From Reformation to restoration: Ireland, 1534–1660*. Dublin, 1987.

——, *Kingdom and colony: Ireland in the Atlantic world, 1560–1800*. Baltimore, 1988.

——. *Making Ireland British, 1580–1650*. Oxford, 2002.

——, *The upstart earl: a study of the social and mental worlds of Richard Boyle, first earl of Cork, 1566 to 1643*. Cambridge, 1982.

——, and Low, A. eds., *The Oxford History of the British empire*. vol. i. *Origins of the empire: British overseas enterprise to the close of the seventeenth century*. Oxford, 1998.

—— and Pagden, A., eds. *Colonial identity in the Atlantic world, 1500–1800*. Princeton, 1987.

Carey, V. *Surviving the Tudors: the 'wizard' earl of Kildare and English rule in Ireland, 1537–1586*. Dublin, 2002.

—— and U. Lotz-Heumann, eds. *Taking sides? Colonial and confessional mentalités in early modern Ireland: essays in honour of Karl S. Bottigheimer*. Dublin, 2003.

Clarke, A. *The Graces*. Dublin, 1967.

——, *The Old English in Ireland, 1625–42*. London, 1966.

——. *Prelude to restoration in Ireland: the end of the commonwealth, 1659–60*. Cambridge, 2003.

Cockburn, J., ed. *Crime in England, 1550–1800*. London, 1977.

——, *A history of English assizes, 1558–1714*. Cambridge, 1972.

Coleman, C. and Starkey, D.R., eds. *Revolution reassessed: revisions in the history of Tudor government and administration*. Oxford, 1986.

Collinson, P. *The religion of Protestants: the church in English society, 1559–1625*. Oxford, 1982.

Cooper, J.P. *Land, men and beliefs: studies in early modern history*, ed. G.E. Aylmer and J.S. Morrill. London, 1983.

Cosgrove, A., ed. *A new history of Ireland, vol ii: Medieval Ireland, 1169–1534*. Oxford, 1987.

Coughlan, P., ed. *Spenser and Ireland: an interdisciplinary perspective*. Cork, 1989.

Crawford, J.G. *Anglicizing the government of Ireland: the Irish privy council and the expansion of Tudor rule, 1556–1578*. Dublin, 1993.

Cross, C., Loades, D. and Scarisbrick, J.J., eds. *Law and government under the Tudors: essays presented to Sir Geoffrey Elton on his retirement*. Cambridge, 1988.

Cullen, L.M. *The emergence of modern Ireland, 1600–1900*. New York, 1981.

Cunningham, B. *The world of Geoffrey Keating: history, myth and religion in seventeenth century Ireland.* Dublin, 2004.

Dean, D.M., and Jones, N.L., eds. *The parliaments of Elizabethan England.* Oxford, 1990.

Donaldson, A.G. *Some comparative aspects of Irish law.* Durham, NC and London, 1957.

Dunlop, R. *Ireland from the earliest times to the present day.* London, 1922.

Edwards, D. *The Ormond lordship in County Kilkenny, 1515–1642.* Dublin, 2003.

——, Duffy, P.J. and Fitzpatrick, E., eds. *Gaelic Ireland, c. 1250–c.1650.* Dublin, 2004.

Edwards, R.D. *Church and state in Tudor Ireland: a history of penal laws against Irish Catholics, 1534–1603.* Dublin, 1930.

—— *Ireland in the age of the Tudors: the destruction of Hiberno–Norman civilisation.* London, 1977.

Ellis, S.G. *Ireland in the age of the Tudors, 1447–1603: English expansion and the end of Gaelic rule.* London, 1998.

—— *The Pale and the Far North: government and society in two early Tudor borderlands.* Galway, 1988.

—— *Reform and revival: English government in Ireland, 1470–1534.* London, 1985.

—— *Tudor frontiers and noble power: the making of the British state.* Oxford, 1995.

—— *Tudor Ireland: crown, community and the conflict of cultures, 1470–1603.* London, 1985.

—— and Barber, S., eds. *Conquest and union: forging a multinational British state, 1485–1707.* London, 1995.

Elton, G.R. *English law in the sixteenth century: reform in an age of change.* London, 1979.

—— *The parliament of England, 1559–1581.* Cambridge, 1986.

—— *Policy and police: the enforcement of the reformation in the age of Thomas Cromwell.* Cambridge, 1972.

—— *Reform and reformation: England 1509–1558.* London, 1977.

—— *Star chamber stories.* London, 1958.

—— *The Tudor revolution in government: administrative changes in the reign of Henry VIII.* Cambridge, 1953.

—— ed. *The Tudor constitution: documents and commentary.* 2nd ed. Cambridge, 1982.

Falkiner, C.L. *Essays relating to Ireland, biographical, historical, topographical.* London, 1909.

Falls, C.B. *Mountjoy: Elizabethan general.* London, 1955.

Fitzgerald, B. *The Geraldines: an experiment in Irish government, 1169–1601.* London, 1951.

Fletcher, A. *Tudor rebellions.* London, 1983.

—— and Stevenson, J., eds. *Order and disorder in early modern England.* Cambridge, 1985.

Ford, A. *The Protestant Reformation in Ireland, 1590–1641.* Frankfurt, 1985.

Gilbert, J.T. *A history of Dublin.* 3 vols. Dublin, 1861.

—— *A history of the viceroys of Ireland.* Dublin, 1865.

Gillespie, R. *The borderlands: essays on the history of the Ulster–Leinster border.* Belfast, 1989.

—— *Cavan: an Irish county history.* Dublin, 1995.

—— *Colonial Ulster: the settlement of East Ulster, 1600–1641.* Belfast, 1985.

—— *Conspiracy: Ulster plots and plotters in 1615.* Belfast, 1987.

—— *Devoted people: belief and religion in early modern Ireland.* Manchester, 1997.

—— *A various country: essays in Mayo history.* Westport, 1987.

——, and Moran, Gerard, eds. *Longford; essays in county history.* Dublin, 1991.

—— and B. Cunningham. *Stories from Gaelic Ireland: microhistories from the sixteenth century Irish annals.* Dublin, 2003.

Grant, A., and Stringer, K., eds. *Uniting the kingdom: the making of the British state.* London, 1995.

Greengrass, M. ed. *Conquest and coalescence: the shaping of the state in early modern Europe.* London, 1991.

Greer, D.S., and Dawson, N.M., eds. *Mysteries and solutions in Irish legal history: Irish Legal History Society discourses and other papers, 1996–1999.* Dublin, 2001.

Guth, D.J. and McKenna, J.W., eds. *Tudor rule and revolution: essays for G.R. Elton from his American friends.* Cambridge, 1982.

Guy, J. A. *The cardinal's court: the impact of Thomas Wolsey in star chamber.* Hassocks, 1977.
_____ *The court of star chamber and its records to the reign of Elizabeth I.* PRO Handbooks, no. 21. London, 1985.
_____ *Tudor England.* Oxford, 1988.
_____, ed. *The reign of Elizabeth I: court and culture in the last decade.* Cambridge, 1995.
Hamilton, E.W. *Elizabethan Ulster.* London, 1919.
Haigh, C. *Elizabeth I.* London, 1988.
——, ed. *The reign of Elizabeth I.* London, 1985.
Hadfield, A. and McVeagh, J., eds. *Strangers to that land: British perceptions of Ireland from the Reformation to the Famine* [Ulster editions and monographs, 5]. Gerrards Cross, Bucks., 1994.
Hand, G.J. *English law in Ireland, 1290–1324.* Cambridge, 1967.
Hardiman, J. *The history of the town and county of Galway.* Dublin, 1820.
Harrington, T. *A diary of coercion being a list of cases tried under the Criminal Law and Procedure Act.* 3 parts. Dublin, 1888–90.
Hart, A.R. *A history of the king's serjeants at law in Ireland: honour rather than advantage?* Dublin, 2000.
Hechter, M. *Internal colonialism: the Celtic fringe in British national development, 1536–1966.* London, 1975.
Heinze, R. *The proclamations of the Tudor kings.* Cambridge, 1976.
Hinton, E.M. *Ireland through Tudor eyes.* Philadelphia, 1935.
Hoak, D. *The king's council in the reign of Edward VI.* Cambridge, 1976.
—— *Tudor political culture.* Cambridge, 1995.
Hogan, D. and Osborough, W.N., eds. *Brehons, serjeants and attorneys: studies in the history of the Irish legal profession.* Dublin, 1990.
Hughes, J.L.J. *Patentee officers in Ireland, 1173–1826.* Dublin, 1960.
Hurstfield, J. *Freedom, corruption and government in Elizabethan England.* London, 1973.
—— *The illusion of power in Tudor politics.* London, 1979.
—— *The queen's wards: wardship and marriage under Elizabeth I.* London, 1958.
Ives, E.W. *The common lawyers of pre-Reformation England: Thomas Kebell, a case study.* Cambridge, 1983.
——, ed. *Law, litigants and the legal profession.* London, 1983.
Jackson, D. *Intermarriage in Ireland, 1550–1650.* Montreal, 1970.
Jackson, V. *St. Patrick's cathedral.* Irish Heritage Series. Dublin, n.d.
James, M.E. *Society, politics and culture: studies in early modern England.* Cambridge, 1986.
Jones, F.M. *Mountjoy, 1563–1606: the last Elizabethan deputy.* Dublin, 1958.
Jones, W.J. *The Elizabethan court of chancery.* Oxford, 1967.
—— *Politics and the bench: the judges and the origins of the English Civil War.* London, 1971.
Kearney, H.F. *Strafford in Ireland, 1633–41: a study in absolutism.* Manchester, 1959, rev. ed., 1989.
Kelly, J. *'That damn'd thing called honour': duelling in Ireland, 1570–1860.* Cork, 1995.
Kenny, C. *The King's Inns and the kingdom of Ireland: the Irish 'inn of court', 1541–1800.* Dublin, 1992.
Knafla, L. *Law and politics in Jacobean England: the tracts of Lord Chancellor Ellesmere.* Cambridge, 1977.
Leask, H.G. *Irish castles and castellated houses.* Dundalk, 1946.
Lehmberg, S.E. *Sir Walter Mildmay and Tudor government.* Austin, TX, 1964.
Lennon, C. *Archbishop Richard Creagh of Armagh, 1523–1586: an Irish prisoner of conscience in the Tudor era.* Dublin, 2000.
—— *Richard Stanihurst the Dubliner, 1547–1618.* Dublin, 1981.
—— *Sixteenth century Ireland: the incomplete conquest.* New York, 1995.
——. *The lords of Dublin in the age of the reformation.* Dublin, 1989.
Loades, D.M. *The Tudor court.* London, 1987.
Loeber, R. *The geography and practice of English colonization in Ireland from 1534 to 1609.* Irish Settlement Studies, no. 3. Athlone, 1991.
MacCaffrey, W.T. *The shaping of the Elizabethan regime.* Princeton, 1968.

—— *Queen Elizabeth and the making of policy, 1572–1588.* Princeton, 1982.
—— *Elizabeth I: war and politics, 1588–1603.* Princeton, 1992.
—— *Elizabeth I.* London, 1993.
McCarthy, D. *Dublin Castle, at the heart of Irish history.* Dublin, 1997.
McCarthy-Morrough, M. *The Munster plantation: English migration to southern Ireland, 1583–1641.* Oxford, 1986.
McCavitt, J. *Sir Arthur Chichester, lord deputy of Ireland , 1605–1616.* Belfast, 1998.
MacCuarta, B., ed. *Ulster, 1641: aspects of the rising.* Belfast, 1993.
MacCurtain, M. *Tudor and Stuart Ireland.* Dublin, 1972.
McEldowney, J.F. and O'Higgins, P., eds. *The common law tradition: essays in Irish legal history.* Dublin, 1990.
McIntosh, M. *Controlling misbehaviour in England, 1370–1600.* Cambridge, 1999.
MacLysaght, E. *Irish life in the seventeenth century.* 2nd ed. Cork, 1950.
—— *Irish families, their names, arms and origins.* Dublin, 1957.
McMahon, M. *Portumna Castle and its lords.* Nenagh, 1983.
Malcomson, A.P.W. *The pursuit of the heiress: aristocratic marriage in Ireland 1750 to 1820.* Belfast, 1982.
Merritt, J.F., ed. *The political world of Thomas Wentworth, earl of Strafford, 1621–1641.* Cambridge, 1996.
Monck Mason, W. *The history and antiquities of the collegiate and cathedral church of St. Patrick's near Dublin.* Dublin, 1820.
Moody, T.W., Martin, F.X. and Byrne, F.J., eds. *A new history of Ireland, vol. iii: early modern Ireland, 1534–1691.* Oxford, 1976.
—— *A new history of Ireland, vol. ix: Maps, genealogies, lists.* Oxford, 1984.
Morgan, H., ed. *Political ideology in Ireland, 1541–1641.* Dublin, 1999.
—— *Tyrone's rebellion: The outbreak of the Nine Years' War in Tudor Ireland.* Royal Historical Society. London, 1993.
Morrill, J.S., Slack, P. and Woolf, D., eds. *Public duty and private conscience in seventeenth century England: essays presented to G.E. Aylmer.* Oxford, 1993.
Morrill, J.S. and Bradshaw, B., eds. *The British problem, c. 1534–1707: state formation in the Atlantic archipelago.* London, 1996.
Nicholls, K.W. *Gaelic and gaelicized Ireland in the middle ages.* Dublin, 1972.
O'Connor, G.B. *Elizabethan Ireland, native and English.* Dublin, 1906.
O'Dowd, M. *Power, politics and land: early modern Sligo, 1568–1688.* Belfast, 1991.
—— and Dudley Edwards, R.W. *Sources for early modern Irish history, 1534–1641.* Cambridge, 1985.
—— and MacCurtain, M., eds. *Women in early modern Ireland.* Edinburgh, 1991.
O'Flanagan, J.R. *Lives of the lord chancellors of Ireland and keepers of the great seal of Ireland.* 2 vols. London, 1870.
O'Grady, S. *Strafford and Ireland: the history of his viceroyalty with an account of his trial.* 2 vols. Dublin, 1923.
Ohlmeyer, J. *Civil War and Restoration in the three Stuart kingdoms: the career of Randal MacDonnell, marquis of Antrim, 1609–1683.* Cambridge, 1993.
—— *Ireland from independence to occupation, 1641–1660.* Cambridge, 1995.
—— ed. *Political thought in seventeenth century Ireland.* Cambridge, 2000.
O Siochrú, M. *Confederate Ireland, 1642–49: a constitutional and political analysis.* Dublin, 1999.
——, ed. *Kingdoms in crisis: Ireland in the 1640s [essays in honour of Donal Cregan].* Dublin, 2001.
Pawlisch, H. *Sir John Davies and the conquest of Ireland: a study in legal imperialism.* Cambridge, 1985.
Perceval-Maxwell, M. *Scots migration to Ulster in the reign of James I.* London, 1973.
—— *The outbreak of the Irish rebellion in 1641.* Montreal, 1993.
Philpin, C.H.E., ed. *Nationalism and popular protest in Ireland.* Cambridge, 1987.
Pollard, M. *Dublin's trade in books, 1550–1880.* Oxford, 1989.

Prest, W. *The inns of court under Elizabeth I and the early Stuarts, 1590–1640*. London, 1972.
—— *The rise of the barristers: a social history of the English bar, 1590–1640*. Oxford, 1986.
Pulman, M.B. *The Elizabethan privy council in the fifteen-seventies*. Berkeley, 1971.
Quinn, D.B. *The Elizabethans and the Irish*. Ithaca, NY, 1966.
Read, C. *Mr. Secretary Cecil and Queen Elizabeth*. London, 1955.
—— *Lord Burghley and Queen Elizabeth*. London, 1960.
—— *Mr. Secretary Walsingham and the policy of Queen Elizabeth*. 3 vols. Oxford, 1925.
Reeves-Smyth, T. *Irish castles*. Belfast, 1995.
Reid, R.R. *The king's council of the north*. London, 1921.
Richardson, W.C. *Tudor chamber administration, 1485–1547*. Baton Rouge, LA, 1952.
Richey, A.G. *Lectures on the history of Ireland, 1534–1609*. London, 1870.
Robinson, P.S. *The plantation of Ulster: British settlement in an Irish landscape, 1600–1670*. Dublin, 1984.
Ronan, M.V. *The reformation in Ireland under Elizabeth, 1558–1580*. London, 1930.
Russell, C. *Parliaments and English politics, 1621–29*. Oxford, 1979.
—— *Unrevolutionary England, 1603–42*. London, 1990.
—— *Causes of the English Civil War*. Oxford, 1990.
—— *The fall of the British monarchies, 1637–42*. London, 1991.
Samaha, J. *Law and order in historical perspective: the case of Elizabethan Essex*. New York, 1974.
Scofield, C.L. *A study of the court of star chamber*. Chicago, 1900.
Silke, J.J. *Ireland and Europe, 1559–1607*. Dublin, 1966.
Simms, K. *From kings to warlords: the changing political structure of Gaelic Ireland in the later middle ages*. Dublin, 1987.
Sharpe, K. *The personal rule of Charles I*. London, 1992.
Slack, P., ed. *Rebellion, popular protest and the social order in early modern England*. Cambridge, 1984.
Smith, A.G.R. *The government of Elizabethan England*. London, 1967.
—— *The emergence of a nation state: the commonwealth of England, 1529–1660*. London, 1984.
Stone, L. *The crisis of the aristocracy, 1558–1640*. Oxford, 1965.
Stubbs, J.W. *The history of the University of Dublin from its foundation to the end of the eighteenth century*. Dublin, 1889.
Thomas, A. *The walled towns of Ireland*. 2 vols. Dublin, 1992.
Treadwell, V. *Buckingham and Ireland, 1616–1628: a study in Anglo-Irish politics*. Dublin, 1998.
Webb, J.J. *Municipal government in Ireland: medieval and modern*. Dublin, 1918.
Williams, P. *The council in the marches of Wales under Elizabeth I*. Cardiff, 1958.
—— *The Tudor regime*. Oxford, 1979.
Wood, H. *A guide to the records in the Public Record Office of Ireland*. Dublin, 1919.
Wrightson, K. *English society, 1580–1680*. London, 1982.
Youngs, F. *The proclamations of the Tudor queens*. Cambridge, 1976.

ARTICLES

Abbott, L. 'Public office and private profit: the legal establishment in the reign of Mary Tudor', in J. Loach and R. Tittler, eds., *The mid-Tudor polity, c. 1540–1560*. London, 1980.
Appleby, J.C. and O'Dowd, M. 'The Irish admiralty: its organisation and development, c. 1570–1640', *IHS*, xxiv (1985), 299.
Baker, J.H. 'Criminal courts and procedure at common law, 1550–1800', in J.S. Cockburn, ed., *Crime in England, 1550–1800*. Princeton, 1977.
—— 'The third university of England: the inns of court and the common law tradition' [Selden Society lecture] London, 1990.
Barnard, T.C. 'Lawyers and the law in later seventeenth century Ireland', *IHS*, xxviii (1993), 256.
—— 'Scotland and Ireland in the later Stewart monarchy' in S.G. Ellis and S. Barber, eds., *Conquest and Union: fashioning a British state, 1485–1725*. London, 1995.

Barnes, T.G. 'The archives and archival problems of the Elizabethan and early Stuart star chamber', *Jn Soc Archivists*, ii (1963), 345.

—— 'A Cheshire seductress, precedent, and a "sore blow" to Star Chamber' in T. Green, ed., *On the laws and customs of England: essays to S.E. Thorne*. London, 1977.

——, 'Due process and slow process in the late Elizabethan and early Stuart star chamber'. *AJLH*, vi (1962), 221, 315.

——, 'Mr. Hudson's star chamber', in D. Guth, ed., *Tudor rule and revolution*. Cambridge, 1982. pp. 285–308.

—— 'Star chamber litigants and their counsel, 1596–1641', in J.H. Baker, ed., *Legal records and the historian*. London, 1978. pp. 8–26.

—— 'Star chamber mythology'. *AJLH*, v (1961), 30.

Beier, A.L. 'Vagrants and the social order in Elizabethan England.' *PP*, no. 64 (1974), 3.

Berry, H.F. 'The sheriffs of the county of Cork: Henry III to 1660'. *RSAI Jn*, xxxv (1905), 39.

Bottigheimer, Karl. 'The failure of the Reformation in Ireland: *une question bien posée*'. *Jn Eccl Hist*, xxxvi (1985), 196.

—— 'The Irish Reformation in European perspective', *Archiv für Reformationsgeschichte*, xcvi (1998), 313.

—— 'Kingdom and colony: Ireland in the westward enterprise, 1536–1660' in N.P. Canny, K.R. Andrews, P.E.H. Hair, eds., *The westward enterprise: English activities in Ireland, the Atlantic and America, 1480–1650*. Liverpool, 1978.

Boynton, L. 'The Tudor provost-marshals.' *EHR*, lxxvii (1962), 437.

Bradshaw, B. 'Cromwellian reform and the origins of the Kildare rebellion, 1533–34.' *TRHS*, 5th ser, xxvii (1977), 73.

—— 'The Elizabethans and the Irish.' *Studies*, lxvi (1977), 38.

—— 'Nationalism and historical scholarship in modern Ireland.' *IHS*, xxvi (1989), 329.

—— 'Native reaction to the westward enterprise: a case-study in Gaelic ideology' in N.P. Canny, K.R. Andrews, P.E.H. Hair, eds., *The westward enterprise: English activities in Ireland, the Atlantic and America, 1480–1650*. Liverpool, 1978.

—— 'Robe and sword in the conquest of Ireland' in C. Cross, D. Loades, J.J. Scarisbrick, eds., *Law and government under the Tudors: essays presented to Sir Geoffrey Elton on his retirement*. Cambridge, 1988.

—— 'Tudor reformation and revolution in Wales and Ireland: the origins of the British problem' in B. Bradshaw and J.S. Morrill, eds., *The British problem, c. 1534–1707: state formation in the Atlantic archipelago*. London, 1996.

Brady, C. 'Comparable histories? Tudor reform in Wales and Ireland' in S.G. Ellis and S. Barber, eds., *Conquest and Union.: forging a multinational British state 1485–1707*. London, 1995.

—— 'Conservative subversives: the community of the Pale and the Dublin administration, 1556–1586', in P.J. Corish, ed., *Radicals, rebels and establishments: Historical Studies XV.* Belfast, 1983, p. 28.

—— 'Court, castle and country: the framework of government in Tudor Ireland' in C. Brady and R. Gillespie, eds., *Natives and newcomers: essays on the making of Irish colonial society, 1534–1641*. Dublin, 1986.

—— 'The decline of the Irish kingdom', in M. Greengrass, ed., *Conquest and coalescence: the shaping of the state in early modern Europe*. London, 1991.

—— 'England's defence and Ireland's reform: the dilemma of the Irish viceroys, 1541–1641' in B. Bradshaw and J. Morrill, eds., *The British problem, c. 1534–1707: state formation in the Atlantic archipelago*. London, 1996.

—— 'Faction and the origins of the Desmond rebellion of 1579'. *IHS*, xxii (1981), 289.

—— 'The O'Reillys of East Breifne and the problem of "surrender and regrant"'. *Breifne*, vi (1985), 233.

—— 'The road to the View: on the decline of reform thought in Tudor Ireland' in P. Coughlan, ed., *Spenser and Ireland*. Cork, 1989.

—— 'Sixteenth century Ulster and the failure of Tudor reform' in C. Brady, M. O'Dowd, B. Walker, eds., *Ulster: an illustrated history*. London, 1989. p. 97.

—— 'Spenser's Irish crisis: humanism and experience in the 1590s.' *PP*, no. 111 (1986), 17.

—— 'Thomas Butler, earl of Ormonde (1534–1614) and reform in Tudor Ireland' in C. Brady, ed., *Worsted in the game: losers in Irish history*. Dublin, 1989.

Brand, P. 'The early history of the legal profession of the lordship of Ireland, 1250–1350' in D. Hogan and W.N. Osborough, eds., *Brehons, serjeants and attorneys*. Dublin, 1990.

Brooks, C.W. 'Litigants and attorneys in King's Bench and Common Pleas, 1560 to 1640' in J.H. Baker, ed., *Legal records and the historian*. London, 1978.

Butler, W.F.T. 'Irish land tenures, Celtic and foreign.' *Studies*, xiii (1924), 291, 524.

—— 'The policy of surrender and re-grant'. *RSAI Jn*, xliii (1913), 47, 99.

Canny, N. 'The attempted Anglicisation of Ireland in the seventeenth century: an exemplar of "British History"' in J.S. Morrill, ed., *The political world of Thomas Wentworth, earl of Strafford, 1621–1641*. Cambridge, 1996.

—— 'Edmund Spenser and the development of an Anglo-Irish identity.' *Yearbook of English Studies*, xiii (1983), 1.

—— 'The formation of the Irish mind: religion, politics and Gaelic Irish literature, 1580–1750' in C.H.E. Philpin, ed., *Nationalism and popular protest in Ireland*. Cambridge, 1987.

—— 'Hugh O'Neill, earl of Tyrone and the changing face of Gaelic Ulster.' *Stud Hib*, x (1970), 7.

—— 'Identity formation in Ireland: the emergence of the Anglo-Irish', in N. Canny and A. Pagden, eds., *Colonial identity in the Atlantic world, 1500–1800*. Princeton, 1987.

—— 'Irish, Scottish and Welsh responses to centralisation, *c.* 1530–*c.* 1640: a comparative perspective' in Grant and Stringer, eds. *Uniting the kingdom: the making of the British state*. London, 1995.

—— 'The marginal kingdom: Ireland in the first British empire', in B. Bailyn, ed., *Strangers within the realm: cultural margins of the first British empire*. Chapel Hill, NC, 1991.

—— 'The permissive frontier: social control in English settlements in Ireland and Virginia, 1550–1650', in N.P. Canny, K.R. Andrews, P.E.H. Hair, eds., *The westward enterprise: English activities in Ireland, the Atlantic and America, 1480–1650*. Liverpool, 1978.

—— 'Protestants, planters and apartheid in early modern Ireland.' *IHS*, xxv (1986), 105.

—— 'Revising the Revisionist' [a review of Ciaran Brady, *The chief governors: the rise and fall of reform government in Tudor Ireland, 1536–1588* (Cambridge, 1994)], *IHS*, xxx (1996). p. 242.

—— 'Rowland White's "Discors touching Ireland", *c.* 1569', *IHS*, xx (1976), 439.

—— 'Rowland White's "The dysorders of the Irisshery", 1571.' *Stud Hib*, xix (1979), 147.

—— 'Spenser and the reform of Ireland', in P. Coughlan, ed., *Spenser and Ireland: an interdisciplinary perspective*. Cork, 1989.

—— 'Why the reformation failed in Ireland: une question mal posée.' *Jn Eccl Hist*, xxx (1979), 423.

Carey, V. 'John Derricke's "*Image of Irelande*", Sir Henry Sidney, and the massacre of Mullaghmast, 1578'. *IHS*, xxxi (1999) 305.

—— 'The Irish face of Machiavelli: Richard Beacon's *Solon his follie* (1594) and republican ideology in the conquest of Ireland' in H. Morgan, ed. *Political ideology in Ireland, 1541–1641*. Dublin, 1999.

Clarke, A. ed., 'A discourse between two councilllors of state, the one of England and the other of Ireland.' *Anal Hib*, no. 26 (1970), 159.

—— 'Patrick Darcy and the Queries' in Jane Ohlmeyer, ed., *Political thought in seventeenth-century Ireland*. Cambridge, 2000. p. 47.

—— 'Sir Piers Crosby, 1590–1646: Wentworth's "tawney ribbon."' *IHS*, xxvi (1989), 142.

—— 'A woeful sinner: John Atherton', in V.P. Carey and V. Lotz-Huemann, eds., *Taking sides? Colonial and confessional mentalités in early modern Ireland: essays in honour of Karl S. Bottigheimer*. Dublin, 2003.

Cockburn, J.S. 'The nature and incidence of crime in England, 1559–1625: a preliminary survey', in J.S. Cockburn, ed., *Crime in England, 1550–1800*. Princeton, 1977.

—— 'The spoils of law: the trial of Sir John Hele, 1604', in D. Guth, et al., eds., *Tudor rule and revolution*. Cambridge 1982.

Crawford, J.G. 'The origins of the court of castle chamber: a star chamber jurisdiction in Ireland'. *AJLH*, xxvi (1980), 22.

Cregan, D.F. 'The Confederate Catholics of Ireland: the personnel of the Confederation, 1642–9'. *IHS*, xxix (1995), 499.

—— 'Irish catholic admissions to the English inns of court, 1558–1625'. *Ir Jur*, n.s., v (1970), 95.

—— 'Irish recusant lawyers in politics in the reign of James I.' *Ir Jur*, n.s., v (1970), 306.

Cunningham, B. 'The composition of Connacht in the lordships of Clanricarde and Thomond'. *IHS*, xxix (1984–5), 1.

—— 'Native culture and political change in Ireland 1580 –1640' in Brady and Gillespie, eds., *Natives and newcomers: essays on the making of Irish colonial society, 1534–1641*. Dublin, 1986. p. 148.

—— and R. Gillespie, 'Englishmen in sixteeenth century Irish annals'. *Ir Econ Soc*, xvii (1990), 14.

Delany, V.T.H. 'The palatinate court of the liberty of Tipperary.' *AJLH*, v (1961), 95.

Donovan, B.C. 'Tudor rule in Gaelic Leinster and the rise of Feagh McHugh O'Byrne' in C. O'Brien, ed., 'Feagh McHugh O'Byrne: the Wicklow Firebrand.' *Journal of Rathdown Historical Society*. Vol. 1 (1998). pp. 118–49.

Edwards, D. 'The Butler revolt of 1569'. *IHS*, xxviii (1993), 228.

—— 'Collaboration without anglicisation: the MacGiollapadraig lordship and Tudor reform' in Edwards, D. et al., *Gaelic Ireland: land, lordship and settlement, c.1250–1650*. Dublin, 2002.

—— 'Ideology and experience: Spenser's *View* and martial law in Ireland', in H. Morgan, ed., *Political ideology in Ireland, 1541–1641*. Dublin, 1999.

—— 'The poisoned chalice: the Ormond inheritance, sectarian division and the emergence of James Butler, 1614–1642' in T. Barnard, J. Fenlon, eds., *The dukes of Ormonde, 1610–1745*. Woodbridge, Suffolk, 2000.

—— 'Recovering Gaelic Ireland, c. 1250–c. 1650' in P. Duffy, D. Edwards, E. Fitzpatrick, eds., *Gaelic Ireland: land, lordship and settlement*. Dublin, 2000.

Edwards, R.D. 'History of the penal laws against Catholics in Ireland, 1534–1691'. *IHR Bull*, xi (1933–34), 185.

—— and T.W. Moody. 'The history of Poynings' law, 1495–1615'. *IHS*, ii (1941), 415.

Ellis, S.G., 'Crown, community and government in the English territories, 1450–1575'. *Hist*, lxxi (1986), 187.

—— 'The collapse of the Gaelic world, 1450–1650'. *IHS*, xxxi (1999), 468.

—— 'Henry VIII, rebellion and the rule of law'. *Hist Jn*, xxiv (1981), 531.

—— 'Historiographical debate: representations of the past in Ireland: whose past and whose present?' *IHS*, xxvii (1991), 289.

—— 'Nationalist historiography and the English and Gaelic worlds in the late middle ages'. *IHS*, xxv (1986), 1.

—— 'More Irish than the Irish themselves? the Anglo-Irish in Tudor Ireland.' *History Ireland*, vii (1999), 22.

—— 'The Pale and the far North: government and society in two early Tudor borderlands' [O'Donnell lecture to National University of Ireland]. Galway, 1988.

—— 'Tudor state formation and the shaping of the British Isles' in S.G. Ellis and S. Barber, eds., *Conquest and Union: fashioning a British state, 1485–1725*. London, 1995.

—— 'Thomas Cromwell and Ireland, 1532–40'. *Hist Jn*, xxiii (1980), 510.

Elton, G.R. 'Crime and the historian', in J.S. Cockburn, ed., *Crime in England,1550–1800*. Princeton, 1977.

—— 'English law in the sixteenth century: reform in an age of change'. [Selden Society lecture] London, 1979.

—— 'Informing for profit: a sidelight on Tudor methods of law-enforcement'. *Hist Jn*, xi (1954), 149.

'Lex terrae victrix: the triumph of parliamentary law in the sixteenth century' in D.M. Dean, and N.L. Jones, eds., *The parliaments of Elizabethan England*. Oxford, 1990.

—— 'The problems and significance of administrative history in the Tudor period.' *Jn Brit Stud*, iv (1965), 18.

—— 'The rule of law in sixteenth century England,' in G.R. Elton, *Studies in Tudor and Stuart politics and government*, vol. 1 Cambridge, 1974. p. 266.

—— 'Tudor politics: the points of contact. II. The council', *TRHS*, 5th ser, xxv (1975), 195.

Fisher, N.R.R. 'The Queen's court in her chamber at Westminster'. *EHR*, cviii (1993), 314.

Flanagan, E. 'Barnaby Rich, Sir John Davies and the failure of reform, 1609–22' in H. Morgan, ed., *Political ideology in Ireland, 1541–1641*. Dublin, 1999.

Fletcher, A. 'Honour, reputation and local officeholding in Elizabethan and Stuart England', in A. Fletcher and J. Stevenson, eds., *Order and disorder in early modern England*. Cambridge, 1985.

Ford, A. 'The Protestant Reformation in Ireland', in C. Brady and R. Gillespie, eds., *Natives and newcomers*. Dublin, 1986.

Frame, R. 'The judicial powers of the medieval Irish keepers of the peace.' *Ir Jur*, n.s., ii (1967), 308.

Garnham, N. 'How violent was eighteenth-century Ireland?' *IHS*, xxx (1997), 390.

Gillespie, R. 'Destabilizing Ulster, 1641–2', in B. MacCuarta, ed., *Ulster 1641: aspects of the rising*. Belfast, 1993.

—— 'Negotiating order in early seventeenth century Ireland' in M.J. Braddick and J. Walter, eds., *Negotiating power in early modern society: order, hierarchy and subordination in Britain and Ireland*. Cambridge, 2001.

—— 'Women and crime in seventeenth century Ireland', in M. O'Dowd and M. MacCurtain, eds., *Women in early modern Ireland*. Edinburgh, 1991. p. 43.

Guy, J. 'Law, faction and parliament in the sixteenth century.' *Hist Jn*, xxviii (1985), 441.

—— 'Law, lawyers and the English reformation.' *History Today*, xxxv (1985), 16.

—— 'The privy council: revolution or evolution', in C. Coleman and D.R. Starkey, eds., *Revolution reassessed*. Oxford, 1986.

Hart, A.R. 'The king's serjeant at law in Tudor Ireland, 1485–1603', in D. Hogan and W.N. Osborough, eds., *Brehons, serjeants and attorneys*. Dublin, 1990.

Herrup, C. 'Law and morality in seventeenth century England.' *PP*, no. 106 (1985), 102.

Hoak, D. 'Two revolutions in Tudor government: the formation and organization of Mary I's privy council', in C. Coleman and D.R. Starkey, eds., *Revolution reassessed*. Oxford, 1986.

Hurstfield, J. 'Political corruption in early modern England.' *Hist*, lii (1967), 16.

Irwin, Liam. 'The Irish presidency courts, 1569–1672'. *Ir Jur*, xii (1977), 106.

——. 'The suppression of the Irish presidency system.' *IHS* xxii (1980), 21.

Ives, E.W. 'Law, history and society: an eternal triangle', in E.W. Ives, ed., *Litigants and the legal profession*. London, 1983.

—— 'Promotion in the legal profession of Yorkist and early Tudor England.' *LQR*, lxxv (1959), 348.

—— 'The reputation of the common lawyers in English society, 1450–1550'. *U of Birmingham Hist Jn*, vii (1960), 130.

Jackson, D. 'The Irish language and Tudor government'. *Eire-Ireland*, viii (1973), 21.

Jefferies, H.A. 'The Irish parliament of 1560: the anglican reforms authorised.' *IHS*, xxvi (1988), 128.

Jones, W.J. 'Conflict or collaboration? Chancery attitudes in the reign of Elizabeth I.' *AJLH*, v (1961), 12

—— 'Due process and slow process in the Elizabethan chancery.' *AJLH*, vi (1962), 123.

—— 'Palatine performance in the seventeenth century' in P. Clark, A.G.R. Smith and N. Tyacke, eds., *The English Commonwealth, 1547 to 1640*. Leicester, 1979. p. 192.

Keane, R. 'The will of the general: martial law in Ireland, 1535–1924'. *Ir Jur*, xxv–xxvii (1990–92), 151.

Kearney, H.F. 'The court of wards and liveries in Ireland 1622–41'. *RIA Proc*, lvii (1955) sect. c., p. 29.

Kenny, C. 'The exclusion of Catholics from the legal profession in Ireland, 1537–1829'. *IHS*, xxv (1987), 338.

—— 'The four courts in Dublin before 1796.' *Ir Jur*, xxi (1980), 107.

—— 'The records of King's Inns, Dublin' in D. Hogan and W. N. Osborough, eds., *Brehons, serjeants and attorneys: studies in the history of the Irish legal profession*. Dublin, 1990.

Knafla, L.A. '"Sin of all sorts swarmeth": criminal litigation in an English county in the early seventeenth century', in E. W. Ives, ed., *Law, litigants and the legal profession*. London, 1983.

Lennon, C. 'The Counter-Reformation in Ireland, 1542–1642', in C. Brady and R. Gillespie, ed., *Natives and newcomers: essays on the making of Irish colonial society, 1534–1641*. Dublin, 1986.

—— 'Political thought of Irish Counter-Reformation churchmen: the testimony of the "Analecta" of Bishop David Rothe' in H. Morgan, ed., *Political ideology in Ireland, 1541–1641*. Dublin, 1999.

—— 'Richard Stanihurst (1547–1618) and Old English identity.' *IHS*, xxi (1978), 121.

—— 'Mass in the manor house: the Counter Reformation in Dublin, 1560–1630', in J. Kelly and D. Keogh, eds., *History of the Catholic diocese of Dublin*. Dublin, 2000. pp. 112–126.

Little, P. 'The English parliament and the Irish constitution, 1641–9' in M. O Siochrú, ed., *Kingdoms in crisis: Ireland in the 1640s: essays in honour of Donal Cregan*. Dublin, 2001.

—— 'The Geraldine ambitions of the first earl of Cork.' *IHS*, xxxiii (2002), 151

McCafferty, J. '"God bless your free Church of Ireland": Wentworth, Laud, Bramhall and the Irish convocation of 1634' in J.S. Morrill, ed., *The political world of Thomas Wentworth, earl of Strafford, 1621–1641*. Cambridge, 1996.

—— '"To follow the late precedents of England": the Irish impeachment proceedings of 1641', in D.S. Greer and N. Dawson, eds., *Mysteries and solutions in Irish legal history*. Dublin, 2001. p. 51.

McCavitt, J. '"Good planets in their several spheares"; the establishment of the assize circuits in early seventeenth century Ireland.' *Ir Jur*, xxiv (1989), 248.

MacCraith, M. 'Gaelic Reaction to the Reformation' in S.G. Ellis and S. Barber, eds., *Conquest and union: forging a multinational British state, 1485–1707*. London, 1995.

MacCuarta, B. 'The plantation of Leitrim, 1620–41'. *IHS*, xxxii (2001), 301.

McGrath, B. 'Parliament men and the confederate association' in M. O Siochrú, ed., *Kingdoms in Crisis: Ireland in the 1640s*. Dublin, 2001.

McLaughlin, J., ed. 'Select documents xlvii: Richard Hadsor's "Discourse on the Irish state, 1604"'. *IHS*, xxx (1997), 347.

Morgan, H. 'Beyond Spenser? a historiographical introduction to the study of political ideas in early modern Ireland' in H. Morgan, ed., *Political ideology in Ireland, 1541–1641*. Dublin, 1999.

—— 'British policies before the British state' in B. Bradshaw and J.S. Morrill, eds., *The British problem, c. 1534–1707: state formation in the Atlantic archipelago*. London, 1996.

—— 'The colonial venture of Sir Thomas Smith in Ulster, 1571–1575'. *IHS*, xxviii (1985), 265.

—— 'The end of Gaelic Ulster: a thematic interpretation of events between 1534 and 1610'. *IHS*, xxvi (1988), 8.

—— 'Extradition and treason trial of a Gaelic lord: the case of Brian O'Rourke'. *Ir Jur*, xxii (1987), 285.

—— 'The fall of John Perrot' in J. Guy, ed., *The reign of Elizabeth I: court and culture in the last decade*. Cambridge, 1995.

—— 'Overmighty officers: the Irish lord deputyship in the early modern British state.' *History Ireland*, vii (1999), 17.

Miller, J. 'Thomas Sheridan (1646–1712) and his "Narrative"'. *IHS*, xx (1976), 105.

—— 'The earl of Tyrconnell and James II's Irish policy, 1685–88'. *Hist Jn*, xx (1977), 803.

Morrill, J.S. 'The fashioning of Britain', in S.G. Ellis and S. Barber, eds., *Conquest and Union: fashioning a British state, 1485–1725*. London, 1995. p. 11.

Murray, J. 'The diocese of Dublin in the sixteenth century' in J. Kelly and D. Keogh, eds., *History of the Catholic diocese of Dublin*. Dublin, 2000. p. 99

Myers, J.P. 'Early colonial experiences in Ireland: captain Thomas Lee and Sir John Davies.' *Eire-Ireland*, xxiii (1988), 8.

Nicholls, K.W. 'Irishwomen and property in the sixteenth century' in M. O'Dowd and M. MacCurtain, eds., *Women in early modern Ireland*. Edinburgh, 1991.
—— 'Land, law and society in sixteenth century Ireland'. [O'Donnell lecture, University College Cork] Dublin, 1976.
O'Brien, C. 'Feagh McHugh O'Byrne, firebrand of the Wicklow Mountains.' *History Ireland*, vii (2000), 13.
O'Dowd, M. 'Women and the Irish chancery court in the late sixteenth and early seventeenth centuries.' *IHS*, xxxi (1999), 472.
—— 'Gaelic economy and society', in C. Brady and R. Gillespie, eds., *Natives and newcomers*. Dublin, 1986.
J. Ohlmeyer, '"Civilizing of those rude partes": colonization within Britain and Ireland, 1580s to 1640s,' in N. Canny and A. Low, eds., Oxford History of the British Empire, vol. 1, *Origins of the empire: British overseas enterprise to the close of the seventeenth century*. Oxford, 1998. p. 124.
—— 'Irish recusant lawyers during the reign of Charles I' in M. O Siochrú, ed., *Kingdoms in crisis: Ireland in the 1640s*. Dublin, 2001.
—— 'Records of the Irish court of chancery: a preliminary report for 1627–1634' in D.S. Greer and N.M. Dawson, eds., *Mysteries and solutions in Irish legal history: Irish Legal History Society discourses and other papers, 1996–1999*. Dublin, 2001.
—— 'Strafford, the "Londonderry Business" and the "New British History"' in J.S. Morrill, ed., *The political world of Thomas Wentworth, earl of Strafford, 1621–1641*. Cambridge, 1996.
Osborough, W.N. 'Ecclesiastical law and the Reformation in Ireland' in W.N. Osborough, *Studies in Irish legal history*. Dublin, 1999. p. 136.
—— 'Executive failure to enforce judicial decrees: a neglected chapter in nineteenth century constitutional history' in J.F. McEldowney and P. O'Higgins, eds., *The common law tradition*. Dublin, 1990.
—— 'The Irish custom of tracts'. *Ir Jur*, xxxii (1997), 439.
—— 'Letters to Ireland: professional enlightenment from the English bench'. *Ir Jur*, xxxi (1996), 228.
—— 'The regulation of the admission of attorneys and solicitors in Ireland, 1600–1860' in W.N. Osborough, *Studies in Irish legal history*. Dublin, 1999. p. 157.
O'Sullivan, M.D. 'Irish lawyers in Tudor England'. *Dublin Review*, clxxix (1926), 1.
Otway-Ruthven, A.J. 'The native Irish and English law in medieval Ireland.' *IHS*, vii (1950), 1.
Palmer, P. 'Interpreters and the politics of translation and traduction in sixteenth century Ireland.' *IHS*, xxxiii (2003), 257.
Patterson, N. 'Gaelic law and the Tudor conquest of Ireland: the social background of the sixteenth century recensions of the pseudo-historical Prologue to the *Senchas mar*'. *IHS*, xxvii (1991), 215.
Pawlisch, H. 'Sir John Davies' law reports and the case of Proxies.' *Ir Jur*, xvii (1982), 368.
Piveronus, P.J. 'Sir Walham St Leger and the first Munster plantation, 1568–69.' *Eire-Ireland*, xiv (1979), 15.
Quinn, D.B. 'Anglo-Irish local government, 1485–1534'. *IHS*, i (1930), 354.
—— 'A discourse of Ireland (circa 1599): a sidelight on English colonial policy.' *RIA Proc*, xlvii (1942), sect. c., 151.
—— 'Government printing and the publication of Irish statutes in the sixteenth century.' *RIA Proc*, xlix (1943), sect. c, 45.
—— 'Ireland and sixteenth century European expansion'. *Historical Studies: I* (1958), 20.
—— 'The Irish parliamentary subsidy in the fifteenth and sixteenth centuries.' *RIA Proc*, xlii (1935), sect c, 219.
—— 'Parliaments and great councils in Ireland, 1461–1586'. *IHS*, iii (1942), 60.
—— 'Renaissance influences in English colonization.' *TRHS*, 5th ser, xxvi (1976), 73.
Ranger, T. 'Richard Boyle and the making of an Irish fortune.' *IHS*, x (1957), 257.
Rutledge, V.L. 'Court-castle faction and the Irish viceroyalty: the appointment of Oliver St John as lord deputy of Ireland in 1616.' *IHS*, xxvi (1989), 233.

Samaha, J. 'The recognizance in Elizabethan law enforcement'. *AJLH*, xxv (1981), 189.

Sheehan, A.J. 'Irish towns in a period of change, 1558–1625', in C. Brady and R. Gillespie, eds., *Natives and newcomers*. Dublin, 1986.

—— 'Official reaction to native land claims in the plantation of Munster'. *IHS*, xxiii (1983), 297.

—— 'The recusancy revolt of 1603: a reinterpretation'. *Arch Hib*, xxxviii (1983), 3.

Simms, K. 'The brehons of later medieval Ireland', in D. Hogan and W.N. Osborough, eds., *Brehons, serjeants and attorneys*. Dublin, 1990.

Starkey, D.R. 'Court and government' in C. Coleman and D.R. Starkey, eds., *Revolution reassessed*. Oxford, 1986.

Treadwell, V. 'The Irish court of wards under James I'. *IHS*, xii (1960), 19.

—— 'The Irish customs administration in the sixteenth century'. *IHS*, xx (1976–77), 384.

—— 'The Irish parliament of 1569–71'. *RIA Proc*, lxv (1966), sect. c, 55.

—— 'New light on Richard Hadsor I: Richard Hadsor and the authorship of "*Advertisements for Ireland*", 1622/3'. *IHS*, xxx (1997), 305.

—— 'Sir John Perrot and the Irish parliament of 1585–6'. *RIA Proc*, lxxxv (1985), sect c, 280.

Walshe, H.C. 'Enforcing the Elizabethan settlement: the vicissitudes of Hugh Brady, bishop of Meath, 1563–84.' *IHS*, xxvi (1989), 352.

—— 'The rebellion of William Nugent, 1581' in R.V. Comerford, et al., eds., *Religion, conflict and coexistence in Ireland: essays presented to Mgr Patrick J. Corish*. Dublin, 1990.

Williams, P. 'The star chamber and the council in the marches of Wales, 1558–1603'. *Board of Celtic Studies Bull*, xvi (1956), 287.

Wood, H. 'The court of castle chamber or star chamber of Ireland'. *RIA Proc*, xxxii (1914), sect. c, 170.

—— 'The office of chief governor of Ireland, 1172–1509'. *RIA Proc*, xxxvi (1923), sect. c, 206.

—— 'The offices of secretary of state and keeper of the signet or privy seal.' *RIA Proc*, xxxviii (1928), sect. c, 51.

Youings, J.A. 'The council of the West.' *TRHS*, 5th ser., x (1960), 41.

Youngs, F. 'Towards petty sessions: Tudor JPs and the division of counties' in D.J. Guth and J.W. McKenna, eds., *Tudor rule and revolution: essays for G.R. Elton*. Cambridge, 1982.

DISSERTATIONS AND UNPUBLISHED PAPERS

Connors, T. 'Survival and anglicization in the west of Ireland: common law and the transformation of the Irish family, 1540–1650'. Paper delivered to the North American Conference on British Studies, Montreal, 1993.

McCafferty, J. 'Bramhall and reconstruction of the Church of Ireland, 1633–41'. Cambridge University Ph.D. dissertation. 1993.

Index

compiled by Helen Litton

CCC = court of Castle Chamber

O'Toole, Phelim McFeagh, 357
O'Toole, Rose, 272
O'Tooles, 42, 100n, 187, 314n
outlaws, 44
Owin Roe of the Grandge, 441
Owre, Thomyne, 426
Oxford University, 105, 108, 110, 118, 338
oyer and terminer, 109, 125, 210, 211: Connacht, 203; Munster, 275

Pacekilbride, Co. Westmeath, 544
Paie, Matthew, bailiff of Wexford, 387, 587–8
Painston, 437
palatinate court, 53–4
Pale, the, 11n, 100, 175, 235. *See also* Old English: abuses by soldiers, 279n; and administration, 181, 211, 222, 306, 341; Baltinglas rebellion, 140, 229–30, 236; Burnell agitator for, 129; cess, 85, 161–2, 218–21, 237; common law resisted, 54; defence of, 177; families, 8–9, 106, 107, 119, 155, 228; general hosting, 217; impartiality of juries, 11; Kildare's control of, 173; lawyers, 27, 359; litigation from, 158n; Mandates, 104, 292–3, 299; oath of uniformity, 248; penal laws opposed, 302; plague, 208; property disputes, 179; recusancy, 247, 320, 321; settlers, 57n; treason trials, 231, 237–8
Pallice, William, 154
Palmer, Peter, judge of common pleas, 129n, 522, 523, 539
paper, wearing of (confession of crimes), 94, 95, 561–2, 565: abduction, 556; conspiracy, 560; forgery, 551; jurors, 498, 501, 536, 564; perjury, 224, 553; slander, 503, 568, 569
Parcelston, Co. Westmeath, 259, 466
Parker, Sir John, master of the rolls, 183
Parker, Robert, 2–3
Parke's Castle, 2–3
parliament, English, 13, 14, 18, 27: Black Oath, 20; house of lords, 390–1, 414; Queries, 12; relations with Irish parliament, 39; Strafford impeachment, 398–401
parliament, Irish, 54–5, 160, 211, 246, 302, 358, 569n: administration of, 18; and CCC, 97, 164; under Chichester, 76–7, 307–8; delegation to James I, 305–6; under Falkland, 1626, 343; high court of, 38–9; house of lords, 102, 407, 408, and Queries, 403, 406, reverses CCC decision, 589; impeachments, 1641, 108; packing of, 302–3; privy council as substitute, 84; prorogued, 1641, 407, 412; Queries, 12, 165–7, 402–6, 408, 409; recusant lawyers petition, 322; reform sought, 419; right of impeachment, 407; speaker's chair dispute, 38, 95–6, 303; under Sydney, 195; under Wentworth, 368–9, 397–8

parliamentary boroughs, 38, 76
Parry, Thomas, marshal, 124, 380, 586n
Parsons, Sir Lawrence, second baron of exchequer, 108, 345, 371n, 578, 581
Parsons, Sir William, chief justice, 317–18, 388n, 390n, 395, 410, 416n, 576n, 589: master of court of wards, 318n, 401–2; plantation policy, 77n; on Queries, 409; surveyor-general, 326, 340n, 512–13; Wicklow plantation, 352
partible inheritance, 37, 147–8
patronage, 29
Patterson, N., 55
Paulee, Symon, 146, 301, 502–3
Pawlisch, Hans, 12, 53, 112n, 290n, 299
Payne, John, 440
Pecke, Daniel, 513–14, 514–15
pedigrees, 127
peerage, 155, 209: and administration, 128, 177, 211: Mandates, 292–3, petition to Chichester, 303–4, Wentworth, 392–3n, 406; ascendancy established, 336; behaviour of, 152, 264–5, 334–5; and CCC, 117, 134; and cess, 161–2; creation of, 18; as litigants, 136–7; property disputes, 176–7, 180–1, 336–9, 355–6; recusancy, 326–7
Pelham, Sir Edmund, chief baron, 110, 288n, 291n, 481–2
Pelham, Sir William, chief governor, 110, 225, 227–8
Pellagh, the, 440
Pemberton, Richard, 124
Pemerton, Myles, curate of Clone and Castleryckard, 514–15
penal laws, 34, 96, 287, 297, 302, 397: in 'Graces,' 358; suspension, 398
Penruddock, Sir Thomas, 340n
Penteney, Richard, 446, 447
Pentnye, Edward, 521–2
Pentnye, John, merchant, 149, 214, 431, 455
Pentnye, Mary, 149, 265, 476
Pentnye, Thomazene, 149, 214, 431, 455
Peppard, Anthony, 456
Perceval, Sir Philip, 19, 394, 412, 557
Perceval-Maxwell, M., 166
perjury cases, 145, 150, 207, 241, 356–7, 552–3, 559–60: charge dismissed, 216; false affidavit, 565–6; Howth case, 152, 223–4; juries charged, 141, 238–9, 251; punishment for, 143; role of CCC, 86
Perrott, Sir James, 340n
Perrot, Sir John, chief governor, 109, 155, 200n, 227, 242, 350, 365n, 456n, 462: Bird forgery case, 65–6, 261–2, 457–9, 463, and CCC, 39, 168; charges against, 245–6, 255–6; Ealand sentence reversed, 64, 460n; end of, 107, 257; forgery of signature, 114, 252–3, 464–5; governorship, 34, 246–56, 258, 259, 391,

The Irish Legal History Society

Established in 1988 to encourage the study and advance the knowledge of the history of Irish law, especially by the publication of original documents and of works relating to the history of Irish law, including its institutions, doctrines and personalities, and the reprinting or editing of works of sufficient rarity or importance.